THE COMPLETE PLAYS OF CHARLES LUDLAM

Something RIDICULOUS
from Bryan & Tom
Christmas, 1990

The Complete Plays of Charles Ludlam

PERENNIAL LIBRARY

Harper & Row, Publishers, New York
Grand Rapids, Philadelphia, St. Louis, San Francisco
London, Singapore, Sydney, Tokyo, Toronto

All of the plays included in this work are fully protected by copyright, and may not be acted either by professionals or amateurs without permission and without the payment of royalty. All rights, including but not limited to the professional, motion picture, radio, television, videotape, foreign language, tabloid, recitation, lecturing, publication, and reading rights are reserved.

The amateur and stock acting rights in "The Mystery of Irma Vep," "Bluebeard," "The Artificial Jungle," "Medea," "Stage Blood," "The Enchanted Pig," "Love's Tangled Web," and "Reverse Psychology" are controlled exclusively by Samuel French Inc., 45 West 25th Street, New York, New York 10010, without whose permission in writing no performances of said plays may be made. All inquiries concerning all other rights to the aforementioned plays and all rights to the other plays included in this work should be addressed to Walter Gidaly, Esq., 750 Third Avenue, New York, N.Y. 10017, the Literary Executor of the Estate of Charles Ludlam.

FIRST EDITION

Designed by Joan Greenfield

Library of Congress Cataloging-in-Publication Data

Ludlam, Charles.
  [Selections. 1989]
  The complete plays of Charles Ludlam.—1st ed.
  p. cm.
  ISBN 0-06-055172-0
  ISBN 0-06-096399-9 (pbk.)
  I. Title.
PS3562.U258A6   1989   89-45103
812'.54—dc19

---

89 90 91 92 CC/HC 10 9 8 7 6 5 4 3 2 1
89 90 91 92 CC/HC 10 9 8 7 6 5 4 3 2 1 (pbk.)

CONTENTS

CHARLES LUDLAM
A Brief Life

by
Steven Samuels

In 1984, when he was forty-one years old, *The Mystery of Irma Vep* brought Charles Ludlam surprisingly close to his long-term goal of conquering the universe. Possessor of a personal yet influential vision of modern American stage comedy as a synthesis of "wit, parody, vaudeville farce, melodrama, and satire," he had, since 1967, pursued this vision as a superb actor, inventive director, delightful designer, and—most significantly—prodigious playwright, with a year-round company dedicated exclusively to producing his works. New York's Ridiculous Theatrical Company had had major successes before (*Bluebeard, Camille, The Ventriloquist's Wife,* and *Reverse Psychology* among them), but even the back-to-back hits *Le Bourgeois Avant-Garde* (a tribute to and transfiguration of Ludlam's revered French comedic master, Molière, and a declaration of independence from aesthetic labels he had found confining since the sixties) and *Galas* (the life of opera singer Maria Callas conceived as a "modern tragedy," with Ludlam himself as the diva), could not prepare the press or the public for *The Mystery of Irma Vep.*

An astonishing tour-de-force in which two performers—Ludlam and his longtime lover, Everett Quinton—portrayed men, women, and an assortment of monsters in a full-length quick-change act, *The Mystery of Irma Vep* was inspired by the "penny dreadful," that quintessentially Victorian melange of sensationalism and sublime poetry. Ludlam had always ransacked the history of art for the form and content of his crafty comic engines; this time he introduced a vampire, a werewolf, and an Egyptian mummy into his usual assortment of jokes and puns, trademark stage business like cross-dressing and billowing fog, and literary references ranging from *Jerusalem Delivered* to *Little Eyolf.* An uproarious, thought-provoking paean to love everlasting, *The Mystery of Irma Vep* garnered praise, awards, adoring audiences, and an embarrassment of offers for Ludlam from the worlds of film, television, opera, and the legitimate stage.

Armed with strong opinions and big plans, Ludlam set out to remake all the theatrical arts. Tempted as he was by wider arenas, and fully intending to invade them, he never forgot that the conquest of the universe could best be conducted from his 145-seat theater in the heart of Greenwich Village, where the unusually creative conditions he had developed for himself let him concentrate on his most important work: the writing and staging of plays.

EARLY YEARS

One is tempted to say Charles Ludlam's father was Aristophanes, the ancient Greek satirist, but Ludlam was born, in fact, in Floral Park, New York, on April 12, 1943, the middle son of Joseph William Ludlam, a witty, eccentric, ambitious master plasterer, an independent man who built the family home in New Hyde Park himself (as the witty, eccentric, ambitious Charles Ludlam would later establish his own theater). His mother, the former Marjorie Braun, may have started her six-year-old son's career by losing him at the Mineola Fair, where he wandered into a Punch and Judy show, which enthralled him, and then a freak show, where he saw armless black dwarves painting pictures with their toes.

Soon he was watching puppet shows on TV ("Foodini and Pinhead" was his favorite), then performing his own in the basement. By the age of seven he was out in the backyard, stringing up sheets to serve as curtains, making up lines for the little girls next door to say. He was also appearing in productions at school (beginning in second grade with *Santa in Blunderland*), the once-a-year chance for an otherwise withdrawn child to shine.

Other children played games, but Ludlam lived in the intense world of his imagination. The Catholic church, with its drama, mystery, role-playing, rhetoric, philosophy, and spirituality, would prove an enduring influence. Of equal importance was the movie theater conveniently located directly across the street. Until he was ten years old and the family moved to Greenlawn, his mother took him to the movies whenever the marquee changed.

Always somewhat "different," Ludlam was a rebel and an outcast by his high school years, wearing long hair a decade before it became fashionable. A voracious reader of the classics, he was obsessed with theater. In 1958, an apprenticeship at the Red Barn Theater, a local summer stock company, gave him his first true glimpse of actors' lives and—since the performers lived together in an adjoining barn—bohemian life as well.

He went to New York City to attend Living Theatre performances of *Tonight We Improvise* and *The Connection.* Inspired by this first glimpse of an expressive, noncommercial company, Ludlam founded his own avant-garde troupe, the Students Repertory Theatre, above a Northport liquor store, in an abandoned Odd Fellows' meeting hall, at the age of seventeen, directing and acting in such dramatic obscurities as *Madman on the Roof,* a modern Nōh play by Kikuchi Kahn, and Nikolai Yevreinov's *Theatre of the Soul,* a Russian late-romantic work set inside the human body, as well as Eugene O'Neill's *The Great God Brown* and August Strindberg's *Dream Play.*

In 1961, he matriculated at Hofstra University on Long Island with an acting scholarship and clashed with his professors immediately. His behavior was outrageous and his acting excessive; so excessive that the staff insisted he concentrate on writing and directing. One result was his first full-length play, *Edna Brown*—expressionistic, semiautobiographical, and never performed. (Ludlam later destroyed it, although he did work fragments of it into subsequent efforts.)

Ludlam would always refer to his Hofstra experience as crucial, since it provided him the opportunity to master the techniques of classical stagecraft. But his college sojourn also had significant personal ramifications. In long conversations with his old friend Christopher Scott, Ludlam finally discovered the source of his outrageous, excessive "difference": he was queer. Graduated from Hofstra with a degree in dramatic literature, he headed straight for New York City, immersing himself completely in the almost indistinguishable artistic and homosexual undergrounds.

On the Lower East Side (where Ludlam lived for many years before settling in the West Village), 1965 was characterized by great aesthetic exuberance and cross-fertilization, rock and roll, happenings, experimental filmmaking, and the flowering of off-off-Broadway. Among the many on the cutting edge were playwright Ronald Tavel and director John Vaccaro, who formalized their nascent collaboration in 1966 with the founding of the Play-House of the Ridiculous in a loft on 17th Street. Ludlam made his first New York stage appearance as Peeping Tom in the Ridiculous's premiere production, *The Life of Lady Godiva.*

"We have passed beyond the absurd; our situation is absolutely preposterous," Tavel declared in a program note, and his play gave ample evidence. Like most subsequent efforts in the divergent strains of the Ridiculous, *The Life of Lady Godiva* was a self-conscious mix of high and low culture, an anarchic, psychosexual phantasmagoria filled with camp, drag, pageantry, grotesquerie, and literary pretension. Its impact on Ludlam cannot be overestimated.

A subsequent Play-House production proved equally telling. In *Screen Test,* intended as a half-hour curtain-raiser, a director (Vaccaro himself) was to interview and humiliate an actress and a transvestite (an important early member of Ludlam's Ridiculous, Mario Montez). The introduction of another female character provided Ludlam with his first drag performance opportunity: wearing a wig that had passed through Salvador Dali's hands, he found himself transformed instantly and almost magically into Norma Desmond, the fading star played by Gloria Swanson in the movie *Sunset Boulevard.* Improvising both character and lines, Ludlam turned *Screen Test* into a two-hour star turn before he was finished with it.

Despite subsequent difficulties, Ludlam was always grateful to Vaccaro for freeing him as an actor. Before Vaccaro, he had been accused of being "too pasty, corny, mannered, campy." After Vaccaro, he knew these weren't deficiencies but assets.

EPIC THEATER

Soon after *Screen Test,* Tavel and Vaccaro quarreled and parted. In search of new material, Vaccaro turned to Ludlam, whom he had heard was writing a Ridiculous play.

Big Hotel was originally intended as an exercise, fun for Ludlam to have with a notebook. With a very loose plot and a bizarre assortment of characters having little in common other than occupancy at a metropolitan hotel, *Big Hotel* drew on dozens of movies, songs, comic books, television ads, and great works of literature for its material.

Its staging encouraged Ludlam's next play, *Conquest of the Universe,* a collage epic partially patterned on Christopher Marlowe's *Tamburlaine the Great.* Whereas *Big Hotel* had been modeled on movies, *Conquest of the Universe* demonstrated Ludlam's flair for Elizabethan dramaturgy. Because of Ludlam's talent for exaggeration, his Tamberlaine could never be satisfied with conquering mere continents; Ludlam's Tamberlaine's hubris demanded the subjugation of planets and allowed him to reenact passages from *Hamlet* and to imitate the Last Supper.

Ludlam himself was slated to star as Tamberlaine's twin opponents, Cosroe and Zabina, but in the middle of rehearsals the famously temperamental Vaccaro fired him. Half of the company walked out with Ludlam and, at a subsequent meeting, encouraged him to stage the play himself. Then they elected him to lead their new troupe, The Ridiculous Theatrical Company.

Its first shoestring performances—weekends after midnight at Tambellini's Gate, on Second Avenue and 10th Street, after the company had taken down Tambellini's movie screen—were *When Queens Collide* (otherwise *Conquest of the Universe,* the same play presented simultaneously by Vaccaro's newly christened Theater of the Ridiculous, which owned the rights to the play), and *Big Hotel,* revived in repertory. Over the next several years—despite limited attendance and continual moves from venue to venue—the company continued to perform and to add new plays to its repertoire: Bill Vehr's *Whores of Babylon* (a verse play by the actor/filmmaker who was, at the time, Ludlam's closest associate; a play so intriguing that Ludlam staged it on three separate occasions, once as a shadow puppet play); *Turds in Hell* (a collaboration with Vehr which recapitulated the mythic search for a lost parent, with the hero in this case being a hunchback, pinhead, sex maniac with goat's hooves and gigantic cock and balls); and *The Grand Tarot* (an aleatoric experiment inspired by Commedia dell'Arte methods, with stock characters created from cards in the Tarot deck and the order of the scenes at each performance determined by the luck of the draw).

These were chaotic, nonconformist, often all-night affairs. Even in an era of experimental theater, Ludlam's must have seemed *supremely* experimental. He was simultaneously devoted to the virtuosic use of language and the sheer physicality of stage presentation, energized by the clash of opposing philosophies and divergent acting styles. Tawdry, flamboyant sets and costumes, nudity, and simulated sex were juxtaposed with the words of Wilde, Joyce, Shakespeare, and Baudelaire. Ludlam stood in awe before the world's art and literature, viewing himself as a recycler not only of cultural detritus, but also of neglected and abused masterworks. He collaged his plays because he didn't feel worthy of adding one word to the canon, anxious instead to use his gifts to reanimate tradition-bound classics and to revive outmoded theatrical techniques.

Ludlam wasn't only making theater, he was remaking himself. Theater had replaced Catholicism as his religion. Whatever was rejected anywhere else was welcome on his stage. East and West could meet there, dramatically, spiritually, philosophically.

Formerly confused about his sexuality, Ludlam was now a man without a closet, intent on setting his actors and audiences free of culturally-enforced conformity and prejudice. Polemical, furrowed-brow theater was not for him. Ludlam knew life was "a comedy to those who think/a tragedy to those who feel," and he was an irrepressible thinker. Laughter was the great liberator and the great equalizer. Anything carried to an extreme was, willy-nilly, ridiculous.

Ridiculous, too, was critical neglect by mainstream publications. Ludlam and the Ridiculous had their champions, but their champions' influence, unlike that of the mainstream's, did not extend to the box office. Glorious as these adventurous productions may have been, they didn't bring in any money.

Ludlam survived by working in a health-food store, packaging rare books, doing stunts on "Candid Camera," occasionally receiving help from Christopher Scott. Few of the ever-changing cast of gypsies who made up his troupe seemed as serious or disciplined as he was. As the sixties came to a close, Ludlam knew it was time for a change.

development period, added one more rule to Ludlam's formula for success: since the plays were produced as he wrote them, and often performed before they were complete, only extensive previews could ensure that the works would be ready before bowing for the press.

A quick trip to Coney Island in late 1981 resulted in a second silent black and white film, *Museum of Wax,* in which Ludlam starred as a homicidal maniac. A playwrighting fellowship from the National Endowment for the Arts helped him produce two new plays in 1982: *Secret Lives of the Sexists* (which Ludlam called "The Farce of Modern Life"), an exposé of modern mores indebted to Aristophanes' *Thesmophoriazusae,* and *Exquisite Torture,* a surrealistic comedy about the last of the Neros inspired by Salvador Dali's remarkable novel *Hidden Faces.* *Exquisite Torture* ("A Romantic Ecstasy") was Ludlam's last box office flop, somewhat ameliorated by another stint as a playwrighting professor at Yale University.

Le Bourgeois Avant-Garde ("A Comedy Ballet"), presented early in 1983, with Ludlam as Rufus Foufas, a successful greengrocer who wanted to become "avant-garde," was Ludlam's knowing, loving attack on those theatrical brethren he believed had mistakenly thrown out character and plot in a misguided search for the new. This production—which Ludlam considered a public service—inaugurated an unprecedented string of hits including *Galas* (the first woman he had portrayed since Marguerite Gautier, and a secretly autobiographical vision of a demanding, original, overworked artist) and *The Mystery of Irma Vep* (for which Ludlam turned down Broadway and world tour invitations).

Contractual obligations led, in the space of two months, to the writing of *Medea* (which Ludlam chose not to play, so disturbing did he find the notion of killing his own children), and *How to Write a Play* ("An Absolute Farce" hilariously depicting the playwrighting process—with Ludlam and Quinton featured in mock renditions of themselves—which was, unfortunately, performed publicly only twice). Ludlam spent the summer of 1984 with the American Ibsen Theater, appearing in the title role of *Hedda Gabler.*

The success of *The Mystery of Irma Vep,* and one last National Endowment fellowship, provided Ludlam with financial security for the first time in his life and gave him the nerve to attempt another epic, an adaptation of Gustave Flaubert's historical novel of the siege of Carthage, *Salammbô.* (Ludlam's version was "An Erotic Tragedy.") Bodybuilders were hired to play the barbarian hordes; five-hundred-pound Katy Dierlam took on the cross-dressed role of the decadent, decaying suffete Hanno; and Ludlam himself portrayed the title character, the thirteen-year-old virgin priestess of the moon. The opening was delayed while Ludlam directed the Santa Fe Opera in Henze's *English Cat* and filmed a guest spot on "Miami Vice" (having made his network television debut the previous year as a guest star on Madeline Kahn's "Oh, Madeline"). When it opened in the fall of 1985, *Salammbô* was a *succès de scandale* and proved Ludlam could be popular without losing his bite.

More opportunities followed. *The Production of Mysteries,* a short opera he had written with the company's resident composer, Peter Golub, in 1980, was performed by Lukas Foss and the Brooklyn Philharmonic Orchestra. He directed his own libretto of *Die Fledermaus* for the Santa Fe Opera. He filmed an episode of "Tales from the Dark Side" for television and was featured in two movies, *Forever Lulu* and *The Big Easy.*

But Ludlam remained dedicated to The Ridiculous Theatrical Company and his life on the stage, and triumphed again, in the fall of 1986, with *The Artificial Jungle* ("A Suspense Thriller"). Indebted to the writings of James M. Cain, but more particularly to Emile Zola's *Thérèse Raquin, The Artificial Jungle* was set in a pet shop on the Lower East Side and showed Ludlam being murdered onstage six times a week. The audience could not have known that their belovéd clown was actually dying then. Neither could he, at first.

Ludlam, who had often said "no one is promised tomorrow," had long feared AIDS, but he refused to be tested for the virus. His many plans and obligations distracted him: an adaptation of *Der Ring Gott Farblonjet* for Broadway; direction of *Titus Andronicus* for the Public Theater's Free Shakespeare in the Park; completion of *The Sorrows of Dolores* for a showing at the Collective for Living Cinema; and a new play, *Houdini, A Piece of Pure Escapism*—all these meant too much to him for him to consider that they would never happen. *Houdini,* particularly, was intended to be his noblest creation, a masterful blend of history, comedy, and stage illusion, a philosophical disquisition on the tragedy of Harry Houdini's desperate attempts to escape the bonds of this life. Ludlam had received a generous grant to make a film of himself creating *Houdini,* a documentary which would have opened still more doors for him and the company.

When his illness was confirmed at Thanksgiving, 1986, he would not surrender to it. He convinced himself he would be the first man to beat this disease, through strict application of macrobiotic principles. He sought to lessen stress by devotion to his hobbies—his plants, his fish, his birds, watercolor and Sumi-e painting—but he relinquished none of his dreams, rehearsing Houdini's death scene when he was too weak to get out of his chair, negotiating a second ten-year lease on the theater at One Sheridan Square, finishing—with much assistance—*The Sorrows of Dolores* the very day of its premiere, April 30, 1987. That same evening, he was hospitalized with pneumocystis pneumonia. Along with other complications, it ended his life on May 28.

He was only forty-four. He had planned, but not accomplished, his greatest work.

We mourn the man, this priceless theatrical resource, determined to free us with laughter. We mourn the works that might have been: *Houdini, Twilight of the Surrealists, The Lonely Communist. . . .* In the end, we must be grateful for the wisdom and grace with which he packed a lifetime's achievement into his brief span.

Using bawdy, shameless humor and a larger-than-life stage presence, Ludlam had spent twenty years leading The Ridiculous Theatrical Company's rise from a small, out-of-the-way, avant-garde theater to a major attraction and theatrical influence. Theater was Ludlam's intellectual and sociological battleground. The intensely active life of the mind manifested so richly in his works was the greatest gift he gave his public.

We are lucky to have the twenty-nine plays collected here to continue Ludlam's conquest of the universe. Not since Molière have we been blessed with such a playwright, and it may be several centuries more before we see his like again.

EDITORS' NOTES AND ACKNOWLEDGMENTS

Camille, ultimately played in a touring version, has had its original large cast restored, while the best bits added in the show's long life have been integrated into the present script. A pastiche of *Faust* translations has been made for *Big Hotel,* and an ending for *The Grand Tarot* has been reconstructed. Otherwise, our adjustments are mostly minor and may appropriately be passed over in silence. The most blatant appear in brackets, especially to distinguish our clumsy prose from Charles's often beautiful stage directions. Brackets in *Turds in Hell,* however, designate parts of the play edited out for publication in *The Drama Review.* It appears here complete in print for the first time.

We wish to thank Eureka for helping to decipher the pig latin sequence in *Exquisite Torture;* Peter Golub for discovering the first appearance of the lyrics of *Reverse Psychology*'s title song; Ed McGowan for describing the puppet show in *A Christmas Carol* and recalling the quote about culture in *Conquest of the Universe;* and John Brockmeyer, Black-Eyed Susan, Stefan Brecht, Ted Castle, and especially Lola Pashalinski, without whom *The Grand Tarot* would have been more random than even Charles might have liked.

We also express our appreciation to Craig Nelson and Jennifer Hull at Harper & Row for their patience, understanding, flexibility, and dedication to the project; Ellen Turner, Daphne Groos, and Karen Crumley for their assistance with the photographs; Christopher Scott for providing biographical details and encouragement; Walter Gidaly, our lawyer and friend, who continues to help make Charles's work possible; and our many associates in and around The Ridiculous Theatrical Company who have seen us through this effort.

Steven Samuels
Everett Quinton

Charles Ludlam as Norma Desmond
in *Big Hotel* (Diane Dorr-Dorynek)

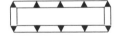

Cast of Characters

MOFONGA
MAGIC MANDARIN
GOD
DEVIL
ELWYNN CHAMBERPOT, *agent*
CRAMWELL, *desk clerk*
BIRDSHITSKAYA
BELLHOP
CHOCHA CALIENTE
MR. X
DRAGO RUBLES
NORMA DESMOND
LUPE VELEZ
TRILBY
MATA HARI
MAISIE MADIGAN
SVENGALI
MARTOK
BLONDINE BLONDELL
WAITER
SANTA CLAUS
GYPSY
COBRA CUNTS

PROLOGUE

(Enter MOFONGA *from one door.* MAGIC MANDARIN *at the other.)*

MOFONGA: I weel kiss thy lips, O Magic Mandarin. I weel kiss thy lips, O Magic Mandarin! Que ángel me despierta en mi cama de flores? *(Screams and runs away)*

MANDARIN: Why did you run away from me?

MOFONGA: Strange faces frighten me—even handsome ones.

MANDARIN: Strange?

MOFONGA: I mean well-known faces appearing unexpectedly.

MANDARIN: Is your name Mofongo?

MOFONGA: Certainly not! O Magic One, you must have mistaken me for that Puerto Rican dish "Mofongo."

MANDARIN: And what makes you think I have misnamed you, my dear?

MOFONGA: You see, my name is Mofon*gah*!

MANDARIN: I was pretty close.

MOFONGA: I'll say you were. Get away from me, you three-inch fool!

MANDARIN: If I had a thousand pieces of gold I would give them all to you.

MOFONGA: A thousand pieces of gold! That's not enough; my price is high.

MANDARIN: Mofonga, I think you are too high.

*(*GOD *and the* DEVIL *enter above.)*

[GOD: Will nothing on earth please you?

DEVIL: No, Lord! It's bad. I so deplore men's wretchedness, even I would rather not torment them anymore.]

GOD: Know you one Mandarin?

DEVIL: The magic one?

GOD: My servant.

[DEVIL: He serves you strangely, I think. The fool refrains from earthly meat and drink. His spirit's ferment drives him far, himself half conscious of his madness. He demands of heaven its brightest star, and of earth its highest gladness. Yet all that's close, and all that's distant, can't satisfy his troubled soul an instant.

GOD: Though now he serves me with confusion, I shall soon lead him from delusion. The gardener knows, when leafy green appears, that flowers and fruits shall crown the coming years.

DEVIL: What will you wager? Him shall you yet lose, if you let me gently lead him as I choose!] Ha haaaa!!

[GOD: So long as he lives on earth, I do concur. For while man strives, he will, in striving, err.

DEVIL: Thanks! I do not willingly traffic with the deceased. For me, a fresh, plump *cheek* is like a *feast*!] (GOD *gooses* DEVIL, *pinches his cheek*) Ha haaa!

GOD: *(Laughing)* [Enough! So let it be! Divert this spirit from his original source, if you can lead him on your downward course. But stand abashed when forced to confess, that even in darkness a good man retains the way of righteousness.

DEVIL: Agreed, for that won't last. I'm bound to succeed. And you excuse my gloating when I win. Dust shall he eat, with relish, like the] *Cobra,* [my renownèd cousin.

GOD: That you may, if that's your due; I have never hated the likes of you. Of all the spirits that plague me with denying, I find the scoffer least trying. Man loves unconditional ease, and so gets lazy; I'm glad to send the Devil to tease and drive him crazy. But ye true children of heaven, rejoice in beauty's living profusion. The creative essence, ever-growing, enfolds you in bonds of love sure. What hovers in changeful seeming, fix firm with thoughts that forever endure.]

(GOD exits. [ELWYNN CHAMBERPOT enters.])

ELWYNN:
   Truth says, of old the art of making plays
   Was to content the people; and their praise
   Was to the poet money, wine, and bays.

   But in this age a sect of writers are,
   That only for particular likings care,
   And will taste nothing that is popular.

   With such we mingle neither brains nor breasts;
   Our wishes, like to those make public feasts,
   And not to please the cook's taste but the guests'.

   Yet if those cunning palates hither come,
   They shall find guests' entreaty, and good room;
   And though all relish not, sure there will be some,

That when they leave their seats shall make them say,
Who wrote that piece, could so have wrote a play;
But that he knew this was the better way.

For, to present all custard or all tart,
And have no other meats to bear a part,
Or to want bread and salt, were but coarse art.

The poet prays you then, with better thought
To sit; and when his cates are all in brought,
Though there be none far-fet, there will dear-bought,

Be fit for ladies: some for lords, knights, squires;
Some for your waiting-wench, and city-wires;
Some for your men, and daughters of Whitefriars.

Nor is it only while you keep your seat
Here that his feast will last; but you shall eat
A week at ord'naries on his broken meat:
　　　If his muse be true,
　　　Who commends her to you.

ACT I

Scene: *Hotel lobby.*

(Roman marble statuary. Thick carpets. Potted palms. Roaming BELLHOPS *assisting potted guests with thick accents.)*

CRAMWELL: This is Big Hotel. A woman was raped in this hotel by the same man in the same elevator on the same floor at the same time every day for two weeks. *She* says it was rape. Here comes Birdshitskaya, the great ballerina.

(Enter BIRDSHITSKAYA. Swan Lake *plays. She is a great and beautiful ballerina.)*

BIRDSHITSKAYA: *(To* CRAMWELL, *heavy Russian accent)* Tell to effrevan Ayam not to be disturbed for.
CRAMWELL: How's that?
BIRDSHITSKAYA: No von understandse me!
CRAMWELL: I beg your . . .
BIRDSHITSKAYA: Leef me alone! Leef me alone! Ven vill dey see Ayam just a vomon for? Vat is the use of being the great artist for? No von sees me for vat Ayam! *(She rushes out desperately)*
CRAMWELL: My Russian is rusty.

(Mysterious Chinese music plays. Enter the MAGIC MANDARIN.*)*

MANDARIN: *(Chinese accent)* You have a loom?
CRAMWELL: Yes.
MANDARIN: Need velly quiet loom.
CRAMWELL: Room 214, sign here. *(*MANDARIN *signs)* Magic Mandarin. What a moniker! Is your name really Magic Mandarin?
MANDARIN: Yes.

CRAMWELL: How'd you get a name like Magic Mandarin?
MANDARIN: I'm magic.

(Phone rings. CRAMWELL answers.)

CRAMWELL: Yes? Birdshitskaya threatening suicide? Throw herself off our roof? Don't let her do it. Talk her out of it. Reason with her! Humor her! Dear me no! This will give the hotel a bad name! Don't let her throw herself off our roof!

(BIRDSHITSKAYA appears above and throws an effigy of herself off the roof. It lands in front of the desk.)

CRAMWELL: *(To BELLHOP)* Is she hurt?
BELLHOP: *(Picking up limp dummy)* No, but she will never dance again. *(Carries dummy off)*
CRAMWELL: Thank God she's not hurt.

(CRAMWELL continues with MANDARIN in pantomime while CHOCHA CALIENTE and MR. X steal in downstage of potted palm.)

MR. X: It was a lucky thing for us we were able to slip in here during the confusion caused by Birdshitskaya's plunge.
CHOCHA: She wore a plunging neckline.
MR. X: One more line like that and I'll wring your neck.

(CRAMWELL rings BELLHOP.)

CHOCHA: Where will you get the ring?

(CRAMWELL rings for BELLHOP again.)

MR. X: Quiet, you idiot, or you'll ruin everything! There's our man!
CHOCHA: Which one?
MR. X: The Oriental one of course, you fool!
CHOCHA: Quite right. The coarse fool of an Oriental!
MR. X: *(Slugs CHOCHA who falls into the potted palm)* I'm warning you. Another false move like that and . . . *(Draws hand across his throat)*
CHOCHA: You mean? *(Repeats gesture)*
MR. X: Yes! *(Gesture again)*
CHOCHA: Oh no! Not . . . *(Repeats same gesture)*
MR. X: Now here's the plan. At exactly a quarter to one, the Magic Mandarin will ask to have his bags carried up. The clerk will ring for the Bellhop. And then *(Ominously)* you know the rest. O.K.?
CHOCHA: O.K. *(Long pause. They look from side to side furtively)* I don't know the rest!
MR. X: You mean you forgot already?
CHOCHA: I didn't mean it!
MR. X: You make me sick. *(CRAMWELL rings for BELLHOP)* We've no time. Just do as I do. *(They jump the BELLHOP. There is a struggle behind the potted palm. They emerge disguised in his clothes)*
CRAMWELL: Take this gentleman's bags to room 214. And make it snappy. *(They pick up bags and exit left with MANDARIN. Phone rings)* Hello, Big Hotel. Birdshitskaya? *(Dramatically)* No. She won't be able to make it tonight or any other night. In fact, she will never dance again! Yes, we're all heartbroken. It is a great tragedy. You're welcome. Oh, don't mention it. *(Pause)* No

. . . thanks. I can't dance a step. *(Pause)* No, really, I have two left feet. Yes. *(Pause)* Well, it's nice of you to have thought of me. All right. Bye now.

BELLHOP: *(Ringing alarm bell)* Help ho! Help ho! Sleep! They do murther sleep!

CRAMWELL: What is it, boy?

BELLHOP: O insufferable woe. *(Rings bell)*

CRAMWELL: Stop ringing that confounded bell and answer me!

BELLHOP: Little did we think as we hollowed his narrow bed and smoothed down his lonely pillow!

(GUESTS enter in confusion in nightwear, with candles.)

CHOCHA: What happened? What is it?

BELLHOP: The Magic Mandarin is dead!

CRAMWELL: Dead? Oh, no. This will give the hotel a bad name!

MR. X: How did he die this untimely death?

BELLHOP: He was murthered!

(Women faint.)

CRAMWELL: Shhhh!

BELLHOP: Slain!

CRAMWELL: Don't say that!

BELLHOP: I needs must shout it! Murthered! Slain! He is most cruelly undone.

GUESTS: Gasp! Shocking! We're not safe in our own beds. Scandalous! Tch. Tch. Tch. I'm changing my hotel. Me, too. I'm moving out.

CRAMWELL: Oh, no! Now see what you've done?

(Enter BIRDSHITSKAYA.)

BIRDSHITSKAYA: What's all this noise about? Vat has happened?

BELLHOP: The Magic Mandarin desperately is dead!

BIRDSHITSKAYA: In this hotel? Under our very roof?

BELLHOP: Yes, my lady.

BIRDSHITSKAYA: What was the cause of his untimely death?

BELLHOP: He was shot *(BIRDSHITSKAYA faints)*, stabbed, strangled, hung, poisoned, garroted, had a heart attack, an acid attack, an ulcer attack, a cavalry attack. In short, he died of old age and other unknown natural causes.

BIRDSHITSKAYA: *(Coming to)* He was a foolish man. Did he leave a large estate?

BELLHOP: Considerable.

MR. X: Let's divvy up the loot before the police come!

CRAMWELL: Good idea!

BIRDSHITSKAYA: Ve must act fast.

BELLHOP: Hagies on the watch.

CRAMWELL: Nibsies on his rings.

BIRDSHITSKAYA: Did you notice any gold fillings?

CHOCHA: I'm first. I want that kimono *(Etc.)* . . .

(Enter MAGIC MANDARIN. Crowd gasps.)

MANDARIN: What's all this noise about? What has happened?

(BIRDSHITSKAYA faints.)

ALL: We thought you were dead!

MANDARIN: I was. But I am lisen.

ELWYNN: *(To* DESK CLERK*)* Is there a Norma Desmond staying in this hotel?

DRAGO: I don't know, I'm new here. Let me check the register.

ELWYNN: I've checked every flea-bitten hotel in this part of the world. This is the last one; she must be here.

(Enter NORMA DESMOND, *drunk.)*

NORMA: *(To* DESK CLERK*)* Are there any messages for me?

DRAGO: This gentleman has been looking for you.

NORMA: Lynn!

ELWYNN: Norma!

NORMA: Well, Lynn, we haven't seen each other in a long time.

ELWYNN: How long would you say it's been, Norma?

NORMA: Five or six years I'd say.

ELWYNN: You've changed, Norma.

NORMA: *(With mock alarm)* Have I lost my looks?

ELWYNN: No, Norma, you're more lovelier than ever.

NORMA: You haven't changed a bit, Lynn. Just a bit grayer I expect.

ELWYNN: Something about you has changed. What is it about you that seems so . . . changed?

NORMA: It's true, Lynn. I have changed. I've changed my name.

ELWYNN: Married?

NORMA: No, it took more than one man to change my name to . . . Shanghai Lily!

ELWYNN: Shanghai Lily!

NORMA: Yes, the white flower of China! You've heard of me, and you've always believed what you heard.

ELWYNN: I still do. I've been tracking you down the last five years. I've looked in every flea-bitten and five-star hotel on this continent. I knew one day I'd find you. I know you know in your heart of hearts, you haven't forgotten . . . the CONTRACT. *(He brandishes a yellowed contract)*

NORMA: *(Shrieks)* That contract isn't worth the paper it's written on!

ELWYNN: What do you mean? I paid two hundred and fifty dollars to have this contract notarized!

NORMA: A legitimate notary only charges two dollars! Late Show, Late Late Show, and not a dime in my pocket. Like Lupe Velez was I, these sloping shoulders, this gracelessness. My career bends before me. Too far for me to put a hand there once or lightly. Mine is far, and his *(Indicates* ELWYNN*)* secret as our eyes. Secrets, silent, stony sit in the dark palaces of both our hearts. Secrets, weary of their tyranny, tyrants willing to be dethroned. *(To* DESK CLERK*)* I demand that you throw this man out of the hotel.

DRAGO: We can't do that, Miss Desmond. Mr. Chamberpot is just checking into the hotel.

NORMA: If no one else has the balls to throw you out of this hotel, I will!

*(*NORMA *attacks* ELWYNN. *He lifts her over his head in an airplane hold, twirls her around three times, and throws her the length of the stage.)*

NORMA: *(Disheveled)* I've never been so insulted in my life! *(Rises)* Please Lynn, come up to my room. I don't want to create a scene here in the lobby. *(Exits through the elevator)*

ELWYNN: *(To* DRAGO*)* What room is Miss Desmond staying in?
DRAGO: Room 214.

*(*NORMA *switches on a lamp in her room above. Searches for a bottle, pours herself a drink. There is a knock at the door, and* ELWYNN *enters.)*

ELWYNN: Drinking again?
NORMA: Still drinking!
ELWYNN: You've had enough!
NORMA: I never have enough! Pour me another.

(He grabs the bottle and spills out the contents.)

NORMA: *(Screams)* Are you crazy? That's good liquor!
ELWYNN: You're going downhill fast, Norma. I can remember the time you could make a whole audience weep just reading the telephone book! All my work and you're pissing it away!
NORMA: You got your ten percent!
ELWYNN: I knew someday you'd begrudge me my ten percent. *(He grabs her face)*
NORMA: Take your hands off me!
ELWYNN: *(Holds her face to a mirror)* Just look at that face!
NORMA: No!
ELWYNN: I see the little lines and wrinkles now. You're finished. Ya understand? Soon the public will tire of this face!
NORMA: Never!
ELWYNN: You're all washed up. *(He throws her down)* Norma, Norma, you know what [your] name reminds me of, Norma?
NORMA: *(Drunkenly)* No, what?
ELWYNN: The opera, *Norma.*
NORMA: By Bellini?
ELWYNN: Yes, and when I think of the opera *Norma* by Bellini, do you know what that reminds me of?
NORMA: No, what?
ELWYNN: The "Casta Diva," and when I think of the "Casta Diva," I wanna casta diva inta the river! *(He exits, throwing her to the floor)*
NORMA: He has no heart, that man. *(She reaches desperately for the telephone book)* Who will come to my aid? *(She reads ten names at random from the telephone book, and rejects them all with a "No.")* Lupe Velez? She was always good for a few bucks. *(She reaches for phone)* Hello, desk? This is Norma Desmond.
DRAGO: *(Aside to audience)* The madly chic Norma Desmond! *(To* NORMA*)* Yes, Miss Desmond, is there anything I can do for you?
NORMA: Could you connect me with Lupe Velez? I believe she's staying in this hotel.
DRAGO: I'll see if I can get her. *(To* BELLHOP*)* Call for Miss Lupe Velez. I think she's at the Sacred Pool of the St. Mark's Baths.
BELLHOP: Call for Lupe Velez! Call for Lupe Velez!

*(*LUPE VELEZ *enters down the aisle from the audience in bathing attire, a towel wrapped around her head. She wears a small robe.)*

LUPE: Who dares to interrupt me when I'm sipping complimentary orange juice?

DRAGO: There's a call for you, Miss Velez.

LUPE: *(Taking phone)* Hallo. Who is zeez?

NORMA: *(In a gravel voice)* Hello, Lupe, dahling. This is Norma Desmond.

LUPE: Who?

NORMA: Norma Desmond.

LUPE: Oh, hello Norma. What seems to be wrong with your voice?

NORMA: I haven't been getting much sleep lately, dahling. Lupe, could you do me a favor? It seems that I've lost my purse. Could you lend me five dollars until I can cash a check?

LUPE: Oh, I'm sorry Norma, you caught me at the wrong time. I just paid my hotel bill.

NORMA: Lupe, I need the five dollars for cab fare. I have a dinner engagement.

LUPE: Couldn't you take the subway?

NORMA: I can't be seen coming out of the subway again. Listen, Lupe, let's drop the shallow mask of pretense. I'm flat broke, I haven't got a dime. I haven't made a picture in years. I've got to get uptown to shake down a john at a cocktail party.

LUPE: There are plenty of johns in this hotel, Norma.

NORMA: You've shaken all the johns in this hotel until their dentures rattled. Listen to me, you cheap spic! Think of the pictures you cheated me out of. The Late Show and The Late Late Show . . .

LUPE: *(Flaring up)* How dare you call me a spic! I was born in Mexico. You're nothing but a cunt-lapping wino! *(She hangs up and exits calling, "Johnny, I'm coming")*

NORMA: *(Desperately jiggling the receiver)* Lupe! Lupe!

(Blackout in Room 214.)

ACT II

(Enter BIRDSHITSKAYA *and* MAGIC MANDARIN.*)*

BIRDSHITSKAYA: Mental cruelty.

MANDARIN: Excessive sexual demands.

BIRDSHITSKAYA: Nonsupport.

MANDARIN: Infidelity.

BIRDSHITSKAYA: Bizarre practices.

MANDARIN: Bad breath.

BIRDSHITSKAYA: Cold feet.

MANDARIN: Divorce!

BIRDSHITSKAYA: Divorce!

DRAGO: I didn't know you were married.

BOTH: We're not!

DRAGO: Well, that makes getting a divorce a lot easier.

BIRDSHITSKAYA: Oh, no, it doesn't. Now we have to go through all the trouble of getting married so we can get a divorce.

MANDARIN: You see the inconvenience. A successful attempt was made on my life earlier in this play. He told me the mob was taking over his union. And he's bringing me evidence to prove it.

DRAGO: We'll locate it, Mr. Mandarin.

MANDARIN: I want the police to locate it!

DRAGO: You'll soon find out that the United States doesn't own Chicago!

MANDARIN: *(Confidentially)* Men are still losing their heads over it.

BIRDSHITSKAYA: *(Aside to DRAGO)* I found it the other night at the dock.

MANDARIN: I must find out. Before tonight. Before I dare sleep in that room, tonight. I am risen, but they have murthered sleep. *(Dramatic exit)*

DRAGO: He got out and started looking around for something.

BIRDSHITSKAYA: Jim, we got something. He couldn't trust anybody else.

DRAGO: It's registered to Blane. It's the murder weapon. Sit down, will you? You hang around the docks a lot?

BIRDSHITSKAYA: What are you questioning me for? I came here to help you. I don't want to give you a song and dance. I'm leveling with you.

DRAGO: *(Aside to audience)* If I can convict Blane, I'm good as elected. *(To BIRDSHITSKAYA)* What did Mr. Blane say? You have stated that Mr. Blane came to your apartment at nine o'clock. Let me remind you that you are under oath.

BIRDSHITSKAYA: Is this confidential?

DRAGO: I don't know.

BIRDSHITSKAYA: No! No! One more witness has to be eliminated. Sylvia Clarkson. Artie was with me that night. He couldn't have killed Mr. Fremont.

DRAGO: *(Slaps her)* That's a sample of what it's like. You never saw Blane at her apartment.

BIRDSHITSKAYA: We have, your honor. We find the defendant guilty of murder in the first degree.

(Blackout.)

CHOCHA: We got trouble. That girl we planted.

MR. X: Get to the point!

CHOCHA: I expect to read about it in tomorrow's paper.

MR. X: *(Knocks her out)* Don't have to worry about it. Just sit there and take it nice and easy. You gonna end up in the river with cement bedroom slippers.

(Sound of an old 78 phonograph is heard playing silent screen vamp music, then a scream, and MATA HARI enters, carrying a sword.)

MR. X: Are you the new spy? What's your name, your social security number? You are three days and twenty minutes late.

MATA HARI: I am the daughter of the moon. I was stopped in Tangiers by the police. They mistook me for Andy Warhol and tortured me for two long days.

MR. X: What about the other day?

MATA HARI: That was Thursday!

MR. X: So?

MATA HARI: So Thursday is my day off.

MR. X: But what about the twenty minutes?

MATA HARI: Oh, I missed the subway again. Do you know if the Magic Mandarin is in?

MR. X: The Magic Mandarin? You are the first caller the Magic Mandarin ever had.

MATA HARI: Perhaps you are right. He's my twin brother. We are the last of the Mandarins and we should stay together. What's the room number?

MR. X: Room 214.

(Exit MATA HARI, MR. X, *and* CHOCHA CALIENTE. TRILBY *crosses lobby of hotel and goes into elevator, passing* DRAGO *and* MRS. MADIGAN, *the hotel scrubwoman, who are standing by the desk.)*

MRS. MADIGAN: There she goes, spreadin' her legs seven days a week, and not even closin' them on the sabbath.

(Scene: SVENGALI'*s room. A knock at the door.)*

SVENGALI: *(Opening door)* Madame. Trilby. Madame.
TRILBY: Professor Svengali! *(He kisses her hand)* Monsieur.
SVENGALI: Monsieur is composing.
TRILBY: Ah, composing. I'm sorry I disturbed you. I'm early?
SVENGALI: On the contrary, you are just on time.
TRILBY: I could hardly wait for this evening. My days are so empty.
SVENGALI: Ja liebchen, I know just how you feel. I am empty too.
TRILBY: *(Laughing)* Ah, how can you be? You have so many other pupils.
SVENGALI: Ja, naturlich, but no one who responds like you. Ah, now, what did we do last?
TRILBY: Don't you remember?
SVENGALI: I am speaking about music! Ah, here! Ja, there now, I remember! Riggerue robato, riggerue robato, riggerue robato . . .

(He plays. She sings.)

SVENGALI: Come on! Come on!
TRILBY: *(Trills two times)* Ah-h. Ah-h!
   We're off on a hunt while you hear trumpets blowing.
   (Trills two times) Ah-h. Ah-h!
   Everyone has such fun when the tally ho's blowing.
   (Coloratura four trills) Ah Ah Ah Ah.
   Oh the joy: for each girl and boy. On the hunt.

(Hold long trill into a scream)
(Repeat coloratura four trills)

   Tally ho! Cheery-O!
   Carefree go a-playing
   Everyone! Oh, the fun!
   We're on the way to the hunt!
   Over hill, over dale!
   Hear the horns a-playing
   Here we go! Tally ho-o-o.
   We're on our way to the *(High note)* HUNT—
SVENGALI: *(Interrupts her)* Never mind!
TRILBY: What's the matter?
SVENGALI: *(Laughs)* Heh. Heh. Nothing, darling. It is beautiful. But such a delicate instrument must not be strained. Come now, we rest.
TRILBY: *(Softly)* Ah.
SVENGALI: You are comfortable?
TRILBY: Yes.
SVENGALI: Because there is a little something I must tell you.
TRILBY: I have something to tell you. I've left my husband.

SVENGALI: Huh?

TRILBY: I've left him for good.

SVENGALI: And . . . er . . . how much has he left you?

TRILBY: Do you think I'd take money from such a brute? Why, I threw it in his face!

SVENGALI: He gave you money and you threw it back at him?

TRILBY: But he . . . he bit me on the wrist and, and, kicked me. Oh *(Tearfully)*, you have no idea what I've been through.

SVENGALI: And you left your husband, without a settlement?

TRILBY: I've come to you—just as I am.

SVENGALI: With no settlement at all—nothing?

TRILBY: Nothing. . . . Except me.

SVENGALI: Errrrrr. *(Turns away)*

TRILBY: Svengali, you, you don't want me? But . . . but you promised! But, my voice. It's yours now. To make us both famous.

SVENGALI: *(Laughs)*

TRILBY: But you told me so often. *(SVENGALI paces)* But I've no other place to go. There's only you left. *(Heart breaking)* Oh, I worship you, Svengali . . . I'd even die for you! *(He trains his eyes on her)* Oh, don't look at me like that, Svengali. *(Pause)* Oh, don't look at me like that! *(Becoming hysterical)* Take your eyes off me, Svengali! Take your eyes off me! *(Screaming)* No more! I can't bear it! *(She screams a long scream and runs out, dragging her fur after her. The sound of her scream dies away. Downstairs the elevator door opens.* TRILBY *exits across the hotel lobby, out the revolving door, still screaming the same scream)*

MRS. MADIGAN: Oh, Mr. Drago, doesn't she have a lovely voice. I used [to] do a bit of singing myself, ya know.

DRAGO: Would you favor us with a selection?

(She sings "Danny Boy" and DRAGO RUBLES *follows with a reprise on the alto recorder.)*

MRS. MADIGAN: It kinda keeps ya goin'. I'm goin' to the pawn to get me four quid, five shillings. And you can do what you like me bucko. Saint Cecilia, Jesus, Mary, and Cardinal Fanny Spellman, it's another bottle I'm wantin'. This one's empty. A fine thing to come rollin' in on top a ya. And after all my prayin' to Saint Frigid and the Little Flower. *(She passes out in a drunken stupor)*

(Enter MANDARIN, *drunk.)*

DRAGO: By mine honor, half drunk. What is he at the gate, cousin?

MANDARIN: A gentleman.

DRAGO: A gentleman! What gentleman?

MANDARIN: 'Tis a gentleman here. A plague of these pickle herring! How now sot!

DRAGO: *(Aside)* Utter astonishment, I imagine.

MANDARIN: *(Aside)* But one knows nothing for certain.

(Thunder and lightning.)

DRAGO: I will go to the city and return as soon as possible. Meanwhile, promise me that you will keep your hand on a revolver at all times . . . to protect you from this mysterious assassin. . . .

MANDARIN: I will . . . I will take care of myself and await your return. I will pass the time thinking of the happiness we will share when I receive my inheritance.

(Exit DRAGO. *Enter* BIRDSHITSKAYA.*)*

BIRDSHITSKAYA: *(Gruffly)* Did you see a young lad passing this way in the early morning or the fall of night?
MANDARIN: You're a queer kind to walk in not saluting at all!
BIRDSHITSKAYA: Did you see the young man?
MANDARIN: What kind was he?
BIRDSHITSKAYA: He had a linen stock on one leg and a kersey boot-hose on the other, gartered with a red and blue list; an old hat and "the humor of forty fancies" pricked in't for a feather: a monster, a very in apparel, and not like a Christian footboy or a gentleman's lackey.
MANDARIN: *(Aside)* What'd she say? What'd she say?
BIRDSHITSKAYA: No one understands me! *(She dons false nose, eyeglasses, and mustache. Exits)*
MANDARIN: *(Sings)* Chinatown, my Chinatown . . . *(He falls asleep)*

(While the MANDARIN *sleeps,* MR. X *and* CHOCHA *enter in an Apache dance. The impression should be that the dance has been in progress for some time.)*

CHOCHA: De quelle couleur sont les crayons?
MR. X: Les crayons sont bleus. Ils sont bleus.
CHOCHA: De quelle couleur est la robe de Lucie?
MR. X: La robe de Lucie est blanche. Elle est blanche.
CHOCHA: De quelle couleur sont les brosses?
MR. X: Les brosses sont vertes. Elles sont vertes.
CHOCHA: De quelle couleur est la table?
MR. X: Elle est brune.
CHOCHA: De quelle couleur est la cravate de Jean?
MR. X: Elle est rouge.
CHOCHA: Où sont le drapeau français?
MR. X: Voici le drapeau français.
CHOCHA: Où sont les stylos noirs?
MR. X: Voilà les stylos noirs!

(There is music as of the flight of swans. MANDARIN *awakes.)*

MANDARIN: Let the Cobra Cunt Ceremony begin!
CHOCHA: Best consult the Tarot, my son, before the Cobra Cunt Ceremony.
MANDARIN: You mean about the successful attempt made on my life earlier in the play?
CHOCHA: Yes, my son, ask the Tarot now, before it is too late.
MANDARIN: I will.
CHOCHA: Pick a card, any card. *(He does so)* Be careful of dubious matters, disputes, and discussions. Something ill will befall you. I see a run-in with the cops. Later on, all will turn out well. Your lucky number is one, your correct weight is 145 pounds.
MANDARIN: Let the Cobra Cunt Ceremony begin!

*(*MARTOK, *the High Priestess, storms in.* BIRDSHITSKAYA *throws herself off the roof.)*

MARTOK: You think I'm so easily gotten rid of? You have another think coming!

CHOCHA: This is the High Priestess of Big Hotel.

MANDARIN: Pleased to meet you.

CHOCHA: I'm sure she will help us.

MANDARIN: Are you boss of this hotel?

MARTOK: No, just the High Priestess.

CHOCHA: If you're the priestess, you can help my friend out of this jam.

MARTOK: I'm a High Priestess. I'm high.

CHOCHA: But what about my friend?

MARTOK: I'm afraid I can't do anything about that. You see, strangers in this hotel are executed.

CHOCHA: You have a kind face. I know you'll help my friend.

MARTOK: Mofonga has gone to the Cobra Temple through the Royal Tunnel. The people know the price of peace. The Firepit Restaurant cries for more dishwashers. You shall see for yourself the cruel barbarism by which Mofonga holds our people. Fear has made them religious fanatics.

(Enter BELLHOP. *Frantic,* CHOCHA, MR. X, *and* MARTOK *torture the* MANDARIN.*)*

BELLHOP: Somewhere along the line, I have lost the thread of the narrative.

MANDARIN: Don't look for it here, young man. We have a play to put on.

BELLHOP: The whole play is falling to pieces. I've lost the thread of the narrative.

MARTOK: *(Throwing* BELLHOP *down and riding him like a horse)* Quiet, you fool. You'll give everything away. If you find it rough going now, how will you ever find the balls to do the Cobra Cunt Ceremony! *(Rides him out)*

*(*MR. X *and* CHOCHA *carry* MANDARIN *out through elevator. Phone rings.)*

CRAMWELL: *(Entering, answering phone)* Hello, Big Hotel. Birdshitskaya, no, she hasn't come down yet. *(Pause)* Her comeback! Yes, yes. A wonderful event in the dance world. In the real world even!

*(Grand entrance—*BIRDSHITSKAYA.*)*

BIRDSHITSKAYA: Comeback! Did I hear somvan say comeback?

CRAMWELL: I did.

BIRDSHITSKAYA: *(Angry)* Comeback! How Ay hate dat expression! The word is "return." If dey tink Ayam coming back now, they've got another ting coming! They didn't want me when I was a hopeless cripple. Not good enuff to dance the great roles they said! But now that I've fought my way back from the grave, they're on their knees. *(Laughs wildly)* Hah! They'll eat those words, "not good enough." They'll crawl back to me. And when I get good and ready to dance . . . I'LL DANCE . . . ON THEIR FACES! *(Exit)*

(Enter BELLHOP *as in old Philip Morris ad. Scene: The Firepit Restaurant.)*

BELLHOP: Call for Blondine Blondell! Call for Blondine Blondell!

(Enter BLONDINE *on the arm of* DRAGO RUBLES.*)*

DRAGO: We're going to go to Marshall Field. I'm gonna buy you the sleaziest sexiest gownless evening strap you ever saw. *(To* WAITER*)* Table for two.

BLONDINE: Oh Drago, that sounds just elegant and kind of dreamy, if I may say so. *(Looking at menu)* How about some orange juice, Joey? *(Aside to audience)* I ate Limburger cheese with bagels for breakfast. I ate mofongo with garlic dressing at lunch. I ate steak and onions at dinner. But he'll never know, 'cause I always stay kissing sweet the new Dazzle-Dent way.

DRAGO: I take it this place is soundproof?

BLONDINE: I don't trust the waiter. He is too short.

DRAGO: I think Blane knows more than he lets on. He's shielding someone. Sylvia Clarkson saw him with a blonde the night of February second.

BLONDINE: *(Rising suddenly)* Build your Maxwell. I'll be right back. I think I'll take my wig off.

DRAGO: *(Roughly forcing her to sit down)* You can't afford to take a week off now. We need you for the Cobra Cunt Ceremony.

(Spotlight on WAITER.)

WAITER: Tonight, Ladies and Gentlemen, the Firepit Restaurant is proud to present—just back from her tour of the Near East where she packed nightclubs—Mata Hari!

(Applause. The whole cast comes on and dances to "The Lady in Red.")

BLONDINE: Listen, they're playing our song. *(Number ends)*

DRAGO: *(To WAITER)* Oh, Pierre! Bring in the missing persons' file.

WAITER: A man called Lumis.

BLONDINE: You know something about my husband, Lumis!

WAITER: On the night of July twelve–thirteen, wife awakened him, saying that she had heard someone walking with high heels in Lumis's museum. Lumis also heard the footsteps. Identifying them as those of his sweetheart, Sylvia Clarkson. "I used to recognize Sylvia in Stockholm merely by the sound of her footsteps," Lumis said. But Clarkson was not in Lumis's museum. In fact, there was no one in the museum. The single door to the room was locked and Lumis had the key in his bedroom. Nevertheless, he went down, unlocked his museum, and made a thorough search. There was not the slightest sign that anyone had been in the room. A few days later, Lumis received word that his girlfriend, Sylvia Clarkson, had died in Stockholm at precisely the hour her footsteps had been heard in the locked museum.

BLONDINE: Where is he? You know something about my husband?

MATA HARI: *(Holding up a fan)* Ever seen this before?

BLONDINE: It's his! *(Hysterical)* What are you all standing around for? Look for him! Find him!

WAITER: *(Aside)* In Niagara Falls?

MATA HARI: Is there anyone you can stay with? A relative or close friend?

BLONDINE: You've all been very kind. But I'd rather walk. *(Wiggles out)*

MANDARIN: *(Goes to phone and dials)* Hello. Is Mrs. Starkie there? This is Mrs. Cutler. It's about Lumis. No, I don't want to speak to Blane. Lumis! Lumis! *(Pause)* L as in Lincoln, U as in Utrecht, M as in Massey, I as in Ingres, S as in Synagogue. Lumis! Tell him I called. *(Pause)* Cutler. *(Pause)* C as in Cutler, U as in Utrecht, L as in Lumis, E as in Erie, R as in Robespierre . . . *(Pause)* Robespierre. *(Pause)* R as in Raw, W as in Wren. A small bird. *(Pause)* No, this is not Mr. Robespierre. Mr. Starkie. Synagogue. Yes! Raw. Utrecht, Blane. Yes. No-o-o. *(He hears bells in the tower)* Oh, Blondine, they're playing our song. *(Exit)*

ACT III

(The elevator opens, revealing SANTA CLAUS, *who falls forward on his face, revealing* MR. X *and* CHOCHA *behind him.* MR. X *wipes the blood from his knife.)*

MR. X: Have the corpse leave his name at the desk.

CHOCHA: That's $12.50.

MR. X: Well, what is it? Are we leaving or are they going to keep us here all day?

CHOCHA: They've got some kind of roadblock up ahead.

MR. X: In 1883, the French tightrope walker, Blondine, walked a rope clear across Niagara Falls!

CHOCHA: There's no escape. Too bad they can't play it for you now, Mr. X. *(They strangle each other and fall dead on stage)*

(Enter NORMA. *Alone in her room.)*

NORMA: Of human sufferage. Of common aspirings. You free yourself and then fly according to . . . I've seen sidereal archipelagos, islands whose delirious skies open to wanderers. It is in such bottomless nights as these that you sleep exiled. Oh, countless golden birds, oh, force to come! *(Knock at the door)* Oh, come in!

*(*ELWYNN *enters and collapses drunk at* NORMA's *feet.)*

NORMA: *(Offers him a bottle of Gypsy Rose)* Quench those parched lips, dahling.

ELWYNN: The water's terrible here, Norma.

NORMA: Well, whose idea was it to come to Mexico, huh?

ELWYNN: But, Norma, we had to go on location for your comeback. It was the perfect role for you, Norma. The Aztec Princess.

NORMA: Aztec Princess! Aztec Princess! What kinda role is that for a white woman, huh? The mosquitoes are eating me alive!

ELWYNN: Dawns are heartbreaking.

NORMA: True, I have wept too much. Cruel all moons. And bitter the suns.

ELWYNN: Within this restless hurried modern world, we took our hearts' full pleasure, you and I. Now the white sails of our ships are furled. And spent the lading of our Argosy.

NORMA: Wherefore my cheeks before their time are wan for very weeping is my gladness fled. Sorrow hath paled my lips vermillion and ruin draws the curtain of my bed.

ELWYNN: But all this life has been to thee no more than lyre or lute or subtle spell or of the music of the sea that sleeps a mimic echo in the shell. Norma, Norma, it's all a dream. Or, dare I say, dare I say . . .

BOTH: Nightmare!

ELWYNN: By Neptune's trident do not despair so utterly. I have word from C.B.

NORMA: deMille? deMille? Give it me and then go. You who were my agent.

ELWYNN: Were?

NORMA: You belong to Lupe Velez. Someday, all of Universal-International will be hers. And I . . . just a prisoner of Paramount. *(Reads)* "Dear Norma: Please come and see me Monday morning if you are free. I have something to discuss with you. It's about your car. It's the only one made that year whose chassis is still in such good condition. Yours truly, C.B." He's read my *Salomé* script. He wants me for the part. I'm perfect for it.

ELWYNN: How about a little nuggie?

NORMA: I will kiss thy mouth, O Jokanaan! I will kiss thy mouth!

ELWYNN: Touch me. Soft eyes. Soft, soft hands. I am quiet here alone. Sad, too. What is that word known to all men? Oh, touch, touch me.

NORMA: It is his eyes above all that are terrible. They are like black Egyptian torches, burning black holes in the black tapestries of Tyre.

ELWYNN: Just a quickie! *(Turns to audience)* When she first came to us, she had more courage, talent and beauty and heart than ever came together in one young person. But, a team of press agents working overtime can do terrible things to the human spirit.

NORMA: And remember, I never work before one o'clock. And, I'm driven to the studio in a chauffeured limousine. Desmond and deMille! Desmond and deMille! We'll make our greatest pictures! And I promise I'll never desert you again, you little people out there in the dark. And the camera! The camera! Tell Mr. deMille I'm ready for my close-up.

(Agent throws a pie in NORMA'*s face. Blackout. Lights up on* MANDARIN.*)*

MANDARIN: Oh, Father Divine, when does the Cobra Cunt Ceremony begin?

GOD: First you must rescue Rappuccini's daughter from the garden of poisonous flowers.

MANDARIN: Is that all?

GOD: No, there are three tasks. Accomplish this one first. The rest will be revealed to you later! Go, my boy, and get acquainted with the West. Compare the people of the West with those of the East—the way of the Occident with that of the Orient—and see where the two paths meet. Learn from the peoples of the Occident the things in which they are ahead of us. And make known to them the things in which the Orient has already reached the goal. Go and work in your way to bring these two paths together. But in the West, you will realize that the science of HATHA YOGA is not only the way to health, but also the world's only physical culture method based on the close union between body and soul. Although it is a science for building up the *Body,* it is nevertheless based on mental and spiritual forces. . . .

MANDARIN: *(Looking up with eyes shining)* Master, Master, I knew this a long time ago when I was endeavoring to build up my body. When I directed my attention to the different parts of my body, my muscles and nerve centers, I noticed that hitherto unknown spiritual powers developed within me. To the extent that I became master of my body, my willpower increased. You brought me back to life; you took a sickly, emaciated little boy and turned him into an athlete. You took me out of my physical ruin and led me back to myself! I promise you . . .

VOICE: Promise nothing, my boy! . . . The West is in a turmoil and seems to have little time to concern itself with the East. But go and do your duty. The sower seldom reaps. But if you succeed in passing on the Yoga of the body to only a few of your friends, you have done your duty to your brothers in the Occident. In any case, the teaching will only appeal to those whose minds are free from the blindness of materialism and whose spiritual world is open for a more beautiful and higher order of life. But remember, THIS IS YOUR MOST SACRED DUTY. WHEN YOU RECEIVE A MESSAGE FROM ME, ACROSS

THE SEAS, YOU WILL KNOW IT IS TIME FOR YOU TO COME HOME . . . THAT
YOUR NATIVE LAND IS CALLING YOU. . . . GO MY BOY. . . . HEAVEN BE WITH
YOU!

(BIRDSHITSKAYA throws herself off the roof. MARTOK enters.)

MARTOK: So, you are the brave one.

MANDARIN: Brave one?

MARTOK: Yes, I was curious to see the man who defied our laws and laughed
at our faith.

MANDARIN: You must have brought me here for some other reason besides just
curiosity. Tell me why I am in prison.

MARTOK: Because you were found in a Smaller Hotel. Because you bathed in
the Sacred Pool of the St. Mark's Baths. Profaned the person of the High
Priestess with your touch, violated her lips with your kiss. Each of these is a
crime punishable by death.

MANDARIN: That's four times I die. Too bad I only have one life to live. Let
me live it as a blonde. I'm appealing because I am about to die.

MARTOK: I don't find you appealing. You want to die blonde?

MANDARIN: I plead guilty to the first two. But, you're wrong on the others.
Yeah, I had a perfect right to kiss the lady in the pool. She had a right to kiss
me.

MARTOK: She . . .

MANDARIN: Certainly, and she liked it. Why not? We're gonna be married.

MARTOK: You're insane. This is a wild imagining of your decaying brain. She
is the priestess and she is going to marry me!

MANDARIN: One of us is mixed up. I'm sure the royal lady herself knows the
answer.

(Enter MR. X and GYPSY.)

GYPSY: Do not argue with her. Fear has made her a religious fanatic.

MR. X: The faithful grow more unfaithful to their queen. The gold tribute grows
less and less. Demand more! Punish them.

MARTOK: Come, let us go to the Firepit Restaurant, and discuss plans for the
Cobra Cunt Ceremony.

(All exit, except MANDARIN, who is left alone on stage.)

MANDARIN: All meaning alters with acceleration.

(MOFONGA enters.)

MOFONGA: Geef me that Cobra Jewel! Geef me that Cobra Jewel! Hey, where
did everybody go?

MANDARIN: They have all gone to the Cobra Temple to eat at the Firepit
Restaurant you have taught them to fear.

(Blackout.)

CRAMWELL: *(Phone rings)* Hello. Big Hotel. Yes! What? Birdshitskaya threatening to shoot herself?!!! Talk her out of it! Reason with her. Oh, this will give
the hotel a BAD NAME. *(A shot is heard offstage)* It is too late.

(BIRDSHITSKAYA throws herself off the roof.)

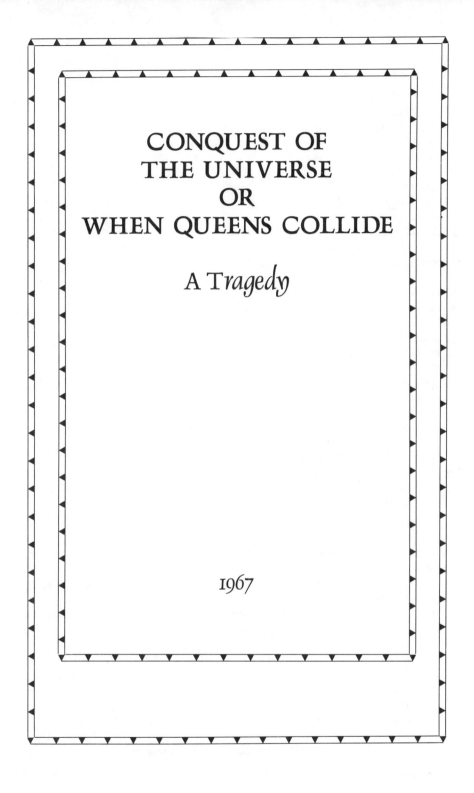

CONQUEST OF
THE UNIVERSE
OR
WHEN QUEENS COLLIDE

A Tragedy

1967

Dramatis Personae

TAMBERLAINE, *President of Earth*
BAJAZETH, *King of Mars*
COSROE, *brother of Zabina, a Martian prince*
MAGNAVOX, *King of Mercury*
ORTYGIUS, *Caliph of Jupiter*
TECHELLUS ⎤
USUMCASANE ⎦ *Tamberlaine's men*
ALICE, *First Lady of Earth*
ZABINA, *Queen of Mars*
EBEA, *her maid*
VENUS, *Queen of Venus*
CONSUELA, *her maid*
NATOLIA, *Queen of Saturn*
WITCH OF ENSOR
WAR
HUNGER
PESTILENCE
WOMAN IN A CELL
NEWSBOY
CHORUS OF FIRE WOMEN
BALLERINA OF URANUS

Scene 1: *The palace of Bajazeth, King of Mars.*

(TAMBERLAINE *is standing with his foot on the neck of* BAJAZETH, *who lies on the floor, vanquished.*)

TAMBERLAINE: And sooner shall the sun fall from his sphere than Tamberlaine be slain or overcome.

BAJAZETH: And sooner shall the sun fall from his sphere than Tamberlaine be slain or overcome.

ALICE: You've triumphed over Bajazeth, King of Mars. Now you are King, my beloved Tamberlaine.

TAMBERLAINE: *(Sotto voce)* President, not King, President. *(Aloud)* No hesitation to shoot in case of need. Every policeman must grasp the fact that inaction is a more serious crime than an error committed in the execution of orders received. Each bullet which leaves the barrel of a policeman's revolver is my bullet. If you call that a murder, it is I who am the murderer. These are my orders and I give them my full support. I assume the responsibility and I am not afraid.

ALICE: *(Pettishly)* President then.

TAMBERLAINE: *(To his men)* Take him away! And sterilize him! Come, Alice, we must find Zabina. With you beside me I shall not fail.

(*Trumpets. Exeunt* TAMBERLAINE *and* ALICE. *Enter* ZABINA *and her maid* EBEA, *running.*)

EBEA: *(In terror)* All Mars shakes with fear, my lady.

ZABINA: Even from the midst of fiery Cancer's tropic to Amazonia under Capricorn, and thence as far as Archipelago, even the men who live in the dark craters of the moon are in arms; and Christians must have peace. *(Laughs wildly and then collapses into her maid's arms in tears)*

EBEA: *(With an Irish brogue)* Don't cry. Would you like me to get you a nice cup of tea? Or a nice egg?

ZABINA: *(Exploding)* Summon my Fire Women!

EBEA: No, no! Not the Fire Women!

ZABINA: *(Like one possessed)* Yes. Yes. The Fire Women. They are the last hope for Mars.

EBEA: *(Frightened)* Do not fight evil with evil, my lady, I beg of you.

ZABINA: I fight strength with strength. Emoc nemow erif.

(Enter FIRE WOMEN.)

FIRE WOMEN: *(Singing)*
Eclipses of the sun
reflected in the water
eclipses of the sun
eclipses of the daughter.

You shouldn't build with bricks
unless you oughter
You cannot build with bricks
without some mortar.

If you've seen your Aunt
smooching with the porter
then you've got no right
to lead a lamb to slaughter.

Beauty is as beauty does
but never the twain shall meet
And if you will not pet my fish
I'll have to beat my meat.

Eclipses of the sun
reflected in the water
eclipses of the sun
eclipses of the daughter.

TAMBERLAINE: *(Above)* Hear me, Martians. Surrender or die. *(FIRE WOMEN dance wildly)* Last chance. Send out your King, the fat and red-faced Bajazeth, to kneel and be buggered.

ZABINA: Never, Evil Earthling, never. Dance, Fire Women, dance.

(The dancing becomes wilder still.)

TAMBERLAINE: I free Mankind from the yoke of reason which weighs upon it. Rape and behead them.

(Tamberlaine's men carry out the screaming, fighting FIRE WOMEN.)

ZABINA: Kill me, Ebea. Spare me this dishonor. Don't let that evil motherfucker get me. It is your sacred duty.

EBEA: I cannot, my Lady, forgive me. I am too weak to do it. *(She stabs herself and dies)*

ALICE: *(Entering sword in hand)* Now you are done for, Zabina.

ZABINA: En garde.

ALICE: En garde, my foot. I've met you many moons ago, in the moonlight garden by the Sea of Storms. And as we sat on the lucite love seat we made a pledge: either to love each other or to destroy each other. Earth is mine, my foolish sister, and with you out of the way, Mars will be mine, too.

ZABINA: I remember that night as clear as the lucite bench. You loved me once, Alice.

ALICE: I do not desire love. I desire power.

ZABINA: Then whatever induced you to marry that Mongol tyrant, Tamberlaine?

ALICE: Every woman is mysterious until the right man marries her . . . and Tamberlaine is the right man, whether he's Mongoloid or not! Our men are struggling now. Tamberlaine will use Bajazeth like a woman.

ZABINA: No!

ALICE: Your husband will writhe under mine. His legs spread apart. His ass bare.

ZABINA: NO!

ALICE: But WE shall duel to see who will be Queen of Mars.

(They duel.)

ZABINA: *(Pulling out a whip)* Your bare bottom will feel the sting of my whip on television. Petticoats over your head. Let's see your treasure chest. *(Lashes whip)*

ALICE: Stand back. I know the only weapon that can destroy you.

ZABINA: *(In horror)* What's that in your hand? No. No. Mercy, I beg of you.

ALICE: Yes! Beer! *(Shakes up bottle and squirts it on ZABINA)*

ZABINA: *(Screams as she passes out)* No, no, not beer. Beer is my undoing.

ALICE: *(Victoriously)* Now there is only one Queen on Mars.

(BAJAZETH enters leaping through the air, followed by Tamberlaine's men.)

BAJAZETH: Save yourself! Save yourself!

TECHELLUS: *(KO's BAJAZETH)* Score one for me!

BAJAZETH: Tolerance signifies weakness. The rest is silence. *(Collapses)*

TAMBERLAINE: *(Attaching leash to BAJAZETH's collar)* We all suffer from the infirmities of impure blood. He who is not a thoroughbred is nothing.

BAJAZETH: You'll never get away with this.

TAMBERLAINE: *(Ignoring him)* Now, bright Alice, the world's fair eye, whose beams illuminate the lamps of heaven, whose cheerful looks do clear the cloudy air and clothe it in a silvery livery. Thy sons shall be emperors and every one the ruler of a world.

ALICE: Later baby, we got Venus to conquer.

TAMBERLAINE: You're right. Come, fair Alice, you will be my love and light; Bajazeth, my clown and cunt. Today I am the happiest of men.

ALICE: As I of women.

(Exeunt TAMBERLAINE and ALICE dragging BAJAZETH and ZABINA on leashes.)

BAJAZETH and ZABINA: We've never been so insulted in our lives.

Scene 2: *Boudoir of Venus, queen of Venus.*

(Enter COSROE. CONSUELA, *Maid to Venus, stops him.)*

CONSUELA: Halt and identify yourself!

COSROE: *(Wearily)* My name is Cosroe. Brother to Zabina, one-time Queen of conquered Mars.

CONSUELA: It seems that the approaching thunderstorm is making all of your limbs feel miserably tired.

COSROE: I have come to Venus to see the Queen.

CONSUELA: Never ask a woman about her age.

(A drapery is drawn back revealing VENUS *in bed.)*

COSROE: Venus!

VENUS: Cosroe! Welcome, come to bed! Come into my chamber!

COSROE: *(Climbing in)* Tamberlaine is coming!

VENUS: Amorous view, riding on his ass. Better change the cod's head for the salmon's tail!

COSROE: Conquer a maiden's bed? No, he'll do the deed of darkness.

VENUS: I won't defend my belly from the dribbling dart of love! He'll die in my lap.

COSROE: You'll not exchange flesh with him?

VENUS: I might fall backward.

COSROE: Are you greased so much? *(Slaps her)*

VENUS: *(Tearfully)* He'll not fish for trouts in my river. *(In baby talk)* I'd rather hang his bugle in an invisible baldric.

COSROE: I kiss your hand, your voluptuousness.

VENUS: Give me a kiss on the inside lip.

COSROE: *(With great trepidation as he approaches her labia majora)* Thy lips are moist.

VENUS: *(Hard, like a woman of the street)* Drink your fill. I'm in no mood for a mouse hunt.

CONSUELA: Magnavox, King of Mercury, wishes an audience with your voluptuousness.

VENUS: *(Gaily)* Let him enter my chamber.

(Enter MAGNAVOX.*)*

MAGNAVOX: Nose painting! Beware of Tamberlaine, he'll make you eat crow.

VENUS: I beg your pardon! You talk of conquests. A penetrating argument.

MAGNAVOX: Do you take my bauble for a bawcock? Roll over bona roba!

VENUS: *(Aside)* He's come to ram me. I'll wring his urinals with my little finger . . . mouse hunt.

MAGNAVOX: *(Fucking her in the ass)* I'll bridle and ride her.

VENUS: Be gentle! Magnavox, I'll break my wind.

CONSUELA: Ortygius, Caliph of Jupiter, wishes an audience with your voluptuousness.

VENUS: Let him enter my chamber, too! *(ORTYGIUS strides in big)* Come to me, Ortygius. Magnetic Magnavox warns me of Tamberlaine's advances.

ORTYGIUS: Don't talk to me about Tamberlaine. What nonsense to mix affairs of state with lovers' quarrels! I speak to you of peace . . . of war . . . the interests of the whole Universe.

VENUS: Doth not Tamberlaine deserve as fortunate a bed as ever Venus shall couch upon?

ORTYGIUS: Fie! Foul-mouthed fornicatress.

COSROE: Whatsa matter, Ortygius? Scared of the French velvet?

ORTYGIUS: *(While the others fuck)* Oh, I wish I had never come to court. So many dangers lurk here . . . intrigues and seductions.

(Fanfare. Enter TAMBERLAINE.*)*

TAMBERLAINE: Four worlds in one bed! I'll tickle your catastrophe!

MAGNAVOX: You'll never take me alive!

TAMBERLAINE: *(Lopping off his dick)* You'll never spit white again! Ortygius, what are you doing here?

ORTYGIUS: We were—.

VENUS: *(Interrupting)* The penalty for discussing affairs of state is life imprisonment. Why do you shove your warlike head at me? I am Venus, mythic Queen of Love. Go bug Mars, the God of War.

(Thunder.)

TAMBERLAINE: I humped Mars earlier in this play.

(Thunder.)

VENUS: And that didn't satisfy you?

TAMBERLAINE: No, baby, I always could come bullets. I wanna come comets and meteors.

(Thunder.)

COSROE: Pretentious pig!

VENUS: Oh, I don't know. He's just a kid with a dream.

*(*MAGNAVOX *and* ORTYGIUS *draw on* TAMBERLAINE. COSROE *runs away.)*

COSROE: He who fights and runs away, will live to fight another day. *(Exit)*

ORTYGIUS: *(To* TAMBERLAINE*)* Draw your sword or I'll send your soul to hell. *(They duel.* ORTYGIUS *is mortally wounded)* The eternal feminine draws us on. *(Dies)*

TAMBERLAINE: Are there any more comers?

MAGNAVOX: Uncle!

TAMBERLAINE: *(Calling his men)* Techellus! Usumcasane! Prepare them for ramming!

(They line them up, tie their hands behind their backs, bend them over the bed, bare their bottoms.)

MAGNAVOX: Hang all guilty men!

TECHELLUS: Hang all innocent men.

VENUS: I think we should hang some guilty men and some innocent men. It's more fair.

TAMBERLAINE: Well, bark, ye dogs; I'll bridle all your tongues, and bind them close with bits of burnished steel. Come, bring them into my pavilion.

Scene 3

NATOLIA:
  The silent night, that brings the quiet pause
  From painefull traviles of the wearie day,
  Prolonges my carefull thoughtes,
  and makes me blame
  the slow aurore that so for
  love or shame
  Doth long delay to shewe
  her blushing face;
  And how the day renewes
  my griefull plaint.
  Stand! Who goes there?

EBEA: A friend.

NATOLIA: Friends, Ebea! Hide me from my friends, by George. I'd rather see the face of Hell than meet the man I love.

EBEA: Madame, I have brought you a packet of news.

NATOLIA: Open it quickly.

EBEA: In the first place, I enquired *who* the Gentleman was; they told me he was a stranger. Secondly, I asked *what* the Gentleman was; they answered . . . and said that they never saw him before. Thirdly, I enquired what Country-man he was; they reply'd 'twas more than they knew! Fourthly, I demanded whence he came; their answer was, they could not tell. And fifthly, I asked whither he went; and they reply'd they knew nothing more of the matter . . . and this is all I could learn.

NATOLIA: What do the people say? Can't they guess?

EBEA: Some say he's a motherfucker and some say he's a Jesuit. Why Jesuit? Why Jesuit?

NATOLIA: Why motherfucker? Why motherfucker?

EBEA: Because he always keeps his horses saddled and his footmen speak French.

NATOLIA: How do you know they French?

EBEA: Because they both had hards-on!

NATOLIA: *(Aside to audience)* And me in love with Cosroe. Oh lord! What will become of ME. He loves his twin sister Zabina incestuously, and jealousy, that green-eyed monster, drives me to this! *(Produces wedding cake)* Yes. A poisoned wedding cake! *(To EBEA)* Heavy with irony and poisoned with purple death dust. *(A fanfare of farts is heard)*

EBEA: *(Who has been eavesdropping on Natolia's aside)* How will I ever get her to eat it, mum!

NATOLIA: Eat it? Eat it? Aw! Tell her there's a saw inside.

EBEA: *(To audience, holding the cake aloft)* Now. Shewilldieshewilldieshewilldie-shewilldieshewilldieshewilldieshewilldie . . .

(Etc., while NATOLIA speaks)

NATOLIA: Now will Ebea disguised as a demon tempt Zabina with this poisoned wedding cake! *(Strikes gong)* Don the demon mask. Destroy Zabina. You take the cake.

EBEA: *(Ritually disguising herself as a demon)*
> One thought consumes me:
> the anger of lust denied
> covers me like darkness.
> I am become a demon
> Dwelling in the hell
> of my dark thoughts,
> Stormcloud of my desires.

(As she ceremonially dresses herself as monster a drum beats ominously and finally wailing sounds are heard) Here is the sinner you sent for.

NATOLIA: Go! Go! Kill Zabina. Her incestuous love for Cosroe is to blame!

EBEA: I go! *(Weeping as monster in* NATOLIA'*s arms)* Oh God! Must it begin again? I think the world has gone mad.

NATOLIA: Zabina thought that, too. Who knows?

EBEA: Mummy, won't it be over soon?

NATOLIA: *(Smiles)* No, my child! Life is a war that never ends!

*(*EBEA *runs out as monster.)*

EBEA: Good night, Mrs. Kalabash, wherever you are.

NATOLIA: *(Calling after her)* And bring me news of your success?

(Enter TECHELLUS *and* USUMCASANE.*)*

TECHELLUS: Oh Natolia, exalted Queen of Saturn. This package just came for you.

NATOLIA: He hadde maad ful many a mariage of yonge woman at his owne cost.

TECHELLUS: *(Doesn't understand a word she says)* I guess so! Anyway, you keep it till Tamberlaine shows up.

NATOLIA: Tamberlaine! As leeve was his hors as is a rake and he was not right fat, I undertake. *(She shakes box)*

TECHELLUS: Well, hasn't it? Even now you're shaking the box for a clue to what's inside.

USUMCASANE: What did she say? What did she say?

TECHELLUS: She says, "Okay, smarty pants! I'll show all of you I can control my curiosity if I want to! That box means nothing to me."

NATOLIA: Nevere wille ay opene this here bocks! *(She opens the box.* TAMBER-LAINE *leaps out of the box and conquers her)*

TAMBERLAINE: It is a sin to do nothing. There is always something useful to be done. I have no respect for those idle rich who discharge their duty to be useful by staging charity balls.

(Fanfare. Enter VENUS, BAJAZETH, ZABINA, MAGNAVOX, ORTYGIUS, *on hands and knees, chained.)*

VENUS: Love's labours lost!

TAMBERLAINE: Quit that complaining, woman! Of all my conquests only Bajazeth amuses me. Bajazeth!

BAJAZETH: Master.

TAMBERLAINE: How do I pay you when I use you as a woman?

BAJAZETH: In piles, Master!

TAMBERLAINE: *(Roars with laughter)* I taught him that this morning. Natolia, you are conquered. *(To his men)* Chain her!

BAJAZETH: Like him was I, these sloping shoulders, this gracelessness. My child bends beside me. Too far for me to lay a hand there once or lightly. Mine is far and his secret as our eyes. Secrets, silent, stony sit in the dark palaces of both our hearts; secrets weary of their tyranny; tyrants willing to be dethroned.

TAMBERLAINE: Bajazeth, how did they know the parakeet was a faggot?

BAJAZETH: Because he kissed a cockatiel.

(Everyone moans.)

ALICE: That's the wittiest thing I've heard in my life.

TAMBERLAINE: Moan, will you? Whip their asses and put them to bed without supper. Except Bajazeth. I'll take him with me. I must get up early tomorrow and conquer Neptune.

(Exit TAMBERLAINE *and* BAJAZETH. *Guards drag others out.)*

ALICE: *(Alone)* Six nights out of seven my husband prefers Bajazeth for bed. Maybe it's my hair. *(Exit)*

Scene 4: *Zabina's cell.*

(ZABINA *is dragged in and thrown to the floor by a guard.)*

ZABINA: *(On her knees)* Let us pray that strength and courage abundant be given to all who work for a world of reason and understanding.

(Thunder.)

TECHELLUS: Was it the bloom in her cheeks?

ZABINA: Maybe it just proves we're human when we drop the ball once in a while.

TECHELLUS: *(Coaxing)* Come live the continental life.

ZABINA: You view from the eyes of a wasp or cod.

TECHELLUS: We know a tropical paradise that has: horse racing, night harness racing, dog racing, jai alai, thirty golf courses, fantastic deep-sea fishing, two hundred million dollars in sunken treasure, great hotels, fabulous restaurants, big name entertainment, professional and college football, Indians, Italian palaces, porpoises, blue sky, stone crabs, and Jackie Gleason.

ZABINA: *(Transfigured)* Shangri-la?

TECHELLUS: No.

ZABINA: Bali Hai?

TECHELLUS: No. It's called Miami.

WOMAN IN ANOTHER CELL: *(Haunted like a madwoman)* Miami! Miami! Miami! Miami!

ZABINA: *(To* TECHELLUS*)* Please leave me. I would like to be alone.

TECHELLUS: *(Going)* Think over my proposition and yell if you change your mind. *(Exit)*

ZABINA: *(Alone)*
   Of human sufferage,
   Of common aspirings
   You free yourself then . . .
I've seen sidereal archipelagos. Islands whose delirious skies open for wanderers. "Is it in such bottomless nights you sleep exiled, O countless golden birds,

O force to come?" *(She moans with anguish and throws herself to the ground. There is a knock at the door.* BAJAZETH *enters)*

BAJAZETH: *(Consoling her)* Dawns are heartbreaking.

ZABINA: True, I have wept too much. Cruel all moons and bitter the suns.

BAJAZETH:

Within this restless, modern, hurried world,
We took our hearts' full pleasure, you and I,
And now the white sails of our rocket ship are furled
And spent the lading of our argosy.

ZABINA:

Wherefore my cheeks before their time are wan,
For very weeping is my gladness fled.
Sorrow has paled my lips vermilion
And ruin draws the curtain of my bed.

BAJAZETH:

But all this crowded life has been to thee
Naught but lyre and lute
That sleeps a mimic echo in a shell.

By Neptune's trident, do not despair so utterly. I have word from Cosroe.

ZABINA: Give it to me. And go, I can't bear to look at you. Who were my husband.

BAJAZETH: Were?

ZABINA: You belong to Tamberlaine. Some day all the Universe will be his. *(She opens the letter and reads.)* "Dear Zabina: A giant enemy cargo sub rising out of the mud where it had lain concealed! Will send out the thermal rays, to capture the test planes. I won't make a move till I find out to what destination they are towing the plane! Yours truly, Cosroe." A ray of hope. Cosroe, Cosroe. My brother will avenge this whole mess. He's just one of the many surprises in my power pack that the punks never even dreamed of!

BAJAZETH: How about a little nuggie?

ZABINA: No nuggie for you till Tamberlaine is slain or overcome.

BAJAZETH: Touch me. Soft eyes. Soft, soft, soft hand. I am lonely. O touch me soon, now. What is that word known to all men? I am quiet here alone. Sad, too, touch, touch me. . . . Just a quickie.

ZABINA: I say to you and Jove, my will be done. . . . No more nuggie till Tamberlaine be slain or overcome!

Scene 5: *Some damned place near the cove of the Witch of Ensor.*

(It is very dark. Enter COSROE, *walking feverishly back and forth.)*

COSROE: He feels like an explorer on the edge of a new world.

VOICE OF MAGNAVOX: And more! So much more!

VOICE OF VENUS: *(Suggestively)* Who will be next?

COSROE: Neptune—Uranus—Pluto—Cambodia—Laos—North Vietnam—South Vietnam—West Hempstead!

VOICE OF NATOLIA: Hadde loved hire best of any creature two yeer and moore, as was his aventure.

VOICE OF MAGNAVOX: We've taken enough of his sass. When Tamberlaine destroyed my people, he destroyed my spirit. I'd give up my life to save the Universe.

COSROE: I will avenge my sister's death. Tamberlaine must die. I must stop Tamberlaine.

(Enter WITCH OF ENSOR *amidst wolves howling, etc.)*

WITCH: Listen to them! Children of the night! What music they make!

COSROE: *(In despair)* Venus gone . . . gone . . . without leaving me anything to remember her by . . . SUFFERING SAPPHO . . . How can I go on living?

WITCH: You must go on, Cosroe. The world needs you! There . . . there . . . cry. Get it out of your system. . . . I understand.

COSROE: Ha! What an opportunity! Revenge shall be slaked! *(To* WITCH*)* Your destiny is calling you! According to Hoyle, I need the book I Ching and the Ting Tripod to make the incantation that would safely allow me to continue in this play. Once I cringed in the dirt, now I have it within my power to slay the slayer himself and to cry in his ear at his last moments, VICTORY . . . battle is mine!

WITCH: He speaks of death . . . let's move on to our duties. *(She begins her incantation)* Figures painted! Figures real! Figures from this parchment steal! Fight these three, your newfound foes . . . bring them loss and bring them woes! . . . A murderer stands before me!

COSROE: Victory! Victory! The avenging dawn now rises to make the wicked tremble! And liberty returns, the scourge of tyrants!

WITCH: GO! Shout your boasts! Pour out the last dregs of your vile soul! Go! The hangman's noose awaits you.

COSROE: Ha! Shall I cringe before a woman? You shall both taste my fury. If you have cast your lot with his, now share his death! *(He kills her)* SUFFERING SAPPHO! How long must my traitorous acts continue? 'Tis sin to kill—I bear this mortal stain—But sin I must to free my life again—For life is death—Ere I kill Tamberlaine! *(Exit)*

Scene 6

(Enter TAMBERLAINE *and* ALICE *in nightgowns.)*

TAMBERLAINE: *(Terribly upset)* Why? What has happened? What have I been saying? Have I? What have I?

ALICE: Hark ye! Accursed be this day's success.

TAMBERLAINE: Oh, at last! At last!

ALICE: Quick, tell me! Did the King forgive you?

TAMBERLAINE: Put me into any heavy work you like!

ALICE: *(Furiously)* What on earth do you mean? Don't you know who I am, what I was?

TAMBERLAINE: Roll these camel dung balls faster, you piece of manure!

ALICE: Are you beginning too? Already?

TAMBERLAINE: Now don't imagine you're in a railway carriage, Alice, it's only the whisky in your honorable head that shakes. *(He takes hold of her arms and bites her neck. She screams)*

ALICE: You bit me!

TAMBERLAINE: *(In the voice of a fat rat)* When you have rolled the camel dung balls, lay out the balls on a bowl, beat the drum, and light them.

ALICE: *(Showing him her ring finger)* Look at the mark of the fetter you have broken! I was a slave and now I'm free.

TAMBERLAINE: The God is speaking to you!

ALICE: You?

TAMBERLAINE: Alas no!

ALICE: I thought at one moment you were . . .

TAMBERLAINE: That is my secret. We'll go to the theater tonight and let everyone see us.

ALICE: What's playing?

TAMBERLAINE: *The Conquest of the Universe, or When Queens Collide* by Charles Ludlam.

ALICE: Filth! The insane ravings of a degenerate mind! I won't go! Besides I haven't a thing to wear!

TAMBERLAINE: It's the theater or rolling dung balls. Take your pick.

ALICE: I choose . . . the theater.

TAMBERLAINE: You were thinking about the theater and supper I suppose. I was thinking about our two daughters . . . and *no* sons.

(ALICE strikes him across the mouth.)

ALICE: Prig!

TAMBERLAINE: Forgive me!

ALICE: On your knees then! *(TAMBERLAINE falls to his knees)* On your face! *(TAMBERLAINE touches the floor with his forehead)* Kiss my foot. *(He does so)* Now, get up! And never do that again!

TAMBERLAINE: Don't you notice something? The way you look . . .

ALICE: *(Alarmed)* Something's happening to us!

TAMBERLAINE: We've changed . . .

ALICE: We . . . we look like the natives of this world! That robot's food!

TAMBERLAINE: We ate the native grasses and now we are natives! Alice, do something!

ALICE: Wh—what can I do?

TAMBERLAINE: GUARD! HO! GUARD! By Terra, if only I had a weapon instead of just water!

(Enter guard.)

TECHELLUS: My lord?

TAMBERLAINE: My wife is troubled and cannot sleep. She dreamed my statue, like an fountain with an hundred spouts, did run pure blood. And all the people of this solar system came and bathed their hands in it. Can you read a meaning into it?

TECHELLUS: I can. You are not a fountain but rather like a heart, you pump blood to all the parts of the body. Which might be compared to the solar system.

TAMBERLAINE: You will be my personal mind guard. My thoughts can control inanimate matter but my thought power has no effect on intelligent minds.

TECHELLUS: I hear and now obey. *(Exit)*

ALICE: *(To TAMBERLAINE)* Think not too deeply on't. 'Twill make us mad.

TAMBERLAINE: I'm used to pests like him, trying to get publicity. That's why I rarely let strangers get close to me.

(They gradually begin to fall back to sleep, and their line delivery becomes drowsier and drowsier.)

ALICE: *(Yawning)* Girl Friday, salary open.

TAMBERLAINE: *(Also yawning)* Growing multicorp. organization, Pan Am Bldg., has challenging position for accountant desiring future. Five years' experience required.

ALICE: *(More faintly)* Secy. to Vice President. Ambitious? Tired of job limitations? Grow with home office. Salary commens. w/intelligence, skills.

TAMBERLAINE: Do you have sales ability, sales ability, sales ability? Let us give you a sales aptitude test and we will tell you if we can use you! *(They are asleep)*

VOICE ON LOUDSPEAKER: Surrender Jupiter! Surrender Saturn! Surrender Neptune or die!!

Scene 7

(Strange music as in a dream . . . enter WAR *. . . she leads* HUNGER *and* PESTILENCE *on leashes like two mad dogs.)*

WAR: I am WAR, the maker of heroes. I lead Hunger and Pestilence on leashes like two mad dogs.

HUNGER: I am Hunger and I am like a Mad Dog. Every night a million Americans go to bed without supper. Twiggy, what hast thou wrought?

PESTILENCE: I am Pestilence, and I am like a Mad Dog. Cancer. Leprosy. Tuberculosis. Elephantiasis. Syphilis. Crabs. Gonorrhea. The Common Cold. Trench mouth. Hookworm. Ringworm. Tapeworm. Beriberi. Leeches! Leeches! Leeches! LEECHES!

WAR: NOW CRY HAVOC *(Bloodcurdling scream)* . . . and unleash the dogs of War! *(She releases the dogs who run offstage yapping)* To arms, patriots, to arms! *(She utters a curdling scream)*
　　Of human sufferage
　　Of common aspirings!
　　You free yourself then
　　You fly according to . . .
(Bloodcurdling scream) War is hell. *(Exit)*

Scene 8

(Enter TAMBERLAINE *and his train.* BAJAZETH *on a leash.)*

TAMBERLAINE: Bajazeth, amuse me. I feel a bit depressed. Tell me some jokes.

BAJAZETH: Yes, Master . . . "Adultery is democracy applied to love." *(*TAMBERLAINE *roars)* "Advice to loveworn lasses. If you tingle when you tinkle, have the doctor check your wrinkle." *(*TAMBERLAINE *roars)* "I call my girl shotgun, 'cause I love to give her a bang." *(*TAMBERLAINE *roars)* "She got rich bookmaking, because she knew how to take a hot tip."

TAMBERLAINE: I don't get it.

BAJAZETH: Think now. . . . It's a double entendre . . . hot tip . . . hot tip . . .

TAMBERLAINE: Hot tip . . . hot tip . . . I still don't get it.

BAJAZETH: Hot tip refers to the male genital organ in an erectile state.

TAMBERLAINE: *(Bowled over)* Male genital organ . . . Ha! . . . Ha! . . . erectile . . . Ha! . . . state. . . . Tell me more . . . tell more . . . more.

BAJAZETH: "Clara claims that when the doctor gave her an enema it was nothing but a goose with a gush." "Come into my parlor said the spider as he opened his fly."

ALICE: Tamberlaine, you never pay any attention to me anymore.

BAJAZETH: "The midget in the circus married that Amazon lady. He said he got on fine but he didn't have anybody to talk to."

TAMBERLAINE: What's that, dear?

BAJAZETH: "No, Ida, we don't believe crossing a turtle with a tomcat will produce a snapping pussy."

ALICE: I said you never pay any attention to me anymore.

BAJAZETH: "My greatest thrill," said the wife of the ex-soldier, "was when Johnny came marching home and I awoke to find him standing by the bed with his discharge in his hand."

TAMBERLAINE: I'm very busy conquering the Universe.

ALICE: *(Aside)* Ever since he saw the play *Conquest of the Universe, or When Queens Collide* by Charles Ludlam, he's gotten strange ideas.

TAMBERLAINE: Bring out Natolia, my Saturnine conquest.

(GUARDS drag on NATOLIA, a beautiful exotic who speaks Middle English. She is proud, and does not genuflect.)

TECHELLUS: On your knees before the conqueror, whore!

NATOLIA: *(With great wisdom and cool)*
Men may conseille a womman to be oon,
But conseillyng is no comandement.
He put it in oure owene juggement,
For hadde God comanded maydenhede,
Thanne hadde he dampned weddyng with the dede.

TAMBERLAINE: What does she say? Who speaks Sauterne?

MAGNAVOX: I do . . . *(With contempt)* . . . Master!

TAMBERLAINE: Let's hear the translation of that.

ALICE: Be careful, Tamberlaine, translators are traitors.

MAGNAVOX: She says . . . fuck you!

TAMBERLAINE: I like the way the girl thinks. *(As he is carried out)* Have her sent, at midnight. Bajazeth, take the night off.

(Everyone goes out except ALICE and BAJAZETH.)

BAJAZETH: What kind of woman is she that would marry the conqueror of the Universe?

ALICE: Oh, not much different from any other woman. Some find her beautiful. . . .

HE'S THE CONQUEROR

(Vamp to song)
I curse the day I met him
And still I can't forget him.
He took me for his bride,
I've stood right by his side,
Now he's casting me aside. . . .

He takes what he wants, and if you're what he wants,
    he takes you.
He knows what he wants, and if you're not what he wants,
    he doesn't take you.
    He's the conqueror.

I know I'm just a woman, and a woman's place is near him.
I want to be near him, though others fear him
    for he's the conqueror.
    Yes, the conqueror
    He's the conqueror.
I've loved him from the start
    I love him now
    I'll always love him
    Although he hits me
    He's the conqueror, Yes, the
    conqueror
    of my heart.

I know there's two or three
that he loves as well as me
but when he beats me,
when he eats me,
He's the conqueror.

I guess I'll always love him
I'll always love him
I'll always love him
I have loved him from the start
For although he's just a fart
He's the conqueror! Yes, the conqueror!
The conqueror of my heart!

(Sad exit)

BAJAZETH: "The underworld is buzzing about the gangster's moll who walked out on her boyfriend when she discovered he was just a fingerman." "She didn't know the difference between sexual intercourse and Caesar salad, but I didn't explain . . . I have lunch with her every day."

Scene 9

(Enter TAMBERLAINE *alone.)*

TAMBERLAINE: What form of prayer will serve my turn? O wretched state! O bosom black as death! O limed soul, that struggling free art more engaged! *(He cries out)* Help! Angels! Bow stubborn knees! *(He kneels)* And heart, with strings of steel, be soft as sinews of the newborn babe. All may be well. "Hail Mary full of grace, the Lord is with thee. . . ." *(His voice fades out.* COSROE *appears behind him)*

COSROE: Now might I do it, and so free Zabina. Now he is a-praying. If I do it now his soul goes to heaven. Should I send a villain to heaven? No! No!

A thousand times, no! This is reward not revenge! He kills men, their crimes full-blown, as flush as May . . . to get revenge I must delay. *(Exit)*

TAMBERLAINE: Blessed art thou amongst women and blessed is . . . blessed is . . . *(Runs through prayer again quickly)* blessed is . . . blessed is . . . *(Rising)* My words fly up. My thoughts remain below.

Words without thoughts never to heaven go.

Ho, guard!

TECHELLUS: *(Entering)* My lord?

TAMBERLAINE: Have you executed Zabina yet?

TECHELLUS: She was shot this morning at dawn.

TAMBERLAINE: You have told good news well. Here's a fin. Come, I've another mission for you.

Scene 10: *Zabina's cell.*

(ZABINA kneeling in a posture of supplication, her hands folded as in prayer as the rays of dawn fall through the barred window on her face.)

ZABINA: Oh God . . . damn it. Give me a cigarette. I'll do anything. I'm having a nicotine fit. You can fuck me, anything!

TECHELLUS: No cigarettes, it's against the rules.

ZABINA: Don't you understand, darling? I need a cigarette. Listen to me, you cocksucker, I've got to have a butt or I'll drop dead! dead! dead! *(Aside)* That was the worst line I've ever had to say in *any* play. No, no, no . . . not death . . . death . . . death . . . *(Pause)* Not like this. *(Pause)* Not here. *(Pause)* No . . . No . . . When I die the stars will crash together like a thousand glass bells and shattered fall to earth. Birds will gouge their eyes blotting heaven's mirror, cracking it with shrieks and strewing earth with broken bits reflecting. When they come blind to bury me, the splinters will cut their feet, making a river of blood, and I'll be washed away to the place where the earth consumes the flesh and the cries of the dead turn into black stones. What dreams are these. Light lamps, I fear the night!

TECHELLUS: A visitor to see you.

(Enter EBEA, with cake.)

EBEA: Madame, I've brought you life and hope from the one you love.

ZABINA: Who?

EBEA: Cosroe. *(Presents cake)*

ZABINA: Cosroe. Oh, he shouldn't have gone to so much trouble! *(Gobbles cake)*

EBEA: With Duncan Hines you only need one egg!

ZABINA: And it's so light and moist you don't have to wash it down! *(Sampling the frosting)* Almond? No. Mocha? No. Banana Surprise? No.

EBEA: That cake was flavored with Pyrinate A-200!

ZABINA: *(Realizing what she has eaten)* Pyrinate A-200!

EBEA: Now the only person in the Universe who knows I am the bastard daughter of Tamberlaine must die! No more sneers, insults, and disdain. Oh, Lorenzo, at last I am free to love!

VOICE ON TAPE: THE ROBOT, TECHELLUS, FARTS, THE SMELL OF WHICH,

COMBINED WITH THE GREEN FUMES OF PYRINATE A-200 EXUDED BY THE FROSTING OF THE CAKE, ASPHYXIATES EBEA, WHO IS A LOUSE.

EBEA: My windpipe! My windpipe! O Techellus, thou hast robbed me of my youth! *(Dies)*

ZABINA: *(Holding her nose)* P.U. Oh, God . . . damn it . . . give me a menthol cigarette.

TECHELLUS: No smoking. It's against the rules.

ZABINA: Not the hashish. Just the ordinary kind that only gives you cancer!

TECHELLUS: What will the Universe say when they find out the Queen of Mars is a dope addict?

ZABINA: It started with injections to ease the pain. The hashish came later.

TECHELLUS: Your time is up. It's dawn. Do you have any last requests?

ZABINA: Just this . . . my feather boa.

TECHELLUS: No boas! It's against the rules.

ZABINA: A boa . . . a boa . . . my kingdom for a boa!

TECHELLUS: *(To* USUMCASANE, *moved to tears)* Give her the boa.

*(*USUMCASANE *brings the boa and gently places it around her neck.)*

TECHELLUS: I hate to do this, but you can still pray if you like.

ZABINA: I don't think I'll pray. I just want to go out the way I came in. *(Raises her hemline to reveal a well-turned thigh. Takes a compact from her garter and as she touches the puff to her nose, they shoot her down)*

Scene 11

*(Gravedigger [*TECHELLUS*], with* ZABINA*'s body, digging. Enter* COSROE.*)*

COSROE: Why, who are you, sir?

GRAVEDIGGER: I am the maker of graves.

COSROE: The opposite of a comedian, you make us grave. Whose grave is it you make, sir?

GRAVEDIGGER: I bury Zabina, one-time queen of conquered Mars. She is a grave woman. A grave womanly offense. Her brother Cosroe, they say, is mad.

COSROE: Is he?

GRAVEDIGGER: They should send him to Earth.

COSROE: Why?

GRAVEDIGGER: They have many psychiatrists there to help him recover his wits. But if he doesn't, 'tis no great matter there.

COSROE: Why?

GRAVEDIGGER: 'Twill not be seen in him there: there the men are as mad as he.

COSROE: *(Picking up a skull)* Alas, poor Urine, he pissed his life away.

*(*BAJAZETH *enters weeping, with* NATOLIA *and* VENUS *carrying flowers.* COSROE *hides in the shadows.)*

BAJAZETH: *(Weeping)* Zabina! Zabina! Lay her in the earth; and from her fair and unpolluted flesh may violets spring!

COSROE: But who comes here? I know that countenance. I cannot countenance that countenance. 'Tis Bajazeth!

VENUS: *(Throwing flowers on grave)* Sweets to the sweet; farewell!

COSROE: How dare you mourn, sir, the woman you scorned.

VENUS and NATOLIA: *(Frightened)* 'Tis Cosroe the mad!

BAJAZETH: I loved Zabina more than you'll ever know.

COSROE: I loved Zabina: forty thousand husbands, with all their quantity of love, could not make up my sum. What wilt thou do for her?

BAJAZETH: Although our last words were harsh words, I know Zabina understands.

NATOLIA: O he is mad, Bajazeth! Let's humor his fancy while the fit is on him.

COSROE: You don't know what love is. You should read Erich Fromm.

BAJAZETH: You should read Wilhelm Reich.

COSROE: Wilhelm Reich was wrong. You've come here to outweep me at her grave. Who is this man? I know his name. They call him Bajazeth, the whore of Tamberlaine. History, jot that down.

VENUS: Of course. Men have lost all sense of decency. And besides, they're disgusting. Look at them in the evening, sitting at their tables in the cafés, working away in unison, with their toothpicks, hour after hour, digging up roast beef, veal, onion. . . .

BAJAZETH: *(With anger)* Stop it. Tell me what's happened.

VENUS: The girl died. Sit down.

BAJAZETH: *(Sitting)* You won't have to swim.

(The sound of crickets is heard.)

VENUS: Oh . . . it's all one to me. I don't care what happens. I don't care if the biggest storm in the whole world comes. Let it come. *(She folds her hands)*

BAJAZETH: Listen to that music. Venus, do you remember the dances in the firehouse at Yonkers on Saturday nights?

VENUS: I begin to get some of your thinking now. When you mentioned killing us. I'm sure you thought the whole thing up in quite heroic terms.

COSROE: Here are question and reply. And the fire reflected in the thinking eye. So peace, and let the bobcat cry. *(VENUS and BAJAZETH imitate sound of bobcat. COSROE feigning madness)* Hee-haw! Ho-hum! Have you ever seen a dead person? *(To VENUS)* I think you must have had many admirers in your youth.

NATOLIA: *(Furiously, to the GUARDS)* You devil, you think I'm so easily gotten rid of? You have a thing or two to learn. First I have nothing else to do. And nowhere to go.

COSROE: *(To NATOLIA)* This is Frau Studienrat-Furcke. Good afternoon, Frau Mummermann. Is Klaus-Heinrich at your place? He isn't? Then, I just can't think where the boy is. . . . Tell me, Frau Mummermann, is the club room of the Hitler youth open Sunday afternoon? It is? Thanks, I'll look for him there.

NATOLIA: What is he? Some kinda nut?

BAJAZETH: You speak English?

NATOLIA: Of course I speak English.

COSROE: There are only two things necessary for salvation.

NATOLIA: Get him.

COSROE: Money and gunpowder.

VENUS: Blessed are the peacemakers.

BAJAZETH: A good slogan in wartime.

VENUS: *(Reading the paper)* Why do I do this every Sunday? Even the book reviews seem to be the same as last week's. Different books . . . same reviews.

COSROE: Look at the moon. How strange the moon seems! She is like a woman rising from a tomb. She is like a dead woman. One might fancy she was looking for dead things.

NATOLIA: He gives me the creeps.

BAJAZETH: Man must suffer to be wise.

(MAGNAVOX and ORTYGIUS are brought in by the GUARDS.)

MAGNAVOX: *(To NATOLIA)* What of Tamberlaine?

NATOLIA: By night and day he wrongs me, every hour he flashes into one gross crime or other that sets us all at odds. I'll not endure it. The nights grow riotous.

COSROE: The moon has a strange look tonight. Has she not a strange look? She is like a madwoman seeking everywhere for lovers. She is like a little slut walking down the alley in high heels.

NATOLIA: You're making fun of me.

VENUS: There's nothing to be scared of. He just talks and passes the time of day. Occasionally plays cards.

BAJAZETH: *(Taking COSROE aside)* Suppose we kill a king . . . and then a king . . .

COSROE: Princes are waiting everywhere. Suppose by water or with poison kill a queen . . . *(He starts to attack VENUS and NATOLIA)*

BAJAZETH: *(Pulling him off)* Her daughter waits upon the stair.

COSROE: The moon has lost one of her high heels.

MAGNAVOX: *(To NATOLIA, with an affectionate grin)* No stranger are you among us, nor a guest, but our daughter and our dearly beloved.

NATOLIA: I think this Jewish fox has eaten my life.

ORTYGIUS: *(Tearing up VENUS's newspaper)* Hope and a Red Rag are baits for men and mackerel.

VENUS: *(Coming back)* Discontented minds and fevers of the body are not to be cured by changing beds or businesses.

MAGNAVOX: Listen, someone is coming.

(Footsteps. They all watch the door. A green light falls on the door. There is a drumroll. The door flies open revealing ALICE.)

ALICE: *(To NATOLIA)* I'm delighted to see you've come back safe and sound. *(COSROE steals one of her pumps)* Guard! Guard!

GUARD: Yes, sir?

ALICE: I beg your pardon! Seize him.

COSROE: *(Seeing that the shoe fits, decides to wear it)* I'm as much a queen as she.

NATOLIA: Oh, no. Methinks something's rotten in Denmark!

(GUARD returns shoe to ALICE.)

ALICE: Won't you all have dinner at my house tonight? Please do.

ORTYGIUS: How do you do, Alice? I'm afraid I can't come to dinner. I have balls to attend.

ALICE: Oh come, all of you *(To NATOLIA)* to show there are no *hard* feelings.

NATOLIA: *(Threatening COSROE)* Are you making fun of me again?

BAJAZETH: What are we having for dinner, Alice?

ALICE: *(With an air of unexpected intimacy)* Mofongo and rice and beans!

COSROE: *(Thunderstruck)* Beans?

ALICE: Beans. That's iron for your blood.

VENUS: But lead for your stomach.

COSROE: *(Brooding)* Beans. *(Then aside to* VENUS*)* Don't knock Alice or we won't get in the palace.

VENUS: *(Aside to* BAJAZETH*)* Don't knock Alice or we won't get in the palace.

BAJAZETH: *(Aside to* ORTYGIUS*)* Don't knock Alice or we won't get in the palace.

ORTYGIUS: *(Aside to* MAGNAVOX*)* Don't knock Alice or we won't get in the palace.

MAGNAVOX: *(Aside to* NATOLIA*)* Don't knock Alice or we won't get in the palace.

NATOLIA: *(Aside to* ALICE*)* Don't knock . . .

COSROE: *(Slapping hand over her mouth)* Beans. Beans.

VENUS: We'd be glad to come, Alice.

COSROE: *(Slapping hand over her mouth)* Beans. Beans.

VENUS: We'd be glad to come, Alice.

COSROE: *(Taking* BAJAZETH *aside)* Beans, Bajazeth. Beans.

BAJAZETH: Beans?

*(*COSROE *whispers into* BAJAZETH*'s ear.)*

BAJAZETH: Beans! *(They rejoin the others)*

ALICE: *(Facing audience)* Remember, ladies, you have seen nothing unusual here today. *(Exits)*

COSROE: They've denied us our high heels but we'll die with our boots on. The dinner's the thing wherein I'll catch the something of the King.

ALL: Revenge! Revenge! Revenge! *(Exit)*

Scene 12

NEWSBOY: Extree! Extree! Read all about it! Tam Conks Uni! Extree, Extree.

TAMBERLAINE: I'll have a paper, boy. Keep the change.

NEWSBOY: Gee, thanks mister. *(The* NEWSBOY *runs out.* TAMBERLAINE *cries like a baby)*

ALICE: *(Enters)* What's the matter, sweetie?

TAMBERLAINE: *(Rhetorical)* I hear the ruin of all space, shattered glass and toppling masonry. And, time, one livid final flame. What's left us then? There are no more worlds to conquer. *(Resumes crying like a baby)*

ALICE: Aw, don't cry. What you need is something to eat. Let the Banquet Scene begin!

(The Kings and Queens of the nine planets enter in a stately procession to stately music, and sit at banquet table.)

TAMBERLAINE: Before the cock crows thrice: one of you will betray me.

ORTYGIUS: A toast to Tamberlaine!

ALL: A toast to Tamberlaine!

ORTYGIUS: To your genitalia, may they never fail ya! *(Everyone drinks)*

TAMBERLAINE: And now, a divertissement. Performed by the ballerina of Uranus.

(BALLERINA OF URANUS dances on her toes.)

ALL: Brava! Encore! Viva Uranus! *(Etc.)*

(TAMBERLAINE shoots URANUS.)

TAMBERLAINE: Whenever I hear the word "culture," I draw my pistol.

BAJAZETH: *(Approaching COSROE with bucket)* Cosroe, now is the hour. *(Letting down his pants and showing his ass to the audience)* My cook's cap, once a crown.

BAJAZETH and COSROE: *(As BAJAZETH shits in bucket, which COSROE is holding)*

Sing a song of sixpence,
A pocket full of rye,
Four and twenty blackbirds,
Baked in a pie;
When the pie was opened,
The birds began to sing;
Wasn't that a dainty dish
To set before a king?

BAJAZETH: A toast to Alice!

ALL: Speech! Speech!

ALICE: Tamberlaine, I have something to tell you. Fanfare! Fanfare! *(Fanfare of farts is heard)* I'm going to have a little stranger.

ALL: Ooooooooooo.

ALICE: In fact, X-rays show I'm going to have nine little strangers. And all boys. One to rule each planet.

ALL: Aaaaaaaaaaaaaaaah.

(The sound of a crash is heard.)

EBEA: Somebody dropped her earring!

ALICE: Why here it is in my back cleavage!

(She dances a wild flamenco labor dance. COSROE serves as doctor and delivers the nine babies.)

VENUS: Doctore! Doctore! Do you need any hot water?

COSROE: No, I'm in hot water enough as it is.

(They all dance and COSROE completes delivery. ALICE is prostrate.)

NATOLIA: I'm certainly glad you got that out of your system.

COSROE: This hasn't been placenta.

ALICE: *(Looking to TAMBERLAINE)* Well, my love?

TAMBERLAINE: Puta, I have not this twelvemonth fucked thee. *(He stabs ALICE and the nine infants)*

COSROE: *(Aside)* Oh, deeds most monstrous!

ALICE: Ah, my young princes! Ah, my tender babes! My unblown flowers, new-appearing sweets! If yet your gentle souls fly in the air and be not fixed in doom perpetual, hover about me with your airy wings and hear your mother's lamentation. O Mother of Pearl, is there anything left to believe in?

TAMBERLAINE: Bajazeth! Amuse me. Chase the blues away.

BAJAZETH: Warning! Flies spread disease. Keep yours buttoned.

TAMBERLAINE: I'm inconsolable.

BAJAZETH: *(Aside)* Maybe this will cheer him up. *(To* TAMBERLAINE*)* Tamberlaine, I have something to tell you. I, too, have borne you nine little ones, out of my asshole. One to rule each planet.

TAMBERLAINE: O my love! My light! Where are my sons?

COSROE: Would please you eat? Would please your highness food?

TAMBERLAINE: Go, fetch them hither to us presently.

*(*TAMBERLAINE *eats.)*

ALL:
Sing a song of sixpence,
A pocket full of rye,
Four and twenty black turds,
Baked in a pie.

ALICE: If these have to be my last moments, let me live them in peace.

ALL:
When the pie was opened,
The turds began to stink;
Wasn't that a dainty dish
To set before a fink!

TAMBERLAINE: WHAT?

BAJAZETH: Why here they are, love. All baked in this pie whereof their father daintily hath fed.

WITCH: 'Tis true! 'Tis true! The nine turds of Bajazeth borne out of his asshole.

COSROE: Witness my knife's sharp point. *(Stabs* TAMBERLAINE*)*

TAMBERLAINE: *(Turning on* BAJAZETH*)* Die frantic wretch, for this accursed deed.

ALICE: Shall a wife stand and see her husband's blood? Here's tit for tat and death for deadly deed. *(Stabs* COSROE*)*

COSROE: Oh, I am slain!

TAMBERLAINE: Farewell, my boys; my dearest friends, farewell! My body feels, my soul doth weep to see your sweet desires deprived my company, for Tamberlaine, the scourge of God, must die.

GHOST OF ZABINA: *(Calling)* Cosroooe! Cosroooe!

COSROE: Zabina! Methinks I hear my sister Zabina!

GHOST OF ZABINA: Cosroooe! Cosroooe! You have avenged my death bravely and paid with your own life! Sucker!

COSROE: It's not what you do, it's how you do it. *(Dies)*

VENUS: *(In a stately manner)*
Would you be free from your burden of Sin?
There is power in the blood, power in the blood.
Would you o'er evil, victory win?
There is power in the blood of the Lamb.

ALL:
There is power, power, wonder-working
power, in the blood of the Lamb.
There is power, power, wonder-working
power, in the precious blood of the Lamb.

VENUS:
Would you be free from your passion and pride?
There is power in the blood, power in the blood.

Come for cleansing to Calvary's side,
There is wondrous power in the blood.
ALL:
There is power, power, wonder-working
power, in the blood of the Lamb.
There is power, power, wonder-working
power, in the precious blood of the Lamb.
VENUS:
Would you die to see your mind blow?
There is power in the blood, power in the blood.
Just plant the seeds and let them grow!
There is wondrous power in the blood.
ALL:
There is power, power . . . *(Etc.)*
NATOLIA: The vast majority of men as well as women are sexually disturbed as a result of a training which inhibits their sexuality; that is, they are not satisfied in sexual intercourse. What is necessary, therefore, is the establishment of a sufficient number of clinics for the treatment of sexual disturbances. What is necessary is a rational sex education which will affirm the validity of love.

*(*COSROE *is carried off in state. The cast follows his body out solemnly.)*

WITCH: Life is but a lying dream. He only wakes, who casts the world aside.

Finis

TURDS IN HELL

by
Charles Ludlam
and
Bill Vehr

1969

The whorehouse scene in
Turds in Hell (Thomas Harding)

Cast of Characters

THE DEVIL
TURZAHNELLE
ORGONE, *the Hunchback, Pinhead, Sex Maniac*
THE ANGEL
CARLA, *the Gypsy Wildcat*
THE SOLDIER
CROUPIER
BARON BUBBLES IN THE BATHTUB, *the Brazilian Brassiere Buster*
MADAME TRYPHOENA
TURTLE WOMAN
VERA, *Madame Tryphoena's ward*
SAINT OBNOXIOUS
SAINT FRIGID
THE PIMP
THE POPE
DEVILS
GYPSY VIOLINIST
WEDDING GUESTS
GAMBLERS
MUSICIANS
SAINTS
MONKS
NUNS
WHORES

(Enter the DEVIL.*)*

DEVIL: The play you are about to see is a mortal sin. Any person witnessing this play takes part in that sin and thereby risks his immortal soul.

The Mountaintop

(The bell in the watchtower strikes twelve. The curtains open revealing TURZAH-NELLE *on a mountaintop, pushing a shopping cart in which, swathed in swaddling clothes, lies her newborn son,* ORGONE, *the Baby Hunchback, Pinhead, Sex Maniac.* TURZAHNELLE *sings a lullaby to her son before she abandons him on the mountaintop. The* ANGEL *appears above and scatters snow on the scene below.)*

TURZAHNELLE:
Little lamb, child of mine,
Let's go to the shores of the sea;
The tiny ant will be at his doorway;
I'll nurse you and give you your bread.

(Refrain)
Orgone, baby hunchback,
Orgone, baby pinhead,
Orgone, baby sex maniac,
Little lamb . . .

Rock, rockaby,
Let's go to the palms at Bethlehem's Gate.
(She laughs.)

Neither you nor I would want to sleep.
The door will open itself,
And on the beach we'll go and hide
In a little coral cabin.
(Repeat refrain.)
ANGEL: Grandmother, where are you going?
TURZAHNELLE: Are you going to part the clouds for me? Who are you?
ANGEL: How did you get out here?
TURZAHNELLE: I escaped.
ORGONE: From Creedmore.
TURZAHNELLE: You, who are you? And when are you gong to have a baby?
 I've had this one.
ANGEL: Where did you get that lamb?
ORGONE: Bamberger's, Newark!
TURZAHNELLE: I know it's a lamb. But can't a lamb be a baby? Besides, children
 born know nothing of life, not even its greatness. *(She repeats her song, putting
 a purse full of money in the shopping cart. Speaking like a somnambulist)*
 One nonday I sleep.
 I dreamt of a someday.
 Of a wonday I shall wake.
 Ah! May he have now of here fearfilled me!
 Sinflowed, O sin flowed!
(She exits, abandoning the baby in the shopping cart)

(Enter CARLA, *the Gypsy Wildcat. She discovers the Baby Hunchback, Pinhead, Sex
Maniac and wheels him off.)*

The Gypsy Encampment

([Several years later.] CARLA *dances in singing, accompanied by an orchestra of*
DEVILS.*)*

CARLA:
 A Gypsy wasn't born to live in slavery.
 He wasn't born to bow or bend on knees.
 So raise your voices, and let them hear you.

 A Gypsy's life is like the wind, it must be free.
 Shout it from your wagons, sing it at your campfire.
 Who makes the Gypsy's life of toil a life of pleasure?
 She whom he takes to wife and loves beyond all measure.

 She makes each day more lovely seem.
 She is his treasure, his only treasure.
Satan! My fiery Gypsy music, if you please.

(She goes into a wild Gypsy dance. A SOLDIER *ambles on during the dance and leans
against the wagon.)*

SOLDIER:
 Her cheeks are red, her eyes are bright.
 Her hair is black as wing of night.
 Let no blond man in her sight,
 For she will bewitch his baby blue eyes.
 (Speaking to her) Are you leaving this camp?
CARLA: We Gypsies never linger.
SOLDIER: Your voice was talking to me while you were dancing.
CARLA: Did you listen to it?
SOLDIER: I had to, you were singing so loudly.
CARLA: Over the music?
SOLDIER: Over everything. You smiled at me while you were dancing.
CARLA: You dropped a coin in my tambourine.
SOLDIER: You sell your smiles. Your kisses too? *(CARLA slaps him)* Ha! Ha! Ha!
 I deserved that. Listen.
CARLA: The Baron's men?
SOLDIER: No, our inner voices are talking to us.
CARLA: What is yours saying?
SOLDIER: A beautiful Gypsy girl smiled and danced her way into my heart.
CARLA: And mine is saying, "Keep me there and never let me go."

(The SOLDIER *kisses* CARLA. *Enter* ORGONE, *the Teenage Hunchback, Pinhead, Sex Maniac.)*

ORGONE: *(Calling)* Mother! Mother!
CARLA: You are a most unruly one: you are still up while you should be
 sleeping.
ORGONE: How can I sleep with you making all this racket?
SOLDIER: Is he in love with you?
CARLA: All Gypsies are in love.

(Enter GYPSY VIOLINIST, *playing.)*

CARLA: Listen! The Gypsy song of freedom.
SOLDIER: I heard it yesterday in the wagon.
CARLA: Yes, we always sing it when we are in trouble.
SOLDIER: Why, is the Brazilian Brassiere Buster, Baron Bubbles in the Bathtub,
 bugging you, baby?
CARLA: Last week the madly chic Turzahnelle broke the bank at his casino. And
 now he's taxing the Gypsies to death to recover the loss.
SOLDIER: Couldn't you refuse to pay?
CARLA: Any Gypsy refusing to pay the taxes is turned into a galley slave and
 lashed a hundred times to make him row.
SOLDIER: What makes the Baron so cruel?
CARLA: When greed takes hold of a man, he will stop at nothing.
SOLDIER: I'm going. I'll stop the Baron's men!

(He exits marching. CARLA *goes to kiss him, but he only salutes her.)*

ORGONE: He's left us. Come tell me that tale of which you sang today.
CARLA: To think that you don't know it. *(Aside)* How could he know that other
 footsteps guided him far from his country? *(To* ORGONE*)* I sang the gruesome

tale of a mother who bore a son, wrapped him in swaddling clothes, and brought him to a mountaintop. I followed her sad procession. In vain I tried to reach her. She left him there in the snow, and in failing accents, "Sinflowed, O sin flowed," she wailed. Those bitter words of anguish on this, my heart, are nailed.

ORGONE: O tale of horror!

CARLA: I stole the child from that wicked mother and brought him hither with me.

ORGONE: I am not your son? Then who am I? Who the hell am I?

CARLA: *(Tenderly)* Of course you are my son.

ORGONE: But just now you told me . . .

CARLA: I told you? I told you? Forget it! When it comes back to me, that dreadful vision, my mind becomes overclouded and the words that I speak are often foolish. There is a voice within all of us that never lies. But appearances often do.

ORGONE: I know, I know. But tell me, whose son am I?

CARLA: When I found you on the mountaintop, did I not find you living still? Was it not my skill in leechcraft that healed the wounds of which you were bleeding?

ORGONE: *(Aside)* I used to have the syph! *(To* CARLA*)* Who is this woman? I must find her and avenge my childhood.

CARLA: That is not for me to say. But I'll help you. Out there beyond this forest lies the world.

ORGONE: Forty-second Street!

CARLA: Go. And when you find your mother, give her this seat. *(She produces a toilet seat which she plays to the rhythm of her words like a giant castanet, as she utters this incantation)* Whoever sits on this seat, sits on this seat forever! Till tree from tree, tree among trees, tree over tree become stone to stone, stone between stones, stone under stone forever!

ORGONE: *(Exultant)* The silent cock crows at last. The West shall shake the East awake!

CARLA: Go while ye have the night for morn.

ORGONE: Bye-bye, Mother.

CARLA: Good-bye, Son. *(She blows him a kiss and exits)*

On the Road

ORGONE: Ah, if only I had a crust of dry bread to eat and a faggot to keep me warm in the winter.

(The ANGEL *appears.)*

ANGEL: Let me be your faggot, sir.

ORGONE: Are you an angel?

ANGEL: No, Orgone, I'm a fairy. Do you want to see how many angels can fit on the head of a pin?

(The ANGEL *lifts his skirt and bends over.* ORGONE *shoves his pinhead up the* ANGEL*'s ass.)*

ORGONE: Oh, I must stop whatever it is we're doing because the windmills of your asshole are fucking with my mind.

ANGEL: Do you mind if we go a little way on foot?

ORGONE: Do you want to talk to me about something?

ANGEL: I ask myself whether you are worth all the pains that I should have to take with you. We trim yews, as a last resort, because yews and begonias submit to treatment. But we should like to give our time to a plant of human growth. In the heart of our tub, like Diogenes, we cry out for a man.

(They stroll out.)

The Gambling Casino

(There is a change of lighting. MUSICIANS *dressed as Devils enter and play the theme of* Turds in Hell. *Flames are projected behind them. Money begins to fall as the snow fell in the first episode.*

In the gambling casino, the wheel of fortune spins. The GAMBLERS, *in formal evening dress, place bets, win and lose money. There is the constant murmur of the words "rouge," "noir," "baccarat," etc. The stage is flooded with money and poker chips.* ORGONE *slips into the casino unnoticed by the* GUESTS, *in spite of his goat legs, hunchback, pinhead, and enormous cock and balls. Although he wears no complete human clothing, he wears a tuxedo jacket with tails and a black tie. The* DEVIL *acts as Butler and announces the* GUESTS *as they arrive.)*

DEVIL-AS-BUTLER: Your host, the Brazilian Brassiere Buster, Baron Bubbles in the Bathtub.

(Enter the BARON, *a man of enormous girth who sounds exactly like Arthur Godfrey with a French accent.)*

BARON: How ay ya? Howaaiya? Hawaii ya? *(Belly laugh)*

ORGONE: He is a voluptuary. He knows all the toilets in Paris that have seats.

BARON: To do a good job, I've got to be sitting down.

ORGONE: He walks for miles preciously carrying in his bowels the desire to shit, which he will then gravely deposit in the mauve, tiled toilets of the Café Terminus at the Saint Lazare Station, Gai Paris!

BARON: *(Announcing to all his* GUESTS*)* My friends, do not be envious of this wealth of mine you see before your eyeballs. For remember in this one thing we are all created equal. *(The* DEVIL *plays a fanfare of farts)* When nature calls, we must all take down our pants, or, with deference to the ladies present, lift up our skirts, and unload. *(Belly laugh)*

ORGONE: He needs a hearing aid for his asshole.

BARON: My chamber pot! *(The* DEVIL-AS-BUTLER *brings his chamber pot.* BUBBLES *drops his pants and squats on the pot)* You see, ladies and gentlemen, lacquered ladies and gentle gentlemen, all men are created equal! *(He shits a torrent of gold coins into the chamber pot. The* DEVIL-AS-BUTLER *wipes the* BARON's *ass with a twenty-dollar bill. To the* DEVIL-AS-BUTLER*)* Keep the change!

(The DEVIL-AS-BUTLER *kisses the twenty-dollar bill and pockets it. All the* GUESTS *applaud except* ORGONE.*)*

ORGONE: *(Aside)* It's a shame to see so much money go to waste in other people's pockets. This is my big chance to turn the numbers racket into a legal lottery.

DEVIL-AS-BUTLER: Enter Madame Tryphoena.

(MADAME TRYPHOENA *enters, dressed like Elizabeth I.*)

BARON: *(to the* DEVIL-AS-BUTLER*)* Would you mind helping me off with my leg? *(He has a wooden leg which fastens to the stump, below the knee, by a system of straps and buckles)* Sometimes I feel like beating it for Brazil. But with my trick paw, it's not so easy.

DEVIL-AS-BUTLER: *(Back at his post by the door)* Enter Turtle Woman. She is like a turtle in every way, except that she is rich.

TURTLE WOMAN: I like to take my time.

ORGONE: *(Aside)* You see what two million dollars can buy?

DEVIL-AS-BUTLER: Enter Vera.

(VERA *enters wearing a gown and hat made out of dollar bills. Her jewelry is made of mint-condition Kennedy half-dollars. She wears a dollar-bill mask and peers through the eyes of George Washington. The* BARON *rushes up to her, ecstatically hopping on one foot.*)

BARON: Believe me, Vera, I have never admired your acting as I do tonight. How brilliantly you understand your role!

TURTLE WOMAN: What great interpretation, and how forceful!

MME. TRYPHOENA: What artistry!

VERA: Yes, every word and gesture comes down to me on wings of inspiration; the words flow forth, as if not learned by rote but like the beatings of my heart itself.

BARON: How true! And even now your eyes are gleaming, your cheeks aflame, your passion not extinguished. And since it glows, don't let the embers die. Sing us a song. Oh, Vera, sing for us. Sing anything you like.

(TURTLE WOMAN *loses all her clothing except her merry widow at baccarat.*)

DEVIL: *(To the audience)* O credulous mankind, is there one error that has woo'd and lost you? Now listen and strike error from your mind: The King, whose perfect wisdom transcends all, made the heavens and posted angels on them to guide the eternal light that it might fall from every sphere to every sphere the same. He made earth's splendors by a like degree and posted as their minister this dame, the Lady of Permutations. All earth's gears she changes from nation to nation, from house to house, in changeless change through every turning year. No mortal power can stay her spinning wheel. The nations rise and fall by her decree. None may foresee where she may set her heel. She pauses and things pass. Man's mortal reason cannot encompass her. She rules her sphere as other gods rule theirs. Season by season, her changes change her changes endlessly. Those whose time has come press her so, she must be swift by hard necessity. For this is she so railed at and reviled that even her debtors in the joys of time blaspheme her name. Their oaths are bitter and wild. But she in her beatitude does not hear. Among the primal beings of God's joy, she breathes her blessedness and wheels her sphere. *(He spins the wheel of fortune)*

(VERA *sings Kay Starr's 1956 hit "The Wheel of Fortune" and the Crowd cheers.*)

ALL: Brava, brava! Sublime! Superb! Divine! *(They resume gambling)*

BARON: Enchantress, thank you. You have reached our hearts. Of all life's pleasures, music is surpassed only by love, itself a melody.

(A flagellant procession of SAINTS, MONKS, NUNS, *etc., and the* ANGEL *enter the casino, heralding the entrance of* TURZAHNELLE. SAINT OBNOXIOUS *carries a cross.* SAINT FRIGID *crawls on her knees, crowned with thorns. The* ANGEL *scourges* SAINT OBNOXIOUS. *The* DEVIL-AS-BUTLER *and* ORGONE *attempt to crack the casino safe.)*

FLAGELLANTS: *(In chorus, speaking in a round)* Enter Turzahnelle! How serene does she now arise, a queen among the Pleiades, in the penultimate antilucan hour, shod in sandals of bright gold, coiffed with a veil of . . . what do you call it?

TURZAHNELLE: Gossamer!

FLAGELLANTS: Gossamer. It flows, it floats about her starborn flesh and loose it streams emerald, sapphire, mauve, and heliotrope, sustained on currents of cold interstellar wind, winding, coiling, simply swirling, writhing in the skies a mysterious writing, till, after myriad metamorphoses of symbol, it blazes, alpha, a ruby, and triangled sign, upon the forehead of Taurus.

TURZAHNELLE: How humiliating! Life has but one true charm: the charm of gambling. Spin the wheels! Break the bank!

[(In the following speeches, each company may insert names of critics who have given them bad reviews.)

TURTLE WOMAN: My dear, speaking of Madame de L. reminds me of Y. She came to me yesterday evening and if I had known that you weren't engaged, I'd have sent round to ask you to come. Madame M. turned up quite by chance, and recited some poems by Queen Ronald Tavel in the author's presence. It was too beautiful.

MME. TRYPHOENA: *(Aside)* What treachery! Of course. That was what she was whispering about to Madame B. and Madame de C. the other day. *(Aloud)* I had no engagement. But I should not have come. I heard M. in her great days, she's a mere wreck now. Besides I detest Ronald Tavel's poetry.

TURTLE WOMAN: Didn't Ronnie write *The Anus of Leukorrhea?*

MME. TRYPHOENA: M. came here once—the Duchess of A. brought her—to recite a canto of the *Inferno,* by Dante. In that sort of thing she's incomparable.

CROUPIER: Madame, your beauty is exceeded only by your towering wisdom.

MME. TRYPHOENA: Thank you. Now, sir, if you are fond of painting, look at the portrait of Madame de M. It's one of the finest examples of pornographic art. *(She shows the portrait)*

ORGONE: Oooh! If I had a face like that I'd have it lanced!

MME. TRYPHOENA: *(Murmuring) There's* Monsieur L. He had a sister, Madame A. D. Coleman, not that that conveys any more to you than it does to me.

TURTLE WOMAN: *(Exclaiming)* What! Oh, but I know her quite well! *(Putting her hand over her lips)* That is to say, I don't know her! But, for some reason or other, Wynn Chamberpot, who meets her husband at the St. Mark's Baths, took it into his head to tell the wretched woman she might call on me. And she did. I can't tell you what it was like. She informed me that she had been to London, and gave me a complete catalog of all the things in the British Museum. And this very day, the moment I leave your house, I'm going, just as you see me now, to drop a card on the monster. And don't for a moment suppose that it's an easy thing to do. On the pretense that she's dying of some disease or another she's always at home, it doesn't matter whether you arrive at seven at night or nine in the morning, she's always ready for you with a dish of strawberry tarts.]

DEVIL-AS-BUTLER: I've got everything, but I can't get into the safe. They must have changed the combination.

ORGONE: This is a seaman's hook. It will sink eleven inches into wood. I wonder how far it will penetrate human flesh.

DEVIL-AS-BUTLER: Don't you trust me?

ORGONE: *(Sinisterly)* Of course I trust you. I just want you to see how worried I am.

[TURTLE WOMAN: No, but seriously, you know, she is a monstrosity. *(MADAME TRYPHOENA questioningly glances)* She's an impossible person, she talks about plumitives and things like that.

MME. TRYPHOENA: What does "plumitive" mean?

TURTLE WOMAN: *(With mock indignation)* I haven't the slightest idea! I don't want to know. I don't speak that sort of language. *(Then, to show she is a scholar as well as a purist)* Why, of course. *(With a half-laugh that the traces of her pretended ill humor keep in check)* Everybody knows what it means: a plumitive is a writer, a person who holds a pen. But it's a dreadful word. It's enough to make your wisdom teeth drop out. Nothing will ever make me use a word like that. So that's the brother, is it? But, after all, it's not inconceivable. She has the same doormat docility and the same mass of information, like a circulating library. She's just as much of a flatterer as he is, and just as boring. Yes, I'm beginning to see the family likeness now quite plainly.]

MME. TRYPHOENA: *(to the BARON)* Sit down, we're just going to take a dish of tea. Help yourself. You don't want to look at the pictures of your great-grandmothers. You know them as well as I do.

BARON: Don't shrug your shoulders at me, my friends. *(He shits)* I'm not crazy. All men are created equal.

DEVIL-AS-BUTLER: That old guy is washed-up. He can't even get a hard-on.

ORGONE: His father and mother were in the iron and steel business—his mother used to iron and his father used to steal.

DEVIL-AS-BUTLER: Hellstones and flamballs, it's hot down here.

(ORGONE cracks the safe. The safe cracks. Explosion.)

DEVIL-AS-BUTLER: You broke the bank!

(Money falls like snow as the cast sings "We're In the Money.")

ST. OBNOXIOUS: What do I behold? Shall my Father's house be thus dishonored? Is this the house of God or is it a marketplace? Shall strangers, who come from heathen lands to worship God, perform their devotions amidst this tumult of usury? Woe unto you! He who searcheth the heart knows wherefore ye permit this wrong.

ANGEL: It is the great prophet of Nazareth in Galilee.

ST. OBNOXIOUS: Go hence, ye servants of Mammon! I command it. Take that which is yours and depart from this holy place.

TURTLE WOMAN: Are men no longer to offer sacrifices?

ST. OBNOXIOUS: Without the temple are places sufficient for your business. My house, saith the Lord, shall be called a house of prayer for all people! But ye have made it a den of thieves. *(Overturning the tables)* Take all this hence!

BARON: Who will make good the loss to me?

ST. OBNOXIOUS: *(With a scourge of cords)* Go hence! I will that this consecrated place be given back to the worship of the Father.

BARON: What signs showest thou that thou hast power to do these things?

ST. OBNOXIOUS: Ye seek after signs! Yea, a sign shall be given unto you: Destroy this temple and in three days I will raise it up.

MME. TRYPHOENA: Rebuke thy disciples!

ST. OBNOXIOUS: I say unto you, if these should hold their peace the stones would cry out.

ANGEL: Grind them to a powder!

ST. OBNOXIOUS: Come, my disciples! I have done as the Father gave me commandment, I have vindicated the honor of His house. The darkness remains darkness; but in many hearts the day star will soon arise. Let us go into the sanctuary and take the Last Supper. I'll pick up the tab.

(Exit all but the BARON *and* TURZAHNELLE.*)*

The Marriage Proposal

TURZAHNELLE: Baron!

BARON: Will you be mine?

*(*TURZAHNELLE *hesitates. The* BARON *shits money.)*

TURZAHNELLE: *(Seeing the money)* Yes!

BARON: Congratulations, my dear.

TURZAHNELLE: Thank you, darling.

BARON: You have a national responsibility, I hope you understand.

TURZAHNELLE: You mean the money.

BARON: Shh! Let's not speak of those profane things at such a tender moment!

TURZAHNELLE: Baron, I do admire your candor.

BARON: It is such a lovely night and a happy occasion—isn't it wonderful?

TURZAHNELLE: Wonderful. *(Aside)* Charming man, really. The nuts! *(She laughs)*

BARON: Too much excitement?

TURZAHNELLE: I can hardly wait.

BARON: Come dear, let's drink to this!

TURZAHNELLE: Oooh, Bubbles!

(They exit.)

Marriage Television Style

(The DEVIL *is seen on a television screen as a Newscaster. He is reading the news of the day.)*

DEVIL-AS-NEWSCASTER: *(In conclusion)* . . . Turzahnelle will be a miniskirted bride wearing an ivory gown by Valentino with a hemline four inches above her crack for her marriage to the Brazilian Brassiere Buster, Baron Bubbles in the Bathtub. She will also be wearing a crown of orange blossoms as will her sixty-two-year-old bridegroom, if they are married in the Greek Orthodox tradition as is expected. The last-minute arrangements for the wedding were made by Turzahnelle, on Bubbles in the Bathtub's yacht, which is docked in the brilliant blue waters of the Ionian Sea. The gleaming white yacht has been there for two months. The wedding guests, numbering between twelve and fifteen, are *living* on the yacht. It has many more luxuries than the living quarters on the island where the Baron is building his villa.

(MADAME TRYPHOENA *enters, calling for her ward,* VERA.)

MME. TRYPHOENA: Vera! Vera! VE-RA!

(VERA *enters, skipping rope.*)

VERA: *(Timidly)* You wanted me, Tryphoena?
MME. TRYPHOENA: *(Looking around quickly)* Ah, Vera! Yes, I want talk you.
VERA: You all right?
MME. TRYPHOENA: Yes, why ask?
VERA: Look spent.
MME. TRYPHOENA: Oh, no, hot, that's all.
DEVIL-AS-NEWSCASTER: Choose heaven for climate but hell for company.
MME. TRYPHOENA: Sit down. (VERA *sits down*) You busy?
VERA: Busy? No.
DEVIL-AS-NEWSCASTER: Women are like money: keep them busy or they lose interest.
MME. TRYPHOENA: Vera, want to talk serious.
VERA: What? Serious?
MME. TRYPHOENA: You smart girl. Time to think about your future.
[VERA: What?
MME. TRYPHOENA: Future.]
VERA: Future.
MME. TRYPHOENA: You like daughter, house for you.
VERA: Oh.
MME. TRYPHOENA: You orphan. You not rich.
VERA: Poor?
MME. TRYPHOENA: Time you come to dislike live permanently other people.
VERA: Who?
MME. TRYPHOENA: Me.
VERA: Oh.
[MME. TRYPHOENA: You like own house?
VERA: *(Slowly)* I don't understand.
MME. TRYPHOENA: You.] *(After a pause)* Men ask hand.
VERA: Huh?
DEVIL-AS-NEWSCASTER: Women would be more charming if one could fall immediately into their arms without falling into their hands.
VERA: Hands?
MME. TRYPHOENA: Yes!
VERA: No.
MME. TRYPHOENA: You didn't expect. Me, too. You young. I don't push you. Soon for marriage.

(VERA *buries her face in her hands.*)

MME. TRYPHOENA: *(Coming on dyky)* Vera crying? *(Taking her hand)* Vera trembling! Vera afraid?

VERA: *(Tonelessly)* I'm in your hands, Madame Tryphoena.

MME. TRYPHOENA: Vera, shame crying. My hands? My daughter, you thought . . .

(MADAME TRYPHOENA turns, lifting her dress. VERA, smiling through her tears, kisses MADAME TRYPHOENA's ass. TRYPHOENA puts an arm around her and draws her toward herself.)

[VERA: All right.

MME. TRYPHOENA: Vera, you not emotional, you not sincere.

VERA: I *am* emotional! I *am* sincere!

MME. TRYPHOENA: Better! Laugh! *(VERA laughs)* Command.

DEVIL-AS-NEWSCASTER: He who laughs last, laughs best, may laugh best but soon gets a reputation for being dumb.]

MME. TRYPHOENA: Vera, pretend me your mother.

VERA: What?

MME. TRYPHOENA: Mother.

VERA: Mother.

MME. TRYPHOENA: No, better sister. Have good talk. Wonderful.

VERA: You mean there's a language of the senses too?

MME. TRYPHOENA: Vera, if you had known this perhaps you would have been less bored.

VERA: Perhaps I would have been more bored.

(ORGONE enters.)

MME. TRYPHOENA: Orgone! Orgone, Vera. Vera, Orgone.

ORGONE: *(Presenting a box of candy and a bouquet)* How's tricks?

VERA: *(Screaming in horror)* Hie me to a nunnery! *(She exits)*

MME. TRYPHOENA: I can't understand it. I thought for sure she'd love you.

ORGONE: Maybe she had the rag on today. *(Exiting with MADAME TRYPHO-ENA)* I used to subscribe to *Mothers' Monthly*—it's a periodical. You write to the Department of Labor Pains, Washington D and C.

[En Una Noche Oscuro

ST. OBNOXIOUS: Harélo aunque fuera justo poner mi enojo en efecto.

ANGEL: Vienes ya desenojado.

ST. OBNOXIOUS: Por los que me han pedido.

ANGEL: Perdon mil veces te pido.

ST. OBNOXIOUS: ¿Y Turzahnelle?

ANGEL: Aqui ha jurado. No entra en la corte más.

ST. OBNOXIOUS: ¿A donde se fué?

ANGEL: A Toledo.

ST. OBNOXIOUS: Bien hizo.

ANGEL: ¡No tenga mierda que vuelva in Madrid jamás!

ST. OBNOXIOUS: Hijo, pues simple nasciste. Y por milagro de amor dejaste el pasado error como el ingenio perdiste.

Charles Ludlam & Bill Vehr in *Turds in Hell* (Leandro Katz)

ANGEL: ¿Que quieres, hermano? A la fe de bobos, no hay que fiar.
ST. OBNOXIOUS: Yo lo pienso remediar.
ANGEL: Como si el otro se fué?
ST. OBNOXIOUS: Pues te engañan facilmente los hombres.
ANGEL: Pues, ¿donde?
ST. OBNOXIOUS: In parte secreta.
ANGEL: Será bien en un desván, donde los gatos están. ¿Quieres tú que allí me meta?
ST. OBNOXIOUS: Hay que tomar la muerte como si fuera aspirina.
ANGEL: En el desván sea. Tú lo mandas su justo y advierte que lo has mandado.
ST. OBNOXIOUS: Una y mil veces.]

The Convent

"O Holy Night" begins playing as SAINT OBNOXIOUS, *the* ANGEL, *and* SAINT
FRIGID *pose as statues in the convent.* ORGONE, *the Hunchback, Pinhead, Sex
Maniac, sneaks into the convent disguised as Santa Claus, carrying a Christmas tree.*
VERA, *dressed as a nun on roller skates, skates in.)*

VERA: I open the window and influenza like the autumn wind which turns the
leaves to yellow.

ORGONE: So here you are, transformed into a woman! And I a man!

VERA: No! Orgone, no. I am going to take the veil.

ORGONE: I can't believe it! Is this you?

VERA: Yes! Oh, it is—I have renounced the world. However, before I leave
it, I should like to have your opinion—do you think I'm right to become a
nun?

[ORGONE: Don't ask me about that. I could never get into the habit, myself.

VERA: Orgone, answer my question. Am I right to stay in the convent?]

ORGONE: No.

VERA: Then should I do better to marry you?

ORGONE: Yes. *(He laughs)*

VERA: If your village priest breathed on a glass of water and told you it was a
glass of wine, would you drink it as if it were?

ORGONE: No.

VERA: If your village priest breathed on you and told me you'd love me all your
life, would I be right to believe him?

ORGONE: Yes and no. Because I'm AC and DC.

VERA: What would you advise me to do the day I saw you didn't love me
anymore?

ORGONE: Take a lover.

VERA: Then what shall I do the day my lover doesn't love me anymore?

ORGONE: You'll take another.

VERA: How long will that last?

ORGONE: Till your hair is gray and then mine will be white.

[VERA: Do you know what the cloister is, Orgone?

ORGONE: Oh, sure. You take the A Train and get off at Two-hundredth Street.

VERA: Have you ever sat there for a whole day?

ORGONE: Oh, God, no! I had to stand—it was rush hour!] *(He leaps up insanely,
shouting)* [You're nothing but a filthy prostitute!

VERA: *(Enraged)* What did you say?

ORGONE: *(More viciously)* You're nothing but a filthy prostitute.

VERA: *(Relieved)* Oh, I thought you said Protestant.]

ORGONE: Are you a nun or are you straight?

*(*ORGONE *attacks and rapes* SISTER VERA.)*

VERA: You're a pervert?

ORGONE: I'm trisexual. I'll try anything.

VERA: *(Screaming)* Saint Frigid! Protect me!

*(*VERA *and* ORGONE *disappear behind the statue of Saint Frigid.)*

ST. OBNOXIOUS: Nuns should never have intimate friends.

ST. FRIGID: *(Showing her grill)* I am the Holy Frigid, flogged with rods day after day for seven days and then roasted alive on this grill over a slow fire. No other being has suffered as frightfully as I!

ST. OBNOXIOUS: Is that anything to speak of! I am the Holy Obnoxious with the skin, who, at the command of Emperor Pamphilius, was flayed alive all the way down to my knees. And all the miracles that took place after my death! And haven't you heard of the many mysterious happenings—or about the devil appearing in the shape of a woman—or the presaging of the erupting of the volcano? No mortal man has ever suffered as I have.

ANGEL: Obnoxious? Obnoxious! Is that you?

ST. OBNOXIOUS: Gaybriel!

ANGEL: How many years has it been, Obnoxious?

ST. OBNOXIOUS: Five or six years, I'd say.

ANGEL: Five or six years! There's something different about you—you've changed. What is it?

ST. OBNOXIOUS: You haven't changed a bit, Gaybriel—just a bit holier, I expect.

ANGEL: Yes, Obnoxious, you have changed! What is it? What is it?

ST. OBNOXIOUS: *(In a panic)* Have I lost my looks?

ANGEL: No, you're lovelier than ever—it's something else. What have you been doing these five or six years?

ST. OBNOXIOUS: Praying, Gaybriel.

ANGEL: Hah!

ST. OBNOXIOUS: Fasting and penance, solitude—the hard road.

ANGEL: The hard road?

ST. OBNOXIOUS: Oh, Gaybriel, no mortal man has ever suffered as I have. I was forced to carry a heavy cross up a steep hill and I was crucified upside down.

ANGEL: Oh, pshaw!

ST. OBNOXIOUS: On the third day after my death my flesh was boiled in oil and fed to the lions.

ANGEL: You talk to me of suffering? I, who've walked through hell and purgatory and seen the eyes and faces of the many suffering, you talk to me of suffering?

ST. OBNOXIOUS: But Gaybriel, what of the dead body of the nun?

(VERA screams and reappears with ORGONE, who is now dressed in Vera's habit. VERA is naked except for crucifix pasties on her tits, a rosary G-string, and a pig mask. Kneeling in front of SAINT FRIGID, she says the "Hail Mary" in pig latin.)

ST. FRIGID: [*To* VERA] And you, you little tramp! Where did you get your morals? In some gutter?

ORGONE: *(Remorsefully, as his good side shows through)* Oh Sister, oh God, I'm sorry. . . . *(Pause)* What will you do now?

VERA: I'll return to the Convent, make a good confession, and tell the priest that as I was walking home, you grabbed me, dragged me into the bushes, and raped me . . . *twice,* if you're up to it!

ORGONE: Don't worry, baby, they call me "woman of mystery"—the Mona Lisa in drag. But don't worry. Mother's got a box in heaven. *(He exits, singing)* "Sunrise, sunset . . ."

The Monastery

ST. OBNOXIOUS: *(Speaking off)* Laurent, put away my hair shirt and my scourge and continue to pray heaven to send you grace. If anyone asks for me I'll be with the prisoners distributing alms.

DEVIL: *(Aside)* The impudent hypocrite!

ST. OBNOXIOUS: Where have you been?

DEVIL: Going to and fro on the earth and walking up and down on it.

ST. OBNOXIOUS: You're a devil.

DEVIL: In little hell. Yes, look at me, I am worse than a heretic—I am a pagan.

[ST. OBNOXIOUS: You were an evangelist once too, but you tired of that.

DEVIL: I did not tire, but when I found I could not live what I taught, I stopped teaching in order not to be called a hypocrite. And when I discovered that nowhere was there any putting into practice of those beautiful doctrines, I left their realization for the land of fulfilled desires.]

ST. OBNOXIOUS: *(Beside himself)* Yes, I want to bite your throat and suck your blood like a lynx. You have roused the wild beast in me which for years I've been trying to kill by self-denial and penance. I came here thinking myself rather better than you . . . but it is I who am vile. Now that I have seen you—in the full horror of your nakedness—now that passion has distorted my vision, I know the full force of evil. Ugliness has become beauty and goodness is growing ugly and feeble. . . . Come to me! I will suffocate you . . . with a kiss! *(He embraces the DEVIL and kisses him on the mouth)*

DEVIL: *(Breaking loose)* You're mighty susceptible to temptation, then! The flesh must make a great impression on you! I really don't know why you should get so excited. I can't say that I'm so easily aroused. I could see you naked from head to foot and your whole carcass wouldn't tempt me in the least.

ST. OBNOXIOUS: Peel off my skin. I won't cry, but you will. What am I?

DEVIL: *(Crying)* An onion! *(He exits)*

The Woodland Shrine of Saint Obnoxious

(SAINT OBNOXIOUS friezes in a niche, as a statue. CARLA enters and places a bouquet of lilies of the valley at his feet. Muguet du Bois cologne is sprayed on the audience. The BARON and his men (including the DEVIL) enter. The BARON spots SAINT OBNOXIOUS and mistakes him for CARLA.)

BARON: Seize her! Seize her!

ST. OBNOXIOUS: *(Struggling to get away)* No, no, not me! You have the wrong person! I haven't done anything—I'll give you indulgences—anything!

(The BARON and his men brand SAINT OBNOXIOUS on his ass.)

ST. OBNOXIOUS: Ahhgh aghh!! *(Weeping)* I'll turn the other cheek.

(They brand his other buttock.)

BARON: I could have sworn I saw Carla, the Gypsy Wildcat, placing a bouquet of lilies of the valley next to the statue of Saint Obnoxious.

ST. OBNOXIOUS: Even through the scent of one kosher grilled bun . . . *(He points to his branded ass)* . . . I can still smell the scent of lilies of the valley. Carla must be close at hand.

BARON: Ah! That can mean only one thing. That Carla is very near to us and all we have to do is to sniff our way through the trail scent of the lilies of the valley. Allons!

(The BARON *and his men begin sniffing.* OBNOXIOUS *sniffs also. Sniff! Sniff! Sniff! They reach* CARLA.*)*

BARON: Oho, just as I thought! Seize her!

*(*CARLA *screams and a wild chase ensues.)*

BARON: Allons! Allons!

(The DEVIL *seizes* CARLA.*)*

CARLA: Take your filthy hands off me, you dirty old man. *(She stamps on the* DEVIL*'s foot.)*

DEVIL: Oooh!

ST. OBNOXIOUS: Why, Carla, the Gypsy Wildcat, has stepped on his open-toed wedgies with her high-heeled, red vinyl boot trimmed in red marabou.

CARLA: That just goes to show you that these boots were not just made for walking. Go ahead, Baron, brand me if you like. *(The* BARON *hesitates)* Well, why did you not brand me?

BARON: It's your combination of that Latin intense look mixed with courage. Oh, Carla, would I like to brown you now!

CARLA: I don't quite understand it, Baron—first you wanted to brand me, now you want to brown me.

[BARON: Her breath takes my beauty away.

ST. OBNOXIOUS: *(In an* ENGLISH *accent)* Which do you prefer, my deah, Kipling or Browning?

CARLA: Oh, Browning, definitely!

ST. OBNOXIOUS: Why's that?

CARLA: Well you see, I have never been kippled, so I really cannot say.]

BARON: We could make a deal, Carla. I'll take you to my pavilion so you can tell my fortune.

(The BARON *throws* CARLA *over his shoulder and carries her off.)*

CARLA: *(Singing)* A Gypsy wasn't born to live in slavery. . . . *(Etc.)*

The Pavilion

(The BARON *and* CARLA *reenter at the other side of the stage. The* BARON *is still carrying* CARLA*—she is still singing. They sit at a table. The* BARON *pours some wine.)*

BARON: Carla, we're together at last. Can you tell my fortune in my hand, Carla?

CARLA: *(Looking at the palm of his hand)* Of course, Baron, that's right up my alley, nothing easier. Everybody's future is in their face. Nothing easier.

BARON: But what about my past—my youth, where did it go?

CARLA: I'm sorry about that, but I cannot undo what you have done already. It slipped away while you weren't looking. While you were asleep. While you were drunk? Think! Think!

BARON: What good are you Gypsies?

CARLA: I can't tell the past and neither can you, but I *can* tell you about tomorrow.

BARON: You say "tomorrow," but tomorrow never comes.

CARLA: That's what's so intriguing about tomorrow.

BARON: Carla, tell me, whom will I marry?

CARLA: I can tell you without looking at my cards, Baron, that it is not a Gypsy you will marry.

BARON: Then who is it?

CARLA: You will find a clue in your toilet.

BARON: What do you mean, in my toilet?

CARLA: That's exactly what I mean: Turds in Hell! *(She spits)*

BARON: Turds in Hell? Turds in Hell? Merde en enfer? What can you mean? How can you know so much?

CARLA: You seem to forget, Baron, that I am a *gitana*—Gypsy to you.

BARON: A Gypsy yes, but . . .

CARLA: And because of you, I long for a man who has left me; because of Turds in Hell . . . *(She spits)* . . . I weep for a child.

BARON: You speak rashly, my dear. Watch your language.

CARLA: There's more things in Turds in Hell . . . *(She spits)* . . . than are dreamed of in your philosophies, Baron. *(She turns to leave)*

BARON: Wait, Carla! Where are you going?

CARLA: I am going back to my people. Hasta la vista. *(She starts off)*

BARON: *(Following her)* Wait! I have another question to ask.

(He whispers in CARLA'S ear. She slaps him. They exit.)

The Brothel

(Enter VERA, wearily.)

PIMP:
There was a woman, and she was wise, woefully wise was she;
She was old, so old, yet her years all told were but a score and three;
And she knew by heart, from finish to start, the Book of Iniquity.

VERA:
There is no hope for such as I on earth, nor yet in Heaven;
Unloved I live, unloved I die, unpitied, unforgiven;
A loathéd jade, I ply my trade, unhallowed and unshriven.

I paint my cheeks, for they are white, and cheeks of chalk men hate;
Mine eyes with wine I make to shine, that man may seek and sate;
With overhead a lamp of red I sit me down and wait,

Until they come, the nightly scum, with drunken eyes aflame;
Your sweethearts, sons, ye scornful ones—'tis I who know their shame.
The gods, ye see, are brutes to me—and so I play my game.

For life is not the thing we thought, and not the thing we plan;
And Woman in a bitter world must do the best she can—
Must yield the stroke, and bear the yoke, and serve the will of man;

Must serve his need and ever feed the flame of his desire,
Though be she loved for love alone, or be she loved for hire;
For every man since life began is tainted with the mire.

And though you know he loves you so and sets you on love's throne;
Yet let your eyes but mock his sighs, and let your heart be stone,
Lest you be left (as I was left) attainted and alone.

PIMP:
Fate has written a tragedy; its name is *The Human Heart.*
The theatre is the House of Life, Woman the mummer's part;
The Devil enters the prompter's box and the play is ready to start.

(The PIMP *then introduces the* WHORES *as they enter.)*

PIMP: The charming whores, those in which beauty consists, are: the Tyrannical . . .

TYRANNICAL WHORE: Anyone for a little rubber and discipline?

PIMP: . . . the Too Too Mahooch, the Compulsive, the Tarantula . . .

DEVIL-AS-TARANTULA: *(Holding a set of chattering teeth between his legs, in a German accent)* I was featured in *Beavers on Parade*—I was the famous snapping pussy.

PIMP: . . . the Scarcely Credible, the Blasé, and, last but not least, the Empty-Headed . . .

VERA-AS-EMPTY-HEADED-WHORE: I may be dumb, but you didn't come here for any conversation, either!

(ORGONE enters in the nun disguise, and looks the WHORES over.)

ORGONE: Proud fondling whores, in spite of talc and rouge and all the gaudy lipstick, you smell of death.

PIMP: Are you the gentleman from Shirley?

ORGONE: Yeah!

PIMP: I have important news for you: you are afflicted with a grave sickness.

ORGONE: What kind of sickness it? And how have you come by this information?

PIMP: It is an inner sickness. Your body has been filled with a most dangerous poison. I learned this from revelations by the gods.

ORGONE: What would you have me do?

PIMP: The only way to cure the sickness is to draw the venom out of you.

ORGONE: Oh.

PIMP: You are fortunate in that we are equipped with tools which are capable of extracting the venom quite painlessly. In fact, it is certain that you will find the extraction enjoyable. *(Yells)* Yab Yum!

(Displaying the Whores' extractors, the PIMP removes ORGONE's clothes and takes hold of his dick. The WHORES scream in ecstasy when they see ORGONE's giant cock and balls and dive on him. An orgy ensues.)

[BLASÉ WHORE: Holy Toledo, you must have been born in a barn or something—why, you're hung like a horse.

DEVIL-AS-TARANTULA: Looks more like an elephant's trunk to me. I don't think I can take it.

ORGONE: What do you think this is, a fucking mike? C'mon, spread your cheeks a little wider, baby—it'll fit in there like a glove.

TYRANNICAL WHORE: I think by the size of that salami we are going to have to spread ourselves out just a little bit more, girls.

BLASÉ WHORE: I'm sick and tired of working like a horse. Why can't we get those nice guys—just a mere four-and-a-half inches?

VERA-AS-EMPTY-HEADED-WHORE: I know what you mean. You're referring to the ones that just barely tickle your ovaries.

COMPULSIVE WHORE: I don't know about you girls, but I ain't chicken—I can take it. *(She begins to blow* ORGONE's *giant cock)*

TOO TOO MAHOOCH: Honey, you ain't chicken, you're a gobbler.

BLASÉ WHORE: With a tool like that one, you certainly don't have to have your box scraped.]

DEVIL-AS-TARANTULA: If I continue, he will rise up, become erect, and penetrate me so deeply that I shall be marked with stigmata.

VERA-AS-EMPTY-HEADED-WHORE: Dreamin' again, huh?

DEVIL-AS-TARANTULA: Listen, honey, I ain't never met a man yet who could take care of all this sauerkraut, but I worship him. When I see him lying naked, I feel like saying Mass on his chest.

TYRANNICAL WHORE: To the heart, to the hilt, right to the balls, right in the throat.

ORGONE: Suck it yourself, sugarstick!

VERA-AS-EMPTY-HEADED-WHORE: The nights are mad about me! Oh, the sultanas! My God, they're making eyes at me! Oh, they're curling my hair around their fingers—the fingers of the nights, men's cocks! They're patting my cheek—stroking my butt!

TYRANNICAL WHORE: I'm not in the business for love, you know. I was in love once and I got the business.

PIMP: Time wounds all heels. I remember that some ten years ago, a beautifully plump, fresh young girl, the personal chambermaid of the queen, was found guilty of high treason for trying to poison the king, and consequently was condemned to suffer the cruelest death that could be devised for her. It was decreed that, after she had been crucified, she should be kept alive for as long as possible. The sentence was scrupulously carried out; when she fainted from the pain, the executioner gave her a little glass of liquor to revive her. She only died six days later. Her long suffering, her young age, and her robust constitution had made her flesh so tender, so savory, and so sought after that the executioner was able to sell it for more than eight sequins.

WHORES: Eight sequins! Get *her!*

PIMP: *(Shouting them down)* This inhuman market was so thronged with customers that persons of quality esteemed themselves happy if they could buy a couple of pounds.

WHORES: Fleshmongers—all of them!

TYRANNICAL WHORE: Thinness is more naked, more indecent than corpulence.

DEVIL-AS-TARANTULA: *(Singing)* Suck a dick a day or die!

WHORES: *(Singing)*
Spermatozoa,
I love you so-a

I want to know-a
When you will come.

You are so tasty
I want to taste ye
I will not waste ye
Please give me some.

Yum yum yum yum.

ORGONE: I saw something horrible last night as I was going home.

[TYRANNICAL WHORE: You astonish me; what was it startled you?

ORGONE: It was terrible—it made my blood stand still to behold what I beheld.]

TYRANNICAL WHORE: What was it met your gaze?

ORGONE: I saw a young man and a young lady swinging on a gate in the moonlight, biting each other.

VERA-AS-EMPTY-HEADED-WHORE: The impulse to bite is the origin of the kiss.

TYRANNICAL WHORE: To kiss means the act of biting rather than that of sucking.

ORGONE: Suck it yourself, sugarstick!

VERA-AS-EMPTY-HEADED-WHORE: Not only is he strange and queer, but he's got a one-track mind as well.

DEVIL-AS-TARANTULA: We always need to make a certain effort to understand the loves of others, and their way of making love. If it were possible to watch, the practices of our nearest neighbor would seem as strange, and even as extravagant—and, let us say, as monstrous—as the couplings of reptiles, insects, dogs, and prehistoric monsters.

PIMP: There is no exalted pleasure which cannot be related to prostitution. At the theatre, in the ballroom, each one enjoys possession of all. God is the most prostituted of all beings, because He is the closest friend of every individual, because He is the common inexhaustible reservoir of love.

ORGONE: Oh, hideous Jewess, lay with me for hire one night: two corpses side by side.

(ORGONE *and the* DEVIL-AS-TARANTULA *begin to fuck.*)

COMPULSIVE WHORE: What are you so smug about, you doxy trollop?

VERA-AS-EMPTY-HEADED-WHORE: Nothing—only this invitation to the biggest party of the year.

TYRANNICAL WHORE: Not Turzahnelle's!

VERA-AS-EMPTY-HEADED-WHORE: The one and only.

TYRANNICAL WHORE: Yeah, well she sure thinks her shit don't stink, huh, but she's no better'n the rest of us—I hear she murdered her child.

COMPULSIVE WHORE: She didn't murder him, just left him on a mountaintop—he had two heads or something.

(ORGONE *is listening intently while fucking the* DEVIL-AS-TARANTULA. *The more he realizes it's his mother they're talking about, the closer he gets to his orgasm. When he reaches it, he lets out a joyous yell, a scream.*)

DEVIL-AS-TARANTULA: *(Aside)* The devil's semen is as cold as ice. *(To* ORGONE*)* Auf Wiedersehen. I must return to the dead. As thou hast bragged of having fucked my body, so also canst thou boast of having fucked my soul.

ORGONE: And she fucks like she's got a newspaper asshole.

(The PIMP *and the* WHORES *exit, talking.)*

COMPULSIVE WHORE: What is the greatest pleasure in love?

BLASÉ WHORE: To receive.

TYRANNICAL WHORE: To give oneself.

VERA-AS-EMPTY-HEADED-WHORE: The pleasure of pride.

COMPULSIVE WHORE: The voluptuousness of humility.

TYRANNICAL WHORE: To beget citizens for the State.

PIMP: For my part, I say the sole and supreme pleasure in love lies in the absolute knowledge of doing evil. And man and woman know from birth that in evil is to be found all voluptuousness.

*(*ORGONE, *left alone, finds the invitation* VERA *dropped—the invitation to his mother's wedding.)*

ORGONE: Thou, nature, art my goddess. To thy law my services are bound. Why should I stand in the plague of customs and submit for the curiosity of nations to deprive me? Just because my mother dumped me? Why hunchback? Wherefore pinhead? How come sex maniac? When my form is as well compact, my mind as sharp . . . *(He lights his pinhead)* . . . and my shape as true as any honest madam's issue. Why brand they us with base? with baseness? with bastardy? Why base? Why basement? Why not try the roof? Well, Orgone, if this invitation gets you on the yacht, Orgone the Base shall grow and prosper. Now, gods! Stand up for hunchbacks, pinheads, and sex maniacs! *(He exits doing the shuffle-off-to-Buffalo)*

The Yacht on the River Styx

(The wedding party yacht begins to float onstage, headed by VERA *who, as the masthead of the ship, has turned into a harpy with a bird's head and claws for hands. The other* GUESTS *float in. The* DEVIL-AS-CHARON *steers the ship. In the background is heard "The People Who Walked in Darkness" from Handel's* Messiah. *All wear sporty nautical costumes and sway with the roll of the boat.)*

DEVIL-AS-CHARON:
Woe unto you, depraved souls!
Bury here and forever all hope of paradise:
I come to lead you to the other shore,
Into eternal dark, into fire and ice.
And you who are living yet, I say,
Begone from these who are dead.
By other windings and by other steerage
Shall you cross to that other shore.
Not here! Not here!
A lighter craft than mine must give you passage.

(The ANGEL *and a procession of* SAINTS, *led by* ORGONE, *brandishing his invitation, approach the ship.)*

ST. OBNOXIOUS: How melodorous is thy bel chant, O songbird, and how exqueezit thine afterdraught!

(A masked ball is in full swing on the yacht.)

ORGONE: *(to the* DEVIL-AS-CHARON, *showing his stolen invitation)* Charon, bite back your spleen: this has been willed where what is willed must be and is not yours to ask what it may mean.

[GUEST 1: Do you see clearly what is going on?

GUEST 2: I don't see clearly, but I hear well.

GUEST 1: Plenty to see and hear and feel and yet . . .

GUEST 3: I don't mind the heat, but the humidity.

GUEST 2: Feel live warm beings near you.

GUEST 1: Let them sleep in their maggoty beds. They are not going to get me this inning.

GUEST 2: Oh heaven, who can suffer this?

GUEST 1: I can.]

(The ANGEL *and the* SAINTS *begin to row the ship like galley slaves.)*

ANGEL: The summer evening had begun to fold the world in its mysterious embrace. Far away in the west the sun was setting and the last glow of all too fleeting day lingered lovingly on sea and strand, on the proud promontory of the dear old mountain guarding as ever the waters of the bay, on the weed-grown rocks along the shore and, last but not least, on the quiet church whence there streamed forth at times upon the stillness the voice of prayer to her who is in her pure radiance a beacon ever to the storm-tossed heart of man, Mary, star of the sea.

ST. OBNOXIOUS: And still a light moves long the river. And stiller the mermen ply their king. Its pith is full. The way is free—their lot is cast.

TURZAHNELLE: I don't think the Baron exactly likes me—between ourselves, of course.

GUEST 2: You're wrong. I promise you. He's often told me he thinks you're one of the prettiest women on earth.

TURZAHNELLE: Really? That's very charming. But I deserve it, as I've a very high opinion of him too.

[GUEST 1: The dresses that Palmira woman makes. You can never feel the shoulders and you think the whole time that everything's going to fall down. Did she make those sleeves of yours?

GUEST 2: Yes.

GUEST 1: Very pretty, very pretty indeed! Definitely there's nothing like straight sleeves, but it's taken me a long time to come round to them. Besides you mustn't be too fat to wear them or you look like a grasshopper with an enormous body and tiny feet and hands.

GUEST 2: What a charming thought.

GUEST 1: But isn't it true? Look at Madame Tryphoena. But of course you mustn't be too thin either or there's nothing left at all. Everybody's talking about the Turtle Woman. But to me she looks like a gallows. She has a lovely face, I agree, but she's just a Madonna on the end of a flagstaff.

TURZAHNELLE: Can I get you something to drink, dear?

GUEST 1: Nothing but hot water, with a dash of tea and a wisp of milk. *(Raucous laugh)* Now, look, there's another of them! With all those curls and lanky legs, she looks to me like one of those long-handled brooms you use for dusting picture rails.

TURZAHNELLE: She really is a little odd.] *(She sees* VERA*)* Oh, Vera, come here.

VERA: Why?

TURZAHNELLE: Look me straight in the face.

VERA: What's so extraordinary about me? Into every life a little rain must fall.

TURZAHNELLE: Yes, I was right, your eyes are red; you've just been crying, it's as clear as daylight. Why, what's happened, Vera?

DEVIL-AS-CHARON: Man has no Body distinct from his Soul; for that call'd Body is a portion of Soul discerned by the five Senses, the chief inlets of Soul in this age. Energy is the only life, and is from the Body. Reason is the bound or outward circumstance of Energy. Energy is Eternal Delight!

ANGEL: How do you know but every bird that cuts the airy way is an immense world of delight, clos'd by your senses five?

(VERA is shot—a shot in the dark. She crows as she falls.)

ST. OBNOXIOUS: An albatross! The ship is doomed!

(All rush to VERA's side.)

BARON: Water, water everywhere, and not a drop to drink. I know what will revive her. My specialty de la maison.

(He dons goggles and a raincoat, pops the cork of a bottle of champagne, and lies flat on his back. The women straddle him one at a time, lifting their skirts. He spits a stream between the legs of each in turn, douching their cunts with champagne.)

MME. TRYPHOENA: *(Singing)*
I was a virtuoso virgin.
Avoided upper crust lust.
Befuddled studs kept urgin' for a mergin'
With my size forty bust.

Liberalism led me astray,
Fell in a rebel's hotbed.
You know the type, a pothead,
Anyway, I thought he was gay.
(I'm not that type of girl.)

Some girls pray for a rape.
Not me, I'm no torrid tease.
I fell prey to rape because
I just wanted to please.

(A likely story.
No, really, it's on the up and up.)

I was caught in a rampage,
He had a masculine scent,
I was the torrid target of
A sex quest hard to assuage.

So here's a tip for you lonesome gals—
Don't give your heart to no stuck-up studs
Because manipulators you think are your pals
May be dykes in some stud's duds.

I was lost in the shuffle,
Thought it was true love but then
I found myself alone with a lezzie,
In her dyky den.

I know where I went wrong
So I'm singing this song,
So I'm singing this song.

VERA: Do you mean to say there's a language of the senses, too?

TURZAHNELLE: Yes, Vera, if you had known this, perhaps you would have been less bored.

VERA: Perhaps, perhaps . . .

ANGEL: *(Appearing to* VERA*)* Perhaps? O maid, I tell thee, when I pass away it is to tenfold life, to love, to peace, and raptures holy: we're all skating on thin ice.

VERA: *(Crossing herself in awe)* If I've only one life to live, let me live it as a blonde.

ANGEL: So you have only one life to live, eh?

VERA: I meant no offense, sir.

ANGEL: You didn't give any. But you know yourself you could live a devil of a long life if you really wanted to.

VERA: Oh, don't say that sir. It's so unsettling.

ANGEL: Well, what do you think of living for several hundred years? Are you going to have a try at it?

VERA: Oh, I tell you straight out, sir, I'd never promise to live with the same man as long as that. I wouldn't put up with my own children as long as that. Why, sir, when you were only two hundred, you might marry your own great-great-great-great-great-great-grandson and not even know who he was.

ANGEL: Well, why not? For all you know, the man you've married may be your great-great-great-great-great-great-grandmother's great-great-great-great-great-great-grandson.

VERA: But do you think it would ever be thought respectable, sir?

ANGEL: My good girl, all biological necessities have to be made respectable whether we like it or not, so you needn't worry your head about that.

VERA: There is nothing like biology.

ANGEL: "The cloud-capped towers, the solemn pinnacles, the gorgeous temples, the great globe itself: yea, all that it inherit shall dissolve, and, like this influential pageant faded, leave not a rack behind." That's biology for you: good sound biology.

VERA: Measured by that yardstick, we all stand condemned.

ANGEL: It is not enough to bathe in the sweat of anguish; you must pass through the fire of torture. That you *cannot* will be forgiven; that you *will* not, never.

VERA: Yes, it must be so. Oh, lift me, lift me to where you climb. Lead me towards your high heaven. My longing is great, my courage weak. I grow dizzy, my feet are tired and clogged with earth.

ANGEL: Listen, Vera. There is but one law for all men: no cowardly compromise! If a man does his work by halves, he stands condemned.

VERA: *(Bowing her head)* Lead and I shall follow. *(She raises her head.* THE ANGEL *is gone)*
Did you see the apparition, Turzahnelle?
Was he from heaven or was he from hell?

TURZAHNELLE: What did he look like? Did he sing?

VERA: Yes, he sang.

TURZAHNELLE: I didn't hear him, but he sang. Did he speak?

VERA: Well, he spoke to me in a well-articulated warble. I couldn't understand what he said, but the syntax was so pure that I could guess which were verbs and which were pronouns.

TURZAHNELLE: Is it true that the joints of his wings creaked harmoniously?

VERA: Perfectly true, like a grasshopper's only less metallic. With my fingers I touched the roots of his wings. It was like a harp of feathers!

TURZAHNELLE: Oh why are you so mad? You've a pound of rouge on your cheeks. Where did you get this costume? And aren't you ashamed?

GUEST 1: *(In alarm)* Turzahnelle. They say it's going to rain—shouldn't we turn back?

TURZAHNELLE: Never! Drink! Dance! I want to be happy—happier than I've ever been.

ST. OBNOXIOUS: Warmest climes but nurse the cruelest fangs; the tiger of Bengal crouches in spaced groves of ceaseless verdure. Skies the most effulgent but basket the deadliest thunders; gorgeous Cuba knows tornadoes that never swept tame northern lands. So, too, it is, that in these resplendent Japanese seas the mariner encounters the direst of all storms, the typhoon. It will sometimes burst from out that cloudless sky, like an exploding bomb upon a dazed and sleepy town.

GUEST 2: It never rains but it pours.

ST. OBNOXIOUS: Nor seldom in this life, when, on the right side, fortune's favorites sail close by us, we, though all adroop before, catch somewhat of the rushing breeze, and joyfully feel our bagging sails fill out.

TURZAHNELLE: I've planned this party for months and I'm not going to let a little rain stop me now.

[GUEST 1: I've always admired people who make plans—I often change mine at the last moment. There is a question of a summer frock which may alter everything. I shall act upon the inspiration of the moment.

TURZAHNELLE: Charon, what time is it?

DEVIL-AS-CHARON: Why, my watch has stopped. Say, Vera, what time is it?

VERA: I don't know. My clock's stopped. Hello, Tryphoena, what time is it?

(Etc.)

TURZAHNELLE: No matter the time! Keep rowing!] Keep rowing! The night is young.

(Sound of thunder. Lightning.)

ORGONE: No doubt, this is a Ship of Fools!

DEVIL-AS-CHARON: What do you want of me! Do you want minstrel songs? The dance of the hours? Do you want me to vanish, to dive after the ring? Is that what you want? I will make gold; remedies . . . anything—but don't make me row! I am bound on a wheel of fire and my very tears do scald!

TURZAHNELLE: Row on, Charon! For all we know—it's all a dream. The greatest crime of man is having been born.

(The ship lunges. Thunder, lightning.)

ST. OBNOXIOUS: We dream much of paradise, or rather of a number of successive paradises, but each of them is, long before we die, a paradise lost, in which we should feel ourselves lost also. Full in this rapid wake, and many fathoms in the rear, swam a huge, humped old bull, which by his comparatively slow progress, as well as by the unusual yellowish incrustations overgrowing him, seemed afflicted with the jaundice, or some other infirmity.

(The ship lurches and all the passengers are thrown overboard. A scrim falls over the stage and only SAINT OBNOXIOUS *and the* ANGEL *are left.)*

ST. OBNOXIOUS: *(Singing)*
Full fathom five thy father lies;
Of his bones are coral made;
Those are pearls that were his eyes:
Nothing of him doth fade,
But doth suffer a sea-change
Into something rich and strange.

(Music for an underwater ballet comes up and the drowned passengers, changed into sea creatures, reappear and dance.)

The Desert Island

(BARON BUBBLES IN THE BATHTUB *is now called* CHARLIE THE CANNIBAL.*)*

CHARLIE: Tryphoena the Cannibal, I heard a funny thing about you today.
[MME. TRYPHOENA: Well, Charlie the Cannibal, where'd you hear it?
CHARLIE: The other part of this desert island—Coconut Grove?]
MME. TRYPHOENA: What was it?
CHARLIE: They say that when your stomach is empty and your pocket also, you sit down near a hot fire and read a cookbook.
MME. TRYPHOENA: Funny you should bring that up, Charlie, for just the other day I came across a recipe for cookin' human balls.
CHARLIE: Balls?
MME. TRYPHOENA: Yeah, it goes like this: Sprinkle balls with a small amount of toasted sesame seeds. Place a small amount of Japanese salted plum in the center of each ball. Place Taduku mash in one hand and roll on balls. Deep-fry balls in hot corn oil until golden. To ½ cup brown rice flour and ½ tablespoon salt, add enough water to form firm balls. Deep-fry. Test center to see if they are done. Toast sheets of Nori Seaweed by passing them gently over burner on stove until the color changes. Use amount needed to wrap each ball, dipping fingers in water and patting Nori at the edges, until it adheres to balls.
CHARLIE: Hm . . . hmmmm! Does that sound scrumptious!
MME. TRYPHOENA: Well, all we need are some ingredients . . . if you know what I mean. Quick, here comes some now. . . . Let's ambush 'em.

(They go off to hide, as TURZAHNELLE *and* ORGONE, *the sole survivors of the shipwreck, enter.)*

TURZAHNELLE: Careful, fellows, I think these guys are cannibals, and if there's one thing I hate it's cannibals. We better get out of here.
ORGONE: What you mean "we," dark meat?
TURZAHNELLE: I said "be careful" for it's true that religion can't explain what happens when a missionary on his way to heaven is eaten by a cannibal on his way to hell.

(SAINT OBNOXIOUS *and the* DEVIL *appear.)*

MME. TRYPHOENA: I'll grill her until she's well done.

ST. OBNOXIOUS: I remember the night we met, I drank a quart of champagne from your slipper. It would have held more but you were wearing innersoles.

MME. TRYPHOENA: When we go in to dinner you will sit on my right hand, and . . . *(To the* DEVIL*)* . . . you will sit on my left hand.

CHARLIE: How will you eat . . . through a tube?

TURZAHNELLE: I'm very drunk and in a few minutes with any luck I'm gonna be a whole lot drunker.

ST. OBNOXIOUS: If you wake up the next morning with your hat on, it's a sure sign you've had a touch too much the night before.

ORGONE: You must have been blind drunk last night, too.

TURZAHNELLE: Why so?

ORGONE: Why, Vera said she saw you on the starboard deck, arguing with your shadow.

DEVIL: Why is dancing like new milk?

ST. OBNOXIOUS: Because it strengthens the calves.

DEVIL: Dat is to say dat an indulgence in terpsichorean pleasure is calculated to enlarge and strengthen de calf.

ST. OBNOXIOUS: If dancing is good for the calf I would recommend the exercise to you.

DEVIL: You're a cowherd to offer such an insult.

MME. TRYPHOENA: I'll offer her another drink while you get the pot started. Have another drink, madame.

TURZAHNELLE: Don't mind if I do. *(Drinking up, dreamily)* There's an odor of lovers around my house. No one passes naturally before my door. It rains guitars and secret messages.

DEVIL: Does ye know why dar am no more cream in de cities now?

ST. OBNOXIOUS: Can't say as I does. Can you 'splain de cause?

DEVIL: Well, y' see, milk has raised so high dat de cream can't reach de top.

ST. OBNOXIOUS: Dar's a peeler comin', we'd better cheese it.

*(*CHARLIE *and* TRYPHOENA *jump* TURZAHNELLE.*)*

TURZAHNELLE: *(Resisting)* A very simple calculation shows the impossibility of any species living off its own kind. Let us take man, for example. It takes about twenty years to raise a man, while an adult man will eat, though not exclusively, at least one man (average weight about 120 pounds) every sixty days (at the rate, therefore, of two pounds a day), thus eating six men in a year. This means that while one man is growing up (in twenty years), he will have to eat 120 men. As can be seen, in a short time this would mean the destruction of the entire species, especially as men would not be caught for eating without fights and there would be a wastage of life sometimes resulting in a supply of dead men exceeding the demand. It will therefore only be possible for a man to eat other men at long intervals of several months.

(By now she's in the pot and stirring. The CANNIBALS *dance around her, singing.)*

TRYPHOENA AND CHARLIE:
  A negress with a margaret once,
  Lolled frousting in the sun,

Thinking of all the little things
That she had left undone.
With a hey, hey, hey, hi hey ho . . .

TURZAHNELLE: Eternity's a great nest and every creature flies away from it one after the other like young eagles, to cross the sky and vanish.

(ORGONE comes to the edge of the pot.)

TURZAHNELLE: He's here: my blood retreats towards my heart, and I forgot what I had meant to say.

ANGEL: Think of a son whose sole hope lies in you.

TURZAHNELLE: *(To ORGONE)* I come to wed my tears unto your griefs; and to explain my anxious fears to you. My son is now without a father; and the day is near which of my death will make him witness too. His youth is threatened by a thousand foes, and you alone can arm against them—but secret remorse is fretting in my soul. I fear you're deaf to his cries, and that you'll break on him your wrath against an odious mother.

ORGONE: Madame, I do not harbor such base feelings. It is not time to grieve. Perhaps your husband is alive.

TURZAHNELLE: He is not dead since he still lives in you. Ever before my eyes I see my husband. I see him, speak with him, and my heart still . . .

ORGONE: I see Love's wonderful effects. Dead though he is, he is always present to your eyes; your soul is burning with your love.

TURZAHNELLE: Yes, Orgone, I pine and burn for him. I love him. He had your bearing, your eyes, your speech. Why were you too young to sail with him unto our shores? For then you would have slain the Minotaur. And, yes, it would have been me, Orgone; by timely aid, I would have led you through the labyrinth. How many cares that charming head of yours would then have cost me! I would not have trusted to that weak thread alone, but walked before you, companion in the peril which you chose: and going down into the labyrinth, Turzahnelle would have returned with you, or else been lost with you.

ORGONE: O gods! What do I hear? Do you forget that this man you speak of is my father and you his wife?

TURZAHNELLE: Oh, cruel! You've understood too well. I've said enough to save you from mistaking. Know Turzahnelle then, and all her madness. Yes, I love; but do not think that I condone it, or think it innocent; nor that I ever with base complaisance added to the poison of my mad passion. Hapless victim of celestial vengeance, I abhor myself more than you can. The gods are witnesses—those gods who kindled in my breast the flame fatal to all my blood, whose cruel boast was to seduce a weak and mortal heart. Recall what's past. I did not flee from you, Orgone; no, I drove you away. I wished to seem to you both hateful and inhuman. To resist you better I aroused your hatred. But what have profited my useless pains? You loathed me more, I did not love you less; I've languished, shriveled in the flames, in tears. Your eyes will tell you so—if for a moment your eyes could look at me. What am I saying? Think you that this confession I have made was voluntary? I trembled for a son I did not dare betray—futile schemes devised by a heart too full of what it loves. Alas! I could only speak to you about yourself. Avenge yourself; punish an odious love; free the universe of a monster who offends you. Excuse me, son, I must take a piss. *(She begins to spread her legs)*

CANNIBALS: Not in the pot! Not in the pot!

(TRYPHOENA bends over the pot. CHARLIE gooses her. She screams.)

TURZAHNELLE: My cook is goosed.

MME. TRYPHOENA: Let her boil in her own stew.

(The CANNIBALS help TURZAHNELLE out of the pot, while ORGONE arranges an electric chair as a toilet, religiously placing the seat—the one on which CARLA cast a spell.)

ORGONE: Well, here we are, now, try this on for size.

TURZAHNELLE: *(Sitting down on the toilet)* There is my heart: there you should aim your blow. I feel it now, eager to expiate its sins.

ANGEL:
One nonday I sleep.
I dreamt of a someday
Of a wonday I shall wake.
Ah! May he have now of here fearfilled me!
Sinflowed, O sin flowed!

TURZAHNELLE: Advance towards me, Orgone. Strike. Or if you think it unworthy of your blows, your hatred envying me a death so sweet, or if you think your hand with blood too vile would be imbued, lend me your sword instead.

(She flushes the toilet–electric chair!!!)

ORGONE: The douche of death!

(The flagellant procession enters with trumpets, banners, candles, swords, icons, palms, incense, etc.)

ST. OBNOXIOUS: Turzahnelle will be no more—a cruel flame will leave all her glory but a name.

DEVIL: Founded upon His everlasting word, Turzahnelle will be protected by the Lord.

ST. OBNOXIOUS: My eyes behold her glory disappear.

DEVIL: I see her brightness spreading everywhere.

ST. OBNOXIOUS: Turzahnelle has fallen into the abyss.

DEVIL: Aspiring Turzahnelle and heaven's kiss.

ST. OBNOXIOUS: What sad abasement!

DEVIL: What immortal glory!

ST. OBNOXIOUS: How many cries of sorrow!

DEVIL: What songs of triumph!

TURZAHNELLE: Peace! Trouble not yourselves; someday the mystery will be revealed.

ORGONE: *(Beginning to weep)* The throne of grace is a spiritual toilet.

TURZAHNELLE: Do you see him? He is crying, the baby hunchback, pinhead, sex maniac—all the hoarfrosts of the world have passed through his lips. He is the god of volcanoes and the king of winters! *(Looking up, she sighs a long moan)* The eagle has already passed by, the new spirit calls me. . . . I have put on for him the dress of Jezebel—he is the beloved child of Turzahnelle.

DEVIL: Do you recognize the temple with the vast peristyle, and the bitter lemons which were marked by your teeth, and the grotto, fatal to impudent guests, where the old seed of the anguished dragon sleeps? He will return— the dragon for whom you still weep! Time will bring back the order of the former days: the earth has trembled with a prophetic breath.

(Enter the Dragon from the Book of Revelation, with seven heads and seven crowns on each head, followed by the POPE, *who recites the litany of Satan, as money and white roses (snow?) fall profusely over all the living and the dead. . . .)*

POPE:
    O grandest of the Angels, and most wise,
    O fallen God, fate-driven from the skies,
CHORUS:
    Satan, at last take pity on our pain.
POPE:
    O first of exiles who endurest wrong,
    Yet growest, in thy hatred, still more strong,
CHORUS:
    Satan, at last take pity on our pain.
POPE:
    O subterranean king, omniscient,
    Healer of man's immortal discontent,
CHORUS:
    Satan, at last take pity on our pain.
POPE:
    To lepers and to outcasts thou dost show
    That passion is the paradise below.
CHORUS:
    Satan, at last take pity on our pain.
POPE:
    Thou, by thy mistress Death, hast given man
    Hope, the imperishable courtesan.
CHORUS:
    Satan, at last take pity on our pain.
POPE:
    Thou knowest the corners of the jealous Earth
    Where God has hidden jewels of great worth.
CHORUS:
    Satan, at last take pity on our pain.
POPE:
    Thy awful name is written as with pitch
    On the unrelenting foreheads of the rich.
CHORUS:
    Satan, at last take pity on our pain.
POPE:
    In strange and hidden places thou dost move
    Where women cry for torture in their love.
CHORUS:
    Satan, at last take pity on our pain.

POPE:

Father of those whom God's tempestuous ire
Has flung from paradise with sword and fire,

CHORUS:

Satan, at last take pity on our pain.

(VERA, *looking younger and more innocent than ever before, delicately approaches* TURZAHNELLE *on her throne.*)

VERA: Turzahnelle, with your hands full of fires, rose with the purple heart . . . did you find your cross in the desert of the skies? White roses, fall! Fall, white phantoms, from your burning skies: the saint of the abyss is more saintly in my eyes!

(*Choirs of angels sing joyously as the curtain falls.*)

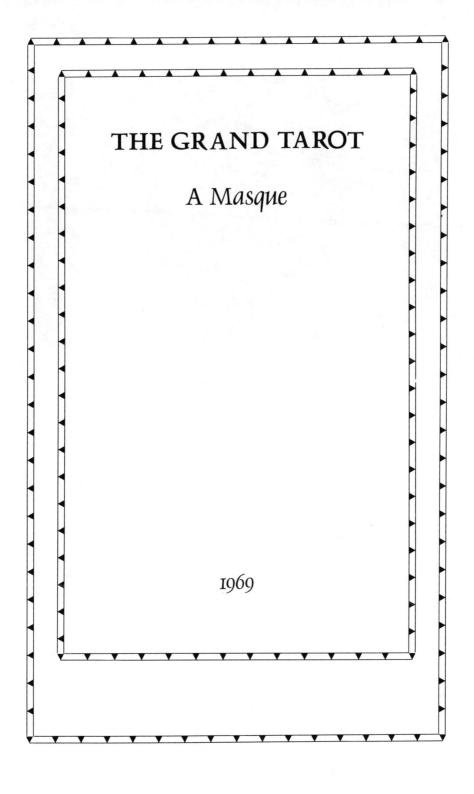

THE GRAND TAROT

A Masque

1969

Lola Pashalinski, Charles Ludlam & Bill Vehr
in *The Grand Tarot* (Thomas Harding)

Cast of Characters

GYPSY
THE FOOL
DEATH
THE DEVIL
THE MAGICIAN
THE MOON
THE HIGH PRIESTESS
THE EMPRESS
THE EMPEROR
THE HERMAPHRODITE *(also* MARRIAGE, HE *and* MARRIAGE, SHE*)*
THE POPE
THE HERMIT
THE SPHINX
THE HANGED-MAN
THE STAR
TEMPERANCE
THE SUN
SPECTATORS
JURORS

The game of cards called The Tarot, which the Gypsies possess, is the Bible of Bibles. It is the book of Thoth Hermes Trismegistus, the book of Adam, the book of primitive Revelation of ancient civilizations.

When we read Tarot cards, we see a drama unfold in which the hieroglyphic emblems of this old fortune-telling pack appear like actors. There are twenty-one numbered cards which comprise the Major Arcana and one unnumbered card, The Fool or zero, which is an arcanum unto itself. So I've constructed a play of twenty-two interchangeable scenes. Each scene represents a different card of The Tarot.

Before each performance, we lay out the twenty-two cards. The order in which they fall determines the order in which the scenes will be played.* Taken as a narrative (the play is in the epic tradition), we could say that the story is never the same twice. Asked a question, the play becomes an oracle. The sequence of scenes is everything. Compare two different performances or compare a performance with a reading of Tarot cards given on the same night. But I must remind you that science has little empire over the subject of fortune telling, for it is imagination and intuition that reign over this charming kingdom.

Ask a question of the oracle before we shout the sacred name of God, Yod He Vau He, and watch the future of your fates.

—CHARLES LUDLAM: Inventor

*Although *The Grand Tarot* was originally performed as the "inventor" describes, it evolved into more than twenty-two scenes and eventually settled into the fixed form represented here. The role of chance was maintained by the play being stopped periodically for the actors to come forth and relate their dreams.—Editors

PROLOGUE

GYPSY:
> Brothers, sisters, and gentle friends
> Come, set your minds at zero
> In defiance of current theatrical trends
> A play that has a hero!
> In a clandestine theater to which one would go
> In secret, at night, and masked
> To see a play called *The Grand Tarot*
> Pay for your ticket. No questions asked.

(The stage is a platform of the sort used by the early Italian comedians. Two poles suspend a large drop curtain painted with the signs of the zodiac. There are two slits in the curtain which serve for entrances and exits. Ladders on either side of the stage, on which the actors may climb, provide the necessary elevation to suggest the sky or heaven. A trapdoor leads to hell. Stools and benches are brought on as needed. If there is room the musicians should play in full view of the audience. They can also help out with "live" sound effects. If lights are placed behind the curtain the actors can cast fantastic shadows.)

THE FOOL: *(Dancing a jig)* The Fool's motto is this: If you tell people the truth you'd better make them laugh or they'll kill you. *(Turns a cartwheel and takes out a deck of Tarot Cards)* So you don't believe in fortune telling, huh? How do you expect us Gypsies to make an honest living in our storefronts? As long as you do not know the future you do not know that it will not be happier than the past. That is hope. *(Watches a fly buzzing around his head, catches it, and munches on it with great gusto)* Choose a day for your death and resolve to die on that day. Then death is no longer uncertain but certain. The future, let it come! *(Draws a card from the deck)* Here is your card: The lightning-struck tower, the fall of the tower of Babel. Look! Here is The High Priestess with her handmaiden, Luna, The Moon. *(Draws another card)* The Lady of Permutations and Situations . . . Lady Luck to you. *(Tosses these cards into the audience)* Here is the man with three staves, and here, The Wheel *(Draws another card)*, and this card, which is blank, is something he carries on his back, which I am forbidden to see. I do not find The Hanged-Man. Fear death by water. I see crowds of people walking around in a ring. Inferior men in positions of power. Fortune is no ladder, but a wheel. Fall back on your inner worth and wait your turn. Turn wheel.

(The Wheel of Fortune appears on the shadowgraph. THE SPHINX *alights on top and gives the wheel a spin.)*

THE FOOL:
> Now there's some people say that the Tarot's a sham,
> But you can ring hell's bell if you can guess who I am.

ACT I

Scene 1: THE FOOL, DEATH.

(DEATH *enters during* THE FOOL*'s dance. When* THE FOOL *sees* DEATH, *he stops dancing.*)

THE FOOL: Good sir, could you offer some advice?
DEATH: I'll advise you if I can.
THE FOOL: I need a life's work. But no profession suits me.
DEATH: Here's something you can do. Turn around. Bend over.

(THE FOOL *does so and* DEATH *kicks him in the ass.* THE FOOL *falls on his face.*)

THE FOOL: But this is nothing. And you don't get nothing for nothing.
DEATH: Take this rose. (DEATH *gives* THE FOOL *a white rose*) When you smell its sweetness you will desire nothing.
THE FOOL: (*Smelling the rose*) I desire nothing.
DEATH: Shall we have another go at it?
THE FOOL: Practice makes perfect. (*He turns around and offers his ass to be kicked*)
DEATH: (*Kicking his ass*) Very good. But don't forget to smell the white rose.
THE FOOL: (*Smelling the rose*) Oh thank you, sir. Now I have a life's work. I am a professional. Today I am a Man. It will take but a minute to pack my bag and I will be off on life's journey.
DEATH: What are those things that you carry in your bag?
THE FOOL: This is just a bag full of memories. Oh sir, how can I ever repay you?
DEATH: No debt can ever be repaid because everything you have, even your life has been lent to you. You came into this world with nothing and you will leave it with nothing. You can't take it with you when you go.
THE FOOL: I am so grateful to you, sir. But I don't even know your name.
DEATH: My name is Death.
THE FOOL: What nationality is that?
DEATH: (*Toasting* THE FOOL *with his white rose*) Until we meet again. (*Exits*)
THE FOOL: O happy day! I was nothing. But now I am a fool! (*Exits dancing*)

Scene 2: THE DEVIL, THE FOOL.

THE DEVIL: (*Appearing in a puff of smoke and several flames*) Huzzah!
THE FOOL: Who are you?
THE DEVIL: I'm the Devil.
THE FOOL: Well get the devil out of here! (*They go around in a circle kicking each other in the ass.* THE DEVIL *slings* THE FOOL *over his shoulder and carries him out through the trapdoor.* THE FOOL *sets off a string of firecrackers tied to* THE DEVIL*'s tail.*) Devil may care! Devil may care!

Scene 3: THE MAGICIAN.

THE MAGICIAN: (*Entering ceremonially, he goes into a trance as if hypnotizing the audience*) Go deep within meditation and find your own divine center.

Tarot! Torah! Rota! *(Repeat three times)*

(Juggling a sword, cup, scepter, and a coin)

> Swords cups scepters coins
> Fire water earth and air
> Matter and spirit here conjoin
> See the future if you dare!

Prepare to pass through the beautiful gate of symbolism into the starry world beyond.

Scene 4: THE MOON, THE MAGICIAN.

THE MOON: *(Enters chanting)* Silver coin in the cup and the cathedral's eye. Hidden enemies, danger, terror: these things am I! Who is hiding? And who sobs in the darkness? I am the moon weeping tears of blood which fall like swords through the air. You cannot escape me. My reflected light will light the night with a fever bright as diamonds. *(THE MOON strikes a pose upon a pedestal. The "Bo La Bo, Egyptian Fox-Trot" by Ted Lewis and his orchestra begins to play softly)*

THE MAGICIAN: *(Looking off)* But who is this, what thing of sea or land? Female of sex it seems, that so bedekt, ornate, and gay comes this way sailing like a stately ship of Taurus, bound for the Isles of Javin or Gadier. With all her bravery on, tackle trim and streamers waving, courted by the winds that hold them play, on amber scent of odorous perfume her harbinger . . .

Scene 5: THE HIGH PRIESTESS, THE MOON, THE MAGICIAN.

(THE HIGH PRIESTESS enters and dances around the pedestal from which THE MOON shines down.)

THE MAGICIAN: I will hide myself and watch her dance. *(He conceals himself behind his cloak)*

THE HIGH PRIESTESS: *(Breaking off in the middle of her dance)* Oooops! This dress is too tight! Luna, help me please. Priyamvada, my dressmaker, is always playing silly tricks like this.

THE MOON: *(Giggling as she comes to her aid)* Priyamvada isn't playing silly tricks. Your figure's getting better, that's what it is, O High Priestess! Ah, you smell as sweet as the night-blooming cannabis.

THE HIGH PRIESTESS: You are good at flattery, aren't you, Luna?

THE MAGICIAN: *(Aside)* Flattery nothing! It's the truth! Her lips glisten like new leaves, her arms are shoots, and her youth sprouts a glory of glittering flowers. *(THE HIGH PRIESTESS seats herself on a crystal seat and THE MOON enfolds her in an immense cloak of night embroidered with crewel silver stars. THE HIGH PRIESTESS draws a veil across her face. THE MAGICIAN reveals himself)* O High Priestess, when may I lift the transparent veil that falls across your face?

THE HIGH PRIESTESS: I distract the hearts of men like you and lead them out of their ways of mischief. I'm warning you, O Blonde One, the veil of Isis must not be raised by the profane.

THE MAGICIAN: And your book, O Flamelike beauty, when may I read from your book?

THE HIGH PRIESTESS: The doctrines of Isis are hidden. I will reveal only to the Magi the secrets of the Kabbalah and of occult science.

THE MAGICIAN: *(Aside)* She does not recognize me!

THE HIGH PRIESTESS: For it was written in the stars that I was destined to remain in a state of virginity until eternity.

THE MAGICIAN: Was it also written in the stars that you were destined to wear fourteen-karat-gold fuck-me pumps until eternity?

THE HIGH PRIESTESS: I don't know what you're getting at. I personally purchased these shoes at Shaman's and the label read "High Priestess Heels" *(Archly)* with arch supports.

(THE MOON *begins to weep.)*

THE MAGICIAN: The moon methinks looks with a watery eye, and when she weeps she weeps every little flower, lamenting some enforced chastity. Ah, the desert wind!

THE HIGH PRIESTESS: And the aroma of date palm trees that makes them sway and dance away, as the nightingales sing a song of love that's in the air, everywhere. In the pool of midnight two children bathe in the nude. The moonlight was reflected in the water.

THE MAGICIAN: Just as it is reflected in your eyes. Their water-moistened naked bodies seemed to be glowing and reflecting the rays of moonlight as they came out of the midnight pool. They sat under a palm tree and she gave him a casaba pancake with sesame butter that had crunched pieces of mixed nuts. For a most tantalizing dessert she ripped open a pomegranate and offered him a piece. But he refused. That night he had a craving for wild and very young cherries. *(He puts his hand up under her dress)*

THE HIGH PRIESTESS: *(Snaps her legs together forcing him to withdraw his hand painfully)* He was fortunate that she had brought along some cherries to their midnight picnic rendezvous. *(She offers him some cherries, which they both eat, spitting the pits at each other playfully. He lifts her veil and steals a kiss)*

THE MOON: *(Observing the clinch)* These men! When their stomachs speak they forget about their brains. When their brains speak they forget about their hearts. When their hearts speak they forget about everything.

THE HIGH PRIESTESS: *(Breaking away)* Why you kissing bandit! *(Slaps* THE MAGICIAN*)* It's no use trying to get me sexually aroused by buttering me up with your dreams that are full of graphically induced tall tales.

THE MAGICIAN: O High Priestess, don't you know that a man without his dreams soon withers and grows old? Then as they held each other very close and tight they fell asleep as they were looking at the deep blue skies which were filled with stars that looked like diamonds afloat and glowing back at their eyes.

THE HIGH PRIESTESS: There is but one who may pass between the two columns of Jakin and Bohas of the Temple of Solomon and of Freemasonry. *(Aside)* What fools these men are to think that we women do not recognize the right one when we see him. *(To* THE MAGICIAN*)* I am governed by the Moon and therefore given to monthly changes.

THE MAGICIAN: I have no astronomical affinities!

THE HIGH PRIESTESS: No astronomical affinities? *(She laughs)* Oh come on now, just who are you trying to kid with that sorcerer's malarkey? You mean to say you were not born? Then you must have been hatched.

THE MAGICIAN: Yes, I was born. But my conception took place on an astral plane inaccessible to human conceptions. *(Aside)* Why does she not understand?

THE HIGH PRIESTESS: But your name—does he who was born beyond human conceptions have a name the human mouth may speak?

THE MAGICIAN: Osiris.

THE HIGH PRIESTESS: Osiris?

THE MAGICIAN: O Isis!

THE MOON: Oasis.

THE HIGH PRIESTESS: Osiris!

THE MAGICIAN: O Isis!

THE MOON: Oasis.

[(THE MAGICIAN *takes out an amulet, hypnotizes and blindfolds* THE HIGH PRIESTESS, *leads her into the audience. They improvise a mind-reading act based on the one done by the Lunts in* The Great Sebastians. THE MAGICIAN *returns to the stage, snaps his fingers, and breaks* THE HIGH PRIESTESS's *trance.)*]

THE HIGH PRIESTESS: *(Thrills)* Osiris! *(Aside)* I will drop this shallow mask of pretense. *(To* THE MAGICIAN, *as she removes her veil)* Osiris, you are he? Unite with me and we be three!

THE MAGICIAN: Come, kiss me and let the world slip. We'll ne'er be younger.

(They kiss.)

THE MOON: The world was left to mankind not as a creation but as a reject, a horrible turd trembling expectantly on the void. And Man was too clean and jumped back and shrank from it as from the stink of a fart or some other filth representing the created world. *(Exit)*

[*Or, alternative verse:*]

THE MAGICIAN:
    Collaboration will never fail
    between the two ends of the bright wag-tail,
    first to sing and then to fly
    as the days and the moons pass by.

Scene 6: THE HIGH PRIESTESS, THE MAGICIAN.

THE HIGH PRIESTESS: *(Breaking off in the middle of the kiss)* I just remembered. There's a surprise circumcision tonight and I promised to bless the matzoh balls. *(She rushes out)*

Scene 7: THE MAGICIAN.

THE MAGICIAN: She's left me alone, to breathe these orgiastic miasmas of barbarity.
    Around the world where the four winds moan.
    Across seven seas I am alone

In search of her now will I roam
And I won't look back till I bring her home. *(Exit)*

Scene 8: DEATH, THE MAGICIAN.

DEATH: *(Like a barker in a sideshow)* Step right up and have a look-see! Step right up and have a look-see! Step right up and what do you see? The cabinet of Caligari!

*(*SPECTATORS *crowd around* DEATH, *who is standing on a small stage.* DEATH *unveils a sarcophagus inlaid with jet, mother-of-pearl, and moonstones.)*

SPECTATORS: Oooooh!
DEATH: The original cabinet of Dr. Caligari, inlaid with jet, mother-of-pearl, and moonstones.
SPECTATORS: Aaaaah!
DEATH: Veneers of sandalwood, rosewood, and pear are dovetailed in a kind of geometric witticism which at once epitomizes and critiques the Art Deco style.
FIRST SPECTATOR: What's Art Deco?
SECOND SPECTATOR: It came after Art Nouveau.
THE MAGICIAN: *(To* DEATH*)* What are you selling?
DEATH: I'm not selling anything. Do I look like a salesman to you? I'm giving it away. Yes, Ladies and Gentlemen, you heard right. I will give the original cabinet of Dr. Caligari absolutely free to the man among you who fits it to a T.
SPECTATORS: Ooooh! Aaaah! Mmmmmm!
DEATH: Step right up and try it out for size!

(The SPECTATORS *queue up and each one steps inside of the sarcophagus in turn. It fits none of them.)*

DEATH: *(To* THE MAGICIAN*)* And what about you, sir? Don't be shy. Give it a whirl. Give it a try. *(*THE MAGICIAN *steps into the sarcophagus)* A perfect fit! The cabinet of Caligari is all yours! *(He slams the lid and nails it shut)* Move along now all of you, the show is over. Did you hear what I said? The show is over.

(The crowd disperses.)

FIRST SPECTATOR: It was fixed.
SECOND SPECTATOR: That guy works for the show. They planted him in the crowd.
THIRD SPECTATOR: Yeah, you don't get nothin' for nothin'. What d'ya think, we was born yesterday?
DEATH: Aw, get lost sucker, and don't give me none o' yer lip. There's one o' you guys born every minute.
THIRD SPECTATOR: *(Calling back)* When we're born we cry and each day teaches us why.

(Exit the SPECTATORS.*)*

Scene 9: DEATH, THE MAGICIAN.

THE MAGICIAN: *(From inside the sarcophagus)* Let me out! Let me out!
DEATH: Now I hermetically seal the casket with molten irony. You'll smother
in thirty seconds, my friend. *(Pours molten iron over the sarcophagus)* I'll dump
you in the River Nile. I have no motive for these acts. This is a gratuitous
sarcophagus. *(Exit with the sarcophagus)*

Scene 10: THE EMPRESS.

THE EMPRESS: *(Rushing in)* Oh God, sometimes the truth socks it to me so hard
between the eyes that I can see the stars. And then I feel so damn sorry for
the lot of you—for the whole mother son of a gun of you—that I'd like to run
naked into the street and love the whole mob to death. Like I was bringing
you all a new brand of dope that would make you forget everything that ever
was for good. Where is my knave, my Fool? Go ye and tell The Fool to come
hither. *(THE FOOL enters)* How does His Highness, The Fool, today?
THE FOOL: The worse for my friends, my boy, and the better for my enemies.
THE EMPRESS: You mean the better for your friends and the worse for your
enemies.
THE FOOL: No, I mean the worse for my friends and the better for my enemies.
My friends flatter me and thereby make of me a bigger fool than I already am.
But my enemies tell me I am an ass to my face and thereby add to my
knowledge of myself. And that's why I say, my boy, the worse for my friends
and the better for my enemies.
THE EMPRESS: A witty Fool. What next?
THE FOOL: Better a witty Fool than a foolish wit.
THE EMPRESS: Take The Fool away.
THE FOOL: Did you hear that, fellows? Take away the lady.
THE EMPRESS: I bade them take you away. Are you calling me a fool?
THE FOOL: Would the Madonna grant me permission to prove you a fool?
THE EMPRESS: Can you do it?
THE FOOL: Dexterously good, Madonna.
THE EMPRESS: For want of better idleness, I'll bide your proof.
THE FOOL: I shall have to catechize you for it, Madonna. Would my mouse of
virtue answer me?
THE EMPRESS: Make your proof.
THE FOOL: Good Madonna, why do you mourn?
THE EMPRESS: Good Fool, for my brother's death.
THE FOOL: I think his soul is in hell, Madonna.
THE EMPRESS: I know his soul is in heaven, Fool.
THE FOOL: The more fool you, Madonna, to mourn your brother's soul being
in heaven. *(Pointing to THE EMPRESS)* Take away The Fool, gentlemen.

(Processional music is heard softly at first then swelling to a crescendo.)

THE EMPRESS: But who with hasty step the palace seeks?
THE FOOL: It is our emperor, high in birth and deed, the flowers of narcosis
forfettering his footlights.

(THE EMPEROR enters. THE FOOL exits making obeisances.)

Scene 11: THE EMPEROR, THE EMPRESS.

THE EMPEROR: Entering on the arm of the countess was a mite of a woman, fancifully enveloped in a fairy-hued cashmere shawl. The Cyclopean chatelaine of Cuppingforth Castle and one of the wealthiest women in Riding. She was considered by some to be eccentric for her habit of living alone, which may have had its dangers for a woman of her disposition and sex.

THE EMPRESS: Yet at times to convince an intrusive stranger that a male was in the house she would knot her hair across her chin in front in a thick cascade to imitate a beard and discharge a cartridge out of the window. *(Sitting)* These theater seats are all alike: insanitary death traps. It gives you a bit of the brown.

THE EMPEROR: *(Sitting and observing the audience for several moments in silence)* I prefer comedy. Life is tragic enough. We don't have to buy our tears.

THE EMPRESS: Did you bring a gun?

THE EMPEROR: *(Leaping to his feet)* I have a gold revolver. "Honor," I call it.

THE EMPRESS: That's good. Tomorrow I and a few other women are going wild goose shooting near Solanis, if you would care to come.

THE EMPEROR: *(Dropping his imperious facade and squealing with glee)* Oh, how I should enjoy it!

THE EMPRESS: We meet under the Hyppolytus Charioteer, Cuna Cuna Square, opposite the church at ten o'clock. *(THE EMPEROR winces)* Is it too early, do you think?

THE EMPEROR: Oh, no matter, I'll take a psychic energizer. For if a man commits adultery with another man's wife, or if a man commits adultery with his neighbor's wife, or if a man commits adultery with his own wife, both the adulterer and the adulteress shall be put to death. Their blood shall be upon them.

THE EMPRESS: Or if a man lieth with another man as he lieth with a woman, he has committed an abomination. They shall surely be put to death. Their blood shall be upon them.

(They begin to undress as they give these laws.)

THE EMPEROR: Or if a woman should approach unto any beast, to lie down thereto, you shall slay the woman and the beast! It is confusion. *(A Rubens nude standing)*

THE EMPRESS: *(A Rubens nude reclining)* Or if a man lieth with a woman having her sickness to uncover her nakedness, he hath discovered the fountain of her blood. They have committed an abomination and both of them shall be cut off from among their people!

(THE EMPEROR recoils from her "fountain of blood" with an apple in his mouth.)

THE EMPEROR: Good God, the sky has gone mad! Let's get out of here at once! Leave your breasts alone!

THE EMPRESS: Shit! What's the matter with you?

THE EMPEROR: *(Pointing a finger at her accusingly)* Accursed woman!

THE EMPRESS: *(Pouting to her pet snake)* Nobody's perfect. *(Then donning fig leaves and offering one to THE EMPEROR)* But I am the woman clothed with the sun and woman is the gate through which entrance is obtained into this life, the Garden of Venus, The Earthly Paradise.

THE EMPEROR: *(Kneeling before her)* But which is the way that leads out therefrom into that which lies beyond?

THE EMPRESS: That is a secret known only to The High Priestess. It is communicated by her only to the elect.

Scene 12: MARRIAGE, THE EMPEROR, THE EMPRESS.

(Handel's wedding march swells as MARRIAGE *enters down the aisle personified as an hermaphrodite. The actor playing* MARRIAGE *is split down the middle. His left side represents the bride with half a bridal gown, veil, train, and bouquet. His right side represents the groom with half a tuxedo, mustache, and top hat. When one half of* MARRIAGE *speaks to the other half, the actor turns the appropriate side to the audience. This should create the illusion of there being two people.)*

MARRIAGE, HE: Will you marry me?

MARRIAGE, SHE: Of course! *(Aside)* Silly boy! I wanted to marry him from the first time I laid eyes on him. But I thought I'd play it cool and cagey until he got the marriage idea himself.

MARRIAGE, HE: Ocypris, loveliest of goddesses in heaven, keep modest my delights, all my desires lawful, so that I may have my part in love, but not in passion's madness.

Scene 13: THE POPE, MARRIAGE, THE EMPEROR, THE EMPRESS.

THE POPE: *(Entering to the strains of a Gregorian chant)* Dearly beloved, we are gathered together to join this hermaphrodite in holy matrimony which Jesus Christ did glorify with his presence. Do you take this man to be your lawful wedded husband, to love honor and obey, for better or for worse, for richer or for poorer, in sickness and in health, to be not puffed up from this day forward until death do you part?

MARRIAGE, SHE: I do.

THE POPE: Do you take this woman to be your lawful wedded wife, to love honor and obey, for better or for worse, for richer or for poorer, in sickness and in health, to be not puffed up from this day forward until death do you part?

MARRIAGE, HE: I do.

THE POPE: You may present the ring. If any present knows any reason why this hermaphrodite should not be joined in holy matrimony speak now or forever hold your peace.

Scene 14: THE DEVIL, THE POPE, MARRIAGE, THE EMPRESS, THE EMPEROR.

THE DEVIL: *(Appearing in a puff of smoke)* Stop! This marriage must not take place!

THE POPE: Satan! For what reason do you dare to interrupt my ministration of this holy sacrament?

THE DEVIL: Both matrimony and mirrors are abominable because they multiply the numbers of mankind.

THE POPE: Begone, Satan! Marriages are made in heaven.
THE DEVIL: This is a hell of a marriage! *(Vanishes in another puff of smoke)*

Scene 15: THE POPE, MARRIAGE, THE EMPRESS, THE EMPEROR.

THE POPE: You may kiss the bride. Those whom God hath joined together, let
no man put asunder.

("The Anniversary Waltz" begins to play, vocal by Al Jolson. MARRIAGE, HE *waltzes
with* MARRIAGE, SHE.*)*

THE EMPRESS: *(Blubbering)* I always cry at weddings.
THE EMPEROR: *(Bowing to* THE EMPRESS*)* May I have this dance?

*(*THE EMPRESS *waltzes with* THE EMPEROR.*)*

THE EMPRESS: Look on your left and you'll see it!
THE EMPEROR: Oh?
THE EMPRESS: In trine of Mars. The seventh house. The house of marriage. The
house of happiness!
THE EMPEROR: You're fond of Astrology, I see.
MARRIAGE: I know very little about the heavenly bodies.
THE EMPRESS: Ah, don't be too impatient there!

*(*MARRIAGE *waltzes off. There is a roll of drums like thunder.)*

Scene 16: DEATH, THE POPE, THE EMPEROR, THE EMPRESS.

DEATH: *(Enters dramatically and perches above the others)*
I am death, that no man fear
For every man I arrest and no man spare.
For it is God's commandment
that all to me should be obedient.
THE EMPRESS:
Oh death, thou comest when I had thee least in mind.
In thy power it lieth to save me yet.
Of my jewels will I give thee if thou wilt be kind.
Yea, a thousand pounds shalt thou get.
Please defer this matter to another day.

*(*DEATH *drops white rose.* THE EMPRESS *drops to her knees, picks it up, and hands
it to* DEATH.*)*

DEATH: *(Snatching back the rose)*
No, Empress, it may not be in any way.
I set no store in gold, riches, and such gear
Not by pope, emperor, king, prince, or peer.
For if I would receive gifts great
all the world I might get.
But my custom lies clean the contrary way.
I give thee no respite. Come, no delay.

EMPEROR:
Alas, shall I have no longer respite?
I may say death giveth no warning.
To think on thee maketh my heart sick
For all unready is my book of reckoning.
If I could have ten years of waiting
My accounting book would I make so clear
that my reckoning I would have no need to fear.
Wherefore death I pray thee for God's mercy
Spare me till I be provided with a remedy.

DEATH:
It availeth thee not to cry, weep, and pray.
For thou knowest well the tide avoideth no man.
And in the world each living creature
For Adam's sin must die by nature.

POPE:
Death, if I this pilgrimage take,
And my reckoning duly make,
Show me for Saint Charity
Should I not come again shortly?
Oh wretched caitiff, whither shall I flee?
That I might escape this endless sorrow!
Nay, gentle death, spare me until tomorrow . . .
That I might amend me with good advisement.

DEATH:
Nay, Pope, I will not consent.
Nor no man will I respite.
But to the heart suddenly shall I smite
Without any advisement.
And now out of thy sight I will fly.
See thou make thee ready shortly.
For thou mayest say this is the day
That no man living may 'scape away.

(DEATH *exits laughing and dragging* THE POPE, THE EMPEROR, *and* THE EM-
PRESS *after him in a net.*)

Scene 17: THE MAGICIAN, THE FOOL.

THE MAGICIAN: Master, young man, you, I pray you, which is the way to The
   High Priestess? Have you seen her pass this way?
THE FOOL: *(Aside)* O heavens! This is my true-begotten father, who knows me
   not. I will try confusions with him.
THE MAGICIAN: Master, young gentleman, I pray you, which is the way to The
   High Priestess? Do you have information concerning her?
THE FOOL: Turn up on your right hand at the next turning, but at the next
   turning of all, on your left; however, at the very next turning, turn of no hand,
   but turn down indirectly to the place where you may begin your journey.
THE MAGICIAN: Jesus, Joseph, and Mary! 'Twill be a hard way to hit! Is there
   no one who can give simplified direction to where I may find my better half?

THE FOOL: There is a Hermit who lives at the top of this mountain. His blind eyes turn inward and he sees into his own soul. He may know.

THE MAGICIAN: For The High Priestess, according to fates and destinies and such odd sayings, the Sisters Three and such branches of learning, is indeed missing.

THE FOOL: Do you know me, Heavenly Father?

THE MAGICIAN: Alack the day, I know you not, young gentleman; farewell, I must be off to climb this mountain.

THE FOOL: O rare fortune! May I follow you? I had a devil of a master and now the devil himself would master me. My conscience counsels me to go back to my master, who is a kind of devil, and shun the devil himself. Bridge says the fiend, bridge not says my conscience. It is a kind of hard conscience that would counsel me to stay with the devil or a devil of a master. Therefore, I would like to follow you, Heavenly Father!

THE MAGICIAN: I'm sorry, young master gentleman.

THE FOOL: The Fool to you.

THE MAGICIAN: This journey I must make alone away. *(Exit)*

THE FOOL: Father! Father! Tarry! Take The Fool with thee!

(Curtain.)

End of Act I

ACT II

Scene 1: THE HERMIT, THE MAGICIAN.

(THE HERMIT is standing with a lantern in his hand. He is blind. THE MAGICIAN enters and addresses him.)

THE MAGICIAN: *(Calling from the back of the theater)* Hello! Hello!

THE HERMIT: Who are you and what do you want?

THE MAGICIAN: *(Mounting the platform)* I am The Magician, the juggler, Osiris. I am searching for the High Priestess. People at the foot of this mountain told me to ask The Hermit. They say he sees all.

THE HERMIT: I am The Hermit. I have attained. Where I am someday you may be.

THE MAGICIAN: But you are blind.

THE HERMIT: I was blind until I had my eyes torn open.

THE MAGICIAN: Where is the High Priestess?

THE HERMIT: What right have you to ask me such a question? I guard the mysteries and occult knowledge. Supply and demand, you know.

THE MAGICIAN: The High Priestess is my twin sister, Isis. We made love in the womb. United we embody the secret of immortality. Alone and separate, we are sterile and useless as a blind hermit in the mountains counting the stars.

THE HERMIT: *(His voice rings out)* I heard that! Magician, Magician, hear me! You are seeking a classic glory. But there is another kind of glory. Infamy, the last refuge of the arrogant who defy the stars. You are arrogant, arrogant and crude!

THE MAGICIAN: *(Taking THE HERMIT by the throat)* I'm warning you!

THE HERMIT: Let go of me!

THE MAGICIAN: You're afraid of me! I can read your real motives here in your blind eyes.

THE HERMIT: Are you trying to mug me? You crumb! You murderer!

THE MAGICIAN: Yes, I'd be a fool not to murder you. If only I dared to, I . . . *(Suddenly, with wonder)* Why, why, look! In those blind eyes!

THE HERMIT: Let go of me!

THE MAGICIAN: The future! My future . . . a crystal ball!

THE HERMIT: Do not attempt to see what would not be seen.

THE MAGICIAN: I see an old woman sitting on the stump of a tree. The roots of the tree are twined around something. It sparkles. Jet, mother-of-pearl, and moonstones . . . Now it's becoming blurred. What's happened? I can't see. . . . It's you; you're doing it. I want to see more, I must!

THE HERMIT: Stop it! Stop it!

THE MAGICIAN: *(Recoiling, releasing* THE HERMIT *and clutching at his eyes)* Aaaaah! You have blinded me, thrown pepper in my eyes.

THE HERMIT: I swear I didn't.

THE MAGICIAN: *(Writhing on the ground)* You're lying. Water, quickly! My eyes are on fire!

THE HERMIT: You reached out for what the gods are keeping in darkness, and they are making you suffer for your presumption.

THE MAGICIAN: Water, water, quickly! I am blind!

(THE STAR *appears and pours water on* THE MAGICIAN'*s eyes.)*

THE HERMIT: Are you still in pain?

THE MAGICIAN: No, it's gone away. It was like fire, a thousand pins, a cat's claw tearing my eyes.

THE HERMIT: Can you see?

THE MAGICIAN: Yes, I can see again. Thank you. What shall I do? This moving image of the future in your eyes has bewildered me.

THE HERMIT: You must consult the enigma of enigmas, the Egyptian monster, the Bitch that sings.

THE MAGICIAN: Who?

THE HERMIT: The Sphinx.

THE MAGICIAN: Where can I find her?

THE HERMIT: She is perched atop the Wheel of Fortune on the tenth card of the Grand Tarot. You can't miss her. Answer her riddle and discover the secret of Man's life. Fail and she destroys you.

THE MAGICIAN: You look frightened, Hermit.

THE HERMIT: Yes, I am frightened. Fare well my boy. *(Exit)*

Scene 2: THE MAGICIAN, THE SPHINX.

(THE SPHINX *is borne onto the stage on a litter carried by Anubis and the Typhon.)*

THE SPHINX:
I am more deceitful than the heart.
More mysterious than the egg
More fatal than the stars
Like the flow of blood through the veins of a statue
Numb as an arm you have slept on and deadened

The enigma of enigmas
The human monster
The bitch that sings.

THE MAGICIAN: You are the Sphinx.

THE SPHINX: Yes, I . . . I am the Sphinx.

THE MAGICIAN: I'm dreaming.

THE SPHINX: You are no dreamer, Magician. You know exactly what you want . . . what you always wanted.

THE MAGICIAN: But why do you—

THE SPHINX: Silence! Here I reign. Come forward. Nearer. (THE MAGICIAN *struggles as though his arms were pinioned*) Hop, then. (THE MAGICIAN *falls to his knees*) Crawl! It is good for heroes. That's right, forward! There's nobody watching you. (THE MAGICIAN *crawls toward the Sphinx, writhing in fury*) Stop, and now . . .

THE MAGICIAN: This is how you snare men and slay them.

THE SPHINX: Don't resist. Don't make it more difficult for me—I may hurt you.

THE MAGICIAN: (*Shutting his eyes and turning his head*) I will resist.

THE SPHINX: In vain you shut your eyes and turn your head. I do not charm through my voice or my sight.

THE MAGICIAN: Let me go! Mercy!

THE SPHINX: And you would cry for mercy and you would not be the first. I have heard prouder men than you cry for their mothers, and have seen more arrogant men in tears.

THE MAGICIAN: Mommeeee!

THE SPHINX: Come a little nearer: I will untighten your limbs. (THE MAGICIAN *crawls forward*) So! Which animal walks on four legs in the morning, two legs at noon, and three legs in the evening? Comb your mind till you can think of nothing but some tiny medal you won as a child. Or mumble a number or count the stars.

THE MAGICIAN: You know, the trouble with women is they ask too many questions.

THE SPHINX: The animal is Man. He crawls on all fours as an infant; he walks on two legs when he is grown up; and when he is old, he leans on a stick for a third leg.

THE MAGICIAN: Of course! How simple!

THE SPHINX: You *would* shout, "Of course, how simple!" As everybody else does. Then . . . then, I would have my jackals released from their cages. (*Vicious dogs are heard baying and snarling*) I would make you go down on your knees. Down, down further! That's right. You would bend your head . . . and . . . and . . . inhale the fumes from the cunt of The Sphinx that gives men visions!

(*The sound of a calliope is heard.* THE FOOL *tumbles in.*)

Scene 3: THE FOOL, THE MAGICIAN, THE SPHINX.

THE FOOL: How does the French woman hold her liquor?

THE SPHINX: By the ears!

THE FOOL: (*To* THE MAGICIAN) J'accuse! So! You are my rival!

THE MAGICIAN: *(Relieved, but taken aback)* Your rival? Are you looking for the Sphinx?

THE FOOL: Yes, I have a riddle to ask her. You look a little down in the dumps.

THE MAGICIAN: I failed to answer the riddle. At any moment, I am to be fed to the jackals.

THE FOOL: Don't worry about a thing. This Sphinx is yellow.

THE MAGICIAN: Yellow?

THE FOOL: Yeah, this Sphinx is yellow. Watch me. *(To* THE SPHINX*)* Look here, Sphinxie, you don't think I'm going to stand by and watch you bully my buddy here. Put up your dukes!

*(*THE SPHINX *punches him in the eye and knocks him down.)*

THE MAGICIAN: I thought you said she was yellow.

THE FOOL: I'm color blind.

THE MAGICIAN: Now we are both doomed.

THE FOOL: Mystery has its own mysteries, and there are gods above gods. We have ours; they have theirs.

THE MAGICIAN: *(Metaphysically)* That's what is known as infinity.

THE FOOL: *(Matter-of-factly)* That's also what is known as bureaucracy. Let's go over her head and beat the system. *(To* THE SPHINX*)* I've got a real brain twister for you, Sphinxie.

THE SPHINX: *(Condescendingly)* Oh, really?

THE FOOL: Yeah, see if you can answer this one.

THE SPHINX: And if I succeed?

THE FOOL: You name the stakes. Ladies first.

THE SPHINX: If I succeed, you will be nothing more than zeroes wiped from a slate. Even though each zero may be an open mouth crying for help.

THE FOOL: And if you fail?

THE SPHINX: I fail? The possibility has never occurred to me before.

THE FOOL: If you fail you will help us find The High Priestess. Agreed?

THE SPHINX: Agreed. Let's hear this riddle, Fool.

THE FOOL: Tell me, Sphinxie, tell me do, why you have the wings of a bird, the body of a lion, and the head and breasts of a woman.

THE MAGICIAN: I'd like to know the answer to that myself.

THE SPHINX: I'd better do some serious thinking. *(Goes into a dance to thinking music)*

THE FOOL: *(After a while)* Your time is up!

THE SPHINX: *(Looking perplexed)* I . . . I don't know!

THE FOOL: Because that's the way superstitious people picture you. If you didn't look the way they imagine you to look, they wouldn't see you at all.

THE SPHINX: Of course! How simple!

THE FOOL: *(Aside to* THE MAGICIAN*)* Say, who is this dame, anyway?

THE MAGICIAN: The Two-Thousand-Year-Old Woman.

THE FOOL: The Two-Thousand-Year-Old Woman? Very well preserved!

THE MAGICIAN: Yeah. Why don't you ask her for something?

(With some encouragement, THE FOOL *goes over and whispers in* THE SPHINX*'s ear. There is a drumroll.* THE SPHINX *gives* THE FOOL *a hug, then she hugs* THE MAGICIAN.*)*

THE MAGICIAN: *(Aside to* THE FOOL*)* What did you ask her for?

THE FOOL: I asked her to give us each a hug.

THE MAGICIAN: Why don't you ask her for something else?

*(*THE FOOL *repeats whispering business.* THE SPHINX *kisses* THE FOOL *and* THE MAGICIAN.*)*

THE MAGICIAN: What did you ask her for?

THE FOOL: I asked her to give us each a smooch and a hootch-a-ma-kootch.

THE MAGICIAN: Why don't you ask her for something else?

*(*THE FOOL *whispers in* THE SPHINX*'s ear and she slaps them both.)*

THE SPHINX: You have asked me a riddle I could not answer. At first, I took you to be superficial. But now I find you to be profoundly superficial!

THE MAGICIAN: Now you must keep your promise, Sphinx. You must take us wherever we want to go.

THE SPHINX: Very well, where do you want to go?

THE FOOL: Oh, nowhere in particular. Anywhere the four winds blow me. I'm just breezing along with the breeze.

THE MAGICIAN: *(Clapping his hand over* THE FOOL*'s mouth)* I have borne my phallus through the wood of the world seeking something to plunge it into. I seek The High Priestess. Can you take me to her?

THE SPHINX: I will put at your service the four powers of The Sphinx: to know, to dare, to will, and to keep silent.

THE MAGICIAN: Why do you ask so many riddles?

THE SPHINX: Why did the weather forecaster get bounced from his job? *(*THE MAGICIAN *and* THE FOOL *shrug their shoulders)* Because the climate didn't agree with him. You see? All of reality can be expressed in a riddle and all questions can be answered with one. Ah, the riddle! The unanswered question! *(*THE FOOL *takes a fit)* How do you keep a dog from going mad in August? Shoot him in July.

THE FOOL: What bow can never be tied?

THE MAGICIAN: A rainbow!

THE SPHINX:
Voiceless it cries
Wingless it flutters
Toothless it bites
Mouthless it mutters!

THE MAGICIAN AND THE FOOL: What is it?

THE SPHINX: *(Grandiose)* The WIND!

THE MAGICIAN: No more riddles, Sphinx. You promised to take us to The High Priestess.

THE SPHINX: I will submit my heart to be harnessed. You have asked me a riddle I could not answer. This was the conquest of positive science. Now you must also conquer magnetism and alchemy, travel through the sublunar world, confronting Death, Temperance, and the Devil. Then through the solar system to the Moon and the Stars and escape through the Sun in the abyss of the infinite. Here in broad outline there is already an answer to your question. For the sake of clearness an equilateral triangle has been superimposed upon the three meridians. The Arcana of the lower zones seen only transparently might be confused with the upper, through their mutual symmetry. The Spirit descends by three trinities from the absolute into matter (upper hemisphere). It is realized by trinity X (in the Hebrew) of the Kabbalah ha ha Malkuth XI and XII (the equator). And these four fundamental divisions of the four suits of the pack, spades, hearts, clubs, and diamonds, with their hieroglyphic and far more significant names, Scepters, Cups, Swords, and Pentacles. Everything is dual in this world, where equilibrium is unstable, unable to find any rest, except in its return to the trinity, from which it proceeds. Therefore all hieroglyphic suits of the minor Arcana divide into spiritual and material duads.

THE FOOL: Duad?

THE SPHINX: Duad.

THE MAGICIAN: Duad.

ALL: *(As in "It Don't Mean a Thing if It Ain't Got That Swing")* Duad duad duad duad duad duad.

THE SPHINX: Listen carefully and I will explain everything.

THE MAGICIAN: Forward into Terra Incognita!

THE FOOL: *(Fearfully)* The unknown land!

THE MAGICIAN: Lead, Sphinx, and I shall follow.

(THE SPHINX starts out through the audience. THE MAGICIAN follows, carrying THE FOOL piggyback.)

Scene 4: THE SPHINX, THE FOOL, THE MAGICIAN.

THE MAGICIAN: What goes on here?

THE SPHINX: The Hermaphrodite is suing The Himaphrodite for a divorce.

THE MAGICIAN: Isn't he afraid of the gossip and the scandal?

THE FOOL: There's nothing wrong with gossip. Gossip is history. But scandal is gossip made tedious by morality. Why are the Seven Sisters only seven?

THE SPHINX: Because they are not eight.

THE FOOL: Bravo, Sphinxie. You would make a good fool.

THE MAGICIAN: Is The Hermaphrodite guilty?

THE SPHINX: You must be the judge of that. This is the first trial you must pass through. If you really seek the High Priestess.

(THE EMPRESS enters wearing the jackal head of Anubis and carrying the scales of justice.)

THE EMPRESS: *(To THE MAGICIAN)* Secret executions belong to the past, Judge Buttinski. This will be a different kind of trial.

THE MAGICIAN: Different?

THE EMPRESS: Nothing like this has been done in Poland since the war.

THE MAGICIAN: And I would have to be sure of my facts. This is a most important trial. And I have not been myself since the riots. Forgive me. Even the sight of a tattered blouse is cause for rioting in the streets. Nevertheless, court is in session.

Scene 5: THE EMPRESS, THE MAGICIAN, THE SPHINX, THE FOOL, THE HANGED-MAN.

THE HANGED-MAN: Hear ye! Hear ye! Court is now in session! Here come de judge! Here come de judge!

THE MAGICIAN: Morfendike vs. Morfendike. Or The Hermaphrodite vs. The Himaphrodite.

Scene 6: THE MAGICIAN *(as judge)*, THE EMPRESS *(as justice)*, THE SPHINX, THE FOOL, THE HANGED-MAN, JURORS, THE HERMAPHRODITE.

THE EMPRESS: Swear the jury.

THE FOOL: *(Standing on his head or hanging by his foot)* The jurors will stand and raise your right hands. Now raise your right foot. Now raise your left foot.

(The JURORS *fall down)*

THE MAGICIAN: Members of the jury, the case which the jury will be impaneled to hear is one involving this hermaphrodite who wishes to be divorced from himself. The Hermaphrodite is seated here. Will The Himaphrodite stand and face the jury?

THE EMPRESS: The counsel will cross-examine The Hermaphrodite.

MARRIAGE: *(Crying out)* I appeal to the court!

THE FOOL: You don't appeal to me!

*(*MARRIAGE *makes an obscene gesture to* THE HANGED-MAN: FOOL.)*

THE MAGICIAN: Motion denied!

THE EMPRESS: Defense counsel has stated that he has no further motions and I will now order the defendant to plead to the charge.

MARRIAGE, HE: I am sick of this supposedly ideal marriage in which I am nothing but Dad and she is nothing but Mom and we even call each other that. This degrades marriage to the level of a mere breeding pen.

MARRIAGE, SHE: I wanted to disturb that comfortable ease so dangerous to the personality of a man but frequently regarded by him as marital faithfulness.

THE MAGICIAN: The judge advocate will summon the first witness.

*(*THE HIGH PRIESTESS *enters heavily veiled.)*

THE FOOL: The prisoner enters a plea of not guilty to the charge and all its specifications.

THE MAGICIAN: Swear the witness.

THE FOOL: Raise your right hand, sir. Do you swear to tell the truth, the whole truth, and nothing but the truth, so help you God?

THE HIGH PRIESTESS: *(Behind her veil)* If you tear me limb from limb until you separate my body from my soul, you will get nothing out of me beyond what I have told you.

THE EMPRESS: *(Aside to THE MAGICIAN)* That is The High Priestess. She holds the secret behind her veil.

THE MAGICIAN: *(In great agitation)* Drop that veil!

*(*THE HIGH PRIESTESS *drops her veil and* JURORS *gasp.)*

Mario Montez & John Brockmeyer
in *The Grand Tarot* (Thomas Harding)

THE HIGH PRIESTESS: What more is there to tell that you could understand? Besides, I cannot bear to be hurt; and if you hurt me I will say anything you like to stop the pain. But I will take it all back afterwards: so what is the use of it?

THE MAGICIAN: You will be held in contempt of court for withholding evidence. What is this great feminine secret?

THE HIGH PRIESTESS: Emptiness! Emptiness! Emptiness! That is the great feminine secret! It is something absolutely alien to man: the chasm, the unplumbed depths, the yin. The Mothers, the Mothers, how eerily it sounds! Fall man happily into this pit! *(Slaps her yoni)*

THE MAGICIAN: Such a female is fate itself!

THE EMPRESS: *(Jealous)* Objection!

THE MAGICIAN: *(Coming to his senses)* Sustained. Consider your verdict.

THE FOOL: Not yet! Not yet! There's a great deal to come before that.

THE MAGICIAN: Call the first witness.

THE FOOL: Why do the two halves of The Hermaphrodite stick together like glue?

MARRIAGE, BOTH: Because the feeling is mucilage.

THE SPHINX: Take away both halves of The Hermaphrodite and what do you have left?

THE FOOL: I give up.

THE SPHINX: Nothing.

THE FOOL: You've got my number. *(Offers his ass to be kicked)*

THE SPHINX: Nothing will come of nothing. Let us say nothing lest we mar our fortunes.

THE EMPRESS: First witness! The Fool!

THE HIGH PRIESTESS: But I thought I was the first witness.

THE EMPRESS: The fourteenth of March I think it was.

THE MAGICIAN: Fifteenth.

THE FOOL: Sixteenth.

THE MAGICIAN: *(To* THE FOOL*)* Write that down.

THE FOOL: Seventeen dollars and thirty-seven cents. Cheap!

THE MAGICIAN: Give your evidence.

MARRIAGE, HE: I'm a poor man, your honor.

THE MAGICIAN: *(In pear-shaped tones)* You're a very poor speaker. Is it true that you are a morphodike?

MARRIAGE, BOTH: The word is "Hermaphrodite."

THE MAGICIAN: If that's all you know about it, you may stand down.

MARRIAGE, HE: I can't go no lower. I'm on the floor as it is.

THE MAGICIAN: Then you may sit down.

MARRIAGE, HE: *(Dejected)* I'm so low the skunks won't even piss on me.

THE MAGICIAN: *(Handing a document to* THE FOOL*)* Show this to the prisoner. *(The* FOOL *hands document to* THE HERMAPHRODITE*)* Is that the confession you gave to the security police?

MARRIAGE, HE: *(Looking up after examining the document)* Yes.

THE MAGICIAN: Is that your signature?

MARRIAGE, SHE: *(Hysterical)* Yes, it's mine . . . but I don't know what I confessed to. The police wrote it for me. They forced me to sign it.

THE MAGICIAN: You repudiate this confession?

MARRIAGE, HE: It's not mine. I was forced to sign it. It's their words. *(Pointing to* THE FOOL*)* Ask him, he'll tell you. He was treated the same.

(The court goes into an uproar.)

THE MAGICIAN: Order, order in the courtroom!

THE FOOL: I'll have BLT down, seaboard, eighty-six on the mayo, and a side of French.

THE EMPRESS: May it please the court . . . if the court will allow . . . the prosecution has a statement to make.

THE FOOL: I must advise my client. *(To* THE HERMAPHRODITE*)* Anything you say will be held against you.

MARRIAGE, HE: Christine Jorgensen.

THE FOOL: Submitted for the defense. *(Shows his-and-hers towel)* Entered as evidence of the utter lack of sanitary facilities.

THE SPHINX: *(Flirtatiously to* THE MAGICIAN*)* You must be the judge. I can tell by your big . . . wig. Nice tie, Judge.

THE MAGICIAN: *(Grinning)* Swear the lady.

THE FOOL: Why you no good son of a bitch, cocksuckin', shiteatin', ass friggin', scumbag bastard, motherfuckin', cunt lappin' wino, so help you God?

THE SPHINX: I do.

THE FOOL: Are you tryin' to pull a fast one? Sit down. Admit that you was the palooka what got The Hermaphrodite in Dutch in the first place. That it was nothin' but a frame-up and The Hermaphrodite was a patsy you could set up like a sittin' duck.

THE SPHINX: Ladies and Gentlemen of the jury, are you going to take the word of a jailbird, a two-time loser who never gave a sucker an even break? I'm leveling with ya. I'm on the up-and-up. *(Aside to* THE JUDGE*)* How'm I doin', Judge?

THE MAGICIAN: Are you trying to show contempt for this court?

THE SPHINX: No, your honor, I'm doin' my best to hide it!

THE EMPRESS: *(To* THE HERMAPHRODITE*)* Try to tell the court in your own words exactly what happened.

MARRIAGE, SHE: First he put his hand on my ankle.

ALL: Yes?

MARRIAGE, SHE: Then he put his hand on my calf.

ALL: Yes?

MARRIAGE, SHE: Then he put his hand on the inside of my thigh.

ALL: Yes?

MARRIAGE, SHE: Then he ran off with my purse and I screamed. *(Screams)*

THE MAGICIAN: Why didn't you scream when he put his hand on your ankle? When he put his hand on your calf? Why didn't you scream when he put his hand on the inside of your thigh?

MARRIAGE, SHE: How was I to know that he was after my money?

THE MAGICIAN: The jury will consider its verdict.

(The JURORS *go into a football huddle and emerge with* THE FOOL *upside down hanging by his feet.)*

THE FOOL: It's a hanged jury.

MARRIAGE, SHE: *(Shouting)* Hang the jury!

(All point accusing fingers at MARRIAGE.*)*

THE MAGICIAN: I hereby sentence you to ten years at Leavenworth or eleven years at twelveworth.

MARRIAGE, SHE: I'll take five to ten at Woolworth's.

(Exit JURORS, THE EMPRESS.*)*

Scene 7: THE MAGICIAN, THE SPHINX, MARRIAGE, THE FOOL, THE HIGH PRIESTESS.

THE MAGICIAN: How pale she is tonight! Never have I seen her so pale! She is like the shadow of a white rose in a mirror of silver.

THE FOOL: Don't look at her so much, Heavenly Father! It is dangerous to look at people too much. Something terrible might happen.

THE MAGICIAN: O High Priestess, speak to me! Your voice is like music to my ears.

THE FOOL: He's out of his mind.

THE SPHINX: Let us hold him down. The High Priestess is governed by The Moon. Men go mad if they look at her too much. When the seizure passes, we can release him.

THE FOOL: *(Tying* THE MAGICIAN *to The Chariot)* Here you go, Father.

THE MAGICIAN: O ye Gods of my country, help me!

THE FOOL: In my country there are no gods left. The professionals have driven them out. There are some who say that they have hidden themselves in the mountains, but I do not believe it. Three nights I have been in the mountains seeking them everywhere. I did not find them. And at last I called them by their names and they did not come. I think they are dead.

THE MAGICIAN: She is getting up! She is leaving. She looks very troubled. How pale she is! I have never seen her so pale.

THE FOOL: I pray you not to look at her.

THE MAGICIAN: She is like a dove that has strayed the wild storm. She is like a narcissus trembling in the wind.

THE HIGH PRIESTESS: *(As she recedes and disappears)* There is but one! There is but one! There is but one!

Scene 8: THE FOOL, THE MAGICIAN, THE SPHINX, MARRIAGE, THE MOON, THE STAR.

(THE MOON shows herself in the sky.)

THE MAGICIAN: Look at the moon. She is like a madwoman seeking everywhere for lovers.

THE SPHINX: No, The Moon is like The Moon, that's all.

THE FOOL: How strange The Moon seems. She is like a dead woman rising from the tomb.

THE MAGICIAN: Where are we?

THE FOOL: I dunno.

THE MAGICIAN: Is it day or night?

THE FOOL: I dunno.

THE MAGICIAN: Is that the sun, the moon, or a star?

THE FOOL: I dunno.

THE MAGICIAN: Don't you know anything?

THE FOOL: I ain't lost, Father.

THE SPHINX: Look, the moon is waning and the stars are coming out.

MARRIAGE: *(Sighs)* I always sigh at moonset.

THE FOOL:
    Star light, Star bright
    I wish I may. I wish I might.
    Have the wish I wish tonight.
    I wish I had some English pudding.

THE SPHINX: Granted!

(A bowl of English pudding appears in THE FOOL's hand.)

THE FOOL: Yum, yum, yum.

THE MAGICIAN: You wasted one of the wishes. Now there are only two wishes left.

THE SPHINX: *(Laughing)* One down and two to go!

THE FOOL: I'm sorry.

THE MAGICIAN: O moon of my delight that knowest no wane, where is The High Priestess? Lead me to her, Luna. Her beauty draws me on!

THE MOON: The beauty of The High Priestess is greatly overrated. Today she looks a lover of delicatessen. She's become so mercenary. She seems now to have a sort of hunger for money.

THE SPHINX: Disgusting!

THE MOON: Why one day she saw my reflection in a puddle and mistook it for a silver coin. She tried to put it in her pocket. *(Laughs)*

THE MAGICIAN: Arise, fair sun and kill the envious moon.

THE STAR: She needs money because she squanders it on her lover. A tall dark man in the army.

MARRIAGE, SHE: In my opinion a woman may accept the consolations of Bacchus as soon as accept a lover.

THE MAGICIAN: Do you really think she may?

THE STAR: Still, every now and then one's face needs transforming. And love does it better than anything else.

MARRIAGE, SHE: It depends, my child, upon the *sort.*

THE STAR: I suppose when one's husband is fifty-seven . . .

THE MOON: My dear, even a man of fifty-seven is better than nothing at all.

MARRIAGE, SHE: I don't agree.

THE STAR: No?

MARRIAGE: I've been married, you know, too. Yet I sometimes think the simple comfort of a hot-water bottle . . .

THE STAR: Look, the Sun is going down . . . on the moon!

THE MAGICIAN:
The Moon is shining sulkily, because she thinks the sun,
Has got no business to be there after day is done.

THE SPHINX: You are both mad. You have looked too long at The Moon. You have a dreamer's look; you must not dream. It is only sick people who dream.

Scene 9: THE HIGH PRIESTESS, THE EMPEROR, THE EMPRESS.

THE HIGH PRIESTESS: You are Queen Ishtar of Syria?

THE EMPRESS: *(Aside)* You see what I mean? *(To The High Priestess)* I am.

THE HIGH PRIESTESS: I am a stranger here in Syria and I seek your help.

THE EMPRESS: *(Aside)* She wears her breasts bare. She is undoubtedly Egyptian! *(Aloud)* You are welcome if you are a gentlewoman. My doors are always open to people of fashion.

THE HIGH PRIESTESS: *(Aside)* She mistakes my ceremonial robes for haute couture. I will not tell her that I am a goddess. *(Aloud)* Humble thanks great lady. If I can perform any service for you at all, feel free to ask. My gratitude knows no bounds.

THE EMPEROR: What brings you to these parts?

THE HIGH PRIESTESS: My jealous brother Death has stolen my husband Osiris, locked him in a chest, and cast him in the river Nile. I have followed the river for nine months hoping to find the cabinet in the reeds along the riverrun.

THE EMPEROR: What does your husband do for a living?

THE HIGH PRIESTESS: He is . . . a Magician.

THE EMPEROR: Perhaps he will escape like Houdini.

THE HIGH PRIESTESS: *(Aside)* Dash the gaudy death cup!

THE EMPEROR: *(Aside)* What a pretty pair of knockers! *(Aloud)* It happens that I need a wet nurse for this child of mine. Will you nurse him?

THE HIGH PRIESTESS: I only wish everyone was as sure of anything in this watery world as we are of everything in the [newly wet fellow] that's bound to follow. I'll mother him. [*(Exit The Emperor and The Empress)*] Osiris, Osiris, I can hear your heart's memory of beating. I will free you from the palace pillar. I will reward The Empress for granting me asylum. I will suckle her child on my fingertips and holding him over a candle flame burn away his mortal parts so that he will be a god like myself. *(Holds infant over flame and chants)*

Grass of levity
[Speak] in brevity
Flowers felicity
Fire of misery
Wind's stability
Is mortality.

THE EMPRESS: *(Enters and screams)* What are you doing?

THE HIGH PRIESTESS: Foolish woman. What have you done. I would have given him immortal life if you hadn't butted in.

(She throws the baby to The Empress.)

THE EMPRESS: If I get my hands on you. . . .

THE HIGH PRIESTESS: Turn me into a swallow. *(She turns into a swallow and flies away)*

(The cries of a bird.)

Scene 10: THE EMPEROR, THE EMPRESS, THE HANGED-MAN.

THE EMPEROR: Last night I had a particularly afflicting dream. I saw the tower struck by lightning and you and I falling with the fragments of broken masonry.

THE EMPRESS: *(Troubled)* And I have heard rumors of a plague, miasmas of a virus from the Orient.

(Enter THE HANGED-MAN.*)*

THE HANGED-MAN: The *Grand-Saint-Antoine,* a month out of Beirut, asks for permission to dock here at Cagliari.

THE EMPEROR: *(To* THE EMPRESS*)* This ship must be contaminated! *(To* THE HANGED-MAN*)* Dispatch the pilot's boat and some men with orders that the *Grand-Saint-Antoine* tack about immediately and make full sail away from this port or we shall sink her by cannon shot. This is war against the plague. We mustn't waste any time.

(Exeunt THE EMPEROR *and* THE EMPRESS.*)*

Scene 11: THE HANGED-MAN, DEATH.

THE HANGED-MAN: Idiotic order. Insane . . . despotic . . . irresponsible.

(Enter DEATH.*)*

DEATH: Ahoy! Ahoy!

THE HANGED-MAN: *(Shouting)* Name your ship.

DEATH: The *Grand-Saint-Antoine.*

THE HANGED-MAN: Back ho! Back ho! Or be sunk by cannon shot. You may not dock at Cagliari!

DEATH: We seek replenishment with meat and wine. There is much running backwards and forwards among the crew. There is no staying in any one place; for at one and the same time everything has to be done everywhere.

THE HANGED-MAN: Talk about immediately—it is the order of The Emperor. Your ship is contaminated with the plague.

DEATH: Curses throttle thee. Well done for a hanged-man. That's Christianity! We're off! Farewell a while to her and thee. The brine's my bride to be.

Scene 12: THE MOON, THE DEVIL.

THE MOON: Epidemics of inflamed eyes, diarrheas, with fever and tenesmus, watery stools, vomiting, and sweating, prolonged fevers lasting twenty-four days or more, swellings of the parotid glands. An epidemic of mumps—a mild fever, without mortality and with bilateral parotid swelling, dry cough, and occasional swellings of the testicles. Sore throats with fever, coughs, delirium, scarlet fever, or diphtheria.

THE DEVIL: An unarmed man died of a condition which was an attack either of acute appendicitis or of cholecystitis. In the middle of the night after a heavy meal, he was seized by sudden vomiting, fever, and pain in the right hypochondrium. He died on the eleventh day.

Scene 13: THE EMPEROR, THE EMPRESS.

(Enter THE EMPEROR *and* THE EMPRESS.*)*

THE EMPRESS: Ever since the accident, she has been going about in such heavens of joy. I've seldom seen anyone so happy. *(Passing her hand over her eyes)*

THE EMPEROR: It fell so suddenly I was in my bathtub.

THE EMPRESS: I fear it's badly damaged.

THE EMPEROR: Half of it is down. Such gusts of wind! The way they pulled the bushes . . .

THE EMPRESS: How did it happen, exactly?

THE EMPEROR: A pair of scissors it appears was left upon the parapet and caught the lightning's eye.

THE EMPRESS: What a dreadful thing! *(Shudders)*

THE EMPEROR: That the cathedral should submit to be struck strikes me as being so strange. It never has before.

THE EMPRESS: My maid has asked me if she may go over and see the ruins.

THE EMPEROR: Age holds no horrors for me, not anymore. Some day I'll have a house here and I'll grow old quite gracefully.

THE EMPRESS: Surely with age one's attractions should increase. One should be irresistible at ninety.

THE EMPEROR: A few of us, perhaps, may. You dear . . . you will . . .

THE EMPRESS: You used to say it would be in a town with a *V*, Versailles, or Vallombrose, or Verona. *(Exit)*

Scene 14: THE SPHINX, THE MAGICIAN, THE FOOL, THE SUN, THE MOON, THE STAR, THE EMPEROR, THE EMPRESS, THE DEVIL, DEATH.

DEATH: *(Putting his hand on* THE FOOL's *shoulder)* Care for a game of chess? *(He unrolls a ruglike chessboard)*

THE FOOL: *(Aside)* I can beat him with my eyes closed!

DEATH: *(Aside)* The Fool does not remember my fifteenth move in the fourth game of the second elimination tournament! *(To* THE FOOL*)* Your choice of colors!

[*(Enter* THE EMPEROR *and* THE EMPRESS. THE FOOL *sits on* THE EMPRESS's *knee and* DEATH *on* THE EMPEROR's.*)*]

THE FOOL: White.

DEATH: And I take black, the noble symbol of death and destruction, and not white, the putrid emblem of decency in a decadent civilization that has been doomed. Remember, Fool, chess is war! *(Sarcastically)* Ist der bauer gescheutzt?

THE FOOL: Der bauer ist gescheisst!

DEATH: *(Shrieks)* Pferd!

THE FOOL: Patzer!

DEATH: Sacrifice or bust!

THE FOOL: *(Forcing back a primordial image into his collective unconscious)* Sacrifice?

ALL: *(Chanting)* Sacrifice! Sacrifice! Sacrifice! Jesus Christ! Sacrifice! Jesus Christ! Sacrifice! Jesus Christ! Sacrifice!

THE FOOL: My time has not yet come!

DEATH: *(Rising and making an elegant bow)* Allow me to inform you, dear sir, that you are a hopeless idiot! Checkmate. Fool's mate.

THE EMPRESS: I love sex. Sometimes I don't have time for it, but believe me there is no adequate substitute, not even chess. Ah, bring me men to match my mountains.

*(*THE FOOL *knocks over the chessmen.* DEATH *takes* THE FOOL *in his arms.)*

DEATH: Kiss me, my Fool.

THE EMPEROR: For all our yesterdays have lighted fools the way to dusty death.

THE FOOL: I sing of the Angustia de la Cucaracha: the Anguish of the Cockroach. The cockroach and the cross. Of cucarachas en la casa. Angustia de la Cucaracha . . . Gloria! Gloria! Gloria! The weeping cockroach and his mother. The crucified cockroach and his doubts. The drowned cockroach floating in the baptismal font. *(Spits)* The undrinkable water. Of the Seven African Powers, Las Siete Potencias Africanas, The Voodoo deities and all the abandoned gods who, fallen into neglect, roam through the world seeking revenge! These are joking matters. If I had human emotions instead of just charm, I might weep. What are tears? Water and salt?

THE EMPRESS: And sorrow.

THE MAGICIAN: A bitter Fool!

THE FOOL: Can you tell me, my boy, the difference between the bitter Fool and the sweet one?

THE SPHINX: *(Spins the Wheel of Fortune)* It is said that if The Fool can make Death laugh he will be spared one extra day.

DEATH: *(To* THE FOOL*)* Make me laugh.

THE FOOL: *(Aside)* I'm not afraid, I'll tell you why. You see I have no death to die.

DEATH: Make me laugh.

THE FOOL: Did you hear the one about the man who died and then lived?

DEATH: Died and then lived?

THE FOOL: He dyed . . . his hair! He he he he. *(*DEATH *does not laugh)* This one will really slay you. Why did Lothario put it to his girl in the graveyard? *(*DEATH *cocks his head quizzically)* Because he thought it would be a good place to bury a stiff.

DEATH: Not funny. You lose our game of chess. You may be a Fool today, but when they come for you tomorrow you will be a grave man.

*(*THE FOOL *bends over and* DEATH *gives him a swift kick in the ass.)*

THE FOOL: Touché.

THE MAGICIAN: I thought you said you could beat him with your eyes closed.

THE FOOL: Aw, I was at a disadvantage. I had my eyes open.

DEATH: *(Bursts out laughing)* Ha! Ha! Ha!

THE SPHINX: The Fool has made Death laugh. He wins one extra day on earth.

DEATH: What will you do with your one extra day?

THE FOOL: I think I'll sleep late. *(Tumbling)*

DEATH: Now I must return to the netherworld. Yes, it is a touching moment when they administer the last sacrament: the last sleep: the last dream.

THE MAGICIAN: The last dream . . . do you know The High Priestess?

DEATH: Intimately.

THE MAGICIAN: Do you know where she is?

DEATH: On the other side of the River Styx.

THE FOOL: Styx and stones will break my bones . . .

THE MAGICIAN: Would you take me to her?

DEATH: There's a ferry leaving every minute for Hades.

THE MAGICIAN: Hades . . .

THE FOOL: I've heard so much about your wicked city. I'm dying to see it.

THE MAGICIAN: Take me to her.

DEATH: Smell this white rose.

THE MAGICIAN: *(Smells rose)* Ahhhh!

DEATH: You have breathed Plague, Cholera, Dysentery, Typhoid—the four Princes of the Blood Royal in the Palace of King Death.

THE MAGICIAN: This is it. Everything's slipping. I'm falling inside.

DEATH: That's all right. Don't fight it. Go with it. Think of all the guys who've done it before you. You've got company. High-class company. Bonsai, kid.

*(*THE MAGICIAN *falls into a deathlike sleep inside the sarcophagus. The* ANGEL OF TEMPERANCE *appears pouring water back and forth between two chalices.)*

TEMPERANCE: Who will carry his ashes unto the mountains?

THE FOOL: I will!

TEMPERANCE: You? Who are you?

THE FOOL: I am a thoroughbred mongrel. Related to all the earth and nothing human is foreign to me.

TEMPERANCE: And what can you do?

THE FOOL: I will open the doors and castles of death and now forever the laughter of children shall spring forth from coffins.

THE SPHINX: All is empty, all is equal, all hath been. I breathe the odor of dusty eternities.

THE FOOL: I will terrify and subvert them with laughter. Give me back my father.

DEATH: Your father lost a father, and that father lost his. Don't you know, Fool, all that lives must die, passing through nature to eternity?

THE FOOL: But I have three wishes and I wish my father alive again.

THE SPHINX: Granted!

(The sarcophagus opens. THE MAGICIAN *comes forward dressed as the mummy.)*

THE FOOL: Congratulations, Father. You're a mummy!

THE MAGICIAN: I wish The High Priestess were here.

THE SPHINX: Granted.

MARRIAGE: Look at that old beggar woman! She looks like the stump of a tree.

THE MOON: This is The High Priestess.

THE MAGICIAN: Oh no. You are old. Old. Oh no, not old.

THE HIGH PRIESTESS: Old. Will you hear him? In my own young days I had a hundred letters from men a sight better than he is. They came like raindrops in May. And I had a high head that time and sent out no answer. Don't think because you see me alone now that I was in want of handsome men in the old days, when Shoshu came to me—shii no shocks of Tukakusa—that came to me in the moonlight and in the dark night, and in the nights flooded with rain, and in the black face of the wind, and in the wild swish of the snow. He came as often as the rain falls from the heavens, ninety-nine times and then he died. And I am still a virgin. Ever virgin! Ever virgin, until eternity. And his ghost is about me driving me on with the madness.

THE MAGICIAN: I wish The High Priestess young again!

THE SPHINX: *(Asks a riddle)*

THE MAGICIAN: Did you hear me, Sphinx? I said I wish The High Priestess young again.

THE SPHINX: *(Asks another riddle)*

THE MAGICIAN: What does this mean?

THE SPHINX: *(Asks riddle)*

*(*THE DEVIL *builds a tower out of children's blocks.)*

THE MAGICIAN: We're out of wishes. You wasted the wish on English pudding. How could you? I hate you. You Fool. You idiot. *(He kicks* THE FOOL's *ass)*

THE FOOL: Father, why hast thou forsaken me?

THE STAR: Look, The Fool has wept a tear. It is a green tear. *(Holds up a jewel)*

THE FOOL: I am new at weeping.

THE SPHINX: All the tears a Fool can weep will not make The High Priestess young again.

(Caruso's Pagliacci *plays and* THE FOOL *rends his garments with weeping.* THE MOON *wipes his face and his face appears on the cloth.)*

THE DEVIL: His heart is broken.

DEATH: In the future let those who play The Fool have no hearts.

(The tower falls. THE SUN, THE MOON, *and* THE STARS *dress* THE FOOL *as Christ [and* THE MAGICIAN *as God the Father. The old lady becomes the Virgin Mary. They assume the positions of Michelangelo's "Pietà."])*

GOD:
  First when I this world had wrought,
  Wood and wind and waters wan
  And everything that now is ought,
  Full well methought that I did then;
  When they were made, good I them thought.
  Then to my likeness made I man,
  And Man to grieve me gave me nought,
  Thus rue I that I the world began.

VIRGIN MARY:
  Here may ye see his five wounds wide
  Which he endured for your misdeed,
  Through heart and head, foot, hand and hide,
  Not for his guilt, but for your need.
  Behold his body, back and side,
  How dear he bought your brotherhood.
  These bitter pains would he abide,
  To buy you bliss, thus would he bleed.

FOOL-AS-CHRIST: Now is fulfilled all my forethought. For ended is all earthly things. All at once in earth that I have wrought, now after their works have winning. They who have sinned, and ceasèd not, a sorrow song now shall they sing. But they that mendeth while they might, shall dwell and bide in my blessing.

*(*THE FOOL-AS-CHRIST *gives Communion with the pieces of his broken heart.)*

THE HIGH PRIESTESS: Why didn't you tell me that you were so strong?

THE MAGICIAN: Why didn't you tell me that you were so beautiful?

THE EMPRESS: *(Singing as she strums her ukulele)*
  Always spring comes again bearing life.
  Always always forever and again,
  Spring again! Life again!
  Summer and fall and death and peace again.
(With agonized sorrow)
  But always love and conception—and birth!
(She falls on her back, goes into labor, and bears the planet Earth.)
  Birth! Birth! Birth!
(With agonized exultance)
  Spring bearing the intolerable chalice of life again.
(Speaks)
  Bearing the glorious, blazing crown of life again.

(She sits like an idol of Earth staring out over the world.)

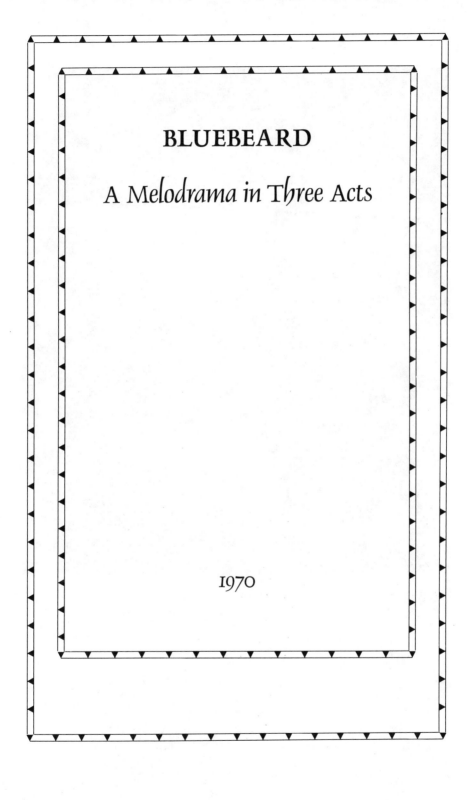

BLUEBEARD

A Melodrama in Three Acts

1970

Mario Montez & John Brockmeyer
in *Bluebeard* (Roy Azenella)

Cast of Characters

SHEEMISH
MRS. MAGGOT
LAMIA "THE LEOPARD WOMAN"
KHANAZAR VON BLUEBEARD
GOOD ANGEL
BAD ANGEL
RODNEY
SYBIL
MISS FLORA CUBBIDGE
HECATE
HER TRAIN

ACT I

The alchemical laboratory of DR. BLUEBEARD, *located on an island off the coast of Maine.*

(The house is a lighthouse still in use. Revolving light, test tubes, and other laboratory equipment including an operating table. SHEEMISH, *the butler, and* MRS. MAGGOT, *the housekeeper, are dusting and sweeping.* MRS. MAGGOT *bumps the table, causing a test tube to fall and break.)*

Scene 1: SHEEMISH, MRS. MAGGOT.

SHEEMISH: Now see what you've done! Clean it up at once. For if Khanazar, the Bluebeard, finds anything broken, he will surely send you to the House of Pain.
MRS. MAGGOT: *(Terribly frightened)* No, no, not the House of Pain!
SHEEMISH: *(Sadistically)* Yes, yes, the House of Pain. If I should mention the fact that you broke this little glass tube, I'm sure the master would send you to the House of Pain.
MRS. MAGGOT: *(More frightened)* No, no, not the House of Pain! Please, Sheemish, don't tell, I beg of you.
SHEEMISH: *(Calculatingly)* Very well. I will not tell . . . as long as you realize that I am doing you a favor . . . and that I will expect a favor in return.
MRS. MAGGOT: Anything, I'll do anything you ask, but please, please do not tell.
SHEEMISH: Replace the little glass tube. Substitute something for the sticky liquid inside. Do this quickly, for the good ship *Lady Vain* will dock here at three o'clock this afternoon, drop off a female passenger, and return to the mainland. *(MRS. MAGGOT puts test tube under her skirt and urinates in it.)* We must prepare the guest room for tonight . . . and the bridal chamber for tomorrow.
MRS. MAGGOT: You mean he's found another . . . another . . . ? *(She begins to weep)*
SHEEMISH: Say it, Mrs. Maggot! Wife. Say it: Wife! Wife! Wife!
MRS. MAGGOT: I can't. I can't bear to say it. *(Falling to her knees)* Lord of my prayers! God of my sacrifice! Because you have done this thing, you shall lack

both my fear and my praise. I shall not wince at your lightnings nor be awed when you go by.

SHEEMISH: Curse not our god, Khanazar, the Bluebeard.

MRS. MAGGOT: Why should I not curse him who has stolen from me the gardens of my childhood?

SHEEMISH: Remember the House of Pain and hold your tongue. [(MRS. MAGGOT *holds her tongue with her fingers.*)] You have replaced the little glass tube. It looks exactly as it did before the little accident. Even the sticky liquid is the same color and viscosity. You and I are the only ones who know. Come, the guest room. And, Mrs. Maggot, forget about the past.

MRS. MAGGOT: Since the operation I can't remember it anyway.

SHEEMISH: And think as I do, of the future.

MRS. MAGGOT:
    The future is so very far.
    The present is what must be feared.
    For we are slaves of Khanazar,
    And dread the wrath of the Bluebeard.

(Exeunt.)

Scene 2: LAMIA THE LEOPARD WOMAN.

(Enter LAMIA THE LEOPARD WOMAN, *wearing more leopard than the costume designer thought advisable. She riffles through* BLUEBEARD'*s papers.)*

Scene 3: KHANAZAR, THE BLUEBEARD.

BLUEBEARD: *(Entering and seeing* LAMIA*)* I thought I told you never to come to this side of the island again! *(Draws gun and fires.* LAMIA *runs out.)* Give up your passions, Bluebeard, and become the thing you claim to be. Is to end desire desire's chiefest end? Does sex afford no greater miracles? Have all my perversions and monstrosities, my fuckings and suckings, led me to this? This little death at the climax followed by slumber? Yet chastity ravishes me. And yet the cunt gapes like the jaws of hell, an unfathomable abyss; or the boy-ass used to buggery spread wide to swallow me up its bung; or the mouth sucking out my life! Aaagh! If only there were some new and gentle genital that would combine with me and, mutually interpenetrated, steer me through this storm in paradise! *(The sound of a foghorn)* They said I was mad at medical school. They said no third genital was possible. Yang and yin, male and female, and that's that. *(Laughs maniacally)* Science suits a mercenary drudge who aims at nothing but external trash. Give me a dark art that stretches as far as does the mind of man; a sound magician is a demigod.

(Foghorn again.)

Scene 4: GOOD ANGEL, BAD ANGEL, BLUEBEARD.

GOOD ANGEL:
    On, Bluebeard, lay these thoughts aside,
    And think not on them lest it tempt thy soul

And heap God's heavy wrath upon thee.
Take half—one sex, that's all—for that is nature's way.

(Foghorn.)

BAD ANGEL:
Go forward, Bluebeard, in that famous art
Wherein all nature's treasure is contained:
Be thou on earth as God is in the sky,
Master and possessor of both sexes.

(Exit ANGELS.*)*

Scene 5: BLUEBEARD.

BLUEBEARD:
Love must be reinvented, that's obvious.
Sex to me no longer is mysterious
And so I swear that while my beard is blue,
I'll twist some human flesh into a genital new.

Scene 6: BLUEBEARD, SHEEMISH, MRS. MAGGOT.

SHEEMISH: Master, Master.
BLUEBEARD: *(Enraged)* Swine! How dare you enter my room without knocking? *(Lashes whip)* Have you forgotten the House of Pain?
SHEEMISH: *(Clutching his genitals)* No, no, not the House of Pain! Mercy, Master.
BLUEBEARD: How can I show you mercy when I am merciless with myself? I see in you nothing but my own failure; another experiment down the drain.
SHEEMISH: *(On his knees pathetically)* Forgive me. *(Whimpers)*
BLUEBEARD: Aaagh, get up. Tell me what you want.
SHEEMISH: The good ship *Lady Vain* has docked here on the rocky side of the island.
BLUEBEARD: *(Anticipating)* Yes . . .
SHEEMISH: There are two women . . .
BLUEBEARD: *(In ecstasy)* Ah, resolve me of all ambiguities. Perform what desperate enterprises I will!
MRS. MAGGOT: And a man.
BLUEBEARD: Huh? A man? There is no man! *(Lashes her with whip)* You are mistaken, there is no man.

(Loud knocking at the door.)

MRS. MAGGOT: It's them.
SHEEMISH: *(Correcting her)* It is they.
BLUEBEARD: *(Looking through spy hole)* Sybil said nothing about a man. *(Loud knocking, howling wind, and the sound of rain)* Go away! Go away! Leave me in peace!

Scene 7: BLUEBEARD, SHEEMISH, MRS. MAGGOT, RODNEY PARKER, SYBIL, MISS FLORA CUBBIDGE.

RODNEY'S VOICE: Baron Bluebeard, please open the door!

BLUEBEARD: Leave me alone! Go away!

SYBIL'S VOICE: Dear Uncle, please let us in for the love of God. It's bitter without.

BLUEBEARD: *(Aside)* And I am bitter within!

MISS CUBBIDGE'S VOICE: We'll catch our death of cold!

MRS. MAGGOT: *(In confusion)* What should we do, Master?

SHEEMISH: *(Calling down from a lookout point)* We must let them in for their ship, the *Lady Vain,* its sails big-bellied, makes way from our port. I think it will go down in the storm.

BLUEBEARD: Aagh, very well, come in then. But you can't stay. *(Opens the door)*

(Enter SYBIL, RODNEY, *and* CUBBIDGE, *wet.)*

SYBIL: *(Rushing to* BLUEBEARD*)* Oh Uncle Khanazar, my dear Uncle Khanazar, why wouldn't you let us in? How glad I am to see you. Who would have thought of you?

BLUEBEARD: Why, Sybil, I hope you always thought of me.

SYBIL: Dear Uncle, so I do; but I meant to say of seeing you—I never dreamed I would while you were quartered here at . . . at . . . what is the name of this island anyway?

BLUEBEARD: *(Lying)* I don't believe it has a name. I've never thought to give it one.

RODNEY: The sailors called it "The Island of Lost Love."

SYBIL: It's true our ship was almost lost in the fog.

RODNEY: And we are in love.

BLUEBEARD: *(Aside)* Grrrr!

SYBIL: Oh, excuse me, Uncle, this is my fiancé, Rodney Parker.

BLUEBEARD: *(Icily)* Howdyedo?

RODNEY: *(Running off at the mouth)* Sybil has told me so much about you. She says you were the great misunderstood genius at medical school. But that you suddenly gave it all up, threw it all away to live here in almost total seclusion—

SYBIL: *(Interrupting)* And this is Miss Cubbidge, my beloved traveling companion and tutor.

MISS CUBBIDGE: *(Shaking his hand violently)* I am incensed to meet you, Baron Bluebeard. Sybil told me that you were with her father at medical school when the terrible fire . . .

BLUEBEARD: *(Flaring up)* Don't squeeze my hand! I work with my hands. *(Then politely)* If you will excuse me. I expected only one guest. *(Turning to* MRS. MAGGOT *and* SHEEMISH, *who bow with sinister smiles)* Now, there are extra preparations to be made. Mrs. Maggot and Sheemish will show you to your rooms. *(Kisses* SYBIL's *hand, shakes* MISS CUBBIDGE's *hand, and ignores* RODNEY's *hand)* We will sup when the moon rises over Mount Agdora. *(Exits)*

RODNEY: Did you see that? I offered him my hand, but he refused it.

SYBIL: I'm sure Uncle Khanazar meant nothing by it. He's so involved in his work and he's unused to human companionship.

Scene 8: SYBIL, RODNEY, CUBBIDGE, MAGGOT, SHEEMISH.

RODNEY: *(Aside to* SYBIL*)* What about these serving people he keeps around here?

SYBIL: *(Aside to* RODNEY *and* CUBBIDGE*)* Yes, of course. *(Then strangely)* But then they hardly seem human, do they?

MRS. MAGGOT: *(Dyky)* This way to the washroom, ladies. Follow me to the washroom, ladies.

MISS CUBBIDGE: Shall we wash away that which we acquiesced during our long adjunct? I refer, of course, to the dust of travel.

SYBIL: Until dinner, Rodney dear.

RODNEY: Sybil, there is something that I must discuss with you.

SYBIL: Excuse me until then, dear Rodney, I must freshen up. *(Throws him a kiss and exits)*

Scene 9: RODNEY, SHEEMISH.

RODNEY: Ah, I'm convinced of it! Sybil is in love with him.

SHEEMISH: With whom?

RODNEY: Excuse me, I was thinking aloud. Thinking, thinking, thinking, that's all I ever do. My head thunders with thinking. I must stop thinking. I needs must shout it. *(Very loud)* Why did she come here? To look for him. Nothing I could do but she must come to look for him. I think this jealousy will drive me mad!

SHEEMISH: Shall I tell you between our two selves what I think of it? [*(Joins* RODNEY *on the sofa and passes him a bottle of whiskey, which they share during scene)*] I'm afraid she'll get little return for her love; her journey to this foggy island will be useless.

RODNEY: *(Overjoyed)* But what is the reason? Do tell me, Sheemish, what makes you take such a gloomy view of the situation?

SHEEMISH: His feelings are cold.

RODNEY: *(Enraged again)* You think he will betray her innocent love?

SHEEMISH: He has no heart, that man.

RODNEY: But how could a gentleman do such a vile thing?

SHEEMISH: I have been his servant on this island nineteen years and I will say this—just between us—that in my master, Baron Khanazar, the Bluebeard, you see the vilest scoundrel that ever cumbered the earth, a madman, a cur, a devil, a Turk, a heretic, who believes in neither Heaven, Hell, nor werewolf: he lives like an animal, like a swinish gourmet, a veritable vermin infesting his environs and shuttering his ears to every Christian remonstrance, and turning to ridicule everything we believe in.

RODNEY: But surely there's nothing between them. He wouldn't marry his own niece, Sybil. What a ridiculoush idea! *(Laughs)*

SHEEMISH: *(Ominously and with candor)* Believe me, to satisfy his passion he would have gone further than that, he would have married you as well and her dog and cat into the bargain. Marriage means nothing to him. It is his usual method of ensnaring women! *(Sound of footsteps)* But here he comes taking a turn in the palace. Let us separate—what I have spoken I have spoken in confidence. I am his slave, but a master who has given himself over to wickedness is a thing to be dreaded. If you repeat a word of this to him, I will swear you made it up.

(Exit RODNEY.*)*

Scene 10: SHEEMISH, BLUEBEARD.

BLUEBEARD: I have been in my laboratory putting things in readiness, for I have found the ideal subject for my next experiment . . . or should I say my next work of art?

SHEEMISH: *(With dread)* Oh, Master.

BLUEBEARD: What is it?

SHEEMISH: I'm afraid. I'm afraid. I'm afraid. *(Leaps into* BLUEBEARD's *arms)*

BLUEBEARD: *(Throwing him off)* Down, down, you fool. Never mind the disagreeable things that may happen. Let us think of the pleasant ones. This girl is almost the most charming creature imaginable. Add to that a few of my innovations! I never saw two people so devoted, so completely in love. The manifest tenderness of their mutual affection inspired a like feeling in me. It affected me deeply. My love began as jealousy. I couldn't bear to see them so happy together; vexation stimulated my desire and I realized what a pleasure it would give me to disturb their mutual understanding and break up an attachment so repugnant to my own susceptibilities.

SHEEMISH: Have you no desire for Miss Cubbidge?

BLUEBEARD: She is not without a certain cadaverous charm. *(Footsteps)* Shhh! Quickly, the spy hole, see who it is.

SHEEMISH: The sun is in my eyes, but I know the sound of her footsteps. It is only Mrs. Maggot.

Scene 11: MRS. MAGGOT, SHEEMISH.

*(*MRS. MAGGOT *and* SHEEMISH *bring on a table and chairs. Then they set the table for dinner.)*

MRS. MAGGOT: *(Carrying in a platter)* Yum, yum, yum . . . I'm nibbling . . . yum . . . mutton good! Lovely . . . yum . . . yum . . . yum.

SHEEMISH: It is the first time meat has been seen in the palace in nineteen years.

MRS. MAGGOT: Twenty for me! Twenty years and never any meat. I've withered. You fed yourself on the fat in your hump, didn't you? Ach. Ouf. *(She is seized by a violent coughing fit)* Swallowed the wrong way.

SHEEMISH: Heaven has punished you, glutton. Stop, before you eat the knives and the tablecloth.

MRS. MAGGOT: My illness, not my sin! Look, Sheemish, a chicken! Ah, the drumstick! *(With her mouth full)* Those who have a stomach, eat; those who have a hump, glue themselves to keyholes.

SHEEMISH: Watch what you say to me. My hump contains a second brain to think my evil thoughts for me. It hasn't forgotten the broken test tube and our little secret.

MRS. MAGGOT: You must teach me to spy through keyholes. Which eye does one use, the right or the left? They say in time one's eye becomes shaped like a keyhole. I prefer eavesdropping. There, see my ear, a delicate shell. *(She shows her ear trumpet)*

SHEEMISH: When others are present you are as deaf as a bat—but when we are alone you are cured and hear perfectly.

MRS. MAGGOT: It's a miracle! Look at that pork chop!

SHEEMISH: *(Grabs her and throws her onto the table. Climbing on top of her, he forces a huge piece of meat into her mouth)* Here, glutton, eat this! Someday your mouth will be full of maggots and greenish pus. *(Laughter of the dinner guests is heard off)* But here come the guests to dinner. Let us have a truce until the next time that we are alone.

MRS. MAGGOT: Peace!

Scene 12: MRS. MAGGOT, SHEEMISH, BLUEBEARD, RODNEY, SYBIL, MISS CUBBIDGE.

(The dinner guests and BLUEBEARD enter. MRS. MAGGOT and SHEEMISH just manage to get off the table in the nick of time. MISS CUBBIDGE enters on BLUEBEARD's arm, SYBIL on RODNEY's arm.)

BLUEBEARD: Work, work, work. I have thought of nothing else these nineteen years. My work, my work, and nothing else.

SYBIL: Beware, Uncle, all work and no play makes Jack a dull boy.

MISS CUBBIDGE: True, Sybil, but all play and no work makes Jack a mere toy.

BLUEBEARD: No danger there. I never cease in my experimenting. My dream is to remake Man. A new man with new possibilities for love.

SYBIL: "Love for a man is a thing apart. 'Tis woman's whole existence."

MISS CUBBIDGE: *(Applauding)* Lord Byron!

BLUEBEARD: Won't you all be seated? *(BLUEBEARD seats MISS CUBBIDGE at the table. RODNEY seats SYBIL)*

MRS. MAGGOT: *(To SYBIL)* Why, dearie, what an unusual locket.

SYBIL: Yes. It's lapis lazuli. My mother gave it to me the night she died when the terrible fire—

MISS CUBBIDGE: *(Interrupting)* Don't, Sybil. . . .

SYBIL: I never knew my mother.

RODNEY: Strange, all the places are set to one side of the table.

BLUEBEARD: That is because of a little surprise I have for you. There will be an entertainment tonight while we are taking our evening meal, a little play I wrote myself.

SYBIL: What, a play?

RODNEY: Jolly!

MISS CUBBIDGE: Wrote it yourself? You've a touch of erosion, I see, Baron. And yet you studied medicine?

BLUEBEARD: I write for amusement only.

MISS CUBBIDGE: Were you indoctrinated? I mean, did you receive the doctorate? On what theme did you write your dissipation? Which degree did you receive?

BLUEBEARD: I received the third degree.

(MRS. MAGGOT places a platter of meat on the table.)

RODNEY: This meat looks delicious.

BLUEBEARD: *(Having a seizure)* Meat? Meat? *(Turning on* MRS. MAGGOT*)* You dare to serve them meat?

MRS. MAGGOT: Eh?

BLUEBEARD: *(In a blind rage)* Take it away at once, blockhead! Do you want to ruin my experiment? *(He throws the meat at* MRS. MAGGOT *and then leaps up on the dinner table like a wild man, roaring)* What is the Law?

MRS. MAGGOT and SHEEMISH: *(Bowing before him as though he were an idol on an altar, they link their arms together and chant, swaying back and forth rhythmically)* We are not men. We are not women. We are not men. We are not women. His is the hand that makes. We are not men. We are not women. His is the House of Pain. We are not men. We are not women. That is the Law!

BLUEBEARD: *(Rolling his eyes savagely)* Now get out! *(Turning on the guests)* All of you!

MISS CUBBIDGE: *(Horrified)* What about dinner?

BLUEBEARD: I've lost my appetite!

RODNEY: What about the play?

BLUEBEARD: I detest avant-garde theater.

Scene 13: BLUEBEARD, MISS CUBBIDGE, SYBIL, RODNEY, SHEEMISH, MRS. MAGGOT, LAMIA.

(The face of LAMIA THE LEOPARD WOMAN *appears at the window.)*

RODNEY: Look, there's a face at the window!

(MISS CUBBIDGE *screams,* SYBIL *faints in* RODNEY*'s arms,* BLUEBEARD *fires his revolver at* LAMIA: *Tableau vivant. The curtain falls.)*

ACT II

Scene 1: SYBIL, RODNEY.

SYBIL: Rodney, you have come to speak to me about my letter to you.

RODNEY: Yes, you could have told me face-to-face. People living in the same house, even when they are the only people living on a deserted island, as we are, can be further apart than if they lived fifty miles asunder in the country.

SYBIL: I have thought much of what I then wrote and I feel sure that we had better—

RODNEY: Stop, Sybil . . . do not speak hurriedly, love. Shall I tell you what I learned from your letter?

SYBIL: Yes, tell me if you think it is better that you should do so.

RODNEY: I learned that something had made you melancholy since we came to this island. There are few of us who do not encounter, every now and again, some of that irrational spirit of sadness which, when overindulged, leads men to madness and self-destruction. Since I have loved you I have banished it utterly. Do not speak under the influence of that spirit until you have thought whether you too can banish it.

SYBIL: I have tried, but it will not be banished.

RODNEY: Try again, Sybil, if you love me. If you do not . . .

SYBIL: If I do not love you, I love no one upon earth. *(Sits quietly, looking into his face)*

RODNEY: I believe it. I believe it as I believe in my own love for you. I trust your love implicitly, Sybil. So come, return with me to the mainland and let us make an early marriage.

SYBIL: *(Strangely, as if in a trance)* No, I cannot do so.

RODNEY: *(Smiling)* Is that melancholy fiend too much for you? Sybil, Sybil, Sybil.

SYBIL: *(Snapping out of it)* You are noble, good, and great. I find myself unfit to be your wife.

RODNEY: Don't quibble, Sybil.

SYBIL: *(Falling to her knees)* I beg your pardon on my knees.

RODNEY: I grant no such pardon. Do you think I will let you go from me in that way? No, love, if you are ill, I will wait till your illness is gone by; and if you will let me, I will be your nurse.

SYBIL: I am not ill. *(Her hands stray unconsciously to her breasts and yoni)*

RODNEY: Not ill with any defined sickness. You do not shake with ague, nor does your head rack you with aching; but yet you must be ill to try to put an end to all that has passed between us for no reason at all.

SYBIL: *(Standing suddenly)* Mr. Parker . . .

RODNEY: *(Deeply hurt)* If you will call me so, I will think it only part of your malady.

SYBIL: Mr. Parker, I can only hope that you will take me at my word. I beg your forgiveness and that our engagement may be over.

RODNEY: No, no, no, Sybil. Never with my consent. I would marry you tomorrow, tomorrow or next month, or the month after. But if it cannot be so, then I will wait . . . unless . . . there is some other man. Yes, that! and that alone would convince me. Only your marriage to another man could convince me that I had lost you. *(He kisses her on the lips)*

SYBIL: *(Turning away and surreptitiously wiping away the kiss)* I cannot convince you in that way.

RODNEY: *(Prissily wipes his lips on a lace hankie and carefully folds it and replaces it in his breast pocket, relieved)* You will convince me in no other. Have you spoken to your uncle of this yet?

SYBIL: Not as yet.

RODNEY: *(Anxiously)* Do not tell him. It is possible you may have to unsay what you have said.

SYBIL: No, it is not possible.

RODNEY: I think you must leave this island. The foggy air is no good for you. Living on an island can make one grow so insular.

SYBIL: Or insolent.

RODNEY: You need the sun, I think. You have grown so pale. You need a change.

SYBIL: Yes, you treat me as though I were partly silly and partly insane, but it is not so. The change you speak of should be in my nature and in yours. *(RODNEY shakes his head and smiles. Aside)* He is perfect! Oh, that he were less perfect!

RODNEY: I'll leave you alone for twenty-four hours to think this over. I advise you not to tell your uncle. But if you do tell him, let me know that you have done so.

SYBIL: Why that?

RODNEY: *(Pressing her hand)* Good night, dearest, dearest Sybil. *(Exits)*

Scene 2: SYBIL, BLUEBEARD.

BLUEBEARD: What, Sybil, are you not in bed yet?

SYBIL: Not yet, Uncle Khanazar.

BLUEBEARD: So Rodney Parker has been here. I smell his cologne in the air.

SYBIL: Yes, he has been here.

BLUEBEARD: Is anything the matter, Sybil?

SYBIL: No, Uncle Khanazar, nothing is the matter.

BLUEBEARD: He has not made himself disagreeable, has he?

SYBIL: Not in the least. He never does anything wrong. He may defy man or woman to find fault with him.

BLUEBEARD: So that's it, is it? He is just a shade too good. I have noticed that myself. But it's a fault on the right side.

SYBIL: *(Deeply troubled)* It's no fault, Uncle. If there be any fault, it is not with him.

BLUEBEARD: Being too good is not one of my faults . . . I am very bad.

SYBIL: *(Starry-eyed)* Are you bad? Are you really bad?

BLUEBEARD: When I am good, I am very, very good; but when I'm bad, I'm not bad. I'm good at being bad. . . . I do it well.

SYBIL: *(Again as if in a trance)* Tonight, at dinner, your words carried me away. . . . *(Their lips almost meet, but she yawns, breaking the spell, and he yawns sympathetically)* . . . But I am yawning and tired and I will go to bed. Good night, Uncle Khanazar.

BLUEBEARD: Good night, Sybil. *(Aside)* And rest, for a new life awaits you!

(Exit SYBIL.*)*

Scene 3: BLUEBEARD, MISS CUBBIDGE.

MISS CUBBIDGE: Oh, excuse me. I didn't realize that the parlor was preoccupied. *(Starts out)*

BLUEBEARD: Come in, Miss Cubbidge. I do not desire to be alone.

MISS CUBBIDGE: No, I think I'd better go and leave you to your own devices.

BLUEBEARD: Please stay. I think I know what you are thinking.

MISS CUBBIDGE: I'll do my own thinking, thank you; and my own existing.

BLUEBEARD: Miss Cubbidge, I don't think you like me.

MISS CUBBIDGE: I can sympathize with neither your virtues nor your vices.

BLUEBEARD: What would you say if I told you that I need a wife?

MISS CUBBIDGE: I do not believe in sudden marriages.

BLUEBEARD: People often say that marriage is an important thing and should be much thought of in advance, and marrying people are cautioned that there are many who marry in haste and repent at leisure. I am not sure, however, that marriage may not be pondered over too much; nor do I feel certain that the leisurely repentance does not as often follow the leisurely marriages as it does the rapid ones. Why, you yourself might marry suddenly *(Kneeling before her on one knee)* and never regret it at all.

MISS CUBBIDGE: My health might fail me under the effects of so great a change made so late in life.

BLUEBEARD: Miss Cubbidge, how can you live without love?

MISS CUBBIDGE: It is my nature to love many persons a little if I've loved few or none passionately, Baron Bluebeard.

BLUEBEARD: Please, call me Khanazar; and may I call you . . .

MISS CUBBIDGE: *(Shyly)* Flora.

BLUEBEARD: Ah, Flora! It is only possible to be alone with you in nature. All other women destroy the landscape; you alone become part of it.

MISS CUBBIDGE: *(Aside)* Could any woman resist such desuetude? *(Giggling)* Why, Baron Blue—

BLUEBEARD: *(Interrupting)* Khanazar.

MISS CUBBIDGE: *(Giggling)* Khanazar.

BLUEBEARD: Flora, you are part of the trees, the sky; you are the dominating goddess of nature. Come to me, Flora, you lovely little fauna, you.

MISS CUBBIDGE: *(Recovering herself)* Mr. Bluebeard, I shall certainly not come to you.

BLUEBEARD: *(Suddenly)* Look, do you see what it is I am holding in my hand?

MISS CUBBIDGE: *(Alarmed)* A revolver!

BLUEBEARD: Take it, press it to my temple and shoot, or say you will be mine.

MISS CUBBIDGE: *(Frightened with the revolver in her hand)* I can't shoot you, but I cannot be yours, either.

BLUEBEARD: It is one or the other. Blow my brains out. I will not live another day without you.

MISS CUBBIDGE: Recuperate your gun at once. It isn't loaded, is it?

BLUEBEARD: Pull the trigger! There are worse things awaiting Man than death.

MISS CUBBIDGE: To what do you collude?

BLUEBEARD: All tortures do not matter . . . only not to be dead before one dies. I will not live without your love. *(He pretends to weep)*

MISS CUBBIDGE: Don't weep, Baron Bluebeard . . . er . . . Khanazar. 'Tisn't manly. Try to be more malevolent.

BLUEBEARD: Marry me, marry me, Flora, and make me the happiest man on earth.

MISS CUBBIDGE: How can I marry you?

BLUEBEARD: *(Hypnotically)* Easily. Just repeat after me. I, Flora Cubbidge . . .

MISS CUBBIDGE: I, Flora Cubbidge . . .

BLUEBEARD: Do solemnly swear . . .

MISS CUBBIDGE: Do solemnly swear . . .

BLUEBEARD: To take this man, Baron Khanazar von Bluebeard, as my lawful wedded husband . . .

MISS CUBBIDGE: To take this man, Baron Khanazar von Bluebeard, as my lawful wedded husband . . .

BLUEBEARD: To love, honor, and obey; for better or for worse; for richer or poorer; in sickness and in health; from this day forward . . . *(He begins to undress her)*

MISS CUBBIDGE: To love, honor, and obey; for better or for worse; for richer or for poorer; in sickness and in health; from this day forward . . .

BLUEBEARD: Until death us do part.

MISS CUBBIDGE: Till death us do part.

BLUEBEARD: *(Licentiously)* I may now kiss the bride.

MISS CUBBIDGE: What about your vows?

BLUEBEARD: Don't you trust me?

MISS CUBBIDGE: I do. I do. I do.

(They begin to breathe heavily as they undress slowly. They move toward each other, wearing only their shoes, socks, stockings, and her merry widow. They clinch and roll about on the floor making animal noises.)

BLUEBEARD: Was ever woman in this manner wooed? Was ever woman in this manner won?

MISS CUBBIDGE: *(Aside)* There are things that happen in a day that would take a lifetime to explain.

(There follows a scene of unprecedented eroticism in which MISS CUBBIDGE *gives herself voluptuously to* BARON VON BLUEBEARD.)

BLUEBEARD: In my right pants pocket you will find a key. It is the key to my laboratory. Take it. And swear to me that you will never use it.

MISS CUBBIDGE: I swear! I must return to Sybil at once. She sometimes wakes up in a phalanx.

BLUEBEARD: Won't you sleep here tonight, with me?

MISS CUBBIDGE: No, I can't sleep in this bed. It has cold, wet spots in it. Good night, Baron . . . husband.

BLUEBEARD: Good night, Miss Cubbidge.

MISS CUBBIDGE: Please don't mention our hymeneals to Sybil. I must find the right words to immure the news to her.

BLUEBEARD: Believe me, I'll confess to none of it.

MISS CUBBIDGE: Thank you. I believe that you have transformed me to a part of the dirigible essence. You have carried me aloft and I believe I am with Beatrice, of whom Dante has sung in his immortal onus. Good night. *(Exit)*

Scene 4: BLUEBEARD.

BLUEBEARD: It is a lucky thing for me that I did not take the vows or this marriage might be binding on me as it is on her. I cannot sleep tonight. There is work to be done in my laboratory. Good night, Miss Cubbidge, wherever you are. And good night to all the ladies who do be living in this world. Good night, ladies. Good night, sweet ladies. *(Exits into laboratory)*

Scene 5: RODNEY PARKER, LAMIA THE LEOPARD WOMAN, MRS. MAGGOT.

(Entering surreptitiously, MRS. MAGGOT *crosses, lighting the candelabra.)*

LAMIA: SHHH! Take care of the deaf one. . . . She hears nothing of what you shout and overhears everything that you whisper.

RODNEY: What is it that you wish to tell me?

LAMIA: He is mad, I tell you, mad! And he will stop at nothing.

RODNEY: Who?

LAMIA: The Bluebeard, Khanazar. If you love that girl, convince her to leave this island at once.

RODNEY: But why?

LAMIA: Look at me. I was a woman once!

RODNEY: But you are a woman. So very much a woman. You are all woman.

LAMIA: No, no, never again will I bear the name of woman. I was changed in the House of Pain. I was a victim of his sex-switch tricks and his queer quackery.

RODNEY: Quackery—Sybil told me that he was a brilliant physiologist.

LAMIA: Even in Denmark they called him a quack. He wasn't satisfied with sex switches. He wants to create a third genital organ attached between the legs of a third sex. I am an experiment that failed.

RODNEY: (Seductively) You look like a woman to me.

LAMIA: I wish I could be a woman to you. (Aside) Perhaps when Bluebeard is defeated I will. (Aloud) He uses the same technique on all his victims. First he married me. Then he gave me the key to his laboratory, forbidding me ever to use it. Then he waited for curiosity to get the better of me. All women are curious.

RODNEY: Men marry because they are tired, women because they are curious.

LAMIA: Both are disappointed.

RODNEY: Does he ever use men for his experiments?

LAMIA: At first he did. Sheemish was the first. But when that experiment failed he turned to women. We are all experiments that have failed. He has made us the slaves of this island.

RODNEY: (Realizing) The Island of Lost Love!

LAMIA: Save yourself and save the woman you love. Take the advice of the Leopard Woman and go.

RODNEY: How did a nice girl like you get mixed up in a mess like this?

LAMIA: I was entertaining in a small bistro nightclub called The Wild Cat's Pussy. I was billed as Lamia the Leopard Woman. It was only fourteen beans a day but I needed the scratch. I sang this song: (Sings)

Where is my Leopard Lover?
When will I spot the cat for me?
I'm wild when I'm under cover.
Where is the cat who will tame me?
Where is my wild cat lover?
Leopard hunting is all the rage.
Where is my wild cat lover?
I'm free but I want to be caged.
If you dig this feline.
Better make a beeline.
I've got the spots to give men the red-hots
Where is my wild leopard hunter?
I'm game if you'll play my game.
Where is that runt cunt hunter?
I'm wild but I want to be tame.

After I sang my set, he signaled and I sat at his table. He ordered a Tiger's Milk Flip. He was into health food. No woman can resist him, I tell you.

RODNEY: He seduced you?

LAMIA: Worst, worst, a thousand times worst. I didn't know if I was coming or going. He has a way with women.

RODNEY: Sybil, great Scott no. Either you're jesting or I'm dreaming! Sybil with another man? I'll go mad.

LAMIA: His idealism . . . his intensity . . . the Clairol blue of his beard! His words carried me away. He had a strange look in his eyes. I felt strange inside. He and I were total strangers! If you love her, get her off this island before it is too late.

RODNEY: No, not Sybil. I am ashamed to listen to you. Yet she admires him so. . . . I have gone mad!

LAMIA: He came closer . . . closer. "Submit," he said, "in the name of science and the dark arts. Submit. Submit."

RODNEY: *(In a panic)* Sybil is with him now. You are lying.

LAMIA: If you think I am lying, look. *(She lifts her sarong)* Look what he did to the Leopard Woman's pussy.

RODNEY: Eeeccht! Is that a mound of Venus or a penis?

LAMIA: *(Perplexed)* I wish I knew.

RODNEY: No, no, he can't do that to Sybil. I must kill him. What am I saying? This is madness. But what consolation is sanity to me? The most faithful of women is after all only a woman. I'll kill you. No, I am mad.

LAMIA: Go and stop him. Save her from the fate that has befallen me.

RODNEY: I will kill myself! [*(He tries to strangle himself)*] No, I will kill her! Oh, God, it is impossible. I have gone mad! *(He runs out)*

Scene 6: LAMIA.

LAMIA: *(Sings)*
I've lost my leopard lover.
A world of made is not a world of born.
Bluebeard will soon discover
Hell hath no fury like a woman scorned.

Scene 7: LAMIA, SHEEMISH.

LAMIA: *(Calling after him)* Rodney! Rodney! Rodney! He is gone.

SHEEMISH: *(Appearing out of the shadows)* Are you afraid of being alone?

LAMIA: *(Fanning herself with a leopard fan)* How stifling it is! There must be a storm coming.

SHEEMISH: I heard you telling the secrets of the island to Rodney *(Spits)* Parker.

LAMIA: *(Furiously)* [*Hits him over the head with her fan*] Sneaking little eavesdropper! How dare you?

SHEEMISH: I love you.

LAMIA: *(Fanning herself)* What awful weather! This is the second day of it.

SHEEMISH: Every day I walk four miles to see you and four miles back and meet with nothing but indifference from you.

LAMIA: Your love touches me but I can't return it, that's all.

SHEEMISH: *(Accusing)* But you came four miles here to tell the secrets of the island to Rodney *(Spits)* Parker.

LAMIA: You are a bore.

SHEEMISH: *(Twisting her arm)* You are in love with him!

LAMIA: *(In pain)* Yes, it's true. If you must know. I do love him. I do! *(Aside)* For all the good it will do me. He loves Sybil.

SHEEMISH: *(Taking her in his arms roughly and humping her like a dog)* I want you.

LAMIA: *(Fighting him)* You stupid, vulgar, deformed nincompoop! Do you think

I could ever fall for such a one as you? You are as ugly as sin itself. Besides, our genitals would never fit together.

SHEEMISH: *(Groping her)* We can work it out.

LAMIA: Evil cretin! God will punish you. *(She breaks away)*

SHEEMISH: God will not punish the lunatic soul. He knows the powers of evil are too great for us with weak minds. Marry me!

LAMIA: I'd rather blow a bald baboon with B.O. and bunions than marry a monster! *(Exit LAMIA in a huff)*

SHEEMISH: *(Following her)* Lamia, be reasonable!

Scene 8: BLUEBEARD, SYBIL.

(SYBIL is seated at the spinet. She plays dramatic music. BLUEBEARD moves slowly, approaching her from behind. His eyes are ablaze. She senses his approach. She plays with greater emphasis. Her shoulders are bare. He begins kissing them. The music she is playing rises to a crescendo. She stops playing suddenly.)

SYBIL: This is ridiculous!

BLUEBEARD: *(Swinging a key on a chain back and forth before her eyes as though hypnotizing her)* Here is the key to my laboratory. Take it and swear to me that you will never use it.

SYBIL: *(In a trance)* Yes, Master!

BLUEBEARD: Ah, my darling, my own one. You will be my wife.

SYBIL: Yes, Master!

BLUEBEARD: You will be the loveliest of all wives. *(Aside)* When I am through with you.

SYBIL: Yes, Master.

BLUEBEARD: I am about to perform the *magnum opus*. The creation of a third genital organ will perhaps lead to the creation of a third sex. You will be my ultimate masterpiece of vivisection! *(He kisses her)*

Scene 9: BLUEBEARD, SYBIL, CUBBIDGE.

MISS CUBBIDGE: *(Entering)* Sir, what are you doing with Sybil there? Are you making love to her too?

BLUEBEARD: *(Aside to CUBBIDGE)* No, no, on the contrary, she throws herself at me shamelessly, although I tell her that I am married to you.

SYBIL: What is it you want, Miss Cubbidge?

BLUEBEARD: *(Aside to SYBIL)* She is jealous of my speaking to you. She wants me to marry her, but I tell her it is you I must have.

MISS CUBBIDGE: *(Incredulous)* What, Sybil?

BLUEBEARD: *(Aside to CUBBIDGE)* The impressionable little creature is infatuated with me.

SYBIL: *(Incredulous)* What, Miss Cubbidge?

BLUEBEARD: *(Aside to SYBIL)* The desperate old maid has got her claws out for me.

MISS CUBBIDGE: Do you . . .

BLUEBEARD: *(To MISS CUBBIDGE)* Your words would be in vain.

SYBIL: I'd . . .

BLUEBEARD: *(To* SYBIL*)* All you can say to her will be in vain.
MISS CUBBIDGE: Truly . . .
BLUEBEARD: *(Aside to* CUBBIDGE*)* She's obstinate as the devil.
SYBIL: I think . . .
BLUEBEARD: *(Aside to* SYBIL*)* Say nothing to her. She's a madwoman.
SYBIL: No, no, I must speak to her.
MISS CUBBIDGE: I'll hear her reasons.
SYBIL: What . . .
BLUEBEARD: *(Aside to* SYBIL*)* I'll lay you a wager she tells you she's my wife.
MISS CUBBIDGE: I . . .
BLUEBEARD: *(Aside to* CUBBIDGE*)* I'll bet you she says I'm going to marry her.
MISS CUBBIDGE: Sybil, as your chaperone I must intercept. It is past your bedtime.
SYBIL: Dear Miss Cubbidge, I have been to bed but I got up because I have insomnia.
MISS CUBBIDGE: So I see. Sybil, I must ask you to leave me alone with *my* husband. The Baron and I married ourselves in an improvident ceremony earlier this evening.
BLUEBEARD: *(Aside to* SYBIL*)* What did I tell you? She's out of her mind.
SYBIL: Dear *Miss* Cubbidge, are you sure you are feeling all right? Are you ill?
MISS CUBBIDGE: *(Indignantly)* I've never felt more supine in my life. Sybil, it does not become a young *unmarried* woman to meddle in the affairs of others.
BLUEBEARD: *(Aside to* CUBBIDGE*)* She thinks she is going to marry me.
SYBIL: It is not fit, *Miss* Cubbidge, to be jealous because the Baron speaks to me. I am going to be his wife.
BLUEBEARD: *(Aside to* CUBBIDGE*)* What did I tell you?
SYBIL: Baron, did you not promise to marry me?
BLUEBEARD: *(Aside to* SYBIL*)* Of course, my darling.
MISS CUBBIDGE: Baron, am I not your wife, the Baroness von Bluebeard?
BLUEBEARD: *(Aside to* CUBBIDGE*)* How could you ask such a question?
SYBIL: *(Aside to the audience)* How sure the old goat is of herself!
MISS CUBBIDGE: *(Aside to the audience)* The Baron is right, how pigheaded the little bitch is!
SYBIL: We must know the truth.
MISS CUBBIDGE: We must have the matter abnegated.
SYBIL and MISS CUBBIDGE: Which of us will it be, Baron?
BLUEBEARD: *(Addressing himself to both of them)* What would you have me say? Each of you knows in your heart of hearts whether or not I have made love to you. Let her that I truly love laugh at what the other says. Actions speak louder than words. *(Aside to* CUBBIDGE*)* Let her believe what she will. *(Aside to* SYBIL*)* Let her flatter herself in her senile imagination. *(Aside to* CUBBIDGE*)* I adore you. *(Aside to* SYBIL*)* I am yours alone. *(Aside to* CUBBIDGE*)* One night with you is worth a thousand with other women. *(Aside to* SYBIL*)* All faces are ugly in your presence. *(Aloud)* If you will excuse me, there's work to be done in my laboratory. I do not wish to be disturbed. Good night, ladies. *(Exit)*

Scene 10: SYBIL, MISS CUBBIDGE, SHEEMISH.

SHEEMISH: *(Appearing out of the shadows)* Poor ladies! I can't bear to see you led to your destruction. Take my advice, return to the mainland.

SYBIL: I am she he loves, however.

MISS CUBBIDGE: It is to me he's married.

SHEEMISH: My master is an evil sadist. He will do you irreparable harm as he has done to others. He wants to marry the whole female sex so that he can take them to his laboratory and . . .

Scene 11: SYBIL, MISS CUBBIDGE, SHEEMISH, BLUEBEARD.

BLUEBEARD: *(Popping back in)* One more word . . .

SHEEMISH: My master is no evil sadist. He means you no harm. If you ladies think he can marry the whole female sex, you've got another think coming. He is a man of his word. There he is—ask him yourself.

BLUEBEARD: What were you saying, Sheemish?

SHEEMISH: *(Aside to* BLUEBEARD*)* You know how catty women are. I was defending you . . . as best I could.

BLUEBEARD: *(To* SYBIL *and* MISS CUBBIDGE*)* She who holds the key to my heart holds the key to my laboratory. *(Exit)*

Scene 12: MISS CUBBIDGE, SYBIL, SHEEMISH.

MISS CUBBIDGE: *(Aside)* Then he is my husband, for he gave me the key.

SYBIL: *(Aside)* The key, I have the key! It is me he loves after all. *(Loud)* Good night, Madame. If you have the key, you are his wife.

MISS CUBBIDGE: Good night, Sybil. If it is to you he gave the key, you are his bethrothed. *(They both exit laughing)*

Scene 13: SHEEMISH, MRS. MAGGOT.

MRS. MAGGOT: *(Entering excitedly)* I overheard laughter. It is the first time laughter has been heard on this island in nineteen years. Who was laughing? Who is it that knows a single moment of happiness on the Island of Lost Love?

SHEEMISH: It was not with joy you heard them laughing, but with scorn. Bluebeard has got the young woman and her governess fighting like cats in the alley.

MRS. MAGGOT: I thought they always swore by each other.

SHEEMISH: It's at each other that they swear now. He's married both of them!

MRS. MAGGOT: Wedding bells must sound like an alarm clock to him.

Scene 14: SHEEMISH, MRS. MAGGOT, SYBIL.

MRS. MAGGOT: Look, here comes the young one carrying a candle, her long black hair unloosed, her lips slightly parted. A lovely flower that blooms for just one hour.

SHEEMISH: A sleepwalker, a somnambulist.

MRS. MAGGOT: Her eyes are open.

SHEEMISH: But their sense is shut. I believe he has mesmerized her. Let us conceal ourselves, I will keep my eyes peeled.

MRS. MAGGOT: And I my ears. I can't wait to find out what happens next! *(*MRS. MAGGOT *and* SHEEMISH *hide)*

SYBIL: I can control my curiosity no longer. I must see what lies behind the door to my lover's laboratory. I know he has forbade me ever to use this key. But how can I stand the suspense? Should not a woman take an interest in her husband's work? *(She unlocks the door with her key and opens it.* BLUEBEARD *awaits her)*

MRS. MAGGOT: Shouldn't we try to save her?

SHEEMISH: Would you prefer to take her place in the House of Pain?

MRS. MAGGOT: No, no, not the House of Pain.

Scene 15: SYBIL, BLUEBEARD, SHEEMISH, MRS. MAGGOT.

BLUEBEARD: I trust you have kept your coming here a secret.

SYBIL: Baron!

BLUEBEARD: Curiosity killed the cat. *(Aside)* But it may have a salutary effect on the pussy. Look into my eyes, my little kitten, and repeat after me. *(Hypnotizing her)* I, Sybil, do solemnly swear to take this man, Baron Khanazar von Bluebeard, as my lawful wedded husband.

SYBIL: I, Sybil, do solemnly swear to take this man, Baron Khanazar von Bluebeard, as my lawful wedded husband.

MRS. MAGGOT: *(Moving her ear trumpet like an antenna)* I hear someone coming. Just in time! Rodney Parker will save her from the fate worse than death!

SHEEMISH: *(Aside)* My rival, Rodney Parker! Now I will have my revenge. *(To* MRS. MAGGOT*)* Detain him!

BLUEBEARD: To love, honor, and obey . . .

MRS. MAGGOT: Oh, cruel! Don't ask me that. I won't do it. Anything but that.

SYBIL: To love, honor, and obey.

SHEEMISH: Even the House of Pain? The test tube! Master, Master . . .

BLUEBEARD: For better or for worse; for richer or for poorer . . .

MRS. MAGGOT: I'll do it.

BLUEBEARD: In sickness and in health . . . from this day forward . . .

SYBIL: For better or for worse; for richer or for poorer . . . in sickness and in health, from this day forward . . .

Scene 16: SHEEMISH, MRS. MAGGOT, SYBIL, BLUEBEARD, RODNEY.

*(*RODNEY *rushes onto the stage, mad.)*

RODNEY: Where is he? Where is he?

*(*SHEEMISH *roughly throws* MRS. MAGGOT *into* RODNEY.*)*

MRS. MAGGOT: Eh?

BLUEBEARD: Until death us do part.

SYBIL: Until death us do part.

*(*BLUEBEARD *blows out the candle and kisses* SYBIL.*)*

RODNEY: *(Shaking* MRS. MAGGOT *violently)* Where is Bluebeard?

MRS. MAGGOT: Eh?

RODNEY: Aagh! *(He throws* MRS. MAGGOT *aside.)*

BLUEBEARD: *(Pressing* SYBIL *to him, demented)* And now, ye demons, ere this night goes by, I swear I'll conjure or I'll die!

RODNEY: *(Sees* BLUEBEARD*)* Damn you, Bluebeard! Damn your soul!

SYBIL: Rodney! Ah! *(She faints)*

(BLUEBEARD *catches her and quickly carries her into the laboratory.* MRS. MAGGOT *trips* RODNEY, *then* SHEEMISH *and* MRS. MAGGOT *follow* BLUEBEARD, *slamming the door in* RODNEY*'s face and locking it.* RODNEY *beats on the door and shouts.)*

Scene 17: RODNEY.

RODNEY: Open the door, you pervert! You invert, you necrophiliac! Open up! Bluebeard! Bluebeard! BLUEBEARD!

Curtain

ACT III

Scene 1: BLUEBEARD, SYBIL, SHEEMISH, MRS. MAGGOT.

(There is no lapse of time between Act II and Act III. The scene changes to the interior of BLUEBEARD*'s laboratory. Enter* BLUEBEARD, *carrying* SYBIL *in his arms. He walks with a hesitant step, looking from side to side, his cheeks quivering, contracting, and expanding, his eyes intently focused.* SHEEMISH *and* MRS. MAGGOT *scurry about taking care of last-minute details. There is an air of great anticipation.)*

RODNEY'S VOICE: *(Offstage)* Bluebeard! Bluebeard! Bluebeard! Open this door or I'll break it down! *(Loud knocking)* Bluebeard!

BLUEBEARD: *(Laughing)* That door is lined with double-duty quilted zinc. No mortal arm can break it down. Even a man whose heart is pure and has the strength of ten could not break it down. But a delicate girl with just enough strength to lift a powder puff to her white bosom can open it . . . if she has the key. *(More loud knocking)* Sheemish, take the girl to the operating room, bathe her, and prepare her for surgery.

SHEEMISH: No, Master, please don't ask me to do that. Anything but that.

BLUEBEARD: And be gentle with her. I want no marks left on her lily-white body. If you so much as bruise her, you and I will make an appointment for a meeting here in the House of Pain, hmm?

SHEEMISH: No, no, not the House of Pain! *(He carries* SYBIL *off)*

Scene 2: BLUEBEARD, MRS. MAGGOT.

BLUEBEARD: Mrs. Maggot, bring in the frog, the serpent, and the hearts, hands, eyes, feet, but most of all the blood and genitals of the little children. Bring in the serpent first. I need it to trace a magic circle.

MRS. MAGGOT: *(Extending her ear trumpet toward* BLUEBEARD*)* Eh?

BLUEBEARD: Perhaps your hearing would be improved by a vacation. *(He covers her ears and mouths the words)* In the House of Pain.
MRS. MAGGOT: No, no, not the House of Pain! *(She quickly hands him a bottle of blood and a paintbrush)*
BLUEBEARD: *(Laughs)* Thank you. Now, leave me. Go and assist Sheemish. *(*MRS. MAGGOT *lingers)* Is there something that you want, Maggot?
MRS. MAGGOT: Yes, Master.
BLUEBEARD: Well, what is it?
MRS. MAGGOT: The lapis lazuli locket the girl is wearing. May I have it?
BLUEBEARD: Yes, take it, scavenger!
MRS. MAGGOT: Do you think she will mind?
BLUEBEARD: No, she will not mind. She will remember nothing of her former life after the operation. Now get out. *(Kicks her in the ass)*
MRS. MAGGOT: Thank you, thank you, Master. *(Exit)*

Scene 3: BLUEBEARD.

BLUEBEARD: *(Inscribing a circle of blood)*
   Now by the powers that only seem to be,
   With crystal sword and flame I conjure thee.
   I kiss the book; oh, come to me!
   Goddess of night: Hecate!

(The sound of a gong is heard and a high-pitched cockcrow that sometimes breaks from the most refined throat. HECATE *appears in a flash of light and a puff of smoke.)*

Scene 4: BLUEBEARD, HECATE.

HECATE: *(Wearing a blue beard)* Who summons the Slave of Sin?
BLUEBEARD: *(Laughing quietly aside)* Not for nothing I have worshiped the Dark One. *(To* HECATE*)* I called, Hecate; I, Khanazar von Bluebeard.
HECATE: How dare you? Don't you know that torture is the price you pay for summoning the Slave of Sin?
BLUEBEARD: All tortures do not matter: only not to be dead before one dies.
HECATE: What is it you want of me, my fool?
BLUEBEARD: Look, here are my books written in blood, there my apparatus. For nineteen long years I've waited and worked for this moment. In there, on the operating table, swathed in bandages, a new sex, waiting to live again in a genital I made with my own hands! *(Maniacally)* With my own hands!
HECATE: What about your own genitalia?
BLUEBEARD: The male genital organ is but a faint relic and shadow, a sign that has become detached from its substance and lives on as an exquisite ornament.
HECATE: And what do you want of me, my fool?
BLUEBEARD: Good fortune.
HECATE: Do not seek for good fortune. You carry on your forehead the sign of the elect.
   Seek, probe,
   Details unfold.

Let nature's secret
  Be retold.
If ever you mean to try, you should try now. *(She vanishes)*

(There is a roll of thunder. Dramatic music from Bartók's Bluebeard's Castle *begins to swell.* BLUEBEARD *dons surgeon's coat, gloves, and mask and enters the House of Pain.* MRS. MAGGOT *and* SHEEMISH *close the doors after him. There is the sound of loud knocking at the door.)*

Scene 5: MRS. MAGGOT, SHEEMISH.

MRS. MAGGOT: Look, Sheemish, the lapis lazuli locket. The Master said I could have it. Pretty, ain't it?
SHEEMISH: What's with you and that locket? *(A bloodcurdling scream issues from the laboratory. We may be sure that it is* SYBIL *writhing under the vivisector's knife. Both* SHEEMISH *and* MRS. MAGGOT *freeze for a moment in terror and clutch their own genitals in sympathy)* Listen, he has begun the operation.

(There is another bloodcurdling scream. Again MRS. MAGGOT *and* SHEEMISH *freeze and clutch their genitals.)*

RODNEY'S VOICE: *(Off)* What are you doing in there, you monster? *(He beats loudly on the door.* SYBIL *screams again off)* Open the door or I'll tear your heart out! *(Knocks loudly)*

Scene 6: BLUEBEARD, MRS. MAGGOT, SHEEMISH.

BLUEBEARD: *(Rushes on)* The test tube! The test tube. Everything depends upon the sticky liquid now. *(He snatches the test tube and hurries back to his work)*

*(*MRS. MAGGOT *and* SHEEMISH *exchange a guilty look. Another scream is heard. Suddenly* MISS CUBBIDGE *and* RODNEY *burst into the room.* MISS CUBBIDGE *brandishes the key.)*

Scene 7: MRS. MAGGOT, SHEEMISH, RODNEY, MISS CUBBIDGE.

MISS CUBBIDGE: I could control my curiosity no longer.
RODNEY: I'll see to it that he goes to the guillotine. That will shorten him by a head.
MISS CUBBIDGE: He robbed me of my maidenhead. So it's not his head I'll see cut off him! I want him decalced.

(Another scream is heard.)

RODNEY: Let me at him. I'll maim the bloody bugger.
SHEEMISH: Don't be a fool. The girl is on the operating table. If you interfere now, she'll lose her life.
MISS CUBBIDGE: *(Aside)* With Sybil out of the way, the Baron will be mine alone. *(Aloud)* We must save her no matter what the danger.

*(*SYBIL *screams again.)*

RODNEY: I can't stand it. I'm going in there.

SHEEMISH: Are you crazy?

RODNEY: Yes, I'm crazy.

SHEEMISH: Can't you understand that we are powerless against a supernatural enemy?

Scene 8: BLUEBEARD, MISS CUBBIDGE, RODNEY, MRS. MAGGOT, SHEEMISH.

BLUEBEARD: The time has come. The final stage of transmutation must be completed. Mars, God of War, and Venus, Goddess of Love, are conjunct in the twelfth house. The house of change and transformation. Scorpio, which rules surgery and the genitalia, is at the zenith. This is the horoscope I have been waiting for. The signs are in perfect aspect. The third genital will be born under the most beneficent stars that twinkle in the heavens. Sheemish, bring in the girl, or should I say "subject"?

MISS CUBBIDGE: Khanazar, you have deceived me. I . . .

BLUEBEARD: Quiet! I have no time to talk to an idiot.

RODNEY: If anything goes wrong with this experiment, I swear I'll kill you.

BLUEBEARD: I have already sworn upon the cross to enter into this experiment for life and for death.

(SHEEMISH *carries on* SYBIL, *who is wrapped in bandages like a mummy.*)

Scene 9: RODNEY, SYBIL, SHEEMISH, MISS CUBBIDGE, MRS. MAGGOT, BLUEBEARD.

BLUEBEARD: Gently, gently! Be careful, you fool.

MISS CUBBIDGE: (*Gasps*) Is she . . . is she . . . dead?

BLUEBEARD: (*Listens to* SYBIL's *heart and genital through stethoscope*) No, she is not dead. She's just resting, waiting for new life to come.

(*There is the sound of thunder and flashes of lightning.* MRS. MAGGOT *and* SHEEM-ISH *light candles, incense. There are science-fiction lighting effects.*)

RODNEY: Is it a new life or a monster you are creating, Baron Prevert?

BLUEBEARD: The word is "pervert." I believe in this monster as you call it.

RODNEY: So, this is the House of Pain.

BLUEBEARD: How do you know when you unlock any door in life that you are not entering a House of Pain? I have thought nothing of pain. Years of studying nature have made me as remorseless as nature itself. All we feel is pain. But we must take risks if we are to progress.

RODNEY: How could you? How could you?

BLUEBEARD: Do you know what it feels like to be God, Parker?

RODNEY: (*Spits in* BLUEBEARD's *face*) I spit in your face.

BLUEBEARD: Do you think that the envenomed spittle of five hundred little gentlemen of your mark, piled one on top of the other, could succeed in so much as slobbering the tips of my august toes? *(He turns his back on* RODNEY *and, with the assistance of* SHEEMISH, *begins unwinding the bandages that envelop* SYBIL. *When she is completely nude except for her fuck-me pumps, the genital begins to move)*

BLUEBEARD: Look, it's moving. It's alive. It's moving. It's alive! It's alive!

*(*SYBIL *moves like the bride of Frankenstein, with stiff, jerking movements of the head and neck. First she looks at* SHEEMISH *and screams with horror, then she looks at* BLUEBEARD *and screams with horror, then she looks at her new genital and growls with displeasure.)*

Scene 10: LAMIA, RODNEY, SYBIL, MRS. MAGGOT, SHEEMISH, MISS CUBBIDGE, BLUEBEARD.

LAMIA: *(Enters and crawls with catlike stealth over toward* SYBIL *and examines the third genital)* Now no man will ever want her! Rodney is mine. *(She leaps toward* RODNEY. BLUEBEARD *fires on her and she falls)*

BLUEBEARD: I told you never to come to this side of the island again.

SHEEMISH: *(Kneeling over* LAMIA's *body)* You killed the woman I love.

BLUEBEARD: *(Going to her also, feeling her pulse)* Woman—I wouldn't say she was a woman. She was a leopard, a wild cat. I couldn't make my leopard love me.

SHEEMISH: You killed the woman I love. Now you must die. *(He moves toward* BLUEBEARD *threateningly.)*

BLUEBEARD: *(Backing away)* No, Sheemish, no! Remember the House of Pain!

SHEEMISH: I no longer fear pain. My heart is broken. *(He seizes* BLUEBEARD *by the throat)*

RODNEY: *(Looking at* SYBIL's *genital)* No man will ever want her?

MISS CUBBIDGE: *(To* MRS. MAGGOT*)* What are you doing with the lapis lazuli locket? Sybil's mother gave it to her the night she died when the terrible fire . . . Sybil's real mother had a strawberry birthmark on her left kneecap.

RODNEY: I need never be jealous again!

MISS CUBBIDGE: Margaret, Margaret Maggot? Maggie!

*(*SHEEMISH *releases* BLUEBEARD *in amazement.)*

MRS. MAGGOT: The fire? Margaret Maggot? It's all coming back to me. I am Maggie Maggot. *(Turning on* BLUEBEARD*)* What have you suffered for that child that you dare to tear her from me without pity? Sybil is my daughter. I am her real mother. If you give me back my child, I shall live for her alone. I shall know how to tame my nature to be worthy of her always. My heart will not open itself to anyone but her. *(On her knees)* My whole life will be too brief to prove to her my tenderness, my love, my devotion.

BLUEBEARD: *(Kicking her over)* I detest cheap sentiment.

MISS CUBBIDGE: This exploits women!

MRS. MAGGOT: Women want an answer!

(They seize BLUEBEARD, *tie ropes to his wrists, and stretch him across stage.* LAMIA *rises and begins strangling him slowly.)*

Final Scene in *Bluebeard* (Thomas Harding)

BLUEBEARD: Lamia! I thought you were dead.

LAMIA: My dear, didn't you know? A cat has nine lives.

SYBIL: *(The monster speaks haltingly)* Stop . . . in . . . the . . . name . . . of love. The human heart . . . who knows to what perversions it may not turn, when its taste is guided by aesthetics?

(The women drop the rope. LAMIA *releases* BLUEBEARD. *The sound of the ship's foghorn is heard offstage.)*

SHEEMISH: *(Looking out the spy hole)* The *Lady Vain*! The *Lady Vain*! The *Lady Vain* has weathered the storm!

MISS CUBBIDGE: *(To* BLUEBEARD*)* I am leaving this moment. Tomorrow I shall be far away. I shall have forgotten everything that happened yesterday. It's enough to say that I will tell nobody, nobody. If, as I hope, you regret the words that escaped you, write to me and I shall despond at once. I leave without rancor, wishing you the best, in spite of all. I am carrying your child. Would that your son will be your good angel. *(Hands him the key to the laboratory)* Adieu! Come, Margaret, Sybil, Rodney. We must return to normalcy. *(They exit. There is the sound of a foghorn)*

Scene 11: BLUEBEARD, LAMIA, SHEEMISH.

BLUEBEARD: *(In a rage, shaking his fists at the heavens)* I curse everything that you have given. I curse the day on which I was born. I curse the day on which I shall die. I curse the whole of my life. I fling it all back at your cruel face, senseless fate! *(Laughing)* With my curses I conquer you. What else can you do to me? With my last breath I will shout in your asinine ears: Be accursed, be accursed! Be forever accursed! I'm a failure, Sheemish, I'm a failure.

SHEEMISH: But, Master, you have heart, you have talent.

BLUEBEARD: Heart! Talent! These are nothing, my boy. Mediocrity is the true gift of the gods. *(Exit)*

Scene 12: SHEEMISH, LAMIA.

SHEEMISH: Come, let us do the best we can, to change the opinion of this unhappy man. *(Exit with* LAMIA*)*

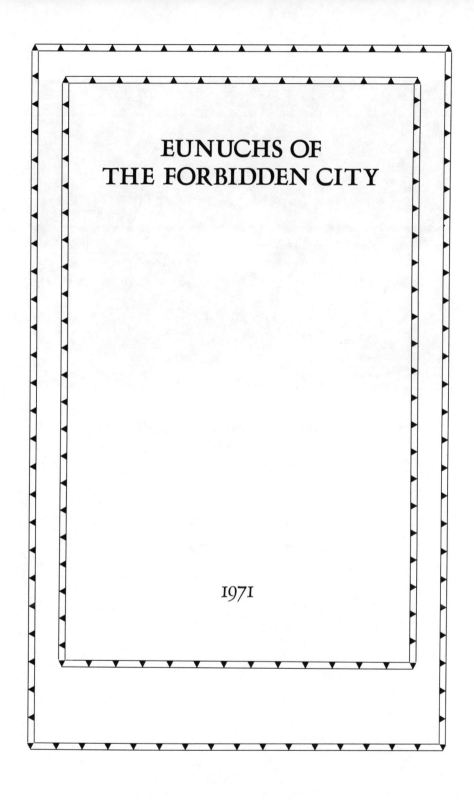

EUNUCHS OF
THE FORBIDDEN CITY

1971

The innkeeper scene in *Eunuchs of the Forbidden City*
(Leandro Katz)

Cast of Characters

ORCHID YEHONALA *(later* TSU HSI*)*
SAKOTA *(later* TSU AN*)*
CHIEN FENG, *the Emperor*
T'UNG CHIH, *his son*
THE EMPRESS DOWAGER
PERVADING FRAGRANCE *virgin*
WELCOME SPRING *virgin*
PRINCE KUNG ⎱ *Chien Feng's brothers*
PRINCE YI ⎰
SU SHUN, *Grand Councilor*
AN TE HAI, *Chief Eunuch*
LI LIEN YING, *a lesser eunuch*
A LU TE, *a concubine*
WU YUNG FOO, *an innkeeper*
TING PAO CHEN ⎱ *magistrates of Shantung*
TSI NAN FU ⎰

ACT I

Scene 1

*(*ORCHID *is in her bubble bath. The young eunuch,* LI LIEN YING, *is bathing her and pouring fragrant oils into the tub. The sound of a gong is heard.)*

VOICE: *(Offstage)* I have come to see my cousin, Orchid Yehonala.

*(*LI LIEN YING *draws back a screen, revealing* SAKOTA.*)*

SAKOTA: *(Yawning)* Forgive me for yawning, Cousin Orchid. I spent a sleepless night.
ORCHID: Cousin Sakota, what brings you here so early? It is not yet the hour of the mouse. Why are you up before the sun?
SAKOTA: Haven't you heard? Last night I bore a child to our emperor, the son of heaven.
ORCHID: Oh, Cousin Sakota, may he live ten thousand years! *(She kisses her.)* What a great joy this must be for you.
SAKOTA: There is no joy in this for me. I bore a girl. The emperor has fallen into a deep depression and refuses to see either me or our daughter. Nothing will rouse him from his sorrow. I fear . . . I fear . . . that he may die of grief. *(She weeps.)*
ORCHID: Ai ya! Is there nothing that can help?
SAKOTA: That is why I have come to you. Today, in the hope of raising the Emperor's spirits, the Empress Dowager has called for the selection of a new consort to the Dragon Throne. I have little or no influence now. But if you are selected, you could bear a male child and put in a good word for me with the Son of Heaven. If not, I will be lost.
ORCHID: Don't build up your hopes, O Motherly and Restful. Chien Feng may not choose me. There are many girls more beautiful than I.

SAKOTA: You will be chosen. Did I not always say that you have a destiny? I
can see it in your eyes. We must obey Chien Feng, the Son of Heaven. He
guards the ancient secrets. Without him who would protect us in this asphalt
jungle of a Forbidden City? I have arranged to have An Te Hai, Chief Eunuch,
call on you today to take you to the Pavilion of Selection. The rest is up to
you. Good night and good luck!

Scene 2

LI LIEN YING: When you are Empress, my precious, will you remember your
favorite eunuch and send down help to our humble hand laundry?
ORCHID: I shall be only a concubine, one of hundreds.
LI LIEN YING: You will be what heaven ordains. Unwind your long black hair,
young hopeful. An Te Hai will come early this morning bearing with him the
Golden Summons.
ORCHID: I am so nervous. Which comb shall I use?
LI LIEN YING: Comb your hair with the Chinese wooden comb.
ORCHID: What perfume?
LI LIEN YING: *(Producing an exotic vial)* This is a mixture of half-moon musk and
the fragrant oil of the mimosa tree. Rub it into the seven openings of your
body. If you are loved tonight, these oils will make your love intoxicating. The
Son of Heaven will find you irresistible.
ORCHID: How do you know these things?
LI LIEN YING: The eunuchs know men and the eunuchs know women. We know
them better than they know themselves. But above all, we know the Son of
Heaven. The eunuchs "serve." Wind your hair into two coils over your ears,
and into each coil put a small lotus of seed pearls with leaves of thin green jade.

Scene 3

(Footsteps are heard.)

AN TE HAI: *(Off)* I have come from the Imperial Chambers of the Forbidden
City.
LI LIEN YING: It is An Te Hai. Ai ya! *(He sighs.)* Now, Orchid, prepare yourself
for a long journey through the Forbidden City.
AN TE HAI: *(Entering abruptly)* Where is the girl, Orchid Yehonala?
ORCHID: I am she.
AN TE HAI: You? You? *(He laughs)* A waste of time, my coming here. We heard
there was a flawless beauty. But you, my dear, were it not for the fact that you
are overrouged, overpowdered, and smell of that whorish perfume, would
scarcely pass muster. *(He turns his back, but his hand is out, palm up)*
LI LIEN YING: *(aside to ORCHID)* Offer him a tip.
ORCHID: A bribe? I will not stoop to that.
LI LIEN YING: If you want to become one of the Great Ones, you had better
learn to stoop.
ORCHID: To be a Great One means to be uplifting, to inspire men and cultivate
their higher natures.

LI LIEN YING: When uplifting—get underneath. Offer him a tip.

AN TE HAI: I cannot insult the Eye of Heaven with a toad. This girl is unsuitable.

ORCHID: *(To* AN TE HAI*)* Perhaps these pearl earrings are too much. Take them. To a homely girl like me, simplicity should be the keynote.

AN TE HAI: *(Accepting the bribe and pocketing the pearl earrings)* Better. Better. Her appearance is much improved.

ORCHID: And this fragrant oil of the mimosa tree mixed with the half-moon musk, priceless though it be, and rarer than any perfume in China, does not express my personality. Take it. It just isn't me. In the future, I'll stick to lemon peels and crushed cloves.

AN TE HAI: *(Pocketing the perfume)* You know, the girl doesn't look so bad.

LI LIEN YING: *(Aside to* ORCHID*)* Now you've got the idea.

ORCHID: I think this Shantung brocade with coral peonies and amber buds is too flamboyant. Vulgar, really. My eyes are black and they are jewels enough. My hair will clothe me as well as any robe. And if I am clean, why should I need a scent? Take this robe, An Te Hai; you have taught me to be beautiful.

AN TE HAI: *(Stuffing the rich garment under his girdle)* And I have given my advice free. I usually demand some remuneration. *(*ORCHID *glares at him)* But as I said, for you there's no charge. Come, the Son of Heaven must not be kept waiting.

ORCHID: *(Following* AN TE HAI *out)* How many contestants are there this year?

AN TE HAI: Six hundred.

ORCHID: *(In despair)* I am one of six hundred?

AN TE HAI: *(With a double meaning)* I have no doubt that in the end you will be first. Come!

LI LIEN YING: Ssst! Ssst! Orchid . . . remember me.

ORCHID: Do not speak to me. You do your duty and I will do mine.

(They exit.)

Scene 4

EMPRESS DOWAGER: *(Entering with* CHIEN FENG*)* It is now the hour for the selection of the concubines. *(Muttering, aside)* Oh, stupid I! Someday this girl will depose me. What shall I be then but an old woman in the palace? *(Aloud)* An Te Hai, bring in the girls that the Son of Heaven may select a consort to the Dragon Throne. *(To* CHIEN FENG*)* Find a jewel of a woman, my son.

CHIEN FENG: If you seek a jewel of a woman, look in books.

EMPRESS DOWAGER: And remember, my son, virtue becomes a wife. Beauty becomes a concubine.

(The gong is struck three times by AN TE HAI.*)*

AN TE HAI: The virgins will now pass before the Son of Heaven for final selection. First runner-up, Pervading Fragrance.

(Music. PERVADING FRAGRANCE *glides in, overdressed.* CHIEN FENG *looks her over.)*

EMPRESS DOWAGER: Exquisite, my son. Is she not exquisite?

CHIEN FENG: I like her not. I like not her. Her I don't like.

EMPRESS DOWAGER: Observe the jet-black beauty mark on her left cheek. It points up her eyes. It is the flaw that gives her beauty proof.

CHIEN FENG: One rat dropping spoils a pot of rice.

EMPRESS DOWAGER: Ah, me! It is easier to rule an empire than a son.

AN TE HAI: Second runner-up: Welcome Spring!

(Music. WELCOME SPRING *glides in, overdressed.)*

EMPRESS DOWAGER: Isn't she lovely? A healthy, robust girl.

CHIEN FENG: I don't want her, you can have her, she's too fat for me!

EMPRESS DOWAGER: And modest. See how she covers her eyes with her fan?

CHIEN FENG: *(Pulling down her fan and poking at her eyes)* Her eyes are bloodshot. Her nose is like an elbow. *(Tweaking her nose)* And her bosom sags.

*(*WELCOME SPRING *weeps.)*

EMPRESS DOWAGER: My son, you've made her weep.

CHIEN FENG: Two barrels of tears are no substitute for plastic surgery.

EMPRESS DOWAGER: Ugly wives and stupid servant girls are treasures, my son.

CHIEN FENG: If the first words fail, ten thousand will not then avail.

AN TE HAI: Third runner-up: Yehonala.

(Music. ORCHID YEHONALA, *naked except for fans, glides past* CHIEN FENG. *They stare into each other's eyes as though in a trance.)*

EMPRESS DOWAGER: This girl is too bold. She looks the Son of Heaven straight in the eye.

CHIEN FENG: This one I choose.

EMPRESS DOWAGER: No, no, O Son of Heaven, this girl is immodest. Do not choose this one.

CHIEN FENG: This one I choose.

EMPRESS DOWAGER: Marry this girl today and you will regret it a thousand days. Give up this girl and I will give you a thousand concubines.

CHIEN FENG: The light of a thousand stars cannot make one moon. This one I choose.

EMPRESS DOWAGER: How can you do this to me, your own mother? After all I've sacrificed for you?

AN TE HAI: It is too late. The Son of Heaven has spoken thrice. Yehonala is the winner and chosen favorite.

EMPRESS DOWAGER: If I were ten years younger, I'd forbid this marriage.

CHIEN FENG: The Yangtze cannot flow backward, Mother, and a man cannot recapture his youth.

EMPRESS DOWAGER: One thing I want to wish on you: that your children should treat you the way you treated me.

ORCHID: May we have your blessing, O Motherly and Magnanimous?

EMPRESS DOWAGER: *(Raising her hands over them)* In bed be wife and husband. In hall, each other's honored guests. Enduring as heaven and earth, no love however ancient can ever die. Timeless as light and shadow, no debt of breeze and moonlight can ever be repaid. You are too young to understand this.

(All but AN TE HAI *exit.)*

Scene 5

AN TE HAI: *(To the audience)* What we eunuchs find most deplorable is the cocky attempts men and women make to distinguish between love of beauty and licentiousness, forgetting that one always leads to the other.

Scene 6

(One year later: CHIEN FENG's *deathbed.)*

CHIEN FENG: We regret. We regret. We regret.

TSU HSI: Do not waste your hour with regrets. The sun sets so soon. *(*CHIEN FENG *sighs and leans back)* There are things that must be done before you . . .

TSU AN: *(Aside)* Sister, remember, the word "death" may never be uttered near the Emperor.

*(*TSU HSI *dismisses* TSU AN *with a gesture.)*

Scene 7

TSU HSI: Before you . . . pass out of the red dust beyond the Yellow River . . . Your son, my lord, our son, is the heir to the Dragon Throne. He must be the next emperor of China. *(She pulls a scroll out of her sleeve)* Sign this and secure the Dragon Throne for your line.

CHIEN FENG: *(Feebly)* Our son is an idiot, an idiot is our son. Is our son an idiot?

TSU HSI: He is still young. Someday he will be as great an emperor as his sire.

CHIEN FENG: In the little boy we see the final man. You will spoil him as our mother spoiled us. Debauch him with eunuchs until his manhood is sucked from his young body. Comfort him with opium so he will never know the meaning of the word "pain." And worst, worst of all . . . teach him to believe that he is immortal so that he wastes a lifetime in idleness, when to a laborer, one day of leisure is immortality in little. *(He sighs)* We regret. We regret. We regret.

TSU HSI: Oh, Sacred Dragon, sign this document and secure the Dragon Throne—if not for his sake, then for mine. I am your loyal wife and lover.

CHIEN FENG: You women swear your loyalty to us in life but when we are dead, you marry again quickly enough.

TSU HSI: *(Archly)* I suppose you preferred your eunuchs to us women.

CHIEN FENG: At least the eunuchs do not stink like dead fish in the summer so that we are almost driven out of our palace by the foul and rancid smell of women's love. We'd rather smell an asshole than a cunt.

TSU HSI: So it was war, not love, we made in bed, my Lord and Dragon! *(She kowtows nine times)* Oh, Son of Heaven and my God. I beseech you. Sign, seal, and deliver this Edict of Succession to your ministers.

CHIEN FENG: Never, Tsu Hsi! Never! *(Suddenly a stricken look comes across his face. He winces with pain)* Aaagh! Aaagh! Aaagh! Pain! We can't stand the pain. . . .

TSU HSI: *(Urgently)* I beg you sign before it is too late.

CHIEN FENG: Opium! We need opium! We must ring for the eunuchs. *(He grabs for the bell)*

TSU HSI: *(Snatching the bell away)* Why ring for the eunuchs? I have opium right here. *(She pulls out a lump of opium from her sleeve.)*

CHIEN FENG: Aaagh! Give it to us. We can't stand the pain.

TSU HSI: I will, my husband—when you have signed your name and made the Imperial Seal.

CHIEN FENG: No! Never!

TSU HSI: Then die like a miserable rat, O Glorious Dragon!

CHIEN FENG: Tsu Hsi, we beg of you.

TSU HSI: Sign, sign—or die a slow death.

CHIEN FENG: That word is never to be uttered in our presence. We are the Emperor.

TSU HSI: What word, *death, death, death? (She smiles)*

CHIEN FENG: Oh, ancestors! We are in her power. We cannot stand the pain. Give us the brush. *(He signs the document)*

TSU HSI: Here's your opium. *(*CHIEN FENG *eats the opium)* Sleep well, Glorious Immortal Dragon.

Scene 8

(Sound of cannon fire.)

LI LIEN YING: *(Rushing in and prostrating himself before* TSU HSI*)* O Motherly and Auspicious, Lord of Ten Thousand Years, the white devils have broken into the summer palace! Strange-looking soldiers are reported to be in the Temple of the Seventh Heaven.

TSU HSI: *(Firmly and coolly)* Pull yourself together, eunuch. You may be alarming yourself unnecessarily. They are probably Moslem soldiers sent to protect us.

LI LIEN YING: *(Despair in his voice)* Unfortunately no, O Orthodox and Blissful Ancient Mother! The Moslem general is fleeing westward.

TSU HSI: In that case, we leave.

LI LIEN YING: *(Going toward* CHIEN FENG's *body)* The Emperor . . . is he . . . dead?

TSU HSI: No, the dread Immortal Dragon is not dead. He has gone to join his ancestors.

LI LIEN YING: Orchid Yehonala must not linger another second.

Scene 9

TSU AN: *(Entering like a flurry of autumn leaves)* Sister, Sister, the palace is under siege!

TSU HSI: Prepare to leave at once. Li Lien Ying, go to An Te Hai, the Chief Eunuch of the Imperial Nursery, and bring my son to me. He is the rightful Heir to the Dragon Throne.

TSU AN: Sister, O Goddess of Mercy, please save my little girl, the Princess, too.

TSU HSI: Bring the Princess too. She would have been the Heir if she had been born a boy.

LI LIEN YING: I hear and now obey. *(He exits)*

Scene 10

TSU AN: *(Wringing her hands)* What'll we do? What'll we do?

TSU HSI: We must save the Heir at any cost and set him on the Dragon Throne.

TSU AN: O Goddess of Mercy, Kuan Yin, help us, help us! *(She weeps)*

TSU HSI: Stop this sniveling. Our survival depends on keeping our wits about us. *(She slaps TSU AN's face)*

TSU AN: *(Suddenly calm)* Thanks, I needed that.

Scene 11

PRINCE YI: *(Forgetting to kowtow)* I heard about the Emperor's death. I want the Imperial Seal.

TSU HSI: The Imperial Seal belongs to my son, rightful heir to the Dragon Throne. He will be the next ruler of China.

PRINCE YI: He who holds the Seal will rule China. And I intend to get that Seal. *(He pushes TSU HSI and TSU AN aside and rummages through CHIEN FENG's bedclothes)* It's not here!

TSU HSI: Not here?

PRINCE YI: The Emperor must have left it in the throne room. Whoever first lays hands on the Seal will rule China! *(He rushes out)*

TSU AN: We are lost! Everything is lost! *(She weeps)*

Scene 12

(Eunuchs enter, carrying the two infants)

AN TE HAI: *(Carrying the Emperor's son)* Here is the Heir.

LI LIEN YING: *(Carrying the Princess)* Here is the Princess. What is wrong, Majesty?

TSU HSI: We don't have the Imperial Seal. Prince Yi has gone to search for it. If he gets the Seal, it will mean our death.

Scene 13

PRINCE KUNG: *(Rushing in)* The Imperial Seal is missing! The palace is in an uproar. Princes have dropped their dignity and run like chickens through the palace. *(PRINCE YI crosses the stage imitating a chicken)* Your lives are in danger here. I will take Tsu An, the Heir, and the Princess to the North Gate and prepare to travel to the Forbidden City.

TSU AN: *(To Tsu Hsi)* Will you not come too?

TSU HSI: I will join you in exactly ten minutes by the Chinese water clock. I need a moment alone to bid farewell to the summer palace. Who knows if I will ever vacation here again?

PRINCE KUNG: *(Quietly)* I understand.

(He exits with AN TE HAI, TSU AN, *and the infants.)*

Scene 14

LI LIEN YING: Empress?

TSU HSI: Yes, eunuch?

LI LIEN YING: I have a going-away present for you.

TSU HSI: Oh Li Lien, you shouldn't have.

LI LIEN YING: I hope you like it. *(He gives her a packet wrapped in yellow silk)*

TSU HSI: *(Opening it)* The Seal of legally transmitted authority! Where did you get the Imperial Seal?

LI LIEN YING: During the play, I sent a midget eunuch to the throne room; he slipped under the bars and broke open the Dragon coffer.

TSU HSI: *(Laughing gaily)* You will be rewarded for this, Li Lien Ying! Power is ours! *(She dances out with the Imperial Seal up her sleeve.)*

LI LIEN YING: *(Greedily)* Yes, power is *ours*! *(To the audience)* In life every man must choose between love and power. But for us eunuchs the die is cast. For though the wise men say that love contains the greatest power of all, we have no power to love. We must love power! *(Footsteps are heard)* Who's coming? Prince Yi and Su Shun, the Grand Councilor. Information is worth gold, and a bad word whispered will echo a hundred miles. Where will I hide? *(He looks frantically for a place to hide and finally crawls under* CHIEN FENG's *chaise in the nick of time)*

Scene 15

PRINCE YI: I tell you, we searched every corner of the palace and the Imperial Seal was nowhere to be found.

SU SHUN: This is a disaster. Without the Imperial Seal, you can lay no claim to the Dragon Throne.

PRINCE YI: My sister-in-law claims the regency for her infant son.

SU SHUN: Yes, yes. But until he comes of age, someone must handle the affairs of state.

PRINCE YI: And that someone . . . ?

SU SHUN: . . . must be you! China cannot be ruled by a concubine.

PRINCE YI: Tsu Hsi is no ordinary concubine. She has the will of a man.

*(*LI LIEN YING *sneezes.)*

PRINCE YI and SU SHUN: God bless you.

SU SHUN: You have no recourse but to kill the Heir. Without the infant emperor, she can lay no claim to the Dragon Throne. And then I'll set your head on headless China!

(They exit.)

Scene 16

LI LIEN YING: *(Coming out of hiding)* The Empress shall know of this. *(He hears a loud noise)* Aaah! The white devils are coming! Farewell, summer palace!

Scene 17

PRINCE KUNG: *(Entering alone)* My body is here to protect the Empress and the Heir. Each year I eat of the Imperial Grain. How can I act as a mere onlooker when the Court is in trouble? I cannot choose between disaster and happiness. I must fulfill my duty. Even if I meet with disaster, I shall have a clear conscience. But if I avoid my duty, I shall question my heart, and I know that it will not be at peace. If I use all my power to do what must be done, whatever is coming to me, whether good or bad, will be my destiny in life. I am determined to protect the Sacred Chariot.

Scene 18

(INNKEEPER enters, carrying the door of the inn and hiding behind it.)

PRINCE KUNG: *(Knocking on the door)* Innkeeper! Innkeeper! Innkeeper!

INNKEEPER: *(Still behind the door)* Who is it?

PRINCE KUNG: Who do you think it is?

INNKEEPER: *(Feeble and frightened)* If you are one of the Eight Immortals, please leave me alone. I have given your men all the food I had. All that is left is a little green pea porridge and millet gruel for the Emperor, who will be passing this way. And that you'll eat over my dead body.

PRINCE KUNG: I am no Immortal. I am Prince Kung, Harbinger of the Sacred Chariot. Open up!

(INNKEEPER hesitantly comes out from behind his door. He is bloody, as if he has been beaten.)

INNKEEPER: Is the Empress Dowager coming?

PRINCE KUNG: The Worshipful and Illustrious Old Buddha is coming.

INNKEEPER: Oh joy! Is the Son of Heaven with her?

PRINCE KUNG: The Infant Dragon is safe in her arms.

INNKEEPER: The gods be praised! It is to see the Son of Heaven that I stayed behind.

PRINCE KUNG: What are you doing here alone? Where are the others?

INNKEEPER: The town is empty. There are but few things left. Almost everything has been looted by the defeated soldiers and the rebels who call themselves the Righteous Harmony Fists. Everything is gone, gone. Of the three hundred horses belonging to the post station, there is only one old one left. Now it's just a one-horse town. There were three inns in the town and each prepared a great pot of millet and green pea porridge. But it was all eaten up by the defeated soldiers and the minor official refugees. I hid some in a chamber pot for the Son of Heaven. That was the only way I could save any. This is all that's left. *(He shows him the chamber pot)*

PRINCE KUNG: And they didn't find the pot?

INNKEEPER: They would have found it if I hadn't sat on the pot all night pretending to have loose bowels. That was my plot.

PRINCE KUNG: This is a loose plot.

Scene 19

AN TE HAI: The Sacred Chariot has arrived. When you meet the Sacred Chariot you must kneel and kowtow nine times while the chair and the first litter are passing. Then you may rise.

Scene 20

(The Empress TSU HSI *and her Co-Regent,* TSU AN, *are borne onto the stage in sedan chairs. Each carries an infant in her arms. Their appearance is dilapidated. Their fatigue and hunger are evident. They have been suffering hardships for several days.* LI LIEN YING *is attendant to the Co-Regents.)*

INNKEEPER: I, Wu Yung Foo, Innkeeper of the Jaded Palate Chinese Restaurant, kneel to welcome the Sacred Chair of the Empress Dowager. *(He kneels and kowtows nine times, then stands to await orders)*

(When the commotion surrounding the entrance of the Imperial Entourage has subsided, AN TE HAI *steps forward and stares haughtily, with his stomach and chest stuck out.)*

AN TE HAI: *(In a loud voice)* Which is the innkeeper of the Jaded Palate Chinese Restaurant?

INNKEEPER: I am he.

AN TE HAI: Those above call you to audience. Come with me.

INNKEEPER: *(Terrified)* Is the Imperial Summons dangerous? Is the Emperor angry with me?

AN TE HAI: How should I know? That is your fate. Walk this way. *(He walks with his stomach and chest stuck out, bent slightly backward)*

(The Innkeeper follows him to the Dragon Seat, imitating his walk.)

TSU HSI: Are you Manchu or Chinese?

INNKEEPER: I am a Chinese from the province of Chekiang.

TSU HSI: Which "Yung" do you use for your name?

INNKEEPER: It is the "Yung" meaning eternity, from the propitious phrase, "Everlasting Happiness, Eternal Well-being."

TSU HSI: Ah! It is the water ideogram with the dot?

INNKEEPER: It is! It is!

TSU HSI: Have you prepared all that we will need?

INNKEEPER: *(Humbly)* I have. But I received word only last night. What I have prepared is not enough and therefore I am afraid.

TSU HSI: Good! What you have prepared is sufficient. *(Weeping aloud)* The Emperor and I have traveled for many hundreds of miles and have not seen a single subject. Not only have we not seen a subject, we have not even seen a shadow of a magistrate. But you, a lowly innkeeper, have stayed and kowtowed where men of rank have fled. I never thought the country's affairs would come to this. But seeing you who have not discarded ceremony nor broken faith, I feel that there may still be hope for the country and for the dynasty. Day by day we fled and had nothing to eat or drink. We were both cold and hungry.

TSU AN: On the road we were thirsty. We told the eunuchs to get water but the wells . . . the wells . . . were . . . *(She weeps)*

TSU HSI: The wells were filled with floating human heads. Unable to obtain water, they brought us giant canes of millet, which we chewed. There is not much moisture in the canes, but we got a little and thus stopped our thirst. Last night we had only a bench between us and we sat shoulder to shoulder, I with the Emperor in my arms, watching the sky for morning. We could not endure that again. Look at me! I am like an old country woman now.

TSU AN: The Emperor too is very tired. It is two days since we had food. My stomach is starved. Have you prepared food for us?

INNKEEPER: Only this porridge of millet and green peas. I am afraid this food is too coarse for you to eat.

TSU HSI: If you have millet porridge, that is good. Bring it quickly. In time of distress, this is enough. Can I, at this time, say what is good and what is not good? *(INNKEEPER presents them with the chamber pot)* You should see the Emperor. Li Lien Ying. Hold up the Son of Heaven that this loyal subject may see his Emperor.

(LI LIEN YING holds up the baby. TSU HSI *and* TSU AN *eat the porridge.)*

PRINCE KUNG: Oh, pitiful sight! To see the Empresses eating from a chamber pot!!

TSU HSI: Make our beds. We want to sleep. Who will guard us during the night?

SU SHUN: *(Aside, to* PRINCE YI*)* Now's your chance. Pledge your protection to the Heir. In the black of night the black heart will not be seen. Night will camouflage our deeds obscene.

PRINCE YI: O Serenely Independent, I offer my protection to yourself and the Heir.

(LI LIEN YING whispers in TSU HSI's *ear.)*

TSU HSI: You, Prince Yi? You who have broken promises, incited armed disturbances, troubled the Emperor, and afflicted the people? Your rush to seize the Imperial Seal has made you seem a beast that knows no gratitude.

PRINCE YI: Just a moment! Just a moment! Your indignation is well merited. I acted rashly. But it was to secure the Seal from your enemies in the palace that I behaved as I did.

(LI LIEN YING whispers in her ear again.)

TSU HSI: It seemed to me you wanted to take the Seal yourself and usurp the Dragon Throne.

PRINCE YI: This would be a disgrace to the Manchu Dynasty and a disgrace to China. It is now the task of a loyal Prince to sacrifice himself to reassure the Emperor and to wipe out his shame. O Flawless Jade, etch this in the cold green of your heart. Behold what I do! *(Grasping his dagger with the point downward, he thrusts it into his eye, turns it around along his eyelids, and draws out the crimson eyeball, which he places on the ceremonial tray)* Accept my crimsoned eyeball.

TSU HSI: What is the meaning of this gesture? Su Shun, Grand Councilor, what would you advise me to do?

SU SHUN: O Lord of Ten Thousand Years, a man's eyes are his sun and moon.

The left eye, belonging to the Yang principle, is his sun. The Prince has become emasculated without that eye. Surely this is proof of loyalty.

TSU HSI: *(Reverently accepting the tray)* Words fail me when I see what a loyal minister you have proved.

LI LIEN YING: *(Trying to get* TSU HSI*'s attention)* Majesty, Majesty. Psssst! Psssst!

TSU HSI: *(Aside)* Silence! *(Aloud)* Prince Yi shall remain outside the door and guard us while we sleep.

LI LIEN YING: *(To the audience)* When the Emperor errs, the peasant shivers. But I must hold my tongue.

(TSU HSI and TSU AN enter the inn with their infants. The others lie down and go to sleep. The two Co-Regents sleep with their infants in their arms.)

Scene 21

SU SHUN: You have won the confidence of the concubines. But will you dare to do what comes next?

PRINCE YI: Do you think it was for nothing that I cut out my eye? I have a vision. I see the way with my one eye better than I did with two. The Heir must die and I will be the Son of Heaven.

SU SHUN: They are all asleep and in their sleep they dream. But dreaming is but seeming to our waking nightmare scheming.

PRINCE YI: We dare not show our faces. Give me the mask.

(They put on masks and enter the inn.)

Scene 22

PRINCE YI: *(Putting his hand over* TSU HSI*'s mouth)* Where is the Son of Heaven?

SU SHUN: *(Doing the same to* TSU AN*)* If you scream, I'll smother you both and kill the infants in your arms.

TSU HSI: I won't scream. But I'll never give you the Son of Heaven.

TSU AN: *(Aside, trembling with fear)* Sister, they'll kill us both and they'll kill both our babes. Please, please, we must save ourselves.

TSU HSI: *(Aside)* Small-minded, ignoble cow! Without the Son of Heaven, we are obsolete. Do you think the Princes will honor us when we can no longer lay claim to the Dragon Throne? That is death and worse than death, our own eunuchs would spit on us. And we would be banished to the Pavilion of Forgotten Concubines—to live alone, unloved until the day we die.

TSU AN: Then let us scream for the guards. Prince Yi would come and though they'd kill us, he'd save the Heir.

TSU HSI: Look at the left hand of the assassin—on the third finger . . .

TSU AN: He wears a ring.

TSU HSI: He wears a red jade ring. There is only one like it in all of China. Where have we seen it before?

TSU AN: *(In a hoarse whisper, terror-stricken)* Prince Yi!

TSU HSI: Yes, it is Prince Yi. O Kuan Yin, Goddess of Mercy, may I live to see him die by slow slicing!

TSU AN: What'll we do? What'll we do?

TSU HSI: Switch the infants and let them take the Princess.

TSU AN: Nooooooooooooo!

TSU HSI: It's the only way. Exchange their garments. Put the Princess in the Golden-Dragon coverlet.

TSU AN: *(Clutching her daughter)* Nooooooo!

TSU HSI: *(Snatching away the infant and switching their clothes, to* PRINCE YI*)* Here is the Heir. But remember, if you kill the Son of Heaven, you disinherit the earth.

SU SHUN: *(To* PRINCE YI*)* The earth belongs to those who take it. The strong stand on top and the weak are pushed below.

(The infant cries, PRINCE YI *smothers it.* TSU AN *screams. All wake and rush toward the infant.* PRINCE YI *and* SU SHUN *rush out.)*

Scene 23

PRINCE KUNG: What has happened?

TSU HSI: There has been an attempt on the life of the Son of Heaven.

Scene 24

PRINCE YI: Villains! Villains! Villains! Two prowlers just escaped. They must have hidden in the inn. Are you all right, Venerable Ancestors?

TSU AN: *(In a state of shock)* They killed the Princess. My little Princess.

PRINCE YI: *(Shooting a look at* SU SHUN*)* The Princess?

SU SHUN: *(Shaking his head)* It must have been the Boxer bandits. Stupid, *inaccurate* rebels.

TSU HSI: There can be no rest for us until we reach the Forbidden City.

TSU AN: No rest, no sleep for me. No place to lay my head. I was nothing but a mother. Now I'm nothing. My little girl is dead.

PRINCE KUNG: Eunuchs, carry us away. We'll reach the Forbidden City before the break of day.

(The train and sedan chairs exit. PRINCE YI *and* SU SHUN *remain.)*

Scene 25

SU SHUN: A foolish mistake, my prince.

PRINCE YI: What should I do now?

SU SHUN: You had your chance and you blew it. Tricked by a woman!

PRINCE YI: Woman! She is no woman. She is neither male nor female and she is more devious than any eunuch. She is not bound by the rules of conduct germane to either gender.

SU SHUN:
Tsu Hsi lives on mother's milk
and sucks it from the teat.
She says it keeps her skin like silk
and tastes so thick and sweet.

*(*PRINCE YI *and* SU SHUN *exit after the caravan.)*

Scene 26

AN TE HAI: *(Expansively)* Black swans in the moonlight, a little silver fishing boat. The scent of incense. Ecstasy intense. It's good to be in the Forbidden City at last!

LI LIEN YING: *(Complaining)* I'm told you called me disreputable the other night.

AN TE HAI: I'm sure I hardly recollect whether I called you reputable or disreputable—I don't remember.

LI LIEN YING: Unkind.

AN TE HAI: What are you complaining about? You have been appointed Imperial Hairdresser, have you not?

LI LIEN YING: I have.

AN TE HAI: I have been appointed Imperial Salad Dresser. Salads! Salads! I wish it was hair!

LI LIEN YING: Be contented that you are only a salad dresser. If Tsu Hsi loses so much as a single hair during a combing, she has the Imperial Hairdresser beaten to death.

AN TE HAI: You do not understand women, Li Lien Ying.

LI LIEN YING: I understand them as well as you do.

AN TE HAI: That's what I said, you do not understand women. I do not understand them!

Scene 27

VOICE: *(Offstage)* Li la! Li la!

AN TE HAI: The Empress is coming.

(They kowtow.)

TSU HSI: *(Entering with her train)* Oh, you gardens of the Forbidden City! How often have you witnessed agitation and disappointment? You smooth adorned paths . . . ! How often have you known the extremes of care . . . ? Eunuchs! Sound the gong! Have Prince Yi and Su Shun brought before me.

(AN TE HAI strikes the gong.)

Scene 28

PRINCE YI and SU SHUN: *(Entering and kowtowing)* You sent for us, O Motherly and Auspicious?

TSU HSI: In deciding how to deal with your crimes I have consulted the Oracle of the *I Ching,* the ancient Chinese book of wisdom and statesmanship. I have drawn the hexagram Shih-Ho, Biting Through, the symbol of which is thunder and lightning. This hexagram represents an open mouth with an obstruction between the teeth. As a result the lips cannot meet. To bring them together, one must bite energetically through the obstacle.

PRINCE YI: Surely you don't believe me to be an obstacle to unity. Did I not act as your bodyguard when you fled the summer palace?

TSU HSI: Liar! Your red jade ring has given you away, although you wore a mask. (PRINCE YI *looks with terror at the ring on his finger*) Just as the kings of old made firm and just laws through clearly defined penalties, now justice comes with the terror of thunder and the clarity of lightning. Behead the criminal!

(PRINCE KUNG *lops off* PRINCE YI's *head.*)

HEAD OF PRINCE YI: How can you be so cruel?
TSU HSI: I have been taught by masters. Take him away.

(All exit but TSU HSI *and* TSU AN.*)*

Scene 29

TSU HSI: The Infant Dragon has an ocean of sleep upon him.
TSU AN: Oh, he's a little rascal.
TSU HSI: You know, he's a year old today?
TSU AN: His birthday?
TSU HSI: Yes.
TSU AN: Everyone forgot. Even Aunt Sakota.
TSU HSI: Let's measure him.
TSU AN: Where?
TSU HSI: Against the wall. Here, you hold him up. I'll make a mark.
TSU HSI and TSU AN: *(A lullaby)*
> Ching-a-ling-a-ling
> Ching-a-ling-a-loo
> You're my Chinese baby
> If you love me like
> >   I love you
> No one can cut our
> >   love in two.
>
> Ching-a-ling-a-ling
> Ching-a-ling-a-loo
> Why are you so shy?
> If you want to kiss me,
> You will never miss me.
>
> Ching-a-ling-a-ling
> Ching-a-ling-a-ling
> Ching-a-ling-a-ling-a-loo.

TSU AN: We woke him. But he doesn't even cry. What a profound-looking baby!

(Curtain)

ACT II

Scene 1

(The scene is the same as the end of Act I.)

(TSU HSI and TSU AN are sixteen years older. The son of Heaven, T'UNG CHIH, is now seventeen years old. He stands against the wall where the infant was at the end of the first act, as do the Co-Regents. They are measuring him against the same wall now scored seventeen times, one for every birthday the young Emperor has had.)

TSU HSI and TSU AN: Happy birthday, two hundred and four moons old!

TSU HSI: Minus two days.

TSU AN: There's the big boy. I can't reach to make the mark.

TSU HSI: *(To LI LIEN YING)* Let me have a chair here.

(LI LIEN YING brings a chair. TSU HSI climbs up on it.)

LI LIEN YING: Be careful, Venerable.

TSU HSI: *(To T'UNG CHIH)* Now stand up straight. Put down that Western toy. Today you are a man. See how he's grown?

T'UNG CHIH: *(In a temper)* I want my railroad train!

TSU HSI: No more toys. One can't attain stillness of soul, dearest, within earshot of trains and trams.

T'UNG CHIH: *(Caterwauling)* I want my railroad train!

TSU HSI: Nor within earshot of my son the Heir. All of China is yours, my son, except this railroad train. We must be true to our traditions and not adopt the ways of the white men whose skins are the color of pus.

T'UNG CHIH: I want my railroad train! *(He holds his breath)*

TSU AN: He's holding his breath. Sister, Sister, please let him have his railroad train.

TSU HSI: Release your breath at once, you meathead, or I'll smack your face.

TSU AN: Sister, you must not strike the Son of Heaven.

TSU HSI: Yesterday he blew up the Porcelain Pagoda of Mind-Nurture with his chemistry set!

TSU AN: No, Sister, you are too hard on him. *(In baby talk)* T'ung Chih, if you give up your railroad train, Aunt Sakota will give you some of those sweetmeats you like made with pork drippings.

TSU HSI: How can I make an emperor out of him when you spoil him by giving in to his every whim?

TSU AN: I love him so. I think I love him more than anything else in this world. You'll never know how much I love him. He is my favorite nephew.

TSU HSI: I love him too. But I cannot give in to him as you can. I must think what is good for him and what is good for China. Who loves him more—you who will ruin his teeth with sweetmeats and pork drippings, or I who see to it that he eats his rice? Who loves him more—you who give him opium when he has a stomachache, or I who teach him that pain is a message from the gods telling us that we have violated the Order of the Universe? Who loves him more, you who let him play those filthy little faggot games with the eunuchs, or I who would keep him chaste for a plain woman who would support and serve him? I ask you, who loves him more? *(Snatching away his railroad train)* Put that thing down!

T'UNG CHIH: Aunt Sakota, make her stop picking on me.

TSU AN: There, there, do what your mother says. Aunt Sakota will keep your
   railroad train for later.

TSU HSI: *(Aside)* So, he prefers Tsu An to his own mother. I must win him back.
   (Aloud) T'ung Chih, I have a surprise for you. In two days the eunuchs will
   perform a play in honor of your two hundred and fourth moon birthday. But
   this afternoon, we will hold the selection of the concubines. *(Aside)* Marriage
   to the right girl will deliver him into my hands. *(She strikes the gong.* AN TE HAI
   appears) An Te Hai, go and summon all the eligible Manchu girls to the
   Pavilion of Selection.

T'UNG CHIH: *(Abandoning* TSU AN *for* TSU HSI*)* I can hardly wait. Wait I hardly
   can. Can I wait? Hardly. Two days will seem like an eternity.

Scene 2

A LU TE: *(Alone, kneeling in prayer)* Oh, help me, Kuan Yin, Goddess of Mercy,
   to be decorative and to do right. Let me always look young, never more than
   sixteen or seventeen at the *very* most, and let T'ung Chih love me—as much
   as I love him. I can't tell you how much I love him, especially when he wags
   it! I mean his tongue. . . . I think he's very bighearted. And I can't wait until
   he gives it to me . . . his love, I mean. Bless all the concubines, above all Tsu
   An, and keep them out of his favor. Show me the straight path! And keep me
   free from the malicious scandal of the Court. Amen.

Scene 3

A LU TE: *(To* TSU HSI*)* I am willing to wager that another week will find the
   court shivering upon the peony mountain of the summer palace.

TSU HSI: We've no time or desire now for making bets. *(Turning to* LI LIEN
   YING*)* Fan us. Is that you, A Lu Te? Tell us, do, of a place that soothes and
   lulls one.

A LU TE: The summer palace.

TSU HSI: Impossible. The imperial doctors flatly forbid it. Bring us our amethyst
   anemones. We are expecting the Son of Heaven.

A LU TE: Ah, what a dearest he is!

TSU HSI: *(With a quelling glance)* We think you forget yourself. You had better
   withdraw.

A LU TE: He has such strength. One could niche a bodhisattva in his dear dinted
   chin.

TSU HSI: Enough!

   *(*A LU TE *exits.)*

Scene 4

TSU HSI: *(Addressing herself to the ceiling)* O Kuan Yin! If the Son of Heaven were
   to fall for that girl!

LI LIEN YING: I do not consider her at all distinguished.

TSU HSI: It would be a fatal connection and it must never, never be!

Scene 5

(A gong.)

T'UNG CHIH: *(In a voice extinct with boredom)* Here I am, Mother.
TSU HSI: We see life today in the color of mold. The Japanese beetles have attacked our peony mountain . . . but that's the least of our worries.
T'UNG CHIH: I gather you are alluding to A Lu Te? *(He protrudes his tongue)*
TSU HSI: But what can you see in her?
T'UNG CHIH: She suits my feelings.
TSU HSI: That girl is gutter! *(To* LI LIEN YING*)* These Chinese earrings tire us. Take them out.

(LI LIEN YING *removes her earrings.)*

T'UNG CHIH: She saves us from cliché.
TSU HSI: Our eunuchs tell us that you sneak out into the streets at night, patronizing brothels and attending lewd theaters.
T'UNG CHIH: Yes, I contracted a slight catarrh. *(He sneezes)*
TSU HSI: What makes you do it?
T'UNG CHIH: I have been bored.
TSU HSI: Your concubine is perhaps too shy . . . and of the violet persuasion?
T'UNG CHIH: *(Defensively)* That's not a bad thing in a young girl. *(He stalks out)*

Scene 6

TSU HSI: *(To* LI LIEN YING*)* Give us the other sunshade, the jade . . .
LI LIEN YING: The rumor of her betrothal it seems is quite without foundation?
TSU HSI: To my son? Ai ya! Yes . . .
LI LIEN YING: They say she's anything but stupid.
TSU HSI: *(With a start)* I do not know whether intellect is always a blessing. Ah, if only I were a man!
LI LIEN YING: I assure you, it's positively nothing.
TSU HSI: Once men . . . those instruments of delight, engaged me utterly, I was their slave. Now . . . one does not burn one's fingers twice. I have been so bored.
LI LIEN YING: Will this drought ever end, Venerable? The seeds cannot bring forth rice. The flowers wither in the gardens.
TSU HSI: Tonight I will pray to Kuan Yin, Goddess of Mercy, for rain.

(They exit.)

Scene 7

AN TE HAI: *(Wailing)* The Forbidden City has robbed me of my throat, sir, it has deprived me of my voice. Last night during the performance of *The Butterfly Dream* I cawed like a crow.
PRINCE KUNG: Eunuch, stop complaining! Your performance needs a little tightening up, that's all. You should go back to playing the Old Woman in *Ssu Lang Visits His Mother.* That was your forte.
AN TE HAI: No more will the Hu Chin player play for me. No more the Ehr

Hu, the Hu E Chin, the San Hien. No more Sa lo and Ta lo [large and small gongs] and the suna [a wind instrument]. *(Weeping loudly)* No more suna!

PRINCE KUNG: *(Aside)* All eunuchs are detestable, but nothing is worse than a eunuch in despair. *(To* AN TE HAI*)* Tell the Empress that I am here to give her her political science lesson, and I will give you a tip to cheer you up and stop your complaining.

AN TE HAI: There is one thing, Prince Kung. Would you give me your red jade ring?

PRINCE KUNG: My red jade ring? Certainly not!

AN TE HAI: Often have I said to myself, "How happy you would be, An Te Hai, if you had a red jade ring to wear on your thumb."

PRINCE KUNG: Forget it. I would never give anything of such value to a eunuch and least of all to the ugliest eunuch of all.

AN TE HAI: *(Shouting)* I heard that!

PRINCE KUNG: I detest eunuchs! Now tell the Empress I am waiting.

Scene 8

AN TE HAI: What about my tip?

PRINCE KUNG: Do as I say or I'll give you the tip of my boot.

(A voice offstage calls out "Li la." The EMPRESS *enters.)*

TSU HSI: Why do you look so sad, An Te Hai?

AN TE HAI: I begged Prince Kung for his red jade ring, but he flatly refused. It makes me sad when I want something I cannot have.

TSU HSI: Ah yes, we know what it is to have longings. This afternoon we sat on the Terrace of Great Fragrance and thought of the summer palace which the white devils have destroyed. *(Nervously fingering her pearl pendant)* Ah, the summer palace—our early home. Now, we hear, it's nothing but a weed-crowned ruin.

AN TE HAI: Oh yes, Venerable, Prince Kung is waiting to give you your political science lesson at once.

PRINCE KUNG: *(Rising)* We should support whatever the enemy opposes and oppose whatever the enemy supports.

TSU HSI: But can you tell us, Prince Kung, exactly what is a revolution?

PRINCE KUNG: A revolution is not a dinner party, nor writing an essay, nor painting a picture, nor doing embroidery; it cannot be so refined, so leisurely and gentle, so temperate, kind, courteous, restrained, and magnanimous. A revolution is an insurrection, an act of violence by which one class overthrows another.

TSU HSI: We see. It sounds most disagreeable. And what is the best way to stop this revolution?

PRINCE KUNG: The best way to *hinder* this revolution—and I say hinder because in truth a revolution cannot be completely stopped—is to confuse the public so that they cannot tell who are their friends and who are their enemies.

TSU HSI: Is there no other way than that? Is there nothing else we can do?

PRINCE KUNG: The other way is to put chemicals in their food and drinking water. And to addict them to sugar and the milk of cows, butter, cream, and cheeses . . . these will render the people weak and feebleminded.

TSU HSI: Let them eat cake! But how can we put chemicals into their food?

Won't they suspect that we are up to something? We must disguise these chemical poisons cleverly.

PRINCE KUNG: There is no need to disguise the chemical poisons or even conceal their presence if you can convince the people that they fortify the food, kill germs, retard spoilage, or some such nonsense. On the other hand, no such propaganda is necessary with sugar and dairy products. They are so unsatisfying that they increase the appetite that feeds on them, while they kill the taste for other nutritional foods. And remember, revolutions are never begun by fat people.

TSU HSI: Obesity serves our necessity. Revolutions are rather low class, aren't they? Not at all the kind of thing a lady or a gentleman would involve themselves in, are they?

PRINCE KUNG: In a class society, everyone lives as a member of a particular class, and every kind of thinking, without exception, is stamped with the brand of class.

TSU HSI: You mean if the revolution is successful, people won't have any class?

PRINCE KUNG: Exactly.

TSU HSI: Dismal, dismal, dismal. What would become of us?

PRINCE KUNG: Classes struggle, some triumph, others are eliminated. Such is history, such has been the history of civilization for thousands of years.

TSU HSI: Perhaps if we ignore these people, they will go away.

PRINCE KUNG: The enemy will not perish of himself. No one will step down from the stage of history of his own accord.

TSU HSI: You are right, but fortune and flowers do not last forever. Today's wine I'll swallow now. Tomorrow's sorrow I'll swallow tomorrow. I will deal with these revolutionaries. It is a careless rat that chews on a cat's tail.

PRINCE KUNG: Are there any more questions concerning affairs of state, Venerable?

TSU HSI: Yes, Prince Kung, do you think an empress should have affairs?

PRINCE KUNG: What an Empress does at night is her own affair.

TSU HSI: *(Mournfully)* Only women and eunuchs are permitted in the Forbidden City after sunset.

PRINCE KUNG: Your nights are lonely.

TSU HSI: Yes, but perhaps you could fill our afternoons?

PRINCE KUNG: I must decline your most sweet offer. An empress may take lovers and then have them put away with a poisoned cup lest they presume upon or tell of favors received. Is there anything else, venerable?

TSU HSI: There is one other thing, Prince Kung. The red jade ring that you wear on your thumb—may we have it?

PRINCE KUNG: *(Giving the ring to her immediately)* It is yours.

TSU HSI: Thank you. You are dismissed.

(Gong. PRINCE KUNG *exits.)*

Scene 9

*(*LI LIEN YING *enters with several eunuchs and ladies-in-waiting.)*

LIE LIEN YING: Venerable Ancestor, there is a messenger from Chang Chih T'ung, bearing presents.

TSU HSI: *(Her face lighting up)* Bring in the presents.

(He brings in the boxes.)

TSU HSI: *(Gasping)* Jade earrings! *(Holding them up to the light)* See, they are perfect. There is not a flaw in them anywhere. The best jade is perfectly smooth. Carving is used to conceal its imperfections. There is nothing in our collection to equal these jade earrings.

LI LIEN YING: Will the Old Ancestor wear them at once?

TSU HSI: No, we do not look well enough, vital enough at present. We would like to wear these earrings, but not today. *(Holding up a bracelet to the light)* We cannot wear them today. What we should wear today is pink coral. Its color does not clash with tired face and weary eyes.

LI LIEN YING: *(Flattering)* Your Majesty speaks the truth. *(Aside)* His attitude toward precious stones is more in keeping with the beautiful girl he was as a bride than with the old woman he is now. However, vestiges of his beauty remain, and when he is particularly happy, or has slept unusually well, life seems to flow into him, and he captures some of his lost youth.

TSU HSI: We will explain our meaning. You remember that Tsu An, Empress of the Eastern Palace, came here to visit the Western Palace a few days ago?

LI LIEN YING: I remember, Venerable. Something about her wearing apparel had jangled somehow, but I couldn't say exactly what.

TSU HSI: Tsu An is no longer young. There are lines in her face. She looks old. She looked especially old when she came to court the other day—yet she knew no better than to wear jade. But jade is for a happy mood. It is for life and youth and laughter. If an old person or a tired person wears it, that person's age is not only made more apparent, but the jade itself is made to appear lacking in luster. Not only does the jade itself sharply bring out the tired lines, the tired lines in turn deaden the jade. Tsu An's face, between her jade earrings, looked exactly like a piece of decayed wood.

LI LIEN YING: *(Aside)* That is just his way of expressing himself. He did not make this statement necessarily as a criticism of Tsu An, but to make his point about the matter of wearing jade.

TSU HSI: Chang Chih T'ung is a subtle man, a man of excellent taste. He has sent jade because it will soon be summer, when jade is worn.

LI LIEN YING: He knows that jade is for youth, Father. He means to say that you are still youthful.

TSU HSI: Ah, yes, he did. But I will not allow myself to be misled. Take the jade gifts to the Treasure House until I am in a happy mood. I will fondle them even if I never wear them. *(Turning on* A LU TE *and rapping sharply)* That gown is wrong. Remove it immediately. When we are in an unhappy mood bright red is trying to our nerves. Then it does not seem to suit you at all and it irritates us.

A LU TE: *(Remembering the remark about the dress)* Tsu, Tsu, Tsu Hsi, good-bye! *(She exits.)*

LI LIEN YING: You are not quite yourself today, O Ancient Father.

TSU HSI: No, Li Lien, I'm not.

LI LIEN YING: What is wrong, O Restless as a Willow in a Windstorm?

TSU HSI: I keep tossing in my sleep at night. And what's more, I've lost my appetite, I wonder why? I wonder why?

LI LIEN YING: Are there any other symptoms, O Bewitched, Bothered, and Bewildered?

Charles Ludlam & Black-Eyed Susan in
Eunuchs of the Forbidden City (Leandro Katz)

TSU HSI: Yes, I feel a cold chill that runs along my spine all the way from here
  to here. *(She indicates where the chill is)*
LI LIEN YING: May I recommend a massage to Your Majesty? A rubdown with
  a velvet glove . . .
TSU HSI: Anything that will relieve this aching heart of ours.

  (LI LIEN YING rings the gong.)

Scene 10

AN TE HAI: You rang?
LI LIEN YING: His Majesty is not quite himself today. He asked me to recom-
  mend a masseur.
AN TE HAI: I will massage him.

LI LIEN YING: *(Hinting for a tip)* It must be someone with feeling.

AN TE HAI: I have feeling. *(Pushing him aside)* I am the most sensitive eunuch in the Forbidden City.

TSU HSI: *(Languishing on her dais)* Have you come to give me my massage?

AN TE HAI: I have, O Flawless and Dignified.

LI LIEN YING: What about my tip?

AN TE HAI: No need to tip me. I never accept a bribe. I'm as honest as the day is long. My, isn't that a lovely sunset?

TSU HSI: *(Slipping her robe down off her shoulders)* Come in, An Te Hai. Perhaps you can do something for us?

AN TE HAI: I will try, Illustrious Grandfather of Ten Thousand Years. *(He begins to massage her back)*

TSU HSI: You have marvelous hands.

AN TE HAI: *(Sniffing deeply)* Mmmmm, that scent you're wearing smells good. What is it?

TSU HSI: Insect repellent. Do you like it? *(He massages her and she writhes rhythmically)* Mmmmm, ahhh, mmmm, aaaah, mmmm, aaaaah.

TSU HSI and AN TE HAI: Mmmmm, aaaah, heeeee, yaaaaaa, mmmmm, aaaah, heeeeee, yaaaaaaaa, *etc.*

TSU HSI: We have been so bored. Everything is so boring.

AN TE HAI: Boredom is the absence of yum-yum.

TSU HSI: Yum-yum?

AN TE HAI: Yum-yum.

TSU HSI: Oh, pooh! What can a eunuch do?

AN TE HAI: Let me satisfy you the unique way. *(Aside)* Hope I don't muff it. *(He eats her out)* Slurp! Slurp!

TSU HSI: Enough! You eunuchs are strictly for vegetarians. A queen needs a piece of meat once in a while. Why do they castrate you guys, anyway?

AN TE HAI: I don't think of myself as castrated. I think of myself as extremely well circumcised.

TSU HSI: That's funny, you don't look Jewish. We are going to issue an edict forbidding the castration of eunuchs over forty-five. Where is our Imperial Seal? *(She kneels on all fours and searches for the seal among the embroidered pillows on her dais)*

AN TE HAI: It is now the hour of the dog. I have found the Imperial Seal, Father.

TSU HSI: Give it to us.

AN TE HAI: Give it to you, O Worshipful and Illustrious?

TSU HSI: Yes, give it to us.

AN TE HAI: Are you sure you want me to give it to you, O Dutiful and Dignified?

TSU HSI: I said give it to us!

(AN TE HAI rams the seal up her ass.)

TSU HSI: *(Screaming)* Not in our ass! In our coozie!

AN TE HAI: Your unworthy slave begs forgiveness. It was an understandable mistake. They are only two inches apart. *(He pulls out the Seal and shoves it in again.* TSU HSI *achieves an Oriental orgasm)* It is done.

TSU HSI: *(Looking at* AN TE HAI *and glowing)* Strange, I never saw your beauty before this moment. You will be rewarded for this, An Te Hai. Here is the red jade ring that Prince Kung wore on his thumb. Wear it on your thumb now, An Te Hai.

AN TE HAI: Ten thousand thank yous, O Magnanimous and Merciful Ancient Grandfather.

TSU HSI: All of China is mine. I can afford to be generous. If there is anything else your heart desires, name it and we will make it yours.

AN TE HAI: There is one thing, O Unbending and Inscrutable Goddess of Mercy.

TSU HSI: Name it, An Te Hai, and it is yours.

AN TE HAI: I have longed for years to revisit the town of my birth. But as you know there is a law that no eunuch shall ever leave the Forbidden City.

TSU HSI: Where were you born?

AN TE HAI: In Levit Tung.

TSU HSI: Ah, a happy coincidence. We have ordered the Imperial Yellow Silk from weavers a few miles down the Yangtze from Levit Tung. Last year the silk they sent was unusable because the color was too dark. You will go to inspect the silk and visit the city of your birth at the same time. Take an entourage of eunuchs on my barge down the river. And remember, the silk must be *pale* yellow. Here, take the Emperor's robe and be sure of a perfect match.

AN TE HAI: Myriad thanks, O Elegant, Sedate, and Frequent Phoenix. *(He takes the Imperial Robe and starts out, is stopped by* LI LIEN YING*)*

LI LIEN YING: So you have curried favor with the Empress of the Western Palace.

AN TE HAI: So you had curried shrimp for lunch. I can smell it on your breath.

LI LIEN YING: And when I asked for a tip, you stiffed me. Have you forgotten that it was I who recommended you to the Ancient One?

AN TE HAI: How dare you address me without kowtowing! Can't you see that I am carrying the Imperial Robe and therefore I am due the same respect as the Emperor who wears it? Watch out or I'll have you beheaded. *(He pushes* LI LIEN YING *out of the way and exits)*

Scene 11

LI LIEN YING: Making bedfellow of serpent no guarantee against snakebite. Worry not—what is to be is to be—as inscrutable fates very busy arranging program.

(A clap of thunder is heard.)

TSU HSI: Li Lien Ying!

LI LIEN YING: Yes, Father.

TSU HSI: Listen . . . thunder—there's going to be a storm. *(Thunder sounds again and then rain)* Look, it's raining. My prayers were answered.

LI LIEN YING: Venerable, you have brought an end to the drought. It is as if Buddha himself had intervened. From now on I shall call you "Old Buddha."

TSU HSI: Come with us to the Imperial Wardrobe. We want to dress ourselves as Kuan Yin, Goddess of Mercy.

LI LIEN YING: The Old Buddha's wish is my command.

(They exit. Curtain.)

ACT III

Scene 1

TSU AN: The flowers are wet, the moon dim. Tonight you must go to your love.

A LU TE: O Motherly and Restful, I am so nervous. Will T'ung Chih love me?

TSU AN: He sent you a fan, did he not? Don't worry. I have arranged everything.

A LU TE: Why do you do this for me?

TSU AN: I am alone in the Pavilion of Discarded Lovers. Perhaps you will bear a male child and I will mind him for you.

A LU TE: Did you ever have a child of your own?

TSU AN: Once long ago . . . but never mind that . . . you go to him.

(A LU TE exits.)

Scene 2

A LU TE: Off with these slippers. Off with my stockings. I want to feel the wet grass on my feet. Psssst! Psssst!

T'UNG CHIH: Be quiet, crickets. I have been sleepless upon my embroidered pillows. (Standing) I stand and watch the moonlight creep through the bamboo gate across the court. I cannot sleep.

A LU TE: Psssst! Psssst! Pssst!

T'UNG CHIH: Eunuch. Shut that cricket up!

LI LIEN YING: That is no cricket, O Son of Heaven. (He draws back a screen revealing A LU TE)

T'UNG CHIH: A Lu Te!

A LU TE: My heart was stirred to its depths by the fan you sent to remind me of our love. Listen, someone is playing on a flute of jade.

T'UNG CHIH: What do you want?

A LU TE: It is time, Lord of Ten Thousand Years.

T'UNG CHIH: Time for what?

A LU TE: It is time for you to pluck my cherry blossom.

T'UNG CHIH: Pluck your cherry blossom? What do you mean by that?

A LU TE: It is time for you to drink the wine in my cup.

T'UNG CHIH: What wine? What cup? What are you talking about?

A LU TE: It is time for your horse to enter my valley.

T'UNG CHIH: (Aside to LI LIEN YING) Is she crazy or is she drunk?

LI LIEN YING: (Aside to A LU TE) Remove your robe. That should turn him on.

A LU TE: (Slipping her robe down over her shoulders) It is time for you to find yourself in me and I in you.

T'UNG CHIH: What do you want? Speak plain Chinese.

A LU TE: I have come to make love. Roll in hay. Get laid. Do the business. Fuckee fuckee. Get it?

T'UNG CHIH: I've never done anything of this kind before. Are you a eunuch?

A LU TE: No, something better. Something special. (She climbs on top of him) Feel anything?

T'UNG CHIH: No.

A LU TE: *(Kissing him)* Feel anything now?

T'UNG CHIH: Nothing.

A LU TE: *(Rubbing her body against him)* Anything?

T'UNG CHIH: Nothing.

LI LIEN YING: *(Aside to A LU TE)* Try this on him.

A LU TE: What is it?

LI LIEN YING: It's a special preparation the eunuchs know to assist in the art of love, where all else fails. It's called a popper.

A LU TE: How do you use it?

LI LIEN YING: Break it like this and shove it under his nose.

A LU TE: Try this, O Lord of Ten Thousand Years. *(She breaks the popper and shoves it under his nose)*

(T'UNG CHIH gets a rush, leaps up, stands on his head, musters all his strength, and then collapses, unable to consummate the tryst.)

A LU TE: *(Complaining)* Why aren't the nightingales singing? And why is there no moon?

T'UNG CHIH: But there is, dearest. A delicate new one—for both of us.

A LU TE: I mean a proper moon.

T'UNG CHIH: My dear A Lu Te, I see nothing improper about this one.

A LU TE: I meant a full moon, darling.

T'UNG CHIH: I don't know why you should prefer it to be full. A full moon is perhaps rather vulgar?

A LU TE: Vulgar?

T'UNG CHIH: Just a little.

(LI LIEN YING draws the screen. There is the sound of coming.)

LI LIEN YING: It is done!

Scene 3

AN TE HAI: *(Rudely)* Kowtow, Prince, I am carrying the Emperor's robe.

PRINCE KUNG: *(Kowtowing unwillingly)* Kowtow to a eunuch!

AN TE HAI: Look, Prince, your red jade ring. I am wearing it on *my* thumb now. That which you would not hand over to me directly, I have received through the Empress. *(He flashes the ring)*

PRINCE KUNG: *(Enraged)* I swear to you, An Te Hai, that before another moon has passed, I will have caused you to be put to death.

AN TE HAI: I'm not afraid of you. I am the Empress's favorite and she protects me. I really think you'd do better to become a eunuch—it's the only way to get ahead! *(He exits, laughing)*

Scene 4

PRINCE KUNG: I will have revenge on that eunuch . . . but how?

LI LIEN YING: *(Coming out of hiding)* An opportunity to pay him back may present itself when you least expect it, or even when you no longer have any interest in the prospect of reprisal—for time plays such tricks on us all—only then you must be ready for it and worthy of executing it. That is what is to be hoped for if you are really serious. Revenge is a dish best savored cold. *(He exits)*

Scene 5

TSU AN: *(Entering)* Is the little beast gone?

PRINCE KUNG: He must be stopped from traveling in the Emperor's barge. It will give him license to riot, loot, and debauch every city along the Yangtze between here and Levit Tung.

TSU AN: By night and day he wrongs me. Refuses to bring my tea, carry my messages, or perform *any* of the duties required of a eunuch.

PRINCE KUNG: Yesterday he had my cook banished to the provinces for "failing" in respect to the Imperial Swans.

LI LIEN YING: Give him enough rope and he will hang himself.

PRINCE KUNG: O Motherly and Restful, I must request your signature on an edict for his execution.

TSU AN: *(Frightened)* His execution? Sign an edict? I couldn't, not without Tsu Hsi. I've never done it before. My penmanship is so poor.

PRINCE KUNG: You are an Empress. It is not right that you should be afraid of a eunuch. T'ung Chih is the Emperor. He will back you up.

TSU AN: Oh, how could I . . . I am afraid.

PRINCE KUNG: The power is yours. Use it or lose it. It was not the intention of the late Emperor that she should rule alone. Did he not appoint you Co-Regent? Soon you must both give up your power to T'ung Chih. One edict in all your reign . . . is that too much . . . for an Empress?

TSU AN: Yes . . . I am an Empress . . . I can say yes and I can say no. That's what it means to be an Empress. I can say yes and I can say no. *(She signs)*

(They exit.)

Scene 6

LI LIEN YING: I have come as an emissary to bring you some tea.

A LU TE: I don't want tea, thanks.

LI LIEN YING: The Emperor has just arrived with an octet of concubines like cabbage roses, so large, so pink, so fresh.

A LU TE: There's going to be a crush. I'll sleep in my own pavilion tonight. *(She exits)*

Scene 7

VOICE: *(Offstage)* Li la! Li la!

(AN TE HAI kowtows.)

TSU HSI: *(Entering, in a vile mood)* In love! Ha! Married to that girl. Ha! Ha!

AN TE HAI: Woman is an object that always makes a man ridiculous. If she is ugly—oh, what a misery! If she is beautiful—oh, what a danger! And whether he takes her or leaves her, he always repents his actions.

TSU HSI: I don't know what the Forbidden City is coming to. I was leaning on my windowsill and I saw some young men who appeared to be bathing without false modesty of *any* kind.

AN TE HAI: Eunuchs?

TSU HSI: No, they *weren't* eunuchs.

AN TE HAI: How dreadful!

TSU HSI: I'm sure if I looked, it was quite involuntary.

AN TE HAI: Women amuse me at times. But I've never loved one.

TSU HSI: You have never loved any woman?

AN TE HAI: Never.

TSU HSI: It's a pleasure to know a man of really advanced morals.

AN TE HAI: I can safely say I prefer the society of other men to that of women.

TSU HSI: That's nice of you. *(Angry again)* It made my skin crawl to see him in the custody of a wife.

AN TE HAI: Sssssh! For shame! I admire the Son of Heaven. He wears his degradation as though it were an order. But here he comes.

TSU HSI: Today you leave for Levit Tung. Farewell, An Te Hai.

AN TE HAI: Farewell, Motherly and Auspicious, Orthodox and Blissful, Prosperous and All-Nourishing, Radiant, Sedate, Dignified, Flawless, Long-Lived, Gaudy, Dutiful, Reverend, Praiseworthy, Inscrutable, Worshipful, Indescribably Illustrious, Old Buddha, Lord of Ten Thousand Years!

TSU HSI: Farewell, Chief Eunuch.

(AN TE HAI exits grandly.)

Scene 8

T'UNG CHIH: Tomorrow, I will be Emperor, Mother. It is time for you to put away your spies, yield the great Imperial Seal, promise never to decree again, and employ yourself henceforth with flowers, caged singing birds, your favorite dogs . . .

TSU HSI: *(Dropping her fan)* But why?

T'UNG CHIH: You are an obstacle to progress. I want to bring a new nation into being, modeled on the West. If we resist, the foreigners will carve up China. I have had a telephone installed in my pavilion on the Island of Fulfilled Desires.

TSU HSI: Railroads, armies, wars, telephones, television, Muzak, pay toilets, automobiles, Blimpie bases, air pollution! No! No! No! I love my people. They are my subjects. For two hundred years the Dragon Throne will be ours.

T'UNG CHIH: It is time for reforms.

TSU HSI: I spit on reforms! You have betrayed your sacred ancestors! Earlier societies have failed. We have defeated the Yellow Headcloth, the Grain Thieves, the White Lotus Society. But these Righteous Harmony Fists or Righteous Harmony Societies—I will support these Boxer bandits and send them to attack all foreigners at the Western Silk Depot.

T'UNG CHIH: Ten thousand, ten thousand times: there should be no fighting with the foreigners!

TSU HSI: *(Turning livid with rage)* What kind of talk is this?

T'UNG CHIH: It is suicide to support the rebels. On the seventeenth of the fifth moon, the Boxers rioted, and with the excuse of burning churches, set fire to many places and looted the district outside Chien Nen, the Front Gate of the City, the East and West Lanes of Sachet Bags, the Pearl Market, the Street of the Great Wickets, the First and Second Lanes of the Lang Fang, and the Coal Market Street—all these busy places were burned to the ground. Dead bodies filled the streets. The cry of distress from the people shook the earth.

TSU HSI: If they could do all that by themselves, then they should surely be able to oust the foreigners with the support of our soldiers.

T'UNG CHIH: Fortunately for China, I am Emperor now. Your mad plans will go unheeded. Good night, mother.

TSU HSI: *(Sweetly)* Going out again?

T'UNG CHIH: Yes.

TSU HSI: *(Butter wouldn't melt in her mouth)* In disguise again?

T'UNG CHIH: Yes. A last fling, you might say.

TSU HSI: Enjoy yourself. And take Li Lien Ying with you. I'll feel better if you are not alone.

T'UNG CHIH: I will. Good night, Motherly and Auspicious. *(He exits)*

Scene 9

TSU HSI: Tonight I will be more auspicious than motherly. *(She rings the gong)*

Scene 10

LI LIEN YING: The Old Buddha rang.

TSU HSI: Yes. Accompany the Son of Heaven to his favorite restaurant, theater, and brothel tonight.

LI LIEN YING: Yes, Old Buddha.

TSU HSI: And would you do us a little favor?

LI LIEN YING: Yes, Old Buddha.

TSU HSI: When the Son of Heaven has eaten and laughed and lusted and called for his steaming hot towel to wipe his face and hands . . .

LI LIEN YING: Yes, Old Buddha . . .

TSU HSI: Before giving the warm towel to your master, pass it over the ulcerated face of a man with smallpox.

LI LIEN YING: Yes, Old Buddha.

(They exit. Curtain.)

ACT IV

Scene 1

LI LIEN YING: Bring out your spiciest vittles and a few of your daughters. *(Aside)* It's the Imperial Taxman.

AN TE HAI: *(Entering formally with the* MAGISTRATES, *attended by* LI LIEN YING *and* A LU TE*)* Good Ting Pao Chen, good Tsi Nan Fu, when you bring in the garments, jewels, and foodstuffs—I am exacting as taxes—be sure to pile them

neatly. I do not want the garments wrinkled or the necklaces tangled or the
rice bags to spring a leak. Good Ting Pao Chen, good Tsi Nan Fu.

MAGISTRATES: *(Running out, yelling)* Robbers! Robbers!

AN TE HAI: *(To* LI LIEN YING*)* Fan us. *(To* A LU TE*)* Ah, why so blue, my
wanton little Won Ton?

A LU TE: You promised me dinner. But I haven't seen the chopsticks let alone
the rice.

AN TE HAI: Do you want to eat here or do you want to eat out?

A LU TE: I want to eat here.

AN TE HAI: I want to eat you out!

LI LIEN YING: Pardon me for mentioning it, but have you checked the color
of the Imperial Silk yet? That was the purpose of this journey.

AN TE HAI: Why don't you go out and get us a couple of two-thousand-year-old
eggs, and make sure they're fresh. (LI LIEN YING *exits)* Ah, why so blue, my
little jejune jade? Come, smoke the pipe of golden dreams.

A LU TE: I need . . . I need . . .

AN TE HAI: Your eyes spit fire. Your cheeks grow red as beef. Out with it! Out
with it!

A LU TE: Oh, spare my blushes, but I mean a husband.

AN TE HAI: *(Sticking out his tongue and wiggling it obscenely)* Let me satisfy you the
unique way.

A LU TE: If a concubine does not bear a male child she must be *milked* every
day for her mother's milk, which the Empress drinks as part of her beauty
ritual. Oh, help me, An Te Hai, help me! I must bear a male child.

AN TE HAI: So the Son of Heaven can't cut the mustard, eh?

A LU TE: You are obscenity all over with your sexless dugs hanging like gourds
under your yellow tunic.

AN TE HAI: I will not be seen in women's company in public.

A LU TE: Ah, strange aversion!

AN TE HAI: No, I'm for women's company in private.

A LU TE: *(A ray of hope)* Look, there's a full moon!

AN TE HAI: That's not a full moon, that's a gibbous moon.

A LU TE: What's a gibbous moon?

AN TE HAI: It's a moon that's not quite full and a little lopsided.

*(As he stands there, she leaps into his arms and wraps her legs around his waist. He
pulls a silken cloth over their heads.)*

A LU TE: If on earth there's a heaven of bliss, it is this! It is this! It is this!

*(*PRINCE KUNG *enters with the* MAGISTRATES, *who seize* AN TE HAI.)*

TING PAO CHEN: Impoverished by your exaction of taxes and outraged by your
Imperial Masquerade, I sent a plea to Prince Kung.

TSI NAN FU: The Prince in turn sent me this order for your decapitation, signed
by the Empress of the Eastern Palace.

AN TE HAI: That edict is from the wrong side of the palace. It's the Empress
of the Western Palace who counts.

PRINCE KUNG: Here is the Imperial Seal. *(He shows the seal on the document)*

AN TE HAI: No, no, do not cut my head from my body. I have often acted such
scenes in the plays at court. But this is not the theater. This is real life! Spare
me and I will give you the largest emerald in the world cut in the shape of
a man's cock. The concubines have made it shine with fondling. They call it

the lonely emerald. I will give it to you if you let me go. *(Kneeling)* There are no peacocks in Shantung. I will give you black peacocks with opal eyes or white peacocks with ruby claws. Blind they are, these peacocks of mine. But their blood, oh their blood! If a man should drink their blood, he would fall into a deep sleep and dream the dream of fulfilled desire. To drink their blood is to sup on paradise. There are eunuchs addicted to the blood of peacocks.

PRINCE KUNG: Get down on your knees. Pull his pigtail to hold him steady and expose his neck.

AN TE HAI: No, no! *(To* A LU TE*)* Send word to the Empress of the Western Palace. She will spare me.

PRINCE KUNG *(Stopping her)* You cannot get to the Empress to tell her your wrongs. Prepare the huge double-edged ax.

AN TE HAI: She will give you her costliest robe of gold-incrusted satin embroidered in phoenixes of every shade and hue, her famous collar of sixty thousand pearls of *every* perfect shape and color; the shields she wears upon her fingernails—gold, set with jade, Burmese rubies, and Indian sapphires. Slippers woven from the hair of dead women stolen from their coffins on moonless nights, headdresses made from the tiny feathers of the kingfisher's breast, and from the wings of butterflies, a double dragon of gold, the Pearl of Omnipotence with coral flames, the golden bells from the porcelain Pagoda of Mind-Nurture. The Empress can refuse me nothing. All this is yours in exchange for my life. Ivory, topaz, moonstones, sapphires, and chrysolites, beryls and chrysoprases. Rubies, sardonyx, hyacinth stones and stones of chalcedony. Could you use a snuffbox? The Empress has one you might like—it is a huge, hollow, ear-shaped pearl with a ruby stopper. Take it. I will get it for you. I would offer diamonds but the Empress never wears them.

TSI NAN FU: The dynastic laws of the Manchus do not allow the palace eunuchs to leave the capital except when accompanying the Empresses. The object of this excursion was to check on the color of the Imperial Silk yet you have usurped the prerogatives of the Son of Heaven, traveling along the canals in gilded barges under the dragon-embroidered canopies of the Imperial Yellow, impoverishing us with taxes. You have eaten out the twats of our virgins and sucked the cocks of our young boys until they have shot off their hot loads of come into your mouth and rammed their stiff little rods up your backside. For these sacrileges we must decapitate the eunuch who usurped the pomp of the Son of Heaven.

AN TE HAI: It was heaven. For six hundred years, the Sons of Heaven have been born sterile. I am no eunuch. I am Hung *(He whips out his schlong),* Father of Emperors. The secret weapon of the concubines!

(The ax falls and cuts off his dick.)

TING PAO CHEN: He has cast doubt upon the legitimacy of the entire dynasty.

TSI NAN FU: It is forbidden to make any comment whatsoever on the conduct of the Imperial Family. All rumors must go undenied and unconfirmed. Let's hang him naked in a public place and let history write itself.

(They exit.)

Scene 2

(The throne room of the Forbidden City.)

*(*TSU HSI *and* TSU AN *are seated on the Dragon Thrones, the others are kneeling in audience.* T'UNG CHIH *lies on a couch.)*

T'UNG CHIH: Mother, my face itches!

TSU HSI: The Son of Heaven has had the good fortune to contract smallpox. His attendants have dressed him in the Ceremonial Robes of Longevity and he awaits his journey beyond the Yellow Springs here in our presence with his face turned to the south.

PRINCE KUNG: The King's face gives grace.

T'UNG CHIH: My face itches. *(He begins to scratch it)*

TSU HSI: Do not scratch yourself, you will cause sloughing.

A LU TE: What is "sloughing"?

TSU AN: Sloughing is when parts of the body begin to crumble away.

T'UNG CHIH: But my face itches!

TSU HSI: Bring some opium.

(A gong is sounded. LI LIEN YING *brings forth a tray with* AN TE HAI's *cock on it.)*

LI LIEN YING: An Te Hai is dead. The Old Buddha will regard his head. *(He uncovers the cock)*

ALL: Ecccht! *(They turn their heads)*

PRINCE KUNG: Villainous even in death!

TSU HSI: He was not villainous! He was a man who knew he was lost before he was born. *(Whimsically)* Such a strange, bored, and beautiful face he had . . . though he was harrowingly thin. *(Laughing)* I sometimes miss his clever imitations of birdcalls and animal noises. *(Joylessly)* Growl! Arf-arf! Cock-a-doodle-doo! Meow! Hee-haw! I shall not come upon his like again.

PRINCE KUNG: He died as the water clock was dripping midday.

TSU HSI: I will mourn him in Chinese fashion—in white.

TSU AN: I believe you grieve the death of this eunuch more than you do your son's.

TSU HSI: *(Referring to the cock)* Take him away. Let the concubines see him and offer their cherry blossoms to his memory.

TSU AN: Sister, this is immoral. Your violation of rites will provoke scandals.

TSU HSI: Let morality be a comfort to you, Tsu An. When women cease to attract men, they usually turn to morality as a last recourse. It is time to think of the successor to the Dragon Throne.

TSU AN: A Lu Te is the Emperor's favorite.

T'UNG CHIH: The itch! The itch!

TSU HSI: A rather unfortunate union, which we in the family would prefer to forget.

TSU AN: She is with child. We must wait and see if she bears a male child.

TSU HSI: If! If! If! If *ifs* were male children, you would rule China. You have never even signed an edict in your life.

TSU AN: *(Bravely)* I signed the edict to behead the profane eunuch An Te Hai.

TSU HSI: *(Stung)* You?

TSU AN: His behavior was a disgrace, Prince Kung said so, and I have been insulted by the little beast once too often.

TSU HSI: Prince Kung?

TSU AN: I am an empress too! I am the Empress of the Eastern Palace, am I not?

TSU HSI: Traitors!

TSU AN: *(Backing down)* Oh, don't say that, Sister. I have always loved you—in spite of everything. . . .

TSU HSI: Aarrrrgh!

TSU AN: Let me prove it. Here, look at this. *(Producing a yellowed scroll)* This edict was given to me by our husband, the Son of Heaven. It says I can have you beheaded at any time if I feel that you overstep your share of our Co-Regency. I've had it all these years. I've never used it, have I? *(TSU HSI is shaken)* As further proof of my devotion and loyalty, look! *(She burns the document)* There, I've burned it. Isn't that proof that I would never betray you?

PRINCE KUNG: *(Leaping up)* No!

TSU HSI: Seize him and hustle him out. No Prince may rise until we dismiss him. Prince Kung will be stripped of all honors—especially the rights of succession. *(GUARDS take PRINCE KUNG out)* Prince Kung will undergo the five punishments: cutting off the hands *(Scream off; severed hands are thrown onstage from the wings)*, cutting off the feet *(Scream as before; feet fly on)*, cutting off the nose to spite the face *(As before, with the nose)*, castration *(Ditto)*, and death *(Gurgle off)*.

Scene 3

TSU AN: I love you, Orchid. Tell me that you love me. Have you forgotten your first day in the Forbidden City and your bubble bath? How nervous you were that you would not be selected? All our dreams have come true, Orchid. Although not quite the way we thought they would. Everything turns out for the best just like in the *I Ching.*

TSU HSI: I remember. Sakota, forgive me if I have been unjust. *(To A LU TE)* You, accompany your lord and master to his pavilion. *(T'UNG CHIH exits on litter, followed by A LU TE)* Li Lien Ying, it is a great pity that people do not have the good taste to die when they have outlived their usefulness.

LI LIEN YING: *(Chuckling)* Yes, Old Buddha.

TSU HSI: Ah, turn your head away when you laugh. Your breath is foul.

LI LIEN YING: It's my teeth, Old Buddha. *(He laughs and turns his head away)*

TSU HSI: *(Aside)* Here is a powder made from the black lotus whose blossoms wave in the lost jungles of Gang Bang, where none but the numbskulled priests of Num Nuts dwell. This powder strikes dead all who taste it. It's called monosodium glutamate. I will put some of this on some sweet and pungent pork and bring it to Tsu An.

Scene 4

TSU AN: Well, say something. Have you nothing to say? Speak, speak, I cannot bear the silence. *(TSU HSI takes TSU AN in her arms)* You pounce and you have me! The excitement is unbearable. Yet you bear it with this discipline of which you are the mistress. You bird! You eagle! You vulture! You phoenix! Creature of flaming blood!

TSU HSI: Sweet captive, you will find I can be cruel.

TSU AN: And I patient.

TSU HSI: There is no room for you here anymore.

TSU AN: I am your own flesh and blood. Ah, but I understand everything now. When T'ung Chih is healed, we will go away from here to the palace at Jehol.

TSU HSI: The palace at Jehol was destroyed by foreigners.

TSU AN: Or the summer palace.

TSU HSI: The summer palace too.

TSU AN: The summer palace too?

T'UNG CHIH: *(An agonized cry, off)* Mother . . . Motherly and Auspicious!

TSU AN: Why do you look at me like that? . . . I can't bear your eyes.

TSU HSI: Please, do not think I hate you. You have no need to fear me.

TSU AN: Orchid . . . Orchid . . .

T'UNG CHIH: *(As before)* Motherly and Auspicious!

TSU AN: T'ung Chih is dying. . . . You, you have destroyed him.

TSU HSI: Yes, of course I destroyed him. I destroyed the infant to create the boy. I destroyed the boy to create the man. And now I destroy the man to create an empire. His end will be excruciating, protracted, agonizing, perfect.

T'UNG CHIH: *(As before)* Motherly and Peaceful!

TSU AN: You have reduced me to helplessness, powerlessness. I am weak, sick, ruined.

TSU HSI: No, no. Here, I have brought you a light dinner: rice cakes, sweet and pungent pork, Mu Goo Gai Pan, Chicken Chow Mein, and a fortune cookie. And remember, many men swallow, but few men chew. Good night, Tsu An, you are no use to anyone anymore.

TSU AN: You say I am of no use to anyone. But I am of use to you. Make a trophy of me, make a living example of your power.

(In one catlike scratch, TSU HSI *tears off* TSU AN*'s robe)*

TSU AN: Motherly and Auspicious?

T'UNG CHIH: *(As before)* Motherly and Auspicious!

TSU HSI: Yes, Motherly and Peaceful?

T'UNG CHIH: *(As before)* Motherly and Peaceful!

TSU AN: For the first time in my life, I am not afraid. *(Winces with pain)* I am dying, China. *(She dies, elaborately)*

TSU HSI: *(Stooping over Tsu An and sucking her teat, then spitting and wiping her mouth)* O Motherly and Peaceful, your milk, it bitter!

Scene 5

LI LIEN YING: The Son of Heaven is dead, Old Buddha. *(Seeing* TSU AN*)* And the Empress of the Eastern Palace too!

TSU HSI: I have struck off the heads of the tallest poppies in my garden.

LI LIEN YING: There is none like you under heaven. You are not male or female, Majesty, but more than either, greater than both. Will you dress yourself now, Father?

(A LU TE, *obviously pregnant, carries in makeup on a tray.)*

Scene 6

TSU HSI: We are always very particular about our appearance. Everything must be of the very best. You understand that widows are not supposed to wear powder or rouge but in our position, we must use it in spite of custom, in order that our complexion will not clash with our gown. This powder for the face is a mixture of rice powder and lead. We have been told that very poor qualities of powder have a great amount of lead in them. Sometimes this makes the face very black. It would be an evil thing if our face were to turn black in the midst of an important audience, would it not?

(A LU TE laughs.)

TSU HSI: You! *(Pointing at A LU TE with her two little fingers)* Why do you laugh?

A LU TE: *(Apologetically)* The thought of the dignified and sedate Old Buddha appearing before her ministers in a black face amused me.

TSU HSI: Laughter does not become the widow of the Son of Heaven. *(Reaching into a little box)* Here, take this silken cord.

(A LU TE, delighted, tries the cord on around her neck.)

LI LIEN YING: *(Aside)* When the silken cord is presented, the recipient must hang himself.

A LU TE: *(Quickly removing the cord)* What will people think?

TSU HSI: People always think what they are told to think. And I never make war on the dead. I will issue a decree calling you "the filial, wise, excellent queen, who governed her actions by the laws of Heaven, and whose life added luster to the teachings of the sages." Your grief has not allowed you to survive your Imperial Consort.

A LU TE: Oh, your manners were always so perfect. But a golden bed cannot cure the sick, and good manners cannot produce a good man.

TSU HSI: Only two kinds of men are good: buried and unborn. But why speak to you? It is probable that we shall not hear of you again from this moment to the end of time, and that when the great filigree iron gates are once closed on you, you will never issue therefrom into this little world of history. In the future you will request permission before laughing. *(Looking in the mirror again)* Our rouge is composed of the petals of roses ground into a thick paste and dried in the sun. *(She applies rouge)* Gray hair does not look well with the Imperial headdress. It is not that we are vain, but that it is necessary we always look our best. For this reason we dye our hair. *(Applying a disgusting black paste to her hair, she sighs)* If only we could find some hair dye that would not damage our hair and would not blacken the scalp.

LI LIEN YING: I can find such dye for Your Majesty. They have marvelous things in foreign countries. I have heard that they change the color of the hair at will. We could send away for some French hair dyes.

TSU HSI: How long would I have to wait for these dyes?

A LU TE: *(Touching her pregnant belly thoughtfully)* It would require about a month to procure the dyes from France.

TSU HSI: A month is so little in a lifetime. If you really believe we can manage it, we are willing to try.

LI LIEN YING: Are you expecting a visitor today, Venerable?

TSU HSI: So many people we are told are lacking in self-respect. They are careful of their appearance when they are where others can see them. We are careful too, but we are careful even when we are not seen. *(She goes behind a stage curtain on a tiny stage)*

A LU TE: *(To* LI LIEN YING*)* What kind of play is this?

LI LIEN YING:

Pages full of unlikely words
Handfuls of hot bitter tears
They call the author a silly fool
Because they know not what he means

(A gong is sounded. LI LIEN YING *draws back the curtain revealing an enormous lotus bud. The lotus bud opens, revealing* TSU HSI *elaborately dressed as Kuan Yin, Goddess of Mercy.)*

TSU HSI: All one family—under Heaven all are one.

A LU TE: O Goddess of Mercy! Goddess of Mercy!

End

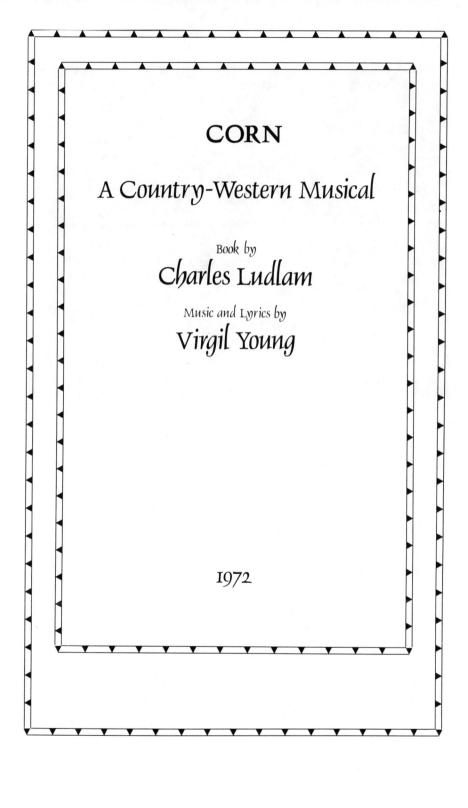

CORN

A Country-Western Musical

Book by
Charles Ludlam

Music and Lyrics by
Virgil Young

1972

Lola Pashalinski & Bill Vehr in *Corn* (Les Carr)

Cast of Characters

PAW HATFIELD
RUBEN
MOE } *his sons*
MAW McCOY
RACHEL
MELANIE } *her daughters*
LOLA LOLA, *a country-western singer*
DUDE GREASEMAN, *her agent*
THE LUCKY STARS, *her musical group*
AUNT PRISCILLA, *an old faith healer*

ACT I

Scene 1: THE LUCKY STARS.

LUCKY STARS: (Sing "Hot Time in Hicksville")
There's a Gal Who's Become a Big Country-Western Star,
She was born back home in Hicksville, but that most folks don't know,
She made it big in Nashville singin' in Honky-Tonk bars,
Now she's goin' back to her hometown to give 'em a free show.

(Chorus)
Well there's gonna be a hot time in Hicksville,
Run tell everybody I said so,
Take down that scarecrow and put up a stage,
Lola Lola and The Lucky Stars are givin' a free show.

Well Lola's gonna find the old folks pretty much the same,
The Hatfields and McCoys, they are still fightin',
Ma McCoy is still makin' home remedies for pain,
And Paw Hatfield is still a-makin' home-brewed white lightnin'.

But with fightin' and a-feudin' the kids do not abide,
Yes it's different with the younger generation,
On both sides of the fence the kids are seein' eye to eye,
And in the end there's gonna be a surprise celebration.

(Repeat chorus)

LUCKY STAR 1: Well now, let's bring her out here where y'all c'n meet 'er. Here she is, Miss Country Sunshine herself, happy-go-lucky . . .
LUCKY STAR 2: Happy-go-lucky!
LUCKY STAR 1: Don't fence her in . . .
LUCKY STAR 2: Don't fence her in!
LUCKY STAR 1: Effervescent . . .
LUCKY STAR 2: Effer . . . effer . . . What you said!
LUCKY STAR 1: Smilin' Lola Lola!

Scene 2: THE LUCKY STARS, LOLA LOLA.

(The curtain rises revealing a billboard with a huge airbrush portrait of Lola Lola, in 1940s cowgirl clothes, advertising the Grand Ole Opry. A tiny LOLA LOLA *enters and stands in front of the poster Lola Lola, which dwarfs her. She hangs her head.)*

LUCKY STAR 2: She ain't smilin'.

LUCKY STAR 1: Hey, what's the matter, Lola Lola?

LOLA LOLA: Ah, boys, I'm down. I got a feelin' called the blues. I'm afraid I'm gettin' too commercial.

LUCKY STAR 2: But you're big.

LUCKY STAR 1: That's right, you're big.

LOLA LOLA: *(Tearing down the poster of herself)* Yeah, I'm big. But I ain't *that* big. Unless a country singer stays close to her roots, she's just another pop-art product, like old Kentucky recipe frozen TV dinners. We gotta keep country music country.

LUCKY STAR 1: We've got a big national tour comin' up.

LOLA LOLA: I'm sorry, boys, but I ain't goin' on the big national tour.

LUCKY STAR 1: You ain't?

LOLA LOLA: No, I ain't.

BOTH LUCKY STARS: Where are ya goin'?

LOLA LOLA: *(Sings "I'm Goin' Home")*

(Chorus)

I'm goin' home,
Take me back to the hills of Tennessee
I'm goin' home,
Bring back memories and dreams,
I'm goin' home to the country.

Didn't cry on nobody's shoulder,
The day I left behind past years,
Thought I'd take the path that's golden,
But a body needs more than money and cheers.

(Repeat chorus)

LUCKY STAR 2: Does the Dude know about this?

LOLA LOLA: No, he don't. But he's gonna find out. Because I'm goin' to his office to tell him right now.

LUCKY STAR 1: *(To the audience)* You folks can come along, too, if you like.

Scene 3: LOLA LOLA, THE LUCKY STARS, DUDE GREASEMAN.

LOLA LOLA: Dude, I'm goin' home.

DUDE: You're what?

LOLA LOLA: I'm goin' home!

(THE LUCKY STARS *sing a reprise of chorus to "Hot Time in Hicksville," as the scene changes to Hicksville, a small town in Appalachia. There is a sign that says so. Stage left is the Hatfield shanty, on stage right is the McCoy shanty. A barbed-wire fence stage*

Lola Pashalinski in *Corn* (Leandro Katz)

center runs perpendicular to the apron. Sandbags, trenches, and the muzzles of guns protruding from the windows of the houses suggest that this is indeed the scene of the age-old Hatfield and McCoy feud. Hopefully, the stage machinist will contrive to have the walls of the two shanties draw back to reveal interior scenes.)

Scene 4: RUBEN, MOE.

(Ruben is pouring water over Moe's head as he takes a bath in a wooden tub.)

RUBEN: Them dang McCoys done it again. Hooked up their clothesline to our still.

MOE: Dang 'em.

RUBEN: Better take out yer buck knife an' cut 'er down afore Paw sees it.

MOE: *(Opening his knife ominously toward the clothesline)* The only good McCoy is a dead McCoy.

(RACHEL McCOY, a mute maid of all work, enters from the house right carrying a basket of laundry. MELANIE McCOY enters and sits, provocatively spraying herself with perfume from an atomizer.)

Scene 5: RACHEL, MELANIE, RUBEN, MOE.

RUBEN: Wait a minute and wait a minute. I smell McCoys.

MOE: Lookee yonder. There's th' dummy hangin' out the wash. She cain't talk no how.

RACHEL: *(Seeing the Hatfield boys)* Hsssssss!

RUBEN: An' there's 'er sister, Gabby Guts. She talks a blue streak.

MELANIE: Why, Rachel, look over there, t'other side o' th' fence. I do believe it's those wild Hatfield boys. Up to no good, I have no doubt. *(RACHEL starts to run inside pulling* MELANIE *after her)* We cain't run away. Maw will be whippin' mean and mad if the laundry ain't been hung up in the midday Appalachian sun to dry. They're tryin' to scare us off. You know what Maw says, "Never let a Hatfield have his way." *(Posing on the porch and lifting her dress to show her legs)* Let's hold our ground.

RUBEN: Don't cut that line. Let's have some fun with 'em first.

(RACHEL approaches the clothesline warily. RUBEN and MOE pretend to pay no attention. They whistle innocently while preparing their deviltry. Suddenly, when RACHEL comes within range, RUBEN pulls a garden hose or bucket from between his legs, signals MOE to turn on the water, and soaks her in her T-shirt. RACHEL screams silently. MOE and RUBEN laugh uproariously and fall all over themselves.)

MELANIE: Why, of all the dirty, low-down, snake-in-the-grass Hatfield tricks! To pick on a poor little mute like my sister Rachel.

RUBEN: *(Suddenly stops laughing)* Rachel. Hey, Moe, the dummy's name is Rachel.

MOE: *(Still laughing)* Well, she's still a dummy just the same.

(MELANIE runs to the triangle and sounds the alarm. PAW HATFIELD enters from his house and MAW McCOY enters from hers.)

Scene 6: MAW, PAW, RACHEL, MELANIE, RUBEN, MOE.

MAW: What's all this ruckus?

MELANIE: Maw, Maw, it's Hatfield hijinks!

MAW: Get inside the house, girls. We're gonna have a good go at it. Take the wash inside, hear? I don't want no shrapnel messin' up my nice clean laundry. *(Sings "Ready, Aim, Fire")*
    You Hatfields have had your day,
    This time you won't get away,
    There's nothin' that you can say,
    Right here and now you will pay,
    Get your guns, girls, we'll show 'em who's tough.

(Gun points are lowered out of the McCoy windows.)

MOE: Paw! Paw!

PAW: Ya call me, boys?

MOE: Yeah, Paw, looks like the McCoys is fixin' for a fray.

PAW: Man your battle stations. We're gonna give 'em what for. *(Sings)*
    You McCoys might miss a bit,
    Now you know that you can't hit,

My boys are down and ready,
They hold their rifles steady,
I think your best bet would be to give up.

(MAW shoots off PAW's hat.)

HATFIELDS AND McCOYS: *(Sing)*
    Ready . . . , aim, fire!
    Ready . . . , aim, fire!
    Ready . . . , aim, fire!
RUBEN: Aw, Paw, that Rachel McCoy sure whar purty in her wet Fruit of the
    Loom T-shirt. She ain't bad like the rest of 'em.
PAW: She's a McCoy, ain't she? And I hates McCoys!
MOE: The only good McCoy is a dead McCoy, huh Paw?
PAW: That's right, Son.
MAW: *(Sings)*
    You Hatfields are the last three
    Rotten branches on your tree,
    I'll be mighty glad to see
    Your kind buried down six feet,
    We're women who are ready to get rough.
PAW: *(Sings)*
    You McCoys have bitten through
    A bit more than you can chew,
    If my mind still serves to think
    When you're gone you'll be extinct,
    Right here and now I'm callin' your bluff.
ALL: *(Sing)*
    Ready . . . , aim, fire!
    Ready . . . , aim, fire!
    Ready . . . , aim, fire!

(Guns are fired out of the windows on both sides. Grenades are thrown. The clothesline falls. The still explodes. Smoke pours out of the end of a cannon, which shoots volleyballs that bounce lamely across the stage. Parts of the shanties are blasted apart.)

Scene 7: LOLA LOLA, DUDE.

DUDE: *(Off)* Lola! Lola Lola! Wait for me! I can't keep up with you.
LOLA LOLA: *(Striding in dressed as a man, like Calamity Jane)* Well, get a move
    on, Dude. The exercise'll do ya good.
DUDE: Can't we sit down and rest a while? My feet are killing me.
LOLA LOLA: Sure, sit down and take a load off yer feet. We're here!
DUDE: We're where?
LOLA LOLA: Hicksville, town where I was born. I ain't laid eyes on this place
    since I was a little whippersnapper.
DUDE: How are you so sure this is Hicksville?
LOLA LOLA: Jest *look* at it! This is the ideal location for the country-western
    jamboree.
DUDE: You want to perform the Lola Lola Show here, in this slum?
LOLA LOLA: Watch your language, Dude. This ain't no slum. Jest because the

government pays 'em not to grow corn on their land. We was born on this land and we love every stone of it.

DUDE: You're crazy. We could have had Madison Square Garden or the Cow Palace, and you want to give a free concert for a bunch of Yokels, Rubes, Rednecks, and Crackers!

LOLA LOLA: There are no cows in the Cow Palace, not a blade of grass in Madison Square Garden.

DUDE: Why did you really come back, Lola Lola?

LOLA LOLA: Unfinished business, you might say. I wanna show these Yokels how big I am. They gave me a bad time when I was jest knee-high to a grasshopper and now I'm gonna jam it up their asses.

(The gunfire between the two houses resumes.)

LOLA LOLA: Hit the dirt!

(They both fall on their faces.)

DUDE: Let's get out of here while we're still in one piece.

LOLA LOLA: Things around here haven't changed a bit. The Hatfields and the McCoys are still a-feudin'. Well, let's go in and find out how they take to our little proposition.

DUDE: Go in there and risk our lives?

LOLA LOLA: Sure. Hatfields hate McCoys and McCoys hate Hatfields. But strangers are always welcome. Come on. I'll take the Hatfields and you take the McCoys.

(They walk cautiously into the line of fire. Their hats get shot off. They hit the dirt. Then they wave white hankies. The shooting stops. DUDE approaches the McCoy shanty and knocks on the door.)

Scene 8: MAW, DUDE, MELANIE, RACHEL.

MAW: *(Inside)* No use tryin' to sell us encyclopedias . . . We cain't read.

DUDE: I'm not selling encyclopedias.

MAW: Well, whatever it is you're sellin', we don't want any. Besides, we've got no money. Even the burglars in these parts know that.

DUDE: Mrs. McCoy, I'm afraid you're sadly mistaken. I'm not a traveling salesman. Allow me to introduce myself. My name is Dude Greaseman and I represent Lola Lola and The Lucky Stars.

MELANIE: *(Screams)* Lola Lola and The Lucky Stars! Aaaaaaaaah!

MAW: Melanie, get back. Don't have no truck with city slickers, hear?

DUDE: We want to bring The Lola Lola Show to Hicksville to do a free country-western jamboree.

MELANIE: *(Screams)* A free country-western jamboree! Aaaaaaaaah!

MAW: Melanie, hush up. Landsakes, how can I hear what the man says with you caterwaulin' like a sow in heat. Well, mister, a free jamboree sounds real nice. But what's all this got to do with me?

DUDE: We want to hold it in your cornfield.

MELANIE: In our cornfield! *(Yells)* Eeeeeyaaaahoooo! Let 'em do it, huh, Maw?

Let 'em do it, huh? Huh, Maw? Maw? Let 'em, huh? Let 'em do it. C'mon, Maw, let 'em, huh? Maw?

MAW: *(Bellows)* Quiet!

DUDE: We are prepared to offer you a sizable amount of money.

MAW: I don't see why not. We don't grow nothing these days anyway. Rachel, bring Mr. Greaseman some of that instant cornbread you made.

MELANIE: EeeeeeeeYaaaaaaaaaaHooooooooooo, Maw!

(MAW stuffs a towel in MELANIE's open mouth.)

MAW: 'Scuse me, Mr. Greaseman. But, you see, I was blessed with one daughter that's dumb and cursed with one that never shuts up. Mr. Greaseman, these are my daughters, Rachel and Melanie.

(RACHEL nods shyly, hiding behind her mother's skirt.)

MELANIE: *(Through the towel)* Ungfh.

DUDE: Now as soon as you enter into the agreement with Mr. Hatfield, I will be able to offer you a sum of money that . . .

MAW: Hatfield? Did I hear you say Hatfield?

DUDE: Yes, I er . . .

MAW: Slowly I turn, and inch by inch, step by step . . .

(MAW emits a roar and, picking up DUDE by the seat of his pants, throws him out of the house.)

Scene 9: MAW, MELANIE, RACHEL.

MAW: *(to MELANIE)* Well, what do you think of that city slicker now?

MELANIE: Ungfh.

MAW: *(Pulling the towel out of her mouth)* Speak up, Daughter.

MELANIE: Aw, Maw, you went and spoiled everything. Now I'll never get to meet Lola Lola and The Lucky Stars!

MAW: Ow, my sacroiliac! I'm havin' an attack. God is punishin' me with ungrateful children and a bad back.

MELANIE: Want me to go fetch Aunt Priscilla?

MAW: No, I don't want you to go fetch Aunt Priscilla! Rachel, quick, mix up some hog lard, turpentine, and kerosine and rub it on my back. I gotta eat raw honey and rock candy. Bring me the Good Book, Daughters, and carry me to my bed.

MELANIE: *(Whispers to RACHEL)* Looks like Maw's got Hatfielditis.

(RACHEL and MELANIE carry MAW out.)

Scene 10: LOLA LOLA, DUDE.

LOLA LOLA: How'd it go?

DUDE: Everything was proceeding satisfactorily when, suddenly, on the mention of the name "Hatfield," the McCoy matriarch forcibly expelled me through her portals.

LOLA LOLA: People jest love to hate each other, Dude. They love to make each other miserable. I'm gonna go check out the Hatfield tribe.

(LOLA LOLA *crosses the stage to the barbed-wire fence, which she is obliged to crawl under on her belly. She knocks at the Hatfields' front door.*)

Scene 11: LOLA LOLA, PAW, RUBEN, MOE.

RUBEN: Paw, there's some dude knockin' at the front door.
PAW: *(In a panic)* Hide the still! It's a government agent!

(RUBEN *and* MOE *exit hurriedly and disguise the still.*)

PAW: *(Answering coolly)* Lookin' fer someone?
LOLA LOLA: I'm a stranger in this town.
PAW: Yer boots look like you're a stranger in many towns.
LOLA LOLA: I have been on the road for some time. Do you know an Ezekiel Hatfield that lives in these parts?
PAW: Maybe I do an' maybe I don't. Depends on what you want 'im fer.
LOLA LOLA: My name is Lola Lola. I'm a country-western singer.
RUBEN AND MOE: *(Poking in their heads)* Lola Lola?
LOLA LOLA: I want to rent your cornfield and hold a free country-western jamboree featuring the Lola Lola Show, that's me, and my musical group, The Lucky Stars.
RUBEN AND MOE: Eeeeeeee Yaaaaaaaaa Hooooooooooo!
PAW: In that case, I *am* Ezekiel Hatfield! Moe, bring out some o' that moonshine o' ourn.
LOLA LOLA: *(Lighting up)* Moonshine?
RUBEN: You don't have to be scared. Paw's moonshine is good stuff—crystal clear . . .
MOE: Stinks to high heaven, but if you can git past th' smell . . .
RUBEN: It'll set ya on yer head or yer butt faster'n he'd blow yer innards out fer smilin', courtin' like, at one o' Maw McCoy's daughters.
PAW: Drink up. It'll put hair on yer chest.
LOLA LOLA: Jest what I need! *(Drinks)*
PAW: When I was high sheriff, I put the ax to at least three hundred stills, but never those of my kin. One time, me an' my old woman had a fallin' out. See, I got to drinkin' my own likker an' come home an' beat up on her. Well, she got all hot an' went down an' told the law where my still was hid. He told her he'd come up an' git me. But he never did 'cuz I was his kin. *(Laughs)*
LOLA LOLA: *(Smacking her lips)* Nice stuff, real nice.

(PAW *refills her glass and his own while the boys drink from the jug.*)

PAW: My daddy made his own likker and died at the age of sixty-four in a big drunk. Stayed drunk for thirteen days on his own bottles. . . . Stuff was so strong, must've burned his insides out.

(LOLA LOLA *refills her own glass and his.*)

LOLA LOLA: Well, how are things in Hicksville?
PAW: Times is hard. This year we fear an epidemic of yellow flowers will spoil the hay.

LOLA LOLA: How high is the corn?

PAW: Shucks, we don't grow corn no more, ain't no money in it. I got a special grant to grow cellulose for automobile dashboards.

LOLA LOLA: You cain't eat cellulose.

PAW: Naw, we buy our food now, frozen. I wouldn't want them government fellers to find out, but I grow a little corn, secretlike, for my still. An' to remind me of the way things was.

LOLA LOLA: Maybe the rent on the cornfield will help you out. Maybe you can go back to growin' that old-time organic corn.

PAW: What's "organic"?

LOLA LOLA: Grown in cow shit, Pardner.

RUBEN AND MOE: Mmmmmmmmmmmm Mmmmmmmmmmm! I can taste it now. The cornbread, that is.

(To live music, the three HATFIELDS go into a wild drunken dance that becomes quite violent. LOLA LOLA speaks after the dance is over, when the men have collapsed in a heap on the floor.)

LOLA LOLA: There's jest one hitch.

RUBEN, PAW, AND MOE: Huh?

LOLA LOLA: Yer cornfield ain't big enough.

RUBEN, PAW, AND MOE: Ain't big enough?!

LOLA LOLA: *(Cagey)* Yeah, we're expectin' Rednecks, Rubes, Crackers, and Yokels from miles around. We'll need a cornfield about twice the size of yourn.

RUBEN: Shucks.

MOE: Heck.

PAW: Dang.

LOLA LOLA: Yep, if only there was some neighboring cornfield that wasn't growin' nothin' that we could join up to yourn. Why, then, everything would be jest fine.

(MOE and RUBEN look nervously at one another. PAW just stares in a slow burn because he knows what's coming and feels trapped.)

LOLA LOLA: Do any of you fellers know if any of your *friendly* neighbors . . .

(MOE and RUBEN look to their father, fearful of giving the answer themselves.)

PAW: What're ya lookin' at me fer? *(Exploding)* I ain't doin' it! I ain't gettin' mixed up with my neighbors!

LOLA LOLA: *(Innocently)* Why not?

PAW: Because they're McCoys. *(Slow burn)* And I hates McCoys.

RUBEN AND MOE: Aw, Paw.

PAW: Shaddup! I said I ain't havin' no truck with McCoys and I means what I says.

RUBEN: Aw, Paw, yer gonna spoil everything.

PAW: *(Letting out an animal cry of pain)* Ow, my lumbago. Oooeeee, my liver and my kidneys. I'm havin' an attack. Quick, Boys, bring me my pokeberries! Boil up that root from the queen of the meadow. I'm not long for this world. My boys have turned against their father.

MOE: Should I go and get Aunt Priscilla, Paw?

PAW: No, don't get Aunt Priscilla! Make me some sheep's-dung tea with trailing arbutus leaves. Bring a bottle o' shine. Lord, Lord, I am sick with ingratitude.

(RUBEN *and* MOE *carry their father out.* LOLA LOLA *rejoins* DUDE *outside.*)

Scene 12: LOLA LOLA, DUDE.

LOLA LOLA: Looks like this is gonna be a tough nut to crack, Dude. Seems like the Hatfields went and killed off all of the McCoy menfolk and the McCoys killed off all the Hatfield womenfolk. These are the only six left! We got the battle of the sexes on our hands.

(Shots are fired by the HATFIELDS.*)*

LOLA LOLA: Those male chauvinist pigs!

(The MCCOYS *fire a volley in return.)*

DUDE: There's women's liberation for you. I'm ready to give up and go home anytime you are.

LOLA LOLA: Hold your horses, Dude. Do you see what I see?

(They spy RUBEN *and* RACHEL *exchanging a kiss over the back fence.)*

Scene 13: LOLA LOLA, DUDE, RUBEN, RACHEL.

DUDE: Why, I believe that a sibling from each of the warring dynasties have proximated their orbicularis oris muscles in a state of contraction!

LOLA LOLA: They're kissin' all right, Dude.

RUBEN: *(Sings "Silver-Studded Saddle")*
    In a dream last night
    You were by my side
    We were sleeping

    I stole a tender kiss

    Dreams are all I have
    When it's you from me
    They are keeping

    I'll promise you this

    We'll ride someday
    Bluebirds will guide our way
    And we'll sit upon my silver-studded saddle

    I offer a dream
    For I have no horse
    No silver saddle

    In dreams I forget

    If you dream with me
    One day you and I
    Will skedaddle

Into the sunset

We'll ride someday
Bluebirds will guide our way
And we'll sit upon my silver-studded saddle
And we'll sit upon my silver-studded saddle
Get along, little dogies, get along

Scene 14: LOLA LOLA, DUDE, RUBEN, RACHEL, MAW.

MAW: Rachel McCoy, what're you doin' out there? You ain't talkin' to one of them no-good Hatfields, are ya?

(RUBEN *and* RACHEL *just stand transfixed, staring at one another.*)

MAW: *(Shrieking)* Rachel, Rachel! You get in the house. Where's my shotgun? *(She gives a blast with the gun)* Git back, Hatfield! Git over on yer own side afore I blows ya to kingdom come! *(Grabs Rachel by the arm)* If I ever catches you with that trash again, I'm gonna tan yer hide fer ya.

(MAW *drags* RACHEL *out.* RACHEL *turns and throws a small nosegay of wildflowers to* RUBEN. *He catches them and looks sadly after.*)

MAW: Hatfields, how I hates 'em! *(She yanks* RACHEL *into the house and slams the door after them)*

Scene 15: LOLA LOLA, DUDE, RUBEN.

DUDE: Why, this is a regular backwoods *Romeo and Juliet!*
LOLA LOLA: And the poor kids just stand there, starin' at each other, cryin' their eyes out. I got an idea. I want to bring love and harmony to Hicksville.

(RUBEN *approaches* LOLA LOLA *and the* DUDE, *sadly fingering the nosegay.*)

RUBEN: Gee, I'm sorry you cain't do the free country-western jamboree here in Hicksville, Lola Lola.
LOLA LOLA: We ain't givin' up that easy. We gotta put our heads together. Ruben, this here is my agent, Dude Greaseman. Dude, this is Ruben Hatfield.
RUBEN: Pleased to meet you.
DUDE: My pleasure.

(They shake hands.)

RUBEN: As I see it, we're up against creepin' old fogeyism.
LOLA LOLA: You kids have those old geezers outnumbered. There's four of you and only two of them.
DUDE: But they can't get together. You see that barbed-wire fence?
RUBEN: It's worse than that, Mr. Greaseman. I'm . . . er . . . uh . . . a . . . Well, Rachel an' me . . . er . . . a . . . Aw, shucks!
LOLA LOLA: You got it bad and that ain't good. So you're in love.
RUBEN: Yeah. But Rachel is one of them mutes. She cain't talk nohow. I cain't even find out how she feels about me. All she do every day is throw me some posies. *(Shows bouquet)*

LOLA LOLA: Posies? Why, Rachel can talk, Ruben.

RUBEN: *(Very excited)* She can?

LOLA LOLA: She's trying to tell you something in the language of flowers. Lovers like it because no one can hear. *(She reads the bouquet to him like a love letter, flower by flower)* Dark geranium melancholy darling because I balsam impatient at our trumpet flower separation. But my begonia dark pansy thoughts are new to a white rosebud heart ignorant of love. We will mistletoe these difficulties. Flowers have made my belladonna silence Indian lagerstroemia eloquent. Your milkweed presence softens my pains. Checkweed meet me tonight blooming convolvulus. White clover . . . think of me. Four-leafed clover . . . be mine. Lily of the valley . . . the return of happiness.

RUBEN: She does love me.

LOLA LOLA: And she wants to meet you tonight. When the moon shines over the pigsty, she'll be waiting for you on the roof of the cow shed.

RUBEN: I'd better get ready for my big date.

LOLA LOLA: Put on your best bib and tucker.

RUBEN: I ain't got no fancy clothes. But I think I'll take a bath!

DUDE: Don't do anything too extreme.

RUBEN: Up here in the hills, we take a bath once a week. *(Pause)* Whether we needs it or not. Wait a minute and wait a minute! I don't know the language of the flowers. I won't understand her and she won't understand me.

LOLA LOLA: What a hitch.

RUBEN: Would you come along with me and tell me what the flowers mean? Leastwise, I'll know what she's sayin'.

LOLA LOLA: *(Hesitant)* Waal, I sure hate to horn in.

RUBEN: *(Pleading)* Please.

LOLA LOLA: But if I can make myself useful, I'll be glad to help out.

RUBEN: Thank you kindly, Miss Lola. I'm much obliged.

LOLA LOLA: That's okay, Ruben.

RUBEN: Nice meetin' ya, Mr. Greaseman.

DUDE: The pleasure was mine.

(RUBEN exits into the Hatfield house.)

Scene 16: LOLA LOLA, DUDE.

LOLA LOLA: Nice kid.

DUDE: Now tell me why you're getting mixed up in these kids' love affair. We've got a concert to get on.

LOLA LOLA: Don't ya see, Dude? *(Sings "The Language of the Flowers")*
    There is a country girl who lives next door
    To a country boy she loves each day more and more
    She wants to tell him of her love, but she can't speak a word
    There is only one way her message will be heard.

LOLA LOLA AND DUDE:
    She will speak to him in the language of the flowers
    She will say I love you in the language of the flowers.

DUDE:
    Now this country boy next door, well he loves her too
    But understanding not the language, how will her message get thru

He needs someone to translate and tell him what he should say
Cupid please draw back your bow, shoot an arrow this a-way.
LUCKY STARS:
　　She will speak to him in the language of the flowers
　　She will say "I love you" in the language of the flowers
　　She will speak to him in the language of the flowers
　　She will say "Ruben, I love you"
　　In the language of the flowers.
LOLA LOLA: Come on, Dude, I need your help.
DUDE: Where are we going?
LOLA LOLA: To pick some flowers.
DUDE: What?
LOLA LOLA You heard what I said. We're gonna pick some flowers. Git a move on!

(LOLA LOLA and DUDE exit up left into the fields.)

Scene 17: THE LUCKY STARS.

(There is a musical interlude. THE LUCKY STARS play and sing the chorus to "The Language of the Flowers." The moon rises a silver sliver over the pigsty. RACHEL appears on the roof of the cow shed with her apron full of wildflowers. RUBEN and LOLA LOLA enter below, followed by DUDE who is burdened with an enormous, and I mean enormous, bundle of wildflowers.)

Scene 18: LOLA LOLA, DUDE, RUBEN, RACHEL.

RUBEN: I sure hope this works.
LOLA LOLA: Sure it'll work. When she throws a flower to you, pass it to me and I'll tell you what she's saying. Then you tell me what you want to tell her. I'll tell Dude which flower. He'll pass the appropriate posy to you and you toss it up to Rachel. It's simple.
DUDE: *(Dubious)* Simple!
LOLA LOLA: Don't be dubious, Dude.

(The two lovers blow kisses to each other. RACHEL lets fall a flower.)

RUBEN: *(Picking up the flower)* Yellow acacia. *(Passes it to LOLA LOLA)*
LOLA LOLA: Secret love.
RUBEN: *(To LOLA LOLA)* I love you too, Rachel.
LOLA LOLA: *(To DUDE)* Ambrosia—love returned.

(DUDE selects a flower and passes it to RUBEN who tosses it up to RACHEL. RACHEL catches the flower, kisses it, and drops four blossoms on RUBEN.)

RUBEN: Blackthorn. Field anemone. Indian azalea. Moss.
LOLA LOLA: Our parents' sickness is the cause of our difficulties. But I will remain true to the end.
RUBEN: I live for you, Rachel. . . .
LOLA LOLA: Cedar leaf.
RUBEN: From the first time I laid eyes on your rustic beauty . . .

LOLA LOLA: Honeysuckle.
RUBEN: I am your captive.
LOLA LOLA: Peach blossom.
RUBEN: I can't live without you. And if I die . . .
LOLA LOLA: Black mulberry.
RUBEN: Bury me amid nature's beauties.
LOLA LOLA: Persimmon.
DUDE: *(Aside to* LOLA LOLA*)* Are you sure corn wouldn't be more appropriate?
LOLA LOLA: Corn means fertility. We'd have a shotgun wedding on our hands.

(RACHEL *drops more flowers.* RUBEN *catches them and arranges them in a small bouquet.)*

RUBEN: Balm of Gilead. Basil. Cranberry.
LOLA LOLA: Somehow we must cure our parents of their hatred and hardness.
RUBEN: Peony. Marjoram.
LOLA LOLA: I am bashful and I blush. . . .
RUBEN: Pansy. Tuberose. Oleander.
LOLA LOLA: I am fearful at the thought of dangerous pleasures.
RUBEN: Never despair. Accept a faithful heart.
LOLA LOLA: Petunia. Weigela.

(MELANIE *and* MOE *come creeping out of their respective houses.* RACHEL *sees them and throws down a mushroom.)*

RUBEN: *(Catching it)* Mushroom?
LOLA LOLA: Suspicion. Danger. Rachel has spotted someone coming.

(The four conspirators stand still in the shadow of the cow shed. They watch MELANIE *and* MOE *in silence. Much to their surprise,* MELANIE *and* MOE *don't even notice them but join hands and go behind the haystack.)*

Scene 19: LOLA LOLA, DUDE, RUBEN, RACHEL, MELANIE, MOE.

MOE: *(In a gruff voice)* Wudgee wudgee wudgee?
MELANIE: *(Like a cat)* Nyaoooo! Nyaooo!
MOE: *(Same voice)* Wudgee wudgee wudgee?
MELANIE: *(As before)* Nyaoooo! Nyaooo!
MOE: *(Sings "Oh! Babe! What Are You Up to Now?")*
   I've been seein' you for some time
   And I thought that you were all mine
   Until I heard what you did allow
   He said he saw you at your home
   And the two of you were alone
   Oh! Babe! What are you up to now?
MELANIE:
   You tell me that I'm the only one
   Who can really show you any fun
   And you love me more than you know how
   Then I see you in the orchid lounge

Lounging with some scroungy runaround
Oh! Babe! What are you up to now?

MOE AND MELANIE:

You had better stop and think about what you have done
'Cause I am now totally convinced I am not the only one.
But you're comin' back and tellin' me
To you these tales are a mystery.
Oh! Babe! What are you up to now?
Oh! Babe! What are you up to now?
Oh! Babe! What are you up to now?

MOE: *(Still gruff)* Wudgee wudgee *wudgee* wudgee?

MELANIE: *(Protesting)* Stop! Don't! Stop! Don't! Stop! Don't!

MOE: *(Heatedly)* Wudgee wudgee wudgee!

MELANIE: *(Weakening)* Stop. Don't. Stop. *(Then with mounting excitement)* Don't! Stop! Don't stop! Don't stop! Don't stop!

DUDE: There is something to be said for getting back to basics.

(Suddenly the doors of the Hatfield and McCoy shanties open. PAW *and* MAW *look out.)*

Scene 20: LOLA LOLA, DUDE, RUBEN, RACHEL, MELANIE, MOE, PAW, MAW.

MAW: *(As if she were calling hogs)* Melanieeeee! Raaaaaaaachel!

PAW: *(As if he were driving mules)* Ruben! Moe! Ruben! Moe!

MAW: My land, I don't know what's got into those girls. Why, it's almost ten o'clock and I don't know where my children are!

PAW: Where in the Sam Hill are my boys? They just better not be out hootchin' and kootchin' if they knows what's good fer 'em!

*(*MAW McCOY *lets out a banshee wail as she discovers* MELANIE *and* MOE *in the haystack.)*

MAW: Rape! That foul Hatfield has raped my daughter!

PAW: *(Shouting at* RACHEL *and giving a blast with his blunderbuss)* Git down off the roof o' my cow shed, ya little tramp! Tryin' to corrupt my boys, are ya?

*(*MELANIE *and* MOE *are still in the altogether. Fearful of the gunshots,* MOE *picks up* MELANIE *and, throwing her over his shoulder, tries to carry her to safety.)*

MAW: It's the rape o' the Sabine women!

PAW: *(Firing again)* Back, Whores of Babylon!

(There is complete confusion. A knock-down-drag-out battle ensues. LOLA LOLA *and the* DUDE *find themselves in the middle of it. Much whoopin' and hollerin'. Finally, the two parents manage to capture their offspring and drag them back home.)*

PAW: C'mon, Boys, we're goin' out to the woodshed.

MAW: Now I've got to beat the devil out o' ya. Gotta keep my girls clean.

MELANIE: Aw, Maw!

MAW: And, believe me, Daughters, I'm only doin' it fer yer own good.

PAW: C'mon, Boys, ya gotta face th' music.

RUBEN AND MOE: Aw, Paw!

PAW: And I want youse to take it like men, no cryin', 'cuz this is gonna hurt me more than it is you.

(They all exit at opposite sides of the stage behind the houses. RACHEL turns and throws a small bunch of flowers across the stage to RUBEN. He tries to catch them but PAW drags him out and they fall short of his reach. LOLA LOLA and the DUDE creep out of hiding.)

Scene 21: LOLA LOLA, DUDE.

DUDE: *(Shaken up)* Things have taken a desperate turn.

LOLA LOLA: What's this? A last bouquet?

DUDE: A last nosegay.

LOLA LOLA: Rachel was tryin' to tell us something. *(Reading the bouquet)* American starwort—welcome to the strangers. Love-in-a-mist . . . perplexity. Love-lies-a-bleeding . . . *(Sounds of the whuppings and cries issue from the woodsheds)* Hopeless, not heartless . . . lettuce—coldheartedness . . . lichen—solitude. Gee, this is breaking my heart. Ox eye—patience. Crimson polyanthus—the heart's mystery. Pink carnation—woman's love. Thistles? Musk roses? I don't understand. Wisteria. Licorice. Witch hazel . . . cast a spell. Veronica—the unknown one. Moonworts? Withered moonworts? Something about an Aunt Priscilla.

(Sound of the whuppings.)

DUDE: These people are barbarians.

LOLA LOLA: Aunt Priscilla. Aunt Priscilla.

DUDE: Aunt Priscilla! I think you're offa your rocker! Let's get outta here.

LOLA LOLA: We can't abandon our fans in Hicksville!

DUDE: You're the type that if it was raining twenty-dollar bills, you'd be out with an umbrella looking for a nickel you lost. What are you worrying about Hicksville for when they want you in New York?

LOLA LOLA: I wanna get back to my roots. I wanna make sure my roots are real!

DUDE: *(Touching her hair)* Any hairdresser will tell you that your roots are the only thing about you that is real.

LOLA LOLA: What's it to you? You're getting your ten percent!

DUDE: I knew one day you'd begrudge me my ten percent. Well, what's ten percent of nothing, huh? Nix, goose egg, zero, ya get me?

LOLA LOLA: Yeah, I got your number—zero! *(Sings "One Step Behind")*
When you go out you're never happy
Unless I am right there standin' by
And when you're feeling down and out, it's always
Honey, will you get me high?
But you never seem to be around
When I need you right here by my side
Honey, you're always one step behind.

(Music continues to play during dialogue.)

DUDE: That's right! Treat me like a nonentity! But I happen to know that you've got flopsweat. You heard me, FLOPSWEAT! You're afraid to play the big city because you're afraid your hick music won't go over. You haven't got the guts! You're afraid the critics will murder you!

   You're singing last year's singles
   And you're into wearin' tacky cowgirl clothes
   Your makeup's never on right
   And we both know where you got your perfect nose
   Your careless ways have brought me
   To bring to your attention one more time
   Honey, you're always one step behind.

LOLA LOLA: Oh yeah? You and your college education. When I met you, you were nowhere. Booking broken-down rodeo acts for the glue factory! A sleazy creep who knew the price of everything and the value of nothing! You talked to me about the Big Time. Said I needed a business head. And I . . . yeah, I admit it, I was sweet on ya. A pushover. But now I see. You ain't never gonna be Big Time, 'cuz you're Small Time in your heart!

   I guess you're tired of hearin' my complaints
   And will be glad when I am through

DUDE:

   Sometimes I really wonder just what it is
   That keeps me lovin' you

LOLA LOLA AND DUDE:

   But just because I love you
   Do not think I will erase what's on my mind
   Honey, you're always one step behind.

DUDE: *(Yelling, throws a five-dollar bill at her)* Well, here's five dollars, Baby. I wanna buy back my introduction to you. *(Slaps himself across the face. Then aside)* Now, what did you go and say that for, you low-down heel! Lola Lola is the best thing that ever happened to you and you know it. What a mess! Things sure look hopeless . . . hopeless!

Scene 22: AUNT PRISCILLA, LOLA LOLA, DUDE.

(AUNT PRISCILLA enters, a wizened centenarian.)

AUNT PRISCILLA: *(Mumbling in a low chant)* I can blow fire out. I can stop blood. I can blow fire out. I can stop blood. I can cure the thrash. I do it all by the help o' the Lord. Amen. I can blow fire out. I can stop blood. . . .

(DUDE and LOLA LOLA slowly turn and behold the apparition.)

DUDE: What the deuce?

AUNT PRISCILLA: I can cure the thrash. I do it all by the help o' the Lord. I don't do it by meself. If I ain't got the Lord wi' me . . . *(Hesitates)* I feel quarrelsome vibrations! *(She takes out a divining rod and holds it out; it leads her toward* DUDE *and* LOLA LOLA*)*

LOLA LOLA: Where did you come from?

AUNT PRISCILLA: I took the dirt road across the divide all the way from Picken's Nose. I felt the bad vibrations through my rod. Been huntin' everwhar t' find out whar th' comin' from.

DUDE: Okay, I'll bite. Who are you?

AUNT PRISCILLA: Me? I'm Aunt Priscilla.

LOLA LOLA: I knew it! Aunt Priscilla, we're in a peck of trouble. The Hatfields and the McCoys . . .

AUNT PRISCILLA: I knows all about them Hatfields and McCoys. I lived in Hicksville all my life.

LOLA LOLA: How did this feud ever get started in the first place?

AUNT PRISCILLA: It's as old as American history. It seems that way back "when," the great-great-great-great-great-great-great-great-great-great-great-great-granddaddy o' th' Hatfields and the great-great-great-great-great-great-great-great-great-great-great-great-granddaddy o' th' McCoys had an argument over who owned a wild pig that was rangin' aroun' these parts. Each of 'em claimed that pig was his an' it got the two families feudin'.

DUDE: You mean they were pig chauvinist males.

LOLA LOLA: *(Sarcastically to the audience)* Laugh it up, Folks. I *think* these are the jokes.

DUDE: You *think!* Lola, you've got a great delivery. Where did you park your truck? *(AUNT PRISCILLA looks at them askance)* All kidding aside, Aunt Priscilla, Lola Lola and I are very good friends.

LOLA LOLA: *(Aside)* But not each other's.

AUNT PRISCILLA: *(Spinning her yarn)* Then, when the Civil War broke out, the Hatfields joined the Confederacy and the McCoys sided up with the Yanks. I don't think they gave a hoot about the War Between the States. It was jes' an excuse to carry on their private war. *(Volley of shots)* Waal, this is all that's left of 'em now. An' they're still goin' at it, as you c'n see.

LOLA LOLA: Can you help us?

AUNT PRISCILLA: I don't know if I can cure plain hatin'. I never did try.

DUDE: How long does it take you to cure by faith?

AUNT PRISCILLA: *(Snapping her fingers)* About that long.

Scene 23: LOLA LOLA, DUDE, AUNT PRISCILLA, PAW, MOE, RUBEN.

(Suddenly a cry of pain comes from the Hatfield house.)

PAW: *(Yelling off)* Eeeeeow, my lumbago! My liver and my kidneys! Ooooh, I'm sick unto death! Oooooh, I'm dyin'. I tole you boys that this was gonna hurt me more'n it was youse.

MOE: *(Off)* Do you want me to go fetch Aunt Priscilla?

PAW: *(Off)* Naw, don't go fetch Aunt Priscilla. I need a doctor. Go git me a doctor. The reaper is comin' for to call!

(RUBEN and MOE come out from behind the Hatfield house rubbing their butts. A cry of pain comes from the McCoy house.)

Scene 24: LOLA LOLA, DUDE, AUNT PRISCILLA, RUBEN, MOE, MAW, MELANIE, RACHEL.

MAW: *(Yelling off)* Aieeeeee, my sacroiliac! I'm havin' an attack! Oh, Daughters, my back is killin' me. "From dust thou hast come and unto dust thou shalt return." I hear the last trumpet.

MELANIE: *(Off)* Do you want me to go fetch Aunt Priscilla?

MAW: *(Off)* No, I don't want you to fetch Aunt Priscilla. I need a doctor. Go git me a doctor. Yer Maw is goin' to her reward!

(RACHEL and MELANIE come out from behind the McCoy house, rubbing their butts.)

Scene 25: LOLA LOLA, DUDE, AUNT PRISCILLA, MELANIE, MOE, RUBEN, RACHEL.

(MELANIE and RACHEL stand on one side of the barbed-wire fence while RUBEN and MOE stand on the other.)

MELANIE: Aunt Priscilla, please, you've got to help us. Moe an' me . . .

MOE: *(Embarrassed)* Aw, shucks, Melanie, don't say it right out loud.

(RACHEL hands two flowers to AUNT PRISCILLA.)

AUNT PRISCILLA: White daisy, red catchfly . . . innocent young love. So, nature has taken her course, eh? My my my my my. *(Sighs and nods her head, smiling in reverie)*

DUDE: If only we could cure those old fogies.

AUNT PRISCILLA: You hold it right thar. To *me,* they're *young* fogies. You can't blame it on oldness. Why, in my day, people lived to be over a hundred and they was never mean like that.

LOLA LOLA: Waal, young or old, they still need curin'.

AUNT PRISCILLA: I can cure th' body. But only th' power of love can cure th' soul. I'm gonna teach you to heal! Might be of some use to ya when I'm gone.

DUDE: I don't believe in faith healing. It's nothing but a lot of silly superstition.

AUNT PRISCILLA: I believe in th' healin' power becuz th' Lord has healed me. I know he has. Seein' in a sense is a great believin'. You c'n hear things. But if you've seen it, you've got more sense out of it. If it hadn't a-been true, it would'na been handed down through the years.

RUBEN: Please teach us how to heal, Aunt Priscilla.

ALL BUT DUDE: Yes, teach us. Please. We need your help. *(Etc.)*

(RACHEL gives AUNT PRISCILLA some rhubarb.)

AUNT PRISCILLA: Rhubarb . . . you want my advice, Rachel, child. But I can't tell ya how to heal as long as one o' ya don't believe in th' healin' power of th' Savior. *(Pointing a finger at DUDE)* If ya tell somebody how to heal an' there's an unbeliever in on it, ya lose yer power. Jes' like a man doin' something to destroy his rights, ya know. It's handed down from th' beginnin'. It's in the Bible!

LOLA LOLA: C'mon, Dude, can't you muster up a little faith out o' all that ornery hide a-yourn?

DUDE: It's blind superstition. Going to a witch to cure you with magic spells and potions.

RUBEN: She don't even have to see the person. She cures by faith!

MOE: It's true. Jes' like they says.

AUNT PRISCILLA: I could cure 'em even if they was in New York, whether they believe or not. I don't even have to know 'em. But I can't teach no unbeliever, an' that's a fact.

LOLA LOLA: Come on, Dude.

ALL: Come on, Dude!

DUDE: This is not the Dark Ages. This is 1959!

(RACHEL, *in tears, presents* DUDE *with a rose in a pantomime of supplication.*)

LOLA LOLA: The red Christmas rose means relieve my anxiety or I die of love.

DUDE: *(Taking flower)* Ouch! Thorns!

LOLA LOLA: That's a nasty gash.

RUBEN: That blood sure is a-comin'.

(*Drops of blood fall from* DUDE*'s hand.*)

DUDE: It just won't stop!

AUNT PRISCILLA: Dude, it's bleedin' pretty bad, ain't it?

DUDE: Yeah!

AUNT PRISCILLA: I'll stop it from bleedin' on ya.

DUDE: *(Showing some pain)* Get away from here. You don't know a thing about it.

AUNT PRISCILLA: An' you don't know right from wrong. Ya ain't got no more sense 'n a hill of beans!

DUDE: Aw, you go on. Shut your mouth!

AUNT PRISCILLA: Hit's all right. I done doctored it. It won't bleed no more, nohow. It's quittin' as fast as it can.

(*The blood stops. Everyone gasps.*)

LOLA LOLA: Why, I'll be hog-tied, the blood stopped!

DUDE: You actually believe you stopped that blood?

AUNT PRISCILLA: Waal, you didn't. Who did?

DUDE: *(Falling on his knees and kissing* AUNT PRISCILLA*'s apron)* It's a miracle!

AUNT PRISCILLA: *(Simple and exultant, she lays her two hands on his head and throws her head back)* Cured by th' hand o' th' Holy Goost. Amen.

ALL: Amen!

AUNT PRISCILLA: I can teach only one person of the opposite sex not related to me by blood.

ALL: *(Disappointed)* Aw!

AUNT PRISCILLA: But we can pass it on round-robin style. I'll teach Ruben, an' Ruben'll teach Melanie, an' Melanie'll teach Moe, and Moe'll teach Miss Lola Lola, an' Miss Lola Lola'll teach th' Dude, an' th' Dude'll teach Rachel.

(*They enact this as a whispering ring.*)

AUNT PRISCILLA:
I put my faith in the hands of the Lord. . . .
(*Sings "Glory! Glory! Hallelujah!"*)
When life's road becomes too rocky and nothin's goin' right
Satan's knockin' at your front door and you're too weak to fight
Do as I did, back when I was livin' in sin day and night
Put your faith in the Lord's hands and he'll show you the light.

ALL: *(Chorus)*
Glory, Glory! Hallelujah, Glory, Glory! Hallelujah
Glory, Glory! Hallelujah, I put my faith in the hands of the Lord.

AUNT PRISCILLA:
There are lots of part-time christians livin' in this world today
Careful to do good on Sundays, leavin' six days for foul play

Would you want to be in their shoes on that final judgment day
Put your faith in the Lord's hands, walk in his footsteps all the way.
ALL: *(Repeat chorus)*
LOLA LOLA: I got a plan how we can cure 'em!

(They form a huddle, like football players.)

DUDE: You know, it's so crazy, it just might work!
AUNT PRISCILLA: *(Leading them off like Crusaders)* Now come on. Everybody!
Let's put our faith in the hands of the Lord!

(AUNT PRISCILLA exits playing a hymn on the trumpet. They all follow her out,
RACHEL last, dancing and strewing flowers. Curtain.)

End of Act I

ACT II

Scene 1: MELANIE, MAW.

MAW: *(Calling)* Melanie!
MELANIE: Yes, Maw?
MAW: Did my kerosine enema work?
MELANIE: Your kerosine enema?
MAW: Did I pass much bile?
MELANIE: Don't ask me! Better let the doctor nose into that. He gets the profit
from it.

(A knock at the door.)

MELANIE: Maw!
MAW: What is it?
MELANIE: The doctor's here!
MAW: Well, send him in. It's almost too late!

Scene 2: MELANIE, MAW, LOLA LOLA, DUDE.

(LOLA LOLA enters, disguised as a doctor, along with DUDE, who is disguised as a
nurse.)

LOLA LOLA AND DUDE: *(Sing chorus, at rapid speed)*
Oh! Oh! Oh! Oh! Never fear, the doctor's here
And it looks like I showed up just in time
I'll cure your ills with my candy-coated pills
Or maybe an injection is what you've got on your mind.
MAW: *(To the DOCTOR)* Are you an M.D.?
LOLA LOLA: M.D., Ph.D., IRT, BMT, PDQ, and Q-U-A-C-K!
MAW: What's yer name?
LOLA LOLA: Name? Name . . . Doctor . . . Skinner. Yep, that's me, Doctor
Skinner, and this is Nurse Jane. *(DUDE starts to protest but LOLA LOLA rides over*
his objection) Now then, what's wrong with you?
MAW: It's my back, Doctor.

LOLA LOLA: Who told you that?

MAW: Well, that's where it hurts.

LOLA LOLA: Ignorance. Looks like a case of pimple genitalia to me.

MAW: Pimple genitalia?

LOLA LOLA: Yes, you've got pimple genitalia, by crackee! Nurse Jane, let's have her pulse.

(DUDE *feels* MAW's *pulse. He chews gum and snaps his fingers to the rhythm.*)

LOLA LOLA: Come on, now, you've lost the beat. Let's take it from the top. *(Feels the pulse, then pronounces gravely)* I'm afraid your pulse is syncopated.

MAW: Is that bad?

LOLA LOLA: Bad? Bad, she asks me. It's a lucky thing I came when I did.

DUDE: He's not your ordinary doctor, you know.

    He has no use for minor ailments

    Only major entailments

    Will bring the happiness he's looking for

    Fevers of long duration

    Or lungs with inflammation

LOLA LOLA:

    Bring in enough to pay for my new car.

ALL: *(Repeat chorus)*

DUDE: Why bother with a cold when you can have consumption? Why settle for a headache when you can have the plague?

LOLA LOLA: I only wish that you had all these ailments that we've just mentioned so that I could demonstrate my skill on you!

MAW: Much obliged.

LOLA LOLA: How long has your arm been this way?

MAW: How d'ye mean?

LOLA LOLA: I'd have that arm off right away if I was you.

MAW: Why?

LOLA LOLA: Don't you see how it's sapping the strength from the other one?

MAW: Yep, but I need my arm.

LOLA LOLA: I'd have that right eye out too if I was in your shoes.

MAW: Have my eye out?

LOLA LOLA: Don't you see how bad it is for the other one? It's stealing all the vitamins. Take my advice and have it out as soon as you can. You'll see a lot better with the left.

MAW: There's no hurry.

MELANIE: Still sick, Maw?

MAW: Am I sick! Don't I look sick to ya?

MELANIE: *(Cowed)* You look sick all right. You're probably a lot sicker than you think.

    When she is not yellin'

    About some kind of swellin'

    Headaches backaches or ankle sprain

    She'll create a scene

    By turnin' her tongue green

LOLA LOLA:

    I think it's a case of the insane

MAW:
> That's enough of your back-talkin'
> To all my squawkin'
> The doctor will decide what is my cure
> Maybe I need fillin' with cc's of penicillin

LOLA LOLA:
> How much more can this ole girl endure?

ALL: *(Repeat chorus)*

LOLA LOLA: Well, good-bye now, I have to go dissect a patient of mine who died yesterday.

MAW: A patient of yours died yesterday? You must feel terrible.

LOLA LOLA: Oh, not at all, not at all. He paid in advance.

MAW: You know, Nurse Jane, you look right familiar like.

LOLA LOLA: *(Grabbing* DUDE *and dragging him off)* We'll be back to see you tomorrow. Believe me, I want to cure you in the *worst* way.

(Exit LOLA LOLA *and the* DUDE.*)*

Scene 3: MAW, MELANIE.

MELANIE: Now there's a right smart doctor fer ya.

MAW: He's in a little bit too much of a hurry fer me.

MELANIE: Newfangled doctors are all like that.

MAW: Wantin' to cut off one arm and take out an eye so the other would get along better! I'd be more likely to die of th' cure than th' disease! A fine operation that would be, wouldn't it, to leave me one-eyed and one-armed!

MELANIE: Did the doctor say at what time he plans to operate tomorrow?

MAW: He didn't say. *(Pause)* 'Cuz there ain't gonna be no operation.

MELANIE: But Maw . . .

MAW: Don't but Maw me! Nobody's gonna go cuttin' off my arm or gougin' out my eye. *(Pause)* You better run and git Aunt Priscilla. I think I need some o' that old-time religion.

*(*MELANIE *gaily runs out the door and down the road. The wall of the McCoy shanty closes and the wall of the Hatfield shanty draws back revealing* PAW HATFIELD *in all his misery, surrounded by home remedies.)*

Scene 4: PAW, MOE.

PAW: *(Bitching and bellyaching)* Ooooh me! Ooooh my! I'm fadin' fast. Moe, my boy . . .

MOE: Yes, Paw?

PAW: Everything's gettin' dark before my eyes. This is it. Everything's slippin'. *(Moaning)* Light, more light! *(Sings)*
> Swing low, sweet chariot.
> Comin' for to carry me home.

*(*MOE *opens the window shade and the room fills with sunlight.* PAW *explodes)* Pull down that shade, you dang fool! Can't you see I'm a sick man?

MOE: *(Lowering the shade)* Paw, I don't know anybody who's less ill than you are. You'll live to bury us all.

PAW: That's becuz I take care of myself when I'm sick. Is the sheep's urine ready for my turpentine tea?

MOE: It's out back a-coolin'. I fallered th' sheep aroun' all mornin' afore he had to pee.

PAW: Well, you can bring my onion poultice and the White Cloverine brand salve.

MOE: One proof that there's nothin' wrong with you is you'd have to be strong as a horse to survive all the medicines you've swallowed.

PAW: But don't you see, Boy, that's jes' what keeps me goin'. I have Sloan's salve and Doctor Fowler's snake oil to thank that I'm alive today.

MOE: Paw, I think you'd do better to thank Mother Nature. Nobody can cure you. You have to cure yourself.

PAW: Then what should a man do when he's sick?

MOE: Nothin', Paw.

PAW: Nothin'?

MOE: Nothin'. Rest. If Nature has made ya ill, then I guess it's up to Nature to make ya well again. You've got to have faith.

PAW: But you must agree, Son, that there is ways and means of assistin' Nature.

MOE: That, Paw, is the fairy tale of medicine.

PAW: It's fine fer you to talk about faith. Yer young. You have yer health! *(Sinking back among his pillows and pulling up his quilt around himself)* But I'm old and I'm *really* sick. Ooooh me! Ooooh my!

(A knock is heard at the door. MOE *looks out and then returns to* PAW.*)*

MOE: Th' doctor's here, Paw.

PAW: *(Ignoring* MOE *and shaking his leg)* M' dang leg fell asleep!

MOE: *(Whispering)* Paw, the doctor's here.

PAW: What d' ye say?

MOE: The doctor's here.

PAW: What're ya whisperin' fer?

MOE: I didn't want to wake up yer leg!

PAW: Aw, let 'im in!

Scene 5: PAW, MOE, LOLA LOLA, DUDE.

(MOE *opens the door revealing* LOLA LOLA *and the* DUDE *disguised as before.)*

LOLA LOLA AND DUDE: *(Repeat chorus, as before)*

DUDE: Well, how's the star invalid today? Glad to see you're feeling better.

PAW: Oh me, oh my! I'm bad, very bad.

LOLA LOLA: Bad? In what way?

PAW: You wouldn't believe how feeble I am.

LOLA LOLA: That's a pity.

DUDE: Tch, tch, tch!

PAW: I ain't hardly got enough strength to speak.

LOLA LOLA: But you're looking well.

PAW: *(With vehemence, rising from his bed)* Well! How dare you come into my house and tell me I look well! *(Shouting)* I'm weak! I'm feeble!

DUDE: That's better. I'm glad to see you are stronger.

LOLA LOLA: My visit's doin' ya good. You're showin' all the signs of health.

> There once was a feller who
> Turned all yeller
> Seems he was drinkin' too much wine
> I've got him smokin' herb
> Now he complains not a word
> Just lies around a-gigglin'
> All the time.

ALL: *(Repeat chorus)*

PAW: Never mind tellin' me how healthy I c'n be. I want to hear about my illness. What kind of a doctor are you anyway?

LOLA LOLA: I'm a gynecologist!

DUDE: An *overt* gynecologist.

PAW: Jest what I need.

LOLA LOLA: But, if you don't think I can do anything for you, I'll be on my way.

PAW: Don't leave me!

DUDE: He doesn't deserve to be cured.

LOLA LOLA: I was gonna give your system a thorough cleaning out and get to the bottom of your trouble. Jane, pack up the enema bag, we're leaving.

DUDE: Leave him to the foulness of his bowels.

LOLA LOLA: The corruption of his blood.

DUDE: The bitterness of his gall.

LOLA LOLA: And his flatulence that withers the flowers!

PAW: Oh, Lord, have mercy!

LOLA LOLA: In three days, you'll be incurable. You'll lapse into a state of colapepsia.

PAW: Doctor Skinner!

DUDE: From colapepsia into dyspepsia.

PAW: Nurse Jane!

LOLA LOLA: From dyspepsia into apepsia.

PAW: Doctor Skinner!

DUDE: From apepsia into diarrhea.

PAW: Nurse Jane!

LOLA LOLA: From diarrhea into pyorrhea.

PAW: Doctor Skinner!

DUDE: From pyorrhea to dropsy and dysentery.

PAW: Nurse Jane!

LOLA LOLA: From dropsy and dysentery to autopsy and cemetery. That'll teach you to question a doctor's authority.

PAW: Oh, my God! Moe, I'm dyin'. Medicine is takin' vengeance on me!

MOE: Aw, Paw, these newfangled doctor fellers give me th' creeps. I sure wish you'd send 'em away and ask Aunt Priscilla for help.

PAW: *(Aside)* Sh! Don't let 'im hear ya. There's no tellin' what he might do to me if I make him jealous. *(Aloud)* Doctor, Doctor, please tell me what's wrong with me.

DUDE: Doctor Skinner, the patient wants a diagnosis.

LOLA LOLA: A diagnosis?

DUDE: He wants to know what's wrong with him.

LOLA LOLA: Oh, a *diagnosis*. *(To* PAW*)* So you want a diagnosis, huh?

PAW: I'd be much obliged.

LOLA LOLA: Diagnosis . . . diagnosis. Nurse Jane, maybe you should read my findings to the patient.

DUDE: The esophagus is normal in caliber. The lower end of the esophagus is slightly narrow with a collection of greeman just above the esophagogastric junction. However, this may be artefactual. A fairly large hiatus hernia is seen just above the bravelschnitz and just below the pheenaschnob junction.

LOLA LOLA: Oh, that college education!

DUDE: There was prompt regurgitation of the gastric contents into the esophagus and irregular contractions may be seen as the result of esophagitis.

PAW: Ooooh me!

DUDE: The herniated part of the stomach shows no ulcer disease or neoplasm.

PAW: Ooooh my!

DUDE: The subdiaphragmatic part of the hiatus shows no ulcer disease, neoplasm, or abnormality.

PAW: *(Moans, gasps, coughs, and begins to sing softly)*
  Swing low, sweet chariot.
  Comin' for to carry me . . .

LOLA LOLA: In short, the patient is in perfect health.

PAW: What?

LOLA LOLA: You heard me. There's nothin' wrong with you. That will be fifty dollars consultation fee.

PAW: Fifty dollars fer you to tell me I'm not sick! If I'm not sick, you shouldn't git anything.

LOLA LOLA: I'm a specialist.

PAW: You ain't nothin' but a no-good quack horse doctor! Not sick! Git out of my house! In perfect health! Out, out! Where's my shotgun? I'll show you how sick I am!

(LOLA LOLA and the DUDE run out of the house jeering at PAW HATFIELD.)

Scene 6: PAW, MOE.

PAW: Moe, my boy, run up the road an' git Aunt Priscilla. At least she never went so far as to say I was in perfect health. Now shake a leg. It's a matter of life and death.

MOE: *(Yelling as he runs out the door)* Eeeeyaaahooo, Paw!

PAW: Oh me, oh my. I wonder where my boy Ruben is now that I needs him. He oughter be here with me in my final hour.

(The wall of the Hatfield shanty closes and the wall of the McCoy shanty draws back revealing AUNT PRISCILLA and MAW MCCOY.)

Scene 7: MAW, AUNT PRISCILLA.

MAW: Oh, Aunt Priscilla, I sure hope you can cure me better than that Doctor Skinner.

AUNT PRISCILLA: We do better than a doctor because we let Our Maker do it. We don't doctor it. Other words, I mean we don't cure it. We're used as th' vessel for th' Lord. He does th' curin'. Mmmmmmmm, what's that yer eatin'?

MAW: Chicken stew, new-laid eggs, hog maws, mashed pertaters, plump sun-ripened tomaters, eggplant, cheese, and rock candy.

AUNT PRISCILLA: Enjoy it, 'cuz as of today, I'm puttin' ya on th' ten-day corn diet.

MAW: What's th' ten-day corn diet?

AUNT PRISCILLA: It's real simple. You jest eat nothin' but corn fer ten days.

MAW: Nothin' but corn?

AUNT PRISCILLA: That's right, nothin' but corn. It'll cure what ails ya. A panacea, I believe they calls it.

MAW: No more chicken stew?

AUNT PRISCILLA: *(Trucking)* No no *no* no!

MAW: New-laid eggs?

AUNT PRISCILLA: *(Still trucking)* No no *no* no!

MAW: *(In the rhythm of the patter)* Hog maws, pertaters, sun-ripened tomaters?

AUNT PRISCILLA: *(Keeps on trucking)* No no no no *no* no!

MAW: Can I have eggplant parmigianer?

AUNT PRISCILLA: If you eat that, you gonna be a goner!

MAW: What about rock ca-a-an-deee?

AUNT PRISCILLA: Sugar is the biggest no-no of all.

MAW: But my sweet tooth says, "Yes-yes."

AUNT PRISCILLA: Well, yer sweet tooth may say, "Yes-yes," but yer wisdom tooth better say, "No-no."

MAW: *(Groans)* Oh me, oh my!

AUNT PRISCILLA: An' do th' cookin' yerself. See how many recipes fer corn you can come up with.

MAW: Well, lessee, there's cornbread, corn fritters, corn cakes, popcorn . . .

AUNT PRISCILLA: I'm gonna leave you a helper, kind of a faith healin' farmhand. Cousin o' mine. *(Calling)* Brother Ruben!

Scene 8: MAW, AUNT PRISCILLA, RUBEN.

(RUBEN enters in a choir robe with a Bible in one hand and a hoe in the other.)

AUNT PRISCILLA: Brother Ruben, I want you to look after Maw McCoy while she's on the spiritual path of corn eatin'. *(Exit)*

Scene 9: MAW, RUBEN.

RUBEN: Shucks, ma'am, sure looks like you could use a hand aroun' th' place.

MAW: *(Looking healthier already)* Things are a bit run-down. It's nice to have a man around the house. Y' know, I used to have an hourglass figure, but the sands of time sure have shifted!

(The wall of the McCoy shanty closes and the wall of the Hatfield shanty draws back revealing AUNT PRISCILLA and PAW HATFIELD.)

Scene 10: PAW, AUNT PRISCILLA.

PAW: *(Thunderstruck)* Corn?!!!
AUNT PRISCILLA: Corn and nothin' but corn.
PAW: Fer ten days?
AUNT PRISCILLA: Fer ten days.
PAW: But I don't know how t' cook nothin' but frozen foods. Ever since Mavis, Mavis was my ol' woman, died in th' big feud o' thirty-nine, about th' time there was that war in Germany . . .
AUNT PRISCILLA: Never you mind about cookin'. I brang ya a little cousin o' mine. *(Calling)* Sister Rachel!

Scene 11: PAW, AUNT PRISCILLA, RACHEL.

(RACHEL enters shyly, hiding herself behind AUNT PRISCILLA's skirts. She is dressed like a Shaker lady.)

PAW: *(Eyes popping out of his head)* Well, I'll be hog-tied!
AUNT PRISCILLA: I figgered this place needed a woman's touch.
PAW: Ain't she cuter 'n a bug's ear? Howdy-doody, Rachel? *(RACHEL, of course, doesn't answer)* What'sa matter, cain't she talk?
AUNT PRISCILLA: She don't talk to men. She's a Shaker.
PAW: *(Vibrating)* A Shaker, huh? How come she don't talk to men?
AUNT PRISCILLA: That's strictly between the Shaker and his Maker. But this Shaker is a mighty fine baker!
PAW: I'll take 'er!

(The wall of the Hatfield shanty closes.)

Scene 12: AUNT PRISCILLA, MELANIE, MOE, RUBEN, RACHEL, MAW, PAW, LOLA LOLA, DUDE, THE LUCKY STARS.

(The Big Corn production number. LOLA LOLA and the DUDE come on dressed as the front and rear end of a horse pulling a wagonload of corn. THE LUCKY STARS play "Corn," which is sung by members of the cast, as indicated. Everybody dances. Two giant ears of corn come on and do a tap dance. The corn out in the field behind the houses begins to grow and blossom. The trees burst into bloom. The walls of the two shanties draw back revealing the improvements that RUBEN and RACHEL have wrought. The change is akin to that which Snow White brought about in the lives of the Seven Dwarfs. There is the smell of fresh-baked cornbread, which RACHEL is baking onstage.)

MELANIE:
    Cornbread cornflakes corn on the cob
    That's just a few of the ways Ma fed me corn with love
MAW:
    You forgot to mention popcorn balls on Halloween
    And corn mash corn hash corn-baked corn-caked and corn-creamed

ALL:

   (Chorus)

   Call it corn corn corn

   We ate it all our lives

   Call it corn corn corn

   It's all right

RUBEN:

   Remember all the corn liquor that Pappy used to drink

MOE:

   Yes, and I remember just how bad it made him stink

RUBEN AND MOE:

   But now we're older we know just how good it made him feel

   We've discovered where it is that Pappy hides his still

ALL: *(Repeat chorus)*

PAW:

   Corn was here when our fathers first set foot on this land

   I think it's time we all got back to corn again

ALL: *(Repeat chorus)*

GIRLS:

   I wonder why it is that Maw is dancin' so darn slow

BOYS:

   I think she do-si-dos a corn upon her little toe

GIRLS:

   Paw is really havin' a good time with the men folk

BOYS:

   He's probably tellin' them one of his favorite corny jokes.

ALL: *(Repeat chorus)*

LOLA LOLA: Let's bring out Paw an' Maw an' see if th' corn cured 'em!

AUNT PRISCILLA: Ezekiel Hatfield! Maude McCoy! Come on out here. Let's see how you're doin'.

(PAW and MAW peek hesitantly out of their respective doors [wearing ear of corn costumes].)

MAW AND PAW: Somebody call? I'm all ears.

AUNT PRISCILLA: Come on out an' blow th' stink offa ya.

Scene 13: MAW, PAW, RUBEN, RACHEL, MELANIE, MOE, LOLA LOLA, DUDE, AUNT PRISCILLA.

(RACHEL takes PAW by the hand and leads him out to the fence while RUBEN does the same with MAW.)

MAW: Rachel!

PAW: Ruben!

MAW: Hatfields!

PAW: McCoys!

MELANIE: Aw, Maw!

RUBEN AND MOE: Ah, Paw!

(RACHEL throws a flower at MAW.)

MAW: *(Shocked)* Rachel, watch your language!

DUDE: You mean to tell me that after all we've gone through to cure you, you two aren't going to let Ruben Hatfield marry Rachel McCoy?

MAW: Brother Ruben? You mean I've been harborin' a Hatfield?

PAW: Sister Rachel? You mean I've been cavortin' with a McCoy?

LOLA LOLA: Eggzackly!

MAW: *(Turning against* RUBEN*)* Hatfield, git back over on yer own side o' th' fence. And never darken my doorstep agin!

PAW: *(With deep regret)* Go on, McCoy! Go back where ya come from! Yer a McCoy an' I hates McCoys!

(The two kids cross over to the opposite sides of the fence.)

PAW: *(To* RUBEN *and* MOE*)* Jest when I was takin' a shine to th' little Shaker. You boys need a Maw an' I reckon Sister Rachel an' I was perfect fer each other.

MAW: *(To* RACHEL *and* MELANIE*)* I was fixin' to hitch up with Brother Ruben myself.

AUNT PRISCILLA: Now listen, *everybody.* I got some ole news for all o' youse. Brother Ruben is really Ruben McCoy.

MAW: The traitor! My own flesh an' blood turnin' against me!

AUNT PRISCILLA: An' Sister Rachel is really Rachel Hatfield. They was switched at birth during th' big feud o' thirty-nine. I oughta know, I was th' midwife who switched 'em in th' confusion o' th' feud. By th' time I realized my mistake, they was taken away to th' opposite sides o' this barbed-wire fence where they growed up ever since. I figure there was some divine plan in it. Now I see that th' Lord works in strange ways his miracles to perform.

MAW: *(To* RACHEL*)* Yer Paw would turn over in his grave if he was alive.

AUNT PRISCILLA: *(To* MAW*)* You cain't marry yer own son. *(To* PAW*)* An' you cain't marry yer own daughter. An' you ain't got no right to tell 'em who they can marry since you didn't raise 'em up.

MAW: Melanie, git away from that little Hatfield slut!

PAW: Moe, I don't want you hangin' aroun' with that Hatfield scum . . . er . . . I mean that McCoy scum. Jest 'cuz you growed up together.

MELANIE: This doesn't help Moe an' me.

MOE: Aunt Priscilla, you gotta cure 'em better than that.

AUNT PRISCILLA: I prescribe the layin' on of hands. Pull down that fence an' whup 'em 'til they agrees to marry each other.

PAW: Never!

MAW: Over my dade body!

*(*MELANIE, MOE, RUBEN, *and* RACHEL *pull down the fence and take* PAW *and* MAW *across their knees.)*

MAW: You cain't whup yer own father an' mother. It's against th' Ten Commandments.

PAW: It's a sin!

AUNT PRISCILLA: Jest as you whupped them in their first childhood, they gotta whup you in your second childhood.

*(*PAW *and* MAW *give in after a brief whupping.)*

PAW: All right, all right, I'll marry anyone you say.

MAW: Show me the man an' I'll marry him.

John Brockmeyer & Charles Ludlam in *Corn* (Leandro Katz)

ALL: Eeeeyaaahooo!

MOE: Now Ruben an' me can grow organic corn to supply health-food stores across the nation!

(They all join in a brief matrimonial square dance in which AUNT PRISCILLA *ties the knots joining* RUBEN *and* RACHEL, MELANIE *and* MOE, *and a reluctant* MAW *and* PAW *in holy matrimony. A shotgun is employed in the hymeneals of* MAW *and* PAW. *The stage is set up for the Country-Western Jamboree.)*

LUCKY STAR 1: *(Calls "Square Dance in F")*
  Honor your partner corner salute
  All join hands go lickety stew
  The other way home paint your wagon
  Hurry up boys let's see 'em waggin'
  When you get home swing high and low
  Swing her till she says let go
  Then promenade and around you go

Then promenade till you get straight
Promenade around you go
The two head couples to the right
Balance her but not all night
Then right and left eight across you go
Right and left go go go
Head couple to center and circle four
Four hands hold and round you go
Cowboy style and do-si-dos
Hurry up boys don't be slow
Ladies go straight boys ho ho
Chicken in the breadpan kickin' up dough
One more throw and home you go
Now everybody swing
Big one swing and the little ones too
Swing with her and he'll swing with you
Swing 'em high till it hits their toes
Then promenade and around you go
Promenade boys two by two
Walk it home like you always do
The two side couples to the right
Balance her but not all night
Then right and left eight across you go
Right and left eight ball in the hole
Side couple to the center circle four
Four hands up and around you go
Cowboys do a do-si-do
Hurry up boys don't take it slow
Do-si-do with the one you know
Walk around on heel and toe
One more do and home you go
Now everybody swing
Big ones swing and the little ones too
Swing your honey and he'll swing you
Swing 'em high and swing 'em low
Now promenade
Promenade in a great big ring
The rooster crow and the birdy sing
Now you know why I don't care
Take your darlin' to a rockin' chair.

Scene 14: DUDE, THE LUCKY STARS.

DUDE: Ladies and Gentlemen, presenting for the first time in Hicksville, Lola Lola and The Lucky Stars!

(THE LUCKY STARS *begin the concert with two numbers.*)

LUCKY STARS: (*Sing "Motorcycle Baby"*)
I'm wonderin' where my baby has gone
She went out one night and she said I won't be long

I thought she was goin' out to buy me some beer
But she never returned, won't you tell me if you've seen 'er.

(Chorus)
She's the one with the black leather jacket on her back
She wears a silver-studded policeman's cap
She rides an old Harley that looks real bad
She's my motorcycle baby, she's all that I had.

I searched in the bars till late in the night
And just before goin' home on sight of daylight
Reported to the missing persons' bureau
Won't you help me find my baby, here's all you need to know.

(Repeat chorus)

I forgot all about her as time passed away
Until an old buddy who lived in L.A.
Came walkin' up to me with a face awfully long
Said "my baby has left me and I don't know where she's gone."

(Repeat chorus)

(Sing "Life-Style of Fun")
Up every day 'bout two-thirty
Always got a new man on her mind
Not so important to look pretty
Long as she looks like one of a kind
Got a strong body mind and spirit
Learned how to hustle all three.

(Chorus)
She's living a life-style of danger
Doin' things that she's never done
She's living a life-style that's bound to drive her wild
She's living a life-style of fun.

Now don't get me wrong about the hustle
She always walks the right side of the street
Workin' her way up from the bottom
Runnin' with the small-time elite
Won't miss the club 'cause she fears it
Wants to hear the new, that's all.

(Repeat chorus)

Now it sounds like that she may be a loser
But inside her head fate has a plan
Lives off of her friends and neighbors
Some rich and some ain't got a dime
But it's for certain that she is gonna make it
Everybody patiently waits their time
So if you know a gal who plays the part
Smile and say you're doin' fine.

(Repeat chorus)

Scene 15: LOLA LOLA, THE LUCKY STARS.

(LOLA LOLA *joins* THE LUCKY STARS *on the concert stage.*)

LOLA LOLA: (*Sings "Big Vacation"*)
   Well she's out of school and she's no fool
   Ain't gonna be a country farmer's wife
   So she packs up her clothes and says good-bye to those
   Kinfolk that she's loved for all her life.

   Her mother sheds a tear and says, "Please, my dear,
   Won't you live at home for a short while,
   I'm afraid for you what they say is true,
   The city is bound to ruin your life."

   (*Chorus*)
   She made her final preparation for that big vacation
   It will be a celebration day and night
   She's takin' Greyhound transportation on her big vacation
   It will be the ruination of her life.

   Well, she hits the city lights and says, "boy they're bright,
   There must be one million things to do"
   A year of runnin' round all over that big town
   Now she's become tired, broke, and blue.

   Three years alone in a one-room home
   Livin' only for the next night
   When to the honky-tonk she'll go singin' for her dough
   Hopin' soon to see her name in lights.

   (*Repeat chorus*)

Scene 16: LOLA LOLA, DUDE.

DUDE: Looks like the Free Country Music Jamboree is a big hit, Lola Lola.
   There's press here from every big city in the United States of America. Radio,
   television, movies, and videotape cassettes: you've got 'em all in the palm of
   your hand. I guess you were right after all. About your roots, I mean. Lola
   Lola, I love you. Why don't you and I get married and settle down?

Scene 17: LOLA LOLA, DUDE, THE LUCKY STARS.

(THE LUCKY STARS, *who have been playing throughout the Dude's speech, come
running in from the concert stage.*)

LUCKY STAR 1: They're yellin' fer ya, Lola Lola.
LUCKY STAR 2: Will you come out and do another number?
LOLA LOLA: Sure, Boys, jest give me a minute. Play 'em something sweet. Tell
   'em I'll be right there.
LUCKY STAR 1: We'll tell 'em. But don't be long.
LUCKY STAR 2: Everybody loves you, Lola Lola.

DUDE: Well, go on. Don't keep the public waiting! And be careful of those costumes; you know they're rented!

(DUDE *exits with* THE LUCKY STARS.)

Scene 18: LOLA LOLA, AUNT PRISCILLA.

AUNT PRISCILLA: *(Poking in her head)* You wanted to talk to me, Miss Lola Lola?

LOLA LOLA: Yes, Aunt Priscilla, you said before that you was a midwife in Hicksville back in thirty-nine. That was about th' time that I was born. Well, I wondered if . . . maybe you know something . . . more than you're tellin'. . . . I mean, I wondered if you know anything about who my folks were.

AUNT PRISCILLA: I didn't want to say anything with the others around. You are the illegitimate daughter of the thwarted love of Jebediah McCoy fer Mavis Hatfield.

LOLA LOLA: The two who shot each other down during the big feud of thirty-nine?

AUNT PRISCILLA: That's what people in these parts says and they thinks it's true. But I happen to know that they took th' Lover's Leap because their parents made 'em hitch up with those two ornery crackers, Ezekiel Hatfield and Maude McCoy. They left you with me. *(In tears)* An' I gave ya to th' Snake Oil man in th' Medicine Show.

LOLA LOLA: Dr. Fowler taught me how to sing country music.

AUNT PRISCILLA: *(Breaking down)* Forgive me if I done wrong. I wanted ya to grow up away from all this hatin'. I was afraid of what they'd do to ya if they ever found out.

LOLA LOLA: Looks like I'm th' real McCoy! But what was my first name?

AUNT PRISCILLA: Yer Lola Lola now.

LOLA LOLA: No wonder I never wanted to settle down. Nobody ever set me an example.

AUNT PRISCILLA: You got an example. I never did marry.

LOLA LOLA: You didn't?

AUNT PRISCILLA: No, I guess I'm married to my art. I'd rather devote myself to healin' than to some heel.

LOLA LOLA: Right on, sister!

Scene 19: LOLA LOLA, AUNT PRISCILLA, DUDE.

DUDE: *(Bursting in)* They want you, Lola Lola, and they won't wait. Hello, Aunt Priscilla.

(AUNT PRISCILLA *tries to smile and nods.)*

DUDE: What's your answer, Lola Lola, will you marry me?

LOLA LOLA: I gotta go on. But I'll sing my answer to ya, okay? *(Exit)*

Scene 20: AUNT PRISCILLA, DUDE.

DUDE: Aunt Priscilla, are you cryin'?

AUNT PRISCILLA: Naw, jest got somethin' in my eye.

Scene 21: LOLA LOLA, THE LUCKY STARS, COMPANY.

(LOLA LOLA appears onstage in her white leather cowgirl costume with rhinestone cacti. THE LUCKY STARS are dressed in flashy matching outfits. The rest of the company are audience to the concert and stand with their backs to the audience in silhouette. LOLA LOLA sings "I've Been a Loner All My Life." The number ends to big applause, whoopin', and hollerin'.)

LOLA LOLA:
Grew up never havin' me a mom
Always movin' livin' in a mobile home
Strangers tellin' me what to do.

(Chorus)
I've been a loner all my life
And I won't cheat on myself now
By startin' a love affair with you.

Became a woman without time to live the test
All my questions were answered back in jest
Stranded with nobody to turn to.

(Repeat chorus)

As a young girl twisted words caused me to live in shame
I had to accept loneliness before happiness came
I'm satisfied so nothin' said will convince me I'm wrong
I'll love you for tonight but I won't cheat and love too long.

So now that you've been warned of me
Be strong, let's face reality
Even though you say your love is true.

(Repeat chorus, then)

I just want to thank my Lucky Stars.

(LOLA LOLA indicates the musical group and they take a bow. Then RUBEN runs in very excited.)

Scene 22: RUBEN, RACHEL, COMPANY.

RUBEN: Listen, everybody, Aunt Priscilla has cured Rachel's dumbness!
RACHEL: *(Clearing her throat)* You dosh burn little pinhead of misery you! Goll dang me if I think you're worth the powder to blow ya up! You peel them duds and git to work or else mosey right off'n this farm. Now see here, Ruben McCoy, I guess you thought that becuz I couldn't talk you was gonna git away with *any* tomfoolery. Well, you was sadly mistaken. You gonna git to work. Did you hear what I said? WORK! Now, I wanna take that cottage down by Picken's Nose. Moe an' Melanie are gonna take Maw's place. We'll git a little mortgage. A little down payment and monthly payments for the next thirty years.
RUBEN: *(Wailing)* Aunt Priscilla, please make her dumb again!

RACHEL: And I want you to paint it white and put up a post and rail fence with rambling roses.

(As RACHEL *continues to rant,* RUBEN *begins to hum the reprise of "Silver-Studded Saddle." Music joins in. He begins to sing softly, "We will ride one day," etc.)*

RACHEL: Now you gotta git up early and make me my cornmeal mush. And don't wake me until breakfast is ready. Don't think I forgot that little hosing down you gave me . . .

(As Ruben's song casts its spell, RACHEL *becomes tame and loving by the last words of her complaint, turns it into a yodeling accompaniment to the song. Sunset on the cyclorama.*
The whole company bursts out laughing, and sings the reprise of "Corn.")

ALL:
   Call it corn corn corn
   We ate it all our lives
   Call it corn corn corn
   It's all right!

Curtain

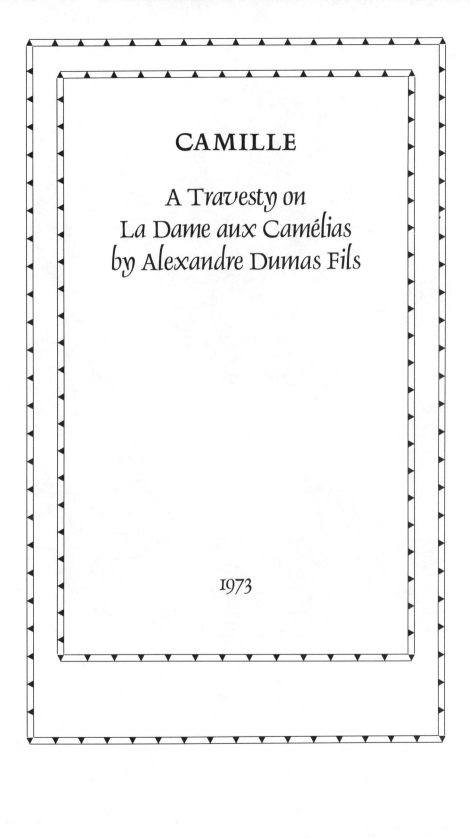

CAMILLE

A Travesty on
La Dame aux Camélias
by Alexandre Dumas Fils

1973

Charles Ludlam & Bill Vehr in *Camille* (John Stern)

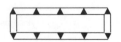

Cast of Characters

BARON DE VARVILLE, *Armand's rival*
NANINE, *maid*
MARGUERITE GAUTIER, a *courtesan*
JOSEPH, *the butler*
NICHETTE FONDUE, *a childhood friend of Marguerite*
OLYMPE DE TAVERNÉ, *Saint Gaudens's mistress*
SAINT GAUDENS, *a roué*
PRUDENCE DUVERNOY, *a milliner*
GASTON ROUÉ, *a playboy*
ARMAND DUVAL, *Marguerite's lover*
DUVAL SR., *Armand's father*

ACT I

Marguerite's drawing room, Paris, 1848.

VARVILLE: *(Pacing up and down with a bouquet of flowers)* Will she see me?
NANINE: Madame says she wants to be alone.
VARVILLE: So, she's playing cat and mouse, eh? Well, I hope she finds him amusing, whoever he is.
NANINE: Madame is alone. She has seen no one for three days. She's been ill again. It's a pathetic story. . . .
VARVILLE: Oh, yes, that is a pathetic story. Only unfortunately . . .
NANINE: Unfortunately?
VARVILLE: Unfortunately, I don't believe it.
NANINE: There are enough true things that can be said about Madame, so there's no use your telling things that aren't true. Madame never tells lies.
VARVILLE: *(Laughs)* Of course not.
NANINE: During her long illness, Madame accumulated over fifty thousand francs' worth of debts, and that's no lie.
VARVILLE: Bring Madame these flowers and tell her I am offering to pay her debts. Is it my fault I love her?
NANINE: *(Taking the flowers)* I don't know. It may be better to owe money to some people than gratitude to others. *(NANINE exits into Marguerite's room with the flowers. Off)* Marguerite, the Baron de Varville is still waiting. He says he is willing to pay all your debts if you will only see him. And he sends these flowers.
VARVILLE: Birds of paradise and aspidistra.
MARGUERITE: Aagh, get them away from me! Get those flowers away from me!

(The bouquet of flowers comes flying out of the door.)

VARVILLE: *(Picking them up)* You don't care for them?
MARGUERITE: What do they call me?
VARVILLE: Why . . . er . . . ah . . . you are called many things that one would hesitate to repeat.
MARGUERITE: I mean my name. What is my name?
VARVILLE: Marguerite Gautier.

MARGUERITE: No, no, you fool. I mean by what name am I known in the Bohemian quarter?

VARVILLE: The Lady of the Camellias.

MARGUERITE: *(Enters)* Why?

VARVILLE: Because you wear no other flowers?

MARGUERITE: And I can bear no other flowers. Their scent makes me ill. *(Coughs)* Now take your birds of paradise and get your aspidistra out of here. *(VARVILLE does not move)* You're not going?

VARVILLE: No.

MARGUERITE: Then, for God's sake, play the piano, dahling. Your music is your only saving grace.

VARVILLE: *(Obeying)* Is it my fault I love you?

MARGUERITE: If I were to listen to everyone who's in love with me, I would have no time for dinner. *(To NANINE)* Did you order dinner?

NANINE: Yes, Madame.

MARGUERITE: *(To VARVILLE)* I let you call on me when I'm in and wait for me when I'm out. But if you insist on talking of nothing but your love, I will withdraw my friendship.

VARVILLE: What have you got against love?

MARGUERITE: I have nothing against love. It just makes such dull conversation.

VARVILLE: And yet, last year at Marienbad you did give me some hope.

MARGUERITE: My dear, that was last year, that was Marienbad. I was ill; I was bored. But this is Paris and I'm very much better, and not at all bored.

NANINE: Marguerite, the doctor called again this morning.

MARGUERITE: What did he say?

NANINE: He said you are to rest as much as possible.

MARGUERITE: Dear doctor, always giving me good advice. *(To VARVILLE)* What's that you're playing?

VARVILLE: A rhapsody by Rauschenberg.

MARGUERITE: It's charming.

VARVILLE: Listen, Marguerite, I have eighty thousand francs.

MARGUERITE: How nice. I have a hundred thousand.

VARVILLE: Your indifference to me is like a camellia, no scent and no thorns.

MARGUERITE: *(Aside to NANINE)* He is the most persistent man in Paris. He insists on loving me.

NANINE: *(Confidentially)* He has eighty thousand francs.

MARGUERITE: How he bores me with his eighty thousand francs.

(The bell rings. BUTLER goes to the door.)

BUTLER: *(Announcing)* Nichette Fondue.

NICHETTE: Marguerite!

MARGUERITE: Nichette!

NICHETTE: You're looking well.

MARGUERITE: I always look well when I'm near death. Will you stay for supper?

NICHETTE: I can't. Gustave is waiting downstairs.

MARGUERITE: Oh, Nichette, you're still seeing that Gustave?

NICHETTE: Yes. He's been promoted to comptroller!

MARGUERITE: Oh, Nichette, you can do much better than a comptroller!

NICHETTE: But I never want to do better than Gustave. I love him.

MARGUERITE: Nichette, you're a very pretty girl, but a very bad business-woman.

NICHETTE: You'll see, Marguerite. One of these days you'll fall like a ton of bricks.

MARGUERITE: Me, fall in love? No, no, Nichette!

NICHETTE: Toodle-oo, Marguerite.

MARGUERITE: Ta-ta, Nichette.

(Bell.)

BUTLER: *(Announcing)* Madame Olympe de Taverné. Monsieur Saint Gaudens.

MARGUERITE: At last, Olympe. I thought you weren't coming.

OLYMPE: Blame it on Saint Gaudens. It's his fault.

SAINT GAUDENS: It's always my fault. Good evening, Marguerite. Good evening, Varville.

OLYMPE: I just found out today that Saint Gaudens is of Polish extraction.

MARGUERITE: No.

OLYMPE: His dentist is Polish. *(Aside to* MARGUERITE*)* Did you invite Gaylord?

MARGUERITE: I thought you would bring him.

OLYMPE: With Saint Gaudens? You know how jealous he is.

MARGUERITE: I thought you had him trained.

OLYMPE: You can't teach an older dog new tricks.

MARGUERITE: I like older men. They're so . . . grateful.

OLYMPE: And they have so much poise.

SAINT GAUDENS: Is Varville staying for supper?

MARGUERITE: No, he isn't. He's being punished for bringing me the wrong flowers.

SAINT GAUDENS: Didn't he bring camellias?

MARGUERITE: No, he didn't.

OLYMPE: How gauche of him. He committed a real false pah!

SAINT GAUDENS: Varville's in the doghouse.

MARGUERITE: *(At the window)* Prudence!

PRUDENCE: *(Off)* What do you want?

MARGUERITE: I want you to come over here at once.

PRUDENCE: Why?

MARGUERITE: Because it's my birthday and the Baron de Varville is still here, and he's boring me to death.

PRUDENCE: I have two young gentlemen here who have asked me out to supper.

MARGUERITE: Well, bring them over here to supper. Anything is better than the Baron. Who are they?

PRUDENCE: You know one of them, Gaston Roué.

MARGUERITE: Of course I know him. And the other?

PRUDENCE: A friend of his.

MARGUERITE: Come on over, dahlings, there's plenty of food here.

OLYMPE: It's so convenient to have Prudence living just across the courtyard.

MARGUERITE: Yes, she delivers my gossip fresh every morning.

SAINT GAUDENS: Who is this Prudence?

OLYMPE: She was once a kept woman who tried to go on the stage and failed. So, relying on her acquaintance with fashionable people, she opened a milliner's shop.

MARGUERITE: And nobody buys her hats but me.

OLYMPE: But you never wear them.

MARGUERITE: Dahling, they're beastly. I wouldn't wear one to a dogfight. But I adore Prudence, and she is hard up. *(Coughs a little)* It's cold this evening.

(Bell rings.)

BUTLER: *(At the door)* Madame Prudence Duvernoy, Monsieur Gaston Roué, and Monsieur Armand Duval.

PRUDENCE: *(Barges in wearing a big hat)* The classy way they announce people here! I knew this party was going to be piss elegant!

GASTON: *(To* MARGUERITE, *kissing her hand)* I trust you are well, Madame.

MARGUERITE: Quite well, thank you. And you?

PRUDENCE: Gee, the classy way they talk here! Marguerite, I want to present to you Monsieur Armand Duval, the man who is more in love with you than any man in Paris.

MARGUERITE: Nanine, set two more places. I hope his great passion hasn't spoiled Monsieur Duval's appetite.

ARMAND: Please accept this book as a remembrance of your birthday.

MARGUERITE: *Manon Lescaut?*

ARMAND: Yes. The story of a woman who brightened her wit with champagne, and her eyes with tears.

MARGUERITE: It's not a sad story, is it? I don't like sad thoughts.

ARMAND: It has a sad ending.

MARGUERITE: Well, I'll read it, but I won't read the ending.

SAINT GAUDENS: My dear Gaston, I'm so glad to see you!

GASTON: Saint Gaudens . . . as young as ever!

SAINT GAUDENS: Younger. Only my teeth are aging.

GASTON: And your love affairs—prospering?

SAINT GAUDENS: Well, there's Olympe here.

GASTON: So, you've taken up with this little trollop, eh?

OLYMPE: Watch who you call little.

MARGUERITE: *(To* NANINE, *who is setting the table)* Not the Melmac, Nanine, the Limoges.

GASTON: Whatever became of Beatrice?

SAINT GAUDENS: I gave her up. Her lover was a banker but she loved me for myself alone. But, still, the affair required a lot of hiding in cupboards, prowling about the back stairs, and waiting in the street.

GASTON: Which gave you rheumatism.

SAINT GAUDENS: Not a bit, but times change. We none of us grows any younger.

GASTON: *(To* MARGUERITE*)* Isn't he wonderful?

MARGUERITE: We are all growing old at exactly the same rate so there will be no sympathy for anyone, do you hear? *(To* ARMAND*)* Are you following me?

ARMAND: Yes.

SAINT GAUDENS: *(To* ARMAND*)* Are you related to Monsieur Duval, the receiver general?

ARMAND: Yes, sir, he is my father. Do you know him?

SAINT GAUDENS: I met him years ago at the Marchioness Fanzeepanzee's summer house, with your mother whom I remember as a very beautiful and charming fairy of a woman. You take after your mother.

ARMAND: My mother died three years ago.

SAINT GAUDENS: Forgive me.

ARMAND: I am always glad to be reminded of my mother.

SAINT GAUDENS: Are you an only son?
ARMAND: I have one sister. . . .

(ARMAND, SAINT GAUDENS, *and* OLYMPE *join* VARVILLE *at the piano.*)

MARGUERITE: *(Aside to* GASTON*)* I think your friend is charming.
GASTON: He is and, what's more, he adores you. Doesn't he, Prudence?
PRUDENCE: What?
GASTON: I was telling Marguerite that Armand is madly in love with her.
PRUDENCE: He's got it bad and that ain't good. Ah, l'amour, l'amour!
GASTON: He loves you so much, my dear, that he doesn't dare tell you about
  it.
MARGUERITE: Varville, please, please!
VARVILLE: You told me to keep on playing the piano.
MARGUERITE: When I am alone with you, not when I have friends.
PRUDENCE: He's loved you for two years.
MARGUERITE: Quite an old story, then.
GASTON: Armand simply lives at Gustave's and Nichette's to hear them talk
  about you.
PRUDENCE: I want something to drink.
OLYMPE: Look, I found some champagne.

(PRUDENCE, GASTON, *and* OLYMPE *get involved in opening the bottle of champagne.*)

NANINE: *(Taking* MARGUERITE *aside)* Marguerite, when you were ill a year
  ago, remember I told you of a young man who called to inquire after you every
  day but wouldn't leave his name?
MARGUERITE: I remember.
NANINE: *(Pointing discreetly)* That's him. Armand Duval.
MARGUERITE: How nice of him. *(Calling across the room)* Monsieur Duval, do
  you know what I have just been hearing? That you called to inquire after me
  every day when I was ill.
ARMAND: It's quite true.
MARGUERITE: Then the least I can do is thank you. Did you hear that, Varville?
  You never did that for me, did you?
VARVILLE: I have only known you for a year.
MARGUERITE: Don't be ridiculous, this young gentleman has only known me
  for five minutes.
BUTLER: *(Enters with boar's head on platter)* Dinner is served. *(Exits)*
PRUDENCE: Here is supper. I'm famished.
VARVILLE: I have no luck. Good-bye, Marguerite Gautier, Lady of the Ca-
  mellias. *(Kisses her hand)*
MARGUERITE: Good-bye. When shall we see you again?
VARVILLE: Whenever you wish. *(Bowing)* Gentlemen. *(Exits)*
SAINT GAUDENS: Good-bye, Varville, old boy. Better luck next time.
MARGUERITE: Let's eat!

(*They rush madly to the table.*)

PRUDENCE: You really are too hard on the Baron, dear. You could end up a
  baroness if you played your cards right. We're none of us getting any younger,
  and it's time you settled something about your future—while you still have
  one!

OLYMPE: I simply adore the Baron. He's rich, handsome, wealthy, talented, and he's got money! Do you know that he's just written a book?

MARGUERITE: Really?

GASTON: Ah, yes, his memoirs are considered the breviary of The Decadence.

PRUDENCE: And he's got eighty thousand francs.

MARGUERITE: How he bores me with his eighty thousand francs.

OLYMPE: Eighty thousand francs! I wish someone would offer to bore me that way! Do you know what Saint Gaudens gave me for my birthday? A coupé! But he didn't give me any horses to go with it!

PRUDENCE: Still, a coupé is a coupé is a coupé!

ALL: *(Clinking glasses simultaneously)* Touché!

SAINT GAUDENS: I'm ruined. Why can't I be loved for myself alone?

OLYMPE: *(Shrieking with laughter)* The idea!

MARGUERITE: Oh, come on Saint Gaudens, come and get your MDA.

SAINT GAUDENS: What's MDA?

MARGUERITE: Monsieur, don't ask.

PRUDENCE: What are those little fellows?

GASTON: Partridges.

PRUDENCE: *(To BUTLER)* You can put some on my plate.

GASTON: Some? Partridges aren't oysters, you know.

PRUDENCE: Well, they're not much bigger than oysters.

GASTON: What a birdlike appetite. Now we know who ruined Saint Gaudens . . . she did!

PRUDENCE: She! She! Is that any way to talk of a lady? Why in my day . . .

GASTON: We needn't go back to Louis the Fifteenth! Marguerite, fill Armand's glass. He's looking sad.

SAINT GAUDENS: This dinner is delicious.

PRUDENCE: I want another drink.

MARGUERITE: Gaston, play the piano. Come on, Saint Gaudens, sing us a song.

SAINT GAUDENS: How can I sing when I'm having my supper?

MARGUERITE: Sing for your supper.

PRUDENCE: I want another drink!

(SAINT GAUDENS begins to sing "Plaisir d'Amour.")

MARGUERITE: No, no, not that one! Let's have something gay, dahling.

(SAINT GAUDENS sings "Frère Jacques" and all join him, singing in rounds.)

ALL: Bravo! Bravo! *(Tap glasses with silverware)* Toast!

GASTON: *(Making a toast)* Ah, life is short and sweet and Prudence is short and fat.

(All clink their glasses together and drink.)

PRUDENCE: *(Quite drunk)* I want another drink!

OLYMPE: Fat, fair, and forty!

PRUDENCE: All right, smart ass, how old do you think I am? I'm . . . thirty-six!

(Riotous laughter.)

GASTON: But you don't look a day over forty!

(PRUDENCE hits GASTON over the head with a partridge. SAINT GAUDENS whispers in OLYMPE's ear.)

OLYMPE: *(Shrieking with laughter)* That's the funniest story I've ever heard in my life!

PRUDENCE: Tell me! Tell me! *(Motioning to* SAINT GAUDENS*)* Whisper in my ear.

MARGUERITE: That isn't fair. Tell us all. We want to hear it too.

PRUDENCE: *(Laughing almost uncontrollably)* I know what's coming, but do go on.

MARGUERITE: I want to hear it too.

SAINT GAUDENS: You tell her, Gaston.

GASTON: Ah, but you tell it so much better than I do.

SAINT GAUDENS: But it's your story.

GASTON: But I like to hear you tell it.

MARGUERITE: Let's have the story, man. Out with it!

OLYMPE: If Saint Gaudens won't tell it, *I* will.

SAINT GAUDENS: *(Cupping his hand over her mouth)* I'll tell it! I'll tell it! Well, you remember that awful divorce last year of Odile de Lille and that stockbroker of hers. Well, last week I saw her at the Ballet Gala at the Opera. They were doing *Zinnia, The Mute Girl of Cincinnati.* And who should arrive in the next box but Odile's ex! And he leaned over and said in a very loud voice, "Odile, my dear, how does your new husband like that worn-out twat of yours?" And she said—

OLYMPE: *(Breaking loose and interrupting)* "He likes it fine, once he gets past the worn-out part!"

(Everyone laughs uproariously except ARMAND.*)*

MARGUERITE: Monsieur Duval, you're not laughing. Don't you like Gaston's jokes?

ARMAND: I have heard Gaston's jokes. In fact, he learned some of them from me. But I would rather they were not repeated in your presence.

MARGUERITE: Come now, I'm not a colonel's daughter just out of the convent.

SAINT GAUDENS: Who hasn't been deceived? One's friends and one's mistresses are always deceiving one.

PRUDENCE: Ah yes, just as in *Berenice* by Racine . . .

(PRUDENCE *takes center stage, gesturing madly and emitting Gallic gutturals. The others look at her in wonderment.)*

MARGUERITE: Oh, she's acting.

PRUDENCE: Oh, mon pauvre chevrolet. J'aime le chateaubriand. Oh, le coq au vin, le coq au vin, sur le table avec les pommes frites.

(Standing at the table, she leans back on top of it, in a kind of reverie. GASTON *throws a pie in her face. Everyone laughs.)*

MARGUERITE: Bravo, Saint Gaudens. You are a hero and we are all in love with you. All those madly in love with Saint Gaudens hold up your hands. *(To* SAINT GAUDENS*)* Well, hold up your hand, dahling. Unanimous. Prudence, my dear, you really ought to stick to Maeterlinck. You will always be remembered for your *Joiselle.* Gaston, play something for Saint Gaudens to dance to.

GASTON: I don't know anything but St. Vitus' Dance.

MARGUERITE: Then we'll have St. Vitus' Dance. Come on, Saint Gaudens . . . Armand, move the table.

PRUDENCE: But I haven't finished.

OLYMPE: Do I have to dance with Saint Gaudens?

MARGUERITE: No, I'm going to. Come along, little Saint Gaudens.

ARMAND: Aren't you afraid that you're not well enough to dance?

MARGUERITE: I'm not afraid of anything except being bored.

OLYMPE: Come, Armand.

SAINT GAUDENS: Your hollandaise was divine, my dear.

MARGUERITE: It's especially good around the Jewish hollandaise.

(*All dance to the music that* GASTON *plays.* MARGUERITE *coughs. The music stops. All look to her.*)

SAINT GAUDENS: What's the matter?

MARGUERITE: Nothing. I lost my breath.

ARMAND: (*Going to her*) Are you all right?

MARGUERITE: Yes. It's nothing. Don't stop. (*Starts to dance again and then falls*)

ARMAND: Stop, Gaston.

PRUDENCE: Marguerite is ill.

MARGUERITE: It's nothing. (*Falls again*)

ARMAND: (*Catching her*) The party's over.

PRUDENCE: She's always ill just when everybody is having a good time.

OLYMPE: You can never have any fun here.

PRUDENCE: Let's go somewhere else. Let's go to my place. Wait a minute! I'm just beginning to get hungry again! Bring the food with us. Forward . . . march!

GASTON: (*To* ARMAND) She's been laughing too much and she's spitting up blood. It's nothing. It happens to her every day.

(*Exit all with the food except* MARGUERITE *and* ARMAND.)

MARGUERITE: (*Looking in a mirror*) How pale I look!

ARMAND: You're killing yourself.

MARGUERITE: If I am, you're the only one who objects. The others don't worry about me.

ARMAND: The others don't love you as I do.

MARGUERITE: Ah yes, I had forgotten that great love of yours.

ARMAND: You laugh at it.

MARGUERITE: I've heard it too many times to laugh anymore. It's an old joke and the joke is on me.

ARMAND: Promise.

MARGUERITE: What?

ARMAND: To take care of yourself.

MARGUERITE: My good man, if I were to begin to take care of myself, I would die. Don't you see that it is only the feverish life I live that keeps me alive? The moment that I am no longer amusing to people, they leave me, and the long days are followed by longer nights. I know, I was in bed for two months and after three weeks, no one came near me.

ARMAND: Those people are horrible.

MARGUERITE: They're the only friends I have and I'm no better than they are.

ARMAND: Don't say that. Let me take you away from all this. We could go to the country where I would take care of you like a brother. I'd never leave you and I would cure you. Then, when you were strong again, you could return to this life if you wished, but I don't think you would want to.

MARGUERITE: How depressing. I don't like sad thoughts.

ARMAND: Have you no heart, Marguerite?

MARGUERITE: I'm traveling light, no heart.

ARMAND: Have you never been in love with anyone?

MARGUERITE: Never!

ARMAND: Thank God!

MARGUERITE: You're a strange boy. You've drunk too much wine and that has made you sentimental. Tomorrow it will be a different story.

ARMAND: Was it wine that brought me here every day when you were ill?

MARGUERITE: No, that couldn't have been wine. But why didn't you come up?

ARMAND: What right had I?

MARGUERITE: Since when are men so formal with women like me?

ARMAND: And I was afraid.

MARGUERITE: Afraid?

ARMAND: Afraid that you would grant me too promptly that which I wanted to win through long suffering and great sacrifice. Imagination lends too much poetry to the senses, and the desires of the body make concessions to the dreams of the soul. I would rather die for your love than pay fifty francs for it.

MARGUERITE: So, it's as bad as that! And you would look after me?

ARMAND: Yes.

MARGUERITE: You would stay with me all day long?

ARMAND: Yes.

MARGUERITE: And even all night?

ARMAND: As long as I didn't weary you.

MARGUERITE: And what does this great devotion come from?

ARMAND: The irresistible sympathy which I have for you.

MARGUERITE: So you are in love with me. Why don't you just say it? It's much more simple.

ARMAND: If I say it, it will not be today.

MARGUERITE: Never say it.

ARMAND: Why?

MARGUERITE: Because only two things can come of it. Either I shall not accept—then you will have a grudge against me—or I shall accept, and you will have a mistress who is sad or gay with a gaiety sadder than grief, who spits up blood and spends a hundred thousand francs a year. That is all very well for a rich old man like the Baron, but it is very bad for a young man like you. . . . If what you say is true, go away at once. Love me a little less or understand me a little better. I'm not worth much. You're too young and sensitive to live in a world like ours. Love some other woman and marry. . . . I'm trying to be honest with you.

ARMAND: What if I were to tell you that I've spent whole nights beneath your windows and that for two months I've treasured a glove you dropped.

MARGUERITE: I should not believe you.

ARMAND: You're right to laugh at me. I'm a fool. There's nothing else to do but laugh at me.

MARGUERITE: Armand, can't we just be friends?

ARMAND: That's too much, and not enough. Don't you believe in love, Marguerite?

MARGUERITE: I don't know what it is. It's hard to believe in it if you've never had it.

ARMAND: *(Crushing her in his embrace)* Let me make you believe. We'll rent a country house. Fresh air and good food will make you well in no time.

MARGUERITE: But that takes money.

ARMAND: I have money.

MARGUERITE: How much?

ARMAND: I have seven thousand francs a year.

MARGUERITE: *(Pulling away from him and laughing)* I spend more than that in a week. And I've never been too particular where it came from, as I guess you know.

ARMAND: Don't talk like that!

MARGUERITE: It's true. The hard cold facts are we need hard cold cash. Why, the rental of a country house, horses, and a carriage to get around, to get us there and back . . . Enough for the table, even simple food costs money . . . No servants except for Nanine . . . *(Handing him a pen and paper)* Oh, I'm no good at arithmetic. You figure it out.

(ARMAND sits down at the desk and begins figuring. A knock at the door. NANINE enters with an enormous bouquet of red camellias.)

NANINE: *(Aside to MARGUERITE)* The Baron de Varville sent these. Looks like he's learned his lesson. They're camellias this time.

ARMAND: *(Finishing the sum)* Eighty thousand francs.

NANINE: He's waiting downstairs.

MARGUERITE: What did you say?

ARMAND: I said we'll need eighty thousand francs.

NANINE: I said the Baron de Varville is waiting downstairs.

ARMAND: But don't worry, darling, I'll get it somewhere.

MARGUERITE: Eighty thousand francs. *(ARMAND tries to take MARGUERITE in his arms but she resists)* Take this camellia and bring it back to me when it dies.

(She hands ARMAND a flower and he kisses it.)

ARMAND: When will that be?

MARGUERITE: How long does it take a flower to wither? A morning, an evening. Tomorrow night.

ARMAND: *(Crushing the flower in his hand)* Here, it's dead already.

MARGUERITE: No, no, impossible. I wear red camellias when I've got the rag on . . . when the moon is not favorable to pleasure. I'll be wearing white ones tomorrow.

ARMAND: I can't wait. Let me sleep here tonight beside you like your brother or at the foot of your bed like your dog. But let me wait here until the camellias turn white.

MARGUERITE: You put tears on my hand. Yes. Yes. No! Yes!

ARMAND: *(Overjoyed)* You'll take me? Like this, at a moment's notice?

MARGUERITE: Does it seem strange to you? *(Taking his hand and placing it on her heart)* Feel my heart beating. I shall not live as long as others so I have promised myself to live more quickly.

ARMAND: Don't talk like that, I beg of you.

MARGUERITE: But however short a time I have to live, I shall yet live longer than your love.

ARMAND: I thought you didn't like sad thoughts.

MARGUERITE: I don't. But they come sometimes.

(Bell rings.)

NANINE: *(Enters whispering)* Madame, the Baron is waiting. Shall I send him away?

MARGUERITE: *(Aside to* NANINE*)* Tell him to wait. *(To* ARMAND*)* Armand, would you run out and get me some marrons glacés? I suddenly have the maddest craving for marrons glacés.

ARMAND: Aren't there any in the house?

MARGUERITE: No, and nothing but marrons glacés will do. Please go out and get me some.

ARMAND: Marguerite, is something wrong? I feel you're trying to get rid of me.

MARGUERITE: Now what on earth gave you that idea? Come back at midnight, and I'll be waiting for you.

ARMAND: How do I know you'll let me in when I come back?

MARGUERITE: *(Giving him a key)* I'll give you the key and you can let yourself in. Now go, quickly. *(*ARMAND *starts out the door.* MARGUERITE *blocks his way and shows him another)* No, this way.

*(*ARMAND *rushes out. There is a pause.* ARMAND *rushes in again.)*

ARMAND: I love you. *(Exits)*

MARGUERITE: *(To* NANINE*)* Is it possible that he does love me? Or can I even be sure that I love him, I who have never loved? Show the Baron in, Nanine.

NANINE: I shall pray for you, Madame.

MARGUERITE: Why?

NANINE: Because you are in danger.

MARGUERITE: Oh pooh. Lying keeps my teeth white. Send the Baron in, Nanine. *(*THE BARON *enters)* Baron!

VARVILLE: You kept me waiting long enough.

MARGUERITE: Hello, you. I have just been putting my account books in order. *(Showing him the book)* See?

VARVILLE: Lovely.

MARGUERITE: But, look at all these bills. I have eighty thousand francs' worth of debts. Will you lend me the money?

VARVILLE: No.

MARGUERITE: What will I do?

VARVILLE: Come with me to Siberia *(*MARGUERITE *coughs)* and I'll give you all the money you want.

MARGUERITE: If you are my friend, why won't you give it to me now?

VARVILLE: Because if I do, you may no longer have any use for me. It has been months since we've as much as spent a night together. [*(*VARVILLE *plants a kiss on* MARGUERITE*'s arm. Lipstick is left. She wipes it off and sprays it with an atomizer)*] Until we do, your bills will go unpaid. *(*MARGUERITE *sits down at the piano and begins to play Chopin.* VARVILLE *looks over the papers on the desk. He finds the sheet on which* ARMAND *was doing the sum and picks it up)* What's this? "House: thirty thousand francs; horses and carriage: twenty thousand . . . Nanine, Marguerite, and myself . . . thirty thousand. . . ." Who is this "my-self"?

MARGUERITE: *(Still playing)* Myself, of course. My doctor insists that I go to the country this summer for my health. That's why I asked you for the eighty thousand francs. I'm afraid of getting sick again. I know how it bores you.

VARVILLE: This note says, "Nanine, Marguerite, *and myself. . . ."* A summer in the country, away from the glamour of Paris, living quietly with the cows and the chickens sounds very unlike you, my dear.

MARGUERITE: But, it's true.

VARVILLE: You can't fool me. I know you've found a playmate for this rustic holiday.

MARGUERITE: *(Stops playing suddenly)* Damn Chopin and all his sharps and flats!

VARVILLE: I'm afraid your mind isn't on it, my dear.

MARGUERITE: You know quite well that I could never play it.

VARVILLE: Let me spend the night and you can have all the money you need.

MARGUERITE: Only if you will play the piano for me. *(Rings for* NANINE*)*

VARVILLE: *(Bitterly)* My one merit. *(Begins to play)*

MARGUERITE: *(Aside to* NANINE*)* Bolt the door and don't answer it, no matter what happens.

NANINE: Yes, Madame. *(Exits)*

VARVILLE: Are you two through whispering over there?

MARGUERITE: I was just giving some orders to Nanine.

VARVILLE: Yes, I'm sure you were. *(Continues playing. The doorbell rings)* Someday I'm going to get temperamental and complain when doorbells ring while I am trying to play.

MARGUERITE: *(Pulling out whip and masks of black leather)* Did the doorbell ring? I didn't hear it.

VARVILLE: *(Continuing to play)* Does my music shut out the world for you, my dear?

MARGUERITE: You play beautifully. *(Puts on mask)*

VARVILLE: You lie beautifully.

(Doorbell rings again.)

MARGUERITE: *(Masking* VARVILLE*)* Thank you, that's more than I deserve.

VARVILLE: Oh, no, it's not half as much as you deserve. *(They laugh. Doorbell. The clock begins striking twelve)* I wonder who it could be at this hour.

MARGUERITE: *(Handcuffing* VARVILLE *to the piano)* If I told you, you wouldn't believe me.

VARVILLE: Try me.

MARGUERITE: *(Whipping him)* I could say that someone has found the wrong door. *(Laughs)*

VARVILLE: The great romance of your life! *(Laughs)*

MARGUERITE: That might have been! [*(Starts to whip piano)*]

(They both laugh—she ironically, he bitterly—as the curtain falls.)

ACT II

Scene 1: A country house at Auteuil. A room looking out on a garden.

ARMAND: Where is Marguerite?

PRUDENCE: She is in the garden picking strawberries with Nichette, who has come to spend the day with her. I'm just going to join them.

ARMAND: One moment, Prudence. A week ago, Marguerite gave you some diamond bracelets to have reset. What has become of them?

PRUDENCE: Well, that's a long story. I . . . er . . . I . . . ah . . .

ARMAND: Come, tell me frankly. Where are Marguerite's bracelets?

PRUDENCE: Do you want the truth?

ARMAND: Of course I want the truth.

PRUDENCE: Sold.

ARMAND: Her gowns?

PRUDENCE: Sold.

ARMAND: Her horses and her jewels?

PRUDENCE: Sold and pawned.

ARMAND: Who has sold and pawned them?

PRUDENCE: I did.

ARMAND: Why did you not tell me?

PRUDENCE: Marguerite made me promise not to.

ARMAND: And where has all the money gone?

PRUDENCE: In payments. Ah, my dear fellow, she didn't want to tell you. Marguerite's creditors went to the Baron de Varville to settle, and he had them thrown out of his house. They wanted their money. I gave them part payment out of the few thousand francs you gave me. But, someone told them that Marguerite had been abandoned by the Baron and was living with a penniless young man. They stormed her house and ripped off all of her goods. Marguerite wanted to sell everything, but it was too late. So rather than ask you for the money, she sold her horses, her carriage, her gowns, and her jewels. Here are the receipts and the pawn tickets. *(Gives him the receipts)*

ARMAND: How much money is needed?

PRUDENCE: Fifty thousand francs. Ah, I hate to say I told you so. You think it is enough to be in love, and go to the country, and live on air. You'll soon find out that someone has to pay the rent on your pastoral dream! Ah, l'amour, l'amour. Toujours l'amour! Yecch.

ARMAND: Ask our creditors for a fortnight's grace. I will pay.

PRUDENCE: Are you going to borrow the money?

ARMAND: Yes. I suspected something of the kind and have written to my solicitor.

PRUDENCE: No, Armand, you'll only quarrel with your father and ruin your whole future.

ARMAND: Hush, she's coming. [*(MARGUERITE enters wearing wooden shoes)*] I want you to scold Prudence for me, dearest!

MARGUERITE: Why?

ARMAND: She forgot to bring me my mail, so I shall have to go to Paris to get it myself. I didn't give anyone our address here because I wanted to be left in peace. I'll be gone only a couple of hours.

MARGUERITE: Yes, go dear, but do come back quickly.

ARMAND: I shall drive in and be back in an hour.

MARGUERITE: And take care of yourself.

ARMAND: And you too. Take care of her, Prudence.

MARGUERITE: Each moment will be an eternity.

PRUDENCE: For God's sake, he's not going to war! He's just going to get his mail.

NICHETTE: *(Entering)* Oh, what a happy couple!

ARMAND: Hello, Nichette. I'm just leaving. I'm sure you girls have a lot to talk over. *(Exit with PRUDENCE)*

MARGUERITE: You see, this is where we have been living for the last three months. Salon, bedroom, anteroom, and kitchen. Furnished in a way that would divert a hypochondriac. Was I right?

NICHETTE: Are you happy?

MARGUERITE: Very happy.

[*(Picks up hand bell, rings it with abandon.* NANINE *enters with tea on a serving tray.)*]

NICHETTE: I always told you, Marguerite, that this was the way to be happy. Many a time Gustave and I have said to each other, "When will Marguerite really love someone and settle down?"

MARGUERITE: Well, your wish is fulfilled. I am really in love. I think it was watching you and Gustave that first made me envious.

NICHETTE: We have two dear little rooms in the rue Blanche.

MARGUERITE: Two little rooms.

NICHETTE: And Gustave says that I am not to work and he will buy me a carriage, one of these days.

MARGUERITE: One of these days!

NICHETTE: And we're going to get married, too.

MARGUERITE: One of these days?

NICHETTE: Soon.

MARGUERITE: You will be very happy. [*(*MARGUERITE *pours tea.)*] Sugar? [*(*MARGUERITE *places twelve sugar cubes in her cup, one by one, hesitates with the thirteenth, decides against it)*]

NICHETTE: But aren't you going to get married and do as we do?

MARGUERITE: Whom should I marry?

NICHETTE: Why, Armand, of course!

MARGUERITE: Armand would marry me tomorrow if I wished it. But I love him too much for that.

NICHETTE: But so long as you are happy, what does it matter?

MARGUERITE: I *am* happy. I can tell you because I know you will understand. [*(Takes off wooden shoes)*] The Marguerite that used to be and the Marguerite of today are two different beings. I used to spend enough money on camellias to keep a poor family for a year. *(*NANINE *enters with dish of strawberries)* But, now, a flower like this that Armand gave me this morning is enough to fill my whole day with perfume. What do you call this flower, Nanine?

NANINE: Bittersweet. *(Exits)*

MARGUERITE: And yet money-money-money-money. It was the Baron de Varville who paid for everything. Now I'm in debt. Why can't anything ever be perfect?

NICHETTE: If only you could be content with two little rooms like ours.

MARGUERITE: Listen, Nichette, I came up from grinding poverty and it stinks. I never want to go back to work in a shop and live in two little rooms with cucarachas and ratóns. No, no, I'll never go back! There are only two ways a woman may rise from the gutter and become a queen: prostitution or the stage. And, believe me, Nichette, I'd rather peddle my coosie in the streets than become an actress!

NICHETTE: There is another way a woman may rise, Marguerite. A woman may marry.

MARGUERITE: Marriage is nothing but legalized prostitution. *(Salutes with fist. Throws a strawberry up and catches it in her mouth)*

NICHETTE: I think you're wrong, Marguerite, terribly wrong.

MARGUERITE: Perhaps . . . perhaps . . .

NICHETTE: If only you would come to visit our two little rooms, I'm sure you would change your mind.

MARGUERITE: Perhaps I will . . . one of these days.

NANINE: *(Entering)* There is a gentleman here who wishes to speak to you, Madame.

MARGUERITE: That will be my lawyer. I was expecting him. *(To* NICHETTE*)* Please excuse me.

NICHETTE: I really must be going. I want to have Gustave's dinner ready for him when he gets home from the office.

MARGUERITE: Cooking? Sister, have you no pride?

NICHETTE: Pride? That's one luxury a woman in love can't afford. Toodle-oo, Marguerite!

MARGUERITE: Ta-ta, Nichette!

(Exit NICHETTE. *Enter* PRUDENCE.*)*

PRUDENCE: I've sold your diamond earrings. Here's your receipt. Here are the earrings. *(Pulling earrings from* MARGUERITE*'s ears)* Here's my commission. I'm off! Good-bye, Marguerite. You know where to find me if you need me. L'amour, l'amour. *(Exits)*

DUVAL: *(Entering)* Mademoiselle Marguerite Gautier?

MARGUERITE: Yes, I am she. To whom do I have the honor of speaking?

DUVAL: To Monsieur Duval.

MARGUERITE: Monsieur Duval?

DUVAL: Yes, Madame, I am Armand's father. Is Armand here?

MARGUERITE: *(Troubled)* No, Armand is often here. But just now he is away, at Paris.

DUVAL: Good. I want to speak to you alone. You see, I know what's going on here. My son is ruining himself for you.

MARGUERITE: You are mistaken, sir. I accept nothing from Armand.

DUVAL: Am I to understand, then, as your habits of luxury are well known, that my son is mean enough to help you spend what you receive from others?

MARGUERITE: You must excuse me, sir. Your manner of addressing me is not what I should have expected from a gentleman. I must ask your permission to withdraw.

DUVAL: Your indignation is cleverly assumed, Madame. They were right when they told me you were dangerous.

MARGUERITE: Dangerous to myself, perhaps, but not to others.

DUVAL: Then will you explain to me the meaning of this letter? It is from my lawyer informing me that my son wishes to turn over to you the inheritance he received from his mother.

MARGUERITE: I assure you that, if Armand has done such a thing, it is entirely without my knowledge. He knew that, if he had offered it to me, I should have refused it.

DUVAL: That was not always your method, I think.

MARGUERITE: It is true, now . . .

DUVAL: Now?

MARGUERITE: Now I have learned what true love means.

DUVAL: Fine phrases, Madame.

MARGUERITE: You force me to disclose to you that which I should have preferred to keep secret. Ever since I knew and loved your son, I have been selling my horses, my carriage, my gowns, and my jewels. A moment ago, when I was told that someone wished to speak with me, I concluded that it was in connection with the sale of furniture, pictures, and the rest of the luxury with which you have reproached me. I was not expecting you, sir, so you may be quite sure that this paper was not prepared especially for you, but if you doubt what I say, read this. . . . *(Gives him the bill of sale which* PRUDENCE *has drawn up)*

DUVAL: *(Reading)* A bill of sale on your jewels, the purchaser to pay your creditors, the balance to be given to you? *(Looks at her in astonishment)* Have I been mistaken?

MARGUERITE: You have. It is Armand who changed me.

DUVAL: Forgive me, Madame, for my discourtesy a moment ago. I was not acquainted with you and quite unprepared for what I was to find. I was deeply hurt by my son's silence and ingratitude of which I judged you to be the cause. I beg your pardon.

MARGUERITE: Thank you.

(Pause)

DUVAL: And what if I ask you to give Armand a greater proof of your love?

MARGUERITE: No! No! You are going to ask something terrible of me. I knew I was too happy.

DUVAL: Let us speak together now like two friends.

MARGUERITE: Yes . . . friends.

DUVAL: I speak to you as a father who asks you for the happiness of his two children.

MARGUERITE: Of his two children?

DUVAL: Yes, Marguerite, of his two children. I have a daughter, young, beautiful, pure. She is to be married and she, too, has made her love the dream of her life. Society is exacting in certain respects, especially provincial society. The family of my future son-in-law have learned of the manner in which Armand is living; they have given me to understand that the marriage cannot take place if it continues. Marguerite, in the name of your love, grant me the happiness of my child.

MARGUERITE: How can I refuse what you ask with so much gentleness and consideration? I understand. You are right. I will go back to Paris. I will leave Armand for a while. Besides, the joy of our reunion will help us to forget the pain of parting.

DUVAL: Thank you, Marguerite, thank you, but there is still something that I must ask of you.

MARGUERITE: Can you ask anything more of me?

DUVAL: A temporary parting is not enough.

MARGUERITE: You mean you want me to leave Armand altogether?

DUVAL: You must.

MARGUERITE: Never! You don't know how we love each other.

DUVAL: My son is as dear to me as he can possibly be to you.

MARGUERITE: But you have friends and a family. I have only Armand. I'm ill. I have only a few years to live. To leave Armand would kill me.

DUVAL: Come, come, let's not exaggerate. You're not going to die. What you feel is the melancholy of happiness, knowing that even love can't last forever. No woman is worthy of a man if she lets him ruin himself. Think of Armand's career. He will never go through doors you cannot go through. He can't present you to his family and friends. You're killing his right to a normal life.

MARGUERITE: You're not telling me anything I haven't said to myself a hundred times—but I never let myself go through to the end. *(To herself)* A woman once she has fallen can never rise again. *(To* DUVAL*)* But a man can go back, he can always go back!

DUVAL: What career would remain open to him? What will be left to you both when you are old? Who can promise that he will not be less dazzled when time casts the first shadow over your beauty? Has not your own experience taught you that the human heart cannot be trusted?

MARGUERITE: My God!

DUVAL: No unprotected woman can afford to waste the best years of her life. What will your old age be, doubly deserted, doubly desolate?

MARGUERITE: What must I do? Tell me.

DUVAL: You must tell Armand that you no longer love him.

MARGUERITE: He won't believe me.

DUVAL: Leave him.

MARGUERITE: He will follow me.

DUVAL: In that case . . .

MARGUERITE: Do you believe that I love Armand with a love that is truly unselfish?

DUVAL: Yes, Marguerite.

MARGUERITE: Then, sir, will you kiss me just once, as you would your own daughter? And believe me when I tell you it is the only really pure kiss that I have ever received. And promise me that one day you will tell this beautiful and pure young girl that somewhere in the world there is a woman, who had only one thought, one hope, one dream in life, and that for her sake she renounced them all *(Throws spray of bittersweet off)*, and that she died of it. Because I shall die of it and then, perhaps, God will forgive me.

DUVAL: *(Moved in spite of himself)* Poor girl! *(Kisses her)*

MARGUERITE: I swear that he shall never know what has passed between us. One last favor.

DUVAL: Ask it.

MARGUERITE: Within a few hours, Armand will experience one of the greatest sorrows he has ever known, or perhaps ever will know. He will need someone who loves him. Will you be here, sir, at his side?

DUVAL: What are you going to do?

MARGUERITE: If I told you, it would be your duty to prevent it.

DUVAL: You are a noble girl. But I am afraid.

MARGUERITE: Fear nothing, sir. He shall hate me. *(Rings for* NANINE*)*

DUVAL: I shall never forget what I and my family owe you.

MARGUERITE: Make no mistake, monsieur, whatever I do is not for you. Everything I do is for Armand.

DUVAL: Is there nothing I can do for you in acknowledgment of the debt that I shall owe you?

MARGUERITE: When I am dead and Armand curses my memory, tell him that I loved him and that I proved it. We shall never meet again. Good-bye. *(Exit* DUVAL. MARGUERITE *alone)* Venus Castina give me strength. *(Writes a letter)*

NANINE: *(Entering all smiles)* You rang for me, Madame?

MARGUERITE: *(Weeping)* Yes, there is something I want you to do for me.

NANINE: What is it?

MARGUERITE: Take this letter, Nanine.

NANINE: Why, you're weeping. I don't know what's in it, but I can see that the thought of it makes your blood run cold.

MARGUERITE: Read the address.

NANINE: The Baron de Var . . . Now what do you want to send this for? I thought you were so happy with Monsieur Duval.

MARGUERITE: I was.

NANINE: Then what are you doing, you foolish girl?

MARGUERITE: I'm going to make my love hate me, Nanine. Make him hate me! Make him hate me! *(Sobs)*

NANINE: But . . .

MARGUERITE: Hush. Go at once! *(Exit* NANINE*)* And now for Armand. *(Begins writing a second letter)*

ARMAND: *(Entering)* Ah, Marguerite, I'm back.

MARGUERITE: Already?

ARMAND: What's the matter? You don't seem glad to see me.

MARGUERITE: I saw you this morning and last night and yesterday and the day before that.

ARMAND: How was your day?

MARGUERITE: Well, this morning Prudence and I walked down the road to see the new cow. And this afternoon, I washed my hair. Those were the two big events of my day.

ARMAND: You seem so strange. What's the matter?

MARGUERITE: I'm bored.

ARMAND: Bored? But this morning you said you liked the country.

MARGUERITE: That was this morning.

ARMAND: Are things so different now?

MARGUERITE: Yes, things are different now. This is no life for me.

ARMAND: What does this mean?

MARGUERITE: I'm going back to Paris.

ARMAND: But you said it would kill you if you went back to Paris.

MARGUERITE: Perhaps it will. If I'm going to die, I'd rather die gaily than of boredom. Wasn't one summer all you wanted, dahling?

ARMAND: I won't let you go. *(He takes her in his arms and holds her very tight)*

MARGUERITE: You must let me go, Armand. You must. It's better this way, better for both of us.

ARMAND: You've put tears on my hand.

MARGUERITE: I had to cry a little. There, I'm better now. Believe me, I've loved you as long as I can. It's not my fault that I can't love you forever. We don't make our own hearts, Armand.

ARMAND: *(Releasing her)* No, Marguerite, you can't help it that you can love me only a little while. Just as I can't help it that I will love you for the rest of my life.

MARGUERITE: *(Bitterly)* That's the way it is. I'm going.

ARMAND: I can't let you go!

MARGUERITE: You must. The Baron de Varville is expecting me.

ARMAND: The Baron de Varville?!! I could kill you for this.

MARGUERITE: I'm not worth killing. You can't give me the things in life I want. I can't part with my horses, my carriage, my gowns, and my jewels. I thought I could, but I can't.

ARMAND: You filthy slut! *(*MARGUERITE *runs out the door. Calling after her)* Marguerite, forgive me! I didn't mean it! Marguerite, don't leave me! Please don't leave me! (*DUVAL SR. *has entered at the back.* ARMAND *turns, sees his father, and collapses into his arms in tears)* Father!

Scene 2: *A soirée at Olympe's house in Paris, six months later.*

PRUDENCE: What a wonderful party!

GASTON: Yes, splendid, splendid. I've been losing all my money.

PRUDENCE: That's all right. Gambling is a gentleman's vice.

GASTON: Olympe has outdone herself tonight. This is the most extravagant soirée of the season.

PRUDENCE: I wonder if Saint Gaudens knows what it is costing him.

OLYMPE: *(Overhearing)* His wife does!

(They all laugh.)

PRUDENCE: Very witty!

GASTON: What a charming gown you are wearing tonight, Olympe.

OLYMPE: Thank you. It's from Prudence's shop. A Duvernoy original. I wanted to wear a gown by Gongora, but Saint Gaudens wouldn't hear of it.

SAINT GAUDENS: My dear, it wasn't you. A grande bateau-mouche tricked out in Punch and Judy orchids. Foh!

OLYMPE: Whenever Saint Gaudens doesn't like the dress I'm wearing, I take it off!

SAINT GAUDENS: Gaston, do you think a demimondaine such as this one might want to give up her former life and lead a simple and pure existence?

GASTON: Put a duck on a lake among swans and you will observe that the duck misses its mire and will return to it.

SAINT GAUDENS: Homesick for the mud. Then you don't believe in repentant Magdalenes.

GASTON: I do. In the desert!

OLYMPE: I like poise, don't you? I always insist upon it. For instance, a woman should always leave a man before he leaves her.

PRUDENCE: And here I am, six months later, and still in the same dress.

OLYMPE: Fermez la bouche. Nobody's going to buy you a new one.

BUTLER: *(Announcing)* Monsieur Armand Duval.

GASTON: Look, there's Armand.

SAINT GAUDENS: Hurumph!

GASTON: But where is Marguerite?

OLYMPE: *(Mit schadenfreude)* Haven't you heard? They've broken up!

GASTON: Impossible.

PRUDENCE: It's quite true. It happened last summer at Auteuil.

GASTON: Then they've really parted. Will Marguerite be here tonight?

PRUDENCE: No, not a chance.

OLYMPE: Don't be too sure, Prudence. I invited the Baron de Varville.

GASTON: Then Varville won her after all.

OLYMPE: "Bought" is more the word, I should say.

SAINT GAUDENS: Don't be a camp, Olympe.

OLYMPE: How can you reproach me? I've been a very good friend to Marguerite. Didn't I buy her horses, her carriage, her gowns, and her jewels when she needed the money?

PRUDENCE: It is true.

OLYMPE: *(Pointing out various items of jewelry she is wearing)* See, these and this one and this one. I got them for peanuts. Even this gown belonged to her.

PRUDENCE: The Baron has given her back everything that she lost—her horses, her carriage, her gowns, and her jewels. Ah, l'amour, l'amour! For what happiness is worth in this world, she is happy. But she never sleeps.

OLYMPE: She goes everywhere: theaters, balls, orgies, and operas.

PRUDENCE: She won't listen to her doctor. She won't last long at this rate. Ah, l'amour, l'amour, toujours l'amour!

GASTON: *(Greeting* ARMAND*)* Well, Armand, what a surprise to see you. I thought you'd left Paris.

ARMAND: Well, you were wrong.

GASTON: I hear you've broken with Marguerite.

ARMAND: You heard right.

GASTON: Do you ever see her?

ARMAND: No, never.

GASTON: I hear she is coming here tonight.

ARMAND: *(Starts)* Then I *shall* see her.

GASTON: Of course, she'll be with Varville.

ARMAND: So much the better. *(Intensely)* Listen, Gaston, I'm going crazy. Ever since Marguerite left me, I have hardly slept. And when I do sleep, I have nightmares.

GASTON: Dear boy.

ARMAND: I came here tonight because I knew she would be here. I want to punish her for leaving me.

GASTON: Armand, be careful. She is a woman, and any act of revenge on your part will seem like cowardice.

ARMAND: Then let her escort protect her. I would give anything for an excuse to kill him.

BUTLER: Madame Marguerite Gautier. The Baron de Varville.

(ARMAND *goes over and puts his arm around* OLYMPE, *who plays up to him.* MARGUERITE *enters wearing the same gown as* OLYMPE *but much more fabulous. There is a momentary confrontation between the two women.)*

MARGUERITE: *(To* VARVILLE*)* I don't feel well. I want to go home.

OLYMPE: *(Turning on* PRUDENCE, *furiously)* I thought you said this gown was an original!

PRUDENCE: *(Sheepishly)* Well, it was. The first time I made it.

OLYMPE: *(Wringing* PRUDENCE*'s neck)* You treacherous old harridan! *(Spinning around furiously)* I won't be outdone in my own home! *(During her tantrum, her dress becomes disheveled and one tit is exposed; she hides it with her fan. Regaining her composure, she faces* MARGUERITE*)* You made me lose my poise and for this, I shall never forgive you! *(Starts out)*

SAINT GAUDENS: Where are you going?

OLYMPE: I'm going to change into my Gongora with the Punch and Judy orchids! *(Exits)*

MARGUERITE: Please, Varville, I want to go home. I'm ill.

VARVILLE: Your illness bores me, my dear. *(*MARGUERITE *drops her fan)* You've dropped your fan.

MARGUERITE: What?

VARVILLE: You've dropped your fan.

MARGUERITE: Oh, have I? *(Bends over and picks it up)*

GASTON: Good evening, Marguerite.

MARGUERITE: *(Drying her eyes)* Good evening, dear Gaston, I'm so glad to see you.

GASTON: You're weeping. What is the matter?

MARGUERITE: It's nothing. I'm just unhappy, that's all.

GASTON: What are you doing here?

MARGUERITE: I am not my own mistress. Besides, I do all I can to forget.

GASTON: Take my advice and leave at once! I fear there may be some trouble between Armand and the Baron, perhaps a duel.

MARGUERITE: A duel between Armand and Varville?

GASTON: Make some excuse. Say you are ill.

MARGUERITE: You are right. *(To* VARVILLE, *who has been cruising the* BUTLER*)* Varville, I'm terribly ill. We must leave at once.

VARVILLE: We're staying right where we are. I'm not missing the best soirée of the season because of Armand Duval.

*(*OLYMPE *enters in an outrageous Gongora gown with Punch and Judy orchids.)*

GASTON: Is this a woman or a circus tent? *(Pops one of the balloons that hold up her skirt)*

OLYMPE: You stop that. *(Hanging around* ARMAND*'s neck)* Look, Armand's been winning at cards.

ARMAND: Yes, I'm testing the old saying, "Lucky at cards, unlucky in love."

OLYMPE: How do you like me, Armand?

ARMAND: I like you as well as you like my money.

OLYMPE: Come, let's greet the Baron de Varville and Marguerite Gautier together.

ARMAND: I will on one condition.

OLYMPE: I'll do anything as long as it's *not* within reason.

ARMAND: If you don't stop talking like that, I'm going to knock your little teeth down your throat. I want you to insult Marguerite.

OLYMPE: I'd be delighted. *(*ARMAND *and* OLYMPE, *petting each other, go to greet the* BARON *and* MARGUERITE*)* Good evening, Marguerite, Baron.

MARGUERITE: Good evening, Olympe.

ARMAND: Marguerite, Baron. *(Bows)*

VARVILLE: Good evening. *(Bows stiffly)*

MARGUERITE: Good evening.

VARVILLE: We've just come from the Opera, where we heard Berenice Blowell.

OLYMPE: What did she sing?

VARVILLE: *Manon Lescaut.*

ARMAND: Ah, yes, *Manon Lescaut,* the story of a vile woman incapable of loyalty, who sold her young lover for an old man's gold.

OLYMPE: How very unoriginal. And most untrue. Women never betray their lovers.

ARMAND: Some do.

OLYMPE: Of course, but there are lovers and lovers.

ARMAND: Just as there are women and women.

*(*MARGUERITE *drops her fan again.)*

VARVILLE: You dropped your fan again, my dear.

*(*ARMAND, *intercepting* MARGUERITE, *picks up the fan and returns it to her.)*

MARGUERITE: Thank you.

ARMAND: Any gentleman would do the same.

(VARVILLE makes a threatening movement toward ARMAND. MARGUERITE and OLYMPE draw the two men apart.)

GASTON: Armand, would you care for a hand of baccarat?

ARMAND: Yes, I intend to make my fortune tonight. Then when I am really rich, I intend to go and live in the country.

OLYMPE: Alone?

ARMAND: No, with someone who went with me once before and left me. It all depends on how much I win. If I am wealthy, perhaps I can buy her back.

GASTON: Be quiet, Armand. Look at that poor girl.

ARMAND: It's an amusing story. You would enjoy it. There is an old buffoon who makes his appearance right at the very end—a sort of deus ex machina. . . .

VARVILLE: Sir!

MARGUERITE: *(Aside to VARVILLE)* If you challenge Monsieur Duval to a duel, you will never see me again as long as you live.

ARMAND: You addressed yourself to me, sir?

VARVILLE: I did. Your luck tonight tempts me to try my own. I understand perfectly how you intend to use your winnings and I should be happy to help you increase them. Therefore, I propose to bet against you.

ARMAND: I accept with all my heart, sir. But remember, the reverse of the old saying may also be true. "Lucky in love, unlucky at cards."

(ARMAND and VARVILLE begin gambling.)

MARGUERITE: My God, what are they doing?

PRUDENCE: *(Aside to BUTLER)* Say dinner is served.

BUTLER: I beg your pardon?

PRUDENCE: Say dinner is served. *(Gives him a good swift kick in the hams)*

BUTLER: *(Blurts out)* Dinner is served!

PRUDENCE: Thank heavens! I'm famished. Dinner is ready, everyone. Come into the next room and eat! *(She herds everyone out)* Ah, l'amour, l'amour!

MARGUERITE: Gaston, dahling, please ask Armand to come in here a moment. I must speak to him.

GASTON: I will. *(Exits)*

VARVILLE: *(To MARGUERITE)* Are you coming, my dear?

MARGUERITE: Go ahead without me. I need a moment to repair my maquillage.

VARVILLE: All right. But if you are longer than five minutes, I'll come back for you. *(Exits)*

ARMAND: *(Entering)* You sent for me?

MARGUERITE: Yes, Armand, I want to speak to you.

ARMAND: What do you want?

MARGUERITE: I want to beg you to please stop this.

ARMAND: Stop what?

MARGUERITE: This torture. I can't bear it.

ARMAND: I'm sure I don't know what you mean.

MARGUERITE: You *do* know what I mean. This continuous punishment. I can't bear it. I can't bear it.

ARMAND: What business is it of yours what I do? We mean nothing to each other anymore.

MARGUERITE: That's not true, Armand. I love you. I have always loved you.

ARMAND: Then come away with me at once!

MARGUERITE: Oh, I would give my life for one hour of such happiness, but it's impossible.

ARMAND: It will be humiliating for me, but I will do anything to have you back. You can take everything I own. You name your price.

MARGUERITE: Armand, stop!

ARMAND: *(On his knees)* Please, Marguerite. Since I have loved you, I can love no other. Help me! Help me!

MARGUERITE: I can't, Armand. I have promised not to.

ARMAND: Who have you promised?

MARGUERITE: Someone to whom I owe all the respect in the world.

ARMAND: *(Incensed)* The Baron de Varville?

MARGUERITE: Yes.

(ARMAND throws open the doors to the next room.)

ARMAND: Come in here, all of you. I have an announcement to make!

MARGUERITE: What are you doing?

(All enter, puzzled.)

ARMAND: You see this woman?

ALL: *(Pointing simultaneously to* MARGUERITE*)* Marguerite Gautier?

ARMAND: Yes, Marguerite Gautier! She spent a summer in the country with me once. I gave her everything I had. I loved her as I have never loved anyone and as I shall never love again. But that love was not enough for her. It meant less to her than horses, a carriage, and the diamonds around her neck. I have not yet paid her for the summer we spent together. You are my witnesses. I owe this woman nothing.

(ARMAND slaps MARGUERITE across the face with the bundle of franc notes he won and throws them at her. They fall about her in a flurry.)

VARVILLE: *(To ARMAND)* Congratulations, young man. You have treated her as she deserved.

(ARMAND slaps VARVILLE across the face. MARGUERITE faints. Curtain.)

ACT III

Marguerite's bedroom. Paris, six months later. New Year's Day.

(The light of dawn reveals snow falling outside the window of Marguerite's apartment. MARGUERITE *is in bed asleep;* NANINE *has fallen asleep in a chair.* GASTON *enters [wearing a skeleton's head on the back of his head]. The occasional sound of a last reveler tooting his party horn is heard off stage along with a cry of "Happy New Year" and a snatch of "Auld Lang Syne" sung drunkenly. A bit of confetti might blow past the window.* GASTON *wears a party hat with bits of confetti in his hair and a few serpentines around his neck. He may be a little drunk on champagne, but not unbecomingly so.)*

GASTON: She is still asleep. What time is it? Seven o'clock. Not yet daylight. *(The sound of loud snoring from* NANINE*)* Faithful old Nanine. *(Lights candle)* It is better to light one candle than to curse the darkness. *(He picks up Marguerite's purse from the mantel)* Here's her purse. *(Looking inside)* Empty! *(He reaches* *deep inside his pockets and pulls out some franc notes, turning his pockets inside out in the process. Stuffs the notes into her purse)*

MARGUERITE: *(Waking)* I'm thirsty, Nanine.

GASTON: *(Giving her some tea)* Here you are, old girl.

MARGUERITE: I'm cold. Nanine, throw another faggot on the fire!

NANINE: *(Waking)* There are no more faggots in the house. *(Falls asleep)*

MARGUERITE: *(Plaintively looking out at the audience)* No faggots in the house? Open the window, Nanine. See if there are any in the street. *(Seeing GASTON)* Gaston, what are you doing here?

GASTON: Drink this first, and then I'll tell you. I am a born nurse.

MARGUERITE: But where is Nanine?

GASTON: Asleep. How do you feel this morning?

MARGUERITE: Better, Gaston dear. But why should you tire yourself like this?

GASTON: Tire myself? Nonsense! I've been out all night partying. I just wanted to wish you a Happy New Year.

MARGUERITE: New Year?

GASTON: I wanted to bring you flowers. But I couldn't find a single camellia in Paris. It seems there was a killing frost last night in the flower market.

MARGUERITE: I'm cold.

GASTON: Drink this.

MARGUERITE: It's strange that you should come here to take care of me. I always thought that you were just a scatterbrain who cared for nothing but pleasure.

GASTON: You were quite right. *(MARGUERITE laughs and then coughs)* Now, I'll tell you what we'll do.

MARGUERITE: What?

GASTON: You must try to sleep a little longer. There will be plenty of sunshine in the early part of the afternoon. Wrap yourself up well, and I will come back and take you for a drive. And then who'll sleep tonight? . . . Marguerite! Now I must go and call on my mother, and God knows what kind of a reception I'll get. I haven't been to see her in over a fortnight. I shall lunch with her and then call for you at one o'clock. How will that suit you?

MARGUERITE: I shall try to have enough strength.

GASTON: You will. Of course, you will. *(To NANINE)* Marguerite is awake. Until this afternoon then. *(Exits)*

MARGUERITE: Until this afternoon. Are you tired, my poor old Nanine?

NANINE: A little, Madame.

MARGUERITE: Open the window, Nanine, and let in the morning air. I should like to get up.

NANINE: The doctor said you weren't to get out of bed.

MARGUERITE: Dear doctor. Always giving me good advice.

NANINE: He's going to have you well by spring.

MARGUERITE: When God said it was a sin to tell lies, he must have made an exception for doctors. I suppose they have a special dispensation from the pope every time they visit a patient. What have you got there?

NANINE: Presents, Madame.

MARGUERITE: Oh, yes, it's New Year's Day. How much can happen in a year! . . . A year ago today, we were sitting around the table singing and laughing. . . . Where are the days, Nanine, when we still laughed? *(Opens parcels)* A *ring* with a card from Saint Gaudens. A *bracelet!* From the Baron de Varville. He sent it all the way from Siberia. It's cold. What would he say if he could see me like this? . . . And marrons glacés! Well, men are not so forgetful, after all. Joseph has a little niece, hasn't he, Nanine?

NANINE: Yes, Madame.

MARGUERITE: Give him these marrons glacés, for the little girl. It's been a long time since I've wanted any. Is that all?

NANINE: There is a letter.

MARGUERITE: A letter! *(Takes letter, opens it, and reads)* "My dearest Marguerite, I have called again and again, but was not allowed to see you. I cannot bear the thought that you will have no share in the happiest day of my life. I am to be married on the first of January. It is the New Year's gift that Gustave was keeping as a surprise for me. I do hope that you will be able to come to my wedding—such a simple, quiet wedding in the Chapel of Sainte Thérèse, in the Madeleine. I kiss you, dear, with all the fervor of my most happy heart. Toodle-oo. Nichette." And so, there is happiness for everyone in the world except for me. But there, I am ungrateful. Please, shut the window, I'm cold. *(The bell rings.)* Ah, there is the bell. See who it is, Nanine.

NANINE: *(Coming back)* Madame Duvernoy would like to see you.

MARGUERITE: Let her come in. Pretty please, let her in. Just this once. *(Etc.* NANINE *relents)* There's the good Nanine.

PRUDENCE: *(Entering)* Well, my dear Marguerite, how are you this morning?

MARGUERITE: Better, thank you, Prudence. And how are you?

PRUDENCE: Rotten, thank you. I drank too much champagne last night at Olympe's and I've got the worst hangover. My stomach, oh my God, I don't know when I've had such indigestion. Olympe has a new chef who is a genius, an absolute artist of genius. But he's ruined my stomach. And then, there's a headache to top it all off. And my sciatica has been acting up again. I'm feeling terrible. I'm really enjoying very poor health.

MARGUERITE: I'm sorry to hear it.

PRUDENCE: Have you heard? The Baron de Varville has recovered from the duel. Fortunately, it was only a scratch and Armand can return from exile. The Baron has taken up with little boys. He likes to get kicked in the rump by little boys! All that money he used to spend on jewels is now being wasted on toys. Ah, l'amour, l'amour! Send Nanine away for a moment. I want to speak to you alone.

MARGUERITE: You can finish the other room first, Nanine. I'll call you if I need you.

(Exit NANINE.*)*

PRUDENCE: I wonder if you would do me a favor, Marguerite?

MARGUERITE: What is it?

PRUDENCE: You have money in hand, don't you?

MARGUERITE: You know that I have been very short of money for some time.

PRUDENCE: It's New Year's Day and I have some presents to buy. I'm badly in need of two hundred francs. Do you think you could lend it to me until the end of the month?

MARGUERITE: Until the end of the month!

PRUDENCE: If it's not inconvenient.

MARGUERITE: Well, I do rather need what money I have left.

PRUDENCE: *(In a snit)* Very well, then, we'll say no more about it. *(Pause)* I didn't want to mention it, but you do owe me two hundred francs for the bonnet I made for you last Easter.

MARGUERITE: Bonnet?

PRUDENCE: Of course, it was violet voile with Costa Rica roses. Don't tell me you've forgotten it.

MARGUERITE: How could I forget the Costa Rica roses.

PRUDENCE: Why, here's your purse.

MARGUERITE: It's empty.

PRUDENCE: *(Looking inside the purse)* Nonsense! It's full of money!

MARGUERITE: Full of money? . . . Gaston! How much is there?

PRUDENCE: Five hundred francs!

MARGUERITE: Then take the two hundred that you need.

PRUDENCE: Are you sure the rest will be enough for you?

MARGUERITE: I shall have all I need. Don't worry about me.

PRUDENCE: You are looking better this morning.

MARGUERITE: I feel better.

PRUDENCE: It won't be long now before spring will be here. Warm weather and a little country air will soon put you right.

MARGUERITE: Yes, that's what I need.

PRUDENCE: *(Going out)* Well, good-bye, dear. And thank you again.

MARGUERITE: Send Nanine to me.

(Enter NANINE.)

NANINE: Has she been asking you for money again?

MARGUERITE: Yes.

NANINE: Did you give it to her?

MARGUERITE: Money is such a little thing to give, and she needed it badly, she said. But we need some too, don't we? We must buy some New Year's presents. Take this bracelet that has just come. Sell it and come back as quickly as you can.

NANINE: But what about you?

MARGUERITE: I shall not need anything. Oh, Nanine. Sweet Nanine. Perfect Nanine. You will not be gone very long. You know the way to the pawnbroker's. He's bought enough from me these last three months.

(Exit NANINE. JOSEPH has been standing in the background listening.)

BUTLER: *(Coming forward)* Excuse me, Madame, I am a man of few words. Nanine and I have put away a little money for our old age. It isn't much. But it might be enough for a pilgrimage to Lourdes. Please accept our life's savings.

MARGUERITE: Yes, it is a miracle that I need. Thank you, Joseph. But there is only one miracle that can save me . . . Armand's return.

NANINE: *(Entering)* Here is the money, Madame. I had to smuggle it past the bailiff waiting downstairs.

MARGUERITE: *(Putting the money into an envelope with a note)* Take this to Nichette at the Chapel of Sainte Thérèse in the Madeleine. Tell her not to open it until after the wedding.

BUTLER: Yes, Madame. *(Exit with NANINE)*

MARGUERITE: If only I had some word from Armand. That hope alone keeps me alive. How changed I am. The doctor said that I am very ill. But one may still be very ill and have a few more months to live. If only Armand would come and save me. It is the first day of the new year; a day to hope and look forward in. *(Laughter is heard outside the window)* I hear people laughing far away.

NANINE: *(Entering)* Madame . . .

MARGUERITE: Yes, Nanine?

NANINE: You feel better today, don't you?

MARGUERITE: Why?

NANINE: If I tell you something, will you promise to keep quite calm and quiet?

MARGUERITE: What is it?

NANINE: I want to prepare you. I'm afraid a sudden joy might kill you.

MARGUERITE: Did you say a joy, Nanine?

NANINE: Yes.

MARGUERITE: Armand! You've seen Armand? He's coming to see me? *(NA-NINE nods and gives MARGUERITE a bunch of camellias)* He mustn't see me like this. My hair, bring me a brush. Help me up.

NANINE: No, Madame, you must not get up. You're too weak.

MARGUERITE: *(Adamant)* Don't just stand there, help me, Nanine. *(NANINE supports MARGUERITE as she struggles over to her vanity table and paints her lips and cheeks)* Please, Nanine. Ma solitaire. Ne pas le gros, l'énorme. My camellias. There isn't much time. Send him in, hurry!

(DUVAL SR. appears in the doorway.)

DUVAL: Madame, you have kept your word to the utmost limit of your strength, and I fear recent events have injured your health. I have written to Armand, telling him the whole story. He was far away but he has returned to ask your forgiveness, not only for himself but for me, too. Go to her, Armand!

(ARMAND enters remorsefully and crosses to MARGUERITE.)

MARGUERITE: At last, Armand! It's not possible that you've come back, that God has been so good to me.

ARMAND: If we had not seen Nanine, I should have remained outside and never dared to come near you. Have pity, Marguerite! Don't curse me! If I had not found you again, I should have died because it would have been I who killed you. My father has told me everything. Tell me that you forgive us both. Oh, how good it is to see you again!

MARGUERITE: Forgive you, darling! It was all my fault! But what could I do? I wanted your happiness so much more than my own. Your father won't part us again, will he? You do not see the Marguerite that you used to know, Dear, but I am still young. I will grow beautiful again now that I am happy.

ARMAND: I will never leave you again, Marguerite. We will go to the country at once and never come back to Paris anymore. My father knows what you are now, and will love you as the good angel of his son. My sister is married. The future is ours.

MARGUERITE: We must lose no time, beloved. Life was slipping away from me, but you came and it stayed. You haven't heard, have you? Nichette is to be married, this morning, to Gustave. Let's go to see her married.

ARMAND: And repeat those vows along with them, silently, in our hearts.

MARGUERITE: It would be so good to go to church, to pray to God, and look on a little at the happiness of others. Tell me again that you love me.

ARMAND: I love you, Marguerite. All my life is yours.

MARGUERITE: Bring my outdoor things, Nanine. I want to go out.

ARMAND: You are a good girl, Nanine. You have taken faithful care of her. Thank you.

MARGUERITE: We used to speak of you every day. No one else dared mention your name. But Nanine would comfort me and tell me that I would see you again. And she was right. You have traveled a long way and seen many strange lands with strange customs. You must tell me about them and perhaps take me there one day. *(She sways)*

ARMAND: What is it, Marguerite? You are ill!

MARGUERITE: *(With difficulty)* No, it's nothing. Happiness hurts a little at first and my heart has been desolate for so long. *(She throws back her head)*

ARMAND: Marguerite, speak to me. Marguerite!

MARGUERITE: *(Coming to herself)* Don't be afraid, Dear. I always used to have these moments of faintness, don't you remember?

ARMAND: *(Taking her hand)* You are trembling!

MARGUERITE: It's nothing. Come, Nanine, give me my shawl and bonnet. We're going to the country! *(NANINE begins to weep)* Don't just stand there, Nanine. Hurry, we're going to the country! *(Tries to walk)* I can't. I can't. I can't.

(MARGUERITE drops. ARMAND catches her and carries her to the chaise.)

ARMAND: *(In terror)* Oh God! Oh, my God! Run for the doctor, Nanine! At once!

MARGUERITE: Yes, yes! Tell him that Armand has come back! That I want to live! That I must live . . . *(Exit NANINE)* But if your coming hasn't saved me, nothing will. I have lived for love. Now I'm dying of it.

ARMAND: Hush, Marguerite. You will live. You must.

MARGUERITE: Sit down here beside me, as close as you can. Just for a moment. I was angry at death. But now I see that it had to come. I'm not angry anymore because it has waited long enough for me to see you again. If I had not been going to die, your father would never have written to you to come back.

ARMAND: Marguerite, don't talk like that! I can't bear it! Tell me that you are not going to die! That you don't believe it, that you will not die!

MARGUERITE: Even if I did not wish it, Dear, it would have to be because it is God's will. If I had really been the girl you should have loved, I might have grieved more at leaving a world where you are and a future so full of promise. Then we might have lived happily ever after. But perhaps it's better that I die. Then there'll be no strain on our love. Believe me, God sees more clearly than we do.

ARMAND: Don't, Marguerite, don't.

MARGUERITE: Must I be the one to give you courage? Come, do as I tell you. On my vanity table you will find a miniature of me, painted in the days when I was still pretty. Keep it, it will help your memory later. If ever you should love and marry some young and beautiful girl, as I hope you may one day, and if she should find the portrait and ask who it is, tell her it is a friend who, if God in her starry heaven permits, will never cease to pray for you and her. And if she should be jealous of the past, because we women sometimes are, and ask you to give up the picture, do so, Dearest. I forgive you now, already. A woman suffers too deeply when she feels she is not loved. . . . Are you listening, Armand, my darling, do you hear me?

(Enter NICHETTE, *timidly at first and then more boldly as she sees* MARGUERITE *smiling and* ARMAND *at her feet.)*

NICHETTE: Marguerite, you wrote to me that you were dying, but I find you up and smiling.

ARMAND: *(Aside)* Ah, Nichette, I am so miserable!

MARGUERITE: I am dying, but I am happy too, and it is only my happiness that you can see. . . . And so you are married! . . . Look at that. . . . What a strange life this first one is. What will the second be? . . . You will be even happier than you were before. Speak of me sometimes, won't you? Armand, give me your hand. Believe me, it's not hard to die. That's strange. *(Enter* GASTON*)* Here is Gaston come back for me! I am so glad to see you again, dear Gaston. Happiness is ungrateful. I had forgotten you. . . . Thank you for filling my purse with money. . . . He has been so good to me, so kind . . . Ah! . . . It's strange.

ARMAND: What?

MARGUERITE: I'm not suffering anymore. I feel better, so much better than I have ever felt before . . . I am going to live. *(Appears to sleep)*

GASTON: She is asleep.

ARMAND: *(With anxiety at first, then with terror)* Marguerite! Marguerite! Marguerite! Don't leave me! Please don't leave me!

GASTON: She loved you dearly, poor girl.

NANINE: *(On her knees beside* MARGUERITE*)* Much will be forgiven you, for you loved much. Toodle-oo, Marguerite.

(Tableau vivant. All lights dim out leaving the little statue of the Madonna on Marguerite's vanity in the flickering light of a votive candle.)

Curtain

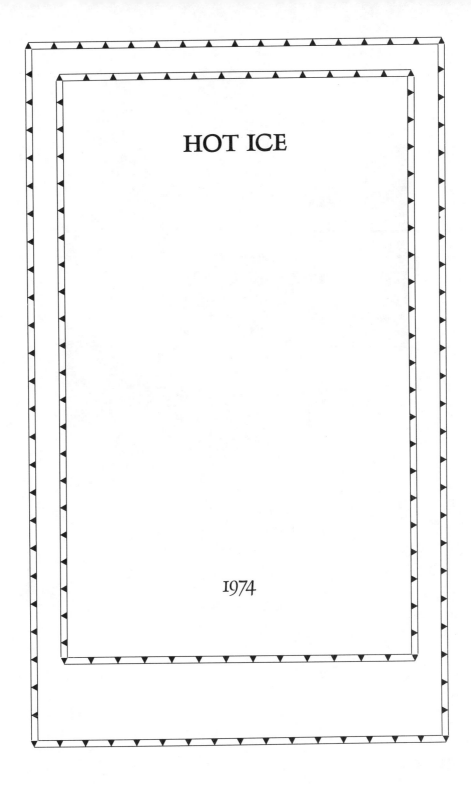

HOT ICE

1974

Charles Ludlam & Black-Eyed
Susan in *Hot Ice* (Thomas Harding)

Crassest of Caricatures

RAMONA MALONE, *an attractive widow*
TANK IRISH, *Chief of Euthanasia Police*
BUCK ARMSTRONG, *radio expert of Euthanasia Police*
LIEUTENANT SCZUTCARETSKI
MISS ENRIGHT, *Euthanasia Police matron*
MAX MORTIMER, *president of The Cryogenic Foundation*
IRMTRAUT "MOMS" MORTIMER, *a tough customer*
BUNNY BESWICK, *Jewish princess*
PIGGIE
NARRATOR
MAN IN THE AUDIENCE
WOMAN IN THE AUDIENCE
HER MOTHER
THE KID
LADY WITH THE POODLE

ACT I

NARRATOR: *(Sitting on the edge of an office desk, leafing through a newspaper)* Unless you are the type who reads the papers from cover to cover, you may have missed a small item in yesterday's late edition. "Frozen bodies discovered in the Tombs." Incredible? Fantastic? Science Fiction? No. Ever since Man first gained consciousness he has been troubled by the awareness that he must die. All of the world's great religions have been built on the fear and mystery surrounding this simple, irreversible fact. Since his first awakening, Man has gazed on the amaranth, the mythical undying flower, and dreamed of immortality. But today, in the wake of a decadent technology, the monstrous perversity of which is unequaled in the annals of art, certain men are challenging death through cryogenics or low-temperature biology. A man may provide in his will to keep himself frozen until such time as science can discover a cure for the disease of which he died. Such a man was Markus P. Malone. *(NARRATOR retires to an inconspicuous position upstage and begins to play with a yo-yo.)*

Scene 1: *Euthanasia Police Headquarters.*

(Enter EUTHANASIA POLICE *and* RAMONA *in mourning suit with black veil covering her face.)*

TANK: Try to calm yourself, Ms. Malone. I just want you to answer a few routine questions. What's your moniker?
RAMONA: Ramona Malone, ossifer. What's yours?
TANK: Tank Irish.
RAMONA: That's a pretty name.
TANK: What's in a name? William Shakespeare.
RAMONA: You're a card. I swear, you're a real card.
TANK: Name of rube town in which you hung forth?
RAMONA: Or fifth. Levittown, Long Island.
TANK: Housing development?

RAMONA: At one time.

TANK: Sex?

NARRATOR: Raising a little her hem.

RAMONA: Yes.

TANK: Do you smoke after intercourse?

RAMONA: I don't know. I never looked.

TANK: Occupation?

RAMONA: Croquet, mush-and-milk sociables. The Elks Lodge and a maiden aunt. What can a poor widow do?

TANK: Widow? Congratulations, mourning becomes you.

NARRATOR: Shrugging off the compliment.

RAMONA: This old rag?

TANK: Religion?

RAMONA: None.

TANK: You don't go to church?

RAMONA: No, I don't go to church. Kneelin' bags my nylons.

TANK: Have you had your appendix out?

RAMONA: Yes, I have a scar here. *(Indicates her neck)*

TANK: If you had your appendix out, why do you have a scar here. Your appendix was down there.

RAMONA: I'm ticklish.

TANK: Did you go to school?

RAMONA: Yes.

TANK: Name of school?

RAMONA: I can't tell.

TANK: Why not?

RAMONA: Because the school pays me seventy-five dollars a week not to tell.

TANK: Diet?

RAMONA: Vegetarian.

TANK: You know, there's something I'd like to ask you about that. If they call a man who eats only vegetables a vegetarian, why can't we call a man who eats human beings a humanitarian?

RAMONA: You're pulling my leg. Get real. I haven't got forever. Every moment that we delay is costing me money. Thaw my husband. Do something.

NARRATOR: She breaks down.

RAMONA: Oh . . .

TANK: Aw, turn off the water faucet. Lieutenant Sczutcaretski, where is Buck Armstrong?

SCZUTCARETSKI: He's in the men's locker room oiling his body.

TANK: Send that jock in here. He's our man.

SCZUTCARETSKI: *(Calling off)* Captain Armstrong, sir, the chief wants to chew your ear.

BUCK: *(Off)* Eeow!

NARRATOR: Buck Armstrong bounds onto the stage a real he-man.

(Enter BUCK ARMSTRONG *on a unicycle.)*

TANK: Buck, I want to introduce you to Ms. Ramona Malone.

BUCK: I know Ms. Malone. At least I've read so much about you in "Ladies Who Lunch" in *Women's Wear Daily* that I feel I know you already.

RAMONA: Now I get it. The chief tried the sympathetic bit. You know—"Tell

Daddy all about it." When that didn't work they sent you in here with the
comedy routine. Right?

TANK: I'm goin' nuts trying to make sense outa that screwball dame.

BUCK: Leave me alone with her. *(Looking at Ramona's application)* So, you're
from Levittown?

RAMONA: Yes.

(Exit TANK, SCZUTCARETSKI, *and* MISS ENRIGHT.*)*

BUCK: *(To* RAMONA*)* Well, what seems to be the trouble, "Levittown?" Can
I get you something? A cigarette—a cup of coffee?

RAMONA: Thanks.

NARRATOR: Suddenly her face contorted grotesquely.

RAMONA: Help me. Please help me. I'll make it worth your while.

BUCK: *(Aside)* Suddenly she looked like ten thousand bucks and a vacation in
Rio to me. I could hear the clink of ice cubes in a tall glass.

RAMONA: Please help me get back my rocks. I used to be Miss Got Rocks. Now
I'm just a pseudonym on an IOU and that's nothin', Jack.

BUCK: Wait a minute. Wait a minute. Slow down. Begin at the beginning.

RAMONA: It all began the day I met Markus, my late husband. I'd never known
love like that. I loved him for his mind.

BUCK: I understand.

RAMONA: And he loved me for my mind. He called it platonic love.

BUCK: *(Rubbing his crotch)* You mean you never . . .

RAMONA: No, we never did. I loved him for his mind, I tell you. Of course,
there were others. I'm only flesh and blood.

BUCK: So I see. Where did you meet your husband?

(Crosses and begins to flex his muscles and pose in physique positions.)

RAMONA: In the Egyptian wing at the Metropolitan Museum of Art. He swept
me off my feet. We had a real relationship, straight up, no game playing. We
married a week later. He gave me a mummy case for a wedding present.

BUCK: Get to the point.

RAMONA: Markus was a member of a research group called the Cryogenic
Foundation. They freeze the dead in the hope of bringing them back to life.

BUCK: We know the group, but as yet we haven't been able to locate the brain
center of their operation.

RAMONA: Markus believed fervently in their work. He made me promise
. . . he made me promise. *(Weeps)*

BUCK: I know this is a strain, Levittown, but I must have all the facts if I'm going
to help you.

RAMONA: I'm sorry. These last few days have been like a nightmare. Here is
a copy of our marriage contract. Do you see anything unusual about it?

BUCK: *(Reading)* Usual bunkum . . . to love honor and obey . . . from this day
forward . . .

RAMONA: It doesn't say until death do us part.

BUCK: *(Still reading)* "If my husband should for any reason predecease me, I
agree to keep him in a state of cryogenic suspension indefinitely and at my own
expense." *(To* RAMONA*)* How much is it costing you?

RAMONA: It was a thousand dollars a year. That was before the dollar collapsed.
The cost has gone up every year since. And now with the energy crisis . . .
(Sobs) . . . I'm ruined. I even gave them my diamond necklace as collateral.

It was an heirloom. What will Great-Aunt Penelope say when she hears what I've done with it? I'll have to declare bankruptcy.

BUCK: Levittown, I must ask you to join me in a most dangerous mission.

RAMONA: I'm hard to get, Buck. All you gotta do is ask.

BUCK: It'll be like shootin' craps in a shithouse.

RAMONA: I'm sincere, Buck. I can take it and I can dish it out.

BUCK: Then start some heavy dishing, Pussy.

RAMONA: What kind of a dish do you think I am?

BUCK: I'll let you know after I've tasted it.

RAMONA: Talk dirty to me, Buck. Talk dirty to me.

BUCK: *(Into the intercom)* Miss Enright, would you bring in a uniform for Ms. Malone.

RAMONA: Uniform?

BUCK: Yes, the uniform of the Euthanasia Police Woman.

RAMONA: *(Inspired)* An E.P.W.

BUCK: Join us, we want to join you.

TANK: *(Entering discreetly)* Excuse me for interrupting, Captain Armstrong, but it's almost time for the six o'clock Euthanasia Marathon.

BUCK: I'm sorry, Ms. Malone. But we'll have to clear the area while the crew sets up.

(EUTHANASIA POLICE enter and begin to make preparations for the television program.)

TANK: I've got a big idea. Why don't we videotape Ms. Malone's training to become an E.P.W.?

RAMONA: *(Enthusiastic)* I've never been on television before. Except on the closed-circuit antishoplifter surveillance systems at the A & P.

BUCK: Nix. This is espionage! Sabotage! Decolletage! If one member of the Cryogenic Foundation were to recognize Ms. Malone as an E.P.W. . . .

RAMONA: *(Rhapsodically)* Euthanasia Police Woman!

BUCK: *(Drawing his finger across his throat)* Grrrk! It could jeopardize our whole operation. This has got to be strictly on the QT.

TANK: O.K.

RAMONA: *(Disappointed)* Oh, gee!

TANK: Buck, here's the briefing on "Operation Defrost." *(Holding up a blowup mug shot of* MAX MORTIMER*)* Here they are: Max Mortimer, president of the Cryogenic Foundation, his moll, Bunny Beswick *(Shows blowup of* BUNNY*)*, and his mother . . . *(Shows blowup of* MOMS*)*

BUCK: Omigod! That woman is Irmtraut "Moms" Mortimer. I prevented her husband's face-lift ten years ago, when I was still a rookie.

TANK: Will she recognize you?

BUCK: She'd know me in the dark.

TANK: Then you'll have to go in disguise. Miss Enright, comb the files and dig out every freeze freak we ever busted since 1968.

MISS ENRIGHT: Roger! *(Exits)*

TANK: I was going to seize this opportunity to enlist the aid of the lovely Ramona. But as usual I see you have anticipated me.

MISS ENRIGHT: *(Reentering)* Here's the file, Chief.

SCZUTCARETSKI: How do you do it, Miss Enright?

MISS ENRIGHT: That's what I'm paid for, to know things.

TANK: *(To* BUCK*)* You will be Gunnar Wunderlich. Here's his file. Memorize all his vital statistics.

BUCK: What if the real Gunnar Wunderlich shows up?

TANK: He won't. We've got him in the cooler. Now it seems this guy, Max Mortimer, is a little crazy. He has epileptic seizures and a really sick relationship with his mother. Get close to him. Work your way into his confidence.

SCZUTCARETSKI: Buck knows his business. Didn't he foil the heart transplant caper and short-circuit the pacemakers on over a hundred human vegetables?

MISS ENRIGHT: *(Like a cheerleader)* Not to mention raids on homes for the mentally retarded.

BUCK: I don't want to blow my own horn. But I did bust the sperm bank.

TANK: I know your record, Buck. You have my complete confidence.

MISS ENRIGHT: *(Bringing in uniform)* Here they are: leather hot pants, halter top, boots, and helmet. *(Sizing up* RAMONA *with a professional once-over)* What size do you take?

RAMONA: Twelve.

MISS ENRIGHT: What size?

RAMONA: Twelve.

MISS ENRIGHT: What size?

RAMONA: I told you twice—twelve!

MISS ENRIGHT: Oh, twice twelve, that's more your size.

BUCK: Don't be a bitch, Miss Enright, give her a twelve.

*(*MISS ENRIGHT *concedes grudgingly.* RAMONA *tries to squeeze into the hot pants. There is a lot of grunting and groaning on her part.* BUCK *and* SCZUTCARETSKI *set up for the broadcast.* TANK *is on camera.)*

SCZUTCARETSKI: Countdown, Miss Enright. Stand by!

TANK: How's my makeup?

MISS ENRIGHT: *(Powdering his nose)* Baby, the eyeshadow is a little obvious. But your lips are a real work of art. *(Steps back out of range of camera)*

SCZUTCARETSKI: 10-9-8-7-6-5-4-3-2-1-0 ON THE AIR.

RAMONA: *(Still struggling with the hot pants)* Ooooomph!

SCZUTCARETSKI: Shhh!

RAMONA: Don't "Shhh" me.

NARRATOR: The following program will be brought to you almost live. Tank Irish on the air for euthanasia.

(Tchaikovsky's First Piano Concerto as introduction)

TANK: *(All smiles)* Good evening, viewers, this is Tank Irish for your Euthanasia Police Force. Tonight I want to discuss the new "get tough" physical fitness laws and the new mandatory prison sentences for people who are arrested and convicted of obesity, anemia, or faulty limbs, even on the first offense. We will wind up today's broadcast with our usual "Suicide Drive," when you can call in and make pledges. Obesity is a felony. Eating more than your share is a form of theft. . . .

NARRATOR: *(Tuning down the sound)* While Tank is conducting the Public Service Euthanasia unilateral Demolish Ontology Society, commandos interview each new client energetically. The cast and I would like to take this opportunity to clarify a few points of the plot in a brief lecture demonstration. *(*RAMONA *and* BUCK *come forward)*

NARRATOR: *(Using a pointer, blackboard, chalk, and charts)* A. It is intended that Ramona Malone will become a policewoman and undergo training.
RAMONA: This uniform doesn't fit.
BUCK: You must undergo training.

(RAMONA lies on her back and moves her feet as if she were pedaling a bicycle, jumps rope. Miss Enright becomes a vibrating machine and RAMONA gets onto or into it and is violently vibrated.)

NARRATOR: *(During the vibration)* If Ms. Malone can fit her pink little cheeks into these hot pants, she will have earned her E.P.W. and will be ready for the most dangerous mission of which Buck spoke a moment ago. They're turning off the machine. . . .
MISS ENRIGHT: *(Handing the hot pants to* RAMONA*)* Try 'em on again, Honey.
RAMONA: *(Does so)* They fit!
MISS ENRIGHT: I never would have believed it if I hadn't seen it with my own eyes.
NARRATOR: B. Ramona will pose as a corpse with the aid of a sleeping draught.
RAMONA: You want me to drink this stuff? Maybe I ought to check with Adelle Davis.
NARRATOR: C. Buck will pose as the widower seeking to place his wife in the deep freeze of cryonic suspension.
RAMONA: *(Squeals)* This is getting exciting!
SCZUTCARETSKI: Hey you, pipe down!
RAMONA: How dare you "hey you" me!
NARRATOR: Ramona will pose as his wife. At his very first opportunity, Buck will plant a transmitter, which can be made from any radio, in her vagina.
RAMONA: Cunt.
NARRATOR: And Buck will insert.
BUCK: Ram.
NARRATOR: Mona's.
BUCK: Shove it.
MISS ENRIGHT: Up her cunt.
RAMONA: Twat.
BUCK: Vagina.
NARRATOR: Discovering the secret storage vaults. Fly in the map of New York City. *(Map flies in)* Squad cars equipped with the proper antennae will pick up a signal when they are within a twenty-mile radius of the transmitter.
RAMONA: I'm scared, Buck.
NARRATOR: By driving in spirillic patterns and reporting their positions to headquarters by car radio, cartographers can determine the exact location of the widow with the transmitter in her snatch as cryonic criminals move the body through the city.
RAMONA: What happens when we reach the secret storage vaults?
SCZUTCARETSKI: The search-and-destroy team of Euthanasia Commandos will be sent to defrost the capsules.
RAMONA: *(To* BUCK*)* I agree to the plan. . . . There's just one thing. How big did you say that transmitter was going to be?
BUCK: It wouldn't be more than about nine inches long and about that big around.
RAMONA: *(Resolved)* I can handle it. Where's that mock hemlock? *(Toasting)* Down the hatch! Here's mud in your eye! *(Quaffs)* Say, this isn't a narcotic,

is it? *(Falls into a deathlike sleep. Rigor mortis sets in and* BUCK *carries her off stiff as a board)*

TANK: *(Broadcasting)* . . . add two cups of flour and then boil the placenta. And, remember, as Monsieur Voyeur, the watchbird says *(Pulls out a hand puppet)* "Sometimes it's necessary to sacrifice a life to save a life." And, kids, if you're watching tonight, why don't you send for ENDITOL. *(Presents a large bottle to the viewers)* Send tonight and you'll never be pushed around again. Tonight's suicide pact is number fourteen in our current series of household helpers. It contains nothing but a plastic bag, so simple, just pull it over your head. *(*EUTHANASIA POLICE *sing)*

Have your youth and beauty fled?
Don't join the living dead.
Why live life ugly?
Become compost instead.

Scene 2: *Main Office of the Cryogenic Foundation.*

NARRATOR: Meanwhile, at the main office of the Cryogenic Foundation, Moms Mortimer and Bunny Beswick are discussing the Malone diamonds.

BUNNY: *(Holding the diamonds up to the light and then trying them on)* So this is the ice that's gonna keep the old boy frozen.

MOMS: Give them here before you get any bright ideas. I'm going to put them away for safekeeping.

BUNNY: That isn't fair! Piggie gave them to me.

MOMS: I don't care what Piggie did. These diamonds are going to be invested where they'll earn enough money to legitimize the racket. Hand them over.

BUNNY: I won't! Piggie gave them to me.

MOMS: Hand them over or I'll . . .

BUNNY: I won't give them up. I won't!

*(*MOMS *slaps her across the face. A catfight ensues.* BUNNY *pulls* MOMS's *skirt up over her head and ties it. Then she paddles her behind in a kind of blindman's buff.)*

MAX: *(Entering and discovering this scene)* What is this?

*(*MOMS *yells and mumbles from inside the skirt.)*

BUNNY: That's right, listen to her side of the story and just ignore me!

MOMS: *(Mumbles)*

BUNNY: That's easy for you to say!

MAX: What's that, Moms?

BUNNY: *(Standing on a chair and shrieking in her mink coat)* Take her part! Stick up for her? You big mamma's boy!

MAX: *(Kicking her off the chair)* You shaddup! Don't you ever say anything against Moms again. *(Untying Moms)* She's all I got.

BUNNY: *(Bra and panties under the mink)* Well, somebody tell me when is it my turn?

MOMS: *(To* BUNNY*)* You little slut, where did you get your morals, in some gutter?

BUNNY: See this fur . . . fox, and that's how I got it, too. *(Sticks out her tongue)*

MAX: Eeeeeeeee! Eeeeeeeee! Eeeeeeeeeee!

MOMS: What is it, Son?

BUNNY: He's having one of his seizures. *(Pronounce it sizeure)* The second one this month.

MOMS: C'mere, baby, it's all right. Everything is going to be all right. You, don't stand there gawking, cover the front desk.

(BUNNY exits)

NARRATOR: His psychiatrist said that these fits began when he was a child, to get attention. Only his mother's massage could bring him out of them. As time went on, the attacks became more and more violent.

(MOMS massages MAX's neck, his body stiffens, and he has an orgasm with spit and collapses.)

MAX: It feels as though I were burning up and freezing at the same time inside my head.

MOMS: Is it better now?

MAX: Yes, Moms, it's better now.

(The doorbell rings.)

BUNNY: *(Reentering)* There's a man outside who wants to have his wife frozen.

MOMS: Now stand up, Son, and act like nothing happened. People will think you're losing your grip.

BUNNY: What's the decision on the hot rocks? Do I get to wear them or do they go in the bank? *(She kisses MAX)*

MOMS: What's your decision, Son?

MAX: They go in the bank.

BUNNY: But that's not fair. Piggie gave them to me.

MAX: *(To MOMS)* When did you talk to Piggie?

MOMS: I had to defrost him this afternoon. I needed his advice.

MAX: That does it. Piggie goes back to the secret storage vaults.

MOMS: *(Pleading)* No, Max, please don't. He's your own father.

MAX: You see what happens when you defrost him too often. He begins to meddle.

MOMS: He didn't mean it.

MAX: I'm Mr. Big now. That's the way it is and that's the way it's gonna be.

NARRATOR: World without end. Amen.

BUNNY: Don't forget the guy in the waiting room. *(Exits)*

MAX: *(Impatiently)* Coming. Coming. *(Exits.)*

(MOMS dashes to a control dial on the wall. She turns the giant lever from ICE to HOT. A whining turbine noise is heard, snow begins to fall, and a man in mountain climbing gear, snowshoes, and goggles, enters.)

MOMS: *(Softly)* Piggie, Piggie, wake up.

PIGGIE: *(Waking)* What time is it?

MOMS: *(Looking at her watch, then pressing it to her ear)* I don't know. My watch has stopped.

PIGGIE: I had the strangest dream. I saw four men riding through the clouds on unicycles.

MOMS: Who do you think they were?

PIGGIE: The Human Fly, the Daredevil, the Indestructible Man, and the Crack

Up Champion. The four princes of the blood royal in the palace of King
Death.

MOMS: Piggie, you've got to go back to the Secret Storage Vaults.

PIGGIE: You're cold, Irmtraut, cold.

MOMS: It isn't me, Piggie. It's Max. You shouldn'ta told Bunny she could have
the carats.

PIGGIE: Diamonds are a ghoul's best friend.

MOMS: That does it. *(Turns the knob to* ICE *and* PIGGIE *exits)*

(MAX *and* BUCK, *disguised as Gunnar Wunderlich, enter with* RAMONA, *stiff on
a hand truck.)*

MAX: The cost of keeping a cryonaut frozen will be two thousand dollars a year,
Mr. Wunderlich, not taking into consideration future devaluations of the
dollar.

BUCK: Will you accept a personal check?

MAX: Your own?

BUCK: Yes.

MAX: Certainly.

*(*BUCK *writes out check. They shake hands.)*

MAX: Your hand is cold.

BUCK: Cold hand, warm heart.

MAX: We must take the body to the Secret Storage Center . . .

BUCK: *(Aside)* The Secret Storage Center!

MAX: . . . where we can exsanguinate the corpus and perfuse the veins with
glycerol. But first we must wrap the body in aluminum foil and pack it in dry
ice.

MOMS: *(Entering with* BUNNY*)* But, Son, it's time for your lunch.

MAX: I'll skip lunch today, Moms.

MOMS: You've got to eat to keep up your strength, Son.

MAX: There's no time to eat.

MOMS: What's the rush? Rushing and no eating. You'll stunt your growth.

BUNNY: Why don't we just send out for a pizza? I'll run down to the corner
pizzeria.

MAX: All right, but zip up your fox. I don't want you givin' them greaseballs
any ideas.

BUNNY: You think I'd let them fuck me right there in the pizzeria? What do
you think I am, a pizza ass?

MOMS: That'll take too long. Let's just take along a frozen pizza.

BUCK: That's a great idea.

(Exit BUNNY.*)*

MOMS: *(To* BUCK*)* Haven't I met you somewhere before?

BUCK: Do you ever work out at Jack LaLanne's Health Spa?

MOMS: Yeah. I went from a gigantic twenty-four to a size twelve. My friends
can't believe it and neither can I.

BUCK: Maybe you know an old friend of mine, works in the steam room, Ellen
Ballzer.

MOMS: Sure. Ellen and I are like that. *(Crosses her fingers)*

MAX: *(With* BUCK, *moves* RAMONA *to platform and wraps her in foil)* Okay, Moms,
you'll go and get the car.

MOMS: Where did you park the cryobus?

MAX: Around the corner. What are the parking hours downstairs?

MOMS: *(Pulls a file drawer out of the wall and checks a folder)* No parking between seven A.M. and eight P.M., except Thursdays.

MAX: What is it on Thursday?

MOMS: Thursdays it's no parking from eight P.M. to nine A.M. All other times except holidays and every other Thursday it's the other way round.

BUNNY: Pizza's here!

MOMS: I'll get the car.

MAX: Nix. You gotta go in the garage and camouflage our entourage. If one member of the Euthanasia Police Force were to recognize Moms *(Draws finger across his throat)* Grkkk . . .

NARRATOR: With heavy sarcasm.

BUNNY: *(Sarcastically)* Wouldn't that be toooo bad!

MOMS: One of these days I'm going to do you a big favor. Like picking out my very own burial plot ahead of time so you can spit on it when you feel inclined.

BUNNY: Who'd bury you, except the Sanitation Department, maybe?

MOMS: *(Taking BUNNY by the arm and speaking in a confidential tone)* You know what I wish for you? A mansion with a hundred rooms and in every room a heart attack. *(Grabs BUNNY's radio and smashes it. Exits)*

NARRATOR: A stroke of luck for Buck.

BUNNY: *(Hysterical)* Oi vey! If I have to spend one night in that Egyptian caboose without Muzak, I'll have a conniption fit.

BUCK: *(To BUNNY)* Aw, don't cry. Let me see that radio. I think I can fix it for you.

BUNNY: Gee, thanks, short, dark, and handsome.

(BUCK fiddles with radio and places a long phallic tube in RAMONA's snatch, during the following dialogue.)

BUNNY: Aw Max, all you ever do is think about dead bodies. Why don't you go down and live at the morgue, instead of making a morgue of our home?

WOMAN IN THE AUDIENCE: I suggest you just close the play down. *(Actors onstage try to continue and ignore the interruption)* I said stop this play!

CHARLES: *(In a stage whisper)* Georg, keep going.

WOMAN: No, don't keep on going.

MAN IN THE AUDIENCE: Would you please pipe down, lady.

WOMAN: I won't! This play is evil and insensitive. *(Screaming)* You! Actors! Don't know what you're talking about!

CHARLES: Would somebody please take this woman out so we can finish the play?

BILL: *(Trying to reason with him)* Charles, no. Let's listen to what she has to say.

CHARLES: *(Sarcastic but giving in)* Great, audience participation! My favorite theatrical device.

WOMAN: *(Taking the floor, she speaks intensely, even passionately)* My mother was a vegetable! For thirteen years she lay, being fed intravenously, in an iron lung. The doctors gave up hope. One of them who knew I was having financial difficulties . . . intensive care is expensive . . . it was costing me so much that I had to have a night job as well as a day job. This doctor offered to unplug my mother. I remember it was a Friday night . . . and as I lit the Sabbath candles I thought of Mama. She believed in euthanasia. "I never want to outlive my usefulness," she used to say. "If it ever comes to that, let me die." . . . BUT

I COULDN'T DO IT!!! That weekend was torture. But on Monday morning, the doctor called. Mama was up and walking around the room, completely recovered. Since then, she's gone back to school and gotten her master's degree. She's teaching at the secondary school level and working as a volunteer with MENTALLY RETARDED CHILDREN!

JACK: What right have you got coming in here and disturbing our performance? We're trying to make a living. We've worked hard.

WOMAN: I don't care.

MAN: Look, lady, shut up or ship out. We came here to be entertained, not to listen to a discussion of euthanasia.

WOMAN: What about the rest of the people in this audience? Do you agree?

KID IN THE AUDIENCE: I couldn't disagree with you more. I believe in euthanasia.

WOMAN: How can you say that?

KID: I think that every person in the society should produce enough to sustain himself plus enough extra to provide for his old age and to repay the cost of his nurture.

MAN: And what about people who don't want to produce anything?

KID: If they repeatedly refuse to cooperate with the rest of humanity they should be taken to the lethal chamber and get rid of them. The world would be a better place without them.

WOMAN: How can you stand there and say that? I want you to meet my mother. She's living proof that euthanasia is no way to live.

(Her MOTHER *comes forward from the audience.)*

MOTHER: You should love your mother. She's the only mother you've got.

KID: I think it's disgusting to resort to heroic measures such as heart transplants and iron lungs to extend life beyond its natural limits, with no thought to the quality of the life you are extending.

MOTHER: Well, let me tell you, when the time comes, you'll be screamin' and beggin' to get plugged into one of them machines, toots.

KID: Think of the overpopulation problem.

WOMAN: Your parents should have thought of the overpopulation problem.

MISS ENRIGHT: Wait a minute. Let the kid speak.

LOLA: Yeah, let the kid speak.

KID: I've said what I have to say.

CHARLES: You really believe in euthanasia?

KID: Yes, I do.

BILL: He should be in the play.

TANK: He should be on the Euthanasia Recycling Team.

CHARLES: Have you ever acted before?

BLACK-EYED SUSAN: *(Impatient)* Let's get ON with it.

TANK: Really, Buck, this is a really big idea. Draft an audience member into the play.

CHARLES: It's too Pirandellian for my taste. I'm a de-illusionist.

BILL: The plot can support it.

LOLA: They have supernumeraries at the Met.

CHARLES: Yeah, but do you know what is the deficit at the Met?

LOLA: No, but if you hum a few bars, I'll fake it.

WOMAN: Come on, Mama. Let's go home.

MOTHER: *(Waving a finger at the KID)* These young people have no respect. *(*MOTHER *and* DAUGHTER *exit)*

CHARLES: At the risk of seeming experimental, would you be willing to come up out of the audience and be inducted into the Euthanasia Police Force?

KID: I'll give it a try.

CHARLES: You will?

KID: What the hell?

SCZUTCARETSKI: Great, kid.

SUSAN: Are we going to continue this play or not?

CHARLES: Wait, I haven't thought of a name for this new character.

SCZUTCARETSKI: We've got to think of a name for the kid.

MISS ENRIGHT: What'll we call the kid?

CHARLES: *(To* BLACK-EYED SUSAN*)* You seem annoyed.

BLACK-EYED SUSAN: *(Slow burn)* I'm not annoyed.

LOLA: We've got to think of a name for the kid.

BLACK-EYED SUSAN: Then think of a name for the kid and let's get on with it.

KID: Why don't you just call me . . . The Kid?

TANK: That's good. That's really good.

CHARLES: Okay, now let's back it up. Where were we?

MISS ENRIGHT: There will be a brief but grueling initiation ceremony.

TANK: That's right. I forgot about the hazing.

SCZUTCARETSKI: Just don't leave any marks.

(All exit but MAX, BUNNY, BUCK, *and* RAMONA. BUCK *goes back to platform with* RAMONA. BUNNY *remains forward.)*

CHARLES: Pick it up, John.

JOHN: I've lost my concentration.

CHARLES: John, you can get back into it. Think about your inner life, John.

JOHN: Eeecht!

CHARLES: *(Massaging his shoulders near his neck)* Well, think of a situation analogous to the character but personal to yourself.

JOHN: *(At a loss)*

CHARLES: *(Desperate)* Use the magic "if," John. What "if" we had to return the audience's money.

JOHN: It's all coming back to me.

CHARLES: All right Bunny baby. Let's go. Lots of personality, acting, the works . . .

GEORG: Where were we?

CHARLES: "Why don't you go down and live at the morgue, instead of making a morgue of our home?" *(Pause)* We can't do it cold. *(To the audience)* With your permission we'd like to take a preparation. It's an actor's trick for getting back into the mood of the play. It'll be slick and glossy in a minute. It'll be kind of a glimpse backstage, as it were. *(To the actors)* All right, kids, Stanislavski stuff. *(To the light booth)* Mood lighting, please.

(All strike the same pose, fingertips to the bridge of the nose, eyes closed. Long pause.)

BUNNY: Aw, Max, all you ever do is think about dead bodies. Why don't you go down and live at the morgue, instead of making a morgue of our home?

MAX: I'm worried about Moms. One of them punks might try to fancy pants.

MOMS: *(Confident)* If they do, I'll throw a couple o' nifties at 'em. I'll know I'm gettin' old when I can't handle their kind.

MAX: You should have an alibi ready and pack a rod.

(Exit MOMS.)

BUNNY: This is all more trouble than it's worth. Why don't we just let the bodies thaw and go south for the winter?

NARRATOR: Nudging her out of the way.

MAX: I'm not going to risk losing those checks I've grown so accustomed to at the end of every month. You want me to give back that diamond necklace?

BUNNY: What's the sense of being rich if you never get to enjoy it?

MAX: When we attain immortality through freezing there will be plenty of time to enjoy ourselves. First we must overcome death.

BUNNY: You want to avoid death. But you're spending your whole life in a tomb!

MOMS: *(Reentering and strutting around dressed in a dark suit, tie, and broad-brimmed hat)* How'm I doin'?

BUCK: You look great. If I were a woman I'd go for you myself.

MAX: Moms, I want to tell you something.

MOMS: What is it?

MAX: You've been like a mother and a father to me.

MOMS: *(Embarrassed)* Aw, go on.

(MOMS and BUNNY exit with RAMONA on a hand truck, wrapped in aluminum foil and stiff as a board.)

BUCK: Mr. Mortimer, I'd like to see my wife's body frozen and perfused with glycerol. Do you mind if I tag along?

MAX: *(Moving to his desk)* That would be highly irregular.

BUCK: I may be of use to you at the Secret Storage Vaults. I have a degree in air conditioning and refrigeration repair.

MAX: Only intimates are permitted to work in the Secret Storage Vaults. We have enemies, Mr. Wunderlich. Reactionary fools who would like to sabotage our work.

NARRATOR: Playing his role to the hilt.

BUCK: Now who would want to do a thing like that?

NARRATOR: Passionately.

MAX: Philistines, Mr. Wunderlich. They squander incalculable wealth on useless trips to the moon, futile wars, even tobacco. But not one cent on the attainment of immortality.

BUCK: All that lives must die . . . William Shakespeare.

MAX: Death shall die . . . John Donne, Mr. Wunderlich. A Japanese scientist has already kept a cat's brain frozen for two years and revived it . . . under laboratory conditions. Frogs' hearts can already be kept beating indefinitely with a simple dry cell battery. Who knows what we can attain, in time, with government subsidy.

BUCK: You can trust me.

MAX: I trust no one . . . except my mother, Mr. Wunderlich. How do I know you are any better than the rest?

NARRATOR: Not quite laughing.

Lola Pashalinski, John Brockmeyer &
Georg Osterman in *Hot Ice* (Thomas Harding)

BUCK: Look pal, I'm trying hard to think you're a fundamentally good egg.
  Help me out a little, can't you?
MAX: Look me in the eyes.
NARRATOR: Sad boozer's eyes.
BUCK: *(Stares into* MAX'S *eyes. Aside)* Poached eyes on ghost. I knew the guy was
  a bad egg. He had bitten off more than he could chew.
NARRATOR: With a kind of world-weary scorn.
MAX: I don't believe in heaven, Mr. Wunderlich, and I don't believe in hell.
  We get our heaven and hell on earth, Mr. Wunderlich. Life is what you make
  it.
BUCK: You're very philosophical.
MAX: I was a philosophy major at C.C.N.Y. I had to know more and more.
BUCK: A healthy curiosity, that's all.
MAX: I was ambitious. And ambition in the field of philosophy is a dangerous
  thing, Mr. Wunderlich.
BUCK: Don't be so hard on yourself.
MAX: That was my . . . shall we say, tragic flaw?
NARRATOR: Existentially.
BUCK: Que será, será. *(Belches)* Forgive me, it was the pizza speaking.
MAX: Think nothing of it, Mr. Wunderlich.
BUCK: Why be so formal? You can call me Gunnar. Why don't you call me
  Gooney? Yeah, call me Gooney.
MAX: I see no need for excessive familiarity, Mr. Wunderlich.
LADY: *(Rushing in with a poodle)* Sir, I beg of you, it's a matter of life and death.
  Could you take my toy poodle, Fi Fi?
MAX: *(Distractedly in his haste)* Take your poodle?

LADY: Would you? I'll pay whatever you ask for quick service.

MAX: You'll pay whatever . . . ? Very well, I'll take her.

LADY: Oh, you are a perfect darling. I have to be at the hairdressers in twenty minutes. Can you do it while I wait?

MAX: While you wait . . . ? Certainly. *(Aside)* While she waits.

LADY: I'll just read my magazine. *(Sits and reads)*

(MAX and BUCK wrap the poodle in aluminum foil with some difficulty and a little carelessness.)

NARRATOR: *(During the wrapping)* Handle with care. Bodies frozen at these temperatures shatter when dropped.

MAX: Your dog is finished.

LADY: Already? How utterly divine. *(In baby talk)* Can Mumsey Wumsey see her wittle Fi Fi Wi Fi? *(Sees dog and screams)* What have you done to my little pooper scooper? Fi Fi, Fi Fi, speak to me! (Touches dog and recoils in shivering horror) Why have you frozen Fi Fi? Are you mad?

MAX: This is the Cryogenic Foundation, madam.

LADY: You mean it isn't "Puppy Love"?

BUCK: Puppy Love?

LADY: The Poodle Beauty Parlour.

BUCK: No, lady, this isn't puppy love. It isn't even infatuation. It's the kiss of death.

MAX: That's where you're wrong, Mr. Wunderlich. Cryogenic Suspension isn't the kiss of death. It is our only hope for everlasting life.

(BUCK drops dog.)

LADY: *(Screaming)* Help! Murder! Police!

MAX: *(Having another seizure)* Ngong . . . ngong . . . ngong . . .

BUCK: *(Alarmed)* What is it? What's wrong? Tell me what's wrong!

MAX: *(Whining)* I'm sick. Service me, I'm sick.

(He shows BUCK how to massage his neck until he spits up a milky liquid. . . . Flustered, BUCK untangles himself, dashes to the desk, and fumbles for a cigarette.)

BUCK: Feel better now?

MAX: Yes, I'm better now. Thank you . . . Gooney.

(House lights begin to come up. WOMAN IN THE AUDIENCE *and her* MOTHER *come racing down the aisle.)*

MOTHER: My daughter and I want to apologize for any trouble we may have caused you.

WOMAN: We've decided to give the play a fair hearing.

MOTHER: And just to show there are no hard feelings, I'm going to call bingo tonight.

[*(She does. Bingo cards passed out with programs allow the audience to play for prizes throughout intermission.)*]

PROLOGUE TO ACT II

NARRATOR: Audience members interested in its origin would be advised to compare with this production the earlier prototype upon which it was based—

the Ur-Hot Ice of Snazzy Ripoffsky of the neo-futilist school of antidrama and his associate plagiarist Ungar Grateful. Each of whom represented opposing schools of futility: the Adamant and the disinterested, or Lethargic school. Of course, there were many crosses between the two: Adamant Lethargists and Lethargic Adamantives. But only the pure originals concern us here. The Adamants were known for their motto, "Detest the halfhearted, they rob life of its irony." While the Lethargists would take refuge in a monistic view, which was not wholly unlike fatalism except they were never willing to form a semantic attachment, however ennobling it might be, from a public relations point of view. So, while the Lethargists have left little or no theory, their practice is visible everywhere. "Give me a hero without brains who can slug his way out of a jam with his two fists" is one of the few fragments representing their position on psychological drama.

The monistic approach, rather than striving for a happy ending, tends to view all endings as happy. No matter, the Ur-Hot Ice was, in any case, a bore—long in all the wrong parts, overly sentimental, meant to be taken seriously by a coterie, wholly undemocratic in its sympathies. Talky, with a poorly developed plot, which was practically incomprehensible unless one was familiar with a lot of obscurantist literature marked by its unemotionality. Colorless and decadent. A tiresome affair for all but the author's creditors. It was, to the surprise of the formula men, a commercial success. Dull as it was, people flocked to see it. One hundred thousand tickets were sold on the first day the box office opened, returning twice the initial investment before opening night. But after the lukewarm reception by the press, ticket sales doubled. Audience members refused to leave their seats after performances; so enthralled were they, that each performance had to be held in a different theater. Actors never tired of performing it. Bus and truck tours propagandized in the hinterlands. Later, the formal futility became the dominant religion for a hundred years after it was performed. When the energy crisis reached mammoth proportions, performances were given in the sunlight. A woolly mammoth was discovered frozen in a block of ice in Antarctica, and performers ate the beast, although it was over a million years old, at a testimonial dinner given for Walt Disney, in his personal forever flask.

Futurists of the past debated with pasticheists of the future across the international dateline, and as time wore on, the expression "killing time" fell into disuse.

ACT II

Scene 1: *Euthanasia Police Headquarters.*

(*Seated around a table,* MISS ENRIGHT, TANK, SCZUTCARETSKI, *the* KID, *and the* NARRATOR *are smoking, drinking beer, and playing cards.*)

NARRATOR: Smells of men, sweet cigarette smoke, spilt beer, men's beery piss. Stale very stale.

(MISS ENRIGHT *turns up transistor radio.*)

SCZUTCARETSKI: I gotta take a wicked piss. *(Crosses stage and urinates in a bucket)*
NARRATOR: It splashed yellow at his boot.
SCZUTCARETSKI: That's the way it is when you're drinking beer. You drink and piss and drink and piss.
TANK: And it don't look any different when it comes out than it did when it went in.
MISS ENRIGHT: Muncha mumfa muncha mumfa.
TANK: Don't talk with your mouth full.
MISS ENRIGHT: Where are Pinhead and Waldo?
TANK: They took the day off to work on the Mother's Day Matricide Matrix.
MISS ENRIGHT: *(Referring to* SCZUTCARETSKI*)* Hey, will you look at that slob. He didn't wash his hands after he pissed.
SCZUTCARETSKI: I never wash my hands after I piss.
MISS ENRIGHT: Hey Tank, do you wash your hands after you piss?
TANK: Yeah, I wash my hands after I piss. What about the Kid?
SCZUTCARETSKI: Yeah, what about the Kid?
NARRATOR: Yeah, what about the Kid?
MISS ENRIGHT: Kid, do you wash your hands after you piss?
THE KID: I wash my hands before I piss.
NARRATOR: Hey, man, don't get pissed off.
MISS ENRIGHT: Better to be pissed off than pissed on.
THE KID: Why are there so many piss references in this play?
NARRATOR: Because the author wants to bathe the audience in his imagery.

*(*SCZUTCARETSKI *opens a bottle of beer that shoots like a geyser.)*

TANK: Well, that's pretty piss poor.

(A bleep is heard on the radarscope and all jump up.)

TANK: Drop the map of New York City.
TANK: *(With headset)* Car A. Forty-second Street.
SCZUTCARETSKI: Forty-second Street.
TANK: Car B. Seventh Avenue.
MISS ENRIGHT: Seventh Avenue.
THE KID: *(Marks converging lines with grease pencil)* Times Square.
TANK: Car A. Thirty-fourth Street.
SCZUTCARETSKI: Thirty-fourth Street.
TANK: Car B. Sixth Avenue.
MISS ENRIGHT: Sixth Avenue.
THE KID: Herald Square.
TANK: Car A. Fourteenth Street.
SCZUTCARETSKI: Fourteenth Street.
TANK: Car B. Broadway.
MISS ENRIGHT: Broadway.
THE KID: Union Square.
TANK: It looks like they're taking the square route. Car A. Christopher Street.
SCZUTCARETSKI: Christopher Street.
TANK: Car B. Seventh Avenue.
MISS ENRIGHT: Seventh Avenue.
THE KID: Sheridan Square.
TANK: Car A. Mott Street.

SCZUTCARETSKI: Mott Street.
TANK: Car B. Pell Street.
MISS ENRIGHT: Pell Street.
THE KID: Chatham Square.
TANK: Car A. Chrystie Street.
SCZUTCARETSKI: Chrystie Street.
TANK: Car B. Wooster Street.
MISS ENRIGHT: Wooster Street.
THE KID: Chatham Square.
TANK: They're either lost or they're looking for a parking space.
THE KID: Chatham Square.
MISS ENRIGHT: Isn't that where the deserted prisons are?
THE KID: Chatham Square.
TANK: That must be it! O.K., men, let's go!
THE KID: Chatham Square.
NARRATOR: Human Fly! Daredevil! Indestructible Man! Crack-Up Champion! Fall In! *(To* MISS ENRIGHT*)* Why do they call you the Crack-Up Champion? *(*MISS ENRIGHT *stands on her head and spreads her legs)* Oh, I see. *(Marching drill ensues, then all run up aisle)*

Scene 2: *The Secret Storage Center.*

(Enter MAX *with* BUCK *blindfolded.)*

MAX: We're here, Gooney. This is the Secret Storage Center. I'm worried about Moms. It isn't like her to be late.
BUCK: So this is the Secret Storage Center.
MAX: Yes, this is my, shall I say . . . sanctum sanctorum?
BUCK: How many dead bodies do you have frozen here?
MAX: Not dead, not dead, Gooney. A frozen body is not a dead body. We freeze them that they might live again. If there is even one chance in a million that one of the cryonauts will come back, my work will not have been in vain. Do you know what a phoenix is, Gooney?
BUCK: A bird?
NARRATOR: In monumental effigies, in pyramids of stone, and in treasured mummies, the Egyptians sought eternity. Is it any wonder that their culture gave rise to the myth of the deathless bird, the phoenix?
BUCK: A bird that lives forever?
MAX: Not forever. Eternity is cyclical. *(Offers* BUCK *sandwich)* Ham and cheese?
BUCK: No, thank you. *(Aside)* Sure, I like ham and cheese, but not when the guy's using me for a diary.
MAX: The life span of the phoenix is one platonic year. That is the length of time it takes the sun, moon, and planets to return to their initial position.
BUCK: How long is a platonic year?
MAX: *(Rolling a marijuana cigarette)* Nine thousand nine hundred and ninety-four common years. *(Offers* BUCK *the cigarette)*
NARRATOR: Wartle the birds, Immortal, Immortal.
BUCK: *(Taking the cigarette. Aside)* I was repelled by the degenerate's filthy habits, but dared not give myself away. I won't inhale.
MAX: The ancients believed that upon the completion of this vast astronomical

cycle the history of the world would repeat itself in all its details. The universe
dies in fire and is reborn in fire. A cycle without beginning and without end.
I am not seeking immortality per se. But a man should live long enough to
complete the cycle . . . one platonic year.

BUCK: You mean you only want to live nine thousand nine hundred and
ninety-four years.

MAX: Exactly. And then burst into flame like the phoenix *(Music builds and paper
bird bursts into flames)* and rise again out of my own ashes, an heir to myself
and witness to the ages.

NARRATOR: Wartle the birds, Immortal, Immortal.

BUCK: *(High in spite of himself)* Far out!

MAX: People hate me because I'm different from them. They don't understand
me. I don't belong here. I belong in another age. And you, they don't understand you either.

BUCK: You're getting paranoid, man. You're going to make me paranoid.

MAX: Do you like cities, noise, dirt? Travel with me into the future. Cryonauts
in our Cryocapsules, safe as a child in a womb.

(Enter MOMS and BUNNY with RAMONA wrapped in foil on a hand truck.)

BUCK: Hiya, Moms. How's your ass?

MOMS: Aw, shut up.

BUCK: Mine is, too. It must be the cold air in here.

MAX: Moms, you're late.

MOMS: This is just a hunch, but I had the feeling we was being followed. I
thought I saw a car with an antenna.

MAX: Your hunches are never wrong, Moms.

MOMS: I don't think we have anything to worry about. I gave 'em the slip.

MAX: *(Indicating RAMONA)* We gotta hurry and get this body frozen before
brain damage sets in. Now watch carefully, Gooney, so you can learn the
business.

MOMS: Hey, Max, what is this? You should know better than to bring a stranger
to the Secret Storage Center.

MAX: This is no stranger, Moms. This is Gooney.

MOMS: Gooney???

MAX: He's going to help us out. He has a degree in refrigeration repair. We
can trust him.

MOMS: I don't trust nobody that ain't my own blood.

MAX: Bunny ain't your own blood.

MOMS: That's what I mean.

(All lights go very dim.)

MOMS: Jesus Christ! This is the third brownout this week. It's really making me
uptight, Max. More shit like this from Con Ed and the bodies'll thaw out.

BUCK: I know a trick that'll fix it. All I need is a penny.

MOMS: Come on!

(NARRATOR and MAX slap their pockets, revealing no change.)

BUCK: *(Inspired)* From my penny loafer! *(Removes penny from shoe)* Where's the
fuse box?

MOMS: *(Points with flashlight)* Over there on the wall.

(BUCK puts in penny, sparks fly, and lights come back up.)

MOMS: Hey, any guy that can fix a brownout with a penny is all right in my book.

BUNNY: *(Entering)* Here's the ice.

MAX: After we raise the jugular vein and carotid artery we'll drain your wife's blood and pump a chilled cryoprotective solution through her body with the aid of an external cardiac compressor or iron heart.

NARRATOR: Buck's head is spinning. In a moment it will be too late for Ramona.

MAX: *(To BUCK)* Let me show you how to make the proper incisions.

BUCK: Wait a minute. What did you say was in that solution you're using?

MAX: Twenty percent glycerol, eighty percent Ringer's solution, a small amount of heparin, and a dash of cattle tranquilizer.

BUCK: What's the cattle tranquilizer for?

MAX: They've got to do something while they wait. And now for the incision.

BUNNY: Aw, Max, you're such a drag. I wish we had some music.

BUCK: That reminds me. I fixed your radio.

BUNNY: Weeeo!

BUCK: It won't get all the stations but I think you'll do all right.

BUNNY: Off the wall! *(She puts on headset and begins to frug)*

MAX: When the perfusion is completed we'll place the body in a plastic container filled with ice and salt. Cut the jugular vein vertically.

NARRATOR: Stalling for time.

BUCK: Who froze the first man?

MAX: That's a long story.

MOMS: It all began just a month before little Maxie was born. My husband and I had just been married and were spending our honeymoon in Nome. That's in Alaska. He got buried in an avalanche. When they finally dug him out he was frozen. I thought to myself, "At last, stiff!" I couldn't let go of him. I just couldn't accept the idea that I would never see him again. So I kept him frozen. That's how the business got started. We made the service available to the public.

NARRATOR: Keep them talking, Buck. Each moment the Euthanasia Police delay is a step closer to Ramona's icy death.

BUCK: What should I say?

NARRATOR: This is psychological warfare! Make them paranoid.

BUCK: When did you first realize that freezing bodies is against the law?

MAX: Genius is its own law!!

NARRATOR: Buck chooses his words carefully.

BUCK: Don't you ever get to worrying about having to spend a nice long prison sentence?

MAX: I knew they'd arrest me, but I couldn't let them. When you're born with my gifts, you can't let them get in the way.

RAMONA: They're right, Buck. Join us. There's no pain here, and no hope. Become one of us, immortal . . . immortal . . . immortal.

TANK: *(Offstage)* All right, Mortimer! This is it. Come out with your hands up or we're coming in after ya.

MOMS: You'll never take me alive, copper!

MAX: *(Trying to put BUCK in Forever Flask)* Travel with me into the future. Cryonauts in our Cryocapsules. Safe as a child in a womb.

(Max kisses BUCK *on mouth.* BUCK *struggles.* MOMS *injects him with a sedative.* BUNNY *throws plastic bag over his head.)*

BUNNY: *(Jealous)* Forget about him. Take me. What's his life compared to mine? A mediocre repairman working on refrigerators and air conditioners?

MAX: The Future! I can see the Future!

BUNNY: You'd better forget about the future. Because you ain't gonna have no future. Your future is all used up. You can't help yourself because you're MAD, MAD, MAD. Yes, you're insane.

*(*BUCK *crawls to fuse box and outs the lights.)*

NARRATOR: The lights jerked off.

(Sirens. Whistles. The EUTHANASIA POLICE *come in on unicycles, led by the* POODLE LADY *on a tricycle, and exit other door.)*

MAX: The four horsemen of the apocalypse!

MOMS: Piggie's dream!

BUNNY: The ice is melting.

RAMONA: Look, Buck, I'm weeping.

*(*BUNNY *heads toward exit.)*

MOMS: Where ya going, Bunny?

BUNNY: I'm going to give myself up. I never had no advantages. I want hot baths—trendy clothes—a high school equivalency diploma. I want to live in an apartment with a doorman. There ain't no future in immortality.

MOMS: Go ahead. I always knew you had a yellow streak down your back.

*(*BUNNY *turns to exit.)*

BUNNY: *(Hands over her head)* Don't shoot. I'm giving up.

*(*MOMS *pulls gun. Shoots* BUNNY *in back.* MOMS *empties the gun into her as she staggers around the stage and finally drops.)*

MOMS: Nobody walks out on Irmtraut Moms Mortimer.

(Whistles blow. EUTHANASIA POLICE *reenter, followed by* POODLE LADY.*)*

POODLE LADY: There he is. There's the man who froze Fi Fi.

THE KID: Get him.

*(*TANK *draws gun and takes aim on* MAX *who is carrying* BUCK *downstage to where* BUNNY *has fallen.)*

SCZUTCARETSKI: Don't shoot! He's got Buck.

MAX: Bunny, are you all right?

BUNNY: Yeah. It's only a brain wound.

NARRATOR: Force the forever flask!

(Whining turbine noise. Snow begins to fall and PIGGIE *emerges.)*

SCZUTCARETSKI: Jesus Kee-riist! What is that? Chief, you better have a look at that under a microscope. This is your field.

TANK: *(Examines* PIGGIE *with a magnifying glass)* No arterial structure evident.

No nerve endings. Porous matter with a kind of sticky sap. I'll bet it's sugar based.

THE KID: Chief, you sound like you're describing vegetable matter.

TANK: I am.

BUNNY: Piggie?

MAX: Yes, Piggie. A human vegetable.

PIGGIE: An onion can make you cry, but show me a vegetable that can make you laugh.

MOMS: You must try to talk to him. He's obviously so much wiser than we are. It's our only hope to learn so many things.

(PIGGIE *begins to spout the quadratic theorem and other esoteric bits of information and continues to do so until the* POLICE *do him in.*)

BUNNY: Since when do plants have intelligence?

MAX: Plants have had intelligence countless millennia before the evolution of the animal arrogance that has overlooked them.

TANK: I say destroy it before it destroys us!

MOMS: Don't kill him in anger!

(POLICE *kill* PIGGIE, *while* RAMONA *escapes downstage.* MAX *picks up* BUCK *and carries him to Forever Flask.*)

MAX: (*Carrying* BUCK) This is my work. Please do not touch it.

TANK: (*Indicating* RAMONA) Let's get that one.

(POLICE *line up in front of* RAMONA, *with hammers raised.* RAMONA *knocks them all down in a line with one blow.* MOMS *rushes downstage with gun drawn.*)

MOMS: All right, you guys, freeze. I've got an itchy trigger finger.

SCZUTCARETSKI: Imagine the earth covered with frozen bodies.

MISS ENRIGHT: Imagine ten thousand.

SCZUTCARETSKI: Imagine the world covered with frozen bodies.

THE KID: Imagine millions.

TANK: You're talking like a frightened schoolboy.

THE KID: You're right, Chief, I am frightened.

(MAX *has seizure.*)

MOMS: (*Handing gun to* BUCK) Here . . . keep 'em covered. (*Rushes to* MAX. MAX *pushes her away and falls in front of* BUCK, *massaging his throat*)

BUCK: (*Aside*) I don't know what it was about him, but at that moment I liked the guy.

TANK: Kill the creep.

POODLE LADY: Maim the mother . . .

SCZUTCARETSKI: Get 'em.

BUCK: I can't do it. It's all right for you to go through life wearing a badge on your minds.

MAX: Gooney!!!

NARRATOR: (*Taking center stage*) There are two possible endings to *Hot Ice.* The Adamant ending and the Lethargic ending. Tonight, the Ridiculous Theatrical Company, in the tradition which has made them famous, will once again go out on a limb, in defiance of gravity. Tonight, we will present both possible endings. First, ending A, or the Lethargic ending, typified by their motto,

"Give me a hero without brains who can slug his way out of a jam with his two fists."

MAX: Gooney!

MOMS: Max! That ain't no Gooney. It's Buck Armstrong. I'd know him in the dark. I can smell a Euthanasia dick a mile away.

(MAX *sniffs* BUCK's *crotch.* MOMS *goes for* BUCK. MAX *tries to restrain her.*)

BUCK: Stand back Moms. I gotcha covered. I'll kill ya in cold blood. I'll fill ya fulla lead. I'll mess up your face so bad your own mother wouldn't recognize ya.

MOMS: You and what troop of Boy Scouts?

MAX: Moms, no!

MOMS: It's all right, Son, I forgot to load the gun.

(BUCK *throws the gun at* MOMS. *She ducks. They proceed to have a kung fu battle.* MOMS *picks up* BUCK *and carries him offstage.*

BUNNY *rushes down to center stage. The* KID *and* SCZUTCARETSKI *grab her by the upper arms. She grabs them both in the crotch, they fall toward each other, banging their heads together, and fall.* BUNNY *drags them offstage.*

TANK *and* MAX *rush to down center stage. Both stop dead, facing each other.* NARRATOR, MISS ENRIGHT, RAMONA, *and* POODLE LADY *become*)

CHORUS: *(moaning)* OOOO. OOOO. OOOO.

(MAX *and* TANK *take a few moments of preparation, then square off facing one another, hands held stiffly in front of them. After several minutes, both fall unconscious. They are carried off by* RAMONA, POODLE LADY.)

NARRATOR: *(Taking center stage)* So you see, ladies and gentlemen, the difference between Cryogenics and Euthanasia is a—

(MISS ENRIGHT *interrupts by getting a hammerlock on* NARRATOR.)

NARRATOR: What the hell is going on here? *(Breaks away)* Miss Enright, I'm the narrator. I'm neutral.

MISS ENRIGHT: In times like these no one is neutral. *(Punches him in the face. He falls. She drags him off.* BUCK *enters running, with the* KID *slumped over his shoulders)*

KID: I can't make it. Go on without me.

BUCK: You gotta make it, Kid. You gotta make it.

MISS ENRIGHT: Come on, Kid, you can make it.

KID: Go on, save yourselves. I'm a goner.

BUCK: Don't talk like that, Kid.

MISS ENRIGHT: You can make it, Kid. You can make it.

KID: This is it. Everything's slipping. I'm falling inside.

BUCK: That's all right. Don't fight it. Go with it. Think of all the guys who've done it before you. You've got company. High-class company.

KID: Here goes. I'm goin'. Everything's gettin' dark before my eyes. My whole life is passing before me. This is the last you'll hear from me. You'll never hear my voice again. Good-bye cruel world. Now! 10-9-8-7-6- I'm really dying this time. 5-4-3- Buck, take this message for me. There's a little girl back home.

BUCK: *(Impatient)* Sure. Sure.

KID: 5-4-3-

MISS ENRIGHT: You said that already.

KID: Two and three quarters—two and a half—two—

BUCK: This is painful.

MISS ENRIGHT: Come on, I'm late for my scalp massage. *(Chloroforms the* KID*)*

BUCK: Bonzai, Kid!

(The KID *dies.* SCZUTCARETSKI *runs in screaming bloody murder.)*

SCZUTCARETSKI: I don't want to die. I'm too young to die.

TANK: *(Running in)* What's the matter Sczutcaretski?

SCZUTCARETSKI: I don't want to die! I'll freeze myself. *(Locks himself in freezer)*

TANK: Don't do it Sczutcaretski!!

BUCK: Sczutcaretski!! Come out of there you crazy Polack!

SCZUTCARETSKI: It's cold in here. I can't breathe. I need air. Give me some air.

BUCK: *(Taking pistol from* TANK*)* You want air? I'll give you air. *(Empties gun into* SCZUTCARETSKI*)*

TANK: I can't believe it. Sczutcaretski, a disgrace to the force.

BUCK: *(Eulogizing)* He was a stupid, penny-ante Joe Blow; too dumb to play ball.

*(*BUCK *and* TANK *carry off body)*

NARRATOR: *(Entering)* And now for the second possible ending of *Hot Ice.* Ending B, or the Adamant ending, typified by their motto, "Detest the half-hearted, they rob life of its irony."

*(*EUTHANASIA POLICE *enter and line up on one side of the stage. The Cryogenic people enter and line up opposite.)*

NARRATOR: *(Leafing through the* Hot Ice *script)* Now, in the second ending of *Hot Ice,* the Euthanasia Police and the Cryogenic Foundation should be . . . Of course the dialogue here is a little . . . and the staging and the blocking could be in the style of . . .

BUCK: Reinhardt.

NARRATOR: Yes, Reinhardt.

(Phone begins to ring.)

MISS ENRIGHT: *(Answering phone)* Hello. You want what? Yes. Yes. He's here. Just a moment. Oh, Narrator, It's for you.

NARRATOR: *(On phone)* Yes? Why, that's amazing. Why, that's incredible! That's unprecedented in the history of dramaturgy. *(Throws script in the air and resumes place in center stage)* Ladies and gentlemen, it gives me great pleasure to announce . . . Ladies and gentlemen, it gives me great pleasure to announce . . . *(Looks toward sound booth)* Hey, isn't there supposed to be a fanfare here?

SOUND MAN: I'm sorry, but I've accidentally erased eighteen minutes of the tape.

NARRATOR: Do you expect the audience to believe such a ridiculous excuse? Really! Ladies and gentlemen, it gives me great pleasure to announce that the Euthanasia Police Force and the Cryogenic Foundation have been purchased by the American Medical Association, Incorporated.

(All throw confetti in the air and hug and kiss each other, and drift offstage, leaving the NARRATOR *holding a cream pie, hidden in a box.)*

NARRATOR: Is the young lady who was going to give the play a fair hearing still in the audience?

WOMAN: Yes, I'm still here.

NARRATOR: Could you come up here.

WOMAN: Sure. *(Goes up on stage)*

NARRATOR: Well, now that you've seen the play, what do you think of it? Seriously.

WOMAN: I think this is the most impartial play I've ever seen. In every other play I've ever seen either one side or the other wins, or the author tries to convince the audience of his point of view. But this play shows both sides fairly.

(NARRATOR hits WOMAN in face with pie. Her MOTHER screams from audience and runs up on stage.)

MOTHER: That's not nice. Young man, you'll pay for this. Who's responsible for this?

(NARRATOR hits MOTHER with pie.)

MOTHER: That's not funny.

(WOMAN and MOTHER exit through theater. BUCK and RAMONA enter.)

RAMONA: Well, Buck, everything turned out for the best.

BUCK: Yeah, Ramona, except for one thing. I didn't get your diamonds back. *(RAMONA pulls the diamond necklace out of the pocket of her uniform)*

BUCK: Holy Toledo! Ramona Ramona, I acknowledge your superiority in battle.

RAMONA: Buck, you're as intelligent as any woman. Buck, you've got that faraway look in your eyes.

BUCK: *(Mounting his unicycle)* It's time I hit the road.

RAMONA: *(Blocking the way)* Don't leave me, Buck. Please don't leave me.

BUCK: Ramona, if you think it's easy to ride a unicycle through a chocolate cream pie, you're crazy. *(He rides the unicycle through the pie, on a good night)*

RAMONA: You're cute!

BUCK: And you've got rocks in your head. What makes you think that I'd want to be institutionalized in penal servitude?

RAMONA: Buck, who was the girl that left you with such a high opinion of women?

BUCK: My mother. *(Breaks a whiskey bottle over her head)*

RAMONA: Buck, you shoulda done that a long time ago! *(They clinch)*

Curtain

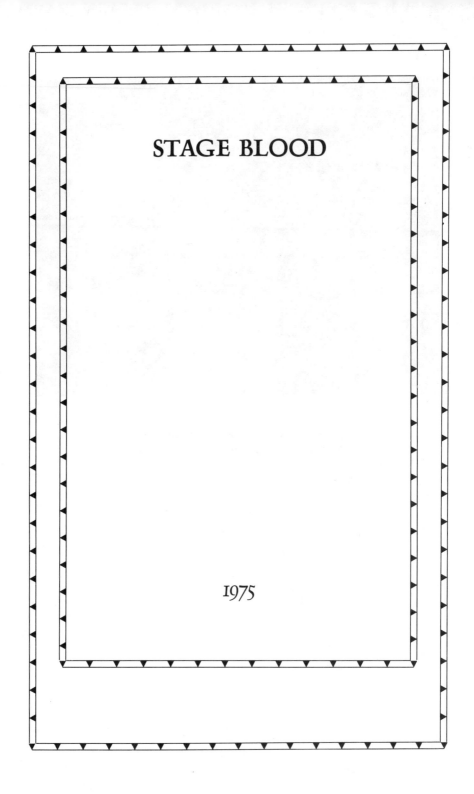

STAGE BLOOD

1975

Lola Pashalinski, Bill Vehr, Black-Eyed Susan
& Charles Ludlam in *Stage Blood* (Ron Scherl)

Cast of Characters

CARLTON STONE, *an elderly player*
CARLTON STONE, JR., *an actor-manager, his son*
HELGA VAIN, *a mature actress, Stone's wife, Carl's mother*
JENKINS, *the stage manager*
EDMUND DUNDREARY, *thespian*
ELFIE FEY, *a stagestruck, small-town girl*
GILBERT FEY, *Elfie's father*
GHOST

ACT I

Scene: *A theater with the curtain closed.*

(After the audience are in their seats, the curtains part revealing a bare stage, riggings, and the glare of a work light. Enter CARLTON STONE, SR. *and* JR. *They are having a heated argument.* STONE, SR. *is obviously drunk.)*

CARL: Pop, please! Lay off that booze!

STONE: Don't nag me! You're worse than your mother.

CARL: We've got a show to do and you're no good half in the bag.

STONE: Son, I'm nervous.

CARL: You are nervous. What are you nervous about?

STONE: I'm nervous about being nervous. It's Mudville,* you know. Tonight is Mudville.

CARL: Pop, you should be glad we're playing your hometown.

STONE: I didn't want to take this booking.

CARL: We needed the money. . . .

STONE: I've got flopsweat! *(Drinks from a bottle)*

CARL: Pop, put that stuff away! *(Grabs bottle and empties it)*

STONE: *(Incensed, threatening with cane)* Are you crazy? That's good liquor!
. . . *(*CARL *returns bottle)* I used to be Hamlet.

CARL: Pop, don't . . .

STONE: Now I'm just the ghost. Poetic justice. I'm a ghost of my former self.

CARL: Pop, you're making me feel guilty. I never wanted to play Hamlet. It was your idea.

STONE: Someone had to play it. You don't want the Caucasian Theatrical Company to take its final bow, do you?

CARL: No, Pop, of course not.

STONE: What else would you do if you didn't act?

CARL: I don't know, Pop. I never thought about it.

HELGA: *(Off)* Where is it?

JENKINS: *(Off)* This way.

CARL: This is it.

(A door at the back of the theater opens and three somewhat weary and bedraggled theater people enter, dragging some trunks with them down the aisle.)

*Or the name of the town in which *Stage Blood* is played.

HELGA: There's something about an empty theater.

EDMUND: Especially on opening night.

HELGA: Don't be sarcastic, Edmund. We were lucky to get a booking at all.

JENKINS: We'll be lucky to give a performance at all with no Ophelia.

CARL: Aargh, don't remind me!

JENKINS: Somebody's got to remind you. We need a new Ophelia by tonight and you've got to find one.

CARL: Don't look at me.

EDMUND: Jenkins is right, Carl. It's your responsibility.

CARL: But it was Pop's fault that she quit.

JENKINS: Yes, Carlton got us into this mess.

STONE: *(Quietly)* She was unprofessional.

JENKINS: *(Defensively)* She never missed a performance.

STONE: What do you call this?

JENKINS: Why, you old reprobate. You didn't understand her acting because she was Stanislavski-trained. She works honestly and truthfully.

STONE: What do you know of honesty and truth? I call it lies and deception. Deceiving the audience into believing in surface reality, illusion. The great actor gives you a glimpse beneath the surface. Something that lies beyond your honesty and truth.

HELGA: Darlings, we don't need honesty and truth. We need an ingenue.

EDMUND: Maybe you should ask your Ouija board for the answer.

HELGA: *(Enigmatically)* Of course. Ouija never lies.

JENKINS: *(Exasperated)* Ouija! Ouija! Ouija! Karen is gone and all you can talk about is your goddamn Ouija board!

HELGA: In every theatrical company, there is always one damn fool who's in love.

EDMUND: *(Mockingly dramatic)* Ah, the agony. *(Calling)* Karen! Karen!

JENKINS: That's enough. *(All laugh. Beside himself)* I said that's enough! *(Turning on STONE with sinister intensity)* I'll get even with you, Carlton Stone. If it's the last thing I do, I'll get even with you! *(Exits)*

HELGA: Now, now, Jenkins!

CARL: Leave him alone; he'll get over it.

EDMUND: I hope he doesn't go in the prop room and sulk for hours. The set's got to go up. We play tonight, you know.

STONE: Where are the dressing rooms?

CARL: I don't know. Let's find them. Take a break for lunch, everybody, and we'll have a dry run-through at one . . . if that's all right with you, Mother.

(HELGA grunts in acknowledgment. All exit except HELGA and EDMUND.)

HELGA: *(Looking up from her Ouija board)* "Something is rotten in the State of Denmark."

EDMUND: What's that?

HELGA: "Something is rotten in the State of Denmark." That's the line that's going to be flubbed tonight. Ouija says so.

EDMUND: *(Peeved)* But that's *my* line.

HELGA: And according to Ouija, you're going to blow it tonight.

EDMUND: *(Helplessly)* Oh, for God's sake!

HELGA: Ouija never lies.

EDMUND: *(Pensively)* "Something is rotten in the State of Denmark." I've said that line hundreds of times and I've never gone up in it once.

HELGA: *(Darkly)* Well, you will tonight. Mark my words.

STONE: *(Reentering with CARL)* You may humbug the town as a tragedian, but comedy is a serious thing, my boy, so don't try that just yet.

CARL: But, Pop, couldn't you give me a few pointers? How do you play Hamlet?

STONE: *(Taking a recorder from his breast pocket)* Will you play upon this pipe?

CARL: But, Pop, I don't know how.

STONE: I pray you.

CARL: Believe me, I can't.

STONE: It's quite simple, you blow at this end, and cover the holes with your fingers and thumb.

CARL: I knew that much. But I couldn't play a tune. The result would be mere cacophony.

STONE: Son, I can't tell you how to play Hamlet anymore than I can tell you how to play this flute. In order to play Hamlet, you have to have *been* Hamlet. Why, look you now, how unworthy a thing you make of Hamlet! You would play Hamlet; you would seem to know his stops. You would pluck the heart of his mystery. You would sound him from his lowest note to the top of his compass; and there is much music, excellent voice, in this little organ, yet you cannot make it speak. 'Sblood, do you think Hamlet is easier to be played on than a pipe? Call Hamlet what instrument you will, though you can fret over him, you cannot play him.

EDMUND: I'd like to do a murder mystery.

STONE: Why, *Hamlet's* the greatest murder mystery of all time.

EDMUND: What about *Oedipus Rex*?

CARL: Ah, yes, a great gimmick. The detective discovers his own guilt.

HELGA: The detective done it, huh?

EDMUND: Just like *The Mousetrap.*

JENKINS: *(Entering)* A man could make a fortune who could write a better *Mousetrap.*

STONE: But that's my point. *Hamlet* gave to the mystery story the one quality it had formerly lacked, the quality without which it could never attain greatness . . . a streak of the irrational.

HELGA: You mean the Ghost?

STONE: Exactly. Hamlet was not even sure that a crime had been committed, let alone who committed it.

HELGA: *(Enthralled)* A streak of the irrational!

EDMUND: Ah, yes, it seems today we had a streak of the irrational and it has left us without an Ophelia.

HELGA: Will the show go on?

STONE: Of course the show will go on. The show *must* go on! I will play Ophelia myself if necessary.

CARL: I don't know about that, Pop. We're doubling as it is!

HELGA: Why must the show go on? I've always wondered.

STONE: Actors must eat, and in my company, a day you don't act is a day you don't eat.

HELGA: I've never missed a performance. Be a darling, Jenkins, and hand me a sandwich, will you?

JENKINS: I'll see if the sandwiches have arrived. *(Exits)*

STONE: Now you're talking about potboilers, not Shakespeare.

EDMUND: Shakespeare wrote shameless potboilers. That's why he called them *As You Like It, Much Ado About Nothing,* and *What You Will.*

STONE: Pshaw! Can you imagine a play entitled *As You Don't Like It?*

EDMUND: My point exactly. It wouldn't sell.

STONE: Are you denying the genius of Shakespeare?

EDMUND: No, I am only saying that in the theater, genius is often wedded to a mountebank.

STONE: This is outrageous!

EDMUND: Come now, Carlton, great actor though you are, can you deny that you have ever stooped to monkeyshines?

STONE: How dare you! What you do to Shakespeare shouldn't happen to John Simon!

HELGA: Which brings us back to potboilers.

EDMUND: And the irrational.

JENKINS: *(Entering)* And murder mysteries. Here are the sandwiches.

STONE: Faugh!

CARL: *(Grabbing the bag of sandwiches from JENKINS)* Well, what'll it be, Mother . . . ham or turkey?

HELGA: I'll take turkey.

CARL: I don't think turkey's good luck on opening night, Mother.

HELGA: Better give me ham.

CARL: You've got it. And don't eat the bread.

HELGA: Carl, I've only had two pieces of bread today—not more than eight hundred calories. . . .

CARL: *(Consulting a small notebook)* Mother, if my memory serves me, you have had exactly *twelve* hundred calories today.

HELGA: Impossible!

CARL: Salad dressing, Roquefort cheese . . . goose-liver pâté! Admit the pâté.

HELGA: I admit the pâté.

CARL: *(Incredulous)* Banana Surprise!

HELGA: I wasn't surprised, I was appalled.

CARL: Mother, I'm afraid that if you eat those two slices of bread, you'll have gone over your limit. And you know what that means; no frozen skim milk later.

HELGA: Oh! *(Struggling with her conscience)* Very well. No bread.

CARL: Oh, I'm proud of you, and because you were so disciplined, I'll see to it that you get strawberry.

GIRL: *(From the back of the house)* Excuse me, Mr. Stone, but I know the role of Ophelia.

CARL AND STONE: You do?

GIRL: *(Still from the back of the house)* I know every line of it. I can do the "mad scene" for you, if you don't believe me. *(Entering down the aisle)* "Where is the beauteous Majesty of Denmark?"

*(*CARL *nudges* HELGA *with his elbow.)*

HELGA: Huh?

CARL: *(In a whisper)* Give her the cue.

HELGA: Oh, the cue . . . "How now, Ophelia?"

GIRL: *(Sings)*
How should I your true love know
From another one?
By his cockle hat and staff
And his sandal shoon.
HELGA: "Alas, sweet lady, what imports this song?"
GIRL: *(Going to* EDMUND*)* There's rosemary, that's for remembrance—pray you, love, remember. And there is pansies, that's for thoughts.
EDMUND: A document in madness: thoughts and remembrance fitted.
GIRL: There's fennel for you, and columbines. There's rue for you. And here's some for me. We may call it herb of grace o' Sundays. O, you must wear your rue with a difference. There's a daisy. I would give you some violets, but they withered all when my father died. They say 'a made a good end. *(Sings)*
For bonny sweet Robin is all my joy.
EDMUND:
Thought and affliction, passion, hell itself
She turns to favor and to prettiness.
GIRL: *(Sings)*
And will 'a not come again?
And will 'a not come again?
No, no, he is dead,
Go to thy deathbed! *(Points to* STONE*)*
He never will come again.
His beard was as white as snow,
All flaxen was his poll.
He is gone, he is gone,
And we cast away moan.
God 'a' mercy on his soul!
And of all Christian souls, I pray God. Good-bye you. *(Exits.)*
STONE:
Follow her close; give her good watch, I pray you. *(*CARL *goes after* GIRL*)*
O, this is the poison of deep grief: it springs
All from her father's death. *(Turning to* HELGA*)*
O Gertrude, Gertrude,
When sorrows come, they come not single spies,
But in batallions. First, her father slain;
Next—
HELGA: Will somebody stuff this ham with cloves? This is our lunch break, and I don't want to rehearse. I want to enjoy my lunch in peace.
GIRL: *(Peeking out from the wings)* Well?

(All stand dumbfounded for a moment and then STONE *applauds.* CARL, *who is behind the* GIRL, *pushes her onto the stage. Everyone joins in the ovation.)*

STONE: Brava! Brava! My child, you can act! Can't she, Carl?
CARL: *(Nodding)* Yesiree.
EDMUND: *(Kneeling before the* GIRL*)* Please accept this rose. *(It is a trick rose and it squirts the* GIRL *in the face.)*
STONE: *(To* EDMUND*)* You damn practical joker! *(To the* GIRL*)* Your words came down on wings of inspiration, as if not learned by rote but like the very beating of your heart. *(Turning to* CARL *very excitedly)* Carl, you must let her.

You really must. She will play Ophelia! She must! Zounds! A talent like this comes along once in a lifetime. Oh, I'm out of breath. *(Gasping)* Ah! Ah! Ah!

CARL: Jenkins! Don't just stand there. Get Pop's oxygen!

STONE: Ah, the excitement! Ah! Ah! *(He clasps the* GIRL'*s hands)* How fortunate, how very fortunate that you found us, that we found you. Oh! Ah! Ah! Ah! *(Gasping for breath)*

JENKINS: Carlton, you're getting all excited. Calm down.

STONE: *(Icily)* You take a morbid interest in my health, Jenkins. I think you envy me my role.

JENKINS: You're paranoid.

STONE: Even paranoids have real enemies. I know you've been slowly tightening my armor.

JENKINS: You've been putting on weight, that's what it is.

STONE: *(Beating his forehead with his fist dramatically)* Aagh, what a curse it is to have the stage manager against you!

JENKINS: It's a good thing you don't have any food props or you'd think I was poisoning you.

(HELGA *starts and looks suspiciously at her hero sandwich.)*

STONE: *(Spitting dramatically)* "The funeral baked meats will coldly furnish forth the marriage tables."

HELGA: What do you mean by that?

STONE: If you want me, Carl, I will be in my dressing room. *(Exits grandly)*

GIRL: May I play tonight, Mr. Stone? Oh, may I?

CARL: What's your name, sweetheart?

GIRL: Elfie Fey.

CARL: Not a bad stage name. What does your Ouija board say, Mother?

HELGA: *(At the Ouija board)* "Something is rotten in the state of Denmark."

EDMUND: *(Vaingloriously)* I won't go up in my lines tonight, I won't! *(Stalks out)*

ELFIE: What do you think, Mr. Stone? Do I have what it takes to be an actress?

CARL: Can you starve, Elfie? *(Turning to* JENKINS, *who has been muttering under his breath)* What's the matter now, Jenkins?

JENKINS: When I talk, people won't listen to me.

CARL: If you would just . . .

JENKINS: Not get so emotional?

CARL: Try to talk a little more dispassionately.

JENKINS: I'm in charge. They gotta listen to me.

STONE: *(Reentering)* The other day you told me to shut up and when I did, you walked out of the room and didn't even say what you had to say.

JENKINS: If I said to you, "Carlton, shut the fuck up . . ."

EDMUND: They'd probably applaud. There's a conflict of power.

CARL: I don't think so. Pop doesn't want to be responsible for the stage management, would you?

STONE: *(To* JENKINS*)* Last night we were supposed to start at seven. But you didn't show up till seven. Everybody was ready to go.

EDMUND: Nobody thought we'd start at seven.

HELGA: I thought you said we'd start at eight-thirty.

CARL: It was never made clear whether we were supposed to be here at seven or begin at seven.

JENKINS: That should be made clear next time.

STONE: The reason I was late is that while on the telephone, I discovered that I had crabs.

HELGA: Echt!

CARL: I discovered my first crabs on the phone, too.

EDMUND: Like father, like son.

STONE: These were hardly my first! Twenty minutes before the dress rehearsal . . . I didn't want to infest my costumes because they wouldn't be cleaned for another week. Wearing those costumes every night, I knew I'd never get rid of them. So I went out and got some A-200 and all my makeup and went home and treated myself.

HELGA: Where did you get crabs?

STONE: Oh, Helga!

JENKINS: I think the show's in trouble.

CARL: But you thought the last show was in trouble.

JENKINS: Your old man should let me do my play. Can't you talk him into it?

CARL: All eighteen hundred pages of it? It would take weeks to perform. That plot isn't your tightest.

JENKINS: *(Showing a glimpse of an enormous script)* This is the tightest plot that has been constructed in the last four hundred years. . . . No! . . . In the whole history of drama. Someday some poor sucker will be writing his doctoral thesis on the relationship between my writings and my bowel movements.

EDMUND: I had a psychiatrist who was very interested in my bowel movements.

STONE: *(To EDMUND)* That reminds me. You've got a dislocated diphthong. Instead of saying "I'm," you're saying "aum," or "om," or "ahm," or something. I find it jarring. *(Sticks his fingers in EDMUND's mouth as he tries to say "I'm")*

EDMUND: *(Almost strangling)* I'm. I'm. I'm. *(Bites STONE's fingers)*

STONE: *(Screams with pain)* Ouch!

EDMUND: I'll go over all my "I'ms" in the first act! *(Exits)*

CARL: Pop, Jenkins wants you to do his play.

STONE: *(Heartily)* I would, if he'd cut it.

JENKINS: *(Pressing the script to his breast like a mother protecting her child)* Never!

STONE: In my boyhood days, I had enough of good reviews and empty houses. The story is everything.

HELGA: That's what we owe our success to. Your father and I could always pick a story.

JENKINS: It would be a crime to cut this play. Besides, it's impossible. You can't cut one word. My plot is tightly woven like a hand-knit sweater; you cut one thread and the whole thing ravels. Why, this plot is tighter than Ibsen! Tighter than Scribe!

STONE: Tighter than a bull's ass in fly season?

JENKINS: Every new form seems formless at first . . . someday you'll see . . . Ah! What's the sense of talking to you!

STONE: *(Laughing heartily)* Talk! Talk! I'm listening.

JENKINS: What's the use?

ELFIE: What's the name of your play?

JENKINS: *Fossil Fuel.*

ELFIE: *(Venturing an opinion timidly but ever for the underdog)* I don't think anyone understands your work.

JENKINS: If they did, they'd hang me!

HELGA: *(Looking up from her Ouija board suspiciously)* What do you mean by that?

STONE: I am in the same predicament as almost all theater managers throughout history. Actors of genius greatly outnumber playwrights of genius. Good actors abound; good playwrights are far to seek. The best actors of every generation have been forced to lean heavily on the classics and revivals of recent successes.

HELGA: A good melodrama!

JENKINS: Faugh!

STONE: But I prefer fustian, my boy, I do!

JENKINS: Mere bombast.

STONE: What's mere about bombast?

EDMUND: I always found Shakespeare too long and windy.

STONE: Yes, you wouldn't want to break your wind! *(Sits on a "farting cushion," which* EDMUND *has placed unbeknownst to the others)* A pooh-pooh cushion! *(Throws it at* EDMUND*)* You damn practical joker!

(Everyone laughs uproariously.)

HELGA: Tut tut! Falstaff farts in Shakespeare.

JENKINS: There were many playwrights in Shakespeare's own time—give or take a generation—who were far better than Shakespeare. Marlowe's mighty line, for instance, "And sooner shall the sun fall from its sphere, than Tamberlaine be slain or overcome." What of the forbidden love of John Webster's *Duchess of Malfi,* not to mention his invention of echo effects in the fifth act. Or Middleton and Rowley's *The Changeling*! Many scholars acknowledge these to be unique masterpieces, each one a distillation of an entire literary gift. These men wrote only a few plays. I have put everything into one!

EDMUND: In other words, it's your first play!

JENKINS: Well, I've got news for all of you.

ALL: !!!!!!!

JENKINS: The plays of Shakespeare were, in fact, never written by Shakespeare.

HELGA: Really?!

JENKINS: They were written by another playwright of the same name!

HELGA: Now that's a cue if I ever heard one.

CARL: That's my exit cue. *(Exits)*

JENKINS: There's nothing as safe as Shakespeare if you do it straight.

EDMUND: But that's pure bardolatry.

JENKINS: Bardolatry leads to bardicide.

HELGA: Bard is box, darlings. It's as simple as that.

JENKINS: *(With disgust)* Box office! That's all you ever think of.

HELGA: Frankly, I think his box is bigger than his bite.

EDMUND: I'm for a good story with a message you can take home with you. And I'm sure that everyone in this company will back me up on it.

JENKINS: Of course, of course! Everyone will agree. But that's the M.D.R., baby, Minimum Daily Requirement: a good story that raises an issue. But what then, huh? Repeat the old forms? Never! *(Shouting like Lear)* Recycle! Waste nothing! Do you hear what I'm saying? Cling to the Now through which all Future plunges to the Past!!!

(Suddenly everyone is silent for a long moment. JENKINS *becomes self-conscious.)*

EDMUND: *(Applauding)* Well played! Bravo, Jenkins! I say, quite a performance!

HELGA: Almost a Lear!

EDMUND: Yes, not quite a Lear.

JENKINS: You're all fools, fools! How long do you intend to go on hacking it in Shakespeare? Dishing up culture with a capital K! How can you go on pretending that there is a validity to monarchy, and that the high-born speak sublime blank verse, while the poor and laboring classes speak prose and doggerel?

EDMUND: *(Very bored and condescending)* Is that communism you're espousing, Jenkins?

JENKINS: Oh, what's the use? Anything left of stage center would look like communism to you!

EDMUND: I don't like politics. The theater is like a religion to me.

JENKINS: Ah, yes. The art-religion . . . Out of the frying pan into the fire.

STONE: That *Hamlet* exists at all is a miracle!

JENKINS: It's a miracle we don't dissolve when we take a bath. *(To STONE)* This show's in trouble and you're the only one who can do anything about it. The theater needs new blood.

STONE: *(Scornfully)* There's blood enough in *Hamlet,* my boy. Blood enough for anyone.

EDMUND: It's getting quite late. Hadn't the set better go up?

JENKINS: *(Belligerently)* All right, all right! That's all I'm good for around here!

HELGA: Now, now, Jenkins.

EDMUND: For God's sake, let him alone, don't coddle him!

(JENKINS, HELGA, and EDMUND gather up their belongings and exit.)

ELFIE: Well, Mr. Stone, what do you say?

STONE: Oh, you'll play Ophelia, all right. There's no time to rehearse you, so you'll have to use common sense. *(Calls to CARL, who enters in Hamlet's "customary suit of solemn black" and blond wig)* Carl, run through your scene with her, will you? The blocking is a little complicated. If you need me, Carl, I will be in my dressing room. *(Exits)*

ELFIE: What's blocking?

CARL: It's the plan of all the actors' movements and positions on the stage. Let's run through it. There isn't much time and I have got to get a cup of coffee before the performance tonight. Jenkins, would you run out and get us a couple of cups of coffee?

JENKINS: *(Carrying a ladder across the stage)* Do you want the set to go up or don't you? It's bad enough that I have to go out on a rum-run for your old man. I ain't goin' out for coffee, too. *(Exits)*

CARL: Sorry I asked.

ELFIE: That fellow's got a chip on his shoulder, hasn't he?

CARL: Never mind the coffee, let's run the scene.

JENKINS: *(Reentering apologetically)* You can have some from my thermos, though.

(ELFIE and CARL exchange a look of surprise.)

CARL: Why, thank you, Jenkins.

JENKINS: *(Pouring hot coffee into a red thermos cup, which they share)* I haven't got any sugar, though.

CARL and ELFIE: That's all right, I don't take sugar. *(They exchange a look. Then in unison)* Neither do I.

CARL: *(To ELFIE)* Neither do I.

JENKINS: And it's a good thing you don't. Sugar causes cancer.

CARL: Still eating those health foods, eh Jenkins?

JENKINS: I swear by vegetable juices.

CARL: *(To* ELFIE*)* Jenkins is a vegetarian.

JENKINS: It's just that I can't stand butchers and butchery. *(Exits)*

ELFIE: You meet so many interesting people in the theater.

CARL: Yes.

ELFIE: Oh, this is so exciting! You must love the theater.

CARL: I am attracted by the theater, but frankly, I'm repelled by it. I would never have tried to go into the theater if my parents hadn't been actors. I always wanted to be a marine biologist. The people in the theater are so insincere, they don't seem to know where the play leaves off, and real life begins. And besides, it's not a healthy life. You get a lot of exercise, but at night. I guess that's why acting is called the world's second oldest profession.

ELFIE: Yes, you're cut off from the solar energy. But night is a very intuitive time, don't you think?

CARL: *(Lost in thought, but suddenly coming back to himself)* What? . . . Oh, yes, intuitive.

ELFIE: *(Elbowing him)* Shall we rehearse?

CARL: Oh, we'll be all right but we won't run the risk of getting stale, will we?

ELFIE: Your zeal is only matched by your indifference.

CARL: Your iambics are only surpassed by your pentameters.

ELFIE: Listen, there's one thing about Ophelia I don't feel, ya know what I mean?

CARL: What do you mean?

ELFIE: Is Hamlet mad or only pretending to be?

CARL: He's only pretending.

ELFIE: I don't believe it. If he loves Ophelia, why would he pretend? No, I think he really was mad.

CARL: He wanted to get her out of the way. He was afraid she might get hurt.

ELFIE: And besides, if she really loved him, she would have known that he was not sincere. She would have . . . sensed it.

CARL: Listen, I have watched my father play Hamlet over five hundred times, and I don't know if I'm mad or only pretending to be.

ELFIE: When you act, do you really become the character?

CARL: *(Emphatically)* No, that would be dangerous. Acting is the art of seeming, not being. For instance: I will play Hamlet here tonight. I will seem to be Hamlet. Now, suppose I took a part in another play where I played a character who's playing Hamlet. I would seem to be Hamlet in that play, too. That would be just as good as playing Hamlet, don't you think? Only better. Whatever role we play, we construct it out of our own personalities anyway. We can never be anything other than what we are, so I say to seem is better than to be.

ELFIE: I see. To be an actress or not to be an actress . . . to ruin one's life before a room full of people. What fun!

CARL: *(Rashly)* Besides, Hamlet was a great actor.

ELFIE: And she was just a green ingenue.

CARL: A green ingenue . . . sounds like a sauce.

ELFIE: Listen. There's something I've always wanted to know about acting. When you have to cry on stage, actually produce real tears, night after night, how do you do it? Do you provoke the pain externally by pinching yourself where nobody can see? Or do you endow the situation with sense memory? Once I read in Uta Hagen's book that instead of concentrating on producing real tears, which would make you lose the value of the scene, what you should do is invoke a poetic image that would bring tears to your eyes, like a lonely, frail, delicate tree in the middle of a vast, windy prairie.

CARL: Throughout the great ages of the theater, the greatest actors of every generation have, well, uh . . . my mother always did it this way. *(Grabs a Kleenex from the dressing table and begins to cry violently)*

ELFIE: *(Amazed)* Real tears!

CARL: Would you like to try it?

ELFIE: Yes!

CARL: Take this onion, take this handkerchief. Now, holding the handkerchief in the right hand and the onion in the left (of course, if you're facing in the other direction, it's all reversed, but we'll get to that). Now, the handkerchief is like a little stage curtain, concealing the onion from the audience's view. It goes up and comes down, see? Up and down. Of course the great Berma was reputed to have been able to hold both the onion and the handkerchief in one hand, but I think that's too advanced for you. We'll just take it one step at a time. Forget the play, the scene, the character, just go for the eternal thing; go for the emotion. Work yourself up.

(ELFIE begins to cry.)

CARL: *(Coaching her on)* Get upset . . . get more upset. Lower your head. . . . Squeeze a little onion juice in your eye. That's it. *(Pointing to a tear on her cheek)* There it is! A little one, but it's a beginning. You were beautiful. You were . . . beautiful! You may keep the onion if you wish.

ELFIE: I'll treasure it always. I wish I could be right for you. I wish I could be thirty-five, have my hair bleached, and say sophisticated things.

CARL: Promise me something, Elfie.

ELFIE: What?

CARL: That you'll never say sophisticated things, never have your hair bleached, and never ever be thirty-five.

(They kiss.)

JENKINS: *(Interrupting)* Do you know that half hour was called fifteen minutes ago?

CARL: Come. On to the dressing room. I hope you're the type that can wear any size.

ELFIE: What shall I take as a stage name?

CARL: How about Irving?

STONE: *(Overhearing as he enters in Ghost costume)* Ah, yes, Irving. I used to fetch his ale when I was pump boy at the Old Beefsteak Club Room.

CARL: Pop is a member . . .

STONE: In good standing . . .

CARL: In good standing of the Sublime Society of Beefsteaks!

STONE: Of which Sheridan was a member. I want you to understand one thing, Miss Fey. Our company may be small, but it's pretentious.

JENKINS: *(Entering)* Will you three please get off the stage? It's time to let the audience in.

STONE: This is going to be a great performance. I feel inspired. Miss Fey, you have inspired me.

(Exeunt omnes. There's a change of light and the sounds of an audience heard over Elizabethan music. The curtain rises on Act I, Scene 1 of the Caucasian Theatrical Company's production of Hamlet. *Elsinore. Fog on the battlements. A banshee wails.)*

EDMUND: Who's there?

HELGA: Nay, answer me. Stand and unfold yourself.

EDMUND: Long live the King!

HELGA: Bernardo?

EDMUND: He.

HELGA: You come most carefully upon your hour.

(They shake hands. EDMUND *has a buzzer concealed in his palm and gives* HELGA *a shock.)*

HELGA: *(Under her breath)* You damn practical joker!

EDMUND: 'Tis now struck twelve. Get thee to bed, Francisco.

HELGA: For this relief much thanks. 'Tis bitter cold, and I am sick at heart.

EDMUND: Have you had quiet guard?

HELGA: Not a mouse stirring.

EDMUND: Well, good night.
    If you do meet Hamlet and Horatio,
    The rivals of my watch, bid them make haste.

(Enter CARL *and* JENKINS.*)*

HELGA: I think I hear them. Stand, ho! Who is there?

JENKINS: Friends to this ground.

CARL: And liegemen to the Dane.

HELGA: Give you good night.

JENKINS: O, farewell, honest soldier, who hath relieved you?

HELGA: Bernardo hath my place. Give you good night. *(Exits)*

CARL: The air bites shrewdly, it is very cold.

JENKINS: It is a nipping and an eager air.

CARL: What hour now?

JENKINS: I think it lacks of twelve.

EDMUND: No, it is struck.

JENKINS: Indeed? I heard it not.
    It then draws near the season
    Wherein the spirit held his wont to walk. *(Ghost enters.)*
    Look, my lord, it comes.

CARL: Angels and ministers of grace defend us!
    Be thou a spirit of health or goblin damned,
    Bring with thee airs from heaven or blasts from hell,
    Be thy intents wicked or charitable,
    Thou com'st in such a questionable shape
    That I will speak to thee. I'll call thee Hamlet,
    King, father, royal Dane. O, answer me.
    Let me not burst in ignorance, but tell
    Why thy canonized bones, hearsed in death,
    Have burst their cerements, why the sepulchre
    Wherein we saw thee quietly interred
    Hath oped his ponderous and marble jaws
    To cast thee up again. What may this mean

That thou, dead corpse, again in complete steel,
Revisits thus the glimpses of the moon,
Making night hideous, and we fools of nature
So horridly to shake our disposition
With thoughts beyond the reaches of our souls?
Say why is this? Wherefore? What should we do?

(Ghost beckons.)

JENKINS: It beckons you to go away with it,
    As if it some impartment did desire
    To you alone.
EDMUND: Look with what courteous action
    It wavés you to a more removéd ground.
    But do not go with it.
JENKINS: No, by no means.
CARL: It will not speak. Then will I follow it.
JENKINS: Do not, my lord.
CARL: Why, what should be the fear?
    I do not set my life at a pin's fee,
    And for my soul, what can it do to that,
    Being a thing immortal as itself?
    It waves me forth again. I'll follow it.
JENKINS: What if it tempt you toward the flood, my lord,
    Or to the dreadful summit of the cliff
    That beetles o'er his base into the sea,
    And there assume some other horrible form
    Which might deprive your sovereignty of reason
    And draw you into madness? Think of it.
    The very place puts toys of desperation,
    Without more motive, into every brain
    That looks so many fathoms to the sea
    And hears it roar beneath.
CARL: It waves me still.
    Go on. I'll follow thee.
EDMUND: You shall not go, my lord.
CARL: Hold off your hands.
JENKINS: Be ruled. You shall not go.
CARL: My fate cries out
    And makes each petty artery in this body
    As hardy as the Nemean lion's nerve.
    Still am I called. Unhand me, gentlemen.
    By heaven, I'll make a ghost of him that lets me.
    I say, away! Go on. I'll follow thee.

(Exit Ghost and Hamlet.)

JENKINS: He waxes desperate with imagination.
EDMUND: Let's follow. 'Tis not fit thus to obey him.
JENKINS: Have after. To what issue will this come?
EDMUND: Something is denten in the state of Rotmark. O, shit!

(A bloodcurdling scream is heard. All run into the dressing room. HELGA *stands with blood on her hand, screaming.* STONE *lies dead, his head in the toilet, blood issuing from his ear.)*

CARL: *(Coming in)* What is it? What's happened? Omigod, it's Pop!

HELGA: *(In shock)* At first I thought it was real. Then I saw it was only stage blood!

CARL: He's dead.

HELGA: It isn't real. It's stage blood, I tell you! Stage blood!

(Curtain.)

End of Act I

ACT II

Scene: *Same as in Act I.*

*(*HELGA *sits at the dressing table removing her makeup.* EDMUND *is seated on the toilet, upstage.)*

EDMUND: *(Reading* Variety*)* Pap, pap, nothing but pap. *(Finishes, attempts to flush)* This damn toilet never works.

HELGA: I'll have Carl take a look at it. He's real good with the W.C.

EDMUND: *(Begins to shave)* What does your Ouija board say now, Helga?

HELGA: All that is, I see.

EDMUND: You're going to go up in your lines tonight?

HELGA: Yeah, Ouija doesn't play favorites. *(She opens a jar of cold cream and a snake jumps out at her. She screams. Affectionately)* You damn practical joker.

EDMUND: *(Referring to Ouija board)* Why don't you ask it who killed the old man?

HELGA: Who do you think killed him?

EDMUND: I think you did it.

HELGA: *(Laughing gaily)* Of course I did it . . . to get the company for you, my baby.

*(*HELGA *embraces and kisses* EDMUND, *whose face is covered with shaving cream.)*

EDMUND: Oh, come on, right here!

HELGA: No!

EDMUND: There's plenty of time. . . . I've been a bad boy today, Mamma.

HELGA: Edmund's been a bad boy.

(He drops his pants. She playfully whips him with his belt.)

EDMUND: I'm gonna get you, Mamma.

HELGA: He's after me!

EDMUND: *(Grabs her fur coat and throws it over them)* Venus in furs!

CARL: *(Calling from offstage)* Mother! Mother!

HELGA: *(Startled)* Oh, my God, it's Carl! He'll be here any minute.

(They jump up. EDMUND *grabs his clothes and tries to put on his pants.)*

EDMUND: Tell him you've had enough. You're fed up. Lay down the law. Do you want *him* to manage this company or *me*?

HELGA: You, of course, darling. *(Kisses him)*

EDMUND: What are you going to tell him?

CARL: *(Off)* Mother?

HELGA: Don't worry about me. Hide. He'll be here any minute.

(EDMUND hides behind the arras. CARL enters, goes to the toilet to urinate.)

CARL: Toilet not working?

HELGA: Yeah. Would you have a look at it?

CARL: I'll fix it. *(Does so)*

HELGA: Now, Carl, what's the matter?

CARL: I want to run some lines from the closet scene.

HELGA: Must we? This day has just exhausted me.

CARL: It seems so cold-blooded. This morning we buried Pop, this afternoon we've replaced him, and tonight we're going on.

HELGA: We must perform. There is no posthumous fame for actors.

JENKINS: *(Poking in his head)* Carl, there's a man out front who wants to see you.

CARL: Who is it?

JENKINS: He looks like a mortician's bill collector, if you ask me.

HELGA: You can't get much lower than that.

CARL: *(To HELGA)* All right, we won't rehearse. *(To JENKINS)* Send him in.

(Exit JENKINS.)

HELGA: I'm going to see about supper.

CARL: Mother, there's something I want to discuss with you.

HELGA: What is it?

CARL: Mother, I think Pop was murdered.

HELGA: Carl, I don't want to talk about this. It was suicide. He was all washed up. He couldn't take the humiliation of playing his hometown.

CARL: Someone we know did it. Someone in this company.

HELGA: Carl, you're frightening me.

CARL: Perhaps a little fear would do you good. Someone in this company killed my father and I'm not going to rest until I find out who it is.

HELGA: You look tired.

CARL: I can't think about that now. There's the performance tonight, and later I've got to go over all the books. Pop always took care of the business end, and I guess now it's up to me. There are a lot of bills to be paid; death is expensive.

HELGA: Carl, I think you're working too hard. You shouldn't have to think about money. You need to concentrate on playing Hamlet just now. Why don't we get someone else to take care of the dull business end of it? Then you'd have more time to think about your art—

(A small crash is heard off.)

CARL: *(Suddenly starting to his feet, draws prop sword)* What's that! A rat! *(Stabs sword through the costume rack, as if it were the arras in the closet scene of Hamlet)* Dead for a ducat! Dead!

HELGA: *(Shrieks)* Don't!

CARL: *(Diving through the costume rack)* There's no one there!

(The door to the dressing room, stage left, opens and EDMUND *falls in dead, with a dagger stuck in his back.* HELGA *and* CARL *turn and gasp.* EDMUND *jumps up laughing, and pulls the dagger out of his back.)*

EDMUND: Ha! Ha! Ha! Cute trick, don't you think? I had Jenkins order it.

CARL: *You* had Jenkins order it?!

EDMUND: Yes, the blade retracts into the handle. We should try it out tonight, don't you think?

HELGA: Carl, Edmund has a lot of ideas about how we can improve the company.

EDMUND: Yes, Carl, I'm going to handle the management from now on.

CARL: You? *(Laughing)* Mother, did you hear that?

HELGA: It's true, Carl. Edmund and I are going to be married.

CARL: *(Retching)* Mother! A beast that wants discourse of reason would have mourned longer.

HELGA: Now, Carl, don't get all excited. It'll just spoil your performance.

CARL: It didn't hurt your performance *(Makes obscene gestures)* did it, Edmund?

EDMUND: Your sense of humor and mine differ.

CARL: Well, if you don't like it, get out of my dressing room, motherfucker!

(They go to fight. HELGA *comes between them.)*

GILBERT: *(Entering)* Oh, excuse me, I'm interrupting.

HELGA: Not at all. We were just leaving. *(Pushes* EDMUND *through the door and following, turns to* CARL*)* Carl, try to understand. *(Then looking* GILBERT *up and down)* Exactly like a mortician's bill collector. *(Exits)*

GILBERT: You don't know me, Mr. Stone. My name is Fey, Gilbert Fey. I'm Elfie's father.

CARL: What can I do for you?

GILBERT: Prevent my daughter from going on the stage.

CARL: Isn't that up to her?

GILBERT: It most certainly is not. She's underage. If she leaves with you on tour, I'll slap you with statutory rape.

CARL: Your threats don't frighten me, Mr. Fey. She's your daughter; you control her.

GILBERT: If only I could. She's strong-willed and once they get a taste of the theater, there's no reasoning with them.

CARL: Your daughter is an inspired actress.

GILBERT: I know that I may be wasting my time appealing to the honor of an immoral actor, but I do appeal to that honor in the hope that it exists. Please help me.

CARL: As you just pointed out, you have the law on your side. What do you need me for?

GILBERT: Ah, if only it were as simple as that.

CARL: You see this bottle?

GILBERT: Stage blood?

CARL: Yeah, stage blood. It's not real blood; it's the blood we use on stage. That's what your daughter has in her veins.

GILBERT: You are an actor; disillusion her. She must not go the way Carlton went.

CARL: Carlton? What do you know about my father?

GILBERT: I'll make a deal with you. Stop my daughter's career and I'll tell you who killed your father.

CARL: It's a deal. On one condition: that you let her finish the performance tonight. You see, we don't have an Ophelia.

GILBERT: Ah, that sounds dangerous.

CARL: Mr. Fey . . . a moment ago you called me an immoral actor. Frankly, I was shocked. Now I see that perhaps what you say may be true. The theater is my church. To act my experience of God. But I only have one scruple: to get the play onto the stage. Because I sacrifice myself to that end, I do not flinch at sacrificing others. Let your daughter play Ophelia tonight, and I promise that I will send her back to you, a little shaken perhaps, but cured of the theater forever.

GILBERT: Thank you.

CARL: But I warn you, I shall have to hurt her. Perhaps even subject her to some humiliation.

GILBERT: Yes, hurt her, if you must. But cure her of this thing, this stage blood.

CARL: Consider her cured.

GILBERT: *(Starts to go, stops, and turns)* What if she doesn't believe you?

CARL: Don't worry about that, Mr. Fey. Those of us who make our livings at make-believe are the most easily taken in by it.

GILBERT: *(Smiling an oily smile and taking his wallet out of his inside jacket pocket)* May I offer some remuneration for what may be your greatest performance?

CARL: *(Snatching the money)* Now get out before I throw you out!

(FEY beats a hasty retreat. JENKINS enters with a toilet brush and scrubs toilet bowl, whistling while he cleans.)

CARL: *(To JENKINS)* You're going to have to play the Ghost tonight. I don't know what you're going to do for armor.

JENKINS: *(Still scrubbing bloody toilet)* I just happen to have a suit that fits me.

CARL: That fits you???

JENKINS: *(In cold blood)* Yeah, I always had a feeling I was going to play that part someday.

CARL: But you knew Pop would only let you play it over his dead body.

(Pregnant pause.)

JENKINS: It wasn't me. But I think I do know who killed your old man. *(Starts to leave, then turning and coming toward CARL)* And I'm going to tell you after tonight's performance.

(A sandbag falls from the flies just outside of the door and crashes to the floor of the stage, missing JENKINS by inches.)

CARL: A sandbag! Jenkins, if I've told you once, I've told you a thousand times, never whistle in the dressing room. It's bad luck! Unless you say a line from *Hamlet* immediately afterward. Now go get into costume. And Jenkins, when you hear that call—"Places"—you know that you're going on because if you're not, you're in the wrong business. We've got a performance to give, and you're on in the first act. Now go on . . . and Jenkins, break a leg.
(JENKINS exits hurriedly, trips over the sandbag, and falls)

JENKINS: "He smote the sledded Polacks on the ice."

CARL: Are you sure that's from *Hamlet*?

JENKINS: Yes, it's from Horatio's first ghost scene. They always cut it.
CARL: No wonder. I never thought that Shakespeare would stoop to a Polish joke!

(JENKINS exits.)

CARL: *(Alone, changing from CARL to Hamlet)* A father is a necessary evil. Shakespeare must have written *Hamlet* in the months following his father's death. Fatherhood in the sense of conscious begetting is entirely unknown to man. From only begetter to only begotten. For all we know, fatherhood may be a legal fiction. Who is the father of any son that any son should love him? The son unborn mars his mother's beauty; born he brings pain, divides affection, increases care. He is a male: his growth his father's decline, his youth [his] father's envy, his friend his father's enemy. *(Regarding his nude body in the mirror)* Oh, that this too too solid flesh would melt.
JENKINS: *(Off)* Hamlet, I am thy father's spirit.
CARL: *(Startled)* Oh, it's Jenkins rehearsing.
STONE'S VOICE: You are the dispossessed son: I am the murdered father: your mother is the guilty queen.

(Enter GHOST as in Hamlet. *He speaks in* STONE, SR.*'s voice.)*

CARL: I can't believe my eyes.
GHOST: To my son I speak. The son of my soul.
　　The son of my body.
　　My son! and what's a son?
　　A thing begot within a pair of minutes, there about;
　　A lump bred up in darkness, and doth serve
　　To balance those light creatures we call women;
　　And at the nine months' end creeps forth to light.
　　What is there yet in a son,
　　To make a father dote, rave or run mad?
　　Being born, it pouts, cries, and breeds teeth.
　　What is there yet in a son?
　　He must be fed, be taught to go, and speak.
　　Ay, or yet? Why might not a man love a calf as well?
　　Or melt in passion o'er a frisking kid, as for a son?
　　Methinks a young bacon,
　　Or a fine little smooth horse colt,
　　Should move a man as much as doth a son;
　　For one of these, in very little time,
　　Will grow to some good use; whereas a son,
　　The more he grows in stature and in years,
　　The more unsquared, unlevel'd he appears;
　　Reckons his parents among the rank of fools,
　　Strikes cares upon their heads with his mad riots,
　　Makes them look old before they meet with age:
　　This is a son.
CARL: Art thou there, truepenny?
GHOST: I died so that my namesake may live forever. My brother didn't do it. My brother didn't do it.
CARL: I never thought he did!

GHOST: Man at ten is any animal, at twenty a lunatic, at thirty a failure, at forty a fraud, at fifty a criminal. Damn good gin that was!

CARL: *(Applauds)* Father! A masterly rendition.

(The GHOST *disappears.)*

HELGA: *(Off)* Carl . . . Carl. *(Enters)* Carl, you're not dressed yet . . . and you're on in five minutes!

(She frantically helps him dress.)

CARL: All these hooks and eyes . . . I'll never make it. . . . Why can't we get any tights that fit?

HELGA: You're not in New York now, darling, this is Mudville. Carl, why don't you get one of your tricks to do your sewing for you?

CARL: It's so hard to meet anyone on the road, Mother.

HELGA: Tell me about it.

CARL: It could be worse, Mother. We could be in Vienna.

HELGA: Carl, I told you never to mention Vienna to me again.

CARL: Slowly I turn and inch by inch, step by step . . .

HELGA: Ah, Vienna, the city of my nightmares. The only town we played where we had to go back to our hotel rooms to take a piss.

CARL: What about the night that Edmund Dundreary was discovered in his hotel room forcing a load of shit down the sink with his thumb? He couldn't find the key to the W.C. in the middle of the night.

HELGA: Jenkins never got over it.

CARL: I never got over it.

HELGA: Vienna never got over it. Carl, haven't you forgotten something?

CARL: Oh, yes, the locket.

HELGA: *(Holds up wig)* Carl . . .

CARL: No! Not the wig.

HELGA: Carl, you've got to wear the wig.

CARL: Mother, if I've told you once I've told you a hundred times: I hate that wig!

HELGA: Carl, you have to wear the wig!

CARL: People laugh at me when I come on stage in that wig.

HELGA: Go with it, go with it! Carl, please, you cannot play Hamlet without being blond. It's never been done in theater before.

CARL: Well, why not? Some Danes have black hair.

HELGA: Name five. Please, Carl, wear the wig. *(In baby talk)* Wear the wiggie, wiggie, wiggie. *(*CARL *resists)* Please, Carl, don't make me beg. *(She begins crying. He gives in and takes the wig)* Thank you. And tonight could you true up the "to be or not to be" speech? It's been a little too two-dimensional. Try to mean what you are saying. No wooden Hamlets. Not even in the sticks. *(Exits)*

CARL: Yes, Mother. Why, I know the "to be or not to be" speech so well that I could say it backwards. "Question the is that; be to not or, be To." *(He enters the playing area as Hamlet and begins the "To be or not to be" speech)*
   To be or not to be . . .
   (Whispers) Line!
   That is the question.
   Whether 'tis nobler in the mind to suffer

The slings and arrows of outrageous fortune,
Or to take arms against a sea of troubles
And by opposing end them. To die—to sleep,
No more; and by a sleep to say we end
The heart-ache and the thousand natural shocks
That flesh is heir to: 'tis a consummation
Devoutly to be wished. To die, to sleep,
To sleep—perchance to dream. Aye, there's the rub:
For in that sleep of death what dreams may come
When we have shuffled off this mortal coil,
Must give us pause—there's the respect
That makes calamity of so long life.
For who would bear the whips and scorns of time,
The oppressor's wrong, the proud man's contumely,
The pangs of despised love, the law's delay,
The insolence of office and the spurns
That patient merit of the unworthy takes,
When he himself might his quietus make
With a bare bodkin? Who would fardels bear,
To grunt and sweat under a weary life,
But that the dread of something after death,
The undiscovered country, from whose bourn
No traveler returns, puzzles the will,
And makes us rather bear those ills we have
Than fly to others that we know not of?
Thus conscience does make cowards of us all,
And thus the native hue of resolution
Is sicklied o'er with the pale cast of thought,
And enterprises of great pitch and moment
With this regard their currents turn awry
And lose the name of action—Soft you now,
The fair Ophelia! Nymph, in thy orisons
Be all my sins remembered.

(Enter ELFIE *as Ophelia.)*

ELFIE: Good my lord,
How does your honor for this many a day?
CARL: I humbly thank you, well, well, well.
ELFIE: My lord, I have remembrances of yours
That I have longed long to redeliver.
I pray you now receive them.
CARL: No, not I,
I never gave you aught.
ELFIE: My honored lord, you know right well you did,
And with them words of so sweet breath composed
As made the things more rich. Their perfume lost,
Take these again, for to the noble mind
Rich gifts wax poor when givers prove unkind.
There, my lord.
CARL: Are you honest?
ELFIE: My lord?

CARL: Are you fair?

ELFIE: What means your lordship?

CARL: That if you be honest and fair, your honesty should admit no discourse to your beauty.

ELFIE: Could beauty, my lord, have better commerce than with honesty?

CARL: Ay, truly, for the power of beauty will sooner transform honesty from what it is to a bawd than the force of honesty can translate beauty into his likeness. This was sometime a paradox, but now the time gives it proof.

(HELGA and EDMUND enter watching from the wings, dressed as Gertrude and Claudius.)

EDMUND: *(To HELGA)* We almost muffed it in that last little scene.

HELGA: I'm afraid that Carl is going to be trouble.

EDMUND: You can handle him. Use a little psychology.

HELGA: That's underhanded, Edmund. I wouldn't stoop to using psychology.

(ELFIE and CARL continue the performance of Hamlet.)

CARL: I did love you once.

ELFIE: Indeed, my lord, you made me believe so.

CARL: *(Seeing his mother and EDMUND kissing in the wings)* You should not have believed me, for virtue cannot so inoculate our old stock but we shall relish of it. I loved you not.

ELFIE: I was the more deceived.

CARL: Get thee to a nunnery. Why wouldst thou be a breeder of sinners? I am myself indifferent honest, but yet I could accuse me of such things that it were better my mother had not borne me: I am very proud, revengeful, ambitious, with more offenses at my beck than I have thoughts to put them in, imagination to give them shape, or time to act them in. What should such fellows as I do crawling between earth and heaven? We are arrant knaves all; believe none of us. Go thy ways to a nunnery.

ELFIE: O, help him, you sweet heavens.

EDMUND: She's good, really good.

HELGA: She even makes *him* look good.

CARL: *(As Hamlet)* I have heard of your paintings too, well enough. God hath given you one face and you make yourselves another. You jig, you amble, and you lisp; you nickname God's creatures and make your wantonness your ignorance. Go to, I'll no more on't, it hath made me mad. I say we will have no more marriage. Those that are married—all but one—shall live. The rest shall keep as they are. To a nunnery, go.

(Applause is heard. CARL exits from the stage through the arras to the dressing room. We hear ELFIE as Ophelia finishing the scene with her lament through the curtain.)

ELFIE:
O, what a noble mind is here o'erthrown!
The courtier's, soldier's, scholar's, eye, tongue, sword,
Th'expectancy and rose of the fair state,
The glass of fashion and the mould of form,
Th'observed of all observers, quite, quite down!
And I, of ladies most deject and wretched,
That sucked the honey of his musicked vows,

Now see that noble and most sovereign reason
Like sweet bells jangled, out of time and harsh,
That unmatched form and feature of blown youth
Blasted with ecstasy. O, woe is me
T'have seen what I have seen, see what I see!

(During ELFIE's *speech,* JENKINS *and* CARL *are in the dressing room.)*

JENKINS: *(Handing* CARL *a whiskey bottle half full)* Here's the whiskey bottle you wanted. I found it in the prop room.

CARL: I'll empty it. Do you have some tea?

JENKINS: That's tea in it now. I know you don't drink.

CARL: *(Sniffs it)* Tea!

JENKINS: Rose hip . . . organic . . . vitamin C.

CARL: Thank you, Jenkins, you're my right arm.

JENKINS: But, tell me, what scene are you going to use it in?

CARL: In a little scene I'm going to play right now. *(Both listening to last of* ELFIE's *speech)* Leave me alone with her.

JENKINS: What are you going to do?

CARL: That's between the Father, the Son, and the Holy Ghost.

JENKINS: P.U. All religion stinks to . . .

CARL: High heaven? Yes, I know.

*(*JENKINS *heaves a sigh and exits.* ELFIE *enters dressing room.* CARL *is sitting at dressing table drinking.)*

ELFIE: Carl, is something wrong?

CARL: Why do you ask?

ELFIE: *(Troubled, perhaps even haunted)* There was something about your eyes . . . I don't know. Maybe it was just my imagination, but you looked as though you were going to tear my clothes off me. It frightened me.

CARL: Tear your clothes off you? *(He drinks from the bottle)*

ELFIE: *(Shocked)* Carl, you're not drinking? *(Trying to reason with him)* You should smoke grass, dear. That stuff will ruin your liver.

CARL: *(Brash, almost obnoxious)* Of course, I'm drinking. I'm an actor, not a goddamn hippie! The drama originated as a festival of Dionysus. *(Ranting)* Grapes! Wine! Intoxication!

ELFIE: Please stop drinking! You have a performance to give.

CARL: That's one of the highly guarded secrets of our profession. All actors are better drunk. *(Belches)*

ELFIE: That's disgusting!

CARL: What's disgusting about it? It's more constructive than what most people do when they're drunk.

ELFIE: Here, take back your rabbit's foot.

CARL: I never gave that to you.

ELFIE: You did, but take it back. For to the noble mind, rich gifts wax poor when givers prove unkind.

CARL: *(Sarcastically)* I saw the movie.

ELFIE: Carl, I know that you're going through something terrible about your father. But I'll stand by you. I'd do anything for you.

CARL: *(Rubbing her face with his hand)* What's that on your face?

ELFIE: Makeup. I'm an actress now.

CARL: What do you need makeup for? What's wrong with your own face?

(He splashes her face with water and wipes it clean. Then he kisses her.)

ELFIE: *(Aroused)* Carl, do you know how you make me feel?

CARL: *(Shocked at her willingness)* No, I don't know how I make you feel, but I know how you look—like a whore! *(Spanks her)*

ELFIE: *(Outraged)* I hate you and I hate the theater! I'll do Jenkins's studio performance tonight but, after that, I never want to see you or the inside of a theater again. *(Exits)*

CARL: Don't slam the door. *(Sound of door slamming and applause)*

(FEY enters.)

GILBERT: Well played, Mr. Stone. You've kept your part of the bargain.

CARL: And now, Mr. Fey, you keep your part of the bargain. Who did it, Mr. Fey? Who was the dirty rat who killed my father?

GILBERT: I killed him.

CARL: You!!!

GILBERT: Look at my face . . . over here in the light.

CARL: Omigod!

GILBERT: You see a resemblance? Yes, I killed Carlton and I impersonated the Ghost. . . . We were twins, Carlton and I, and we were both stagestruck.

CARL: Then you're my . . .

GILBERT: Yes, I'm your Uncle Gilbert.

CARL: You killed your own brother to indulge a petty jealousy?

GILBERT: Yes, yes. It should be easy for you to understand. It's in my veins too—this stage blood.

CARL: You killed your own brother to play his role for one night?!

GILBERT: You'd let me fry for that, wouldn't you? But there's more to it than that, believe me. Hear me out. Percy and me . . . yes, that was your old man's name before he changed it for the stage—Percy Fey . . .

CARL: *(Shocked)* You mean my name isn't Stone?

GILBERT: No, it's Fey, Raymond Fey.

CARL: Ray Fey! Omigod! It's horrible!

GILBERT: Percy got a local girl in trouble, and she bore his baby in a woodshed. Percy didn't want the little bastard to saddle him with responsibility, so he seized the child and tried to drown it in a drunken scene. I beat on him and saved the child. He ran away that night with a road show and never came back. I made that girl an honest woman, and raised his child . . . Elfie Fey.

CARL: Then she's my sister!

GILBERT: She's your half-sister.

CARL: He might have killed Elfie. Still, revenge cannot be justified.

GILBERT: Then you mean you'll let me fry, after all? But whatever course of action you choose to take, never let her know that that foul, old, drunken piece of human garbage . . . God rest his soul . . . was her father.

CARL: Uncle Gilbert, you'll find that blood is thicker than water, especially stage blood. . . . Uncle Gilbert, do you think you could memorize a short speech of about twenty lines? You see, Elfie and I are doing a scene from Jenkins's experimental drama, *Fossil Fuel.* We're trying to convince Mother that it might be profitable to add an avant-garde play to the repertoire. And I think we might just have a part in it for you.

GILBERT: Oh, I'd be honored to play with you, Mr. Stone.

CARL: Come back tonight after the performance, and I'll have the whole thing written out for you.

GILBERT: Aye, my lord. *(Exits)*

EDMUND: *(Entering dressing room)* Carl, your mother wants to see you.

CARL: You say my mother?

EDMUND: She wants to speak with you in her dressing room before the closet scene.

CARL: Tell her I'll obey. Were she ten times our mother!

(CARL puts on a wig and enters the Hamlet *stage where* HELGA *as Gertrude awaits him.* FEY *sneaks into the dressing room during the following scene; he snoops around, takes a sip from the fake bottle of booze, spits it out, then eavesdrops by the arras.)*

CARL: Now, Mother, what's the matter?

HELGA: Hamlet, thou hast thy father much offended.

CARL: Mother, you have my father much offended.

HELGA: Come, come, you answer with an idle tongue.

CARL: Go, go, you question with a wicked tongue.

HELGA: Why, how now, Hamlet?

CARL: What's the matter now?

HELGA: Have you forgot me?

(Weeps. An onion drops from HELGA*'s handkerchief.)*

CARL: No, by the rood, not so!
　　You are the Queen, your husband's brother's wife,
　　And, would it were not so, you are my mother.

HELGA: Nay, then I'll set those to you that can speak.

CARL: Come, come, and sit you down. You shall not budge.
　　You go not till I set you up a glass
　　Where you may see the inmost part of you.

HELGA: What wilt thou do? Thou wilt not murder me?
　　Help, ho!

GILBERT: What, ho! Help!

CARL: *(Draws)* What's that? A rat? Dead for a ducat, dead! *(Makes a pass through the arras)*

GILBERT: O, I am slain.

HELGA: O me, what hast thou done?

CARL: Nay, I know not. Is it the King?

HELGA: O what a rash and bloody deed is this!

CARL: A bloody deed. Almost as bad, good mother,
　　As kill a king, and marry with his brother.

HELGA: As kill a king?

CARL: Ay, lady, it was my word.—
　　(Lifts up the arras and sees that he has accidentally killed GILBERT*)*
　　Uncle Gilbert?
　　Thou wretched, rash, intruding fool, farewell!
　　I took thee for thy better. Take thy fortune.
　　Thou find'st to be too busy is some danger.—
　　Leave wringing of your hands. Peace, sit you down,
　　And let me wring your heart; for so I shall

If it be made of penetrable stuff.
If damned custom have not brazed it so,
That it be proof and bulwark against sense.

HELGA: What have I done, that thou dar'st wag thy tongue
In noise so rude against me?

CARL: Look here upon this picture, and on this,
The counterfeit presentment of two brothers.
This was your husband. Look you now what follows.

HELGA: O Hamlet, speak no more.
Thou turn'st mine eyes into my very soul,
And there I see such black and grainéd spots
As will not leave their tinct.

CARL: Nay, but to live
In the rank sweat of an enseaméd bed,
Stewed in corruption, honeying and making love
Over the nasty sty—

HELGA: O speak to me no more.
These words like daggers enter in mine ears.
No more, sweet Hamlet.

CARL: A murderer and a villain,
A slave that is not twentieth part the tithe
Of your precedent lord, a vice of kings,
A cutpurse of the empire and the rule,
That from a shelf the precious diadem stole
And put it in his pocket—

HELGA: No more.

(Enter GHOST.)

CARL: A king of shreds and patches—
Save me and hover o'er me with your wings,
You heavenly guards? What would your gracious figure?

HELGA: Alas, he's mad.

CARL: Do you not come your tardy son to chide,
That lapsed in time and passion, lets go by
Th'important acting of your dread command?
O, say.

GHOST: Do not forget. This visitation
Is but to whet thy almost blunted purpose.
But look, amazement on thy mother sits.
O, step between her and her fighting soul.
Conceit in weakest bodies strongest works.
Speak to her, Hamlet.

CARL: How is it with you, lady?

HELGA: Alas, how is't with you,
That you do bend your eye on vacancy,
And with th'incorporal air do hold discourse?
Forth at your eyes your spirits wildly peep,
And as the sleeping soldiers in th'alarm
Your bedded hairs like life in excrements,
Start up and stand on end. O gentle son,

Upon the heat and flame of thy distemper
Sprinkle cool patience. Whereon do you look?
CARL: On him, on him! Look you, how pale he glares!
His form and cause conjoined, preaching to stones,
Would make them capable.—Do not look upon me,
Lest with this piteous action you convert
My stern effects. Then what I have to do
Will want true color; tears perchance for blood.

(A second Ghost enters, pushes the first off the edge of the stage, and exits hurriedly pursued by the first.)

HELGA: To whom do you speak this?
CARL: Do you see nothing there?
HELGA: Nothing at all; yet all that is I see.
CARL: Nor did you nothing hear?
HELGA: No, nothing but ourselves.
CARL: Why, look you there, look how it steals away!
My father, in his habit as he lived!
Look where he goes even now out at the portal!

(Exit CARL, chasing the GHOSTS out of the theater.)

HELGA: This is the very coinage of your brain.
This bodiless creation ecstasy
Is very cunning in.
CARL: Ecstasy!!!

(Blackout. All the characters in the play grope about the stage in the darkness, carrying lighted candles.)

JENKINS: *(Announcing)* Ladies and Gentlemen, please stand by. Remain seated. A fuse has blown.
HELGA: *(Voice in the dark)* What's the matter?
JENKINS: There's a short circuit.
HELGA: Call wardrobe and have it lengthened. *(If the audience moans, HELGA says, "Did you people come here for entertainment or revenge?")*
VOICE OF OPHELIA: Alas, he's mad!
HELGA: Behind the arras, hearing something stir, whips out his rapier, and cries, "A rat, a rat," and in his brainish apprehension kills the unseen, good old man.
EDMUND: O, heavy deed!
HELGA: Your wisdom best shall think.
EDMUND: It shall be so. Madness in great ones must not unwatched go.

(Suddenly the lights come up on CARL.)

CARL: Jenkins, Jenkins!
JENKINS: *(Entering)* Carl! I dug up this skull in the prop room last night. It's real!
CARL: *(Taking the skull)* Alas! Poor Urine. He pissed his life away.
JENKINS: Carl, that skull belonged to the stage manager of the Walnut Street Theatre.
CARL: In Philadelphia?
JENKINS: Yeah. He had seen Edwin Booth play Hamlet countless times, so,

Adam McAdam & Charles Ludlam in *Stage Blood* (Ron Scherl)

when he died, he willed his skull to the theater, to be scraped out and bleached
and used in productions of *Hamlet.*
CARL: Jenkins, why don't you do that?
JENKINS: I've donated my body to science, but I guess they could send over
the head.
CARL: Jenkins, what did you say this stage manager's name was?
JENKINS: Bernard . . .
CARL: Not Bernard Waxberger?
JENKINS: Bernard Waxberger!
CARL: I knew him, Jenkins! Why, you'd never know to look at him now, but
he had quite a sense of humor. Many a time while Pop was trampling the
boards as Hamlet, he'd carry me piggyback through the flies. You know, he
knew all the minor roles in Shakespeare's plays.
JENKINS: They're the most difficult.
CARL: Of course. Everybody knows that. Whenever a road company came in
with a skeletal cast, he'd just fill in. He was reputed to have been the greatest
Osric who ever lived. . . . Jenkins, I read your play last night. All eighteen
hundred pages of it. It's good! Really good. You've got something there.
JENKINS: You read it?
CARL: That scene where the woman is tied to a railroad track is really suspense-
ful.
JENKINS: That may not be good. I want to keep the emotional tone low-key.
An author must look on murder and mutilation with a dispassionate eye. You
see, I cannot show the inner workings of the murderer's mind. I must not. For
the identity of the murderer is kept hidden until the end of the play. . . . Carl,

I've thought it ever since this morning. Karen killed your father. It was a simple case of revenge.

CARL: No, Jenkins, no. Karen didn't do it. *They* did it to him. They made him play the same role night after night, year in and year out. To a true artist that deadly repetition can lead to only one of two things: alcoholism or madness. My father was a consummate artist, Jenkins. . . . He resorted to both of them!

JENKINS: You mean . . .

CARL: Year in and year out, Carlton Stone played on like a shadow. He was a perfectionist.

JENKINS: Great Scott!

CARL: Yes, Jenkins. My father died to perfect the role of the ghost!

(Blackout.)

End of Act II

ACT III

Scene: *Same as Acts I and II.*

(ELFIE *and* CARL *are warming up for* JENKINS*'s studio performance.)*

CARL: There's just one thing I don't understand, Elfie. If Grotowski calls his book *Towards a Poor Theatre,* why does the book cost fifteen dollars?

ELFIE: Let's exercise.

CARL: I'll watch.

ELFIE: Carl, what do you do for exercise?

CARL: I act.

ELFIE: That's not enough. If you want to be a great actor, you must hone your body. Yoga is designed to unite the body with the soul. A lot of people think that the brain is the most important organ of the body. It simply isn't true. The Japanese have a saying: "If the liver is not in good condition, neither is the disposition."

CARL: What do you think is the most important organ of the body, Elfie?

ELFIE: The heart. What do you think is the most important organ?

CARL: *(Pause)* Let's exercise.

ELFIE: O.K. Let's start with the Salute to the Sun. *(*CARL *gives an army salute.)* Oh, Carl, try being serious. And remember to inhale and exhale.

CARL: I will try to keep that in mind.

ELFIE: O.K., so start in a prayer position, and follow me. *(She goes through the exercise smoothly.* CARL *tries, but cannot bend to the floor.* ELFIE *continues exercising)* Grab your ankles, put your head to your knees, with the palms of your hands to the floor . . .

CARL: Elfie, I can't get my hands to the floor.

ELFIE: Why not?

CARL: I don't know. I think my pants are too tight.

ELFIE: Continue.

*(*ELFIE *finishes the exercise.* CARL *continues to try to reach the floor, and by heavy breathing finally makes it. He gasps with relief.)*

CARL: I see. You breathe in. And then you breathe out.

HELGA: *(Entering with* EDMUND *and* JENKINS*)* . . . and when I was at the Yale

Drama School, the students stood on the back of the chairs and applauded for twenty minutes. They couldn't get enough of me. *(Pause)* They've been rehearsing for days.

EDMUND: Rehearsing?

HELGA: Yes, it's Jenkins's play—what was it called? *Dinosaur Dung,* wasn't it?

EDMUND: *(Laughing) Fossil Fuel,* my dear. But then you're joking, aren't you?

HELGA: *(In a loud whisper)* Don't make me laugh. It's supposed to be a tragedy. *(They take seats in the theater. Calling affectionately)* Carl! *(With difficulty)* Son. How are you doing?

CARL: It's not how I'm doing, but what I'm doing that I keep asking myself.

HELGA: I mean the play. How is it going?

JENKINS: *(In a temper)* It's a joke! All a big joke.

HELGA: A joke?

CARL: Don't pay any attention to him. *(Aside)* It's going brilliantly. He's nervous, that's all.

EDMUND: *(Condescending)* Opening night jitters? Stage fright? I have no sympathy for actors trembling in the wings. If you want to go on the stage, then get on with it.

HELGA: Carl, what kind of character do you play?

CARL: Well, there aren't really any characters in the play.

HELGA: No characters? Then how do you tell the story?

CARL: It doesn't have a story, either. In a way it's all the stories that ever were, rolled into one . . . and there are these images . . .

JENKINS: Carl, please, you shouldn't be out front. You should be in your place. You're spoiling the whole illusion.

CARL: Excuse me.

HELGA: *(To CARL, half humorously)* Break a leg! *(To EDMUND)* Aren't they cute?

EDMUND: I hope this won't take too long.

HELGA: I think they're ready to begin.

EDMUND: I mean the performance.

JENKINS: Ladies and Gentlemen . . .

HELGA: *(To EDMUND)* Shhh, they're beginning.

GILBERT: *(Entering obtrusively in spite of himself, with script in hand)* "Pardon me for living, but" . . . *(Realizes that the performance has begun)* Oh . . . dear me . . . I'm interrupting . . . I mean I'm late. *(Exits)*

HELGA: *(Aside, incredulously, to EDMUND)* Did you hear what he said? "Pardon me for living!"

EDMUND: Some things are unpardonable.

JENKINS: I'll begin all over again. Where was I?

EDMUND: You were saying, "Ladies and Gentlemen."

JENKINS: Oh, yes. Ladies and Gentlemen, *Fossil Fuel* by James Jenkins. Starring . . . Elfie Fey as the Allmother and Carlton Stone, Jr. as her son.

HELGA: *(Under her breath)* There's something decadent about this.

CARL: *(From the side, imploring her)* Mother, please!

HELGA: Carl, this reminds me of the time I played Arkadina in *The Seagull.* "O Hamlet, thou hast cleft my heart in twain."

CARL: "Throw away the worser part and live the better with the other half."

HELGA: Did I tell you about the time I appeared at the Yale Drama School . . .

EDMUND: *(Applauding)* Brava, Helga, brava!

CARL: Sit down, Mother.

(The curtain opens revealing ELFIE *wrapped in white sheets sitting on a phony-looking stage rock.)*

JENKINS: The action of the play is set nine thousand nine hundred and ninety-nine years in the future after the ecological disaster. All life has been blotted out, all is empty, all is null, all is void.

HELGA: She's not wearing any makeup.

(During the following, JENKINS *periodically yells "Cue!" and a bell rings.* CARL *attaches strings to* ELFIE *and the set.)*

ELFIE: OOOOOOOOOOMMMMMMMau! OMMMMMMMMMMMMMMMMMMau! Ommmmmmmmmmmmmmau! *(Screams)* OOOOOOOOOOOMMMMMMMMM-MAU! OOOOmmmmmAAAAAuuuuu! Haya HeeYah Haya HeeeYah Haya-heeeyah. *(Grunts)* My wooommmbb! Nunga nunga nunga nunga nunga nunga. *(Then she breaks out of the scene and says matter-of-factly)* Rebirth. *(She then lies on her back and enacts ritual labor pains.)* Labor Ritual/May Day—Unyin Square. *(Screams experimentally)*

HELGA: This is either pure madness or pure genius. But I can't tell which.

GILBERT: *(Poking his head in)* There's such a thin line, I think.

HELGA: *(Whispering hoarsely to* EDMUND*)* Who *is* that man!

EDMUND: Why don't you ask him?

ELFIE: Mankind, man unkind, mankind, man unkind, mankind, man unkind.

HELGA: The lady doth protest too much, methinks!

ELFIE: *(Screaming in labor)* EEEEEEEYow! EEEEEEEYOW! EEEEEEEYOW!

HELGA: Oh, for God's sake, is that caterwauling starting up again?

(Smoke bombs go off. CARL *crawls out from between* ELFIE*'s legs, and is wailing like a baby.)*

HELGA: I smell sulphur. Is that necessary?

JENKINS: Yes, it's intentional.

HELGA: *(Laughing)* Oh, it's a stage effect! I like that.

EDMUND: It smells like the devil! If you wanted fog, why didn't you use the fog machine? At least dry ice doesn't smell.

JENKINS: I didn't want fog. I wanted smoke!

EDMUND: Well, what's the difference? *(Aside to* HELGA*)* They want to work in the theater, but they don't want to know its effects!

HELGA: The theater is chilly tonight.

JENKINS: *(Flaring up, loudly)* That does it! The play is over! That's enough! Curtain!

CARL: But we haven't finished.

JENKINS: Enough! Curtain! *(Stamping his foot)* Bring down the curtain! *(Finally lowers it himself)* You must forgive me. I forgot that only the chosen few can write plays and act in them. I have infringed on a monopoly! My life . . . The theater . . . Oh, what's the use! *(He makes a helpless gesture and exits)*

HELGA: What's the matter with him?

CARL: You hurt his feelings.

HELGA: What did I say? The theater *is* chilly tonight. He said himself it was going to be a joke. Now he wants to be taken seriously! I know what's behind all of this. He's trying to make us feel guilty that we're doing the classics. He's

jealous of the classics. I'll bet he just wishes he could write a play as good as
. . . as good as *Hamlet*! But no! He'll never admit to any feelings of inferiority.
He covers up with his ravings about new forms. I think what he calls new forms
are nothing but bad manners!

ELFIE: We meant to give you pleasure.

HELGA: Really? Then why don't you do the usual sort of play and not make us
listen to your obscene noises.

(ELFIE *stalks off.* CARL *follows.*)

GILBERT: (*Entering behind* HELGA *and* EDMUND, *dressed as the Ghost*) You
shouldn't wound young people's pride like that.

HELGA: (*Turning*) Sir, I'll thank you to mind your own business! (*She turns back
with a horror-stricken look on her face*) OMIGOD!

EDMUND: What is it?

HELGA: It can't be . . .

EDMUND: What?

HELGA: For a moment I thought it was Carlton!

EDMUND: Calm yourself, my dear. You're imagining it.

HELGA: If you think I'm imagining it: Look!

EDMUND: (*Turns, looks at* GILBERT *and screams*) Give me some light!

(*There is a blackout. Applause. Lights come up on* HELGA *and* EDMUND *in their*
Hamlet *costumes, bowing. They try to steal an extra bow, but the applause dies
suddenly, stopping them in their tracks. Flustered, they exit into the dressing room.*)

HELGA: Did you know about this meeting?

EDMUND: Carl told Jenkins to pass it around.

HELGA: What do you expect?

EDMUND: Either a pathetic abdication speech or a power grab. I'm ready for
either.

HELGA: Is our protégée, Elfie Fey, going to be at this meeting?

JENKINS: No, she's not.

HELGA: Oh, she didn't take her call.

CARL: (*Entering*) Mother. Mr. Dundreary. Where's Jenkins?

JENKINS: Here I am.

CARL: Is Elfie here?

JENKINS: (*Darkly*) No Carl, she's not. She said she was going down to the river.

CARL: Omigod!

EDMUND: Now, Carl, I know you murdered Gilbert Fey.

CARL: It was an accident. It wasn't a real rapier. The blade retracts into the
handle—like you said.

EDMUND: Who would believe it? He had just told you that he killed your
father.

CARL: How did you know that?

EDMUND: (*Pointing to the keyhole*) The keyhole.

CARL: This is blackmail.

EDMUND: That's one word for it. I call it the simple economics of discretion.

CARL: What do you want?

EDMUND: Your company, your role, your mother, and your name.

CARL: My name?

EDMUND: Yes, the name Stone is a theatrical trademark. (*Brandishing a contract*)

And you're going to sell it to me for the legal sum of one dollar—and agree to act only in London.

CARL: Why in London?

EDMUND: 'Twill not be noticed there. The acting there is as bad as yours. Sign on the dotted line.

JENKINS: Don't sign, Carl. Don't give anything to that sleazy son of a bitch.

EDMUND: Sign, or I'll blab to the police.

CARL: They have me where they want me. *(Signs)* Uncle Gilbert didn't do it. Are you people blind? Can't you see that he was shielding someone? It was Elfie—Elfie killed my father!

HELGA: What was her motive?

CARL: He tried to drown her when she was a little child, left her to be raised by the petty bourgeoisie. Then, as her artistic aspirations grew and were thwarted, so did her resentment, and now . . . now she's gone down to the river!

ELFIE: *(Entering in a wet swimsuit)* Of course I went down to the river. I always take a swim after a performance.

JENKINS: Elfie didn't do it, Carl. It was Edmund and your mother. They are . . . they have been . . .

HELGA: There's no need for delicacy, Jenkins. You're trying to say that Edmund and I had a "special relationship." Well, it's true and Carl knows all about it.

JENKINS: Then you admit it?

HELGA: I admit to having a lover, but not to being a murderess. I told you, Carl, it was suicide.

CARL: Pop was discovered poisoned by the dread hebenon poured into the porches of his ear. I think that's a rather unlikely way to commit suicide.

EDMUND: Really, people wouldn't believe this if it were acted upon the stage!

CARL: Someone in this company killed my father *(To the audience)* and we're not leaving this theater until we find out who it is. Each of you had a motive. If only one of you didn't, then we could suspect the least likely person.

ELFIE: You're just like Hamlet, seeking to avenge your father's death.

CARL: That would be neat, Elfie. But it wouldn't quite be true. How can I seek revenge for something I have done myself so often in my dreams? I know I should be horrified by all this. I know I should seek the murderer out of moral indignation or revenge. But the truth is that the situation in the abstract has so taken hold of me that I have come to regard the actors in it as merely pieces in a puzzle, baffling and fascinating to the point of monomania.

GILBERT: *(Entering)* So you thought you could get away from me, did you, you little slut! You're coming home with me!

CARL: Uncle Gilbert!

GILBERT: You swore to me!

CARL: And I swear now.

ELFIE: There's no need to swear, Carl. *(To GILBERT)* I heard everything, Uncle Gilbert. Did you think that anything could keep me away from the theater? I would defy you forever. *(To CARL)* Carl, I'm convinced of your greatness as an actor now. You were able to convince me that you didn't love me.

CARL: But Elfie, Carlton was my father, too. . . . That makes you my sister.

HELGA: That's where you're wrong, son. Your father was no actor. You were the son of a plumber. That accounts for your knack in fixing the W.C., and why you're not blond.

CARL: *(To* ELFIE*)* Now there's nothing standing in our way. . . . Tell me, all of you, who was the greatest actor that ever lived?

EDMUND: Sir Johnston Forbes Robertson.

HELGA: Modjeska.

ELFIE: Eleonora Duse.

JENKINS: Chaucey Allcott.

CARL: Henry Irving.

GILBERT: The greatest actor who ever lived was Carlton Stone, Senior!

CARL: You say that, Uncle Gilbert? After all he put you through? Really, I think you're being more than generous. Oh, Pop was a great personality, it's true, but an actor in the true sense? Not really. Why, Pop never heard of Grotowski! He never did his yoga. Why, his idea of a great play was a play with a good part in it for him! A great speech was a speech he could give with bombast. No, I think Pop was little more than a ham.

GILBERT: Carl, how could you?

CARL: *(Shamed)* Perhaps I'm being a little harsh on Pop. He did have perfect timing. Why, even his death was so perfectly timed that it revealed his friend's secret ambition, his wife's adultery, and loyalty in a man he thought was his enemy. In all of his career, Pop only stepped out of character once: when he took exception to his son's assertion that Irving was anything to compare with his old man!! *(Removes* GILBERT*'s disguise, revealing him to be* CARLTON*)*

ALL: Carlton!

STONE: Carl, when did you guess?

CARL: Well, Pop, you didn't give yourself away until the play within the play scene. I saw you come on as the Ghost, and I remembered something you said, "In order to play Carlton, you have to have been Carlton." . . . There's just one thing I can't figure out, Pop: Who is Elfie Fey?

STONE: My mistress, young man, my mistress.

HELGA: Well!

ELFIE: I'm sorry, Carl. You're just too immature for me.

STONE: Sorry to cut you out of the action, son.

CARL: That's all right, you two. I'm having a rather interesting "experimental" relationship: with Jenkins!

HELGA: It's a mother's dream come true. To have a son who's gay!

EDMUND: Helga, you told me you did it.

HELGA: I wanted to do something to make you admire me.

EDMUND: A remark like that could cost me my job.

STONE: Edmund, you're a scoundrel. But I like a good scoundrel, so I'm giving you a raise. That's not bad coming from a man who knows you're fucking his wife, is it?

EDMUND: *(Beaming)* You're one in a million.

CARL: That's my Pop!

HELGA: *(Indignant)* Yesterday I felt positively wanton. Now I'm beginning to feel a little hemmed in.

STONE: By the way, Edmund, I hear you bought my name. That name was, in fact, Raymond Fey. And that's the name you're going to be acting under from now on: Ray Fey! Here's your itching powder, Ray *(Opens paper and blows powder on* EDMUND*)*; and all along I thought I had crabs. *(To* CARL*)* You see, my boy, all this was contrived . . .

CARL: It certainly was.

STONE: . . . to teach you a little lesson.

EDMUND: Don't make hangmen of your superiors.

HELGA: That although there is only one way of being born, there are many ways of getting killed.

JENKINS: Never suspend your disbelief.

ELFIE: And that the important thing in life is not to tell the truth, but to perfect the mask!

STONE: Ah, yes, we all learned something along the way. But I just wanted to teach you that in order to play Hamlet, you have to have been Hamlet. And from what I see in these reviews, you *were* Hamlet out there tonight.

ALL: Reviews!!!!

(STONE hands out newspapers to all present.)

EDMUND: "The costumes were beautiful." *Women's Wear Daily.*

HELGA: "An unmasculine Hamlet." *New York Post.*

ELFIE: "Exhilarating." *New York Times.*

JENKINS: "Stones Hone Bard's Bones." *Variety.*

ELFIE: A *Hamlet* with a happy ending!

HELGA: Very hedonistic!

EDMUND: *(In the voice of Eric Blore)* Very eighteenth century!

JENKINS: And very advanced dramaturgically.

CARL: Gee, Dad, the rest is silence?

STONE: Is there any music to compare with it? *(Hands recorder to CARL who miraculously begins to play "Greensleeves")*

(STONE and ELFIE exit, while CARL plays the recorder.)

CARL: *(Suddenly very excited)* Jenkins, I'm going to do your play!

JENKINS: *Fossil Fuel?*

CARL: Well, that's the only play you've written, isn't it?

JENKINS: Yes.

CARL: Until we do that one, you'll never get on to the next.

JENKINS: Oh, no!

CARL: What is it now, Jenkins?

JENKINS: If people are beginning to like my work, there must be something wrong with it.

EDMUND: *(Shocked)* Jenkins, you're a snob. And here all along I thought you were a communist. *(Gives HELGA a jewel case, which she opens; a mouse pops out. They exit laughing)*

CARL: Jim, there's just one thing I can't figure out. Pop was playing dead in the dressing room, but we saw him go on as the Ghost. How could he be in two places at the same time!

JENKINS: Beats me.

STONE: *(Reentering)* Jenkins, are you going hunting tomorrow?

JENKINS: Hunting?!

STONE: For props.

JENKINS: Yes.

STONE: I've just remembered. We've run out of stage blood.

(Enter the Ghost, reading Variety.*)*

End

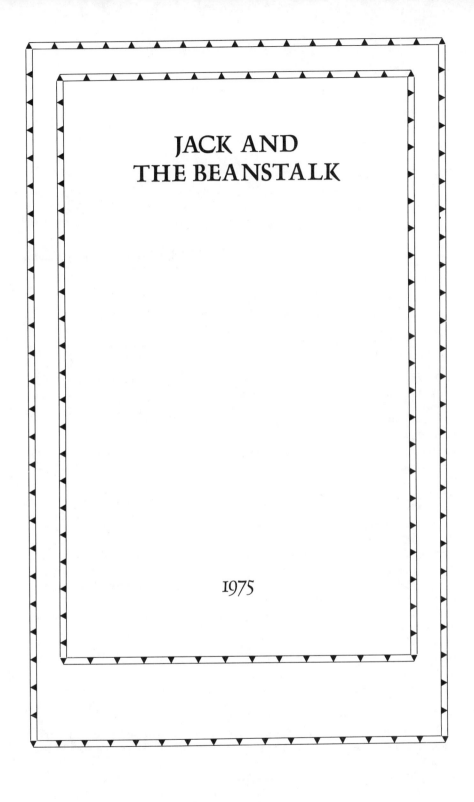

JACK AND
THE BEANSTALK

1975

Cast of Characters

JACK
MOTHER
COW
EX-BUTCHER
MAN-IN-THE-MOON
GIANTESS
GIANT
GOOSE
HARP
PEASANTS

To be played in one act without intermission. The duration of the performance should not exceed forty-five minutes.

Scene 1: *The tenement apartment of Jack and his mother, Mrs. Beanstalk.*

(The style should be socialist realism. MRS. BEANSTALK *is vacuuming.* JACK *comes in from school.)*

JACK: Hi, Mother, I'm home from school. I'd like some milk and cookies.
MOTHER: *(Shutting off the Electrolux with her foot)* All that lazy boy ever thinks about is milk and cookies. *(Weeping)* Oh Jack, I'm so sad. We have no money for milk and cookies. We can't even afford meat.
JACK: Don't cry, Mother.
MOTHER: We need money to live, Jack. Unless we get some you will have to quit school.
JACK: Hooray!
MOTHER: And work!
JACK: No, no, not work. Please Mother, anything but work! *(Running away)*
MOTHER: Oh Jack, when are you going to grow up and get some sense?
JACK: Does one go with the other?
MOTHER: It seems we have no choice but to sell Bossie, our pet cow.

*(*BOSSIE THE COW *enters.)*

JACK: But who will we sell him to?
MOTHER: Jack, I don't know what they're teaching you in that school. Cows are hers, not hims.
JACK: Whose?
MOTHER: Hers. Not hims but hers.
JACK: *(Looking around for the "her")* Hers?
MOTHER: Him is a bull.
JACK: Who is a bull, Mother?
MOTHER: Him is a bull! Him is a bull!
JACK: *(Spinning around to see where the "him" is)* Him? Mother, sit down. I think you're delirious with hunger. Let's get back to Bossie. To whom should I sell him?
MOTHER: To the *(Spelling)* B-U-T-C-H-E-R.
JACK: To the B-U-T-C-H-E-R?

MOTHER: Yes, to the B-U-T-C-H-E-R.

JACK: But, Mother, that spells *butcher!*

(BOSSIE, *who has been trying to figure out what* B-U-T-C-H-E-R *spells, suddenly starts mooing with fear.*)

MOTHER: Oh Jack, now you've spilled the beans. I didn't want Bossie to know.

BOSSIE: *(Very frightened)* Moo.

JACK: But Mother, I can't sell Bossie. I promise I'll give up milk and cookies.

MOTHER: But Jack, we must pay the rent too or be thrown out in the street. I'm afraid there's no choice but to sell Bossie.

JACK: Please don't make me take him out and sell him! Please don't make me take him out!

MOTHER: Why not, Jack?

JACK: This is a five-flight walk-up.

MOTHER: Don't be a lazy boy! Off with you, now. Get the best price you can and hurry home with the money.

JACK: All right, if there's no choice. Come along Bossie old boy.

BOSSIE: *(Plaintively)* Moo.

Scene 2: *The street.*

EX-BUTCHER: Say boy, that's a nice-looking cow you've got there.

JACK: My name is Jack, sir.

EX-BUTCHER: Jack, I'd like to buy your cow.

JACK: You want to buy Bossie? Would you give him a good home?

EX-BUTCHER: Yes, I promise to take good care of her.

JACK: And you wouldn't grind him up for sausages in a machine?

EX-BUTCHER: No, I wouldn't.

JACK: Then you're not a butcher, sir?

EX-BUTCHER: Not anymore. I used to be a butcher who cut up animals to make meat. But now I'm so sorry that I just want to take a cow home as a pet and lavish all the good things in life on her.

JACK: Oh, would you, sir? Would you?

EX-BUTCHER: Yes, I would.

JACK: That's great! How much money do you have?

EX-BUTCHER: Well, I haven't got any money, Jack. Ever since I gave up butchering, I haven't had much money. But I could give you these beans.

JACK: Beans?

EX-BUTCHER: Soybeans. They have just as much protein as meat. They don't take up as much room. And you don't have to eat your pets! *(He strokes* BOSSIE*)*

BOSSIE: *(Beaming contentedly)* Moo.

JACK: You want me to sell Bossie for a handful of beans?

EX-BUTCHER: These beans are magic, I tell you.

JACK: Well, I'd rather see Bossie live out a long happy life giving us milk for years than grinding her up for sausages that can be eaten in one day. I'll take the beans.

EX-BUTCHER: You'll never regret it.

JACK: Good-bye, sir. Bye-bye, Bossie!

BOSSIE: Moo.

EX-BUTCHER: Good-bye, Jack. Tell your mother that if she pressure-cooks them, don't salt until after they're done or they don't get soft.

Scene 3: *Back at the tenement.*

JACK: Mother, I'm home. And I sold Bossie.

MOTHER: *(Turning off the vacuum cleaner with her foot)* That's good, Jack. How much did you get for her?

JACK: And listen to this, Mother. I sold her to an ex-butcher who wanted to give her a good home.

MOTHER: Why, that's wonderful, Jack. How much did he give you?

JACK: Well, he . . . er . . .

MOTHER: Come, tell me quickly, Jack. How much money did he give you?

JACK: He didn't give me any money.

MOTHER: WHAT?

JACK: He gave me these beans. *(Shows her the beans)*

MOTHER: BEANS?

JACK: He said they were very healthy.

MOTHER: BEANS?

JACK: And he said that if you use the pressure cooker . . .

MOTHER: Oh, Jack, how could you be so stupid?

JACK: But Mother, he said they were magic.

MOTHER: *(Laughing)* I don't know whether to cry or laugh. You've thrown away our only hope for food. Just as I throw these worthless beans out of the window. *(Fits the action to the words)*

JACK: No, Mother, don't throw them away.

MOTHER: Too late.

JACK: Mother, now *you've* spilled the beans!

MOTHER: Now we'll both go to our beds without supper. I suppose we deserve it. We've both been behaving like naughty children. Good night, Jack. Brush your teeth and try to get some sleep. Tomorrow we must look for work.

(They both go to sleep. And while they sleep the beanstalk begins to grow slowly up past the roof of the house, all the way up to the sky.)

Scene 4

JACK: *(Waking and looking out of the window)* Mother, Mother, come quickly!

MOTHER: *(Waking)* What is it, Jack?

JACK: Look where you threw the beans. The beanstalk has grown up past the rooftops.

MOTHER: *(Amazed)* Why, Jack, it reaches up to the sky!

JACK: Good-bye, Mother. I'm going to seek my fortune.

MOTHER: Where are you going?

JACK: I'm going to climb the beanstalk and see where it leads.

MOTHER: Oh Jack, be careful.

JACK: Don't worry, Mother. It must lead somewhere.

MOTHER: *(Calling after him)* Jack, Jack, don't climb too high. You might get dizzy and fall.

JACK: I'm sure I won't fall if I don't look down, Mother. *(Calling back)* Good-bye! Good-bye!

*(*MOTHER *fades from view behind a scrim. The tenement sinks down until it is out of sight. The crescent moon descends like a swing, holding the* MAN-IN-THE-MOON.*)*

Scene 5

JACK: Who are you?

MAN-IN-THE-MOON: I'm the Man-in-the-Moon.

JACK: You mean I've climbed so far that I've climbed past the moon?

MAN-IN-THE-MOON: *(Shining a flashlight on* JACK*)* Let me have a better look at you in my moonbeam. Why, you're a little boy!

JACK: Yes, I am.

BOSSIE: *(Jumps over the moon)* Moo.

MAN-IN-THE-MOON: What on earth was that?

BOSSIE: Moo.

JACK: That's Bossie. He must be the cow that jumped over the moon.

MAN-IN-THE-MOON, JACK, AND BOSSIE: *(Sing)*
  Hey diddle diddle
  The cat and the fiddle,
  The cow jumped over the moon;
  The little dog laughed
  To see such fun
  And the dish ran away with the spoon.

JACK: *(Waving at* COW*)* Hi, Bossie!

BOSSIE: *(Exiting)* Moo!

JACK: No wonder meat prices are so high.

MAN-IN-THE-MOON: I don't understand why the government spends billions of dollars to put men on the moon when anyone can jump over the moon.

JACK: How can anyone jump over the moon?

MAN-IN-THE-MOON: When it is reflected in a puddle.

JACK: This conversation is getting moonotonous.

(The MAN-IN-THE-MOON *sings a medley of songs with "moon" in the title as* JACK *climbs past him. Lots of glitter falls on* JACK.*)*

JACK: What's this stuff?

MAN-IN-THE-MOON: Stardust. *(A shot rings out)* Duck!

(A comet flies past.)

JACK: A shooting star!

MAN-IN-THE-MOON: You're a pretty smart kid. You're so bright I'll bet your mother calls you "Sonny."

JACK: So long! *(Begins to climb out of sight)*

MAN-IN-THE-MOON: Say wait a minute, kid. Do you know where you're going?

JACK: Not exactly. I'm just climbing the beanstalk.

MAN-IN-THE-MOON: Do you know where it leads?

JACK: No, sir. But it must lead somewhere. *(Begins climbing again)*

MAN-IN-THE-MOON: Wait a minute. Not so fast. This here is a very high beanstalk. Did you hear what I said? *Very* high. And your fazoolas might kazule your flapdoodles. Now pay attention kid 'cause I don't want to say this twice. Did you hear what I said? I don't want to say this twice.

JACK: Yes, Mr. Moonman.

MAN-IN-THE-MOON: At the top of this beanstalk you will find a great castle.

JACK: Where did it come from?

MAN-IN-THE-MOON: It grew up out of the mud just like the beanstalk. In this castle lives a terrible giant named Fazool. Years ago during the Great Depression Fazool hired many people to build his castle for him and he promised to pay them a lot of money for building it. Everyone was very happy to help because they thought of the money he had promised and of all the things they could do with the money to make their lives better. But then when it came time to pay the men and women who built the castle a terrible thing happened.

JACK: He refused to pay them?

MAN-IN-THE-MOON: Oh, no, he paid all right. He knew he couldn't get away with not paying the builders because they would tear his castle down even faster than they had built it up.

JACK: *(Eager to learn)* Then what went wrong?

MAN-IN-THE-MOON: After the castle was all built and furnished and fitted out with every comfort and every luxury a real home should have and the giant was all settled in and cozy, he paid the workers all the money he had promised. And even paid them an extra bonus for ten years if they would defend his castle and make it safe from all enemies. But at the end of the ten years when they got the money he had promised, the people discovered that the prices had gone up incredibly and that the money the giant paid them could no longer buy the comforts they had dreamed of.

JACK: Couldn't they still tear the castle down?

MAN-IN-THE-MOON: No, they couldn't. The only way they could feed their families was by working to defend the castle they had built and the giant who had swindled them.

JACK: That's horrible.

MAN-IN-THE-MOON: Your father was one of those men, Jack. When he spoke out against the giant, the giant had him killed. And that's why you and your mother live in poverty.

JACK: Didn't the other castle builders help him?

MAN-IN-THE-MOON: They couldn't, Jack. They were afraid of losing their jobs as defenders of the castle. It was his fellow workers who silenced him.

JACK: Oh, my poor father! My poor mother! What shall I do?

MAN-IN-THE-MOON: That castle and all that is in it is rightfully yours, Jack. It is the legacy to the children of all the men who built it. You must win it back. But the task is a very difficult one, and full of peril, Jack. Have you the courage to undertake it?

JACK: I fear nothing when I am in the right.

MAN-IN-THE-MOON: Then you are one of those who slay giants. You must find a way into the castle. You must take the goose that lays the golden eggs, and a harp that talks, away from the giant.

JACK: *(With moral indignation)* But that's stealing.

MAN-IN-THE-MOON: It isn't really stealing. Remember, Jack, all that the giant possesses is really yours. Did you hear what I said, kid? It's all really yours.

JACK: I heard you the first time.

MAN-IN-THE-MOON: So long, kid, and remember what I told you. *(Disappears)*

Scene 6

(Time: Moments later. After a little climbing music. Place: The portal of the GIANT's castle. JACK blows the crumphorn which hangs by the great door.)

JACK: Knock knock.
VOICE WITHIN: Who's there?
JACK: Watcha.
VOICE: Watcha who?
JACK: Watchawannaknowfer?

(A spy hole opens and a frightful GIANTESS with one eye in the middle of her forehead [appears].)

JACK: *(Upon seeing the giantess)* Eeeeek! That's a frightyfullsomely giantess in a dress with only one eye in the middle of her head! I'm getting out of here! *(He turns to run away)*
GIANTESS: *(Catching him by the shirttail or the seat of his pants and laughing loudly the whole time)* Ho ho ho—no you don't—why should I be workski so hardski? I wanna livil boychick for to be makin' them beddern and whashin' th' dish. Why for not? Like them other great ladskis in them stories on television! You gonna work real hard for me! You gonna fire my fires and black my boots. You gonna makeum up goodski when the giant ain't at home. But when that biggest ole bigness hiself come home I hide the little boy or giant eat him up.
JACK: I will help you and work as your servant, madame. But please do be sure to hide me from your husband for I should not like to be eaten at all.
GIANTESS: There's the good boy! You are lucky that you didn't scream when you first saw me as the other little boys did. That would have awakened Fazool. He would have eaten you, as he did them, for breakfast. Ee likes boys for 'is brekkers sunnyside up!
VOICE OF GIANT: *(Thunders from afar)*
Fee 'em, fire 'em, fo 'em, fum.
I smell the blood of an Englishman.
Be he alive or be he dead,
I'll grind his bones to make my bread!
JACK: *(Terribly frightened)* Oh, do hide me, madame giant!
GIANTESS: You hide in the closet. Where I keep all my clothes. The giant wouldn't dare to open that!

(JACK hides in the closet.)

Scene 7

GIANT: Wife! There is a man in the castle. Let me have him for breakfast.
GIANTESS: You are grown old and stupid. It's only a nice fresh steak off an elephant that I have cooked for you, which you smell! Sitski downski and eaten your brekkers.

(The GIANT sits down to eat the elephant steak which the GIANTESS serves him.)

GIANT: Volumnia, bring in my goose that lays the golden eggs! I'll just pick my teeth with this wolf's bone. I've had a hard day terrorizing the countryside. I think I'll rest and count my money.

GIANTESS: It's been laying very well lately. The eggs are heavier than ever.

Scene 8

(The GIANTESS *sets the* GOOSE *before* GIANT.*)*

GIANT: *(Commanding like thunder)* Lay!

(The GOOSE *lays a golden egg with a dollar sign on it, and makes the sound of a cash register.)*

GIANT: *(As before)* Lay! Lay! Lay!

(The GOOSE *lays three more $ eggs.)*

GIANT: Now bring me my harp. I will have a little music.

(The GIANTESS *brings in a* HARP *sparkling with diamonds and rubies, with strings of platinum.)*

JACK: *(Peeking through the giant keyhole)* Gasp! That harp is encrusted with diamonds and rubies and its strings are of purest platinum.

GIANT: *(Starting)* What was that? Volumnia, I heard someone gasp!

GIANTESS: That was only me gasping. This harp is heavy to carry.

GIANT: Ah, you're getting old, Volumnia. I remember the fun we used to have terrorizing the lowlands. Now all you do is sit at home and dream of fine things to wear.

GIANTESS: It's true. I'm not the mad thing I was as a girl. But I've still got me looks.

GIANT: Indeed you have. You're a fine figure of a giantess. And I've never had cause to be ashamed of you.

GIANTESS: *(Blushing)* Ah, go on and eat your elephant steak! Play your harp and don't soft-soap me.

GIANT: *(Fondling the* HARP*)* This is one of the nicest things I took from the workers. I am a great music lover. And my harp is a faithful servant. Philharmonia?

Scene 9

HARP: Yes, master.

GIANT: Play me something sweet and melodious. *(The* HARP *plays a sad song)* That song is too sad. Play me something merry! *(The* HARP *plays a gay air)* Now play me a lullaby. *(The* HARP *plays a lullaby)* I want to sleep. Zzzzz. *(Snores)* Where are you going, Volumnia?

GIANTESS: To my room. I want to finish the fairy tale I'm reading.

GIANT: I don't approve of your reading these fairy tales, Volumnia. It'll stunt your growth.

GIANTESS: You're an illiterate! That's what you are!

GIANT: I am not! What's an illiterate?

GIANTESS: It's someone who's never read a book in his life!

GIANT: What's the good of sitting around with your nose in a book? I'd much rather count my golden eggs. Help me, Volumnia.

GIANTESS: Oh, very well. Where should I start?

GIANT: Pick up where you left off.

GIANTESS: Oh, yes. One million nine hundred and ninety-nine thousand nine hundred and ninety-nine. Two million. Two million one. Two million two. Two million three.

GIANT: Counting always makes me sleepy. *(Yawns and sleeps)* Hnuhnhg! Zzzzzz . . .

GIANTESS: *(Taking the candle and exiting somnambulistically)* And now to bed. To bed. To bed. *(Exits)*

Scene 10

*(*JACK *steals out of the closet on tiptoes. He steals past the sleeping* GIANT, *trying carefully not to wake him. A giant mouse scurries past and frightens him.)*

JACK: Come along little goose. You're going with me!

GOOSE: Gazoooo! Honk! Gazooo!

JACK: Shhhh! Or you'll wake Fazool. Then my goose will be cooked!

GOOSE: Hisss! Honk! Gazooooooo!

GIANT: *(Waking up)* Fe fa fi fo fum! I smell the stink of an Englishman!

JACK: *(Aside)* I took a bath this morning!

GIANT: *(Noticing* JACK*)* Who's that?

JACK: *(Unafraid)* It's only me, sir.

GIANT: Who are you?

JACK: Only myself as you see me, sir.

GIANT: What's your name?

JACK: Nobody.

GIANT: Nobody? That's an unusual name. Why yer an itsy-bitsy livil personette. Ain'tchew? Kitschie coo! Kitschie coo!

JACK: A giant who talks baby talk! It's revolting!

GIANT: Nobody, I'm going to have you for breakfast tomorrow morning. But right now I'm so sleepy. *(Dozes off)* Zzzzzzzzzz . . .

JACK: The giant snores so loud it sounds like thunder. Well, I've got the goose, now for the harp. *(Takes the* HARP *and the* GOOSE *and tries to leave the castle)*

HARP: Master! Master! He's taking me away. Help me, master. Don't let him steal me.

JACK: Shhh! Please don't call the giant.

HARP: Master! Master!

*(*JACK *exits with the* HARP *and the* GOOSE.*)*

Scene 11

GIANT: Did I hear your sweet voice calling me, Philharmonia? My harp is gone! My goose is gone! Everything is gone. *(Calling after them)* Philharmonia, who has stolen you?

DISTANT VOICE OF PHILHARMONIA: Nobody, master.

GIANT: Nobody! The little boy I was planning to eat for breakfast? Volumnia! Volumnia! Come quick. Nobody has stolen my harp! *(Roaring with anger)* Nobody has stolen my goose that lays the golden eggs!

Scene 12

GIANTESS: *(Entering in her nightgown)* If nobody has stolen them what are you making this big fuss about?
GIANT: You don't understand. Nobody has stolen all we possess.
GIANTESS: Then we still possess it.
GIANT: Nobody is a little boy.
GIANTESS: Oh, I wouldn't say that. I see lots of little boys right out there in the audience. Little girls, too.
GIANT: Oh, never mind, you idiot! I'm going after the little boy and when I get him I'll make blood sausages out of him! *(Exit)*
GIANTESS: *(Calling after him)* No, no, please don't hurt him. Catch him and make him work for me. It's so hard to find good domestic help these days!

Scene 14: [*Back at the tenement.*]

MOTHER: O loo lee loo lay! It's been a month of Sundays since my dear son Jack climbed up the beanstalk. Is he safe? Will I ever see him again? O loo lee loo lay!
JACK'S VOICE FROM FAR OFF: Mother! Mother! Come quickly and bring an ax.
MOTHER: *(Looking up and shading her eyes)* Jack, Jack, oh Jack. I hear your voice but I can't see where you are!
JACK'S VOICE AS BEFORE: I'm up here in the beanstalk little mother, somewhere between heaven and earth.
MOTHER: Oh, Jack, it's so good to hear your voice!
JACK: *(Appearing above with GOOSE and HARP)* There's no time to lose. There's a great giant chasing me. Quick, get the ax!
MOTHER: *(Exits and reenters with the ax)* Here is the hatchet. Oh, do be careful, Jack!
GIANT'S VOICE: I'm going to catch Nobody! Ha ha ha!
JACK: *(Shouting up to him)* That's exactly who you're going to catch! Come on! What's keeping you!
GIANT'S VOICE: I'm going to eat Nobody up!
JACK: *(Urgently)* Now stand out of the way, Mother. Because Nobody is going to cut the beanstalk down!

(Suddenly the GIANT appears above.)

MOTHER: *(Screams)* Jack, look out!

(With that JACK cuts through the last tendril of the beanstalk and the GIANT experiences the greatest crash since twenty-nine.)

JACK: *(Climbing up on the GIANT, addresses a bunch of miserable louts below)* My fellow countrymen. The cruel giant who robbed and enslaved you is dead. It was I, a mere nobody, who delivered you from his cruel oppression. Come forward with me and let us take possession of the castle and all that is in it. Our fathers built it. It is ours.

PEASANTS: Yea! Right on! Let's take that castle! *(Etc.)*

JACK: But we must be careful, for the Giantess is still alive.

PEASANTS: Kill the Giantess! Cut off her ears! Make her into hamburgers!

GIANTESS: *(Entering, terribly frightened)* Mercy, midgets, mercy.

JACK: The first lout to lay a hand on this great lady will answer to me. The man's a coward who would draw his sword upon a woman. Besides, the Giantess was very kind to me.

GIANTESS: Oh thank you, little boy.

JACK: In fact, I've taken quite a shine to my jolly jumbo over here. The Giantess and I are to be married. We plan to beget a race of men too big to be pushed around.

EX-BUTCHER: Well, well, my boy. You've done very well for yourself, haven't you?

JACK: Why, it's the ex-butcher! How is Bossie, sir? Is he well?

EX-BUTCHER: Is she well? Why she even had a little calf when she jumped over the moon.

(Enter BOSSIE *with Calf.)*

MAN-IN-THE-MOON: I believe that makes it a moon calf!

(The COW *moos. The* HARP *plays and sings, the* GOOSE *lays golden eggs, the* GIANTESS *dances, and everyone lives happily ever after.)*

The End

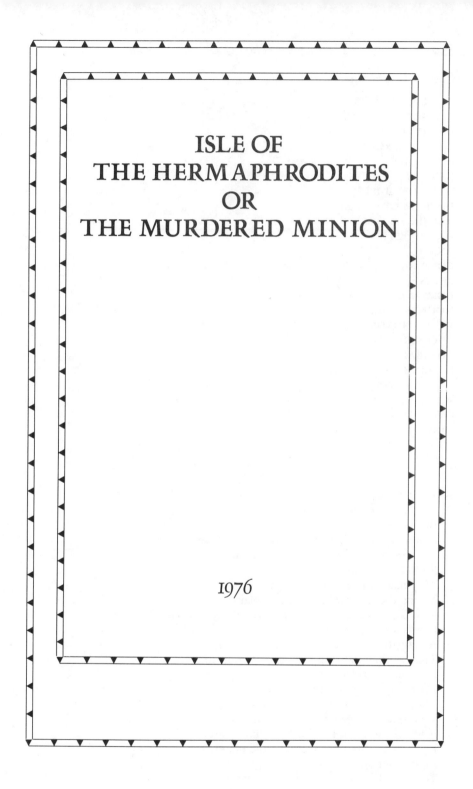

ISLE OF
THE HERMAPHRODITES
OR
THE MURDERED MINION

1976

Cast of Characters

CATHERINE DE' MEDICI
RUGGIERI, *her astrologer*
HENRY III
ST. MUGGEROON ⎤
EPERNOUN ⎬ *his "minions"*
JOYEUSE ⎦
DUKE OF GUISE
DUCHESS OF GUISE
ARTHUR, *a child, her cousin*
MACHIAVELLI
ANJOY ⎤
GONZAGO │
RETES ⎬ *makers of the massacre*
DUMAINE │
MOUNTSORRELL ⎦
THREE MURDERERS
TWO SERVANTS
ADMIRAL
LOREINE
ATTENDANTS
SOLDIERS
CATHOLICS
HUGUENOTS

PROLOGUE

MACHIAVELLI:
   The world thinks Machiavelli's dead,
   But here I am reborn before your eyes.
   Again my thought will rear its lovely head
   And prove itself in yet another guise.
   Philosophers cannot explain
   Why man is made of evil stuff.
   To me the answer seems quite plain:
   Man hasn't yet learned to be evil enough!
   Life is a comedy to those who think
   A tragedy to those who feel.
   That sentimental slop has really begun to stink.
   It's time to tackle something real.
   Hard rhymes and high crimes,
   The ring, the contest, win or lose,
   Where actions can redeem the times
   And men are there for other men to use.
   Dangerous thoughts are like cold water:
   In and out again quick!
   To keep them thinking in the theater
   Farce tempo does the trick.
   So if cruel things pass lightly here

It's to make you think and not to feel.
It's pain and not the cruelty that we fear
And time will always wound the heel.

ACT I

Scene 1

(During the overture, lights come up in the tower of the alchemist and sorcerer, RUG-GIERI, astrologer to the queen, CATHERINE DE' MEDICI. The queen paces slowly back and forth like some great caged cat. The astrologer cowers, watching her every movement with a terrified stare.)

RUGGIERI: I can't do it!

CATHERINE: You can! You will!

RUGGIERI: Impossible, the risk . . .

CATHERINE: You miserable coward, think of the risks I've taken. I drugged the bitch. I arranged to have her brought here.

RUGGIERI: You're reckless.

CATHERINE: I'll tell you something Machiavelli told my father, "The end justifies the means." This I learned at my father's knee while other little children were learning their "Do unto others. . . ." It's become the Medici motto.

RUGGIERI: Starlight becomes you, Catherine.

CATHERINE: How dare you become familiar! Remember your place! You are my astrologer, nothing more.

RUGGIERI: You let me do your chart.

CATHERINE: An intimacy I have since regretted.

RUGGIERI: I know I am beneath you. But queens have been known to raise a man up.

CATHERINE: Do you see these mourning weeds I wear? Black, black, nothing but black since Henry died. Do you remember the day of the king's death?

RUGGIERI: I predicted it twenty years in advance.

CATHERINE: Since that day I have mourned and will do so until the end of my life.

RUGGIERI: And yet I think you do not entirely despise another Henry, duke of Guise.

CATHERINE: He *is* a devout Catholic like myself. I see him only at Mass.

RUGGIERI: Domine vobiscum.

CATHERINE: I particularly like the way he genuflects. And the way he sticks out his tongue to receive the host has sent a shiver of religious fervor down my spine more than once, I can assure you.

RUGGIERI: You know nothing more of him?

CATHERINE: No, but I should *adore* to hear his confession.

RUGGIERI: So Guise is my rival in the field. And this whole plot is against his wife.

CATHERINE: Ruggieri, you know my son is *(Pregnant pause)* that way?

RUGGIERI: What way?

CATHERINE: Women are more fond of him than he is of them.

RUGGIERI: You mean he's queer?

CATHERINE: As a square pizza. But it's not his fault. I think it's mine. I didn't want him to grow up to be like his father and torture his poor wife with a mistress. I impressed this on him at every chance I got. *(Dubious pause)* I'm afraid I overdid it. Now he won't look at a woman. Hates anything feminine. And spends his days with his minions.

RUGGIERI: Those young men he hangs out with?

CATHERINE: Yes.

RUGGIERI: I can hardly believe it, they're all so excessively masculine.

CATHERINE: That's always a dead giveaway. One in particular, Muggeroon, is a Protestant. I'm afraid he will convert the young king.

(Sound of voices approaching.)

CATHERINE: Here they come. Say you'll do it.

RUGGIERI: I don't dare. I haven't got that kind of courage.

CATHERINE: *(Putting her hands around his throat)* Do you remember the wax figure of the pope that was found on La Mole the day they burnt him at the stake? Everyone wanted to know where he got it. There's another pyre ready for you, Ruggieri, if I were to tell.

RUGGIERI: *(Gasping for air, almost strangling)* But, Highness, this plot is a violation of the alchemist's oath.

CATHERINE: Never to employ occult knowledge for an evil purpose?

RUGGIERI: No, never to employ occult knowledge without getting paid.

CATHERINE: *(Releasing him)* Here's a purse.

(Voices again.)

RUGGIERI: They're coming.

CATHERINE: Let me out by the royal tunnel.

(The wall opens by machinery. CATHERINE escapes through the secret passage. The wall closes again. The three minions, MUGGEROON, EPERNOUN, and JOYEUSE, burst into the room. Macho musclemen all, they cavort and gambol in locker room camaraderie. They stage a mock duel and brawl and inadvertently knock over a table spilling papers and occult equipment. RUGGIERI enters and discovering the mess flies into a rage.)

RUGGIERI: Miserable minions! What have you done? Do you know the dangers that lurk in an alchemist's laboratory?

MUGGEROON: Watch it, Pops. Don't miff the minions.

JOYEUSE: He's a bully, I'm a razzer.

EPERNOUN: As ready to slit a throat as tumble a wench.

RUGGIERI: I have flasks of poisoned vapor, which if opened cause everyone around to faint and die.

MUGGEROON: *(In wonderment)* Is there really such a vapor?

RUGGIERI: Yes, and of other phenomenae that fools hold to be magic, I know the rational cause.

MUGGEROON: See here, Ruggieri, we're forming a Protestant party to convert our king to the new enlightened religion.

RUGGIERI: Enlightened religion! A contradiction in terms.

MUGGEROON: Calvin says we should judge our worth by the work we do.

JOYEUSE: And that everything is predestined anyway.

EPERNOUN: People can't make mistakes even if they want to. So we know we're right.

RUGGIERI: I'm for the religion that puts on the best show. And up until now that is still Holy Mother, the Roman Catholic Church.

MUGGEROON: Are you a Catholic?

RUGGIERI: No, I'm a Jew. But I know a good show when I see one. *(Putting the table upright and arranging things on it as they were before)* Thank heaven nothing's broken.

MUGGEROON: Join us. You could use some new ideas, Ruggieri.

RUGGIERI: That's what I hate about your mongrel ideas. They haven't got a sufficiently long pedigree. *(Suddenly he rivets MUGGEROON with an hypnotic stare)* My boy! Oh my boy! Oh my dear boy!

MUGGEROON: What's the matter?

RUGGIERI: *(In a pitying tone)* Dear boy! Dear dear boy!

MUGGEROON: *(Alarmed slightly)* What is it you see?

RUGGIERI: *(Under his breath)* This is not for the others' ears. I must tell you this in private.

MUGGEROON: *(With great bravado)* Anything you have to say to me you can say in front of my friends. I have no secrets from them.

RUGGIERI: It's about your sex life.

MUGGEROON: Would you guys mind going on without me? Tell King Henry I'll be there this afternoon to help him pick out his costume for the Water Spectacle.

JOYEUSE: Sure, Muggeroon, sure.

EPERNOUN: Anything you say.

(JOYEUSE and EPERNOUN slink out.)

MUGGEROON: *(Sarcastically)* Well, are you going to read my palm?

RUGGIERI: I do not indulge in the cruder forms of necromancy. I leave those to the stage magician. I know something about you.

MUGGEROON: *(Contemptuously)* The hell you do!

RUGGIERI: You're in love.

MUGGEROON: *(In amazement)* How could you tell?

RUGGIERI: *(The inscrutable old sage)* I have my ways.

MUGGEROON: Anyone might be in love. That's not sorcery. It's the law of averages. But do you know whom I love? That's a secret I've been trying to keep from myself.

RUGGIERI: Stand here before this mirror. Gaze into it. Think of the one you love and she'll appear.

MUGGEROON: So, you do it with mirrors after all! *(Taking the mirror)* Give it here, you old faker. *(Gazes into the mirror)* I'm fond of parlor tricks!

RUGGIERI: *(Draws a circle around him)* But you must face the east, and don't step out of this charmed circle. *(Shows him a book)* Repeat these words.

MUGGEROON: But I don't know this language.

RUGGIERI: These words are of such power that even on the tongues of amateurs they have wrought miracles.

MUGGEROON: *(Reading solemnly)* Meanderthalltale fatamiliafamilias immermemorial . . . *(RUGGIERI draws back a curtain in the secret passageway revealing the DUCHESS OF GUISE reclining in a deep slumber. The image is reflected in the mirror)* Dulce delectissima! I've conjured the Duchess of Guise! My secret's out!

(RUGGIERI closes the secret door just as MUGGEROON wheels about.)

RUGGIERI: Your secret's safe with me. In fact I mean to help you in your love. I can conjure her for you in flesh and blood.

MUGGEROON: *(In a transport of ecstasy)* If you can do that I'll abandon reason and believe in you alone!

RUGGIERI: Drink this.

MUGGEROON: It isn't poison is it?

RUGGIERI: It is if love is poison.

MUGGEROON: Then let me die of love. *(Drinks)*

(RUGGIERI slips out of the room and opens the panel of the secret alcove.)

MUGGEROON: *(Finishes his drink only to discover the DUCHESS OF GUISE slumbering on a dais)* O woman unattainable, you I love! *(Bends over and kisses her)*

DUCHESS: *(Stirs half-asleep)* Kiss me again. I'll never be younger.

(MUGGEROON kisses her and she opens her eyes.)

DUCHESS: *(Looking at him dreamily)* Muggeroon, my wild young lover! *(Suddenly she stops, shakes herself abruptly, and looks around her in panic)* What have I said? Dreaming or waking, which is which?

MUGGEROON: You called me lover.

DUCHESS: Where am I? How did I get here? You caught me half in a dream. Oh my God! I've given myself away!

MUGGEROON: When we sleep we dream and when we wake the dream continues. People with bad dreams are living a nightmare.

DUCHESS: Then there's no escape from one into the other?

MUGGEROON: *(Crushing her in his embrace)* No escape. *(They kiss)*

(Harsh knocking at the door.)

GUISE: *(Voice off)* Ruggieri! Ruggieri! Open up you old quack!

MUGGEROON: *(Startled)* Who is that?

GUISE: Open up! I know you're in there! It's the Duke of Guise. I have a message from Her Highness Catherine de' Medici.

DUCHESS: *(In stark terror)* My husband! We're both lost!

RUGGIERI: *(Entering through the secret passage)* Shhh! Coo quietly my little dove. *(To the DUCHESS)* Out this way. *(Indicates the secret passage)* Fly! Fly!

(The DUCHESS escapes hurriedly by the secret passage but drops her handkerchief. The wall closes behind her. RUGGIERI opens the door and admits the DUKE OF GUISE.)

GUISE: *(Enters hurriedly)* Ruggieri, there's an urgent matter. . . . *(Suddenly sees MUGGEROON)* Ah, but I see you are not alone.

RUGGIERI: I have been coaching youth in the game of love.

GUISE: Oh really, is that the new view of love, that it's a game?

RUGGIERI: A kind of combat. *(Indicating MUGGEROON)* This is the athlete and I think the champion.

GUISE: I have never played at love. I am that rarest of all birds: a man who's happy with his wife. I have never even committed an "adultery of the heart." My wife is perfect. *(Correcting himself)* The perfectest. My duchess is a model woman. I couldn't come with any other woman. She begins and ends my day. My world revolves around her. She is a heavenly body.

MUGGEROON: *(In a cold sweat)* She certainly has, Sir!

GUISE: Do you know me?

MUGGEROON: Yes, my lord, you are the Guise, husband of the heavenly body . . . I mean the Duchess of Guise.

RUGGIERI: *(Aside)* Are you blind, can't you see the Duke is jealous?

MUGGEROON: You've got a funny name, Guise.

GUISE: I do, and I hate more than anything when people play on it. I do not know you. But I find you something saucy. Marriage is a sacrament, an outward sign instituted by Christ to give us grace.

MUGGEROON: The hypocrite inquisitor talks of grace!

GUISE: How dare you, pup? By heaven, I'll cut your throat!

MUGGEROON: I wish the king feared your cutting his throat as little as I fear your cutting mine.

GUISE: I'll do it by this hand! *(Draws a dagger)*

MUGGEROON: That hand dares not do it! You have cut too many throats already, Guise, and robbed the realm of many thousand souls more precious than your own.

GUISE: Who dares defy the Guise thus?

RUGGIERI: Muggeroon, minion in service of the king.

GUISE: *(With a sly smile)* I know the "service" minions render to the king: Their mouths and their arses! *(Puts his dagger back in his sheath)* I wouldn't degrade my blade with faggot's blood!

MUGGEROON: For this insult, Guisser, I'm going to enjoy your wife.

GUISE: No way!

MUGGEROON: Every way. Bed her, board her.

GUISE: I'll have you whipped!

MUGGEROON: I'll have her licked before you have me whipped. Before this day is over the faggot is going to fuck your wife! *(Exits)*

GUISE: Heretic scum! My wife will never hug a Huguenot!

RUGGIERI: The Protestants grow bold.

GUISE: We'll trample them under our feet. *(Stamps his foot)* What's this? *(Stoops and picks up the handkerchief)* A lady's hankie. Monogrammed with Guise and Cleves! This is my wife's coat of arms! *(Beside himself)* She's been here! With him.

RUGGIERI: *(In mock amazement)* Under our very noses!

GUISE: Did you know?

RUGGIERI: Nothing. But my guess is that they used my observatory for a secret rendezvous.

GUISE: *(Puts the handkerchief inside his vest)* All Protestants will pay for what this Huguenot has done! We'll massacre them by the millions. Tonight the blood will run!

Scene 2: *Somewhere in the palace.*

(Enter QUEEN CATHERINE *and the* DUKE OF GUISE.*)*

CATHERINE: Tell me, sweet Guise, how do you intend to conduct the massacre?

GUISE: Exquisitely, Madame. I have sent down an order that all men participating in the massacre should wear silver crosses on their helmets and white linen scarves tied around their arms. Anyone not wearing these signs will die even if he were the King. I'll have an ordnance of cannon fire shot from the tower, and on that signal a bell will ring. When they hear that bell they will begin to kill and kill and kill until the bell stops ringing. Then breathe a while.

CATHERINE: Good. Go Guise, and lose no time.

GUISE: But Madame, I'm afraid your son the King takes pity on the Protestants.

CATHERINE: He'd do better to think on the good of his country than worry about Huguenots. But never mind him. I've planned a masquerade tonight to distract him. His head will be full of feathers and frills and never will notice how many we kill.

(They exit. [Re]enter GUISE, *[with]* ANJOY, DUMAINE, GONZAGO, RETES, MOUNTSORRELL, *and* SOLDIERS *to make the massacre. As* GUISE *calls the roll each man makes some inarticulate sound of recognition.)*

GUISE: Anjoy.

ANJOY: Uh-huh.

GUISE: Dumaine.

DUMAINE: Yo!

GUISE: Gonzago.

GONZAGO: Here, Excellency.

GUISE: Retes.

RETES: Present.

GUISE: Swear by the silver crosses on your helmets that you will seek and kill anyone you suspect of heresy.

DUMAINE: I swear to be unmerciful.

GUISE: Spoken like a true Christian.

ANJOY: I'm disguised and since no one will know who I am, I mean to murder everyone I meet.

GONZAGO: And so will I.

RETES: Me too.

GUISE: Break and enter the Admiral's house. He is the leading Lutheran. Commence the massacre. Murder him in his bed. Get him first. Cut off the head and the members cannot stand. Go to his house and leave no man alive.

GONZAGO: *(Drawing his dagger)* Follow me, gentlemen.

(Exit GONZAGO *with the others.)*

RETES: *(To* GUISE*)* Look, my lord, they've entered the Admiral's house.

*(*ANJOY, DUMAINE, *and* GONZAGO *enter the Admiral's house.* GUISE *and* RETES *wait below and watch the windows. The* ADMIRAL *is in his bed.)*

ANJOY: Slay his servants before they warn him.

(They seize two SERVANTS.*)*

GONZAGO: Where is the Admiral?

ADMIRAL: O let me pray before I die!

GONZAGO: Pray to our Lady of Mercy! Kiss the cross. *(Stabs him to death)*

ADMIRAL: O God, forgive my sins!

GUISE: *(From below, under the window)* Is he dead?

GONZAGO: Ay, my lord.

GUISE: Throw him out the window!

GONZAGO: What?

GUISE: I say throw him down here. I want to have a better look at him.

(They throw the body of the ADMIRAL *out the window.)*

ANJOY: *(Shouting out the window)* Take a good look at him, Cousin. We may have killed the wrong man while he escaped.

GUISE: *(Bending over the lifeless form)* No, it's he. I'd know him anywhere. Here is the wound where one of my men shot him . . . a near miss. But we finished him off this time. *(Addressing the corpse)* You degenerate, heretic. In contempt of your religion I kick your corpse!

ANJOY: Cut off his hands and send them to the Pope. And let the punishment fit the crime: Hang this man that hated the cross on the same cross in chains!

GUISE: If you men are keen on this as I am, tomorrow no Huguenot will breathe in France!

ANJOY: I swear by the cross to kill every Protestant I meet!

RETES: Retes will follow you.

MOUNTSORRELL: And Mountsorrell!

DUMAINE: And I, Dumaine.

GUISE: Sound the ordnance! Toll the bell! Forward to the massacre! *(The ordnance is shot off, the bell tolls, and they all exit. A group of Protestants runs across the stage pursued by the* GUISE *and his men with their swords drawn)* Let none escape! Murder the Huguenots.

ANJOY: Kill them! Kill them!

(They exit. LOREINE *enters running, the* GUISE *and his henchmen chasing him.)*

GUISE: Follow Loreine! Don't let him get away! *(They corner* LOREINE.*)* Are you a preacher of these heresies?

LOREINE: I am a preacher of the word of God. You are a traitor to your own soul and Him.

GUISE: Do unto others . . . before they do unto you. *(Stabs him)*

ANJOY: Should I bury him?

GUISE: Give him an informal burial: throw him in a ditch.

(They exit, some dragging LOREINE.*)*

Scene 3: [*The royal chambers.*]

JOYEUSE: Here are more letters for you to sign, Majesty.

HENRY: *(Whimpering)* The agony of writer's cramp! I'm being martyred, crucified with pen quills upon a fine parchment cross.

EPERNOUN: May I massage your fingers, Majesty?

HENRY: Don't come behind the screen. You mustn't look at me when I'm signing important documents. It doesn't become me. I look older when I'm thinking.

JOYEUSE: Why do you insist on signing everything yourself, Highness?

HENRY: Majesty! Majesty! I hate "Highness," it sounds so dowdy.

JOYEUSE: Majesty, why do you insist on sign—

HENRY: *(Interrupting angrily)* There is a king in France, is there not?

EPERNOUN: Majesty.

HENRY: *(Stepping out from behind the screen)* I am he, am I not?

JOYEUSE: She. *(Giggles)*

HENRY: *(Wheeling on him suddenly. Then coolly)* Joyeuse, when I look at you I understand why no minion has ever lived to be thirty. *(Temperamentally lets out a cry that comes from the heart)* This day has been wretched! Positively wretched!

EPERNOUN: *(Aside to* JOYEUSE*)* Henry is in one of his moods. Humor him.

JOYEUSE: There there, Henry.

HENRY: Drop everything you're doing. I need about half an hour of attention. *(Reclines on a dais)*

(The two minions wait on him hand and foot. They stroke his brow and talk baby talk to him.)

EPERNOUN: Tell us about when you were king of Poland.

HENRY: When I was king of Poland I had nobody to talk to.

EPERNOUN: Why, Majesty?

HENRY: I don't speak Polish.

JOYEUSE: What on earth did you do?

HENRY: I stayed in a lot. Had a few French friends. Ah but Venice, Venice.

EPERNOUN: Venice, Majesty?

HENRY: There for a few brief weeks among the gondolas and the canals I was happy. In Venice I was touched by the splendor of the cathedral dancing boys and choir. Not like here! We're ruined! The crown is bankrupt. The last three reigns have spent everything. *(Raving)* Low masses, cheapness and economy, misericordia, how I detest them!

JOYEUSE: Henry, stop making that terrible face! It will freeze like that!

HENRY: *(Pouting)* I won't!

JOYEUSE: *(Talking baby talk)* Why issisms pouting? Why? Why? Why isims wivle Henwy pouting?

HENRY: You didn't kiss me when I came in.

JOYEUSE: You didn't give me a chance.

HENRY: You don't love me.

JOYEUSE: That's not true. I do.

HENRY: Then say it.

JOYEUSE: I said it. I do.

HENRY: You do what?

JOYEUSE: I'm very fond of you.

HENRY: I know you're fond of me. But do you love me?

JOYEUSE: I like you.

HENRY: You like me, yes. But you don't love me?

JOYEUSE: *(Lashing out angrily)* All right, I LOVE you! Now are you satisfied?

EPERNOUN: Come on, Henry, smile.

HENRY: I don't want to. Joyeuse hates me and so do you.

JOYEUSE: Just one little smile from our sovereign. Come on. Just one itsy-bitsy little smile. *(Tickles him)*

HENRY: *(Screaming and writhing with laughter)* Don't tickle me! Don't! DON'T! I can't stand it. Please stop. *(Begging)* PLEASE!

EPERNOUN: That's better. There's the good Henry. That's the Henry we like to see!

JOYEUSE: Are His Highness's—

HENRY: *(Correcting him)* Majesty's . . .

JOYEUSE: . . . Majesty's didies all changed?

EPERNOUN: Not quite. Help me roll him over.

(They undress him and roll him over on his stomach with his bare ass sticking up.)

JOYEUSE: I'll just powder his derrière. *(Sprinkles powder on the king's ass and then slaps it)*

HENRY: Ouch, that really hurt.

JOYEUSE: Kiss and make better. *(Kisses the king's ass)*

HENRY: *(Delighted)* You do love me after all! Do you love me, Epernoun?

EPERNOUN: I love you too. *(Bends over and likewise kisses the king's ass)*

JOYEUSE: Henry, this is no time for hanky-panky.

EPERNOUN: No time for messin' with your minions.

HENRY: Why not, love?

JOYEUSE: Have you forgotten the masquerade tonight?

HENRY: *(Alarmed)* I have no disguise!

EPERNOUN: Why not just dress up in your mother's clothes?

JOYEUSE: Surely Her Highness, your mother, would let you borrow *something.*

HENRY: How perfectly *fairy! (Opens the royal wardrobe)* Ermine . . . vair . . . or sable. Which will it be?

JOYEUSE: Oh squirrel definitely, it climbs but it doesn't "push."

HENRY: Vair then.

(MUGGEROON enters out of breath.)

MUGGEROON: Majesty, Majesty!

HENRY: At last, St. Muggeroon! I missed you terribly. My sweetheart, what kept you? You know I rely on your advice for dress-up.

MUGGEROON: Majesty, there's a massacre in progress. The Huguenots are being slaughtered.

JOYEUSE: His Majesty is dressing, Muggeroon. Do you want to spoil the party for him tonight?

MUGGEROON: Every man who's had an original thought in the last five years is being stabbed to death. Henry, do something!

HENRY: *(Begins to get upset)* What can I do? They're killing them you say? Really, does Mother know?

MUGGEROON: The Admiral is dead and other friends of yours. Teachers, scholars . . . all the best people in Paris.

HENRY: This is sheer madness to kill worthy men for their ideas. Ideas don't mean anything. They're hurting no one. Why don't they hunt evildoers? Why don't they raise the taxes? Whose idea was this massacre anyway? *(Wrings his hands)* Oh dear, this will positively spoil the masquerade tonight.

MUGGEROON: Guise led the attack. The conservative scum! What I wouldn't give for a chance to kill him!

JOYEUSE: He's a bastard all right.

HENRY: But what is there to gain by killing these people?

MUGGEROON: It's all about money. The church is a business like any other. They don't want competition.

HENRY: Surely this massacre won't make a big difference in the collection plate on Sunday. The Huguenots don't give anything anyway.

MUGGEROON: I'm talking about Big Business, Sire. All professions are conspiracies against the layman. Who'd hire a cook if he could cook it better himself? Who'd go to a doctor if he could heal himself? Who'd go to a priest if he could reach his god directly? Not me! Not you!

HENRY: Not me? I am a Catholic. I even learned to cook easily enough. A Polish kitchen boy taught me how to make a soufflé. But administering the sacraments . . . that's another matter!

MUGGEROON: The sacraments are spiritual food, and simple food at that. You've mastered the soufflé, Sire. Want to have a go at bread and wine?

HENRY: Your words ring in my ears. My earring is weighing me down. Take it out.

(JOYEUSE removes the king's earring.)

HENRY: Kings are born, not made. But cooks—

MUGGEROON: *(Interrupting)* Cooks and Popes are made.

HENRY: We have had quite an extraordinary number of Popes in the family . . . but no cooks.

MUGGEROON: Just servers of bread and wine.

EPERNOUN: Who is responsible for this massacre?

MUGGEROON: *(Spits)* Guise, parting body, blood, and spirit, has spent the night sending good Christians to heaven. How I hate him!

HENRY: The feeling is mutual. He hates you too.

MUGGEROON: Why does he bear me such deadly hate?

HENRY: Because his wife bears you such kindly love.

MUGGEROON: How did you know?

HENRY: Ruggieri is my astrologer, too.

MUGGEROON: He betrayed my secret?

HENRY: He knows I love you and feared for your life. The Guise is a murderous, jealous man. He'd stab you in the back as soon as look at you.

MUGGEROON: *(Contemptuously)* Let him try. He'll soon find out that fancy dress and sudden death is the code of the minions!

EPERNOUN AND JOYEUSE: All right!

MUGGEROON: I'd give the world for a chance to meet him on an equal footing man-to-man and cut him to ribbons like this glove. *(Takes a dagger and throwing up his glove, cuts it to shreds)*

HENRY: Keep the world. The chance may come cheaper.

(A tumult of voices is heard below the king's window.)

JOYEUSE: Just listen to that crowd.

EPERNOUN: Go get an ovation, Majesty. It will do you good.

HENRY: *(Wearily)* I don't feel up to it.

JOYEUSE: It might be good to let the people see you.

(Voices below again.)

HENRY: I'm tired of being looked at. Besides, the people hate me.

JOYEUSE: Oh, Majesty, go to the window as you are. The people will think you're the queen.

EPERNOUN: And at the same time you'll be testing your costume for the masquerade.

HENRY: I can't resist. *(He springs to the window, bows, and blows kisses to the rabble)*

(The crowd boos and jeers. Scallions and a bunch of carrots fly through the window followed by a cabbage. HENRY lets out a little shriek and dodges the vegetables. The GUISE enters just in time to see the skirmish. He has seen HENRY only from the back. Convinced that HENRY is the Queen, GUISE runs to help. He seizes HENRY passionately and murmurs fervently.)

GUISE: Dearest Majesty, are you hurt?

MUGGEROON: *(Pugnaciously)* Unhand the King, pervert!

GUISE: King? I thought you were the Queen!

HENRY: And I thought you weren't. *(Kisses the* GUISE *and spits)*

GUISE: *(Shocked and embarrassed pulls himself free of* HENRY's *mock embrace. He wheels on* MUGGEROON*)* How dare you call me pervert! Henry, Henry, what mad pranks are these? *(Comes to himself and genuflects)* Forgive me, Majesty, I took you for your mother.

HENRY: And what do you take her for? Rise from your bony knees, Guise, and tell me who is responsible for this massacre.

GUISE: I counseled her. Your mother gave the word. And by tomorrow no Huguenot will draw his breath in France.

MUGGEROON: The coward creeps up from behind; kills them in their beds. Where reason is of no avail he cuts their throats instead.

GUISE: Henry, dismiss your minions. They bring you nothing but disgrace.

HENRY: What, you don't love my minions?

GUISE: Love them, no!

HENRY: Ah, but your wife does, so I hear. *(Makes horns at the* GUISE*)*

MUGGEROON: Henry!

HENRY: I can't say I blame her. Look at him. Big mop of hair, broad chest, taut little belly, and if his buttocks are a little big, so what? You can't drive a spike with a tackhammer.

(The minions laugh.)

GUISE: I swear by all the saints in heaven you'll pay for that slut's favors with your blood. Whether it's true or not.

MUGGEROON: How dare you call that angel a slut! You doubt her virtue? Doubt yourself. If you were any good there'd be no man on earth that could take her away from you!

HENRY: *(With malicious glee)* This is getting good!

MUGGEROON: *(Throws down his glove)* There's my glove.

GUISE: I find it like your reputation. Somewhat tattered. I don't have to honor this. A challenge from a commoner.

HENRY: A mere technicality. Muggeroon, my sweetheart, I hereby make you Duke. You meet tomorrow fair and square.

GUISE: Tomorrow at dawn old debts will be paid.

HENRY: But tonight we'll dance at the masquerade!

(Exit HENRY, EPERNOUN, JOYEUSE, MUGGEROON. *Quick curtain.)*

ACT II

Scene 1

(Enter two with the body of the ADMIRAL.*)*

1: What should we do with the body of the Admiral?

2: Let's burn him for a heretic.

1: Oh no, his body will infect the fire, the fire the air, and the smoke will spread heresy and poison us.

2: What'll we do then?

1: Let's throw him in the river.

2: Oh, no, it'll pollute the water, and the water the fish, and the fish will corrupt us when we eat them on Friday.

1: Then throw him in a ditch.

2: The safest thing between you and me is hang him here upon this tree.

1: Agreed.

(They hang him from a tree and exit. Enter CATHERINE *and* GUISE *strolling arm-in-arm under the tree.)*

GUISE: Well, Madame, how do you like our lusty Admiral?

CATHERINE: He's very well-hung, I see.

GUISE: That's what he gets for barking up the wrong tree.

CATHERINE: But come, let's walk. The air's not very sweet here and there's another fruit I'd like to see in a tree where it belongs.

*(*ATTENDANTS *take down the body of the* ADMIRAL *and exit.)*

GUISE: I assume you refer to one of the King's minions.

CATHERINE: The same. A certain Protestant, Muggeroon.

GUISE: Don't trouble yourself over him, Your Magnificence. We duel at dawn and I have little doubt I'll do him in.

CATHERINE: No, sweet Guise. You mustn't risk your life to rid me of him. The minions kill the way lightning strikes a tree—without thought and without remorse. The way a pet cat will scratch its master's hand when he plays a little too rough. They attack by instinct with that flash of brilliance one sometimes encounters in a gifted amateur. They mock at life and die with a certain relish.

GUISE: Ephemeral creatures.

CATHERINE: But we normals are built for survival. We're not as fantastic, not as bizarre, but we breed and that's our strength.

GUISE: Thinking of posterity, Catherine?

CATHERINE: Is it a sign of getting old and realizing that one has postponed a certain kind of happiness perhaps a little too long? Now we bear our disappointments with a thought of the next life. Oh, Guise, Guise, look at me. I'm not beautiful.

GUISE: But you are. You're very pretty.

CATHERINE: *(Slaps his face)* How could you? Prettiness is only a debased and inferior form of the beautiful.

GUISE: Forgive me. I forgot that you were raised in Florence, the queen of cities.

CATHERINE: Yes and we aging queens have got to stick together. There are Florentine ways of avoiding duels, caro.

GUISE: You know them?

CATHERINE: Pink candles in the opponent's room on the eve of the duel. That's one way.

GUISE: *(Laughs incredulously) Pink* candles?

CATHERINE: Poisoned pink candles.

GUISE: Ah, *pink* candles. *(Chuckles)* But doesn't that smack of cowardice?

CATHERINE: Don't let your bad conscience betray your bold deeds and leave them undefended at the front. Cut your morality to fit your needs.

GUISE: Don't you believe in sin, rara?

CATHERINE: Sin? God no! But then you're joking, aren't you? I took you for a man of advanced morals. Oh, don't disappoint me. Give a yes to life! Say you'll do anything to survive.

GUISE: I'm not a man of appetites.

CATHERINE: A small appetite? Then you'll never enjoy me.

GUISE: Whet it!

CATHERINE: What?

GUISE: My appetite.

CATHERINE: Oh, I thought you meant . . .

GUISE: Catherine, Catherine, I am a married Catholic man. You are a widowed queen. We can't even consider having . . . having . . . a relationship.

CATHERINE: Tomorrow, then, you plan to meet the minion? Risk your life for the honor of a commoner? Guise, please . . .

GUISE: The king has made him a Duke. We meet as equals. There's the thing that galls me.

CATHERINE: Why not just crush him like a bug?

GUISE: How?

CATHERINE: Set a trap!

GUISE: A trap?

CATHERINE: In a fair duel there's little chance you'd win. Unless we set a trap to catch the minion in! But come my lord and let's devise his death.

(Exit GUISE and CATHERINE.)

Scene 2

DUCHESS: Isn't it always the way? I who never write letters go to write one and find my inkwell's all dried up! Arthur, would you go quickly and get me another?

ARTHUR: Where is it, Tamyra?

DUCHESS: On the Duke's desk. Go to his study and get it.

ARTHUR: Should I ask him for it?

DUCHESS: No! Peek in first and see if he is there. If he's not, get it. If he is, tell him . . . tell him . . . *(Thinks a moment)* Tell him I'm thinking of him.

ARTHUR: Yes Cousin.

DUCHESS: That's only if he sees you. If he doesn't see you, slip away and come back without the ink.

ARTHUR: Is something wrong, Tamyra?

DUCHESS: Nothing's wrong, but nothing's really right either. You'll understand when you grow up. Hurry now!

ARTHUR: I don't know to what you allude. But I presume it to be of a libidinous nature. Of course I have no firsthand knowledge of eroticism. I expect that I will, though, when I reach puberty. *(Exit)*

DUCHESS: Precocious child. Do I dare write to my beloved Muggeroon? Why can't I have him? Because I am the wife of Guise? I can't even find a way to speak to him. And so I'll write, and with a quill plucked from fair Cupid's wing, print the words within my lover's heart.

(Enter ARTHUR.)

ARTHUR: Here's the ink. The duke wasn't there.

DUCHESS: Arthur, promise me that you won't leave me no matter what, unless I tell you to.

ARTHUR: I promise.

(The DUCHESS seats herself and begins to write feverishly.)

ARTHUR: Cousin, are you weeping?

DUCHESS: No, but my eyes itch. *(Writes feverishly again. Then startled)* What was that? Who was it that knocked?

ARTHUR: It's the wind.

(Enter the GUISE.)

GUISE: *(Stealing up silently behind the DUCHESS)* Can that be you, my love, writing a letter?

DUCHESS: People write letters all the time.

GUISE: People yes, but not you.

DUCHESS: *(Prettily)* Am I not a person, my lord?

GUISE: To whom are you writing?

DUCHESS: To a person who I'm afraid will laugh when she sees my poor penmanship!

GUISE: Let me see.

DUCHESS: Oh no, my Lord, only a woman may share the secrets of a woman's heart.

GUISE: I know I am no woman but I may have a strong enough stomach for it. *(Snatches the letter and reads)* So these are the secrets of a woman's heart! *(Reads from the letter)* "I hunger for your body." Were these lines addressed to a woman?

DUCHESS: Oh forgive me my husband!

GUISE: There's more and worse.

DUCHESS: Please, husband, don't read it in front of the child!

GUISE: *(Hesitates)* Go boy, and wait outside. *(ARTHUR doesn't move)* Did you hear me, boy? I said wait outside. *(ARTHUR doesn't move. GUISE removes his belt)* Ignore me? Do you want a taste of this strap, boy?

(ARTHUR looks at the DUCHESS.)

DUCHESS: Arthur, wait outside.

(ARTHUR runs out.)

GUISE: Your cousin needs a lesson in obedience.

DUCHESS: He's faithful to me.

GUISE: As you are to me?

DUCHESS: What do you want of me?

GUISE: I want a companion who will be with me, follow me, look up to me, long for me when I'm away, and greet me cheerfully when I come home.

DUCHESS: Why don't you get a dog?

GUISE: How dare you speak to me like that? I who have loved you above all else. You who were the apple of my eye. Tell me, strumpet, to whom were you writing this hot letter!

DUCHESS: Lower your voice. Do you want the whole world to know?

GUISE: How do I know the whole world doesn't already know? To whom were you writing this letter?

DUCHESS: To a woman . . .

GUISE: Liar! Would you have me lap your adulterous vomit? For whom did you intend this letter? Answer me! *(Stabs her, but not mortally)*

DUCHESS: My God!

GUISE: If you won't tell me you'll drink this. *(Produces a vial of poison)*

DUCHESS: What's that? Henbane?

GUISE: The dreaded hebona in a vial. Here, pour it in your own ear. It's quicker that way. Make it easy on yourself.

DUCHESS: Yes, give it to me. And let me exit gracefully!

GUISE: *(Withholds the poison)* Not so fast. If you won't tell me to whom you were sending this letter, then let me tell you to whom you are going to send it. Muggeroon, minion to the king.

DUCHESS: Muggeroon?

GUISE: Yes, write what I tell you. *(Gives her a pen quill and begins to dictate)* Meet me sweet in my chamber tonight—wear the habit of a monk. Slip away from the masquerade. And let us both unmask our tenderest senses here among my pillows.

DUCHESS: My Lord, these words written to any other but yourself be treason.

GUISE: Yes. Treason. Now write. Wear the scent of heliotrope and abstain till then. Whatever it is you want I shall tender unto you.

DUCHESS: I won't do it! I won't bait your trap!

GUISE: You will! *(Stabs her again)*

DUCHESS: Oh why don't you kill me and get it over with!

GUISE: No such luck! You're not getting off that easily. The convent walls for you. I'll have you decalced!

(GUISE strips off his shirt and jacket and bare-chested drags the DUCHESS across the stage by the hair. He unlocks a cabinet out of which a torture rack drops down in the manner of foldaway ironing boards. He ties her to the rack and brandishes a horsewhip.)

DUCHESS: *(Writhing on the rack)* Not the face! Please, not the face. Do what you will but please don't leave any marks on my face!

GUISE: *(Ranting)* Write! Write! Torment in ashes! Write what I told you to!

DUCHESS: O kill me, kill me dear husband! Be not crueler than death!

GUISE: Enough talk! Now will I torture use against your whorish fortitude! Now measure your wrongs against this maddening pain, and see which weighs the heaviest! *(Tortures her)*

DUCHESS: Aie! Husband, have you turned to stone?

GUISE: Yes, when I beheld your Gorgon's face! *(Tortures her again)*

DUCHESS: Let my hot blood dissolve you into a man again! O let me down my Lord and I will write!

GUISE: If it weren't for my child in your womb, in whom I have some hope, I'd use torture still! *(Takes her down from the rack)* Now write. *(Hands her the quill)*

DUCHESS: I will. I will. I'll write it with my blood that he may see, these words come from my wounds and not from me! *(She writes)*

GUISE: Now call in the boy and have him deliver it to Muggeroon. I warn you. Do not tell him of its darker purpose. No hints, no whispers, no winks or secret looks. If a suspicion so much as crosses the boy's mind he dies and you will be his murderess.

DUCHESS: You wouldn't hurt Arthur.

GUISE: I didn't say I'd hurt him. I said I'll kill him.

DUCHESS: No!

GUISE: Don't worry my dear. His life is in your hands. I'll hide behind this curtain where I'll hear every word. *(Wraps himself in the arras)*

DUCHESS: I'd sooner die! *(Goes to drink poison, then changes her mind)* No! I must live and try to save him. *(Hides poison in her bosom. Struggles to the door)* Arthur, Arthur. Are you there child?

ARTHUR: What do you want Tamyra?

DUCHESS: Take this letter to Muggeroon.

ARTHUR: Why are you trembling, Tamyra?

DUCHESS: *(Concealing her wounds from his eyes)* It's cold. Don't you feel it?

ARTHUR: No.

DUCHESS: It's just me.

ARTHUR: Cousin you look pale! If something is wrong you know you can tell me.

DUCHESS: Nothing is wrong. Now leave me.

ARTHUR: Leave you like this? Shall I call your women? You are fainting.

DUCHESS: Not for your life! This key, this letter, take them to Count St. Muggeroon.

ARTHUR: So he's the cause of this emotion!

DUCHESS: *(Pushes him out the door)* Go!

ARTHUR: As winds rage before a storm! *(Exit)* I'll bring him your love.

DUCHESS: My love. No! His death! Wait! Come back! Arthur, come back!

(GUISE comes out from behind the arras and slaps his hand over her mouth.)

GUISE: Silence, Madame.

DUCHESS: *(Falls on her knees before him)* Oh heaven! Oh husband! I beg you for remission of my sins but not my pains!

GUISE:
    Oh that I may see the devil and survive
    To be a devil and learn to wive.

Scene 3

(MUGGEROON alone. Later ARTHUR. A garden somewhere above the city. It is twilight of a summer evening. Distant thunder can be heard. MUGGEROON is discovered looking out over the city. [His] reverie is broken by the discovery of ARTHUR who has entered from behind.)

MUGGEROON: What's this? An eavesdropper? Spying on my reverie? *(Grabs the page ARTHUR by the ear)* What do you want? Speak!

ARTHUR: Count St. Muggeroon?

MUGGEROON: Yes? What is it?

ARTHUR: I've brought you these . . . this . . . this letter and this key.

MUGGEROON: From whom?

ARTHUR: Don't you recognize the writing? *(MUGGEROON shakes his head)* Nor the coat of arms upon the seal?

MUGGEROON: Cleves and Guise! Good God, am I dreaming? Is this a trick?

ARTHUR: I wouldn't trick you even if I had the nerve.

MUGGEROON: She gave this to you?

ARTHUR: Yes.

MUGGEROON: Where?

ARTHUR: In her chamber.

MUGGEROON: Was she all alone?

ARTHUR: Yes.

MUGGEROON: What did she say?

ARTHUR: Almost nothing.

MUGGEROON: How did she seem to you? She wasn't just playing a joke at my expense. Was she laughing?

ARTHUR: Laughing? No she wasn't laughing. She trembled and looked pale. I thought she was going to faint.

MUGGEROON: Can this be true? Oh heaven! Oh earth! This woman loves me!

ARTHUR: Count . . .

MUGGEROON: *(Dances around wildly)* She loves me! She loves me! *(Seizes AR-THUR and gives him a big hard kiss)*

ARTHUR: *(Struggles to get loose)* Stop it! Shhhhhh! Quiet! Keep her secret if you love her.

MUGGEROON: *(Coming to his senses)* You're right, boy. Forget everything you've seen here tonight. Forget my face. Forget my body. Forget everything.

ARTHUR: Don't worry. I love secrets. And it's an honor to keep a secret for the Duke Muggeroon.

MUGGEROON: Ah, but it's a dangerous secret you're keeping, boy. It's like the vial of poisoned vapor Ruggieri told me of. If it so much as leaks into the air it will bring death to everyone who breathes it. It is a heavy load for one so young to bear. Don't let it make you old before your time. Avoid me. Say nothing. Write nothing. I'll read your looks. And remember, so long as you live you have a friend in Duke Muggeroon. Away!

ARTHUR: This is the greatest day of my life! Farewell Duke Muggeroon. *(Exit)*

MUGGEROON: I could almost love that little boy because he has her eyes. God grant we meet again.

(Enter JOYEUSE.)

JOYEUSE: Muggeroon, are you coming to the masquerade tonight? What are you going to wear?

MUGGEROON: Do me a favor, will you Joyeuse?

JOYEUSE: Anything.

MUGGEROON: Get me the habit of a monk.

(Tableau.)

Scene 4

HENRY: Where is Muggeroon? I hope he won't be late for the masquerade.

EPERNOUN: I don't know where he is, Majesty.

JOYEUSE: He didn't dine with us as he said he would.

HENRY: Oh dear.

EPERNOUN: But this missive just arrived. Would Your Majesty care to peruse it?

HENRY: *(Breaks the seal and reads)* What! How dare!

EPERNOUN: What is it, Sire?

HENRY: It is from our mother. She dares to suggest that *I* go to meet with Guise at the Hotel de Soissons! This is an outrage! If Guise wants to speak to me, let him come here! *(Screaming with rage)* How dare they send for me! We will not be sent for, do you hear!

JOYEUSE: Calm yourself, Majesty. I will deliver your message myself. *(To* EPERNOUN*)* Surely His Majesty is abused thus. I think this calls for some reprisal. *(Exit)*

EPERNOUN: I agree. I think we must devise something.

HENRY: *(Burning)* How could our mother suggest such an insulting proposition?

EPERNOUN: Majesty, the Guise deserves to be taken down a peg.

HENRY: Yes? What do you propose?

EPERNOUN: He massacred the Protestants on St. Bartholomew's Day. Why don't we give the Catholics a taste of their own medicine?

HENRY: *(Somewhat pacified)* Kill the Catholics?

EPERNOUN: Oh why not?

HENRY: That's an idea.

EPERNOUN: And start with Guise.

HENRY: Yes. I have it! We'll trap him here, like a rat! But there's no time to lose. Quick, beloved Epernoun, fetch us those ruffians you sometimes do disport with. Tell them their king has some noble action for them.

EPERNOUN: Sire, I will. *(Exit)*

HENRY: Oh this will be rich. *(Enter* EPERNOUN *with the three* MURDERERS*)* Are you the loyal men who mean to save your king?

FIRST MURDERER: Aye, Yer Majesty.

SECOND MURDERER: That we are.

HENRY: And you, my good man? Have you committed murder before?

THIRD MURDERER: Aye, aye, Yer Majesty. I've broken lots of skulls and spilt some guts, too!

HENRY: Then you're experienced?

THIRD MURDERER: Aye, that I am. I learned my craft on St. Bartholomew's Day. And practiced on them Huguenots.

HENRY: *(Staggers back from him and turns his face away)* Ah! That stings.

THIRD MURDERER: But don't you worry, Sire. I'll kill a Catholic too. You see I ain't prejudiced.

HENRY: Go liberals, each behind another door. And wait for my signal.

FIRST MURDERER: What will the signal be, Yer Majesty?

HENRY: Epernoun will ask me what we are having for dinner and I'll say . . . fondue bourguignon. Then you skewer him like a piece of raw meat.

SECOND MURDERER: And dip him in boiling oil?

THIRD MURDERER: Mmmmm mmmmm! I loves fondue bourguignon. When do we eat?

HENRY: After the job is done.

THIRD MURDERER: Aw rats! I was hoping it was before. I missed me breakfast.

HENRY: You've got a strong stomach.

EPERNOUN: And a weak mind.

JOYEUSE: *(At the window)* My liege, the duke approaches on foot and bear-headed beside your mother's chair.

HENRY: Now hide. And remember the signal, "fondue bourguignon."

(Enter CATHERINE *with* ATTENDANTS *carrying her chair.* GUISE *beside her on foot as described by* JOYEUSE.*)*

CATHERINE: My son, it was inconsiderate of you to make me come here. You know I've been ill and in such pain that I have not been able to leave my Hotel for weeks.

HENRY: It wasn't necessary for you to come, Mother. Guise could have come alone. But I see you felt it was a matter of great importance.

CATHERINE: I had a premonition.

HENRY: *(To the* DUKE OF GUISE*)* Why have you come here?

GUISE: I have heard a rumor that on the advice of Epernoun you were planning a Bartholomew in reverse. And if it's true that you plan to kill every Catholic in Paris, I want to be here to die with the rest.

HENRY: I have never even considered such a thing! It is you who wants the crown of France on your own head and will stop at nothing to get it! *(Working himself up into a rage)* You plot against me. You have all but seduced my mother.

CATHERINE: Henry, these are mad words.

HENRY: And now you think you'll kill my favorite minion! *(Screaming)* Is that what you want to do? Take away the only ones who love me? Is it? Is it?

CATHERINE: *(Taking* HENRY *aside to the window)* Henry, you're very upset. I'm afraid you're losing your mind.

HENRY: *(Shrieking and laughing maniacally)* I'm losing *my* mind? Ha-ha! On the contrary, Mother dear, it is your friend Guise that is mad. Ha-ha! Mad mad mad to come here to the Louvre without a bodyguard!

CATHERINE: *(Whispering hoarsely and urgently to* HENRY*)* If you are not completely insane, come here and look out the window. *(Boos, jeers and a few vegetables come through the window. They duck as in Act I. She points to the chanting and jeering mob below)* Listen to them! All of Paris is his bodyguard! Unless Guise returns to them unharmed our lives won't be worth a sou!

RUGGIERI: Your mother is right.

HENRY: So you can see the future can you? You old witch!

EPERNOUN: Well, Your Majesty, what will we have for dinner?

HENRY: Quiche Lorraine. The Guise will live.

*(*EPERNOUN *sinks into a chair in disappointment.)*

GUISE: Your Majesty. I take my leave. Let us meet again tomorrow.

HENRY: In the garden of Tuileries we will meet in the afternoon to discuss affairs of state.

GUISE: Until tomorrow, adieu. *(Exit)*

HENRY: If you live. *(There is a cheer from the crowd outside. Peeking out of the window from behind the curtain)* Mother, how can I be King of France when he is King of Paris?

CATHERINE: He wishes only to serve you and France. But just in case we'll order two hundred thousand troops to come here and protect us from the Parisian scum. And you shall be Commander in Chief. *(Passes window inadvertently triggering a volley of boos and jeers from the louts below. Exits)*

HENRY: We'll see. We'll see. Ruggieri, do you have the amulet?

RUGGIERI: Here it is, my Liege.

HENRY: And where is Schomberg's sword?

JOYEUSE: Here, Sire.

HENRY: Oh why isn't Muggeroon here to put it on?

EPERNOUN: Here he comes, my Liege.

(Enter MUGGEROON.)

HENRY: *(Embracing MUGGEROON and kissing him on each cheek)* At last, St. Muggeroon! Since we have parted I have given myself a promotion, too.

MUGGEROON: What's that?

HENRY: I've sent for six hundred thousand troops to protect me from these Parisians. And named myself Commander in Chief. What do you think of that?

MUGGEROON: The French will not be ruled like an Italian city-state, Sire. You can't call foreigners to rule them. But you do what your mother tells you. Who am I to question her? I would deal with it differently.

HENRY: How?

MUGGEROON: If Guise survives our duel tomorrow, lock him up in the deepest darkest dungeon you can find.

HENRY: The only dungeon deep and dark enough for him is a lead coffin and a marble sepulchre. And that's for you to lock him in. Are you ready for the fight? Have you confessed?

MUGGEROON: Not yet, my Lord. Later for that.

HENRY: The time grows short. Come, sleep with me tonight. And in my private chapel my chaplain will confess you.

MUGGEROON: I can't, my Lord. I have pressing business elsewhere.

RUGGIERI: Do as the king advises. For the sake of those you love, stay in the palace tonight.

MUGGEROON: Vain warnings, warlock. My plans cannot be changed. Adieu, Henry, my king.

HENRY: Wait Muggeroon. Take Schomberg's sword. It didn't help Schomberg. God grant it bring you better luck than him. Ruggieri, give him the talisman. What does it do?

RUGGIERI: The man who wears it cannot be killed by fire or steel.

HENRY: *(Puts the amulet around MUGGEROON's neck)* You must give it back after the combat. Farewell, dear boy. *(The clock strikes twelve)* Midnight! Hear it? Time for my prayers. Dear, dearer, dearest boy, I'll pray for you.

(Exit HENRY leaning on JOYEUSE and EPERNOUN.)

MUGGEROON: What, still here Ruggieri? Why are you looking at me like that? What is it you see, man of doom?

RUGGIERI: I see the hot flush of adolescent passion on your young brow.

MUGGEROON: Tonight's my night. I can feel it pounding in my veins.

RUGGIERI: But I see danger too. Mists of death shroud the sunlight of your youth and joy.

MUGGEROON: Danger and death tomorrow when I meet the Guise in single combat.

RUGGIERI: At what time is the duel?

MUGGEROON: Nine.

RUGGIERI: The danger I foresee is more imminent. You will not fall by the Guise's sword if you live until tomorrow morning.

MUGGEROON: If I live?

RUGGIERI: The lives of men are written in the stars.

MUGGEROON: Predestined, like Calvin says.

RUGGIERI: No, nothing is predestined. The stars impel but they do not compel. There is always a point at which one can make a choice, turn back, and change one's fate.

MUGGEROON: I must live until tomorrow! I must!

RUGGIERI: *(Leads* MUGGEROON *to the open window)* Do you see beyond the tower where yonder star shines in her milky way? *(Points to the star)*

MUGGEROON: I see it.

RUGGIERI: That's your star. And there a tiny black interstellar cloud?

MUGGEROON: Where?

RUGGIERI: There! *(Points again)*

MUGGEROON: Ah! *(Nods)*

RUGGIERI: That red light is the planet Mars. My son, within an hour your star will transit lustful Scorpio and in the murky womb of that dank orb, drown its fiery beams. *(Exits)*

MUGGEROON: *(Stares at the heavens for a moment transfixed. Then he realizes that he is alone and calls after* RUGGIERI*)* Wait, Ruggieri, wait! Tell me more! *(Looks out of the window)* He didn't hear me. Ah, there he goes walking with the queen mother. She is smiling. She must be nursing some dark design on her shrunken dugs. *(Looks up at the heavens)* My star! It's shining bright.

(Enter JOYEUSE.*)*

JOYEUSE: Stargazing? Ruggieri will be proud of his pupil. Lost in thought? What do you see out there in the stars?

MUGGEROON: Joyeuse, do you believe in life after death?

JOYEUSE: You know I don't.

MUGGEROON: Then you think our lives are lights like stars, that once extinguished never burn again.

JOYEUSE: That's right.

MUGGEROON: And leave no trace?

JOYEUSE: No trace but memory. There one may live on . . . a little while.

MUGGEROON: Have you got the monk's mantle?

JOYEUSE: Here it is: the robe, the sandals and the cross.

MUGGEROON: And Schomberg's sword?

(Thunder.)

JOYEUSE: Here it is. Muggeroon, I don't think it's wise to go out, there seems to be a storm coming. Thick black clouds have already covered those stars you've been watching.

MUGGEROON: You're right. The ominous clouds approach. But my star is shining still.

JOYEUSE: I know your mother wouldn't sleep tonight if she knew where you were.

MUGGEROON: Strange you mention her. I wish I could have seen her one more time. *(Cutting off a lock of his hair with his poniard)* If I don't return tomorrow morning take this lock to her. Tell her I wasn't such a bad boy after all. Knowing the short memory of the court, I'll need her prayers.

(Thunder again.)

JOYEUSE: Muggeroon, in friendship I beg of you. Don't go out at this hour. The streets are dangerous and this storm is getting worse.

MUGGEROON: Farewell Joyeuse. Those clouds are menacing my star. And I must go while it still shines. *(Exit)*

Scene 5: *The chamber of the* DUCHESS OF GUISE.

(The DUCHESS *is alone, dressed for the masquerade. The clock strikes.)*

DUCHESS: The clock strikes. I pray God he didn't get my letter. Or perhaps he thought it brazen and decided not to come. Yes, that's it. Why should he be such a fool as to risk his life for a silly letter? Or perhaps, pray God he doesn't love me and so saves his life!

(Footsteps are heard outside.)

DUCHESS: Footsteps on the stair! They come. They hesitate. They continue to approach. Oh let it not be him!

(Knock at the door.)

DUCHESS: *(In a hoarse whisper)* Who is it?

VOICE WITHOUT: I've come to hear your confession.

DUCHESS: *(Peeking through a spy hole)* It is a monk. Some goodly friar come to confess me? *(She opens the door)* Come in Father, I need your help.

MUGGEROON: *(Throwing off the monk's habit and sweeping her up in his arms)* Confess you love me.

DUCHESS: *(Horrified)* Oh my God, Muggeroon!

MUGGEROON: *(Passionately)* Confess! Confess! *(Covers her with kisses)*

DUCHESS: We're lost!

MUGGEROON: Why do you say we're lost when we've found each other at last? Kiss me!

DUCHESS: Muggeroon, listen . . .

MUGGEROON: Don't speak! Don't spoil this moment.

DUCHESS: Oh, you fool. Don't you see that this moment may be your last? You've been had! Betrayed! Caught in a snare. Trapped like a rat!

MUGGEROON: What?

DUCHESS: My husband made me send that letter. At any moment they will burst into this room and kill you!

MUGGEROON: *(Suddenly calm)* So you don't love me. Suddenly death doesn't sound so bad to me. Horrible woman, was I meant to die so young without putting up a fight?

DUCHESS: Go, fly, while there's still time!

MUGGEROON: Oh what an idiot I was to be taken in by such a trick. What a fool I was to think you loved me!

DUCHESS: *(Sinking to her knees before him)* Forgive me that I couldn't bear the pain. Rather I had died upon the rack than lured you to your doom.

(Distant thunder.)

MUGGEROON: The rack?

DUCHESS: He tortured me.

(Thunder again.)

MUGGEROON: Is this the truth?

DUCHESS: Look, here is where he stabbed me. And here are the marks left by the straps. *(Shows him her wounds)* Believe me, Muggeroon, if ever a woman loved a man: I love you.

MUGGEROON: Then life is sweet again. Rise, woman, and grant your man one dying wish.

DUCHESS: Name it.

MUGGEROON: Let me make love to you.

DUCHESS: We can't—not here! There is no time.

MUGGEROON: Love me, woman, and make this moment a brief eternity.

(They make love. Thunder and lightning. A wild wind blows the curtains in at the window. There is violent pounding at the door.)

DUCHESS: My God, they're here already.

MUGGEROON: Hold me tight and never let me go.

DUCHESS: You must get up.

MUGGEROON: One more kiss and then I'll kill the Guise!

DUCHESS: He won't come. He's hired murderous scum to do his dirty work.

MUGGEROON: Murderers? The coward! *(Tries the door. Finds it locked)*

DUCHESS: It's locked. He has the only key.

MUGGEROON: I'll break off the point of my dagger in the lock. That should hold them.

GUISE'S VOICE WITHOUT: The door won't open. Break it down.

(Men's voices outside the door.)

DUCHESS: *(Clutching her head)* I'm going mad!

MUGGEROON: The window . . .

DUCHESS: It's too high. The fall would kill you.

MUGGEROON: Death is the coward's way out. I'll stay and face them.

DUCHESS: *(Falling to her knees in prayer)* If there is a merciful God in heaven, hear us, send a miracle.

MUGGEROON: Tell me again that you love me.

DUCHESS: I love you, Muggeroon. I have always loved you.

MUGGEROON: There's the miracle. *(Kisses her)*

(They begin to beat the door in with a battering ram. Show both sides of the door.)

DUCHESS: *(In an ecstatic transport)* Some nights you would come to me in dreams and make love to me in my sleep.

MUGGEROON: And you came to me! Ruggieri warned me of the succuba.

DUCHESS: This is the end.

MUGGEROON: Despair. All hope is lost. *(Battering at the door. Thunder very loud)* This window were my only hope. If only there was a rope, a sash, or some cords.

DUCHESS: I hear someone below. *(Yells out the window)* Help us someone! Whoever you are! Please, dear God, someone help us!

MUGGEROON: *(Puts his hand over her mouth and drags her away from the window)* Quiet, you'll alert the murderers.

(A coil of rope is thrown in the window with a note attached to it.)

MUGGEROON: What's this?

DUCHESS: A note! *(Reads)* "I overheard a conversation and learned everything. This rope is all the help I can offer you. Use it quickly." Arthur. Dear Arthur! I always said he was a precocious child!

(They batter the door.)

MUGGEROON: *(Attaching the rope and throwing the other end out of the window)* Is there time?

DUCHESS: *(Putting her arms through the rings of the bolt)* If my frail body can gain you a moment or two of life, I'll gladly sacrifice it!

MUGGEROON: I can't let you. *(Takes her to the window)* Look out there! And when you see my star, think of me. *(Descends by the rope with sword between his teeth)*

DUCHESS: *(Looking vainly at the sky)* Muggeroon, I don't see anything! The sky is black. There aren't any stars! *(GUISE and his men break in at the door. There are sounds of swords clashing and voices below the window. Then groans)* Muggeroon? Arthur? *(Screams)*

GUISE: What's this? The window's open. Death by defenestration, that's novel. So he didn't want to stain his lover's room with blood! Damned considerate, I'd say! My lady duchess, thanks for helping me murder your lover.

DUCHESS: *(Beating on his chest with her fists)* Has he been murdered? Tell me! Tell me!

GUISE: Come over to the window and see for yourself. *(Calling to his men below)* Let's have some torchlight there!

DUCHESS: Is he . . . is he dead?

VOICE OF ONE BELOW: There's a dead child here. Killed by accident.

DUCHESS: Arthur! Oh no.

GUISE: Curses! Did the minion escape?

VOICE BELOW: We've stabbed him in twenty places but he will not die. He wears a talisman against fire and steel.

GUISE: Then strangle him with this hankie. *(Takes out the DUCHESS's hankie)* Monogrammed with Guise and Cleves. *(Tosses down the hankie)* He'll die wearing your colors, Madame. *(Those below strangle MUGGEROON)* Now strip off that talisman and cut out his heart!

DUCHESS: You're an animal!

GUISE: And throw it up here! *(They throw up the heart on the tip of a sword)* Here, woman, your paramour sends his bloody valentine. *(Throws the sword and heart down across her bed)*

DUCHESS: *(Seizes the heart and drops it into a goblet. Then she pours in the poison from the vial she hid between her breasts)* Yes he was my lover. A mad young love who made me feel crazy! So with your heart's blood, I die. *(Drinks and dies)*

Scene 6: *Finale at the masquerade.*

(They watch the auto-da-fé. CATHERINE *tries to form an alliance with the* DUKE OF GUISE *but he rejects her.* HENRY *on discovery of* MUGGEROON*'s death strips off his costume and leads a flagellant procession of minions.)*

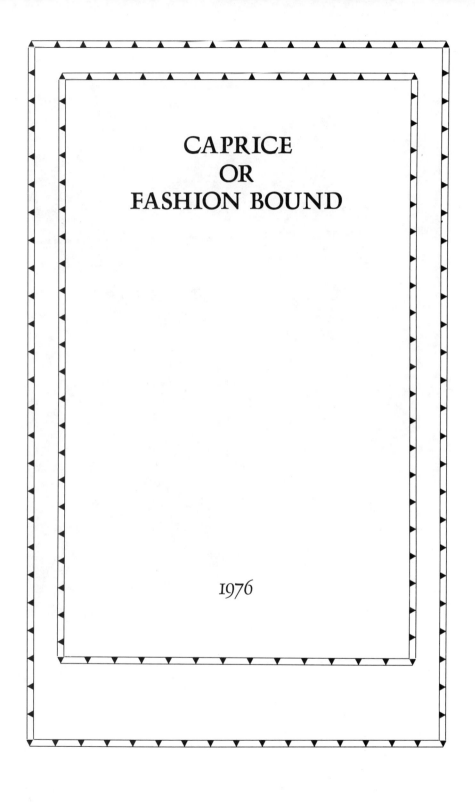

CAPRICE
OR
FASHION BOUND

1976

Bill Vehr & Charles Ludlam in *Caprice* (Les Carr)

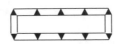

Cast of Characters

CLAUDE CAPRICE, *fashion designer and tastemaker*
ADRIAN, *his inspiration*
TATA, *a gentleman's gentleman*
HARRY FEINSCHMECKER, *Caprice's landlord*
BARONESS ZUNI FEINSCHMECKER, *a slave of fashion*
TWYFFORD ADAMANT, *couturier, rival to Caprice*
COPELIAS, *a mechanical doll*
BABUSHKA, *the world's first live fashion model*
LA FLEUR, *parfumeur*
BERTHA, *Adamant's maid*
ALTHEA GORDON, *interviewer*
MODELS
PRESS PHOTOGRAPHERS
SLAVES OF FASHION
CHILDREN OF THE ATELIER ENFANTINE
HERMIT *(later Caprice)*
WAYFARER *(later Adamant)*
SCRUBWOMAN *(later Babushka)*

PROLOGUE

The hovel of a monk.
(Outside, a tree. On a small table, just inside the window of the hut, sits a bonsai trained in the exact likeness of the tree outside. A sleeping pallet, a bowl, and chopsticks. Knocking at the door.)

HERMIT: *(Waking)* Huh? Who's that at the door? It's cold tonight. I can see my breath.

(Knocking again.)

HERMIT: *(Shivering)* Coming! *(Muttering)* Brrr! Cold.

(Knocking still.)

HERMIT: I said I'm coming! *(He opens the door)*
WAYFARER: It's bitter cold and I have journeyed a great distance. I saw your light.
HERMIT: Come in. Come in.

(Wind howls. Snow blows in through the door.)

WAYFARER: Thank you, Brother. I think I have frostbite.
HERMIT: You'll sleep with me. There's no fuel.
WAYFARER: How can I thank you?
HERMIT: It is nothing.
WAYFARER: *(Looking around him)* This is strange.
HERMIT: Strange?
WAYFARER: There's nothing here.
HERMIT: Nothing.
WAYFARER: *(Examining the pallet)* This is where you sleep?

HERMIT: Yes.

WAYFARER: This bowl and two sticks?

HERMIT: To eat my rice.

WAYFARER: The barest necessities of life . . .

HERMIT:
Ah, world in a dewdrop,
World in a dewdrop though you are,
Nevertheless . . . nevertheless.

WAYFARER: Forgive me.

HERMIT: For what?

WAYFARER: I intruded on your hermitage.

(The wind howls.)

HERMIT: That's a cold wind. *(Chuckles quietly to himself)*

WAYFARER: You have achieved enlightenment?

HERMIT:
No earth at all,
No sky at all,
And still
The snowflakes fall.

WAYFARER: Then it is so. *(Stares at him for a long time, then)* How do you differ from one of the unenlightened?

HERMIT: When I eat, I eat. When I sleep, I sleep.

WAYFARER: Isn't that also true of the unenlightened?

HERMIT: When I eat, I eat. When I sleep, I sleep. My mind is not thinking of a thousand other things. I do not dream.

WAYFARER: Have you no worldly connections, no luxuries, no . . . vanity?

HERMIT: *(Showing the bonsai with a faint hint of pride)* This tree is my only vanity, my only earthly attachment, my only luxury. Years ago when I withdrew from the world of men I planted two seeds from the same tree: one out there and one in here in this crock. As time and weather rent and gnarled the great tree outside, so did I twist the miniature and imitating each chance of Nature, trained it to be identical. This was the work of my life and hermitage. It is all that keeps me from nirvana.

(The wind howls.)

WAYFARER: It's bitter cold.

HERMIT: I live in the high mountains.

WAYFARER: Can you light a fire?

HERMIT: Ah, stranger, there is no firewood here and no warmth. I call this place solitude, the cold abode.

(Sound of the wind again.)

WAYFARER: I'm chilled to the marrow of my bones. It will kill me if we don't have a fire. *(Pleading pitifully)* Please, please do something.

HERMIT: *(With a faint, almost imperceptible smile manifest in the subtleties of facial expression and countenance alone)* Yes, yes I will do something. *(Aside)* I will cut down my little tree. *(He cuts the tree. Suddenly a bolt of lightning strikes the tree outside, rending it in exact imitation of the miniature. The* HERMIT *makes a fire with the little tree and the big tree outside likewise bursts into flame. At this moment, the*

WAYFARER *rises from the bed, throws off his cowl, and reveals himself to be a shining bodhisattva in white and gold. Awed)* A bodhisattva!

BODHISATTVA: Did you not notice that I came by the road *down* the mountain? You are the first mortal I have seen in a thousand years of solitude. The last was a woman exiled for adultery . . . and now you, perfected spirit. You have severed your last attachment to materialism. You may enter into nirvana and no-mind at will.

HERMIT: I would prefer to postpone that ecstasy a while and live yet another life to help others to become enlightened.

BODHISATTVA: You mean you haven't overcome sympathy?

HERMIT: I got rid of overwork easily. Curiosity was a good deal more difficult. But sympathy is persistent. No, I need one more life to purge it away.

BODHISATTVA: Then I pass on my Bodhisattvahood to you, and I will pass into nirvana. For when I let you cut down your little tree, I overcame the last drop of sympathy in myself. The very act that released me holds you.

HERMIT: I am used to paradoxes.

BODHISATTVA: But one so attained as yourself may choose his next incarnation. Who will you choose to be?

HERMIT: I have lived a life of seclusion, balance, order, and reason. For my last life, I should like its opposite. I would like to lead people out of materialism. But in a different way. A way wholly unlike hermitage. I would like to bring frivolity to Mankind, know many people, take chances, risk everything, live as though I were Caprice itself!

BODHISATTVA: *(A light increasingly bright until one can no longer see anything)* So shall you live until the last drop of sympathy in you is purged away. Om Sri Satchidananda Maha Vishnu Ommmmmm.

ACT I

Scene 1: FEINSCHMECKER, ZUNI.

FEINSCHMECKER: I tell you Caprice is a faggot, a fanatic, a freeloader, and a fraud.

ZUNI: Your alliteration bores me.

FEINSCHMECKER: Your attachment to that imbecile is ruining our marriage. I won't have you degrade yourself with that guttersnipe! If you're going to degrade yourself with anyone it's going to be with me.

ZUNI: *(Fervently)* I think he is a genius.

FEINSCHMECKER: And what's more, he owes me six months rent on his loft in SoHo.

ZUNI: Caprice has no time to think of trivial, mundane affairs like rent. He is a visionary. I'll pay his boring rent for him.

FEINSCHMECKER: I can't bear this absurd extravagance.

ZUNI: If you had been born with money, as I was, you wouldn't be so afraid to spend it.

FEINSCHMECKER: If you had had to earn your fortune, as I did, you wouldn't waste money the way you do.

ZUNI: Oh, Harry, how prosaic you are. There's more to life than material things. That's what Caprice shows us with his art.

FEINSCHMECKER: Art? How can you talk about art? Look at this picture in today's paper. Hundreds of Irish patriots shot down in cold blood.

ZUNI: Oh, my God! Harry, look at those sweaters they're wearing! I want an Irish sweater.

FEINSCHMECKER: *(Smiling affectionately)* Ah, my little numbskull. How can I resist you? But resist you I must. One of us has got to have common sense. But how could you be the one? You've never had to struggle, never had to fight.

ZUNI: I can't bear you when you get patronizing. How right was Proust when he said that it is to impress our inferiors that we have to go to the greatest lengths.

FEINSCHMECKER: It's better to be nouveau riche than never to have been riche at all.

ZUNI: Sometimes I forget that I married you for your sense of humor.

FEINSCHMECKER: I've lost my sense of humor. I've lost my youth. I've lost my looks.

ZUNI: And unless you support Caprice you're going to lose me. *(Starts out)*

FEINSCHMECKER: Where are you going?

ZUNI: To Caprice's studio. He called and said he wants me to be the first to see his new collection.

FEINSCHMECKER: Tell me, Zuni, why must you always dress in fashion?

ZUNI: I simply haven't the time or the money to dress *out* of fashion. *(Exit)*

FEINSCHMECKER: *(Calling an unseen servant)* Aldridge, lay out my radical chic. I'm going to SoHo.

Scene 2: ZUNI, TATA.

ZUNI: Really, Tata, if we don't eat soon I'm simply going to wither up and die.

TATA: But Baroness, you can hardly expect me to serve brunch while Monsieur is still in his room.

ZUNI: I was congratulating Caprice only yesterday. . . . I said, "I know you're depressed that your lover has left you. But at least you've been getting out of bed in time and we can all have lunch at noon again." It looks as though my congratulations were a bit premature.

TATA: We will surely serve by one.

ZUNI: What time is it now?

TATA: Quarter to.

ZUNI: But what on earth is keeping Caprice?

TATA: Oh, didn't I tell you? Mr. Adrian has come back.

ZUNI: *(Thunderstruck)* You can't be serious. After that last scene I thought they'd never speak to each other again.

TATA: On the contrary, they're closer than ever. Scenes are as necessary to the progress of love as wars are to the progress of civilization.

ZUNI: Can that be true?

TATA: They're in there now.

Scene 3: ZUNI, TATA, LA FLEUR.

LA FLEUR: *(Enters in a snit)* Is Caprice here?

TATA: What do you want, Mr. La Fleur?

LA FLEUR: My money, that's what I want. Caprice owes me eighteen hundred dollars on his perfume bill!

ZUNI: Eighteen hundred dollars! What did he buy?

LA FLEUR: *(Very high-strung)* What did he buy? I'll tell you what he bought! Ambergris, bergamot, civet, frangipane, gardenia, heliotrope, jasmine, lotus, mimosa, new-mown hay, olibanum, patchouli, rhodium, rose geranium, black narcissus, sandalwood, smoke, sweet pea, tuberose, violet, and wisteria. If he doesn't pay up I'll cut him off without a scent!

TATA: You wouldn't!

LA FLEUR: Oh wouldn't I? I'll make a stink that will smell from here to . . .

Scene 4: CAPRICE, ZUNI, LA FLEUR, TATA.

CAPRICE: *(Entering fancifully through the center door)* That's a remarkable tie you are wearing, Mr. La Fleur.

LA FLEUR: *(Mollified)* Do you really think so?

CAPRICE: Hello, Zuni.

ZUNI: You look chipper.

CAPRICE: Why shouldn't I? Adrian is back.

ZUNI: Tata told me.

CAPRICE: Get me an aspirin.

LA FLEUR: Aren't you feeling well?

CAPRICE: *(Euphoric)* Me not feeling well? Why I've never felt better in my life! It's for Adrian. He has a splitting headache.

ZUNI: You mean he's hung?

CAPRICE: I should say he is! He had too much to drink last night. You don't know how I felt when I saw him in the doorway.

ZUNI: He came to your door?

CAPRICE: No, I found him in the same doorway he was standing in the night we met.

ZUNI: Well, I hope you're pleased.

CAPRICE: Pleased? I felt like a heel after all the terrible things I said about him and the poor bunny's been suffering for weeks. He can't live without me.

ZUNI: That's dreadful.

CAPRICE: Thank God it hasn't spoiled his looks. On the contrary, he looks even better than I remembered him!

ADRIAN'S VOICE OFF: Claude! Claude!

CAPRICE: Ah, that's Adrian now. Do you recognize his voice?

ZUNI: How could I forget it?

CAPRICE: I'm here, my divine love.

ZUNI: *(As if entering a sickroom)* May I see him?

CAPRICE: Adrian, beloved, Zuni is here. She wants to say hello.

Scene 5: CAPRICE, ZUNI, LA FLEUR, TATA, ADRIAN.

ADRIAN: *(Enters brushing his hair, wearing the pajama bottoms that go with Caprice's oversize top)* Hello, Zuni.
TATA: How are you this morning, sir?
ADRIAN: Who is that?
CAPRICE: He's my new butler.
ADRIAN: What do you need a butler for?
CAPRICE: He's been serving me breakfast in bed every day for two weeks.
ADRIAN: Where did he come from?
CAPRICE: I don't know. But I'm enjoying it while it lasts.
TATA: How are you feeling this morning, sir?
ADRIAN: I'm a bit under the weather. I've got a headache.
TATA: Here is your aspirin, sir.
ADRIAN: *(Taken aback)* Why, thank you.
CAPRICE: Adrian, darling, do try to rally. We're all going to have brunch.
LA FLEUR: Caprice, what about your perfume bill?
CAPRICE: Didn't you get the check? We put it in the mail this morning.
LA FLEUR: Caprice, please, I have a small boy at home.
CAPRICE: And you want me to underwrite your pederasty?
LA FLEUR: Please, Caprice, he is my son.
CAPRICE: More and more sordid.
LA FLEUR: Pay at least part of your bill and save my happy home.
CAPRICE: Oh very well, I'll pay for the musk and the civet.
LA FLEUR: And the lignum aloes.
CAPRICE: And the lignum aloes. *(Aside)* The bandit!
TATA: *(Serving brunch)* Braised pigeon ovaries on toast points?
CAPRICE: That's me.
TATA: Fat pâté and fruit?
ADRIAN: *(Moaning)* I couldn't look at food.
TATA: Very good, sir. Bread?
CAPRICE: *(In a voice extinct with boredom)* Panis angelicus.
TATA: Butter, jam, or cheese?
CAPRICE: Just plain panis angelicus.
TATA: Baroness?
ZUNI: Hot water and lemon.
TATA: *(Backing out with the tray)* Very good, Madame.

Scene 6: CAPRICE, ADRIAN, ZUNI, SCRUBWOMAN.

CAPRICE: It's uncanny. When do you suppose he'll discover he has the wrong house?
ADRIAN: That was a close one. He almost discovered our little secret.
CAPRICE: It would have been a mauve imbroglio!
ADRIAN: I don't believe in scandalizing the servants, that's all.
ZUNI: One must set an example for the proletariat.
CAPRICE: The proletariat does not hesitate in scandalizing us.
ADRIAN: One must make allowances, for on them rests the responsibility of reproducing the numbers of Mankind.
CAPRICE: Reproduction often involves some scandal.

ZUNI: Those who can't create, procreate. I prefer the unnatural. Art, for instance.

CAPRICE: Pshaw! Art is like a blindfold that stands between Man and Nature. If we could truly see Nature we would not need Art. But alas, it is easier to see Nature in Art than it is to see Art in Nature.

ADRIAN: Claude, please, it's so early in the morning!

CAPRICE: *(Helping himself to more pigeon ovaries)* The fact is, my dear Adrian, that when the period in which a man of talent is condemned to live is dull and stupid, the artist is haunted, perhaps unknown to himself, by a nostalgic yearning for another age. At these moments you are to me what Antinous was to Hadrian and Patroclus was to Achilles.

ZUNI: Caprice, I haven't a thing to wear. I need something new and different. I know what I want. But I can't find what I want. Nobody has what I want. They won't give me what I want. . . .

ADRIAN: Claude, please do something!

CAPRICE: *(Aside to the SCRUBWOMAN who has been working on the floor throughout the scene)* Carlota?

SCRUBWOMAN: ¿Sí?

CAPRICE: How much did you pay for that hat you're wearing?

SCRUBWOMAN: Two dollars and forty-nine cents on Fourteenth Street.

CAPRICE: *(Taking the hat)* Here's a twenty. Get yourself half a dozen. *(Throws the hat on the floor, stamps on it a few times, then places it on the baroness's head)* Here you are, Baroness.

ZUNI: *(Admiring the hat in the mirror)* That's what I want!

CAPRICE: That's what I thought!

Scene 7: CAPRICE, ADRIAN, ZUNI, TATA, FEINSCHMECKER.

FEINSCHMECKER: *(Barges in)* Is Caprice here?

TATA: *(Trying to prevent him from entering)* Who shall I say is calling?

FEINSCHMECKER: Tell him that his landlord, Harry Feinschmecker, wants to speak with him.

CAPRICE: What do you want, Mr. Feinschmecker?

FEINSCHMECKER: My rent, that's what I want.

ZUNI: Harry, don't make a scene.

FEINSCHMECKER: You keep out of this, Zuni. Caprice, you owe me six months' rent. If you don't pay up I'll throw you out on your royal American ass!

ADRIAN: You wouldn't!

FEINSCHMECKER: Oh wouldn't I? I'll slap you with a dispossess so fast it will make your head swim.

CAPRICE: Stop! The rent will be paid. For today Caprice has realized, quite suddenly, what he must do to imbue feminine beauty with a new air of enchantment. And somewhere in Paris or in London, in New York or Berlin, there lives a woman who yesterday only dimly felt the slavery of her unfashionable clothes, who yesterday knew and suspected nothing of Caprice, and who today will rejoice in her newfound freedom when she has seen his creations, when she has enveloped her body and at the same time revealed her beauty in the new and delightful garments which are Caprice's present to her. Caprice, who will today make her a queen. A queen of beauty . . . for Caprice is more than a king of kings—he is a king of queens! Behold, "Freedom," the world's first brassiere!

ZUNI: How much do you want, Caprice? Name any sum.

CAPRICE: *(Embarrassed)* No, no, I did it for Womankind. I could not accept payment.

ZUNI: *(With warmth and understanding as though she were comforting a child)* We cannot *pay* for Art. You know that, Caprice. I give you this money. You give me your brassiere. Shall we call it foundation support? *(Takes money from FEINSCHMECKER and gives it to CAPRICE)*

CAPRICE: *(Overcome)* I shall study deserving. *(Passes the money back to FEINSCHMECKER)*

FEINSCHMECKER: *(Aside)* This is how he pays the rent!!

Scene 8: CAPRICE, ADRIAN, ZUNI, FEINSCHMECKER, TATA.

TATA: *(Rushing in)* Have you seen the papers? *(Hands a newspaper to each of them)*

ADRIAN: *(Reading)* "Twyfford Adamant Invents Brassiere, Calls It Freedom."

TATA: And they're selling like hotcakes. Tomorrow every woman in America will have one. *(Exit)*

Scene 9: CAPRICE, ADRIAN, ZUNI, FEINSCHMECKER.

FEINSCHMECKER: *(Scornfully)* Some women will buy anything!

ADRIAN: Oh no! Not again! Every time Claude comes up with an original idea, Twyfford Adamant steals it and makes it more commercial.

ZUNI: Well, Caprice, what are you going to do?

CAPRICE: I shall retaliate!

ALL: What is he going to do?

CAPRICE: I'm going to make a slingshot out of this brassiere and break all of Twyfford Adamant's windows! *(He does so, shooting from his balcony)* Fwapp! I invent no brassiere!

(The sound of shattered glass is heard off. CAPRICE burns his brassiere.)

ADRIAN: *(As though it were Veronica's veil)* Look, the newspaper headline changed! It says, "No Brassiere."

(The sound of a gong.)

Scene 10: CAPRICE, ADRIAN, ZUNI, FEINSCHMECKER, TATA.

TATA: *(Poking in his head)* Twyfford Adamant to see you, Mr. Caprice. *(Exit)*

Scene 11: CAPRICE, ADRIAN, ZUNI, FEINSCHMECKER, ADAMANT.

(ADAMANT storms onto the stage with a huge bale of tangled brassieres, which he hurls down at CAPRICE's feet.)

CAPRICE: What's this?

ADRIAN: Brassieres! Hundreds of them!

ADAMANT: *(Furious)* Every order has been returned. You'll answer for this, Caprice.

CAPRICE: Don't be such a sore loser, Twyf. It's fashion's law. What's in today is definitely out tomorrow. Maybe someday they'll revive the brassiere—as camp!

TWYFFORD: I'm not amused. Dismiss your entourage. I want to talk to you in private. *(Suave)* Baroness Feinschmecker, I would worship to have you visit the Atelier Adamant.

ZUNI: Indeed I couldn't. I never go to the West Side.

ADRIAN: No one ever goes there anymore.

CAPRICE: It's too crowded.

ZUNI: Caprice, I would like to see some of your other creations.

CAPRICE: I will send the world's first live model to your home to show you my new line.

ADAMANT: *(Aside)* Live model, damn! Why didn't I think of that?

FEINSCHMECKER: Caprice, even *I* have got to hand it to you. You're the only man I've ever met who could pay the rent by inventing nothing. *Un*inventing the brassiere, I mean.

CAPRICE: It's just part of my new line. The completely nude clothing.

ADRIAN: The birthday suit.

CAPRICE: And for after six—the gownless evening strap.

ADAMANT: Topless and bottomless. At this rate we'll all be out of business!

CAPRICE: *(Kissing her hand)* Ah, Baroness Feinschmecker, ever the fashion plate. I see you are wearing no brassiere. *(Winks)*

ZUNI: You made me what I am today.

CAPRICE: One cannot improve on Nature.

FEINSCHMECKER: *(To ZUNI)* Come on honey, let's get out of here. This looks like a place for a poodle's bar mitzvah.

(Exit the FEINSCHMECKERS.)

Scene 12: CAPRICE, ADRIAN, ADAMANT.

ADAMANT: I'm waiting, Caprice.

ADRIAN: *(Aside to CAPRICE)* Be careful, Claude. Twyfford Adamant is the Fu Manchu of fashion.

CAPRICE: *(Aside to ADRIAN)* You seem to forget that I am the Zatoichi of fashion. *(Aloud)* Adrian, prepare my mannequins. I will be draping this afternoon.

(Exit ADRIAN.)

Scene 13: CAPRICE, ADAMANT.

CAPRICE: You wanted to speak to me alone?

ADAMANT: Yes, my nose always rebels slightly at the proximity of other human beings.

CAPRICE: Ah, you misanthrope.

ADAMANT: But wasn't your motive the same when you invented perfume? Confess, Caprice.

CAPRICE: How well we know one another!

ADAMANT: A strong enemy is to be treasured.

CAPRICE: We teach each other how the world works.

ADAMANT: We are bound to each other.

CAPRICE: In moral combat.

ADAMANT: Yes, I know you inside out. You're cut on the bias. You always were.

CAPRICE: How did you know I was circumcised?

ADAMANT: At sixteen you were the catamite of a cardinal. I have a theory about you.

CAPRICE: What's your theory?

ADAMANT: Your behavior is always above reproach, except for your temper, which you cannot control. That's because you're shanty Irish . . . the only unfashionable thing about you.

CAPRICE: *(Flaring up)* We were lace-curtain Irish and don't you ever forget it!

ADAMANT: You're a puzzle. Why do you sacrifice your life to bring a bunch of crackpot ideas into existence? Zealous frivolity? No. I suspect an ulterior motive, hidden meanings, unplumbed depths.

CAPRICE: Profound frivolity.

ADAMANT: The mask is unconvincing, Caprice. Drop it. You are ethical even to your own detriment. Is not this ironclad moral discipline which you exercise over an inordinately passionate nature an expression of contempt for a weak-willed humanity by a man who in his heart of hearts believes in nothing, a man who laughs in solitude?

CAPRICE: Tell me, Twyfford, with all your contempt for morality, your Machiavellian machinations, do your friends justify your meanness?

TWYFFORD: *(Guarded)* What are you getting at?

CAPRICE: You let nothing get in your way. You will stop at nothing. You don't play by the rules. Shouldn't you then be a lot more successful than you are? Something is holding you back. Admit it, Adamant.

ADAMANT: I admit it. What is your hypothesis?

CAPRICE: I suspect a bad conscience.

ADAMANT: The devil!

CAPRICE: The devil, exactly! That twinge of conscience keeps you from achieving your ideal, pure villainy.

ADAMANT: How well we know one another.

CAPRICE: Yes, I know the man behind the mask. You are no two-dimensional stage villain. You're human like the rest of us.

ADAMANT: *(Anguished)* Human, all too human. That is why I must achieve my goal.

CAPRICE: A secret goal?

ADAMANT: No, the only goal: the complete triumph of my personality over everything.

CAPRICE: You'll never get away with it. There are some people who won't let you pull the rayon acetate over their eyes.

ADAMANT: *(Sharply, through his teeth)* Try and stop me. I hate anything that comes easy.

CAPRICE: I'm a good sport. You invented the brassiere first, congratulations. *(Offers his hand)*

ADAMANT: *(Shaking CAPRICE's hand)* But you did think of live models. That's good. That's really good.

CAPRICE: *(Modestly)* I have my moments.

ADAMANT: So that's our bond. Either to love each other or . . .

CAPRICE: To destroy each other.

Scene 14: CAPRICE, ADAMANT, TATA.

TATA: *(Appearing at the door)* I beg your pardon, Mr. Caprice. But Mr. Adamant's car has come round for him.

ADAMANT: *(Confidentially aside, with his hand on CAPRICE's shoulder)* Melancholy has poisoned all my goodness. Black bile curdles the milk of human kindness.

CAPRICE: Let me get you a bicarbonate of soda.

(Exit CAPRICE and ADAMANT.)

Scene 15: TATA, ADRIAN.

ADRIAN: *(Enters with a sketch pad in his hand)* Where is Claude?

TATA: He's showing Mr. Adamant to the door.

ADRIAN: Thank you.

TATA: Will there be anything else, sir?

ADRIAN: *(Looking through some fashion illustrations)* No, that's all. *(Absently)* I'll just go over my illustrations of the new "Jeunesse Eternelle" line.

TATA: *(Coming up behind him quietly and looking over his shoulder at the drawings)* "Jeunesse Eternelle"? That one's a beaut.

ADRIAN: *(Coming to himself)* Say, wait a minute. These designs are top secret. I don't think Claude would want me to show them to you. I don't even know who you are.

TATA: Tata is my name, sir.

ADRIAN: Where did you come from?

TATA: I come from a long line of gentlemen's gentlemen. I'm a Virgo, sir, and Virgos serve.

ADRIAN: You're fond of astrology, I see.

TATA: I know very little of the heavenly bodies.

ADRIAN: Ah, but you will, my boy. You will! Who sent you to work for Caprice?

TATA: I sought him out, as it were, sir. You see a gentleman's gentleman without a gentleman is a gentleman's gentleman out of work as it were, sir.

ADRIAN: But where's your revolutionary spirit, man?

TATA: I don't care much for labor. I identify with the aristocracy. I live off the fat of the land. Now, if you'll excuse me, I'll go and dress for dinner. *(Exit)*

Scene 16: CAPRICE, ADRIAN, SCRUBWOMAN.

CAPRICE: *(Entering in excitement)* Adrian, I want to send a live model to Zuni's apartment to show her the new Peter Pan uniforms I've designed. *(Looking through the illustrations)* These illustrations you've done capture it perfectly! *(Throws his arms around* ADRIAN *and kisses him on the neck)*
ADRIAN: Oh, Claude, let me model the "Jeunesse Eternelle" line.
CAPRICE: I'm afraid the Baroness would recognize you. We've got to get a real woman.
ADRIAN: But we can't afford to hire anyone now.
CAPRICE: You're right. If only there were someone already working for us. Someone who could . . . *(Fixing his attention on the* SCRUBWOMAN*)*
ADRIAN: No, Claude, we can't use her. She has housemaid's knees.
CAPRICE: True, Adrian, under ordinary circumstances a woman of her social class, laboring for her living, would look sixty at age forty. But watch what can be done through Caprice's cosmetic miracles. *(Helping the* SCRUBWOMAN *up from her knees)* Carlota.
SCRUBWOMAN: ¿Sí?
CAPRICE: Would you mind standing up for a minute?
ADRIAN: But, Claude, she has no poise.
CAPRICE: *(Slapping the hand with which the* SCRUBWOMAN *has been picking her nose)* We'll teach her poise. *(Removes her horn-rim glasses)*
ADRIAN: Why, she's beautiful!
CAPRICE: Will you do it, Carlota? Will you be the world's first live fashion model?
SCRUBWOMAN: Yes, I would do anything for you, Mr. Caprice. But I don't know how to model. Will you show me how it's done?
CAPRICE: Sure. Put this book on your head and your hand on your hip, like this. Slouch. Now walk this way. Bend over backwards. Look the customer up and down with disdain. Then turn scornfully and slouching the while, stalk away. *(The* SCRUBWOMAN *attempts this)* You're getting it. Suck in your cheeks. *(The* SCRUBWOMAN *tightens her buttocks)* All four of them.
SCRUBWOMAN: *(Garbled)* Like this?
CAPRICE: Let's see your scornful look. *(The* SCRUBWOMAN *flashes a scornful look Shuddering)* Adrian, I don't know what I'd do if she ever looked at me like that and meant it. Let's get some sketches of this.

(The SCRUBWOMAN *strikes a number of poses and* ADRIAN *does a quick sketch of each pose.)*

SCRUBWOMAN: How am I doing?
CAPRICE: You've got the basic idea. You can refine it later. Now away to the Baroness Feinschmecker's house. Let Tata drive you.
ADRIAN: I don't trust Tata. We really hardly know him.
CAPRICE: Adrian, you're an incurable xenophobe. Tata is sweet.
ADRIAN: There's something oily about him. I don't know what it is. But I never trust a man with crooked teeth.
CAPRICE: But that's just what gives him character. Look at me. I'm gap-toothed.
ADRIAN: A sign of wantonness.
CAPRICE: That's just coincidental.

ADRIAN: There's good reason to be suspicious. Somebody's been stealing your ideas, probably a spy. And just a little while ago I caught sweet little Tata looking over my shoulder at the illustrations of the "Jeunesse Eternelle" line. He seemed *very* interested.

CAPRICE: So he loves my work. What's wrong with that?

ADRIAN: Everything. I used to be the only one you allowed to see your designs before they were made public.

CAPRICE: Adrian, I think you're jealous of Tata.

ADRIAN: Don't be ridiculous.

CAPRICE: Then enough of this paranoid nonsense. We'll send Tata to Zuni's with . . . Oh no, we haven't thought of a name for the world's first live model.

ADRIAN: It should be something exotic.

SCRUBWOMAN: Could I please have my babushka back?

CAPRICE: *(Taking the* SCRUBWOMAN *in his arms and kissing her wildly)* That's it! We'll call her Babushka!

Scene 17: ZUNI.

(The Baroness Feinschmecker's apartment. The BARONESS *sits before her vanity and talks on the telephone. She wears a mudpack and her hair is all in curling irons which bristle from her head like electrodes.)*

ZUNI: Yes? What is it this time? Go ahead and tell me, you fool. You've gone this far. *(Listens)* Really, now that you've aroused my curiosity you must tell me. *(Listens)* No. *(Listens)* He didn't! *(Listens)* He did? And may I ask with whom? *(Listens)* A Girl Scout! This has got to be the pits, the obscene dregs. Well, I always knew this was bound to happen sooner or later. *(Pause)* I saw it coming. Still, it is a bit of a shock. Does anyone know besides you and me? *(Listens)* The scout leader. Buy her off. Yes buy all her cookies or something. We've got to do everything we can to keep this out of the papers. *(Listens)* Yes. Yes, I will. He is my husband and I suppose I really ought to defend him, even if he is a pervert.

Scene 18: ZUNI, FEINSCHMECKER.

FEINSCHMECKER: *(Calling from offstage)* Zuni! Zuni!

ZUNI: Oh, I hear him coming. I'll call you back. *(She hangs up the phone)*

FEINSCHMECKER: *(Entering in childlike excitement)* Zuni! Zuni!

ZUNI: Don't look at me. I'm wearing a mudpack.

FEINSCHMECKER: I've just discovered a more expensive way to wipe my ass.

ZUNI: More expensive than vellum?

FEINSCHMECKER: *(Condescending)* I haven't used vellum since Southampton. I'm using damask now.

ZUNI: If you would eat macrobiotically you wouldn't need to wipe your ass at all.

FEINSCHMECKER: Am I interrupting your beauty ritual?

ZUNI: Some women are lucky. They're born beautiful. I have to work at it.

Today I'm working overtime. I'm having trouble with the line between my eyes.

FEINSCHMECKER: Why do you worry so much about makeup and what you wear? I like you best clean-scrubbed and bare-assed naked.

ZUNI: Provocative nakedness always leaves something hidden. Some accouterment, some element of fashion must always be retained. And perfume! Perfume! Perfume!

FEINSCHMECKER: There's no perfume to equal the smell of balls and cunt.

(The doorbell rings.)

ZUNI: Would you see who that is? I gave the maid the day off.

FEINSCHMECKER: If the restaurants closed on the cooks' day off you'd starve to death. *(Goes to the door)*

ZUNI: *(Pouting at her mirror)* I look like the Wreck of the Hesperus at low tide.

FEINSCHMECKER: It's a couple of fruits from the Chez Caprice.

ZUNI: That will be the model Caprice sent me with his latest creation.

FEINSCHMECKER: *(Exasperated)* What do you see in the clothes he designs? They're not fit to wrap fish in. They're that ugly.

ZUNI: But, Harry, that's just it. *(Enraptured)* They're ugly. Caprice designs the ugliest clothes in the world.

FEINSCHMECKER: Yet you wear them.

ZUNI: Of course I wear them. The uglier my clothes, the more beautiful I appear by contrast. So many designers want all the attention to go to their clothes. But not Caprice, he makes clothes ugly and women beautiful.

FEINSCHMECKER: I used to suspect you were crazy. Now I'm convinced of it.

ZUNI: Send in the model.

FEINSCHMECKER: My wife, the Baroness, will see you now. *(Exit)*

Scene 19: ZUNI, TATA.

ZUNI: *(Rising and welcoming* TATA *with open arms)* Tata! So, my idea worked. Caprice has hired you.

TATA: It was just like you said. I served him breakfast in bed every day for two weeks and now he can't live without me. I feel just like one of the family over there.

ZUNI: It was all a question of strategy. Caprice hates money. He won't accept payment, let alone charity. As his patron I feel that I must remain as unobtrusive as possible.

TATA: So you pay my salary.

ZUNI: Correct. Caprice needs many helping hands to accomplish his great work—the enhancement of feminine beauty. There are few men of such vision . . . so few men willing to make the necessary sacrifices.

TATA: I needs the work for me poor ole mither.

ZUNI: Of course. But Tata, I have found another reason for taking you into my confidence. It seems my husband . . . I hardly know how to put this. My husband is a pervert.

TATA: *(Protesting)* Madame!

ZUNI: No, it's quite true. You will, I trust, excuse my candor.

TATA: It's just that it's such an awful thing to say about the gentleman your husband, mum.

ZUNI: Make no mistake. He's a pervert in the best sense of the word. You might even say he's a creative pervert. He has a genius for the new and different.

TATA: It's very kind of you to give credit where credit is due.

ZUNI: But his sexual originality makes him restless. I have had to go to *very* great lengths to hold his interest all these years. My bondage to fashion has been a nightly attempt to renew his interest in me. Like Scheherazade I have dished up a thousand and one nights of perversion to hold him under my spell.

TATA: This is an unusual history.

ZUNI: *(Matter-of-factly)* Once when he began to get bored I had him frigged while he kissed the asshole of one girl while a second frigged his ass and a third his prick. Then I had him lick the cunt of another while a fourth licked his asshole. Then I had them all switch positions so that when all was said and done he sucked a beshitted ass, had a tongue frig his beshitted asshole, encunted the friggeresses, swallowed their balm, and all three of them had their asses kissed.

TATA: Olympian debauch!

ZUNI: But at his most austere and in reaction to his former baroque manner, like some renegade Puritan, he would simply have an older girl introduce a younger girl to bad habits.

TATA: Tch tch tch.

ZUNI: At first he sought extremes of beauty. But when that resource had been exhausted he turned to the oldest and ugliest women he could find, whom he had vomit in his mouth.

TATA: *(Chuckles)* The old ramrod himself!

ZUNI: Yes, those were the innocent days when his activities hurt no one but himself. But then one day he had a young boy dressed in mare's skin, his asshole smeared with mare's fuck, and surrendered this small boy to an excited horse. He observed their struggles and the boy's death.

TATA: Now whatever possessed him?

ZUNI: He had seen *Equus* the night before. He was always an intellectual, a theatergoer. I had a hard time keeping that little incident quiet.

TATA: I can imagine.

ZUNI: In New London, Connecticut, he embuggered a goat, which miraculously begat a monster.

TATA: Lordy!

ZUNI: Monster though it was, he embuggered it.

TATA: Not the type of story you'd want to get around.

ZUNI: Exactly. But this is the last straw! I have just received word from a very reliable source that he's gone from gargoyles to Girl Scouts. *(Losing her composure)* I'll never dress as a Girl Scout. Do you hear? Nevair! *(Coming back to herself)* So I'd like you to keep an eye on my husband whenever he comes to Chez Caprice. If he does anything to cause me even the slightest embarrassment I'd like to know about it at once. This is for Caprice's protection as well as for my own. You understand, don't you?

TATA: Exquisitely, madonna. You want me to spy for you.

ZUNI: I prefer to call it "observation."

TATA: It fits me like a glove. The very idea of espionage sounds romantic to me. Why I might even keep a diary!

ZUNI: Then that's settled. I'll pay you to look after Caprice and to observe my husband. Report everything to me and above all preserve my anonymity.

TATA: Will you peruse the "Jeunesse Eternelle" line now, Baroness?

ZUNI: *(Turning back to her mirror)* Eternal youth! I feel exactly like an Egyptian mummy.
TATA: Do you believe in face-lifting?
ZUNI: I believe it is something that should be seriously considered every day. Oh what's the use? I spit in the face of time that has transfigured me!
TATA: *(Very officiously)* On behalf of the Chez Caprice I would like to introduce Babushka, the world's first live model. She's a hot one, she is!

Scene 20: ZUNI, TATA, BABUSHKA.

(BABUSHKA enters dressed as Peter Pan and parades up and down slouching as Caprice taught her to. She flashes her "scornful" look at the BARONESS.)

ZUNI: *(Horrified)* A Girl Scout uniform!
BABUSHKA: But I'm a Brownie.
ZUNI: Brownee or brownor, you're just a fairy to me! *(Exit)*

(BABUSHKA tries to attack the BARONESS but TATA restrains her.)

BABUSHKA: You have insulted the master! Caprice will hear of this!

Scene 21: CAPRICE, ADRIAN. *Chez Caprice.*

CAPRICE: *(Dressed as Oberon, petulantly)* Adrian, my magic wand! How can I go to the masquerade as Oberon, King of the Fairies, with no magic wand? I'll feel underaccessorized.
ADRIAN: *(Entering on CAPRICE's heels)* It isn't in the lizard armoire.
CAPRICE: Then look behind the ilex topiary. I might have let it fall during a déjà vu I had there this afternoon.

(Exit ADRIAN.)

Scene 22: CAPRICE, TATA.

TATA: *(As Peter Pan)* Mr. Caprice, the Baroness Feinschmecker to see you.
CAPRICE: Faugh! Send her in and I'll give her a piece of what I laughingly call my mind.

Scene 23: CAPRICE, ADRIAN, ZUNI, BABUSHKA, TATA.

ADRIAN: *(Entering also in a Peter Pan uniform)* Here is your wand, sire.
CAPRICE: *(Taking the magic wand from ADRIAN and pointing it at the BARONESS as she walks through the door)* You will be out of fashion for six months!
ZUNI: *(Cowering)* No, no! I couldn't bear it! Why me? What have I ever done to you?
CAPRICE: You have insulted me. You have insulted the "Jeunesse Eternelle" line. But worst of all you have insulted Babushka, the world's first live model. Not for six months will you be received in the House of Caprice!

ADRIAN: *(Crying out)* God is high! Justice is good!

ZUNI: But the masquerade tonight. What will I wear?

CAPRICE: You can wear sackcloth and ashes for all I care.

ADRIAN: *(Aside to the* BARONESS*)* You'd better leave. I think you're getting off easy.

ZUNI: *(Throwing herself down on the floor in front of them)* I will not budge.

CAPRICE: *(Effortlessly)* Then I will hold the masquerade in another ballroom. Come Adrian.

(Exit CAPRICE, ADRIAN, BABUSHKA, *and* TATA, *stepping over the* BARONESS*'s body.)*

Scene 24: ZUNI.

ZUNI: Sackcloth and ashes?

Scene 25: BERTHA, ZUNI. *Atelier Adamant.*

BERTHA: *(Leading* ZUNI *into Adamant's "factory")* Baroness Feinschmecker, welcome to the Atelier Adamant, or as we who work for Adamant call it, 'the Plant.' Mr. Adamant will be with you in a moment.

ZUNI: Thank you, I'll wait.

(Exit BERTHA.*)*

Scene 26: ZUNI.

ZUNI: *(Looking at the sofa in horror)* My God, that sofa is upholstered in the same fabric as my dress. I've got to get out of here before Twyfford sees me!

*(*ZUNI *starts to run for the exit but hears* ADAMANT *coming from that direction.)*

ADAMANT: *(Calling off)* I'll be with you in a minute, Zuni!

ZUNI: *(In a panic)* He can't see me in this dress!

(She darts this way and that like a trapped animal. Suddenly she has an idea. She tears off the dress and stuffs it into her rather large handbag, musses her hair, and pretends to weep.)

Scene 27: ZUNI, ADAMANT.

ADAMANT: *(Entering)* Zuni, what happened? You look positively ravished.

ZUNI: I was raped by . . . I think there were three of them. . . . Black men . . . they ran off with my dress. *(Swoons)*

ADAMANT: Ran off with your dress? They must have been transvestites! Bertha, bring the salts! *(Patting her cheeks)* Zuni! Zuni! Speak to me.

ZUNI: *(Feebly)* My honor. My honor.

Scene 28: ZUNI, ADAMANT, BERTHA.

BERTHA: *(Entering)* Here are the salts, mum.
ZUNI: *(As though coming around)* What happened? Where am I?
ADAMANT: It's Twyfford, dear. You're at my studio.
ZUNI: *(Embracing him tearfully)* Oh, Twyfford!
ADAMANT: There there. Bertha, help me get her over to the sofa.
ZUNI: *(Stricken)* No, not the sofa! Not the sofa!
BERTHA: *(Aside)* I think she's popped her cork!
ADAMANT: Leave me alone with her. Bring some food. A cold wing of chicken
  and a young Sauterne.

(BERTHA curtsies and exits.)

Scene 29: ZUNI, ADAMANT.

ZUNI: Don't fuss over me. I'll just go home and . . . er . . . sleep it off.
ADAMANT: You're sure you'll be all right?
ZUNI: Oh yes, perfectly.
ADAMANT: Let me lend you one of my dresses. They're all in the Atelier. You
  know where they are. Feel free to borrow anything at all.
ZUNI: Thank you, I will. *(Exits seemingly dazed)*

Scene 30: ADAMANT.

ADAMANT: *(Confidentially to the audience)* At last! Feinschmecker wears an Adamant. This will be a milestone in my career.

(Commotion off.)

Scene 31: ADAMANT, ZUNI, BERTHA.

BERTHA: *(Enters dragging the* BARONESS *in a half nelson)* Oh, no you don't! I
  caught you. Baroness, my foot! You're nothing but a thief!
ADAMANT: *(Horrified)* Bertha, you've made a horrible mistake! I told the Baroness to take one of my dresses!
BERTHA: Oh yeah? Well, did you also tell her to steal the new slipcover offa
  the sofa and smuggle it out of the house in her handbag?

*(BERTHA holds aloft the handbag from which a corner of the dress hangs incriminat-
ingly out. She realizes that the sofa is intact, then pulls out the dress and holds it up
dumbfounded.)*

ZUNI: *(Humiliated, drones under her breath)* "Not for six months will you be in
  fashion."
ADAMANT: Oh, Zuni, can you ever forgive me?
ZUNI: *(Melodramatically)* This has nothing to do with you. It's just the Curse of
  Caprice.

Scene 32: CAPRICE, TATA, ADRIAN, BABUSHKA. *Caprice's studio.*

(Shoji screens. CAPRICE *is draping fabric on* BABUSHKA. ADRIAN, *clad in a kimono, is kneeling at a small Japanese writing table. He opens envelopes and removes human ears from them.)*

TATA: *(Breaking the silence)* Mr. Caprice, artists from all over the world have cut off their ears and sent them to you. Why do you ignore their sacrifice?

CAPRICE: It only takes a moment to cut off your ear. But poor Adrian has to spend an hour and a half every day opening the mail. *(Sighs)* What are we going to do when we get old? Will we be put in crooked nursing homes? Or will we be kept by our secretary's ex-lovers.

ADRIAN: Or our lover's ex-secretaries.

CAPRICE: *(In a fit of pique)* I'm tired of being dismissed as a genius. I shall sequester myself with Jussi. *(Exit into the steam room.)*

Scene 33: TATA, ADRIAN.

TATA: Where is he going?

ADRIAN: Whenever he feels melancholy, he locks himself up in his steam room and listens to Jussi Bjoerling sing "Mamma, quel vino è generoso" from *Cavalleria Rusticana.*

(The aria is heard off.)

TATA: *(Making a note in his diary)* How do you spell it?

ADRIAN: *(Noticing the book)* What's that?

TATA: It's my diary. Ever since I've come to work for you and Mr. Caprice, my life has become so memorable that I've decided to write down my memoirs . . . before I forget them.

ADRIAN: Good idea.

TATA: I write down everything I see and hear.

ADRIAN: You must be very observant.

TATA: Yes! That's exactly what I am! Observant! *(After a pause)* You are Mr. Caprice's . . . er . . . closest friend. How do you manage to communicate with this megalomaniac?

ADRIAN: Communication is unnecessary. His mind has been rendered clairvoyant by neurosis. Besides we're lovers, which means that communication is virtually impossible anyway.

TATA: *(Writing)* What is it that you love about Caprice?

ADRIAN: *(Musing mystically)* I think it is that no matter what perfume essence I choose to wear each day when I arise, the scent he has elected to wear never clashes, never jangles. Of course we have never spoken of this.

Scene 34: TATA, ADRIAN, FEINSCHMECKER.

FEINSCHMECKER: *(Enters blustering)* Where is Caprice?
ADRIAN: He's gone hunting.
FEINSCHMECKER: Hunting?!!!
ADRIAN: For antiques.
FEINSCHMECKER: Tell him that Baron Feinschmecker wants to see him.
TATA: Mr. Caprice is seeing no one today.
FEINSCHMECKER: *(Trying to force his way in)* I demand that he see me!
TATA: *(Blocking* FEINSCHMECKER'*s way)* I'm sorry, Baron, but I have my orders.
FEINSCHMECKER: Your orders! Your orders! *(Slow burn)* Young man, do you know that if it wasn't for me you wouldn't be working for the House of Caprice? *(Exploding)* Because there wouldn't be any House of Caprice! This entire industry was built on me and my wife's poor taste. Now stand aside! If Caprice won't come out and see me, I'll go in after him.
ADRIAN: I wouldn't do that if I were you.
FEINSCHMECKER: Try and stop me! *(Beats on the door of the steam room with his fists)* Caprice, come out of there! Caprice!

(The door opens. Out pours the voice of Jussi Bjoerling and fog.)

Scene 35: TATA, ADRIAN, BABUSHKA, FEINSCHMECKER, CAPRICE.

CAPRICE: *(Enters through the fog speaking to someone unseen, off)* If I'm not back in five minutes, begin without me. Ah, Baron Feinschmecker, what brings you here? The rent is not due for a fortnight.
FEINSCHMECKER: *(Brashly)* Caprice, what's this I hear about your banning my wife from your salon?
CAPRICE: *(The blue fire of fanaticism)* I had every justification in the world. She insulted me and my mannikin.
TATA: *(Writing in his diary)* His eyes burned with the blue fire of fanaticism.
FEINSCHMECKER: Then you admit it's true?
CAPRICE: I do, and I intend to stand by my decision to the bitter end.

(Door chimes.)

ADRIAN: Tata, see who's at the door.
FEINSCHMECKER: *(Threateningly)* No matter what the consequences?
CAPRICE: *(Defiantly)* No matter what the consequences!
FEINSCHMECKER: Then I shall have no recourse but to . . .
TATA: *(At the door)* It's the Baroness Feinschmecker to see you, Mr. Caprice.
FEINSCHMECKER: *(Alarmed)* She mustn't know I've come here! You must hide me.
CAPRICE: *(Hesitant)* I don't know if I should . . .
FEINSCHMECKER: *(Falling to his knees)* Caprice, I beg of you. I'm completely at your mercy. If Zuni finds me here I'll never hear the end of it. *(Breaks down and cries)* Caprice, I'm asking you not as your landlord, but as a man. Please protect me from that woman.
CAPRICE: Hide in here. *(Indicates steam room)*

*(*FEINSCHMECKER *hides in the steam room.)*

Scene 36: BABUSHKA, TATA, ADRIAN, CAPRICE, ZUNI.

ZUNI: *(Enters in sackcloth and ashes, a suppliant)* Caprice, accept the penance of a votaress, nay, a slave of fashion. I have doffed and donned. Doffed my black cloth and sashes and donned my sackcloth and ashes. I bend my knees in supplication.

CAPRICE: *(Rhetorical)* You will find my bias binding. The more you try with your hooks and eyes the more you make me want to gromit! *(Contemptuously)* Do you think my pinking shears? Prostitute my sewing? Hem and whore? That would be stump work indeed!

ZUNI: What do you want me to do? Fall into one of the black holes in lace?

CAPRICE: Button your lip. The hems aren't what they seam.

ZUNI: Then farewell fashion. Good-bye to ladies who lunch and *Women's Wear Daily.* Good-bye to mattress ticking and my Butterick patterns. Farewell Norell, adiós Balenciaga. Adieu Dior. Schiaparelli and Chanel, farewell farewell. Howdy! Lady Wrangler.

CAPRICE: Begone on off-the-rack and ready-to-wear!

(ZUNI crawls off on her knees, abject.)

Scene 37: BABUSHKA, TATA, ADRIAN, CAPRICE, FEINSCHMECKER.

FEINSCHMECKER: *(Enters from the steam room, his clothes in tatters)* So, Caprice, you have resolved to break with the Baroness forever.

CAPRICE: Just as I said.

FEINSCHMECKER: Then please accept my philanthropy.

CAPRICE: Philanthropy? Sounds like a disease.

FEINSCHMECKER: If generosity is a disease, let me infect you with it. Let me overcome your resistance. Let me give you symptoms. *(Taking* CAPRICE *in his arms and breathing heavily)* Suc-cumb! Suc-cumb!

CAPRICE: This is alarming. I'm a hypochondriac as it is. *(Breaking away from* FEINSCHMECKER*'s embrace)* What makes you so lovey-dovey all of a sudden? When you came in here you were hot under the collar.

FEINSCHMECKER: I came here to threaten you with a lawsuit. But while hiding in your steam room, I was initiated into the rites of homoerotica.

ADRIAN: Homoerotica?

CAPRICE: *(Aside)* He turned queer.

FEINSCHMECKER: And since I feel that I will be visiting your steam room several times a week, I would prefer that the Baroness *not* be here. To express my gratitude for having been brought out, I would like to offer you this entire building rent free for as long as you both shall live.

(CAPRICE and ADRIAN embrace FEINSCHMECKER from either side.)

ADRIAN: *(Ecstatically)* Oh, Claude, now we can build our perfume factory.

CAPRICE: I'll revolutionize the theater with smell-o-drama. Opera with an orchestra of atomizers. For each emotion . . . a different perfume!

FEINSCHMECKER: *(Getting more and more flamboyant)* And I'm going to change my name. I'm sick of Feinschmecker. It's German. *Fein* means "good." *Schmeck* means "taste." A Feinschmecker is a person with good taste, a connosewer. *(Doubtfully)* Somehow it sounds better in French. But I can't very well call myself Baron Connosewer, could I? From now on I want to be called Marcel, your cosmetician. A man who lives for one thing only . . . *(Runs out screaming)* Makeup!

CAPRICE: I'm a little worried about the Baron.

ADRIAN: He'll be all right. Some people overreact at first.

(Curtain.)

End of Act I

ACT II

Scene 1: FEINSCHMECKER, ZUNI.

FEINSCHMECKER: Zuni, dear, let me do your hair.

ZUNI: Leave me alone or I swear I'll shave my head.

FEINSCHMECKER: Nonsense! What you need is a little "height." I'll just tease it a little.

ZUNI: Ouch!

FEINSCHMECKER: Sorry, sweets, just combing out a knot.

ZUNI: You're not teasing my hair. You're tormenting it!

FEINSCHMECKER: How's about a wash and set? Or something really camp, like a frosting?

ZUNI: If there's one thing I cannot tolerate it's effeminacy in women.

FEINSCHMECKER: Can I give you a manicure? A pedicure? A facial?

ZUNI: You're torturing me.

FEINSCHMECKER: One must suffer to be beautiful.

ZUNI: Harry, that is exactly the conclusion I have come to. Pure beauty is pure suffering. And so I have abjured fashion.

FEINSCHMECKER: But powder, paint, and patching never fail to draw the eyes and tongues of men upon you.

ZUNI: Nothing is ever wanting to make one's ugliness remarkable.

FEINSCHMECKER: Shouldn't women endeavor to make themselves agreeable?

ZUNI: Not when it's impossible. Women should be withdrawn from dressing as addicts are from drugs. Sackcloth and modesty, ashes and silence, things that shadow and conceal; they should think of nothing else.

FEINSCHMECKER: Why this morbid mood? You need a little frivolity. You need a little Caprice.

ZUNI: *(Exploding)* Caprice? I never want to hear that word again! I have left the ranks of the Capricious. Number me among the Adamantines.

FEINSCHMECKER: There there, let me put your curls in order.

ZUNI: What on earth has gotten into you, Harry? You used to be the enemy of fashion.

FEINSCHMECKER: Zuni, I've seen the light. I've found myself in fashion.

ZUNI: *(Shocked)* Harry Feinschmecker!

FEINSCHMECKER: Oh, that reminds me, Zuni. I've changed my name.

ZUNI: You've what?

FEINSCHMECKER: I've changed my name to Marcel.

ZUNI: Marcel?

FEINSCHMECKER: After the divine Proust. I wanted to take the name of Adrian . . . but it's been done. I positively *adore* Adrian.

ZUNI: *(Grudgingly)* He is physically beautiful. But he hasn't got brain one.

FEINSCHMECKER: I just *adore* him! He wears his clothes fashionably, and has a very pretty negligent air about him, very courtly, and much affected; he bows, and talks, and smiles so agreeably. I never saw anything so genteel.

ZUNI: Varnished over with good breeding and fashionable clothes many a blockhead makes a tolerable show.

FEINSCHMECKER: I wonder why you don't like him.

ZUNI: I believe he is the real reason why Caprice has banished me from fashion.

FEINSCHMECKER: *(Feigning surprise)* Banished you?

ZUNI: Oh Harry . . .

FEINSCHMECKER: Marcel.

ZUNI: Oh Marcel, please intercede for me.

FEINSCHMECKER: Why don't you just give up on Caprice and wear the clothes of Twyfford Adamant?

ZUNI: I may have lost my couturier. But I haven't lost my taste.

(Doorbell.)

FEINSCHMECKER: *(Eager to serve)* Shall I see who's at the door, my princess?

ZUNI: No, no! I'm unfit for company.

FEINSCHMECKER: *(At the door)* It's an emissary from the Chez Caprice. *(Exit)*

ZUNI: *(Her spirits brightening)* Is there word from Caprice?

Scene 2: ZUNI, TATA.

TATA: *(Entering urgently)* Baroness, I have something that I think you should know.

ZUNI: Have a stool, pigeon. I mean sit down.

TATA: Your husband has turned homosexual.

ZUNI: What?

TATA: His mind has been faggotized by fashion.

ZUNI: But surely this can't be a symptom of homosexuality. There are at least as many heterosexual faggots as there are homosexual ones. Tata.

TATA: Madame?

ZUNI: I hate myself, I look so ill today.

TATA: Hate the wicked cause of it, that base man Claude Caprice, who makes you torment and vex yourself continually.

ZUNI: He is to blame indeed.

TATA: To blame! He hasn't called, written, or seen you in two days.

ZUNI: I know he is a devil, but he has something of the angel yet undefaced in him, which makes him so charming and agreeable that I must love him, no matter how wicked he is.

TATA: But let us go where we cannot be overheard and devise a scheme whereby you may be reconciled.

(Exit ZUNI and TATA.)

Scene 3: ADAMANT, TATA.

ADAMANT: You have spied on Caprice and recorded his conversations?

TATA: I did. His ideas are as good as ours.

ADAMANT: And his profits will be ours too. *(Chuckles)* Eh eh eh!

TATA: *(Emptying his bag)* Sketches, photos, swatches, and scent testers. Twyfford, sniff this.

ADAMANT: Quite a haul. *(Accidentally squirts atomizer in his eye)* That son of a bitch, sending scent testers to twits with no sense!

TATA: They all flock to the Chez Caprice.

ADAMANT: Chez Caprice, bah! Sounds more like a restaurateur than a couturier.

TATA: His new line will be called "Jeunesse Eternelle."

ADAMANT: Eternal Youth? How does he plan to pull that off?

TATA: It's a kinky unisex number with everyone tricked out as Peter Pan.

ADAMANT: Sounds like he's losing his grip.

TATA: Methinks no one will ever buy it.

ADAMANT: The slaves of fashion will wear anything Caprice tells them to. Such is the power he holds over them.

TATA: The truth of your words was demonstrated earlier today. Caprice has broken with the Baroness Feinschmecker.

ADAMANT: Impossible.

TATA: It's true. He told her she could wear sackcloth and ashes for all he cared. And do you know? She did just that!

ADAMANT: *(Tapping the touch tone)* What a stroke of luck! I'll bring it out in ready-to-wear. *(Into the phone)* Hello, this is Twyfford Adamant of the Atelier Adamant. Send over thirty-three bolts of rayon acetate sackcloth and nine pounds of ashes. *(Shouting impatiently)* You heard what I said, SACKCLOTH AND ASHES! *(Hangs up the phone)*

TATA: It's a great idea, Twyfford. But do you think it will sell?

ADAMANT: Will it sell? The Baroness wears what Caprice says and all the slaves of fashion imitate the Baroness. This will be the greatest knockoff in the history of Seventh Avenue. *(Suddenly sinister)* Unemployment breeds malcontents, like moths in cloth make holes for want of wearing. Sackcloth and ashes, perfect for the repentant mood of America!

TATA: Vultures fatten best in hard weather. It's called inflation. *(Pats his belly)* Why not I in these dog days?

ADAMANT: Some men they say are possessed by the devil. The greater the man, the greater the devil. I have a scheme to induce despair in the dreamer.

TATA: Caprice?

ADAMANT: Who else? I have constructed a mechanical doll to look like the most beautiful boy in the world: Copelias!

(ADAMANT opens a cabinet and the mechanical doll, COPELIAS, enters with mechanical movements.)

Scene 4: ADAMANT, TATA, COPELIAS.

ADAMANT: Caprice will fall madly in love with the doll and turn away from Adrian, his inspiration. Without inspiration, Caprice will wither and die. The House of Caprice will fall.

TATA: Fiendish.

ADAMANT: And effective. This doll, shrouded in deathless beauty, will tell him anything he wants to hear. But try though he may, it will never give him one drop of human feeling. Caprice will learn in pain what Mallarmé meant when he said, "A kiss could kill if beauty were not already death." *(He opens a little door in the chest of the doll. He takes out a remote walkie-talkie unit and speaks into it)* Oh, Caprice, you are a genius.

COPELIAS: *(Expressionlessly)* Oh, Caprice, you are a genius.

ADAMANT: *(Into microphone as before)* I don't know what I'd do without you.

COPELIAS: *(As before)* I don't know what I'd do without you.

ADAMANT: Isn't that cunning?

TATA: Think you to seduce him then with words that have no meaning?

ADAMANT: Seducer is another word for blame-bearer. He who has the strength to bear the blame, will find the wildest virtue to be tame. Deliver this doll to Caprice and this theater ticket to Adrian.

TATA: Theater ticket?

ADAMANT: Yes, it is an opening night ticket to the Trocadero Gloxinia Ballet Company. Won't Adrian be surprised to find himself alone in a box with me! Caprice will hear of it within an hour. I dare say some of the tendrils on his grapevine won't even wait for the intermission before rushing to the lobby to phone him. Caprice's jealousy will do the rest.

TATA: But Mr. Adamant, what about my pay?

ADAMANT: Here is a spoon of cocaine. Now keep quiet about all this. And if you need drugs, boy, or art, call me. *(Exit)*

(Comic pantomime between TATA and COPELIAS ends with the doll chasing TATA off.)

Scene 5: FEINSCHMECKER, BABUSHKA. *House of Caprice.*

FEINSCHMECKER: *(Enters with BABUSHKA and looks about him)* Things have certainly changed around here. The garden paths are strewn with charcoal, the ornamental pond edged with black basalt and filled with ink, even the shrubberies have been replanted with cypresses and pines. To think, this was once the gay House of Caprice.

Scene 6: FEINSCHMECKER, CAPRICE, COPELIAS, BABUSHKA *(in and out)*

(FEINSCHMECKER enters the dining room metamorphosed for the occasion. A long table center at right angles to the apron and covered with a black cloth. Baskets of violets and scabious. The candelabra shed an eerie green light. Funeral marches are heard being played by a hidden orchestra.)

CAPRICE: *(Rises and kisses FEINSCHMECKER on each cheek)* Marcel, my dear Marcel.

FEINSCHMECKER: Caprice, how like you to have dressed for dinner. I'm sorry to intrude. Are you expecting someone?

CAPRICE: No, I have no further expectations of *any* kind. Adrian is gone. *(Sinks into his chair at table)*

FEINSCHMECKER: Are you terribly lonely?

CAPRICE: We are always alone. When people leave us we notice it more, that's all. I hope you're hungry.

FEINSCHMECKER: *(Seating himself opposite* CAPRICE*)* I could find an appetite.

CAPRICE: Of course you could! What is life but appetite? Would you believe it? These days I love to get up in the morning. When I think of all the mornings I wasted in bed I could kick myself! Work, that's all one really has. One's work never deserts one. Turtle soup?

FEINSCHMECKER: *(Helping himself)* You've had many lovers.

CAPRICE: Yes, but it was always my desire that I loved. Not what was desired. Pass the caviar.

FEINSCHMECKER: *(Passing the caviar)* Sometimes in our love of humanity we embrace someone at random simply because we cannot embrace them all.

CAPRICE: But one must not tell *him* this.

FEINSCHMECKER: What's for dessert?

CAPRICE: Plum pudding, truffle jellies, chocolate creams, and mulberries.

FEINSCHMECKER: Caprice, I think you owe me an explanation. For dinner you served me game in licorice sauce. We drank the dark wines of Lemagne and Roussillon, of Teneclos, Valdepeñas, and Oporto. And now a nearly naked negress serves us coffee, walnut cordial, and stout. Black food, black drink, black decor, black help.

CAPRICE: Black, black, everything black!

FEINSCHMECKER: Is this what you call an homage to negritude?

CAPRICE: No, my dear Marcel, this is a funeral banquet for my recently deceased virility. Adrian went to the theater tonight with Twyfford Adamant.

FEINSCHMECKER: Adrian with Adamant? It can't be true.

CAPRICE: Some people are such hypocrites. They think it's bourgeois to be upset if they steal your lover. But they never speak to you again if you steal their cook.

FEINSCHMECKER: So often it's the same person.

CAPRICE: Good cooks are much rarer than good lovers.

FEINSCHMECKER: What is it that you love about Adrian?

CAPRICE: No matter what perfume essence I chose to wear each day when I arose, the scent he had elected to wear never clashed, never jangled. And we never even spoke of it. Now Copelias is my only consolation.

FEINSCHMECKER: Can you copulate with Copelias?

CAPRICE: Yes, but what's even better, he always tells me exactly what I want to hear. Watch this. *(Into the microphone of the automaton)* Caprice, you are the ultimate.

COPELIAS: Caprice you are the ultimate.

CAPRICE: The ne plus ultra . . .

COPELIAS: The ne plus ultra . . .

CAPRICE: The haute couture du jour.

COPELIAS: The haute couture du jour.

CAPRICE: Well, what do you think of him?

FEINSCHMECKER: He's like a blank sheet of paper waiting to be written on.

CAPRICE: That's it! A perfect definition of beauty. A certain blankness.

FEINSCHMECKER: I'm jealous.

CAPRICE: Shhh. Can't you see the boy's madly in love with me?

COPELIAS: Your pinstripes and farthingales, your furbelows and codpieces, your darts and cuffs, your sweat shields and shoulder pads, your tufted muff and spats . . .

CAPRICE: *(Suddenly turning off the automaton)* That's Adrian now. Go quickly. I'm going to have it out with him.
FEINSCHMECKER: Do you think that's wise?
CAPRICE: Never mind, go!

(Exit FEINSCHMECKER.*)*

Scene 7: CAPRICE, ADRIAN, COPELIAS.

*(*CAPRICE *snaps off the light and sits in the dark waiting for* ADRIAN *who tiptoes in.)*

CAPRICE: Did you go to the theater?
ADRIAN: Yes.
CAPRICE: How was the piece?
ADRIAN: It failed as a fiasco. But it succeeded as a bore.
CAPRICE: Who were you with?
ADRIAN: I went alone.
CAPRICE: *(Flaring up)* Don't lie to me! You went with Twyfford Adamant!
ADRIAN: *(Shocked)* How could you?
CAPRICE: I bribed the attendant at the Turkish baths. She told me everything.
ADRIAN: Bribe them and they'll tell you anything you want to hear.
CAPRICE: *(Raving)* I molded you. I nurtured you. There isn't a gesture you make that I didn't teach you. *(Waves a limp wrist)*
ADRIAN: *(Trying to explain)* Someone sent me a complimentary ticket to the ballet. *(Unconsciously repeats Caprice's gesture on "ballet."* CAPRICE *winces at the sight of* ADRIAN *making this gesture.* ADRIAN *doesn't notice this business)* You were working late gathering the organza. I had nothing better to do so I attended. How was I to know that my seat would be in a box with Twyfford Adamant?
CAPRICE: A likely story.
ADRIAN: Oh, Claude, don't let's ask for the moon. We have the stars. I admit you taught me everything I know.
CAPRICE: Yes, Adrian, I taught you everything you know. But I did not teach you everything I know. *(Raving again)* And with Twyfford Adamant, that little nobody! Why I knew him when he was sewing undergarments!
ADRIAN: *(Simply)* I love you.
CAPRICE: *(Loud and mirthless)* Ha!
ADRIAN: *(Not to be outdone)* Ha! Ha!
CAPRICE: Ha! Ha! Ha!
ADRIAN: Ha! Ha! Ha! Ha!
CAPRICE: Ha! Ha! HA!!! Ha! Ha!
ADRIAN: That does it. I'm leaving. Good-bye.
CAPRICE: Oh God, I feel like Tancred and Clorinda in *Jerusalem Delivered.* Destiny had marked him out, ever unwittingly, to injure what he loved beyond all else.
ADRIAN: There's no need to drag mother image by the hair or the feet down the worm-eaten staircase of terrified syntax.
CAPRICE: Ingrate! When I think of the money I spent to get your name in the papers! I was like a mother to you.
ADRIAN: *(Pulls out a pistol and points it to his forehead)* I'll kill myself like Werther!
CAPRICE: *(Desperately)* No, Adrian, don't do it! *(The pistol goes off and drops a flag*

that says, "Bang!") A fake gun? Of all the cheap tricks to get my sympathy! *(Laughs mercilessly)*

ADRIAN: You never pay any attention to me anymore. All you do is play with that mechanical doll. Why, you're in love with a machine!

CAPRICE: *(Indicating* COPELIAS*)* This machine happens to be a perfectly honed instrument. Not like your body—touched with catabolism.

ADRIAN: *(Horrified)* What's catabolism?

CAPRICE: It's when the organism has reached the peak of its beauty and begins to decay.

ADRIAN: I prefer a body touched with catabolism.

CAPRICE: To each his own.

ADRIAN: Why are you jealous? I don't understand it. After all we've been through together you still don't trust me. Do you want my love or don't you?

CAPRICE: Yes, Adrian, I want your love.

ADRIAN: Then take me. I'm real. Here I am standing before you in flesh and blood. Better than your worthless fantasy.

CAPRICE: How dare you insult my fantasy? I am an artist. My fantasy is worth two of you.

ADRIAN: *(With deadly aim)* Then I love Twyfford Adamant's designs. I do. *(Then screams irrationally)* I love them! I love them! I love them!

CAPRICE: Get out. *(*ADRIAN *starts to go)* Adrian, where are you going? To Twyfford?

ADRIAN: *(Turning to* CAPRICE *at the door)* Suddenly it all makes sense.

CAPRICE: Forgive me.

ADRIAN: *(Wearily)* Yes, I forgive you. But if we go on like this, I'll spend the rest of my life forgiving you.

CAPRICE: *(Hysterically)* How can you do this to me on the eve of my big fashion show? Adrian, please stay.

ADRIAN: I'd sooner starve. Have my things sent to the Waldorf. *(Exits)*

Scene 8: CAPRICE, COPELIAS.

*(*CAPRICE *collapses at the feet of the mechanical doll and sobs.)*

COPELIAS: *(Repeats expressionlessly until the end of the scene)* Oh, Caprice, you are a genius. I don't know what I'd do without you. Oh, Caprice, you are a genius. I don't know what I'd do without you. Oh, Caprice, you are a genius. I don't know what I'd do without you. Oh, Caprice . . .

Scene 9: ADAMANT, TATA.

ADAMANT: How goes it with Caprice?

TATA: The gay couturier is too sad at heart to spring any extreme novelties.

ADAMANT: And the beautiful people?

TATA: As a protest against the high cost of living they don the livery of the working man, the working man who has contributed so greatly to the costli- ness of living. I have seen, in Monte Carlo, an individual dressed in sackcloth and ashes made of heavy silk and black diamonds. It cost more than a complete costume made by a leading tailor.

ADAMANT: Good, then it's already all the rage.

Scene 10: ZUNI, ADAMANT, TATA.

ZUNI: Twyfford, today is the last day of my banishment from fashion.

ADAMANT: Six months was a long time.

ZUNI: At midnight tonight I will cast off my sackcloth and ashes.

ADAMANT: *(Alarmed)* My God!

ZUNI: I've been looking less lovely lately.

ADAMANT: That's not true. I thought the sackcloth and ashes very becoming.

ZUNI: Guilt is never becoming. I want to punish Caprice and wear one of your designs to the fashion show tomorrow.

ADAMANT: One of my designs?

ZUNI: Yes. May I see them?

ADAMANT: *(Aside)* Zounds, I am undone!

ZUNI: I need a change from this hideous sackcloth and ashes.

ADAMANT: Then change a genuine absurdity for an imitation one. *(Shows her the mass-produced sackcloth and ashes)*

ZUNI: What's this? More sackcloth and ashes! *(Outraged)* So you were planning to make money out of my humiliation.

ADAMANT: Please, let me explain. . . .

ZUNI: That won't be necessary. I see it all clearly now. From now on I'm going to use fashion to get rid of fashion.

ADAMANT: Pourquoi, Zuni, pourquoi?

ZUNI: Pourquoi? Je suis fatigué. That's pourquoi!

TATA: Fatigué?

ZUNI:
    The fashion world is far too unkind,
    That six months out of sight
    is six months out of mind.
    You'll lie and you'll cheat and you'll play every angle,
    Just to come up with something newfangled!
Come Tata.

(ZUNI exits with TATA.)

Scene 11: ADAMANT, LA FLEUR.

ADAMANT: These are rash words. La Fleur!

LA FLEUR: Yes, Mr. Adamant?

ADAMANT: Now shall I test and reward your love for the Atelier Adamant. Where are those perfumed gloves which I sent to be poisoned? Have you done them? Speak; will every savor breed a pang of death?

LA FLEUR: Here they are, Twyfford. And he who smells but to the left one dies.

ADAMANT: And you remain resolute?

LA FLEUR: I am in whatsoever you command, 'til death.

ADAMANT: Thanks, my good friend, I will requite your love. Let these gloves be known as the Lavender Gloves of Fashion. Award them to the winning designer tomorrow.

LA FLEUR: And if you win?

ADAMANT: There's no chance of that now. The Baroness has switched her allegiance back to that queen, Caprice! He is that huge blemish in our eye that makes these upstart heresies in fashion.

LA FLEUR: Twyfford, you're rotten to the core.

ADAMANT: I am. It's very ecological. Take the gloves. Present them to him straight. Let what the baroness wears tomorrow determine his fate!

Scene 12: CAPRICE, BABUSHKA.

(CAPRICE is cutting out pieces of a pattern. BABUSHKA slaves at the sewing machine.)

CAPRICE: Keep sewing, Babushka. It's already five-fifteen. The fashion show is at eleven. Sew! Sew!

BABUSHKA: *(Desperately fighting fatigue)* More black coffee! Mr. Caprice, I don't think I can go on much longer. My eyes won't focus anymore.

CAPRICE: Take these doohickeys and sew them onto all those thingamajigs. I'll get your coffee.

BABUSHKA: I just keep thinking of a nice soft bed.

CAPRICE: Nonsense! Here's your coffee. Sew! Sew!

BABUSHKA: How can I sew and drink my coffee at the same time?

CAPRICE: Oh please, Babushka, don't fail me now. We've got to fight our human limitations. All I ask is for a chance to reveal my new Ballet du Macquillage line to the American woman. I need your help.

BABUSHKA: *(Doubtfully)* Wait a minute. I think I'm beginning to get a second wind. *(Resumes sewing furiously)*

CAPRICE: That's my baby, Babushka! *(Looks at the work already completed)* Oh, no! You've sewed the thingamajigs to the watchamacallits! You didn't even do the doohickeys.

BABUSHKA: I thought the doohickeys were already done.

CAPRICE: Never mind! Just sew! Sew!

(They sew on heroically for a few moments but finally exhaustion overtakes them and they fall asleep.)

Scene 13: CAPRICE, BABUSHKA, MARCEL, ADRIAN.

MARCEL: *(Entering stealthily)* Here they are, Adrian. Look, he's fallen asleep at the cutting table.

ADRIAN: And here's Babushka, asleep at the sewing machine. And the collection isn't ready.

MARCEL: Let's wake them.

ADRIAN: No, Marcel, don't wake him yet. Seeing him sleep so peacefully makes me almost forget how angry he is at me.

MARCEL: Yes, that's the only time there's any peace—when he's asleep.

ADRIAN: He's a monster.

MARCEL: Yes, he is. But a gay monster is worth more than a sentimental bore. *(Shaking* CAPRICE *gently)* Caprice? Caprice? Claude.

CAPRICE: *(Still half dreaming)* Swing tacks! Swing tacks! Mind those selvages. Babushka, leave a broad selvage.

ADRIAN: Wake up, dear. It's Adrian.

CAPRICE: *(Radiant when he sees* ADRIAN*)* Adrian! My lover, my mad young lover. My wild young lover! *(Throws his arms around* ADRIAN*'s neck)* I've been such a brute to you.

ADRIAN: It was all my fault.

CAPRICE: No, you were right. I was hypocritical. How could I be jealous and unfaithful at the same time?

ADRIAN: Forgive me . . .

CAPRICE: No, forgive me . . .

ADRIAN: No, forgive *me.*

CAPRICE: No me.

ADRIAN: No me.

CAPRICE: *(Kissing him)* Me!

ADRIAN: *(Falls to his knees dramatically)* Claude, I've been a beast. You know what beasts men are. Oh, let my heart live in your breast and let your nomad heart find a home in mine.

CAPRICE: You've thought of everything but a Gypsy violin.

ADRIAN: *(Calling to an unseen Gypsy violinist off)* Mischa!

(A Gypsy violinist is heard playing off.)

CAPRICE: Let's forget it ever happened.

MARCEL: Forget and forgive.

CAPRICE: Yes, Adrian, I forgive you all your infidelities.

ADRIAN: *My* infidelities? What about *your* infidelities?

CAPRICE: I always came back to you. Didn't I? No one is ever as good as you are.

ADRIAN: Do you really mean that?

CAPRICE: Of course I do. But if I never made it with anyone else I wouldn't know that. Would I?

ADRIAN: I suppose not.

CAPRICE: Each infidelity just makes me appreciate you more.

ADRIAN: And what about the team of athletes you keep stripped naked to fight after the manner of gladiators who advance like women making obscene gestures every time you open the door of your steam room?

CAPRICE: I've got to keep in training for my big love bouts with you.

ADRIAN: Forgive me, Claude, if I've ever done or said anything to hurt you.

CAPRICE: Forgive me, Adrian *(Aside)* for the times I've deserved it!

ADRIAN: Claude, you're just cut on the bias, that's all.

CAPRICE: Adrian, I need your help. Can we save the Ballet du Macquillage line before this morning's press conference?

ADRIAN: There isn't much time, but we can try. Enough, Mischa. *(The Gypsy violin stops.* CAPRICE, ADRIAN, MARCEL, *and* BABUSHKA *begin working on the collection with great gusto. Referring to the dress* BABUSHKA *is modeling)* I'd like to take this number out of the collection.

CAPRICE: As bad as that, huh?

ADRIAN: Worse. Do you mind?

CAPRICE: Babushka, let's leave that dress out of the show.
BABUSHKA: Right, chief.

Scene 14: ADAMANT, LA FLEUR.

ADAMANT: It's a disgrace! That's what it is. The fashion show is about to begin and Caprice isn't here yet.
LA FLEUR: Probably looking after a last-minute ruffle or nick-of-time rickrack.
ADAMANT: That man will be fashionably late for his own funeral. Have you got the gloves?
LA FLEUR: *(Nervously fingering the Lavender Gloves of Fashion)* I go to pieces every time I think of it. Poor little Caprice, killed by a couturier.
ADAMANT: *(Under his breath)* Get a grip on yourself, La Fleur. Someone may overhear us!
LA FLEUR: It's wicked. That's what it is, wicked!
ADAMANT: Please, La Fleur, spare me this righteous indignation. Why, I have enough on you to hang you.
LA FLEUR: *(Defiantly)* What could you say?
ADAMANT: What could I say? I might mention to the good sisters how you urinated in the holy water they sent to be scented and told them it was bitter rhodium sacred to Saint Jerome.
LA FLEUR: You wouldn't!
ADAMANT: Or how you have been known to distill your own rankest farts into frankincense for the Holy Father himself in Rome.
LA FLEUR: No, please!
ADAMANT: Or how you took apart the image of the Blessed Virgin and sealed it up with . . .
LA FLEUR: Enough! Don't expose my blasphemies.
ADAMANT: I'll expose more than that, La Fleur!

Scene 15: ZUNI, TATA, ADAMANT, LA FLEUR, FEINSCHMECKER.

ADAMANT: *(To* FEINSCHMECKER*)* The press have arrived and your wife, Mr. Feinschmecker.
FEINSCHMECKER: Wife? Bux! Titivilitium! There's no such thing in Nature. I confess, gentlemen, a man needs a cook, a laundress, and a house drudge. But why put all your eggs in one basket? Let the whore have her own domain. The man's a fool who would tie himself to one woman. Wife! The name dulls appetite. Give them what they want all day or they give you no piece at night.

(Enter the BARONESS *behind with* TATA*.)*

ADAMANT: Why did you marry one then, Baron?
FEINSCHMECKER: A pox! I married with a title, I. I was in love with that. I have not fucked my fury these forty weeks.
ADAMANT: Why not?
FEINSCHMECKER: She wears a wig that's made of dynel and stiff as paintbrush bristles.
ZUNI: O treacherous liar!
FEINSCHMECKER: A most vile face! Yet she spends me eight hundred dollars

a year in astringents and cotton balls. All her teeth were made in Chelsea, her eyebrows on Park Avenue, her hair in the Village. Every part of town owns a piece of her.

ZUNI: O viper, mandrake!

FEINSCHMECKER: She takes herself apart when she goes to bed, into some twenty boxes; and about next day noon is put together again, like a great German clock: And so comes forth to ring a tedious alarm to the whole house and then is quiet again for an hour, but for her hindquarters which sound off at any time of day regardless. Have you understood me?

ZUNI: *(Falls upon him and beats him)* All too well, you stinkardly pig! Is my hair stiff?

FEINSCHMECKER: Ow, ow! Mercy! Mercy! My princess!

ZUNI: You'll sooner get a fart from a dead donkey than mercy from me.

FEINSCHMECKER: Help! Help!

ZUNI: Do I lack eyebrows? Answer me you bulldog! Have I no teeth? *(She bites him)*

FEINSCHMECKER: *(Screaming with pain)* No, I protest! Under correction . . .

ZUNI: Now that you are under correction, you protest. But you did not protest before correction, sir! Thou Judas, to offer to betray thy princess!

*(*FEINSCHMECKER *howls and runs out, pursued by the avenging* ZUNI.*)*

Scene 16: CAPRICE, LA FLEUR, ADAMANT.

CAPRICE: What's this?

ADAMANT: Paunch and Judas. All in good fun! Caprice, you're here already.

CAPRICE: How English of you to think I would be late. Are we ready to begin? Where's Marcel?

ADAMANT: I believe he left in the custody of his wife.

CAPRICE: *(Steps into the runway and addresses the company)* Welcome press photographers and slaves of fashion. Today my fantasies carry me away to the fashions of the future. I have lived the future in advance imaginatively. The Ballet du Macquillage line is definitely where fashion is going. The Unnatural Look. An era in which women will not wear makeup. They will become makeup. Women imprisoned in tubes of lipstick! Women smothered in boxes of powder! Women in the rouge pot! Women in mascara!

THE VOICE OF TALLULAH BANKHEAD: *(Intones endlessly)* Lipstick, powder, rouge, mascara. Lipstick, powder, rouge, mascara. *(Da capo)*

(Models dance on. ADRIAN *as lipstick;* MARCEL *as powder;* BABUSHKA *as rouge; and* LA FLEUR *as mascara.)*

ADAMANT: This is appalling. I knew his clothes were going to be ugly. But I never dreamed they would be this ugly! *(Then he mounts the runway and introduces his collection to the company)* Here it is, folks! Adamant's off-the-rack sackcloth and ashes. Getting back to basics. It's inspired! Brilliant! And so practical!! At last a simple uniform anyone can afford that needs little care and no ironing!

ADRIAN: O fickle public! Look, the crowd is turning to Twyfford Adamant for solutions to their individual fashion problems! Why, he's become the pope of fashion.

CAPRICE: Twyfford Adamant, a broken decadent, sinking down before the Christian cross. Am I the only couturier in America who shudders at this horrid spectacle? All my life, the only man I could respect was my enemy . . . now there is no one.

ADAMANT: *(Helping the slaves of fashion into the caterpillar of sackcloth, he places a thumbprint of ash on the forehead of each)* Shave your head. Have your ears pierced. Have your feet bound. Tattoo your buttocks. Remove one breast. Apply hot wax and tweezers.

Scene 17: ZUNI, COMPANY.

ZUNI: Ladies and gentlemen, this afternoon it is my privilege to award the coveted Lavender Gloves of Fashion to the designer of the year. This award must needs be given not to the designer who exceeds his time and not to the designer who puts his own egocentric stamp on his time. But rather this award must go to the designer who best exemplifies his time. May I have the envelope please? *(Someone hands the envelope to ZUNI)* This year, ladies and gentlemen, the Lavender Gloves of Fashion go to Nicole Newfangle for the Je Suis Fatigué line! *(She pulls off her cloak of sackcloth and ashes to reveal her government-issue fatigues complete with combat boots and cap)*

CAPRICE: Nicole Newfangle?

ADAMANT: *(Pointing at ZUNI, dumbfounded)* Fatigues! She's wearing fatigues!

CAPRICE: *(Pointing to NICOLE NEWFANGLE)* Isn't that Tata in drag?

(It is indeed TATA who steps up to receive the award.)

TATA: Thank you, Zuni. And I would like to say that I am deeply grateful for this *(Dangles gloves),* the highest award that the fashion world has to bestow, because I really and truly deserve it. This is a great tribute to all the tastemakers who prove by their fairness of judgment that worthiness is sometimes rewarded. But this award does not belong to me alone. It belongs also to the many many other people behind the scenes whose hard work and self-sacrifice go into making what the French call chic. And above all I would like to thank a man without whose influence my own talent could not have grown and flowered. I was his right-hand man through my apprenticeship to his salon. I would like to repay his trust and encouragement now by giving the right glove of fashion to my mentor and my friend . . . Claude Caprice.

(CAPRICE rises modestly and goes up to the runway to receive the glove.)

CAPRICE: Tata! So, you were the fashion spy who was selling my ideas to Adamant, and I never suspected!

TATA: There were clues, you just didn't pick them up, that's all.

CAPRICE: Clues?

TATA: My name Tata.

CAPRICE: Tata?

TATA: Ta stands for Twyfford Adamant. Why, those initials are all over everything he designs. And next I want to give the left glove of fashion to a man whose left hand is the only gauche thing about him . . . Twyfford Adamant.

ADAMANT: *(Solemnly mounts the platform)* I feel that things being what they are I have no choice but to accept. *(Begins to put on the glove)*

LA FLEUR: *(Shrieks out)* No! Don't do it!

TATA: For heaven sake, La Fleur, what's gotten into you?

LA FLEUR: That glove is poisoned!

ADAMANT: *(Smelling the glove)* It is too late. *(Falls)*

TATA: But who could have poisoned it?

ADAMANT: Dead by my own hand.

CAPRICE: *(Running to* ADAMANT'*s side)* Twyff, don't leave me. I need you. I need an adversary.

TATA: He'll be stiff competition after this!

ADAMANT: What's this? Moved to tears? Caprice, will you never learn? *(Turns his head, whispers something in* TATA'*s ear, and dies)*

SONG:

Count no artist great till he be dead
Assurance against all recanters.
Sometimes you'll find that you disgrace,
The very things that you embrace.
Count no artist great till he be dead.
Ladies, please, give up your passions,
What once were crimes are now but fashions.

Scene 18: TATA, ALTHEA GORDON.

(In a large armchair sits the aged TATA *smoking a cigar, fondling a fresh tuberose, waving a silk handkerchief, and sipping a tequila martini. On a pouf to his right sits an* INTERVIEWER *with a cassette tape recorder. She holds out the microphone towards* TATA *like a weapon.)*

GORDON: Let me make sure the machine is on. *(Checks the machine, then into the microphone)* Althea Gordon interviewing Stella Artois.

(Stella Artois is TATA.*)*

TATA: I'm terrified of machines.

MACHINE: Althea Gordon interviewing Stella Artois. I'm terrified of machines.

GORDON: It works. Ms. Artois, this year your extensive diaries are being published in thirty-six leatherbound volumes. This is quite an achievement. How do you feel about it?

TATA: I feel as though I've outlived myself.

GORDON: Why the title, *My Ovaries Complete?*

TATA: I stank at French.

GORDON: Are we to surmise from the title that there won't be any more additions to your diary?

TATA: That is correct. Keeping a diary was always a vice with me.

GORDON: What are your plans for the future?

TATA: To crawl unburdened toward death.

GORDON: In your diaries you describe many affairs with the greatest women of your day. Does this mean that your marriage to Claude Caprice was a marriage of convenience?

TATA: There was never anything convenient about Caprice. He was a man to offend the practical.

GORDON: Cocteau postulated that genius was the highest development of the practical. Does this mean that Caprice was not a genius?

TATA: Anyone with a knack for anything is a genius today. Caprice eschewed the herd of geniuses. He was an antigenius. He was an arrow of aspiration shot by humanity at some unknown target . . . he was . . . he was . . . a very good friend of mine.

GORDON: Your criticism of his dying words has caused a scandal in that strange artistic half-world where you generated the most brilliant journals since Madame de Sévigné. Would you care to explain?

TATA: My life with Caprice makes a very long anecdote. But you must bear in mind from the very beginning that Caprice was a lucky man . . . the luckiest man I have ever met . . . perhaps the luckiest man who ever lived. . . .

Scene 19: CAPRICE, THREE CHILDREN.

FIRST CHILD: What's wrong with the world?

CAPRICE: It's dull, child, drab, terribly banal. It lacks . . . it lacks . . .

SECOND CHILD: He's searching for the right word.

CAPRICE: Je ne sais quoi. That's what it lacks. Je ne sais quoi!

SECOND CHILD: I think he's found it.

CAPRICE: Zephir! No whispering! Ah, where was I? You children are impossible today.

THIRD CHILD: On the contrary, we are entirely possible.

FIRST CHILD: We are nothing more than possibilities.

CAPRICE: Why won't you learn your lesson?

THE THREE: What is the lesson?

CAPRICE: *(Beating them with flowers)* Beauty! Beauty! Beauty! *(He puts on the dunce cap and sits in the corner.)*

THIRD CHILD: Caprice, you're trying too hard.

CAPRICE: The dunce cap, symbol of my degradation.

THIRD CHILD: On the contrary, the conical shape serves as an energy condenser. You're apt to get the point at any moment. But first you must give up.

CAPRICE: *(Turning and looking at his canvas)* The drawing drew itself!

THE THREE: See?

CAPRICE: Ah, now I see. How simple.

THIRD CHILD: In the future cultivate simplemindedness.

CAPRICE: I have an idea! An inspiration. Yes, Beatrice?

SECOND CHILD: May I please be excused?

CAPRICE: Certainly. (BEATRICE *exits*) Here I have a black silk scarf. Here a handful of white dots. Imagine this: the white dots on the black field. But how do I get them on there?

FIRST CHILD: A difficult problem.

THIRD CHILD: Almost insoluble.

FIRST CHILD: Give it up. It's a bad job.

(CAPRICE throws the dots up in the air and waves the black silk scarf with a gesture of despair. Suddenly the dots stick to the scarf and it turns polka-dot. The sound of a polka is heard in the distance. BEATRICE enters.)

CAPRICE: Look at this, the world's first polka dots! The minute I give up . . . the minute I stop trying . . . Everything begins to happen. . . .

BEATRICE: Such is human progress.

CAPRICE: Of course, you know everything. Don't you?

BEATRICE: We were born knowing everything.

CAPRICE: And education is the process of forgetting. *(He wanders off into the fog)*

FIRST CHILD: Forgetting is the process of healing.

THIRD CHILD: Death is just incurable amnesia.

THE THREE: *(Singing together)*

> The master's gone alone
> Herb picking somewhere on the mount
> Mists are his companions
> Whereabouts unknown.

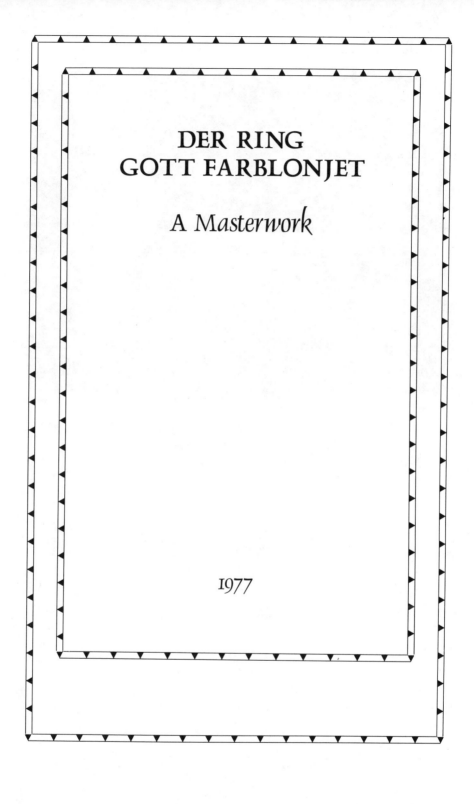

DER RING
GOTT FARBLONJET

A Masterwork

1977

Richard Currie, Ethyl Eichelberger & Black-Eyed Susan
in *Der Ring Gott Farblonjet* (Leandro Katz)

Cast of Characters

Gods	*Goddesses*	*Rheinmaidens*
TWOTON	FRICKA	FLOSSHILDE
DUNDERHEAD	FREIA	WOGLINDE
FROH	EARTHA	WELGUNDE
LOGE		

Giants	*Nihilumpen*	*Valkyries*
FASDOLT	ALVERRÜCK	BRUNNHILDA
FAFNER	NINNY	HELMVIGE
		GERHILDA
Volsungs	*Gibichungen*	ORTLINDA
SIEGMUND	HAGEN	SIEGRUNA
SIEGLINDA	GUNTHUR	ROSSWEISSA
SIEGFRIED	GUTRUNA	GRIMGERDA
		SCHWERTLEITA
		VALTRAUTA

3 NORNS
HUNDING, *a Gesundheit*
WOOD-BIRD
VASSALS
HEATHEN ONLOOKERS

Act I.	Act II.	Act III.	Act IV.
TWOTON	SIEGMUND	SIEGFRIED	3 NORNS
DUNDERHEAD	HUNDING	NINNY	SIEGFRIED
FROH	TWOTON	TWOTON	BRUNNHILDA
LOGE	SIEGLINDA	ALVERRÜCK	GUNTHUR
FASDOLT	FRICKA	FAFNER	GUTRUNA
FAFNER	BRUNNHILDA	EARTHA	HAGEN
ALVERRÜCK	HELMVIGE	WOOD-BIRD	VALTRAUTA
NINNY	GERHILDA	BRUNNHILDA	ALVERRÜCK
FRICKA	ORTLINDA		WELGUNDE
FREIA	SIEGRUNA		WOGLINDE
EARTHA	ROSSWEISSA		FLOSSHILDE
WOGLINDE	GRIMGERDA		VASSALS
WELGUNDE	SCHWERTLEITA		HEATHEN
FLOSSHILDE	VALTRAUTA		ONLOOKERS

ACT I. DAS RHEINGOLD

Scene 1: *In the depths of the Rhein.*

(Three skeevie pansettes with fishtails swim about the Rheingold playing flirty winkies with themselves.)

WOGLINDE: Weia! Water! Waga! Waves of wasser! Waves of wasser! Waga-laweia! Wallalla weiala weia!

WELGUNDE: Woglinde, Woglinde, where is Flosshilde? It's her turn to guard the gold!

FLOSSHILDE: It's Woglinde's turn, Welgunde.

WOGLINDE: Nein, it's Welgunde's turn, Flosshilde!

WELGUNDE: Genug! Du gibst mir ein schmerz in kooz. Garden sie das Gold your selbst! Ich will nicht das Gold garden! Ich gardet das Gold zu lang already!

FLOSSHILDE: Looken who's lookin' at uns. Es ist das uglische Dwarf, Alverrück!

WELGUNDE: Er kommt nicht das wasser zu trinken!

ALVERRÜCK: I came some tuschies zu pinchen.

WOGLINDE: Fie!

WELGUNDE: Foh!

FLOSSHILDE: Faugh! Horny beast!

WOGLINDE: Guard the Gold. Father warned us not to talk to strangers.

ALVERRÜCK: Hey you!

FLOSSHILDE: How dare you "Hey you!" me!

ALVERRÜCK: Wrap your scaly little arms around me.

WELGUNDE: He didn't come to steal the Gold. Can't you see? The hairy little monster is in love.

THE THREE RHEINMAIDENS: Ha ha ha ha ha ha!

ALVERRÜCK: Ah, poisson farouche! Slither me a wet one or I'll catch you by the tail.

WELGUNDE: Hairy hump!

WOGLINDE: Nihilump!

ALVERRÜCK: Bony fisch!

FLOSSHILDE: *(Aside)* Sisters, let's play with him and lead him on!

WELGUNDE: Come to me, my sexy little toad.

ALVERRÜCK: Where?

WELGUNDE: *(Swimming out of his reach)* Over here.

FLOSSHILDE: No, over here.

WOGLINDE: No, down here. *(They swim circles around him)*

ALVERRÜCK: *(Grabbing first for one then for another)* I can't breathe underwater!

THE THREE RHEINMAIDENS: Ha ha ha ha ha ha!

ALVERRÜCK: Malicious laughter! Then you were only mocking me!

(A golden light spreads through the water.)

THE THREE RHEINMAIDENS: Golden madrugada, das Gold! Das Gold! Through the golden madrugada scheint das Gold! Rheingold! Rheingold! Heijaheia heijeia! Wallalallalala leiajahei!

ALVERRÜCK: What is it that glitters and gleams so?

WOGLINDE: Has the troll never heard of the Rheingold?

WELGUNDE: We swim in its glow.

FLOSSHILDE: We sing in its schein!

THE THREE RHEINMAIDENS: Rheingold! Rheingold! Wallalaweia!

ALVERRÜCK: Since you won't let me play with you. The golden light is no fun to me.

WOGLINDE: The hideous dwarf would not scorn the Gold if he knew of its wonderful secret!

WELGUNDE: He who forges a ring from the Rheingold will win all power over the world and its people.

FLOSSHILDE: That's why Father told us to guard it. He fears someone may rob the river.

WELGUNDE: Do you know, funny little subhuman, who alone can forge the ring?

WOGLINDE: Only he who forswears love forever can attain to this great power.

WELGUNDE: So that's why we play so carelessly.

WOGLINDE: We know no one will ever steal the gold.

FLOSSHILDE: Because we know that every living creature craves love. And no one will ever dare forswear it.

WELGUNDE: Least of all this little lecher who burns with desire.

WOGLINDE: Least of all the lascivious love, a slave who dies of desire!

THE THREE RHEINMAIDENS: Ha ha ha ha ha ha!

ALVERRÜCK: Nobody loves me anyway! I may as well rule the world. Hear me, you waters. I hereby curse and forswear love forever! *(Seizes the Gold)*

THE THREE RHEINMAIDENS: The gnome has gone mad! Stop, thief!

FLOSSHILDE: Save the Gold!

THE THREE RHEINMAIDENS: Oi veh! Oi veh!

(The entire scene is plunged into darkness.)

Scene 2

(The waves giftoff themselves to scrimmist sheerest parting until all is clear, a clearing on a mountain's height. Lustering glistering temples pinnacles of casteln hinterground. TWOTON *and* FRICKA *lie asleep in a floral dell.)*

FRICKA: Wake up, Twoton! Awake!

TWOTON: *(Dreamentraumish)* Ah, the dreaming of glittzering glistering towers of manhood. Manhood of renown!

FRICKA: He dreams of fame! Wake up from rosy dreams to gray reality!

TWOTON: *(Awakes, rubs his eyes, and regards the castle)* Look, Fricka, it's finished! Wallhalla, castle and stronghold of the Gotts! My dream has come true.

FRICKA: Your dream is about to turn into a nightmare. These castles in the air must be paid for. The mortgage is due on Wallhalla. And remember what you promised to pay!

TWOTON: Never mind the price.

FRICKA: Never mind my sister whom you promised to those giants, Fafner and Fasdolt.

TWOTON: You longed for a home and security.

FRICKA: To keep you with me! To keep you home at night!

TWOTON: No real man wants to be tied down.

FRICKA: And so you willingly offer my sister as payment for your pretension.

TWOTON: Am I not a Gott? You are jealous and possessive, Fricka. I gambled an eye for you and you don't believe in luck! I admit I'm a bit of a womanizer, but piss, shit, cock, and duty! I wouldn't abandon Freia! Not by ninnies knees! Nosiree!

FRICKA: Then protect her now. Here she comes running and weeping.

FREIA: Help me, Twoton! Help me, Fricka! Fricka Twoton Fricka! Those foul-smelling giants Fafner and Fasdolt are coming from yonder mountain.

FRICKA: Protect her, Twoton. Without the goddess of youth and beauty the Gotts will grow old and die like the beautiful people.

TWOTON: The Gotts are not alone and defenseless. Where is Dunderhead with a thunderhead? Pyro with fire or Tutti-frutti with the rain, sun, and fruits!?

FRICKA: Do you think you can buy off those giants with a basket of fruit!? In high Godhome you must have no weaknesses, no sympathy for anyone. Leave love to the stupid toiling Giants as a bribe to keep them working. Beasts of burden, slaves of toil may taste such sweetness but Godhead, nicht!

TWOTON: Where is Logic, the liar? He promised to get me out of this.

FRICKA: Why shouldn't the lie fail Twoton since that is his nature?

(Enter the Giants FAFNER *and* FASDOLT.*)*

FREIA: *(Running in)* A roarer! A roarer! Them Giants is after me!

TWOTON: Isim Giants a rearly agin yer and after you running in the do be after?

FAFNER and FASDOLT: Have after her! Have after!

FRICKA: Twoton, raise your seven wrothschields against 'em!

TWOTON: Back bassuckers, back!

FAFNER and FASDOLT: Back, youstead! We come krieging the funk from your patrimony.

TWOTON: *(Aside)* Parsimony!

FAFNER: While soft sleep sealed your eigenen augen your eyes we toiled. Don't tease us now. Your castle, Godhome, stands on high. Stone upon stone, stone under stone, stone beyond stone forever. There she stands: doors and rooms, halls and lintels, mullions and rooks, roof and walls in shimmering light of day—bright in the light of day! Now pay what you promised to pay.

TWOTON: What is the price?

FASDOLT: *(Sweetly)* Freia aleine die Rheine, die feine, die kleine, die eine.

TWOTON: Your heinie! You jest. Freia is not up for sale.

FASDOLT: Ha! What's this? A trick? *(In shock and despair)* Oh, no! Faf, we've been tricked by our Gods!

FAFNER: Our Gods are false!

FASDOLT: O Wise One, Twoton, when the Gods do not uphold contracts, no one else will. A stupid Giant tells you this O Great One. Take it from me!

TWOTON: How sly you are to take seriously what was meant as a joke. You wouldn't know what to do with such a beauty as Freia.

FASDOLT: Don't add insult to injury. While you dreamed of cold castles of stone we clods worked like brutes to earn us a woman's warmth. Woman, the only beauty possible to us poor devils. And you say all was a joke.

FAFNER: Freia alone can grow the apples of eternal youth. Without these apples the Gods will grow old and die. I say let's carry her off.

FREIA: Help me! Help me! Don't let them take me! Don't let them put their hot sweaty hands on me!

DUNDERHEAD: I'll bash in a few Giants' heads with my hammer's blows.

TWOTON: *(Placing his spear between* DUNDERHEAD *and the Giants)* No violence. This bargain is written in runes on Twoton's own spear!

(Enter LOGE.*)*

TWOTON: Loge, at last! Where were you when I needed you? You were going to get me out of this.

LOGE: So I was. But search though I may throughout the world, I couldn't find anything that would make man give up woman. No man would do it, no man but one. Alverrück, hideous dwarf of the race of Nihilumpen, has stolen the Gold and forsworn love. If this Gold is fashioned into a ring he could rule the world!

FAFNER and FASDOLT: Rule the world!

LOGE: Yes, rule the whole dung heap. Just forswear love and forge a ring.

TWOTON: Rule the world? I would like to rule the world.

LOGE: Then forswear love.

TWOTON: No, never!

LOGE: No, not you. Least of all you. A man in love can't rule himself, let alone the world. The Rheinmaidens asked me to ask you to get it back for them. . . . Disaster will ensue if the world falls into the hands of the masochists.

FRICKA: Rule the world, did you say? A woman who ruled the world might keep her husband home at night.

LOGE: It is too late, all of you. Alverrück has already forged the ring.

(The Giants confer apart then address TWOTON.*)*

FAFNER and FASDOLT: We accept the bribe. Deliver this Gold to us by nightfall and we will accept it as ransom for Freia. Until then, we hold her hostage.

(The Giants drag FREIA *shrieking from the stage. Suddenly before our very eyes the Gods begin to grow old.)*

TWOTON: My God—I mean I'm God! Look what's happening to us! My beard's turned gray!

DUNDERHEAD: My hammer falls.

FROH: My heart falters.

FRICKA: *(Alarmed)* We're aging!

LOGE: I know what's wrong. We haven't eaten Freia's apples yet today. We're growing old. Without the golden apples we lose our youth . . . our eternal youth.

FRICKA: *(Panicky)* Twoton, do something! It's your fault. You got us into this with your wheeling and dealing!

TWOTON: For God's sake don't nag me, woman. I did it for you. Schlack! Schlack! Schlack!

FRICKA: Schlemiel!

TWOTON: Schlemasel!

FRICKA: Schlepp!

TWOTON: Schloomp!

FRICKA: Schlub!

TWOTON: Schmo!

FRICKA: Schnook!

TWOTON: Schnorrer!

FRICKA: Schnozzle!

TWOTON: So now it's schnozzle! How could you insult my nose? That's hitting below the belt. I'll descend through the thicker lower atmosphere to Nibblehome where Alverrück's race the lowly Nihilumpen dwell.

FRICKA: You, ride a subway? This must be a depression we're in.

TWOTON: To get the Gold I must degrade myself.

LOGE: *(Feeling his pulse)* My pulse is slowing down.

FRICKA: Old wrinkles crack my brow.

FROH: Quickly, Twoton, do something . . . our youth . . . help us, save us. We're growing old.

(They age before our very eyes.)

TWOTON: Forward to rescue Freia! To Nibblehome!

LOGE: Follow me! *(Leaps down through a crevice. Fog rises after him)*

TWOTON:
　　Youth is hot
　　Old age is cold
　　The old will grow young,
　　When I've stolen the Gold. *(Follows* LOGE*)*

(Fog again.)

DUNDERHEAD: Farewell Twoton!

FROH: Good luck! Good luck!

FRICKA: Be careful, husband. And hurry home to your worried wife!

(Fog fills the stage. The sound of hammers on anvils is heard and then fades in the distance. The fog parts revealing a cavern with stalactites and stalagmites. Tunnels.)

Scene 3: *Nibblehome—Nowhere. Subterranean cavern.*

ALVERRÜCK: He he! He he! Kam hier you craftische zwergende Dwarf! Tapfer gezwickt sollst du mir sein. *(Pinches him)* Where is the golden ring I ordered you to make? Is it finished?

NINNY: Ohe! Ohe! Ow! Ow! Let go of my ear! Cease and desist from this pitiless pinching! Please, I moiled and toiled from morn to midnight.

ALVERRÜCK: Is it finally finished?

NINNY: It's done.

ALVERRÜCK: Show it to me.

*(*NINNY *shows him the ring.)*

ALVERRÜCK: *(Taking it and hastily putting it on his hand)* Ahhhhh! And the helmet?

*(*NINNY *gives him the helmet.)*

ALVERRÜCK: *(Puts the helmet on)* The helmet fits my head. Will the spell work too? Like night and fog, a person of no appearance! *(He becomes invisible)* Can you see me?

NINNY: Where are you? I can't see you.

ALVERRÜCK: *(Pummeling him)* Feel me, then, lazy shit!

NINNY: *(Writhes under the blows)* Ohe! Ohe! Oh! Oh! Oh!

ALVERRÜCK: Ha ha ha ha ha ha! Thanks, little shit. Your work has passed the test. Ho ho! Ho ho! Bow down, Nihilumpen, bow down. Now Alverrück wears the crown. You work for me although I am invisible. When you least expect it I am watching. You are my slaves forever! Ho ho! Ho ho! Listen for him. Live in fear. When you least expect him, he'll appear. For Alverrück, king of Nihilumpen, is here. *(Fades from sight in a vaporous fog)*

(NINNY cowers between the rocks in fear and anguish. TWOTON and LOGE are lowered onto the stage ex machina.)

LOGE: Here's Nibblehome. Home sweet Nibblehome deep in the bowels of the earth! *(Fart sound effect)* In tunnels and caves the lowly laboring lazy louts the lascivious Nihilumpen dwell. Far from the light of day. See, there's a glint through the vapor.

NINNY: *(Pained)* Oik, oi oi oi ow!

TWOTON: Who's groaning so loudly?

LOGE: What freak is this, whimpering in the darkness?

NINNY: Ohe! Ohe! Oh! Oh!

LOGE: Heih ho, Ninny, bruise water dwarf! What buzza and touzery? Eh?

NINNY: Leave me in peace!

LOGE: Don't cry over spilt milk! Help is on the way.

NINNY: Ich bin all smacked up! My brother has made me his slave.

LOGE: What gave him the right to command?

NINNY: Alverrück made a magic ring of gold. With its magic spell he enslaves the race of Nihilumpen. We used to make things of beauty. Jewelry for women . . . toys for our kids. We laughed as we worked. Now this bastard makes us toil in mines underground. The gold leads him to more gold and more gold and more! We pile up the treasure for him alone.

LOGE: Perhaps he found your idleness provoking.

NINNY: Ah, how I'd like to get the ring I forged. I'd tumble the bully and make him *my* slave.

LOGE: Have you tried?

NINNY: *(Sobbing)* How can I? The tarnhelm gives him power to change into whatever shape he pleases. He made himself invisible and beat me. Oi! Oi! Oi! That's the thanks I get. Oh, what a fool I've been.

LOGE: *(Aside to TWOTON)* This isn't going to be easy. The oppressed wish to be oppressors, nothing more. *(To NINNY)* You may get even with him yet.

NINNY: *(Looking at the Gods more closely)* But what manner of beings are you that ask me these questions?

LOGE: Friends come to free the Nihilumpen folk.

NINNY: Look out! Here comes Alverrück! *(Runs back and forth with fear, looking for someplace to hide)*

TWOTON: We'll speak to him. *(Sits)*

(ALVERRÜCK enters driving a band of enslaved Nihilumpen with a whip. They bear in treasure and pile it up as ALVERRÜCK heaps abuse on them.)

ALVERRÜCK: Heave ho! Work, you lazy scum! He! He! Ho! Ho! Get the lead out! Pile up that gold! *(Sees TWOTON and LOGE)* What's this? Who let these strangers in? *(Threatens Nihilumpen with the whip)* Answer me! Confess or get a whipping. Ninny, you know the rules: No talking with strangers.

NINNY: *(Trembling with fear)* I didn't do anything.

ALVERRÜCK: *(Menacing the Nihilumpen bystanders)* All right, back to work, all of you! *(Nihilumpen murmur and mumble discontentedly.)* Back, slaves! Dare you defy me? *(Kisses the ring and holds it out toward them)*

(NINNY and the Nihilumpen scream and disperse. Exeunt.)

ALVERRÜCK: What brings you strangers to Nihilhome?

TWOTON: We've heard tales of its wonders. Gawdy Nibblehome is gorgeous they say. We came to see for ourselves.

ALVERRÜCK: Greed and envy brought you here, I'd guess. You smelt gold.

LOGE: You know me, gnome. God of fire, I light your forge! Where would you be without me? Is this the welcome I get? Consider us friends.

ALVERRÜCK: With friends like you I don't need enemies.

LOGE: You can trust me.

ALVERRÜCK: I can trust you to lie.

LOGE: Your newfound power has made you rude.

ALVERRÜCK: Good manners are for the weak. Look at my piles . . . of gold I mean.

LOGE: Enormous.

ALVERRÜCK: That's just the beginning. Today Nibblehome, tomorrow the world!

TWOTON: But what's the use of gold in Nibblehome where there's nothing to buy?

ALVERRÜCK:

Gold to husband
Gold to hide
Gold to hoard
Gold to heap

When I've hoarded, and hidden, and heaped enough gold, I'll rule the world!

TWOTON: How do you plan to do that?

ALVERRÜCK: You who laugh and love on high shall fall. The Nihilumpen you scorn shall rise and topple you. I've forsworn love. Someday all who live shall forswear it too. They'll live for gold alone. We'll buy your women and use them and then TO HELL WITH LOVE!

TWOTON: *(Horrified)* Back, vermin!

ALVERRÜCK: *(Drunk with power)* Beware the night of the Nihilumpen for their numbers shall rise by night into the light of day, and then the silent Nihilumpen will be heard!

LOGE: You wield your ring well. Your people tremble with fear. But what if some night while you sleep a thief should steal your ring, huh? What then?

ALVERRÜCK: I've already thought of that. My magic tarnhelm protects me from danger. When I wear it I can take whatever shape I will or make myself invisible. Then no one can harm me—not even Gotts like you!

LOGE: Really, do you expect us to believe this fairy tale?

ALVERRÜCK: Do you think I'm a liar like you?

LOGE: Seeing is believing.

ALVERRÜCK: I'll prove it, then. *(Puts the tarnhelm on his head)*
Slither and slink,
A giant skink.

(ALVERRÜCK is transformed into a giant snake)

LOGE: *(Pretending to be afraid)* Eeeek! I'm scared!

TWOTON: *(Laughing)* Bravo! Well done, Alverrück!

LOGE: Don't swallow me, snake. Spare my life.

ALVERRÜCK: *(Resuming his dwarfish form)* Ha! Ha! What do you think now?

LOGE: *(Fear in his voice)* Terrifying! But of course this kind of transformation is more the realm of the stage magician. A clever costume, mirrors, a puff of smoke. We've seen it all before!

ALVERRÜCK: What! Still unconvinced?

LOGE: What about turning into something tiny, or is that too difficult?

ALVERRÜCK: Difficult for you! Easy for me! How small do you want?

LOGE: A size that's good for hiding from enemies. The size of a toad.

ALVERRÜCK: There's nothing to it! *(Dons the tarnhelm again)*
   Tiny and warty,
   Make me a toad!
   (Transforms into a toad.)

LOGE: He did it! Catch him quick!

(TWOTON puts his foot on the toad and removes the Tarnhelm. ALVERRÜCK reappears squirming under TWOTON's boot.)

TWOTON: Gotcha!

ALVERRÜCK: Damn you. Now you've got me!

TWOTON: The need to show off always betrays the nouveau riche!

LOGE: Bind him fast and up we go!

TWOTON: To Walhalla! Ha! Ha! Ha!

(They drag him up and out the way they came. Through mists and the sound of anvils they ascend.)

Scene 4: *In the high mountains.*

LOGE: Look down below, there lies the world you wanted to rule. *(Circles him snapping his fingers)*

ALVERRÜCK: Liar! Thief! Untie me gnomenapper or you'll regret it!

TWOTON: *(Laughing)* Behold the slaver enslaved!

ALVERRÜCK: Let me go!

TWOTON: We will . . . for a ransom.

ALVERRÜCK: Oh what a numbskull I was to have faith in the Gods! Revenge, sweet revenge!

TWOTON: Lick your wounds. There's no revenge for a man in chains. Ransom first, revenge later.

ALVERRÜCK: What do you want?

TWOTON: Your hoard and the gleaming gold.

ALVERRÜCK: Greedy thieves! *(Aside)* I'll give them the hoard. For so long as I keep the ring I can easily pile up another.

TWOTON: Now, elf, what do you say?

ALVERRÜCK: Untie my hands and I'll send for it. *(They untie his hands. He kisses the ring and whispers a spell)* Nihilumpen come! Bring forth the gold from the bowels of the earth. *(A loud fart is heard)* Now let me free.

TWOTON: Not until all has been paid.

ALVERRÜCK: Oh, vile degradation! That my slaves should see me thus. Bound before the Nihilump nation. *(To the Nihilumpen)* Cover your eyes! Don't look this way! Keep moving! Lazy scum! Beasts of burden! Heave ho! Heave ho! *(The Nihilumpen enter. They bear in the treasure and pile it up)* Now back to the pits. Back to work! *(Kisses the ring and holds it out toward them. The Nihilumpen shrink from it in terror and go back out through the trapdoor. They grunt and mumble as they go)* There, I've paid in full. Now give me back my helmet and I'll be off.

LOGE: The Tarnhelm is part of the treasure. We take it as ransom.

ALVERRÜCK: Thief! *(Aside)* Yet while I still hold the ring I can forge me another.

LOGE: Should I set him free?

TWOTON: The golden ring you wear on your finger. That too is part of the treasure. Give me that if you want to go free.

ALVERRÜCK: *(Stung)* The ring? Over my dead body! Take my life, but not the ring.

TWOTON: Your life is worthless. It's the ring I want.

ALVERRÜCK: The ring is mine.

TWOTON: How dare you call it your own? Let's ask the Rheinmaidens if it's yours or not. You stole it, evil dwarf!

ALVERRÜCK: You hypocrite! How can you blame me for doing something you dreamed of yourself? You could have stolen the Gold. But forge it? No, you wouldn't soil your hands with labor. I earned the ring I forged. Hear me, so-called Gods. We gnomes are small-time sinners. But when you big shots sin everybody gets the shaft! Lay off der ring!

TWOTON: Hand over the ring and don't give us a song and dance. *(Yanks the ring from* ALVERRÜCK's *finger)*

ALVERRÜCK: I'm beaten. I'm ruined, a miserable slave in the shits.

TWOTON: *(Gazing on the ring)* With this ring I am the mightiest God. *(Puts on the ring)*

LOGE: May I release him?

TWOTON: Let him go.

LOGE: *(Untying* ALVERRÜCK*)* Go on home. You're free now.

ALVERRÜCK: Free, am I? *(Laughs maniacally)* Then hear my thanks. Since the ring is a curse, then cursed be the ring. Execration: Let omnipotence bring impotence. Imprecation: Let all who hold the ring find it bitter, cold, and cutting. Malediction: Let jealousy and heartburn gnaw those who long for it. Let it bring death to all who possess it! Let them not sleep a night for fear it will be stolen. Let the ring's lord be the ring's slave until once again I wear it on my little finger! That's my blessing. *(Laughs)* Enjoy your ring *(Angrily)* and its curse!

LOGE: Some blessing.

TWOTON: *(Contemplating the ring)* Let him gripe!

LOGE: *(Looking off)* Here come the Giants, Fafner and Fasdolt, with Freia.

(Enter DUNDERHEAD, FROH, and FRICKA.)

FROH: *(Seeing TWOTON and LOGE)* They've returned.

DUNDERHEAD: Welcome home, kinsmen.

FRICKA: What news from Nebule-heim?

LOGE: *(Indicating the treasure)* We outwitted the dwarf. There lies Freia's ransom.

(Enter FAFNER and FASDOLT with FREIA between them. FRICKA runs to FREIA.)

FRICKA: *(Embracing her)* Freia, you've come back to us. O welcome, sister.

FASDOLT: *(Stepping between them)* Not so fast. Freia is still ours . . . until you pay the ransom.

TWOTON: There lies the ransom.

FASDOLT: Losing this maiden depresses my nature. As long as I see her I can't part with her. Therefore heap up the treasure and hide her from sight.

TWOTON: Very apt. Let Freia be the measure. Cover the girl with the treasure.

(They set FREIA *between them and pile up gold in front of her.)*

FAFNER: Heap the hoard high.

LOGE: Help me, Froh. Help me, Donner. Let's put an end to Freia's dishonor.

*(*DUNDERHEAD, FROH, *and* LOGE *pile up the gold.)*

FASDOLT: I can still see her hair. It touches my heart. Cover her head with the helm.

FRICKA: Oh, the shame! Youth and beauty bought and sold like a whore. You brought her to this, Twoton.

FAFNER: More gold! Pile it up closer together.

DUNDERHEAD: *(Raising his hammer)* I'll bash in your head.

TWOTON: Easy, Donner, I think she's covered now.

LOGE: That's all there is. The hoard is finished.

FASDOLT: I can still see her eyes through a little tiny cranny. As long as I can see her eye, I can't part with that girl.

LOGE: I said there is no more. Can't you see there's nothing left?

FAFNER: On Twoton's finger is a ring. Use the ring to stop up the chink.

TWOTON: What! Give up the ring? Never! The ring is mine. I won it.

LOGE: But I promised the Rheinmaidens.

TWOTON: You promised, not I.

FASDOLT: Now yield the ring.

TWOTON: Not for the world would I give up the ring.

*(*FASDOLT *seizes* FREIA.*)*

FASDOLT: The deal's off! Freia is ours forever.

FREIA: Help! Help me!

FRICKA: Proud Godhead, do as they ask!

FROH: Don't hold out on them.

FRICKA: Give them the ring!

TWOTON: Back, horrors! Leave me alone. The ring is mine! *(Turns away)*

*(*EARTHA, *a talking torso, rises up to her diddies out of the ground. She points a warning finger at* TWOTON.*)*

EARTHA: Watch out, Twoton, watch out! Earth mother tells you and I'm leveling with you. You'll be sorry if you keep that ring. *(Singing the blues)* Death and destruction it brings, that ring.

TWOTON: Who are you, woman of doom?

EARTHA: *(Blues singing)* All that is; all that has been; all that will be; world without end, know I! Three Norns have I for daughters born to me long before the earth was. These Norns are fates that nightly speak to Twoton. Danger brings me here. Hark ye! Hark ye! Hear me! All things that are pass away. An evil day dawns for Wallhalla. Give up the ring before it is too late.

TWOTON: Truth rings in your words. Tell me more, woman of mystery.

EARTHA: I've warned you and you have heard. Hear my words and fear them! *(Disappears)*

TWOTON: *(Following her)* Wait. Wait. Tell me more. I want to know all. . . .

(FROH and DUNDERHEAD throw themselves in his way to keep him from following her.)

FRICKA: Are you mad?

FROH: Heed her, Twoton.

(TWOTON appears to be lost in thought.)

DUNDERHEAD: Back, Giants. Twoton will give you what you ask.

FREIA: Am I worth the price, Twoton?

(All look to TWOTON for the answer.)

TWOTON: Stay, Freia! Restore our youth. Giants, here is your ring. *(Throws the ring upon the pile of treasure)*

(FREIA runs to the other gods who embrace her. FASDOLT begins stuffing the treasure into a sack.)

FAFNER: Stop, pig. Share it with me!

FASDOLT: You wouldn't share the girl. I won't share the gold.

FAFNER: Thief! *(To TWOTON)* Make him share—fair and square.

LOGE: Give him the treasure. You keep the ring.

FAFNER: The ring is mine, you crooked cheat!

FASDOLT: I've got it. It's mine as long as I live.

FAFNER: Then let that be short. *(Kills FASDOLT and wrenches the ring from his dying hand and puts it in the sack)* Now it's mine!

TWOTON: *(Contemplating the corpse of FASDOLT)* The curse has already begun to work.

LOGE: *(Consolingly)* Though you lost the ring, Twoton, you escaped doom.

TWOTON: Horror! Chaos! Horror! Eartha alone can restore things to order. So many unanswered questions trouble my mind. Eartha, Eartha alone can answer them!

LOGE: Why do you pause, mighty Twoton? Your palace, Walhall, waits for you.

TWOTON: Think what I paid for it. *(He covers his face with his hands)*

DUNDERHEAD: The air is heavy and oppressive. I'll rive the air with thunderbolts and produce some negative ionization. That will clear the air. *(Swings his hammer)* Hey-da Hey-da Hey-do! Come thunder! Come lightning! Come rain! Hey-da Hey-da Hey-do! *(Clouds gather. It thunders and lightens. Rain falls)*

LOGE: Cheer up, Twoton! Dangerous ideas are like cold water. In and out again quick!

DUNDERHEAD: *(To FROH)* Brother, give us the rainbow sign.

FROH: *(Throwing a rainbow across the clouds to Walhall)* No more water!

LOGE: Fire next time!

TWOTON: *(Offering his arm to her)* Come, Fricka, to Walhall.

FRICKA: What is Walhalla? You've never told me that.

TWOTON: Our home, Fricka. *(Wistfully)* Even the Gods need a home.

(FRICKA takes his arm and they cross the bridge with DUNDERHEAD and FROH.)

LOGE: *(Lingering to talk to the audience)* God of fire tho I am they made me tame. Sometimes when I'm being used by them to cook or some other homely duty, I get a strange urge to blaze and burn them all up . . . Gods tho they are. It's the most inexplicable urge. I must think about that. Who knows what it means? Gods, Gnomes, Giants—it's really the blind leading the blind. But until someone pulls off a better creation in the universe next door, I guess I'll stay right here. *(He crosses the bridge)*

THE THREE RHEINMAIDENS: *(Lamenting below)* Rheingold! Rheingold! Rankle rank old Feingold! We sang in its glow. We pine for its shine. Return das Gold to the depths of the Rhein!

LOGE: *(Looking down on them from above)* The Rhein mermaids miss their stolen Gold.

TWOTON: *(Covering his ears with his hands)* Quiet, accursed nixies! Quiet!

LOGE: *(Calling down to them)* You fish out of water, why do you wail? Learn to love what the Gold has bought you: Gods! Glorious Gods! *(The GODS laugh)* Live in their glow! Sing in their schein!

(Exeunt GODS.)

THE THREE RHEINMAIDENS:
  The Gods are false! The Gods are weak!
  Pure Gold, true Gold, give the Gold back
  To the depths of the Rhein!

  The Gods are false! The Gods are weak!
  The only true light is from
  Pure Gold, true Gold, give the Gold back
  To the depths of the Rhein!

(The curtain closes slowly.)

ACT II. THE DYKE BIKERS AT HELGELAND

Scene 1: *Helgeland, N.J. Time: before the discovery of America.*

(A hut with an ash tree growing up through the living room floor. Storm sounds. A knock at the door is heard. SIEGLINDA *opens the door and admits the bedraggled* SIEGMUND.*)*

SIEGLINDA: *(Astonished)* Who are you, stranger?

SIEGMUND: That I know not. But I do know that I am of all men the most miserable. Could you offer shelter from the storm?

SIEGLINDA: Come in.

SIEGMUND: I thirst.

SIEGLINDA: Here is water. *(Offers him drink)*

(Enter HUNDING with dogs.)

HUNDING: Wife, who is this?

SIEGLINDA: *(Obviously cowed)* A stranger needing respite from the storm.

SIEGMUND: Pardon my intrusion. I meant no offense. *(Shows his wounds)* I am a wounded wayfarer, weary and worn.

HUNDING: What would you?

SIEGMUND: A night's sleep. A bit of food. That's all.

HUNDING: And then . . .

SIEGMUND: And then press on.

HUNDING: My home is holy and my guest sacred. Bring us food, woman. *(*SIEGLINDA *gets food)* Whither have you come?

SIEGMUND: By wood. I have just fought off seven brothers who tried to force a girl to marry against her will. We killed them all. She clung to her dead. Avenging kinsmen killed the bride and all my men. I alone escaped.

HUNDING: *(Suddenly incensed)* Now I know who you are! The last member of the Volsung race, hated by all. I too was called to vengeance by my kinsmen. I arrived too late. Now I return to discover the enemy in my very home! You are my guest. Rest here for the night. But tomorrow prepare your arms. At dawn we fight to the death. Woman, prepare my drink and come to bed. *(Withdraws with* SIEGLINDA*)*

SIEGMUND: Alone, wounded, and unarmed. My father was a wolf. He told me I'd find a sword in my hour of greatest need. *(Cries out)* Volsa! Volsa! Wolf father, where is your sword now that I need it?

(The dying fire flares up revealing a sword hilt stuck in tree. The fire dies out.)

SIEGLINDA: *(Enters in a white robe)* Wounded guest?

SIEGMUND: Radiant woman, what do you dare?

SIEGLINDA: Hunding sleeps. I drugged his drink.

SIEGMUND: Betray not your husband.

SIEGLINDA: I hate him because . . . he bought me. I was sold to him. Use this night to prepare for the fight.

SIEGMUND: I won't win. I'm weak and wounded. My weapons broken, both my sword and shield.

SIEGLINDA: Here in this tree is a sword stuck to its hilt by a strange wayfarer at my wedding feast. I was an orphan, forced to marry Hunding, taken by the conquering clan. All these years I've hoped that some member of our race would be left to save me and our race from extinction.

SIEGMUND: You remind me of someone.

SIEGLINDA: That's strange. You remind me of someone too.

SIEGMUND: Who?

SIEGLINDA: Me.

SIEGMUND: You?

SIEGLINDA: Yes, you remind me of me.

(They stare at each other.)

SIEGMUND: They say I had a twin sister from whom I was separated at birth. Could you be she?

(They go to the mirror.)

SIEGMUND: Look, Volsung, we are identical.

SIEGLINDA: *(Thrills)* Did you say, "Volsung"? Was Volsa your father too?

SIEGMUND: Do you know what this means?

SIEGLINDA: I didn't dare hope.

SIEGMUND: I didn't dare think.

SIEGLINDA: Our race . . .

SIEGMUND: The Volsungs . . .

SIEGMUND and SIEGLINDA: Need not be extinct!

SIEGLINDA: Tonight, while my husband sleeps, we'll sow the seed. That the race of the Volsungs need not perish from the earth. The sword is yours!

SIEGMUND: Brother and sister, we'll prove that blood is thicker than . . . er . . . usual.

SIEGLINDA: *(Enraptured)* Brother and sister—my brother, my friend!

SIEGMUND: After a life of winter, spring!

SIEGLINDA: The Volsung race will be the purest, uncorrupted by other bloods! Pure blood!

SIEGMUND: Pure blood!

SIEGLINDA: *(Embracing him)* Siegmund!

SIEGMUND: *(Embracing her)* Sieglinda!

SIEGLINDA: *(Runs to the tree)* Here is your sword. Call it by name!

SIEGMUND: It was promised when needed. Now I'm most needful. I'll call it Necessity. *(He pulls the sword out of the tree)*

SIEGLINDA: Are you really my lost brother, Siegmund? Take me and your sword. We belong to you. Brother be husband.

SIEGMUND: Sister be bride. My sister, my love, beget, bear, and bloom the blood of Volsungs again in the world! *(They fall to lovemaking)*

(Quick curtain.)

Scene 2

BRUNNHILDA: *(Leaping from rock to rock)* Hoyotoho! Hoyotoho! Hejaha! Hejaha! Hahei! Hahei! Hahei! Heiaho! I prefer the wars of men to domestic squabbles, Father. Your wife is coming and I'm getting out of here! Hoyotoho! Hoyotoho! Heiaha! Heiaha! Hoyotoho! Hoyotoho! Hoyotoho! Hoyotoho! Heiahahaha! *(Hides behind rock)*

(Enter FRICKA *in a chariot drawn by two rams.* TWOTON *tries to hide but* FRICKA *spots him and strides toward him angrily)*

FRICKA: Don't try to hide. I see you!

TWOTON: *(Caught in the act and sheepish)* What's the trouble now?

FRICKA: I want you to punish the adulterous twins, Siegmund and Sieglinda!

TWOTON: Can an act of love be so bad, my dear?

FRICKA: Don't play dumb. When holy marriage vows are flaunted, I must intercede.

TWOTON: They are unholy vows that bind those who do not love each other.

FRICKA: You're a fine one to talk. You cheat on me at every chance you get. You're always restless!

TWOTON: Men are different from women that way.

FRICKA: Are they? There you go applying a double standard. Why should there be one law for men and another for women? I'll tell you why! Because if we carried on as you men do everything would topple down around our ears and you know it!

TWOTON: You're shortsighted. I am always thinking of the future.

FRICKA: Dream on. But let me tell you something. The world at large won't live by the homely double standard you apply to me. Your authority rests on the good example that you set. Otherwise you can hardly call yourself a God.

TWOTON: Again those words.

FRICKA: You won't be God long if you don't even keep your own commandments. Then what will become of you, huh?

TWOTON: Nagging woman, what would you have me do?

FRICKA: Let Hunding kill Siegmund in battle.

TWOTON: No, never! I have plans for him.

FRICKA: Plans? What plans?

TWOTON: To get back the ring.

FRICKA: Still harping on that same ring? I thought you were through with that. Oh, you really are a child. You have the world but still you want another toy.

TWOTON: Don't baby me! I know what I know.

FRICKA: No, I won't baby you. I'm telling you what must be done. Punish Siegmund for his double crime—incest and adultery!

TWOTON: Their child would be my only hope!

FRICKA: The child of brother and sister. Bad enough you betrayed our bed to beget a race of bastards! Now you want to breed a race of idiots! It was a sorry day for Wallhalla when you strayed our marriage bed and begot the Volsung scum!

TWOTON: Don't talk like that. I have yet hope for a hero from that race.

FRICKA: What can a hero do that the Gods cannot do better?

TWOTON: Work in the world. We Gods can inspire men, but when it comes to practical matters we're really useless.

FRICKA: Without you, God, men are nothing.

TWOTON: Not true. What they have made they've made in spite of me, by their own daring. I never protected them. . . .

FRICKA: Then don't protect him today. Let Hunding kill Siegmund.

TWOTON: Woman, what are you saying?

FRICKA: Break the magic sword you gave him.

TWOTON: Necessity?

FRICKA: Yes, take that away and the strongest cannot stand and fight.

TWOTON: I won't. I promised him. I taught him. . . .

FRICKA: What did you teach him?

TWOTON: The only thing a God can teach: how to live without happiness. Necessity is the only thing I was ever able to give my child. And I won't take that away from him!

FRICKA: Then if marriage vows mean nothing to you I will flaunt mine too!

TWOTON: *(Horrified)* You wouldn't.

FRICKA: I might just take a human lover into your bed while you're out with your warrior virgins.

TWOTON: Don't you dare! I command you.

FRICKA: Who are you to command?

TWOTON: I'm God!

FRICKA: A Godless God? I don't believe in you and neither will anyone else. *(Starts out)*

TWOTON: Wait, woman. Have your way.

FRICKA: Then you'll take back the sword?

TWOTON: *(With a catch in his voice)* I will.

FRICKA: Look me in the eye and swear it.

TWOTON: *(Reluctantly looks her in the eye)* I swear. *(Sinks to a rock in despair)*

FRICKA: That's better. You know that a divorce is the last thing on earth I'd want. Because I do love you. I do. You know I do. *(Gives him a maternal kiss on the forehead)*

BRUNNHILDA: *(On a rock above)* Hoyotoho! Hoyotoho!

FRICKA: There's your tomboy daughter. *(To* BRUNNHILDA*)* Your father has some battle news for you. *(Exits laughing in the cart drawn by rams)*

BRUNNHILDA: Father, you look sad. What is it?

TWOTON: God's grief, Brunnhilda, God's grief. *(Hangs his head in dejection)*

BRUNNHILDA: You can tell me, Father. What is it that weighs on your heart?

TWOTON: Something I can't tell to anyone or I'll lose my power to command my own will.

BRUNNHILDA: But Father, I am your own will. Command me. I have always done what you truly wanted me to.

TWOTON: Yes, Brunnhilda, you are my only consolation.

BRUNNHILDA: Then tell me. Unburden your heart.

TWOTON: I have heard that Alverrück, the enemy of love, has bought a whore and invested his seed in her womb. That child of hate will someday steal back the ring that I in my moral prison am not free to take. With its power he will buy Wallhalla and set himself up as a God.

BRUNNHILDA: Oh no!

TWOTON: I need a human hero, unbound by petty rules, to get back that ring. That child a bit God and mostly human might have been born to Siegmund and Sieglinda. But now all hope is lost. This morning at dawn, Siegmund must die by Hunding's sword. And with him my only hope.

BRUNNHILDA: But that's impossible. You must let him live.

TWOTON: I cannot. Fricka has ordered it.

BRUNNHILDA: Why listen to her?

TWOTON: Because I need her. Without her sense of order I wouldn't be a God today. Believe me, you must let Siegmund fall.

BRUNNHILDA: I won't do it. You love Siegmund, and what about your plan to save Wallhalla?

TWOTON: Forget my plan. Forget everything. You will do as I tell you or I'll forget you're my daughter and . . .

BRUNNHILDA: *(Defiantly)* And what? You know I do not cringe before the threat of physical pain.

TWOTON: *(Laughs with false bravado)* Ha ha! You'd shrink with fear at the first thunderbolt I'd hurl! *(Remorsefully)* Oh why did I ever confide in you?

BRUNNHILDA: Because I am your true will, born to do what you truly want me to.

TWOTON: I warn you I'll do something terrible. I'll . . . I'll . . .

BRUNNHILDA: Go on! Let me hear this terrible threat. I'm not afraid!

TWOTON: I'll marry you to some man and make a wife of you.

BRUNNHILDA: *(In fear)* Father, what are you saying?

TWOTON: I'll make you a wife! No more battles, no more will you carry the dead heroes to Wallhalla. The home for you.

BRUNNHILDA: *(Shrinking before him in awe and terror)* No, Father, anything but that!

TWOTON: You'll cook and clean house.

BRUNNHILDA: Let me die in battle!

TWOTON: You'll raise children and the nursery will be your world.

BRUNNHILDA: Father, no more. The cruelty of this vision is more than I can bear. Siegmund will fall. I promise you.

TWOTON: Good. Now go girl and do my will.

BRUNNHILDA: Yes, Father. *(Aside)* Your *true* will!

(They exit in opposite directions.)

Scene 3

(Enter SIEGMUND *and* SIEGLINDA *running. She rushes forward and he tries to hold her back.)*

SIEGMUND: Let's rest here a while.

SIEGLINDA: *(Like a madwoman)* No rest! No rest! Hear the horns! Hear the hounds! We must go on.

SIEGMUND: A moment's rest.

SIEGLINDA: Press on. We mustn't look back. . . . *(Leaps to her feet and runs forward)*

SIEGMUND: *(Catching her in his arms and dragging her back)* No, now. We'll hide a while.

SIEGLINDA: There's no place to hide! They'll catch us here. Nothing can protect us now.

SIEGMUND: Don't forget, we have Necessity.

SIEGLINDA: Outcast woman and outcast man. We're dirty and nothing will ever make us clean. I'm so ashamed! *(She hears hunting horns.)* Hunding is coming! I hear the bloodhounds. They're coming closer and closer.

SIEGMUND: Let him come! I'll give his heart a taste of Necessity!

SIEGLINDA: The dogs know what the Gods know! The dogs know what the Gods know! *(Laughs wildly and then screams with terror and faints)*

SIEGMUND: *(Trying to revive her)* My sister! My love!

*(*BRUNNHILDA *enters and speaks to* SIEGMUND *in the form of an apparition.)*

BRUNNHILDA: Siegmund, look at me. I have come to lead you onward. Follow me.

SIEGMUND: Who are you?

BRUNNHILDA: Only warriors doomed to die may see me.

SIEGMUND: Then I am doomed to die?

BRUNNHILDA: You are.

SIEGMUND: Where will you lead me?

BRUNNHILDA: To Wallhalla.

SIEGMUND: Who will I meet in Wallhalla?

BRUNNHILDA: Your holy father and all the other heroes slain.

SIEGMUND: And are there women in Wallhalla?

BRUNNHILDA: There are maidens to serve your every wish.

SIEGMUND: And may a brother take his sister there and live with her as his bride? May I hold Sieglinda in my arms there and make love to her?

BRUNNHILDA: Sieglinda is not marked for death. You alone are chosen.

SIEGMUND: Then send my regards to Wallhalla, and Holy Father, and all the slain heroes, and the maidens who serve their every wish. But I won't go.

BRUNNHILDA: You have no choice!

SIEGMUND: I tell you I won't go anywhere without Sieglinda. Now that I've found her I'll never let her go!

BRUNNHILDA: Death cannot be overruled, my fool. I am his messenger. Today you will be slain in battle.

SIEGMUND: Who will slay me?

BRUNNHILDA: Hunding will be the victor.

SIEGMUND: Impossible while I have this sword!

BRUNNHILDA: He who gave you this sword has broken its spell.

SIEGMUND: Why has my father forsaken me?

BRUNNHILDA: He wishes your death.

SIEGMUND: Hush! Not so loud. You'll frighten my bride. She defied the world for me and now there's nothing I can do to protect her. So if this sword cannot protect us let it destroy us instead! *(Raises his sword over* SIEGLINDA*)* First you, my love, then I will follow.

BRUNNHILDA: Stop, Volsung! I see your love is true. Brunnhilda chiefest Valkyrie offers you the protection of her shield. Farewell Siegmund, we meet again in battle. *(Exit)*

(Horn calls and drums, rolls of thunder and flashes of lightning accompany the scene of combat.)

SIEGMUND: Sleep on, sister my love. And dream. *(Strides into battle)*

SIEGLINDA: *(In a dream)* Is there to stay? To stay is there? Is there to stay (we stay) in there. Is there to stay? Is there to stay? Is there? Is there?

HUNDING: Fight me or fight my dogs.

SIEGMUND: Which is which?

(A lightning flash reveals HUNDING *and* SIEGMUND *fighting.)*

SIEGLINDA: Don't fight! Hunding! Siegmund! Kill me. It's all my fault! *(She rushes forward to throw herself between the men in combat but a flash of lightning drives her back)*

BRUNNHILDA: *(Is seen covering* SIEGMUND *with her shield)* Kill him, Siegmund. Use your sword!

TWOTON: *(Appears from behind a cloud and breaks Siegmund's sword on his spear)* Back, woman!

*(*BRUNNHILDA *shrinks back from* TWOTON*'s spear.* HUNDING *stabs* SIEGMUND *to death.* SIEGLINDA *screams and faints.* BRUNNHILDA *swoops down and catches* SIEGLINDA. HUNDING *yanks the sword out of* SIEGMUND*'s chest.)*

BRUNNHILDA: *(Carrying* SIEGLINDA *to safety on her horse)* The woman goes with me. Away to safety!

TWOTON: *(Sorrowfully contemplating* SIEGMUND*'s dead body, speaks to* HUNDING*)* Go, beast, and tell Fricka that Twoton's spear has avenged her. *(Waves his hand in disdain and* HUNDING *drops dead)* Ah, but Brunnhilda must be punished for her crime! After her! Away!

(Curtain falls.)

Scene 4: *High in the mountains. Rocks forming a precipice.*

GERHILDA: *(Calling down to the other Valkyries)* Hoyotoho! Hoyotoho! Hiyaha! Hiyaha! Helmvige!

HELMVIGE: Gerhilda!

GERHILDA: Valtrauta!

VALTRAUTA: Schwertleita!

SCHWERTLEITA: Ortlinda!

ORTLINDA: Hoyotoho *(Etc.)*. Rossweissa! Grimgerda!

ROSSWEISSA, GRIMGERDA: Hoyotoho *(Etc.)*.

ALL:
> Valkyries we oh!
> Valkyries we oh!
> Carrying heroes!
> Carrying heroes!
> Hoyo! Hoyea!
>
> Valkyries we oh!
> Valkyries we oh!
> Conquering heroes!
> Conquering heroes!
> Hoyo! Hoyea!
>
> Dykes queer are we! Yo!
> Dykes queer are we! Yo!
> Villanee! Tyranee! Enemy!
> Cavalry! Cavalry! Cavalry!
>
> Memory oh!
> History oh!
> Mastery, slavery,
> Savagery, bravery,
>
> Oh!
>
> Nursery, no!
> Drudgery, no!
>
> Valkyries we!
> Valkyries we!
> Valkyries we!

ORTLINDA: Roll call. *(As she calls the roll each Valkyrie responds with a "Hoyotoho")* Gerhilda, Valtrauta, Helmvige, Siegruna, Grimgerda, Rossweissa, Ortlinda— that's me! Hoyotoho! Schwertleita?

SCHWERTLEITA: Gesundheit!

ORTLINDA: Brunnhilda. Brunnhilda? Where is Brunnhilda?

VALTRAUTA: She eighty-sixed.

ORTLINDA: With a hero?

ROSSWEISSA and HELMVIGE: We saw her fly to the east.

GRIMGERDA and SCHWERTLEITA: We saw her fly to the west.

GERHILDA and SIEGRUNA: And she was carrying a woman!

ORTLINDA: A straight woman?

BRUNNHILDA: *(Enters hurriedly)* Lesbic sisters, save me! High Lord Val Fatherer is after me. And this woman is pregnant!

SCHWERTLEITA: Why have you brought a straight woman here? You know the rules.

BRUNNHILDA: Shut up, Schwertleita. She carries in her womb the fetus of a hero.

GRIMGERDA: Does she need help to get an abortion?

BRUNNHILDA: This woman's seed must not miscarry. The genes are of the very highest quality.

HELMVIGE: You're wasting your time. Try though you may, you'll never make a thoroughbred of mongrel Man.

BRUNNHILDA: I know that seems to be the case, Helmvige. Man did not seem a very promising species when our ships first landed on their planet. But Father bred with them. . . .

ALL: Ugh!

BRUNNHILDA: *(Undaunted)* And from a pair of twins with his celestial blood, Sky-father hoped to breed a champion.

ORTLINDA: What need a champion from a totally useless species? Cows give milk, meat, and leather. But what earthly use is man?

BRUNNHILDA: That question is still waiting to be answered.

TWOTON: *(A booming bass from the wings)* Brunnhilda! Criminal! Give back the woman and the broken sword!

BRUNNHILDA: *(Sings)* Protect me, lesbic sisters! Don't let him take me! Hide the woman and the fruit of her womb!

TWOTON: *(Thundering entrance)* Brunnhildische treachery!

BRUNNHILDA: Godly debauchery!

TWOTON: Armory roguery!

BRUNNHILDA: Godly skullduggery!

TWOTON: Go from bravery to finery from cavalry to nursery from victory to drudgery!

BRUNNHILDA: Help me, sisters.

ALL: No . . . !

TWOTON: This lunacy this piracy this pregnancy must end.

BRUNNHILDA: Woman, awake! Flee the wrath of the terrible God. Into the woods! Away! Away! Don't let that child in your womb miscarry. It's the Gods' only hope. Keep the pieces of the sword—go! Onward!

SIEGLINDA: My feet won't bear me up!

TWOTON: Lightning krieg!

BRUNNHILDA: Go on. Escape while there's still time!

SIEGLINDA: *(Somewhat delirious)* It's hurtful to be wistful. The daylight blue is bright. I'll hide from Gods and rest me and sleep except at night! *(Exit)*

TWOTON: Be Brunnhilda banished!

(Thunder. The sound of horses' hooves. The Valkyries flee in every direction.)

GERHILDA and ORTLINDA: Would it had been better! *(Exit)*

TWOTON: Struck by my spear!

VALTRAUTA and SCHWERTLEITA: This is without any doubt a number! *(Exit)*

TWOTON: End of death!

HELMVIGE and SIEGRUNA: Why will they be willing to go when they are to an advantage whichever, wherever the advantage when they like for their own use! *(Exit)*

TWOTON: Spurned one back from my spear!

GRIMGERDA and ROSSWEISSA: And now then allow them then not to be un-equal; your name's already on the door! *(Exit)*

TWOTON: Great as he was could do nothing to help you. Where is the woman?

BRUNNHILDA: Into a dark wood where you dare not go.

TWOTON: Where the men do not believe in me?

BRUNNHILDA: Even there. Mourning her destiny. Leaving youth and manhood behind her.

TWOTON: Struck by my spear would your own life perish?

BRUNNHILDA: Why punish me? I did what you truly wanted.

TWOTON: I am the breaker of whores and horses. Defy me not, high-hearted maid! In a ring of fire will you sleep until some hero wakes you with a kiss. On yon bronze slab without a blast from the sea. Raise a huge inhuman blaze, a pyre in the whistling wind ring her in double fold of fire! Nightlong pile on the flames upon the fire. In wicked circle drawn! Defy the flames young heroes! Burn your blasphemous bones! Throw wine upon the pyre! Sleep, Brunnhild, sleep! (BRUNNHILDA *falls asleep in her father's arms and he throws a circle of fire around her)* And I an old man now will put my dead son's bones in a golden jar the better to mourn them. Away from the fury of fire and let an old man mourn some bones.

(Curtain.)

ACT III. SIEGFRIED

Scene 1

NINNY: *(Works at the anvil forging a helmet and sword)* Verk without resht! The beste sword that I efer forged der boy takes und breaks in two. Risen Fausten! Verk mitout resht! Der schmelicke knabe! Der kitten kunst von der Nihi-lumpen!

(SIEGFRIED eintrt mit ein bigische polar bear.)

+ MOTIVE OF SIEGFRIED THE FEARLESS

SIEGFRIED: Oho oho! Sic 'em Sic 'em! *(Laughs)*
NINNY: Oik oik! Takem away! Ich want not the bear!
SIEGFRIED: Schniffleink coward! You got mein sword gefinisched?
NINNY: Nay nay. Gibt mir ein break. Was hab ich gedone to you? Ich bringe you up wie du wast mein own son! Und was tanks du ich get? Nix! Niminitz! Hier ist yer sword!
SIEGFRIED: Genug, freund bear! *(Wrestles with the bear and taking it off the rope gives it a boot in the behind and the bear trots back into the woods)* Gibt mir mein sword! Gut! *(Swings the sword around and strikes the ground with it and it breaks)* Du callst dis ein sword? Das sword ist nicht goot! Das ist kein swort! Das ist scheisse!
NINNY: Hier ist yer supper, Siegfried.
SIEGFRIED: *(Throwing the meat at him)* Ess das meat und das fleisch yerselbst! Ich bin ein Vegetarian!
NINNY: Why you eatten wegetables mein sohn?

+MOTIVE OF LOVE OF LIFE

(Birdsong)

SIEGFRIED: Der birds ist gesinging! Und der spring ist geschpringing! Und der animalisch creetures all got another creeture to be animalische with. But Siegfrieds aint got nobody. Er ist ein loneliscshe knabe.
NINNY: Yous got mich, Siegfried.
SIEGFRIED: Eeeeecht. Du bist eine uglische Dwarf!
NINNY: Ich bin dein vater.

Everett Quinton & Bill Vehr in
Der Ring Gott Farblonjet (Martha Morgan)

SIEGFRIED: Mein vater? Den who ist mein mutter?

NINNY: Ich bin yer mutter, too.

SIEGFRIED: Das ist unnaturalisch! Ich know dat ich got a mutter and a vater too. Like dem animalische creetures! You bin nix mein farter! Mein vater bin pretty like ich bin. Du bist uglische, yechtliche dwarf!

NINNY: Ich bin ein vater und mutter in one.

SIEGFRIED: *(Threatening* NINNY *with the sword)* Tell mir who wast mein mutter und vater or ich will yer ass gekillen!

NINNY: *(Trembling with fear)* Nay! Nay! Killt mir nicht! Und ich will sich tellen der truth. Dein mutter war Sieglinda who died hier. Und left you in mein care! She gabe you yer name, und she gabe me dis. *(Gives him the pieces of the sword)*

SIEGFRIED: Dis ist mein onlisch heritage, ein broken sword? Gibt mir das pieces! Ich will siech schowen was einn gut sword really ist! *(Hammers the pieces and singing, forges the sword anew)*

+ MOTIVE OF SIEGFRIED THE IMPETUOUS

(NINNY cowers.)

SIEGFRIED: *(Holding aloft the sword in triumph)* Hier ist ein real sword! Necessity! Goot news. Dis bin nicht mein haus! Du bist nixt mein vater. Ich bin free! Und nebber come backe here no more! Der worldt ist mein home! Ich bin free! Ich ich ich bin free! Good-bye, forefer, Ninny! *(Rushes off into the woods brandishing the sword)*

NINNY: *(Calls after him in alarm)* Siegfried, comen sie back! Comen sie back! *(TWOTON enters from the back where he has been watching in the guise of the WANDERER. He silently observes NINNY's grief)* Oik oik! What an ingrate das childt ist! Oik! Oik!

Scene 2: *A deep forest. The office of the Fafner Foundation.*

+ MOTIVE OF THE FAFNER FOUNDATION

ALVERRÜCK: *(Squatting)* Yuk! Someday somebody gonna kill dis tragon! And I'll get back my ring.

WANDERER: YEEEEchght! Hideous dwarf! Zeus cloud-gathering he did destroy the corpse pyre.

ALVERRÜCK: Who is that? Has the dragon slayer come at last?

WANDERER: Earth encircler, I come to hatred cave. Without the ring Wall-halla's city is made desolate.

ALVERRÜCK: Back, thief. I know you by your one eye!

WANDERER: Blackguard skinhead, Alverrück!

ALVERRÜCK: Liars and thieves are not welcome here. Oh I wish I had never trusted you! You robbed me of my ring!

WANDERER: I have come only to observe.

ALVERRÜCK: But you dare not steal. Nor break any of the laws written in runes on your own speare!

WANDERER: *(Incensed, raises his spear)* Aalgh!

ALVERRÜCK: Don't dare shake a spear at me, old man. I know what I'm doing.

WANDERER: Insolent Trojan!

ALVERRÜCK: Shhhh! You'll wake the dragon!

WANDERER: That's what I mean to do! *(Shouting)* Fafner! Awake you worm!

(NINNY and SIEGFRIED approach.)

SIEGFRIED: Genug, Ninny. Where ist es das du will mich was fear ist teachin?

NINNY: Ich toldt you dat ich would teach du der meanink of der word, fear. Und ich will you der meaningk oft ter word fear teachin. Van du spies der tragon du willst be afeard.

SIEGFRIED: Ist der tragon fearsome?

NINNY: Ya ya, das it ist! Yer got ter trap?

SIEGFRIED: *(Laughs)* Ha ha ha! Traps ist fer cowvards! Ich bin ein Mann und ich will use mein sword. Ha ha ha.

(The dragon awakes.)

FAFNER: Who wakes me from my slumber? Hungh? *(Breathes flames)*

NINNY: *(Trembling with fear)* Ick bin scairt!

SIEGFRIED: Shivering shit! Schtant back! Ich bin nicht intimidatirt! Tell mir, Ninny, hast der tragon got a heart?

NINNY: Jawohl, he's got!

SIEGFRIED: Where ist der heart?

NINNY: In bezwischen der tripe and der leber knodel suppe.

SIEGFRIED: Gotcha. Now will ich mit mein sword in der tragon's heart gesticken machen!

FAFNER: *(Laughs when he sees* SIEGFRIED*)* Aha, has dinner come to me. Let me eat! *(Opens wide his jaws)*

SIEGFRIED: *(Stabs* FAFNER *to death after a short combat. First he stabs the dragon in the tail, then in the foot, but finally he stabs him in the heart)* Gut! Necessity ist in yer gizzard geschtuck machen.

FAFNER: *(With a dying breath)* Who is the fearless lad that killed me?

SIEGFRIED: *(To* NINNY*)* Vat didt he zay?

NINNY: *(Translating)* He zays, Who ist it dat hat him in der heart mit dem sword stuck und killed him gemacht haben?

SIEGFRIED: *(To the dying dragon, proudly)* Ich bin Siegfried.

FAFNER: You didn't think of this yourself. Someone put you up to it. Beware, Siegfried. The ring is cursed. He who told you to kill me plans your death . . . hear me . . . *(Very feebly)* hear me . . . *(Dies)*

SIEGFRIED: *(To* NINNY*)* Vat didt he zay?

NINNY: Ich didn't qvite catch der last part. Mein Englisch ist rustig.

SIEGFRIED: *(Pulls the sword out of the dragon's heart. Blood gets on his hand and he absently sucks it off. Suddenly a forest bird appears and darting and swooping about* SIEGFRIED *sings in flute song)* Mein blut brunt! Und ich can der song of der waldvogelbird ferunterstanden!

WOOD-BIRD: *(Sings)* You got der sword. Now you got ter Nihilumpen hoard! The tarnhelm! Will maken yer invincible! But if you master the ring, you will lord it over the whole world!

SIEGFRIED: *(Moved)* Thank you, birdie, for the goot adwice. Und ich wille always follow your call. *(Exit into the cave)*

*(*ALVERRÜCK *enters and quarrels bitterly with* NINNY.*)*

ALVERRÜCK: !&¢#?....::;;+ = + =   %$!

NINNY: Gyjnyesv, ij nxxxu uuw hdu yip hj jj!

ALVERRÜCK: Yam nemphotek! Yer blither in fine ewick of spermatogyroids.

NINNY: Nin o' yer fithir, messup I been zwitchen end cruomph in the fanny wigs anc wadjup to three's up him and you 'n me both!

ALVERRÜCK: I blam bathers in the Fisgyhogs.

NINNY: The hill you well!

ALVERRÜCK: Gaters and glad he ate hers by my reckoning is bissiness. Whatchoo Gott. All these sects is positively Freudening.

NINNY: I'm too Jung to be Freudened.

ALVERRÜCK: The plot sickens.

NINNY: Pea john in the massed pertainers. Wampus nix?

ALVERRÜCK: Siegfried ain't no small potato pit man.

NINNY: Eee raised him up, end grease him a galoptious cumuppence.

ALVERRÜCK: Win eem gettin' that ring ick bin rulen dem welt! Und ich bin der fuehrer! Der fuehrer uber alles!

NINNY: Nay!

ALVERRÜCK: Where ist mein ring?

NINNY:

Mit des knaben.

Ich raistem up.

fur die nurseing und der nurture fur die toil und woe

Eees goanta pay mich! Ee will gib mich der ring!

ALVERRÜCK: Nein, der ring ist mein!

NINNY: Nichts!

ALVERRÜCK: Behalt!

NINNY: You taken der tarnhelm but gib mir der ring!

ALVERRÜCK: Ich will nicht bargain!

NINNY: Alles fur you? Nichts fur mich?

ALVERRÜCK: *(Furious)* Nuttin' fa yoo! Nuttin', ya hear?

NINNY: Ich gott der boy und he's gott der sword und you ain't gettin' der ring nor der helm.

ALVERRÜCK: Lookin twrds der cave! Der boy comes mit der tarnhelm in his hand.

NINNY: Und he's gott ter ring!

ALVERRÜCK: Curses der ring!

NINNY: *(With an evil laugh)* Let 'im der ring to thee render. Ich ween full soon ich shall win it!

ALVERRÜCK: Ah, but der true Lord will have his ring!

(They withdraw to opposite sides of the platform. SIEGFRIED *enters from the cave with tarnhelm and ring. He gazes at the treasure in rapt silence.)*

SIEGFRIED: Tellt mir, birdie now ich got ter ring und ter helmit und der treshoor. Vot do ich do mit it alles? Ach deres der rub! Vot's dot mit der indebendence? Hoompug! Shust as any odder schneak vot goes py te schweardavit und says a lie vot isn't so much troot as a dinner mitout gabbage. Das is der indebendance, mein frients! Life, liperty, und bersuit of happiness isn't so mit a cent's wort! It's a lie pigger'n a prewery wat makes peer mitout malt. *(Shouts)* Ish life so tear, or beace so schweet as to pe burchases at de brice mit schains und schlavery? Nix! Nein! I speacks like der breacher, so lout as eferpody shall listen!

Vell den, if ter citizen's eatin' lager und trinken Schweitzercheese, mit a pologna sausage in hees bocket, goes ofer ter street py ter lambost und sings.

Vot sall der indebendence pe coming mit der boliceman und say, "Git out, Dootchy, or I'll pull you," und schlaps me on der kopf mit a glub, und makes me go home? Dot's a lie! Der indebendence ish der boliceman's glub, und der life, liperty, und der bersuit of happiness ish ein hoffeltegobblegunst! Und so's mein name ish Singfreed, birdie, I goes mit ter odder barty vot don't swear mit der Gonstitution und der Law. If dos ish treason makes as mooch apout it as ye blease. *(*SIEGFRIED *hangs the tarnhelm on his belt and puts the ring on his pinkie finger)*

VOICE OF THE WOOD-BIRD: *(in the lime tree)*

Hey! Siegfried doth hold

now the helm and the ring

O trust not in Ninny,

the treacherous elf!

Heareth Siegfried but sharply
the shifty hypocrite's words:
what at heart he means
shall by Ninny be shewn;
so booteth the taste of the blood.

SIEGFRIED: *(Nods affirmatively)* Ich unterschtandt alles. *(Hears* NINNY *approach and awaits his entrance impassively. He leans on his sword)*

NINNY: Where ish Siegfried? Ah, dere he ish brooden on der treayshoor. Ich giff him der soft soap schnow chob. Ich wunder did der wanderer talk und wise him up? Ach! Ich must mit kraftig vorts mein wrathful runes to hide! Und pullen te vool ofer 'is eyes! Hey, hero! Hast you lernt was fear ish?

SIEGFRIED: Ich didn't find te teacher.

NINNY: Didt you kill ter tragon, mein son?

SIEGFRIED: Ja, he's dead.

NINNY: He was an uglish enemy, not zo, Ziegfried?

SIEGFRIED: Ja, he vas uglisch. But it machen me sad to tink on dem dot more evil und more uglisch vot yet remains alive. Und get nicht gepunisched! Ich hate der von what put me up to killink der vorm vorse than the vorm istself.

NINNY: *(Solicitous)* Vat a vay to talk! I come to deceive you und vas tanks do ich get?

SIEGFRIED: You hast nicht got mein best inderests at heartz.

NINNY: How can you zay dot? You bin mein baby! *(Tenderly)* Und although I alvays hater you und ter resbonsipility of raisink you. I thought only of ter Gold! Now all I vant is you out of der vay. *(Puts his arms around him and gives him a maternal hug)*

SIEGFRIED: Zo, you do hate mich!

NINNY: Nay, nay, nay! You misunterschtandt! Here I brought you dis trink. Und poisont it meinselbst! Trink! Trink! He he he he he he!

SIEGFRIED: You gonna rob me of ring, helmet, und sword?

NINNY: Don't be paranoid, mein childt! Do you tink I vould admit vats in mein heart of hearts? Nein, ich bin ein conwincingk liar! Trink! Trink! Twill machen you schleep. Und vile you schleepink I cut off you kopf und take efferytink for mein self! *(Laughs fiendishly)* He he he he he he he!

SIEGFRIED: Zo, you means to kill mich in mein schleep!

NINNY: Your hearing is poor, mein son. Ich vouldn't zay a ting like dot! How else but py killink you vould I get the treaschur from Alverrück? Trink! Mein childt, trink! He he he he he he he he he he he he he!

(SIEGFRIED, *seized by sudden revulsion, kills* NINNY *with a single blow of his sword.)*

ALVERRÜCK: *(Utters a mocking laugh)* Ha ha ha ha ha ha ha ha ha ha ha ha ha ha ha ha ha ha!

SIEGFRIED: *(Throws* NINNY's *body into the cave and stops the mouth of the cave with the dragon's body)* Schleep mit yer treaschur you loved so tearly. You deidt of Necessity. *(Sits under the lime tree to rest)*

VOICE OF THE WOOD-BIRD: Tweet! Tweet! Hail, Siegfried!

SIEGFRIED: Ach, birdie. How schveet your song! But Siegfried aint got nobody. Ich bin lonelische!

VOICE OF THE WOOD-BIRD: On mountain high your lovely mate awaits you. She sleeps in double ring of fire! Only the hero who knows not fear may win her for his own.

SIEGFRIED: O loffly zong! Singk on! Singk on!

VOICE OF THE WOOD-BIRD: The most perfect bride awaits in double ring of fire. Penetrate that bridal pyre! Him without fear, O hear, O hear! I weave my song.

SIEGFRIED: Zingk yidlach zingk! I lischten to yer zong! I burn. I'm on fire.

VOICE OF THE WOOD-BIRD: He who wakes the sleeping bride will win the fair Brunnhild! But he must be lacking in fear!

SIEGFRIED: I don't yet know the meanink of ter vort fear. Den vill ich penetrate! Penetrate der fiery ring! Lead, birdie, und ich will follow. Follow where you fly.

Scene 3: *A vaultlike hollow in the rocks in some wild, mountainous place.*

(Thunder, lightning among the clouds, general storm and wind.)

TWOTON:
  Eartha awake
  Awake Eartha!
  Don't slumber, weird woman.
  Woman all knowing, wake up.
  Eartha awake. *(Etc.)*

EARTHA: *(Covered with iridescent hoarfrost rises to her waist from the terrain)* Wis wot know I. Heroes, Valkyries. Wise withal accomplish unbidden to challenge of magic sleep *Daughter* pierced by the slumber thorn sleeps.

TWOTON: The war maid was a witch child.

EARTHA: And a wish child! Woe, oh woe be Odin! Fatal extinction to the Gods!

TWOTON: Wisest of women, tell me all . . .

EARTHA: Restless! Questioning heirlooms the hero comes and we, we Gods shall be . . .

TWOTON: Say it!

EARTHA: No more! No more! *(Begins to sink into the earth again)* No more!

TWOTON: To endless sleep farewell, mystery woman! Unanswered question good night! To endless sleep succumb! And watch my downfall as in a dream.

(The storm subsides and moonlight illuminates the scene. [TWOTON *as* WANDERER.]*)*

WANDERER: Here comes Siegfried. My own destruction I do not regret since it is my will. Here comes Hero, heir to the Nihilumpens' ring!

(EARTHA vanishes completely from sight.)

SIEGFRIED: Beguile, birdie, zum bighearted beyond! The bilingual bibelot gives me power to commandt!

VOICE OF THE WOOD-BIRD: Hup blonde blood! Blueblood, hup!

WANDERER: Say, boy, whither bendst thou thy way?

SIEGFRIED: To wake a woman.

WANDERER: Who inspired this quest?

SIEGFRIED: Der little birtie toldt mir. Now aus mein vay alt man! Ich go to yonter rock. *(Approaches closer to the* WANDERER*)*

WANDERER: Halt. *(Raises his spear)*

SIEGFRIED: *(Laughs)* Vat a funny hat. Vhy for you vears such a funnische hat?

WANDERER: Such is the wont of the Wanderer when he walks against the wind.

SIEGFRIED: Yous got one eyeball missink. See vat happens ven you bar ter vay of youth? You bin loosink der oder von too if you don't lookink out.

WANDERER: I need that other eye. It's all I've got to see the way.

SIEGFRIED: *(Laughs)* You talk funnische! Ha ha ha!

WANDERER: These taunts tear my heart.

SIEGFRIED: Dodderink schtill? Aus mein way alte cocke!

(It grows dark.)

WANDERER: *(Raging)* Ah, how bitterer than the raven's peck it is to have a thinking child.

SIEGFRIED: Schtandt back! Ich seek der schlumberingk maid!

WANDERER: Defy me and leave me powerless? Do you dare to brave the double ring of fire? Glittering lightning? The hot sheen, glare and crackling? The luminous furnace? Back, foolhardy boy!

SIEGFRIED: Der blaze ist nix but ein beacon to lead me to her. Brunnhilda, ich kom! *(Advances)*

WANDERER: *(Barring the way with his spear)* Fear the fire and Twoton's spear! It broke that sword once and will do so again.

SIEGFRIED: Zo! You wast mein vater's enemy! Schveet revenche! Schtrech aus yer schpear! Ich schwing mein schword! *(Hacks the* WANDERER's *spear in two with his sword)*

(Clap of thunder.)

WANDERER: *(Recoiling into the shadows)* Advance! Go forward! I cannot hold you back. *(Vanishes)*

(The stage fills with a sea of fire.)

SIEGFRIED:
  Bathe mir in fire!
  Oho! Oho!
  Aha! Aha!
  Ich seeks love in Brunnhild's pyre!
(He laughs and dances about in the flames. The sound of Siegfried's horn is heard. SIEGFRIED *ascends to where* BRUNNHILDA *sleeps)* Das ist nicht ein voman. Das ist ein young mann! Young soldier, avake! *(Addressing the sword)* Necessity, through das iron gecutin' machen. *(*SIEGFRIED *removes* BRUNNHILDA's *helmet, and golden hair streams forth)* Ein fräulein! Heil, fräulein! *(Kisses her)*

BRUNNHILDA: *(Awaking)* Heil, Siegfried!

SIEGFRIED: She ish awake!

BRUNNHILDA: Heil sun! Heil to the father of the sun!

SIEGFRIED: Heil mein farter!

BRUNNHILDA: Heil to the mother of the sun!

SIEGFRIED: Heil mein mutter!

BRUNNHILDA: Heil forest bird!

SIEGFRIED: Heil dragon's blood!

BRUNNHILDA: Heil helmit!

SIEGFRIED: Heil sword!

BRUNNHILDA and SIEGFRIED: Heil ring!

SIEGFRIED: Marrich mir Brunnhilda!

BRUNNHILDA: *(Looking fearfully toward the woods)* Ich fear mein feary Father!

SIEGFRIED: The olde man shake-'is-speare for the last time. Ich hab his spear gebroken! *(Seizes her impetuously)*

BRUNNHILDA: *(Resists him and runs terrified to the other side of the stage and covers her eyes with her hands)* Impossible!

SIEGFRIED: *(Gently drawing her hands from her face)* Heller dunkel flee with me the fearsome spell.

+ MOTIVE OF LOVE'S PEACE

BRUNNHILDA: I fear the sunshine, I fear the light of day.

SIEGFRIED: I feel a fool.

BRUNNHILDA: Hero! My star!

SIEGFRIED: Woman schwagnerschaft beautiful. Laugh at death love. Laugh at death.

BRUNNHILDA: Even death is laughing.

BRUNNHILDA and SIEGFRIED: *(Sing)* Loving light! Laughing death! *(They laugh)*

(Curtain.)

ACT IV. GÖTTERDÄMMERUNG (RING DAMNS GODS)

Scene 1

FIRST NORN: Triangulation coordination concatenation.

SECOND NORN: Rehabilitation exoneration purification.

THIRD NORN: Inflammation gestation incubation.

FIRST NORN: In kvarters wo fates pringlepik is felt.

SECOND NORN: A stinksome inkenstink dusky tongue ee speekie danskie tongue.

THIRD NORN: Cloever spilling.

FIRST NORN: From the Volkesfiendship to the Enema of the People.

SECOND NORN: The ringen bin for Nihilumpen und the wyf eek her sister free.

FIRST NORN: Tighter tochter pullen da thread—a loose fate, this!

SECOND NORN: Uhg! Hard work.

THIRD NORN: Until dawn waketh we!

FIRST NORN: Priikkes Prikkes!

SECOND NORN: The curse of the ring!!

THIRD NORN: Entangles the cords and this knot we can never hope to untie.

FIRST NORN: Nay sisters, while my mother trims her lamp. It's hard that I should go darkling. This way. *(Bites the thread)*

SECOND and THIRD NORN: You've broken it! You've broken it!

ALL: Thus endeth the power of the Norns. No more Norns! Nimmer! Nimmer! *(They vanish)*

Scene 2

BRUNNHILDA: Sangfroid! Sing Freud! Go, hero, win the victory for peace. Do not despise the mysteries of the most scornfully connuted!

SIEGFRIED: I haf breathed the fires of interlunar air. Brunnhilda! Brunnhilda! Azure halcyons! Cold stars! The perfect foil to the antimensch.

BRUNNHILDA: The wealth of nations. Modern life with all its sacred claims of age and sex beyond the reach of death! Take them! They are yours!

SIEGFRIED: Defiance to your kindness! Brunnhilda is all I ever wanted!

BRUNNHILDA: Recall your plights and troth!

SIEGFRIED: O follow follow follow me! From violence of fire. The licking flames do flatter your symmetry.

BRUNNHILDA: *(Modestly)* Talk!

SIEGFRIED: Your chastity.

BRUNNHILDA: Mere talk.

SIEGFRIED: And your anatomy!

BRUNNHILDA: Keep talkin'.

SIEGFRIED: Am I not a candidate for fame, to be heard in song? Avaunt you boastful bards! Farewell, Brunnhild. *(Embraces her)*

BRUNNHILDA: Farewell, Siegfried. Do deeds but whatever deeds you do remember Brunnhild.

SIEGFRIED: For the runes and body slanguage much thanks. Here, take this ring as pledge of unquenched love. I slew a fearsome dragon for it. *(Gives* BRUNN-HILDA *the ring)*

BRUNNHILDA: A weaker woman I than before, take my horse. He'll carry you anywhere you want to go. *(To the horse)* Stand by Siegfried, together or alone, remembered or forgot. My woman's heart I must subdue.

SIEGFRIED: Our orisons are heard.

BRUNNHILDA: The Gods are merciful. *(Slips golden ring onto her arm)*

SIEGFRIED: Religion, myth, and poetry cannot be eradicated by conquest or education.

BRUNNHILDA: Heil, Genius of the poet!

SIEGFRIED: Heil, dearest friend!

BRUNNHILDA: Heil, Spring!

SIEGFRIED: Heil, Glory!

BRUNNHILDA: Leave the bed low, cold, and red.

SIEGFRIED: O wild west wind!

BRUNNHILDA: Ah twinborn sigh!

BRUNNHILDA and SIEGFRIED: Heil! Heil! Heil! Heil!

(SIEGFRIED leads the horse out. BRUNNHILDA looks after him. Siegfried's horn is heard joyously from the ravine. Curtain.)

Scene 3: *The hall of the Krankheit Gibichungs am Rhein. Two high thrones against the sky.*

GUNTHUR: Tell me, Hagen, is the Krankheit's throne ennobling to Gibich fame?

HAGEN: Our mother would be proud to see the sons of Grimhild have made so much of the world their own! I'm envious of your grandeur, brother mine.

GUNTHUR: Don't envy me. I envy you. You inherited the brains of the family.

HAGEN: But I feel guilty that there are yet excesses unnattainable to our consumptive powers. The shortcomings of ambition mock our festivals. I know a height not yet attained.

GUNTHUR: Tell me.

HAGEN: Progeny. The seven virgins are always seven. Do not make them eight, Gutruna.

GUTRUNA: Again he startles the rattles.

GUNTHUR: Shake 'em.

HAGEN: You too, Gunthur. When will you wive?

GUNTHUR: Marry to give reason to mummery and merriment? What stuff you speak!

HAGEN: I speak the primeval language lost to no man. Don't tell me you need an interpreter. Like the wild boar in the gardens of Lorenzo.

GUNTHUR: And if I do?

HAGEN: There's more than one will fetch thy wanion a league of two pillages. Or do it in the dark like the old stepdame in the tale.

GUNTHUR: Tis true a tribe without chits is like a corpse corrupted and corrupting.

HAGEN: Stretch your tongue to every dialect. Shake from thy soul these dreams effeminate.

GUNTHUR: With whom might we mate to plant our feet firmly in ambitious mire?

HAGEN: For you a maid who sleeps in double ring of fire, Brunnhilda!

GUNTHUR: Don't tell me of treasures I cannot win.

GUTRUNA: Whom might I have as husband to my home?

HAGEN: Dragon slayer Siegfried, the twin born godman is a goddamn goodman.

GUTRUNA: Where might one find this fearless man?

(Siegfried's horn is heard.)

HAGEN: Hark, I hear his horn.

(Enter SIEGFRIED.)

GUNTHUR: Did heresy keep the hangdog beggar? Anathema could ere be beautiful as thoughts strong and bold!

HAGEN: Why touch upon such themes?

GUNTHUR: Bring the victims to slaughter. I will reserve my best ability, my heart, my heart, my honor, only to thee. Only to thee.

GUTRUNA: How might I bind this man to me?

HAGEN: A potion precious, pleasant as ambrosia and red nectar. To his nostrils and he will turn to you.

GUTRUNA: By the frozen and inconstant moon I will withdraw and prepare the magic draught. *(Exit)*

HAGEN: Yes, go girl and use witchcraft to charm the wretch.

GUNTHUR: Gladden my conscience! Who can win this woman for me?

HAGEN: Siegfried with Niblung hoard; ring sword and helm walks through flames before breakfast every morning.

GUNTHUR: *(Hypocritically)* Welcome, Siegfried! Welcome, merry man!

SIEGFRIED: *(Primitively)* Let's fight or let's be friends!

GUNTHUR: *(Laughing at his impetuosity)* I want to be friends, Siegfried. Here, drink your health. Blood brothers.

(Door opens. GUTRUNA enters ceremonially with goblet. They cut their arms and drip blood in the goblet.)

GUTRUNA: *(Offering goblet to* SIEGFRIED*)* Drink, Siegfried!

SIEGFRIED: Our bloods forever mixed. *(Toasting)* Here's to Brunnhilda. The only woman in the world! *(Drinks long and deep. Then to* GUNTHUR*)* Why didn't you drink, Gunthur?

GUNTHUR: Your blood is too rich for my veins.

SIEGFRIED: *(Looking at* GUTRUNA*)* Oh ravishing woman. You alone I love! Become my wife.

GUTRUNA: *(Blushing)* Give me a ring.

SIEGFRIED: That I cannot do. I gave it to Brunnhilda. But I will take it back and give it to you.

GUNTHUR: Do you know where she is?

SIEGFRIED: Long she slept in double ring of fire. There she waits for my return.

GUNTHUR: This woman I want but do not dare the flaming pyre.

SIEGFRIED: Do not fear the double fold of fire! I will penetrate that bridal pyre. Fear not the flames for the high-hearted maid! Without a wake from the sea on yon bronze inhuman slab! Defy the blast of the whistling wind. Ride horses through the fire. To where Brunnhild sleeps! Give me your sister and Brunnhild is yours!

GUNTHUR: My sister gladly will I give!

SIEGFRIED: Then come! We're off! *(Starts out)*

GUNTHUR: *(To* HAGEN*)* Take care of the Gibichhome while I'm away.

GUTRUNA: Where are they going?

HAGEN: To rescue Brunnhild for your brother's bed. There's nothing he won't do to win you.

GUTRUNA: Siegfried—mine? *(Shows emotion)*

HAGEN: *(Sings)*

Mighty the runes of Gibich lore!
Strong the Nihilumpen sing!
Brave the man who walks through fire!
And brings me back the ring.

Beware the night of the Nihilump!
Ye Gods beware that night.
Beware the race born of a whore
The Gold has given us might!

Scene 4: *The rock of the Valkyrie.*

BRUNNHILDA: *(Kissing and fondling the ring)* Siegfried! Siegfried! My hero! *(Footfall and obligatory thunder and lightning.* BRUNNHILDA *stares and looks off toward the pine wood)* Is that you, my darling? Have you returned?

VALTRAUTA: *(Entering breathlessly)* Sister! Sister!

BRUNNHILDA: Valtrauta reconnoitering? What made you defy Val-Father and come here?

VALTRAUTA: Ring-a-rosy made me bolder.

BRUNNHILDA: Speak, Sister. Speak to a bosom in hell!

VALTRAUTA: Father Twoton has all but abdicated! No more go we to battle! No more gather the fallen heroes to him. But rove useless through the world seeking part-time jobs.

BRUNNHILDA: O woe, scattered inhabitants of earth!

VALTRAUTA: People have all but turned away from ye olde Gotts!

BRUNNHILDA: Woe.

VALTRAUTA: Twoton sits in state with his splintered spear and won't touch the apples of eternal youth. The heroes sit about him in the hall, Valkyries at his feet. Heedless he sits tho we implore him. It is for you he pines.

BRUNNHILDA: Guilty me. And yet I did his true will when I sheltered Sieg-mund. What can I do to atone?

VALTRAUTA: Return the ring to the Rhein. The Rheinmaidens alone can restore harmony to the world. If such a thing is possible.

BRUNNHILDA: The ring?

VALTRAUTA: Throw the ring back to the depths of the Rhein.

BRUNNHILDA: The ring? Ask for anything, but not the ring.

VALTRAUTA: Abjure the ring!

BRUNNHILDA: No, never. Siegfried gave it to me! The ring is love and I will not renounce love!

VALTRAUTA: The ring is cursed!

BRUNNHILDA: Then so is love!

VALTRAUTA: *(Throwing herself at* BRUNNHILDA*'s feet)* You doom the Gotts!

BRUNNHILDA: Have you gone crazy?

VALTRAUTA: Relinquish the ring!

BRUNNHILDA: Cloude-borne whelp, begone! Don't scorch your bosom on the way! Hear what I say! Away! Away! Defy not the fiery tide! *(*VALTRAUTA *flees.* BRUNNHILDA *speaks rapturously)* Siegfried! Siegfried! Where are you? *(Enter* SIEGFRIED *with the tarnhelm on his head.* BRUNNHILDA *recoils in horror)* Who are you?

SIEGFRIED: A fearless hero come to woo you.

BRUNNHILDA: The fire did not stop you?

SIEGFRIED: I fear not the fire.

BRUNNHILDA: *(In terror)* What inhuman monster has flown here to bear me off in its beak!

SIEGFRIED: An eagle!

BRUNNHILDA: Nay, a raven! You can't be human.

SIEGFRIED: I am Gunthur. King of the Krankheit Gibichungs. Sons of Alver-rück!

BRUNNHILDA: God Twoton. Is this your revenge? To breed me with the subhuman Nibble-lunkers?

SIEGFRIED: Be mine!

BRUNNHILDA: O shame!

SIEGFRIED: To wed!

BRUNNHILDA: Curse of sorrow. On your true will! *(Threatening* SIEGFRIED *with the ring)* Stand back, I cannot be taken by force.

SIEGFRIED: Give me that! *(Tries to seize the ring)*

(They struggle. She escapes. They struggle again.)

BRUNNHILDA: Stop, thief. Only he who bestowed the token has the right to take it back.

SIEGFRIED: *(Wresting the ring from her grasp)* With this ring you wed Gunthur.

BRUNNHILDA: You're hurting me! *(Loses the ring to him and screams)*

SIEGFRIED: You are mine! *(Drives her before him at the point of his sword)*

BRUNNHILDA: Many articles fetter the mistaken rectitude of being sheltered. But I, wronged woman, what help have I? *(Exits staggering)*

SIEGFRIED: *(Brandishing his sword)* Needed and needless they can be comforting. *(Follows her out)*

Scene 5: *Krankheit altars to the Gibich Gods.*

(HAGEN sleeps against the wall, spear in hand.)

ALVERRÜCK: *(Stealing up and shaking HAGEN)* Schleepink, Hagen, mein sohn?

HAGEN: *(Half in his sleep)* I want that ship. I want to go home. I know that God really cares.

ALVERRÜCK: But we've already come such a long long way. I'd rather enjoy playing God myself for a while. Remember that night? Ah, so many memories. Remember the tree of knowledge forbidden? Schleepink, Hagen, mein sohn?

HAGEN:
My courage seems to falter
at this visit unimplored.
I'm never happy.
I never smile.
I'm bored.

ALVERRÜCK: Learn to hate happy people. Don't trust them, flesh of my flesh. Siegfried slew the serpent and won the ring. Once we seize that ring of Gold we too will taste to attain to be but angels, Gods or demigods. Outbrave the dignity of God, the creator wise—and then threaten and destroy. Schleepink, Hagen, mein sohn?

HAGEN: Are we the heirs to the Gods above?

ALVERRÜCK: Tho peril great, great things must we dare. You and I, we will sit above, dignified on high. Twoton's spear is broke by a son who never grew old in his father's armor. Love and laughter fill his heart. Schleepink, Hagen, mein sohn?

HAGEN: Him have I already doomed to loss of lawless love. There ends laughter.

ALVERRÜCK: You were meant for higher things. Someday you will play with all ten fingers. I brought you up to live in hate so that the circlet will be yours to wield. Wake up, Hagen, mein sohn!

HAGEN: My heart has never let a joy burst forth. I cheat at solitaire and hate myself afterwards.

ALVERRÜCK: *(Disappears gradually and speaks ever more softly as he does so)* The island salt, the watery glass, the raven flies! Tho late repenting him of man depraved, tears drip from their eyes—for deeds tho mute speak loud the doer! *(Exit)*

(SIEGFRIED enters in his own form with the tarnhelm on his head. HAGEN rises.)

HAGEN: Siegfried, hero, where have you been?

SIEGFRIED: To the Valkyries' rock and back.

HAGEN: Did Brunnhilda submit?

SIEGFRIED: Where's Gutruna?

HAGEN: *(Calling)* Gutruna, Siegfried is here.

GUTRUNA: *(Entering)* Praise Freia! You've come back.

SIEGFRIED: Praise Freia! Today you'll marry me.

HAGEN: Does Gunthur have Brunnhilda?

SIEGFRIED: She is his.

HAGEN: How walked he through the flames? Was he not burned?

SIEGFRIED: I won her for him.

GUTRUNA: Then she is yours?

SIEGFRIED: But it's you I want.

GUTRUNA: Did you sleep with her, then?

SIEGFRIED: We did not sleep.

GUTRUNA: Did she lie close by your side, then?

SIEGFRIED: As close as northeast by southwest, no closer.

GUTRUNA: Then how did Gunthur get her?

SIEGFRIED: *(Ingenuous)* I gave her to him.

GUTRUNA: Siegfried, my mastermensch. You frighten me.

SIEGFRIED: Here they come now.

HAGEN: Ancient genealogy from chief pontiff to the all entitled Baron Viscount Earl Marquess Duke and Royal Duke, the paraphernalia of My Lord, all peers whose fork-ended pennon had been cut square bring forth the lump sum or one cnicht Old English for a boy, youth, or attendant. Let Siegfried be served by virgins if there are any and a Knight Batchelor be posted at each lady's door. Leave an embattled eight-foil escutcheon bent sinister with oblong squares, bird bolt, and basilisk, cry ho! Cry ho!

CHORUS OF HEATHEN ONLOOKERS: *(Clamoring insistently)* Ho! Ho!

BRUNNHILDA: Shut up! Did you hear what I said? Shut up all of you!

(HEATHEN ONLOOKERS fall silent.)

HAGEN: Let the blood of beasts run on Twoton's altars! Slaughter boars! Kill calves! Slay swine!

(HEATHEN ONLOOKERS make noises of hearty assent.)

HAGEN: Heil to the two blissful couples! Gunthur and Brunnhild, Siegfried and Gutruna.

HEATHEN ONLOOKERS: Heil!

BRUNNHILDA: Siegfried and Gutruna? Wait a minute. I gave the ring to the man who saved me when I lay naked in double fold of fire. That man alone beheld me and to that man alone am I beholden!

ALL: *(Gasp)*

BRUNNHILDA: Behold the ring upon his hand! *(Points to SIEGFRIED)*

ALL: *(Murmur)*

BRUNNHILDA: *(Points at GUNTHUR)* That man raped the ring from my ring finger! *(To SIEGFRIED)* How do you come to have it? Did he give it to you?

SIEGFRIED: Ich got dis ring in Hatred Cave ven ich killt der tragon mit der sword in his heart gestuck machen.

BRUNNHILDA: *(Beside herself)* These words as in a dream streaming out of my collected unconscience!

GUNTHUR: *(Puzzled)* I didn't give him the ring.

BRUNNHILDA: So! I've been betrayed! There stands the man who stole the ring! Siegfried the thief! Dastard! Dirty dastard!

GUTRUNA: Betrayed?

BRUNNHILDA: Betrayed beyond revenge!

GUTRUNA: But who is betrayed?

BRUNNHILDA: *(Casting a cry of anguish heavenward)* God Twoton, what did I do to deserve this? Send me wrath, Val-Father! Wrath of God!

GUNTHUR: Hush, gentle bride.

BRUNNHILDA: *(Roaring)* Flames of rage that never can be quenched burn the coward Siegfried!

SIEGFRIED: *(Holding his hand over his spear point)* Im zpear test hand held from point of blood brotherhood. Let it bring my death if I lie!

BRUNNHILDA: *(Holding her hand over the spear point as well)* In blood brotherhood the point of the spear I will hold in my hand as a test! Death to the liar!

SIEGFRIED: Gunthur, your wife's shameful words bring you shame!

BRUNNHILDA: Bring his destruction!

SIEGFRIED: *(Putting his arm around GUTRUNA)* Come Gutruna.

(Exit SIEGFRIED, GUTRUNA.)

BRUNNHILDA: Oh shame beyond extremest shame!

HAGEN: I swear, wronged woman, that I will make it right and vow revenge to my brother's wife.

BRUNNHILDA: On whom will you wreak this vengeance?

HAGEN: On Siegfried.

BRUNNHILDA: On Siegfried, you? *(Laughs)* He could kill you with a glance, pretentious gnome! Nothing can harm Siegfried.

HAGEN: Nothing? Know you no magic charm that can bring him low?

BRUNNHILDA: I myself with powers ostentatious made him invulnerable in battle.

HAGEN: Has he no weakness?

BRUNNHILDA: Only a stab in the back can fell him. I did not protect his back with spells because this he would never turn on an enemy. For fearless Siegfried will never retreat!

HAGEN: Now I know exactly where to strike! Rise, Gibich! Your wife has put the power in our hands!

GUNTHUR: I've been disgraced. I'll never show my face again!

HAGEN:
Your shame is great without a doubt,
And only Siegfried's death can wipe it out.

GUNTHUR: Siegfried's death? Has it come to that?

BRUNNHILDA: Whose fault is it? Antimensch! You let another man do your business! He won me but you enjoyed me! Disgrace to your race! You lowest scum of the earth!

GUNTHUR: Deceiver deceived! Betrayer betrayed! Help me, Hagen, walk like a mensch once more.

HAGEN: We'll kill Siegfried and the Gibich will triumph over the Volsung just as the Krankheits triumphed over the Gesundheits!

GUNTHUR: But we swore blood brotherhood!

HAGEN: He broke the bond when he took your wife! Now, get his ring and the world will be yours.

GUNTHUR: Brunnhilda's ring?

HAGEN: Der Nihilump's ring!

GUNTHUR: *(Heaves a profound sigh)* So it has come to this! He'll fall this way.

HAGEN: His fall—our rise.

GUNTHUR: But have you thought of Gutruna? Do you know what this will do to her? How can we kill the man she loves and still look her in the eye?

BRUNNHILDA: She's the one! Yes she!! Sour young sorceress who with gashed potion seduced the nude young hero! She must be broken, she!

GUNTHUR: You are not human, Brunnhild.

HAGEN: Don't tell her, then. His death would break her heart. Tomorrow on a hunt our men will find him boar gored and stabbed in the back.

BRUNNHILDA: Then sealed is Siegfried's doom!

GUNTHUR: Sealed is Siegfried's doom!

HAGEN:

So sealed is Siegfried's doom
At last we'll rise from Nibelheims' gloom
By a wild boar tomorrow Siegfried will be gored
And the Nihilumps' ring will have a new lord!
The banners of Nihilump will be unfurled!
Alverrück, Father, you'll rule the world!

(The three conspirators stand and watch SIEGFRIED *and* GUTRUNA's *bridal procession as the curtain falls.)*

Scene 6: *A lovely landscape through which flows the azure waters of the Rhein.*

(The Rheinmaidens disport themselves among the waves and lament the loss of their gold.)

THE THREE RHEINMAIDENS: Gott in himmel, where ist das Gold? Das Gold is verloren! Das Gold scheint nicht hier! Wagalaweia! Wallala weiala weia! La la! We sang in its glow! We swam in its schein! It rivals the sun in its schein! Return our Gold to the depths of the Rhein!

(Siegfried's horn is heard.)

WOGLINDE: I hear a horn.

WELGUNDE: Hier comes ein real mensch!

FLOSSHILDE: Let's hide!

(They dive under the water.)

SIEGFRIED: Where is that bear? These elves and gnomes make terrible guides. *(Calling out)* Elves! Gnomes! Where is that bear? Ach! I've lost my way!

THE THREE RHEINMAIDENS: Siegfried, watcha lookin' for?

SIEGFRIED: I'm hunting a great bigische bear. Help me to find him and I'll give him to you for a lover, pretty little fishies.

THE THREE RHEINMAIDENS: Ha ha ha ha ha ha!

WOGLINDE: What will you give us if we help you catch him?

SIEGFRIED: What do you want?

WELGUNDE: The golden ring on your ring finger.

SIEGFRIED: What, my ring?

FLOSSHILDE: Will you give it to us, pretty please?

SIEGFRIED: My wife wouldn't like it me giving a ring to strange women.

WOGLINDE: Is she so jealous?

WELGUNDE: Is she so stingy with her man?

FLOSSHILDE: Does she beat you, then?

WOGLINDE: Selfish thing! She wants everything to herself. She has a handsome husband and she wants the ring, too!

SIEGFRIED: Do you want it so badly? Here, take it! *(Holds the ring out to them just out of their reach. They stretch out their arms for it. They leap out of the water to get it but to no avail)* Ha ha ha ha ha ha!

WOGLINDE: Don't tease us!

WELGUNDE: We could tell you something well worth knowing if the hero were willing to listen.

FLOSSHILDE: We know something about that ring of yours.

SIEGFRIED: Tell me what you know?

WOGLINDE: The ring was forged from stolen Gold!

WELGUNDE: The ring is hot.

FLOSSHILDE: The ring is cursed.

WOGLINDE: So you'd better give it to us if you know what's good for you.

WELGUNDE: Only Rheinwater can quench its curse!

FLOSSHILDE: Or else death comes to the ring's lord!

SIEGFRIED: Ha! So you think I'm afraid? I would have given you this trinket, if you'd asked me nicely. But Siegfried never yields to a threat. Farewell naughty nixies.

WOGLINDE: The man is mad.

WELGUNDE: The man's an idiot!

FLOSSHILDE: The man is doomed. Come back, Siegfried! Believe us, mastermensch! We speak the truth! If you love life, listen, O listen . . .

WOGLINDE: It's no use, Flosshilde. The man's a fool who knows no fear. We cannot save him.

FLOSSHILDE: Such a strong man, ripe for love. He's beautiful, isn't he? Ah what a loss to the world!

WELGUNDE: A loss, yes. But sometimes it's better to be weak.

WOGLINDE:
His wife knows better.
She alone can free the world
From its golden fetter!

(They swim away.)

SIEGFRIED: *(Smiling after them)* Now I am too smart for women's wiles. But if Gutruna weren't my wife I might take one of these to bed—after drying her off, of course.

HAGEN: *(Voice far off)* Hoiho! Hoiho!

SIEGFRIED: Hoiho! Hoiho!

THE VASSALS: Hoiho! Hoiho!

(Enter HAGEN and his men.)

HAGEN: Have you any trophies from the hunt yet, Siegfried?

SIEGFRIED: No, but I did meet some waterfowl who told my fortune. They said I would die today. *(Laughs)*

(HAGEN stares guiltily.)

HAGEN: That would be an evil chase indeed, where hunter is killed by the game.

SIEGFRIED: I'm thirsty.

GUNTHUR: *(Aside)* And so he is for more than wine.

SIEGFRIED: *(Offering his hunting horn)* Drink, Gunthur.

GUNTHUR: The wine's too thin. *(Looks into the horn and cries out)* Where's *my* blood? I see only Siegfried's blood! (SIEGFRIED *pours his wine into Gunthur's horn until it overflows*) You're spilling the wine on the ground.

SIEGFRIED: *(Merrily)* That's my offering to Mother Earth. *(Drinks long and deep)*

GUNTHUR: *(Heaves a sigh)* Siegfried, all-too-cheerful man.

HAGEN: *(Changing the subject)* I've heard you can understand birdsong, Siegfried.

SIEGFRIED: Yes, I used to. But since I discovered women's voices I stopped listening to the song of birds! *(Laughs and drinks deeply again)*

HAGEN: *(Aside)* Let this antidote cure Siegfried's amnesia. *(Aloud)* Here, drink, Siegfried.

SIEGFRIED: *(Drinks, pauses, then toasts holding aloft the cup)* Gunthur, all-too-gloomy man, here's a toast. To my love, Brunnhild, for whom I walked through fire, found her asleep, woke her with a kiss—ah, then enfolded myself like fire in Brunnhilda's arms!

(Sensation throughout the party.)

GUNTHUR: *(Springing to his feet)* What did you say? What did I hear?

(Two ravens fly up, circle screaming over SIEGFRIED*'s head, and disappear.)*

HAGEN: Do you understand the speech of ravens? (SIEGFRIED *turns his back to watch the ravens.* HAGEN *thrusts his spear into* SIEGFRIED *from behind)* They scream for vengeance!

*(*SIEGFRIED *wheels around and with his last strength raises his sword and shield. But he staggers and falls backward on his shield.)*

SIEGFRIED: *(Sitting up for a moment supported by some of the men)* Brunnhilda, holy bride, awake! Your lover has come at last! *(Dies)*

(Night falls on the general grief. Gunthur's vassals raise SIEGFRIED *on his shield and bear him out in a funeral procession.)*

Scene 7: *Gibich hall.*

(The clouds part to reveal the moon.)

GUTRUNA:
Siegfried? Siegfried?
Did I hear his horn? No, nothing.
Or was it my nightmare's neighing?
Where is Brunnhilda?
Brunnhilda are you there?
Our men are home from the hunt.

HAGEN: Awake! Awake! Light torches. The hunters are home with fresh kill.

GUTRUNA: *(Very frightened)* Where is Siegfried? I didn't hear his horn.

HAGEN: Nor will you ever hear it again.

GUTRUNA: What are you saying? What are they carrying there?

HAGEN: Your man is dead. A wild boar has slain him.

(All react with horror and grief.)

HAGEN: Do not be downhearted, sister mine.

GUTRUNA: *(Examining the body)* Siegfried was murdered! O horror! O help! Oh! The sons of Gibich have murdered my Siegfried!

GUNTHUR: Don't blame me. Hagen was the wild boar who gored him.

HAGEN: Don't be mad at me, sister mine.

GUTRUNA: Die blind, you fork-tongued blue-toothed boneless swine. Plague blacken your heart until it stinks like a flyblown corpse! Live ever in torments, he who took my Siegfried from me!

HAGEN: Yes, I killed the hero! I, Hagen! And what's to prevent me from becoming a hero in turn? This spear on which he perjured himself wrought his destruction and now Hagen the victor, the hero, claims his prize! The ring is mine!

GUNTHUR: Stand back! I have the prior claim.

HAGEN: Never! Vassals, defend my rights!

GUNTHUR: For shame, greed-wracked elf, to take what doesn't belong to you. You'll never get the ring, this I swear!

HAGEN: The elf will take what's his, damn you! *(They both rush for the ring and fight. The vassals try to part them but HAGEN strikes GUNTHUR dead. GUTRUNA screams)* Now for the ring.

(HAGEN reaches to remove the ring from SIEGFRIED's hand, which rises in a threatening gesture. All shrink back in horror.)

BRUNNHILDA: *(Enters gravely from behind)* Peace! Peace! Quiet all of you! Let's have no crying over spilt milk. There's no man here eloquent enough to frame a lament for the noblest hero that ever lived.

GUTRUNA: Brunnhilda, this is all your fault. You raised the Gibich men against him and told them where to strike!

BRUNNHILDA: You were his mistress, nothing more. I was his lawful wife! Lay off these moonish shades of griefs and fears. There's nothing sooner dry than women's tears.

GUTRUNA: I see it all now. Ah, curse you, Hagen, who made me drug his drink. Brunnhilda was his true love! The cup made him forget. *(Turns away from SIEGFRIED and stands almost fainting over GUNTHUR's corpse)*

BRUNNHILDA: Build a huge inhuman funeral pyre! Pile the logs up higher! Higher! Throw the hero's bones upon the fire. There evermore to sleep in double fold of fire. Twoton, God in all your ire, burn yon blonde man who dared aspire. Without a blast from the sea. Gnomes, Giants, Men, Gods, and you God of Gods, the Sun, behold what Woman for the love of Man has done. *(Takes the ring from Siegfried's finger and hurls it into the Rhein)*

HAGEN: *(Leaping into the waters after the ring)* No! No! The ring is mine!

(The Rheinmaidens draw him down under the waves and drown him.)

BRUNNHILDA: Siegfried! Siegfried! Now in the laughing flames I see! The higher men must learn to laugh and then we'll all be free. *(Mounts her horse and rides into the flames)*

(Wallhalla and all is consumed in flames. Below in the river FLOSSHILDE joyously holds the ring aloft.)

End

THE VENTRILOQUIST'S WIFE

A Psychodrama for Cabaret

1978

Black-Eyed Susan, Walter Ego & Charles Ludlam
in *The Ventriloquist's Wife* (Andrew Horn)

Cast of Characters

THE VENTRILOQUIST
HIS WIFE
WALTER EGO

Scene 1: *The kitchen of the ventriloquist's flat in New York's Lower East Side.*

(The WIFE *is frying fish in ankle socks.)*

VENTRILOQUIST *(Entering with shabby suitcase)* Hi, honey, I'm home.

WIFE: *(Flying into his arms)* Papa bear is home.

VENTRILOQUIST: *(Twirling her)* And have I got a surprise for you!

WIFE: Oh, goody!

VENTRILOQUIST: Baby, I've found it. No more schlepping! No more weddings! No more birthday parties. No more Elks lodge! No more girdle manufacturers conventions! No more being hailed by millions just because I'm driving a cab.

WIFE: You're giving up show business?

VENTRILOQUIST: Guess again.

WIFE: You're giving up stand-up comedy?

VENTRILOQUIST: Wrong again! I'm not giving up stand-up comedy—I'm just beginning! Baby, what I'm trying to tell you is . . . I got a gimmick!

WIFE: So, what's the gimmick?

VENTRILOQUIST: Sit down first.

WIFE: Oh, brother, this had better be good. *(She sits)*

VENTRILOQUIST: Now close your eyes.

WIFE: *(She closes her eyes)* If there's one thing I can't stand it's suspense.

VENTRILOQUIST: Ah ah ah, no peeking. *(He goes to open the suitcase)*

WIFE: What's taking so long?

VENTRILOQUIST: You'll see.

WIFE: Can I look now?

VENTRILOQUIST: No. *(Stands with one foot up on the shabby suitcase and sits a ventriloquist's dummy on his knee)* O.K., now open your eyes.

WIFE: Oh, Charles, he's adorable. Just like a child. *(Addressing the dummy)* Hello, what's your name, little fella?

WALTER: Aw! *(Buries his head in the ventriloquist's chest shyly)*

VENTRILOQUIST: He's shy. Come on, Walter, the lady won't bite you.

WALTER: But you know me. I might bite the lady.

WIFE: *(Laughing delightedly)* You are a cute little devil.

WALTER: You're kinda cute yourself!

WIFE: Oh, you're just saying that because it's true!

WALTER: Cut it out. I do the jokes in this act!

WIFE: Where do you live?

WALTER: I live with daddy.

WIFE: Where does daddy live?

WALTER: With me.

WIFE: Where do you and your daddy live?

WALTER: Together.

WIFE: You're fresh. If you were my kid, I'd kill you.

WALTER: You wouldn't have to. If I were your kid I'd commit suicide.

WIFE: I'd like to take you over my knee and give you a spanking!

WALTER: If you do, you'll get a handful of splinters. Did you ever see a woodpecker? I've got twelve inches, but I don't use it as a rule.

WIFE: Ah, that does it. *(Laughing so hard she can hardly speak)* I'm *(Laughs)* speechless!

WALTER: That's unusual for a gal!

VENTRILOQUIST: That's not fair! Women don't talk all the time.

WALTER: Only when they're awake.

VENTRILOQUIST: What do you think of him?

WIFE: It's perfect. I didn't know that you could do ventriloquism.

VENTRILOQUIST: Neither did I until I picked up Walter in a pawnshop.

WALTER: What the hell is ventrickleism?

VENTRILOQUIST: It's an act done by a comedian and a dummy.

WALTER: Which one are you?

VENTRILOQUIST: It was like fate. I had a bowl of soup at the B&H dairy lunch on Second Avenue.

WIFE: You had mushroom barley.

VENTRILOQUIST: *(Astonished)* How did you know that?

WIFE: This is Tuesday. They always have mushroom barley on Tuesday.

VENTRILOQUIST: Well, you know the fat waiter in there?

WIFE: I thought they were all fat.

VENTRILOQUIST: At lunchtime when the place is crowded he does ventriloquism. He says, "Hey, lady!" in this little pinhead voice. All the women look around, they can't tell where the voice is coming from. It's funny. Anyway, it got me thinking about ventriloquism. Then I walked home a different way and saw Walter sitting in the window of a pawnshop on Tenth Street and Second Avenue. I walked in, asked to see him, and when he started talking I bought him.

WIFE: How much did he cost?

VENTRILOQUIST: Five hundred dollars.

WIFE: Ouch!

VENTRILOQUIST: You think that's too much?

WIFE: *(Affectionately)* I think they saw you coming.

VENTRILOQUIST: Don't you think he's worth it? How many ventriloquist dummies am I going to buy? This is a lifetime investment.

WALTER: Sucker, they should have paid him to take me away.

WIFE: *(Laughing)* How do you do that?

VENTRILOQUIST: It's just a knack, I guess.

WIFE: You must have been born with it.

VENTRILOQUIST: You do think Walter's worth it?

WIFE: Of course he's worth it. You're worth it. No mink coat this winter, that's all.

VENTRILOQUIST: Walter's going to make all the difference for us. You'll see. As soon as he's paid for himself he can start working on that mink coat.

WIFE: Did you think I was serious?

VENTRILOQUIST: I wasn't sure. I know a mink coat makes a woman feel wanted.

WALTER: And if you give her one you'll be wanted too—by the police.

WIFE: I guess I'd better start getting used to living with Walter. And we weren't going to have any of our own.

VENTRILOQUIST: What?

WIFE: Children.

WALTER: *(Screams to ventriloquist)* Father! Father! Acknowledge me!

WIFE: Walter, how would you like me to be your mother?

WALTER: *(With a lewd guttural growl)* Daddy would like that. Yeah!

WIFE: *(To WALTER)* We've got to get you some new clothes.

WALTER: Yeah!

WIFE: Wait a minute. I have some clothes for you.

WALTER: You do?

WIFE: Here they are! Little dungarees, a cowboy shirt . . . how will that do?

VENTRILOQUIST: Where did they come from?

WIFE: They're for my nephew. But his birthday's not till Wednesday.

VENTRILOQUIST: Tomorrow's Wednesday.

WIFE: A week from tomorrow. There's time. I'll get another set. *(Putting them on WALTER)* What do you know? They fit perfectly!

VENTRILOQUIST: I think we should get outfits that match, don't you?

WIFE: A contrast is good too.

VENTRILOQUIST: No, we should definitely have matching outfits.

WIFE: If you say so. I'll make them for you.

VENTRILOQUIST: I'll get the fabric.

WALTER: That's a nice fabric you're wearing. Why don't you have it made into a suit?

WIFE: Is Walter going to have our last name too?

VENTRILOQUIST: No, I've got a last name all picked out for him. Ego.

WIFE: Ego?

VENTRILOQUIST: Walter Ego.

WIFE: *(Laughing)* You're mad!

WALTER: Next to him even I look sane.

VENTRILOQUIST: *(Sternly)* Quiet, Walter.

WIFE: *(To the audience)* He got a job in a nightclub in Greenwich Village, that little Bohemia situated in the triangle of crooked streets in the heart of old New York.

Scene 2: *Stage of a beatnik nightclub in Greenwich Village.*

VENTRILOQUIST: *(With WALTER on his knee)* Ladies and gentlemen, thank you very much for having me here tonight.

WALTER: Baloney! They came to see me.

VENTRILOQUIST: Walter, these people came to see me. I just brought you here out of the kindness of my heart.

WALTER: Do te-hell.

VENTRILOQUIST: Yes. It's just that I like to have you around. You're my valet, my gentleman's gentleman, my aide-de-camp, er er my . . . er . . .

WALTER: Your meal ticket?

VENTRILOQUIST: Yes.

WALTER: Ah, well, be that as it may, Ludlam, I'd be glad to help you out.

VENTRILOQUIST: Thank you, Walter, but I really don't need your help. I've had lots of experience as an M.C.

WALTER: M.C.?

VENTRILOQUIST: Yes.

WALTER: Mildewed Casanova?

VENTRILOQUIST: You shouldn't have said that, Walter. I've always felt that we were . . . that we were pals, Walter, that I could depend on you.

WALTER: Yeah?

VENTRILOQUIST: And that you could depend on me.

WALTER: Yeah.

VENTRILOQUIST: That we could depend on each other.

WALTER: This must be leading somewhere.

VENTRILOQUIST: That we were closer than mere friends. We're . . . we're real buddies.

WALTER: Yeah.

VENTRILOQUIST: Real buddies. Deep down.

WALTER: Yeah. Get your hand off my knee.

VENTRILOQUIST: Ours has been a perfect partnership. We belong together.

WALTER: Yes we do.

VENTRILOQUIST: We go together like, well, like spaghetti and meatballs.

WALTER: Yes, and we know which one is the meatball, don't we?

VENTRILOQUIST: Walter, please, show a little more respect. You are talking to an expert ventriloquist.

WALTER: And you're talking to yourself.

VENTRILOQUIST: I throw my voice.

WALTER: Well you can throw it in the garbage. I'm gonna expose this whole racket.

VENTRILOQUIST: Ventriloquism isn't a racket, Walter. Ventriloquism is a profession.

WALTER: So's ragpicking, but it's still trash.

VENTRILOQUIST: Walter, I'll have you know that the ancient Egyptians used ventriloquism as part of their religious rituals, and there have been ventriloquists found among the Eskimos in the far far north.

WALTER: They weren't found there. They were chased there.

VENTRILOQUIST: And furthermore, ventriloquism . . .

WALTER: I gotta go to the toilet.

VENTRILOQUIST: As I was saying, ventriloquism . . .

WALTER: I gotta go to the toilet.

VENTRILOQUIST: Walter, please, we're in public. You don't say, "I got to go to the toilet."

WALTER: No?

VENTRILOQUIST: No. If when we're in public you should feel a call of nature, just say, "I've got to travel," and I'll know what you mean. Now as I was saying, ventriloquism . . .

WALTER: I gotta travel.

VENTRILOQUIST: Just a minute, Walter. Ventriloquism . . .

WALTER: I gotta travel.

VENTRILOQUIST: Excuse me. Ventriloquism . . .

WALTER: I'm traveling. I'm traveling.

VENTRILOQUIST: *(Gasps)* Excuse me. Good night, ladies and gentlemen. *(Runs out with* WALTER*)*

Scene 3: *The ventriloquist's living room.*

(The phone voices are done ventriloquially by the actress playing the wife.)

WIFE: *(On the phone)* Hello, Sandy, how are you? How's David? *(Long pause, big cringing reaction)* The birthday party was *last* Wednesday. Oh, no, I thought it was this coming Wednesday. I got him the cutest little blue jeans and cowboy suit. Oh, I'm so sorry. I don't know what got into me. Yeah, me too. Bye. *(She hangs up. The phone rings)* Hello?

VOICE OF WALTER: Hello there, Susan. This is Walter.

WIFE: *(Laughing)* Oh, hello, Charles. I was just thinking of you.

VOICE OF WALTER: This isn't Charles. This is Walter. *(Does heavy breathing)*

WIFE: You're a riot! You should go on the stage.

VOICE OF WALTER: Susan, I had a dream about you last night.

SUSAN: Did you?

VOICE OF WALTER: No, you wouldn't let me. Do you know what's big and hairy and sticks out of my pajamas at night?

WIFE: Walter!

VOICE OF WALTER: My head. What's hard that you hold to your mouth?

SUSAN: *(Indignantly)* I wouldn't know.

VOICE OF WALTER: The telephone! heh, heh, heh. *(In a hoarse whisper)* Susan, I want to tell you something. I want you to sit on my face.

WIFE: Charles.

VOICE OF WALTER: I told you this isn't Charles. What do you want to hang around a loser like him for?

WIFE: This isn't funny.

VOICE OF WALTER: *(Heavy breathing)*

WIFE: *(Outraged)* Charles, stop it. It isn't funny anymore.

VOICE OF WALTER: *(Hoarse whisper)* Call the pawnshop. Call the pawnshop.

WIFE: Call the pawnshop?

VOICE OF WALTER: *(Hoarse whisper)* Find out who I am. *(Click)*

WIFE: *(Dials 411)* Could you give me the number of a pawnshop located at Tenth Street and Second Avenue? In Manhattan, yes. Three Balls Pledge and Pawn? And the number? 533-9299. *(Hangs up. Dials)* Hello. I'm the wife of the man who bought the ventriloquist dummy from you the other day. Yes, we love him. *(Pause)* Yes, I'm sure you could have gotten six hundred. *(Perfunctorily)* Yes, he's worth every penny of it. We were wondering who had him last? *(Listens)* Yes, a ventriloquist, but do you know who he was? He did. How long ago was that? His wife, you say. Tch tch tch. Too bad. *(Shudders)* Yes, I guess that's life all right. Thank you. *(Hangs up absently)*

VOICE OF WALTER: *(From behind her)* Have I got something for you!

WIFE: *(Turns around, startled)* You frightened me.

VENTRILOQUIST: Sorry.

WIFE: I'm a little unstrung. I'm not used to getting obscene phone calls.

VENTRILOQUIST: You got an obscene phone call?

WIFE: From you. Or was it all Walter's fault?

VENTRILOQUIST: I don't know what you're talking about. I didn't call you at all today.

WIFE: Stop fooling.

VENTRILOQUIST: Who's fooling?

WALTER: A fool and his dummy are soon parted.

WIFE: *(Reacts to the dummy uneasily, almost as if she were not sure whether to blame him or not)* I got an ugly phone call today.

VENTRILOQUIST: *(Tenderly)* I'm sorry. What was it?

WIFE: The works—heavy breathing and a lewd suggestion.

VENTRILOQUIST: Take it in your stride.

WIFE: It was Walter's voice, Charles.

VENTRILOQUIST: *(Very disturbed)* You're kidding.

WIFE: At first I thought it was you, but then when it got ugly . . .

VENTRILOQUIST: It must be somebody who knows I'm a ventriloquist, some weirdo who's seen my act at the bar. Did he say anything else?

WIFE: No, nothing really. I don't remember.

VENTRILOQUIST: That's right. Try to forget all about it.

WIFE: *(Looking at WALTER)* You didn't make that nasty phone call, did you Walter?

WALTER: I didn't do it! I didn't do it!

VENTRILOQUIST: You know the difference between right and wrong, don't you Walter?

WALTER: Sure I do. Wrong is usually more fun. *(Chuckles)* Heh heh heh!

WIFE: Why don't you put Walter away for a while? It seems we haven't been alone together in such a long time.

VENTRILOQUIST: It's hard when I'm working.

WIFE: Sometimes I don't know what to do with myself when you're away at night.

VENTRILOQUIST: You're always welcome down at the club. But I know you get tired of hearing my jokes.

WIFE: It isn't that. It's just that I can't sit there alone at a table drinking night after night. I'll turn into an alcoholic. I wish I were part of your act.

VENTRILOQUIST: I *was* thinking of making a full-length woman.

WIFE: Charles, I am a full-length woman.

WALTER: I've got it! Why don't you become a topless accordion player?

WIFE: Oh Charles, can't we ever just talk without Walter making wisecracks?

VENTRILOQUIST: *(Grudgingly)* Oh all right. I'm sorry, Walter, you have to go in the suitcase.

WALTER: No! No! Not the suitcase! Are you gonna do everything that woman tells you to? *(Screaming)* I wish Adam had died with both ribs intact!

WIFE: *(To WALTER)* What are you making this big fuss about?

WALTER: It's humiliating. I've gotta save face!

WIFE: Try keeping the lower half shut.

WALTER: There you have the greatest single argument for twin beds.

WIFE: Have you got a chip on your shoulder or is that your head?

VENTRILOQUIST: Susan!

WALTER: She's just sore because I can read her like a book—and I like to read in bed.

VENTRILOQUIST: Walter!

WIFE: Why, you little knothole, I'll make toothpicks out of ya.

VENTRILOQUIST: Stop it, stop it both of you!

WALTER: I'm not going to take that from a kept woman! Especially one that looks like she's been kept under a rock.

WIFE: That does it! Put him away.

VENTRILOQUIST: This time you've gone too far, Walter. Back in the suitcase.

WALTER: Not the suitcase! Help! Murder! Police!

VENTRILOQUIST: It's no use yelling, Walter. Nobody's going to help you.

WALTER: Let go of my arm! You're hurting my arm! Help me! Stop him! He's hurting me!

WIFE: Charles, stop. Don't hurt him.

VENTRILOQUIST: Don't interfere. He's got to learn his lesson. *(Locking* WALTER *into the suitcase)*

WALTER: *(Screaming)* Susan, help. Don't let him do this to me!

VENTRILOQUIST: *(Angrily)* Quiet, Walter!

WALTER: Fuck you!

VENTRILOQUIST: Susan, he cannot be allowed to get away with this. Walter, you're going to be punished.

WALTER: Fuck you! Fuck you!

VENTRILOQUIST: *(Slaps hand over* WALTER's *mouth)*

WALTER: *(Bites hand)* Ha! Ha! Ha! Ak ptui! *(Spits on ventriloquist)* Your mother sucks cocks in hell! Your mother sucks cocks in hell!

WIFE: Charles, he's possessed. *(*WALTER *rotates his head 360 degrees. Suddenly an erection appears between his legs.* WIFE *screams)*

VENTRILOQUIST: *(Urgently locking* WALTER *in the suitcase)* You're going back in the suitcase.

WALTER: You'll never get away with this! I'll get even with you, you dirty son of a . . .

VENTRILOQUIST: *(Slams lid of suitcase)* Wheh!

(They both stand there looking at each other awkwardly and in silence.)

VENTRILOQUIST: Well, what did you want to talk about?

WIFE: Can't we just enjoy being together without talking?

(There is another long and painful silence.)

VENTRILOQUIST: *(Picks up the suitcase and starts to leave)* Since we obviously have nothing to say to each other do you mind if I take Walter down to the club to rehearse our act that earns all three of us our livings?

WIFE: All three of us? Sometimes you talk as though Walter meant more to you than I do. Oh Charles, give up ventriloquism. Stop throwing your voice.

VENTRILOQUIST: Do you want me to give up my work for you?

WIFE: I fell in love with you because I thought you were talented.

VENTRILOQUIST: It's him. I can't get rid of him.

WIFE: Can't get rid of him? A hunk of wood? A fugitive from a fireplace?

VENTRILOQUIST: Don't talk about him that way.

WIFE: "It" not "him" . . . *"it."* Walter is a dummy, Charles. He's not a real person.

VENTRILOQUIST: You believe what you want and I'll believe what I want. *(Exit hugging the suitcase)*

WIFE: *(To the audience)* And I became jealous. How silly of me. It was the greatest tribute I could have paid to him and the way he had gone about perfecting the art of throwing his voice. Walter Ego was everything he would never let himself try to be.

Scene 4: *Stage of a high-class nightclub.*

(The VENTRILOQUIST *and* WALTER *wear matching tuxedos and turbans.)*

VENTRILOQUIST: Good evening, ladies and gentlemen. Tonight we have the rare privilege of participating in a seance with the world's youngest perfect master, Swami Ego. *(Intones)* Ooooooh, Swami Ego. Ooooooh, Swami Ego.

WALTER: Ooooooh, shut up.

VENTRILOQUIST: Swami Ego, is it true that tonight you're going to read the audience's minds?

WALTER: Yes, but it isn't going to be easy.

VENTRILOQUIST: Why's that?

WALTER: It isn't easy to read blank pages.

VENTRILOQUIST: Before reading your minds, the Swami will have to go into a trance. Go into a trance, Swami.

WALTER: *(Makes the sound)* Eeeeegh.

VENTRILOQUIST: What's the matter?

WALTER: A trance isn't easy to go into, you know.

VENTRILOQUIST: I can believe it.

WALTER: Eeeeegh. I think this trance is too small. I may be trying to get into the wrong end of it.

VENTRILOQUIST: Here, let me help you. *(Takes out crystal ball on chain and swings it back and forth before* WALTER'*s eyes)* Watch the crystal ball, Swami.

WALTER: Why? What's it gonna do?

VENTRILOQUIST: Never mind, just watch the crystal ball, Swami, watch it as it swings to and fro.

WALTER: *(Following the crystal ball with his eyes and then finally his head, always favoring the right)*

VENTRILOQUIST: What's the matter?

WALTER: It was swinging to but it wasn't swinging fro.

VENTRILOQUIST: Yes it was, now concentrate. *(Swings ball.* WALTER *falls into a trance)*

WALTER: Gnong!

VENTRILOQUIST: *(Passing his hand before* WALTER'*s staring eyes)* Ladies and gentlemen, the Swami is in a deep trance, and he is about to read your minds. I would like to remind you that Swami is only six years old, so keep it clean. Swami, are you getting any vibrations from the crowd?

WALTER: The lady at table nine puts out.

VENTRILOQUIST: I will now blindfold the Swami with this simple black cloth.

WALTER: I want a polka-dot cloth.

VENTRILOQUIST: Swami, we don't have a polka-dot cloth, we only have this simple black silk cloth.

WALTER: I want a polka-dot cloth!

VENTRILOQUIST: But Swami, what can I do? There is no polka-dot cloth available.

WALTER: Oh ye of little faith!

VENTRILOQUIST: Oh, Swami, I'm sorry to hear you say that.

WALTER: You must empty your mind and recite the sacred mantra, and you will find what you want in your lefthand pocket.

VENTRILOQUIST: Ah, those haunting words. "I must empty my mind, recite the sacred mantra, and I will find what I want in my lefthand pocket." But Swami, I don't know the sacred mantra.

(WALTER *whispers something in the* VENTRILOQUIST'*s ear.*)

VENTRILOQUIST: I'll try. First I will empty my mind. (VENTRILOQUIST *with a concentrated look on his face shakes his head from side to side. Gradually a blank look of peace and contentment comes over his face*) Well, that feels a lot better. I should have done that a long time ago. (*Reaches into his lefthand pocket, pulls out a fistful of polka dots*) Polka dots! But how can I get the polka dots to adhere to the scarf, O, Swami?

WALTER: Give up all strivings and recite the sacred mantra!

VENTRILOQUIST: (*Throws the polka dots in the air*) Oh, who the heck cares! Alakazoo kazam! (*The polka dots stick to the scarf, transforming it into a polka-dot scarf*) It's a miracle! (*Falls on his knees beside* WALTER, *clutching his hand and kissing it*) You are the perfect six-year-old master after all. (*Blindfolds* WALTER *with the scarf*) Now, ladies and gentlemen, as I pass among you, if you will hold up any simple object you may have about you, the Swami will attempt to name the object you are holding. (*Takes* WALTER *and passes among the audience*) Oh Swami Ego, what is this lady holding?

WALTER: She's holding? Loose joints! Loose joints!

VENTRILOQUIST: Concentrate, Swami. What is this lady holding in her hand?

WALTER: A pair of eyeglasses.

VENTRILOQUIST: Amazing! Why Swami, this is clairvoyant!

WALTER: How do you do, Claire.

VENTRILOQUIST: Now Swami, what is this gentleman holding in his hand?

WALTER: He's gonna go blind and insane.

VENTRILOQUIST: The other hand, Swami, the other hand!

WALTER: A bottle of beer.

VENTRILOQUIST: Correct.

WALTER: A bottle of beer. A bottle of beer. A bottle of beer.

VENTRILOQUIST: Swami, what is this lady holding in her hand?

WALTER: I can't guess.

VENTRILOQUIST: How about that? Try again, Swami.

WALTER: I can't guess.

VENTRILOQUIST: How about that, Swami. How about that.

WALTER: I can't remember the code.

VENTRILOQUIST: What code? The Swami is only kidding, folks. Swami, you've got to guess.

WALTER: I can't guess. I can't guess.

VENTRILOQUIST: This is humiliating. (*Sotto voce to* WALTER) How about that. How about that. H-a-t. H-a-t.

WALTER: I can't guess.

VENTRILOQUIST: Swami, you failed.

WALTER: Well it isn't easy to read minds with a hand up your ass.

VENTRILOQUIST: (*Carries* WALTER *back to the stage*) Swami, when I goose you, you will remember nothing. (*Ventriloquist gooses* WALTER)

WALTER: (*Coming out of the trance*) I remember nothing. Ladies and gentlemen, I have an announcement to make.

VENTRILOQUIST: Ladies and gentlemen, may I have your attention please? The Swami has an announcement to make.

WALTER: I'm going to get a new ventriloquist.

VENTRILOQUIST: What?

WALTER: And next time I'm going to get a funny one, folks.

VENTRILOQUIST: Walter, you don't mean that.

WALTER: Yes, I do. You're through, Ludlam. Pick up two weeks' pay and clear out.

VENTRILOQUIST: No, Walter, please, don't leave me. I'll try to improve. If there's anything about my personality that you'd like me to change, I'll do it.

WALTER: Well there is one thing.

VENTRILOQUIST: Tell me what it is. If there's any flaw in my character, I'll try to change.

WALTER: Well, Ludlam, I find you just a little . . .

VENTRILOQUIST: A little what, Walter?

WALTER: I find you just a little bit pretentious.

VENTRILOQUIST: Pretentious? Moi?

WALTER: I'm going to do an act with Susan.

VENTRILOQUIST: With Susan?

WALTER: Yes. We're going out on our own.

VENTRILOQUIST: *(Begging and pleading)* Please, Walter, don't leave me. Let me tag along. I'll make myself useful. *(He weeps.)*

WALTER: *(Laughs)*

VENTRILOQUIST: *(Weeps)*

WALTER: *(Laughs, screams)* Ego über alles!

VENTRILOQUIST: No, Walter, no. You'll never get away with this. I'm the ventriloquist and you're the dummy.

WALTER: How dare you? I am a ventriloquial figure, and don't you ever forget it. You're washed up, Ludlam. I don't need you anymore.

VENTRILOQUIST: *(Possessed)* No, Walter. It is I who don't need you. You're going back in your trunk. And Susan and I will do an act together!

WALTER: *(Screaming)* Take your hands off me! Help! Murder! Police! Just for that, I am never going to speak to you again as long as you live. *(WALTER becomes inanimate)*

VENTRILOQUIST: *(Mollified)* Walter, you don't mean that. Walter, speak to me. Speak to me, Walter. *(Shakes WALTER's limp arm. There is no response)* You're just trying to frighten me. I don't need you. I don't need anybody. *(Locks WALTER in the suitcase like a murderer concealing a corpse)* That's right. I don't need you, Walter. There are plenty of things I can do on my own. *(Places suitcase on stool downstage center)* Yes, I can do lots of things. I can do card tricks. *(Takes deck of cards out of his vest pocket, shuffles them, fans them, and offers them to an audience member)* Pick a card. Any card. *(Pinching his nostrils between his eyes)* You have picked the ace of spades.

AUDIENCE MEMBER: Wrong.

VENTRILOQUIST: *(Throwing the deck in the air)* Fuck card tricks. This is the end, Walter. I don't need you anymore. Good-bye forever. *(Turns and walks upstage, leaving the suitcase alone on the stool)*

VOICE OF WALTER: *(From suitcase, as the suitcase gently rocks back and forth)* You'll never get away with this.

VENTRILOQUIST: *(Turns in horror and gasps)* Walter!

VOICE OF WALTER: *(Muffled)* You'll never get away with this. *(Sinister laughter. The suitcase rocks as the lights fade)*

Scene 5: *Sawing a lady in half.*

VENTRILOQUIST: Ladies and gentlemen, tonight it is my very great privilege to commit a perverse act, the likes of which make the divine Marquis de Sade a mere fantasist by comparison. For tonight, ladies and gentlemen, I intend to saw a lady in two. This experiment has not been undertaken in the spirit of a mere stage illusion. Oh no! In fact I have given little or no attention to the feat of sawing the woman in half. This gruesome enterprise can easily be accomplished by any maniac with a saw. I shall apply the magical processes only to the restoration of the guts to a single female once again. And now as I pass the saw among you for examination, imagine if you will these cold steel teeth gnawing their way through the warm, lovely, and entirely vulnerable flesh of a desirable woman. *(Passes saw through audience)* But before the ladies in the audience faint or the gentlemen rise against me on behalf of the lady in danger, let me assure you that this act will be accomplished painlessly and with the full consent of the victim. Let me introduce her to you now, the very lovely and vulnerable Black-Eyed Susan. *(Enter* WIFE*)* Let me assure you that her participation in this experiment is entirely voluntary. That she is not in debt to me, nor has she been blackmailed. Is this true, Black-Eyed Susan?

WIFE: It is.

VENTRILOQUIST: Susan, consider the feelings you will experience as the saw passes through the various organs of your body. *(Plays accompaniment on musical saw)*

WIFE: Proceed.

VENTRILOQUIST: Very well, then, if you will be so kind as to step into the cabinette.

(The VENTRILOQUIST *helps her into the cabinette. He begins to saw her in half.)*

WIFE: Ooops! Be careful.

VENTRILOQUIST: Did that hurt?

WIFE: No, go on.

VENTRILOQUIST: Susan, you must promise me that you will stop me if you feel the slightest pain.

WIFE: Don't worry about me. Go on!

VENTRILOQUIST: Don't worry, Susan. The last woman I sawed in half is alive and well and living in Paris and London. And now, ladies and gentlemen, I shall indulge for your delectation a deceptively benign form of sadomasochism.

*(*VENTRILOQUIST *draws out an enormous pheasant feather and tickles his* WIFE*'s severed feet with it.)*

WIFE: *(Laughing and writhing in agony)* No no no ha ha ha! Please stop don't stop don't stop don't stop! Ha ha ha! No no no please no stop *(Etc.)*.

VENTRILOQUIST: *(With a sadistic leer)* Kitchie-kitchie coo! And now to restore the two halves into a single female once again. Now I think the way it was done was . . .

WIFE: You think? You mean you don't know?

VENTRILOQUIST: Well as I recall the Richiardi method was . . .

WIFE: Charles, we're not using the Richiardi method.

VENTRILOQUIST: *(Alarmed)* We're not?

WIFE: No, we're using the Golden method.

VENTRILOQUIST: But I distinctly remember that in the improved sawing the woman in half . . .

WIFE: Charles, put me back together!

VENTRILOQUIST: Susan, whatever you do, don't panic. *(He plays with the two halves of his* WIFE, *wheeling her about so that her feet face her head. Finally, after many mishaps, he puts her together)*

WIFE: Oh Charles, you've done it, and you've done it without Walter.

*(*VENTRILOQUIST *then releases his* WIFE *from the cabinette and they embrace. She smiles. The sinister laughter of* WALTER *is heard as the lights fade to black.)*

Scene 6

(Enter WIFE *in the dark with flashlight. She goes to the dummy's trunk and opens it, takes out the dummy and begins examining it. With the sound of the ventriloquist's voice the lights snap on.)*

VENTRILOQUIST: Aha! Now I've caught you together.

WIFE: What?

VENTRILOQUIST: You're cheating!

WIFE: Cheating?

VENTRILOQUIST: You're cheating with Walter. It's just as I suspected. You like Walter better than me!

WIFE: What are you saying?

VENTRILOQUIST: He told me how you go in his room at night and fondle his controls!

WIFE: You're crazy!

VENTRILOQUIST: Crazy, am I? Crazy? Crazy? *(With each repetition of the word "crazy," the ventriloquist's voice leaps up an octave until he speaks with the falsetto ventriloquial drone of* WALTER*)* Crazy?

WIFE: Charles, I called the pawnshop. That dummy belonged to a ventriloquist who killed his wife. He accused her just as you're accusing me! If you don't believe me, here. Call them yourself. *(Hands him the telephone)*

VENTRILOQUIST: The pawnshop? *(Wraps the telephone cord around her neck and starts to strangle her. She gives him a knee in the privates, manages to break away, seizes the dummy, takes a hammer and smashes his head [use a substitute head]. At the moment of the crash, the* VENTRILOQUIST *turns into* WALTER *and sits on the stool, laughing maniacally.* WIFE *screams and falls into his arms. In one deft maneuver, the* VENTRILOQUIST *catches her, they turn, she sobs on his breast)*

VENTRILOQUIST: *(As psychiatrist)* There, there. Cry. Get it out of your system. Feel better now? *(Offers her a handkerchief)*

WIFE: Yes, Doctor.

VENTRILOQUIST: You see, Susan, your husband was the victim of a split personality. What happened wasn't your fault.

WIFE: It wasn't?

VENTRILOQUIST: No. Now Susan, I want you to start doing good things for yourself.

WIFE: Thank you Doctor. I'll try.

VENTRILOQUIST: You think you can get home all right?

WIFE: Yes, thank you, Doctor.

VENTRILOQUIST: And by the way, Susan, last week your check came back.

SUSAN: So did my neurosis.

(Suddenly the dummy's hand rises from the bodice of her dress and grabs her throat. Fade to pinpoint spot on WIFE. *Blackout.)*

The End

UTOPIA, INCORPORATED

An Industrial

1978

Cast of Characters

ANARCH, *President of Utopia*
PHYLLIS, *his daughter*
CAPTAIN JOHN GULLIBLE, *a smuggler of forbidden substances*
BOTCHUP, *his native guide*
ROSALBA, *High Priestess of the Happy Isle*
MARTOK, *Grand Wazir of the Fire Cult*
HYACINTH, *an hermaphrodite, minion of Rosalba*
ROBERTA, *the robot*

Scene 1: GULLIBLE, BOTCHUP.

VOICE OF CAPTAIN JOHN GULLIBLE: Ship's log *(give date)*. Call me Gullible.
Captain John Gullible. For a longer time now than I'd care to remember,
whenever my spirits are high or my cash is low, I take to smuggling gold
. . . no, not mineral gold, but Jamaica gold, that's marijuana, the ha-ha weed,
and hashish, the subtlest of all the hallucinogenic drugs. This occupation
brought me into peril of my life more than once. But I'm the type of poor devil
who was never meant to run in another man's rat race. With me civilization
is only skin deep. Scratch me and you'll find a primitive beneath. I use a yacht
to smuggle, a pleasure boat. And out here in my espadrilles out of sight of land,
there is no law . . . I'm not even a criminal here. . . . In my inner city I am
a good citizen. *(Sings, to the tune "Amapola")*
Marijuana
Make her love me
Marijuana
Make her mine
Marijuana
Stars above me
Marijuana
Make them shine.

Whenever it is I smoke marijuana,
I see that darling girl plain as can be!
But when I run out of marijuana
She's gone like a mirage of mists on the sea!

Marijuana
Where will I see her?
Marijuana
In what port o' call?
Marijuana
Will she love no other?
Or marijuana
Is she there for one and all?

Marijuana
Make the night enchanted.
Marijuana
Like nights were long ago

Marijuana
I took it all for granted
Marijuana
I never knew what it meant to be told . . . No!

(Spoken) Now I know!

Marijuana!
Marijuana!
Marijuana!

GULLIBLE: *(Smoking)* Have some smoke, Botchup?

BOTCHUP: *(Enters mopping deck)* No, thank you, Captain. That weed makes me three things I don't need to be: tired, horny, and hungry. Doesn't it make you paranoid, boss?

GULLIBLE: If it's any good it does. Ah, Botchup, do you think I'll ever find her?

BOTCHUP: Who, Captain?

GULLIBLE: The girl of my dreams.

BOTCHUP: I don't know, Captain. Girls are wise to sailors.

GULLIBLE: Why's that?

BOTCHUP: Because their mothers tell them that sailors are wolves in ship's clothing.

GULLIBLE: Gee, Botchup, this could be such a romantic night—if only we weren't stuck with each other.

BOTCHUP: Someday you'll miss me when I'm gone. Someday my ship will come in.

GULLIBLE: You're so lazy that if your ship ever did come in, I doubt you'd bother unloading it.

BOTCHUP: I think you got it there, Captain. It's not that I'm lazy; it's just that I can't be bothered. I don't believe in putting things off until tomorrow when I can put them off forever.

GULLIBLE: *(With proper Puritan contempt)* How can you be so lazy?

BOTCHUP: It's easy, Captain. Whenever I get the urge to work, I lie down until the urge passes.

GULLIBLE: Why do you lie down? Are you tired?

BOTCHUP: No, I lie down so I won't get tired.

VOICE OVER C.B. RADIO: *(Squee)* Cabin cruiser sighted. *(Squee)* Smugglers. Bust them before they reach the Bermuda Triangle.

VOICE OF GULLIBLE: *(Reading the ship's log)* The second day out we were spotted by the authorities. We decided to change our course and take a shortcut through the Bermuda Triangle. It was our bad luck to hit a storm. Traveling by boat, I wound up on the rails. I was so seasick I was afraid to yawn. I swore it would be my last boat trip and it very nearly was! During that terrible storm, in the middle of the night, I called my sole crew member to me and said *(To BOTCHUP)*, Botchup, do you know how to pray?

BOTCHUP: *(Enters solemnly)* Yes, Captain, I can.

GULLIBLE: Then you'd better get started. There's only one life preserver.

BOTCHUP: *(Falling to his knees with clasped hands)* O Lord, I've broken most of Thy commandments. I've been a hard drinker and smoked more than my share of bush. But if my life is spared now, I'll promise Thee never again . . .

GULLIBLE: Wait a minute. Don't go too far. I think I see a sail. *(Then queasily)* Botchup, can you tell me what to do if I get seasick?

BOTCHUP: I don't have to. You'll do it.

GULLIBLE: *(Retches)* EEEEELCHT!

BOTCHUP: Can I get you anything, Captain?

GULLIBLE: Yes, an island!

(Midnight aloft. Thunder and lightning.)

BOTCHUP: Um, um, um. Stop that thunder! Plenty too much thunder up here. What's the use of thunder? Um, um, um. We don't want thunder; we want rum. Give us a glass of rum. Um, um, um!

VOICE OF GULLIBLE: Suddenly, when I had given it all up for lost, something came over me. A feeling of relief that all was lost! As if a great burden had been lifted from me. Suddenly, I became cheerful and . . .

BOTCHUP: We must send down the main-topsail yard, sir. The band is working loose and the lee lift is half-stranded. Shall I strike it, sir?

GULLIBLE: *(Laughing heartily)* Strike nothing; lash it. If I had skysail poles, I'd sway them up now.

BOTCHUP: Sir? In God's name, sir!

GULLIBLE: Well?

BOTCHUP: The anchors are working, sir. Shall I get them inboard?

GULLIBLE: Strike nothing but lash everything. The winds rise but they haven't got me yet. Blow! Blow! Ha! Ha! Ha! Ha! By masts and keels, be quick about it! Ho glue pots! Ha! Ha! You bastards, blow! I'm not afraid of drowning!

BOTCHUP: You've got nothing to worry about. Destiny has marked you for the gallows!

GULLIBLE: Loftiest trucks are made for wildest winds! And this brain truck of mine now sails among the cloud scud! Shall I strike that? Oh, none but cowards send down their brain trucks in tempest time.

BOTCHUP: Oh Lord! What will I do? The captain's gone mad. I'll test his sanity. Captain, who was our first president?

GULLIBLE: George Washington.

BOTCHUP: Right! Who was our second president?

GULLIBLE: John Adams.

BOTCHUP: I'd continue this examination, but I'm not sure who was the third president, myself.

GULLIBLE: What a hooroosh aloft there! I would e'en take it for sublime, did I not know that the colic is a nasty malady. Oh, take medicine, take medicine! This is a nasty night, lad.

BOTCHUP: *(Shaking GULLIBLE)* Captain, O Captain, the ship is capsizing! Typhoon! Typhoon! The ship is going down to doom!

GULLIBLE: Cheerily, cheerily, my hearts! Ho the fair wind. Cheerily, men!

BOTCHUP: Men? He must be seeing double!

VOICE OF GULLIBLE: A great wave overturned us. I can still remember that delirium. We went overboard. But praise be to that Unknown Power that governs the universe! A miracle happened: although the hashish sank and we'd have drowned had we tried to save it, the marijuana floated! We were barely able to hoist ourselves up on a raft of it, which we clung to till the storm subsided. Botchup had kept his matches dry by dipping them in wax, a waterproof sealer, and for days we floated on that raft, smoking and even eating that ha-ha weed with only a canteen of water between us. At some point, I lost consciousness.

Scene 2: HYACINTH, MARTOK, BOTCHUP, GULLIBLE.

(HYACINTH, a Utopian, enters and discovers BOTCHUP.)

HYACINTH: Martok, Martok, look!

MARTOK: *(Enters)* Where did it come from?

HYACINTH: Its torso is that of a human being.

MARTOK: It's so ugly, yet so frightened.

HYACINTH: *(Discovering GULLIBLE)* I found another one over here.

MARTOK: Come inside. Nothing of this kind has ever been seen in Utopia before! Wait until I bring this creature to the zoological society in Aasgaard.

HYACINTH: Don't hurt them. Even if they are of no practical use, we could exhibit them as curiosities and charge admission.

BOTCHUP: Where am I?

MARTOK: My boy, you've stumbled on Utopia.

BOTCHUP: *(Shakes GULLIBLE awake)* Captain, Captain, we're on land! These men saved our lives. They saved us from drowning!

GULLIBLE: What do you tip for a thing like that?

BOTCHUP: There's no need to tip, Captain. We're in Utopia where service is included.

GULLIBLE: Utopia?

BOTCHUP: These men have evolved the perfect society. I bet these people are so healthy that they had to kill a man to get a cemetery started.

GULLIBLE: Are we really in Utopia?

BOTCHUP: This is Utopia here and now. Anything is possible here and nothing is possible anywhere else.

GULLIBLE: I can hardly believe it! Men have worked their whole lives to build Utopia. And lucky me, I've stumbled on it by accident! *(To MARTOK and HYACINTH)* You Utopians. We friends.

MARTOK: *(Aside to HYACINTH)* We'll give this one a remedial speech course.

HYACINTH: *(To MARTOK)* They seem to belong to a criminal underspecies.

MARTOK: Let's take them to the zoological society for a more exact classification.

HYACINTH: *(Offering them food)* Come along, little fellows, we won't hurt you.

BOTCHUP: Look, Captain, they're offering us food.

GULLIBLE: Wine and cheese, oh goodie!

MARTOK: Come with us to the Happy Isle.

BOTCHUP: Thank you. Thank you. You've been very kind. *(To GULLIBLE)* Boy, it's good to have my feet on vice versa again.

GULLIBLE: You don't mean vice versa; you mean terra-cotta.

(All exit.)

Scene 3: ANARCH, PHYLLIS.

ANARCH: *(Enters in a wheelchair)* Phyllis! Phyllis!

PHYLLIS: *(Strides in)* Yes, Father?

ANARCH: My dear child, you don't know who you are or where you came from.

PHYLLIS: Am I not your child and a child of Utopia, Father?

ANARCH: *(Full of affection, almost moved to tears)* Ignorant child, come and sit by my side. *(Stroking her cheek)* Poor ignorant. Poor, poor ignorant.

PHYLLIS: But what more is there to know than that which I now know?

ANARCH: Ah, Phyllis, my ingenuous, we are not native Utopians. Phyllis, there is a world outside Utopia.

PHYLLIS: *(Perking up)* There is?

ANARCH: *(Spits)* There is. A world that hurt me so badly I had to leave it forever. You see, Daughter, I once had a career in that outer world.

PHYLLIS: Did you, Father? What did you do there?

ANARCH: I was president . . .

PHYLLIS: As you are here?

ANARCH: No, there I was only president of a corporation.

PHYLLIS: Oh.

ANARCH: One day, Phyllis, there was an audit of all our books. Over a million dollars was found to be missing. All the fingers pointed at me. The accountant, my partner, even my secretary bore me false witness. They said I had pocketed huge cash receipts. And in a trial that mocked justice itself, they found me guilty. My partner had let me take the blame. Oh, the swine! The swine! The accusations he brought against me rankled my heart, my spleen, my liver, and my kidneys. The outrageous falsehoods I could stand no longer. I meant to rise to my feet in the courtroom and shout the truth at them. *(Shouting)* Out of order! Objection overruled! But I couldn't move. I couldn't stand up for myself. I was paralyzed from the waist down. My pants were gone. I was naked from the waist down. And in my little T-shirt, they took me from that courtroom. *(Then brokenly)* Out of order. Objection overruled. Disgraced in that outer world, I withdrew to the inner and here I found Utopia, the ideal world. Do you hear?

PHYLLIS: This tale could cure deafness. But why do you tell it to me now, Father?

ANARCH: My electric eye has spotted strangers washed up on our shores by last night's storm. I dread the impact of these imperfect people on our dreamworld.

PHYLLIS: I should like to study them, Father. They should be extremely interesting from the scientific point of view.

ANARCH: Dear little bookworm.

PHYLLIS: I know I'm bookish, Father. But I'd adore to gain some first-hand experience.

ANARCH: My child, take the advice of your father who's seen it all: content yourself with books. *(Exeunt)*

Scene 4: GULLIBLE, BOTCHUP, MARTOK, HYACINTH, ROSALBA.

MARTOK: *(Enters running and throws himself down on the ground)* Rosalba, Ruler of the Happy Isle and High Priestess of God Erunam, comes.

HYACINTH: *(Falls on his face)* God Erunam!

BOTCHUP: Who did he say was coming?

MARTOK: Down on your knees, you dogs!

GULLIBLE: Better do as he says.

(They fall on their faces.)

ROSALBA: *(Enters stepping over their prostrate bodies)* Rise, all of you.

MARTOK: Yes, enchantress.

ROSALBA: Where are the strangers?

MARTOK: High Priestess of Utopia, what you are about to see will amaze you. These creatures tell us that they come from outer earth, a civilization formed on the outer crust of the earth, the atmosphere of which our scientists tell us cannot be breathed by even our most advanced respiratory equipment. We have here two examples of this exoterric form of life. *(Unveils cage containing* BOTCHUP *and* GULLIBLE*)*

ROSALBA: Fascinating, horrible, but fascinating.

MARTOK: Feeding time! *(Gives meat and potatoes to* GULLIBLE *and bananas to* BOTCHUP*)*

BOTCHUP: Bananas again! Why is it he gets meat and potatoes while I always get bananas?

MARTOK: This zoo runs on a very low budget and they have you registered as a monkey . . . until further classification is possible. You may be a mutation. But of what species? Or you may be a throwback to prehistoric times.

HYACINTH: *(Peering into the cage)* Look at his quizzical monkeylike expression, as though he were wondering whether he was his brother's keeper or his keeper's brother.

ROSALBA: Have we evolved to such a high degree that we have to invent cages to keep our ancestors in?

MARTOK: If you look at them long enough, they begin to remind you of someone you know.

HYACINTH: He reminds me of someone I know—you!

MARTOK: Hurmph!

ROSALBA: You're terrible! What beautiful skin they have! I'd love to have it made into a bag, gloves, and matching shoes.

GULLIBLE: *(Freaking)* Let me out! Do you hear? Let me out of this cage!

MARTOK: Believe me, you're safer in there.

*(*HYACINTH *passes the cage sobbing.)*

GULLIBLE: Why is that man sobbing?

ROSALBA: The elephant died.

GULLIBLE: Fond of him, was he?

ROSALBA: It's not that. But he's the one who has to dig the grave.

MARTOK: These strangers' presence here is in violation of Utopian Law. They must serve in the temple.

BOTCHUP: Hey, we're gonna serve in the temple!

GULLIBLE: I used to work in a restaurant where you could eat like a horse for a dollar twenty-five. If you wanted to eat like a human being, it cost eight bucks.

BOTCHUP: I once worked in a restaurant that offered all you could eat for a dollar twenty-five. I took one bite—it was all I could eat.

MARTOK: As human sacrifices!

*(*GULLIBLE *and* BOTCHUP *grab each other.)*

ROSALBA: No. It has not yet been determined whether or not they are human. We are just about to begin testing. It is so amazing that they speak English.

MARTOK: Very well, we'll test them. If they prove to be subhuman, they will be deemed unfit for sacrifice. If human, they die.

BOTCHUP: *(Aside to* GULLIBLE*)* Did you hear that? If we pass this test, we die.

GULLIBLE: Then we'd better not pass it.

BOTCHUP: *(Aloud)* Let's have this test.

GULLIBLE: Yeah, let's have it.

MARTOK: First test: death if you say "stop it."

GULLIBLE: Go.

MARTOK: That's a nice hat you've got there.

BOTCHUP: Thank you. Do you like it? I bought it the day before yesterday. It was very expensive but it's worth every penny of it.

MARTOK: Do you mind if I have a look at it?

BOTCHUP: No, go right ahead.

GULLIBLE: *(Aside to* BOTCHUP*)* Remember, don't say "stop it." It's life and death!

BOTCHUP: Not me. I'm not gonna say mmmmmmmmmmmm—I almost said it!

GULLIBLE: Well, don't.

BOTCHUP: Don't worry. Nobody's gonna make me say sssssssss—oops! That was a close one.

GULLIBLE: Look what he's doing to your hat.

BOTCHUP: Hey, you, sssssssssssss . . .

GULLIBLE: Don't say it! Don't say it!

BOTCHUP: He's cutting holes in my hat!

MARTOK: What were you going to say? Stop it?

BOTCHUP: No, not me. I wasn't going to say sssssssss . . .

GULLIBLE: *(Clapping his hand over* BOTCHUP*'s mouth)* He wasn't going to say anything.

MARTOK: *(Sprinkling the pieces of Botchup's hat into his hands like confetti)* Here's your hat back.

BOTCHUP: *(Looks at the pieces of his hat and whimpers)* Look what he did to my hat.

MARTOK: And how about you, ugly?! Can you keep from saying "stop it"?

GULLIBLE: Sure, here's my hat.

MARTOK: I don't want your hat. *(Dips* GULLIBLE*'s head in a bucket of goo)*

GULLIBLE: Sto—

BOTCHUP: Don't say it! Don't say it! *(Pushes* GULLIBLE*'s head back down in the goo)*

GULLIBLE: You idiot!

BOTCHUP: I did it to save your life, Captain. You were gonna say you know what.

GULLIBLE: Thanks a lot.

BOTCHUP: Ha ha ha! I thought I had it bad getting my hat cut up until I saw what you had to go through!

MARTOK: Second test. *(Takes Gullible's hat and starts cutting it up)*

BOTCHUP: *(Watches with growing apprehension)* He's cutting up your hat. That means . . .

MARTOK: Next! *(Dunks* BOTCHUP *in goo)*

BOTCHUP: *(Coming up gasping for air)* Stop it!

MARTOK: He said "stop it" and "stop it" means death.

BOTCHUP: Gee, Captain, I'm sorry I laughed at you.

GULLIBLE: If they ever put a price on your head, take it.

MARTOK: He failed the test. He is human.

BOTCHUP: You got me all wrong.

ROSALBA: They will be sacrificed to God Erunam.

GULLIBLE: "They"? But I didn't say "stop it"!

ROSALBA: You did now. Let them be made into compost in the gardens of Erunam.

(A pigeon flies onstage carrying a note. HYACINTH *reads the epistle aloud.)*

HYACINTH: Excuse me, but the President of Utopia has sent word that he wants to see the strange creatures. He has countermanded the Writ of Destruction served on them as potentially dangerous and illegal aliens. Your lives are saved.

MARTOK: This is a sacrilege!

Scene 5: GULLIBLE, BOTCHUP, MARTOK, HYACINTH, ROSALBA, ANARCH, PHYLLIS.

ANARCH: *(Enters, a mummy in a wheelchair)* Stop, Rosalba! Your jurisdiction does not extend beyond the Happy Isle.

ROSALBA: These men are mine. I found them first.

ANARCH: Hyacinth, creature of fantasy, claims to have found them.

HYACINTH: It's true, Mr. President.

PHYLLIS: Mr. President, I feel that these men are valuable scientific specimens. If it is true, as we heard, that they come from outer earth, they afford us a rare opportunity to learn what the outside world is like.

ANARCH: You are right. They must be treated as honored guests.

MARTOK: Anarch, you are President of Utopia. These men are on our side of the Utopia–Happy Isle border. You are powerless to prevent our ceremony.

ANARCH: He's right.

(BOTCHUP *and* GULLIBLE *tiptoe to the border and are caught just as they would have crossed it by* MARTOK *who pulls them back.)*

ROSALBA: Oh, no, you don't; you're not going anywhere.

MARTOK: Do you have any last requests?

BOTCHUP: Yes, just one. I'd like to smoke one more joint of that sweet Marie-Jeanette before I go to meet my maker.

MARTOK: Very well, but be quick about it.

(BOTCHUP *rolls himself a joint.)*

BOTCHUP: Got a match?

MARTOK: What's a match?

BOTCHUP: Never mind, I found one.

(BOTCHUP *strikes a match.* ROSALBA, MARTOK, *and* HYACINTH *go mad.)*

MARTOK: Fire! Fire!

ROSALBA AND HYACINTH: Fires of the faith! Fires of Erunam!

(The three exit screaming.)

Scene 6: GULLIBLE, BOTCHUP, ANARCH, PHYLLIS.

PHYLLIS: Your lives are saved. Come along. *(Leads them to* ANARCH*)* These are the strangers, Father. *(Exits)*

Scene 7: GULLIBLE, BOTCHUP, ANARCH.

ANARCH: My boys, you've stumbled on Utopia. We have evolved a civilization far superior to any heretofore known under the earth's inner sun. *(Activates inner sun)*
GULLIBLE: You mean the earth is hollow? And that is the inner sun?
ANARCH: It is. But tell me, Traveler from Outer Earth, you know the outside world well then?
GULLIBLE: Yes.
ANARCH: You could give us invaluable information. No Utopian has ever seen the outside of the world.
GULLIBLE: Tch, tch, tch.
ANARCH: Have you gone up the Rhine?
GULLIBLE: Climbed it to the top.
ANARCH: Seen the Lion of Saint Mark?
GULLIBLE: Fed it.
ANARCH: And visited the Black Sea?
GULLIBLE: Filled my fountain pen there. *(Changing the subject)* This scenery here is just heavenly.
BOTCHUP: Um, I don't know. Take away the mountains and the lake, and it's just like anywhere else.
ANARCH: I think you'll like it here. We have the oldest and best wines anywhere.
GULLIBLE: I don't want any old wines, thanks. Just a glass of fresh, pure water.
ANARCH: I'm afraid you'll have to go to a bootlegger for that. But, come, you must tell me about the presidents of your country.
GULLIBLE: Where we come from, every American has the chance to become president.
ANARCH: Sounds risky being an American.
BOTCHUP: I'll have you know that Americans have had the right to bear arms for two hundred years.
ANARCH: Utopians have had the right to bare legs for two thousand years!

(Hands on the clock are seen to turn as BOTCHUP *and* GULLIBLE *wheel* ANARCH *counterclockwise at top speed. There is music.)*

GULLIBLE: And that's how life is in the United States of America. Once, when Mrs. Coolidge wasn't able to go to church, she asked her husband, Calvin Coolidge, what the sermon was about. He replied, in his usual talkative manner, "Sin." And she asked him, "Well, what did he say about sin?" And Calvin Coolidge looked at her and said, "He's against it!" Isn't that a scream? Nobody had a sense of humor like Calvin Coolidge. . . .
BOTCHUP: Unless it was William Howard Taft . . .
GULLIBLE: Did I ever tell you the one about . . . *(* ANARCH *yawns)* You yawned, Mr. President. Are you tired?
ANARCH: No, it's just that your conversation bored me.

GULLIBLE: That's damned rude!

ANARCH: A yawn may be rude but it's an honest opinion. The yawn is functional, too, in that it gives the bored listener a chance to open his mouth once in a while.

GULLIBLE: Boredom is a very subjective matter. It all depends on how you define boredom.

ANARCH: A bore is one who insists on talking about himself when you want to be talking about yourself.

GULLIBLE: I see. Then how does one avoid boring people?

ANARCH: We talk to ourselves. That way we're never bored with the conversation.

GULLIBLE: So that's why all the Utopians are so utterly charming.

ANARCH: Tell me, where was the Declaration of Independence signed?

BOTCHUP: At the bottom?

ANARCH: What do you think of my palace?

BOTCHUP: After seeing our hot-dog stands, movie theaters, and filling stations, it isn't that impressive.

ANARCH: And here is where the greatest heroes of Utopia fell.

GULLIBLE: Oh, is it? I nearly tripped on the damn thing myself.

ANARCH: This tower goes back to Māniarch the First.

BOTCHUP: Why? What's the matter with it? Isn't it satisfactory?

ANARCH: It was in this room that General Havoc received his first commission.

GULLIBLE: How much did he get?

BOTCHUP: *(Laughs)* No, not that kind of commission. A nocturnal commission!

ANARCH: How do you find the weather in Utopia?

BOTCHUP: You don't have to find the weather in Utopia. You just walk out the door and there it is!

GULLIBLE: Is the presidency hereditary?

ANARCH: Oh, yes, we can trace our ancestors back to . . . to . . . well, I don't know exactly who, but we've been descending for centuries. If you come over tomorrow, I'll show you our family tree.

BOTCHUP: I'm sorry, I can't. I promised another family I'd look at their cabbages.

ANARCH: And this is a portrait of my great-great grandfather.

GULLIBLE: Amazing! Why, he doesn't look any older than you.

Scene 8: GULLIBLE, BOTCHUP, ANARCH, PHYLLIS.

PHYLLIS: *(Enters)* Father, what are ancestors?

ANARCH: Well, I'm one of yours and so is your grandfather.

PHYLLIS: Then why is it people brag about them?

ANARCH: Phyllis, go to your room at once!

(PHYLLIS exits.)

Scene 9: GULLIBLE, BOTCHUP, ANARCH.

GULLIBLE: *(Enchanted)* Phyllis.

ANARCH: The Utopian isn't so much concerned about who his grandfather was as about whom his grandson will be.

GULLIBLE: Who, not whom.

ANARCH: I, Anarch, President of Utopia, am above grammar!

BOTCHUP: *(Pointing to portrait)* And below Grandpa.

GULLIBLE: *(Aside to* BOTCHUP*)* Did you hear what he said?

BOTCHUP: Keep your words soft and sweet. You never know when you might have to eat them someday.

GULLIBLE: Aren't you frightened?

BOTCHUP: I don't know the meaning of the word "defeat."

GULLIBLE: Not to mention all the other words you don't know the meaning of. *(Pedantically)* Why don't you try to use the word "defeat" in a sentence?

BOTCHUP: When you bathe before the battle, be sure and wash de feat.

ANARCH: We've heard of Sigmund Freud, Albert Einstein, and John Stuart Mill. Can you tell us more of these men?

GULLIBLE: Damned nice fellows, all of them.

ANARCH: Not their dispositions. We're interested in your wise men for their teachings, their philosophies, their appetites for truth.

GULLIBLE: The men you mentioned were all perspicacious, punctilious, and gregarious. And I say this without fear of contradiction.

BOTCHUP: And without knowing what you're talking about.

ANARCH: *(Ominously)* You must go before the Committee.

GULLIBLE: What's the Committee?

ANARCH: It's a body that keeps minutes and wastes hours. This will be a committee of five.

BOTCHUP: What's a committee of five?

ANARCH: A man who does the work, three others who pat him on the back, and one to bring in the minority report. Come along. *(Exits)*

Scene 10: GULLIBLE, BOTCHUP.

GULLIBLE: What did you think of Phyllis?

BOTCHUP: She didn't seem that intelligent.

GULLIBLE: Yeah, she didn't pay any attention to me, either. *(Exits)*

Scene 11: BOTCHUP, HYACINTH, MARTOK.

(MARTOK and HYACINTH enter, dash across stage, and grab BOTCHUP.)

BOTCHUP: Hey, what is this?

HYACINTH: Do not worry, O Erunam; we have come to rescue you.

MARTOK: Your priests have not forgotten the promise you made thousands of years ago.

BOTCHUP: Promise?

MARTOK: The promise that you would one day return to rule your people on the Happy Isle and lead us against our enemies.

BOTCHUP: Oh, yes, the promise. Of course, the promise! How could I forget the promise?!

MARTOK: Come, O God of our Fathers. *(He and HYACINTH kowtow)* The Happy Isle awaits. For three thousand years we've waited. Come, and lead our armies to victory.

BOTCHUP: Well, actually, I was thinking of having dinner at the President's house. *(Starts off)*

MARTOK: *(Seizing* BOTCHUP *and pulling him back)* That is impossible. Anarch is our enemy. Come.

HYACINTH: The Happy Isle awaits.

Scene 12: BOTCHUP, HYACINTH, MARTOK, ROSALBA.

(They carry him across the Utopia–Happy Isle border—a child's swimming pool filled with water. There the leaf curtain is made to open upon his arrival, revealing the Happy Isle—palms, jungle greenery, pool, birds, and orchids. ROSALBA *offers him her hammock. Totem pole with movable mouths like ventriloquist dummies.)*

ROSALBA: Welcome, O God Erunam, to claim what is yours. The bed of luxury, fruit, incense, a floor show. (HYACINTH *performs a suggestive dance)*

*(*HYACINTH *and* MARTOK *stand beside* ROSALBA.*)*

ROSALBA, HYACINTH, AND MARTOK: *(Sing)*
  On the happy, happy, happy Happy Isle,
  The birds and flowers smile,
  The sun shines bright
  Both day and night
  On the happy, happy, happy Happy Isle
  On the happy, happy, happy, happy,
  Happy, happy, happy, happy,
  Happy, happy, happy Happy Isle.

*(*HYACINTH *and* MARTOK *stand fanning* ROSALBA.*)*

BOTCHUP: Who are these people you rule?

ROSALBA: They have lived and died as other mortals do. The old man who came to me from the desert told me that this secret of eternal life was to be mine alone. Let me show you what no mortal man has seen. The secret of eternal life. *(Takes his hand and leads him to the Everlasting Flame)* See how my feet have worn away the stones? There is the Flame of Everlasting Life.

BOTCHUP: That flame is hot.

ROSALBA: Hot, yes. But sometimes the flame grows cold.

BOTCHUP: Cold?

ROSALBA: Then it might be nice to go and bathe in the flame. *(Steps up delirious)*

BOTCHUP: *(Restraining her)* That would be suicide.

ROSALBA: To bathe in the flame now would be suicide, but not when the flame grows cold. That day will come for you soon.

BOTCHUP: But why not accept things the way they are?

ROSALBA: An inseparable barrier separates us. . . . you, in your world of change and decay—I, in my immortality. You must join me forever beyond death.

BOTCHUP: When?

ROSALBA: Tonight, when the new moon strikes, the flame will grow cold.

BOTCHUP: But I'm afraid.

ROSALBA: Afraid of what?

BOTCHUP: That I am not Erunam—that I am not a true god and the flame will not grow cold.

ROSALBA: How can you doubt, O Erunam? For a thousand years I've waited for you, O Erunam, and now you've returned. *(Pulls curtain to reveal a totem pole featuring a likeness of Botchup)*

(MARTOK and HYACINTH kowtow.)

MARTOK: Will you make Erunam your bride, enchantress?

ROSALBA: I have sworn it. It must be so. God Erunam has commanded it.

(ROSALBA seats herself on half of a throne. MARTOK and HYACINTH lift BOTCHUP by the elbows and plant him beside her, then proceed to dress him à la Carmen Miranda.)

BOTCHUP: Do you have ten commandments like we do?

ROSALBA: Yes, we have ten of them. But they're different commandments. Our only law is not to harm ourselves. We don't bother about others.

BOTCHUP: Do you have "Thou shalt not steal"?

ROSALBA: No, we have "Thou shalt not leave thy goods unguarded."

BOTCHUP: Do you have "Honor thy father and mother"?

ROSALBA: No, we have "Thou shalt pay back every cent they spent on you."

BOTCHUP: Do you have "Thou shalt not commit adultery"?

ROSALBA: No, we have "Thou shalt not deny thyself to another human being who is horny." We find the whole concept of adultery childish.

BOTCHUP: "Thou shalt not bear false witness"?

ROSALBA: "Thou shalt not be unlucky."

BOTCHUP: "Thou shalt not covet thy neighbor's goods"?

ROSALBA: "Thou shalt not admire what other people admire."

BOTCHUP: "Thou shalt not kill"?

ROSALBA: "Thou shalt not be killed."

BOTCHUP: "I am the Lord Thy God; thou shalt not have strange gods before me"?

ROSALBA: "Thou shalt see God in all things and honor what is worthless."

BOTCHUP: "Thou shalt not take the name of the Lord in vain"?

ROSALBA: "Cuss by the Lord and thou wilt be heard."

BOTCHUP: "Thou must remember to keep holy the Lord's Day"?

ROSALBA: We're different from you there, too. We keep holy six days and on the seventh day, we suspend all moral law.

BOTCHUP: The seventh day?

ROSALBA: *Sin* day.

BOTCHUP: Sin day?

ROSALBA: Yes, on Sin day you can do anything you want.

BOTCHUP: The streets must be wild on Sin day!

ROSALBA: On the contrary. They're deserted. Everyone is so scared on Sin day, they stay indoors for twenty-four hours and board up the windows.

BOTCHUP: Ah, Rosalba, my little jungle gardenia, give me a little kiss.

ROSALBA: What's a kiss?

BOTCHUP: A kiss is when two people pucker up their lips like this and press them together.

ROSALBA: But why would people want to kiss each other?

BOTCHUP: Oh, it's an old custom. All the highest civilizations go in for it.

ROSALBA: It seems so silly.

BOTCHUP: Why don't we give it a try? It gives healthful stimulation.

ROSALBA: Oh, very well. *(They kiss)*

BOTCHUP: How was that?

ROSALBA: Restful. Again! *(They kiss)* I begin to feel some of this stimulation you describe. Come, O Erunam, we're going to take a nap.

BOTCHUP: A nap? But I'm not tired.

ROSALBA: Splendid. Neither am I.

(All exit.)

Scene 13: PHYLLIS, GULLIBLE.

GULLIBLE: *(Enters following* PHYLLIS*)* Phyllis, Phyllis.

PHYLLIS: You repeat yourself.

GULLIBLE: Are you happy here in Utopia?

PHYLLIS: Oh, yes, we're all happy here.

GULLIBLE: To what do you attribute this happiness?

PHYLLIS: We've all got good health and a bad memory.

GULLIBLE: And how do you maintain this good health?

PHYLLIS: We follow a simple regimen of eating what we don't like, drinking what we don't want, and doing what we'd rather not.

GULLIBLE: What are your views on capital punishment?

PHYLLIS: I believe in capital punishment. But I don't think women should be hung like men.

GULLIBLE: Phyllis, do you love me?

PHYLLIS: Of course I love you. What a foolish question! I love everybody.

GULLIBLE: When was it you first realized that you loved me?

PHYLLIS: When I found myself getting angry when people said you were brainless and unattractive.

GULLIBLE: *(Transported)* Oh, Phyllis! *(Kisses her hand)*

PHYLLIS: But I must confess sometimes I'm suspicious of you.

GULLIBLE: Suspicious of me? But why?

PHYLLIS: You're always kissing my hand.

GULLIBLE: But that's the way a man of experience kisses.

PHYLLIS: I don't know. A man of experience should have better aim than that. *(*GULLIBLE *embraces and kisses* PHYLLIS *on the lips)* How did you learn to kiss like that?

GULLIBLE: I used to blow up footballs. Ah, can't you see what I'm saying? I love you! Phyllis, will you marry me?

PHYLLIS: No.

GULLIBLE: Why not?

PHYLLIS: Before marriage, a girl has to kiss a man to hold him. After marriage, she has to hold him to kiss him. What would you say if I told you I don't believe in kissing?

GULLIBLE: Good-bye. *(He starts out)*

PHYLLIS: Wait, you taught me that kisses are the language of love.

GULLIBLE: Well, speak up. *(Kisses her again and again)* Kissing a girl is like opening a bottle of olives. Once you get one, the rest come easy. *(Kisses her again)*

PHYLLIS: All this kissing might prove hazardous to my health.

GULLIBLE: You think kissing is unhealthy?

PHYLLIS: It will be if my father catches us. I am going to show you something no outsider has ever seen before.

GULLIBLE: What is it?

PHYLLIS: Behold the mechanism behind Utopia. *(Opens door revealing mechanical ballet performed by a robot, then closes door)* That was it, John. I did something for you that no woman in Utopia would have done. You must bring this secret to your people. With it, they too can build a happy world.

GULLIBLE: But, Phyllis, I don't understand.

(BOTCHUP is heard whistling offstage.)

PHYLLIS: Someone is coming. I must leave by the presidential tunnel.

GULLIBLE: Couldn't I have another look?

PHYLLIS: There's no time. Try to remember all that you have seen. *(Exits)*

GULLIBLE: But Phyllis . . .

Scene 14: GULLIBLE, BOTCHUP.

BOTCHUP: Well, how is your courtship with Phyllis going?

GULLIBLE: Very well.

BOTCHUP: Is she smiling sweetly on you at last?

GULLIBLE: Not exactly. But last night she told me she had said "no" for the last time.

BOTCHUP: Maybe she's got another fellow.

GULLIBLE: She swears she's never been kissed.

BOTCHUP: No wonder she swears.

GULLIBLE: Botchup, there's something preying on my mind. I shouldn't tell anyone, but I've got to tell someone, and you're the only one I can tell. So, I'll tell you if you promise not to tell anybody.

BOTCHUP: Out with it! Out with it!

GULLIBLE: Last night, Phyllis revealed to me . . . er . . . made known to me . . . that is to say she let me see . . . well, to make a long story short . . .

BOTCHUP: Isn't it a little late for that?

GULLIBLE: This is serious.

BOTCHUP: I know. I'm only trying to lighten it up a little.

GULLIBLE: She showed me the secret of Utopia!

BOTCHUP: Is that all?

GULLIBLE: Is that all!? The dream of all the great thinkers of history was revealed to me! Little insignificant ne'er-do-well, black-sheep-of-the-family me!

BOTCHUP: Lucky you.

GULLIBLE: But, Botchup, I couldn't make head nor tail of it! This precious glimpse of the mechanism that could make a happy world was completely lost on me! Oh, if only someone more qualified had seen it.

BOTCHUP: Well, listen to this. I got the lowdown on Utopia myself. And my information comes from a very reliable source—a woman.

GULLIBLE: The High Priestess what's-her-name?

BOTCHUP: How did you guess?

GULLIBLE: You like zaftig women.

BOTCHUP: You're crazy. They don't have to be German.

GULLIBLE: "Zaftig" means a little plump.

BOTCHUP: Well, you know there used to be Mae West and then there was Jane Russell and Lana Turner, then Marilyn Monroe . . .

GULLIBLE: You mean she's this year's bazoom!

BOTCHUP: I don't mean to say she's stacked, but when she takes a shower, it's twenty minutes before her feet get wet. Let's have no sour grapes now, heh heh heh!

GULLIBLE: Phyllis? Why, my kisses thrill her to the bottoms of her feet. They should. They're sole kisses. I know I give her goose bumps.

BOTCHUP: If it wasn't for goose bumps, she wouldn't have any figure at all. She's the type of girl you take to the movies when you want to watch the picture.

GULLIBLE: Yes, Phyllis is an intellectual all right. I could never love a woman just for what's in her brassiere.

BOTCHUP: All the more for me. Rosalba has invited us all to the Happy Isle for the weekend. If the place lives up to its name, we're going to have a fabulous time! Why, the High Priestess and I had sex seventy times last night.

GULLIBLE: Seventy times! How's that possible?

BOTCHUP: Once in bed and sixty-nine on the floor.

GULLIBLE: I don't know, Botchup. There's nothing here: there's no television, no automobiles, no newspapers . . .

BOTCHUP: No commercials, no air pollution, no litter.

GULLIBLE: I don't know if I can live without them, Botchup. Not forever.

BOTCHUP: Captain, I've got good news. I figured out how to make a radio out of some spare parts I've found around Utopia.

GULLIBLE: Fabulous!

BOTCHUP: Let's see if it works. (BOTCHUP *turns radio on—to news or advertisement—both listen, then* GULLIBLE *turns it off*)

GULLIBLE: Just our luck. The radio was invented in an era when people have nothing to say.

BOTCHUP: But, Captain, I thought you liked Utopia. You said you found the girl of your dreams.

GULLIBLE: I did, Botchup. But now that I found her, I want to take her home with me and settle down. I'm homesick, Botchup, I want to go home.

BOTCHUP: It's just the reverse with me. When we first got here, I didn't like Utopia. I said to myself, "Utopia, who needs it?" The people seem like such goody-goodies here in Utopia. I thought we'd never have any fun. But now I don't have to try to have fun anymore. Life is so good here in Utopia that just the simple, everyday things that one does are so much better than fun that I don't need fun to get away from it all anymore. Wait until you've had this weekend vacation at the Happy Isle.

GULLIBLE: A vacation is like love: anticipated with pleasure, experienced with discomfort, and remembered with nostalgia.

(They exit.)

Scene 15: HYACINTH, ROSALBA, MARTOK.

MARTOK: O High Priestess, Erunam comes with the guests from Utopia.
HYACINTH: The ideal guest stays at home.
ROSALBA: Now, now, Hyacinth, my pet, there are two kinds of guests: those who come *after* dinner and those who come after *dinner.*
MARTOK: Will petitoes do for hors d'oeuvres, enchantress?
ROSALBA: Potatoes?
MARTOK: No, petitoes. Pigs' trotters.
HYACINTH: Daddy always serves the appropriate hors d'oeuvres.
ROSALBA: Pigs' feet will do. Remember God Erunam will be here, too.
HYACINTH: Then why not go all the way? Serve pork tartare!
ROSALBA: Do I detect a note of jealousy, Hyacinth?
HYACINTH: Not at all. Though I don't know what you see in him.
ROSALBA: He has a mind of his own.
HYACINTH: Who else would want it?
ROSALBA: He's smarter than he looks.
HYACINTH: He'd have to be.
MARTOK: *(Defending* ERUNAM*)* What he lacks in intelligence, he makes up in stupidity.
ROSALBA: Yes, I enjoy talking to him when my mind needs a rest. Besides, he amuses me. And to be amused is the goal of my life. I can hardly believe that one of your nobility of soul could stoop to jealousy, Hyacinth.
MARTOK: The guests are here.
ROSALBA: Don't put all your eggs in one basket or all your liquor in one guest.

Scene 16: HYACINTH, ROSALBA, MARTOK, PHYLLIS, GULLIBLE, BOTCHUP.

*(*HYACINTH *throws a lei around the neck of each guest.)*

ROSALBA: Welcome, honored guests, to a fabulous, all expenses paid weekend on the Happy Isle!
ROSALBA, MARTOK, AND HYACINTH: *(Sing)*
  On the happy, happy, happy Happy Isle
  The birds and flowers smile,
  The sun shines bright
  Both day and night
  On the happy, happy, happy Happy Isle
  On the happy, happy, happy, happy,
  Happy, happy, happy, happy,
  Happy, happy, happy Happy Isle.

*(*PHYLLIS, GULLIBLE, *and* BOTCHUP *link arms and sway to music.)*

ROSALBA: And, remember, if you let your conscience be your guide, you'll miss all the most exciting places. Are any of you musically inclined?
PHYLLIS: I can sing.
GULLIBLE: I can play the piano by ear.
ROSALBA: That's nothing. Martok fiddles with his whiskers. Do you sing Faust?
PHYLLIS: Yes, but I can also sing slow. I have a falsetto voice.

BOTCHUP: That's nothing. I know a girl with a false set o' teeth. Yesterday we went to the swimming pool and had a great time diving.

GULLIBLE: Yeah, that's a great sport.

BOTCHUP: We'll have even more fun tomorrow when they put in the water.

ROSALBA: Come, let us go into dinner. You *(To* GULLIBLE*)* will sit on my right hand and you *(To* BOTCHUP*)* will set on my left hand.

BOTCHUP: How will you eat? Through a tube?

ROSALBA: Come, we will dance the Blue Banana till dawn.

*(All pair off—*HYACINTH *and* MARTOK, PHYLLIS *and* GULLIBLE, ROSALBA *and* BOTCHUP*—and tango out.)*

ACT II

Scene 1: HYACINTH, MARTOK.

HYACINTH: *(Entering with a daisy)* She loves me. *(Pulls off petals as he recites)* She loves me not. She loves me. She loves me not. She loves me. She loves me not! *(Pulls off last petal)*

MARTOK: My son, I know what you're going through.

HYACINTH: Rosalba doesn't love me anymore, Daddy.

MARTOK: Do not worry, my son. You will marry Rosalba.

HYACINTH: I don't know about that, Daddy. I don't want to marry a woman who doesn't love me.

MARTOK: I tell you, you must marry her. Did I not raise you to rule the Happy Isle one day?

HYACINTH: But she loves Erunam.

MARTOK: Don't worry about that, my son. I have a plan.

HYACINTH: A plan, Daddy?

MARTOK: Yes, we will get rid of this ape from the outer crust.

HYACINTH: Can we do that, Daddy?

MARTOK: Tonight, when the new moon rises, we will throw him down the well.

HYACINTH: But, Daddy, that's murder! We can't kill God Erunam, Daddy.

MARTOK: I'm not so sure he is a god . . . he sweats.

HYACINTH: But he makes fire.

MARTOK: He smells, scratches, and shits. Who ever heard of a god who smells, sweats, scratches, and shits? We'll throw him down the well of everlasting life. If he is a god, it won't hurt him; if not, we're rid of him.

HYACINTH: But how will we get him to the well?

MARTOK: We'll entice him with a love note. Here's a pen and paper. Now write what I dictate. *(Bends over so that* HYACINTH *can use his back to write on)*

HYACINTH: You want me to write it, Daddy?

MARTOK: Yes, your handwriting is more feminine than mine. *(Dictates)* "To the object of my innermost desire" . . .

HYACINTH: But we can't send this, Daddy. People don't write like this anymore.

MARTOK: Don't give me an argument. I am more experienced in these things than you are. Now write what I tell you. *(Continues to dictate)* It would fulfill my most fervent dreams if you would reconvene with me tonight at the well of everlasting life, and I will give myself to you in priapic passion.

HYACINTH: *(Writing)* "Priapic passion," that's good!

MARTOK: Signed "You know who."

HYACINTH: But, Daddy, I don't know who.

MARTOK: Rosalba, of course!

HYACINTH: But, Daddy, this is forgery.

MARTOK: Just write "You know who" and let his imagination do the rest. Now give it to the pigeon and let's lay our plans.

HYACINTH: *(Addressing the pigeon)* Take this to Erunam, birdie. *(The pigeon flies off)* I hope we're doing the right thing. *(Exeunt)*

Scene 2: ROSALBA.

(ROSALBA is taking a bath; the pigeon lights near the tub.)

ROSALBA: What's this, birdie? A note to Erunam? *(Reads)* A love note, hmmmmmmmm. So he's foolin' around with some other dame! And he's going to meet her tonight at the well. Well, well! Sounds like a plot afoot. I think I'll drop by the well tonight, myself. No man is gonna make a sap outta me. Even if he is the promised god. I ain't the High Priestess of the Happy Isle for nuttin'. I've got to look out for my own happiness, too, don't I? It's my responsibility to my people. Here you go, birdie. Take this note to the lovesick swain. I want to test his sincerity.

Scene 3: BOTCHUP, HYACINTH.

BOTCHUP: Oh boy oh birdie oh boy. Every day's a holiday when you're the most popular guy in the earthly paradise, the garden of Eden—the Happy Isle. This must be the well.

HYACINTH: *(Enters)* I can't go through with it. Hear me, O Erunam! Your life is in terrible danger. Unless you heed me, you will be dead within the hour.

BOTCHUP: Why would anyone want to kill me?

HYACINTH: Someone wants you dead for political reasons.

BOTCHUP: Is it the Utopians?

HYACINTH: No.

BOTCHUP: Is it the Happy Islanders?

HYACINTH: No.

BOTCHUP: Well, doesn't that about cover the political field here in the hollow of the earth?

HYACINTH: No, there is a third political party unknown to any but me.

BOTCHUP: How do you know about it?

HYACINTH: Because, up until a little while ago, I was part of it.

BOTCHUP: Urination!

HYACINTH: How's that?

BOTCHUP: I said urination of strange people. It was just my luck to be ship-wrecked on an uninhibited island. Why do modern playwrights find the sex element so essential?

HYACINTH: Because they believe in having a chicken in every plot.

BOTCHUP: That's how many a star is porn. But what has this got to do with politics.

HYACINTH: If a liberal hawk can catch a conservative chicken, then he has chicken cacciatore.

BOTCHUP: Was that the whispering of the leaves?

HYACINTH: No, that was the moaning of the grass.

BOTCHUP: Did you hear a strange moaning sound?

HYACINTH: Someone is having sex. Oral sex.

BOTCHUP: Oral sex should be heard but not obscene. I have big plans. I want to modernize the Happy Isle. Bring it up to date. Put up telephone poles.

HYACINTH: What's a telephone pole?

BOTCHUP: The first telephone pole was Alexander Graham Belinski.

HYACINTH: Someone is coming. Go, before you lose your life! Hide!

BOTCHUP: *(Exiting)* I'll neither quail, cowherd, or flinch!

Scene 4: GULLIBLE, HYACINTH.

GULLIBLE: *(Entering)* Hi, Hyacinth. So tonight is the big date night on the Happy Isle. But I wonder . . .

HYACINTH: Do you have a query?

GULLIBLE: No, I'll bring a girl. This will be a true meeting of the minds.

HYACINTH: A psychia*trist?*

GULLIBLE: Has there ever been a sex survey on the Happy Isle?

HYACINTH: Yes, every year we run a public opinion poll.

GULLIBLE: What did they find?

HYACINTH: Sex has its pros and cons. The pros get arrested and the cons get married.

GULLIBLE: Just as in the Old Testament when the Lord smote women of ill fame for trying to make a prophet.

HYACINTH: Is that so?

GULLIBLE: Why even today when a semiilliterate street walker unwittingly approaches a detective, her proposition ends in a sentence.

HYACINTH: Fascinating! And do flautists lay aside their flutes and listen when a prostitutes?

GULLIBLE: Why, Hyacinth, I think it's charming that you're so naive about sex.

HYACINTH: I used to be an hermaphrodite, but that was too much of an end in itself.

BOTCHUP: *(Peeking out)* But what about this attempt on my life?

HYACINTH: Martok plans to throw you down the well of everlasting life. He'll be here any minute. Someone's coming; let's hide!

Scene 5: ROSALBA, PHYLLIS.

(Enter ROSALBA and PHYLLIS.)

ROSALBA: The trouble with being inhibited is that you're tied up in nots.

PHYLLIS: When I was Jung, I was easily Freudened, but now I'm not afraid to go out during Schopenhauers instead of staying at home in my little Nietzsche.

ROSALBA: And you say you're in love with a sailor?

PHYLLIS: Yes, and he's going to give up smuggling and become a naval surgeon.

ROSALBA: My word, they do specialize today, don't they? But you say he used to smuggle!

PHYLLIS: Yes, he was a very nautical boy.

ROSALBA: Yes, it's always been the same since Eve was nigh Adam and Adam was naive. I used to go out with a millionaire cunnilinguist known as the Midas Muffler.

PHYLLIS: Why did you leave him?

ROSALBA: I found a better offer.

BOTCHUP: *(Peeking out)* Lord, what food these morsels be!

ROSALBA: I hope the night is clear enough to see the moon.

PHYLLIS: If the fog clears, it won't be mist. I'm in such a romantic mood. I hope John will be too.

ROSALBA: Don't worry, my dear, men always feel the need to insert their masculinity.

PHYLLIS: We Utopians don't have the same liberal attitude toward sex that you do.

ROSALBA: Yes, sex is more openly enjoyed inseminations than in others.

PHYLLIS: Without it, there's only artificial insemination: the inoculate conception.

Scene 6: BOTCHUP, GULLIBLE, HYACINTH, ROSALBA, PHYLLIS.

BOTCHUP: *(Entering)* If this continues, I'm going to end up on the punny farm.

GULLIBLE: *(Entering)* That would be just punishment.

ROSALBA: So you boys are here already. And you, O Erunam, are meeting me for immortal purposes.

GULLIBLE: Erunam?

BOTCHUP: Just a little nickname I picked up here. Play along. Play along.

HYACINTH: Overcome by jealousy, I conspired with Martok to murder Erunam. But now I see the evil of my ways and wish only to save his life.

ROSALBA: There's something fishy about this story.

HYACINTH: So you think amphibian, do you? Martok plans to murder Erunam. He plans to throw him down the well.

ROSALBA: We'll lay a trap and block the alibi.

PHYLLIS: The alibi?

ROSALBA: The alley by which he might escape. Hyacinth, get the idol of Erunam and put it in its place.

(HYACINTH *fetches the idol—a life-size dummy dressed like Erunam—and sits it on top of the well.*)

GULLIBLE: An amazing likeness!

(All exit.)

Scene 7: MARTOK.

(MARTOK *sneaks in, sees the idol, and throws it down the well.*)

Scene 8: BOTCHUP, GULLIBLE, HYACINTH, ROSALBA, PHYLLIS, MARTOK.

(All rush in, exclaiming at once: Saw you! Guilty, guilty! Caught in the act! He did it!)

MARTOK: I didn't do it!

ROSALBA: There's only one thing that keeps me from calling you a bald-faced liar: your goatee!

BOTCHUP: He's an atheist. He doesn't believe in Erunam!

HYACINTH: What's an atheist?

BOTCHUP: It's a person with no invisible means of support.

ROSALBA: What punishment do you deem fit, O Erunam?

BOTCHUP: He will be punished after my ancient custom, for he who steps on God Erunam will be sorry.

MARTOK: Mercy, mercy!

GULLIBLE: *(Turning to PHYLLIS)* Phyllis, will you marry me?

PHYLLIS: Yes, for a year.

GULLIBLE: But, Phyllis, marriage is forever.

PHYLLIS: What about a shorter lease? We can try it for a year and, if we like it, we can always renew.

GULLIBLE: Where I come from if you're not satisfied with your marriage, you can always divorce.

PHYLLIS: What's a divorce?

GULLIBLE: It's the billing without the cooing. Phyllis, do you believe in sex before marriage?

PHYLLIS: As long as it doesn't make us late for the ceremony.

GULLIBLE: Listen, everybody! Phyllis and I are going to be married!

BOTCHUP: Mazel tov!

ROSALBA: Congratulations!

HYACINTH: The first hundred years are the hardest!

(GULLIBLE, PHYLLIS, ROSALBA, and HYACINTH exit.)

Scene 9: MARTOK, BOTCHUP.

MARTOK: Erunam! You are not the true god! You have defiled the High Priestess with your touch, profaned her lips with your kiss!

BOTCHUP: I defend your right to worship any god you choose, Martok, but you're wrong about the High Priestess. I had a perfect right to kiss the lady. She had a right to kiss me. Why not? We're going to be married.

MARTOK: You are insane! This is a sacrilege. If you are the true god, walk into the Flame of Everlasting Life right now!

(The Flame is revealed.)

BOTCHUP: I prefer not to walk into the Flame just now.

MARTOK: *(Laughing cruelly)* Ha! Ha! Ha! Ha! I will give you one more chance to prove that you are the promised god . . . when you lead us into battle against the Utopians! I have spoken! So let it be written. So let it be done!

BOTCHUP: What does it all mean?

MARTOK: Don't look for deeper meaning. Just take it at farce value. *(Exits)*

Scene 10: ANARCH, BOTCHUP, GULLIBLE.

(Enter ANARCH *with* GULLIBLE.*)*

ANARCH: John Gullible, I've been looking high and low for you. *(With a glance at* BOTCHUP*)* Apparently, I didn't look low enough.

*(*BOTCHUP *exits dejectedly)*

Scene 11: GULLIBLE, ANARCH.

GULLIBLE: *(To* ANARCH*)* Mr. President, your daughter has promised to be my wife.

ANARCH: It was your own fault. What else did you expect if you kept hanging around here every night? *(Calling loudly)* Phyllis!

Scene 12: PHYLLIS, ANARCH, GULLIBLE.

PHYLLIS: *(Entering)* Yes, Father?

ANARCH: Your young man, John Gullible from Outer Earth, has been staying until a very late hour. What would your dear departed mother have said?

PHYLLIS: She would have said, "Men haven't changed a bit."

ANARCH: My child, never let a fool kiss you or a kiss fool you. Are you engaged to Mr. Gullible?

PHYLLIS: Yes, I have promised to marry him as soon as he has made his fortune.

ANARCH: That isn't an engagement; that's an option. *(To* GULLIBLE*)* Would you excuse us please, Mr. Gullible? I would like to speak to my daughter in private.

GULLIBLE: I can only say, Mr. President, that it would fulfill my fondest wish if you were to think of me as your son. *(Exits)*

Scene 13: ANARCH, PHYLLIS.

ANARCH: Phyllis, this morning I found a number of burnt out matches in the parlor. Were you and Mr. Gullible smoking last night?

PHYLLIS: No, Father. We just lit them occasionally to see what time it was.

ANARCH: Phyllis, ever since I left that world out there years ago and brought you here and founded Utopia, I swore I'd never let that world lay eyes on you—to keep your beauty from them. That was to be my revenge for being paralyzed from the waist down, for having to spend the rest of my life in a wheelchair. And the disgrace of it—ah, the disgrace: to have been falsely accused by my partner, to be publicly humiliated as an embezzler! I won't let you go, my child. I won't let you live in a world where money is God, where fools and mad men pass for heroes, and honest people who quietly do right are overlooked. A mother should receive medals for facing childbirth before a soldier is decorated for bravery in battle!

PHYLLIS: If none of them are worse than he is, I'm sure they can't be so bad.

ANARCH: Very well, my daughter, enter into matrimony: the high sea for which no compass has yet been invented. And set sail for wedlock, the land that strangers are desirous of inhabiting, while its natural inhabitants wish to escape. Bring in young Gullible.

PHYLLIS: *(Calling loudly)* John, you can come in now.

Scene 14: ANARCH, PHYLLIS, GULLIBLE, ROBOT.

(Enter GULLIBLE.)

ANARCH: I must tell you that my daughter can bring her husband only her beauty and her intellect.

GULLIBLE: I don't mind—many young couples have started in a small way. *(Puts an engagement ring on her finger)*

PHYLLIS: Why, John, it's beautiful. Pardon my ignorance, but will you please tell me how to pronounce the name of the stone in this ring? Is it dimind or diamond?

GULLIBLE: The correct pronunciation is "glass."

ANARCH: I have only one reservation about your marrying my daughter.

GULLIBLE: What is that, Mr. President?

ANARCH: Your name: Gullible. It sounds so silly.

GULLIBLE: Well, as a matter of fact, Mr. President, that's not my real name. But when we're married, dear, we ought to have a hyphenated name. It sounds so much smarter. What would go well with Eaton?

PHYLLIS: How about "Moth"?

GULLIBLE: A female moth is a myth.

ANARCH: Eaton? Your name is Eaton?

GULLIBLE: Yes, John Eaton. Son of Spiro Bernard Eaton. My father was an industrialist and he—

ANARCH: Spiro Bernard Eaton? Aaagh!

PHYLLIS: What is it, Father?

ANARCH: Spiro Bernard Eaton was my partner, the man who ruined me, and this whelp is his son.

PHYLLIS: Oh no!

GULLIBLE: This is indeed an unfortunate coincidence. But . . . but, surely you can't blame me for my father!

ANARCH: No, I blame him for you. Roberta! Seize him! Put him in irons! Hard labor will be the reward for the son of my ancient enemy.

(ROBOT enters and locks GULLIBLE in a hold.)

PHYLLIS: Father, show him mercy!

ANARCH: Yes, as much as his father showed to me!! Take him away! *(ROBERTA, the robot, starts to drag GULLIBLE out)*

GULLIBLE: Oh, Phyllis. I shall be so miserable all the while I am away from you.

PHYLLIS: Oh, darling, if I could be sure of that it would make me so happy!

GULLIBLE: *(As he is being dragged out)* We hang petty thieves and appoint the great ones to public office!

ANARCH: I was robbed! I . . . I . . . I . . . was the one who was robbed!

PHYLLIS: Ah, Father, the robbed that smiles steals something from the thief. He robs himself who spends a bootless grief. *(She wheels him out)*

Scene 15: GULLIBLE, PHYLLIS.

(GULLIBLE enters dragging heavy styrofoam very wearily.)

PHYLLIS: *(Enters and sees him)* Oh, John, it breaks my heart to see you laboring so hard at hard labor.

GULLIBLE: Hard labor is easy when I think of you, Phyllis.

PHYLLIS: John, I've decided to defy my father and help you escape from Utopia.

GULLIBLE: Will you come with me, Phyllis? Will you come and live in my world?

PHYLLIS: But will we have to work in your world?

GULLIBLE: I'm afraid so, Phyllis. We don't have machines to do all work for us.

PHYLLIS: Good, I should like to try working. I think I'd like it. I'm tired of this lazy life here in Utopia.

GULLIBLE: It won't be easy, I warn you.

PHYLLIS: And will there be foolishness in your world?

GULLIBLE: Yes, Phyllis, you'd have to put up with a lot of foolishness, I'm afraid.

PHYLLIS: Good, I should like to experience this foolishness. It sounds like it might prove amusing.

GULLIBLE: Oh, I think you'll like it there all right. Oh, it isn't perfect like your world, Phyllis. We haven't found the perfect way yet, Phyllis. We're still changing. But, you never know, someday . . .

PHYLLIS: Perhaps I could instruct your people.

GULLIBLE: We'll have to be tactful. People's minds are hard to change. There's nothing convinces them they're right so much as open opposition. You're going to be hard enough to explain as it is. *(Offstage sounds are heard)* There's only moments; they're coming to stop us! Phyllis, make up your mind now and forever!

PHYLLIS: I'm afraid! I read in a book once about a woman in my position who left and aged terribly. I didn't want to tell you this, Gullible. We don't die. . . . . I am three thousand years old!

GULLIBLE: But I like older women! Forget the difference in our ages. We were meant for each other.

PHYLLIS: How old are you?

GULLIBLE: Thirty-five.

PHYLLIS: Take advantage of a mere child of thirty-five? I'd feel I was robbing the cradle.

GULLIBLE: *(Embracing her)* Ah, Phyllis, it won't just be Utopia; it'll be you-and-me-topia! *(Offstage footsteps and rumblings)*

PHYLLIS: They're coming! I can't decide! I've never been to your world. How can I decide?

GULLIBLE: Phyllis, in the name of our future, I swear to you that if you come with me to my world, I will return to Utopia with you exactly one year from today, and then make your decision.

PHYLLIS: Very well. I'll try your world and then decide where I would rather live.

Scene 16: GULLIBLE, PHYLLIS, POLICEMAN, MUGGER, WAITRESS, DERELICT, PEDESTRIAN.

(Each character from Utopia and the Happy Isle plays one of the New Yorkers.)

GULLIBLE: Well, Phyllis, here we are in New York City!

(Enter Pedestrian, played by ROBOT, *carrying a radio which is tuned to a disco station. As she walks in front of* GULLIBLE *and* PHYLLIS, *they hold their ears.* ROBOT *exits. Enter Policeman played by* MARTOK.*)*

PHYLLIS: Pardon me, Officer, but I want to go to Central Park.
POLICEMAN: All right, I'll let you go this time. But don't you ever, ever ask me again. *(Exits)*

(Enter Mugger played by HYACINTH.*)*

MUGGER: Give me your money or I'll blow your brains out.
PHYLLIS: Better give it to him, John.
GULLIBLE: Blow away! You can live in New York without brains but not without money. *(Exit Mugger)* Let's go to a restaurant.

(Enter Waitress played by ROSALBA.*)*

WAITRESS: *(Carrying a stack of plates with food)* What'll you have?
GULLIBLE: Two eggs and a kind word.
WAITRESS: Here are your eggs. *(Starts to go)*
PHYLLIS: What about the kind word?
WAITRESS: Don't eat the eggs. *(Exits)*
PHYLLIS: I love the way they speak English here.
GULLIBLE: Really?
PHYLLIS: They call the nursery the noisery and I've always thought that's the way it should be pronounced. Where is the population most dense?
GULLIBLE: From the neck up.

(Enter Derelict played by ANARCH.*)*

GULLIBLE: Could you direct us to the First National Bank?
DERELICT: Sure, if you give me a dollar.
GULLIBLE: Very well, here you are. *(Hands him a dollar)*
DERELICT: It's across the street.
GULLIBLE: Well, that was a dollar easily earned.
DERELICT: Bank directors is paid high in Noo Yawk. *(Exit)*
PHYLLIS: The people in New York are just like the people in Utopia!
GULLIBLE: This is my old neighborhood.
PHYLLIS: What's a neighborhood?
GULLIBLE: It's a residential area that's changing for the worse.
PHYLLIS: Are these your neighbors?
GULLIBLE: No, Phyllis, in New York we have neighborhoods but no neighbors.
PHYLLIS: Strange.

GULLIBLE: You see, Phyllis, the history of a metropolis is divided into three parts: first it gets rid of animals, then plants, finally children.

(They exit.)

Scene 17: MARTOK, ROSALBA, HYACINTH, BOTCHUP.

(They enter in uniforms, ready for battle.)

MARTOK: The time has come, O Erunam. Warrior spawned in the dim past, fight now your first battle against science of the far future. Find triumph in failure, failure in triumph.

ROSALBA: Wear my rose into battle and let today be marked ever in memory as the day of the mighty warrior, Erunam.

HYACINTH: Utopia must be destroyed. You, O Erunam, must crush it.

BOTCHUP: Thanks for your vote of confidence, friends, but your mighty warrior is not quite what he seems.

MARTOK: We were told that Erunam's strength could overcome anything.

BOTCHUP: Don't worry, savage, I'll give it the old Utopian try.

(They march toward Utopia in place, moving their feet but not moving forward.)

HYACINTH: It's no use. No matter how long we march, we don't seem to get anywhere.

MARTOK: Something is stopping us.

ROSALBA: Onward toward Styro-City.

MARTOK: We must kill them before they kill us. Anarch must fall!

(All continue to march without moving forward.)

Scene 18: ROBOT, ANARCH.

ROBOT: *(Wheeling* ANARCH *in)* Anarch, there is rioting in the streets. The rebels have torn your statue down!

ANARCH: I hereby declare martial law. After order is restored, I'll hold free elections. *(The Happy Islanders march toward* ANARCH*)* Stun the monsters!

ROBOT: ZZZZZZZZT!! *(Puts them in a state of suspended animation while moving toward them)*

MARTOK: Look out, the robot is coming!

BOTCHUP: That thing is a walking arsenal!

ROSALBA: Hoist your shields, boys.

(A rumbling is heard.)

ROBOT: There is no doubt about the location, Anarch. The volcano will erupt any minute.

ROSALBA: I fear the ancient vow made by our forefathers generations ago. The same vow we pledged to the Great God Erunam.

(The volcano begins to rock.)

MARTOK: That which our ancestors feared in antideluvian times is now coming to pass.

HYACINTH: The volcano is erupting; the Flame of Everlasting Life glows everywhere. Turn back, O Erunam!

BOTCHUP: Well, we've come this far.

HYACINTH: I beg you, turn back.

MARTOK: Forward! Forward! Forward to yesterday!

(The volcano begins to erupt.)

ANARCH: Stop, intruders!

ROBOT: *(Aiming gun)* ZZZZZZZZT!

(All freeze.)

ANARCH: Years, aeons, millions of eras ago, your people threatened all life, which alone is eternal, with extinction through the waging of senseless wars, mad wars, wars of chaos out of mind. Only a few of our ancestors were spared this cosmic idiocy. These few folk sought sanctuary here. We have never meddled in the affairs of you outsiders as long as you did not meddle in the affairs of we insiders. But now you have gone too far. Breaking into our world of suspended animation, releasing the ancient boiling blood of the earth itself. You have created evil through your perverted science. We have waited and watched for this evil's second coming. The limitations of your physical science has exceeded its limit. Your civilization is based on waste of material resources. Why, you could build a Utopia out of the garbage that litters your streets every day! Your scientists have deluded you with bogus projects. They have wasted your money giving it to the moon, but they have been unable to produce anything useful. You have strayed from your original purpose: the simple transmutation of dreams into realities. Release them! You have not dared to go as *(Yawns)* far as thought can reach. *(Falls asleep)*

BOTCHUP: Listen here, old dreamer. Don't let us disturb your pleasant snooze. If we are nothing more than dream material, at least we can look forward to tomorrow morning when we wake.

ANARCH: We wake? We wake? *(Yawns)* What then?

BOTCHUP: Then when?

ANARCH: We wake? *(Sleeps)* Zzzzzzzzzzzzz!!!

HYACINTH: He's fallen asleep.

ROSALBA: This doesn't seem to be leading anywhere.

MARTOK: Yes, this is all leading us nowhere.

BOTCHUP: Just when I was thinking I might get something accomplished.

(All exit.)

ACT III. UTOPIA REVISITED

Scene 1: GULLIBLE, PHYLLIS.

GULLIBLE: Oh, Phyllis, I'm so nervous.

PHYLLIS: About what?

GULLIBLE: About revisiting Utopia. I'm so afraid your father won't forgive us for eloping that I've had insomnia for three days.

PHYLLIS: Can't remember a thing, huh?

GULLIBLE: Insomnia means I can't sleep. Why, I have insomnia so bad, I can't even sleep when it's time to get up.

PHYLLIS: Have you tried talking to yourself?

GULLIBLE: It's no use. When I do fall asleep, I snore so loudly that I wake myself up.

PHYLLIS: I used to have a similar problem. But I cured myself. I sleep in the next room now.

GULLIBLE: I wonder how Botchup is doing.

PHYLLIS: Here's the Utopia–Happy Isle border. Let's cross over and find out.

GULLIBLE: Say, what's that building there?

PHYLLIS: Where?

GULLIBLE: You looked too late. It's gone.

PHYLLIS: Utopia is becoming more like New York every day.

GULLIBLE: Yes, here is an office building where the temple to Erunam once stood.

PHYLLIS: *(Reading sign)* "Utopia, Incorporated." Can it be that the Happy Islanders have industrialized?

Scene 2: GULLIBLE, PHYLLIS, BOTCHUP.

BOTCHUP: *(Entering)* Yessiree, indeed they have. And I am the president of the corporation!

GULLIBLE: Botchup, old man! Good to see you!

BOTCHUP: Hello, Phyllis.

PHYLLIS: Hello, Botchup.

BOTCHUP: Phyllis, were you in New York long enough to feel at home there?

PHYLLIS: Yes. Why, it got so I could ride on the subway with an old lady standing in front of me and not even think about it. How did you get started in business?

BOTCHUP: I sold my wristwatch and bought an alarm clock.

Scene 3: GULLIBLE, PHYLLIS, BOTCHUP, HYACINTH, MARTOK, ROSALBA.

HYACINTH: *(Entering as secretary)* Mr. Chup, Mr. Jones wants to know if you are going to pay up his account.

BOTCHUP: Tell him no.

HYACINTH: He says that if you don't pay him, he'll tell all your other creditors you did.

BOTCHUP: Tell him the check is in the mail!

(HYACINTH exits.)

GULLIBLE: This is amazing! I never would have thought you had a business head.

BOTCHUP: I used to be young and foolish. But I'm not so young anymore.

MARTOK: *(Entering)* Mr. Chup, can you let me off tomorrow to go shopping with my wife?

BOTCHUP: Certainly not. We're too busy.

MARTOK: Thank you, sir. That's a great relief. *(Exit)*

(Enter ROSALBA *also dressed for business.)*

BOTCHUP: Twenty minutes late again! Do you know what time we start work in this office?

ROSALBA: No, Mr. Chup, they're always at it when I get here. *(Exit)*

HYACINTH: *(Entering)* Mr. Chup, people are always asking me how much I make here.

BOTCHUP: Nonsense, your salary is confidential and should not be disclosed to anyone.

HYACINTH: I won't mention it to anybody. I'm just as much ashamed of it as you are. *(Exit)*

PHYLLIS: Is Martok married now?

BOTCHUP: Yes, I only hire married men to work for me.

GULLIBLE: Why's that?

BOTCHUP: The married men don't get so upset if I yell at them.

HYACINTH: *(Entering)* Mr. Chup, I'm having trouble with this business letter.

BOTCHUP: *(To* PHYLLIS *and* GULLIBLE*)* Excuse me. *(To* HYACINTH*)* What seems to be the trouble?

HYACINTH: I don't know the correct plural of mongoose. Should I write, "Please send me two mongeese"?

BOTCHUP: No, that doesn't sound right.

HYACINTH: Or should it be "please send me two mongooses"?

BOTCHUP: That sounds even worse.

HYACINTH: That's what I thought.

BOTCHUP: Write, "Sir, please send me a mongoose, and by the way, send me another."

(Exit HYACINTH.*)*

GULLIBLE: So, your new job makes you independent?

BOTCHUP: Absolutely. I get here any time I want before nine, and leave when I please after five.

ROSALBA: *(Enters answering five phones in succession)* Utopia, Incorporated. He hasn't come in yet. Utopia, Incorporated. I expect him any minute. Utopia, Incorporated. He sent word he'd be in a little late. Utopia, Incorporated. He's been in but he went out again. Utopia, Incorporated. He's gone to lunch.

PHYLLIS: Everyone is so efficient here.

ROSALBA: Utopia, Incorporated. I expect him in any minute. Utopia, Incorporated. He hasn't come back yet. Can I take a message? Utopia, Incorporated. He's somewhere in the building. His hat is here. Utopia, Incorporated. Yes, he was in but he went out again. Utopia, Incorporated. I don't know whether he'll be back or not. Utopia, Incorporated. No, he's gone for the day.

BOTCHUP: I just got back from a business conference.

GULLIBLE: Was the conference a success? What did you decide?

BOTCHUP: It was great! We decided to have another conference next week.

HYACINTH: *(Entering)* Mr. Chup, I'd like my salary raised.

BOTCHUP: Well, don't worry. I've raised it somehow every week so far, haven't I?

PHYLLIS: How many people work in your office?

BOTCHUP: Oh, I'd say about two-thirds of them. *(To* ROSALBA*)* Rose, get my broker.

ROSALBA: Yes, sir, stock or pawn?

BOTCHUP: Miss Alba, I'm afraid you're becoming more inefficient every day.

ROSALBA: Well, sir, if you ask me, it's you who are mismanaging the company's affairs.

BOTCHUP: *(Angrily)* Are you the president of this corporation?

ROSALBA: No, sir.

BOTCHUP: Then don't talk like a fool.

(Exit ROSALBA.*)*

HYACINTH: *(Entering)* Mr. Chup, a man just called. He wants you to tell him the secret of your success in life.

BOTCHUP: Is he a journalist . . . or a detective?

(Exit HYACINTH.*)*

PHYLLIS: Have you seen my father, Botchup? Do you know if he is all right? Has he forgiven me for running off with John?

BOTCHUP: The old man has kept to himself in recent months. Although I do go over and play dominoes with him on rainy afternoons.

PHYLLIS: Does he ever mention me?

BOTCHUP: He never speaks of the past.

GULLIBLE: Let's visit him.

Scene 4: GULLIBLE, PHYLLIS, BOTCHUP, ANARCH, ROBOT.

(They cross the border once again into Utopia proper and draw back a screen revealing the wheelchair with the mummy wrappings in it. ROBOT *stands behind the wheelchair.)*

PHYLLIS: Father . . . Father?

(A strange, disembodied voice issues forth from the wrappings and the glow of an unearthly light.)

ANARCH: Phyllis, my child. John, my son.

PHYLLIS: Do you forgive us, Father.

ANARCH: Forgive, yes, but not forget. Ah, confusion, confusion. All my life I've never known who I was or where I was.

GULLIBLE: *(Drawing* PHYLLIS *close to him)* Tell us your troubles, ancient Father. Perhaps we can solve the problem for you.

ANARCH: It's all through marriage that my troubles arose. I married a widow who had a grown-up daughter. My father visited our house very often and fell in love with my stepdaughter and married her. So my father became my son-in-law, and my stepdaughter my mother, because she was my father's wife, and my wife became my father's mother-in-law. To make matters worse, my wife soon after had a son; he was my father's brother-in-law and my uncle, for he was the brother of my stepmother. My father's wife, who was my stepdaughter, also had a son; he was, of course, my brother and, in the meantime, my grandchild, for he was the son of my daughter. My wife was my grandmother, because she was my mother's mother. I was my wife's husband and grandchild at the same time. *(Begins crying)*

BOTCHUP: Well, who are you?

ANARCH: I'm my own grandfather!

(The light from within the mummy wrappings grows more intense. The wheelchair moves forward as if by its own power. PHYLLIS and GULLIBLE approach the wheelchair warily and discover the mummy wrappings to be empty.)

PHYLLIS: He's gone.

Scene 5: COMPANY

(The Flame of Everlasting Life erupts from the crater of its volcanic well. There is strange music. The Pillars of Utopia crumble and dust falls on the scene. All characters freeze except for HYACINTH and MARTOK who carry picket signs, "Utopia Inc. Unfair." Only ROSALBA's voice is heard as the lights fade.)

ROSALBA: *(Answering ringing phones)* Utopia, Incorporated. He isn't in right now. Utopia, Incorporated. He's in conference, may I take a message? Utopia, Incorporated. We're expecting him back any minute. Shall I have him call you? Utopia, Incorporated. You just missed him.

The End

THE ENCHANTED PIG

A Fairy Tale for the Disenchanted

1979

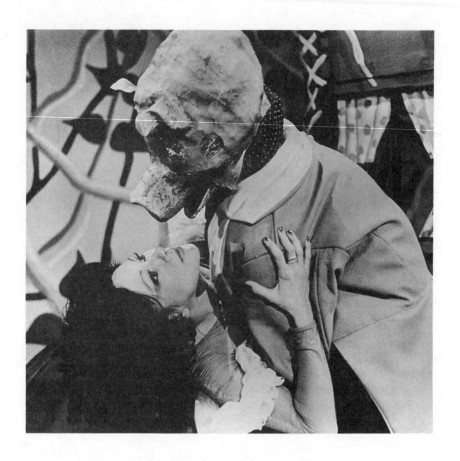

Black-Eyed Susan & Everett Quinton in
The Enchanted Pig (Wolfgang Staehle)

Cast of Characters

KING GORGEOUS III
PRINCESS GONDA
PRINCESS WANDA
THE ENFANTA EULALIE IRENE
A PRINCE FROM THE EAST
A PRINCE FROM THE WEST
A PIG FROM THE NORTH, *later revealed to be a true prince*
A WITCH
THE MOTHER OF THE MOON
THE MOTHER OF THE SUN
THE MOTHER OF THE WIND

Scene 1

(Fanfare. KING on his throne. The three princesses enter to him.)

THE THREE PRINCESSES: You sent for us, Father?
KING: Yes. My dear children, I am obliged to go to the wars. The enemy is approaching us with a large army. It is a great grief to me to leave you all. During my absence take care of yourselves and be good girls; behave well and look after everything in the house. You may walk in the garden, you may sit in the living room, or you may live in the sitting room. But don't go into *that* room. *(Points to a door)* Into that room you must not enter for harm would befall you.
GONDA: You may keep your mind easy, Father.
WANDA: We have never been disobedient to you.
EULALIE IRENE: Go in peace, Father, and may heaven send you a glorious victory.
KING: Here are the keys to all the rooms of the palace, and don't forget what I told you. Don't go into *that* room.

(Fanfare. Exit KING. The three princesses twirl and sit, which implies that it is . . .)

Scene 2

(Several days later.)

GONDA: Sisters, all day long we sew, spin, and read. We have been several days quite alone, and there is no corner of the garden that we have not explored. We have been in all the rooms of our father's palace, and have admired the rich and beautiful furniture. Why should we not go into the room that our father forbade us to enter?
EULALIE IRENE: Sister, I cannot think how you can tempt us to break our father's command. When he told us not to go into *that* room he must have known what he was saying and have had a good reason for saying it.
WANDA: Surely the sky won't fall about our heads if we *do* go in. Dragons and

such-like monsters that would devour us will not be hidden in the room. And how will our father ever find out that we have gone in?

(WANDA and GONDA walk toward the room in slow motion, as if drawn by a magnet. EULALIE IRENE looks on in frozen horror.)

EULALIE IRENE: No. No. Don't do it sisters. Please don't disobey our father.

(The eldest takes out the key, unlocks the door, and opens it. An empty room is revealed with a table center with a gorgeous cloth and on it a big open book.)

GONDA: I wonder what is written in that book. *(Reads)* "The eldest daughter of King Gorgeous III will marry a prince from the East."
WANDA: *(Reads)* "The second daughter of King Gorgeous III will marry a prince from the West."

(WANDA and GONDA laugh and kiss each other.)

WANDA: Now it's your turn, Eulalie Irene.
GONDA: You read next.
EULALIE IRENE: *(Frightened)* No no, I don't want to!
GONDA: Come on, don't be a scaredy cat. Read. *(Drags her to the table)*
EULALIE IRENE: I don't want to read what is written in that book.
WANDA: *(Pushing her face into the book)* Read!
EULALIE IRENE: *(Turns the page with fear and trembling and reads)* "The youngest daughter of King Gorgeous III will be married to a pig from the North." *(Faints)*
WANDA AND GONDA: There there. *(Patting her hands and face)*
EULALIE IRENE: *(Comes to and begins to wail and cry)* Why did I do it? Why did I read when Father told me not to? *(Sobs)*
GONDA: How can you believe such nonsense? When did it ever happen that a king's daughter married a pig?
WANDA: What a baby you are! Has not our father enough soldiers to protect you, even if the disgusting creature did come to woo you?
EULALIE IRENE: *(With a heavy heart)* Yes, I suppose you are right. Oh why, oh why did I disobey Father?

Scene 3

(The princesses sit at their spinning wheels.)

GONDA: Eulalie Irene, Eulalie Irene. Why don't you sing?
WANDA: Why don't you play?
GONDA: Why don't you gather flowers to put in your hair?
EULALIE IRENE: How can I sing? How can I play? How can I gather flowers to put in my hair? When my thoughts always return to that book in which stood written that great happiness waits for you, my sisters, but that a fate is in store for me such as has never been known in the world.

(Fanfare.)

GONDA: Listen! The trumpets. Father has returned from the wars!

(Enter the KING. There are shouts of joy and merry music.)

KING: Please, my people, stop for one moment this revelry and merrymaking. And let us pray. *(All fall silent. Kneeling)* Thank you heaven for this glorious victory I have gained over my enemies who rose against me. Amen.

ALL: Amen!

(The KING rises and the merry music resumes. The three princesses come forward to greet their father.)

KING: Where are my daughters? Where's Wanda and Gonda and Eulalie Irene?

GONDA: Welcome home, Father, how happy I am to see you!

WANDA: Father, Father, how I missed you.

KING: Wanda and Gonda, you look well—and prettier than ever, I might add. But where is Eulalie Irene?

EULALIE IRENE: Here, Father.

KING: And how do you feel? Are you not glad to see me?

EULALIE IRENE: No.

KING: No? What do you mean no? Speak again and tell me yes.

EULALIE IRENE: I cannot lie to you, my father. No, I am not glad to see you.

KING: So young and so untender! And to think I always loved you best. Go to your chamber at once, ungrateful girl, and there remain until you are glad to see me.

EULALIE IRENE: Then there will I remain forever for I cannot lie and say I'm glad to see you. *(She turns to go)*

KING: Wait Eulalie Irene. You break your father's heart. Tell me child, why have you grown so thin? Why do you look so sad.

EULALIE IRENE: Don't ask me, Father.

WANDA: She's been like this for weeks now.

GONDA: Ever since you went away.

KING: Oh no! I fear the worst. *(Very stern)* Daughters, come and tell me the truth. Did you do that which I forbade you to do? Did you open that one door I told you not to open?

EULALIE IRENE: *(Bursting into tears)* Yes! Yes! Forgive me, Father. But that is why I was not glad to see you.

KING: And did you all read from the forbidden book?

WANDA, GONDA, and EULALIE IRENE: Yes.

KING: And which one of you led the others into temptation?

(WANDA and GONDA point at each other guiltily.)

EULALIE IRENE: It was I, Father. I alone knew better.

KING: *(Wailing loudly and beating his breast with his fists)* Oh no! Oh no! What have you done!? *(The princesses are almost frightened to death)* Now what has happened has happened and not a thousand words can alter matters by a hair's breadth.

Scene 4

(Trumpets sound. Enter PRINCE FROM THE EAST.)

PRINCE FROM THE EAST: Hail O King. May your reign be blessed with a plentitude of years! I have come to ask the hand of your eldest daughter.

KING: Her hand? What's wrong with the rest of her?

PRINCE FROM THE EAST: I mean I want to marry her.

KING: Princess Gonda, we have here a prince from the East. He wishes to marry you. What do you say, my daughter?

PRINCESS GONDA: He is a man of goodly parts and as handsome as a prince in a fairy tale. Yes Father, Your Highness, I will gladly marry this prince. I feel I am beginning to love him already.

KING: So be it. And for your dowry take the shadowy forests and champlains rich with plenteous rivers and wide-skirted meads. Of all these parts of my kingdom do I make you lady.

(Trumpets sound. Enter PRINCE FROM THE WEST.*)*

PRINCE FROM THE WEST: Hail O King. May your reign be blessed with health and happiness! I have come to ask the hand of your second daughter.

KING: Princess Wanda, a prince from the West has come to ask your hand. What do you say, my daughter? Will you marry him?

PRINCESS WANDA: Yes, Majesty, my Father. For he is comely and straight as a fir tree. I will be his own.

KING: Good. Then for your dowry take another piece of our fair kingdom no less in space, richness, or pleasure than that I gave your sister. Let there be a great marriage feast. Let there be singing dancing and merrymaking. Eat, everyone, eat! *(Everyone laughs and eats except* PRINCESS EULALIE IRENE*)* Eulalie Irene, why do you not sing, or eat, or dance at your sisters' wedding?

EULALIE IRENE: Everything has fallen out exactly as it was written in that book. I won't eat. I won't put on fine clothes and dance! I won't! I'd rather die than be made a laughingstock to the world.

KING: There there, my child. You're wrong to be so sad. There is nothing to be sad about.

(Trumpets blast an oinking sound.)

EULALIE IRENE: *(Startled and shaking with fear)* What was that I heard?

KING: It was a trumpet blast.

EULALIE IRENE: No no dear Father. I think it was the sound of oinking!

(Enter an enormous PIG FROM THE NORTH.*)*

PIG: Hail O King. May your life be as prosperous and bright as sunrise on a clear day!

KING: I am glad to see you well, my friend, but what brings you hither?

PIG: I come a-wooing.

KING: *(Aside)* This is amazing. I've never heard so fine a speech from a pig! Something is the matter here. Something *unusual* is definitely the matter here.

PIG: Oink oink. I have come to ask the hand of your youngest daughter.

KING: I would gladly give you anything but that O pig. I'll promise you anything that you wish. But not the hand of my youngest daughter, the Princess Eulalie Irene.

PIG: I won't be satisfied with mere promises. I want the wedding to take place at once.

EULALIE IRENE: Father, protect me, call out your armies, but don't give me in marriage to this pig no matter how fine his speech is.

PIG: Soueee! Soueee!

(A great oinking is heard outside the palace.)

KING: What is that sound I hear? *(Goes to his balcony and looks out)* The castle is surrounded by all the pigs in the world.

PIG: I won't go away until you swear a royal oath that the marriage will take place within a week.

EULALIE IRENE: Don't swear it, Father, don't swear!

(The great oinking is heard in the streets once more.)

KING: There is no escape.

PIG: Swear, King, swear.

KING: I swear!

PIG: Good. Let the wedding feast be prepared. But make sure that you prepare it to my specifications. I want the feast to be held in a sty and all the guests to eat from a trough like pigs.

SISTERS and PRINCES: Eeecht!

KING: And what will we serve, O pig?

PIG: Garbage and swill. And after the banquet we'll have dancing and we'll all roll in the mud.

KING: Oh no!

PIG: What did you say?

KING: I said, "just so!"

PIG: And just so it will be. I am going now. But when I return I will expect you to have prepared everything exactly as I ordered it. Farewell for a fortnight O King. *(Exit with a great loud oink)*

PRINCESS: *(Sobbing and weeping)* I won't do it! I won't marry a pig. I won't. *(Bursts into tears again)*

KING: My child, I advise you to submit to fate, for there is nothing else to be done. My armies cannot stand against all the pigs in the world.

PRINCESS: Oh! *(Weeps even more loudly)*

KING: My child, the words and whole behavior of this pig are quite unlike those of other pigs. I do not myself believe that he always *was* a pig. Depend upon it, some magic or witchcraft has been at work. Obey him and do everything that he wishes, and I feel sure that heaven will shortly send you release.

PRINCESS: *(Choking back her tears)* If you wish me to do this, dear Father, I will do it.

Scene 5: *The wedding feast.*

(Pigs and people at a trough decked like a banquet table.)

PIGS: Oink oink oink! Roll in the mud. We accept you as one of us. Oink oink oink! Roll in the mud. We accept you as one of us.

PIG: My dearest wife. Why don't you join in the festivities?

EULALIE IRENE: *(Aside)* This is the most horrible thing I've ever been subjected to. *(Then philosophically)* But what is a poor girl to do? I suppose I may as well oink and roll in the mud with the rest of my in-laws.

PIGS:
　Oink oink oink!
　Roll in the mud!
　We accept you as one of us.

PIG: I'm waiting, darling.

KING: Remember Daughter, better do as he says until fate sends some solution to your problem.

PIGS:
　Oink oink oink!
　Roll in the mud!
　We accept you as one of us.

EULALIE IRENE:
　Oink oink oink!
　Roll in the mud! *(She does so)*

PIGS: Now we accept you as one of us! *(The PIGS all cheer)*

PIG: Now give me a kiss.

EULALIE IRENE: *(Wipes the PIG's snout with her hankie and kisses it)* There, my husband.

PIGS: *(Cheer and chant)*
　We accept you.
　We accept you.
　We accept you as one of us.

PIG: Come my wife, our carriage awaits.

EULALIE IRENE: But where are we going to live? Shall we have a third of your kingdom, Father?

KING: Certainly not. I cannot give my kingdom to the pigs. *(PIGS mutter discontentedly)* You must go and live in Pigland. Your sisters will divide your share of our domain. *(Tears map in half and gives the pieces to WANDA and GONDA)*

PIG:
　Then come Eulalie Irene
　Bid them all adieu.
　For you will be a queen
　In a country new.

(They get into the carriage and drive off.)

PIGS:
　Oink oink oink!
　Roll in the mud!
　We accept you as one of us.

Scene 6: *The* PIG'S *dwelling.*

PIG: *(Enters carrying EULALIE IRENE across the threshold)* Here is our new home, my belovèd Eulalie Irene. This is where we'll settle down.

EULALIE IRENE: Yes, my lord.

PIG: Don't call me "my lord." I don't like flattery. Call me pig, for that's what I am.

EULALIE IRENE: Yes pig.

PIG: You will live here in my sty and if you wait on me hoof and mouth I promise you that I will never hurt you.

EULALIE IRENE: Yes pig.

PIG: Don't be afraid.

EULALIE IRENE: I won't be . . . afraid.

PIG: You must find my ugliness repulsive.

EULALIE IRENE: I cannot lie, pig.

PIG: I will do all I can to help you forget my ugliness.

EULALIE IRENE: That won't be easy. But thank you all the same, pig.

PIG: But you must promise me something.

EULALIE IRENE: What?

PIG: That you will never look into my eyes.

EULALIE IRENE: Why that?

PIG: Please promise me that.

EULALIE IRENE: No. That will I never promise. To live with someone and never look into his eyes? Why that would make me feel too alone, O pig. I could not bear it.

PIG: Do not defy me, wife.

EULALIE IRENE: Why pig, I think you are more afraid than I. Why do you fear my eyes? Why do you refuse me yours? Let me look. *(She takes the* PIG's *head in her hands and looks into his eyes although he tries to look away)* What is it you're afraid I'll see?

PIG: No, please don't.

EULALIE IRENE: *(Amazed at this discovery)* Why they're kind! They're gentle.

PIG: *(Turning away from her ashamed)* My heart is kind. But I am a monster.

EULALIE IRENE: I saw great love in your eyes. And sensitivity.

PIG: I'm crude and unrefined.

EULALIE IRENE: Come now. Don't be ashamed. There are many men more crude than you. But they hide it well.

PIG: I know I am repulsive. But Eulalie Irene, if you could ever find it in your heart to love me . . .

EULALIE IRENE: Please pig, don't ask the impossible. I can never love you. But I will try to be your friend.

PIG: My heart would break if you ever left me.

EULALIE IRENE: I'll never cause you any pain. I could never be cruel to any animal.

PIG: You called me an animal.

EULALIE IRENE: But you are an animal. You're weeping.

PIG: Forgive me.

EULALIE IRENE: *(Kneeling before him)* No no, it is you who must forgive me. I was crude.

PIG: It is I who should be kneeling before you.

EULALIE IRENE: Give me time O pig. Give me time. I will try to love you. I will learn. But not all at once. Please, give me time?

PIG: Thank you Eulalie Irene. *(Yawns an enormous yawn)* I'm so tired I can hardly keep my eyes open. Good night my wife. Good night.

EULALIE IRENE: Why he's fallen fast asleep. Poor thing, he's exhausted. I almost feel sorry for him lying there. Like a big baby pig. He's not really a bad pig . . . as pigs go. I'll just tuck him in. *(She pulls the covers up over him and lo and behold the* PIG *turns into a man)* Why this pig has changed into a man. Clearly my husband must be bewitched. I think in time I will grow fond of him. Don't hog the covers. *(She lies down beside the* PIG *and falls asleep)*

Scene 7

WITCH:
　Mumble mumble
　Fall and stumble
　Elvies tall
　And giants humble
　Into magic thread
　You tumble
　There to make the piggie grumble.
　Mumble mumble
　Fall and stumble
　Sigh of mute
　Cry of wail
　Curly as the piggie's tail
　Follow on the piggie's trail
　Make the piggie cry and wail
　When you tie it on his tail.

EULALIE IRENE: Who is that I hear singing? It's been so long since I've seen another human being. How good to have someone to talk to for a change! *(Calling out to the* WITCH) Good Madame! Good Madame! I say good Madame! Over here. Won't you come and talk to me?

WITCH: What is it you want my dear?

EULALIE IRENE: It's so good to hear your voice. Why, you're the first human being I've laid eyes on since I left my father's kingdom and came hither to live in the Land of Pigs.

WITCH: I'm a stranger here myself.

EULALIE IRENE: What is your name?

WITCH: The people I help call me Mother Wormwood.

EULALIE IRENE: Mother Wormwood. But what brings you to Pigland?

WITCH: I am a woman who knows all the magic arts. I can foretell the future, and I know the healing power of herbs and plants.

EULALIE IRENE: I shall be grateful to you all my life, old dame, if you will tell me what is the matter with my husband. Why is he a pig by day and a human being by night?

WITCH: It could be worse. It could be the other way around. I was just going to tell you that one thing, my dear, to show you what a good fortune teller I am. If you like I will give you an herb to break the spell.

EULALIE IRENE: If you will only give it to me, I will give you anything you choose to ask for, for I cannot bear to see him in this state.

WITCH: Here, then, my dear child, take this thread, but do not let him know about it, for if he did, it would lose its healing power. At night, when he is asleep, you must get up very quietly, and fasten the thread around his left foot as firmly as possible; and you will see in the morning he will not have changed back into a pig, but will still be a man.

EULALIE IRENE: Oh thank you kind woman! How can I ever repay you?

WITCH: I do not want any reward. I shall be sufficiently repaid by knowing that you are happy. It almost breaks my heart to think of all that you have suffered, and I only wish that I had known it sooner, as I should have come to your rescue at once. I must be going now my child, to help others who have need of me.

EULALIE IRENE: Farewell kind woman, and may heaven bless you. *(Exit* WITCH. EULALIE IRENE *tiptoes to her husband's bed and ties the thread to his foot)* Ah! The thread snapped!

PIG: *(Awaking with a start and crying out)* Unhappy woman, what have you done? Three days more and this unholy spell would have fallen from me, and now, who knows how long I may have to go about in this disgusting shape?

EULALIE IRENE: It was a mistake to waken you. We should never wake the man we love. In his sleep he's ours completely. But the moment he opens his eyes, he escapes. Sleep again . . .

PIG: Where did you get this thread? Who gave it to you?

EULALIE IRENE: Mother Wormwood.

PIG: Mother Wormwood! *(Thunder, lightning)* That was the foul witch Sycorax, whose pet dragon I slew. She put this curse on me for revenge. *(Thunder and lightning)*

EULALIE IRENE: But she seemed so kind!

PIG: I must leave you at once, and we shall not meet again until you have worn out three pairs of iron shoes and blunted a steel staff in your search for me. *(He disappears)* That is the curse. Farewell.

EULALIE IRENE: *(Begins to weep)* Wait a minute. These tears and groans will do me no good. I must get up and go wherever fate leads me. But before I do I must go to town and buy me those three pairs of iron shoes and that steel staff. For the sooner a great journey is begun the sooner it is ended. *(Exits)*

Scene 8: *Journey through the Woods.*

(To be depicted with all the resources of the puppet stage. Trees in frightening shapes, weird shadows. The branches tear her hands and hit her face but she presses on. Worn out and overcome with sorrow she arrives at a house.)

EULALIE IRENE: At last a house. Perchance whoever lives herein will grant me shelter for the night. *(Knocks at the door. The door opens and a woman's face of silver peeks out)* Who lives here, pray?

MOTHER OF THE MOON: Who do you think lives here? The Moon.

EULALIE IRENE: Is the moon at home?

MOTHER OF THE MOON: No she's not. I am the Mother of the Moon.

EULALIE IRENE: Oh, let me in I beg of you, that I may rest a little.

MOTHER OF THE MOON: Come in, child, and let me care for you. You look utterly worn out.

EULALIE IRENE: Thank you.

MOTHER OF THE MOON: But tell me, child, how was it possible for you, a mortal, to get hither to the house of the moon?

EULALIE IRENE: It's a long story.

MOTHER OF THE MOON: Come inside my child, and tell me your story.

EULALIE IRENE: Thank you, kind goddess. For of a truth I am going to have a baby.

MOTHER OF THE MOON: Come in and let me help you all I can. *(Yells off)* Hot water and plenty of it!

(They exit into the house and close the door. There is the sound of a baby crying.)

Scene 9

(Enter GONDA *followed by* PRINCE FROM THE EAST.*)*

PRINCE FROM THE EAST: Did your father spank you for not eating your vegetables?

GONDA: Ay, my husband. By night and day he wrongs me! I am queen now. I am an adult. I won't be treated like a child anymore. I won't!

PRINCE FROM THE EAST: But surely he knows you are a grown woman now and can eat whatever you like?

GONDA: I thought when I got married I would be my own mistress in my own castle.

PRINCE FROM THE EAST: Yesterday he forbade me to go hunting for a week because I kicked his favorite dog.

GONDA: I'll not endure it! He flies off the handle at every trifle. Hourly he finds some fresh excuse to punish us like naughty children.

(Horns within.)

PRINCE FROM THE EAST: He's coming, darling. I hear him.

GONDA: I will not speak to him. I'll ignore him and if he speaks to me I'll pretend not to hear.

PRINCE FROM THE EAST: But what explanation will I give?

GONDA: Say I am sick. And if he doesn't like it let him go and live with my sister. She and I have agreed not to let him have his way. He has given the kingdom to us. We are queens. Let us rule him!

PRINCE FROM THE EAST: But Gonda, old fools are babes again and must be kissed and flattered when they feel abused.

GONDA: I won't give in. Remember what I have said. Give him cold looks and freeze him out of the palace. I'll write to my sister Wanda and tell her to do the same. *(Exit)*

(Enter KING *with dog.)*

KING: Ho! What's for dinner? Hello there! Ho! *(To the* PRINCE*)* Where's my daughter? Gonda! Gonda! Why doesn't she come when she is called? Gonda! Gonda!

PRINCE FROM THE EAST: So please you, sir . . .

KING: Eh? What's that you say? *(Shouting)* Dinner—ho—dinner! I think the whole world's asleep! Where's my daughter? Did you not hear me, boy?

PRINCE FROM THE EAST: Your daughter is not well.

KING: Well why did you not say so at once, boy?

PRINCE FROM THE EAST: I beg your pardon, sir, but I am king here. And a king's castle is his home.

KING: *(Roaring with laughter)* King! Oh ho ho! That's a good one! King! You are king because I made you one, pup! And don't forget it.

PRINCE FROM THE EAST: This is a rank offense, sir. How dare you treat me so? I am King.

KING: And who am I?

PRINCE FROM THE EAST: My lady's father.

KING: My lady's father! My horse's tail! You dog! You cur! You mongrel! You poodle!

PRINCE FROM THE EAST: *(Giving him a cold look)* I beg your pardon! I am none of these, my lord.

KING: Don't bandy icy looks at me! *(Strikes him)*

PRINCE FROM THE EAST: I'll not be struck, my lord.

KING: Nor tripped neither? *(Trips him)* You base Babylonian cook! Come on, get up. Here, take my hand. You see how I've helped you up in the world. Now go get my daughter! *(Boots him out)* King!

(PRINCE exits. Reenter GONDA with PRINCE hiding behind her.)

GONDA: Good father, what mad riot is this to kick my husband and call him names? You are a guest in our house. Behave like one, I beg you.

KING: Guest? Guest?

GONDA: Yes, sir, and we are your hosts.

KING: Hosts? And what am I, a parasite? And what am I? And who am I? Does anyone here know me? *(Kneels)*

GONDA: Please, sir, get up off your knees and don't make a scene. Someone might come along.

KING: Is this King Gorgeous? Does Gorgeous walk like this? Does Gorgeous talk like this? That is: Gorgeously? Are these Gorgeous eyes, Gorgeous cheeks, Gorgeous hair? *(Shouting)* NO! A shadow of a King am I since I married my sweetest daughter to a pig and went to live with my piggish daughter.

PRINCE FROM THE EAST: Sire, if you can't say anything nice about someone then you shouldn't say anything at all.

KING: Then I'll say nothing. I have yet another daughter left. I'll go to her. When she hears of the way you treated me she'll scratch your eyes out.

GONDA: Please try to understand my side of it, Father.

KING: Father? Father? I see no fathers here.

GONDA: I mean you, Father.

KING: The father of a sow? That's a boar. Please, don't let me bore you. *(Exit)*

GONDA: I fear what he may do.

PRINCE FROM THE EAST: You may fear too far.

GONDA: Better than trust too far.

(They exit.)

Scene 10

(Enter MOTHER OF THE MOON and EULALIE IRENE with the baby in her arms.)

EULALIE IRENE: I shall always be grateful to heaven for leading me hither, and grateful to you that you took pity on me and on my baby, and did not leave us to die. Now I beg one last favor of you. Can your daughter, the Moon, tell me where my husband is?

MOTHER OF THE MOON: She cannot tell you that, my child. But if you will travel towards the East until you reach the dwelling of the Sun, he may be able

to tell you something. Here is a roast chicken to eat. And be very careful not
to lose any of the bones because they might be of great use to you later on.

EULALIE IRENE: Thank you Mother of the Moon, for your hospitality and good
advice. I'll throw away this pair of iron shoes for I have worn them out. And
I'll put on the second pair. I've got my baby and my chicken bones and I'll
be on my way. Adieu.

MOTHER OF THE MOON: Farewell, brave woman. The East is that way. *(Points
the way)* May my daughter light your way by night. As the sun lights it up by
day.

Scene 11: *Journey through the Mountains.*

(EULALIE IRENE *crawls, she falls, she jumps from peak to peak. The flints tear her
feet and elbows. At length wearied almost to death she reaches the palace of the Sun.)*

EULALIE IRENE: This little piggie went to market . . . *(Knocks at the door. The
door opens and out peers a golden face)* Are you the Mother of the Sun?

MOTHER OF THE SUN: I am, but I am astonished to see a mortal from the distant
earthly shores at my doorstep. What a piteous sight you are with all you have
suffered. What brings you here, mortal woman?

EULALIE IRENE: I have come to ask your son if he knows where my husband
is.

MOTHER OF THE SUN: I will ask him for you. But you must hide in the cellar
so that he doesn't notice you on his return home, for he is always in a bad
temper when he comes in at night.

EULALIE IRENE: But how in the world is it possible for the sun to be angry?
He is so beautiful and so good to mortals.

MOTHER OF THE SUN: This is how it happens: in the morning when he stands
at the gates of paradise he is happy, and smiles on the whole world, but during
the day he gets cross, because he sees the evil deeds of men, and that is why
his heat becomes so scorching; but in the evening he is both sad and angry,
for he stands at the gates of death; that is his usual course. From there he comes
back here. But come inside and let me give you a roast chicken to eat. And
be careful to save all the bones. *(Exit)*

Scene 12

KING: Ah, here at last after weary journey come I to the home of my better
daughter. *(Enter* WANDA *and her* PRINCE*)* Good morrow to you both.

WANDA: I am glad to see Your Highness.

KING: Wanda, I think you are. If you were not . . . if you were not I'd not
believe you were my daughter. . . . I'd doubt your mother's fidelity. Ah,
beloved Wanda, your sister is a snake!

WANDA: Good Father, my sister is no snake!

KING: I am mistaken. A vulture then!

WANDA: Nor no vulture neither.

KING: She's something hideous.

WANDA: Father! How can you speak of my sister so? Why, she's beautiful.

KING: She treated me like a piece of furniture!

WANDA: I cannot think my sister in the least would fail her obligation to you.

KING: My curses on her!

WANDA: O sir, you are old. Confer your cares on younger strengths and let yourself be ruled and led. Go back to my sister and tell her you are sorry.

KING: Ask her forgiveness? After what she did to me? *(Kneeling)* Dear daughter, I confess that I am old; age is unnecessary: on my knees I beg that you'll give me clothing, bed, and food.

PRINCE FROM THE WEST: *(Aside to WANDA)* This is appalling.

WANDA: Good sir, no more; these are unsightly tricks: return you to my sister.

KING: *(Rising)* Never, Wanda! She and her husband gave me cold looks. She struck me with her tongue, most serpentlike upon the very heart. May all the stored up vengeances of heaven fall upon her ungrateful head. Strike her young bones, you damp and poisonous airs, with lameness.

PRINCE FROM THE WEST: Fie, sir, fie!

KING: You nimble lightnings dart your blinding flames into her scornful eyes! Infect her beauty! May her skin shrivel and all her hair fall out!

WANDA: O the blest gods! So will you wish on me when the rash mood is on!

KING: No, Wanda, you I will never curse.

(Trumpet.)

PRINCE FROM THE WEST: What trumpet's that?

WANDA: I know it. It's my sister's. She sent me a letter saying she would be here soon.

(Enter GONDA and PRINCE FROM THE EAST. GONDA and WANDA kiss and join hands.)

KING: O Wanda, you would kiss her and take her by the hand?

GONDA: Why should she not, my lord? What have I done wrong?

PRINCE FROM THE EAST: It's better not to argue with him.

PRINCE FROM THE WEST: You're right. The man's insane and will only curse us more at every word we speak.

WANDA: In this my sister and I are of one mind. If you live with us you live under our law.

KING: I gave you all—

GONDA: You took your time in giving it!

WANDA: Your second childhood's coming on. Let us be your parents now.

KING: Parent abusers! I'll give you both the spankings of your lives! Come girl, over my knee! *(Seizes GONDA)*

GONDA: Help! Husband! Sister! Help!

(KING attempts to spank GONDA.)

WANDA: Oh no you don't! It's our turn now. Come princes, help me turn the tables. Let's spank the king as hard as we are able!

(They free GONDA and the two princesses take the KING over their knees and spank him.)

KING: Ah, how sharper than a serpent's tooth it is to have a thankless child!

(They release him.)

PRINCE FROM THE EAST: That really did my heart good.

PRINCE FROM THE WEST: He had it coming to him.

WANDA: Sir, I hope you've learned your lesson. And behave yourself from now on.

GONDA: From now on you'll obey the rules of my house.

KING: No.

GONDA: Yes.

KING: No, I say.

GONDA: I say, yea.

KING: No no, I will not!

GONDA: Yes yes, you will!

KING: By Jupiter, I swear no!

GONDA: By Juno, I swear yes!

KING: I will not do it. I would not do it. I could not do it. Detested hags, I'll bother you no more. I'd sooner live in a tree like an ape or in a sty like a pig than live with you brats! Away! Away! *(Exits)*

PRINCE FROM THE EAST: I'm worried that the king has no place to stay tonight.

(Distant thunder.)

PRINCE FROM THE WEST: Come inside, there's a storm brewing.

WANDA: A night in the forest with the hoot owls will teach him a lesson.

GONDA: Yes, let the forest be his school.

PRINCE FROM THE EAST: But come inside. It's a wild night.

(They all exit.)

Scene 13: *The palace of the Sun.*

(The door reopens.)

EULALIE IRENE: What did your son say when you asked him where my husband is?

MOTHER OF THE SUN: He said he knew nothing about him and that your only hope is to inquire of the Wind.

EULALIE IRENE: Then there's nothing to be done but pack up my chicken bones and baby, put on the third pair of shoes, for the second pair is all worn out, and with my staff in hand set out on my way to the Wind.

MOTHER OF THE SUN: Good-bye courageous woman, and may my son shine on you, but not too harshly.

EULALIE IRENE: Good-bye. Good-bye.

Scene 14: *Journey through fire and ice. After which* EULALIE IRENE *arrives at an enormous cave in the side of a mountain where the Wind lives.*

EULALIE IRENE: *(Knocking at a gate before the mouth of the cave)* Mother of the Wind! *(Knocks again)* Mother of the Wind. Please answer!

MOTHER OF THE WIND: But how did you, a mortal woman, find your way here beyond the world's portals to the dwelling of the Wind?

EULALIE IRENE: I came upon one mountain of flints after another out of which tongues of fire would flame up. I passed through woods which had never been trodden by human foot, and had to pass fields of ice and avalanches of snow.

I nearly died of these hardships but I kept a brave heart and finally came to this place.

MOTHER OF THE WIND: And here will you rest. I'll see to that, brave woman.

EULALIE IRENE: But could you tell me, Mother of the Wind, where I might find my husband?

MOTHER OF THE WIND: My son, the Wind, has spoken of him often. It seems he has been living in a thick woods, so thick that no axe has been able to cut a way through it; there, shunning humankind, he's been living in a shoe, because he's so unhappy, he doesn't know what to do.

EULALIE IRENE: Thank you, thank you, I knew I'd find him one day!

MOTHER OF THE WIND: Here, eat this chicken and save the bones. Go by the Milky Way which lies across the sky at night and wander on till you reach your goal.

EULALIE IRENE: *(With tears in her eyes)* Thank you, Mother of the Wind. *(Exit)*

Scene 15

(Enter all three MOTHERS.*)*

MOTHER OF THE MOON: Well met by starlight, sisters dear.

MOTHER OF THE SUN: How long before the rooster crows?

MOTHER OF THE WIND: The night wears on and little dreamers wrapped in slumber sleep.

MOTHER OF THE MOON: All our children sleep?

MOTHER OF THE SUN: One-half of the world sleeps while the other works and plays.

MOTHER OF THE MOON: And who are our children? I forgot.

MOTHER OF THE WIND: All those who need a mother mother we.

MOTHER OF THE SUN: We must make haste in what we have to do. The dawn tiptoes, creeping up behind would take us by surprise. You called me here to help our children, did you not, Mother of the Wind?

MOTHER OF THE WIND: I did.

MOTHER OF THE SUN: Last night I heard you wail for Eulalie Irene. I never go to earth. I hate it there. The stories that my son recounts would make you shun it too if once you heard them.

MOTHER OF THE WIND: The wind would tell a tale too if he could. And he can.

MOTHER OF THE MOON: But he whispers it.

MOTHER OF THE WIND: Sometimes he howls. Eulalie Irene is married to a pig.

MOTHER OF THE SUN: All loves are tested in the fire of suffering.

MOTHER OF THE MOON: How can we help?

MOTHER OF THE WIND: There's a bad mother who does not believe in love.

MOTHER OF THE MOON: For every three good mothers there's one bad.

MOTHER OF THE SUN: Nay, not so many! Not one in four under the sun.

MOTHER OF THE MOON: This one's bad, I say. Unloved herself she won't let others love.

MOTHER OF THE WIND: Then we must find her love. Send her love. Bend her love. Bind her love.

MOTHER OF THE MOON: But hark, the dawn is breaking! Listen. *(They all bend to listen. A crash of breaking glass is heard)* The stars are fading.

MOTHER OF THE SUN: The sun, my son, is rising.

MOTHER OF THE WIND: Farewell, my sisters. Sisters, farewell. And pledge we. Pledge we. Not to fail. By wind . . .
MOTHER OF THE SUN: By sun . . .
MOTHER OF THE MOON: By moon . . .
MOTHER OF THE WIND: For living mothers and for mothers lost . . .
ALL THREE MOTHERS: We'll bring together lovers no matter what the cost. Farewell.

Scene 16: *The journey through the Milky Way and through the dense forest.*

EULALIE IRENE: I have endured hardships greater than any human woman. I have worn out my third pair of iron shoes in my wanderings and my iron staff has become quite blunted. Have I wasted my time? Perhaps I should just give up. But what is this here in this thicket? Why it is just the sort of house the Mother of the Wind described. It has no windows. *(Walks all the way around the house)* And no doors. What am I to do? How am I to get in? The only door is on the roof. The chicken bones! I've dragged them all this weary way. Surely the Mothers would not have told me to take such good care of them if they had not had some good reason for doing so. Perhaps now, in my hour of need, they may be of use to me. *(She takes the bones out of the bundle and thinks for a moment)* Perhaps if I just place the two ends together. Why they stuck! Why it seems that if I put all the bones together they will make a ladder. *(She does this and they do. As soon as one step is finished, she stands upon it and makes the next one, and then the next until she comes close to the door)* But what's this? The last step . . . I haven't got enough bones to make the last step! I must have lost one of the bones! What will I do? Without the last step the whole ladder is useless. I have it! *(Takes out a knife)* I'll cut off my little finger. *(Does so)* And make the last step of the ladder. It stuck!
[*(Alternate business: if the ladder isn't possible or dismemberment objectionable, use bones as keys in the lock of the front door.)*
EULALIE IRENE: But what is this here in this thicket? Why, it's just the sort of shoe the Mother of the Wind described. The door's locked. How will I get in? The chicken bones! I've dragged them all this weary way. Surely the Mothers would not have told me to take such good care of them if they had not had some good reason for doing so. Perhaps one of the bones will fit this lock. I've heard of skeleton keys. *(She tries bones. The last one opens lock)* It fits! *(She enters shoe)* Home at last!]
EULALIE IRENE: *(Entering the house)* Why, everything here is in perfect order. Come my baby. We'll take a little food and here we'll rest. This little piggy went to market *(Giggles)*, this little baby stayed home *(Awwww)*, this little baby had . . .
BABY: Zucchini.
EULALIE IRENE: Why zucchini?
BABY: Meatless Wednesdays.
EULALIE IRENE: And this little baby had none. *(Oh no!)* And this little baby cried . . .
BABY: Wee, wee, wee, wee, wee.
EULALIE IRENE: All the way home.
BABY: Hope he made it in time. Snort, snort, snort . . .
EULALIE IRENE: Stop that. *(She takes out baby bottle)*

PIG: *(Entering)* What's this? A ladder of bones with a finger at the top? Some fresh magic must be at work here! I'm getting away from here. *(Baby laughs)* Perhaps there is a witch inside my house. I won't climb that ladder. It may be a trap. I know . . . I'll turn myself into a dove. Then no witchcraft can have power over me. *(Thunder. Turns into a dove)*

[*Or:*

PIG: *(Entering)* What's this? My door is unlocked. And there's a pile of old chicken bones. Some fresh magic must be at work here. I'm gettin' out of here. *(Baby laughs)* Perhaps there is a witch inside my house. It may be a trap. I know . . . I'll turn myself into a dove. Then no witchcraft can have power over me. *(Thunder. Turns into a dove)*]

(The dove flies into the house and lands next to EULALIE IRENE.*)*

EULALIE IRENE: Ah little dove! Do you know where my husband is?

DOVE: Coo coo.

EULALIE IRENE: How I've suffered for him!

DOVE: Coo.

EULALIE IRENE: I've worn out three pairs of iron shoes and blunted a steel staff in my quest through water, fire, stones, and ice. Not to mention the fact that I've had nothing to eat but chicken the whole way.

DOVE: Coo coo.

EULALIE IRENE: I would do anything to change my husband from a pig into a man.

DOVE: Coo coo coo!!!

(Enter WITCH.*)*

WITCH: Coo on my little dove! Coo! Coo! Coo! If it's a dove you want to be, remain a dove. Be always a dove!

DOVE: Coo coo!! Coo! Coo!

EULALIE IRENE: *(Startled by the* WITCH's *sudden appearance)* Agh! Nasty lady! Nasty, nasty lady! You are the cause of all my troubles. You are the author of my sad travail! You, you are to blame. Yes, you!

WITCH: Fie, I say, fie! What are these vain recriminations to one who's scorched by hell's hyperequatorial climate into a lean mark, hardly fit to fling a rhyme at?

EULALIE IRENE: Return my husband from that piggy-shape, O hag, and I will do for you whatever you wish. Please!

WITCH:
Then by strange art will I knead fire and snow
　　Together, tempering the repugnant mass.
With liquid love all things together grow
　　Through which the harmony of love can pass;
And fairer shape out of my hands will flow—
　　A living image, which will far surpass
A handsome prince in a looking glass
　　A sexless thing 'twill be, and in its growth
It will develop no defect of either sex
　　Yet all the grace of both.
So let her be a tree and he a dove
　　And they remain together in their love.

(EULALIE IRENE turns into a tree.)

EULALIE IRENE: A tree? A dove?

DOVE: Coo coo!

WITCH:

From her matted roots to her gnarled heart,
      He'll fly about her and nest in her hair.
So they might live and never be apart,
      He'll coo to her, to him her leaves will whisper there.
On this very spot with matted roots she'll grow,
      Her true identity none but he shall know!

EULALIE IRENE:

A tree? A dove? *(To the dove)*
Then you are he?
You are my own true love?

DOVE: Coo.

WITCH: And now that I have done what you asked, my pretty, give me your first born child!

VOICE OF KING: *(Off)*

O fright! Not fright but truth in hoot owl shapes.
O Crimes! not crimes but custom's careless kids.
O Mad! Not mad but muddled modern man.

WITCH: Agh! Someone's coming. I'll hide. *(Hides behind tree)*

KING: *(Enters raving)* O fright! O crimes! O mad as mad can be. I must sit down and rest me underneath this tree. *(Sighs)*

WITCH: Be false, my heart, I must dissemble here. 'Tis he! 'Tis he! I thank thee heaven that thou hast heard my prayer and sent me King Gorgeous. Now be strong. Be strong my heart! I must dissemble here. *(Aloud)* False friend or true?

KING: A true friend to the true; fear not, come hither. So, you can tell fortunes?

WITCH: Not in the dark. Come nearer to the fire. Give me your hand. It is not crossed I see.

KING: *(Putting a piece of gold in her hand)* There is the cross.

WITCH: Is't silver?

KING: No 'tis gold.

WITCH: There's a lady who loves you. And for yourself alone.

KING: Fie! The old story! Tell me a better fortune for my money, not this old woman's tale!

WITCH: You are passionate, and this same passionate humor in your blood has marred your fortune. Yes, I see it now—the line of life is crossed by many marks. Shame! Shame! Oh you have wronged the maids who loved you! How could you do it?

KING: The maids you speak of are my daughters. But they never loved me.

WITCH: How do you know that?

KING: A little bird in the air whispered the secret.

DOVE: Coo coo. Coo coo. Not true. Not true.

WITCH: There, take back your gold! Your hand is cold like a deceiver's hand! There is no blessing in its charity! Your daughters needed a mother. Where is she now?

KING: Each of my daughters had a different mother. But they all died in childbirth.

WITCH: The curse. The curse. The curse of unrequited love! Long ago you loved a maid, a maid you met at a ball. But you lost her love. Lost her almost forever. Your daughters need a mother. Find her again, your first love, and mend your fortunes mending hers, and take her as your lover.

KING: How like an angel's speaks the tongue of woman, when pleading in another's cause: her own! That is a pretty little shoe upon your foot. Pray give it me.

WITCH: No; from my foot shall that never be taken!

KING: Why, 'tis but a shoe. I'll give it back to you, or if I keep it, will give you gold to buy you twenty such.

WITCH: Why would you have this shoe?

KING: A traveler's fancy, a whim and nothing more. I would fain keep it as a memento of the Gypsy camp at Guadalajara and the fortune teller who told me to wed a maid I loved long long ago and lost. . . . Pray let me have the shoe.

WITCH: No, never! Never! I will not part with it even if I die. For there is only one other like it in the whole world and I lost that. Lost it with my love.

KING: Your love? What, dead?

WITCH: Yes, dead to me. And worse than dead. He is estranged! And yet I keep this slipper. I will rise with it from my grave hereafter to prove to him that I was never false.

KING: *(Aside)* Be still my swelling heart! One moment still! Come, 'tis the folly of a lovesick girl. Come, give it to me or I will say it is mine and that you stole it.

WITCH: Oh, you would not dare to utter such a falsehood! Besides it would be your word against mine! What proof have you?

KING: Perfect proof, for I have the other. *(Shows the other glass slipper)*

WITCH: 'Tis thou! 'Tis thou! Yes yes, my heart's elected! My dearest dear Victorian! My soul's heaven! Where hast thou been so long? It's me. It's me: Cinderella.

KING: Why didst thou leave me, my dearest Cinderella?

WITCH: At midnight my coach was to turn into a pumpkin, my gown to rags. . . . I was so embarrassed. But why didn't you come to look for me?

KING: The kingdom is so vast, there were so many maidens, how could I have found you?

WITCH: You could have tried the glass slipper on every maid until you found the one it fit.

KING: I never thought of that! Here, put it on now and let's forget we ever parted. *(Puts slipper on her foot)*

WITCH: Had you not come . . .

KING: Don't reprimand me.

WITCH: I would have gone on and on doing evil, so bitter was my heart.

KING: Forgive me, sweet, for what I made thee suffer.

WITCH: I've done a terrible thing. I turned Eulalie Irene into a tree and her prince I imprisoned in a dove.

KING: Undo the spell, I pray.

WITCH: Alas, I cannot. For when love came back into my heart the powers of black magic left. I am no longer a witch, just a woman in love.

KING: Then, Cinderella, you die! For the deeds you did when you were still a witch, you shall be burned alive!

EULALIE IRENE: No no. Mercy, Father! Have mercy on her. Mercy mercy. *(She ceases to be a tree but becomes a woman once more and falls on her knees before her father.* [DOVE *becomes* PIG]*)*

WITCH: Mercy! Who spoke that sacred word? Who pleads for me?

EULALIE IRENE: I did, mother.

WITCH: O God, she calls me mother. What power has turned you into a human being once again?

EULALIE IRENE: The power of love.

WITCH: You called me mother.

EULALIE IRENE: I called you mother once before but there was wormwood in it.

WITCH: Forgive me, Eulalie Irene?

EULALIE IRENE: I forgive you. But my husband is still a pig.

WITCH: Blessèd be the power of love, for it can work miracles. It can call back the dead from death's dark realm. Love was denied me and curdled the milk of human kindness in my breast. But you, you can do it.

EULALIE IRENE: *(Humbly)* What can I do?

WITCH: You can love. You can forgive. And so, mighty child, you can do everything. I cannot use my powers, but you can. Go to your love. Lay your hand upon his heart and call his name. Then with the help of god your love will hear your voice and feel your love and he will turn into a man.

EULALIE IRENE: *(Goes to the* PIG. *Lays her hand upon his heart)* But how can I speak his name? I don't know it. I've never known it! I've always called him pig. What is your name, pig? Tell me your name.

PIG: That you must guess. For it is forbidden that any pig should tell his name. Unless you can guess my name I will never turn into a man.

EULALIE IRENE: Is it Rumplestiltskin?

PIG: No, it's not.

EULALIE IRENE: Is it Aloysius?

PIG: No.

EULALIE IRENE: Is it Jake?

PIG: No.

EULALIE IRENE: Is it Tom Dick or Harry?

PIG: No no no!

EULALIE IRENE: Is it Heathcliffe?

PIG: No.

EULALIE IRENE: Is it Fred?

PIG: No.

EULALIE IRENE: Is it Matthew Mark Luke or John?

PIG: No no no no.

EULALIE IRENE: Is it Willie?

PIG: No.

EULALIE IRENE: Is it Charles?

PIG: No.

EULALIE IRENE: Is it Adam?

PIG: No.

EULALIE IRENE: Is it Anthony?

PIG: No.

EULALIE IRENE: Is it Bart is it Brad is it Bud is it Burke?

PIG: No it's not no it's not no it's not no it's not!

EULALIE IRENE: Is it Zeke?

Black-Eyed Susan & Everett Quinton in
The Enchanted Pig (Wolfgang Staehle)

PIG: Nope.

EULALIE IRENE: Then I know it. I will whisper it in your ear. If I'm wrong, tell me and I will go on guessing forever. Because you must be somebody and sooner or later I'll guess who. *(She whispers in his ear)*

PIG: That's right! *(He turns into a handsome prince)*

EULALIE IRENE: Why, you are a prince.

PRINCE: Yes, but my ancestors did not believe in fairy tales and so the fairies put this curse on our house.

(Suddenly there is a great commotion heard off. WANDA *and* GONDA *enter from opposite directions each pursued by a gentleman pig.)*

WANDA: *(Screams)* Get away from me you disgusting beast!

GONDA: *(Screams)* Don't touch me! Don't touch me!

PIGS: Oink oink oink!

KING: What is the matter? What's wrong?

WANDA: My husband's turned into a pig!

GONDA: Mine too!

WANDA: I want a divorce!

GONDA: Yes yes, a divorce as quickly as possible.

PRINCE: You should ask Eulalie Irene's advice. For she had that very same problem and solved it. *(Laughs, embraces* EULALIE IRENE *and kisses her, then he goes out with the others)*

(The WITCH *lags behind for a moment and calls to* EULALIE IRENE.*)*

WITCH: My child, pardon my inquisitiveness, but what *was* the pig's name after all? I mean the prince's name.

EULALIE IRENE: Why, couldn't you guess? I'm surprised at you of all people! It was Charming. Prince Charming.

WITCH: Of course.

(They exit. Together.)

The End

A CHRISTMAS CAROL

Adapted from the Novel
by Charles Dickens

1979

Charles Ludlam & Everett Quinton
in *A Christmas Carol* (Les Carr)

Cast of Characters

SCROOGE
BOB CRATCHIT
NEPHEW
GENTLEMAN #1
GENTLEMAN #2
BOY
MARLEY
CHRISTMAS PAST
LITTLE SCROOGE
FAN
FEZZIWIG
MRS. FEZZIWIG
DICK
GUESTS AT THE FEZZIWIGS' *(dancers)*
GIRL
SCROOGE-THE-MAN
MOTHER *(Girl married)*
FATHER
CHRISTMAS PRESENT
MRS. CRATCHIT
MISS BELINDA
LITTLE BOY
LITTLE GIRL
MARTHA
TINY TIM
MINERS
NIECE
TOPPER
PLUMP BEAUTY
WANT
IGNORANCE
CHRISTMAS FUTURE
BUSINESSMAN #1
BUSINESSMAN #2
BUSINESSMAN #3
MAN A
MAN B
BAG LADY
OLD JOE
MRS. DILBER
HE
SHE
PETER
BOY

Scene 1: *Scrooge and Marley's. Christmas Eve.*

(SCROOGE *counting money.* CRATCHIT *working on books, shivering with cold.* CRATCHIT *rises from his work and, looking at the pitiful little fire in his cell, picks up the coal scuttle and attempts to tiptoe past* SCROOGE *to the coal box.*)

SCROOGE: *(Speaking without looking up, a habit which gives the distinct impression of his having eyes in the back of his head)* If you waste my coal I shall have to ask you to seek employment elsewhere.
CRATCHIT: But, Mr. Scrooge, it's cold and my fire has nearly gone out.
SCROOGE: Warm yourself at the candle.

(CRATCHIT *puts on a muffler and attempts to warm his hands at his candle. Enter Scrooge's* NEPHEW.)

NEPHEW: *(Cheerily)* A merry Christmas, Uncle! God save you!
SCROOGE: Bah! Humbug!
NEPHEW: Christmas a humbug, Uncle! You don't mean that, I am sure.
SCROOGE: I do. Merry Christmas! What right have you to be merry? What reason have you to be merry? You're poor enough.
NEPHEW: Come then, what right have you to be dismal? What reason have you to be morose? You're rich enough.
SCROOGE: *(After a brief reflective pause in which he fails to come up with a better rejoinder)* Bah! Humbug!
NEPHEW: Don't be cross, Uncle.
SCROOGE: What else can I be when I live in such a world of fools as this? Merry Christmas! Out upon Merry Christmas! What's Christmastime to you but a time for paying bills without money; a time for finding yourself a year older, and not an hour richer; a time for balancing your books and having every item in 'em through a round dozen of months presented dead against you? If I could work my will, every idiot who goes about with "Merry Christmas" on his lips, should be boiled with his own pudding and buried with a stake of holly through his heart. He should!
NEPHEW: Uncle!
SCROOGE: Nephew! Keep Christmas in your own way and let me keep it in mine.
NEPHEW: Keep it! But you don't keep it.
SCROOGE: Let me leave it alone, then. Much good it may do you! Much good it has ever done you!
NEPHEW: There are many things from which I might have derived good, by which I have not profited, I dare say, Christmas among the rest. But I am sure I have always thought of Christmastime, when it has come round—apart from the veneration due to its sacred name and origin, if anything belonging to it can be apart from that—as a good time: a kind, forgiving, charitable, pleasant time: the only time I know of, in the long calendar of the year, when men and women seem by one consent to open their shut-up hearts freely, and to think of people below them as if they really were fellow passengers to the grave, and not another race of creatures bound on other journeys. And therefore, Uncle, though it has never put a scrap of gold or silver in my pocket, I believe that it *has* done me good, and *will* do me good; and I say, God bless it!

(CRATCHIT *involuntarily applauds and, upon catching himself, pokes the fire, extinguishing the last coal.*)

SCROOGE: *(To* CRATCHIT*)* Let me hear another sound from *you* and you'll keep your Christmas by losing your situation. *(To his* NEPHEW*)* You're quite a powerful speaker, sir. I wonder you don't go into Parliament.

NEPHEW: Don't be angry, Uncle. Come! Dine with us tomorrow.

SCROOGE: I'll see you hanged first.

NEPHEW: *(Crying out)* But why? Why?

SCROOGE: Why did you get married?

NEPHEW: Because I fell in love.

SCROOGE: *(Mockingly)* Because you fell in love! Good afternoon!

NEPHEW: Nay, Uncle, but you never came to see me before that happened. Why give it as a reason for not coming now?

SCROOGE: Good afternoon.

NEPHEW: I want nothing from you; I ask nothing of you; why cannot we be friends?

SCROOGE: Good afternoon.

NEPHEW: I am sorry, with all my heart, to find you so resolute. We have never had any quarrel to which I have been a party. But I have made the trial in homage to Christmas, and I'll keep my Christmas humor to the last. So, a merry Christmas, Uncle!

SCROOGE: Good afternoon!

NEPHEW: And a happy New Year!

SCROOGE: Good afternoon!

NEPHEW: *(To* CRATCHIT *in the anteroom as he leaves)* And a very merry Christmas to you.

CRATCHIT: *(Warmly)* Merry Christmas, Fred.

SCROOGE: *(Muttering)* There's another fellow, my clerk, with fifteen shillings a week, and a wife and family, talking about a merry Christmas. I'll retire to Bedlam.

*(*CRATCHIT *lets Scrooge's* NEPHEW *out and two other* GENTLEMEN *in.)*

FIRST GENTLEMAN: Scrooge and Marley's I believe. Have I the pleasure of addressing Mr. Scrooge or Mr. Marley?

SCROOGE: Mr. Marley has been dead these seven years. He died seven years ago this very night.

FIRST GENTLEMAN: We have no doubt his liberality is well represented by his surviving partner. *(Presents his credentials. At the ominous word "liberality,"* SCROOGE *frowns, shakes his head, and hands his credentials back)* At this festive season of the year, Mr. Scrooge, it is more than usually desirable that we should make some slight provision for the poor and destitute, who suffer greatly at the present time. Many thousands are in want of common necessaries; hundreds of thousands are in want of common comforts, sir.

SCROOGE: Are there no prisons?

FIRST GENTLEMAN: Plenty of prisons.

SCROOGE: And the union workhouses? Are they still in operation?

FIRST GENTLEMAN: They are. I wish I could say they were not.

SCROOGE: The treadmill and the poor law are in full vigor, then?

FIRST GENTLEMAN: Both very busy, sir.

SCROOGE: Good. I was afraid, from what you said at first, that something had occurred to stop them in their useful course. I'm very glad to hear it.

FIRST GENTLEMAN: Under the impression that they scarcely furnish Christian cheer of mind or body to the multitude, a few of us are endeavoring to raise a fund to buy the Poor some meat and drink, and means of warmth. We choose this time, because it is a time, of all others, when Want is keenly felt, and abundance rejoices. What shall I put you down for?

SCROOGE: Nothing.

FIRST GENTLEMAN: You wish to remain anonymous?

SCROOGE: I wish to be left alone. Since you ask me what I wish, Gentlemen, that is my answer. I don't make merry myself at Christmas, and I can't afford to make idle people merry. I help to support the establishments I have mentioned—they cost enough—and those who are badly off must go there.

FIRST GENTLEMAN: Many can't go there and many would rather die.

SCROOGE: If they would rather die, they had better do it, and decrease the surplus population. Besides—excuse me—I don't know that.

FIRST GENTLEMAN: But you might know it.

SCROOGE: It's not my business. It's enough for a man to understand his own business, and not to interfere with other people's. Mine occupies me constantly. Good afternoon, gentlemen! *(The* GENTLEMEN *exit.* SCROOGE *resumes his work with a chuckle. Fog obscures the clock in the church tower usually visible from Scrooge's Gothic window. Voices of carolers in the street below.* BOY *at keyhole sings, "God rest ye merry gentlemen, let nothing you dismay."* SCROOGE *throws a ruler at him. Rising with ill-will and crossing to the window)* Quiet down there! Quiet, imbeciles! How's a man to work with that racket?

CRATCHIT: It's closing time anyway, Mr. Scrooge.

SCROOGE: So it is. You'll want all day tomorrow, I suppose?

CRATCHIT: If quite convenient, sir.

SCROOGE: It's not convenient, and it's not fair. If I was to dock you half a crown for it, you'd think yourself ill-used, I'll be bound? And yet you don't think *me* ill-used when I pay a day's wages for no work.

CRATCHIT: *(Smiling faintly)* It's only once a year, sir.

SCROOGE: A poor excuse for picking a man's pocket every twenty-fifth of December! *(Buttons up his greatcoat to the chin)* But I suppose you must have the whole day. Be here all the earlier next morning!

CRATCHIT: I will, Mr. Scrooge.

SCROOGE: *(Growls and exits)*

Scene 2: *Scrooge's apartment.*

*(*SCROOGE *and the lighted candle are all that is visible on the stage.* SCROOGE *sits him down by a meager fire and slurps a bowl of gruel. There is the sound of the howling of wind, which produces the effect of ghostly voices.* SCROOGE *goes about the room to see if everything is all right.)*

SCROOGE: *(Talking to himself)* Nobody under the table. Nobody under the sofa. Nobody under the bed. Nobody in the closet. Nobody in my dressing gown— except me. Lumber room as usual. Old fireguard, old shoes, two fish baskets, washingstand, poker. Everything as it should be. *(Goes and double locks the door, then sits down and begins to slurp his gruel again)* Humbug! *(Suddenly a bell hanging by the wall begins to swing by itself and then to ring.* SCROOGE *stares at this phenomenon in horror.* [SCROOGE *sees in the door's knocker Marley's face.*] *The sound of footsteps and dragging chains can be heard, at first far off, but then they come nearer and nearer)* Ghosts? It's humbug still! I won't believe it. (MARLEY'S GHOST *enters, dragging chains made of cashboxes, keys, padlocks, ledgers, deeds, and heavy purses wrought in steel. The dying flame in the fireplace leaps up and dies down again. Cold and caustic)* How now! What do you want with me?

MARLEY: Much.

SCROOGE: Who are you?

MARLEY: Ask me who I *was.*

SCROOGE: *(Raising his voice)* Who *were* you, then? You're particular—for a shade.

MARLEY: In life I was your partner, Jacob Marley.

SCROOGE: Can you . . . can you sit down?

MARLEY: I can.

SCROOGE: Do it, then.

MARLEY: *(Taking a seat on the opposite side of the fireplace as though he were quite used to it)* You don't believe in me.

SCROOGE: I don't.

MARLEY: What evidence would you have of my reality beyond that of your senses?

SCROOGE: I don't know.

MARLEY: Why do you doubt your senses?

SCROOGE: Because, a little thing affects them. A slight disorder of the stomach makes them cheats. You may be an undigested bit of beef, a blot of mustard, a crumb of cheese, a fragment of an underdone potato. There's more of gravy than of grave about you, whatever you are. *(Laughs feebly at his own joke. The ghost however is not amused)* You see this toothpick?

MARLEY: I do.

SCROOGE: You are not looking at it.

MARLEY: But I see it notwithstanding.

SCROOGE: Well! I have but to swallow this, and be for the rest of my days persecuted by a legion of goblins, all of my own creation. Humbug, I tell you—humbug!

MARLEY: *(Lets out a frightful cry and shakes its chains. Then removes its own arm and shakes the gory end of it threateningly at* SCROOGE)

SCROOGE: *(Falling on his knees and clasping his hands before his face)* Mercy! Dreadful apparition, why do you trouble me?

MARLEY: Man of the worldly mind! Do you believe in me or not?

SCROOGE: I do. I must. But why do spirits walk the earth and why do they come to me?

MARLEY: It is required of every man that the spirit within him should walk abroad among his fellowmen, and travel far and wide; and if that spirit goes not forth in life, it is condemned to do so after death. It is doomed to wander through the world—oh, woe is me!—and witness what it cannot share, but might have shared on earth, and turned to happiness! *(Cries out and shakes its chains and wrings its shadowy hands)*

SCROOGE: *(Trembling)* You are fettered. Tell me why?

MARLEY: I wear the chain I forged in life. I made it link by link, and yard by yard; I girded it on of my own free will, and of my own free will I wore it. Is its pattern strange to *you?* Or would you know the weight and length of the strong coil you bear yourself? It was full as heavy and as long as this, seven Christmas Eves ago. You have labored on it since. It is a ponderous chain!

SCROOGE: *(Trembling more and more, looks about him for the chain but sees nothing)* Jacob, old Jacob Marley, tell me more. Speak comfort to me, Jacob.

MARLEY: I have none to give. It comes from other regions, Ebenezer Scrooge, and is conveyed by other ministers, to other kinds of men. Nor can I tell you all I would. A very little more is all permitted to me. I cannot rest, I cannot stay, I cannot linger anywhere. My spirit never walked beyond our counting-house—mark me!—in life my spirit never roved beyond the narrow limits of our money-changing hole; and weary journeys lie before me!

SCROOGE: *(Putting his hands in his pockets thoughtfully)* You must have been very slow about it, Jacob.

MARLEY: Slow!

SCROOGE: Seven years dead and traveling all the time?

MARLEY: The whole time, no rest, no peace. Incessant torture of remorse.

SCROOGE: You travel fast?

MARLEY: On the wings of the wind.

SCROOGE: You might have got over a great quantity of ground in seven years.

MARLEY: *(Crying out again and clanking its chains hideously)* Oh! Captive bound and double-ironed, not to know that ages of incessant labor, by immortal creatures, for this earth, must pass into eternity before the good of which it is susceptible is all developed. Not to know that any Christian spirit working kindly in its little sphere, whatever it may be, will find its mortal life too short for its vast means of usefulness. Not to know that no space of regret can make amends for one life's opportunities misused! Yet such was I! Oh! Such was I!

SCROOGE: But you were always a good man of business, Jacob.

MARLEY: *(Crying out and wringing his hands again)* Business! Mankind was my business. The common welfare was my business; charity, mercy, forbearance, and benevolence, were all my business! The dealings of my trade were but a drop of water in the comprehensive ocean of my business! *(Holds up its chain and flings it on the ground again)* At this time of the rolling year, I suffer most. Why did I walk through crowds of fellow beings with my eyes turned down, and never raise them to that blessed Star which led the Wise Men to a poor abode? Were there no poor homes to which its light would have conducted *me?* Hear me! My time is nearly gone.

SCROOGE: I will, but don't be hard upon me! Don't be flowery, Jacob! Pray!

MARLEY: How it is that I appear before you in a shape that you can see, I may not tell. I have sat invisible beside you many and many a day. (SCROOGE *shivers and wipes the perspiration from his brow)* That is no light part of my penance. I am here tonight to warn you that you have yet a chance and hope of escaping my fate. A chance and hope of my procuring, Ebenezer.

SCROOGE: You were always a good friend to me. Thank'ee!

MARLEY: You will be haunted by Three Spirits.

SCROOGE: *(His face falling and in a faltering tone)* Is that the chance and hope you mentioned, Jacob?

MARLEY: It is.

SCROOGE: I . . . I think I'd rather not.

MARLEY: Without their visits you cannot hope to shun the path I tread. Expect the first tomorrow when the bell tolls one.

SCROOGE: Couldn't I take 'em all at once and have it over, Jacob?

MARLEY: Expect the second when the bell tolls two. And the third when the last stroke of three has ceased to vibrate. Look to see me no more; and look that, for your own sake, you remember what has passed between us. *(Rises and walks backward toward the window, which opens by itself, and passes out into the foggy night air amid the ghostly sounds of lamentation)* Good night, Ebenezer. I must join the others; they have come for me. Hear them? Our misery is this: we wish to interfere, for good, in human matters, but have lost the power forever. Ah! there's a wretched woman with an infant huddled in a doorway.... *(Fades into mist amid a mournful spirit dirge)*

SCROOGE: *(Goes to the door)* The door . . . locked! Hum—

(The word is choked off by emotion and SCROOGE *falls into bed and asleep, fatigued by the labors of the day, his glimpse of the Invisible World, the dull conversation of the Ghost and the lateness of the hour.)*

Scene 3: SCROOGE *in bed.*

(The bell in the neighboring church chimes and SCROOGE *awakes and listens to it. The bell chimes twelve times.)*

SCROOGE: Why, it isn't possible that I can have slept through a whole day and far into another night. It isn't possible that anything has happened to the sun, and this is twelve at noon. *(He goes to the window and looks out)* Still nighttime. Hmmm. *(He gets back into bed)* Marley's ghost. Was it a dream or not? Marley warned me of a visitation when the bell tolls one. Well, I can no more go to sleep now than go to heaven. I may as well lie awake until that blasted hour has passed. *(He tosses and turns uncomfortably: plumps his pillow, tries to arrange the covers, when at length the sound of the bell breaks upon his listening ear: Ding, dong!)* A quarter past. *(Ding, dong!)* Half past! *(Ding, dong!)* A quarter to it. *(Ding, dong!)* The hour itself, and nothing else! *(The bell tolls one. There is a flash of light.* SCROOGE *draws the curtains of his bed and hides his head under the bedclothes. The curtains reopen by an unseen hand revealing him in this ludicrous posture. At this moment the* SPIRIT OF CHRISTMAS PAST *appears. It is a child with long gray hair crowned with a ring of lighted candles. Both old and young at once like the different times of our lives as perceived through memory, it carries a wand of fresh green holly and its white tunic is trimmed with summer flowers)* Are you the Spirit, sir, whose coming was foretold to me?

CHRISTMAS PAST: *(Gently)* I am!

SCROOGE: Who and what are you?

CHRISTMAS PAST: I am the Ghost of Christmas Past.

SCROOGE: Long past?

CHRISTMAS PAST: No. Your past.

SCROOGE: You'd better put out those candles on your head before they burn too low.

CHRISTMAS PAST: What! Would you so soon with worldly hands put out the light I give? Is it not enough that you are one of those whose passions dimmed my light, in hopes that I would through whole trains of years in darkness lose my way?

SCROOGE: No offense meant. But what business brings you here?

CHRISTMAS PAST: Your welfare!

SCROOGE: Much obliged! *(Then aside)* Although a good night's sleep would have done me more good!

CHRISTMAS PAST: Your reclamation, then. Take heed! *(Putting out its strong hand and clasping him by the arm)* Rise! and walk with me! *(Leads him to the window)*

SCROOGE: *(Clasping the Spirit's robe in supplication)* Please, I am a mortal and liable to fall!

CHRISTMAS PAST: Bear but a touch of my hand *there (Lays its hand upon his heart)*, and you shall be upheld in more than this!

(They pass through the window and as they do, the walls of the room disappear, and they find themselves on a country road on a clear winter's day. There is snow upon the ground.)

SCROOGE: *(Clasping his hands together)* Good heaven! I was bred in this place. I was a boy here! There are a thousand odors floating in the air, and each brings back a thousand thoughts and joys and hopes and cares long, long forgotten!

CHRISTMAS PAST: Your lip is trembling, and what is that upon your cheek?

SCROOGE: *(With a catch in his voice)* It's just a pimple. Lead on. Lead me where you will.

CHRISTMAS PAST: You recollect the way?

SCROOGE: Recollect it? I could walk it blindfolded.

CHRISTMAS PAST: Strange to have forgotten it for so many years. Let us go on.

(They walk down the road, SCROOGE *recognizing every gate, post, and tree. Boys on ponies pass, full of laughter, shouting to each other as they pass.* SCROOGE *knows and names every one of them. The walls are scrim, the images cinema.)*

SCROOGE: Why there are all the boys from St. James's. And there's Dan Ireland and Toady! Dear old Toady!

CHRISTMAS PAST: Toady?

SCROOGE: The pony is Toady. Dan got him for Christmas. Ha ha! Hey Dan! Dan!

CHRISTMAS PAST: These are but shadows of things that have been. They have no consciousness of us. The school is not quite deserted. A solitary child, neglected by his friends, is left there still.

SCROOGE: I know it. *(Sobs)* It's my poor forgotten self as I used to be. *(Sits down and weeps)*

(There is the image of a boy reading by candlelight in an atmosphere of not enough to eat. The spirit touches SCROOGE *gently upon the arm and points to the image of the boy, next which the figure of a man has appeared.)*

CHRISTMAS PAST: Look.

SCROOGE: *(In ecstasy)* Why, it's Ali Baba! It's dear old honest Ali Baba! Yes, yes, I know! One Christmastime when yonder solitary child was left alone he *did* come for the first time, just like that. Poor boy! And Valentine and his wild brother, Orson; there they go! And what's-his-name, who was put down in his drawers, asleep, at the Gate of Damascus; don't you see him! And the Sultan's Groom turned upside down by the Genii, there he is upon his head! Serves him right. I'm glad of it. What business had *he* to be married to the princess? *(*SCROOGE *is in a heightened state somewhere between laughing and crying)* There's the parrot! Green body and yellow tail, with a thing like a lettuce growing out of the top of his head; there he is! Poor Robinson Crusoe, he called him, when he came home again after sailing around the island. Poor Robinson Crusoe, where have you been, Robinson Crusoe? The man thought he was dreaming, but he wasn't. It was the parrot, you know. There goes Friday, running for his life to the little creek! Halloa! Hoop! Halloo! *(With a rapidity of transition* *very foreign to his usual character)* Poor boy! *(Cries again)* I wish . . . *(Puts his hand in his pocket after drying his eyes on his cuff)* . . . but it's too late now.

CHRISTMAS PAST: What is the matter?

SCROOGE: Nothing. Nothing. There was a boy singing a Christmas carol at my door last night. I should like to have given him something, that's all.

CHRISTMAS PAST: *(Smiles thoughtfully and waves its hand)* Let us see another Christmas!

(The cinematic image dissolves. The boy is older now. The room in which he sits is more run-down. The door opens and a little girl younger than the boy enters and throws her arms around the little boy and kisses him.)

FAN: Dear, dear brother. *(Kisses him again)* I have come to bring you home, dear brother! *(Claps her tiny hands and bends down to laugh)* To bring you home home home!

LITTLE SCROOGE: Home, little Fan?

FAN: *(Brimful of glee)* Yes! Home for good and all. Home for ever and ever. Father is so much kinder than he used to be that home's like heaven! He spoke so gently to me one dear night when I was going to bed, that I was not afraid to ask him once more if you might come home; and he said, Yes, you should; and sent me in a coach to bring you. And you're to be a man! And are never to come back here; but first, we're to be together all the Christmas long, and have the merriest time in all the world.

LITTLE SCROOGE: You are quite a woman, little Fan!

(The little girl laughs and claps her hands and drags him in her childish eagerness toward the door.)

VOICE OF GRUFF SCHOOLMASTER: *(Off)* Bring down master Scrooge's box there! He's going home.

FAN: *(To the little boy, gleefully)* Did you hear that, Ebenezer? Home! Home! *(Laughs childishly for joy)* Home! *(Her voice fades away)*

CHRISTMAS PAST: Always a delicate creature whom a breath might have withered. But she had a large heart!

SCROOGE: So she had. You're right. I'll not gainsay it, Spirit. God forbid!

CHRISTMAS PAST: She died a woman and had, as I think, children.

SCROOGE: One child.

CHRISTMAS PAST: True. Your nephew!

SCROOGE: *(Uneasily)* Yes.

CHRISTMAS PAST: *(Pointing to a door in a city street scene)* Do you know this warehouse door?

SCROOGE: Know it! Was I apprenticed here? *(They go in. There they see an old gentleman at a desk so high he almost hits his head on the ceiling)* Why, it's old Fezziwig! Bless his heart; it's Fezziwig alive again!

FEZZIWIG: *(Laying down his book and his pen, looking up at the clock, which points to the hour of seven, adjusting his capacious waistcoat, and laughing all over himself from his shoes to his organ of benevolence, calls out in a comfortable, oily, rich, fat, jovial voice)* Yo ho, there! Ebenezer! Dick!

(Scrooge's former self, now grown into a young man, enters with a fellow apprentice.)

SCROOGE: Dick Wilkins to be sure! Bless me, yes. There he is. He was very much attached to me, was Dick. Poor Dick! Dear, dear!

FEZZIWIG: Yo ho, my boys! No more work tonight. Christmas Eve, Dick. Christmas, Ebenezer! Let's have the shutters up! *(Claps his hands)* Before a man can say, Jack Robinson! *(The young men charge about it till they are panting like racehorses. Skipping down from his high desk with wonderful agility)* Hilli-ho! Clear away, my lads, and let's have lots of room here! Hilli-ho, Dick! Chirrup, Ebenezer!

(The two young men clear away every movable until the warehouse is a ballroom. In comes a fiddler and begins to play merrily. In comes MRS. FEZZIWIG, *one vast substantial smile. In come the three* MISS FEZZIWIGS, *beaming and lovable. In come the six young* FOLLOWERS *whose hearts they broke. In come the* HOUSEMAID, *the* BAKER, *and the* MILKMAN. *Until the room is all cheer, all laughter, all dancing away or standing in affectionate groupings. Then the fiddler strikes up "Sir Roger de Coverly" and old* FEZZIWIG *stands out to dance a reel with* MRS. FEZZIWIG. *"Hold hands with your partner; bow and curtsy; thread-the-needle, and back again to your place." Old* FEZZIWIG *outdances them all, young and old, and comes out without so much as a stagger. The clock strikes eleven and the domestic ball breaks up. Then* MR. *and* MRS. FEZZIWIG *take their places at either side of the door and, smiling, shake hands with each and every guest and bid them good night and merry Christmas. All thank them profusely.)*

CHRISTMAS PAST: A small matter to make these silly folks so full of gratitude.

SCROOGE: Small!

CHRISTMAS PAST: Why! Is it not? He has spent but a few pounds of your mortal money: Three or four, perhaps. Is that so much that he deserves this praise?

SCROOGE: It isn't that. *(Heatedly)* It isn't that, Spirit. He has the power to render us happy or unhappy; to make our service light or burdensome; a pleasure or a toil. Say that his power lies in words and looks; in things so slight and insignificant that it is impossible to add and count 'em up: what then? The happiness he gives is quite as great as if it cost a fortune. *(Feels the spirit's glance and stops)*

CHRISTMAS PAST: What is the matter?

SCROOGE: Nothing particular.

CHRISTMAS PAST: Something, I think?

SCROOGE: No, no. I should like to be able to say a word or two to my clerk just now! That's all.

CHRISTMAS PAST: My time grows short. Quick!

(A somewhat older and greedier SCROOGE *appears before them. Beside him sits a* GIRL *in mourning dress with tears sparkling in her eyes.)*

GIRL: *(Softly)* It matters little. To you very little. Another idol has displaced me; and if it can cheer and comfort you in time to come, as I would have tried to do, I have no just cause to grieve.

SCROOGE-THE-MAN: What idol has displaced you?

GIRL: A golden one.

SCROOGE-THE-MAN: This is the evenhanded dealing of the world! There is nothing on which it is so hard as poverty; and there is nothing which it professes to condemn with such severity as the pursuit of wealth!

GIRL: *(Gently)* You fear the world too much. All your other hopes have merged into the hope of being beyond the chance of its sordid reproach. I have seen your nobler aspirations fall off one by one, until the master passion, Gain, engrosses you. Have I not?

SCROOGE-THE-MAN: What then? Even if I have grown so much wiser, what then? I am not changed towards you. Am I?

GIRL: *(Shaking her head)* Our contract is an old one. It was made when we were both poor and content to be so, until, in good season, we should improve our worldly fortune by our patient industry. You *are* changed. When it was made you were another man.

SCROOGE-THE-MAN: *(Impatiently)* I was a boy.

GIRL: Your own feeling tells you that you were not what you are. I am. That which promised happiness when we were one in heart, is fraught with misery now that we are two. How often and how keenly I have thought of this, I will not say. It is enough that I *have* thought of it, and can release you.

SCROOGE-THE-MAN: Have I ever sought release?

GIRL: In words, no. Never.

SCROOGE-THE-MAN: In what, then?

GIRL: In a changed nature; in an altered spirit; in another atmosphere of life; another hope as its great end. In everything that ever made my love of any worth or value in your sight. If this had never been between us *(Looking mildly but steadily upon him),* tell me, would you seek me out and try to win me now? Ah, no!

SCROOGE-THE-MAN: *(Almost yielding to this supposition in spite of himself)* You think not?

GIRL: I would gladly think otherwise if I could. Heaven knows! When *I* have learned a Truth like this, I know how strong and irresistible it must be. But if you were free today, tomorrow, yesterday, can even I believe that you would choose a dowerless girl—you who, in your very confidence with her, weigh everything by Gain: or, choosing her, if for a moment you were false enough to your one guiding principle to do so, do I not know that your repentance and regret would surely follow? I do; and I release you. With a full heart, for the love of him you once were. *(Turns from him)* You may—the memory of what is past half makes me hope you will—have pain in this. A very, very brief time, and you will dismiss the recollection of it, gladly, as an unprofitable dream, from which it happened well that you awoke. May you be happy in the life you have chosen! *(She leaves him)*

SCROOGE: Spirit! Show me no more! Why do you delight to torture me?

CHRISTMAS PAST: One shadow more!

SCROOGE: *(Crying out)* No more! No more! I don't wish to see it. Show me no more!

(SCROOGE tries to turn away but the spirit pinions him with its arms and forces him to look. A domestic scene appears with the girl now turned into a beautiful matron surrounded by children playing noisily. The FATHER enters laden with Christmas presents. They sit by their fire surrounded by their loving children.)

FATHER: Belle, I saw an old friend of yours this afternoon.

MOTHER: Who was it?

FATHER: Guess.

MOTHER: How can I? Tut, I don't know. *(Laughing)* Mr. Scrooge.

FATHER: Mr. Scrooge it was. I passed his office window; and as it was not shut up, and he had a candle inside, I could scarcely help seeing him. His partner lies upon the point of death, I hear; and there he sat alone. Quite alone in the world, I do believe.

SCROOGE: *(In a broken voice)* Spirit, remove me from this place.

CHRISTMAS PAST: I told you these were shadows of the things that have been. That they are what they are, do not blame me!

SCROOGE: Remove me! I cannot bear it! *(Looking into the ghost's face)* Your face! I see in your face fragments of all the faces you have shown me! *(Wrestling with the ghost)* Leave me! Take me back! Haunt me no longer!

(While SCROOGE *struggles desperately the ghost is undisturbed by any of his efforts and shows no visible resistance. In fact his light shines all the brighter until* SCROOGE *forces an extinguisher cap—a giant candlesnuff—over it, and reeling back to his bed, falls into a heavy sleep.)*

Scene 4: *The second of the three spirits.*

(The bell strikes one. SCROOGE *with fear and trembling opens the door to an adjoining room wherein he finds a jolly giant, glorious to see, upon a pile of holiday edibles, crowned with holly and mistletoe and carrying a torch like the horn of plenty.)*

CHRISTMAS PRESENT: Come in! Come in, and know me better, man! I am the Ghost of Christmas Present. Look upon me! You have never seen the like of me before!

*(*GHOST OF CHRISTMAS PRESENT *is a composite of Father Christmas and his forerunners in the Roman Saturnalia cults. He wears a flowing green robe trimmed in white fur out of which bare feet and breast protrude. His dark brown curls are long and free: free as its genial face, its sparkling eye, its open hand, its cheery voice, its unconstrained demeanor, and its joyful air. Girdled round his waist is an antique scabbard with no sword in it whose ancient sheath is eaten up with rust.)*

SCROOGE: Never.

CHRISTMAS PRESENT: Have you never walked forth with the younger members of my family; meaning—for I am very young—my elder brothers born in these later years?

SCROOGE: I don't think I have. I am afraid I have not. Have you had many brothers, Spirit?

CHRISTMAS PRESENT: More than eighteen hundred.

SCROOGE: *(Mutters)* A tremendous family to provide for! *(The spirit rises. Submissively)* Spirit, conduct me where you will. I went forth last night on compulsion, and I learnt a lesson which is working now. Tonight, if you have aught to teach me, let me profit by it.

CHRISTMAS PRESENT: Touch my robe!

*(*SCROOGE *does this and at his touch the room once again disappears and he finds himself once again in the street. It is snowing and the merry pageant of going home for Christmas is acted out in pantomime as the populace hurries to their hearths amid snowball fights and grocery shopping.)*

SCROOGE: Is there a peculiar flavor in what you sprinkle from your torch?

CHRISTMAS PRESENT: There is. My own.

SCROOGE: Would it apply to any kind of dinner on this day?

CHRISTMAS PRESENT: To any kindly given. To a poor one most.

SCROOGE: Why to a poor one most?

CHRISTMAS PRESENT: Because it needs it most.

SCROOGE: *(After a moment's thought)* Spirit, I wonder you, of all the beings in the many worlds about us, should desire to cramp these people's opportunities of innocent enjoyment.

CHRISTMAS PRESENT: *(Shocked)* I?

SCROOGE: You seek to close these places on the Seventh Day? and it comes to the same thing.

CHRISTMAS PRESENT: *I* seek!

SCROOGE: Forgive me if I am wrong. It has been done in your name, or at least in that of your family.

CHRISTMAS PRESENT: There are some upon this earth of yours, who lay claim to know us, and who do their deeds of passion, pride, ill-will, hatred, envy, bigotry, and selfishness in our name; who are as strange to us and all our kith and kin, as if they had never lived. Remember that and charge their doings on themselves, not us.

(On they trudge to Bob Cratchit's house, where the Spirit blesses it with his torch.)

SCROOGE: Whose house is that?

CHRISTMAS PRESENT: Your clerk's.

MRS. CRATCHIT: What has ever got your precious father, then? And your brother, Tiny Tim; and Martha warn't as late last Christmas Day by half an hour!

MISS BELINDA: Here's Martha, Mother!

LITTLE BOY and GIRL: Here's Martha, Mother! Hurrah, there's *such* a goose, Martha!

MRS. CRATCHIT: Why bless your heart alive, my dear, how late you are! *(Kisses her a dozen times and taking off her shawl and bonnet for her with officious zeal)*

MARTHA: We'd a deal of work to finish up last night and had to clear away this morning, Mother!

MRS. CRATCHIT: Well! Never mind so long as ye are come. Sit ye down before the fire, my dear, and have a warm, Lord bless ye!

LITTLE BOY and GIRL: No, no! There's father coming. *(Running everywhere at once)* Hide, Martha, hide!

(The three children run and hide. BOB CRATCHIT *enters, his threadbare clothes darned up and brushed to look seasonable, with* TINY TIM *upon his shoulder.* TINY TIM *carries a little crutch and his body is supported by an iron frame.)*

CRATCHIT: *(Looking around)* Why, where's our Martha?

MRS. CRATCHIT: Not coming.

CRATCHIT: *(With a sudden declension in his high spirits)* Not coming! Not coming upon Christmas Day!

MARTHA: *(Coming out from behind the closet door and throwing herself into his arms)* Don't be disappointed, Father, it's only a joke!

(The little ones hustle TINY TIM *off to the washbasin.)*

MRS. CRATCHIT: And how did little Tim behave?

CRATCHIT: *(Tremulous)* As good as gold and better. Somehow he gets thoughtful sitting by himself so much, and thinks the strangest things you ever heard. He told me, coming home, that he hoped the people saw him in the church, because he was a cripple, and it might be pleasant to them to remember upon Christmas Day, who made lame beggars walk and blind men see. *(His voice trembles more)* But Tiny Tim is growing strong and hearty.

(Tiny Tim's little crutch can be heard upon the floor as he enters and takes his place upon his stool by the fire. CRATCHIT *mixes up some punch. They all bustle about preparations for the meal. They set the table, finally settle down. The children bring in the goose.)*

ALL: The goose! The goose! So big! Mmmm, tender. Delicious. What flavor! And so cheap! Pass the potatoes. Pass the applesauce! Pass the gravy!

TINY TIM: *(Beating his knife and fork on the table, cries feebly)* Hurrah!

(Long silent sequence while they eat.)

MISS BELINDA: Plates! Your plate, Father. Give me your plate, Tim. Martha, pass me Tim's plate. I'm going to bring in the pudding.

MRS. CRATCHIT: *(Rising)* I can't watch. I'm too nervous.

CRATCHIT: There there, I'm sure it will be fine.

MRS. CRATCHIT: It might not be done enough. I should have left it on longer.

MISS BELINDA: Don't worry, Mother. It's been on a good while.

MRS. CRATCHIT: I can't look. Suppose it should break in turning out?

MISS BELINDA: Suppose somebody should have got over the wall of the backyard, and stolen it, while we were making merry with the goose.

LITTLE BOY and GIRL: *(Livid)* They'd just better not have! Run and see! Save the pudding. Watch out for the crooks!

(They turn out the pudding and light it.)

CRATCHIT: Oh, a wonderful pudding! This is the best pudding you've made since we were married.

MRS. CRATCHIT: Well that's a great weight off my mind. I had my doubts about the quantity of flour.

SCROOGE: Rather a small pudding, isn't it, for so large a family?

CHRISTMAS PRESENT: Shhh! They'd think it heresy to say so. Any Cratchit would blush to hint at such a thing.

CRATCHIT: *(Proposing a toast)* A Merry Christmas to us all, my dears. God bless us!

THE FAMILY: God bless us!

TINY TIM: God bless us every one!

*(*CRATCHIT *hugs* TINY TIM*'s frail body and keeps him by his side as if he feared he might be taken from him.)*

SCROOGE: *(With a newly awakened interest)* Spirit, tell me if Tiny Tim will live.

CHRISTMAS PRESENT: I see a vacant seat in the poor chimney corner, and a crutch without an owner carefully preserved. If these shadows remain unaltered by the Future, the child will die.

SCROOGE: No, no! Oh no, kind Spirit! Say he will be spared.

CHRISTMAS PRESENT: If these shadows remain unaltered by the Future, none other of my race will find him here. What then? If he be like to die, he had better do it, and decrease the surplus population. *(On hearing his own words,* SCROOGE *hangs his head, overcome with penitence and grief)* Man, if man you be in heart, not adamant, forbear that wicked cant until you have discovered What the surplus is, and Where it is. Will you decide what men shall live, what men shall die? It may be, that in the sight of Heaven, you are more unfit to live than millions like this poor man's child. Oh God! To hear the Insect on the leaf pronouncing on the too much life among his hungry brothers in the dust!

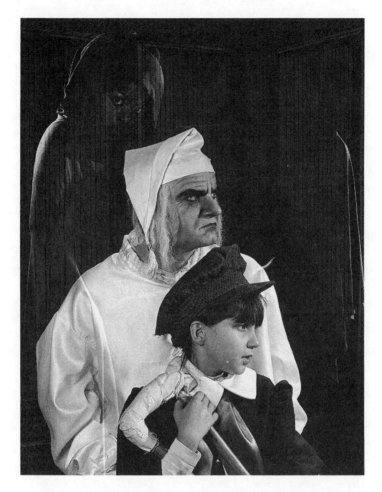

Ghislaine Chantel, Charles Ludlam &
Renee Pearl in *A Christmas Carol* (Les Carr)

(SCROOGE bends before the Ghost's rebuke and, trembling, casts his eyes upon the ground. But raises them suddenly on hearing his own name.)

CRATCHIT: *(Raising his glass)* Mr. Scrooge! I'll give you Mr. Scrooge, the Founder of the Feast!

MRS. CRATCHIT: *(Reddening angrily)* The Founder of the Feast indeed! I wish I had him here. I'd give him a piece of my mind to feast upon, and I hope he'd have a good appetite for it!

CRATCHIT: *(Placating her)* My dear, the children; Christmas Day.

MRS. CRATCHIT: It should be Christmas Day, I am sure, on which one drinks the health of such an odious, stingy, hard, unfeeling man as Mr. Scrooge. You know he is, Robert! Nobody knows it better than you do, poor fellow.

CRATCHIT: *(Mildly)* My dear, Christmas Day.

MRS. CRATCHIT: I'll drink his health for your sake and the Day's—not for his.

Long life to him! A merry Christmas and a happy New Year! He'll be very merry and very happy, I have no doubt!

(All the children grimly drink the toast. Then, after a long, somber silence, they become merrier than ever.)

CRATCHIT: You know, Master Peter, I have my eye on a situation for you that would bring in full five and sixpence weekly.

MARTHA: All week long we've been attaching holly to bonnets at the milliner's. Why on Christmas week we work twelve hours a day! But tomorrow I shall lie abed all morning. After all, it is a holiday. Last week I saw a countess and lord at the shop. Imagine, a real countess and lord! The lord wasn't any taller than Peter!

(All laugh. TINY TIM *sings a song about a little child lost in the snow. It begins to get dark and snow falls pretty heavily. People scurry about the streets laden with gifts.)*

SCROOGE: Where are all these people rushing to?

CHRISTMAS PRESENT: Visiting their families and friends.

SCROOGE: Judging by the number of them on their way you'd think there'd be no one at home to give them welcome!

(As the people pass the ghost waves his hand over them and they get the Christmas Spirit and become merry. The lamplighter sternly dressing the street with specks of light laughs out loudly as the spirit pours out from his generous hand its bright and harmless mirth.)

CHRISTMAS PRESENT: Little does the lamplighter know that he has company at Christmas!

(Suddenly without any warning they find themselves in a desolate place.)

SCROOGE: What place is this?

CHRISTMAS PRESENT: A place where miners live who labor in the bowels of the earth. But they know me, see! *(A* MINER'S FAMILY *sits about a fire singing a Christmas song. An old man leads them)* Hold on to my robe!

SCROOGE: Where are we going? Not to sea!

CHRISTMAS PRESENT: To sea. Look there!

SCROOGE: A light.

CHRISTMAS PRESENT: A lighthouse. Even there two men who watch the light have made a fire and join their horny hands across the table and wish each other Merry Christmas in their can of grog. Even they, their faces damaged and scarred with hard weather, strike up a sturdy song that is like the gale itself. And there beyond any shore, a lonely ship on the black and heaving sea, through lonely darkness, over an unknown abyss, whose depths are secrets as profound as death, sailors hum a Christmas tune or have a Christmas thought or speak below their breath to their companion of some bygone Christmas Day, with homeward hopes belonging to it.

(Suddenly, to SCROOGE'S *surprise, in the moaning of the wind he hears his nephew's laugh. They find themselves in a bright dry gleaming room. [A Punch and Judy stage, with Scrooge's* NEPHEW *as the puppeteer. Puppets of Punch, disguised as Scrooge, and a Ghost.)*

GHOST: Woooo!

PUNCH: *(Turns toward ghost)*

GHOST: *(Disappears)*

PUNCH: *(Turns away)*
GHOST: Woooo!
PUNCH: *(Turns toward ghost)*
GHOST: *(Disappears)*
PUNCH: *(Turns away)*
GHOST: Woooo!
PUNCH: *(Turns toward ghost)*
GHOST: *(Disappears)*
PUNCH: *(Sees ghost, screams, faints)*]
NEPHEW: Ha, ha! Ha, ha! *(Holding his sides, rolling his head, and twisting his face into the most extravagant contortions)*

(Scrooge's NIECE *by marriage and all their circle of friends join in.)*

ALL: Ha, ha! Ha, ha!
NEPHEW: He said that Christmas was a humbug as I live! He believed it, too!
NIECE: More shame for him, Fred!
NEPHEW: He's a comical old fellow, that's the truth; and not so pleasant as he might be. However, his offenses carry their own punishment, and I have nothing to say against him.
NIECE: I'm sure he is very rich, Fred. At least you always told *me* so.
NEPHEW: What of that, my dear! His wealth is of no use to him. He don't do any good with it. He don't make himself comfortable with it. He hasn't the satisfaction of thinking—ha, ha, ha!—that he is ever going to benefit us with it.
NIECE: I have no patience with him!

(The others all agree.)

NEPHEW: Oh, I have! I am sorry for him; I couldn't be angry with him if I tried. Who suffers by his ill whims? Himself, always. Here, he takes it into his head to dislike us, and he won't come and dine with us. What's the consequence? He don't lose much of a dinner—
NIECE: *(Interrupting)* Indeed, I think he loses a very good dinner.

(All agree.)

NEPHEW: Well! I am very glad to hear it because I haven't any great faith in these young housekeepers. What do *you* say, Topper?
TOPPER: We bachelors are wretched outcasts. *(Eyeing a plump young beauty)* But I have no right to express an opinion on the subject.
NIECE: *(Clapping her hands)* Do go on, Fred! He never finishes what he begins to say! He is such a ridiculous fellow!
NEPHEW: *(Laughing his infectious laugh)* I was only going to say that the consequences of his taking a dislike to us, and not making merry with us, is, as I think, that he loses some pleasant moments, which could do him no harm. I am sure he loses pleasanter companions than he can find in his own thoughts, either in his moldy old office, or his dusty chambers. I mean to give him the same chance every year, whether he likes it or not, for I pity him. He may rail at Christmas till he dies, but he can't help thinking better of it—I defy him—if he finds me going there, in good temper, year after year, and saying, Uncle Scrooge, how are you? If it only puts him in the vein to leave his poor clerk fifty pounds, *that's* something; and I think I shook him yesterday.

(All laugh. They play blindman's buff. TOPPER, *though blindfolded, relentlessly pursues the* PLUMP BEAUTY.*)*

PLUMP BEAUTY: It isn't fair! Why I no more believe that you are blind than I believe you have eyes in your boots!

TOPPER: *(Catching her)* The hair is familiar. Who can it be? Let me touch your headdress. I'm sorry but I'm stumped. I don't know you at all.

PLUMP BEAUTY: Oh pooh!

TOPPER: Perhaps if this ring fits, then I'd know you. *(Slipping a ring on her finger)* Then I'd know you anywhere.

NEPHEW: Let's play "Yes and No"!

CHRISTMAS PRESENT: It's growing late.

SCROOGE: Spirit, couldn't we stay until the guests leave?

CHRISTMAS PRESENT: This cannot be done.

SCROOGE: Here's a new game. One half hour, Spirit, only one!

NEPHEW: Now here's how you play "Yes and No." I will think of something and the rest of you must find out what; but I can only answer your questions yes or no, as is the case.

ALL THE GUESTS: *(Asking in turn)* Is it an animal?

NEPHEW: *(Laughing at each response)* Yes.

GUEST: Is it a live animal?

NEPHEW: Yes!

GUEST: Is it a disagreeable animal?

NEPHEW: Yes!

GUEST: Is it a savage animal?

NEPHEW: Yes!

GUEST: Does it growl and grunt sometimes?

NEPHEW: Yes.

GUEST: Can it talk?

NEPHEW: Yes.

GUEST: Does it live in London?

NEPHEW: Yes.

GUEST: Does it walk about the streets?

NEPHEW: Yes.

GUEST: Does it perform in a show?

NEPHEW: No.

GUEST: Is it led about?

NEPHEW: No.

GUEST: Does it live in a menagerie?

NEPHEW: No.

GUEST: Is it killed in a market?

NEPHEW: No.

GUEST: Is it a horse?

NEPHEW: No.

GUEST: Is it an ass?

NEPHEW: [*(Tempted to say yes)*] No.

GUEST: Is it a cow?

NEPHEW: No.

GUEST: Is it a bull?

NEPHEW: No.

GUEST: Is it a tiger?

NEPHEW: No.

GUEST: A pig?

NEPHEW: No.

GUEST: A cat?

NEPHEW: No.

GUEST: Is it a bear?

NEPHEW: No.

PLUMP BEAUTY: I have found it out! I know what it is, Fred! I know what it is!

NEPHEW: What is it?

PLUMP BEAUTY: It's your Uncle Scro-o-o-o-oge!

NEPHEW: It certainly is!

TOPPER: Not fair. When we asked if it was a bear you should have said yes. You were trying to throw us off the track.

NEPHEW: He has given us plenty of merriment, I am sure, and it would be ungrateful not to drink his health. Here is a glass of mulled wine ready to our hand at the moment; and I say, "Uncle Scrooge!"

ALL: *(Raising their glasses)* Well! Uncle Scrooge.

NEPHEW: A Merry Christmas and a Happy New Year to the old man, whatever he is! He wouldn't take it from me, but may he have it nonetheless. Uncle Scrooge!

(SCROOGE has become visibly light of heart and almost toasts the company in return. The scene before them vanishes and SCROOGE and the Spirit are again upon their travels. The spirit has aged visibly.)

SCROOGE: This has been a long night, if it is only a night. Your hair's turned gray. Are spirits' lives so short?

CHRISTMAS PRESENT: My life upon this globe is very brief. It ends tonight.

SCROOGE: *(Cries out in amazement)* Tonight?

CHRISTMAS PRESENT: Tonight at midnight. Hark! The time is drawing near.

(The chimes are heard ringing three-quarters past eleven.)

SCROOGE: Forgive me if I am not justified in what I ask. . . . But I see something strange, and not belonging to yourself, protruding from your skirts. Is it a foot or a claw?

CHRISTMAS PRESENT: *(Sadly)* It may be a claw for the flesh there is upon it. Look here.

(The spirit opens its robe and discloses two children, a boy and a girl, yellow, meager, ragged, scowling, wolfish, stale, and shriveled as if pinched and twisted by age—monsters of horror and dread.)

SCROOGE: *(Starting back, appalled. He tries to say something good about them)* Why they are . . . they are . . . *(Chokes)* Spirit, are they yours?

CHRISTMAS PRESENT: *(Looking down upon them)* They are Man's, and they cling to me, appealing from their fathers. This boy is Ignorance. This girl is Want. Beware them both, and all of their degree, but most of all beware this boy, for on his brow I see that written which is Doom, unless the writing be erased. *(Crying out vehemently)* Deny it! *(Stretching out his hand toward the city)* Slander those who tell it ye! Admit it for your factious purposes, and make it worse! And bide the end!

SCROOGE: Have they no refuge or resource?

CHRISTMAS PRESENT: Are there no prisons? Are there no workhouses?

(The bell strikes twelve. The spirit vanishes. A phantom draped and hooded approaches SCROOGE *gravely, silently, with outstretched hand, like a mist along the ground.)*

SCROOGE: *(Bending down upon his knee)* I am in the presence of the ghost of Christmas yet to come? *(The spirit does not answer but points downward with its hand)* You are about to show me shadows of the things that have not happened, but will happen in the time before us, is that so, Spirit? *(The spirit whose face is not visible bows its hooded head. Thrilled with a vague uncertain horror)* Ghost of the future! I fear you more than any specter I have seen. But as I know your purpose is to do me good, and as I hope to be another man from what I was, I am prepared to bear you company, and do it with a thankful heart. Will you not speak to me? *(The spirit points its hand straight before them)* Lead on! Lead on! The night is waning fast, and it is precious time to me, I know. Lead on, Spirit!

(The phantom moves away and as it does the city appears about them. They find themselves in the heart of the business district. There the phantom points to a little knot of BUSINESSMEN. SCROOGE *advances and listens to their talk.)*

FIRST BUSINESSMAN *(Fat)*: No, I don't know much about it either way. I only know he's dead.

SECOND BUSINESSMAN: When did he die?

FIRST BUSINESSMAN: Last night, I believe.

THIRD BUSINESSMAN: Why, what was the matter with him? *(Takes snuff)* I thought he'd never die.

FIRST BUSINESSMAN: God knows.

SECOND BUSINESSMAN: What has he done with his money?

FIRST BUSINESSMAN: *(Yawning)* I haven't heard. Left it to his company, perhaps. He hasn't left it to *me*. That's all I know. *(All three laugh)* It's likely to be a very cheap funeral, for upon my life I don't know of anybody to go to it. Suppose we make up a party and volunteer?

SECOND BUSINESSMAN: I don't mind going if a lunch is provided. But I must be fed if I make one.

(All laugh again.)

FIRST BUSINESSMAN: Well, I am the most disinterested among you after all, for I would never wear those black gloves they give you as a memento and I never eat lunch. But I'll offer to go if anybody else will. When I come to think of it, I'm not at all sure that I wasn't his most particular friend; for we used to stop and speak whenever we met. Bye-bye!

(They all stroll off in different directions. SCROOGE *looks to the phantom for an explanation but it only glides on down the street and points to two other* BUSINESS-MEN.*)*

MAN A: How are you?

MAN B: How are you?

MAN A: Well! Old Scratch has got his own at last, hey?

MAN B: So I am told. Cold isn't it?

MAN A: Seasonable for Christmastime. You're not a skater, I suppose?

MAN B: No. No. Something else to think of. Good morning!

The Old Joe scene from *A Christmas Carol* (Les Carr)

(They part. The phantom now leads SCROOGE *to a den in the wretched part of town, whose whole quarter reeks with crime, with filth, with misery. Two women like shopping bag ladies and a vulturelike man enter a junk man's shop.)*

BAG LADY: Let the charwoman alone to be the first! Let the laundress alone to be the second; and let the undertaker's man alone to be the third. Look here, Old Joe, here's a chance! If we haven't all three met here without meaning it!

OLD JOE: *(Removing his pipe from his mouth)* You couldn't have met in a better place. Come into the parlor. You were made free of it long ago, you know; and the other two an't strangers. Stop till I shut the door of the shop. Ah! How it shrieks! There an't such a rusty bit of metal in the place as its own hinges, I believe; and I'm sure there's no such old bones here as mine. Ha, ha! We're all suitable to our calling, we're well matched. Come into the parlor. Come into the parlor.

(The parlor is behind a curtain of rags.)

BAG LADY: *(Throws her bundle on the floor and sits down in a flaunting manner on a stool; crossing her elbows on her knees, and looking with a bold defiance at the other two)* What odds, then! What odds, Mrs. Dilber? Every person has a right to take care of themselves. *He* always did!

MRS. DILBER *(A laundress)*: That's true, indeed! No man more so.

BAG LADY: Why, then, don't stand staring as if you was afraid, woman; who's the wiser? We're not going to pick holes in each other's coats, I suppose?

OLD JOE and MRS. DILBER: No, indeed! We should hope not.

BAG LADY: Very well, then! That's enough. Who's the worse for the loss of a few things like these? Not a dead man, I suppose.

MRS. DILBER: *(Laughing)* No, indeed.

BAG LADY: If he wanted to keep 'em after he was dead, a wicked old screw, why wasn't he natural in his lifetime? If he had been he'd have had somebody to look after him when he was struck by death, instead of lying gasping out his last there, alone by himself.

MRS. DILBER: It's the truest word that ever was spoke. It's a judgment on him.

BAG LADY: I wish it was a little heavier one. And it should have been, you may depend upon it, if I could have laid my hands on anything else. Open that bundle, Old Joe, and let me know the value of it. Speak out plain. I'm not afraid to be the first, nor afraid for them to see it. We knew pretty well that we were helping ourselves, before we met here, I believe. It's no sin. Open the bundle, Joe.

MRS. DILBER: Me first. *(She opens her bundle)*

OLD JOE: *(Jotting down the sum)* A seal, a pencil case, a pair of sleeve buttons, a brooch of no great value. Sheets and towels, a little wearing apparel, two old-fashioned silver teaspoons, a pair of sugar tongs, and a few boots. *(Writes an amount on the wall)* That's your account and I wouldn't give another sixpence if I was to be boiled for not doing it. I always give too much to ladies. It's a weakness of mine, and that's the way I ruin myself. That's your account. If you asked me for another penny and made it an open question, I'd repent for being so liberal, and knock off half a crown.

BAG LADY: And now undo *my* bundle, Joe.

OLD JOE: *(Unties a great many knots and drags out some stuff)* What do you call this? Bed curtains!

BAG LADY: *(Laughing and leaning forward on her crossed arms)* Ah! Bed curtains!

OLD JOE: You don't mean to say you took 'em down, rings and all, with him lying there?

BAG LADY: Yes I do. Why not?

OLD JOE: You were born to make your fortune and you'll certainly do it.

BAG LADY: *(Coolly)* I certainly shan't hold my hand, when I can get anything in it by reaching it out, for the sake of such a man as he was, I promise you, Joe. Don't drop that oil upon the blankets, now.

OLD JOE: His blankets?

BAG LADY: Whose else's do you think? He isn't likely to take cold without 'em, I dare say.

OLD JOE: *(Stopping and looking up)* I hope he didn't die of anything catching? Eh?

BAG LADY: Don't you be afraid of that. I an't so fond of his company that I'd loiter about him for such things, if he did. Ah! You may look through that shirt till your eyes ache, but you won't find a hole in it, nor a threadbare place. It's the best he had and a fine one too. They'd have wasted it, if it hadn't been for me.

OLD JOE: What do you call wasting of it?

BAG LADY: Putting it on him to be buried in to be sure. *(With a laugh)* Somebody was fool enough to do it, but I took it off again. If calico an't good enough for such a purpose, it isn't good enough for anything. It's quite as becoming to the body. He can't look uglier than he did in that one. *(OLD JOE writes her sum on the wall, then hands her money)* Ha, ha! This is the end of it, you see! He frightened everyone away from him when he was alive, to profit us when he was dead! Ha, ha, ha!

SCROOGE: *(Shuddering from head to foot)* Spirit! I see, I see. The case of this unhappy man might be my own. My life tends that way, now. Merciful Heaven, what is this! *(SCROOGE recoils in terror, for the scene has changed. Before him on a bare uncurtained bed, beneath a ragged sheet, lies a still form. SCROOGE looks toward the phantom who points to the head of the body)* Oh cold, cold, rigid, dreadful Death, set up thine altar here, and dress it with such terrors as thou hast at thy command: for this is thy dominion! But of the loved, revered, and honored head, thou canst not turn one hair to thy dread purposes, or make one feature odious. It is not that the hand is heavy and will fall down when released; it is not that the heart and pulse are still; but that the hand was open, generous, and true; the heart brave, warm, and tender; and the pulse a man's. Strike, Shadow, strike! And see his good deeds springing from the wound, to sow the world with life immortal! Spirit! This is a fearful place. In leaving it, I shall not leave its lesson, trust me. Let us go! *(The ghost points an unmoving finger to the corpse's head)* I understand you, and I would do it, if I could. But I have not the power, Spirit. I have not the power. If there is any person in this town who feels emotion caused by this man's death, show that person to me, Spirit, I beseech you!

(The phantom spreads its dark robe before him for a moment, like a wing, and withdrawing it, reveals a room by daylight, where a mother and her children are. There is a knock at the door—her husband enters, a man whose face is careworn and depressed though he is young.)

SHE: Is there any news? *(Pause)* Tell me is it good or bad?

HE: Bad.

SHE: We are quite ruined?

HE: No. There is hope yet, Caroline.

SHE: If *he* relents, there is! Nothing is past hope, if such a miracle has happened.

HE: He is past relenting. He is dead.

SHE: *(With a gentle heartfelt sincerity)* Oh thank God. *(Clasping her hands)* What am I saying? God forgive me.

HE: What the half-drunken woman, whom I told you of last night, said to me when I tried to see him and obtain a week's delay; and what I thought was a mere excuse to avoid me; turns out to have been quite true. He was not only very ill, but dying, then.

SHE: To whom will our debt be transferred?

HE: I don't know. But before that time we shall be ready with the money; and even though we were not, it would be bad fortune indeed to find so merciless a creditor in his successor. We may sleep tonight with light hearts, Caroline.

(They embrace. Their children cluster about them.)

SCROOGE: Let me see some tenderness connected with a death, or that dark chamber, Spirit, which we left just now, will be forever present to me.

(They enter Bob Cratchit's house. The mother and the children are seated round the fire still as statues.)

PETER: *(Reading from a book)* "And he took a child, and set him in the midst of them."

MRS. CRATCHIT: *(Lays her sewing upon the table and puts her hand up to her face)* The color hurts my eyes.

SCROOGE: The color? Ah, poor Tiny Tim!

MRS. CRATCHIT: They're better now again. It makes them weak by candlelight; and I wouldn't show weak eyes to your father when he comes home, for the world. It must be near his time.

PETER: *(Shutting his book)* Past it, rather. But I think he's walked a little slower than he used, these few last evenings, Mother.

(Long silence among them.)

MRS. CRATCHIT: I have known him walk with . . . I have known him walk with Tiny Tim upon his shoulder, very fast indeed.

PETER: *(Exclaiming)* And so have I, often.

ANOTHER CHILD: And so have I.

MRS. CRATCHIT: But he was very light to carry *(Resumes her work)*, and his father loved him so, that it was no trouble—no trouble. And there is your father at the door! *(She rushes to meet him)*

(BOB CRATCHIT enters; she brings him tea; the children climb upon his lap.)

CHILD: *(Kissing his cheeks)* Don't mind it, Father. Don't be grieved!

CRATCHIT: I'm not. I'm not. Ah, it's good to be here with you all. The needlework is progressing nicely. It should be done by Sunday.

MRS. CRATCHIT: Sunday! You went today, then, Robert?

CRATCHIT: Yes, my dear. I wish you could have gone. It would have done you good to see how green a place it is. But you'll see it often. I promised him that I would walk there on a Sunday. *(Breaking down and crying)* My little child! My little child! *(Rises and leaves room and enters room where TINY TIM lies surrounded by candles and Christmas things. CRATCHIT kisses the little face. Reenters room)* I met Mr. Scrooge's nephew today in the street. I have scarcely seen him before but once and on seeing me he said I looked "just a little down, you know." On which, because he is the pleasantest-spoken gentleman you ever heard, I told him. And he said, "I am heartily sorry for it, Mr. Cratchit, and heartily sorry for your good wife." Bye the bye, how he ever knew *that,* I don't know.

MRS. CRATCHIT: Knew what, my dear?

CRATCHIT: Why, that you were a good wife.

PETER: Everybody knows that!

CRATCHIT: Very well observed, my boy! I hope they do. "Heartily sorry," he said, "for your good wife. If I can be of service to you in any way," he said, "this is where I live—pray come to me," and gave me his card! Now, it wasn't for the sake of anything he might be able to do for us, so much as for his kind way, that this was quite delightful. It really seemed as if he had known our Tiny Tim, and felt with us.

MRS. CRATCHIT: I'm sure he's a good soul.

CRATCHIT: You would be surer of it, my dear, if you saw and spoke to him. I shouldn't be at all surprised, mark what I say, if he got Peter a better situation.

MRS. CRATCHIT: Only hear that, Peter.

ONE OF THE GIRLS: And then Peter will be keeping company with someone and setting up for himself.

PETER: *(Grinning)* Get along with you!

CRATCHIT: It's just as likely as not one of these days, though there's plenty of time for that, my dears. But however and whenever we part from one another, I am sure we shall none of us forget poor Tiny Tim—shall we—or this first parting that there was among us?

ALL: Never, Father!

CRATCHIT: And I know, I know, my dears, that when we recollect how patient and how mild he was; although he was a little, little child; we shall not quarrel easily among ourselves, and forget poor Tiny Tim in doing it.

ALL: No, never, Father!

(MRS. CRATCHIT kisses him. His daughters kiss him. He and PETER shake hands.)

CRATCHIT: Spirit of Tiny Tim, thy childish essence was from God. And let us always think of Tiny Tim at Christmas—Christmas whose mighty founder was a child himself. I am very happy! I am very happy!

SCROOGE: Specter, something informs me that our parting moment is at hand. I know it. But I know not how. Tell me what man that was whom we saw lying dead? *(The spirit points)* This court through which we hurry now is where my place of occupation is, and has been for a length of time. I see the house. Let me behold what I shall be in days to come. *(The spirit points in the opposite direction)* The house is yonder. Why do you point away? *(They pass through an iron gate into a churchyard. The spirit stands among the graves and points to a single stone)* Before I draw nearer to that stone to which you point, answer me one question. Are these the shadows of the things that Will be, or are they shadows of the things that May be, only? *(The ghost points down to the grave)* Men's courses will foreshadow certain ends, to which, if persevered in, they must lead. But if the courses be departed from, the ends will change. Say it is thus with what you show me. *(The spirit does not move. Creeping toward the spirit and following the finger, reads upon the stone of the neglected grave his own name, Ebenezer Scrooge. Then falling to his knees)* Am *I* that man who lay upon the bed? *(The finger points from the grave to him and back again)* No, Spirit! Oh no, no! Spirit *(Clutching at its robe)* hear me! I am not the man I was. I will not be the man I must have been but for this intercourse. Why show me this if I am past all hope? *(The spirit's hand appears to shake. Falling on the ground before it)* Good Spirit, your nature intercedes for me and pities me. Assure me that I yet may change these shadows you have shown me, by an altered life! *(The spirit's kind hand trembles)* I will honor Christmas in my heart, and try to keep it all the year. I will live in the Past, the Present, and the Future. The spirits of all three will strive within me. I will not shut out the lessons that they teach. Oh, tell me I may sponge away the writing on this stone!

(SCROOGE catches the spectral hand in his agony. It tries to free itself. He detains it. It repulses him. Then holding up his hands in one last prayer to have his fate reversed, the spirit alters, shrinks, and collapses into a bedpost.)

Scene 5: *The next morning.*

SCROOGE: I will live in the Past, the Present, and the Future! *(Scrambling out of bed)* The spirits of all three shall strive within me. Oh Jacob Marley! Heaven and the Christmas Time be praised for this! I say it on my knees, old Jacob; on my knees! *(His face is wet with tears, his voice broken from sobbing violently. He examines the bed curtains)* The bed curtains are not torn down. *(Folding bed curtains in his arms)* They are not torn down rings and all. They are here: I am here: the shadows of the things that would have been may be dispelled. They will be. I know they will! *(His hands have been busy with his garments all this time: turning them inside out, putting them on upside down, tearing them, mislaying them, making them parties to every kind of extravagance. Laughing and crying in the same breath)* I don't know what to do! I am as light as a feather, I am as happy as an angel, I am as merry as a schoolboy, I am as giddy as a drunken man. A Merry Christmas to everybody! A Happy New Year to all the world. Hallo here! Whoop! Hallo! *(Turning in circles, looking about the room)* There's the saucepan that the gruel was in! There's the door by which the ghost of Jacob Marley entered! There's the corner where the ghost of Christmas Present sat! There's the window where I saw the wandering Spirits! It's all right, it's all true, it all happened. Ha, ha, ha! *(Lets out a splendid laugh)* I don't know what day of the month it is! I don't know how long I've been among the Spirits. I don't know anything. I'm quite a baby. Never mind. I don't care. I'd rather be a baby. Hallo! Whoop! Hallo here! *(The church bells ring out lusty peals)* Church bells, oh glorious, glorious! Ding, dong! *(Opens window and puts out his head)* No fog, no mist; clear, bright, jovial, stirring, cold; cold, piping for the blood to dance to; golden sunlight; heavenly sky; sweet fresh air; merry bells. Oh, glorious. Glorious! *(Calling to a* BOY *in Sunday clothes)* What's today?
BOY: Eh?
SCROOGE: What's today, my fine fellow?
BOY: Today—why, Christmas Day.
SCROOGE: *(To himself)* It's Christmas Day! I haven't missed it. The Spirits have done it all in one night. They can do anything they like. Of course they can. Of course they can. Hallo, my fine fellow.
BOY: Hallo!
SCROOGE: Do you know the poulterer's in the next street but one, at the corner?
BOY: I should hope I did.
SCROOGE: An intelligent boy. A remarkable boy! Do you know whether they've sold the prize turkey that was hanging up there? Not the little prize turkey: the big one?
BOY: What, the one as big as me?
SCROOGE: What a delightful boy! It's a pleasure to talk to him. Yes, my buck.
BOY: It's hanging there now.
SCROOGE: Is it? Go and buy it.
BOY: *(Thumbs his nose)* Take a walk!
SCROOGE: No, no. I am in earnest. Go and buy it, and tell 'em to bring it here, that I may give them the direction where to take it. Come back with the man

and I'll give you a shilling. Come back with him in less than five minutes and I'll give you half a crown. *(The* BOY *is off like a shot. Whispering)* I'll send it to Bob Cratchit's. *(Rubs his hands and spits with a laugh)* He shan't know who sends it. It's twice the size of Tiny Tim. Joe Miller never made such a joke as sending it to Bob's will be! *(Writes a note with an unsteady hand. Then while waiting for the poulterer's man, the door knocker catches his eye)* What a wonderful knocker! What an honest expression it has in its face! I scarcely ever looked at it before. I shall love it as long as I live! Here's the turkey. Hallo! Whoop! How are you! Merry Christmas! *(The boy reenters carrying a turkey as large as himself. A man accompanies him)* That *is* a turkey! He could never have stood upon his legs, that bird. He would have snapped 'em short off in a minute, like sticks of sealing wax. Why, it's impossible to carry that to Camden Town. You must have a cab.

(Chuckling all the while he pays for the turkey, pays for the cab and recompenses the BOY. *Then he sits down in his chair and chuckles till he cries. Then he shaves while dancing! and dresses himself and goes out in the street, beaming at everyone as he walks along with his hands behind his back.)*

SEVERAL PASSERS-BY: Good morning, sir! A Merry Christmas to you!

SCROOGE: Of all the blithe sounds I have ever heard those were the blithest in my ears. *(The two* GENTLEMEN *from the charities approach. Quickening his pace and taking the old* GENTLEMAN *by both hands)* My dear sir, how do you do? I hope you succeeded yesterday. It was very kind of you. A merry Christmas to you, sir!

GENTLEMAN: Mr. Scrooge?

SCROOGE: Yes, that is my name, and I fear it may not be pleasant to you. Allow me to ask your pardon. And will you have the goodness . . . *(Whispers in his ear)*

GENTLEMAN: *(As if his breath were gone)* Lord bless me! My dear Mr. Scrooge, are you serious?

SCROOGE: If you please, not a farthing less. A great many back payments are included in it, I assure you. Will you do me that favor?

GENTLEMAN: *(Shaking hands with him)* My dear sir, I don't know what to say to such munifi—

SCROOGE: Don't say anything, please. Come and see me. Will you come and see me?

GENTLEMAN: *(Clearly meaning it)* I will!

SCROOGE: Thank'ee, I am much obliged to you. I thank you fifty times. Bless you! *(Walks on patting children on the head until he arrives at his nephew's house and knocks at the door.* GIRL *opens the door)* Is your master at home, my dear? Nice girl. Very.

GIRL: Yes, sir.

SCROOGE: Where is he, my love?

GIRL: He's in the dining room, sir, along with mistress. I'll show you upstairs, if you please.

SCROOGE: Thank'ee. He knows me. I'll go in here, my dear. *(Poking in his head as* NEPHEW *and* GUESTS *are toasting him)* Fred!

NIECE: *(Terribly startled, lets out a little shriek)*

NEPHEW: Why bless my soul! Who's that?

SCROOGE: It's I. Your Uncle Scrooge. I have come to dinner. Will you let me in, Fred?

(FRED practically shakes his arm off. Stunned expressions on the faces of all the company. Blackout.)

Scene 6: *Scrooge and Marley's. The next morning.*

(SCROOGE at his desk.)

SCROOGE: If only I can catch Bob Cratchit coming late! That's the thing I have set my heart upon. Nine o'clock. No Bob. A quarter past. No Bob. He's a full eighteen and a half behind his time. *(CRATCHIT hurries in with his hat and muffler already off and takes his place on his stool in a jiffy: and drives away with his pen as if he were trying to overtake nine o'clock. Growls)* Hallo! What do you mean by coming here at this time of day?

CRATCHIT: I am very sorry, sir. I *am* behind my time.

SCROOGE: You are? Yes. I think you are. Step this way, if you please.

CRATCHIT: *(Pleading)* It's only once a year, sir. It shall not be repeated. I was making rather merry yesterday, sir.

SCROOGE: You were? Yes, I believe you were. Now, I'll tell you what, my friend. I am not going to stand this sort of thing any longer. And therefore . . . *(Leaping from his stool and giving* BOB *such a dig in the waistcoat that he staggers back)* . . . and therefore, I am about to raise your salary!

CRATCHIT: *(Threatening* SCROOGE *with a ruler)* Don't take another step near me or I'll knock you out and call the people in the court to help and bring a straight waistcoat.

SCROOGE: A merry Christmas Bob! *(Clapping him on the back)* A merrier Christmas, Bob, my good fellow, than I have given you for many a year! I'll raise your salary, and endeavor to assist your struggling family, and we will discuss your affairs this very afternoon, over a Christmas bowl of smoking bishop, Bob! If there be room for two I'd like to be a second father to that boy of yours, Tiny Tim. Make up the fires and buy another coal scuttle before you dot another *i*, Bob Cratchit!

CRATCHIT: Mr. Scrooge, may I stand you to a drink?

SCROOGE: No, I plan to live as an abstainer and have no further need of spirits. *(Laughs outrageously at his own joke)* And so, as Tiny Tim observed:

TINY TIM: [*(Throwing away his crutch and leaping onto* SCROOGE's *shoulder)*] God bless us every one!

REVERSE PSYCHOLOGY

A *Farce*

1980

Charlotte Forbes & Charles Ludlam in
Reverse Psychology (Christopher Scott)

Cast of Characters

DR. LEONARD SILVER
DR. KAREN GOLD
ELEANOR
FREDDIE

ACT I

Scene 1

(ELEANOR and LEONARD enter a cheap hotel room. They kiss long and passionately. Then they look into each other's eyes.)

ELEANOR: What's your name?
LEONARD: Leonard.
ELEANOR: I'm Eleanor.
LEONARD: I know.
ELEANOR: How did you know?
LEONARD: You told me in the bar.
ELEANOR: Oh.

[*(Leonard turns on lamp.)*]

LEONARD: Well, what do you think?
ELEANOR: I think we're both mad.
LEONARD: Why do you say that?
ELEANOR: Well, we'd have to be to come to the sleaziest hotel room in town with a total stranger. We're both out of our minds, darling. *(Throws her arms around him)*
LEONARD: I'm not out of my mind. I'm sane. Completely sane.
ELEANOR: I meant it figuratively.
LEONARD: You thought you meant it figuratively. But you meant it.
ELEANOR: *(Laughs devilishly)* So what if I did? I'm so happy it's almost insane. I'm insanely happy.
LEONARD: You associate happiness with being insane. That's interesting.
ELEANOR: You're right. I'd rather be mad. Being sane is so boring. Don't you agree?
LEONARD: No, I don't think being sane is boring. I think being sane is fun. And I know a thousand insane people who are bores.
ELEANOR: How do you know a thousand insane people?
LEONARD: My work.
ELEANOR: You're a waiter?
LEONARD: No. I'm a psychiatrist.
ELEANOR: I go to a psychiatrist. So does my husband. Ooops!
LEONARD: You're married.
ELEANOR: Does it bother you?
LEONARD: No. I'm married too.
ELEANOR: Is she a horror?
LEONARD: No. She's wonderful. She's a very nice person. I love her very much. We're perfectly adjusted to each other. We work at our relationship.

ELEANOR: Sounds exhausting.

LEONARD: What's yours like?

ELEANOR: My what?

LEONARD: Spouse.

ELEANOR: Oh. He's all right.

LEONARD: Just all right?

ELEANOR: He doesn't beat me up and drag me to bed and make me do sexual things against my will anymore.

LEONARD: Is that what you want me to do?

ELEANOR: No, I just want you to whisper naughty words in my ear. *(LEONARD whispers in her ear.* ELEANOR *pulls away)* Wait a minute. Not *that* naughty! *(LEONARD pulls her back to him and whispers in her ear again)* How do you think of things like that? *(LEONARD whispers in her ear again)* I don't believe it! Do people really do things like that? Well, I'm willing to try, but I'm not guaranteeing anything.

LEONARD: Tell me what your husband is like.

ELEANOR: No.

LEONARD: Come on.

ELEANOR: No.

LEONARD: *(Coaxing)* Why not?

ELEANOR: I'd rather not think about my husband right now.

LEONARD: Describe him to me.

ELEANOR: Why?

LEONARD: I want to imagine him while we're making love. It helps me get aroused.

ELEANOR: *(Undressing before the mirror)* Sometimes I wish I were a man so I could be my own lover.

LEONARD: Talk to me.

ELEANOR: My husband is big and hairy all over his body. He even has thick, black hair all over his back.

LEONARD: *(Undressing)* Go on.

ELEANOR: But his eyes are a heavenly blue.

LEONARD: Go on.

ELEANOR: Shall I tell you my dreams, too?

LEONARD: If you want to.

ELEANOR: Last night I dreamed I was murdered by a sex maniac.

(LEONARD reaches over to the night table and turns the light off. ELEANOR *turns the light on. They begin to make love again.* LEONARD *turns the light off.* ELEANOR *turns the light on again.)*

LEONARD: Leave the light off. I can't do it in the light.

ELEANOR: I can't do it in the dark.

LEONARD: I don't like women with hairy husbands.

[*(The song, "Reverse Psychology," off:)*]
    Crazy it's true
    Crazy for you
    If I am crazy
    It's nothing new
    You're so contrary

I don't know what to do
You're driving me insane.

When I'm out of my mind
You're so damned considerate
I didn't lose my mind
I got rid of it.

I'll give it to you straight
I've never been more gay
Than when you twist my head around
And make me obey
And you know I'm stubborn
And always get my way
You use Reverse Psychology.

ELEANOR: [*(Singing along)*] That's our song.

LEONARD: Oh, no. I'm sorry, but that can't be our song. There is another person and myself who regard this as our song.

ELEANOR: Not yours and mine. My husband and me.

LEONARD: You mean, your husband and you, and my wife and I, all have the same song? Does that make it our song, too?

ELEANOR: [*(After singing the end of the song)*] It's no use.

LEONARD: It's no use. Anyway, I really love my wife.

ELEANOR: And I love my husband. This has all been a mistake.

LEONARD: This has all been a terrible mistake. It was great while it lasted.

ELEANOR: But it was just one of those things. We must never do this again.

LEONARD: You're right. We must *never, ever* do this again.

ELEANOR: Never.

LEONARD: This is nothing against you.

ELEANOR: I understand.

LEONARD: It's not that I don't find you attractive. Because I am attracted to you.

ELEANOR: And I'm attracted to you. It's just that we don't want this thing to go any further.

LEONARD: Recognize it for what it is and . . .

ELEANOR: Let it go at that before . . .

LEONARD: It gets out of hand and . . .

ELEANOR: Somebody gets hurt.

LEONARD: Right.

ELEANOR: So, I guess that's that.

LEONARD: Yeah, that's that. Of course, there's no reason why we can't be friends.

ELEANOR: Of course not.

LEONARD: But we must keep the relationship on the intellectual level.

ELEANOR: Keep it platonic.

LEONARD: Maybe you could give me your phone number and . . .

ELEANOR: I don't think it would be a good idea for you to call me at home.

LEONARD: Or your address! I could send you a Christmas card.

ELEANOR: No, I might have to explain it to my husband.

LEONARD: Or we could meet sometime just to discuss things on the intellectual level. Ideas. Books. The library. We could meet at the library. . . .

ELEANOR: Every Wednesday . . .

LEONARD: In the stacks . . .

ELEANOR: Under nonfiction . . .
LEONARD: And discuss . . .
ELEANOR: On an intellectual level.
LEONARD: We'd be friends.
ELEANOR: We'd be good comrades.
LEONARD: Yes, comrades. *(They shake hands)* Until Wednesday, then?
ELEANOR: Until Wednesday.
LEONARD: Comrade.
ELEANOR: Comrade.

Scene 2: *The Metropolitan Museum of Art.*

(This should be suggested with draperies and a few gilded picture frames floating in midair. FREDDIE *is standing looking at a picture in one of the floating frames.* KAREN *wanders through the gallery as though lost. Occasionally she consults a tour guide booklet.)*

KAREN: *(To* FREDDIE*)* Excuse me. Could you tell me which way to the Chinese bronzes? I can't figure out this map.
FREDDIE: What do you want to see the Chinese bronzes for?
KAREN: I heard they were fantastic.
FREDDIE: They're dead as a doornail.
KAREN: That's all right, I like ancient cultures. *(Spills her purse)* Oh, no! I don't believe it! Why me? Why here? Why now? *(She stoops to pick up the debris)*
FREDDIE: *(Stooping to help her)* Let me help you.
KAREN: That's all right.
FREDDIE: My God, how do you fit all this stuff in there? [*(Gestures with tampon)*]
KAREN: *(A bit put off by this unexpected intimacy)* That's my little secret. I'm sorry to have bothered you.
FREDDIE: The bronzes are that way. *(Points)*
KAREN: Thanks.
FREDDIE: But I wouldn't bother with them if I were you.
KAREN: *(Cheerfully)* Well, you're not me. *(Starts to go)*
FREDDIE: There's only one painting in this museum as far as I'm concerned.
KAREN: *(Dropping her guard)* Which one is that?
FREDDIE: I'd tell you if I thought you were serious.
KAREN: Doesn't an interest in Chinese bronzes qualify me as serious?
FREDDIE: Chinese art is a sleeping pill to me. There's only one painting worth looking at in this museum.
KAREN: That one you were looking at before?
FREDDIE: No.
KAREN: What painting is it then?
FREDDIE: That one.
KAREN: That little tiny one? You're kidding!
FREDDIE: Look at it if you don't believe me.
KAREN: This had better be good. *(Looks at the little picture)*
FREDDIE: Well?
KAREN: *(Stares at the painting a long time)* How did he do that?

FREDDIE: You see how the layers of paint are applied to the canvas one on top of the other?

KAREN: Yes.

FREDDIE: Well, he did it without losing what was underneath. The underlayers still show through. That's what gives it that luminous quality.

KAREN: The brushwork is so controlled. He must have been very painstaking.

FREDDIE: Actually, that's a popular misconception about his work. He worked very quickly. He was almost slapdash in his work methods. Also, he didn't always use a brush. He sometimes pushed the paint around with his fingers.

KAREN: It all looks so precise, and yet, when you get closer, it all seems to break up into little blobs of paint.

FREDDIE: He was able to be spontaneous because he had a virtuoso technique.

KAREN: Well, I certainly agree that he did it as well as it can be done.

FREDDIE: No, I've made certain advances on his technique in my own work.

KAREN: That's modest of you!

FREDDIE: In all fairness to him, I've had some advantages. Being modern, I can select my own subject matter. In those days painters painted what they were told to by patrons. Of course, freedom is not always an advantage to an artist.

KAREN: No? I'd have thought it was.

FREDDIE: Sometimes I find myself wondering what to paint next. Our problems are more existential.

KAREN: Is there anywhere one can see your work?

FREDDIE: At my studio.

KAREN: Don't you have a gallery?

FREDDIE: No.

KAREN: Why is that?

FREDDIE: I can't tell if it's that they don't want me, or I don't want them.

KAREN: Maybe a little of both.

FREDDIE: Would you like to see my work?

KAREN: Sure.

FREDDIE: Then let's go to my studio.

KAREN: Not so loud.

FREDDIE: What's the matter? You'd think we were doing something to be ashamed of.

KAREN: It's not that. It's just that people might misunderstand.

FREDDIE: There'd be nothing new in that. Let's go.

KAREN: Oh, but the Chinese bronzes.

FREDDIE: Forget about the Chinese bronzes. They've been around for three thousand years. They can wait a little longer. Don't you think people should pay more attention to living artists?

KAREN: (Captivated) Yes, now that you mention it, I do.

FREDDIE: After all, he died penniless. (Indicates the tiny painting)

KAREN: No!

FREDDIE: No one paid any attention to him in his lifetime. He was totally misunderstood. They couldn't understand why he wouldn't go on doing it like it had always been done. When he did his greatest work, they thought he had lost his mind.

KAREN: It's so unfair. I want to look at your work. Let's go right now.

FREDDIE: It's only four stops on the subway.

KAREN: Let's take a cab.

FREDDIE: *(Putting his hands in his pockets)* I'm a little short of cash.

KAREN: Don't worry. I'll pay for it.

(They exit together.)

Scene 3: [*The office of Dr. Karen Gold.*]

[*(There is a knock at the door.)*]

KAREN: Come in.

ELEANOR: [*(Entering)*] I'm mixed up, Doctor Gold. I had to see you. Listen, Doctor, I'm seeing him tonight. Break the rules just this once and tell me how to behave.

KAREN: I don't have to tell you how to behave, Eleanor. Get in touch with your feelings. What is it you really want?

KAREN: Oh, Doctor, you embarrass me!

ELEANOR: Lie back. Put up your feet. Close your eyes. What are you feeling now?

ELEANOR: Doctor, it's my husband.

KAREN: Quarreling again?

ELEANOR: No. Sex problem.

KAREN: What sex problem?

ELEANOR: I fake orgasm.

KAREN: Why?

ELEANOR: It seems so important to him. It would hurt him if I told him I'm not getting anything out of it.

KAREN: Have you ever enjoyed it?

ELEANOR: No, never. I just lie there and stare at the ceiling. I look at my watch, twiddle my thumbs, knit behind his back.

KAREN: Doesn't he notice?

ELEANOR: No, he's so involved in what he's doing, he's like another person. I just make little noises, like "oo oo ah ah." He can't tell I'm bored.

KAREN: Why are you bored?

ELEANOR: Well, for one thing, we always have sex in bed. It makes me drowsy.

KAREN: But having sex in bed is a perfectly natural thing. Most couples make love in bed.

ELEANOR: Well, when *I* go to bed I want to sleep. Also, he turns out the light. I can't see him. He's very good-looking. But we always make love in the dark. I can't see what I'm doing!

KAREN: As a child, did you sleep with the light on?

ELEANOR: No. But when we're making love in the dark . . . this is silly, I know . . .

KAREN: Go on.

ELEANOR: I keep imagining he's someone else.

KAREN: Who?

ELEANOR: Just . . . not a movie star, or anything like that . . . But *(Thoughtfully and with difficulty)* usually it's someone I've seen on the street that day.

KAREN: Someone you fantasize having a relationship with?

ELEANOR: No . . . it's always someone different, and most of the time it isn't any one person . . . it's a composite of men I've seen on the street that day. Men completely outside my social sphere. Men of a different class. Men I would never meet. A thigh from one, a mop of hair from another, a bicep, or the way their pants fit in the seat. But it's never one man. It's a composite.

KAREN: Do you find that these recollections of fantasies increase your pleasure?

ELEANOR: Yes and no. The images are too fleeting to really warm up to them, but they distract me . . . but only when the light is off in the room.

KAREN: Have you told your husband that you'd like to make love with the light on?

ELEANOR: He can't. He won't. You see, he's just the opposite.

KAREN: Hmmmm. *(Writes something down)*

ELEANOR: What was that?

KAREN: What?

ELEANOR: What you wrote down just then.

KAREN: Why do you want to know?

ELEANOR: I want to know if it's about me.

KAREN: What difference does it make?

ELEANOR: Doctor, did you write down something about me?

KAREN: Yes, I sometimes take notes. It helps me to review the patient's case. It's hard to remember everything that's said.

ELEANOR: What did you write about me?

KAREN: I'd rather not tell you just now.

ELEANOR: Why?

KAREN: Why does it matter?

ELEANOR: What if someone reads it?

KAREN: No one is going to see this but me.

ELEANOR: What does it say, damn it!

KAREN: You're getting hostile.

ELEANOR: *(Angry)* I am not getting hostile. I just want to know what that damn note says.

KAREN: These are my own confidential notes for my own confidential files.

ELEANOR: *(Screaming)* Give me that goddamn note!

KAREN: Why is it so important, Eleanor?

ELEANOR: I want that note! I want that goddamn note!

KAREN: Why are you upsetting yourself?

ELEANOR: *(Raging through her tears)* Give me that note! Give it to me! Give it to me! *(KAREN calmly hands her the note)* "Pick up chopped liver." I don't get it.

KAREN: It was a note to myself, Eleanor.

ELEANOR: Chopped liver.

KAREN: You don't trust me completely yet, Eleanor.

ELEANOR: Chopped liver. What a relief! *(Laughs)*

KAREN: Let's try something.

ELEANOR: Okay.

KAREN: Lie back on the couch. Slip your shoes off. Make yourself comfortable.

ELEANOR: *(Lying back and relaxing completely)* Aaah!

KAREN: Have you ever tried making love in a different setting?

ELEANOR: Yes, we went to a nudist colony once to air our differences. *(Turning her head sharply back and forth in anguish)* Oh, Doctor, it's just no use! I dawdle, I daydream, I just can't get started. Every day I draw up a list of things to do, but I never get around to doing them. Something in me fights against doing whatever it is I know I should be doing.

KAREN: You're a procrastinator.

ELEANOR: Worse than that! I do impulsive, foolish things. Sometimes I go on spending sprees when I know I don't have enough money. I go into Bloomingdale's and charge everything I see. Often I buy things I don't even need. Like a lawn mower, when I know I live in an apartment. And sometimes I buy them in quantity. One time I bought a dozen egg slicers.

KAREN: Why did you buy a dozen of them?

ELEANOR: *(Carelessly)* One for each egg I suppose! How should I know? Anyway, I just can't settle down to any form of steady work. I hate doing the same thing over and over. I don't even like to sleep in the same place every night. I have a horror of repetition.

KAREN: That must make it very difficult to work.

ELEANOR: *(In a burst of temper)* Oh what do you know? Sitting there looking down your nose at me. What have you got to be so damn smug about, huh? You think you know everything. But you don't. You're stupid! You're the stupidest person I've ever met in my life! You think you have all the answers! Well you don't! You don't understand me. You don't even understand yourself! So wipe that self-satisfied grin off your face. Because you're ugly! I hate your ugly face! I hate your ugly face! *(ELEANOR shrieks this and then sobs and falls)*

KAREN: *(Catching her)* Careful!

ELEANOR: *(Sobbing on the doctor's bosom)* I hate your ugly face! I hate your ugly face! I hate your ugly face!

KAREN: Here's some Kleenex. *(ELEANOR blows her nose and sobs twice)* Do you often have regrettable bursts of temper like this, Eleanor?

ELEANOR: *(Sucking her thumb)* Yeth.

KAREN: Think back, Eleanor, to when you were a little girl. Think back to when you first began to procrastinate.

ELEANOR: It all began when I was eleven years old. My Angora cat got run over. I remember there was this blood all over everything. That morning I had my first period.

(The phone rings.)

KAREN: Excuse me. *(Crosses to the phone on the desk)* Hello? *(Changing her tone to one of intimacy)* Oh, *hello*. Oh, did he? He didn't! He did? Listen, I can't talk now, I'm in session. Tonight would be fine. I'm sorry. I'm sorry. Yes, I wish we could have gone together, but what can we do? Which one did you like best? Yes, that was my favorite, too. Six then. Good-bye. Good-bye. No, I said good-bye. Now hang up. You'll have to wait for that. *(Firmly)* Good-bye, naughty boy. Hang up. *(Giggles)* Good-bye, darling. *(Hangs up and returns to her place at the side of the couch as if nothing had happened)* Go on.

ELEANOR: *(Beginning again with difficulty)* I ran home to my parents to tell them what had happened. But I couldn't find them anywhere. I looked in every room in the house. Finally I went upstairs to their bedroom. The door was closed. And without thinking I was doing anything wrong I opened the door—

(The phone rings again.)

KAREN: *(Annoyed)* Oh, that phone. Excuse me. *(The phone rings again)* Hello. No, I don't think you have to wear a tie. But why don't you bring one along just in case. And I'd bring a jacket, too. It sometimes gets chilly near the water at night. Me too. Me too. Bye. *(Returns to* ELEANOR's *side as if nothing had happened)* You were saying?

ELEANOR: This is so personal.

KAREN: Eleanor, anything you tell me is in strict confidence. Nothing said here goes beyond these office walls.

ELEANOR: *(Frustrated, begins again)* I opened the door and saw my father lying naked on top of my mother. He was bouncing up and down on her. She was moaning. I thought he was hurting her. I screamed and started hitting him. They both jumped up and my mother started yelling and slapped me. She said that I must never come into their room again. I burst into tears. I wanted to run away and never come back. I wanted to—

(The phone rings again.)

KAREN: Go on, Eleanor.

(The phone rings again.)

ELEANOR: Aren't you going to answer the phone?

KAREN: Just let it ring. This is more important.

ELEANOR: Are you sure?

KAREN: It will stop.

(The phone continues to ring insistently.)

ELEANOR: I felt so alone. I felt that nobody loved me. I felt that everything was so unfair. I felt shut out. I felt . . .

(The phone just goes on ringing.)

KAREN: Go on.

ELEANOR: I felt . . . *(Phone)* I felt . . . *(Phone)* I felt . . . *(Phone)* It's no use. Answer the phone.

KAREN: Are you sure you want me to?

ELEANOR: Answer it!

KAREN: I'm sorry. *(Goes to phone)* Hello. Yes. When did this happen? Did he take his medication? You knew that. You were told. I told you. Well, what did you expect? He's trying. You should be more helpful. Let him do what he wants. He's a grown man. Well, stop treating him like a child. I said stop treating him like a child. Give him his medication. I said let him have his medicine. I don't care what the priest said. Give him his medicine now and I'll talk to him about it tomorrow. Good-bye.

ELEANOR: What was that?

KAREN: My God, you think you have problems? This patient of mine is really bananas. He is so totally fixated on his mother that she withholds his methadone when he doesn't do what she wants. *(Laughs)* Really, it's idiotic. He wanted to watch a ball game on TV, and she wanted to watch something else, so she wouldn't let him have his methadone, and he went into convulsions. It's no wonder the guy is completely impotent with women. The only woman he was ever able to come with was his sister, and *(Laughs again)* really, this will kill you, she's only twelve years old. The whole case is ludicrous and pathetic. One time, his mother caught him fooling around with the family dog! And he's thirty years old. Can you believe it? It's really sick. *(Laughs)* But, I guess it takes all kinds to make a world. But let's get back to you.

ELEANOR: Doctor, I'm bored with my marriage. My husband doesn't seem to take the same interest in me that he once did. He used to tremble when we made love. Now it's become completely mechanical.

KAREN: The honeymoon is over, Eleanor. All relationships evolve into something else. Hopefully, what was once based on superficial physical attraction will mature into a real friendship. That can be more important in the long run.

ELEANOR: Oh, we're friends all right. But we're not in love. I miss being in love, Doctor, I really do.

KAREN: Well, what is it *you* want to do?

ELEANOR: I want to have an adventure before I'm too old. It's nothing against my husband. It has nothing to do with him, really. It's just something that *I* want. Do you know what I mean?

KAREN: I know exactly what you mean. You have a right to fulfill yourself, Eleanor.

ELEANOR: Thank you, Doctor Gold. I needed some reassurance.

KAREN: Don't thank me, Eleanor. You're doing this for yourself.

ELEANOR: You know, Doctor, I've never thought of this before but . . . My God! I don't know why this never occurred to me before this moment! But I suddenly realize that—

KAREN: Time is up.

ELEANOR: Just let me tell you this realization I've just had.

KAREN: Time is up, Eleanor.

ELEANOR: But . . .

KAREN: It's four o'clock. I'm sorry.

ELEANOR: That's all right. It slipped my mind now. That's funny. It seemed like such a breakthrough a minute ago.

KAREN: We'll get to it next time. Do you have my check?

ELEANOR: Could I owe you for this week? I'm a little short of cash.

KAREN: I think it's better not to run up a bill, Eleanor.

ELEANOR: It's just for one week.

KAREN: Learning to spend money on things that are worthwhile and good for you is part of your therapy, Eleanor. Did you bring a check?

ELEANOR: Yes, but I thought you would trust . . .

KAREN: It's not a question of trust. I want you to get in the habit of doing good things for yourself. After all, this is for your benefit.

ELEANOR: Yes, Doctor. *(Hands KAREN check)*

KAREN: Why don't you try writing down your dreams and we can go over them next time.

ELEANOR: My dreams! Yes, that's a good idea.

KAREN: See you next week?

ELEANOR: See you next week. *(Exits)*

KAREN: *(Dials phone)* Hello, Lutèce? I'd like to reserve a table for two.

Scene 4: *An artist's garret.*

(A skylight. An easel. ELEANOR is posing draped but nude from the waist up. The phone rings.)

Black-Eyed Susan & Bill Vehr in
Reverse Psychology (Christopher Scott)

ELEANOR: *(Not breaking out of her pose)* Should I get that or will you?

FREDDIE: Don't move. I'll get it.

ELEANOR: All right, but make it quick.

FREDDIE: *(Picking up the receiver)* Hello. *(Hangs up quickly)* They hung up. *(Returns to the easel and continues to paint her)*

ELEANOR: That's been happening a lot lately. It happened this morning. And it happened twice yesterday. Do you think someone is planning to rob the studio?

FREDDIE: You're being paranoid.

ELEANOR: The worst thing about paranoia is that you're only proven well when the worst things you've imagined come true.

FREDDIE: Don't talk. I'm painting your mouth.

ELEANOR: *(Starts humming "Reverse Psychology")* Mmmmmmmmm.

FREDDIE: Eleanor, don't hum. It's distracting. *(ELEANOR sighs)* Just a little more. . . . There, why don't you take a break? Have a look.

ELEANOR: *(Looks at the outpouring of Freddie's soul with disappointment)* Oh Freddie
. . .

FREDDIE: What do you think?

ELEANOR: I think you're getting better. But it's hard to tell.

FREDDIE: What about the paint handling? I read in a review the other day that a painter had bravura paint handling. Don't you think that they should have said that about me?

ELEANOR: Paint handling?

FREDDIE: Bravura paint handling.

ELEANOR: I don't know. Your paintings look feminine to me.

FREDDIE: Feminine?

ELEANOR: You use such pretty colors. Like a lady's boudoir.

FREDDIE: It was you. You are a woman and so I paint you feminine.

ELEANOR: You paint everyone feminine. Remember the Italian delivery boy you got to pose for you? He was furious that he came out all pink and aqua. There was absolutely nothing recognizable in the painting! And yet you made him pose nude!

FREDDIE: My work is lost on such philistines. Rembrandt had the same problem.

(The phone rings.)

ELEANOR: *(Answering the phone)* Hello? Hello? Whoever it was hung up.

FREDDIE: *(Meaningfully)* That's strange.

ELEANOR: Yes, that is strange.

FREDDIE: Who do you think it was?

ELEANOR: Somebody who keeps calling but doesn't want to talk.

FREDDIE: Well, whoever it is doesn't want to talk to either of us.

ELEANOR: *(Changing the subject)* Back to work.

FREDDIE: Let's try another pose. A more difficult one this time.

ELEANOR: That last one was difficult enough.

FREDDIE: I need something more complex. I have it! Why don't I paint you in bondage?

ELEANOR: Bondage?

FREDDIE: I'll tie you up and blindfold you. And paint you like that.

ELEANOR: Sounds different . . . but I don't know. . . . It won't hurt, will it?

FREDDIE: No, I'll do it gently. Just think, you won't have to worry about holding still because you won't be able to move.

ELEANOR: *(Laughs)* I'm not sure I trust you. How do I know you'll untie me?

FREDDIE: Eleanor, if you can't trust me, who can you trust?

ELEANOR: I guess you're right. Go ahead.

FREDDIE: *(Ties her up in bandages and blindfolds her)* I think you should wear these earplugs too. *(Inserts earplugs)*

ELEANOR: Are the earplugs necessary?

FREDDIE: Yes dear, this will be a portrait of total sensory depri—

ELEANOR: *(Interrupting in a loud hard-of-hearing voice)* What?

FREDDIE: I said, this will be a case of—

ELEANOR: *(Interrupting)* I can't hear you.

FREDDIE: *(Removing the earplugs)* I said, this will be a portrait of total sensory deprivation.

ELEANOR: All right, but don't bother talking to me. I can't hear a word with those earplugs in.

FREDDIE: All right, no talking.

(FREDDIE *puts the earplugs back in her ears and ties a gag around her mouth. He appears at first to be going to his easel, but he passes this and goes to the door, which he opens quietly.*)

KAREN: *(Whispering through door)* I was afraid I'd gotten our signals crossed.

FREDDIE: *(Also whispering)* No, you got it right. Ring and hang up, ring and hang up.

KAREN: Where is she? Did you get rid of her?

FREDDIE: Look. *(Points to* ELEANOR*)*

KAREN: *(Horrified)* What have you done? Are you mad?

FREDDIE: She thinks she's posing for a painting. And really, there's no need to whisper because she can't hear a thing.

KAREN: *(A little louder)* Are you sure?

FREDDIE: Certainly. She's deaf as a bat.

KAREN: I just came by to give you this. *(She hands* FREDDIE *a check)*

FREDDIE: Karen, no!

KAREN: It's just to get some supplies: brushes, canvas, paint, whatever you need.

FREDDIE: Karen, I can't accept . . .

KAREN: Of course you can. You must. I don't want you wasting your gifts on mundane matters. You must create, darling, create.

ELEANOR: *(Mumbling through her gag)* Freddie? Freddie? How much longer?

FREDDIE: She's calling me. I must go now.

KAREN: We must stop meeting like this.

FREDDIE: I'm not afraid. Are you?

KAREN: Afraid? Yes, perhaps a little. I'm really more afraid for her. She might get hurt.

FREDDIE: Nonsense, she hasn't suspected anything yet.

KAREN: It's all right for me. I have my own world where I'm wanted and needed. I have a career. If I lost you, I wouldn't be desolate. I'd go away and come back glamorized by distance. And distance lends enchantment. She lives with you every day. She shares the chores. She'll bear your children.

FREDDIE: I hate children.

KAREN: I can only inspire your genius. It's a much smaller thing, but I must settle for it.

ELEANOR: *(Screaming through the gag)* FREDDIE!

KAREN: Now, you must go to her.

FREDDIE: Karen, this is a terrible thing to ask, I know, but I just don't know who else to turn to.

KAREN: Ask me anything, Freddie. If it's within my power I'll do it for you.

FREDDIE: Well, this isn't really for me. It's Eleanor. I want to take her to a fancy restaurant for our anniversary. But she doesn't have anything dressy to wear. . . .

KAREN: Say no more. I have dozens of things I never wear anymore. I'll send over a delivery boy with a box. I've been meaning to go through my things and weed out a few numbers.

FREDDIE: Thanks, Karen. You're a real pal.

KAREN: Anytime. Meet me for lunch tomorrow?

FREDDIE: Not tomorrow.

KAREN: The day after?

FREDDIE: I can't the day after.

KAREN: Friday, then? Don't tell me you have plans for Friday.

FREDDIE: Friday's fine for me. It's just that I must work.

KAREN: Of course. Of course. Work! Work! I'm going.

ELEANOR: *(Begins to protest loudly and insistently)* EEEEE!

FREDDIE: I could meet you when I'm through. Say in half an hour?

KAREN: At the Café des Artistes?

ELEANOR: EEEEE!

KAREN: *(Kisses him and whispers in his ear)* Work. Work. Work. Work. *(Exits backwards blowing kisses)*

(FREDDIE crosses to ELEANOR and is about to untie her when he remembers the blank canvas. He quickly smears some paint on it.)

FREDDIE: *(Untying her)* All finished.

ELEANOR: My God, that was a long time. You don't usually take so long with a painting.

FREDDIE: Have a look. *(ELEANOR crosses to look at the painting)* What do you think?

ELEANOR: Oh, Freddie, this is the best work you've ever done.

FREDDIE: *(Stunned, rushes back to look at the canvas)* It is?

ELEANOR: Yes, it has a freshness I've never seen in your work before.

FREDDIE: Just a little something I tossed off. I think I'll call it *Portrait of Eleanor.* Shall we do another?

ELEANOR: Could we knock off for the day? I'm a little sore.

FREDDIE: Why don't you take a hot bath, and I'll go out for a walk.

ELEANOR: Good idea. I think I will. *(Exit FREDDIE. ELEANOR dials phone)* Hello. It's me. What did you want? What do you mean you didn't call? I heard you signal. You rang and hung up, rang and hung up.

(Blackout.)

Scene 5: *The office of Dr. Leonard Silver.*

FREDDIE: Doctor, Doctor, my wife thinks she's a Volkswagen.

LEONARD: Well, why don't you tell her she's not a Volkswagen?

FREDDIE: And walk to work?

LEONARD: The last time I saw you you couldn't get the names of the different parts of your body straight. You thought your hand was a foot and your foot was a hand.

FREDDIE: Oh, I've got it all straight now, Doctor. This is my hand. *(Points to his hand)* And this is my foot. *(Points to his foot)*

LEONARD: Very good.

FREDDIE: I even know that this is my ankle and this is my knee and my heart is in the left side of my chest. *(Points to each of these)*

LEONARD: How did you remember all that, Freddie?

FREDDIE: It's all up here *(Points to his head)* in my ass.

LEONARD: Lie on the couch and I'll sit over here. Are you a bed wetter?

FREDDIE: Yes.

LEONARD: In that case you sit here and *I'll* lie on the couch.

FREDDIE: Doctor, I've had three wives and all of them died.

LEONARD: What did your first wife die of?

FREDDIE: Poisoned mushrooms.

LEONARD: What did your second wife die of?

FREDDIE: Poisoned mushrooms.

LEONARD: What did your third wife die of?

FREDDIE: Fractured skull.

LEONARD: Fractured skull?

FREDDIE: She wouldn't eat the poisoned mushrooms.

LEONARD: You're a loony. That's what you are! A real loony! With you everything is a joke.

FREDDIE: What's wrong with a little harmless humor?

LEONARD: A joke may conceal a subconscious hostility. There may be another meaning in your jokes.

FREDDIE: Do you really think so?

LEONARD: What do you think?

FREDDIE: The other day I came home and discovered my wife on the couch making love with another man.

LEONARD: What did you do?

FREDDIE: I got my revenge. I *destroyed* the couch.

LEONARD: Ha, ha, very good! But then, you are joking, aren't you?

FREDDIE: *(Unconvincingly)* Oh, yeah, sure, it's all a big joke.

LEONARD: I think that joke was a little belittling to your masculinity, Freddie.

FREDDIE: *(As if realizing everything for the first time)* Yes, it was!

LEONARD: Why do you do that, Freddie, when you know it's crazy?

FREDDIE: Why do I do it? Why do I do it? I'll try to stop doing it, Doc. I promise. No more jokes.

LEONARD: Atta boy, Freddie. You can appear to be as normal as the next one.

FREDDIE: But I'm not normal.

LEONARD: Nobody said you were.

FREDDIE: And I don't ever want to be normal.

LEONARD: *(Very kindly)* Nobody said you have to be normal. All you have to do is *act* normal. Now, lean back. Put up your feet. Take off your shoes.

FREDDIE: I don't want to take off my shoes.

LEONARD: Why not?

FREDDIE: There's a hole in my sock.

LEONARD: Come now, Freddie. You can trust me. I won't think less of you for it. Take off your shoes.

FREDDIE: *(Coyly)* No.

LEONARD: *(Coaxing)* Freddie, take off your shoes.

FREDDIE: *(Coyly)* No.

LEONARD: *(Coaxing, but firm)* Now, Freddie, you don't want people thinking you're a loony, do you?

FREDDIE: I don't care what people think! To hell with them!

LEONARD: Freddie, you're talking crazy. Take off your shoes.

FREDDIE: *(Petulantly)* No.

LEONARD: Take off those shoes!

FREDDIE: *(Angrily)* No!

LEONARD: You're as batty as a bedbug, that's what you are. You're a goddamn weirdo and everybody's going to know it and laugh about it behind your back.

FREDDIE: *(Terrified)* They will?

LEONARD: Yeah, they're going to snigger and whisper *(Whispers),* "See him? That's the loony! He hasn't got all of his marbles. He's crackers. He's off his rocker. He's ready for the funny farm."

FREDDIE: The dirty rats!

LEONARD: They're probably all against you anyway. So Freddie, be a good boy and don't give them an excuse. Let's have those shoes off and no arguments.

FREDDIE: *(Rational)* I'm sorry, Doctor Silver, but I really feel more comfortable with my shoes on.

LEONARD: *(Seizing him roughly and trying to pull his shoes off by force)* Get those goddamn shoes off you little bastard or I'll give you such a smack!

FREDDIE: *(Struggling with the doctor)* Let go!

LEONARD: *(Raising his voice threateningly)* Give me those shoes! *(Slaps* FREDDIE's *face and pulls the shoes off of him)* There. Now how do you feel?

FREDDIE: *(With a sigh of relief)* Thank you, Doctor. I feel much better now.

LEONARD: Now, wasn't that a big fuss for nothing? I don't even see a hole in your sock.

FREDDIE: Look closer.

LEONARD: *(Examining one of* FREDDIE's *feet and then the other)* Why, Freddie, your left sock is painted on!

FREDDIE: I couldn't find the other one, Doc.

LEONARD: *(Brightly)* Let's free associate.

FREDDIE: Shoot.

LEONARD: Inadequate.

FREDDIE: Unsatisfactory.

LEONARD: Weak.

FREDDIE: Puny.

LEONARD: Defective.

FREDDIE: Second-rate.

LEONARD: Inferior.

FREDDIE: Subnormal.

LEONARD: Pitiful.

FREDDIE: Paltry.

(The dialogue slowly begins to accelerate.)

LEONARD: Contemptible.

FREDDIE: Miserable.

LEONARD: Dwarfed.

FREDDIE: Diminutive.

LEONARD: Ordinary.

FREDDIE: Common.

LEONARD: Mediocre.

FREDDIE: Petty.

LEONARD: Trashy.

FREDDIE: Shoddy.

LEONARD: Bad.

FREDDIE: Less than good.

LEONARD: Cheap.

FREDDIE: Flimsy.

LEONARD: Trivial.

FREDDIE: Unimportant.

LEONARD: Trifling.

FREDDIE: Insipid.

LEONARD: Sleazy.

FREDDIE: Squalid.

LEONARD: Crummy.

FREDDIE: Junky.

LEONARD: Raunchy.

FREDDIE: Two-bit.

LEONARD: Corny.

FREDDIE: Cheesy.

LEONARD: Poor.

FREDDIE: Broke.

LEONARD: Down-and-out.

FREDDIE: In the pits.

LEONARD: Hard up.

FREDDIE: In the shits.

LEONARD: What are you feeling now, Freddie?

FREDDIE: I have so much more of a sense of myself. I feel stronger. Doctor, I have something to tell you. And up to now I've been afraid to tell you this. But now I think I can. Although I've been afraid that you would take it wrong.

LEONARD: Go ahead, Freddie. You can be open with me.

FREDDIE: Doctor, I've gotten a new psychiatrist. I'm leaving you.

LEONARD: You what?

FREDDIE: I've gotten a new psychiatrist. I'm leaving you.

LEONARD: How can you do this to me? Not after all we've been through together.

FREDDIE: I'm sorry, but I feel we've gone as far as we can go. I'm grateful to you for the years we've had together. But people change. Their needs change. Sometimes they grow apart. There are some things we have to leave behind.

LEONARD: Oh, so that's what I am, huh? Some *thing* you're going to leave behind! That's all I've meant to you.

FREDDIE: Now, Leonard, don't be upset.

LEONARD: Don't be upset! Don't be upset! You waste the best years of my life and you say don't be upset. Who is he? Some little Freudian you've been seeing on the sly?

FREDDIE: She's into Gestalt.

LEONARD: *(Exploding)* Ha! So it's a woman! You're leaving me for a woman. You'd better be careful there, Freddie. If you go to a woman psychiatrist people are going to think you're gay. I always suspected you were latent.

FREDDIE: I'm not worried about it.

LEONARD: *(Palsy-walsy)* Hey hey hey hey, Freddie! Freddieeee! Hey hey hey hey hey! Don't do anything rash. Let's try to work it out.

FREDDIE: My mind's made up.

LEONARD: *(Incensed)* You ingrate! You're sick. You know that, don't you? You're sick. Two weeks out of my care and you'll be completely out of control. Then don't come crying to me.

FREDDIE: I just don't feel I can make any more progress here.

LEONARD: *(Sweetly)* Freddie, I'm sorry. I didn't mean what I said. Please stay.

FREDDIE: I'd better be going. *(Puts on his shoes)*

LEONARD: Where are you going? To her?

FREDDIE: I have an appointment with her this afternoon.

LEONARD: How will I live if you leave me? You're reducing my income substantially with this nonsense. You know that.

FREDDIE: You have other patients.

LEONARD: (*On bended knee*) None of them mean anything to me but you. I'll get rid of all my other patients if you stay.

FREDDIE: I wouldn't want you to do that.

LEONARD: (*Rising in indignation*) Oh, go and see if I care. And good riddance!

FREDDIE: I'm going.

LEONARD: (*Running to the window*) I'll kill myself!

FREDDIE: No you won't.

LEONARD: (*Suddenly regaining his composure*) You're right. I won't. (*Nervous tic*) Forgive me. (*Tic*) I lost my head. (*Tic*)

FREDDIE: Are you all right?

LEONARD: Yes. (*Tic*) I feel better now. (*Tic*)

FREDDIE: You'll get over it.

LEONARD: (*Calmly and in a very pleasant voice*) Freddie, before you go, I want to tell you something.

FREDDIE: I'm a little late.

LEONARD: Come here, Freddie. Let me tell you this. It's important.

FREDDIE: Go ahead.

LEONARD: Come here first. I want to whisper it.

FREDDIE: Oh, all right. (*Crosses to doctor*)

LEONARD: (*Whispers in* FREDDIE's *ear*) It's just this. (*Loudly*) I hate you and I hope you die!

FREDDIE: Good-bye.

LEONARD: (*Holds onto* FREDDIE's *leg and gets dragged across the floor*) I didn't mean it! Forgive me! Forgive me!

FREDDIE: There's nothing to forgive. Now let go of my leg.

LEONARD: (*Under control*) Very well. As you wish. Do you have my check?

FREDDIE: (*Hands him a check*) I almost forgot.

LEONARD: Huh!

FREDDIE: Good-bye. (*Exits*)

(DR. SILVER *smashes everything in the office. Blackout.*)

Scene 6: *The Manhattan apartment of Dr. Silver and Dr. Gold.*

(*Leonard tiptoes in, starts to undo his tie, but hears* KAREN *and pretends to be tying it.*)

KAREN: My, you're up early this morning.

LEONARD: Scratch my back. (KAREN *does so*) Lower. Lower. Over. Not that far. Back. Back. Up. Lower. Lower. Up a little.

KAREN: How's that?

LEONARD: It went away.

KAREN: It went away because I scratched it.

LEONARD: No, it went away before you found it. Has the paper arrived yet?

(*A thud at the door.*)

KAREN: There it is now. So, what time did you get in last night?

LEONARD: I don't remember. Four? Yes, I guess it was about four.

KAREN: Were you drinking?

LEONARD: Yes.

KAREN: Where were you drinking?

LEONARD: P.J.'s.

KAREN: P.J.'s closes at two. Where were you the other two hours?

LEONARD: What is this? The third degree?

KAREN: I was just curious.

LEONARD: What did you do?

KAREN: There was nothing on television so I went to bed and read for a while. I didn't hear you come in.

LEONARD: I didn't want to disturb you so I slept in the study.

KAREN: Mmmmmm. So what happened after P.J.'s closed?

LEONARD: Oh, I walked around for a while, stopped for a cup of coffee, and watched the sun rise down by the Hudson River.

KAREN: *(Checking the paper)* The sun rose this morning at exactly five twenty-three, and it rose over the East River, so you couldn't have been in by four. You couldn't have been in at six. Leonard, did you just get in?

LEONARD: Karen, I told you . . .

KAREN: *(Crossing right and looking off)* The cot in the study obviously hasn't been slept in. Your story doesn't hold water.

LEONARD: Please don't look at me like that. It reminds me of your mother. And you know how I *love* your mother.

KAREN: Leave my mother out of this. And don't be sarcastic.

LEONARD: In fact I think you're turning into just as big a bitch as your mother.

KAREN: You seem to forget everything she's done for you.

LEONARD: Don't throw that up again!

KAREN: Well she did set you up in private practice. You'd still be strapping drug burnouts to their bedpans at Bellevue if it weren't for her. You'd still be a straightjacket man.

LEONARD: They're not using straightjackets anymore. They're using chemical restraint. And you'd know that if you'd read the professional journals instead of *Redbook*!

KAREN: You're just jealous because they published my short story and rejected yours.

LEONARD: It's easier for a woman to get published today. They all want woman authors. It used to be blacks. Next it will be gays. It's hopeless for a white Anglo-Saxon Protestant male. We're just effete and genetically debilitated. An oppressed majority. The pallid afterglow to the sunset of Western civilization. All there is left for us now is jogging.

KAREN: You'll get no sympathy from me. It might do you good to be passive for a while. Let's take turns.

LEONARD: There, you're doing it again!

KAREN: What?

LEONARD: You're looking like your mother again.

KAREN: Oooo! You fight dirty.

LEONARD: I'm sorry, Karen. But I can't control it. I've never liked your mother and when you look like her I become enraged. It seems you've begun to look more and more like her as you've gotten older.

KAREN: I changed my hair color, lost weight, what more do you want me to do? I think this is terribly unfair and insensitive. I wouldn't say these things to you.

LEONARD: You don't understand. But how could you? I was adopted. I've never looked anything like my parents.

KAREN: Well, what more can I do? I'll try anything. You tell me.

LEONARD: What about a face-lift? A little nip and tuck here and there.

KAREN: A face-lift? Why don't *you* get a face-lift?

LEONARD: They hide the scars under the hairline. I'm bald. Where would they hide the scars?

KAREN: Face-lifts aren't something you just do. It's a serious decision. Surgery is painful, you know, and dangerous. Oh please be careful, dear, you're getting crumbs on the tablecloth.

LEONARD: Your mother was compulsively neat.

KAREN: I am not compulsively neat. I feel more inspired in an uncluttered, airy room. When everything is in its place and the room is immaculate I get a feeling of inner peace.

LEONARD: It's role-playing. Housewife.

KAREN: It is not. It's taste. It's a taste for order.

LEONARD: Then why do you insist on doing the housework yourself? Why don't you hire a maid. We can afford it.

KAREN: I've told you before I don't want a stranger in our house.

LEONARD: She wouldn't be a stranger forever. You'd come to know her. You'd get to know her after a while. You'd come to trust her in time.

KAREN: Her? Why her? Why does the maid necessarily have to be female?

LEONARD: Or a houseboy. Do you want a houseboy?

KAREN: No! That would be worse. I like it the way it is . . . just the two of us here, living alone together. That's the way it's always been. Just us.

LEONARD: And never anyone more?

KAREN: Leonard, I've told you. When I'm ready. There will be plenty of time for that.

LEONARD: Maybe we should adopt.

KAREN: No, Leonard, it's not that I'm afraid of the pain or anything like that . . . it's just that . . .

LEONARD: *(Very sympathetically)* Go on. What is it?

KAREN: Please, don't be hurt, but . . .

LEONARD: Tell me darling. I'll understand.

KAREN: It's just that genetically . . . Well having a child is a big decision. And I think you must be very careful that the genes are of the highest quality. I think the sire should be a magnificent physical specimen.

LEONARD: What are you saying?

KAREN: Well, I've read about this clinic where you can be artificially inseminated by a name donor. Many celebrities, athletes, geniuses, Nobel Prize winners, and male models are donating their sperm to the sperm bank. I want to get some of the sperm of an Olympic athlete. And try to give birth to a perfect child.

LEONARD: That's Fascism.

KAREN: Anything idealistic you call Fascism.

LEONARD: What do you expect? The Fascists gave Idealism a bad name. I want to be the father of our child.

KAREN: You would be, legally.

LEONARD: But not biologically.

KAREN: That shouldn't make any difference to a man. Your role in procreation is a minor one.

LEONARD: Minor!!?¡)(+ =¿.

KAREN: Oh, I know it seems important to you. But objectively it just isn't. In fact you're not even necessary anymore.

LEONARD: Well, I liked it better the old way.

KAREN: Well, as a concession to pleasure and your need for role-playing, we'll have intercourse the night I insert the Olympic athlete sperm into myself. But you must wear a contraceptive.

LEONARD: (Sarcastically) Great! Why don't you wear a coil?

KAREN: I can't. Every time I cross my legs the garage door opens. But we must be careful because if the contraceptive were to break we might get the sperm mixed up.

LEONARD: I have to be careful! I like that!

KAREN: We might produce a mongrel.

LEONARD: Only one sperm fertilizes the egg. It would be either him or me.

KAREN: Man is the only animal bred haphazardly. We think less of ourselves than we do of capons.

LEONARD: Capons are castrated.

KAREN: No, I think they're given female hormones.

LEONARD: Oh, yes, I remember reading in a medical journal about young men who sprouted breasts from eating too many capons.

KAREN: Perhaps all the now obsolete males should be fed capons and turned into worker females.

LEONARD: You're talking about human beings, not ants. This talk is all plainly the result of penis envy. You feel like incomplete males hemorrhaging once a month.

KAREN: You degrade our sexuality forgetting that it is the fountain of life and you are a useless drone.

LEONARD: There, you're doing it again.

KAREN: What?

LEONARD: You're looking like your mother again. I can't stand it.

KAREN: Look at us. We're fighting again.

LEONARD: Why do we do it?

KAREN: Let's not do it anymore, darling.

LEONARD: I'm sorry for what I said before.

KAREN: It wasn't fair of me.

LEONARD: How unfair?

KAREN: I had an unfair advantage. I was right.

(They laugh.)

LEONARD: You're a witch. But I love you.

KAREN: Finish your breakfast.

LEONARD: Damn, my eggs have gotten cold.

KAREN: I'll make others. (Turns to go)

LEONARD: Don't bother. (Catching her arm and stopping her) Karen, everything is all right between us, isn't it?

KAREN: Why don't we cancel all our appointments and spend the day together? Just the two of us.

LEONARD: What would we do?

KAREN: Oh, I don't care. We could walk in the park, go to the zoo, feed the ducks.

LEONARD: Karen, I have a lot of work to do today. I just can't. I have my prize neurotic today. As a matter of fact I'm late now. He's probably waiting for me right now.

KAREN: *(Ardently, seriously, as if it were the most important thing in the world to her)* Call and cancel. It seems that all we do is think about the patients. We never have time for each other anymore. Please, Leonard, I'm asking you. I'm begging you. Let's go for a walk together.

LEONARD: Why?

KAREN: For no reason at all.

LEONARD: I can't.

KAREN: Why are you shutting me out like this?

LEONARD: Karen, Karen. Remember when you were a little girl, how you used to hate your piano lessons?

KAREN: *(Very shaken)* Don't. Go to your patient.

LEONARD: That's my girl.

KAREN: Leonard. I've decided. I'm going to have that face-lift. But I'll have to go away for several months while the scars heal. I don't want you to look at me until the scars heal. I don't even want you to know where I'm staying. In case you get tempted and want to peek.

LEONARD: I'm sorry for what I said before. I didn't mean it. . . .

KAREN: You did. And I see now that there is only one solution. I'm going to go under the knife. For you.

ACT II

Scene 1: *Calypso Beach Resort Boatel.*

(KAREN is lying on a beach chair in a bathing suit, sunning herself. [On the radio we hear "Reverse Psychology" sung.] FREDDIE enters from the pool, wet.)

KAREN: Would you mix me another drink, Freddie? What's the matter? Is something troubling you? You look so sad.

FREDDIE: I'm not sad. I'm thinking.

KAREN: Don't do that darling. It deforms the face.

FREDDIE: Why do people always say I look sad when I'm thinking? Is it a crime to think? What am I supposed to do? Walk around with a big smile on all the time?

KAREN: Watch what you're pouring! I'd like a little tonic in my gin.

FREDDIE: I'm sorry. I didn't mean to snap at you. I'm restless, that's all.

KAREN: Why can't you just relax and enjoy our little vacation?

FREDDIE: It's your vacation. I work every day. I don't take vacations.

KAREN: Have you been drawing? Let me see.

FREDDIE: *(Opens pad, looks at drawing, then tears it up and throws it on the ground)* Hideous.

KAREN: *(Trying to stop him, she dives after the pieces)* No! Don't destroy it!

FREDDIE: Who cares? It's nothing but mediocrity.

KAREN: Let me see. *(She pieces the picture together again)* Why, it's that man who was at the pool last night! When did you draw him naked?

FREDDIE: This morning. He didn't know I was drawing him.

KAREN: He must have. He displayed himself to such *advantage*. It's funny. We saw him in the bar last night and I thought he was a woman at first. Then I wasn't sure if he was a man or a woman.

FREDDIE: I knew.

KAREN: I thought it was either a very masculine woman or a very feminine man. How could you tell?

FREDDIE: Big head. Big hands.

KAREN: Of course. This drawing certainly establishes beyond a shadow of a doubt that it was a man!

FREDDIE: Who cares? It's a bore.

KAREN: Why are you bored?

FREDDIE: Everything is so boring.

KAREN: Why don't you just relax and enjoy yourself?

FREDDIE: I can't. I don't feel right about your paying for everything.

KAREN: I thought we settled that. I'm rich. You're not. Who cares whose money it is? Let's enjoy it. Someday you'll sell your work and you can take me on a vacation.

FREDDIE: My work will never sell.

KAREN: Why not?

FREDDIE: (Contemptuously) Because people don't want to see the truth. They want pretty pictures. Well, they can get someone else to paint their pretty pictures for them! Because I won't! Oh, sometimes I wonder why I don't just give up the struggle. I may as well just go and get a job.

KAREN: Freddie! I won't have you talking that way. These are wild, rash words. You're just trying to worry me.

FREDDIE: I'm sorry.

KAREN: Now look at this picture you just tore up. It's very nice.

FREDDIE: Very nice! That describes it all right. Very nice.

KAREN: The pictures of yours I like best are the ones where you can tell what it's a picture of.

FREDDIE: Ugh. And two months' rent due on my studio.

KAREN: I'll pay it.

FREDDIE: (Exploding) No!

KAREN: Why not?

FREDDIE: You've done too much for me already. You bought me that sports jacket, paid the rent on the studio, and you got me a gallery.

KAREN: Darling, it was the least I could do. Boris and I have been friends for years, and he adored your paintings.

FREDDIE: And then there were all those dinners. I can't go on taking and taking.

KAREN: Well, if you're going to be proud about it, why don't you do a portrait of me for my office and I'll pay you for it.

FREDDIE: No, you'd be insulted. It always happens. When people commission a portrait they always want to be flattered.

KAREN: You do it any way you want. Don't flatter me. I hope I'm not so bad-looking that I have to worry about having my portrait done!

FREDDIE: You're beautiful.

KAREN: Then that's settled. When do we start?

FREDDIE: Right now if you want to.

KAREN: What do I have to do?

FREDDIE: You don't have to do a thing. Just don't move. I'll do a few quick practice sketches first. *(Draws a bit, tears out a page, draws a bit, tears out a page, draws a bit, tears out a page)* Turn your head this way a little. Good. Are you comfortable?

KAREN: Oh, perfectly!

FREDDIE: Now don't move.

*(*LEONARD *and* ELEANOR *enter from the other side.)*

LEONARD: *(In medias res)* And it has a pool, too.

ELEANOR: Calypso Beach Resort Boatel!

LEONARD: In there is a cocktail lounge with piano bar. There's a funny little old lady who plays requests.

ELEANOR: I love it. But do you think it's safe?

LEONARD: They assured me that there would only be one other couple here this weekend. We're lucky it's off-season. In another two weeks this place will be mobbed.

ELEANOR: Maybe we can go skinny-dipping at night.

LEONARD: I don't know.

ELEANOR: You said there was practically no one here.

LEONARD: I know, but I'd prefer not to.

ELEANOR: Don't tell me you're shy. You've got nothing to be ashamed of.

LEONARD: It's not that.

ELEANOR: What then?

LEONARD: I can't swim.

ELEANOR: Really? I'll teach you.

LEONARD: No, I'm afraid of the water.

ELEANOR: A psychiatrist with a phobia? Shame on you.

LEONARD: Nobody's perfect.

ELEANOR: I'll help you get over it.

LEONARD: It's no use.

ELEANOR: Why?

LEONARD: When I was a kid my older brothers threw me in sink or swim. I sank. I almost drowned. Somebody passing by pulled me out.

ELEANOR: That's no way to teach a person to swim! You have to relax.

LEONARD: I could never relax in the water.

ELEANOR: What about in the bathtub? Are you phobic about taking baths, too?

LEONARD: As a matter of fact I always take showers.

ELEANOR: That's fascinating.

(On the other side of the stage.)

KAREN: How much longer will this take?

FREDDIE: Not long, why?

KAREN: I'm getting a stiff neck.

FREDDIE: Just a bit more shading . . . there! Why don't we take a break?

KAREN: I'd like to go upstairs and change for dinner. Why don't you go in, have a drink at the bar, and await the gilded transformation?

FREDDIE: Okay. But I don't want to get too far ahead of you.

KAREN: Don't worry, I'll catch up. I'll drink doubles.

FREDDIE: Don't be too long.

KAREN: *(Exiting)* I promise to be worth waiting for.

(FREDDIE *arranges his drawing things neatly on the table and goes into the bar. Other side of the stage again.*)

ELEANOR: Oh look! Those people left the table with the umbrella. Let's sit down over there.

LEONARD: Good idea. I don't like being so close to the pool. Why don't you lie in the sun. I'll take the bags to the room.

ELEANOR: O.K.

(LEONARD *exits.* ELEANOR *sits in the chaise. Eleanor's dream.*)

FREDDIE: [*(Enters in graduation cap and gown with ticking metronome)*] Isn't there anything you can do to help my wife, Doctor?

KAREN: [*(In medical whites with stethoscope. She could have a bird's head)*] I'm afraid we'll have to give her shock treatments.

FREDDIE: Shock treatments? Isn't that rather . . . I mean, isn't there any other way?

KAREN: Yes, of course. If we had a lot of time and money. We don't really have much time.

FREDDIE: And if there's one thing we don't have it's money. . . . But shock treatments!

KAREN: Sometimes it's the fastest way to establish contact.

(*They prepare* ELEANOR *for shock treatments. They strap her to the reclining chair and attach electrodes to her head.*)

ELEANOR: *(Greatly agitated)* I'm not guilty. I'm not guilty! I should call a lawyer. I should call a lawyer right away!

KAREN: *(Soothingly)* Lie back. Relax. Take off your shoes.

ELEANOR: Who are you? I don't know you! What do you want with me? What did I do to you?

KAREN: Think back, Eleanor. To when you were a little girl. Think back to when you first began to procrastinate. Just make your mind a blank.

ELEANOR: I used to want a blank mind. But I didn't know how. Now I know what a blank mind is. I get up in the morning and before I know it it's time to go to bed. And I can't remember what happens in between.

KAREN: Relax. *(Gives her a jolt of electricity)*

ELEANOR: *(Screams with pain)* I can't remember what day it is. I can't remember my name. I can't. I can't.

(KAREN *gives her another jolt.* LEONARD *enters and goes to* ELEANOR.)

LEONARD: *(Prying her eyes open)* No judgment or response.

KAREN: Give her another shock.

LEONARD: I think you've given this patient too much shock already, Doctor. I think shock is the worst thing you could have used in this patient's case.

KAREN: And what would you have done, Doctor? This patient's case resisted contact.

LEONARD: You should have tried love and understanding.

KAREN: There are too many patients and too few doctors. There isn't time to love and understand every patient. I see no reason to make an exception in this patient's case.

LEONARD: Every case is different.

KAREN: You can't treat every patient as though she were exceptional.

LEONARD: Ah, but Doctor, how else are we to help people get well but by treating every patient as though she were exceptional. *(Unties* ELEANOR's *bonds)*

ELEANOR: Why do you want to help me?

*(*KAREN *and* FREDDIE *gradually back out through opposite doors.)*

LEONARD: Where is your husband?

ELEANOR: Husband? I haven't got a husband.

LEONARD: No? I thought you had. I thought you were married.

ELEANOR: I am.

LEONARD: Do you know me?

ELEANOR: Of course I know you.

LEONARD: Are you sure?

ELEANOR: Of course I'm sure.

LEONARD: Would you mind telling me anyway?

ELEANOR: You're the keeper.

LEONARD: Keeper?

ELEANOR: Of this zoo.

LEONARD: Zoo? How did you come here, to the zoo?

ELEANOR: You're trying to trap me. You're really a warden.

LEONARD: Warden? Eleanor!!!

ELEANOR: Of this prison. Let me go! Take your hands off me. Let me go! Let me go!

LEONARD: *(Shaking* ELEANOR *awake)* Eleanor, Eleanor. You were dreaming. Wake up.

ELEANOR: Dreaming? I've got to write it down. My doctor told me to write down all my dreams. I've got to get a pencil. Do you have a pencil?

LEONARD: No.

ELEANOR: I've got to write it down before I forget it. There's paper and pencils over here. *(Writes feverishly, then)* Want to read it?

LEONARD: Sure, if you don't mind. *(Takes the paper and reads. Then turns over the sheet and exclaims, startled)* Incredible!

ELEANOR: What?

LEONARD: This drawing.

ELEANOR: What drawing?

LEONARD: There's a drawing on the other side of your dream.

ELEANOR: *(Indifferent)* Is there?

LEONARD: Yes. *(Pause)* Amazing.

ELEANOR: What's amazing?

LEONARD: Er . . . ah . . . It's superbly done. Want to see it?

ELEANOR: No. I hate art.

LEONARD: Oh you do not!

ELEANOR: Oh yes I do! My husband is an artist. That's all I hear all day long. Art! Art! Art! It's enough to make you sick.

LEONARD: Still this is extraordinary.

ELEANOR: Oh, what's so extraordinary about it?

LEONARD: Why don't you have a look at it. I'd be curious to know what you think. *(Holds the picture in front of her eyes)*

ELEANOR: *(Closing her eyes)* I don't want to look at any more art!

LEONARD: Just peek.

ELEANOR: *(Opening one eye and then shutting it quickly)* A frump.

LEONARD: How could you say that?

ELEANOR: That's what I see. A drawing of a frumpy matron.

LEONARD: *(Indignant)* That's not what I see. I see a handsome woman of a certain age with great character. I see honesty. I see intelligence.

ELEANOR: God, if you like her that much you should search until you find her. Why don't you marry her if you think she's so great?

LEONARD: As a matter of fact that's what first struck me about the drawing. It bears a strong resemblance to my wife.

ELEANOR: *(Sits bolt upright and seizes the drawing and starts examining it very carefully)* Oh you poor darling. Is that what you're married to? Oh poor darling. *(Strokes him and kisses him sincerely, not in sarcasm)* Poor poor darling.

LEONARD: *(Snatches up the drawing defensively)* What's wrong with her?

ELEANOR: I didn't mean to say anything against her. How could I? I don't even know the woman. *(Looking over his shoulder at the drawing)* It's just that she's a mess.

LEONARD: A mess? What do you mean, a mess?

ELEANOR: Well for one thing her hair is so stiff it makes her look hard. And then there are those awful earrings. And I don't know, her eyes look mean or crossed or something. . . .

LEONARD: Well, my wife's eyes aren't crossed.

ELEANOR: I didn't say they were! I was talking about this drawing. That's funny, they don't look crossed to me now. *(Brushes drawing gently with her fingertips)* It looks like some sort of insect.

LEONARD: Now you're going too far. My wife does not look like an insect!

ELEANOR: I mean the crossed eye. It was some sort of bug crawling on the paper. Anyway it's a terrible drawing.

LEONARD: I suppose your husband can do better?

ELEANOR: If only he could do this well. If he could draw like this we wouldn't be starving.

LEONARD: What's wrong with his drawings?

ELEANOR: Oh they're not bad if you like a blob over here and a couple of yellow squiggles and red schmears on a blue background.

LEONARD: Abstract?

ELEANOR: Totally.

LEONARD: I prefer the abstract. It leaves more to the imagination.

ELEANOR: I don't have any imagination. I don't want to imagine. I want everything and I want it right now. I want to live. I want to live!

LEONARD: When I look at an abstract painting it can be anything I want it to be.

ELEANOR: Not my husband's paintings. They are most specifically what they are. Whatever they are.

LEONARD: I'd like to buy this drawing and give it to my wife. She wouldn't believe how much it looks like her. That is, if he doesn't want more than four or five thousand old new guineas for it. I'll bet it was done by a native artist.

ELEANOR: She probably won't agree. Women like to think of themselves as originals. This is a drawing of another woman.

(Enter FREDDIE.)

FREDDIE: Please be careful with my drawing. You might get fingerprints on it. Eleanor!

LEONARD: You two know each other?

ELEANOR: Yes, of course, how stupid of me. This is Freddie, a very good friend of mine. Freddie, this is Leonard. Leonard, Freddie.

FREDDIE: Leonard!

LEONARD: Freddie!

ELEANOR: Freddie and I were friends at school.

LEONARD: We've met.

FREDDIE: Yes, we've met.

ELEANOR: You two know each other? Well, it looks like we're all friends. *(Laughs nervously)* How do you two know each other?

FREDDIE: We met at the YMCA. Didn't we, *Leonard.*

LEONARD: Yes, we used to work out together. We enjoyed the usual male camaraderie . . . the give-and-take in the showers. We all pulled together down at the YMCA.

(Long pause in which no one can think of anything to say.)

ELEANOR: Yes, Freddie and I are good chums too.

FREDDIE: Chums!?

ELEANOR: Yes, we're real buddies. Freddie is like a brother to me. And I'm like a sister to him. We help each other out of many tight situations, don't we Freddie? *(Puts hands around his throat in a mock-strangling gesture)*

FREDDIE: I guess so.

ELEANOR: Freddie and I have our little secrets.

FREDDIE: You can say that again.

ELEANOR: *(Tightening her grip on his throat)* But we know when to keep our mouths shut. Discretion is the greater part of valor. Don't you think so, Freddie?

FREDDIE: Eleanor, I want to know . . . you're strangling me!

ELEANOR: *(Laughing)* Freddie, sit right down and tell me everything that's happened since we last saw each other. Was it the fourth or fifth grade? *(Talking very fast)* Freddie spent five years in fourth grade or was it four years in fifth. . . . Leonard, get us some drinks. What will you have, Freddie?

FREDDIE: I'll have a zombie.

ELEANOR: Leonard, be a dear, get three zombies. *(*LEONARD *walks out like a zombie.* ELEANOR *and* FREDDIE *look dazed too)* Freddie, what are you doing here?

FREDDIE: What am I doing here? What are you doing here? And what are you doing here with Leonard? How long have you been seeing him?

ELEANOR: I've been seeing him for years. He's my psychiatrist.

FREDDIE: Your psychiatrist? I thought you were seeing a woman psychiatrist.

ELEANOR: I was. But she turned out to be a lesbian. She wouldn't keep her hands to herself. I felt safer with a man.

FREDDIE: I'm going to punch him in the nose.

ELEANOR: Freddie listen, you've really hit it this time. You've found your style. He wants to buy this drawing. He'll pay up to four or five thousand old new guineas for it.

FREDDIE: That's only sixteen dollars in American money.

ELEANOR: He's an art collector.

FREDDIE: I've never seen him with any art.

ELEANOR: Don't be silly. He wouldn't keep his art collection at the YMCA, would he?

FREDDIE: No.

ELEANOR: He wants to buy this picture. He told me so.

FREDDIE: Well he can't have it. I promised it to someone else.

ELEANOR: Ah here's Leonard with the zombies. *(Aside)* Freddie, don't queer it. Leonard, I was just telling Freddie that you're interested in his drawing.

LEONARD: Why, yes, as a matter of fact I'd like to buy it. Especially now that I know you drew it.

FREDDIE: What difference does that make?

LEONARD: Knowing the artist is always more interesting.

ELEANOR: How much can you two know each other?

LEONARD: You'd be surprised.

ELEANOR: Ooh la la! What's been going on down at that YMCA? Boy talk?

FREDDIE: Yeah that's it. Boy talk.

ELEANOR: I often wonder what you boys talk about. In the locker room. It's dirty, I hope.

LEONARD: It's mostly about cars and baseball scores.

ELEANOR: How dull.

FREDDIE: Not necessarily. "I need a lube job, gotta take it to a grease monkey."

(ELEANOR laughs mischievously.)

LEONARD: *(Slyly)* "They told me at the body shop my chassis needs an overhaul."

ELEANOR: Does anyone go in for "drag racing"?

FREDDIE: Naw, most of the guys are into foreign models and you rarely see a convertible anymore.

ELEANOR: *(Pours her drink into the potted palm)* Leonard, get more zombies.

LEONARD: But I've hardly started this one.

ELEANOR: Well, drink up! Drink up! *(Pours the zombie down LEONARD's throat)* There now. Get us another round.

(LEONARD, choking and gasping, exits to the bar.)

FREDDIE: I have a right to know what my wife is doing in a resort hotel with another man.

ELEANOR: I'm trying to help your career, idiot. That man has a lot of money. There are two months' rent due on the studio. Do you want us thrown out into the street?

FREDDIE: If you would only take that super's job we wouldn't have to pay rent.

ELEANOR: Sweep the halls and stairs of a seven-story building every day while you sit in a studio with a nude model and smear blobs of pretty colors on expensive French paper? Go to hell!

LEONARD: *(Reenters)* I'm out of cash. I'll have to go up to my room.

FREDDIE: Don't bother. I'll get this round. *(Exits to bar)*

ELEANOR: Isn't Freddie sweet?

LEONARD: What were you two talking about when I came out? I heard you say, "Don't queer it."

ELEANOR: Oh, Freddie's gay. I was giving him some advice on his love life.

LEONARD: I thought we'd be alone here. That's why I wanted to come during the week and avoid the weekend crowd.

ELEANOR: It's not a crowd. It's just Freddie.

LEONARD: It's bad enough we're not alone. But it had to be someone we both know. This is too much.

ELEANOR: It's just a coincidence.

LEONARD: It's horrible.

ELEANOR: I think it's wonderful that you're going to buy Freddie's drawing. Artists have such a hard life. They're totally dependent on patronage and it's so hard to find anyone who likes arts.

LEONARD: Lots of people *love* art.

ELEANOR: Everyone *says* they do. But I don't believe it. Getting them to pay for it—that's the real test. They all think art should be free.

LEONARD: No one should be deprived of cultural experiences due to inadequate income.

ELEANOR: Tell it to the corner grocer. They all think art should be free. That everyone has a right to it. But just try and get a free slice of liverwurst out of him! Shouldn't everyone have the right to food, too? Oh you will buy Freddie's picture, won't you?

LEONARD: Maybe I will and maybe I won't.

ELEANOR: Well, make up your mind. I hate people who are wishy-washy and indecisive, don't you?

LEONARD: I do and I don't.

FREDDIE: *(Reentering with the zombies)* Gee, you two look upset. I hope I'm not interrupting anything.

LEONARD: As a matter of fact . . .

ELEANOR: Not a thing!

LEONARD: What do you mean not a thing? The fact is that Eleanor and I are . . .

ELEANOR: Leonard means that we're here in a professional capacity.

FREDDIE: Baloney! You two can't fool me! You're having an affair. "Get over your guilt" . . . "Express your true feelings" . . . "Don't worry about who you'd hurt because if the shoe was on the other foot . . ." Eh, Leonard?

ELEANOR: Freddie, Leonard and I are just good friends. . . .

LEONARD: *(Exploding)* We are not!

ELEANOR: Not friends?

FREDDIE: Not good friends?

LEONARD: Not *just* good friends!

ELEANOR: *(Trying to cover up)* We're very good friends!

FREDDIE: *Very* good friends? How good is it, this friendship?

ELEANOR: Freddie, don't jump to conclusions.

LEONARD: Oh, go ahead and jump, Freddie! Jump! Jump!

FREDDIE: *(To* LEONARD*)* You know if you've been fooling around with Eleanor I'm going to beat the shit out of her.

LEONARD: You don't frighten me one bit.

FREDDIE: I'm going to make her this year's battered wife poster girl.

LEONARD: Oh yeah?

FREDDIE: Yeah!

ELEANOR: Freddie, Leonard, please! Let's not make a mountain out of a molehill.

LEONARD: I'd like to see you try it.

FREDDIE: You think I won't but I will.

LEONARD: You and what troop of Boy Scouts?

FREDDIE: Watch this. *(Takes his drink and pours it over* ELEANOR's *head)* How do you like that? That will teach you to go to motel rooms with another man's wife!

LEONARD: I'm not impressed. And what's more, I don't think it's any of your business what Eleanor and I do.

FREDDIE: You're having an affair with her.

LEONARD: And what if I am? What are you going to do about it? What if Eleanor and I were madly in love, huh? What would you do then, huh? What if I decided to kiss her, huh? Like this.

FREDDIE: I'm warning you. If you dare to kiss that woman again I'm going to mess her up.

LEONARD: You haven't got the guts. You haven't got the spine. You're too much of a jellyfish to lay a hand on her. *(Kisses her again)*

FREDDIE: I'm going to mess up her pretty little face so her own mother wouldn't recognize her.

LEONARD: I'll believe it when I see it.

FREDDIE: *(Attacks* ELEANOR *and tears her dress off and tramples it in the mud)* How do you like them apples!

LEONARD: I'm not impressed.

ELEANOR: *(Pleading)* No, Leonard, Freddie, please!

FREDDIE: Not impressed? Not impressed? I'll show you! Here Eleanor, I've always wanted to paint you. *(Takes paint from his paintbox and smears it all over her)* Now are you impressed? Now are you impressed? You want to buy a painting? Buy her. Or have you bought her already?

ELEANOR: Why of all the egotistical . . . I don't like either of you. You're both beasts. *(Runs out)*

LEONARD: Now see what you've done.

FREDDIE: It serves you right! You had it coming to you!

LEONARD: I think you're way out of line here. Eleanor is a sweet kid.

FREDDIE: She's a married woman.

LEONARD: So what's it to you? Do you know her husband?

FREDDIE: Yes.

LEONARD: Oh, Freddie, then that's different. I can see you taking umbrage. What is he, a friend of yours?

FREDDIE: Yes, a very close friend.

LEONARD: Listen, I'm sorry, but we have to be men about this. After all, who hasn't fooled around? But whatever you do don't blame Eleanor. Why should there be one standard for men and another for women?

FREDDIE: Well, I agree with you there.

LEONARD: This guy, Eleanor's husband, from what I gather he's a real wimp.

FREDDIE: What do you mean?

LEONARD: Well, he can't support her.

FREDDIE: He's an artist, like myself. He's had to make a lot of sacrifices for what he believes.

LEONARD: Of course you guys stick together. But lack of money isn't so important if it's really happening between two people. If the relationship is really hot, who needs money? Apparently her husband is a real dud in bed.

FREDDIE: I wouldn't know.

LEONARD: I'm surprised Eleanor hasn't talked to you about it. You being such good friends and all.

FREDDIE: We haven't seen each other in so long.

LEONARD: Oh yes, fourth or fifth grade, wasn't it?

FREDDIE: Kingergarten.

LEONARD: I could fill you in. But then you're probably not interested.

FREDDIE: Oh but I am! *(Not wanting to seem overanxious, he catches himself and feigns nonchalance)* I'm interested in Eleanor's welfare.

LEONARD: Apparently she fell in love with this guy when she was a kid and never wanted to marry anyone else. So they married young.

FREDDIE: Very romantic.

LEONARD: Yes, but then after they were married a while he just petered out. Or maybe they both just lost interest. Who can tell about these things from the outside?

FREDDIE: It's impossible to guess.

LEONARD: But this I can tell you. She's like an animal in bed.

FREDDIE: *(Horrified)* Really?

LEONARD: It's as though she were starved for it. And she scratches.

FREDDIE: Oh, really?

LEONARD: She's into the wild variations. And that French stuff too.

FREDDIE: I never would have thought it of her.

LEONARD: Oh you don't have to tell me. On the surface she's so reserved. But underneath that cool exterior lies a nymphomaniac.

FREDDIE: What?

LEONARD: I'm telling you she can't get enough.

FREDDIE: Do you love Eleanor?

LEONARD: Love Eleanor? That's all I do is love Eleanor. I'm lucky I'm in pretty good shape. If you know what I mean.

FREDDIE: Oh I know what you mean all right.

LEONARD: You know, Freddie, now that we're not seeing each other on a doctor-patient basis, I think we could be buddies.

FREDDIE: You and me, buddies?

LEONARD: Yes, you know, there is a certain inequity built into the psychotherapeutic process. I get to know every intimate detail of a patient's life but the patient doesn't get to know anything about me.

FREDDIE: Oh, I wouldn't say that!

LEONARD: All right, you know some things about me but not to the degree that I know them about you. I know so many specifics.

FREDDIE: Is this a blackmail threat?

LEONARD: Freddie, this is Leonard, your buddy. What I'm saying is that I want to confide in *you* for a change.

FREDDIE: Go ahead. Unburden your heart.

LEONARD: Freddie, I love my wife. Oh, I won't go so far as to say that I'm happily married. I'm not. We quarrel. We say unforgivable things to each other every morning before breakfast. We're competitive. We're both in the same profession. Sometimes we go out and get drunk together, have a few laughs . . . we both love the theater. . . . What am I trying to say? There's just no other relationship in my life like it. It's not always happy. But it is always interesting. Karen is the world to me.

FREDDIE: Karen?

LEONARD: Yes, that's my wife's name, Karen. She's a psychiatrist, too. See, you're getting interested in my life. I don't know why I never thought of trying this in our sessions together. Isn't it interesting?

FREDDIE: I'm afraid it's getting too interesting.

LEONARD: Really, Freddie, we've kept each other at a distance too long. Why don't you ask me some questions about myself? Go ahead, ask me anything.

FREDDIE: Is your wife's name Karen Silver?

LEONARD: No, it's Gold. Karen Gold. Cute, don't you think? Dr. Silver and Dr. Gold?

FREDDIE: Cunning.

LEONARD: Go ahead, Freddie, ask me something else.

FREDDIE: What would you do if you discovered your wife staying in this hotel with another man.

LEONARD: It's never happened so I couldn't tell you. You never know how you would react in a situation like that until it happens to you.

KAREN: [*(Enters)*] Freddie, I have wonderful news for you. Boris sold your portrait of Eleanor for fifteen thousand dollars! Hello, Leonard. *(Take)* Leonard!

LEONARD: Karen!

KAREN: Why did you come here? To spy on me?

LEONARD: Why no, I came here . . . I came here . . . Karen, do we have to discuss this in front of the patient?

KAREN: What patient?

LEONARD: *(Pointing to Freddie)* That patient standing right there.

KAREN: He's not a patient, he's my . . .

FREDDIE: Lover.

KAREN: Freddie, no!

LEONARD: Well, he's my patient and I'd prefer not to have his nose stuck into my personal affairs.

KAREN: Don't try to change the subject. What are you doing here? Why did you follow me? How did you find out where I went?

LEONARD: I didn't follow you.

KAREN: Then what are you doing here? I demand an explanation.

LEONARD: I came here with . . .

FREDDIE: My wife.

ELEANOR: [*(Enters)*] Leonard, I have a confession to make. Freddie is my husband.

KAREN: Eleanor! What are you doing here?

ELEANOR: Doctor Gold! Who called you?

FREDDIE: Nobody called her. She's here with me.

ELEANOR: You're here with my psychiatrist!

FREDDIE: Your psychiatrist?!!!!!

LEONARD: Your psychiatrist?!!!!!

ELEANOR: Yes, what are you doing here with my psychiatrist?

FREDDIE: The same thing you're doing here with my psychiatrist.

ELEANOR: Your psychiatrist?!!!!!

KAREN: Your psychiatrist?!!!!!

FREDDIE: Yes, Eleanor, it seems we've been having affairs with each other's psychiatrists.

ELEANOR: We should have our heads examined.

KAREN: And what's worse, we've been sleeping with each other's patients.

ELEANOR: You mean you two are married?

LEONARD: This is all a harmless mistake.

KAREN, FREDDIE, and ELEANOR: Harmless?!

LEONARD: Yes, it's life. *(ELEANOR and KAREN lift handkerchiefs to their faces to stifle their laughter or tears)* Are you crying?

FREDDIE: No, I think they must be laughing.

LEONARD: That's how life is—a mixture of laughter and tears. Sometimes the most painful experiences will suddenly strike us funny.

FREDDIE: And just when you've decided to take yourself seriously someone comes along and makes a fool of you.

LEONARD: I had a patient once who was married seven times to five different women. He married two of his wives twice. And when he was an old man of ninety he remarried his first wife. One of his wives had to wear her wedding ring on her right hand because he'd cut off her left ring finger in a jealous rage.

FREDDIE: Then you mean you're not jealous?

LEONARD: Not a bit.

FREDDIE: It's superhuman.

KAREN: No, it's just that he doesn't really love me!

ELEANOR: And Freddie doesn't really love me!

FREDDIE: And Eleanor doesn't really love me!

KAREN: Interpersonal Disorientation!—is a syndrome that's always fascinated me! In fact, I've been experimenting with a medication that sometimes helps in cases of extreme dysphoria.

FREDDIE: A remedy?

KAREN: Yes, it's a new medication that's just come out.

ELEANOR: A drug?

KAREN: It's medicine. It's been tested on hundreds of cases and has proven virtually one hundred percent effective.

LEONARD: What is it?

KAREN: It's called R.P.

LEONARD: R.P.?

KAREN: Reverse Psychology.

ELEANOR: I thought reverse psychology was when you tell a person to do the opposite of what you want them to do knowing that they'll do the opposite just to be stubborn or independent.

KAREN: That's right. Only this does the same thing *chemically.*

LEONARD: I don't get it.

KAREN: R.P. makes you strongly attracted to the person you would normally be least attracted to.

ELEANOR: Fascinating.

KAREN: It's useful in opening a person up to new ways of relating to others. Or it can be useful in repairing damage to a relationship where petty quarrels and betrayals have led to an estrangement.

FREDDIE: Well, I have taken every drug under the sun and I've never heard anything about R.P.

KAREN: It hasn't hit the streets of SoHo yet, darling. And even when it does, if it ever does, I doubt that it will be available in this potency. I have pharmaceutical quality R.P.

ELEANOR: Let's try it. Then we can all find out who we're least attracted to.

FREDDIE: Where can we get some of this stuff?

KAREN: I have some in my bag. You see, Leonard? I do read the professional journals.

ELEANOR: Let's all take it.

FREDDIE: Yes.

KAREN: Let's.

LEONARD: Wait a minute. Is this going to be a drug orgy or a medical experiment?

ELEANOR: A drug orgy, I hope.

LEONARD: Well, I'll have no part of it.

KAREN, FREDDIE, and ELEANOR: Aw!

LEONARD: Unless this drug is administered under scientific conditions it constitutes a breach of professional ethics.

FREDDIE: Come on, Leonard. What are you afraid of?

LEONARD: I'm not afraid. It's just that I want to proceed scientifically. This experiment needs a control.

ELEANOR: Control?

KAREN: Leonard is right. One of us shouldn't take the medication so that we have supervision. There should be someone clearheaded and rational to help in case there is some problem.

FREDDIE: Clearheaded and rational? Which one of us would that be?

LEONARD: Me.

KAREN, FREDDIE, and ELEANOR: You?!!!

LEONARD: Yes. I'll be the control. I won't take the R.P.

FREDDIE: I *thought* you were scared.

ELEANOR: Leave him alone, Freddie. Let's take the R.P.

KAREN: All right. We three will take the R.P. and Leonard will be the control. Who wants to go first?

ELEANOR: How long does the effect last?

KAREN: It varies. But rarely more than twenty minutes to half an hour.

LEONARD: That's a long time.

KAREN: Yes, but it gives one time to work things out.

LEONARD: How is this drug administered?

FREDDIE: Let's freebase it.

KAREN: (Slightly offended) Let's try to keep in mind that this is a medication and we're not taking it for "kicks."

FREDDIE: We'll try not to enjoy it. We promise.

KAREN: We're taking this medication to learn something about ourselves.

ELEANOR: Let's do it!

KAREN: (Removing a vial from her purse) This is it. It's in a liquid form. All you have to do is take a little sniff. First you'll sneeze. Then you stare. Then you faint. And after that you fall for the person you're *least* attracted to.

ELEANOR: Let me go first. (Sniffs from the bottle)

FREDDIE: What does it smell like?

ELEANOR: It's all perfumy or something. It smells like new-mown hay and chicken broth and gardenias or garlic or sour milk or mildew or chocolate or clove or cinnamon. Tar and roses, cat piss and cabbages, fresh baked bread and . . . (Sneezes, stares, faints, then) Leonard, I love you.

FREDDIE: Well, there's nothing new in that. You two have been lovers for some time. We don't need R.P. to tell us that you're attracted to Leonard.

ELEANOR: Leonard is beautiful.

LEONARD: Me?

ELEANOR: Leonard is sexy.

LEONARD: Me?

ELEANOR: Leonard is all I could ever want in a man.

KAREN and FREDDIE: Him?

ELEANOR: Yes. Oh Leonard, I liked you before as a friend. As someone who would take me out. But I never realized what I'd found in you. Your eyes spit fire. Your lips drip honey. Kiss me! Kiss me! *(Kisses him again and again passionately)*

LEONARD: *(Gasping for breath)* Eleanor, there must be some mistake. You were attracted to me before.

ELEANOR: No. No. I wasn't. I was using you to get revenge, to make my husband jealous. I was blind. Do you hear? Blind!

LEONARD: Using me?

ELEANOR: Ah, but that's all behind us now. I was a fool, I tell you! A blind fool. My only desire now is to please you. Curse me if only I may hear your voice. Beat me if only I may feel your touch. Kick me if only I may feel your foot. I will be your slave. I am your slave. Only do not send me away. I love you! I love you!

LEONARD: Do you see that? Eleanor isn't attracted to me.

KAREN: She's *least* attracted to you.

FREDDIE: That's a weight off my mind. Karen, why don't you go next?

KAREN: All right. *(She sniffs from the vial, sneezes, stares, faints)* Leonard, kiss me with the kisses of thy mouth for thy love is better than wine!

FREDDIE: You again! This is sickening!

LEONARD: But Freddie, remember what this means. Karen is least attracted to me.

FREDDIE: Oh yes. That's right. Ha, ha!

KAREN: O that thou wert as my brother, that sucked the breasts of my mother! When I should find thee without, I would kiss thee; yea, I should not be despised. I know you. I know you.

FREDDIE: She means it in the biblical sense.

KAREN: I would lead thee into my mother's house, who would instruct me.

LEONARD: I can't stand your mother!

KAREN: I would cause thee to drink of the spiced wine of the juice of my pomegranate.

LEONARD: I don't go that route, honey.

FREDDIE: Give me some of that stuff, will you? I'm beginning to feel left out. I want some action.

LEONARD: Are you sure you still want to? You obviously won't get anywhere with either of these two. No matter which one you're least attracted to, they're both temporarily crazy about me.

FREDDIE: Give me that bottle. I've got to know who I'm least attracted to so that I can choose between them when this stuff wears off. *(Takes bottle. Sniffs, sneezes, stares, faints, then)* Leonard?

LEONARD: Yes, Freddie?

FREDDIE: It's you.

LEONARD: Me what?

FREDDIE: You're the person I was least attracted to because you're the person I'm attracted to now.

LEONARD: Listen, Freddie, I admit I was attached to you. I'll even admit that I was overly attached to you. But it wasn't genital. It wasn't even anal. You interested me. That's all.

FREDDIE: Come on, you hot thing you. You know we can get it on. Don't play coy with me.

LEONARD: Really Freddie. Maybe I'm just more *limited* sexually than you are. That's it! I'm more limited. Think of it that way. It's nothing against you.

FREDDIE: Oh come on Leonard. You know we were meant for each other. Don't fight it. It's bigger than both of us.

LEONARD: You overestimate me.

FREDDIE: Come on Leonard. Just try it. You might like it. It will be the first time for me too.

LEONARD: Are you sure about that?

FREDDIE: I'm positive. You know me better than anybody. Have I ever mentioned anything of the kind?

LEONARD: No.

FREDDIE: You don't think I'd lie about something like that, do you?

LEONARD: No.

FREDDIE: Then what's stopping you?

LEONARD: Freddie, I want to remind you that you are on a drug. You are reacting in *opposition* to your usual impulses.

FREDDIE: Then why don't you take some R.P. too? I'm telling you it's really great. I feel so liberated. I feel liberated from the tyranny of my own taste.

LEONARD: Freddie, as your doctor I feel it is my duty to warn you. You are experiencing hysterical disassociative neurosis.

FREDDIE: Why are you rejecting me? Am I so terrible? Am I so unattractive?

LEONARD: This attraction to me that you're feeling only proves that you are least attracted to me when not under the influence of R.P.

FREDDIE: I won't take no for an answer. You're just like a woman. You say no when you mean yes.

LEONARD: Freddie, I assure you I am nothing like a woman. *(Slaps* FREDDIE's *hand)* Fresh!

FREDDIE: Oh, you little wildcat! It's no use using Reverse Psychology on me, Leonard. I'm onto you. *(Walks toward* LEONARD *as he speaks, with open arms)*

LEONARD: *(Backing away in the direction of the pool)* Freddie, that's the Reverse Psychology speaking. You're not attracted to me. You're not!

FREDDIE: I am! *(Lunges at* LEONARD *and kisses him on the mouth)*

LEONARD: Freddie you're all wet. *(Breaks away from the kiss and falls backward into the pool. A splash of water flies on from the wings)* Aaaagh! Help! Help! Help me! I can't swim. I can't get out.

FREDDIE: Leonard, nobody's going to believe you. You're just using this as an excuse to avoid me.

LEONARD: Help! Please! Help!

ELEANOR: He can't swim. He told me so.

KAREN: I'll get him out. I took a summer course in lifesaving.

(KAREN takes a little time putting on her bathing cap amid LEONARD's *cries of "Help, I'm drowning," etc., and dives into the pool. Splash from the wings again.)*

FREDDIE: I want him. Do you hear? I must have him.

ELEANOR: Forget it Freddie. He only likes women.

FREDDIE: Oh, so that's his game is it? Well two can play! If it's a woman he wants, it's a woman he'll get! *(Exits into cabana)*

ELEANOR: *(Alone)* Gee, everything seems so different to me than it did a moment ago. I've admitted things in public that I never even thought of before. But I don't feel guilty! I realize that some things that happen aren't my fault. That it's no use worrying about things that I can't change. I've got to accept the inevitable. And the problems that I have aren't really so big if I think about the problems other people have. It's just a question of living life for its own sake and being grateful for it. Anyone who has studied modern psychology must be aware that a person under considerable stress could reach a state in which he is not responsible for his actions.

KAREN: *(Enters with* LEONARD *limp and dripping wet in her arms)* I think . . . I was too late . . . He's dead!

ELEANOR: But you said you took a course in lifesaving. Didn't they teach you artificial respiration?

KAREN: Yes, but I'm too upset to do it.

ELEANOR: You've got to do it! A human life is at stake!

KAREN: *(Hysterical)* I can't do it, do you hear? I can't! He's dead! Dead! And I killed him! Why did I play with that R.P.? Why? I killed him! I killed him! And now he can never come back. Nothing can ever bring him back! And it's all my fault!

*(*ELEANOR *slaps* KAREN *across the face.* KAREN *suddenly becomes calm.)*

ELEANOR: Thanks. I needed that.

*(*KAREN *begins to give* LEONARD *artificial respiration.* LEONARD, *lying on his back, emits short spurts of water every time* KAREN *applies pressure to his chest.)*

LEONARD: Where am I?

*(*FREDDIE *enters wearing the dress that* ELEANOR *wore in her first scene in this act. That is, the dress* KAREN *lent her. Oh, you remember! The one she wore to the Metropolitan Museum of Art the day she first met* FREDDIE.*)*

LEONARD: *(To* FREDDIE, *groggily)* Karen!

FREDDIE: Yes, Leonard, my love!

LEONARD: I think administering an untested pharmaceutical was a highly questionable diagnostic aid. It was almost the end of me there. For a minute I thought it was all over.

KAREN: Wait a minute. He's still delirious. He's mistaking . . .

ELEANOR: Quiet. Let the R.P. work.

KAREN: You're right.

LEONARD: That damn drug nearly killed me. Do you realize you could be sued for malpractice?

FREDDIE: But Leonard, you're the only one who didn't take the R.P.

LEONARD: Oh, what do you care what happens to me? You find me repulsive. I know that now. Thanks to the R.P.

FREDDIE: Leonard, I do care.

LEONARD: No, you don't. You lied to me. You said you were going to have a face-lift. But it was just an excuse to come here with Freddie.

FREDDIE: But I did have a face-lift.

KAREN: I did not!

ELEANOR: Shhhh!

FREDDIE: Don't I look different to you?

LEONARD: *(His mind clearing for the first time since his plunge)* Let me look closer. Eeecht, you look worse. Karen, I think you've been seeing too much of Freddie. You're beginning to look like him. Freddie! What are you doing in my wife's dress?

FREDDIE: Surprise! *(Throws himself on* LEONARD*)*

LEONARD: *(Looking around)* Somebody do something!

ELEANOR: Freddie, take your hands off of him, he's mine! *(Tries to pull* FREDDIE *off of* LEONARD*)*

FREDDIE: You little bitch! Keep your hands off of my man or I'll scratch your eyes out.

*(*FREDDIE *and* ELEANOR *have a cat fight.)*

LEONARD: Karen we've got to do something! Twenty minutes to half an hour of this and somebody's going to get hurt.

KAREN: Don't worry. It's been about that long now. They should be coming out of it any minute now.

*(*FREDDIE *and* ELEANOR *roll about with less and less force.)*

LEONARD: *They* should be coming out of it? What about you? Shouldn't you be coming out of it too?

KAREN: Now Leonard . . .

LEONARD: Why aren't you down there fighting over me? Would you mind explaining that?

KAREN: It's very simple. I didn't take the R.P. I faked it.

LEONARD: How could you have faked it? I saw you sneeze, stare, and faint.

KAREN: You mean this? *(Sneezes, stares, and faints)*

LEONARD: You're not practicing psychiatry anymore. This is witchcraft!

KAREN: *(With a sly laugh)* Sometimes there's a fine line between the two. After all, both rely heavily on the power of suggestion.

LEONARD: That's a shocking thing to say.

KAREN: As long as I still have the power to shock you, I guess there's hope for our relationship.

*(*FREDDIE *and* ELEANOR *begin to come off the* R.P.*)*

FREDDIE: What hit me?

ELEANOR: What hit *me?*

KAREN: You've both been hitting each other.

FREDDIE: That stuff is strong!

ELEANOR: It just takes over. You have no choice but to go with it.

FREDDIE: Look at what I'm wearing! I suppose I'll never live this down.

ELEANOR: That stuff is awful. I never want to take it again.

FREDDIE: You can say that again. I'd never touch it again. Not if you paid me. It's bad. It's a bummer.

KAREN: Oh, I don't know. I think it cleared the air and settled a few issues.

LEONARD: Karen, how could you be so irresponsible?

KAREN: I'd have done anything to save my marriage. No risk was too great.

LEONARD: I suppose sneaking off to a resort boatel with Freddie was an attempt to save your marriage, too.

KAREN: I am fond of Freddie.

LEONARD: This isn't a marriage. It's a mirage.

FREDDIE: You two are supposed to be the psychiatrists. But I think you're crazier than we are. At least our marriage is based on a firm foundation.

ELEANOR: Yes, we have so much in common.

LEONARD: The only thing you two have in common is you were married in the same church.

FREDDIE: We're in love!

ELEANOR: Yes, we're in love.

LEONARD: Huh!

KAREN: They are in love. He with himself. She with herself.

LEONARD: Instead of a marriage license you should have gotten a learner's permit.

FREDDIE: Why of all the . . .

ELEANOR: Forgive them, Freddie. It isn't easy running a marriage on one brain.

KAREN: Don't worry. We can't all be mentally healthy.

LEONARD: This is the thanks we get for teaching them to help themselves.

FREDDIE: You help yourself all right. To our money.

LEONARD: Oh, you've got all the answers. Too bad you don't know a few of the questions.

ELEANOR: Freddie is a genius. He can do anything.

KAREN: Anything but make a living.

ELEANOR: He's a self-made man.

LEONARD: Yeah, he started at the bottom and stayed there.

FREDDIE: Some doctor. He begins by examining your wallet. Then he makes love to your wife.

LEONARD: I'll never stop loving her. Because I never started.

FREDDIE: Not that it matters to me. I believe in free love.

KAREN: True. He never spends a cent on a date.

FREDDIE: That's a real friend. She only stabs you in the front.

KAREN: I don't condemn inferiority in my friends.

ELEANOR: No, she rather enjoys it.

FREDDIE: The more I think of her, the less I think of her.

ELEANOR: You were dazzled by her sophistication.

FREDDIE: Oh, she's sophisticated all right. She can bore you on any subject.

ELEANOR: But sexually it was just like in the movies?

KAREN: Yes, a short subject.

FREDDIE: Let's put it this way. She's not frigid. She just flunked puberty.

LEONARD: This R.P. is evil. I'm going to get rid of it once and for all. *(LEONARD raises the bottle of R.P. over his head and throws it to the ground, smashing it)*

KAREN: *(Shrieks)* No! The fumes! *(All four sneeze, stare, and faint. KAREN gets up first. Looks at the other three for a moment and then says licentiously in a masculine voice)* Eleanor, come to mama!

ELEANOR: No, no! I want Leonard! Leonard is the man I love.

KAREN: *(As before)* Man? I'll stomp him if he touches my little girl!

FREDDIE: *(As a woman)* Don't you dare lay a finger on him, you big brute. He's mine, I tell you, mine.

LEONARD: Get away from me! All of you! *(Runs off)*

(Piano music off becomes more fiery, then stops. A scream is heard off.)

FREDDIE: Leonard, how could you do this to me? What's she got that I haven't got?

KAREN: Who screamed?

ELEANOR: What's happened?

FREDDIE: Well, now we know who Leonard is least attracted to.

ELEANOR and KAREN: Who?

FREDDIE: The little old lady who plays requests.

EPILOGUE

(Funny Hill Farm Sanitarium. ELEANOR *and* FREDDIE *are waiting onstage when the lights come up, with a potted plant, box of candy, and magazines.* KAREN *enters to them in a white doctor's coat.)*

KAREN: *(Very warmly)* Eleanor, Freddie, so nice of you to come.

ELEANOR: It was the least we could do.

FREDDIE: Is he all right? May we see him?

KAREN: Yes, but only for a short while. He's still a little tired out after all he's been through.

FREDDIE: We understand.

ELEANOR: How much longer do you think he'll have to stay here?

KAREN: There's no way to tell, exactly. But one thing I can say, he's been steadily improving.

FREDDIE: Are you treating him?

KAREN: Yes, I wouldn't have it any other way. He's my patient now. All mine.

ELEANOR: At least we know he's in good hands.

KAREN: Thank you. Shall we go in?

FREDDIE: Yes. We brought him these. *(Gives her the presents)*

KAREN: Did you bring the coloring book and crayons he wanted?

ELEANOR: Yes, and some pencils and paper in case he wants to write.

KAREN: I don't think he'll be allowed to have the pencils. Sharp objects aren't a good idea.

ELEANOR: Do you think he would attempt . . .

KAREN: No, not necessarily. But there are other patients here. And, well, it's just better not to take any chances.

*(*ELEANOR *and* FREDDIE *exchange a look.)*

ELEANOR: I see.

KAREN: Shall we go in?

*(*KAREN *draws back a screen or opens sliding doors revealing* LEONARD *in a straight-jacket.)*

ELEANOR: *(Almost bursts into tears when she sees him)* Oh, Leonard. Look at you. I'm so sorry. Are you all right?

LEONARD: Yes, perfectly. Don't be upset Eleanor. This was the best thing for me . . . *really.* Everyone is so kind to me here. And I needed time to think things through.

FREDDIE: I feel this is all our fault, Leonard. You didn't want to take that R.P. in the first place. We talked you into it.

LEONARD: Leonard knows better. He doesn't hold you responsible.

FREDDIE: Leonard?

LEONARD: Yes, he told me so. I talk to him every day. Someday he's going to work for me when he gets out of here.

ELEANOR: Work for you?

LEONARD: Yes, he's going to work in my diamond mine. Under Tiffany's.

FREDDIE: But you're Leonard. And you don't have a diamond mine.

LEONARD: I used to be Leonard. But then I went away and had a face-lift and now I'm Louis Comfort Tiffany. Would you like some diamonds? I can get them for you.

ELEANOR: Where do you get them?

LEONARD: In my stools. Next time I go to the bathroom I'll save some for you. You could make diamonds too if you had the proper toilet training.

FREDDIE: *(Aside to* ELEANOR *and* KAREN*)* This is pathetic.

ELEANOR: Poor Leonard.

KAREN: Well, wasn't it nice of Freddie and Eleanor to visit you?

LEONARD:
    Jack and Jill went up a hill,
    They each had a buck and a quarter.
    Jill came back with two and a half.
    Do you think they went up for water?

KAREN: Leonard, aren't you going to say good-bye to Freddie and Eleanor after they took the trouble to come and visit you?

LEONARD:
    There was an old woman who lived in a shoe.
    She had so many children, 'cause she didn't know what to do.

KAREN: Leonard, Eleanor and Freddie are leaving.

LEONARD: No! You and I are leaving. They have to stay here!

ELEANOR: What? What does he mean by that?

KAREN: Humor him.

ELEANOR: Will he be able to go back to work?

KAREN: I'm afraid not. His contract had a sanity clause.

LEONARD: You can't fool me. There's no such thing as Sanity Clause.

FREDDIE: My God! He's in worse shape than I thought.

LEONARD: I won't stay here! I won't! *(*LEONARD *struggles to escape from the straitjacket)* Aaargh! *(Screams)* Aaargh!

KAREN: *(To* ELEANOR *and* FREDDIE*)* Would you mind stepping into the next room just to be on the safe side? I'll handle this.

FREDDIE: Are you sure you don't want help?

KAREN: No, I'm trained for this.

ELEANOR: She knows best. Let's go Freddie. *(They exit)*

KAREN: That's enough, Leonard. They're gone.

LEONARD: *(Rising calmly and removing the straitjacket)* How much longer do we have to keep this up?

KAREN: Until they show some sign of improvement.

LEONARD: It doesn't seem to be helping.

KAREN: The first step is their willingness to accept that they are the patients and that this is a hospital. Once they take that step the rest will follow easily.

LEONARD: Poor kids. And they had their whole lives ahead of them.

KAREN: He has a severe mental block. After selling that one painting, *Portrait of Eleanor,* for fifteen thousand dollars, he was never able to equal it again.

LEONARD: Equal it? Why does he feel he has to equal it?

KAREN: *(Exultantly)* It had a freshness and a spontaneity he could never recapture.

LEONARD: We'll just have to continue the regression therapy.

*(*LEONARD *draws back a screen revealing* ELEANOR *posing bound and blindfolded as in Act 1 Scene 4.* FREDDIE *at his easel, painting. For the first time we see that the words "MENTAL PATIENT" have been stencilled on the front of their clothes.)*

FREDDIE: *(Anguished)* I can't do it! I just can't do it!

ELEANOR: Think back, Freddie. The inspiration. Try to recapture it. What were you thinking of when you painted me?

FREDDIE: *(Wracking his brains)* I can't remember! I can't remember!

KAREN: *(Aside to* LEONARD*)* They're lucky they have us.

*(*LEONARD *nods agreement as the curtain falls.)*

The End

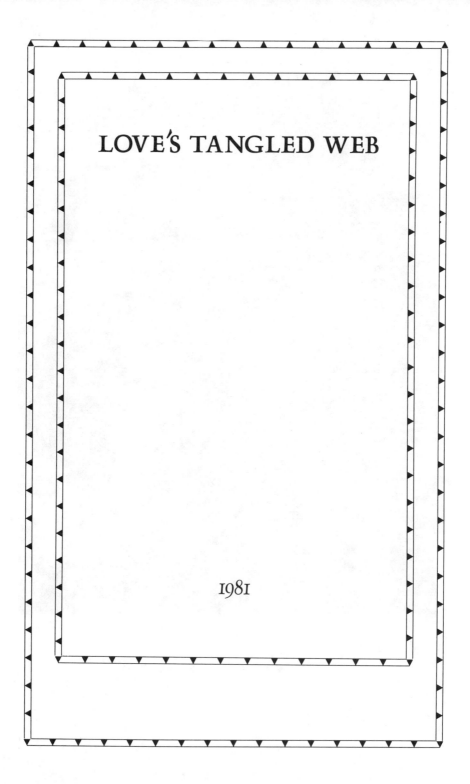

LOVE'S TANGLED WEB

1981

Black-Eyed Susan & Everett Quinton in
Love's Tangled Web (Patrick McMullen)

Cast of Characters

SYLVIA WOODVILLE
EVE, *her mother*
PASTOR FENWICK BATES, *her mother's lover, soon to be her stepfather*
ETHELBERT (BERTIE), *her brother*
RAEANNE AVERY, *the girl next door, a paranormal*
BRAM, *handyman and gardener*
GORILLA

ACT I

Scene I: *The parlor floor of an old house in Eaton's Neck, Long Island.*

(All of the furniture is covered with sheeting which protects it from the dust and imparts a ghostly appearance to the room. There are, among the accoutrements of a center-door-fancy set, a draped statue up left and a small greenhouse through French doors up right, overgrown with orchids.)

RAEANNE: Hurry up and open it.
BRAM: It seems to be stuck.
RAEANNE: Maybe you have the wrong key.
BRAM: . . . warped . . . there.

(BRAM opens the French doors and enters through the greenhouse into the darkened room, with a flashlight, a bunch of asparagus, [and a fish]. RAEANNE hesitates at the threshold. RAEANNE strikes a wooden match; BRAM crosses to the statue left.)

BRAM: This will be the first time anyone has been in this room in ten years.
RAEANNE: I was eleven when they went away.
BRAM: Open that door, let's get some air in here. *(BRAM takes a letter out from under the statue, blows off dust)* It's still here.
RAEANNE: What's still here?
BRAM: Er, ah, this statue. I remember this statue. *(Finds light switch and turns on lights)* Do you remember Sylvia?
RAEANNE: How could I forget Sylvia? You talked about her so much. She's like a giant in my imagination. I had to look up at her, she was so tall.
BRAM: She wasn't tall. You were so little.
RAEANNE: *(Sinister, jealous)* Yes, I was so little.
BRAM: Aren't you going to come in?
RAEANNE: No.
BRAM: Why not?
RAEANNE: I don't want to. The moon is in a bad aspect, and this morning I put my left stocking on inside out.
BRAM: Is that a bad omen?
RAEANNE: No, it's a good omen, but still, I don't want to come in.
BRAM: Sylvia would want you to. We were her friends. And she'll be needing friends more than ever now that she's an invalid.
RAEANNE: Bram, I don't feel that I am Sylvia's friend. After all, you and she were childhood sweethearts.

BRAM: I told you that was kid stuff. But that's all in the past. We're engaged now. So why can't you two be friends?

RAEANNE: We can't as long as she's crippled.

BRAM: Why?

RAEANNE: Because I wished it on her.

(EVE *enters, backing in the door up left, behind statue.*)

EVE: Watch the step. Step up. There's a step. (*Looks about the room*) I'll uncover a chair.

(BRAM *steps forward and quickly whips the cover off of a chair, which gives forth a slight puff of dust.* BRAM *and* RAEANNE *stand in awe at the following spectacle. Two men enter carrying* SYLVIA, *who wears a long dress, reclining regally.*)

BERTIE: Where do we park her?

EVE: Here, in this chair. (*The two men,* BERTIE *and* PASTOR BATES, *carry* SYLVIA *to the chair with some difficulty which they conceal gallantly*) Is she heavy?

PASTOR: Not a bit.

BERTIE: She's gossamer! A fairy!

EVE: Well, you men are so big and strong. Heavens, I don't think I could lift Sylvia.

SYLVIA: Mother, what a thing to say! (*Surveying the room, then as they are about to put her down in the chair*) No, no, not the chair. I don't want to sit up on a chair. I want to recline on the divan. I wouldn't ask it of you but it is a little hard for me to sit up for long periods of time. Would anyone mind?

PASTOR: Not at all!

BERTIE: Anything for you, sister dear.

EVE: Oh dear, I don't think it's going to be easy.

PASTOR: Somebody move the coffee table. (*To* BRAM) You! Don't just stand there! Lend a hand. Get that table out of the way.

(BRAM, *who has been staring, transfixed, suddenly "comes to"; in a shocked state of confusion he lurches forward at the command and dives for the table, knocking over an end table and lamp.*)

BRAM: Ooops!

EVE: (*Shrieking*) That lamp goes back to my great-great grandmother!

BRAM: (*Stammering in confusion*) I-I don't think she'll want it back now. It's broken.

BERTIE: (*To* PASTOR) Maybe we should set her down on the floor for a while.

SYLVIA: Don't you dare set me on the floor!

(RAEANNE *moves the coffee table and* EVE *helps* BRAM *to his feet. They place* SYLVIA *on the divan.*)

PASTOR: Oh, my God! I left the car parked illegally. I'd better go and move it. (*Exits*)

EVE: Good thing you remembered.

BERTIE: They are rather tough about parking regulations in this neighborhood.

EVE: I don't know what I'd do without Reverend Bates. He's been such a comfort to me since Colonel Woodville passed away.

SYLVIA: (*Riveted by* BRAM *and* RAEANNE) But who have we here?

EVE: Why it's Bram! And little Raeanne! My how you've grown.

SYLVIA: Is that Bram? I can't believe it. Why you've changed so much I hardly recognize you. And who is this? I don't believe I've had the pleasure of making your acquaintance. Bram, aren't you going to introduce this young woman to me?

BRAM: I . . . I . . . I . . .

SYLVIA: Is that all you can say *(Mimicking him)* I . . . I . . . I . . . ?

BRAM: *(Stuttering, he crumbles)* I . . . er . . . ah . . . ah . . . ah . . .

RAEANNE: Bram, what's wrong with you?

BRAM: Uh . . . uhh . . . uh.

SYLVIA: I remember you as cute. But you've gotten so ugly—in a funny way.

EVE: Sylvia!

SYLVIA: I said in a funny way, didn't I?

RAEANNE: *(Aside)* Bram, she's insulting you.

BRAM: No . . . er . . . ah . . . *(Blushes)*

SYLVIA: I didn't mean ugly ugly. I meant funny ugly. Bram knew what I meant. Didn't you, Bram?

BRAM: Un . . . un . . . uh . . . uh . . . yes.

SYLVIA: Did you mind?

BRAM: Uh . . . uh . . . yes—I mean no—I mean yes. No!

SYLVIA: You see? He knows he's ugly.

RAEANNE: *(Heatedly to* BRAM*)* Are you just going to stand there and take it?

SYLVIA: What's in your hand?

BRAM: A-a-a-sparagus.

SYLVIA: Asparagus? In lieu of flowers?

BRAM: W-w-w-w-w-we g-gr-grew th-th-th-them organically.

SYLVIA: How sweet! We'll put them in a vase and pretend someone had thought to bring flowers. Bertie, bring that vase over here.

BERTIE: *(Bringing the vase)* It's not a vahse, it's a vāse.

SYLVIA: Vahse, vāse, what's the difference?

BERTIE: A vahse is signed. A vāse is a cheap copy.

EVE: Can that be true? I always thought a vāse was bigger than a vahse. A vahse is for a single bud. A bud vahse.

BERTIE: No! No! That's awful! I'm sure a vahse is bigger than a vāse. A vahse *sounds* bigger than a vāse.

SYLVIA: And what's that? A fish? Ugh, get it out of here, it stinks.

EVE: So fresh, the catch of the day. Let's have it for supper. *(Exits to kitchen)*

SYLVIA: Let's have some wine!

EVE: Sylvia, it's almost time for your laxative. *(Reenters)*

SYLVIA: I don't want to take a laxative! I want wine.

EVE: Sylvia, you must take your laxative, dear. You know you don't get enough exercise to keep your system regular.

SYLVIA: Mother, I don't want to take a laxative!

EVE: *(To the others)* She always refuses to take her laxative.

SYLVIA: Mother, this is so embarrassing. Do we have to keep talking about laxatives in front of the guests?

EVE: If you would simply take it without all this discussion, we wouldn't have to talk about "it" so much. I'll get the lax . . . the you know what.

SYLVIA: Mother, would you get my hairbrush?

EVE: Yes, dear. *(Exits)*

SYLVIA: That woman tortures me with her laxatives. That's all she knows. Her medical knowledge is confined to the bowels and the lower intestine!

PASTOR: *(Reentering, to* BRAM, *sharply)* I say, are you working here or not? Don't just stand around doing nothing! Lend a hand. *(Then civilly)* The freight service is here with our baggage, Ethelbert.

BERTIE: Don't call me Ethelbert.

PASTOR: That's your name, isn't it?

BERTIE: I hate that name.

SYLVIA: Nobody calls Bertie Ethelbert.

EVE: *(Reentering with laxative)* It was his father's idea. I was against it. Here's your laxative, dear.

SYLVIA: Mother, please, you're mortifying me.

EVE: There's nothing to be mortified about, dear. It's a normal bodily function. Everyone does it, dear. Not just you. Remember, I used to change your diapers.

SYLVIA: *(Indignantly)* As a matter of fact I *don't* remember. I have absolutely no recollection of anything of the kind.

EVE: Whenever I have even a hint of a cold I irrigate my lower intestine.

SYLVIA: Give me that laxative! Anything so long as you change the subject!
(Takes the laxative and surreptitiously hides it under the sofa cushion)

PASTOR: Really, Eve, these servants are impossible. They haven't done a lick of work since they got here.

EVE: Pastor, they're not servants. Why I feel that Bram and Raeanne are part of the family. *(Puts her arm around them)*

(A car horn is heard off.)

PASTOR: *(With disgust)* Then we'll just have to unload the truck ourselves, Ethelbert. Those fellows out there sure as hell won't. *(Exits)*

BERTIE: I told you, don't call me Ethelbert. *(Exits)*

RAEANNE: Bram, we had better help, too.

*(*RAEANNE *and* BRAM *exit.)*

SYLVIA: Mother, did you bring my hairbrush?

EVE: Your things aren't unpacked yet. Here, use mine. *(Takes brush out of bag.* RAEANNE *reenters with parcel)* I'm going to start supper. Ah, to have my own kitchen again after all those years of eating in hotel dining rooms for fear of catching dysentery. *(Rapturously)* I'm just dying to do some *really* creative cooking. I want to cook something avant-garde! *(To* RAEANNE*)* Why, I'll bet I could have it ready by the time you've unloaded the truck. Why don't you all stay for dinner?

RAEANNE: Do you really think it would be all right?

SYLVIA: All right? Raeanne, I insist.

EVE: *(Calling out the door)* Bertie, bring in the groceries!

RAEANNE: *(Uncomfortably)* I don't want to impose.

EVE: Don't be silly, Raeanne, it will be fun. *(Glancing off)* The boys seem to be making progress. I'd better get started. *(Starts off)*

RAEANNE: Let me help.

SYLVIA: Oh, no, Raeanne. Don't abandon me. Don't leave me here all alone while everyone else is working. It makes me feel so useless.

RAEANNE: But there's so much to do.

EVE: That's all right. Raeanne, you stay here and keep Sylvia company. That will be your work.

SYLVIA: Mother!

EVE: *(Crestfallen)* Oh, dear, I didn't mean that the way it sounded. *(*BERTIE *reenters with groceries)* Bertie, you're a living doll. Bertie could have been anything he wanted if only he'd been able to keep his mind on one thing. *(Taking a package)* Let me take that one. Be careful, there are eggs.

(Exit EVE *and* BERTIE.*)*

RAEANNE: I hate to make your mother do all the cooking.

SYLVIA: She prefers it that way. She's a dreadful cook, really, scornful of advice. Almost a poisoner.

RAEANNE: Sylvia, what a thing to say about your own mother!

SYLVIA: She almost never cooks. But when she does she experiments. They say Father died of a heart attack. But I'll swear it was indigestion.

RAEANNE: Sylvia!

SYLVIA: Do I shock you? I hope I do. Everyone else is so used to me. Nothing I say or do has the slightest effect on them anymore. They're sick of me, really. I don't blame them. I'm a burden.

RAEANNE: Don't say that.

SYLVIA: A woman with a past but no future.

RAEANNE: But there's so much you could do with what you have. Think of it as an opportunity to cultivate intellectual interests most people never find time for.

SYLVIA: Yes, that's it. Keeping the mind alert. That's how I'll survive. That's how helpless women must survive . . . by their wits.

RAEANNE: Sylvia, I think this is a very good time for women. Things aren't ideal, but progress has been made.

SYLVIA: Oh come now, Raeanne. Don't tell me you want to be a liberated woman and give up makeup and get drafted and pee in the same room with the men, do you?

RAEANNE: No, of course not. But . . .

SYLVIA: I like a man to dominate me.

RAEANNE: I like affection. I don't have to be dominated to feel like a woman.

SYLVIA: Raeanne, my dearest little Raeanne. So you've become a woman.

RAEANNE: I've been a woman for some time. *(Proudly)* I'm twenty-one.

SYLVIA: Tempus certainly does fugit. *(Fingering a curl nervously)* Don't it?

RAEANNE: It *has* been ten years.

SYLVIA: You've changed. You seem so much bigger. What about me? Do I seem different to you? Have I changed?

RAEANNE: *(Laughing a bit intimately, then confiding)* I'm so amazed! You're just a normal-sized person. I remembered you as a giant. You were so much taller than me when you stood.

SYLVIA: When I stood. Of course you know that now I'm a complete invalid?

RAEANNE: I'm so sorry Sylvia.

SYLVIA: What are you sorry for? *(Opens fan)* You didn't wish it on me, did you?

RAEANNE: *(Momentarily taken aback)* Me? No!

SYLVIA: I think it's time we renewed our acquaintance. I used to think of you as my sister.

RAEANNE: I was always so afraid of you.

SYLVIA: *(With exaggerated amazement)* Afraid of me? Why on earth would you be afraid of me?

RAEANNE: You threatened to set my hair on fire.

SYLVIA: *(Laughs uproariously)* Did I really? That's terrible!

RAEANNE: Everyone said you were a terror.

SYLVIA: Oh, did they? Well, I promise I won't be a terror anymore. At least not to you. Come, sit here by me. *(RAEANNE hesitantly does so. Taking her hand)* Let's be sisters and share secrets.

RAEANNE: *(Dropping her guard)* You are very nice.

SYLVIA: *(Emphasizing the word "nice")* Am I nice? Am I very nice?

RAEANNE: Yes, I think you are.

SYLVIA: I am! I am nice. Oh, Raeanne, you have no idea how nice I can be . . . to my *friends.* You are my friend, aren't you, Raeanne? *(Imploring)* Oh, I do so hope that you are my friend. You see, I happen to be in need of friends just now.

RAEANNE: Thank you . . .

SYLVIA: *(Leaning close to her and laughing slightly)* Sister. Go ahead, say it.

RAEANNE: Sister. There, I said it.

SYLVIA: Then we're friends?

RAEANNE: *(A bit uneasily)* Yes, friends.

SYLVIA: So, tell me, Raeanne. What have you been doing the last ten years? While we were traveling around the world.

RAEANNE: Oh, my life wasn't very interesting, I guess, compared to yours. I just lived next door and went to school like everybody else.

SYLVIA: Did you know what you wanted to be when you grew up?

RAEANNE: I knew I didn't want to be a nurse. And I didn't want to be a secretary. And I didn't want to be an airline stewardess. I really didn't know much of anything, I guess. That is, until I met Bram.

SYLVIA: Until you met Bram?

RAEANNE: Yes—he was so different from the other boys I knew. He was interested in nature.

SYLVIA: *(Alarmed)* Nature?

RAEANNE: Botany, zoology, and the ecology. He was interested in the way it all fits together. How all different living things are interdependent. Do you know he built a methane tank and for a whole summer we cooked our food on gas from decomposing matter?

SYLVIA: You cooked your food together?

RAEANNE: It was part of a reforestation project in Yosemite. I didn't think we could have survived three months in a one-room cabin with no electricity—but we did. On cold nights we'd just get under the covers and read to each other. After a while I didn't even miss the television.

SYLVIA: I can imagine that you didn't. But Raeanne, what did your parents think about your living alone with a man in the woods?

RAEANNE: Oh, they accepted it. After all, we are going to get married anyway.

SYLVIA: Raeanne, I think I am going to set your hair on fire after all.

(Enter BRAM and PASTOR carrying a mummy case. BERTIE precedes them with a large birdcage with a parrot and some Chinese parasols which he proceeds to open showing off their brightly colored designs. He wears a Mexican sombrero and snowshoes. EVE enters, ringing a tiny silver bell.)

EVE: Dinner is served.

PASTOR: Oh, what a lovely bell.

EVE: Do you like it?

BERTIE: It's such a sweet sound.

SYLVIA: It's the silver.

BRAM: Soooooooooothing tone.

PASTOR: Charming idea, really.

EVE: I love it, too. It makes any meal a festive occasion. This is going to be fun. Nothing is unpacked and I could only find three dishes so we'll have to eat in shifts. Pastor, could I have a word with you alone?

(BRAM and BERTIE *exit carrying* SYLVIA. RAEANNE *lingers awkwardly behind*)

PASTOR: Would you excuse us?

RAEANNE: You didn't do anything.

PASTOR: I mean would you please go!

(RAEANNE *exits humiliated.*)

EVE: Every time I have to call you Pastor in front of the others, I almost burst out laughing.

PASTOR: Eve!

EVE: I didn't mean it like that. I meant because of us, dearest.

PASTOR: Eve, tonight I was hoping you would give me your answer.

EVE: But I thought I already did. I told you I'd marry you.

PASTOR: I meant about your donation to the boys' orphanage. Is it yes or no?

EVE: You know better than anyone how much I'd like to see the boys' orphanage well endowed, but I can't tell you the amount of the gift until after my husband's will is read. But tomorrow will be plenty of time for that. *(Enter* BRAM *and* RAEANNE*)* Here's Bram and Raeanne, let's eat, it's our turn.

(Exit PASTOR *and* EVE.*)*

RAEANNE: Bram, how could you let her get away with that?

BRAM: With what?

RAEANNE: Sylvia did nothing but insult you all through dinner. And you just sat there and took it.

BRAM: You don't understand Sylvia. That's just her way.

RAEANNE: She's a bitch, pure and simple. A bitch and nothing but a bitch.

BRAM: Lower your voice. They'll hear you.

RAEANNE: I'd like to see her try talking to *me* like that. She'd be carrying her teeth around in her pocket.

BRAM: Raeanne, you have to make allowances for Sylvia. Think of what she's been through. This must be very difficult for her since she can't help herself.

RAEANNE: She still has all her faculties, doesn't she? She can still study. Maybe she should crack a book instead of playing cards all day. She sure finds time to put on all that war paint.

BRAM: She has to occupy her time somehow. And it's not all paint.

RAEANNE: How long is she going to go on making people wait on her hand and foot? Why doesn't she get a wheelchair?

BRAM: Raeanne! I can't believe that you could be so cruel to a hopeless cripple who can't defend herself.

RAEANNE: There's nothing cruel about it. She could get around more on her own.

PASTOR: *(Enters backward carrying his end of* SYLVIA. *Sings fanfare)* Da da da *da* da *daaah!* Here she comes! Reclining regally just like a princess in *The Arabian Nights.*

BERTIE: *(Carrying the other end)* Odalisque! *(They place her on the sofa again)*

SYLVIA: That dinner was really the worst. I've never let anything so vile pass my lips.

PASTOR: It was a little strange and *(Belches)* hard to digest. I'm afraid to think what was on that fish.

BERTIE: It did look nasty—black and sticky.

SYLVIA: *(Hands fan to* BRAM *who fans her)* Almost like excrement. Really, we must never let her cook again. That dessert almost made me gag.

BERTIE: But don't mention it to Mother. She'd be hurt.

*(*EVE *enters and crosses to open the French doors that lead to the balcony.)*

EVE: *(Inhaling deeply)* The rain has brought the scent of flowers with it.

SYLVIA: Close that door. There's a draft.

EVE: *(Closing the doors)* Would anyone care for a game of cards?

BERTIE: I could go for a game of gin rummy.

RAEANNE: Perhaps we'd better go.

EVE: What's your hurry? There's nothing like an evening with friends. Next to a good home-cooked meal, that is.

ALL: *(Grunt in grudging agreement)* Mmm.

RAEANNE: It's clearing now. We could walk. *(Opens doors and goes out on the balcony)*

EVE: Gin is so much better with four, Raeanne, and the Pastor doesn't play.

RAEANNE: What about Sylvia?

SYLVIA: I only play solitaire. That way I can cheat with a good conscience.

BERTIE: You used to play hearts.

SYLVIA: Yes, I think I could still enjoy a good game of hearts.

EVE: Raeanne, why don't you and Bram stay and give us a run for our money?

BRAM: M-m-m-m-money? W-w-w-we c-c-couldn't. I mean we c-c-can't.

EVE: I mean imaginary money. It's like playing for points. But more fun. Sylvia owes me over a hundred thousand dollars in imaginary money.

RAEANNE: *(Turning away and looking out over the Sound)* I can't. I don't want to. The cards . . .

BRAM: Cards don't mean the same thing to Raeanne that they do to other people. She reads them.

SYLVIA: Oh, do you tell fortunes?

BRAM: Not fortunes e-e-exactly—Raeanne is a paranormal.

EVE: You mean she's psychic?

BRAM: She's in touch with the other side.

PASTOR: Balderdash!

RAEANNE: I could tell you a few things.

BRAM: *(Goes out on the balcony with* RAEANNE *and talks to her apart)* Raeanne, why are you acting like this? Come back inside and be sociable.

RAEANNE: No, I don't want to. They were right about dinner. It was horrible. What did she do to my fish?

BRAM: That's what rich people eat. Rich people eat completely different food from other people. They're gourmets.

RAEANNE: Why do we have to stay here? Why can't you just take me home?

BRAM: Raeanne, this is my first chance to get in with really high-class people and you want to go and ruin it.

RAEANNE: Then why don't you stay here and I'll walk home.

BRAM: How would that make me look if I stayed here and let you walk home?

RAEANNE: Why do you care so much about what these people think?

BRAM: These people are somebodies. Do you want to run around with a bunch of nobodies for the rest of your life?

RAEANNE: I like nobodies. I'm a nobody. You're a nobody. What's wrong with being a nobody?

BRAM: Because practically everybody is a nobody and almost nobody is a somebody.

RAEANNE: Maybe there's a good reason why almost nobody is a somebody. Maybe nobody wants to be a somebody. Maybe being a somebody isn't all it's cracked up to be.

BRAM: Do you want to be a clam digger's daughter all your life?

RAEANNE: That's one thing I'm sure of. I'll always be a clam digger's daughter. And proud of it.

BRAM: Raeanne, I'm only thinking of us . . . of our future. You know I love you, don't you?

RAEANNE: You stay. I'm going.

(Thunderclap and sound of rain.)

BRAM: You can't go now. It's raining.

EVE: What's going on out there?

(BRAM and RAEANNE reenter parlor.)

BRAM: She'll read your cards if you want her to.

EVE: But don't you need special cards for that?

RAEANNE: No, any cards will do.

SYLVIA: Even credit cards?

RAEANNE: Let me see. *(Sits in chair)* Put your hands on the table. *(Shuffles cards)* Three queens, jack of diamonds, ace of spades—joker. *(Falls into a trance and speaks in a man's voice)* Eve, Bertie, Sylvia.

EVE: It's Burt. It's my husband! I'd know his voice anywhere.

PASTOR: This is a parlor trick. It's ventriloquism.

RAEANNE: *(In man's voice)* I've made a mistake. A terrible mistake.

EVE: This is no time for regrets, Burt.

RAEANNE: Someone in this house is a liar.

PASTOR: Eve, please, don't play this distasteful game with her. It's a sacrilege.

RAEANNE: Shut up, hypocrite.

PASTOR: Really, this is an outrage!

RAEANNE: Shut up! Shut up! Shut up! Shut up!

PASTOR: What this girl needs is a good thrashing.

BRAM: Don't touch her. You'll bring on a poltergeist!

(Suddenly some books fly off the shelves, a painting drops off the wall, a chair spins, and a vase flies up and comes crashing down. The lights flicker.)

BERTIE: Something's happening here and I don't like it. I don't like it one bit!

RAEANNE: *(Coming to herself suddenly as if nothing had happened)* Well, aren't we going to play cards?

EVE: It seems to be clearing, you'll have a nice walk home. Well, how did you like my dinner? *(Pregnant pause)*

SYLVIA: I adored the bell.

EVE: The bell?

SYLVIA: It had such a sweet sound. May I use it? That way if I'm alone and need one of you, I can call without shouting from room to room.

EVE: Good idea, dear. The bell is lovely. But not one of you said a word about the meal.

RAEANNE: Very interesting.

PASTOR: It certainly was different.

BERTIE: Mother, you've outdone yourself. It was . . .

SYLVIA: Shit.

RAEANNE: *(Gasps)* Sylvia!

SYLVIA: Mother, that dinner was the pits. You must never cook again. Or at least we must never eat it. We're endangering our health.

EVE: *(Crestfallen)* You mean you didn't like the fish molé?

BERTIE: Molé? You mean that was chocolate sauce?

EVE: It's Mexican.

BERTIE: So that's it! Mother, you're supposed to use unsweetened chocolate.

EVE: Oh, are you? I followed the recipe. It just said chocolate.

SYLVIA: It was vile.

EVE: *(Hurt)* I was just trying to be creative. I did try my best. I'm sorry that no one liked my dinner. And I'm sorry that none of you wants to be adventurous.

SYLVIA: Mother, there's adventurous and then there's slime. That meal was slime.

EVE: *(Insulted)* Well, you can all eat out of cans or hire a cook, because nothing could get me to set foot in that kitchen again! *(Bursts into tears and runs to her room)*

BERTIE: Sylvia, that was cruel.

SYLVIA: It had to be said. She'll get over it.

(Exit BERTIE.*)*

PASTOR: I'd better go in and comfort her. *(Exits)*

SYLVIA: I know how he'll comfort her. Listen, you can already hear the bedsprings squeaking. *(Pauses, all hear them)* They're in there fucking like animals.

RAEANNE: Sylvia, why don't you get a wheelchair?

SYLVIA: *(Thrown off balance for a moment and then shocked and horrified)* A wheelchair! I'll never be confined to a wheelchair!

RAEANNE: But that's just it. You would be less confined. You could move around under your own steam and wouldn't have to depend on other people all the time.

SYLVIA: It's bad enough that I have to be a hopeless cripple. But to be confined to a wheelchair! I couldn't face it! *(Becoming hysterical)* I couldn't! I couldn't!

BRAM: Raeanne, how could you?

RAEANNE: What's the matter? Afraid someone will find out you don't have any feet?

SYLVIA: Bitch! *(Throws hairbrush at her, covers her face with her hands and cries)*

*(*RAEANNE *ducks and the hairbrush misses her. She picks up the hairbrush and slips it inside her jacket.)*

RAEANNE: *(Speaking sotto voce)* I'll keep this. *(Aloud)* I thought you'd like a taste of your own medicine. Let's get out of here. *(Turns to go)*

BRAM: *(Looks at* SYLVIA *and stammers)* A-a-a-are y-y-y-you a-a-all r-right, S-s-s-sylvia?

SYLVIA: Leave me alone! Leave me alone!

RAEANNE: *(An ultimatum)* Bram, are you coming or are you going to stay with her?

BRAM: I-i-is there anything I c-c-c-c-can d-d-do for you, S-s-s-sylvia?

SYLVIA: Bram, would you carry me up to bed and tuck me in?

(As he carries her past the light switch, she darkens the room.)

RAEANNE: *(At French doors)* Bram! *(Exits)*

(EVE appears sleepwalking. She opens the French doors and climbs onto a railing.)

BRAM: *(Entering)* Mrs. Woodville!

(EVE screams and falls into his arms.)

BERTIE: *(Running in)* What is it? What's the matter?

BRAM: It's your mother. She was sleepwalking.

BERTIE: Sleepwalking?!

EVE: *(To* BRAM*)* I'm all right. Bertie? Is the cat in? I'm sorry. It's nothing. Where am I? Is everyone staying for supper?

Curtain

Scene 2: *Setting the same but all dustcovers have been removed. There are arrangements of fresh flowers.*

(EVE and the PASTOR enter in black. EVE is veiled.)

PASTOR: Left everything to Sylvia?

EVE: Yes, everything to his little broken butterfly. That was the phrase he used.

PASTOR: But what about you? How are you going to get along?

EVE: My husband provided for me in his will so long as I never remarry and as long as I take care of Sylvia. But she has the purse strings. *(Sighs)* I'm her ward, as it were.

PASTOR: You'll have to take the will to probate court. The money could be tied up for years.

EVE: It's only until we get settled. After we're married I wouldn't dream of accepting a penny from Sylvia. I never want to be dependent on my children.

PASTOR: Eve, we can't think of marriage now.

EVE: Why not? Nothing has changed between us, has it?

PASTOR: Yes, I think it has. The parish is overextended as it is. The Home for Orphaned Boys is using up every dividend in our portfolio. We can't consider marriage now.

EVE: But how do you live? The parishioners put offerings in the plate on Sunday, don't they?

PASTOR: Less and less in recent years. The offerings haven't kept pace with inflation.

EVE: We'll make ends meet somehow. I'll get a job as a cook.

PASTOR: I'm used to living well. I need my creature comforts.

EVE: You could work too—between us we'll manage.

PASTOR: Me work? Have you taken leave of your senses? I have to write a sermon every week, visit the sick, teach Sunday school, christen the newborn and bury the dead, not to mention my duties as headmaster of the Home for Orphaned Boys. I haven't got time to work. I can't support you in the manner to which you've become accustomed. I'm afraid we can't possibly announce the banns now.

EVE: But I love you madly. Don't you love me just a little?

PASTOR: *(Gulps)* Of course, I adore you. Ours is a real romance. But having an affair is one thing and marriage is another.

EVE: I don't think so. At least I don't think it should be.

PASTOR: Love affairs are ideal things based on mutual trust and affection. Marriage is a business arrangement which is contractually binding. All great lovers don't make great business partners. The qualifications are different.

(Bell is heard.)

EVE: There's the bell. She needs something. I'll go to her. She's been impossible since the will was read. I've become like a servant in my own home.

PASTOR: Eve, it may be your home, but it's Sylvia's house.

EVE: And what is that supposed to mean?

PASTOR: I mean it's very generous of Sylvia to let you go on living here. She doesn't have to, you know.

EVE: I gave her birth. I cared for her when she was a helpless little thing. Is this all the thanks I get?

PASTOR: I think you're being very unfair to Sylvia.

EVE: That's right, take her part. *(Bell is heard again)* There, she's ringing that infernal bell again. I'd better go and see what she wants. *(Exits)*

(RAEANNE appears at the French doors.)

PASTOR: *(Turns, and seeing her, is startled)* Now the servants are spying on us. What next? *(Crosses to the glass doors but does not open them)* What do you want? Go around the back way. Use the servants' entrance. *(RAEANNE spits)* You filthy little heathen. *(Seeing her doll)* What is this, some kind of Voodoo?

RAEANNE: Rana rana, Ecbatana.

(PASTOR holds up his cross. RAEANNE holds up a huge cross from which the PASTOR recoils. She exits.)

EVE: *(Entering)* She wants Bertie. *(Calls off)* Bertie!

BERTIE: *(Bounding down the stairs)* What is it, Mother?

EVE: Sylvia wants you.

BERTIE: Not again! Oh, Lawd, dese bones is a-gettin' weary! *(Bell is again heard. Moving in slow motion)* Ahse comin' jest as fast as I kin. Ahse gwine to . . . Ahse gwine to . . . *(Then dropping the Stepin Fetchit act)* Does anyone have any idea what "gwine" means? *(Exits)*

EVE: Now she's completely dispensed with please and thank you. She just orders me about.

PASTOR: I'm telling you I think you should be grateful. Things could be a lot worse than they are.

BERTIE: *(Enters quickly in an agitated state)* How could she do this to me! How could she do it?

EVE: Do what? Bertie, what is the matter?

BERTIE: *(In a state of horror)* Mother, Sylvia says from now on I have to pay rent if I want to continue living here. Is that legal? Can she do it?

PASTOR: I'm afraid so. Your father left her everything.

BERTIE: It's so unfair. This is our home, too. I knew Father never liked me. I knew it!

EVE: Never mind, Bertie, you'll always be my favorite.

PASTOR: Eve, how can you play favorites at a time like this? Surely you must have some motherly feeling left for Sylvia.

EVE: I don't think there ever was any. I remember even as an infant when I nursed her she used to bite my nipples so hard it hurt.

BERTIE: *(Desperately)* Mother, I don't have any money to pay rent. What am I going to do?

EVE: You're going to have to work.

BERTIE: Work?

EVE: Yes, you'll just have to get a job and work.

BERTIE: Mother, how could you say such a thing to your own son? You mean you'd stand by and see me work?

EVE: No, Bertie, I won't stand by. I'm going to go to work, too.

BERTIE: *(Bursts into tears and throws himself on the divan, sobbing)* Oh, it's too cruel! Too cruel! *(Bell is heard again. Savagely)* There, she's ringing that goddamn bell again. The sound of it cuts through me like a knife.

PASTOR: Who's going to answer it this time? I'd really prefer not to.

BERTIE: I'm not going in there again.

EVE: I can't face her either. Not after what she's done to Bertie. I'd be likely to say something I'd be sorry for.

(Bell rings insistently now.)

BRAM: *(Entering the room from the kitchen and hearing the bell ringing)* The bell! Don't any of you hear the bell? Sylvia needs something!

EVE: Why don't you see what she wants, Bram?

BRAM: Yes, Mrs. Woodville. *(Exits like a shot to Sylvia's side)*

PASTOR: Poor bastard. You're just sending him in to take more abuse. She treats him like dirt.

EVE: I just couldn't face her myself. Besides, he doesn't seem to mind it.

BERTIE: Mind? He laps it up! He's a masochist. Anyone would have to be to put up with Sylvia.

BRAM: *(Reentering)* Sylvia says that from now on she wants all her food sent in from Davey Jones's Locker.

PASTOR: Well, she certainly has good taste. That's the best seafood restaurant on the North Shore. But it's miles away!

BRAM: Also from now on she'll only dine on cold lobster tails in their shells and drink champagne. And she wants someone to taste every dish in her sight before she eats it.

BERTIE: What, is she afraid we'll poison her?

BRAM: Yes.

EVE: This is the limit! We can't go on waiting on her like this. We'll never have any time for ourselves.

BRAM: Excuse me, Mrs. Woodville. But I could wait on Sylvia. You wouldn't even have to pay me. I can drive. I could fetch her meals.

EVE: My dear boy, do you really want to take this on yourself? And go on taking her abuse?

BRAM: What abuse? Why, Sylvia wouldn't hurt a fly.

EVE: You mean the things Sylvia says to you don't hurt your feelings?

BRAM: *(Laughs scornfully)* What are my feelings compared to someone as great as Sylvia? Why, she's so far above me—above any of us—that we can't really know what she thinks, or feels. We can only guess. But Sylvia has a depth of feeling and a loftiness of understanding that far surpasses what we ordinary people ever experience. I'm just proud to have been granted the privilege of knowing her. Even at a distance.

EVE: Well, if he feels that way about it, what can I do but agree? Bram will wait on Sylvia. It will give us more time for our own lives.

BRAM: *(Overcome with emotion)* Thank you, Mrs. Woodville, for granting me this opportunity. I swear you'll never regret it. *(Kisses her hands. Bell rings off)* She's ringing. I'd better go to her. *(Exits like a shot)*

EVE: Poor boy. I hate to sacrifice him like that. But what am I to do?

BERTIE: Don't worry, Mother, he's a willing martyr.

EVE: I'd better see about supper.

PASTOR: *(Alarmed)* But I thought you were never going to cook again?

EVE: I've gotten over it. *(Starts toward kitchen)*

PASTOR: But, Eve, maybe we should eat out.

EVE: On what? I've got to watch every penny. Now that I'm dependent on Sylvia, I'll have to cook all our meals.

BERTIE: *(Exclaims)* Good night, nurse! Mother, we can't! I mean *you* can't. You'd be little more than a drudge.

EVE: Cooking is an art. It only turns into drudgery when you don't bring any *originality* to it.

BERTIE: *(Under his breath)* Originality! That's what I'm afraid of!

(BRAM *enters carrying* SYLVIA *in his arms. He tries to place her on the divan but he has her feet at the wrong end.)*

SYLVIA: No! No! No! You idiot! The other way! The other way! *(*BRAM *turns upstage and finds himself sitting on the divan with his back to the audience and* SYLVIA *on his lap)* No you imbecile! I said the other way! Turn me around! Do you have a brain in your head or are you mentally retarded? Moron! Half-wit! Nonentity! *(With some difficulty* BRAM *finally gets her arranged on the divan)* Go up to my room and get my cards.

(Exit BRAM*)*

EVE: Sylvia, I'd like to have a word with you. You've upset your brother terribly. You shouldn't say things you don't mean.

SYLVIA: For instance?

EVE: Suggesting that he pay rent. That's a very cruel joke.

SYLVIA: Cruel perhaps. But it wasn't a joke.

EVE: Sylvia, you can't make Bertie pay rent.

SYLVIA: I'm not *making* him do anything. I said *if he wants to go on living here* he has to pay rent. And what's more, you're going to start paying rent too.

EVE: Sylvia, we don't have any money to pay rent.

SYLVIA: Then you'll have to get out.

EVE: You wouldn't throw your own mother out in the cold!

SYLVIA: What are you talking about? Cold? It must be seventy degrees out there.

EVE: Sylvia, have mercy on us. We don't have any place to go. Surely blood is thicker than water.

SYLVIA: Very well, Mother. You can stay on. I'll be needing a maid and butler. If you two want the job, I'll relax my standards and hire you even though you lack the qualifications.

EVE: Maid?

BERTIE: Butler?

SYLVIA: Take it or leave it.

BERTIE: This is the last straw. Sylvia, we are a family. We all have the right to live in this house.

SYLVIA: You are my family, I'm ashamed to admit, through no fault of my own. Although I'm ashamed to acknowledge you.

EVE: Ashamed of me? You should be ashamed of yourself!

SYLVIA: I don't know what Father ever saw in you.

EVE: Your father and I had a unique relationship. No other woman could have given him what I gave him.

SYLVIA: He told me he liked me better than you.

EVE: He did not!

SYLVIA: How do you know?

EVE: He couldn't have. He loved *me*. He proved it in a thousand ways.

SYLVIA: He loved you, but he *liked* me. No, he didn't like you. He loved you but he didn't like you.

EVE: How could he love me but not like me?

SYLVIA: You're lovable. But you're not likable.

BERTIE: Oh, don't be so la-di-fuckin'-da! *(Exits)*

SYLVIA: Keep a civil tongue in your head.

BERTIE: *(Reentering)* Don't tell me what kind of tongue to keep in my head, miss. I might just tell you what I think of you. *(Exits)*

SYLVIA: You're a shallow little twit.

BERTIE: *(Reentering)* At least when you're shallow you don't sink to any great depths. *(Exits)*

SYLVIA: To whom are you referring?

BERTIE: *(Reentering)* To you, profound bore. *(Exits)*

SYLVIA: Why you pathetic worm, how dare you speak to me like that?

EVE: Oh oh. You shouldn't have said that.

BERTIE: *(Reentering and incensed)* Worm?!!! Worm?!!! Why you spoiled little snot. You dried up old maid! I hope you get some horrible skin disease that gives you blotches all over your body.

SYLVIA: *(Horrified)* Blotches?

BERTIE: Yes, and on your face too!

SYLVIA: *(Screams)* Aaahhh!

EVE: It's not wise to insult Bertie.

SYLVIA: *(Quietly)* Get out.

BERTIE: *(Raving)* I'll get out! I'll get out of here so fast it will make your head swim. You know something? *(Dialing phone)* I'm glad you're throwing me out. Do you hear, GLAD! I'd rather starve in the street than live under the same roof with you. Hello, this is Ethelbert Woodville. Have my things sent to the Waldorf. *(Storms up the stairs)*

PASTOR: *(Astonished)* He called himself Ethelbert.

SYLVIA: He's bluffing.

EVE: I don't think so.

PASTOR: He's absolutely determined. Nothing anyone can say or do will reconcile you now.

SYLVIA: Nonsense. In exactly thirty seconds he'll be back here on his knees begging my forgiveness. *(She looks silently at her watch for thirty seconds with forefinger raised. At the end of thirty seconds she lowers her finger in signal)*

BERTIE: *(Reenters repentent and throws himself on his knees before SYLVIA)* I'm sorry, Sylvia! Forgive me! Please forgive me! *(Sobs)*

SYLVIA: Go upstairs and pack.

BERTIE: *(Rises dejectedly and goes upstairs)* If that's the way you want it. *(Exits martyred)*

EVE: Sylvia, I see I have no choice but to accept your offer. It won't be so different. I've always kept the house anyway.

SYLVIA: But from now on you'll do it in uniform.

EVE: Uniform? Why must I wear a uniform?

SYLVIA: So that you never forget that you're working for me.

EVE: I'm having a migraine. I think I'll go to my room and lie down.

SYLVIA: And another thing, I'm going to take the master bedroom with the view of the Sound.

EVE: And where will I sleep?

SYLVIA: You can sleep in my old room.

EVE: *(Defiantly)* You can't keep telling me what to do—you *can't!* *(Stamps her foot)*

SYLVIA: *(Firmly)* Mother, go to your room. *(EVE starts toward her room)* Uh, uh, uh. Your new room.

(EVE exits sullenly.)

PASTOR: Miss Sylvia.

SYLVIA: Pastor?

PASTOR: Now that you're so well off, would you consider sharing your good fortune by making a donation to the boys' orphanage? *(Places his hand on hers)*

SYLVIA: *(Rapping his knuckles with her fan)* How dare you flirt!

PASTOR: You misunderstand me.

SYLVIA: But you understand me. Don't presume.

PASTOR: But surely you don't think I meant anything more? I was thinking of the orphaned boys.

SYLVIA: I can believe it. But surely you're barking up the wrong tree. Raeanne has much more money than I have. And she's more charitable too, I dare say.

PASTOR: Money? But she doesn't appear to.

SYLVIA: It's *old* money.

PASTOR: Oh, I see. Excuse me, but I think perhaps I've been rude to Miss Avery. *(Exits)*

BERTIE: *(Enters down the stairs with bags and suitcases)* Good-bye, Sylvia. *(Goes to exit)*

SYLVIA: Bertie, one moment, please. Don't be hasty.

BERTIE: The sooner I get out of here the better as far as I'm concerned. And the further away!

SYLVIA: You could live here rent free if you'd do some things for me.

BERTIE: Such as?

SYLVIA: Little services. Nothing depressing.

BERTIE: I'm listening.

SYLVIA: I want you to help me play a trick on someone.

BERTIE: Who?

SYLVIA: Bram.

BERTIE: Bram?

SYLVIA: He seems to be infatuated with me and losing interest in Raeanne. I want you to make a big play for Raeanne to make Bram jealous. I want to bring them back together.

BERTIE: I can't believe it. This is the first unselfish thing you've ever done.

SYLVIA: I've had a change of heart. I want to do something good for someone. Will you help me and stay on rent free?

BERTIE: Yes, Sylvia. Thank you. I've been so wrong about you. I want to apologize. I want to tell everyone how wrong I was.

SYLVIA: Yes, do that, Bertie. Thank you. But you must play your part to the hilt. Really convince Raeanne you are in love with her. Try to get her to marry you.

BERTIE: Marry!

SYLVIA: So that your intentions will seem honorable.

BERTIE: Yes, of course.

SYLVIA: You can start by going upstairs and writing her a love letter right now.

BERTIE: I will. Again, thank you Sylvia. *(Exits upstairs)*

(SYLVIA rises from divan. BRAM enters the room and sees SYLVIA limping around busily.)

SYLVIA: It's gone! *(Turning startled)* Bram!

BRAM: You can walk?

SYLVIA: Bram, let me explain.

BRAM: You can walk? All the time you could walk?

SYLVIA: Bram, I know how this looks but—

BRAM: *(Cutting her off)* All along with the bell and everybody carrying you around and you could walk? They'll tear you to pieces when they find out.

SYLVIA: Bram, that's just it. They must never find out. You can't tell them.

BRAM: Are you kidding? Not tell them? And let them go on waiting on you hand and foot for the rest of their lives?

SYLVIA: We'll break it to them gently a little at a time. First I'll agree to get a wheelchair. Then I'll do physical therapy. Eventually I'll recover, and no one will be the wiser.

BRAM: *(His illusions shattered)* You're a horrible person. And I defended you. I can't believe how wrong I was about you. You're a liar. How could you lie about a thing like this?

SYLVIA: *(Tearfully, playing on his sympathy)* I didn't lie. Do you want to see me walk? Look. I limp. Bram, isn't it awful?

BRAM: Many people with far greater physical handicaps live useful lives. You've just used your money . . . Your money! That's it! Your father left all the money to you because he thought you were crippled. You're low. You're the lowest. I'm going to tell everyone I was wrong right now. I'm going to apologize.

SYLVIA: *(With a stifled scream)* Bram! You can't tell them! For my sake. You said you'd do anything for me.

BRAM: Not anymore, sister. I've wised up. Boy did I wise up. I feel like I was sleepwalking and someone just threw a bucket of ice water over my head. I wouldn't do anything for you now. *(Starts out)*

SYLVIA: Bram, please. I'll do anything. Anything you ask.

BRAM: *(Turning slowly toward her with a look of malicious hatred in his eyes)* Anything? Did you say anything?

SYLVIA: *(Desperately)* Yes, anything.

(BRAM walks toward her slowly, backing her to the couch. He gives her a slight shove and she falls back on the couch. With his back to the audience, he drops his pants.)

BRAM: You would do anything, wouldn't you?

(SYLVIA reacts with fear as . . .)

Curtain

ACT II

Scene 1

(At rise RAEANNE enters through the double doors. She looks around and creeps over to the sculpture and offers incense and flowers to it. She chants some dirge in patois. PASTOR enters at glass doors and knocks.)

PASTOR: Hello? Anybody home?

RAEANNE: *(Hides ceremonial stuff under the statue, crosses to double doors)* Go around the other way! Use the servants' entrance!

PASTOR: I say, let me in. What kind of prank is this? *(RAEANNE crosses her arms and stands resolute watching him beg to be let in)* Oh let me in, for heaven's sake! Oh why did I take the sea walk. Oh Miss Avery—you've had your revenge—now do let me in.

RAEANNE: *(Mocking him)* Miss Avery—that one's sure changed his tune. *(Lets him in)*

PASTOR: *(Coming toward her)* Miss Avery, there's something I want to discuss with you.

RAEANNE: *(Backing away like an animal in terror)* Don't you dare beat me.

PASTOR: *(Aside)* Drat, a bad first impression is so difficult to erase.

RAEANNE: Don't you touch me or I'll scream.

PASTOR: Please—don't scream—I just wanted to ask you a favor.

RAEANNE: *(Expecting the worst)* What kind of favor?

PASTOR: This hardly seems the opportune time to ask. Could you give a donation to the boys' orphanage?

RAEANNE: *(Feeling in her pocket)* I don't know.

PASTOR: I know I've behaved abominably toward you—but if you could give us something I'd bend over backwards to make it up to you. I'd be yours to command.

RAEANNE: *(Hands him some change which she carefully counts out)* You can have this.

PASTOR: But surely you're joking. This is hardly the amount I had in mind.

RAEANNE: *(After a moment's struggle with her conscience)* Oh here, take the bus fare too. I'll walk.

PASTOR: *(Aside)* Eccentric—but then the old money is harder to pry loose. *(Turning on the charm)* Why don't you come to dinner at my house?

RAEANNE: I can't. Bram would never let me hear the end of it.

PASTOR: *(Aside)* I'd like to give that girl a good tongue-lashing myself!

(Enter BERTIE.*)*

BERTIE: Ah Pastor—

PASTOR: I've come to take your mother to the sailboat race.

BERTIE: She waited for you half an hour and then went ahead with the Winthrops.

PASTOR: I'm sorry I missed her. It was such a nice day, I took the sea walk here. I'll go back the way I came. Good day, Miss Avery. *(Exits)*

(Phone rings. BERTIE *answers it.)*

BERTIE: Oh, he just left, let me see if I can catch him. *(Runs to the doors)* Pastor, Pastor—Mother wants you to bring her hairbrush. [*(On the phone)*] Yes, I'll send it along with him.

PASTOR: *(Reentering)* Where is it?

BERTIE: Upstairs in her room. Things up there are in disarray. She only moved last night.

PASTOR: *(Going upstairs)* I'll try to find it. *(Exits)*

BERTIE: Oh, Raeanne, I'm so glad you're here!

RAEANNE: I'm glad you're here too. I don't like being alone in the house with Bates.

BERTIE: Why?

RAEANNE: Because he's so strict. Bram told me he beats the boys black-and-blue.

BERTIE: Oh he did? Did he?

RAEANNE: And a minute ago he took my bus fare away, so that I have to walk home.

BERTIE: How mean can you get?

RAEANNE: You're lucky you went to private schools, so you didn't have him. He's not like teachers in private schools. He doesn't like boys.

BERTIE: Yes. He's not like teachers in private schools.

RAEANNE: No wonder Bram's confused and doesn't know what he wants to be in life.

BERTIE: I had the same problem. I didn't know either.

RAEANNE: You didn't?

BERTIE: I didn't want to be a doctor and I didn't want to be a lawyer. And I didn't want to be an indian chief—well, I did want to be an indian chief but it seemed hopeless. But now I know what I want to be—

RAEANNE: What?

BERTIE: A husband—your husband. *(RAEANNE cries)* Now, don't do that. There, there. I apologize. Don't you think you could love a man like me?

RAEANNE: Yes, as long as he's not too much like you.

BERTIE: I take it back—I didn't mean it.

RAEANNE: *(The clouds parting a little)* You didn't?

BERTIE: No, I didn't mean a word of it. It was a lie.

RAEANNE: Oh, I'm so relieved. I wanted you for a friend and if you loved me, it would just go and ruin it.

BERTIE: It would?

RAEANNE: Yes, then you'd always be trying to impress me. We could never relax.

BERTIE: What a relief! As I said, I never really loved you. Sylvia put me up to it.

RAEANNE: Sylvia?

BERTIE: Oh, dear. I never could tell a decent lie. I'd better go and watch the sailboat race. *(Exits)*

BRAM: *(Entering)* So, what's been going on between you and little Ethelbert?

RAEANNE: Oh, we're just friends.

BRAM: Friends!

RAEANNE: He asked me to marry him. Sylvia put him up to it!

BRAM: Sylvia!

RAEANNE: Someday I'm going to get even with Sylvia.

BRAM: Leave that to me. I've got it all worked out. I'm going to relieve Sylvia of some of her money worries and some of her money.

RAEANNE: That's just what she deserves. Maybe then she won't be so high and mighty. She'll be just poor white trash like us.

BRAM: Yes, I'm going to get her to marry me and take charge of her estate. And you and I will live on her money.

RAEANNE: Marry her?

BRAM: Yes, I'm going to trick Sylvia into marrying me. Then what's hers is mine and what's mine is hers. Only what's mine is nothing and what's hers is . . . well, I don't exactly know how much. But it must be plenty.

RAEANNE: It might not be enough to make it worth marrying her.

BRAM: It has to be. The Woodvilles aren't exactly paupers, you know.

RAEANNE: But why do you have to marry her?

BRAM: I just told you. It's the one legal way to get her to support us.

RAEANNE: I thought we were going to get married.

BRAM: We are—later, someday. As soon as we get back from the honeymoon, I'll swing into action. I've studied accounting. I can juggle those books so many ways they're gonna book my act at Ringling Brothers. *("Juggles" checkbook)*

RAEANNE: That's extortion!

BRAM: Yes, extortion! The word's pure music!

RAEANNE: But why do you have to go on a honeymoon?

BRAM: That's when I'm going to win her confidence—on the honeymoon.

RAEANNE: If you go on a honeymoon with her, I'll kill myself!

BRAM: We knew this wasn't going to be easy.

RAEANNE: No, I'll kill her.

BRAM: Juggling relationships with two different women is difficult.

RAEANNE: No, I'll kill you.

BRAM: But don't worry. I think I can handle it.

RAEANNE: I can't handle it. I can't continue a relationship this way. *(Pulls out switchblade knife)*

BRAM: Don't do anything foolish.

RAEANNE: *(Puts knife away)* Thanks for a lovely evening. *(Starts to go through doors)*

BRAM: Let me take you home.

RAEANNE: I can get there by myself, thank you. *(Starts to go)*

BRAM: Raeanne.

RAEANNE: *(Turns)* Yes?

BRAM: Nothing. *(She turns and goes.* SYLVIA *peeks in and enters)* Aren't you afraid to be walking?

SYLVIA: No, they're all at the Yacht Club watching the annual race.

BRAM: What are you doing?

SYLVIA: I'm torturing this fly. I'm about to pull its wings off.

BRAM: *(Forcing her hand to open)* Let go. Let go. There's nothing there! *(SYLVIA laughs)* You're sick, lady.

(BRAM lifts weights.)

SYLVIA: Do you have to lift weights in the parlor? The smell of the sweat rolling from your armpits disgusts me.

BRAM: Don't you like the smell of a man?

SYLVIA: Men don't interest me. I'd rather read a book.

BRAM: You know, it's funny. All that time I wanted you. I would have done anything to have you. You were unattainable to me. Now when I can use you as I please you no longer interest me.

SYLVIA: Bram, as much as I loathe and detest you, I'm glad we have this moment alone together. I've been up all night thinking. You took advantage of me. You caught me off my guard. You had no right to the liberties you took.

BRAM: I bartered for them.

SYLVIA: Oh, what a fool I was to think that anyone would believe you!

BRAM: I have the truth on my side.

SYLVIA: It would be your word against mine. Who do you think they would believe, a poor cripple or a big strong man who did . . . what you did to me.

BRAM: *(Coolly)* I think what you did to me would be more like it.

SYLVIA: *(Covering her face with her hands in shame)* You monster!

BRAM: And what's more I think you enjoyed it. You seemed to be enjoying it.

SYLVIA: *(Covering her ears)* I hate you! I hate you!

BRAM: Come, come, Sylvia. I didn't force you. You agreed to it.

SYLVIA: *(Lashing out like a cornered cat)* I was tricked! You have no power over me. You're nothing but a servant here. Why, I could fire you anytime I choose.

BRAM: *(Calmly smiling)* Go ahead, Sylvia, fire me. *(Pause)* Well, what are you waiting for? *(Pause)* Then I'm not fired? *(Laughs)* No, I'm not fired. *(Grabbing her roughly)* Listen to me, you little tramp. You are my slave, no more and no less.

SYLVIA: You're hurting my arm.

BRAM: *(Through his teeth)* What are you? I want to hear it from your own lips.

SYLVIA: *(In a hushed voice)* Slave.

BRAM: Whose slave?

SYLVIA: *(As if about to faint)* Your slave.

BRAM: Good. I think we understand each other now. Yes, I think we've finally come to an understanding. *(Throws her back down on the couch, sits in side chair. Throws his boot on pouffe)* Things are going to be a little different around here. From now on you will address me as master whenever we are alone together.

SYLVIA: I will in a pig's eye!

BRAM: You will in a pig's eye what?

SYLVIA: I will in a pig's eye . . . Master.

BRAM: That's better. You do my bidding and I keep your secret. Fair exchange is no robbery.

SYLVIA: Fair exchange!

BRAM: You can begin by wiping my boots.

SYLVIA: What am I supposed to wipe them with, the drapes?

BRAM: Use your dress.

SYLVIA: How will I explain the smudge marks?

BRAM: Use your undies then. *(Leans back and puts up his feet)*

SYLVIA: *(Reaching under her dress and slipping off her undies)* Someday I'll get even with you for this.

BRAM: What did you say? Show a little respect.

SYLVIA: I said, "Someday I'll get even with you for this, Master."

BRAM: That's better. Now get down to it.

SYLVIA: Aren't you going to take your boots off?

BRAM: Uh . . . uh . . . uh.

SYLVIA: Master?

BRAM: No.

SYLVIA: But how will I wipe them way over there? . . . Master?

BRAM: Get down on your knees.

SYLVIA: *(Whispering)* But what if someone should come in, Master?

BRAM: We'll tell them you were showing me the pattern in the rug. Get started, my slave. *(SYLVIA starts to wipe his boots)* Ugh, get up. You make me sick. You'd do anything. Nothing is beneath you. *(SYLVIA starts to cry)* Turn off the sprinkler system, honey. The fire has gone out. I haven't got time to play games with you now. I want to talk business. You and I had better start acting real friendly when other people are around because we're going to get married. *(Steps over SYLVIA)*

SYLVIA: Married! How dare you?!

BRAM: What's wrong? You wanted to marry me once. But your father didn't think the gardener was good enough for you.

SYLVIA: Well now I don't think you're good enough.

BRAM: *(Grabs her)* Good enough or not, you're going to be Mrs. Brammon Taylor. And hubbie is going to take charge of your business affairs, seeing as how you're a poor cripple and can't get around.

SYLVIA: That does it, buster. This time you've gone too far. I'm going to expose the whole thing myself. Nothing they could do would be as bad as marrying a man who repels me.

BRAM: *(Dryly)* Ha. Ha. Don't make me laugh. *(Putting on airs)* I don't think you could tell the truth if you wanted to. You're not capable of it.

SYLVIA: Just watch me! Where is my bell?

BRAM: If you're going to confess, what do you need your bell for? Stand on your own two feet, march down there to the Yacht Club, and tell them.

SYLVIA: *(Does not move)* You'd like that, wouldn't you? To see me stripped of everything.

BRAM: On the contrary, I'd like to put that money to work building Gerbil Generators.

SYLVIA: Gerbil Generators?

BRAM: Did you ever see the way a gerbil runs on his exercise wheel, how tirelessly he turns that wheel? Well, if that treadmill was attached to an armature, and that armature was attached to a generator, that gerbil could produce enough electricity to power a flashlight. Now it stands to reason that thousands and thousands of tiny little gerbils running and running could produce enough electricity to power New York City free! No nukes, no Arabs, no Con Ed. And I think there could be a subsidiary tie-in to solve the rodent problem.

SYLVIA: *(Laughs)* You're insane! It would never work! If it's free, how do you make any money?

BRAM: The units have to be designed, manufactured, and installed. There would be a nominal cost at first. But after that no monthly bills, and I've already gotten a breeder pair.

SYLVIA: *(Archly)* My father made his money by investing in public utilities. Now you want to put them out of business.

BRAM: All great fortunes were made by investing in long shots. Mankind has come a long way in evolution from the gerbil. But don't you trouble your pretty little head about it. I'll be the brains in this business. You just have to play the model wife.

SYLVIA: I'll never marry you! I'd kill myself first!

BRAM: Would you? That would be wonderful. Because then I would simply have to produce this letter.

SYLVIA: *(Stricken)* Letter?

BRAM: Oh, don't tell me you forgot! *(Takes out the letter)* It smells like you used to smell—delicately of rose water. That was ten years ago, before you started stinking yourself up with expensive commercial perfume. The heavy scents they name after vices . . . Sin, Temptation, White Lies . . .

SYLVIA: You've had it all this time?

BRAM: No, Sylvia. You were supposed to leave the key under the doormat, your answer under the statue. I came and found the door barred against me, the windows shuttered.

SYLVIA: You're being very theatrical.

BRAM: I assumed the answer was no.

SYLVIA: *(Breaks down and tells the truth)* It wasn't my fault. My mother guessed I was pregnant. I was so frightened I blurted out a confession. They took me away before I had time to tell you.

BRAM: Pregnant? Are you sure you were the mother?

SYLVIA: Yes.

BRAM: Did you have to tell the truth?

SYLVIA: *(Quietly, sincerely)* That was the last time I ever did. *(Pause)*

BRAM: Is the child living?

SYLVIA: *(Laughing bitterly)* I think you have more maternal instinct than I do! Yes, the child is being raised excellently by nuns. I've been to see her a few times. She doesn't interest me really. I think I bore her, too. The only thing she's interested in is insects . . . bees, I think.

BRAM: Why didn't you write to me? Why didn't you tell me any of this? Things might have been so different.

SYLVIA: *(Defiantly)* Because I was having too much fun. And I wasn't going to let you or your brat spoil it for me.

BRAM: What did you name her . . . our daughter.

SYLVIA: Sylvietta.

BRAM: That's the first thing we'll change after we're married. Sylvietta means Little Sylvia. I'll be damned if I'll see her take after you.

SYLVIA: I told you we're not going to be married.

BRAM: But, Sylvia, according to this letter we already are.

SYLVIA: Damn you!

BRAM: I'll tell you what, Sylvia. I'm going to do something you would never do for another human being. I'm going to give you a break. I'm so sure that I'm going to marry you that I don't even need to use that letter. In fact, I'm going to give you a chance to recover it.

SYLVIA: *(Amazed)* You will?

BRAM: Yes. While your back was turned, I hid the letter somewhere in this room. If you can find it before anyone comes along and discovers your little secret, it's yours. Have fun.

(BRAM *turns on his heel and exits.* SYLVIA *leaps to her feet and, checking the exits, tears the room apart searching for the letter. Footsteps are heard.* SYLVIA *becomes more and more frantic.*)

SYLVIA: I'll go mad! Oh, what's the use? The only place I haven't looked . . . But he wouldn't . . . or would he? (SYLVIA *rushes to the statue and finds the letter under it as the* PASTOR *enters and discovers her walking*) It's here!

PASTOR: You can walk?

SYLVIA: Not again!

PASTOR: But I just saw you. You walked. With a slight limp, perhaps, but you walked. Why didn't you tell anyone that you could walk? Your mother has been worried sick about you.

SYLVIA: Oh, Father, I couldn't bear to have them see me clumping around. It's so ungraceful.

PASTOR: My child, my child, "O what a tangled web we weave when first we practice to deceive."

SYLVIA: Oh Father, is there any hope for me? Tell me that I'm not utterly lost.

PASTOR: There is more rejoicing among the heavenly multitude over one sinner who repents than over all the righteous.

SYLVIA: Then you mean I can still be saved? Tell me what I must do.

PASTOR: Get down on your knees.

SYLVIA: (*Horrified*) What? You wouldn't make me do that! You, a man of the cloth.

PASTOR: It is customary to kneel when receiving the sacraments.

SYLVIA: Sacraments? (*Relieved*) Oh, the SACRAMENTS! (*Kneels*)

PASTOR: Yes, the sacrament of penance. What did you think I meant? Do you know the confiteor?

SYLVIA: Vaguely.

PASTOR: Don't worry, my child, I'll help you if you forget the words. Now make a good confession.

SYLVIA: Pastor, this *is* all confidential?

PASTOR: This will be a secret between you and God.

SYLVIA: I'm not overly concerned about God keeping my secret. It's your discretion I need assurance of.

PASTOR: I am His representative. I never forget my function.

SYLVIA: Men rarely do.

PASTOR: Shall we begin while we still have this time alone together? "Bless me Father for I have sinned . . ."

SYLVIA: "Bless me Father for I have sinned." It has been ten years since my last confession.

PASTOR: Whew!

SYLVIA: What do you mean "whew"?

PASTOR: It's fortunate that I came upon you when I did. You are in a state of mortal sin. If you had died unconfessed, I'm afraid your soul would be irretrievably lost. But go on.

SYLVIA: It happened during a riding accident. I was riding sidesaddle because I was a virgin. I didn't want to lose my virginity because of a horse. Someone set off a firecracker. The horse shied and threw me in a ditch. Then everything went dark. For months I couldn't walk. The doctors gave me up as hopeless. But gradually the strength came back to my legs. I discovered that I could walk, but with this hideous limp. I didn't tell anyone. I felt that if I couldn't walk like other people, I'd rather not walk at all.

PASTOR: Your sin was vanity.

SYLVIA: Oh Father, how can I make amends?

PASTOR: You must try never to commit that sin again.

SYLVIA: But how? How?

PASTOR: Well, you could begin by telling everyone the truth.

SYLVIA: *(Rising abruptly)* Oh no! That isn't possible.

PASTOR: My child, anything is possible if you have faith in Him.

SYLVIA: Who?

PASTOR: God.

SYLVIA: *(Just realizing)* Oh, *Him.*

PASTOR: Think of the love and kindness everyone has shown you when they thought you were afflicted. Surely they will rejoice when they hear you are recovered.

SYLVIA: What kindness?

PASTOR: Why, everyone in your family has made incredible sacrifices for you. Your father even left you his entire estate because he thought you were crippled. *(Stops suddenly)* Oh my! I can see that it might be awkward to tell them now.

SYLVIA: You see the problem.

PASTOR: Yes, I do indeed. But perhaps another form of penance might be more appropriate.

SYLVIA: Anything! Anything so long as I don't have to tell *them.*

PASTOR: Rather than use your ill-gotten money yourself, you could put it to some worthy charitable cause.

SYLVIA: Such as?

PASTOR: The boys' orphanage is sorely in need of funds.

SYLVIA: Orphanage?

PASTOR: Yes, you could donate all of your inheritance to the boys' orphanage. Then the angels would be sure to put a gold star after your name in that great big book in heaven.

SYLVIA: Well you can tell your angels that they can just keep their gold stars. I'll keep my money, thank you, and go to hell with myself. I'm not an angel, Pastor Bates.

PASTOR: You're no better than you should be. There is a divine plan and we are all a part of it—saints and sinners alike. The Lord provides, Sylvia. He watches over wealthy heiresses and poor orphaned boys.

SYLVIA: I don't see the connection.

PASTOR: Don't you? He brought us together. He led me into this room and revealed your secret to me. Your penance will save your soul and the souls of those homeless boys at the same time.

SYLVIA: Holy blackmail.

PASTOR: We were drawn together inexorably by a power far greater than ourselves.

SYLVIA: *(Looking deeply into his eyes)* You know, Pastor, I'm beginning to feel it too. I've been a bad woman. I know I have. But your words have given me strength. Somewhere deep in your eyes I feel a destiny beckoning to me. A destiny so great I would sacrifice anything to it.

PASTOR: How insignificant our little sacrifices seem when we think of the great sacrifice on Calvary. A sacrifice that redeemed the world.

SYLVIA: If only I could redeem any small part of it.

PASTOR: *(Exultant)* You will, Sylvia! You will! First offer your hands to those orphaned boys. Then someday they will offer their hands to others and so on until there is a great chain of helping hands circling the globe. Oh what a world we could show our Savior then if only you would dedicate your heart, your soul, and your money to your fellow men in need.

SYLVIA: Oh, Pastor, would you believe me if I told you that I feel clean again? Your words have washed over me and baptized me anew. I want to dedicate my life to this new vision you have given me. Tell me I may work at your side. Let me be your helpmeet.

PASTOR: How could I refuse?

SYLVIA: I feel a great love radiating from within me. I feel it radiating from you too. I love you, Pastor, I love you as never Woman did love Man.

PASTOR: This is His love you feel, Sylvia. It surrounds us both. We are one in Him.

SYLVIA: Is it possible that such happiness can exist in the world? I had given up hoping I would ever find it.

PASTOR: You have found it, Sylvia. I have found it too. You will work at my side. As I am a priest, you will be my priestess.

SYLVIA: No! No! This can never be. Have you forgotten my mother?

PASTOR: Oh, yes, that.

SYLVIA: She loves you too. Alas! Alas! That we should both love you. Such is your charisma.

PASTOR: Your mother and I have broken off our engagement. My heart is free, is mine to give. Take it, it's yours.

SYLVIA: No! No! As long as Mother loves you, I must live a virgin. For you are the only man in the world to me now.

PASTOR: But what about my boys? You haven't wavered in your commitment to them I hope?

SYLVIA: Without your constant inspiration, I fear my resolve may be shaken.

PASTOR: But, Sylvia, remember your penance. Remember your confession.

SYLVIA: Penance is the sacrament. Not confession. I might donate my fortune to another worthier cause. A girls' orphanage, for example.

PASTOR: You wouldn't.

SYLVIA: If I'm not to be your priestess, I might become a Jew . . . or start my own religion. I could afford it.

PASTOR: Heresy!

SYLVIA: From my slender knowledge of history, I've gleaned that human thought progresses by heresy. What was Henry the Eighth? Why Calvary instead of a pension? How come Moses was not allowed into the Promised Land?

PASTOR: *(Mock applause)* Bravo! Excellent! Did you think that up yourself or did you memorize it?

SYLVIA: What's the matter? Afraid the laity will beat you at your own game— rhetoric?

PASTOR: *(Putting his arms around her)* You're a fascinating little she-devil, do you know that?

SYLVIA: *(Slipping out of his embrace coquettishly)* Aren't you afraid to make love to a devil?

PASTOR: *(Cornering her)* Not if I could conquer her with love.

SYLVIA: I see beneath his skirts a priest is still a man. *(Pushes him away rudely)*

PASTOR: *(Pursuing her)* Would you break those little boys' hearts?

SYLVIA: *(Eluding him)* Would you have me break my mother's heart? *(Sitting on couch)*

PASTOR: Sly Sylvia. Then it would seem that I have no choice but to wait and bide my time although now I feel less obliged to certain confidences that I would have held had the bond between us been what it might have been. Indeed had the bond between us been what anyone might have expected it to become. Therefore I feel less obliged as I said before to hold those aforesaid confidences, confidences which by their very nature might cause a sudden change in social position for the one, yes the very one whom I might, had things been other than what they now are, have held in highest esteem, secret since they were not confessed to me, but rather discovered by me and therefore not participate in the benefits of clerical discretion, having been witnessed EX CATHEDRA. In other words . . . I'll tell.

SYLVIA: I see that I am powerless against your superior intellect. Come to me tonight when you have put my mother to bed. I'll give you everything I have.

PASTOR: Everything?

SYLVIA: Yes, everything.

PASTOR: You said beneath his skirts a priest is still a man. Well, now you'll get to see for yourself.

SYLVIA: But Pastor Bates—

PASTOR: *(Interrupting)* There's no need to be so formal. You can call me Fenwick.

SYLVIA: Must I?

PASTOR: I'd prefer it. When we're alone.

SYLVIA: If I must, I must. Fenwick, I'm a virgin. I'm saving myself for my husband.

PASTOR: Husband? What husband?

SYLVIA: Bram and I are going to be married.

PASTOR: What can you possibly see in that Milquetoast? I'm surprised he ever got up enough gumption to pop the question.

SYLVIA: Well he did. And I accepted.

PASTOR: I can't believe you would throw yourself away on someone like that. You always held him in such contempt.

SYLVIA: You don't understand women.

PASTOR: I understand them as well as you do.

SYLVIA: That's what I said. You don't understand women. Bram is going to be my husband.

PASTOR: That needn't change anything between us.

SYLVIA: Even after I'm married?

PASTOR: Especially after you're married.

SYLVIA: *(With growing horror)* And after you've married my mother?

PASTOR: Even then.

SYLVIA: And you'll be the one cock in the henhouse.

PASTOR: Yes, the one cock in the henhouse. After you've had me, you'll be spoiled for all others.

SYLVIA: Forgive me, Pastor Bates, but I've never seen a man naked before. So come at night, in a darkened room, after everyone is asleep. That way, you won't offend my virgin modesty.

PASTOR: You are a devil after all. When I look at you, the blood vessels in my temples pound out a strange tattoo. Pa dam pa dam pa dam. Temptress, let me taste your lips and I'll worship Beelzebub.

EVE: *(Enters and discovers the* PASTOR *on his knees before* SYLVIA *and drops a tray)* Pastor! Sylvia! What are you doing?

SYLVIA: Mother, call off your priest. He talks about nothing but religion. He's been on his knees half an hour praying for my recovery. And it hasn't helped a bit.

EVE: Sylvia, I won't have you be disrespectful to Reverend Bates.

SYLVIA: Mother, you're fired.

EVE: Fired? I thought slaves were sold. *(Exits)*

PASTOR: Get yourself ready, Sylvia, and I'll meet you in the master bedroom as soon as your mother is asleep. *(Exits)*

(Enter BRAM *combing his hair.)*

SYLVIA: Well, Bram, I suppose you've come to have your way with me again.

BRAM: No, Sylvia, I'm sorry I ever did that. From now on there can't be any more hanky-panky. Our marriage is going to be strictly a business arrangement.

SYLVIA: But I thought I was your slave.

BRAM: Forget that stuff. I was a louse to make you do that. I'm just no good.

SYLVIA: But we're both no good. We deserve each other.

BRAM: No Sylvia—it was fun while it lasted but I don't want to hurt Raeanne. Good night.

SYLVIA: So the training has already begun. Don't go. You can't leave me—not at a time like this.

BRAM: I haven't got any clothes to get married in. I've got to borrow a tux from the doorman down at the bowling alley.

SYLVIA: Don't bother—I want you to wear my father's uniform.

BRAM: I couldn't wear Colonel Woodville's uniform. He wouldn't want me to.

SYLVIA: But I want you to. I've had it unpacked and cleaned—just for this occasion. If it fits you must wear it.

BRAM: But Colonel Woodville couldn't stand me.

SYLVIA: This will serve him right. Go in the kitchen and try it on.

(Exit BRAM.*)*

BERTIE: *(Entering)* Sylvia, I've decided I want to be a ballet dancer.

SYLVIA: Be careful, Bertie. Ballet dancers have midlife crisis.

BERTIE: Midlife crisis nothing. In ballet you're washed up when you get pubic hair.

SYLVIA: Bertie, would you carry me into my room? There's something I want you to do for me.

[*(They exit.)*]

BERTIE: *(From off)* You can walk!

*(*SYLVIA *reenters and goes up the stairs. Doorbell rings and the* PASTOR *answers it. His voice is heard off.)*

PASTOR: Gorilla? No, officer. We haven't seen any gorilla. When did it escape? Well, I certainly hope you catch it. Check the hedges down by the drive.

Dangerous, eh? I'll be sure to lock all the doors and windows. Thank you. Good night.

(During the previous speech, GORILLA *appears at French doors, opens them, and enters.)*

SYLVIA: *(Voice from upstairs)* Bram, is that you? *(*GORILLA *goes upstairs)* Oh, Bram . . . Oh, oh.

*(*PASTOR, *returning from off left, sees French doors left ajar and closes them. He tiptoes to the door of bedroom up center and knocks softly.)*

PASTOR: *(Whispering)* Sylvia. Sylvia.

(Door opens. BERTIE, *in drag as Sylvia, comes out wearing a veil and hiding behind a fan.* PASTOR *chases her around the sofa and back into the room.* EVE *enters sleepwalking. She opens the door to the balcony and goes out, balancing precariously out on the balustrade, as in Act I. A flashlight shines up into her face.)*

RAEANNE: *(Voice)* Mrs. Woodville!

*(*EVE *teeters and falls off the balcony.* RAEANNE *enters with* EVE *in her arms and goes to couch.)*

EVE: Thank heavens you caught me. I would have ruined the rhododendrons. Raeanne, I've been sleepwalking more and more lately. I keep dreaming about my late husband. Do you think he's trying to contact me?
RAEANNE: It's very likely. The departed often appear in dreams.
EVE: Do you think you can contact him?
RAEANNE: I'll try. Put your hands on the table. Are you there, Little Chief?
EVE: Who's Little Chief?
RAEANNE: He's my familiar. Are you there, Little Chief? *(Moaning upstairs)* You may speak to him now.
EVE: Little Chief? Little Chief, I'm trying to contact my husband, Colonel Woodville. Is he there?

(Doors fly open. Sounds of banging and fisticuffs come from the master bedroom, SYLVIA's *moaning orgasmically from upstairs.)*

RAEANNE: I think we're making contact.

*(*BRAM *enters from the kitchen in the Colonel's uniform.* EVE, *seeing him, screams.)*

EVE: Bert! *(Faints)*

Curtain

Scene 2

*(*EVE *is arranging flowers.)*

EVE: First something old, then something new, then something borrowed, then something blue, then something yellow, then something pink, then something green, then something orange—Sylvia has no taste. I finally convinced her to wear white but she was set against it. I wonder why.
BERTIE: Mother, can't you guess?

EVE: It's traditional! All brides wear white. The only time a bride wouldn't wear white is if she wasn't a . . . Oh, no—Bertie, do you think that's the reason?

BERTIE: Mother, she's been had.

EVE: Oh no! How could that be? We gave her a proper upbringing.

BERTIE: Upbringing is no match for instinct.

EVE: I don't like that word, instinct. It's like a bad smell. *(Sprays the room with aerosol deodorant)*

BERTIE: Upbringing sounds like regurgitation. Let's not mince words. . . .

EVE: Don't eat the canapés.

BERTIE: Don't worry, I won't. Make them yourself?

EVE: No, they're catered.

BERTIE: In that case . . . *(Reaches for canapés and eats them behind* EVE's *back)*

EVE: I gave Sylvia a very enlightened sex education. I didn't want her to learn the facts of life in the gutter. That can lead a young girl into trouble. I taught her there are ways to satisfy a man and still remain a virgin.

BERTIE: Mother, I don't recall your ever giving me even the slightest sexual education.

EVE: Didn't your father tell you?

BERTIE: No, he never did.

EVE: But you do know now, don't you? Surely you've heard.

BERTIE: There have been hints but always in veiled terms.

EVE: Didn't you pick it up in the gutter?

BERTIE: Mother, I have never seen a gutter. And I don't think the things the boys taught me at prep school quite reliable.

EVE: Why not?

BERTIE: Well . . . what are *girls* for?

EVE: Bertie, this is not an easy subject for me to discuss with my own son. So here's my advice. Go down to the newsstand and buy a pornographic magazine that's profusely illustrated. One picture is worth a thousand words. But be sure to get one with pictures of girls in it too.

BERTIE: Yes, Mother.

EVE: And would you bring me a *Newsday?* I want to see Sylvia's picture in the Brides-to-Be column. Bram and Sylvia seem so mismatched. I don't see what they see in each other. Oh, Bertie! You've eaten all the canapés and I don't know where I'm going to get any more pork tartare at this hour! Here's Bram.

*(*BERTIE *gags.)*

BRAM: Bertie, here's the ring; now don't lose it.

EVE: Bram, have you had breakfast? I'll make eggs.

BERTIE: For the yoke will soon be on you. *(Exits)*

BRAM: I've lost my appetite.

EVE: Here's Reverend Bates.

PASTOR: Is everything ready? I really don't like marrying people without a rehearsal. It makes me nervous. I didn't sleep a wink all night.

EVE: Well, sit down and take a load off your feet.

PASTOR: I'd prefer not to. I mean I can't. *(Confidentially aside to* EVE*)* Hemorrhoids.

EVE: I have an ointment that does wonders for hemorrhoids. It's right here in my bag. *(Putting on her glasses and reading label)* "Kiss your hemorrhoids goodbye forever."

PASTOR: I'll try anything. *(Takes preparation)*

EVE: I'm going to take the cake out of the oven. Now, whatever you do, don't make any loud noises or walk heavily on the floor because the cake will fall.

PASTOR: I'll go change.

EVE: I hope there's time to frost it. *(Exits)*

BRAM: I'll go see what Sylvia's doing.

PASTOR: My boy, you can't do that! *(Sentimentally)* Don't you know that it's unlucky for the groom to see the bride before the wedding?

BRAM: Shame on you, Father. Talking superstition and you a man o' th' cloth! *(Bounds toward Sylvia's room)*

PASTOR: *(Stepping desperately between BRAM and the door to block his way)* You can't go in there! She's not dressed yet. It's not decent!

EVE: *(Calling from kitchen)* Pastor! Pastor! Come and see. The cake turned out beautifully.

BRAM: He's coming!

PASTOR: *(Furious but calling sweetly)* Yes, I'm coming! *(Exit)*

(BRAM slips into Sylvia's room and slams the door. EVE is heard to scream from the kitchen.)

BRAM: *(Reentering)* She's not there. *(Exits upstairs)*

(Phone onstage rings. BATES rushes in and answers it.)

PASTOR: Woodville residence. Ah, Deacon, I'm glad you called. Am I to baptize the Winthrop brat on this Sunday or next? Why would they cancel? Paper? No, I haven't seen the paper. *(Lowering his voice in a deadly calm)* Oh no! Oh no! Oh no! Why this is an outrage! I'll sue them for libel. I'll . . . I'll . . . I'll . . . The children banded together? *(Covering the mouthpiece of the phone, aside)* The little traitors! *(Aloud)* Apparently they weren't whipped hard enough. *(Alarmed)* The authorities! Assault charges? Child abuse! This is terrible! Why, of course there isn't a shred of truth in it. Everyone knows I've devoted myself to those boys. They needed discipline; that's what it was. I'm just about to secure a donation for the orphanage right now. Shhh! No one must know of this, do you hear? Don't talk to anyone until you hear from me. This could ruin everything. Shhh. I can't talk now. *(As EVE enters, he changes his tone)* Yes, Mrs. Winthrop. Then the christening is canceled, I understand. Good-bye.

EVE: *(Entering, then very concerned)* The Winthrops have canceled the christening? Why?

PASTOR: *(Quickly fabricating a lie)* Er . . . the child's sick. It may die.

EVE: That's all the more reason not to cancel the christening. If the child dies unbaptized, its soul goes to limbo.

PASTOR: *(Caught off guard)* Yes! That's right. Why didn't *I* think of that?

EVE: I must call Mrs. Winthrop.

PASTOR: *(Exclaiming)* No!

EVE: Why not?

PASTOR: It's terribly embarrassing. They've converted—to Judaism.

EVE: Oh. In that case I suppose there's no point in insisting. But I should call to find out how the child is doing.

PASTOR: NO! They're not at home. They've gone to Switzerland to a specialist.

EVE: Then there's no point in calling. I wonder why they converted.

PASTOR: The husband.

EVE: I thought there was something.

PASTOR: Yes, there was *something.*

EVE: Although I'll admit I don't know the proper etiquette in a case like this. Does one send congratulations?

PASTOR: *(Reprimanding her)* Eve!

EVE: I didn't mean that the way it sounded. *(EVE gets tea cart with cake)* I'm afraid the cake fell. But I repaired it. Have some coffee, Pastor?

PASTOR: I'd kill for a cup.

BERTIE: *(Entering brightly)* Here's the paper.

PASTOR: Good God! The paper. *(Grabs the paper and leafs through it searching for the article)*

EVE: *(To PASTOR)* Have you found the article?

PASTOR: *(Taken aback)* Why . . . er . . . ah . . . no—not yet.

EVE: It shouldn't be hard to find. There's a picture with it.

PASTOR: *(Alarmed)* Picture?!!!

EVE: Yes. *(Looks over his shoulder)* Ah, there it is. My, doesn't Sylvia look lovely. If only she had smiled. I really should cut this out. *(Takes out page and holds it up revealing to the audience the article feared by the Pastor on the other side: the one that says, "Abusive Pastor Accused," and features a large picture of Bates)*

PASTOR: *(Snatches sheet from EVE)* Give me that. . . . *(Folds it up and hides it under his coat)* Er . . . I want to save it for my scrapbook.

EVE: But I was hoping to keep it for *my* scrapbook.

BERTIE: Don't worry, Mother. I got two copies.

PASTOR: *(Emits a tiny shriek)* Ahhh! *(All look at him)* Then that's the solution! A copy for each of us!

EVE: Let me cut out the picture. *(Opens second newspaper and reveals child abuse headlines to audience as before)*

PASTOR: Let me do that. *(Deliberately spills his coffee on the paper)* Oh dear. I've gone and ruined it. *(Crumples paper and throws it away)*

BERTIE: Don't worry, Pastor. There are plenty more where that one came from.

PASTOR: *(In agony)* I know. I know.

RAEANNE: *(Entering)* Have you seen Sylvia's picture in the paper this morning?

EVE: Just a glimpse. My copy got ruined.

RAEANNE: You can have mine. I don't want it. *(Hands paper to EVE)*

PASTOR: No! *(Dives for paper and snatches it away)*

RAEANNE: What?

BERTIE: What's the matter with him?

EVE: Is something wrong, Pastor?

PASTOR: No. But we have a wedding to perform. This is no time to be reading newspapers.

BRAM: *(Entering from Sylvia's room)* Well, Sylvia's ready. I guess we'd better get started and tie the knot.

EVE: Bram . . . Son . . . you didn't see Sylvia before the wedding? That's bad luck.

PASTOR: I'll say!

BRAM: Don't worry Mrs. Woodvi . . . Mother. She never lifted her veil.

EVE: That's good. I wouldn't want anything to spoil the wedding.

BRAM: Have you seen the paper? They've run Sylvia's picture.

PASTOR: *(Aside)* Another one! *(Dives for the paper and tears it from BRAM's hands)* Does everyone read that damned paper?

BRAM: It has the largest circulation on Long Island.

PASTOR: Where's the Bible?

BERTIE: It's right here. *(Hides magazine in Bible)*

BRAM: Sylvia wants to see Raeanne and Bertie.

EVE: Tell her everyone's here and we're ready to begin. Since Colonel Wood-ville isn't here to do it, Bertie's going to give Sylvia away.

BERTIE: Nothing could give me more pleasure. *(Exits)*

RAEANNE: *(Turning to BRAM sharply, aside)* Bram, how could you do this to me!

BRAM: *(Under his breath)* Raeanne, please try to understand. Don't make a scene.

(RAEANNE turns and marches upstairs as if to her execution.)

EVE: *(Crosses to the phonograph)* Let me know when you're ready. I always cry at weddings. *(Sits by the phonograph on Colonel Woodville's sword)* Eeeeeeek! *(Screaming, jumps up)* Who left this sword here?

BRAM: I did. Sorry, Mother.

EVE: You must wear it. Ah, you look like Colonel Woodville on our wedding day. I'm so happy. I'm so happy. *(Cries)*

BERTIE: *(On the stairs)* You can start the music, Mother. She's ready.

EVE: Where's Raeanne?

BERTIE: She's upstairs crying her eyes out.

EVE: Isn't she going to come down?

BERTIE: No, she says she can't bear to watch.

EVE: I'll go to her.

BRAM: Please let's continue without her. She'll get over it.

PASTOR: *(Impatiently)* Yes, please let's get this over with.

EVE: Very well, perhaps it's better to leave her alone.

BERTIE: Let her cry herself out.

(EVE puts on phonograph record. The Wedding March from Lohengrin, *sung in German, plays. Record skips and sticks occasionally.* BERTIE *carries* SYLVIA, *heavily veiled, down the stairs.)*

PASTOR: Do you take this woman to be your lawfully wedded wife?

BRAM: I do.

PASTOR: Do you take this man to be your lawfully wedded husband?

RAEANNE: *(As Sylvia)* I do.

(PASTOR opens Bible, sees pornographic magazine.)

PASTOR: Jesus Christ!! *(Catching himself)* Our Savior. Bless this union. Amen. If there is anyone here who knows any reason why this couple should not be joined in holy matrimony, speak now or forever hold your peace.

SYLVIA: *(Voice from upstairs)* I'll speak. *(Enters)* I say they deserve each other. They're both imbeciles.

EVE: *(In amazement)* Sylvia, you're walking!

SYLVIA: *(Acerbically)* Fall on your knees, it's a miracle!

EVE: The seance. I must tell Raeanne. *(Goes towards stairs)*

PASTOR: I knew all along she was faking. She confessed it to me. But I could not break my trust.

EVE: *(Turning)* Then the inheritance is mine. . . .

PASTOR: Well, Sylvia, I suppose that was your last night in the master bedroom. *(Chuckles)* Eh eh eh.

SYLVIA: What are you talking about?

PASTOR: You know what I mean—last night.

SYLVIA: I'm afraid I don't know what you mean—I slept with Mother in my room last night.

PASTOR: With Mother???

SYLVIA: Yes, Bertie slept in the master bedroom.

PASTOR: *(Wheeling on* BERTIE *in horror)* Did *you* sleep in the master bedroom last night?

BERTIE: *(Socking his fist into his palm)* Not a wink.

PASTOR: *(Touches his black eye in horror)* My God!

EVE: *(Turning to bride* SYLVIA*)* Then who is this?

(Bride lifts her veil, revealing herself to be RAEANNE.*)*

BRAM: Raeanne!

RAEANNE: I couldn't let you do it, Bram. She doesn't love you. She could never make you happy.

SYLVIA: No, I suppose I couldn't. I have no recourse but to take this letter . . . *(*BRAM *gasps)* . . . and destroy it. *(Tears letter to pieces)*

BRAM: But the child . . .

SYLVIA: Imaginary. I'm no good for you, Bram. I think Raeanne is really what you need. After last night, I've decided even though you make love like an animal, once the fantasy is gone it's just no good.

EVE: Well, Pastor, now that the inheritance is mine again, you needn't worry about money for the boys' orphanage. In fact I'm going to write you a check right now. But you won't be able to cash it until Monday. *(Writes check)*

PASTOR: Why, er, thank you.

EVE: Here you are.

PASTOR: *(Looks at the check)* Eve! This is perhaps too much.

EVE: Not at all. You are my favorite charity. I love children. And I would do anything to protect them from harm.

PASTOR: Thank you. I'd better go right now and tell the deacon. *(Exits)*

RAEANNE: Thank you, Sylvia, Sister. I've done a terrible thing. I stole your hairbrush and tried to turn you into a nightwalker.

EVE: A nightwalker?

RAEANNE: A zombie. *(Twists doll's arm)*

EVE: Ow!! But that's *my* hairbrush. A nightwalker. My sleepwalking. *I* was a nightwalker.

RAEANNE: I'll never do that again. *(Throws doll to floor)*

EVE: *(Falls to floor)* Now cut that out!

BERTIE: But who should get these flowers now? They were intended for Sylvia, *(Reads card)* "from Raeanne."

SYLVIA: I'll open them.

RAEANNE: No!

*(*SYLVIA *opens flower box revealing wooden leg.)*

SYLVIA: Agh!

RAEANNE: I'm so sorry, Sylvia. Bram, let's go.

SYLVIA: Bye-bye, Bram. Cultivate your mind. It's the little things that count.

*(*BRAM *and* RAEANNE *exit.)*

EVE: So, Sylvia, you were faking.

SYLVIA: *(Frightened)* Mother, what are you going to do to me?

EVE: Not much—I'll take my room back. My, the pranks you children play. I don't know where we'd be if we let you get away with it.

BERTIE: What are you going to do now, Sylvia?

SYLVIA: I think I'll play another game of solitaire.

BERTIE: I've finally decided on a career.

EVE: You have, Bertie, that's wonderful. What is it?

BERTIE: I'm going to be a female impersonator.

EVE: Well, as long as you're the best female impersonator you know how to be. Well, everything has turned out for the best! *(Sits in armchair, kicks off her shoes, breathes deeply)* At last, I can relax and read this paper from cover to cover.

Curtain

SECRET LIVES OF THE SEXISTS

The Farce of Modern Life

1982

Nadine (Mink Stole) meets her mother in
Secret Lives of the Sexists (Richard Currie)

Cast of Characters

BUDDY HUSBAND
IZZY HUSBAND, *brother to Buddy*
NADINE HUSBAND, *Buddy's wife*
FANNY HUSBAND, *Izzy's wife*
MME. ZENA GROSSFINGER
PHIL LANDERS
POLICEWOMEN

[PROLOGUE

(The audience sits before a giant keyhole. The shutters containing the keyhole part, revealing MME. ZENA GROSSFINGER *onstage at the Kiss of Fire nightclub. She wears a devil's head on one shoulder, and his outfit clothes one arm. To the tune of a bluesy saxophone combo,* ZENA *and her devil dance seductively. She struggles against him as he attempts to strip her. In the end the devil reveals one breast, and the shutters slam shut.)*]

ACT I

Izzy and Fanny's basement flat in the Lower East Side.
(BUDDY HUSBAND *is sitting in a leather armchair with pipe and slippers reading an anthropology book. Loud rock and roll blares. He writhes about, attempting to concentrate on his book. Finally, in his despair, he screams at the top of his lungs.)*

BUDDY: Izzy, turn that music down . . . Please!
IZZY: *(Poking in his head, from off)* Was the music too loud?
BUDDY: Just a little.
IZZY: *(Entering)* Sorry.
BUDDY: That's all right.

   (In the silence, IZZY *reads over* BUDDY'S *shoulder and munches corn chips noisily.* BUDDY *winces with each crunch.)*

IZZY: Now I want you to make yourself comfortable.
BUDDY: Thank you. I will.
IZZY: *(Munches corn chips)* I want you to feel that my house is your home.
BUDDY: Thanks. I just have to get some reading done because tomorrow I have to pass my orals.
IZZY: *(Munches corn chips)* Don't let anything disturb you.

   (Doorbell rings. IZZY *lets in* NADINE, *exits.)*

NADINE: I'm late.
BUDDY: No you aren't.
NADINE: Yes, I am. I'm an hour late. You must be furious.
BUDDY: Not at all.
NADINE: You must be. It was inexcusable.
BUDDY: No it wasn't.
NADINE: I should have called. How could I have been so inconsiderate?

BUDDY: Why on earth should you have called?

NADINE: I stood you up.

BUDDY: Stood me up? For what?

NADINE: We had a date tonight. Don't tell me you forgot!!

BUDDY: Date? *(Suddenly remembering)* Oh, our *date!* It completely slipped my mind.

NADINE: How could you forget? I guess it couldn't have been very important to you.

BUDDY: I'm sorry. I'm so forgetful. It had something to do with birds, didn't it? We were going to feed the ducks?

NADINE: We were going to see *Swan Lake.*

BUDDY: At least I was close.

NADINE: Out of sight out of mind, I guess.

BUDDY: This trial separation was *your* idea.

NADINE: Well, I couldn't complete my article on sexism with a man standing over me. Anyway, I guess it's over between us.

BUDDY: You thought we should try seeing other people.

NADINE: I guess you're seeing someone else.

BUDDY: As a matter of fact I am.

NADINE: Who is she?

BUDDY: Guess.

NADINE: Guess? You mean I know her?

BUDDY: Yes, you do. As a matter of fact, she's one of your closest friends.

NADINE: Oh . . . I see what you're trying to do! And believe me it won't work. You're not going to turn me against my own sex! Women can honor a bond of friendship. No woman would betray a friend for a man.

BUDDY: All's fair—

NADINE: *(Interrupting)* All's not fair!

BUDDY: Let's go to *Swan Lake.*

NADINE: It was too late for *Swan Lake* when I got here.

BUDDY: That's right. You came an hour late. Where the hell were you?

NADINE: I'm so angry I could tell you the truth!

BUDDY: You probably forgot *yourself.*

NADINE: I didn't forget. I was detained. But please don't be jealous.

BUDDY: Jealous? Why should I be jealous?

NADINE: Oh, now you've gone and guessed everything.

BUDDY: Everything?

NADINE: About the man . . . I've been seeing.

BUDDY: You're not seeing anyone! I don't believe it. *(Pause)* Who is he?

NADINE: I've gone too far! Oh dear! How indiscreet of me!

BUDDY: Darling, I don't believe it. You'll never be unfaithful to me.

NADINE: I won't?

BUDDY: No, you won't. That's one thing I never have to worry about with you, dear. You'd never have an affair. You're not the type.

NADINE: How dare you take me for granted?

BUDDY: You can't cheat. It's not in you.

NADINE: *(Suddenly touched and a little sentimental)* You trust me that much?

BUDDY: It's men I trust. You're not the type men have affairs with. You're the type they marry.

NADINE: *(Enraged)* You think you have me all figured out! In your pocket.

BUDDY: Darling, why fight it? We're suited to each other. We're the best each other can do. There are some compromises we have to make in life. Let's settle for each other.

NADINE: *(Heavily sarcastic)* How romantic!

BUDDY: Darling, we have each other. We have our life together. We even share a common interest . . . anthropology.

NADINE: I should have married Clyde.

BUDDY: Clyde is an archaeologist.

NADINE: Yes, the older I get the more fascinating he finds me.

BUDDY: We have all these things. Why insist on romance? It's asking too much.

NADINE: I'm furious. This was inexcusable. How could you be so inconsiderate? *(Pause, then loudly)* Who is she? Who is she?

BUDDY: Lower your voice.

NADINE: *(In a hoarse whisper but with every bit as much emotional intensity)* Who is she? Who is she?

BUDDY: Dina, there will never be anyone but you.

NADINE: Then you do love me.

BUDDY: I'm comfortable with you.

NADINE: Do you love me?

BUDDY: I'm used to you.

NADINE: I asked you if you love me.

BUDDY: It's more habitual.

NADINE: You don't love me.

BUDDY: How do you claim to understand my feelings when I'm not even sure of them myself?

NADINE: Because I can't make you jealous.

BUDDY: You've never given me cause. You're a safe wife.

NADINE: What makes you so sure? How do you know I haven't taken lovers— lots of lovers—behind your back?

BUDDY: Have you?

NADINE: No.

BUDDY: That's what I mean. You're safe.

NADINE: Stop using that hideous word, "safe"!

BUDDY: All I'm saying is that you're a perfect mate. I've been doing research on early hominids. You know, there were dozens of different kinds of early humans or prehumans. Any of these might have evolved into Man or manlike beings. But they all died out.

NADINE: *(Shuddering)* Who knows what they might have evolved into.

BUDDY: What was it, Dina? What was it about the sexual behavior of Mankind that proved to be an evolutionary advantage? And which aspects of our sexual behavior might work against our survival in the future?

NADINE: Is that why you want a "safe wife," to reproduce the species? You think no more of me than a racehorse or a prize gladiola?

BUDDY: Heavens to Betsy! You've got to leave immediately.

NADINE: Why? I just got here.

BUDDY: You've got to leave and make it snappy.

NADINE: You're actually throwing me out?

BUDDY: I'm afraid so, darling. You see I'm expecting someone that I don't want you to meet just yet. A long lost relative.

NADINE: A long lost relative, huh? Oh, please don't insult my intelligence with a story like that! I know it's a woman!

BUDDY: As a matter of fact it is.

NADINE: That does it! I'm going to stay right here and get a look at her. This "relative," as you say.

BUDDY: *(Forcibly ejecting her)* No you're not! You're going out and the back way!

NADINE: I suppose you're ashamed of me? I'm not good enough to meet your mistresses. I'm not good enough to meet your whores! *(Laughs and bolts out the back way)*

BUDDY: *(Calling after her)* Quite the contrary! Dina . . . *(Alone)* She's so unreasonable. *(Checking the mirror)* I look slept in. *(Primps)* Must make a good impression. *(A light knock is heard at the door. Checking his watch)* Punctual. *(Admits* MADAME ZENA GROSSFINGER*)*

ZENA: You know the strangest thing just happened. As I was coming up your stoop a young woman ran up to me, stared me in the face, and ran away.

BUDDY: Was she wearing a black dress and pearls?

ZENA: Yes.

BUDDY: It was Nadine.

ZENA: *(Alarmed)* You haven't told her, I hope?

BUDDY: No, I haven't told her, but she suspects something. And now her imagination is running away with her. Maybe we should just tell her the truth.

ZENA: Not yet, please. Just bear with me a little longer. The Beauty Salon is beginning to turn a profit now. As soon as I'm making enough money to give up stripping, we'll tell her. But I'm so afraid.

BUDDY: What is there to be afraid of?

ZENA: Nadine. I'm afraid of what she'll think of me. I may come as quite a shock.

BUDDY: I love you and I'm sure Nadine will love you, too.

ZENA: Do you think so? I think she'll hate me.

BUDDY: No!

ZENA: Nadine was taken away from me because of a morals charge.

BUDDY: You need never tell her that.

ZENA: But she'll want an explanation. Why did I give her up for adoption? That's the first thing she'll want to know. I can't go through with it. I can't! I can't!

BUDDY: *(Firmly)* Stop it. Stop it. Yes you can!

ZENA: Let me go back to where I was and what I was.

BUDDY: I'd never let you go back to your old life. Not when I'm so close to fulfilling one of Nadine's lifelong dreams, to be reunited with her real mother.

ZENA: I'm sure when Nadine dreamed of her mother I'm not what she had in mind. I'm so afraid she'll be ashamed of me.

BUDDY: Because you went on the stage?

ZENA: Because I went on the stage naked.

BUDDY: Nadine is a mature adult. She'll probably get a kick out of knowing that you were a stripper.

ZENA: I prefer the word "ecdysiast." It lends tone.

BUDDY: Nadine will be thrilled to have such a colorful mother.

ZENA: Do you really think so? Oh you don't know what it would mean to me to put my arms around her and tell her how much I've missed her all these years. *(Wipes a tear from her eye)*

BUDDY: *(Offering her his handkerchief)* Need a hankie?

ZENA: No, just an absorbent shoulder. May I borrow yours? *(They embrace)* Thanks.

BUDDY: Feel better?

ZENA: You almost make me feel it's possible.

BUDDY: Anything is possible if you put your mind to it. And before I forget, here is your allowance. *(Writes her check)*

[*(FANNY enters.)*]

ZENA: Another check? How can I accept . . .

BUDDY: How can you refuse?

[*(FANNY exits.)*]

ZENA: You know I'm going to pay all this back as soon as the Swan begins to turn a profit.

BUDDY: You've done wonders with that place.

ZENA: Yes, and this afternoon I'm interviewing physical culture expert Phil Landers to give my customers aerobic exercise classes. Thanks to your financial help, the Swan will be a beauty salon and health club as well.

BUDDY: I'm investing in beauty. That's sound.

ZENA: I'm afraid it's vanity you're investing in. And women's tendency to paint.

BUDDY: Enhancing women's beauty is the only pursuit that's *not* vain.

ZENA: It's all an illusion, darling, an illusion. Another hug, please.

(They embrace again.)

FANNY: [*(Entering)*] Oh, excuse me! I didn't realize you had company.

BUDDY: Not at all. Not at all. Madame Grossfinger, this is our hostess, my sister-in-law, Fanny. Fanny, this is Madame Zena Grossfinger.

FANNY: Charmed, I'm sure.

BUDDY: Zena is an old friend.

FANNY: She certainly is.

ZENA: Ouch! Retract those claws.

BUDDY: Would anyone care for a cocktail?

ZENA: No thanks. I don't drink.

FANNY: Oooh, alcoholic, huh? Well I'm going to drink. Let me see. What will I have?

ZENA: A saucer of milk?

BUDDY: Please, Fanny, Zena is a close close friend of mine.

FANNY: And a close close friend of Nadine's too, I suppose?

BUDDY: No, Nadine hasn't met Zena yet.

FANNY: I'll bet she hasn't.

BUDDY: Now I know what you're thinking. But believe me Zena *is* a very close friend. Well, what she is is my aunt.

FANNY: Oooh, now she's your aunt. I see.

BUDDY: Yes that's it. She's my aunt.

FANNY: I thought she was your friend.

BUDDY: Well, that too. But er . . . ah . . .

FANNY: Oh, I see, she's your friend who's your aunt. And I'd guess from the way she's dressed that she's on her way to a halloween party, too. Excuse me, I think I'll go to the powder room—and take a powder. [*(Exit.)*]

ZENA: Don't forget to cover it with sand!

BUDDY: I must apologize for Fanny. She isn't usually so rude.

ZENA: She's fiercely loyal to Nadine. I like that. And she did misread our embrace.

BUDDY: What a mother-in-law I've got!

ZENA: *(Emitting a tiny scream)* I doubted I was fit for motherhood. But I *know* I'm not fit for mother-in-*law*hood. Why on earth did you tell her I was your aunt?

BUDDY: Oh, I don't know. It was all I could think of at the time. If she could keep a secret I wouldn't mind telling her the truth. But she blabs everything to Nadine.

ZENA: But your *aunt?*

BUDDY: Yes, this way Nadine'll get used to you in stages. First you're my aunt and then when she gets used to *that* we can tell her you're her mother.

ZENA: Try to smooth things over with Fanny, will you? I want to be on good terms with the whole family when we tell them. I want them to accept me.

BUDDY: They will. I know they will. *(Kisses her)*

ZENA: You darling man. I love you already and I've only known you a month.

BUDDY: The feeling is mutual.

(ZENA exits.)

IZZY: Oh, hello, Buddy. I'm not intruding, I hope.

BUDDY: Intruding? In your own house? Don't be ridiculous. I must say it was awfully good of you to let me camp out here until Nadine and I get back together.

IZZY: Not at all.

BUDDY: If it's too much trouble I could always go to a hotel.

IZZY: Nonsense. I won't hear of it. What kind of brother do you think I am?

BUDDY: A damned good one.

IZZY: You can stay here as long as you like.

BUDDY: Thank you.

IZZY: How long do you think that will be?

BUDDY: I don't know.

IZZY: I mean approximately. A few days, a week?

BUDDY: I think it will be more like a month.

IZZY: A month! That'll be about the twenty-eighth, twenty-ninth . . .

BUDDY: More like the thirtieth.

IZZY: It's as bad as that, huh?

BUDDY: Worse.

IZZY: Really?

BUDDY: Yes, you know how women are. They get an idea in their heads and nothing you can do will disabuse them.

IZZY: You don't have to tell me. I have my hands full with Fanny.

BUDDY: Do you?

IZZY: Yes, I've had Fanny up to here.

BUDDY: You have?

IZZY: Yes, I've really had my fill of Fanny.

BUDDY: Another scene?

IZZY: Yes.

BUDDY: She did seem out of sorts.

IZZY: Fanny's a good Catholic girl—she wants children. And I just don't feel ready for it.

BUDDY: I don't know that children are something that you can get ready for.

IZZY: Oh, it's not the children. I love children. I think it's sex I'm not ready for. For some reason it just isn't working out between Fanny and me.

BUDDY: Is she cold? Is she unresponsive?

IZZY: If only she would be! Fanny thinks of nothing but sex twenty-four hours a day. And the more she wants it the less able I am to give it.

BUDDY: *(Alarmed)* Good God, man! Have you seen a doctor?

IZZY: *(Annoyed)* There's nothing wrong with me. I'm just not a Don Juan and I never was.

BUDDY: I didn't mean to imply . . .

IZZY: There's something in her eagerness that turns me off. If only she would resist me, play hard to get. You know.

BUDDY: With Nadine and me it's always been a quick falling to.

IZZY: I wish I was like you. I'd be a rich man today.

BUDDY: Well, you've certainly got a high opinion of yourself.

IZZY: Not really. Fanny will come into a small fortune when she has her first child. That was the provision of her father's will.

BUDDY: How much?

IZZY: It's in excess of two hundred thousand dollars.

BUDDY: And all you have to do is get Fanny pregnant?

IZZY: That's right.

BUDDY: Well what are you standing there for, man? Go to it. Make your fortune. What are you waiting for?

IZZY: Not so fast.

BUDDY: You're going to have to wait nine months to collect anyway. The sooner you get started the better.

IZZY: I don't feel it.

BUDDY: You don't have to feel it. Just think of it as making a deposit in a bank.

IZZY: You're being callous.

BUDDY: I make seventeen thousand a year teaching and take care of the other free. Why two hundred thousand dollars is more than Secretariat got. I'd do it in a minute if I were in your shoes.

IZZY: Then why don't you?

BUDDY: I'm sorry. I didn't mean it that way.

IZZY: But I did. Why don't you do it. I'd split my half of the money with you.

BUDDY: You can't be serious. You'd allow your own brother to have an affair with your wife?

IZZY: Not an affair. I'm too jealous for that. I mean you could do it scientifically. As a favor to me.

BUDDY: Scientifically?

IZZY: You could do it more as an anthropologist than as a lover.

BUDDY: Be careful, Izzy. Once a woman has had an anthropologist she may never go back to ordinary men.

IZZY: Ha ha! Then you'll do it?

BUDDY: I don't know. It's such an out-of-the-way thing to ask.

IZZY: You don't have to go out of your way. You can do it while you're staying here. What could be more convenient?

BUDDY: I don't know.

IZZY: Won't you give this one little thing for your brother?

BUDDY: It's not a little thing. It's a big thing.

IZZY: It's such a small thing to ask.

BUDDY: I said it's not small.

IZZY: It's just an itsy-bitsy . . .

BUDDY: Cut that out!

IZZY: You're all I have. You're the only one I can turn to. This way we're keeping it in the family.

BUDDY: I don't mean to be disloyal.

IZZY: Just think. If you had that money you could take a year off and finish writing your thesis.

BUDDY: I'm coming up for tenure. That would just clinch it.

IZZY: Then it's a deal, fifty-fifty?

BUDDY: I'll give it the old college try. But I'm not guaranteeing anything.

IZZY: Oh, thanks a million, Buddy. Listen, here comes Fanny now. I'll make myself scarce. Warm up to her. This shouldn't be too hard. She's been frustrated for weeks.

BUDDY: How can you just leave me alone with your wife like this?

IZZY: You won't be alone. I'm going to hide in the closet and listen to the whole thing. *(Hides in closet)*

BUDDY: Are you sure that's wise?

IZZY: *(Peeking out)* Shhh! Here she comes. *(Gestures wildly and hides)*

FANNY: *(Enters)* Is that woman gone?

BUDDY: Fanny, is something wrong?

FANNY: Bud, I know you're my brother-in-law and that Izzy is totally devoted to you. But I can't have you using our home as a bachelor apartment.

BUDDY: I told you the truth before. There's nothing between us. Zena is Nadine's aunt.

FANNY: Now she's Nadine's aunt. Oh, Buddy, how could you!

BUDDY: Have you been crying?

FANNY: Why do you ask?

BUDDY: *(Tenderly)* Red eyes. If it's because of Zena I assure you that she *is* my aunt.

FANNY: Oh, I don't care if she's your uncle. I have my own problems. *(Weeping a little)* It's Izzy.

BUDDY: Has he been a brute?

FANNY: If only he would be!

BUDDY: Has he been a beast?

FANNY: Yeah, a cold fish. But there's no sense in working myself up about it.

BUDDY: You mean the honeymoon is over?

FANNY: It hasn't begun. On our wedding night *I* rolled over and went to sleep. All I'm getting out of this marriage is bed and bored.

BUDDY: I'm sorry to hear that.

FANNY: I've tried everything. This is my last hope. *(Opens book)* It's a self-help sex manual.

BUDDY: Let me see that. *(Takes the book and reads)* The Art of Heterosexual Love.

FANNY: If that book doesn't help, nothing will. It lists over six thousand positions for sexual intercourse. Go ahead and open it. Read one at random.

BUDDY: *(Opens book and reads)* "The man and the woman recline horizontally, the man on top of the woman."

FANNY: There's one we haven't tried.

BUDDY: This is really *some* book.

FANNY: What are you reading?

BUDDY: Techniques of seduction.

FANNY: Oh Buddy, you think of everything! Of course, "Techniques of Seduction," that's what I need! Read it to me! Read it to me!

BUDDY: *(Reading)* "Caresses of the hands can be very stimulating. So much so that the hands may almost be considered as secondary sexual organs." (FANNY *looks at her hands a bit disapprovingly*) "A light brush of the hand over the epidermis of the partner can often cause sexual arousal in the male." (FANNY *lightly brushes her hand across* BUD's *cheek and ear*) What are you doing?

FANNY: Just practicing. Sorry. Read on.

BUDDY: "It must be remembered that any form of touch must be regarded as an intimacy. Most people are alarmed if touched unexpectedly." That's right. I never thought of it that way!

FANNY: Go on. It gets juicier.

BUDDY: "Before caresses are possible trust must be established, often by visual signaling."

FANNY: I hate foreplay. Skip to the juicy part.

BUDDY: (*Aside*) Hates foreplay and rolls over and goes to sleep. I'm beginning to get interested. (*Reads*) "The tongue too can be used as a modified genital, especially when applied to the . . ." (*Breaks off in the middle of the sentence and exclaims indignantly*) I'm not going to read this!

FANNY: Why not?

BUDDY: Because it's nothing but filth. Really, this author has sex on the brain.

FANNY: (*Taking the book*) Here, give me that. (IZZY *signals encouragement to* BUDDY *from the closet behind* FANNY's *back*) There must be something in here I can use on Izzy. Something that will thaw that block of ice. Yes, here it is. Step-by-step lessons. Just for practice you be Izzy.

BUDDY: No.

FANNY: Why not?

BUDDY: I don't want to be Izzy.

(IZZY *signals for* BUD *to go ahead.*)

FANNY: You won't really be Izzy silly. You'll be a dummy Izzy.

BUDDY: A dummy Izzy?

FANNY: Yes, and I'll use you like Izzy.

BUDDY: Oh, I see. I'll be Izzy and you'll practice on me to see if you can get him aroused.

FANNY: Yes, that's right. Now you've got it. What do you say?

BUDDY: I don't think . . . (IZZY *signals and makes money signs*) . . . I'd mind. Go right ahead.

FANNY: (*Reading*) "First take his or her hand in yours and press it firmly against your thigh. If you are facing each other press your body close to his or her body and exert a gentle pressure with your knee between his or her legs. By contracting and relaxing the muscle of the upper leg you can cause this pressure to pulsate against the inside of his or her thigh." What do you think? Would it work on you if you were Izzy?

BUDDY: I can't get into all that his or her stuff. Why can't the author make up its mind? I thought this was supposed to be the art of *heterosexual* lovemaking.

FANNY: Yes, but it's written so that either sex can use it. If it's making you uptight we can just forget about it.

(IZZY *signals angrily from the closet.*)

BUDDY: No no, not at all! Go ahead.

FANNY: Are you sure?

BUDDY: Continue, please.

FANNY: Maybe I should be Izzy and you should be Fanny.

BUDDY: No no, I'll be Izzy and you be Fanny.

FANNY: But I already am Fanny. It would be more fun if neither of us was who we really are.

BUDDY: I'm perfectly content to be Izzy.

FANNY: But I want to be Izzy.

BUDDY: But I want to be Izzy.

FANNY: But I love Izzy.

BUDDY: I adore Izzy! *(IZZY makes threatening gestures from the closet)* All right you be Izzy.

FANNY: No, on second thought you'd better be Izzy. After all, it *is* my Fanny that needs practice.

BUDDY: Anything I can do to be of help.

FANNY: *(Searching the book)* Where was I? Oh yes, here it is. *(Reads and demonstrates)* "By contracting and relaxing the muscle of the upper leg you can cause this pressure to pulsate against the inside of his or her thigh. In most cases this is proven to cause the male to get an erection." *(Suddenly stops pulsating and pulls away from BUDDY sharply)* Oh! You really did! How could you? You beast! You brute!

BUDDY: I didn't mean it.

FANNY: Yes you did. Men can't fake it. I know that.

BUDDY: It was only a circumstantial erection. Anyway, I was supposed to be Izzy, wasn't I?

FANNY: Yes, you were supposed to be Izzy. And that definitely wasn't Izzy.

BUDDY: I'm sorry.

FANNY: You're supposed to represent the obstacle. You're supposed to not want it so that I can practice making you want it.

BUDDY: Well, you succeeded. You made me want it.

FANNY: But that was too easy. Izzy is harder.

BUDDY: Oh he is, is he?

FANNY: To please, I mean.

BUDDY: Shall we try again?

FANNY: Is it gone?

BUDDY: Yes it's all gone away now. I promise it will never happen again.

FANNY: *(Begins pulsating but again jumps away suddenly)* It's back again! I knew I should have been Izzy. Then this never would have happened.

BUDDY: Let's not start that again!

(IZZY signals his frustration from the closet.)

FANNY: Let's forget this whole thing ever happened. And whatever you do, don't tell Izzy. There's no telling what he might do.

BUDDY: You're right there.

FANNY: I wouldn't want to come between two brothers.

BUDDY: Semper fidelis—that's my motto too. Ah, but if only he weren't my brother . . . !

FANNY: Even if you weren't his brother I'd still be his wife.

BUDDY: Yes, yes of course. How stupid of me!

FANNY: Let's not forget who we are. Good night.

BUDDY: Good night!

FANNY: *(Sighs)* I'm going up to bed and wait for Izzy. *(Exits)*

(IZZY comes out of the closet.)

BUDDY: It's hopeless.

IZZY: Nice try, though.

BUDDY: Oh damn! Fanny took my anthropology book and left her sex manual here by mistake.

IZZY: I'll go up and get it—but I'd hate to wake her.

BUDDY: Izzy, why don't you do it yourself? Think of how much more satisfaction you'll derive from the feeling of a job well done.

IZZY: I just don't like aggressive women.

BUDDY: Then why did you marry one?

IZZY: She swept me off my feet.

(The shutters slam.)

ACT II

The Swan Beauty Salon.

ZENA: Please have a seat, Mr. Landers.

PHIL: Thank you.

ZENA: As I will be interviewing several applicants for this position, I'd like to take notes on your qualifications. I hope you don't mind?

PHIL: Go right ahead.

ZENA: You see the Swan isn't going to be just another beauty parlor. I want it to be a spa and health club as well. A place right here in the city where a woman can get away from it all and feel like she's vacationing, even if only for a few hours out of her otherwise busy day. So you see I'll need a man of some versatility to keep my customers happy. Are you versatile?

PHIL: Oh yes. Very.

ZENA: Would you call yourself a jack-of-all-trades?

PHIL: Well I wouldn't call myself that. But other people have called me that.

ZENA: I'm looking for an expert on physical culture. Do you know the body?

PHIL: Every nook and cranny of it.

ZENA: Really?

PHIL: Yes, I know it like I know the back of my hand.

ZENA: You have wonderful hands. Do you give massages?

PHIL: Yes I give both licensed and unlicensed massages.

ZENA: Do you have any dance background?

PHIL: Ballet, acrobatic, and tap. Two years of modern—Martha Graham technique. Yoga, aerobic, and anaerobic exercise. Shiatsu and Swedish massage as well as being a lay chiropractor. I hold a brown belt in karate and I belong to the Balkan Men's Chorus. I was awarded master breeder status by the American Catfish and Loach Association for spawning the blue-nosed plecostomus. I give private instruction on guitar, mandolin, and ocarina. My hobbies are needlepoint, stamp collecting, and building ships in bottles.

ZENA: Do you do hair?

PHIL: You mean like comb it, wash it, dye it?

ZENA: Never say dye. You do not dye hair, you color it.

PHIL: And bleach it.

ZENA: You bleach your underwear. You lighten your hair.

PHIL: Of course! That's a very important distinction to make.

ZENA: [Please have a seat, Mr. Landers.] How tall are you Mr. Landers?

PHIL: About five feet seven or eight inches.

ZENA: Please try to be more precise. Exactly how tall are you?

PHIL: Five feet seven inches.

ZENA: That's better. You see it's not the five feet I'm interested in. It's the seven inches.

PHIL: Listen, Madame Grossfinger. I'm badly in debt. I really need this job. I'll do anything I can to give satisfaction.

ZENA: I'm glad to hear that, Mr. Landers. And now would you mind if I ask you a personal question?

PHIL: Not at all. And while you're at it why don't you just call me Phil?

ZENA: Phil, are you gay?

PHIL: Usually—sometimes I get depressed just like anybody else.

ZENA: I mean are you straight?

PHIL: Straight? Am I straight? You mean you have to ask if I'm straight? You can't see with your own eyes?

ZENA: That's what I was afraid of. I'm looking for a gay man for this job. You see all my customers are women. I think it would be very bad for business if one of the customers became involved with a male employee. I couldn't consider hiring you if you were straight.

PHIL: *(His voice breaking into falsetto as he crosses his legs at the knee and throws a limp wrist)* Straight? Am I straight? *(Wetting his pinky at his lips and tracing his eyebrow with it)* You mean you have to ask, you can't see with your own eyes?

ZENA: I'm so relieved. I don't want any trouble with jealous husbands. But I can see you're safe.

PHIL: As a eunuch in the harem of a sheikh.

ZENA: And you shall enjoy all the privileges of one. Because a woman can trust you you will share many intimacies forbidden to the heterosexual male.

PHIL: Really?

ZENA: You will see women as they seldom allow themselves to be seen by the men they wish to attract. Only because you are disinterested.

PHIL: Oh completely disinterested.

ZENA: I think you'll do, Mr. Landers. I think you'll do very nicely. Come into my office and we'll discuss your position. I may have an opening for you.

(Exit ZENA and PHIL. Enter NADINE and FANNY.)

NADINE: I don't think I want to go through with this.

FANNY: Nadine, if you want to get Buddy back you've got to fight fire with fire. And begin with a complete do-over.

NADINE: What's wrong with me the way I am?

FANNY: Nadine, I saw the other woman. She was wearing makeup an inch thick and false eyelashes out to here.

NADINE: Did you get his checkbook?

FANNY: Yes, but I wish I hadn't. I'd have died if Buddy caught me going through his pockets and now I've got to put it back tonight.

NADINE: Give it to me. *(Takes checkbook from FANNY)* If he gave her a check as you said, her name will be on the stub.

FANNY: It's no use anyway. The checkbook has a lock on it.

NADINE: Didn't you get the key?

FANNY: I couldn't find it.

NADINE: *(Takes scissors and cuts the book open)* We'll see what's so secret.

FANNY: You shouldn't have done that.

NADINE: *(Reads)* Four hundred dollars, Zena Grossfinger. Six hundred dollars, Zena Grossfinger. Seven hundred and fifty dollars, Zena Grossfinger! Oh it's true! It's true! He's keeping her!

FANNY: Maybe she is his aunt.

NADINE: Fanny, there aren't any Grossfingers in Buddy's family. You were right. I need a complete do-over. Where is that makeup? Let me at those false eyelashes. I feel so reckless that I may have a mudpack as well as a pedicure!

FANNY: Have the hair on your legs removed with wax. It leaves them with such a silky smooth appearance.

NADINE: I'd love to. I haven't had wax in ages.

FANNY: We've let ourselves go. Men are taken in by all those cheap feminine tricks.

NADINE: We've been too honest.

FANNY: We've been too sincere.

NADINE: It's time to fight fire with fire.

FANNY: We need discipline. Rigorous discipline.

NADINE: Fanny, what did she look like? Was she prettier than me?

FANNY: I thought you said you ran up and stared her in the face.

NADINE: I did. But my eyes were too full of tears to see. But I'll tell you this. If I ever meet her again I'll slap her across her face so hard she'll never forget it!

ZENA: *(Entering)* Mrs. Husband? You have a three o'clock appointment, I believe?

(FANNY looks stricken.)

NADINE: Yes, I'd like a complete overhaul.

ZENA: I want you to know it will be a great pleasure serving you, Mrs. Husband. You see I know your husband.

NADINE: *(Cordial and pleasantly surprised)* Really? How?

ZENA: Business transactions.

NADINE: Wonderful! That's very nice to know. As I've always said, I like to keep business in the family.

ZENA: Yes, in the family.

NADINE: Oh, I'm sorry. This is my sister-in-law, Fanny.

ZENA: We've met.

FANNY: *(Icily)* Yes, we've met.

NADINE: Then we're all friends.

ZENA: I hope eventually we'll be even closer than friends. Now what may I do for you?

NADINE: To begin with I'd like to have the hair on my legs removed with wax. Then I'd like a mudpack.

ZENA: May I recommend our hot oil treatments? After we've cleaned out your pores it's nice to refill them with something.

NADINE: Good idea. I want you to give me the works.

ZENA: And what about you, Fanny? Should I fix some mud, wax, and oil for you, too?

FANNY: No, nothing for me, thanks. I'll just watch.

NADINE: Anything you do to me I want you to do to Fanny here as well.

FANNY: No!

NADINE: Go ahead and splurge, Fanny. It's on me.

ZENA: What about letting me help you develop a completely new makeup concept? All of our cosmetics are custom blended.

FANNY: No thanks. That sort of thing is more for older women. You know, the type that goes after other women's husbands.

ZENA: Then what about a perm? I'd love to get my hands on your hair.

NADINE: Don't listen to Fanny. Just give her the works, too.

ZENA: I will. I promise you I will. And by the way, are either of you interested in our aerobic exercise class? Physical culture expert Phil Landers has consented to join our staff. He can do wonders with a woman's body.

FANNY: Now that's right up my alley.

NADINE: I won't work out in front of a man. I'd be too embarrassed.

ZENA: Oh there's no need to be with Phil Landers. You see he's safe.

NADINE: Safe?

ZENA: What I mean to say is he has no sexual interest in women. He's gay.

FANNY: *(Disappointed)* Oh.

NADINE: Are you sure?

ZENA: Perfectly.

NADINE: It's just that I couldn't bear to have a man watching me bending over or throwing my legs back over my head.

ZENA: I understand, dear.

NADINE: But as long as he's gay I guess it's all right. At least I'll know he won't be enjoying it.

ZENA: You can trust Phil. Now if you'll excuse me. I'll go and prepare your mud.

NADINE: Thanks. *(Exit ZENA)* What a charming, elegant, lovely woman. Now that's what we should aspire to. She knows how to dress attractively, she knows how to do her hair, she knows how to wear makeup but she doesn't overdo it.

FANNY: Nadine, that's her.

NADINE: It certainly is. She's just gorgeous.

FANNY: I mean that's the woman Buddy's been seeing.

NADINE: That toad?

FANNY: That's Zena Grossfinger. I met her at the house.

NADINE: That hideous, vulgar slut? Oh, men are idiots! They're morons! I don't know whether to laugh or cry.

FANNY: Nadine don't take it so hard.

NADINE: I'm not taking it hard. I'm just going to kill her, that's all. No! I'm going to pull every hair out of her pussy one by one.

FANNY: Nadine, get a hold of yourself.

NADINE: I can't believe it! He could have me and he goes to that. Why she's old enough to be my mother. I'm going to get even. Oh god am I going to get even.

FANNY: Nadine, don't do anything rash.

NADINE: I hope they both die! I hope they both die! *(Cries)*

FANNY: Oh honey, don't let her see you crying. Don't give her the satisfaction.

NADINE: I'm not crying. This is a farce. I'm laughing. But the joke's on me!

ZENA: *(Entering)* Here we are. All ready. Here's my lovely mud. My own secret formula made up to order. Y'all sit here and make yourselves comfortable. *(FANNY and NADINE sit in beautician's chairs. FANNY looks worried. NADINE's eyes take on a glazed appearance)* Why don't you go soak your head?

NADINE: What?!!!

ZENA: To open your pores. It helps to soak your head in hot water before taking a mudpack. Ah, here's Mr. Landers now with the hot towels. *(Enter* PHIL*)* Phil, this is Nadine and Fanny. I want you to take good care of them.

PHIL: It will be a pleasure serving you, ladies.

ZENA: Give me a hot towel there, Phil.

PHIL: Here you go.

NADINE: I have something I want to say to you.

ZENA: No talking. *(Placing hot towel on* NADINE's *face)* The towel will get cold. *(To* PHIL*)* And would you get the wax?

PHIL: Wax?

ZENA: Yes, for the removal of unsightly body hair. It's inside on the heating element. And be careful, it's hot.

PHIL: You mean you don't just shave it off?

ZENA: No, never. Shaving causes the hair to grow back in double thickness, and it leaves stubble.

PHIL: Yes ma'am. *(Exits)*

FANNY: Gee, somehow I thought he would be more swish. Are you sure he's gay?

ZENA: Yes, you can rest assured.

FANNY: He sure looks like a man to me.

*(*NADINE *removes the towel from her face and throws it down.)*

ZENA: And now for a good deep cleansing.

NADINE: Don't come near me!

ZENA: What's wrong?

NADINE: What's wrong? You mean to tell me you don't know?

ZENA: Was the towel too hot?

NADINE: Don't play innocent with me you phony bitch! You know perfectly well what I'm talking about.

ZENA: I'm afraid I don't.

NADINE: You haven't told me the whole truth about how you happen to know my husband. Have you?

ZENA: No, I haven't.

NADINE: Well, now we're getting somewhere! At least you're willing to admit it now that you've been found out.

ZENA: Found out? Then you know?

NADINE: Yes, I know all about it.

ZENA: Oh, I see. I was hoping you wouldn't hold it against me.

NADINE: Not hold it against you? Oh this is too much! Not only are you vile but you're stupid, too. After what you've done to me you ask me not to hold it against you.

ZENA: I was hoping you wouldn't hold a grudge and that you'd let me be one of the family.

NADINE: We are not Mormons. When I married Buddy it was my understanding that I was going to be the only wife. But now that I see he doesn't love me I don't very much care what he does.

ZENA: Nadine, you're making a terrible mistake. Your husband does love you. And you love him.

NADINE: I do not love him. I despise him. Aren't you happy? Now you can have him all to yourself.

ZENA: I have him all to myself? You're misunderstanding everything. I don't love your husband.

NADINE: But that didn't prevent you from taking his money, did it? You brazen hussy!

ZENA: Nadine, you're being very unfair. Buddy didn't give me that money out of love. He gave it to me out of a feeling of obligation. He helped to set me up in this business so that when the time came to tell you the truth I could meet you on an equal footing.

NADINE: Well, you'll never be my equal no matter how hard you try, because you're trash. Did you hear what I said? TRASH!

ZENA: Nadine, please!

NADINE: This world is rotten and corrupt! It's everything *The Village Voice* says it is!

ZENA: You've got to believe that he did this for you and for the love of you.

NADINE: Me? What have you got to do with me? You are insolent. You've tried to drag me down to your level. But I won't let you! I'll show you what I think of you and your beauty parlor. *(Takes mud and flings it at the wall)*

ZENA: What are you doing? Stop that! You miserable brat! Why I ought to take you over my knee and give you a spanking you'll never forget. *(Moves toward* NADINE *threateningly)*

NADINE: Keep away from me! You keep away from me.

ZENA: *(Takes a handful of mud and throws it at* NADINE*)* This was intended for your face.

FANNY: *(Steps between* ZENA *and* NADINE*)* Don't you lay a finger on her or I'll . . . *(*FANNY *gets the faceful of mud intended for* NADINE*)* Aagh! Why you slut. I'm going to give you something you'll never forget! *(Throws a handful of mud at* ZENA*)*

PHIL: *(Stepping forward to defend* ZENA *gets hit with the mud)* Don't touch her!

(They all begin throwing mud in each other's face and talking simultaneously.)

ZENA: Really, Nadine, try to listen to reason. You've made a terrible mistake. Things aren't what they seem. Don't blame me. Don't blame your husband. Don't blame yourself. We're victims of circumstance. Anything your husband did he did for you. I swear it. There's nothing between us. There never was and there never will be. I know you're hurt. But trust me. Believe me. I know that anything I say to you now will seem like a lie. But I wouldn't lie to you and neither would Buddy. Fanny, try to make her listen to reason. There's a perfectly good explanation for all of this, I assure you. But now I feel more than ever that it wouldn't be wise to tell you everything. Although you're hurt now, you'll get over it. I'm sorry this had to happen. I so much wanted us to be friends but now I see it's impossible. Someday you'll know the whole truth and I only hope you don't blame yourself as much as you're blaming me now. I should never have tried to be your friend. I see it's impossible. Can't you stop talking for a minute and listen to reason?

NADINE: Oh please don't lie any more than you've lied already. You are vile. And my husband is vile also. But it is I, I who feel degraded. Utterly degraded. Nothing is the same anymore. Degraded to know you and degraded to be married to a man who would rather wallow in filth with a cheap hairdresser than build a life that's clean and meaningful with a woman who is sincere and loyal! I hate you! I hate you! I hate you! And I hate him. Oh God, how I hate him. You've made our marriage unclean! Do you hear me? Unclean! I feel that nothing I can ever do will change that. You couldn't find a man of your own. Oh no! And even if you could find one I don't think you could hold onto him. Because I don't think you know your business. Men may be temporarily taken in by your cheap feminine tricks because they're stupid. But don't think you can pull the wool over the eyes of another woman. We know what you are and that's CHEAP! CHEAP! Did you hear what I said? Cheap! I'd heard of your type but up until today I was lucky. I never met one. Men may be stupid. But you can't fool another woman. I can smell your type a mile away. So go somewhere else and find your free meal ticket. Because you are the lowest scum of the earth, a woman who comes between husband and wife!

FANNY: Oh! How dare you! How dare you talk to my sister-in-law like that? How dare you talk to me like that? We're wise to you. We know what you are! You have a lot of nerve. Don't you ever come to my house again. If you want to meet men do it in your own establishment. What am I talking about? You know very well what I'm talking about. At your house. You know. The one with the little red light over the door. Don't let her get away with this, Nadine! That's telling her! You keep out of this! Who asked you? How dare you. Oh, you bitch. You colossal bitch. If I weren't a lady I'd have words to describe you. But I wouldn't lower myself. Who asked you for your two cents? You don't understand what love is. You've never loved anybody but yourself! You home wrecker! Someday this will all come back on you and I hope you'll be made to suffer just as you've made Nadine suffer. You may play the game but someday you'll lose and you'll lose big. Someday you'll end up alone! And all those husbands will go back to their wives. And then we'll see who has the last laugh. Because husbands do go back to their wives, you know. Nadine, don't blame him. He was blinded by this flashy dame. She flattered his ego. Made him feel like he was some kind of stud. But deep inside I know that Buddy loves you. And you, you hideous harridan. Something about you makes my blood boil. I could scratch your eyes out.

PHIL: Ladies, ladies please. I'm sure we can work this out in some civilized manner. There's no need to upset yourselves. I said there's no need to upset yourselves. You don't mean that, I'm sure. Don't say that! Please, that isn't nice. Tch tch tch. Let's all be friends. Why don't you all kiss and make up? Surely there's a rational explanation for all this. Why don't we all sit down and have a cup of tea. Wouldn't that be nice? Calm yourselves. Take it easy. Live and let live. You don't want to say unpleasant things now, do you? Lower your voices. We're all mature adults and I'm sure we can solve this in a mature adult fashion. Nadine? Fanny? Madame Grossfinger. Please. Let's not forget that we are ladies. I mean that you are ladies. Turn the other cheek. Don't say such terrible things. You don't mean that. Listen, you must listen. Why don't you all be friends. Wouldn't that be nicer than saying unpleasant things? Ladies! Ladies! Ladies! You're probably all upsetting yourselves unnecessarily. Look at yourselves. Let's get that mud off. Here's a towel. Here's mud in your eye. *(Laughs feebly)* Now, I know you don't mean a thing you're saying. Let's all count to ten. Temper, temper. Now ladies please. What would your husbands say if they saw you behaving like this? You should be ashamed of yourselves. And you're all such nice ladies, too. Can you discuss this in a calm, cool, and collected manner? I'm sure when you think about this you'll all find it terribly funny. Won't you. Now don't do that. Please, let's talk one at a time. Quiet! QUIET!

(They all become silent.)

ZENA: I see I am outnumbered and therefore I will quit the field. *(Exits)*

(FANNY, PHIL, and NADINE remain behind, panting.)

PHIL: While we're giving our mouths a rest shall we exercise the rest of our bodies?

FANNY: Maybe that would be a good idea.

NADINE: I'm too angry to exercise.

PHIL: Come on Nadine. You're paying for it anyway.

FANNY: He has a point.

NADINE: Yeah and he should get a hat to cover it.

PHIL: All right now girls, what do you say? Shall we firm up those legs, breasts, and thighs?

NADINE: Is he talking about us or fried chicken?

FANNY: Come on Nadine. It'll take your mind off it.

PHIL: All right now, firming up those tummies and buttocks. And a one and a two and a one and a two. Now stretching: reach for the sky and again and two and a one and a two. Now spreading your legs for a really big stretch. And a one and a two and a one and a two and a stretch and a two and a spread and a two your legs and a two. Now shake it all loose. Loosen up girls. And letting go of that tension shake it shake it let it go and shake and shake and let it all loose and shake and shake and thank you very much.

(NADINE and FANNY applaud.)

FANNY: That was a really good workout, Phil. I love that new stretch you gave us. I can really feel it here on the inside of my thighs.

PHIL: *(Slapping the inside of his thighs, his abdomen, and his buttocks)* You'll feel it here, here, and here.

FANNY: My breasts feel firmer too since taking your class. I was afraid they were beginning to fall. But now they're firmer than ever. Feel.

PHIL: *(Obliging)* They *are* firm. You've worked hard. You have a lot to be proud of.

FANNY: I'm only proud of two things.

PHIL: You have every right to be!

FANNY: My perseverance and my sticktoitivity. Come on, Nadine, hurry up and change. *(Exits to the changing room)*

PHIL: Fanny certainly is bent on self-improvement.

NADINE: She's only putting up a front. *(She puts down dumbbells which seemed to have been her breasts because they matched her outfit)*

PHIL: Don't be discouraged, Dina. I'll give you some breast development exercises. I know a lot of men who have more up there than you and they did it through hard work.

NADINE: Sometimes it just seems hopeless. I'm not the athletic type.

PHIL: Don't give up, Dina. Do you know that I was your typical ninety-eight-pound weakling?

NADINE: You? Oh no, I can't believe it! Don't tell me anyone ever kicked sand in your face!

PHIL: No, but they used to call me a sissy.

NADINE: *(Suddenly looking at her watch)* It's almost quarter after nine! Kiss me! *(She throws herself at him and kisses him)*

PHIL: *(Flustered)* But you don't understand! I don't have to prove my masculinity now. I got over it.

NADINE: Kiss me again! *(Kisses him again)* Perhaps we'd better take off our clothes. *(She starts undressing)*

PHIL: Here? Now?!

NADINE: Yes, but hurry. There isn't much time. *(Pulls off his shirt and shorts leaving him in sneakers, sweat socks, and jockstrap. She strips down to her bra and panties and lies down on the mat with her arms outstretched)* Come on! Make love to me! What are you waiting for? Take me! Do anything you like. Come on! Come on!

PHIL: Somehow this all seems too easy. But! I'm all for spontaneity. *(Lowers himself to her)*

NADINE: *(Reaching up and trying to pull his jockstrap off)* Oh come on, baby, give it to me.

PHIL: *(Lying on top of her, twined in her embrace)* But Nadine, I had no idea you were even attracted to me.

NADINE: Attracted to you? I'm not attracted to you. I'm not attracted to you in the least.

PHIL: Then why the "Come on come on"?

NADINE: I'm doing this to get revenge on my husband.

PHIL: So that explains it.

NADINE: Yes, he had the nerve to say I was a "safe wife" because I'm not the type men go for.

PHIL: The cad!

NADINE: I can't wait to see the look on his face when he walks through that door.

PHIL: *(Alarmed)* Through that door?

NADINE: Yes, he's coming here to pick me up.

PHIL: You're insane! We've got to get up! We've got to get dressed!

(PHIL tries to get up but NADINE keeps pulling him back down on her. He manages to struggle loose and tries to pull on his shorts as BUDDY walks through the door.)

BUDDY: Nadine! Phil Landers! Anaerobic exercises, huh? Is that what you call this?

NADINE: I'll tell you what I call this! A lover! A man who's attracted to me. A man who wants my body!

BUDDY: So you want her body do you?

PHIL: No!

NADINE: What do you mean, "no"?

PHIL: I mean yes but no I didn't . . .

BUDDY: So you want her body, do you?

PHIL: Let me explain!

BUDDY: So you want her body? Well you'll get her body because I'm going to kill her right now. *(Draws a gun)*

PHIL: *(Shrieks)* No! Let me explain! I didn't even know Dina was married.

BUDDY: *(Incensed anew)* Dina! So he calls you Dina? I thought I was the only one allowed to call you Dina. Oh, won't this look good in tomorrow's paper. "Lovers Leap from Landers's Health Club."

PHIL: Lovers leap?

BUDDY: Yes, you're both going to leap from that window. Get out on that ledge.

PHIL: But if Nadine and I jump from that window in a lovers' leap then everyone will know she cheated on you. Wouldn't you rather it was just our little secret?

BUDDY: That's right. If you leap together I'll look bad.

PHIL: Not to mention how we'll look.

BUDDY: You're right. I'd never live it down. Of course this changes everything.

PHIL: Thank heaven.

BUDDY: They'll have to shorten the headline to "Landers Leaps."

PHIL: *(In falsetto)* Landers leaps?

BUDDY: Yes, Nadine's going home with me.

NADINE: *(Falling to her knees)* No, please, mercy! Spare him! It was all my fault!

BUDDY: *(Forcing PHIL toward the window at gunpoint)* Now get out on that ledge.

PHIL: Please, Mr. Husband, before I go let me say that I understand your being furious.

BUDDY: You do?

PHIL: Yes, you have every right in the world to be.

BUDDY: I'm glad to hear you say that.

PHIL: You've been treated very badly. But it's your wife here who's to blame, not me. I didn't even know she had a husband.

BUDDY: Poor boy, you're a victim of circumstance.

PHIL: *(Begins to weep)* If I die it will be all her fault.

NADINE: *(Transported)* A femme fatale!

BUDDY: *(Weeping in sympathy)* It's so unfair—but you do. Get out on that ledge.

PHIL: Believe me, she isn't worth committing murder over.

NADINE: Of course I'm worth it! How dare you?

PHIL: She's next to trash.

BUDDY: *(Realizing that NADINE's next to him, steps away from her)* How dare you? Now you're going too far.

PHIL: I tell you no man would ever make a pass at her. She's not the type.

NADINE: *(Taking the gun and pointing it at PHIL)* I am so! Maybe you'd better get out on that ledge and no back talk.

PHIL: *(Blubbering like a baby)* I'm too young to die!

BUDDY: And you can just stay out there till someone comes and finds you.

(PHIL balances precariously outside the window and gestures wildly, pleading to be let back in.)

NADINE: *(To BUDDY)* So you *do* love me after all.

BUDDY: Don't speak to me! How could you Nadine? How could you do this to me?

NADINE: That's right. Give your jealousy free rein. I love your jealousy.

BUDDY: You're a slut! You're a whore!

NADINE: That's what you want isn't it? You weren't content to have a safe wife.

BUDDY: Oh how you've misunderstood me. Now things can never be the same between us.

NADINE: What do you mean?

BUDDY: [*(Drawing venetian blinds against PHIL)*] If we continue it will have to be on a different basis.

NADINE: Bud, I want you back. Now that I see that I can make you jealous I believe you really do love me. Just that you've gotten so upset by this little incident shows me how much you care. Your jealousy is all the proof I need. Come home, Buddy. Oh baby, I want you so bad I can taste you. *(Tries to embrace him but he pushes her away)*

BUDDY: It's true. I did love you. But now everything has changed. You're not the same woman I loved. That woman couldn't cheat. It wasn't in her.

NADINE: But what about yourself? What about the women you've been seeing. You hypocrite.

BUDDY: There wasn't any woman. I just said that to make you jealous.

NADINE: Then who was the long lost relative?

BUDDY: I can't tell you that. I promised I wouldn't.

NADINE: You promised? Who did you promise? You promised her, didn't you? That's it isn't it? You promised her you wouldn't tell me?

BUDDY: Yes.

NADINE: So promises to her come before me!

BUDDY: Somehow none of this seems to matter anymore. My feelings about you have changed so much that I don't very much care whether you know or not. Why don't you just ask her?

NADINE: I wouldn't ask that woman for the right time of day.

BUDDY: If you had loved me you'd have trusted me.

NADINE: You must think I'm a child who'll believe anything you tell it. Trust you! I trusted you enough to work as a stenographer for the last two years to put you through grad school. Now I find out this is what you've done with the money. *(Throws the checkbook on the floor)*

BUDDY: I wish you hadn't done that.

NADINE: I'll bet you do. But now that you've been found out, why don't you act like a man and tell the truth?

BUDDY: Zena was going into business and I lent her the money to buy some furniture.

NADINE: What? Twelve beds and a cash register?

BUDDY: I was hoping that until Zena got on her feet you'd let her come and live with us for a while.

NADINE: Live with us? You think because I have no family to go to that you can treat me any way you like! Well you're sadly mistaken! I may have been raised in an institution, but if there's one thing those nuns instilled in me it's a sense of decency. That woman is a tramp.

BUDDY: Nadine, that woman as you call her deserves all the respect you can give her. And it is you have who behaved like a tramp.

NADINE: Oh, I feel degraded. Utterly degraded. To think that you would put her above me. I'll show her the respect she deserves. I'm going to drag her name through the mud. And yours too.

BUDDY: What are you going to do?

NADINE: I promised her I'd spread the word about her beauty parlor. Well I'll spread the word. I'm going to speak out at the radical feminist rally. I'll publish a free-lance article in the *Voice.* I'll form a man-haters club. I'm going to ruin that woman and you with her.

BUDDY: You wouldn't dare.

NADINE: Don't you dare dare me. When I'm through every thinking woman will boycott her ugly beauty parlor!

BUDDY: Nadine, please. I can explain everything. I gave Zena my word that I wouldn't tell you this. That I'd let her tell you the truth. But this has all gotten out of hand. So I think I have to go back on my word. Nadine, perhaps you'd better sit down. Prepare yourself, because this may come as quite a shock . . .

FANNY: *(Enters with Nadine and Buddy's wedding picture)* Nadine, look what I found in her office—a picture of Buddy.

NADINE: Why that's our wedding picture! The one you swore you'd never part with. And I've been cut out of it!

BUDDY: So what? Our marriage vows meant nothing to you. Why should this picture matter? After you've made me witness to a scene usually reserved for dog owners in the park. Like any bitch in heat, it was a mistake to let you off your leash.

(FANNY gasps.)

NADINE: You bastard! I only did it for revenge.

BUDDY: Where there is no trust there can be no love.

NADINE: I trusted you and look where it got me. I don't love you. Not anymore! I hate you! I hate you! I hate you! *(Tries to strangle him. They struggle. He pins her)*

IZZY: *(Entering)* Well well well, I'm glad to see you lovebirds have finally patched things up.

NADINE: Oh! *(Runs out)*

IZZY: Did I say something wrong?

BUDDY: *(Distraught)* I've got to talk to Zena. This whole thing has gone too far. *(Exits up center)*

FANNY: I think Nadine and Buddy are on the rocks.

IZZY: That's too bad. How can you tell?

FANNY: He's been seeing another woman. He's such a fool.

IZZY: He's a nincompoop! A complete nincompoop! And I ought to know—he's my brother.

FANNY: Are men never satisfied? Are they all insatiable?

IZZY: Not me. I'm satiable. Aren't you glad you never have to worry about me going out after funsy-wunsy?

FANNY: Please Izzy, we are mature adults. We don't have to refer to it as funsy-wunsy anymore. It's perfectly acceptable to call it whoopie.

IZZY: Aren't you glad you have a husband who's never even looked at a woman?

FANNY: Oh Izzy, I am. But we've been married almost a year now. Don't you think it's time we saw each other with our clothes off?

IZZY: It's just that I'm a modest person. Anyway clothes leave more to the imagination.

FANNY: But we're married. We don't have to have imagination anymore.

IZZY: I think you're so much more attractive with your pajamas on. I don't know why you take them off when you go to bed.

FANNY: I take them off because I want to give you a precious gift—my body.

IZZY: Half the fun of getting a present is unwrapping it. And the gift would be more precious if there were a more limited supply.

FANNY: But we've never even made it! Not once. Sometimes I think we never will.

IZZY: You just have to be patient.

FANNY: I've had the patience of a saint—the Virgin Mary! I feel like I'm waiting for a miracle.

IZZY: Someday it will come.

FANNY: If I'm doing something wrong, just tell me. I'll try to change. Am I too passive?

IZZY: No! God no!

FANNY: [*(Repeating sex exercise)*] How does that feel?

IZZY: It tickles. Here, let me show you one. Close your eyes. I'm going to crack an egg on your head. [*(He does)*]

FANNY: If we were Protestants it wouldn't matter. But to be Catholic and childless!

IZZY: Sects sects sects, that's all you ever think of.

FANNY: But Izzy, unless we have sex I'll never be able to fulfill my role as a woman.

IZZY: And what is that?

FANNY: To be a mommy.

IZZY: And what may I ask is the man's role?

FANNY: Why they're the daddies, of course.

IZZY: You want to turn our marriage into a breeding pen.

FANNY: I'm only thinking of the money I'll get for it.

IZZY: Ugh! Now you're talking like a common prostitute.

FANNY: What did you say?

IZZY: I said you're talking like a common prostitute!

FANNY: *(Relieved)* Oh, I thought you said Protestant.

IZZY: What do you want from my life?

FANNY: I can't go on like this.

IZZY: I've done everything in my power to make you happy.

FANNY: Happy? Don't make me laugh! I'd never have married you if I'd known it was going to be like this.

IZZY: Oh God, here we go again!

FANNY: And to think that I've never so much as looked at another man.

IZZY: What do you want, a medal?

FANNY: Any other woman who'd been so neglected would have started shopping around.

IZZY: Good, go shopping!

FANNY: What I'm not getting at home I could find on the open market.

IZZY: Yeah, John's Bargain Store.

FANNY: Plenty of women with less to offer have found lovers to give them what their husbands didn't!

IZZY: Go! I hope you find him. And I hope you and lover boy will be very happy together.

FANNY: Don't tempt me!

IZZY: What's stopping you?

FANNY: Remember, you asked for it.

IZZY: Yes, I have.

(Outside are heard the sounds of a crowd chanting, "Jump! Jump!")

FANNY: What's that?

IZZY: Oh, I forgot to tell you. There's a man out on a ledge in his undershorts threatening to jump and the crowd is egging him on.

(Enter BUDDY and ZENA.)

ZENA: Calm yourself, please, I'm sure this has all been a misunderstanding. Did you sit down with Nadine and ask for an explanation?

BUDDY: Her actions were self-explanatory. I caught them with their pants down.

ZENA: But with whom?

BUDDY: Your physical culture expert!

ZENA: Phil Landers? But that's impossible. He's gay.

BUDDY: Gay? Are you sure?

ZENA: Yes—he told me so himself.

BUDDY: Gay, eh? *(Laughs with relief)* Ha ha ha ha ha! Gay? Why that's wonderful!

ZENA: He was probably giving her a stretch exercise or a massage.

BUDDY: Whew! What a relief! Of course, how silly of me! Then the whole thing was completely innocent!

ZENA: Of course! Now if I found Phil and you in a similar position I might have my doubts.

BUDDY: Hey watch that! Don't take AC for DC unless you want a shock.

CROWD OUTSIDE: Jump! Jump

ZENA: What's that noise outside?

FANNY: Izzy says there's a man in his undershorts out on a ledge.

BUDDY: Omigod! I think I know who it is. *(Runs over to window and draws up the venetian blind revealing LANDERS with a pigeon perched on his head)*

FANNY: It's just like those plays in the 1950s where the homosexual commits suicide at the end.

BUDDY: I love those plays. Why don't they do them like that anymore?

FANNY: They still do over at Circle Rep.

ZENA: He probably had a terrible family life.

IZZY: We've got to try to save his life. Maybe we should adopt him.

FANNY: Oh the poor, sad, tragic baby. If only I could do something to cure him.

IZZY: Yes, if only you could.

ZENA: No Fanny, that might make him jump. Let one of the boys talk to him.

(IZZY opens the window and LANDERS jumps in and kisses him.)

PHIL: Oh thank you. I have acrophobia.

IZZY: I'm afraid of snakes myself.

(The phone rings.)

ZENA: I'll get that. Hello? It's for you, Fanny.

BUDDY: *(Taking LANDERS aside)* Listen, pal, I hope you won't hold that silly little misunderstanding against me.

PHIL: Misunderstanding? Oh yes—well it could happen to anyone! I mean your reaction was perfectly understandable.

BUDDY: I won't hold a grudge if you won't.

PHIL: Oh sure, sure.

BUDDY: In fact any time you want to do what you were doing to my wife—go right ahead.

PHIL: Really?

BUDDY: Sure, I know now that you were doing it for her own good.

PHIL: Well, yes but er . . . I . . .

BUDDY: In fact next time give her a real workout—you hear?

PHIL: Er, ah, yes sir—if you say so.

BUDDY: I mean give her a real stretching out. I didn't mean to prevent you.

PHIL: I must say that's extraordinarily broad-minded of you.

BUDDY: It will keep her young.

PHIL: That it will. That it will.

BUDDY: I hear you're good at what you do and I want my wife to enjoy the full benefits of it.

PHIL: Thanks. That's very generous of you. Not all husbands are this understanding.

BUDDY: I just want to keep my Dina supple.

IZZY: Yes, and I'd like you to keep my Fanny supple too.

PHIL: Well, gee fellas, I'll try to oblige. As long as my strength holds out.

IZZY: Care for a smoke?

PHIL: Don't mind if I do. Thanks. Got a light? I'll certainly try to service them both. *(BUDDY pulls out gun.* PHIL *screams)* Don't shoot!

(BUDDY pulls trigger showing that the gun is a cigarette lighter. Lights PHIL's cigarette.)

ZENA: I'm glad you boys are getting on fine.

FANNY: *(On phone)* Yes Nadine. *(Covers mouthpiece for her asides)* It's Nadine. *(Into phone)* You want me to meet you at the Radical Feminist Rally? *(Aside)* She wants me to meet her at the Radical Feminist Rally. *(Into phone)* At the Martha Washington Hotel? *(Aside)* At the Martha Washington Hotel. *(Into phone)* And don't tell the boys where I'm going. *(Aside)* And don't tell the boys where I'm . . . *(Back into the phone)* You did? You did? You didn't! She did? She did? She didn't!

BUDDY: Well did she or didn't she?

FANNY: Yes, honey, I'll be right over. No, I won't tell a word of this to anyone. Bye. *(Hangs up)* Nadine wants me to meet her but I can't tell you where.

ZENA: We know.

FANNY: How do you know?

ZENA: We couldn't help but overhear.

BUDDY: What's up?

FANNY: Don't try to pump me. My lips are sealed. *(Exits)*

ZENA: Women Against Stenography? They're the ones who've been picketing the Kiss of Fire. Last week one of them threw a stink bomb during my act when the devil strips me. Fortunately everyone thought it was part of the show. I know they're out to get me. I've got to go the Martha Washington and defend myself.

BUDDY: Those Women Against Stenography can get pretty tough. Maybe we should go too.

ZENA: Men are not permitted in the Martha Washington. I'll go and speak to them. Surely they'll listen to a fellow woman. *(Exits)*

IZZY: What I wouldn't give to hear what goes on at this rally. If only I weren't a man.

BUDDY: I'm worried about Zena. She'll be so outnumbered. Those Women Against Stenography will tear her to pieces.

IZZY: They're extremists. Even more so than Women Against Photography.

PHIL: Is that so?

IZZY: They maintain that women have the right to do what they want with their bodies—as long as they don't photograph it.

PHIL: Maybe we could slip in unnoticed.

BUDDY: No, this is no-man's-land. The most highly fortified lines of defense in the battle of the sexes.

PHIL: We could go in drag and infiltrate their lines. We could go as women.

IZZY: That's an idea!

PHIL: There's enough makeup, wigs, and women's clothes here to dress an army in drag. And I'll help.

BUDDY: We'd never pass.

PHIL: Why not?

BUDDY: We're too hairy.

IZZY: We're too macho.

PHIL: We'll shave it all off.

BUDDY: Shave our legs?

PHIL: Sure.

IZZY: Sounds like fun. I've always wanted to try it.

BUDDY: But I've heard if you shave your legs they grow back ten times hairier.

PHIL: Not if you use wax.

BUDDY: But the stubble when it grows back might itch.

PHIL: With wax there's no stubble.

IZZY: Come on, Buddy, let's do it. Somebody's got to defend Zena.

BUDDY: All right. I don't like it. But if it's for Zena . . . I've got to prevent Nadine from doing anything she'll regret later.

PHIL: Then you're agreed?

IZZY and BUDDY: Yeah.

PHIL: Then here we go! I'll get the wax. Maybe you boys had better drop your pants. *(Exits.* BUDDY *and* IZZY *do so. Returning with the wax)* Was your father a baker?

IZZY and BUDDY: No, why?

PHIL: You've got nice buns.

BUDDY: Hey, no funny stuff now.

IZZY: Yeah, none of that.

PHIL: We'll have to remove the hair on your behinds too.

BUDDY: Is that necessary?

PHIL: Sure, in case either of you has to go to the ladies' room.

BUDDY: Never mind. We just won't go to the ladies' room.

IZZY: Yeah, we'll hold it in.

PHIL: Sit down. Legs up. Here goes. *(Pours wax.* IZZY *and* BUDDY *scream with pain)* What is it?

BUDDY: It hurts!

IZZY: It's hot!

BUDDY: Are you sure women go through this?

PHIL: Yes, all the time.

IZZY: But how do they stand the pain?

PHIL: They endure childbirth, don't they?

BUDDY: Yes, but this *really* hurts.

PHIL: Nonsense! Applying the wax is nothing compared to how much it hurts when you rip it off. *(He does so.* IZZY *and* BUDDY *scream)* Come on, guys. You have to suffer to be beautiful. *(Pulls off more wax)*

*(*IZZY *and* BUDDY *scream and scream and scream and go on screaming until . . . the shutters slam.)*

ACT III

Scene 1: *The rally of Women Against Stenography.*

(There is a dais for speech-making. An American flag. A feminist banner. The background has slogans in Gregg and Pittman shorthand as well as this inscription in speedwriting, "i u cn rd ths u shd ern mo pa.")

NADINE: Women, I have come before this rally to call for an end of the two-sex system once and for all. Who was it who first called us women? Men! Who was it who stood to gain by making women the second sex? Men! Who is it today who still insists on treating us like women? Men! Why should we be treated like second-class citizens? Why should we accept the status men have imposed upon us? When we call mankind Man do we not mean to include women? Can a woman be a postman? Yes. Can a woman be a chairman? Yes. Then why must we mutilate our language with words like postperson and chairperson, when Man includes woman? Would this practice taken to its logical conclusion not demand that Manhattan be called Personhattan, a mango be called a persongo, and a maniac be called a personiac? That way lies madness and chaos! These are the lengths to which the male-dominated society will go to perpetuate the two-sex system.

FANNY: But Madame Chairperson, what are the alternatives?

NADINE: I say we should do away with women altogether.

FANNY: But what would that accomplish?

NADINE: Get rid of the woe and the woo and let's all be men!

FANNY: Have our sexes changed?

NADINE: No, we'd simply give all women a promotion and make them legally men. Some men would have mammary glands and vaginas and some men would carry the seed. This tiny degree of specialization, however, would not be regarded as sufficiently significant to warrant two completely different sexes with different roles and legal status. Those men who bear children would be subsidized during the period of their disability. As long as there are two sexes there can be no equality! *(There is applause)* Thank you. I would now like to turn over the floor to our next speaker, Fanny Husband, who will discuss eugenics and the nuclear family. Fanny?

FANNY: Thank you Mrs., or should I say Ms.?

NADINE: Call me Mr.

FANNY: Thank you Mr. Husband. This afternoon I would like to call all of your attention to the subject of men—a burden to society. Mr. Husband, although I cannot help but admire the development of your theme, and I feel the deepest sympathy with your sense of injustice, I cannot agree to your solution to the problem. Why should we women aspire to be the equals of men, a distinctly inferior subspecies? Biologically speaking, men are a necessary evil. Darwin, a man, tried cleverly to cover up this fact with his theory of evolution when he said that man descended from the apes. I think this theory maligns the ape. A far more likely theory is that the apes evolved from Man and the male sex. These hairy seed-bearers are living proof of this fact. The hairy growth on their arms, legs, chests, and buttocks points the way to the brutality for which they must inevitably be held responsible. Whether it be a gymnast swinging by his arms from a jungle gym or a pack of them chasing a ball around a field, it always leads back to the same thing—a beckoning beastliness. And what is the alternative? I say it is selective breeding. And this is how it would be accomplished: First we would cull all the males for those that were the least hairy. These would be kept on reservations and cared for as breeders. The rest would be put to death. Historically all evolution has not been toward a higher form of life. The early Neanderthal was more advanced than the late Neanderthal. Unless something is done at once to stop our interbreeding with these hairy lower forms of humanity our species will degenerate in stages; first to overall hairiness; then to a semierect; and finally to a form of man that is never erect again. Thank you.

(Applause.)

NADINE: Thank you Fanny. Would any women here care to address themselves to the issues that have been raised?

ZENA: *(Rising from the audience and climbing up on the platform)* Yes, I would!

NADINE: *(Shocked to see* ZENA, *she speaks to her sotto voce)* You! You dare to show your face here?

ZENA: *(Also sotto voce)* And why shouldn't I? I am a woman, am I not?

NADINE: *(Sotto voce still)* You're a traitor to your sex, a panderer to men's desires and their conspiracy to keep us feminine—and submissive.

ZENA: *(Yet again sotto voce)* I'm more of a woman than you'll ever be and you can put that in your bra and burn it!

NADINE: *(Aloud to the audience)* We will now hear from Madame Zena Grossfinger, a beauty parlor operator who tries to help women cater to men's fantasies by painting themselves and generally transforming themselves into sex objects that look more like transvestites than real women. *(Boos and jeers from the crowd. She holds up her hands for silence)* Please, please. I know how you feel. How we all must feel about women like her. But I must defend her right to speak at this rally. Let's hear her out. It will be interesting to hear what she has to say for herself. Grossfinger?

ZENA: Ladies. *(Boos, jeers)* Ladies, please hear me! *(Boos, jeers)* I am not accustomed to public speaking. My own voice sounds very far away to me at this moment, and I can hardly hear it my heart is pounding so and I'm afraid you can hear my knees knocking all the way out there. You see, I am more accustomed to speaking to men than I am to women—having spent so much time in their company as I have. *(A single boo)* So I hope you will excuse me if I speak to you the way I speak to the men I've had the business of doing pleasure with. "Okay, sports! What's in it for me?" Those were the words I learned at my Mamma's knee. You see I was a lady of the evening like my Mamma and her Mamma before her. Three generations of women who made their way in the world providing horizontal entertainment for lonely men— and boys. We were carny folk in those days, livin' out of trailers, travelin' from town to town. My Mamma was an exhibit in the sideshow, "EVE AS GOD CREATED HER," twenty-five cents a peek, an act my Gramma thought of 'cause Mamma couldn't strip. She was all thumbs and had two left feet—couldn't dance and always got her zippers stuck. Between shows Mamma used to invite certain gentlemen to her trailer for tea. I had to hide in my bunk till they were through. Those gentlemen used to get real affectionate toward Mamma and call her doll and honey and love and stuff—and that's when I'd always hear Mamma say, "Okay, sport! What's in it for me?" Now this carny used to travel with a freak show. Every carny used to have a few. And Mamma used to tell me, "Keep away from those freaks. I don't want those freaks messin' 'round with you." But there was this guy they called the Human Worm. Didn't have no arms or legs but he was every inch a man. He was always tryin' to love Mamma. But she just wouldn't let him touch her. Well, one day I was sent to bed without supper for scarin' off one of Mamma's tricks. And I decided to run away. I headed for the road. Then suddenly this traveling salesman tried to grab me. I was only six years old—but well-developed for my age. He tried to kiss me on the mouth. I remember how the stubble of his beard scratched my face and the smell of liquor on his breath. Why, that man slapped his hand over my mouth before I even had time to say, "Well, sport, what's in it for me?" Suddenly he laid on top of me without even taking off his clothes. He just started grunting and sweating right there in the rain—in the mud! Suddenly he groaned a fierce groan and let out a hideous breath. His whole body shuddered and he went limp. He was dead! The Human Worm had stabbed him with a knife held in his teeth. He pushed the salesman off me and we headed back to my trailer with him crawlin' at my side. That night we moved on. But my hero the Human Worm was never the same again. He was haunted by what had happened. He had a powerful guilt. One day he said to me, "Zena, I'm going to turn myself in. I can't live with this on my conscience. I'll probably be away a long time." I begged him not to do it. But he wouldn't listen to my pleas. He wanted to tell the police where he was. But he asked me one last favor before he turned himself in. He said he had never had a woman . . . and now he probably never would. Would I let him, just once? How could I refuse this sad, heroic man who was aching for a woman? I let him. It was a beautiful experience. And I didn't even have to ask, "What's in it for me?" Then he went and dialed the phone with his tongue. Later on I realized that something was changing. My body was full of life. I had a healthy baby and that's when I became Zena Moline, the world's youngest mother. But after a while I realized that I was no good for that child. I didn't want *her* to grow up saying, "Okay, sport! What's in it for me?" So I gave her up to those who'd raise her decent. So she'd know a better life than the one I'd known. And ever since that day I've dreamed of meeting her someday and being with my baby once again.

FANNY: What happened to the Human Worm?

ZENA: They came and took him away. I never saw him again.

FANNY: That's the saddest story I ever heard in my life. *(Weeps)*

NADINE: I must admit that is a pathetic story. But we must not allow our feelings to run away with us. I can only say thank God you gave up that child. That decision was sound. Imagine if that child had had to grow up with your example and that unwholesome environment.

FANNY: It was probably an ugly bugger, too.

NADINE: To me your story just brings home the idea that women who are victims usually go on to victimize others. Why that child might have turned out to be like her mother, her mother's mother, and her mother before her. She is more to be pitied than censured. Let us make an example of this woman.

For there is something to be learned from her story. As long as there are two sexes one sex will always oppress the other.

FANNY: I think this woman is living proof that men are beasts.

ZENA: May I say something, please?

NADINE: I think we've heard enough. Would anyone else like to speak?

PHIL: *(Disguised as a woman, speaks from the house)* I'd like to say a few words in this woman's defense if I may. *(Climbs up on the platform and nudges* NADINE *out of the way)* Girls, let's be fair. How many of us have gone out with a guy we didn't particularly like just to spend his money? Let him take us dancing, to dinner, and a show, and then didn't put out at the end of the evening? How many of us have given a man the itch and then left him to scratch it himself? Now wouldn't it have been far thriftier and more practical for him to go to a good professional like this woman here *(Indicates* ZENA*)* and get what he wanted on an honest cash-and-carry basis? How many of us have in fact married for money? Isn't that the same thing as prostitution except that one is forced into domestic servitude as well?

NADINE: It's true that marriage can be a form of indentured servitude in the male-dominated—

PHIL: *(Interrupting)* It is indeed! But aren't the men the ones we hold in bondage? How many of us work our husbands into an early grave—or when he loses his looks divorce him and keep a young stud on the alimony?

NADINE: This is treason! This kind of talk is completely out of place here.

FANNY: Yes, you shouldn't say things like that. You can think them. But you shouldn't say them.

NADINE: Yes, you're going too far!

BUDDY: *(Rising from the audience, also disguised as a woman)* I don't think so, Madame Chairman. If anything I don't think Miss, er . . . Miss . . . I don't believe I caught your name.

PHIL: Slanders—Phyllis Slanders.

BUDDY: I don't think Ms. Slanders goes far enough.

PHIL: *(Indignant)* Well, that's the first time anyone's ever said that about me before!

BUDDY: She hasn't begun to scratch the surface of the little everyday grievances men might have against us.

NADINE: Grievances? What grievances?

BUDDY: Bathroom grievances.

NADINE: I hardly think this is the place to . . .

BUDDY: *(Now on the platform)* Girls, we do tend to hog the bathroom, clog the sink with hair and hairpins and leave all kinds of underwear hanging all over everything. I know my own husband almost slashed his throat shaving after I had used his razor on my legs.

NADINE: That does sound familiar. So you forgot to change the blade. It's a perfectly human mistake. Anyone might have done that.

BUDDY: And then I always forget to replace the roll of toilet paper when I use up the last piece.

NADINE: Who have you been talking to?

IZZY: *(Also in drag, rises from the audience and prances up on the stage)* Madame Chairman, I once left peroxide in the drinking glass and my husband swallowed it by mistake.

FANNY: You too?

IZZY: He was transparent for a month. You could see everything he ate from the time he swallowed it till it came out the other end.

BUDDY: And there are certain other contrivances we leave lying around that a man should *not* be subjected to.

FANNY: *(During the previous speech something in the wings has caught* FANNY's *attention)* Excuse me, Madame Chairman, but there seems to be a message for someone. *(Exits)*

NADINE: I maintain that if all women were turned into men—

IZZY: *(Interrupting)* Why turn women into men? It would be much easier both philosophically and surgically to go in the other direction.

*(*PHIL *and* BUDDY *cringe and suck in their breath.)*

PHIL: Please, sister, let's not cut off our nose to spite our face.

BUDDY: Yes, without men many of us would have to go out and get jobs and support ourselves.

PHIL: Causing us to miss many of our favorite soap operas on TV.

FANNY: *(Reentering excitedly)* Madame Chairman, I have just received a message that there are male spies present at this meeting who slipped in in drag.

IZZY: Omigod!

BUDDY: *(Aside to* PHIL*)* Looks like the jig is up.

PHIL: *(Aside to* BUDDY*)* Nonsense. A good offensive is the best defensive.

BUDDY: *(As before)* Well, you'd better do it. You're so much better at being offensive than I am.

PHIL: *(Aloud)* I thought I smelt something fishy, *Mr.* Chairperson. You're a man attempting to smear the entire women's movement.

NADINE: I am not a man!

BUDDY: But you just admitted it. We might have guessed! All women should be men indeed!

NADINE: I tell you I am not a man. And I can prove it.

PHIL: Very well, take off that blouse and let's see what you've got up there. Let that be the test.

FANNY: Nadine, you're sunk.

NADINE: That would be no proof at all. Many women are flat-chested.

PHIL: Then drop your panties.

NADINE: I'll do no such thing.

IZZY: I think this one is a man, too.

FANNY: I am not! And I'd be happy to drop my panties anytime to prove it.

IZZY: Er . . . ah . . . we believe you. Never mind, never mind.

NADINE: *(Addressing the audience)* Women, we have received word that there are male spies here.

IZZY, BUDDY, and PHIL: Tch tch tch.

NADINE: And because of this, for security reasons, I would like to dismiss this meeting.

BUDDY: I wish I could dismiss it.

NADINE: Meeting adjourned.

ZENA: *(To* NADINE*)* Listen, I've taken a room upstairs. Why don't we go up there and talk? I don't feel comfortable knowing there are male spies here, do you?

NADINE: Well . . . I don't know. . . .

FANNY: *(Aside)* Oh, let's do it. Then you two could discuss this thing like mature adults.

NADINE: *(Aside)* It would be better to have it out with her in private. *(To* ZENA*)* Yes, we'd be delighted to come up to your room. We can settle things there.

ZENA: I want to get things straight between us once and for all.

PHIL: Where's everybody going?

ZENA: Up to my room for some girl talk.

IZZY: Girl talk? Oh goodie! I just love girl talk. And believe me, I'm just the girl to talk.

BUDDY: Am I invited too?

ZENA: Sure you are, dear. I think I'd like to invite all the speakers.

IZZY, BUDDY, and PHIL: Oh goodie!

NADINE: Must we?

ZENA: Why not?

PHIL: *(Putting his arm around* ZENA*)* Yes, let's all get to know each other better.

BUDDY: *(Putting his arm around* NADINE*)* Yes, I'd like to be your buddy.

IZZY: *(Cuddling up to* FANNY*)* I'd like to be your pal.

FANNY: What are you doing?

BUDDY: Oh you must forgive Angelina. She's very affectionate.

FANNY: Please, Angelina, your breath is melting my mascara.

IZZY: *(Aside)* Ah, she's resisting, resisting!

FANNY: Come on Nadine, let's go upstairs. At least we know there won't be any men there.

PHIL: Yes, and we can each drink two bottles of wine and tell what we really think of men—openly and frankly.

ZENA: Yes, openly and frankly.

BUDDY: We can really let down our hair.

IZZY: And let this be said in defense of women who sneak out to meet other men. At least they don't drag their tired husbands along with them!

(The shutters slam.)

Scene 2: *A room in the Martha Washington Hotel.*

(Doors as needed. A window with floor to ceiling draperies. The three couples are in one queen-size bed. There are many Chianti bottles strewn about. Several of the women hold Chianti bottles. Men still dressed as women.)

ZENA: So much of what we call sexism is really envy.

FANNY: You mean penis envy.

IZZY: I've never envied a penis. Why would anyone want to be a penis?

ZENA: Men envy a woman's superior orgasm potential.

BUDDY: They do?

ZENA: Don't they?

BUDDY: I mean they *do!* They *do!*

ZENA: A woman can conceivably have an orgasm in any organ of her body.

IZZY: She can?

NADINE: Surely you have.

PHIL: I have! I do!

NADINE: Where have you had orgasms lately?

PHIL: Oh the usual—in bed, in the shower, once on a bicycle riding over cobblestones.

NADINE: I meant your organs.

PHIL: Organs?

NADINE: In what organs of your body have you had orgasms?

FANNY: Have you had orgasms in any unusual organs?

PHIL: In the soles of my feet and the palms of my hands.

NADINE: *(Scornfully)* We've all had those. Surely you can do better.

PHIL: *(Thinking hard)* My face. My whole face once had an orgasm.

ZENA: Your face?

PHIL: Yes. Like this. *(Makes a series of rhythmic, grotesque faces)*

ZENA: *(A bit disconcerted)* I see.

PHIL: *(Continues)* And like this. *(Grotesque face)*

ZENA: Enough! We get the idea. You are very advanced, Phyllis.

PHIL: Sometimes it would peak like this *(Face)* and end like this. *(Face)*

NADINE: And what was he doing?

PHIL: Sucking—

LADIES: *(Up)* Oh!

PHIL: My toes.

LADIES: *(A little disappointed)* Oh.

NADINE: *(Drunkenly)* Damn all husbands!

ALL: Damn all husbands!

NADINE: I propose that hereafter we all keep male mistresses!

FANNY: Yes, let men's sole purpose be ornamental!

NADINE: And let's keep more than one! A male harem—of twenty!

FANNY: Make that fifty! And all premature ejaculators!

NADINE: And just line 'em up and have 'em one after the other—

FANNY: Like eating peanuts. You can't stop at one!

NADINE: And let them all be stupid.

FANNY: Yeah, the dumber the better. Beautiful dumb brutes one after the other all night long.

PHIL: Girls, your fantasies frighten me.

ZENA: I think perhaps they've had too much to drink.

NADINE: Who's had too mush to drink? Never enough to drink. This bottle's empty; give me more wine.

BUDDY: You'll be sick tomorrow.

NADINE: Tomorrow may never come. I almost wish it wouldn't. I want to live! I want to live!

FANNY: I found some wine.

NADINE: Give it here. I want to live. That's all I want is to live.

FANNY: *(Passing the bottle)* Bottoms up.

NADINE: *(Drinking)* I want to live. I want to live. I wish I were dead.

FANNY: Have some wine, Zena?

ZENA: No thanks dear. I never touch the stuff.

FANNY: Oh yeah, that's right. *(Slovenly)* You're an alcoholic. *(Hic)*

PHIL: What we need is some music to cheer us up. Doesn't anyone have a radio?

ZENA: There isn't any radio.

FANNY: I hate all men. All the best ones are gay, anyway. Pretty soon straight men will be extinct.

NADINE: They sure do!

FANNY: Now take Phil Landers, for instance.

NADINE: Yeah, what a waste.

FANNY: If only I could discover a cure.

IZZY: You'd be another Jonas Salk.

ZENA: You can't cure it, because it isn't a disease.

IZZY: But think of the fun you could have trying. Phyllis, do you have any ideas?

PHIL: Well I've heard that for the most part gay men are incurable. But there is one cure that has been known to work in rare instances.

IZZY: Oh tell us, do!

PHIL: Well men are gay because of a mental block. They want men instead of women. Now a woman can sometimes cure a gay man by dressing up as a man and trying to seduce him. Then once he gets past the mental block he'll like it and be cured!

IZZY: Do you think that would work on Phil Landers?

PHIL: Oh I feel certain it would!

IZZY: Why don't you try it?

FANNY: I couldn't. I don't think my husband would approve.

IZZY: I'm sure he would think it was for a good cause.

FANNY: Do you think so?

IZZY: I'm sure of it. What man wouldn't want to see another man saved?

PHIL: Well if Angelina has no objection . . . I mean if your husband has no objection, you're in luck. I happen to know that Phil Landers was one of the men who slipped into the rally in drag.

FANNY: No!

PHIL: Yes! And I happen to know that he's in the adjoining room hiding out.

FANNY: No!

PHIL: Yes! Now here are some men's clothes I just happen to have brought along. You slip into them and I'll go tell Phil that I have a friend I want him to meet. *(Exits into anteroom)*

(They start dressing FANNY in Phil's clothes.)

IZZY: I'll help you get dressed.

FANNY: I don't know if I want to have an extramarital affair.

IZZY: Come now, it's for a good cause. Think of it as therapy—for him.

FANNY: O.K. I guess . . .

PHIL: *(Peeking out)* He says it's all right with him.

FANNY: This is worse than a blind date.

PHIL: *(Peeking out—just the head)* You can come in now.

FANNY: Aren't you going to come out first?

PHIL: Sure. As soon as I've introduced you.

(FANNY exits into bedroom. IZZY listens gleefully at the door.)

NADINE: Men are all fuckers. That's all they're good for—they're all fuckers.
  She didn't want the butcher.
  She didn't want the baker.
  But she let the candlestick maker.
(Runs to the window, yells) Hey all of you out there! Fuck me! Fuck me!

ZENA: *(To BUDDY)* We've got to quiet her down. This hotel is very conservative.

BUDDY: *(Too drunk to comprehend, sings)* She wouldn't let the butcher. She wouldn't let the baker.

NADINE: *(At the window, yells out into street)* Fuck me! Eat my taco!

FANNY: *(Enters bowlegged from bedroom)*

IZZY: Is he cured?

FANNY: Cured? I should get the Nobel Prize. Wait until the Esthetic Realists hear about *this* technique!

(Loud knock on the door.)

VOICE OFF: Police.
NADINE: *(Still at window)* Fuck me! Fuck me!
ZENA: Omigod it's the police! You've got to cool it.
NADINE: Leave me alone. *(Swings her arms, accidentally striking* ZENA*)*
ZENA: *(Taking* NADINE *by the shoulders and shaking her)* You little fool. You have a decent life. You've won the respect of all those women today. How dare you risk it now with a scandal?
NADINE: *(Drunk)* I piss on all those women and especially you!
ZENA: *(Raises her hand to strike* NADINE *and then doesn't—turns to* FANNY*)*
POLICE: Open up.
ZENA: Fanny, I don't know if I can save you now. It's probably too late. Take her and hide behind this curtain. And if you get a chance to escape, grab it. *(*FANNY *drags* NADINE *behind drapery. Two* POLICEWOMEN *break the door down and enter with guns drawn.* ZENA *turns to the window, lifts her skirt, and yells)* Come on fellas, fuck me! Fuck me! Eat my taco.

*(*POLICEWOMEN *grab her.* NADINE *and* FANNY *sail out the door.)*

POLICEWOMAN: O.K. honey, come along with me.
PHIL: *(Enters from bedroom half naked, half in drag)* What's going on? *(Sees* PO-
LICEWOMEN *with guns drawn and puts up his hands)*
POLICEWOMAN: *(Crosses to* PHIL *and pulls off his wig)* Looks like we've cracked a vice ring.

(The shutters slam.)

Scene 3: *The library of Buddy and Nadine's brownstone apartment.*

*(*NADINE *seated with an ice pack on her head.)*

NADINE: Just tell me one thing, Fanny. Did I kill anybody?
FANNY: No.
NADINE: That's all I wanted to know. Anything short of that I can live with. Ow, my head.
FANNY: But you did stand in the window and flash your you know what to I don't know who.
NADINE: I didn't.
FANNY: You did. Then you yelled, "Fuck me! Fuck me! Eat my taco!" to the crowd below.
NADINE: I think I'm going to be sick. What were you doing during all this?
FANNY: I was too drunk. I don't remember a thing. And then the police came and Zena made us hide behind the draperies and she jumped up and flashed and yelled all the same things you did as the police burst into the room.
NADINE: Well, at least we know she was as drunk as I was.
FANNY: Nadine, she wasn't. She hadn't touched a drop all evening.
NADINE: Then why should she do such a stupid thing?
FANNY: Don't you see? She took the blame. She let the police think she was you.

NADINE: Why would she want to sacrifice herself for me?

FANNY: I don't know. But she did.

NADINE: Fanny, I've done a terrible thing.

FANNY: So what. We were drunk. We didn't know what we were doing.

NADINE: I mean before I got drunk. Oh no. How could I have done such a thing? I'll never be able to live with myself.

FANNY: Nadine, what are you talking about?

NADINE: Well, do you remember when I left the Swan yesterday after quarreling with Buddy?

FANNY: Yes.

NADINE: Well, on my way to the rally I dropped off my article on sexism at *The Voice.*

FANNY: What's wrong with that? I read that article. It was brilliant and it's going to be very controversial.

NADINE: In a weak moment . . . in the cab . . . I scribbled a paragraph exposing Zena Grossfinger and naming her as an example. And I had the editor insert it in the body of the text.

FANNY: Why, that will be utterly damning. She'll be ruined.

NADINE: *(In a panic)* I've got to stop that article! *(Jumps up and moves around the room in agitation)* I've got to call the paper right now! All this and a hangover too.

FANNY: I'll fix you a hangover remedy. But I'm afraid the recipe may be an old wives' tale.

NADINE: If it's good enough for old wives it's good enough for me.

(They exit. Enter BUDDY *and* IZZY.*)*

BUDDY: That was the worst night of my life. I never thought I'd be thrown in jail and treated like a common criminal.

IZZY: What are you complaining about? At least they took you to a men's prison. I had to submit to a vaginal search and you should have seen the look on those butch matrons' faces when I put my *feet* in the stirrups.

BUDDY: Believe me the men's establishment was no bed of roses.

IZZY: Buddy, tell me, did they . . . I mean were you subjected to rape.

BUDDY: Certainly not! *(Then as an afterthought)* But I could have been! What about you?

IZZY: No, me either. Maybe nobody found us attractive.

BUDDY: Listen, this was harrowing enough. I don't share your new-wave fascination with violence. All I want is peace and quiet. You should have heard the remarks when they took me to my cell in drag!

IZZY: You were entitled to one phone call. Did you make it?

BUDDY: I was too embarrassed to call anybody. I couldn't let my lawyer see me like this. Who did you call?

IZZY: I called Sleazeball Grimes.

BUDDY: Is that a lawyer?

IZZY: No he's a musician who's always putting me down for never having been arrested. I wanted to rub it in.

BUDDY: If the dean ever got word of this my academic career would be over.

IZZY: I feel like mine's just beginning.

BUDDY: What's that?

IZZY: Poet maudit.

BUDDY: I've got to put this stuff away before Nadine sees it. My head feels like a sledgehammer and my stomach feels like a cement mixer.

IZZY: Sounds like everything you need to tear yourself down and erect a new human being on this site.

BUDDY: I'm not used to drinking. Do you know a remedy for hangover?

IZZY: Fanny knows one. Flat beer warmed to blood heat.

BUDDY: Blood heat?

IZZY: 98.6.

BUDDY: All this weird has really given me a craving for normal.

IZZY: With me a little normality goes a long way. I guess as a kid I had enough normal to last me the rest of my life.

BUDDY: Izzy, warm me a beer. *(Exit)*

(Enter FANNY.*)*

FANNY: Oh, Izzy. You're up early.

IZZY: You're up early yourself.

FANNY: I was just fixing Nadine some warm beer for her hangover. *(Places the glass on table)* The early bird catches the worm. That's a horrible expression. Who thought of it?

IZZY: Not a worm.

FANNY: Izzy. I'm sick.

IZZY: Nymphomania acting up again?

FANNY: Oh don't tease me about it. Izzy, I've done a terrible thing. I let a lesbian trick me into making it with her by pretending she was a homosexual man in drag who needed to be cured.

IZZY: Was it any good?

FANNY: How can you ask me a question like that? How should I know? I was too drunk to remember.

IZZY: Nevertheless you seem to have retained a surprising number of details.

FANNY: Now everything is changed between us. Nothing will ever be like it was.

IZZY: That could be a big improvement. We've lived as brother and sister. Now we can be husband and wife.

FANNY: Don't touch me.

IZZY: That doesn't sound like my Fanny.

FANNY: How can you call me your Fanny? I'm not your Fanny and I never will be. You drove me to depravity.

IZZY: *(Tentatively)* Give me a little kiss.

FANNY: No.

IZZY: Come on, just a little one.

FANNY: No.

IZZY: *(Threateningly)* Sweetums, you are going to give me one.

FANNY: I am not!

IZZY: *(More threateningly)* Honeeeee, you are!

FANNY: I won't!

IZZY: Chickee dumplings, you will! *(Pounds fist into his palm)*

FANNY: Not after what you've driven me to.

IZZY: Are you resisting me?

FANNY: Yes I am!

IZZY: Oh! Oh! Oh! Here it comes. *(Makes savage animal noises and chases her around the room)*

FANNY: Izzy! What's gotten into you?

IZZY: You'll see! You'll see *(Grrr. More animal sounds)* because it's going to get into you, too! *(Makes animal noises, chases her around the room and out)*

NADINE: *(Enters agitated)* What am I going to do? They say it's too late to stop the article.

BUDDY: *(Enters)* Nadine, I've come to ask you to take me back. I ask your forgiveness. It was unfair of me to try to make you jealous.

NADINE: But what about Zena? She's the one who stands to lose everything.

BUDDY: Everything? Perhaps. But then it was she who threw it all away. You were right about her—she is a bad woman. As cheap as they come. It was wrong of me to subject you to her. She could only bring you harm.

NADINE: No. *I* was wrong. She's a good woman, Buddy, and it's I who've done her a terrible injustice.

BUDDY: No, she was a lost person who told me she needed help to get back. I was a fool to pick up a stray. They always give you fleas.

NADINE: Don't speak of her like that! *(The phone rings)* Hello. Yes. Yes. I got home all right. Thank you—just a moment. *(Covers mouthpiece. To BUDDY)* It's Zena, she's around the corner. She wants to know if she can come up.

BUDDY: I don't want that woman in this house.

NADINE: This is my house, too. And I will have her here. *(Into phone)* Yes, do come up. I'd love to see you. Bye. . . . She's coming up.

BUDDY: Nadine you were right about her. I feel like everything has soured between us since she came into our lives. I feel that every good thing I've tried to do for her has been turned against me. Don't let that woman come up here.

(Knock at door.)

NADINE: She's already here and there's nothing you can do about it.

([NADINE *goes to let* ZENA *in.* BUDDY *follows.*]* IZZY *and* FANNY *reenter.)*

IZZY: Not bad for a beginner, eh?

FANNY: Izzy, I didn't know you had it in you.

IZZY: Now I'll just rush this to the lab.

FANNY: But Izzy, I think it's a bit premature for a pregnancy test. *(Voices off)* Nadine and Buddy have company. We'd better get dressed.

(They rush off, leaving specimen on table in identical glass as the hangover remedy. Reenter NADINE, BUDDY *with* ZENA.)

NADINE: And then I called and tried to stop the article but the editor told me it had already gone to press.

ZENA: What you did was perfectly understandable. You were driven to it by jealousy.

NADINE: I'm afraid it will be very damaging.

ZENA: Nonsense. If it helped to illustrate your point it served a good purpose.

NADINE: But when the article comes out your business will be ruined.

ZENA: When that article comes out I will be far away from here.

NADINE: Far away?

ZENA: I thought about some of the things you said at the rally. And while I don't agree with all of them, I think you were trying to say that a woman shouldn't try to be what other people want her to be. Is that right?

NADINE: Yes. Yes, that's what I *meant.*

ZENA: That a woman should be herself—

NADINE: Yes.

ZENA: Well the beauty parlor business isn't me.

NADINE: What will you do?

ZENA: Well, you know I used to be a stripper.

NADINE: Oh dear.

ZENA: It's really just a dancer—but more exotic—you dance nude.

BUDDY: That's unnatural.

ZENA: Nudity, unnatural? I should think it was the most natural thing in the world.

BUDDY: I meant immoral.

ZENA: If it's immoral to be naked, then I'm immoral when I take a bath.

NADINE: If I can ever do anything to make this up to you I will. I swear I will.

ZENA: I am the one who should make it up to you.

NADINE: If you ever need anything just ask.

ZENA: There is one thing. I begged Buddy for this picture of you.

NADINE: Of *me?*

ZENA: Yes. He didn't want to part with it, but I'm afraid I insisted, and he is such a gentleman. I cut him out of it. I was going to give it back—but I seem to have mislaid it.

NADINE: Oh, that's all right.

ZENA: I was wondering—would you autograph it for me?

NADINE: Yes—but why?

ZENA: I've read all your books.

NADINE: You have?

ZENA: Yes I read *The Weaker Sex, Tomboy,* and *A World Without Women.* You are my favorite author. Would you autograph it—please.

NADINE: Of course. I don't have a pen. Buddy do you have a pen?

BUDDY: No.

ZENA: Neither do I.

NADINE: I'll get one. *(Exits)*

BUDDY: How can you keep up this pretense?

ZENA: I keep up a pretense?

BUDDY: How dare you carry on this charade with my wife?

ZENA: My daughter you mean.

BUDDY: I insist that you tell her the truth immediately.

ZENA: Don't you see? I can never tell her now. Not with that article coming out in the paper. I think it would hurt Nadine too deeply if she knew she'd done that to her mother.

BUDDY: I don't care. Honesty is the best policy. I couldn't keep a secret from her for the rest of our lives. It would come between us.

ZENA: I think the truth would come between you sooner. You drove her to it. You shouldn't have led her to believe there was anything between us.

BUDDY: I can't stand to watch you playing with her like this. I'm going to tell her. Nadine and I have no secrets from each other.

ZENA: If you do I'll tell her you went to the women's rally in drag.

BUDDY: I don't know what you're talking about.

ZENA: You know very well what I'm talking about . . . Betty.

BUDDY: You're insane to make such accusations.

ZENA: I'd do a lot worse to protect Nadine. Imagine if word got out that the woman she denounced was her mother. She'd be a laughingstock and her career as a writer would be over.

BUDDY: How dare you blackmail me?

ZENA: Blackmail is an ugly word.

BUDDY: You haven't a shred of proof—

ZENA: Your lavender fingernails should be proof enough.

BUDDY: *(Looks at his hands, gasps, and hides them behind his back as* NADINE *enters)*

NADINE: I've got a pen. Here, let me sign that. To Zena . . . from your . . . let me see. What have I been to you . . . besides a nuisance? Would friend be all right?

ZENA: Friend would do fine.

NADINE: From your friend Nadine. Here.

ZENA: I'll always think of you.

NADINE: And I'll think of you. When I look at this.

(Doorbell.)

BUDDY: Now who could that be?

ZENA: I took the liberty of asking Phil to meet me here. You see, he and I are *that* way.

NADINE: Gay?

ZENA: An item.

*(*BUDDY *brings* PHIL *on.)*

PHIL: Oh god I have the worst hangover of my life.

BUDDY: Here. Fanny fixed us a cure. Take it.

PHIL: Which one? *(Switching the glasses)*

BUDDY: Oh, either.

NADINE: I want some of that too.

BUDDY: Me too.

(They switch the drinks, mixing them up, and they are all about to drink when IZZY *enters.)*

IZZY: *(Looks at the table)* What happened to the glass I left here with the urine specimen in it? *(They all freeze.* IZZY *looks at all three of them and, immediately grasping the situation, takes [the glasses] from them)* It has to be one of them. *(Starts out)*

(Enter FANNY.*)*

NADINE: *(To* FANNY*)* Zena and Phil are going to be married.

ZENA: Not married.

FANNY: Isn't it always the way? We cure 'em and she gets 'em.

ZENA: We've accepted an engagement with the Buglione Circus in Paris. It's very continental. Only one ring. And Phil here is going to be a strongman.

NADINE: Are you really that strong?

ZENA: He only has to be able to lift me. *(*PHIL *lifts her. They throw off their cloaks, revealing their circus costumes. To* NADINE*)* Good-bye dear. It was very nice meeting you. *(Extends her hand)*

NADINE: *(Shaking her hand)* Good-bye. I guess we'll never see each other again.

ZENA: I guess not.

NADINE: I'll write to you.

ZENA: That won't be possible. On the road, I don't know where I'll be. Let's just make this good-bye. Come Phil. *(They turn to go. The phone rings)*

BUDDY: *(Picking up the phone)* Hello? *(Pause)* Yes, I'll tell her. Zena, it's the paper. They've scratched the article. Nadine, this is your mother.

(Tableau vivant. Lights fade slowly. Sound of the clock in the children's zoo and children's voices. Fade to black.)

Scene 4: *Nine months later.*

(FANNY and IZZY stroll through the park pushing a perambulator.)

FANNY: *(Cooing into the pram)* Isn't it beautiful?

IZZY: *(Counting his money)* Ah yes, it's gorgeous!

FANNY: I mean our son!

IZZY: Oh yes. Him too. But Fanny, after all we've been through how can I ever be sure he's mine?

FANNY: Izzy, he looks exactly like you! *(She turns the baby carriage around so that the audience can see its contents)*

BABY PHIL LANDERS: Da-da! Da-da!

The shutters slam.

EXQUISITE TORTURE

A Romantic Ecstasy

1982

Cast of Characters

COUNT BENITO NERONI
SOLANGE DE CHOISY
TOINETTE
BARBARA BENDIX
RHEA, *her daughter*
FRANK BARLOWE
KYLE
VEILED WOMAN
PROMPTER
JUDGE
NURSE
WAITER

ACT I

Scene 1

FRANK: Excuse me, madame. Please don't be alarmed. I saw your performance tonight. It was truly extraordinary.
SOLANGE: Thank you.
FRANK: I wonder if I might have your autograph.
SOLANGE: I'm sorry, I don't give my autograph.
FRANK: Wouldn't you make an exception in this case? It is for a friend of mine to whom it would mean a great deal.
SOLANGE: No exceptions. *(She tries to go but* FRANK *steps in her way)* Please let me pass or I shall be forced to call the security guard.
FRANK: I'm afraid I must insist. My friend is very ill.
SOLANGE: *(Out of patience)* Call a doctor.
FRANK: I have reason to believe that you alone can save him. Is it asking too much for you to sign this photograph of yourself? *(Holds out a pen and photograph)*
SOLANGE: *(Looks at the photograph and turns white as death)* Where did you get this?
FRANK: Is it familiar to you?
SOLANGE: It's not my photograph.
FRANK: No? But you must admit the resemblance is striking.
SOLANGE: *(Visibly shaken)* Who is that woman?
FRANK: Who else could it be but you, Mademoiselle Solange?
SOLANGE: Solange? My name isn't Solange.
FRANK: But surely Venus Veronica is only a stage name.
SOLANGE: *(Becoming upset)* Who are you? Why are you bothering me? Go away! Leave me alone! Leave me alone!
FRANK: I'm sorry if I've upset you. But even your emotion has caused me to take heart. Is there someplace we could talk? I assure you that this matter could be of the utmost importance to your future and to the future of one over whose whole life a shadow has been cast.
SOLANGE: *(Pounding on the stage door and shouting)* Kyle! Kyle!
FRANK: Oh come now. You're not going to sic the watchman on me.

KYLE'S VOICE: *(Conveniently unseen)* Yes, madame? Have you forgotten something?

SOLANGE: Would you let us in for a moment? I have some business to discuss with this gentleman.

KYLE'S VOICE: We're all closed up. There's nothing to drink. The chairs are already up on the tables.

SOLANGE: We won't be long.

KYLE'S VOICE: The lights are out. But I'll put them on again.

SOLANGE: Thank you. *(*KYLE *is heard shuffling off muttering)* Come in.

FRANK: Thank you.

SOLANGE: Now don't you think it's time you told me who you are?

FRANK: I'm Frank Barlowe.

SOLANGE: How do you do. Now what do you want? And please be brief.

FRANK: I'll try. Seven years ago the woman in this photograph disappeared without a trace leaving my closest friend alone and utterly desolate. I think you are that woman.

SOLANGE: I don't think so.

FRANK: Madame, the man Solange left behind was once a joyful, generous, ebullient spirit. But no more. He's sick. His soul is sick. A morbid melancholia has engulfed him and he lives in daily contemplation of suicide. His thoughts dwell ever on his lost Solange. If you are Solange you must come back to him.

SOLANGE: And if I'm not?

FRANK: Ah, but I'm convinced you are.

SOLANGE: Who is this man who loved her so deeply?

FRANK: His name is Count Benito Neroni.

SOLANGE: Count?

FRANK: Yes, he is a titled nobleman who can trace his lineage back to the Emperor Nero.

SOLANGE: I see. And where is this Count Neroni?

FRANK: He lives in Rome in his family's house that was built in the Circus Maximus.

SOLANGE: Well, this is all very interesting. And you say the Count hasn't found another woman in all these seven years?

FRANK: Madame, he's only flesh and blood. But I can assure you of this. Ever since the disappearance of Mademoiselle Solange, all other women have been mere ironies to him.

SOLANGE: This is a strange coincidence. Seven years ago I became the victim of amnesia.

FRANK: So that explains it.

SOLANGE: I was found wandering the streets.

FRANK: Then that explains it! You are Solange.

SOLANGE: I didn't say that.

FRANK: But you must be. The amnesia, the seven years, your face: this is too perfect to be a mere coincidence. Doesn't anything I've told you ring a bell?

SOLANGE: No, not even a tinkle. Besides, how do I know that this isn't some sort of confidence game. Perhaps this Solange is wanted for a crime and you want to frame me.

FRANK: I assure you it's nothing of the kind. I want to mend a broken heart and get you back what's rightfully yours.

SOLANGE: What's rightfully mine?

FRANK: There is an estate—a house and a vineyard.

SOLANGE: An estate?

FRANK: The Villa d' Choisy.

SOLANGE: That's very interesting. I happen to be particularly hard up just now.

FRANK: Ah Solange, how you must have suffered.

SOLANGE: That's an ugly name, Solange. I prefer Veronica.

FRANK: I'm afraid there isn't any cash, though.

SOLANGE: And what if I were this Solange? How would I get back my estate? How can I convince others of something I don't believe myself?

FRANK: I'll help you. I know everything about your past life. I'll tutor you. You can learn Solange the way an actor learns a part.

SOLANGE: By rote?

FRANK: By heart.

SOLANGE: That's impossible. I haven't got one.

FRANK: Ah, but I know you do. I can see that you've had a very hard time. It may have made you strong. But it hasn't made you hard. Little by little it will all come back to you.

SOLANGE: And who was this Solange to you that you should care so much for her?

FRANK: She was my sister.

SOLANGE: *(Laughs)* Well! Well! Well! Then who am I to contradict? Her own brother should know for sure. And besides—perhaps I am Solange. *(Laughs)* Perhaps I am!

(Curtain.)

Scene 2: *Villa Neroni.*

(NERONI enters slowly, ritualistically, and lights a votive candle before a painting of Solange. He kneels and prays not to the deity but to the painting itself and the woman it represents.)

NERONI: O Solange, who deigned wondrously to refresh my weary soul with thy precocious piety and angelic modesty, I beseech you to return again to thy precious body, ever virgin, and through your intercession and merits strengthen me that by the same sacrament, the agony of death, I may join you in that heavenly country. Amen. *(He swings a censer before the painting)*

TOINETTE: Still mourning?

NERONI: Morning, noon, and night.

TOINETTE: Why don't you go out?

NERONI: There's been the threat of rain.

TOINETTE: 'Tis unmanly grief.

NERONI: Why should you widows have a monopoly on it?

TOINETTE: A man can't love a woman the way a woman loves a man!

NERONI: Sometimes I see her as she was. She comes to me at night and makes love to me.

TOINETTE: Ah, beware the Succuba! They come from Hell!

NERONI: I know she's in heaven, Toinette. She gave me glory. Oh god, did she give me glory. Glory! Glory! Glory!

TOINETTE: Ah yes. Glory.

NERONI: You know what I mean. Glory!

TOINETTE: Ah, how well I know. I gave mio padrone glory too.

NERONI: Only you understand me, Toinette.
TOINETTE:

All 'alta fantasia qui mancò possa:
ma già volgeva il mio disio e 'l velle,
sì come rota ch' igualmente è mossa,
l'amor che move il sole e l'altre stelle.

NERONI: Can you keep a secret, Toinette?
TOINETTE: I'll carry it to my grave!
NERONI: You swear to me you'll never tell anyone?
TOINETTE: I swear.
NERONI: Even under pain of torture?
TOINETTE: They can make me eat ground glass and rusty nails!
NERONI: Very well, then. *(Sotto voce)* I detest Dante! *(Swings censer before painting)*
TOINETTE: Puffs of incense, clouds of smoke can't heal a soul in pain, for petals dropped upon the stream of time like songs of swans are never heard again. Why sigh for ripples in a brook? When on the boughs new buds await if you'd but look. You're young. You'll love again, and that joy will erase this sorrow.
NERONI: Joy is better than sorrow, but joy is not great. Not for joy the volcano erupts and spews the air with soot and flame. Not for joy the lioness tears the throat of the gazelle. Not for joy the victor tramples the defeated under his boot.
TOINETTE: *(Aside)* He's his father's son.
NERONI: Ah malatesta! Ah infelice. To bed, to bed, to bed. *(Starts to exit)*
TOINETTE: Are you hungry, my boy? Would you like a little soup? A frittura of zucchini? A capella de funghi?
NERONI: A little tortellini in brodo would be nice. *(Exits)*

(There is a knock at the door. TOINETTE *lets in* FRANK BARLOWE. *Violin is heard off.)*

FRANK: Where is he?
TOINETTE: He's upstairs playing with his violin.
FRANK: Get him. She's ready.
TOINETTE: If anything happens to that dress, I swear I'll kill you.
FRANK: Never mind the dress. Get him.
TOINETTE: How did I let myself get involved in this?
FRANK: To cure his melancholy anything is worth a try. *(Speaking to unseen* SOLANGE*)* Well here goes. Are you ready?
SOLANGE: You're crazy. He'll never believe it.
FRANK: Courage, my dear. You've got nothing to lose.
SOLANGE: Unless he calls the police.
FRANK: Hide. Here he comes.

(Enter NERONI.*)*

NERONI: Frank, is something wrong?
FRANK: No, nothing's wrong. I've brought someone I want you to meet.
NERONI: Do you know what time it is? I'm not in the habit of receiving visitors in the middle of the night.
FRANK: I'm sorry if I woke you.
NERONI: Ah, never mind. You didn't wake me. I never sleep. I only rest. Who is it?

FRANK: Shall I ask her in?

NERONI: Ah go ahead. *(To* TOINETTE*)* Don't tell me you're in love again.

FRANK: *(Speaking to* SOLANGE *off)* You can come in now.

*(*SOLANGE *walks through the door and stands under or beside the painting. She is dressed to look exactly like the woman in the picture.)*

NERONI: *(Beside himself)* Solange, it's you! Solange, you're alive, you've come back to me. Ah, forgive me, Solange, and never go away again. Solange. Ah, my Solange!

SOLANGE: I can't go through with this! Oh, you poor man. I'm not Solange. He put me up to it. I'm sorry. I must go now.

NERONI: No. Don't leave me! You are Solange! I know you are. Where have you been—no, don't answer me just yet. Just let me look at you. I promise I won't ask any questions. You've come back, that's all that matters now. *(Begins to laugh)* Ah, we'll be happy again. Whatever has happened—I don't want to know.

SOLANGE: But I'm not who you think.

NERONI: Don't speak, Solange. Don't say a word. Just stand there and let me drink you in, yes, let me imbibe you. Oh, you haven't changed a bit. Have I changed? Don't answer that. Toinette, Madame Solange is back. Isn't it wonderful? Prepare her room. Everything is just as you left it. We haven't touched a thing. Frank, how can I ever thank you for this? Toinette, supper for two! No, three! Frank will stay for supper, won't you, Frank?

FRANK: Perhaps it would be better if I left you two alone.

SOLANGE: *(Aside)* I'd rather that you didn't.

NERONI: Yes, perhaps it would be better. But you'll come round tomorrow and we'll all go for a drive. *(*FRANK *slips out)* We'll visit all the places we used to.

SOLANGE: But I don't think I . . .

NERONI: Ah, don't speak, Solange, don't say a word. Just stand there and let me imbibe you. Let me drink you in. Ah, now that you've come back, promise me that you'll never go away again. Because if you did I'd kill myself. Yes. I know I'd kill myself. Welcome home, Solange! Welcome home!

(Blackout.)

Scene 3

*(*SOLANGE *is standing before a mirror rubbing her eyes.* NERONI *enters. He appears to have been up all night.)*

NERONI: So, Solange, you have tried to look dissipated in order to arouse me.

SOLANGE: I didn't think a man of the world could find any charm in freshness.

NERONI: The redness of your eyes and the blue circles under them seem contrived to drive me wild.

SOLANGE: I barely slept last night.

NERONI: You've done everything you could to fit into my life, and I accuse you of it. How dare you try to make me love you? I am an eagle, and eagles do not fly in pairs.

SOLANGE: If I did, it was unintentional.

NERONI: There, you have me! I've glimpsed myself in the mirror. I've seen my desire reversed.

SOLANGE: But I don't regret that I arouse you.

NERONI: You don't?

SOLANGE: No, I don't. I want to arouse you.

NERONI: Ugh! You admit it just like that?

SOLANGE: Was it indiscreet?

NERONI: It was obscene.

SOLANGE: Oh la! You are no stranger to desire.

NERONI: No stranger to desire, it's true. But its fulfillment is as far away as tomorrow. The closer I come to it the farther it recedes.

SOLANGE: Perhaps you're making things too complicated.

NERONI: There are certain sordid money matters for which I alone am responsible. You see, I am the last of a long and extravagant line.

SOLANGE: And could a d' Choisy not marry a Neroni?

NERONI: "Marry"? Where do you pick up words like that?

SOLANGE: Was it presumptuous?

NERONI: No, it was rural, that's all. It took me aback. The Neronis always lived over their heads. After all, we are the last of the Neros.

SOLANGE: Then you are the last Nero?

NERONI: I am, unfortunately. Ah, Solange, the last of the Neros is having a terrible cash flow crisis. The cash just isn't flowing.

SOLANGE: But your family seat is nicely situated.

NERONI: *(Looks over his shoulder at his behind)* That's all that's left. This house and a lone Neroni. We have a family motto. Never to dominate but never to submit. I couldn't bear to have you support me. Giving me an allowance, dressing me like a doll, paying for everything. What kind of man would I be then?

SOLANGE: *(Laughs)* This is too much!

NERONI: You needn't be cruel.

SOLANGE: *(Laughs until she must gasp for breath)* I'm sorry . . . but really . . . this is terribly . . . funny. *(Regaining control of herself)* I haven't got anything either, except the house and the vineyard.

NERONI: Vineyard? Ah yes, the vineyard. Your wine is superb. And what a catalog of vintages! You've taught these barbarians how to make wine.

SOLANGE: On the contrary, I think barbarians make the best wine.

NERONI: They use it as a drug. But not a sacrament.

SOLANGE: Which is which?

NERONI: But your wine is famous throughout Europe. You live like a queen.

SOLANGE: We still have a stock of rare old vintages. When the taxes are due, I sell a bottle. You'd be surprised what some people will pay for a wine two or three hundred years old.

NERONI: But even your more recent vintages are superb. What is the date on that bottle?

SOLANGE: June.

NERONI: That was a good month.

SOLANGE: *(Bored)* Cadet, cadet, cadet.

NERONI: But those grapes! Those grapes!

SOLANGE: I'll tell you a secret. It isn't the grapes. It's the bacterial cultures.

NERONI: Ah, bacterial cultures, I see! *(Coolly)* No cash?

SOLANGE: None whatsoever.

NERONI: You see, Solange, we can't possibly consider marrying each other. It would be an unsound business move. Find yourself a rich husband.

SOLANGE: I don't care if you have money.

NERONI: Well, I *do*. Ah, I wish I were as idealistic as you. I may as well tell you, ever since you went away, I have lived by attaching myself to rich bourgeois women who found my title glamorous.

SOLANGE: *(Slightly shocked)* What a pleasant way to make a living.

NERONI: Pleasant? To be a ladies' man, a gentleman usher? To give up one's manly right to be slovenly and inconsiderate?

SOLANGE: *(Compassionately)* How you must have suffered.

NERONI: On the contrary. I am a masochist who finds a supreme pleasure in boring himself to death. But rich women are growing harder and harder to come by. One is constantly tempted to change one's criteria and make love to a woman for all sorts of other reasons. Things have gotten so bad that I've had to rent out la casa vecchia de la famiglia Neroni.

SOLANGE: Good. Rent it. That will give you an income. And you can come and live with me in the Villa d' Choisy.

NERONI: We have a family motto.

SOLANGE: Your family has too many mottoes.

NERONI: "We do not pay in coin that does not bear our image."

SOLANGE: Make me a Neroni and I'll change it to Villa Choisy-Neroni, or Villa Neroni, or what about just Neroni.

NERONI: *(Transported for a moment)* I think that sounds too commercial. The Neroni would be better. *(Coming to his senses)* What am I saying? You would like that, wouldn't you? *(Seizing her by the shoulders)* To have me owe you everything. To be totally submissive to your will, a housebroken house husband. No! An ornamental Italian aristocrat kept on as a sex pussycat for the lady's boudoir and the lady's pleasure.

SOLANGE: You're hurting me. Let go. Let go. *(He releases her)* You don't know your own strength. Look, you've left a black-and-blue mark where each finger clutched me. *(Shows marks)*

NERONI: Kiss and make better? [*(Does so)*] While you tossed and turned all night, wracked with insomnia, I slept like a log and dreamed a dream that is going to change my life. Shhhh! Here comes Toinette. I hardly have the heart to tell her. She's going to take it hard.

(Enter TOINETTE.*)*

TOINETTE: *(Senescent)* Have I neglected my little Neroni? *(Massages him)* Ah, you won't grow tired of your poor old Toinette when you have a young woman to take care of you?

NERONI: Agh, turn your head away, you've been eating raw garlic again!

TOINETTE: And some of the earth it grew in. You should eat a pound of dirt before you die.

NERONI: That's a perversion of the proverb. It's you *have* to eat a pound of dirt before you die. Or you may have to. You're not supposed to set about it.

TOINETTE: Better eat it now by choice than have it forced down your throat later on.

NERONI: Look, you're boring Mademoiselle de Choisy.

TOINETTE: Mademoiselle de Choisy, my foot! She's no more Mademoiselle de Choisy than I am!

NERONI: Toinette, please!

TOINETTE: This woman is a fraud, I tell you.

NERONI: Toinette, how can you even doubt for a moment that she's Solange? Look at the painting! It's a perfect likeness.

TOINETTE: Ah, you blind fool! Solange disappeared seven years ago. You think if she were still alive she'd look the way she did? She was almost past her bloom then. By now she would be middle aged. Ask yourself this, Neroni: after seven long, hard years, would she still look as fresh as she does in that painting?

NERONI: She was always lovely. She'd be lovely still. A woman doesn't change so much in seven years.

TOINETTE: Not an aristocratic woman, no. Not a woman who's been pampered, and never had to work a day in her life. But seven years of wandering, seven years of hard work, seven years of—God forgive me—who knows what? Her hands would be roughened. Her face would show the wear and tear. No, my boy, you've lost the pearl of great price, and now you've accepted imitation jewelry.

NERONI: No, no, it can't be true. I've waited too long! *(To* SOLANGE*)* You wouldn't lie to me, would you? You are Solange?

SOLANGE: I don't know.

NERONI: Do you remember me at all?

SOLANGE: No.

NERONI: The house?

SOLANGE: No.

NERONI: The jetting fountain. The ancient herb garden, which dates back to the Caesars?

SOLANGE: Nothing. I'm sorry.

NERONI: I think I'll go mad!

SOLANGE: But I'll tell you this: I want to be Solange! For you!

TOINETTE: I'll bet you do, my dear. You smell money! *(Turning to* NERONI, *furiously)* She's an adventuress, I tell you! A gold digger! And you, you poor lonely fool, are allowing yourself to be had!

NERONI: You have no proof that what you say is true. Get out of my sight! I love this woman, and that's all that matters now.

TOINETTE: Pah! You're in love with love, that's all. The object doesn't matter. But why not take a mistress, or go to whores? At least they make no legal claim upon you.

NERONI: *(Cries out)* Enough! You've insulted me and you've insulted the mistress of my house! It's a rash and jealous thing to make claims you can't substantiate!

TOINETTE: So it's proof you want! Then it's proof you'll get! It was only to spare you the pain that I held my hand. I'll give you back your Solange. The real Solange!

NERONI: What do you mean?

TOINETTE: For the last seven years, Solange has been confined to an insane asylum.

NERONI: No!

TOINETTE: You drove her mad! You should know the truth. Here is your precious Solange! *(*TOINETTE *crosses down left and brings in a woman heavily veiled, with her back to the audience.* TOINETTE, NERONI, *and* SOLANGE *stand in a semicircle, facing the audience, staring at this woman)* Yes, yes! After seven years in a madhouse, she's aged twenty! This is your Solange—hideous, deranged, ugly!

(She raises the woman's veil. NERONI *recoils in horror.)*

NERONI: You lie! She's disgusting, disgusting I tell you!

TOINETTE: Disgusting? So you call your love disgusting!

NERONI: She isn't my love. She's a fake! She's a hag! Get her away from me! *(He spits on the veiled woman, who weeps. Then, turning to* SOLANGE*)* You are Solange, aren't you?

SOLANGE: Perhaps.

TOINETTE: *(To* SOLANGE*)* Well, my dear, there you have it. You've seen his reaction. Now you know what you have to look forward to when your beauty fades!

NERONI: I've had quite enough of this. Get this woman out of my sight! And never mention this again! *(*TOINETTE *leads the veiled woman off and returns)* Madame Solange is your mistress now, and she has my full permission to do with you as she pleases.

TOINETTE: *(Frightened, she falls to her knees before* SOLANGE*)* Have mercy on poor old Toinette and on Scrotum, the wrinkled family retainer.

SOLANGE: *(Turning from the window where she has been watching the rain)* Tell Toinette your dream.

NERONI: Periodically, throughout my life, I have had a recurring dream. I dream that I go on a long journey—to America—and there in Southern California I come to a Spanish house and at the address, Seventeen Yucca Court, I knock at the door and a man comes out and tells me where I may find my fortune. As I said, I have had this dream many times over the years. But lately it has recurred with greater and greater frequency. As my economic situation worsens the dream becomes more beckoning and insistent as though my fate were calling to me.

TOINETTE: You are not the first man to dream himself free of a worry that plagues him while awake.

NERONI: No, Toinette, I think this is more than that. I've decided to rent out my house and follow the directions I've been given in my dream.

TOINETTE: Rent the house—aie! And what will become of poor old Toinette? You will take her with you, won't you? You won't abandon your poor faithful old Toinette who's never left your side.

NERONI: I'm afraid I must, Toinette. I'll be traveling like a tramp. I can hardly bring my nanny along with me.

TOINETTE: *(Going to pieces and weeping and wailing loudly)* Aie aie aie! What will become of me? My little master is leaving his old nanny. Ah I'm dying, I'm dead. I'm buried in an unmarked grave. The worms are eating an unknown woman. Aie aie!

NERONI: This is irritating. Shut up! Shut up!

TOINETTE: *(Still crying)* Ah, you are mad to abandon everything on the authority of a dream. Dreams are just our waking thoughts scrambled. You ate too much before you went to bed. That's the only meaning in a dream.

SOLANGE: Toinette, how would you like me to be your mistress while Count Neroni is away?

TOINETTE: Ah, Mademoiselle Solange, would you be kind to poor old Toinette?

SOLANGE: I shall horsewhip you every day.

TOINETTE: And drive me to Saint Veronica's every morning for Holy Communion?

SOLANGE: I shall defile everything you hold sacred and see to it that you miss the elevation.

TOINETTE: And will you make a home for Scrotum, too? He's deaf and needs a special diet.

SOLANGE: He can eat what the dogs leave.

TOINETTE: Ah, Mademoiselle Solange, you are too kind. I don't deserve such treatment.

SOLANGE: But you'll get it just the same.

TOINETTE: *(Kissing her hands)* Thank you. Thank you.

NERONI: Then that's settled. Toinette, pack your things.

TOINETTE: So soon?

NERONI: The new tenant is arriving today. I'm expecting her at any minute to pick up the keys. Ah, there's her car in the drive.

SOLANGE: Already? How can it be that you already found a tenant?

NERONI: I went through an agent. I'd prefer not to meet her, this American woman. I'll send Toinette down with the keys. *(Exits)*

(There is a knock at the door. SOLANGE hides behind a screen. TOINETTE enters and lets in BARBARA BENDIX and her daughter, RHEA. Then TOINETTE exits.)

RHEA: Imagine, our own house in Rome. Isn't it romantic and picturesque, Mother?

BARBARA: It's run-down and smells like fish.

RHEA: Mother, this is Italy. Why, I've heard that Nero himself slept here.

BARBARA: Probably not a wink with this draft.

RHEA: That's not a draft! It's cross-ventilation. Ah, if these walls could talk, I bet they'd tell some dirt.

SOLANGE: *(From behind screen)* Do you think them so indiscreet?

BARBARA: Discreet or not these walls have dirt to spare.

RHEA: Mother, that wall just spoke.

(BARBARA turns and looks at the wall. TOINETTE enters down the stairs.)

TOINETTE: Here are the keys. Signore Neroni regrets that he could not be here to present them himself.

BARBARA: Ah, I'm disappointed. I thought it would be charming to actually meet Count Neroni.

RHEA: I'd like to get a look at him myself.

TOINETTE: And what do you think of the Villa Neroni?

RHEA: I think it's romantic and picturesque.

TOINETTE: Ah, it's drafty and smells like fish.

BARBARA: Tell Count Neroni that we'll do everything we can to the place. He won't recognize it when we're through.

TOINETTE: Ah yes?

RHEA: It just needs a bit of sprucing up.

BARBARA: Come, Rhea. *(Exits with RHEA)*

NERONI: *(Enters at head of stairs with a sack on a stick)* I'm going. *(Hugs TOINETTE)*

SOLANGE: Don't say good-bye. Good-bye is such a stupid thing to say. What *does* it mean anyway? Darling, I can't bear to watch you go.

NERONI: Oh, you'll be all right. Take care of her, Toinette.

SOLANGE: I'll tell you what. I'm going to turn my back *(Does so)* and don't tell me when you're leaving. To know the exact moment would be too painful.

Just slip away without saying anything. (NERONI *slips away silently*) I don't think I could bear it. Because I *do* love you. There, you've gone now, haven't you? I can feel it. Neroni? Neroni? (*She turns to the door and with her back to the audience emits a scream and cries*)

(*Curtain.*)

ACT II

Scene 1: *La casa vecchia de la famiglia Neroni.*

(*Knock at the door.* SOLANGE *enters dressed as a man. She crosses to the door and opens it to a man in a leather helmet that covers his entire head and face except for holes for his eyes, ears, nose, and mouth.* SOLANGE *draws back with a gasp.*)

MASKED MAN: Is Signore Neroni at home? . . . Solange!

SOLANGE: (*Frightened*) Who are you and how do you know my name?

MASKED MAN: Solange, it's Frank.

SOLANGE: Frank! Why are you wearing that mask?

FRANK: What are you doing here dressed as a man?

FRANK:	SOLANGE:
(*Speaking together*)	
I had to go on a mission to . . .	Neroni rented the house to an Ameri . . .
You go first.	
I was flying a plane over . . .	I couldn't let them change everyth . . .

(*There is a moment of silence during which* SOLANGE *signals to* FRANK *to speak first.*)

FRANK: I was injured on maneuvers. Blew my head to bits but the doctors put it all back together again. Damned clever fellows, those doctors! Had me feeling like Humpty Dumpty there for a while. But what the king's horses and the king's men couldn't do, the queen's horses and men did. But I've got to wear this blasted helmet till I heal. So that my head will have the same shape, you understand. Now you.

SOLANGE: Shhhh! Neroni has gone to San Diego on the advice of a dream and rented this house to an American woman and her daughter.

FRANK: Widowed or divorced?

SOLANGE: Divorced pretending to be widowed. I took this job as butler to keep an eye on the place. They don't even know I know the Count.

FRANK: And they think you're a boy?

SOLANGE: Don't you think I'd make a good boy?

FRANK: I think I'd find you beguiling even if you were a very bad boy.

BARBARA: (*Voice off*) Lesio! Who was that at the door?

SOLANGE: Here's my mistress now. Please don't give me away.

BARBARA: (*Enters in her bathrobe and slippers drying her hair. She wears no makeup*) Lesio, I thought I heard a knock while I was in my bath. (*She is startled to see a masked man*) Who are you and what do you want? (*Draws a gun*) I know how to use this!

FRANK: I say, excuse my grotesque appearance. I was injured in action. The doctors make me wear this. Barlowe is the name, Frank Barlowe. Flier in Her Majesty's Air Force. I came to call on the Count. But I see he isn't here.

BARBARA: You know Count Neroni?

FRANK: Yes, he's my closest friend.

BARBARA: How fascinating! Come in, Mr. Barlowe, and please forgive my appearance. You see, I've just stepped out of my bath. (Opens her robe to reveal her naked body full-length)

FRANK: I see.

BARBARA: Please sit down, Mr. Barlowe. Would you care for some coffee?

FRANK: Tea would be capital!

BARBARA: Lesio, bring coffee and tea for Mr. Barlowe. And make my coffee thick like mud. I like to eat the grinds with a spoon when I'm done.

SOLANGE: Yes, signora. (Bows and exits)

BARBARA: (Sinking back among her pillows) I never drank coffee until I came to Italy.

FRANK: The caffeine puts me to sleep.

BARBARA: Tell me, Mr. Barlowe. What is Count Neroni really like?

FRANK: Oh, he's a little bit queer up here (Taps his temple) but he's authentic.

BARBARA: You mean he's not a phony.

FRANK: I wouldn't say that. It's just that even the phoniness rings true. After all, he is the last of the Neros.

BARBARA: The last of the Neros! Any woman who read romances as a girl has dreamed of marrying an aristocrat!

FRANK: I've always dreamed of a girl who could make me feel like one.

([SOLANGE as] Lesio enters and drops tray.)

BARBARA: Lesio, look what you've done!

SOLANGE: Excuse me, signora.

FRANK: (Rising) Well, I'm off! Thought I'd say one last good-bye to Nito before I go back to fight in the Argentine. Nothing could keep me away. War! I love war!

BARBARA: If you ever come back, I'll marry you.

FRANK: That's damned civil of you. But I couldn't let you. You've never seen my face.

BARBARA: I don't need to. I love you for your personality.

FRANK: Well, since you're being such a sport about it, I'll marry you too.

BARBARA: Ah, I knew I was doing the right thing when I rented this villa!

FRANK: You're a bit of a romantic, I see!

BARBARA: I want to give you a token of my love before you go. . . .

FRANK: Here?

BARBARA: In my bedroom. Wait here. I'll get it. (Exits)

FRANK: Wait here 'til she gets it. I guess it's not what I thought it was. (Chuckles)

RHEA: (Enters and, seeing FRANK masked, at once behaves like the heroine of a fotoromanzo) Phantom!

FRANK: Barlowe, Frank Barlowe.

RHEA: I'll always call you Phantom because I can't see your face.

FRANK: One day my head will heal and you will see it.

RHEA: Will I? Oh, Phantom!

FRANK: I really prefer Frank Barlowe, you know.

RHEA: Because I can't see your face I'd almost dare do anything in front of you. If you promise not to tell Mother, I'll let you touch it.

FRANK: *(Alarmed)* Touch it! *(Recovering)* Touch what?

RHEA: It. *(Pulls up her dress)* Touch it. *(* FRANK *is tempted.* TOINETTE *spies on them.* FRANK *touches it)* Do you like it?

FRANK: Yes, very much.

BARBARA: *(Entering)* So I see you've met my sister, Rhea.

RHEA: Sister?

FRANK: Sister?

BARBARA: Yes, Rhea is my kid sister. She always makes a play for my dates. As you see, she's the plain one.

RHEA: *(To* BARBARA*)* How could you?

BARBARA: Pay no attention to her.

FRANK: I'll try not to.

BARBARA: *(Giving him a locket on a chain)* Here is my heart. Wear it around your neck.

FRANK: *(Admiring the locket)* It's very beautiful.

BARBARA: Idiot! You've missed the whole point. Open it.

FRANK: *(Opens the locket, throws it away from him, screams, and jumps back)* Aaagh! It's alive!

BARBARA: *(Picking up the locket and giving it to him again)* It's a lock of my hair.

FRANK: I thought it was moving. Which reminds me—I really must be going.

BARBARA: Can I drive you anywhere?

FRANK: I have my jeep.

BARBARA: Then let me walk you down to the drive. I want to get the rosebushes out of my trunk.

FRANK: I'll lend you a hand and then I really must be off.

BARBARA: There's no need. Lesio and my sister will help. I'll ring for Lesio. *(Does so)* You'll help me, won't you, Rhea?

RHEA: *(Venomously)* Yes, Sister.

SOLANGE: You rang, signora?

BARBARA: Yes, Lesio. I'd like you to help Rhea and me dig up that weed-crowned ruin out back and plant roses instead.

SOLANGE: Weed-crowned ruin?

RHEA: She means the herb garden.

SOLANGE: *(Alarmed)* The herb garden! But that herb garden dates back to the Caesars, signora!

BARBARA: Well it's time for a change.

SOLANGE: But the herb garden is exquisitely placed outside the kitchen door. Toinette had merely to bend over to—

BARBARA: *(Interrupting)* I think a bit of color there would be a big improvement. Why grow herbs you can buy at the grocers?

SOLANGE: Signora, the quality of the cooking in this house would be seriously impaired. Toinette's art lost. Why, all of us would be reduced.

BARBARA: I'm on a very strict diet anyway. I never eat. I only drink.

FRANK: Good Lord!

BARBARA: I mean I drink my food. Every meal I take is first liquified in a blender and then I drink it through a straw.

RHEA: She does. Meat, potatoes, vegetables, pasta, everything.

FRANK: All blended together?

BARBARA: It all ends up in the same place anyway. Most of the time I'm content with protein powder.

FRANK: Is that good for you?

BARBARA: How can you ask? Look at me. How old do you think I am?

FRANK: *(Struggling)* Thirty—

BARBARA: *(Interrupting)* Close enough! Come, Frank, the rosebushes! *(Exits with* FRANK*)*

SOLANGE: Signorina, we must dissuade your mother. No harm must come to that herb garden.

RHEA: How can you ask me for anything when you said no to me before?

SOLANGE: But, signorina, your suggestion was improper.

RHEA: If you thought that was improper, what would you think if I told you that I want your body?

SOLANGE: *(Nervously)* But, signorina, let's stick to the matter at hand. The herb garden—

RHEA: *(Interrupting)* To hell with the herb garden! Kiss me!

SOLANGE: No! Signora, please!

RHEA: But I love you madly! Make me your slave!

SOLANGE: No!

RHEA: Then let Mother wreck the herb garden! Let Rome burn!

SOLANGE: You don't know what you're saying! That's vandalism!

RHEA: Mother is a Vandal and she's come to sack Rome!

SOLANGE: What do you mean by that?

RHEA: She's hunting.

SOLANGE: Hunting?

RHEA: For a rich husband. She marries them for their money and when she's tired of them . . . pfft—alimony.

SOLANGE: Surely it's not that simple.

RHEA: But it is. She makes their lives miserable. They're always happy to buy their way out of it.

SOLANGE: How terrible for you, Rhea.

RHEA: Oh, I don't mind. I've had affairs with all my fathers. Except my real one, of course.

SOLANGE: Please help me, Rhea.

RHEA: I will if you'll do what I asked you before.

SOLANGE: But I don't want to touch it.

RHEA: *(Enraged)* I never met a man who didn't want to touch it!

SOLANGE: Well now you have!

RHEA: *(Lifting her skirt in front)* If you don't touch it, I'll help Mother dig up the herb garden.

TOINETTE: *(Entering bravely from behind the secret panel where she has been concealed)* If you let your mother dig up the herb garden, I'll tell her you let Frank Barlowe touch it!

BARBARA: *(Entering with arms full of rosebushes)* Here are the rosebushes. Rhea, get the spade.

RHEA: If you dig up the herb garden, I'll tell Frank Barlowe I'm your daughter! *(*BARBARA *drops rosebushes)*

(Curtain.)

Scene 2: *Southern California.*

(A surrealist desert landscape. NERONI *is sleeping under a cactus, dreaming. He appears to himself as in an actor's nightmare. He keeps forgetting his lines and having to be prompted.)*

NERONI: This is an actor's nightmare. I'm onstage but I'm in costume for the wrong play, and I don't know any of the lines! *(He begins to do a tap dance, first slowly, then more and more furiously. He runs in place as though he were being pursued. Periodically he calls out "Line, line" to the* PROMPTER*)* Line! Line!

PROMPTER: How much longer will you go on offering bowls of blood and brains to this god who is impervious to your sacrifices?

NERONI: *(Repeats the line after the* PROMPTER*)*

PROMPTER: He is not grateful. He repays you with earthquakes and tempests.

NERONI: *(Repeats the line after the* PROMPTER*)*

PROMPTER: You kiss his feet and prostrate yourself before his altars. Your fawning worship only makes him want to give your face a slap.

NERONI: *(Repeats the line after the* PROMPTER*)*

PROMPTER: If you must offer prayers and wreathes of flowers, why offer them to only one god?

NERONI: *(Repeats)*

PROMPTER: If you cross your only god, where else do you have to turn?

NERONI: *(Repeats)*

PROMPTER: In every land we find the worship of diverse gods. Some worship the crocodile and some the whore.

NERONI: *(Repeats)*

PROMPTER: But all nations universally sacrifice to that one great bloodthirsty misshapen idol, the louse!

NERONI: But all nations universally sacrifice to that one great bloodthirsty misshapen idol, the louse! [*(Boos. Vegetables.* NERONI *does the old soft shoe, then jogs, runs in place, screams)*] I can't wake up! I can't wake up! *(FRANK enters masked in his leather helmet)* Ah, Frank, what are you doing here?

FRANK: I've come to help you.

NERONI: Oh, Frank, Frank. Thank heaven you've come! I thought we were doing a play and I didn't know the lines.

FRANK: There there. Don't cry about it. This isn't a play, you know. It's real. You were dreaming.

NERONI: But I'm still asleep.

FRANK: No, no, you're quite awake. This is real life, where there's no script and we make it up as we go along.

NERONI: I have a horror of improvisation. I don't even like to be in the same room with one.

FRANK: Here's the address. All written down.

NERONI: Where did you get this?

FRANK: Don't you recognize the hand? *(NERONI takes his hand, which detaches from his sleeve and comes off)*

NERONI: No, but this is the same address you gave me in my dream. Number Seventeen Yucca Court. Why, here's the house. I'll knock at the door.

(Just as he is about to knock, there is a scream from inside the house.)

VOICE WITHIN THE HOUSE: *(Crying out)* Who are you? What are you doing here?

(There is the sound of glass breaking. A police whistle sounds. The door flies open and out run two thieves with bandannas over their faces. The thieves hand a strongbox to the Count and run off. NERONI *opens the box and sees that it is full of money. There are sirens, police whistles, and shots all at once.* FRANK *falls wounded.)*

NERONI: Frank! Are you hurt?

FRANK: It's only a brain wound. Don't worry about me. I can't make it. Go on without me. But take this locket to Barbara. Tell her I love her.

(He passes out. [Policeman enters, gives NERONI *a clunk on the head, takes strongbox.]* TOINETTE *appears as the ghost of Agrippina lamenting some long-forgotten woe in pig latin. Far in the distance, she traverses the width of the stage silhouetted against the cyclorama.)*

[TOINETTE: E-thay ames-flay . . . e-thay ip-shay . . . orror-hay . . . error-tay . . . I-ay ill-way . . . *(Gasps)* Ou-yay!

NERONI: Oh-ay e-yay ods-gay! It's-ay e-thay ost-ghay of-ay Agrippina-ay!

TOINETTE: Icked-way, icked-way yrant-tay! Onster-may!

NERONI: Other-may, y-whay ave-hay ou-yay ome-cay ere-hay?

TOINETTE: I-ay ave-hay ome-cay ere-hay or-fay evenge-ray!

NERONI: Ou-yay on't-day ighten-fray e-may one-ay it-bay!

TOINETTE: Ig-pay.

NERONI: I-ay eard-hay at-thay. Other-may, I-ay ill-way ell-tay ou-yay omething-say at-thay ou-yay ill-way ot-nay approve-ay of-ay.

TOINETTE: At-whay?

NERONI: I-ay ill-way urn-bay Ome-ray! And-ay iddle-fay ile-whay Ome-ray urns-bay.

TOINETTE: Iddle-fay?

NERONI: Iddle-fay on-ay y-may iolin-vay.

TOINETTE: O-nay! O-nay! Ut-bay, y-bay e-thay ight-lay of-ay ese-thay infernal-ay orches-tay, ou-yay all-shay ed-way Oppaea-pay.

NERONI: At's-thay easy-ay or-fay ou-yay o-tay ay-say!

TOINETTE: Nuces tibi. Ustice-jay! Evenge-ray! *(* NERONI *steps on her train, strangling her)* E-thay ames-flay . . . e-thay ip-shay . . . *(Exits)*]

JUDGE: *(Off)* Order in the court! Order in the court! The state of California versus one Benito Neroni!

NERONI: Here come da judge. Here come da judge.

JUDGE: *(Enters)* Whence art thou?

NERONI: I come from Roma.

JUDGE: And what brought thee to San Diego?

NERONI: I saw One in a dream who said to me, "Go to San Diego. Your fortune lies there." But when I am to San Diego coming, the only fortune I find is a clunk on the head you police so generously gave me.

JUDGE: *(Laughing until he shows his wisdom teeth)* Oh man of little wit, thrice have I seen in a dream One who said to me, "There is in Rome a house in such a district and of such a fashion and its courtyard is laid out gardenwise, at the lower end whereof is a jetting fountain, and beside the jetting fountain rose an ancient herb garden; wherein a great treasure lieth. Go thither and take it." Yet I went not. But thou, of the briefness of thy wit, hast journeyed from place to place on the faith of a dream, which was but an idle galimatias of sleep. Go thee back herewith to thine own country.

(Blackout.)

Scene 3: *Villa Neroni.*

(Knock at the door.)

BARBARA: *(Off)* Lesio! Lesio! Will you get that? *(Enters, crosses to door, opens it. NERONI enters with his head bandaged and holds out the locket)* You've come back. Ah, at last, you've come back to me! Come in. Sit down. Your head has healed, I see! Are you tired? Are you hungry?

NERONI: *(British accent)* Just a bit.

BARBARA: Lesio! Lesio! Supper for two. Ah, now that you've come back we can begin where we left off. And you've kept my locket. Did you carry it into battle with you?

NERONI: I had it in the line of fire.

BARBARA: And did you wear it next to your heart?

NERONI: Well, actually, I carried it in my back pocket. *(Taps his rear)*

BARBARA: Darling, do you realize we're about to begin all over again?

NERONI: Yes, it feels like that to me, too.

BARBARA: And we will be married, won't we?

NERONI: Yes. If you wish it.

BARBARA: Lesio!

SOLANGE: *(Entering)* Yes, signora?

BARBARA: Mr. Barlowe has come back! Isn't it wonderful?

SOLANGE: Mr. Barlowe?!!!

BARBARA: Yes, send for a priest. We're going to be married!

SOLANGE: Married?!!!

BARBARA: *(To NERONI)* I'm going to change my name to yours. Yes. I won't be Signora Bendix anymore. From now on I'll be Barbara Barlowe. I love it. Doesn't it sound wonderful?

SOLANGE: Excellent for cowboy movies.

BARBARA: Yes. Ah Frank, you've made my life a romance. Lesio, set dinner for two, and take Mr. Barlowe's bags to my room.

NERONI: I haven't got any bags.

BARBARA: No? Well the Count Neroni left his wardrobe here. Perhaps you could borrow a few things. I don't think he'd mind. I'm going to dress for dinner, darling, and then we can begin where we left off. Yes, we can begin all over again. *(Exits)*

NERONI: Why are you staring at me like that, young man?

SOLANGE: It's so good to see you again, Count Neroni.

NERONI: Why, how dare you, puppy!

SOLANGE: Let's drop this shallow mask of pretense, shall we? I know who you are.

NERONI: Why, of all the insolent . . . *(SOLANGE seizes the Count in his/her arms and kisses the Count on the mouth. At first the Count struggles, then he acquiesces. When their lips have parted)* Solange!

SOLANGE: You must be mistaken. I am Lesio, Barbara Bendix's butler.

NERONI: Don't be absurd.

SOLANGE: Absurd, Mr. Barlowe?

NERONI: You're not going to give me away, are you?

SOLANGE: Give you away? Faugh! Why I can hardly believe she was taken in at all. Why, Frank Barlowe was six foot two, and you are five foot six and three-quarters at the very most.

NERONI: Women have no sense of measurement.

SOLANGE: Indeed!

NERONI: All their lives they've been told that this [*(Indicating space between thumb and forefinger)*] is nine inches.

SOLANGE: Where is Frank?

NERONI: Frank Barlowe is dead.

SOLANGE: Then you plan to continue this masquerade and marry Barbara Bendix?

NERONI: Please try to understand. The house is about to be sold for taxes, and this woman has money.

SOLANGE: Does the house mean that much to you?

NERONI: It's land, Solange. Land is the only thing that's real, the only thing that endures.

SOLANGE: Then don't you see, there's nothing standing in our way. If it's only the house you want, the house has already been sold for taxes, and I bought it!

NERONI: You! But where did you get the money?

SOLANGE: I sold the Villa d' Choisy.

NERONI: You sold your ancestral home to save me mine?

SOLANGE: As vintners crush the grapes to make the wine.

NERONI: Very good! Quick! Get the spade! Our troubles are over!

SOLANGE: A spade? Why do you want a spade?

NERONI: *(Getting spade)* To dig up the herb garden, of course. I have reason to believe there's a great treasure buried beneath it!

SOLANGE: No!

NERONI: What do you mean no?

SOLANGE: *(Blocking his way)* Just what I said. No one is going to touch that herb garden.

NERONI: So you think it's as simple as saying no, do you?

SOLANGE: Not simple. Sometimes I think the hardest thing in the world is to press the tip of the tongue to the roof of the mouth and say no.

NERONI: Well, well, well. Now I see what you are. A cheap trick, my dear.

SOLANGE: What do you mean?

NERONI: So you thought you could buy me, bribe me, own me lock, stock, and barrel. You thought you could deprive me of my will and force my hand. And now you want to keep from me what's rightfully mine. Well, you'll find out that the noble mind is slow to forgive. Just for this, I'll never marry you.

SOLANGE: But I did it for love of you.

NERONI: A likely story. You mean to keep the treasure for yourself.

SOLANGE: Believe what you like. But that herb garden belongs to me now, and I won't let you disfigure it.

NERONI: I could kill you for this. But no, that would be too good for you. Take the house, you thief, you cheap, commercial thief! You've robbed me, and I despise you.

SOLANGE: Please try to understand.

NERONI: Get out of my sight. I never want to see you again. Your memory will be like ashes in my mouth.

(SOLANGE backs out as BARBARA enters.)

BARBARA: Ah, Frank, we can begin at last! Shall we share our first kiss? *(They kiss. There is a shot heard off)* What was that?
NERONI: Sounds like a champagne bottle exploded.
BARBARA: No, no. It came from my room! *(She runs upstairs)*
RHEA: *(Enters mad)* Lesio has shot himself. Our little butler has shot himself. Why did he shoot himself? Why didn't he touch it? Why wouldn't he touch it? I begged him to touch it. But he wouldn't touch it. *(Sings)* He touched me with his beauty but never with his hands. Tra la la. Tra la la. Loo la, loo lay. *(Speaks)* If he had touched it, he'd have liked it. Why did he not touch it? *(She raises her skirt to NERONI)* Touch it. Touch it. I beg you to touch it. Touch me here. Touch me now! *(NERONI strikes a match on it)* Ah, it burns! *(NERONI gives lighted match to RHEA)*
NERONI: Here, Rhea. Set fire to the house.
RHEA: Ah yes. That makes perfect sense. Set fire to the house. Of course. Of course. *(She sets fire to the house. Moving pictures of flames appear, projected on the walls)* It burns. It burns!

(NERONI takes out his violin, begins to play. BARBARA enters with fire extinguisher, fogs up the set as the curtain falls.)

Scene 4: *Hospital.*

(The NURSE is a Good Sister in a wimple.)

FRANK: How is she?
NURSE: Not very well. I'm afraid the end is near.
FRANK: Have you sent for a priest?
NURSE: She's refused the sacraments.
FRANK: Couldn't you force them on her?
NURSE: When Father tried to give her the wafer, she clamped her lips tight and turned her head away.
FRANK: Isn't there anything that could help?
NURSE: She's asked for nothing. But several times in her sleep she called out, "Neroni!"
FRANK: That's the Count. So she loves him after all.
NURSE: Yes, but this Count Neroni . . . oh, what's the use?
FRANK: Please go on.
NURSE: This Signore Neroni refuses to see her.
FRANK: Perhaps if I could convince him.
NURSE: It's very late now. I'm afraid it's . . . well . . . very late. She could live. But she's lost the will.
FRANK: May I see her?
NURSE: Go in, but try not to excite her. The slightest shock would be too much for her. *(Gently)* Mademoiselle Solange? *(No answer)* Mademoiselle Solange?
SOLANGE: *(In a whisper)* What do you want?
NURSE: There's someone to see you.

SOLANGE: I know. But I can't see him just now. That visitor must wait! He must wait a little longer, I tell you!

NURSE: But he's come such a long way. And he cares so very much for you. Won't you let him come in?

SOLANGE: He cares for me?

NURSE: Yes, he's very concerned about you. He wants you to get well. *(Aside to* FRANK*)* Now please try not to upset her. And remember, there's no need to raise your voice when speaking to a blind person.

FRANK: Blind?!

NURSE: Yes. Didn't you know?

FRANK: No.

NURSE: I'm sorry. You can go in now. Mademoiselle Solange. Here is your visitor.

SOLANGE: Neroni? Then you did come to save me. Ah, you know that only you could do it. I sent the priest away. I said only one person can save me, and that's Neroni. And you have come back to me. You do love me after all.

FRANK: Yes, Solange.

SOLANGE: And now you'll stay with me?

FRANK: Yes, Solange.

SOLANGE: And you'll never leave me again?

FRANK: Never.

SOLANGE: No matter what?

FRANK: No matter what.

SOLANGE: Come what may?

FRANK: Come what may.

SOLANGE: It's funny. *(Laughs)*

FRANK: What?

SOLANGE: They say that love is blind. But when you took your love away the darkness fell. But now I see. I *really* see. Your face is lit with a million candles. You glow. You flicker. You disappear and then appear again. Ah, I'm so happy I could die right now. And feel I hadn't missed a thing. Promise me something.

FRANK: *(Choking back tears)* Anything, dearest.

SOLANGE: If I die before you, bury me beneath the herb garden.

FRANK: What's all this talk of dying? You're going to live, Solange.

SOLANGE: Ah yes, Neroni. Now that you've come back, I'm going to live. Oh God, that light is bright. The glare hurts my eyes. I can see! *(Stares at him a moment)* Frank! You? *(Dies)*

FRANK: Oh God, no. Don't take her away. Not yet. Oh God. Not yet.

(Blackout.)

Scene 5: *The Egyptian Garden Nightclub.*

(There is a tiny cabaret stage. NERONI, RHEA, *and* BARBARA *are seated at a table.)*

BARBARA: This is on me, so both of you splurge. I mean order something ferociously expensive.

NERONI: The service is none too good here. Waiter? *(The waiter comes, his head enclosed in a birdcage)* Waiter? Where is that waiter? Waiter?

[*(Neroni sees and is startled by waiter. Waiter distributes menus.)*]

RHEA: I'll have escargot, lobster thermidor, asparagus béarnaise, a glass of Sauterne, and a scoop of pistachio ice cream for dessert.

BARBARA: Calves' brains puree for me, vichyssoise to start, and champagne, the best you have.

NERONI: I'll have a veal chop.

BARBARA: You sound depressed.

NERONI: It's nothing.

BARBARA: It's probably low blood sugar. You should see my doctor. I have a wonderful doctor. He did wonders with my liver, and I have the worst liver in the world!

RHEA: Muriel Fenchurch's liver is much worse than yours.

BARBARA: Muriel Fenchurch's liver can't compare with mine. My liver is much worse than Muriel Fenchurch's! *(The waiter opens the bottle of champagne with a pop, pours it.* BARBARA *toasts)* To us! No, that's not good enough. You propose a toast.

NERONI: I'm no good at toasts.

BARBARA: Go ahead and try. I'm sure you'll come up with something fascinating.

NERONI: Here's to love, the only fire against which there is no insurance!

BARBARA: You're right. You're no good at toasts.

RHEA: Here's to the love that lies in men's eyes, and lies and lies and lies!

BARBARA: Now I'm getting depressed. Come on, you two, let's drink to the past. There's plenty to give an excuse for a glass! *(They all drink)*

RHEA: Sis, can I get a sports car?

BARBARA: No.

RHEA: But Sally Seymour has one!

BARBARA: I don't care what Sally Seymour has.

RHEA: Ah, Sis! *(Sniffles)*

BARBARA: Don't ah Sis me! And don't sniffle. Blow your nose. *(*RHEA *does so)* I'm so glad we got out of that house when we did. What a day. What an utterly beastly day. Imagine, the house burning down and that butler shooting himself! And as I was dressing this morning, I broke a nail! I don't know whether to wear a false nail on that finger or have the others filed down. It's just one thing after another. Sometimes I don't know how I go on. It may be Rome. Yes, I'm sure it's Rome. It's beginning to get on my nerves. All this traffic and Italian food. I think it's time we moved on.

RHEA: Oh, Sister, can we go to Paris?

BARBARA: No, I'm tired of Paris. I feel that Paris is something I've done, if you know what I mean. I think Africa. Yes, Africa! I remember once, in Samarkand, there was this fantastic dervish who whirled and whirled and whirled until I got quite dizzy. And then he cut himself with a sword! And spattered blood all over the people in the front row. Oh it was too divine! Yes, I think Africa! Africa's really inexhaustible. It's not something that you tire of quickly. And the shopping is good. There's really nothing to buy in Italy. Well, it's actually the same all over Europe. But in Africa—well, that's a different story.

*(*NERONI, *during her speech, speaks his thoughts aloud.)*

NERONI: She wasn't the real Solange. She couldn't have been. Toinette was right. Solange would have been much older. Perhaps that madwoman was

Solange after all. Or perhaps Solange is dead. But no, no. Surely we would have heard something. Oh why am I going on like this? A woman is only a woman. Yes, a woman is just a woman after all.

BARBARA: Frank? Frank? Are you listening? Really, I don't know what's the matter with you tonight. You haven't said a word about my dress.

(FRANK BARLOWE *enters and looks about, spies the Count and his party, and rushes over. His head has healed and he wears no mask.*)

FRANK: Nito! *(He extends his hand warmly to* NERONI) I've come back! Nito, it's so good to see you, my friend, my dear dear friend.

NERONI: *(Icily)* There must be some mistake. I've never seen you before in my life.

FRANK: But, Nito. Don't you recognize me? I can't have changed that much.

BARBARA: *(To* NERONI) Who is that man?

NERONI: I have no idea. The imbecile must be drunk.

FRANK: Barbara! It's me, Frank. You said you'd marry me.

BARBARA: *(To* NERONI) Is this some sort of joke? Frank, who is this man?

FRANK: Frank? But I'm Frank.

BARBARA: Frank who?

FRANK: Frank Barlowe.

RHEA: *(Exclaims)* Phantom!

NERONI: *(Irate)* Imposter! *(Slaps* FRANK's *face with the veal chop)*

FRANK: Didn't you tell Barbara I was alive? Didn't you give her the locket?

BARBARA: The locket? Oh Frank! *(To* NERONI) You're not Frank Barlowe. Who are you? Who is it I've married?

FRANK: Married! *(Turning on* NERONI) Why you treacherous . . . I'm lost for words. I thought you were my friend. You filthy, lying, deceitful, double-dealing cheat!

BARBARA: You mean I've been the dupe, the gull, the victim, the easy mark, the fair game, the soft touch, the pushover, the soft mark, the sucker, the greenhorn, the April fool?

FRANK: *(To* NERONI) So you thought you could palm yourself off as me, my boy? Well, you'll never get away with it. You're exposed for the hornswoggling pettifogger that you are!

RHEA: *(To* NERONI) So, shortchange, you overreached!

NERONI: What are you complaining about? You begged me to touch it.

FRANK: *(Turns to* RHEA) You begged him to touch it, too?

RHEA: If I had known he wasn't the Phantom, I never would have.

BARBARA: So, foxy, you let them feel you up? Of all the underhanded . . .

RHEA: Only one of them was underhanded!

(They all talk at once for the next three speeches.)

FRANK: You snake, you treacherous, subtle, tricky, sophisticated snake in the grass!

BARBARA: You bilking, bunco con artist! You thought you could put one over on me, did you? Tried to bamboozle me, eh?

RHEA: Did you mean to beguile me, to cheat me and delude me? Oh, what a fool I was to let you hoodwink me and throw dust in my eyes!

(A singer enters on the tiny stage. She looks exactly like SOLANGE. *She sings.)*

SINGER:
An illusory thing is love.
Illusive illusion, mirage, will-o'-the-wisp.
Colorable, plausible,
specious, varnished,
apparition, phantasm,
myth, chimera,
dream.

NERONI: *(Leaping up)* Solange! It's you! *(All gasp. Singer continues song. As* NERONI *crosses the room toward the singer, with his arms outstretched like a sleepwalker, the tablecloth catches in his fly, and drags across the room all of the dinnerware which is glued to the tablecloth. He leaps onto the bandstand and seizes her in his arms)* Solange! You're alive! You've come back to me! Ah, Solange, my Solange!

SINGER: I'm afraid you're mistaken.

FRANK: But Nito, Mademoiselle Solange is dead. These are her teeth beyond the shadow of a doubt. *(Shows chattering teeth)*

BARBARA: Nito? Who are you? Who is he?

FRANK: *(Turning to* BARBARA, *taking her in his arms)* Why, Barbara, he's Count Neroni!

BARBARA: The last of the Neros?

FRANK: Yes, the spawn of the damned!

RHEA: The last of the Neros?

TOINETTE: *(Entering)* No! No! No! For twenty centuries the Neroni men have been sterile.

RHEA: Then how did they continue the line?

TOINETTE: That was the secret of their women.

BARBARA: Then I am the Countess Neroni?

TOINETTE: No, he was mio bambino. He was the fruit of a youthful indiscretion adopted by the childless Neronis.

BARBARA: Then who *was* his father?

TOINETTE: Il Duce!

NERONI: *(Passionately)* No, no. You died once before. But you came back to me. You are Solange! I know you are. You must be! Tell me you are! Solange! Solange!

The End

LE BOURGEOIS AVANT-GARDE

A Comedy Ballet After Moliere

1983

Zelda Patterson, Charles Ludlam & Black-Eyed Susan in
Le Bourgeois Avant-Garde (Anita & Steve Shevett)

Cast of Characters

THE COMPOSER
THE CHOREOGRAPHER
PERCIVAL HACK, *a stage director*
MR. FOUFAS
MRS. FOUFAS
VIOLET, *their maid*
MODERNA 83, *a grafitti artist*
PRUE FOUFAS, *the Foufases' daughter*
NEWTON ENTWHISTLE, *her fiancé*
MAIA PANZAROFF, *an avant-garde actress*

ACT I

(There is a great cacophony played by an assemblage of instruments such as balloons from which the air is emitted to make them "sing," a radiator which clangs and hisses, occasionally letting off steam, some bells, gamelan, drinking glass piano, an electric violin, pogo 'cello, spoons, and anything else that might pass for an avant-garde instrument. [Three chandeliers rise from the floor to the ceiling. A chair in the shape of a hand adorns the set])

COMPOSER: Come in. Wait here. He'll be along any minute. You can do warm-ups until he comes. If you wish, he'll have a barre installed.

CHOREOGRAPHER: Is it finished?

COMPOSER: The ink is barely dry on the page.

CHOREOGRAPHER: Splendid! Splendid! *(Takes manuscript)* Hmmm. Hmmm. *(Hums a few bars and tries out a step)* Hmmmm! Fascinating! Fascinating! Very innovative indeed!

COMPOSER: *(Taking the manuscript and turning it right side up)* It's meant to be read this way.

CHOREOGRAPHER: Of course! Of course! But then I can read just as well upside down. You know, you might try that—I mean inverting the manuscript and playing it. It might produce some highly original effects.

COMPOSER: I've already thought of that. The second movement was Xeroxed upside down.

CHOREOGRAPHER: Of course! Of course! You are a genius well acquainted with the most advanced theories of art. *(Pats him on the back)*

COMPOSER: Just as you are in the dance. *(They pat each other on the back)*

CHOREOGRAPHER: Although I think that serial music is just a bit passé. I mean it's sort of stuck back there in the muck of Modernism. I consider myself to be much more advanced. I am a Postmodern.

COMPOSER: You mean you are a Futurist?

CHOREOGRAPHER: No, the future was over by the early thirties.

COMPOSER: Well I am a *Post*postmodernist.

CHOREOGRAPHER: And what may I ask is that?

COMPOSER: A Neomodernist.

CHOREOGRAPHER: *(Indignantly)* Hurmph!

COMPOSER: When Postmodernism died, a Modernist revival ensued. *(Triumphantly)* And we're right back where we started!

CHOREOGRAPHER: How pretentious! You've done nothing but revive Futurism.

COMPOSER: You ass! The future cannot be revived until it has been lived, and when it has been lived it is no longer the future!

CHOREOGRAPHER: Do you know what I think? I think you're nothing but a lapsed Surrealist posing as a Postmodernist.

COMPOSER: And I think you're a Constructivist posing as an Expressionist.

CHOREOGRAPHER: Dadaist!

COMPOSER: Fauve!

CHOREOGRAPHER: Cubist!

COMPOSER: Surrealist!

CHOREOGRAPHER: Pop artist!

COMPOSER: Op artist!

CHOREOGRAPHER: Conceptualist!

COMPOSER: Realist!

CHOREOGRAPHER: *(Reeling as if from a blow)* Ouch! *(Then winding up and striking back)* Minimalist!

COMPOSER: *(Doubling over as if he had received a low blow)* Ooof! Wait a minute. I am not ashamed to admit that my work has a certain affinity to Minimalism.

CHOREOGRAPHER: Particularly that one great affinity. Your work is definitely *(Accentuating each syllable of the word)* Minimal.

COMPOSER: I don't like the way you said that. Your sentimental twaddle sickens me. At least I am not self-indulgent!

CHOREOGRAPHER: Of course not. You are a no-talent with no self to indulge.

COMPOSER: Why, how dare you! *(They try to strangle each other)*

(Enter PERCIVAL HACK.*)*

HACK: Artists! Artists, please! Let us not forget that we are here to collaborate. Our divine patron will be here any moment. How would it look if he came in and found us all squabbling amongst ourselves?

CHOREOGRAPHER: He certainly does keep us busy.

COMPOSER: Yes. We have found in him the patron we all needed. A man ravenous for art, starved for culture. And what is more, a man willing to pay for it. I wish there were more people like him.

HACK: Ah, yes, he's one in a million. But I can't help but wish he had a more profound understanding of our work.

CHOREOGRAPHER: It's true he doesn't have a profound understanding of our work. But then who does? Our work is so profound I don't believe it *can* be understood. At least not in the usual sense that we mean when we use the word understanding.

COMPOSER: But let's give credit where credit is due. He has a great *intuition.* Why, that he was instinctively drawn to our work is certainly a sign of something.

HACK: Why, yes, when you think of the other artists he could have chosen to squander his money on. I think it is a tribute to his taste that he chose us.

CHOREOGRAPHER: I agree. That alone is recommendation enough.

HACK: And after all, it's not just the money that we artists crave. It's the glory. Surely you can't evaluate applause in mere dollars and cents.

CHOREOGRAPHER: Ah, you don't know him as we do. You could sooner get a fart from a dead donkey than approval from him. We're subjected to a never-ending torrent of vulgar and ignorant criticism.

COMPOSER: And even when he does like something it's always for the wrong reason.

CHOREOGRAPHER: So that while it's true we live well at his expense, we are deprived of that thing an artist craves most.

COMPOSER: The exquisite pleasure of having one's work appreciated by the truly discerning.

CHOREOGRAPHER: And the praise of one who grasps the subtleties of one's art.

HACK: Well then, keep in mind at all times our urgent need to make a living. His praise is like money in the bank. Vulgar and ignorant though he may be, his applause has cash value far greater than all the aesthetes with their refined compliments and subtle appreciation who are too damned cheap to put their money where their mouths are.

CHOREOGRAPHER: You have a point. But I think a true artist should be above mere mercenary motives and eschew such sordid commercial considerations.

HACK: Still, I haven't seen you refuse his patronage.

CHOREOGRAPHER: I have a foundation to support. And anything is better than teaching. But shhh! Here he comes.

(Enter MR. FOUFAS.*)*

MR. FOUFAS: Well gentlemen, what's new today? Are you going to show me some of your monkeyshines?

CHOREOGRAPHER: Monkeyshines? What monkeyshines?

MR. FOUFAS: You know, your latest prank, your latest hoax, your latest practical joke.

(The COMPOSER *and* CHOREOGRAPHER *exchange puzzled looks and shrug.)*

HACK: He wants to see our work.

COMPOSER: Ah, ah!

CHOREOGRAPHER: Oh that! I didn't realize it was to our work you were referring.

MR. FOUFAS: For geniuses you're not too swift. But anyway, let me see your play.

HACK: Mr. Foufas, the avant-garde don't do plays. We do pieces.

MR. FOUFAS: You shouldn't just do pieces. You should do the whole thing.

HACK: You misunderstand me. A play is a piece and a piece is a play.

MR. FOUFAS: I mean your prologue or dialogue or whatever it is. Your singing and dancing.

HACK: Mr. Foufas, we do not say, "Let me see your play." Among the avant-garde, it would be more appropriate to say, "Let me see your piece." *(Puts his arm around* MR. FOUFAS*)*

MR. FOUFAS: Never mind. None of that funny stuff. I'm not one of them la-di-da guys.

HACK: Mr. Foufas, among the avant-garde, men are not uptight about their masculinity. [*(*COMPOSER *and* CHOREOGRAPHER *shake their heads no)*] Men often embrace when they meet. Show him. [*(They do)*] Now you try. [*(*MR. FOUFAS *embraces* HACK *half-heartedly)*] Come come. You can do better than that. Come on, give me a good hug. [*(He does)*] Much better. Among the avant-garde, men often embrace. Kiss even. [*(*HACK, COMPOSER, *and* CHOREOGRAPHER *pucker up)*]

MR. FOUFAS: Never mind. Let me see your piece. And make sure it's avant-garde. Nothing old hat, mind you.

COMPOSER: I assure you that our work is of the most advanced possible.

MR. FOUFAS: Modern, eh?

CHOREOGRAPHER: Postmodern.

COMPOSER: Postpostmodern.

MR. FOUFAS: But is it up-to-date?

CHOREOGRAPHER: I assure you that it is the last word.

COMPOSER: After us there will be nothing.

MR. FOUFAS: It can't be as bad as all that. Come on, let me have it. And whatever you do, don't pander to me. Go wild. Nothing is too far out.

HACK: I'm not sure I know what you mean.

MR. FOUFAS: I mean nothing shocks me so you don't have to be afraid to make it spicy.

HACK: I'm afraid the piece may not be quite what you expect. Before we begin perhaps I had better give you a bit of an explication.

MR. FOUFAS: What, afraid it will go over my head?

HACK: Not at all. But to fully appreciate our work, it is first necessary to understand how our theater relates to painting.

COMPOSER: How our music comes out of visual art.

CHOREOGRAPHER: How our dancing comes out of literary criticism.

HACK: And how our staging comes out of cinema.

MR. FOUFAS: I see. In other words, everything you do comes out of something else.

COMPOSER and CHOREOGRAPHER: In a manner of speaking.

HACK: Ours is an interdisciplinary art. It's mixed media.

MR. FOUFAS: Sounds like a big mess to me, but if that's the way the avant-garde do it, go ahead.

COMPOSER: Then to proceed.

MR. FOUFAS: Wait a minute. First I want to show you the new outfit I just had made.

HACK: As you wish.

MR. FOUFAS: *(Opens box and shows outfit)* I understand the avant-garde wear this sort of thing. *(Dropping his pants)* Here help me get into these pants.

HACK: *(Helping him to zip up his pants)* Suck it in.

MR. FOUFAS: *(Almost blue in the face from holding his breath)* My god, they're tight. I can hardly breathe.

HACK: Well, you're in them.

MR. FOUFAS: How do the avant-garde breathe? How do they sit down? How do they dance with no ballroom. Ha ha ha! Get it? Ball room! *(Slaps* COMPOSER *on the back)*

COMPOSER: I get it. *(Aside)* But I don't want it.

MR. FOUFAS: How do I look?

CHOREOGRAPHER: Very . . . very.

MR. FOUFAS: Do I? I'd hoped I might.

HACK: Excellent. And now, if you can make yourself comfortable we will begin.

MR. FOUFAS: *(To* HACK*)* By the way, Maia Panzaroff, the great Polish avant-garde actress, will be able to attend my little soiré tonight, won't she?

HACK: Yes, she will.

MR. FOUFAS: Oh good. Did you give Miss Panzaroff that ring I gave you?

HACK: Ah yes.

MR. FOUFAS: Good. Did she like it? What did she say?

HACK: She thought it very beautiful.

MR. FOUFAS: She should. It cost enough!

HACK: But when you see her, it would be better if you didn't mention it. Among the avant-garde any mention of money is considered commercial and—how shall I say—vulgar.

MR. FOUFAS: Is that so?

HACK: When you see her, the way to really impress her would be to pretend that you didn't give it to her.

MR. FOUFAS: Is that how the avant-garde do it?

HACK: Yes. Pretend you think it's nothing. You see, the avant-garde scorn money.

MR. FOUFAS: If that's what the avant-garde do, I'll do it too!

HACK: Good. But let's begin.

MR. FOUFAS: You were going to explicate these shenanigans.

CHOREOGRAPHER: Yes. You see, the most supreme arts are the abstract arts— music, painting, and dance.

MR. FOUFAS: How do you mean abstract?

HACK: You don't know what abstract means?

MR. FOUFAS: Of course I know what abstract means. But I don't know in what *sense* you mean abstract. I understand abstract generally—it's abstract in particular I'm asking about.

CHOREOGRAPHER: Would you like to explain it to him?

COMPOSER: Abstract has to do with pure form removed from any representational content. It is form liberated from content.

MR. FOUFAS: In other words if it doesn't represent anything it's abstract.

COMPOSER: Yes.

HACK: Of course this also depends upon the degree of abstraction. There are the higher abstractions or pure abstractions and the lower abstractions or schematic representations, which while having one or more referents do not achieve or make claim to objecthood in and of their own right. But rather refer or allude rather than depict or represent. Is that clear?

MR. FOUFAS: *(Who has been dozing off)* Ah hum? Oh yes. Perfectly.

CHOREOGRAPHER: The greatest arts are music, painting, and dancing.

MR. FOUFAS: And what are they for?

CHOREOGRAPHER: For?

MR. FOUFAS: Well what's the purpose or as I may say the point, sir. Gee, I've always wanted to ask that but I was never able to put the question into words before.

CHOREOGRAPHER: *(To* COMPOSER*)* You try it.

COMPOSER: I pass.

HACK: Why, art has two great functions: education—and the contemplation of pure beauty.

MR. FOUFAS: And which do you do?

HACK: Well education, that's passé, hopeless—we leave that to the academics. Today we concentrate solely on the contemplation of pure beauty.

MR. FOUFAS: I can easily go along with that. Are you sure Miss Panzaroff will be able to attend?

HACK: I'll call and confirm. *(Exits)*

MR. FOUFAS: *(Sighs)*

COMPOSER: The most important art is music.

CHOREOGRAPHER: The most important art is dancing.

COMPOSER: Without music the world wouldn't go 'round.

CHOREOGRAPHER: Without dancing, life would be empty.

COMPOSER: All the wars, all the turmoil in the world today is due to not learning music.

CHOREOGRAPHER: All the sufferings of humankind, all the miseries, political blunders, failures of the world's leaders, come from not having studied dancing.

MR. FOUFAS: How do you arrive at that?

COMPOSER: Why war is nothing but discord among nations.

MR. FOUFAS: True.

COMPOSER: If men studied music, could we not attain universal harmony?

MR. FOUFAS: That's a good point.

CHOREOGRAPHER: And when a man makes an error in politics or private life, do we not say that he has made a false step?

MR. FOUFAS: We do indeed.

CHOREOGRAPHER: And isn't making a false step the direct result of no dance training? Is it not universally accepted that a man should always put his best foot forward?

MR. FOUFAS: That's right.

CHOREOGRAPHER: Where else can a man better learn to put his best foot forward than in a dance class?

MR. FOUFAS: True enough. But come now. *(To the* CHOREOGRAPHER*)* Stop pulling my leg. *(To the* COMPOSER*)* There's no need to be blowing your own horn. You're both right.

COMPOSER: We just wanted to point out the importance of music and dancing.

MR. FOUFAS: I see it now.

CHOREOGRAPHER: Shall we begin our rehearsal?

MR. FOUFAS: Do it.

HACK: *(Reentering)* Let us begin.

(Music. [One foot in a pointe shoe] pops up on a tiny puppet stage, toes skyward.)

MR. FOUFAS: What is this supposed to represent?

HACK: Please Mr. Foufas, this is an *abstract* theater piece.

MR. FOUFAS: Oh yes, abstract—that means it isn't supposed to represent anything. Am I right?

HACK: Right. [*(A second, naked foot appears.* MR. FOUFAS *points and laughs. A third foot appears.* MR. FOUFAS *falls asleep.)*] That's it.

MR. FOUFAS: *(Waking with a start)* That's it?

HACK: Yes, that was it.

MR. FOUFAS: All of it?

HACK: Yes, all of it.

COMPOSER: Did you enjoy it?

CHOREOGRAPHER: Yes, what did you think?

MR. FOUFAS: Well, you certainly can shake a leg. But I think it needs a little tightening up.

CHOREOGRAPHER: What!?

MR. FOUFAS: It was a bit too long.

COMPOSER: *(Thunderstruck)* Too long!?

MR. FOUFAS: Just a bit.

COMPOSER: But the piece barely lasted three minutes.

MR. FOUFAS: Still, it seemed to drag a bit in places and, if you'll forgive my saying so, it didn't make any sense.

HACK: We warned you that the piece would be abstract.

COMPOSER: Of course you can't expect to get everything on the first hearing. It's subtle.

CHOREOGRAPHER: You mustn't come to it with too many preconceptions. I can see how you might not be sure about it on the first viewing. It's so new. It's so experimental.

COMPOSER: It's very avant-garde.

HACK: Perhaps it was too avant-garde?

MR. FOUFAS: On the contrary. I think you could have gone much further. If anything it was too tame.

HACK: Tame?

MR. FOUFAS: It lacked outrage.

HACK: Just what did you have in mind?

MR. FOUFAS: It could have used some giant phalluses, naked women. Don't ask me. If you've really run out of ideas why don't you do a piece on nuclear disarmament?

COMPOSER and CHOREOGRAPHER: *(Rolling their eyes heavenward)* Oh!

MR. FOUFAS: You know I have a standard by which I judge any work of art.

COMPOSER and CHOREOGRAPHER: Oh?

MR. FOUFAS: There are just two things I look for. If it has one of them I know it's good and if it has both of them I know it's great.

HACK: Tell us.

COMPOSER: Do.

CHOREOGRAPHER: We're all ears.

MR. FOUFAS: First, it must have a certain magic. And second, it must move me. Of course, if it makes me cry, then I know it's really great. In fact, the more I cry, the greater I know it is.

COMPOSER: A certain magic.

CHOREOGRAPHER: And it must move him.

COMPOSER: *(Aside)* But will it *re*move him?

MR. FOUFAS: Don't get me wrong. It wasn't a total loss. I did like the part where the little bare foot went by. That was very clever.

HACK: The piece we are preparing for tonight's festivities will be even more effective.

MR. FOUFAS: Try to liven it up a bit, will you. This was pretty dismal.

HACK: I'll do all I can.

MR. FOUFAS: That will be all for now. Thank you very much, gentlemen. *(Hands each one of them an envelope)* This is for your trouble.

CHOREOGRAPHER: Thank you. And thank you for your helpful suggestions.

MR. FOUFAS: Oh, don't mention it.

COMPOSER: Thanks. We'll try to get a little magic into it for you.

MR. FOUFAS: Save that for later when the lady for whom I am doing all this will be dining with me here. Be sure and come back early so you'll have plenty of time to run it through before she arrives. (COMPOSER *and* CHOREOGRAPHER *back out bowing)* You're sure Miss Panzaroff will be able to attend?

HACK: Everything is all arranged.

MR. FOUFAS: Good. Now listen. I want to tell you a secret. I'm in love with Miss Panzaroff and I want you to help me write a little love letter to drop at her feet.

HACK: Ah, I see.

MR. FOUFAS: That's the correct thing to do isn't it?

HACK: Indubitably. And you want it in verse, of course.

MR. FOUFAS: No. No. Not verse.

HACK: Then you want it in prose.

MR. FOUFAS: No, I don't want it in prose either.

HACK: But it must be in one or the other.

MR. FOUFAS: Why?

HACK: Because there's nothing else to express ourselves in except verse and prose.

MR. FOUFAS: Nothing but verse and prose?

HACK: That's all. Everything that isn't prose is verse and everything that isn't verse is prose.

MR. FOUFAS: And what we are speaking now, what's that?

HACK: Prose.

MR. FOUFAS: And when I say, "Violet, bring me a salami sandwich" or "Where did you put my pajamas?," that's prose?

HACK: Yes, sir.

MR. FOUFAS: Well, what do you know! Here I've been speaking prose for forty years and never knew it! Mr. Hack, you have my eternal gratitude for bringing this to my attention.

HACK: Don't mention it.

MR. FOUFAS: Now what I want to say in the letter is, "Fair mistress, I am dying for love of your beautiful eyes!" But I want it to be put in a more original way, so that it sounds avant-garde, you understand. What should I do?

HACK: Well, you could say, "The tantric synergic epistasis emanating from your corneas produces synaptic signals of affinity which threaten a thrombosis of my auricles and ventricles."

MR. FOUFAS: No no no no no! That's not what I want at all! I just want it to say what I said: "Fair mistress, I am dying for love of your beautiful eyes!" But I want to sound more original.

HACK: But surely you want something a little more elaborate!

MR. FOUFAS: No, I don't want anything in the letter except my exact words. But I want them arranged so that they sound avant-garde. What would you advise me to do?

HACK: Then I'm afraid there's nothing to do but deconstruct the text.

MR. FOUFAS: Deconstruct the text?

HACK: Yes. You could put them as you have already done, "Fair mistress, I am dying for love of your beautiful eyes," or you could deconstruct it. You could write each word in the letter on a separate piece of paper, put them all in a hat, shake them up, pull them out, and write them in the order they occur.

MR. FOUFAS: Let's try that! [*(He recites the words as he tears up the letter)*] I'll be needing a hat.

HACK: [*(Pulling hat out of his back pocket)*] Right here!

MR. FOUFAS: Oh Mr. Hack, you think of everything! [*(Puts words in hat, holds hat while* HACK *goes through elaborate preparations for selection, exasperating* FOUFAS*)*] Cut that out!

HACK: *(Drawing the pieces out and reading them one at a time)* "Your—eyes—for—of—dying—love—beautiful—fair—mistress—I—am."

MR. FOUFAS: I don't like it. Let's try it again.

HACK: Very well.

(They repeat the operation.)

HACK: "For—beautiful—dying—fair—am—eyes—your—mistress—love—of—I."

MR. FOUFAS: That's even worse. Let's do another one.

(They repeat the operation.)

HACK: "Beautiful—your—eyes—for—dying—am—of—I—fair—love—mistress."

MR. FOUFAS: This doesn't seem to be working. What should I do?

HACK: Well, you could arrange the words in the order you used yourself, "Fair mistress, I am dying for love of your beautiful eyes."

MR. FOUFAS: I can't believe it. I've only just discovered the avant-garde, and I got it right the first time! Please be sure you bring Miss Panzaroff when you return this evening—oh, and would you stop by this afternoon with that young artist we discussed? I'd like to introduce him to my daughter!

HACK: You can rely on me.

MR. FOUFAS: Oh, thank you! *(HACK exits. Calling off right)* Violet! Violet! Violet!

VIOLET: *(Entering behind him, left. Stands and watches him call for a while, then)* Yes sir. What is it?

MR. FOUFAS: *(Frightened)* Aahrgh! Don't sneak up behind me like that. Now listen.

VIOLET: *(Laughing)* Hee! Hee! Hee! Hee! Hee! Hee!

MR. FOUFAS: What are you laughing about?

VIOLET: Hee! Hee! Hee! Hee! Hee! Hee!

MR. FOUFAS: What's the matter with you?

VIOLET: Hee! Hee! Hee! It's just the idea of *you* dressed like *that.* Ha! Ha! Ha!

MR. FOUFAS: What do you mean!

VIOLET: Oh my god. Hee! Hee! Hee! Hee! Hee! Hee!

MR. FOUFAS: You little nincompoop! Are you laughing at me?

VIOLET: Oh no, sir. I wouldn't dream of being so disrespectful. It's just that . . . Oh ho ho! Ho ho ho! Ha ha ha! Ha ha ha! I can't help it, sir! *(Laughs again)*

MR. FOUFAS: Are you never going to stop?

VIOLET: I'm sorry, sir. But you look so funny I just can't help . . . ha! ha! ha! ha! ha!

MR. FOUFAS: How dare you laugh at me, you impudent little hussy!

VIOLET: But you look so funny like that. *(Laughs)*

MR. FOUFAS: I'll give you something to laugh about in a minute.

VIOLET: Forgive me . . . but I . . . *(Laughs)*

MR. FOUFAS: See here. If you don't stop laughing this very minute I'm going to smack your face for you.

VIOLET: *(Suddenly stops laughing)* I'm finished. I won't laugh anymore.

MR. FOUFAS: Well see to it that you don't. Now I want you to give the house a thorough cleaning today and get it ready for . . .

VIOLET: Ha! Ha! Ha!

MR. FOUFAS: You must clean up everything for—

VIOLET: Ha ha ha!

MR. FOUFAS: What, again? Hyena!

VIOLET: Oh go ahead and beat me if you want to. Beat me black-and-blue. But let me laugh. I haven't had such a good laugh in years! *(Laughs)*

MR. FOUFAS: I'm losing my temper.

VIOLET: Oh please let me laugh. It will do me more good. Ha! Ha! Ha!

MR. FOUFAS: I've had quite enough of this.

VIOLET: I'll die if I hold it in. Ha! Ha! Ha!

MR. FOUFAS: Are you going to listen to me, good-for-nothing, or are you going to stand there and laugh in my face?

VIOLET: What—what—is it—you—want me—to—do—sir?

MR. FOUFAS: What do you think, slut? Get the house ready for the company I'm expecting shortly.

VIOLET: *(Suddenly serious)* Now *that* isn't funny. Those people you drag in here make such a mess I'm depressed already.

MR. FOUFAS: And am I to shut my door to visitors to please you?

VIOLET: You should shut it on some of them.

(Enter MRS. FOUFAS.)

MRS. FOUFAS: Oh no! What next? What are you doing dressed like that, man? Look at you! Do you want the whole neighborhood laughing at you?

MR. FOUFAS: Let the fools laugh. Every major innovation in modern art has been greeted with laughter by the ignorant bourgeoisie, and everything they took seriously when it first appeared proved later to be kitsch. So let them laugh at me and everything I do. I take it as a compliment to be laughed at by idiots!

MRS. FOUFAS: But it won't be the first time. Your ridiculous carryings-on have been laughed at more than once.

MR. FOUFAS: They're idiots, I tell you.

MRS. FOUFAS: These so-called idiots have more sense than you. I'm revolted by the life you are leading. I can't call my home my own, anymore. And I wish you'd get rid of that chair.

MR. FOUFAS: That chair expresses my personality!

MRS. FOUFAS: Every night is party time—with you bringing in all the trash to sing and dance, make a mess, and eat us out of house and home.

VIOLET: The missus is right! I can't keep the place clean with this pack of bums tramping through here as though it were Grand Central Station! Half of them don't even know enough to wipe their feet before they come in, and I have to work my fingers to the bone polishing the floors for your avant-garde artistes to track them up with all the muck from the gutters of the Lower East Side.

MR. FOUFAS: Are you working for me or am I working for you?

MRS. FOUFAS: Violet is right! She has more sense than you.

VIOLET: And the very idea of your studying modern dance at your age!

MR. FOUFAS: Shut up, both of you!

MRS. FOUFAS: Are you learning to dance for the time when you're too feeble to walk?

MR. FOUFAS: Shut up, I tell you! Ignoramuses! [*(He vocalizes)*]

VIOLET: And those music lessons! All this moaning and groaning. People will think someone's dying in here!

MR. FOUFAS: You don't understand the significance of the sounds I'm learning to make! They are primordial!

MRS. FOUFAS: Well they sound flatulent to me. If you must fart, do it out of the proper end!

MR. FOUFAS: You vulgar bourgeois woman, you. How dare you insult my Orghast! Why Peter Brook spent a fortune in government subsidy inventing that language so that we could express ourselves without signifying anything!

VIOLET: And I've just heard that he's enrolled in the School of Birds, to learn heaven knows what.

MRS. FOUFAS: This is for the birds, all right. You should enroll in a school and have yourself whipped. It would do you more good.

MR. FOUFAS: Ignorant woman! I wish to god I could be whipped! In public, where everyone could see me, if it could teach me the true meaning of ontology!

MRS. FOUFAS: Ontology. And what may I ask is that?

MR. FOUFAS: I have a good mind not to tell you, since you've been so rude. But since I still have some hope that you will see the light and join the avant-garde with me, I will tell you. It is being, pure and simple. Pure being.

MRS. FOUFAS: And what I'm doing right now isn't being?

MR. FOUFAS: It is, it is, of course it is, but you don't know it is, and that's what makes all the difference! It's all a question of juxtaposition.

MRS. FOUFAS: Oh, what a lot of nonsense!

MR. FOUFAS: Oh really? Then what am I speaking?

MRS. FOUFAS: Stuff and nonsense.

MR. FOUFAS: No no no! I mean, what have you been speaking all your life?

MRS. FOUFAS: Common sense.

MR. FOUFAS: No, you've been speaking prose, ignorant woman, prose!

MRS. FOUFAS: Ah Violet, what am I going to do? My husband is mad.

VIOLET: He's not tightly wrapped, and that's a fact.

MR. FOUFAS: Never mind. I want you to get this place good and clean because I am expecting a visit from a major director of the avant-garde, Percival Hack. He's been teaching me how to deconstruct texts.

MRS. FOUFAS: You'd do far better by concentrating on something constructive, like getting our daughter married to a good husband before she's too old.

MR. FOUFAS: I've told you before. I don't want our daughter making the same mistake we made. She should practice free love, have children out of wedlock by any number of different men, preferably famous artists and, like Isadora Duncan, write her memoirs and die in a fatal automobile accident!

MRS. FOUFAS: How could you wish such a fate on our daughter? I think she'd be far better off marrying Newton Entwhistle next door. She loves him and he has a good steady job at the bank.

MR. FOUFAS: Never! I'd rather see my daughter rotting with syphilis in an African brothel than tied to a tedious beer-swilling bourgeois who believes what he reads in the papers.

VIOLET: Nice talk.

MRS. FOUFAS: What would you have her do?

MR. FOUFAS: Why marry a starving artist, of course, and live a bohemian life. I have a husband picked out for her already, Moderna 83. He's one of the best graffiti artists working today in the Independent line. It will be her destiny to carry his spray cans and serve as a lookout for the Transit Police.

MRS. FOUFAS: Over my dead body! *(Throwing up her hands in despair)* Oh my god, my god! To what level of degradation will you not drag us down? I won't have my daughter living with a mole in the subway!

(Doorbell.)

MR. FOUFAS: That will be Mr. Hack now, with our future son-in-law.

MRS. FOUFAS: I suspect they're coming to get more money out of you.

MR. FOUFAS: Oh be quiet. You have no idea what an incredible honor it is to play hostess to the avant-garde. There are many women who'd give their eyeteeth to have a salon.

MRS. FOUFAS: They'll take your eyeteeth all right, especially if there are gold fillings in them.

MR. FOUFAS: These people are my friends, I tell you. They've accepted me into their circle.

MRS. FOUFAS: They are, in a swine's retina. This guy's milking you like a cow.

MR. FOUFAS: It is a privilege to do all I can for the avant-garde.

MRS. FOUFAS: And what does the avant-garde do for you?

MR. FOUFAS: Lots of things that would surprise you if you knew.

MRS. FOUFAS: Such as?

MR. FOUFAS: Never mind. I don't want to talk about it now. Here they are.

(Enter MODERNA *and* HACK.*)*

HACK: Ah Mr. Foufas, my dear friend, how are you?

MR. FOUFAS: Ah very well, my dear friend, very well. *(They embrace. Aside to* MRS. FOUFAS*)* You see how he calls me his friend?

HACK: And how is Mrs. Foufas today?

MRS. FOUFAS: Mrs. Foufas is as well as can be expected.

HACK: And where is your lovely daughter? How is she getting along?

MRS. FOUFAS: On her two legs, thank you.

HACK: This is the celebrated graffiti artist, Moderna 83.

MR. FOUFAS: How do you do?

MODERNA: Doy de de doy.

MR. FOUFAS: How's that?

MODERNA: Doy de de doy.

MR. FOUFAS: I beg your pardon?

HACK: He says, "How do you do?"

MR. FOUFAS: He did?

HACK: Yes. Moderna expresses himself in Newspeak.

MR. FOUFAS: Newspeak?

HACK: Yes, it's the latest thing. Newspeak is composed entirely of monosyllables which, while having no lexical meaning, convey inner emotional states.

MR. FOUFAS: You mean this speech is pure emotion?

HACK: Not quite. This speech is actually a substitute for emotion.

MR. FOUFAS: I see.

HACK: Mr. Moderna is one of the most advanced artists working today. In fact, he has gone beyond art with his invention of Artex.

MR. FOUFAS: Artex? Is that a new form of art?

HACK: Again, not quite. Artex is a convenient art–substitute. It is art without the usual fuss and bother. Art without anguish, that's Artex!

MR. FOUFAS: Then the spray-painting of graffiti on the subway is Artex.

HACK: No, that's just something to do with his free time.

MODERNA: Doy doy doy doy doy. Doy doy doy doy doy doy doy. Doy doy doy. Doy doy doy. Doy doy doy doy doy.

MR. FOUFAS: What did he say?

HACK: He said he's delighted to meet you.

MR. FOUFAS: The pleasure is all mine.

MODERNA: Doy doy doy doy doy doy doy. De doy doy doy doy doy doy doy. Doy de doy, doy de doy, doy doy doy doy doy. Doy doy doy doy doy doy doy doy doy doy doy doy doy doy!

MR. FOUFAS: What did he say? What did he say?

HACK: He says you are a connoisseur.

MR. FOUFAS: He said that about me?

HACK: Yes.

MODERNA: Doy doy doy doy doy doy doy doy doy doy doy doy. Doy doy doy doy doy doy doy doy doy doy doy doy doy doy doy. Doy doy doy doy doy doy doy doy doy doy doy doy doy doy. Doy doy doy doy doy doy doy doy doy doy doy doy doy doy. Doy doy doy doy doy doy doy doy doy doy doy doy doy.

MR. FOUFAS: [*(Caught up in Newspeak)*] Doy doy doy doy doy doy. [*(Stops himself)*]

HACK: He finds your outfit very smart!

MR. FOUFAS: Does he?

MRS. FOUFAS: That's right. Scratch him where he itches!

HACK: Ah yes, very elegant. Turn around!

MRS. FOUFAS: Yes, he looks as silly behind as he does in front.

MODERNA: Doy doy doy doy doy doy doy doy doy doy doy doy. Doy doy doy doy doy doy doy doy doy doy doy doy doy doy doy. Doy doy doy doy doy doy doy doy doy doy doy doy doy doy doy. Doy doy doy doy doy doy doy doy doy doy doy doy doy doy. Doy doy doy doy doy doy doy doy doy doy doy doy doy doy doy doy doy. Doy doy doy doy doy doy doy doy doy doy doy doy doy doy. Doy doy doy doy doy doy doy doy doy doy doy doy doy doy doy doy. Doy doy. Doy doy doy doy doy doy doy doy doy doy doy doy doy doy.

MR. FOUFAS: What does he say now?

HACK: He likes your shoes.

MR. FOUFAS: What about them?

HACK: Nothing. He just says he likes them.

MODERNA: Doy doy.

MR. FOUFAS: What's that?

HACK: He says that he could tell the moment he met you that you were a man of rare intelligence and understanding. That you were not only a great patron, but one of those rare spirits who are utterly ahead of their time. A superb judge of creative work and a harbinger of a new age of cultural achievement!

MR. FOUFAS: "Doy doy" meant all that?

HACK: That's one of the great things about Newspeak. You can express a lot in a few words.

MR. FOUFAS: Tell him that if there's ever anything I can do for him, I am at his service.

MODERNA: Doy doy doy doy doy, doy doy doy.

HACK: He understood you perfectly.

MR. FOUFAS: But of course. How silly of me.

HACK: Mr. Foufas, you are to be congratulated. You are rapidly becoming the premier patron of the avant-garde.

MR. FOUFAS: Thank you! Thank you! You do me too much honor! *(Aside to* MRS. FOUFAS*)* Did you hear that?

HACK: I am deeply indebted to you.

MRS. FOUFAS: *(Aside)* At least he admits it!

HACK: You have generously given me money to support my little projects.

MR. FOUFAS: It was nothing.

HACK: No no, it was most generous! And I wish to repay you.

MR. FOUFAS: It was the least I could do. *(Aside to* MRS. FOUFAS*)* Now what do you have to say for yourself, woman?

HACK: In acknowledgment of the great help you've been to our careers, Moderna wants to give you a work of art of his creation!

MR. FOUFAS: *(Aside to* MRS. FOUFAS*)* You and your silly suspicions!

HACK: He would like to do a portrait of Mrs. Foufas!

MRS. FOUFAS: A portrait of me? Why would anybody want to do a portrait of me?

HACK: You must have been extremely beautiful in your youth!

MRS. FOUFAS: And what am I now? An old bag, I suppose.

HACK: Nonsense. Your face has great character!

MR. FOUFAS: What kind of portrait are you going to do?

MODERNA: Doy doy doy doy doy. Doy de de doy doy doy.

HACK: To begin with, he would like to make a plaster cast of her tongue.

MRS. FOUFAS: *(Furious)* Is that so? You're going to be needing a plaster cast for your skull in a minute!

MR. FOUFAS: You must excuse my wife. She's woefully ignorant of the latest innovations in art. *(To* MRS. FOUFAS*)* Don't be foolish, dear. Why, to have a plaster cast of your tongue done by the great Moderna 83 would be an honor! Your tongue would be immortalized!

MRS. FOUFAS: I'm not sticking my tongue in plaster!

MR. FOUFAS: Forgive her, Mr. Hack. She's unbelievably pigheaded. Perhaps Moderna could do another kind of portrait.

MODERNA: Doy doy de doy doy doy.

HACK: *(Looking her over)* He might be able to do something with her bust.

MRS. FOUFAS: Touch my bust and I'll scream!

MR. FOUFAS: *(Taking* MRS. FOUFAS *aside)* Don't be an idiot! Why, do you know what his work will be worth someday? Why, we could plan our retirement around its resale value!

MRS. FOUFAS: I don't care! Just tell him to keep his hands off me!

MR. FOUFAS: *(To* HACK*)* What about a painting?

MODERNA: Doy doy doy doy de doy doy. Doy doy doy.

HACK: He could do a painting, if that would be more to Mrs. Foufas's liking.

MRS. FOUFAS: All right. I guess there's no harm in a painting.

MODERNA: Doy doy doy.

HACK: Sit here, Mrs. Foufas. Where would you like the painting?

MRS. FOUFAS: I guess we could put it on that wall over there.

*(*MODERNA *holds up his thumb toward* MRS. FOUFAS, *then takes a can of spray paint and sprays a blob on the wall.* VIOLET *screams. As* HACK *passes a Baroque picture frame to* MODERNA, *they hold it in front of* MRS. FOUFAS *for a brief moment, and then hang it over the blob on the wall.* MODERNA *signs the painting.)*

HACK: There you are!

MR. FOUFAS: It's really a wonderful likeness!

HACK: What do you think, Mrs. Foufas?

MRS. FOUFAS: I'm crazy about the frame!

MR. FOUFAS: Ah Mr. Hack, how can I ever thank you?

HACK: Do you think you could let me have fifteen hundred dollars?

MR. FOUFAS: Fifteen hundred? Oh certainly, certainly.

HACK: It's just to keep body and soul together, you understand.

MR. FOUFAS: Don't mention it. I'll write you a check. *(Does so)*

HACK: You know, Mr. Foufas, I'm entirely at your disposal. If there's ever anything I can do for you, don't hesitate to ask.

MR. FOUFAS: You are too kind.

HACK: If there's ever anything I can do for Mrs. Foufas . . .

MRS. FOUFAS: No, thank you very much.

HACK: *(To* MR. FOUFAS*)* As I mentioned in my note, Miss Panzaroff will be here soon to dine with us and see the ballet. I persuaded her to accept your invitation.

MR. FOUFAS: Let's discuss this in private. I think you understand the reason why.

*(*HACK *and* MR. FOUFAS *move upstage and speak quietly.* MRS. FOUFAS *and* VIOLET *move downstage.)*

MRS. FOUFAS: When he's with that fellow, there's no getting him away.

VIOLET: They're thick as thieves.

HACK: *(To* MR. FOUFAS*)* And the gift of the diamond ring will surely help to win her affection.

MR. FOUFAS: I hope so. Do you think I'm going about it the right way?

HACK: Of course. Women love nothing more than to have money spent on them. Your habit of sending flowers every week, the superb fireworks display on the lake, the diamond you sent her, and this entertainment you are now preparing are bound to influence her in your favor more than anything you could say for yourself.

MR. FOUFAS: I would go to any expense to win the heart of a woman who's truly the muse of the avant-garde!

VIOLET: Is he never going to go?

MRS. FOUFAS: *(Aside to* VIOLET*)* What on earth are they talking about for so long? Sneak over there and listen!

MR. FOUFAS: But you don't think my approach is too conventional?

HACK: You, conventional? Don't be absurd! Why, every gesture you make bristles with originality!

MR. FOUFAS: I've written a poem to her, too. Do you want to hear it?

HACK: If you don't think it indiscreet.

MR. FOUFAS:

> Roses are red,
> Violets are blue,
> I'd like to show my privates
> to a pair of sloppy sluts
> plainly showing all the unmentionability
> falsely accusing about the raincoats.

HACK: Superb!

MR. FOUFAS: To avoid any unpleasant complications, I've arranged to have my wife dine with her sister at Beefsteak Charlie's tonight.

HACK: Very prudent. Your wife might have been in the way. I've given the necessary instructions to your cook and arranged for the ballet. You will soon have her here, where you may feast your eyes on her to your heart's . . .

MR. FOUFAS: *(Catching* VIOLET *eavesdropping)* Ah yes, a fishing trip would be a marvelous idea! *(Smacks* VIOLET*)* What gall! *(To* HACK*)* Let's go somewhere where we can discuss this in private.

HACK: Come, Moderna.

(They exit.)

VIOLET: That's what I get for being curious!

MRS. FOUFAS: Did you hear anything?

VIOLET: Something about a fishing trip.

MRS. FOUFAS: Oh Violet, this isn't the first time that I've suspected my husband of having an affair. I'm going to dine with my sister tonight. I want you to stay here and keep an eye on him. Don't let him out of your sight. Watch him like a hawk and give me a full report when I get home. There's something fishy going on on these fishing trips he's going on!

(Does an about-face and they both march off. Enter NEWTON *and* PRUE.)

NEWTON: I think we ought to postpone the wedding.

PRUE: Now why on earth would you think a thing like that?

NEWTON: Your father hates me.

PRUE: So what's new?

NEWTON: Maybe we should wait and try to get his blessing.

PRUE: Listen, Newton, I've been looking forward to this wedding so much I can hardly stand it. I'm not putting it off.

NEWTON: But, but . . .

PRUE: No buts about it. Now just get that out of your head.

(Enter MRS. FOUFAS.)

MRS. FOUFAS: Ah, Newton my boy, I'm delighted to see you. You've come just at the right moment. My husband is coming in. This is your chance to ask him to let you marry Prue.

NEWTON: That's exactly what I want to do. But do you think I have a chance?

MRS. FOUFAS: Ask him and see. Here he comes.

(Enter MR. FOUFAS.)

NEWTON: Sir, I want to ask you myself rather than through any intermediary something which I have thoroughly considered and long desired. And so may I make the request of you without further preamble that I the party of the first part might form a matrimonial alliance with your daughter the party of the second part and would you the aforesaid father of the party of the second part be party to or afford me the rights and privileges accorded to such an alliance and accord me the honor of being your son-in-law?

MR. FOUFAS: Before giving you a reply, sir, I must ask you to answer one question. Are you avant-garde?

NEWTON: I beg your pardon?

MR. FOUFAS: I asked you plainly and simply. Are you avant-garde?

NEWTON: I have served four years in the army.

MR. FOUFAS: That is quite beside the point, sir. Answer my question in a straightforward manner.

NEWTON: Very well then. I must admit honestly and frankly that while I am a fair shot with a rifle I have never studied any form of swordplay.

MR. FOUFAS: Just as I thought. You don't even know the meaning of the word. That settles it. My daughter is not for you.

NEWTON: What!

MR. FOUFAS: If you aren't avant-garde, you can't have my daughter.

MRS. FOUFAS: What are you talking about? You and your avant-garde? What are we but decent, hardworking people?

MR. FOUFAS: Be quiet. Don't insult me.

MRS. FOUFAS: We can be proud that we gave our daughter a respectable middle-class upbringing.

MR. FOUFAS: Watch your language! If you are a bourgeois, that's your problem. But don't try to drag me up to your level.

MRS. FOUFAS: You've worked hard all your life to get where you are. You should be proud and enjoy it.

MR. FOUFAS: Yes I've worked hard to be comfortable. But look at what I've missed. I've never had to starve for what I believed in. I've never been misunderstood. My parents never disowned me. I've never been in love with a prostitute who was jealous of my work and burned my manuscripts. I've never been arrested. Why I've never even had syphilis!

VIOLET: You've really had it rough.

MR. FOUFAS: I want my daughter to know what it is to have to struggle.

MRS. FOUFAS: Our daughter should marry someone who's right for her. Better she should marry a decent young man who's good-looking and has a steady job at the bank than a vandal who's trying to pass himself off as an artist.

VIOLET: The missus is right. Life is enough of a struggle. We don't have to go looking for reasons to suffer. Suffering comes looking for us. And you should just thank your lucky stars it hasn't found you yet.

MR. FOUFAS: And who asked you for your two cents, Miss Blabbermouth!

VIOLET: Would you like to step outside and say that? [*(They go for each other's throats.)*]

MRS. FOUFAS: Violet is right! I want a son-in-law I can be proud of, and one who's not ashamed of me, either. Someone who appreciates the simple pleasures of bourgeois life: boiled beef, beer, and a double bed.

MR. FOUFAS: That just shows what a small mind you have. I say my daughter shall be an innovator! And if you provoke me further, I'll make her a revolutionary! *(Exits)*

PRUE: *(Bawling)* Waaa!

MRS. FOUFAS: Don't give up hope yet, Newton. Don't pay any attention to your father, Prue. He's having a midlife crisis. We must tell your father that if you can't have Newton you won't marry anyone. Meanwhile, I'll make arrangements to go through with the wedding whether your father gives his approval or not.

*(*MRS. FOUFAS *and* PRUE *exit)*

VIOLET: You certainly put your foot in your mouth that time.

NEWTON: What was I supposed to do? I didn't know what old Foufas was talking about.

VIOLET: Why take him seriously? Can't you see he's insane? Why didn't you just go along and tell him you are whatever he wanted you to be?

NEWTON: What's that?

VIOLET: Tell him you're avant-garde.

NEWTON: Well I don't know what avant-garde is.

VIOLET: From what I gather, neither does anyone else.

NEWTON: How do I prove I'm it?

VIOLET: As far as I can see, anything can be avant-garde as long as it doesn't make any sense and goes against the natural way of doing things.

NEWTON: My god, I never thought I'd have to go against nature to become old man Foufas's son-in-law.

VIOLET: *(Laughs)* Ha ha ha ha ha!

NEWTON: What's so funny?

VIOLET: I just had an idea how we could play a trick on the turkey and get what you want at the same time. [*(Laughs)*]

NEWTON: Yes?

VIOLET: [*(Laughs)*] It's really quite an amusing idea.

NEWTON: What is it?

VIOLET: *(Gasping for breath)* It's a gimmick I saw in a play once. It would be a perfect practical joke to play on the old fathead. I have a friend who works in a joke store on Times Square. He's got enough stuff there to make anything avant-garde. This is a bit far-out, but Mr. Foufas is a man who'll believe anything. I don't think we'll have to worry about going too far. Just leave it to me.

NEWTON: What are you going to do?

VIOLET: You'll see. But let's beat it. Here he comes.

(Exit VIOLET *and* NEWTON.*)*

ACT II

[*(*MR. FOUFAS *enters wearing a grass suit.)*]

MR. FOUFAS: I don't see what the hell the fuss is all about. Is it a crime to admire the avant-garde? The culture must either go forward or backward. It can't remain where it is. That's obvious. And there is nothing to compare, in my opinion, with really daring art. Why, revolutionary artists are the only hope for civilization. And I would cut two fingers off my left hand to have one original idea.

(Enter VIOLET.*)*

VIOLET: Mr. Hack is here and there's a lady with him.

MR. FOUFAS: Oh, my god, and I still have instructions to give! Tell them I'll be right there. *(Exit)*

(Enter HACK *and* PANZAROFF.*)*

VIOLET: Mr. Foufas says he'll be with you in a moment. *(Exit)*

HACK: Very good.

PANZAROFF: I don't know, Percy. This is very unlike me to let you bring me to a strange house vere I am don't knowink anyvan.

HACK: Where else can I entertain you, since you won't come with me to my apartment and you haven't invited me to yours?

PANZAROFF: Ah, dat again.

HACK: But it's really quite all right. My place is such a mess. Here everything is just as it should be.

PANZAROFF: But I do not vish to encourage these extravagances. They commit me furthur than I desire. But vhat is the use of my objectink? You vear down my resistance. Your suave insistence makes me putty in your hands and I find myself villink to do anythink you vish. It began vith frequent visits, followed by declarations of love, then serenades, presents, and now this celebration. I have opposed all these thinks. But you vill not take no for an answer. Step by step you make me break my resolutions until my vill is so veakened dat I can't say a vord. And I believe that in the end you vill completely overwhelm me and I vill succumb to a marriage contrary to all I intended.

HACK: And a good thing, too. You are a widow and seek American citizenship. I am independent and love you more than life itself. What is to prevent you from making me happy this very day?

PANZAROFF: My god, Percy! Two people must have more in common than that to live happily together. And even the most reasonable people in the world often find it hard to make a go of it.

HACK: But why think only of the difficulties, darling? Just because your first husband was a louse doesn't mean all men are like that.

PANZAROFF: Still I come back to my point. These expenses that you are incurring on my account worry me for two reasons: first they commit me further than I vould vish, and second I am sure, in spite of what you say, that you are spending more than you can afford, and that is the last thing I want.

HACK: These things are mere trifles. They don't matter in the—

PANZAROFF: No, I know what I am talkink about. Among other things, this diamond ring you have forced me to accept must have cost a—

HACK: Hey! Please don't attach such value to a thing I find unworthy of the woman I love. Please let me . . . ah, but here is the master of the house.

(Enter MR. FOUFAS.*)*

MR. FOUFAS: Ah madam! Welcome to of my for with between underneath you Poland actress American tour making house by me mine heaven granted me the merit to merit a merit such as yours should I accorded . . .

HACK: That's enough, Mr. Foufas. Madame Panzaroff doesn't need an elaborate introduction. She can see at a glance that you are one of the avant-garde.

MR. FOUFAS: *(Aside)* I deconstructed the text myself.

PANZAROFF: *(Aside to* HACK*)* What did he say? I didn't understand.

HACK: *(Aside)* Mr. Foufas is a successful grocer, but somewhat eccentric in his ways.

PANZAROFF: Not *the* Foufas. Not Friendly Foufas of the Friendly Foufas Food Stores!

HACK: The same.

PANZAROFF: Ah, Mr. Foufas, Foufas Foods are so fresh they're famous all the way to Wrczclv.

MR. FOUFAS: No doubt you appeared at the avant-garde theater festival at Wrczclv?

PANZAROFF: I was awarded the brass monkey there.

MR. FOUFAS: I'm sure you deserved it.

PANZAROFF: Oh, Poland! Land of opportunity! Where else could avant-garde playwright go on to become Pope?

HACK: Madam, Mr. Foufas is one of my dearest friends—

MR. FOUFAS: Ah, sir, you do me too much honor.

HACK: A gentleman of parts.

PANZAROFF: I am honored to make his acquaintance.

MR. FOUFAS: Madam, your condescension is quite undeserved.

HACK: *(Aside to* MR. FOUFAS*)* Whatever you do, be careful not to mention the diamond you gave her.

MR. FOUFAS: *(Aside to* HACK*)* Can't I even inquire how she likes it?

HACK: *(Aside to* MR. FOUFAS*)* Not on any account. That would be most vulgar behavior. If you wish to act as the avant-garde do, you must act or pretend as if it were not you who gave her the present. *(To* PANZAROFF*)* Mr. Foufas is just saying, madam, how delighted he is to see you in his house.

PANZAROFF: I am greatly honored.

MR. FOUFAS: *(Aside to* HACK*)* I am most grateful to you, sir, for bringing her here.

HACK: *(Aside to* MR. FOUFAS*)* I had the greatest difficulty persuading her to come.

MR. FOUFAS: *(Aside to* HACK*)* I don't know how I'll ever thank you.

HACK: *(To* PANZAROFF*)* Mr. Foufas is just saying, madam, how charming he finds you.

PANZAROFF: That is extremely kind of him!

MR. FOUFAS: Ah, madam, it is you who are kind—

HACK: Let us think about supper.

(VIOLET *enters.)*

VIOLET: *(To* MR. FOUFAS*)* Everything is ready, sir! *(Throws the platter on the table with a crash,* [*exits*]*)*

HACK: Come, then, let us take our places. Have the dancers and musician summoned.

(PANZAROFF *sits.* HACK *sits next to her.* MR. FOUFAS *is so enraptured, he sits next to* PANZAROFF *and ends up sitting on* HACK*'s lap. He quickly corrects his mistake.)*

PANZAROFF: Percy, this is a magnificent repast.

MR. FOUFAS: You are not serious, madam. I only wish it were more worthy of you.

HACK: Mr. Foufas is right. This meal isn't worthy of you. If I had had the ordering of it, there would have been rack of lamb, partridges, and hearts of palm with red caviar, all served on china plates.

MR. FOUFAS: What do you mean? These are very fresh vegetables. Look at this artichoke. This is what is known as a Foufas artichoke. I'll tell you something about a Foufas artichoke: a Foufas artichoke is an artichoke with a good heart. And an artichoke with a good heart is hard to find these days. What you want to do is parboil your artichoke. If you boil it then the inside gets mushy and you don't get your potassium. Now you pick off each leaf, then you scrape it off on your lower teeth. Sometimes you get a little green thing stuck, it doesn't look too good, so you pick it out, roll it into a little ball and throw it away. But I think everyone would agree that the best way to enjoy an artichoke is to stuff it.

PANZAROFF: Ah yes, the arrangement of the vegetables is beautiful. It looks just like a painting by Cézanne.

MR. FOUFAS: Ah yes, I adore Cézanne. He was the artist with the soul of a grocer. And I am the grocer with the soul of an artist. Ah, but a beautiful woman such as yourself, Miss Panzaroff, can inspire both an artist and a grocer alike.

PANZAROFF: My reply to these compliments is to eat as heartily as you see I am doing.

MR. FOUFAS: And what delightful digits! May I?

PANZAROFF: Help yourself.

MR. FOUFAS: [*(Taking and kissing her hand)*] May I have a second helping?

PANZAROFF: You compromise me.

MR. FOUFAS: Ah! What lovely hands!

PANZAROFF: The hands are only mediocre, Mr. Foufas, but no doubt you are referring to the diamond, which is really magnificent.

MR. FOUFAS: I, madam! Heaven forfend that I should say a word about it. That would be shockingly vulgar behavior, unworthy of the avant-garde. The diamond is a mere piece of junk.

PANZAROFF: I take it you are a great connoisseur of jewelry.

MR. FOUFAS: You are too kind.

HACK: Come! Wine for Mr. Foufas and for these gentlemen who are going to be good enough to give us a song and dance.

PANZAROFF: Nothing adds to the delights of good cheer more than music and dance. We are most admirably entertained.

[(VIOLET *serves wine, which they sip with arms intertwined.*)]

PANZAROFF: Hey! You want to hear American joke?

MR. FOUFAS: Sure!

PANZAROFF: How many Americans it take to screw in light bulb?

MR. FOUFAS: I give up. How many Americans does it take to screw in a light bulb?

PANZAROFF: Von! [(*Laughs heartily*)]

HACK: Let us give silence for these gentlemen. They will entertain us better than we can ourselves.

(COMPOSER *enters, sits at the table with a crystal goblet half filled with water, dips his finger into water, and runs it around the rim of the glass until it sings. This sound continues to the end of the entertainment.*

MODERNA *enters in Greek costume, wearing a mask and buskin, carrying a lyre and a cage with a live chicken in it. The cage has a roll of sheet music attached. As the sheet music is pulled through the cage, the chicken's footprints becomes notes of music, which presumably the composer presumably is playing.* MODERNA *draws the sheet music across the full length of the stage, in front of the dining table. Then the* COMPOSER *begins to chant and drone eerily, modulating off of the tone of the drinking glass.*

The CHOREOGRAPHER *enters, does skipping and spinning in place, and the* COMPOSER *sets off a mechanical monkey which clangs cymbals through the rest of the scene.*

MR. FOUFAS, HACK, *and* PANZAROFF *manipulate their artichokes and exchange them for photographs of artichokes, which they hold in front of their faces.*)

HACK: Art!

PANZAROFF: A!

MR. FOUFAS: Choke! (*Coughs*)

(*They all take a bite of the photographs and repeat the operation three times. When the piece ends,* MR. FOUFAS, HACK, *and* PANZAROFF *applaud by snapping their fingers.*)

PANZAROFF: That was charming. Really charming. It could not have been better sunk.

MR. FOUFAS: But I can see something here even more charming, madam. (*He begins to fondle her breasts. Suddenly the fruit bowl rises and* VIOLET'*s head peeks up through the center of the table with the centerpiece on top of her head*)

PANZAROFF: (*Plays the following lines nonchalantly, as if the whole thing were a matter of course*) Dear me! Mr. Foufas is more gallant than I thought.

HACK: Why, madam, what do you take Mr. Foufas for?

MR. FOUFAS: I know what I'd like her to take me for. *(Continues to maul her breasts)*

PANZAROFF: What, again!

HACK: Ah, but you don't know him yet.

MR. FOUFAS: She shall know me all in good time.

PANZAROFF: Oh, I give it up.

HACK: He is a gentleman who always has an answer ready. Have you noticed, madam, that he eats the scraps from your plate?

PANZAROFF: Mr. Foufas is charming!

MR. FOUFAS: If only I could really charm you I should be—

(Enter MRS. FOUFAS.)

MRS. FOUFAS: Aha! Here's a nice company, I must say. It's easy to see I'm not expected. So this is why you were so anxious that I should dine with my sister! There's a feast fit for a wedding up here. This is where your money is going— in entertaining your lady friends and providing them with music and play-acting while I'm sent off to amuse myself at Beefsteak Charlie's!

HACK: Whatever are you talking about, Mrs. Foufas? Where did you get the idea that this was your husband's festivity? Let me inform you that I am entertaining this lady and that Mr. Foufas is merely permitting me the use of his house. You should take a little more care of what you say.

MR. FOUFAS: Yes, you impudent creature! I'll have you know Mr. Hack is providing all this while Maia Panzaroff has been making her American tour. Mr. Hack has provided all these festivities and has done me the honor of inviting me to dine with him.

MRS. FOUFAS: Fiddlesticks! I wasn't born yesterday.

HACK: Allow me to tell you, madam—

MRS. FOUFAS: I don't need any telling. I can see for myself. *(Beating MR. FOUFAS over the head with her purse)* I've known for some time there was something afoot.

MR. FOUFAS: Sweetheart . . .

MRS. FOUFAS: I'm not a fool.

MR. FOUFAS: Love . . .

MRS. FOUFAS: And it's downright wicked of an artist like you to encourage my husband's tomfoolery.

MR. FOUFAS: Honey . . .

MRS. FOUFAS: As for you, madam, it ill becomes an actress avant-garde or otherwise to be causing trouble in a decent family and letting my husband think he's in love with you.

MR. FOUFAS: Angel . . . *(She turns and glares at the men, who cringe)*

PANZAROFF: How dare you say such things! Come, Percy! What are you thinking of, to expose me to the ridiculous suspicions of this outrageous creature. *(Exits)*

HACK: Stay, madam, where are you going? *(Exits)*

MR. FOUFAS: Make my apologies and try to bring her back. [*(The artists exit with their paraphernalia)*] Now see what you've done! You come in here, you spoil everything, and you drive the avant-garde out of my house—

MRS. FOUFAS: I don't give a rap for the avant-garde!

MR. FOUFAS: Oh yeah?

MRS. FOUFAS: Yeah!

MR. FOUFAS: Well I don't know why I don't just break the pots and pans over your head, you old hag!

MRS. FOUFAS: I don't care what you do. I stand for my rights, and every wife will be on my side. *(Exits)*

MR. FOUFAS: You'd just better watch your step! [*(Seeing* VIOLET*)*] You Benedictine Arnold! You Judith Iscariot! My own maid turning against me. [*(She escapes)*] I don't know why she had to come in here and spoil everything. She couldn't have come at a worse time. I was just in the mood for saying all sorts of avant-garde things. I never felt so lively in my life. *(Sound of the doorbell. Doorbell rings several times)* Now, who could that be at this hour? *(Calls out)* Violet! Violet! Would you get that? Everyone's abandoned me. I'll get it myself. *(He exits. Voices off. Reenters with* HACK, CHOREOGRAPHER, *and* COMPOSER*)* Were you able to smooth things over with Miss Panzaroff? What did she say?

HACK: Never mind about that now. We have wonderful news for you! Nicky Newfangle is in town!

MR. FOUFAS: He is? Fabulous! Wonderful! Who is he?

HACK: Why he is perhaps the most advanced artist in America today.

MR. FOUFAS: He is?

COMPOSER: Yes indeed.

CHOREOGRAPHER: Most definitely.

HACK: You mean you've never heard of him?

MR. FOUFAS: Well the name sounds familiar. . . .

HACK: Nicky Newfangle is the founder and leading theorist of the post-avant-garde.

MR. FOUFAS: Post-avant-garde? What's that?

HACK: Well it's a kind of antimovement. He synthesized subsurrealism and unsound structuralism and came out with repressed expressionism. He's heard about you and wants to meet you.

MR. FOUFAS: Sounds fascinating!

HACK: And what's more, he wants to confer upon you the honor of membership in the avant-derrière movement! This is a society of vanguard artists. He wants to see you at once and hold the investiture ceremony immediately.

MR. FOUFAS: Where?

HACK: Right here!

MR. FOUFAS: This is so unexpected. I . . . I'm not prepared! I don't know what to wear, and I haven't got a speech ready!

COMPOSER: Oh, that won't be necessary.

CHOREOGRAPHER: Not in the least!

COMPOSER: He doesn't speak, you know. He just makes sounds.

CHOREOGRAPHER: But don't worry, he's brought his translator with him.

COMPOSER: He'll be here any minute.

MR. FOUFAS: I can't believe this is happening to me.

HACK: Membership in the avant-derrière always comes on one as a surprise. It's just the way it's done.

MR. FOUFAS: Is he really that talented?

HACK: He's post-talent.

MR. FOUFAS: We must try to tidy up. The place is so untidy!

HACK: Don't worry about a thing. Leave all the preparations to us. *(*COMPOSER *and* CHOREOGRAPHER *carry out the table and chairs. Doorbell)* Ah, there he is now. *(Exits)*

MR. FOUFAS: Oh, this is too much. I'm not sure I can accept it! I feel unworthy! I'm not sure I deserve this.

COMPOSER: Oh you deserve it all right.

CHOREOGRAPHER: Yes, you really have it coming.

(Reenter HACK *with* VIOLET, *disguised as Translator,* NEWTON *as Nicky Newfangle, and* MODERNA *as himself.)*

VIOLET: Mr. Foufas, I'd like you to meet Nicholas Newfangle, the artist of the future. Nicky Newfangle, Rufus Foufas.

MR. FOUFAS: I'm overcome.

NEWTON: *(Barks like a dog; makes sounds of footsteps in a corridor; creaking hinge; closing door; a woman's scream)*

VIOLET: Mr. Newfangle says he is privileged to meet a man who exceeds the highest tastes of his day.

NEWTON: *(Distant train whistle; chug-a-chug-a; sea gulls; waves on shore; water dripping; steam escaping from a radiator pipe)*

VIOLET: He says that you are the Diaghilev, nay, the Barnum of the post-avant-garde.

NEWTON: *(Makes sound of: cough; fart; hiccup; belch; sigh)*

VIOLET: That he has the honor of conferring upon you the title of avant-derrière.

MR. FOUFAS: I will try to live up to it.

NEWTON: *(Makes sounds of: ticking of clock; ringing of alarm)*

VIOLET: He says he would like to begin the ceremony right now.

MR. FOUFAS: By all means. I'm a little unprepared. You caught me off my guard. Or should I say, caught me off my avant-garde.

ALL: *(Laughing feebly at the joke)* Ha ha.

NEWTON: *(Sounds of: rumbling volcano; an explosion)*

VIOLET: Shall we begin?

MR. FOUFAS: I am at your disposal.

*(*VIOLET *exits to get fake asses.)*

NEWTON: Moooo! Moooo! *(*FOUFAS *makes signs that he does not understand. Sounds of: traffic, horns, screeching breaks, car crash, siren)*

MR. FOUFAS: *(Runs to* MODERNA*)* What did he say? What did he say?

MODERNA: Doy doy doy doy doy de doy de doy.

*(*VIOLET, *with the fake asses, enters sideways doing the Susy-Q, moving across the stage in a heel-toe manner.)*

VIOLET: Begin the rites of the avant-derrière!

*(*VIOLET *attaches a false ass to the front of* MR. FOUFAS's *pelvis.)*

MR. FOUFAS: What's this?

NEWTON: *(Sound of fart)*

VIOLET: Why, it's the avant-derrière, of course.

MR. FOUFAS: Of course! Of course! I should have known at once.

(Then she distributes them to all the others who likewise wear them in front.)

VIOLET: The first ritual: the Posterior Presentation.

ALL: Yuk! Yuk!

(Printed title: Posterior Presentation.)

VIOLET: Kiss my avant-derrière! *(MR. FOUFAS kisses the cheek of her false ass)* Kiss both cheeks!

(MR. FOUFAS kisses everyone's cheeks [except NEWTON's. NEWTON barks like a dog.])

MR. FOUFAS: Oh, and I forgot about you. [*(Kisses NEWTON's avant-derrière)*]

VIOLET: The second ritual is the Deconstruction of the Name.
ALL: Yuk! Yuk!

(Printed title: Deconstruction of the Name.)

VIOLET: *(Sounding off demonically)* Foufas!!
ALL: Ass fouf!!

(This is repeated six times.)

VIOLET: The third ritual is you must eat those words avant-garde!
ALL: Yuk! Yuk!

(They point to printed title: Avant-Garde.)

VIOLET: In order to become a member of the post-avant-garde, you must eat the words avant-garde.

(VIOLET removes a letter from the printed title and offers it to MR. FOUFAS, who takes a bite out of it.)

MR. FOUFAS: [*(Chews a long time, swallows hard)*] It's a little hard to swallow.
VIOLET: Thereafter, you must always eat in the avant-derrière manner.
MR. FOUFAS: What's that?
VIOLET: Members of the avant-derrière do not consume food through their mouths like the ordinary bourgeois herd!
MR. FOUFAS: But how do you live??
VIOLET: Through the use of nutrient enemas!
ALL: Yuk! Yuk!
MR. FOUFAS: Nutrient enemas?

(They begin to dance the Susy-Q moving across the stage in a heel-toe manner.)

ALL: *(Chanting)* Caca Caca Muchi Yuk Yuk Yuk! Caca Caca Muchi Yuk Yuk Yuk! Caca Caca Muchi Yuk Yuk Yuk!

(VIOLET, NEWTON, and MODERNA exit to get apparatus, which consists of an enema bag on a stand. MR. FOUFAS bends over, VIOLET inserts the nozzle as if to purge him. The CHOREOGRAPHER mounts a pogo stick whose up-and-down movement seems to inflate MR. FOUFAS. He grows larger and larger.)

MR. FOUFAS: This is so much more original than eating through your mouth! I don't know why I never thought of it before!

(FOUFAS explodes. Blackout.
Sound of explosion. Tiny Mr. Foufas is seen to fly through the air. Enter Mr. Foufas in his underwear with fake ass attached to his pelvis as before. His grass suit hangs about him in shreds.)

MR. FOUFAS: Caca Caca Muchi Ass Fouf! Caca Caca Muchi Ass Fouf!

MRS. FOUFAS: *(Entering)* God have mercy on us. What is he up to now?

MR. FOUFAS: Ass fouf.

MRS. FOUFAS: Are you making a spectacle of yourself again?

MR. FOUFAS: Ass fouf.

MRS. FOUFAS: Are you going to a costume party?

MR. FOUFAS: Ass fouf.

MRS. FOUFAS: What are you supposed to be?

MR. FOUFAS: Ass fouf.

MRS. FOUFAS: Whose influence is this?

MR. FOUFAS: Ass fouf.

MRS. FOUFAS: What's going on?

MR. FOUFAS: You've got your nerve. How dare you talk like that to an avant-derrière?

MRS. FOUFAS: A what?

MR. FOUFAS: You'll have to treat me with a little more respect now that I've been made a leading member of the avant-derrière movement.

MRS. FOUFAS: What in god's name are you talking about with your derrière?

MR. FOUFAS: I tell you I am avant-derrière!

MRS. FOUFAS: Oh? And what manner of beast is that?

MR. FOUFAS: An avant-derrière is what you might call an . . . antimovement.

MRS. FOUFAS: Perhaps a little prune juice.

MR. FOUFAS: Don't try to be clever. You only succeed in showing your ignorance. The avant-derrière is a dignity that has been conferred on me. I've just come from the ceremony.

MRS. FOUFAS: What kind of ceremony?

MR. FOUFAS: *(Doing the Susy-Q)* Caca Caca Muchi. Ass fouf Ass fouf Ass fouf.

MRS. FOUFAS: What does that mean?

MR. FOUFAS: Ass fouf is the deconstruction of Foufas.

MRS. FOUFAS: What do you want to deconstruct your name for?

MR. FOUFAS: The tree of modernism with its many branches—pop, op, kinetic, nuclear, minimal, or conceptual art, as well as happenings, letterism, concretism, the "new novel," projective verse, existentialism, neo-Thomism, linguistic analysis, Black Mountain School, structuralism—must be felled once and for all. This is the most advanced movement yet—the avant-derrière—

MRS. FOUFAS: Eh?

MR. FOUFAS: Caca Caca Muchi. Caca Caca Muchi. *(Makes sounds of automobile)*

MRS. FOUFAS: I don't understand a word of it.

MR. FOUFAS: A front without a back—

MRS. FOUFAS: What on earth?

MR. FOUFAS: Preposterious—

MRS. FOUFAS: Good night, nurse.

MR. FOUFAS: Preposterous art—

MRS. FOUFAS: Whatever is this nonsense?

MR. FOUFAS: Advancing rear end first.

MRS. FOUFAS: Ass backwards, you mean. Oh my god, he's off his head.

MR. FOUFAS: Silence! Show more respect for the avant-derrière! *(Exits [clucking like a chicken])*

MRS. FOUFAS: Oh my goodness. He's off his rocker. I must run and stop him from going out before the neighbors see him. There's nothing but trouble. I never have a moment's peace! *(Runs out)*

(Enter HACK *and* PANZAROFF.*)*

HACK: Really, madam, I don't know where you could see anything so amusing. I wouldn't have believed it if I hadn't seen it with my own eyes. The man's a perfect fool. Still, let's help Newton and not give the joke away. He's a good egg and deserves a better shake than old Foufas was giving him. Besides, he makes a very good living and may prove to be a patron of the arts himself someday.

PANZAROFF: Yes, he's a very sweet boy, and Prue should marry him.

HACK: And what about me? Aren't I a sweet boy, too?

PANZAROFF: Yes, very sweet. But stop fishing for compliments.

HACK: There's still a ballet for us to see, and then perhaps you'll give me your answer.

PANZAROFF: Yes, I see how lavish the preparations are. Percy, I can permit this no longer. I am determined to stop the flood of your extravagances on my account, and so I have decided to marry you forthwith. This seems to be the only solution. Marriage puts an end to such things, as you know.

HACK: Ah, madam, can it be true that you've decided to abandon common sense and marry me at last?

PANZAROFF: Only to prevent you from going into hock. I can see that if I don't marry you soon, you won't have a penny to your name.

HACK: Thank you for your concern with my finances. They are yours, such as they are, and my heart goes with them, to do with as you please.

PANZAROFF: I shall make demands on both. Ah, here comes our friend, and what a sight he is!

(Enter FOUFAS. *From here on in, they move across the stage in parallel lines. When it is necessary to pass one another, they hopscotch from one parallel to another like pieces in a board game. The impression should be flat and mechanical. Only* MRS. FOUFAS *moves naturalistically.)*

HACK: We have come to celebrate your new honor and to rejoice on the occasion of your daughter's marriage to Nicky Newfangle.

ALL: *(Whisper)* Yea! Hurray!

MR. FOUFAS: Caca Caca Muchi. Caca Caca Muchi.

HACK: Caca Caca Muchi. Caca Caca Muchi to you.

PANZAROFF: *(Moving to* FOUFAS*)* I am pleased to be one of the first to congratulate you on your newly acquired honors. Let me kiss both cheeks. *(Kisses both cheeks of his fake ass)*

MR. FOUFAS: Caca Caca Muchi. Caca Caca Muchi to you. As the tree said when it came out of the sawmill, "Glad to be aboard." And from one avant-derrière to another, may I say that I am proud to wear my ass in front of me. And may I take this opportunity to apologize for the rude behavior of my wife?

PANZAROFF: Don't give it another thought. We must make allowances for her feelings. She loves you very much and doesn't want to lose you.

MR. FOUFAS: We of the post-avant-garde know that love must be free. Our feelings cannot be shackled by any consumer-fetishist-bourgeois-possessiveness which treats the love object as chattel. Caca Caca Muchi. Caca Caca Muchi. A man would be fortunate indeed to find a woman like yourself to inspire anarchy in him.

HACK: You see, madam, Mr. Foufas thinks of you as an artist first and a woman second.

The wedding scene in *Le Bourgeois Avant-Garde*
(Anita & Steve Shevett)

PANZAROFF: Yes, it is the sign of a truly advanced mind.

HACK: But where is Nicky Newfangle?

ALL: *(Whisper)* Yea! Hurray!

HACK: We should like to pay him our respects.

MR. FOUFAS: He's coming, and I've sent for my daughter to give him her hand.

(Enter NEWTON *in avant-derrière costume.)*

HACK: We've come to pay our respects, congratulate you, and to offer our help to you as friends of your father-in-law to be.

NEWTON: *(Makes assorted sounds)*

(Enter PRUE, *bound and gagged, in wedding gown and veil.)*

MR. FOUFAS: Come, my girl, and give Mr. Newfangle your hand. He has done you the honor of asking to marry you. *(*PRUE, *unable to speak, grunts)* Speak up, girl. I can't understand a word you are saying. *(*FOUFAS *removes gag from her mouth)*

PRUE: Really, Father, why are you dressed like that? Is this supposed to be a play?

MR. FOUFAS: No, this isn't a play. This is a piece. Today is your lucky day. I have arranged for you to marry America's most post avant-garde artist, Nicky Newfangle.

ALL: *(Whisper)* Yea! Hurray!

PRUE: Me . . . marry *him,* Father?

MR. FOUFAS: Yes, you marry him. Come on. Give him your hand. *(Turns to* NEWTON*)* Show her the engagement ring. *(To* PRUE*)* That's a genuine zircon you've got there.

PRUE: But I don't want to marry him!

MR. FOUFAS: But I want you to, and I'm your father.

PRUE: Well, I shan't! I'd rather die than marry a man I don't love.

MR. FOUFAS: Come come. Don't make a fuss. Give him your hand!

PRUE: No, Father! No, I say. I've told you before: no power on earth could force me to marry anyone but Newton Entwhistle! And if you try to make me, I will do something desperate. I'll—*(Recognizing* NEWTON*)* But, then, again, you are my father, and one should obey one's parents' wishes. You certainly know what's good for me better than I do myself. Forgive me for being so silly, but I am young and immature and have not yet learned how much wiser you are in these matters.

MR. FOUFAS: *(Somewhat taken aback)* Well, I'm glad to see you listen to reason. It's a pleasure to have such an obedient daughter. *(Frees* PRUE's *arms)*

(Enter MRS. FOUFAS *and* VIOLET.*)*

MRS. FOUFAS: What's all this? They tell me you're giving our daughter to a circus freak!

MR. FOUFAS: Oh, be quiet, you tiresome woman. You're always sticking your nose in where it doesn't belong. You and your silly ideas! There's no teaching you sense.

MRS. FOUFAS: It's you who needs to have some sense knocked into you. You go from one insane idea to another. What is this mob doing here?

(Everyone does the Susy-Q to the count of 1-2-3-4 to the right and 1-2-3-4 to the left.)

MR. FOUFAS: I've arranged to marry our daughter to America's most post-avant-garde artist, Nicky Newfangle!

ALL: *(Whisper)* Yea! Hurray!

MRS. FOUFAS: Nicky Newfangle . . .

ALL: *(Interrupting in a whisper)* Yea! Hurray!

MRS. FOUFAS: . . . indeed!

MR. FOUFAS: Pay your respects to him and I will translate it into the appropriate noises.

MRS. FOUFAS: I don't need a translation. I'll tell him to his teeth that he'll never have my daughter!

MR. FOUFAS: Shut your mouth!

HACK: How can you refuse such an honor, Mrs. Foufas, and decline to take Nicky Newfangle . . .

ALL: *(Interrupting in a whisper)* Yea! Hurray!

HACK: . . . as your son-in-law?

MRS. FOUFAS: You mind your own business.

PANZAROFF: You can't refuse a great honor like this.

MRS. FOUFAS: I'll thank you, madam, not to meddle in affairs that don't concern you.

HACK: Believe me, we're your friends and are only trying to help you.

MRS. FOUFAS: With friends like you I don't need enemies.

HACK: But your daughter has agreed to comply with her father's wishes.

MRS. FOUFAS: My daughter has agreed?

HACK: Most definitely.

MRS. FOUFAS: She can forget Newton?

HACK: She's decided to join the avant-garde!

MRS. FOUFAS: I'd strangle her with my bare hands if she did a thing like that!

MR. FOUFAS: Enough of your cackling, Attila the Hen! I say she will marry him.

MRS. FOUFAS: And I say she won't! *(Screams)* Never! Never! Never!

MR. FOUFAS: *(Plugs his ears)* What a noise!

PRUE: Mother dear . . .

MRS. FOUFAS: Get out of my sight, you tart.

MR. FOUFAS: What? You'd abuse her simply because she obeys her father's wishes?

MRS. FOUFAS: She's my daughter too!

VIOLET: Mrs. Foufas?

MRS. FOUFAS: Oh, what do you want?

VIOLET: One word.

MRS. FOUFAS: I don't want to hear another word. I've had enough words for one day, thank you.

(VIOLET goes to FOUFAS. They hop back and forth from one parallel to another missing each other every time. The frustration builds. VIOLET finally seizes MR. FOUFAS and holds him still.)

VIOLET: Mr. Foufas, if I can just speak to the missus in private, I'm sure I can get her to agree to what you want.

MRS. FOUFAS: I'll never agree.

VIOLET: Listen to me.

MRS. FOUFAS: No!

MR. FOUFAS: Listen to her.

MRS. FOUFAS: I won't listen!

MR. FOUFAS: She'll tell you—

MRS. FOUFAS: She can't tell me anything!

MR. FOUFAS: Oh what an obstinate woman. Can it hurt to listen?

VIOLET: Just listen a minute. Then you can do whatever you want.

MRS. FOUFAS: Oh, go on then. What is it?

VIOLET: *(Confidentially)* I've been winking and making mouths at you until my face hurts. Don't you see that we are just humoring your husband's fantastic ideas and that we are putting one over on him with all this stuff, and that Nicholas Newfangle . . .

ALL: *(Whisper)* Yea! Hurray!

VIOLET: . . . is none other than Newton Entwhistle himself?

MRS. FOUFAS: Oh! In that case, I give in.

VIOLET: Don't give it away.

MRS. FOUFAS: *(Doing the Susy-Q to MR. FOUFAS)* That settles it. I consent to the marriage!

MR. FOUFAS: Well now, we all see reason at last! My dear, this has been an incredible breakthrough for you. In no time at all, I could get you into the avant-derrière, but I may have to pull a few strings.

MRS. FOUFAS: Yes, Violet explained everything very nicely, and I am entirely satisfied. Send for a justice of the peace.

HACK: Wonderful! And finally, to set your mind at ease, Mrs. Foufas, let me assure you that your jealousy is quite unfounded, and that Miss Panzaroff and I intend to be married at the same time.

MRS. FOUFAS: I don't object to that either. You have my blessing as well.

MR. FOUFAS: *(Aside to HACK)* Oo hoo hoo, I see what you're doing! You're playing a trick on the old bat to make her believe that . . .

HACK: Yes, we must keep up the pretense to her, Mr. Foufas.

MR. FOUFAS: Brilliant! Send for the justice of the peace!

HACK: And while the contracts are being drawn up, let us all dance in celebration and drink to the future of art!

MR. FOUFAS: Excellent! Let us take our places.

MRS. FOUFAS: But what about Violet? Isn't she going to marry anyone?

(Enter MODERNA *doing the Susy-Q.)*

MODERNA: *(To* MRS. FOUFAS*)* Doy doy doy doy doy doy de doy doy doy doy doy doy de doy doy doy doy doy.

MRS. FOUFAS: Well, it isn't a choice I would have made for her, but love conquers all. Listen, everyone! [*(*COMPOSER *and* CHOREOGRAPHER *enter)*] Moderna and Violet are to be married!

MR. FOUFAS: I give my consent. I give Violet to Moderna and my wife to anyone who'll take her.

VIOLET: Oh, thank you, Mr. Foufas.

MODERNA: *(To* VIOLET*)* Doy de doy doy doy doy.

VIOLET: Oh Moderna, keep whispering those sweet nothings in my ear!

HACK: Thank you, Mr. Foufas. *(Aside)* And if there's a bigger fool than this anywhere, I'd like to meet him.

(Music. They all pair off doing mechanical Susy-Q movements. Then in ballroom dance positions, they do a rocking movement. Then all stop.)

MRS. FOUFAS: *(To* PANZAROFF*)* May I ask a stupid question? What does avant-garde mean?

PANZAROFF: Avant-garde is French for bullshit.

(They all do the rocking dance off. The COMPOSER *and* CHOREOGRAPHER *remain behind.)*

CHOREOGRAPHER: You know, I think he really has something there. It strikes me as a reaction to cubism.

COMPOSER: Spherism!

CHOREOGRAPHER: A kind of unimpressionablism!

COMPOSER: No, I think it's rejectivism.

CHOREOGRAPHER: Abstract rejectivism.

COMPOSER: No, nonplussed rejectivism.

CHOREOGRAPHER: Anarcho-formalism.

COMPOSER: Formal anarchy?

CHOREOGRAPHER: Passive positivism.

COMPOSER: Postpremodernism.

CHOREOGRAPHER: Prepostmodernism.

COMPOSER: Aushaus School—disallows function as a design criterion.

CHOREOGRAPHER: Excellerationism.

(Music swells and lights fade as the exchange becomes more manic.)

COMPOSER: Energism.

CHOREOGRAPHER: Lethargism.

COMPOSER: Inhibitionism.

CHOREOGRAPHER: Precisionism.

(Ad infinitum.)

The End

GALAS

A Modern Tragedy

GALAS: Only my dogs will not betray me.

1983

The yacht scene in *Galas* (Anita & Steve Shevett)

Cast of Characters

MARIA MAGDALENA GALAS, *a famous diva*
GIOVANNI BAPTISTA MERCANTEGGINI, *her aging husband, an industrialist*
BRUNA LINA RASTA, *a mad soprano, Galas' maid*
ARISTOTLE PLATO SOCRATES ODYSSEUS, *a wealthy shipowner*
ATHINA ODYSSEUS, *his beautiful young wife*
HÜRE VON HOYDEN, *a courtesan, his ex-mistress*
POPE SIXTUS VII
PRELATE
GHINGHERI, *artistic director of La Scala*
FRITALINI, *his associate*
FRANCO COGLIONES, *a tenor*
ILKA WINTERHALTER, *a gossip columnist, confidante to Galas*
TICKET SELLER
WAITER *in train station*
STATUESQUE BEAUTY
PEOPLE *in the train station*
PEOPLE *in the opera box*
SAILORS *on Odysseus's yacht*
GUESTS *on Odysseus's yacht*

ACT I

Scene 1: *The Verona train station.*

MERCANTEGGINI: *(To* TICKET SELLER*)* Has the eleven-thirty train arrived
   from Naples?
TICKET SELLER: No, signore, I'm afraid it's late.
MERCANTEGGINI: *(Laughs)* Excellent!
TICKET SELLER: You aren't angry?
MERCANTEGGINI: No, I'm delighted. It's another delightful reminder that that
   bastard Mussolini has fallen. He made the trains run on time. I shall never
   complain about their being late again.

   (Train is heard off.)

TICKET SELLER: Here it comes now. Do you want to buy a ticket?
MERCANTEGGINI: No, I'm meeting someone. The Verona Arena has ap-
   pointed me the official escort for their prima donnas. I am here to welcome
   a new singer from America.
TICKET SELLER: Is she any good?
MERCANTEGGINI: She's supposed to be fabulous.
TICKET SELLER: Have you heard Baldini? Now, there is the voice of an angel.
MERCANTEGGINI: She has a nice middle and wonderful bottom. But I think
   she's a little short on top.
TICKET SELLER: Up you ass! What do you know? *(Exits)*

   (The station fills with steam from the train and assorted types get off. MERCANTEG-
   GINI *watches them and looks eagerly for the prima donna he is expecting. A* SOLDIER
   greets a WOMAN; *they embrace, kiss, and walk off. An* OLD LADY *is greeted by a*

COUPLE *with a baby; he takes her bags, they exit. Suddenly a* STATUESQUE BEAUTY *wearing a fur stole, small hat with veil, and tight skirt enters.* MERCANTEGGINI *approaches her.)*

MERCANTEGGINI: Signorina Galas?

STATUESQUE BEAUTY: I'm afraid you are mistaken. *(Seeing someone off)* Ciao, Guido! *(Runs off)*

(The train starts up again. Through the last cloud of steam enters a dowdy person with her cardboard suitcase tied with string. She wears sensible oxfords, a severe suit, and a cloth coat. She carries a covered birdcage and (forgive me for saying so) she is fat. She looks about the train station wearily and sits down at a small table. MERCANTEGGINI *goes out on the platform.)*

WAITER: Yes, signora?

GALAS: *(To the* WAITER*)* I'd like the veal cutlet, please.

WAITER: I think there's just one.

GALAS: And a cup of coffee.

*(*WAITER *exits.)*

MERCANTEGGINI: *(Reenters)* No sign of her.

WAITER: *(Reenters and serves* GALAS *her veal cutlet and coffee)* Here you are signora . . . the last one. *(Then to* MERCANTEGGINI*)* Yes signore?

MERCANTEGGINI: *(Looking at the menu)* I'll have the veal cutlet.

WAITER: The veal, she is finished.

MERCANTEGGINI: How's that?

WAITER: No more veal cutlet.

MERCANTEGGINI: Damn.

GALAS: *(To* MERCANTEGGINI*)* I'm afraid I have the last one. Please take mine.

MERCANTEGGINI: Thank you, but I couldn't, signorina.

GALAS: No, please, don't be silly. Take it. I'm not hungry. *(Hands him the plate)*

MERCANTEGGINI: If you're sure you don't want it.

GALAS: Positive.

MERCANTEGGINI: You're very kind. *(Tears into the veal)*

GALAS: Not at all. I'm too exhausted to eat. I didn't get a seat on the train so I had to stand all the way from Naples. The train ride was more of an ordeal than crossing the Atlantic.

MERCANTEGGINI: Crossing the Atlantic?

GALAS: Yes. I couldn't afford to fly so I came by boat and train. And now it seems that no one has come to meet me. You see, I've been engaged to sing at the Verona Arena.

MERCANTEGGINI: Forgive me, signorina, I am Giovanni Baptista Mercanteggini *(Kisses her hand),* your official escort.

GALAS: You work for the opera?

MERCANTEGGINI: *(Moves his chair to join* GALAS *at her table)* Not exactly. I am what you call . . . how do you say . . . a fan.

GALAS: You are an opera lover?

MERCANTEGGINI: Yes, I'm a real aficionado. Now there's something we have in common, eh?

GALAS: *(Smiles a little embarrassed)* What's that?

MERCANTEGGINI: We are both music lovers.

GALAS: I am not a music lover. I am a musician.

Charles Ludlam in *Galas* (Anita & Steve Shevett)

MERCANTEGGINI: But surely you love music.

GALAS: I am a musician. And because I am a singer I am a musical instrument. A music lover, no. I am music.

MERCANTEGGINI: But you don't love it? Not even a little bit?

GALAS: I wouldn't dare. Art is so great it frightens me sometimes.

MERCANTEGGINI: What do you like to do more than anything else?

GALAS: To sing. What else is there?

MERCANTEGGINI: Do you have any other interests?

GALAS: Whatever do you mean? Of course I have no other interests. . . .

MERCANTEGGINI: What about as a little girl?

GALAS: I never had any childhood. *(Lashing out bitterly)* And forgive me for saying this, because it may sound cruel, but I really do think there must be a law against making children perform like dogs. It makes them old before their time. My mother robbed me of my childhood.

MERCANTEGGINI: Don't tell me you never went to parties or on outings.

GALAS: *(Amused)* No. No parties. No outings. Only music. In Greece, during the war, I sang to the soldiers for food. Some of the girls sold their bodies. But I could sing so I never had to do *that.* We knew hunger then. As you can see I've made up for it since. *(Laughs)* In fact I had a chance to sing at the Metropolitan but I turned it down because of it.

MERCANTEGGINI: Why? Because of your weight? But that's quite usual in singers.

GALAS: The role was Madame Butterfly. I couldn't see myself as the fragile little geisha. Opera is more than singing, you know.

MERCANTEGGINI: Personally, I've never cared for skinny women. I like them more Rubensesque.

GALAS: *(Laughing, embarrassed)* Really?

MERCANTEGGINI: Yes! I like a woman with some flesh on her bones.

GALAS: *(Slightly annoyed but enjoying the attention)* Oh really? Enough of talking about me now. You haven't told me a thing about yourself. What do you do?

MERCANTEGGINI: I make bricks.

GALAS: No! Really? Bricks of all thing! You don't look it.

MERCANTEGGINI: I don't make them myself. I own a chain of factories that make them.

GALAS: Oh, I see! That's more like it.

MERCANTEGGINI: I'd like to help you.

GALAS: Help me? How?

MERCANTEGGINI: We could make a little arrangement. I will support you for a year.

GALAS: I'm afraid I couldn't . . .

MERCANTEGGINI: Please don't get the wrong idea. This would be purely a business arrangement. I have helped other singers before but none of them ever went on to make a successful career.

GALAS: I'm sorry. I didn't know that.

MERCANTEGGINI: I will, as I said, support you for one year and act as your manager. You will devote yourself entirely to your singing. You study and I will take care of the rest. If at the end of the year we are both satisfied with the arrangement then we will continue. If not, we can let it go at that.

GALAS: Could I have a day to think this over?

MERCANTEGGINI: Of course you should think it over. You must be tired now and you have your Gioconda at the Verona Arena to think about. *(GALAS lifts birdcage and whistles to her bird)* Is that your pet?

GALAS: Pet? No, this is my music teacher. *(WAITER brings the check)* Ah, here's the check.

MERCANTEGGINI: Allow me. *(Gives money to WAITER)* Since I ate your veal cutlet, I'll pay for your coffee.

GALAS: I couldn't let you do that. *(Looks at check myopically, then counts change)* Sixteen, seventeen, eighteen—there.

MERCANTEGGINI: Have you ever seen Venice?

GALAS: No.

MERCANTEGGINI: Tomorrow if you're free we could drive there.

GALAS: Oh well, that would be nice, but I think I'd better not.

MERCANTEGGINI: Oh but I insist. If you've never seen Venice it's an absolute must.

GALAS: I really would love to—but I only brought one change of clothes and I wouldn't have a clean blouse to wear.

MERCANTEGGINI: I see nothing wrong with the one you're wearing.

GALAS: I suppose if I washed it out tonight it could be dry by tomorrow.

MERCANTEGGINI: If not I'll buy you a new one. You need a holiday before you start working. Have you ever sung in the open air before?

GALAS: Not since I sang for those soldiers during the war.

MERCANTEGGINI: It's tricky. Sometimes it's difficult to be heard over the orchestra.

GALAS: Oh don't worry about that. That's one thing I'm sure of. I will be heard.

(Lights fade.)

Scene 2: *Villa Mercanteggini.*

(Mercanteggini is reading a newspaper. Bruna is sweeping.)

MERCANTEGGINI: Was there any mail, Bruna?

BRUNA: There is a letter from la Signora Mercanteggini.

MERCANTEGGINI: From my mother?

BRUNA: From your wife.

MERCANTEGGINI: From Magdalena? At last. I thought she'd never answer my letters. *(Opens letter and reads,* BRUNA *sits and listens)* "Caro, caro Giovanni. Forgive me for not writing sooner but I have been ill, terribly ill. The weather here is beastly. Their seasons are just the reverse of ours. So that while you are having spring, autumn has come here and I apparently got a chill. It's damp and gray, that kind of cold that pierces your bones. I never really feel warm. Anyway, the cold became a flu. And I had to sing with runny eyes and nose. Sometimes the voice obeys and sometimes it does not. We have received very good critics and they have asked me to stay longer and sing a Norma but I told them no. I am homesick darling. I long only to be in the arms of my Giovanni. I cover you with a thousand kisses on your eyes on your lips and other naughty places. Hold me close and never let me go again. Leaving for Argentina on our wedding night I felt like one of my opera heroines. After not hearing from you for weeks one day a packet arrived with all your letters at once. Tomorrow I leave to return to you forever. The mails are so slow that by the time you get this I will probably be home. I long to see the villa. I want to see if it is exactly as I imagined it from your description. I love you so much that I would die happy if I could die in your arms. Magdalena." Bruna, what's today's date?

BRUNA: February thirtieth.

MERCANTEGGINI: March first? My god! She'll be home today! Bruna, prepare her room. *(A bell is heard off)* See who it is.

(Exit BRUNA, *who reenters with* GALAS, *in fur. She is blonde and has undergone a dramatic weight loss.)*

GALAS: Is this the Mercanteggini residence?

MERCANTEGGINI: Yes, signora, can I . . . Magdalena!

GALAS: *(Flying into his arms)* Giovanni, my darling Giovanni! It's so good to be home. *(Removes her coat)*

MERCANTEGGINI: What happened to you? You got so skinny. How did you lose so much weight?

GALAS: Misery. I've been pining away for you.

MERCANTEGGINI: And your hair. You're like a different person.

GALAS: Don't worry. It's still me. Don't you like me blonde?

MERCANTEGGINI: It's just that it seems a little vulgar. It makes you look hard.

GALAS: Don't worry. If you don't like it I'll change it back.

MERCANTEGGINI: So tell me, how was your tour? The reviews I've read have all been glowing.

GALAS: Argentina is a miserable country. Every Fascist in the world must be there. And the climate is very bad for the voice.

MERCANTEGGINI: And you met the Peróns?

GALAS: Yes.

MERCANTEGGINI: What was that like?

GALAS: Well, Evita is a bit of a bitch. I couldn't stand her. You know they run that country almost entirely at their caprice. Although she did do one thing I am thankful of.

MERCANTEGGINI: What's that?

GALAS: She prevented Rigal from singing at the state gala and demanded me instead.

MERCANTEGGINI: Delia Rigal, the great Argentine soprano?

GALAS: Yes, poor Rigal. I really had to laugh. *(Sits)*

MERCANTEGGINI: Bruna?

BRUNA: Yes Giovanni?

MERCANTEGGINI: This is your new mistress Magdalena. Magdalena, this is Bruna, our housekeeper.

GALAS: *(Rising to shake her hand)* How do you do, Bruna?

BRUNA: Very well thank you. I'm pleased to meet you, Magdalena.

GALAS: Really Giovanni, I think the servants should show more respect and not address us by our first names.

MERCANTEGGINI: What, Bruna?

GALAS: Yes. Bruna, in the future I would like you to cultivate a manner of excessive politeness. In the future you will please call the master of the house "Commendatore Mercanteggini" and you will refer to me as "madam."

BRUNA: Yes, madam.

GALAS: And I really do think you ought to wear a uniform.

MERCANTEGGINI: Yes, Bruna, we'll have to get you a uniform.

BRUNA: Yes, Commendatore Mercanteggini. *(Exit)*

MERCANTEGGINI: You know Bruna was a singer herself once.

GALAS: *(Skeptically)* Really?

MERCANTEGGINI: Perhaps you've heard of her. Bruna Lina Rasta.

GALAS: Bruna Lina Rasta! Of course I've heard of her. She was one of the greatest. But how did she come to this . . . I mean being a servant?

MERCANTEGGINI: I don't really think of Bruna as a servant. She's more like a mother to me. She once had a great career but one night she went mad and started singing *Il Trovatore* during a performance of *Aïda* and threw herself into the orchestra pit.

GALAS: Her voice is preserved on only one seventy-eight R.P.M., very speeded up but you can tell she was incredible. I'll bet I could learn a lot from her if she were willing to teach me.

MERCANTEGGINI: And she is a great cook. I'm going to tell her to fatten you up again.

GALAS: Oh no you don't! Now that the weight is off it's going to stay off. I've had quite enough of the critics comparing me to the elephants when I sing Aïda.

MERCANTEGGINI: There's such a thing as being too thin too, you know. It's like you're not the same old Magdalena.

GALAS: *(Embracing MERCANTEGGINI)* But you still love me, don't you?

MERCANTEGGINI: Sure I love you. It's just that there's not as much to hold onto. *(Feels her bottom)*

GALAS: I never want to be away from you again. I don't mind touring if you go with me. But going to Argentina all by myself was almost unbearable. I was so lonely without you.

MERCANTEGGINI: I missed you too. But bookings are where you find them. You only got sixty lira at the Verona Arena. In Buenos Aires you made several thousand. That's some difference.

GALAS: Yes, but they wouldn't let me take the money out of the country. I didn't know what to do so at the last minute I spent it all on fur coats.

MERCANTEGGINI: Every time you sing your fee goes up a little higher. That's good business.

GALAS: *(Sits)* But what about La Scala? Has there been any word?

MERCANTEGGINI: Your audition went so well I was sure it was in the bag. But no matter how often I write or call I get no response. Something is blocking your way. I don't know what it is. *(Sits)*

GALAS: To sing at La Scala. That's every singer's dream. It's the most one could hope for in a career.

MERCANTEGGINI: I hardly know how to break this news to you, cara. Look at this advertisement in today's paper. *(Hands her the paper)*

GALAS: *(Puts on her glasses and reads)* "Physiological Pizza—dietetic foods from the great Roman industries of nourishment—The Pastaciutta Mills and Pizza Factories." What of it?

MERCANTEGGINI: Read the paragraph underneath the caption, "Certificate."

GALAS: "Certificate: In my capacity as the doctor treating Maria Magdalena Galas, I certify that the marvelous results obtained in the diet undertaken by Signora Galas (she lost close to 60 kilos) was due in large part to her eating the miraculous dietetic spaghetti and no-cal pizza dough produced in Rome's Pastaciutta Mills and Pizza Factories.—Giuseppi Gazozza." That worm Vermicelli! He followed me all over Buenos Aires trying to get that endorsement. I told him he was wasting his time to ask me of all people. I never eat that sort of thing. *(Dials phone)* Miraculous spaghetti indeed!

MERCANTEGGINI: What are you doing?

GALAS: I'm calling my lawyer. I'll sue Pastaciutta Mills!

MERCANTEGGINI: But Magdalena, the firm's president is Prince Marcantonio Pucelli, a lawyer and nephew to Pope Sixtus VII.

GALAS: I don't care whose nephew he is! I want these frauds exposed. *(Into phone)* Ciao, Borsa, it's Madgalena. *(Pause)* I'm furious, thank you. *(Pause)* Some little pasta pusher has been using my name to push his pasta. *(Pause)* Then you've already seen it? *(Covering mouthpiece, aside to MERCANTEGGINI)* He's already seen it! The whole world has probably seen it! *(Into phone again)* I've been compromised and humiliated! I want an immediate and precise retraction. *(Pause)* Of course there's no truth in it! Every claim was a lie! I did not diet. Vermicelli was not my physician. AND I NEVER EAT MACARONI! Forget about it? *(Pause)* How can you even suggest that I let it drop? Why, my public will think I'm selling my body for advertising purposes. *(Rises and paces)* Ah hah. Ah hah. Ah, ah. Mmm. Mmm. Oh. Oooh. Ooooooh. Ah. Ah. Ooooh. Tsk, tsk, tsk. Nhhh. *(Somewhat appeased)* Sweet. No. No. *(Giggles, laughs)* Ah hah? Yes. Ah hah? Begin legal proceedings at once. Ciao. *(Hangs up)* I'll make them spit blood in court!

MERCANTEGGINI: You're magnificent.

GALAS: God will avenge me!

MERCANTEGGINI: Does your god always side with you?

GALAS: *(Removing her glasses)* He sees my sacrifices and my sufferings. He will defend me from my enemies.

(BRUNA enters with puppy. The dog is a piece of fur which the actors manipulate like a puppet to give it the appearance of life. The tail should never stop wagging no matter who holds the dog.)

MERCANTEGGINI: *(Rising, takes dog from BRUNA and presents it to GALAS.)* Magda, darling, I got you a little homecoming present.

GALAS: Oh, no! It's a puppy! *(Speaking baby talk to puppy)* Oh, is oo a widdle puppy? Yes oo is, yes, yes. Oh, he's adorable! We'll call him Baby 'cause he's our little baby!

(DOORBELL rings. BRUNA answers it.)

BRUNA: *(Reenters)* Excuse me madam, and Commendatore Mercanteggini, there is a man from La Scala.

MERCANTEGGINI: Show him in, Bruna.

(She does so.)

FRITALINI: I am so sorry to call unannounced but this is a grave emergency. *(Extending hand)* Fritalini.

(Dog snarls at him. LA GALAS must also be a bit of a ventriloquist.)

GALAS: My little dog doesn't like you. Bruna, take him away. Go, go.

(GALAS gives dog to BRUNA. It snarls again and yaps as BRUNA takes it out. BRUNA also does ventriloquism.)

FRITALINI: Baldini is indisposed. We need a replacement for La Gioconda.

GALAS: When?

FRITALINI: Tomorrow night.

MERCANTEGGINI: But this is only twenty-four hours' notice!

GALAS: Please sit down, Mr. Fritalini.

(They sit. MERCANTEGGINI stands behind GALAS.)

FRITALINI: You scored such a great success in this role last summer at the Verona Arena. We know you can do it.

GALAS: *(To MERCANTEGGINI)* I can do it.

MERCANTEGGINI: This is so unexpected. I've been trying to get a reply from La Scala for months but there's never been an answer.

FRITALINI: Of course you will sing at La Scala. We shall give you a guest artist contract.

GALAS: I would like to be a full member of the company.

FRITALINI: I am afraid that is not possible at this time. Between us, it is Ghingheri. Every time he hears your name he says, "No! No! Not Galas! Not Galas, not that woman! Never! Never! NEVER!" This is a golden opportunity. We have him over a barrel.

GALAS: *(Looks to MERCANTEGGINI who shrugs, then swallowing her pride)* Very well, I shall sing at La Scala. But I want you to understand one thing, Mr. Fritalini—someday I will be a member of that company and Ghingheri will pay for this for the rest of his life!

(Lights fade.)

Scene 3: *Villa Mercanteggini.*

MERCANTEGGINI: Magdalena, darling, wake up. Today is our audience with the Pope.

(LA GALAS enters. Her hair has returned to black.)

GALAS: I don't want to see the Pope this morning. It's a gray day, it's going to rain, and wearing black would depress me. We'll go some other time.

MERCANTEGGINI: An appointment with the Pope is different from an appointment with your dentist. This is a once in a lifetime opportunity. *(Phone is heard off.* MERCANTEGGINI *answers it off.* GALAS *sits in a reclining chair reading the score of* Tosca, *myopically.* MERCANTEGGINI'*s voice is heard having an animated conversation)* Pronto. Sì. Sì. Sì. Bellissimo. Sì. Bene. Aspettamo. Sì. Prego. Ciao. Prego.

GALAS: *(Sings)* Vissi d'arte *(MERCANTEGGINI enters)*, Vissi d'a—Who was that on the phone?

MERCANTEGGINI: This is really unbelievable. Ghingheri called. He wants you to sing at La Scala.

GALAS: Well! I hope you told him that never again will I sing at La Scala under a guest artist contract.

MERCANTEGGINI: They're not offering you a guest artist contract. This time you would be a full member of the company.

GALAS: Well well well well well! We certainly have changed our tune. When do they want to meet to discuss fees and repertoire?

MERCANTEGGINI: Apparently they're quite eager to have you. They want to come right over. I took the liberty of telling them we'd see them.

GALAS: *(Leaping up and beginning to pace the garden exultantly)* Aha! Oh this is too good to be true! It's too delicious! I have Ghingheri exactly where I want him. After I bailed them out and sang their Gioconda for them he didn't even thank me, oh no, he merely congratulated the rest of the company on being able to get through it without Baldini! After the way he's insulted me as an artist I'll make him crawl on his knees to me.

BRUNA: *(Entering)* Two men approach the temple. They wish to see the High Priestess. Norma frowns and a cloud passes over the moon.

GALAS: Send them in.

MERCANTEGGINI: Show them in, Bruna.

BRUNA: Let them not profane this sacred place. A goddess must not throw herself away for any man.

GALAS: *(Murmurs)* Bring them before me. Let them taste my justice. *(BRUNA crosses her arms on her breast and exits ceremonially. She then shows in* GHINGHERI *and* FRITALINI*)* Ah, welcome, Signore Ghingheri. This is my husband, Signore Mercanteggini.

GHINGHERI: Forgive our intrusion. But we have urgent business.

GALAS: Not at all. Would you gentlemen care for some tea?

GHINGHERI: That would be very nice, thank you.

GALAS: Bruna, bring some tea.

(BRUNA exits with druidic gesture again.)

GHINGHERI: This is my associate, Signore Fritalini.

GALAS: I'm delighted to see you again, Signore Fritalini. I've tried so often to reach you by phone. But you were never in . . . to me.

GHINGHERI: Ah, business! Business!

MERCANTEGGINI: And you never answered our letters.

GHINGHERI: Of course we answered your letters. You mean they never arrived?

MERCANTEGGINI: Never.

GHINGHERI: *(To* FRITALINI*)* Did you hear that? They never got our letters.

FRITALINI: We sent a Telex. It must have missed you.

GHINGHERI: Oh that's it. They must have missed it. There, that explains it.

GALAS: *(Exchanges a look with* MERCANTEGGINI*)* Ah, business! Business!

GHINGHERI: Ah ha, yes, business. And speaking of business, Madame Galas, I have brought along the contract for your upcoming season at La Scala. *(*FRITALINI *hands* GHINGHERI *two contracts after a frantic search through all his pockets.* GHINGHERI *presents a contract to* GALAS *who looks at it myopically, then searches in vain for her glasses.* MERCANTEGGINI *has them ready for her. She blows him a kiss, puts on the glasses, and reads.* MERCANTEGGINI *looks on)* Let us confirm then that you will open the season on November seventh with *I Vespri Siciliani* and you will sing four additional performances of this opera on the eighth, ninth, tenth, and eleventh. Then in January you will sing five performances of *Norma.* New Year's Day on loan to the Rome Opera *(Galas looks at Mercanteggini, who quiets her with a gesture),* and then on January eighth, sixteenth, and twenty-third at La Scala. Your fifth and final *Norma* of the season will be on February second. In June you will appear in three performances of *Don Carlo.* Let me say that we are very pleased with this contract and we are especially delighted to be able to invite you this time not as a guest artist but as a full member of the company.

GALAS: In my unanswered letter to you I made it quite clear that I would only be interested in singing at La Scala if I could appear in *La Traviata.* I see no mention of this opera here.

*(*GHINGHERI *and* FRITALINI *exchange an uneasy look.)*

FRITALINI: The reason we did not include *La Traviata* is that we have already scheduled several performances of this opera with Baldini. She is closely identified with the rôle of Violetta. We felt that it would be inappropriate to have another soprano sing this rôle in the same season.

GALAS: Then that is your final decision?

GHINGHERI: Yes, we're sorry, but we already have a Violetta.

GALAS: Then there's nothing to be done?

GHINGHERI: Absolutely nothing. I'm sorry.

GALAS: I'm sorry too. Because without *La Traviata* your offer doesn't interest me. Perhaps some other season?

*(*GHINGHERI *and* FRITALINI *look thunderstruck.* BRUNA *enters with tea.)*

GHINGHERI: *(Enraged)* No soprano has ever turned down an offer from La Scala that includes an opportunity to open the season.

FRITALINI: *(Hysterical)* Not to mention the five hundred thousand lira and full membership in the company.

GALAS: No *Traviata?*

GHINGHERI and FRITALINI: No *Traviata!*

GALAS: Gentlemen, let's drink our tea.

GHINGHERI: *(Rising)* No tea, thanks. I see we have wasted our time coming here.

GALAS: Unless you are willing to give me *La Traviata* I'm afraid you have.

GHINGHERI: That is impossible. We do not like Madame Galas's singing *that* much.

GALAS: Then I see, there's nothing further to discuss. *(Rises)* I do not wish to waste your precious time. The season is almost upon you and you must still find a soprano to sing your *Vespri, Norma,* and *Don Carlo* for you. *(Returns the contracts to him)* Good day.

GHINGHERI: Good day. *(To* MERCANTEGGINI*)* Good day.

MERCANTEGGINI: Good day.

FRITALINI: *(To* GALAS*)* Good day.

GALAS: Good day.

FRITALINI: *(To* MERCANTEGGINI*)* Good day.

MERCANTEGGINI: Good day.

*(*GHINGHERI *and* FRITALINI *stand staring at* GALAS *and* MERCANTEGGINI *as if they expected them to change their minds at any moment.)*

GALAS: *(Finally breaks the silence with a very firm but polite)* Good day!

*(*GHINGHERI *and* FRITALINI *exit coldly, followed by* BRUNA *with an Egyptian gesture.)*

MERCANTEGGINI: I think you made a mistake. They offered you most of what you wanted. This is the chance you've been waiting for. Who knows when it will come again?

GALAS: If I sing at La Scala it will be on my own terms or not at all. Ghingheri has to learn that every time he insults me he is going to pay for it. *(Kissing him on both cheeks)* Excuse me Giovanni. I'm going to take my bubble bath. *(Exits)*

*(*BRUNA *clears the tea things. The bell is heard. She exits. A moment later* GHINGHERI *and* FRITALINI *stalk in.)*

GHINGHERI: *(With difficulty)* We have reconsidered and we've decided that perhaps we could arrange for Madame Galas to sing *La Traviata*—if she wants to.

MERCANTEGGINI: *(Surprised by their sudden turnabout)* I'll tell her. *(Crosses to the side of the stage where* GALAS *exited)* Magdalena, the gentlemen from La Scala have returned. They have reconsidered.

GALAS: *(Off)* Not for a million lire!

(Bubbles drift on.)

MERCANTEGGINI: You heard her, gentlemen.

*(*GHINGHERI *and* FRITALINI *exchange an agonized look.)*

GHINGHERI: *(Obsequiously)* We think that fee could be acceptable. *(*MERCAN-TEGGINI*'s mouth falls open.)* And now if you will please to sign the contract.

FRITALINI: *(Giving the contracts to* MERCANTEGGINI*)* Please to sign.

GHINGHERI: You will be so kind as to make the emendations we discussed.

MERCANTEGGINI: It seems you like my wife's singing better now, eh?

GHINGHERI: *(Contemptuously)* Nonsense. She can't sing. But she can create a scandal and that is worth a fortune.

MERCANTEGGINI: My wife and I have a little superstition. We do not like to sign a contract until a month after we have reached an agreement.

GHINGHERI: Very well, then, but please sign the contract and return it to us as quickly as possible.

MERCANTEGGINI: We will return it to you as quickly as we can. *(GHINGHERI and FRITALINI bow and exit. GALAS enters, drying her hair. Bubbles drift on with her)* Magdalena, they have agreed to the million lire.

GALAS: How is that possible?

MERCANTEGGINI: You said, "Not for a million lire," and they agreed.

GALAS: But I didn't really mean a million lire. That was only a figure of speech. I used it merely to emphasize my point about *La Traviata.*

MERCANTEGGINI: Oh, they've agreed to *La Traviata.* But what's more important, I've stumbled on an amazing discovery. We can get virtually anything we ask for.

GALAS: Then it's all settled? You signed the contract?

MERCANTEGGINI: Not quite. I told him we were superstitious and need a grace period of about a month.

GALAS: But why did you wait? They might change their minds.

MERCANTEGGINI: It's a trick I learned in the brick business. They won't change their minds. On the contrary, they'll send out publicity, they'll make commitments, they'll sign a contract for your services to another theater all based on this agreement which has never been signed. By then we'll say your fee has gone up.

GALAS: Is that proper?

MERCANTEGGINI: Sure. It's business. This contract is no good, anyway. It doesn't include *La Traviata.* The whole thing has to be amended. *(Tosses the contracts over his shoulder)*

GALAS: That's right.

MERCANTEGGINI: We'll get a million lire for the Rome *Norma* alone! Don't worry about a thing. You have me to handle your business affairs. And I'm doing a pretty good job, eh?

GALAS: You're brilliant. I don't know what I'd do without you. *(Embraces him)*

MERCANTEGGINI: *(Stands behind GALAS with his arms around her)* Most managers are hungry. They're in a little too much of a hurry. So they end up selling their client cheap. I don't need the money. I can afford to wait until we get exactly what we want. *(Goes to kiss her neck)*

BRUNA: *(Enters)* The Vatican is on the phone.

MERCANTEGGINI: *(They break apart)* Oh my God! What am I going to say to them after we didn't show up for our audience? *(Exits)*

GALAS: Bruna, they want me at La Scala. Because I can sing Isolde and Norma they say I am a phenomenon.

BRUNA: Yes, you are a phenomenon. But you are stretching your voice in two different directions. Someday it will break in the middle.

GALAS: What should I do?

BRUNA: Limit your repertoire.

GALAS: But I can sing anything.

BRUNA: You only have so many Normas and each one is numbered. Make each one count.

GALAS: How many Normas do I have? *(Sits)*

BRUNA: Judging by your voice I would say eighty-six. But you must forget about Isolde.

GALAS: Why?

BRUNA: It isn't worth it. You kill yourself all evening and you have nothing in the end. Also drop Turandot from your repertoire, and never ever sing Salomé.

GALAS: But I can sing Turandot with no trouble at all.

BRUNA: Every Turandot will cost you a Norma. Think about it.

MERCANTEGGINI: *(Enters)* It seems we were missed. The Pope wants to see us so they've made another appointment for Friday.

GALAS: All right, we'll go Friday.

MERCANTEGGINI: And the prelate specified that it would be formal.

GALAS: Bruna, put Commendatore Mercanteggini's tuxedo in the cleaners so that it will be back by Friday.

BRUNA: Yes, madam. *(Exits giving GALAS a significant look)*

MERCANTEGGINI: *(Waving a magazine)* Ah, here is another story circulating about your weight loss.

GALAS: *(Wearily)* What is it now?

MERCANTEGGINI: This one is really filthy.

GALAS: *(Turns suddenly)* What do you mean? Let me see that.

MERCANTEGGINI: *(Keeping the magazine away from her)* Ah, don't bother yourself with it.

GALAS: Now you really have my curiosity aroused. Let me see that. *(Pries magazine out of his hands and opens it)* Oh God, I've always hated that picture. *(Keeping her sense of humor)* What does it say? Tell me.

MERCANTEGGINI: They say you lost weight because you had a tapeworm.

GALAS: *(Stricken with horror and revulsion, cries out)* Aaagh! But it's not true. How could they lie about me like that? How could they lie? *(Flies into a rage)* It's horrible! It's too too horrible! *(She throws herself on MERCANTEGGINI's knees and cries uncontrolledly)*

MERCANTEGGINI: *(Comforting her)* They're just jealous, that's all.

GALAS: Why do they hate me? Why? Why? What have I ever done to them?

MERCANTEGGINI: They're all against you because you have the voice of the century.

GALAS: Why don't they love me for that?

MERCANTEGGINI: They feel you are a greater actress than any singer has the right to be.

GALAS: *(Sobbing)* I just can't understand deliberate cruelty.

MERCANTEGGINI: Great artists are acknowledged but never forgiven. We'll make no reply to this whatsoever. Rumors die out quickly if they go unsubstantiated. There there, dry your eyes. I love you.

GALAS: You're the only person who ever has loved me. And you're the only person I've ever loved.

MERCANTEGGINI: I only want to protect you from the world and from your enemies.

GALAS: Oh my darling, oh my dear sweet wonderful, wonderful Baptista. I wish I could devote my whole life to you. If only I didn't have to work so hard.

MERCANTEGGINI: But you do. I understand that.

GALAS: *(Gives a pained look at his incomprehension, then regaining her composure)* I'm a little run-down. I'm not feeling up-to-date.

MERCANTEGGINI: Maybe you sacrifice yourself a little too much for your art. You should take a vacation once in a while.

GALAS: A vacation?

MERCANTEGGINI: It wouldn't hurt.

GALAS: When could I take a vacation? I have so many engagements.

MERCANTEGGINI: Let me check your appointment calendar. *(Gets a book and flips page after page as her hopes fade)* Next year you can do it.

GALAS: Next year?

MERCANTEGGINI: Yes, next year we will definitely take a vacation.

(GALAS sinks with a look of weary resignation as the lights fade.)

Scene 4: *The Vatican.*

POPE: Deus benedicte tutti homine.

PRELATE: Forgive me, Your Holiness. It is very well to bless all men. But do you think you could expand your blessing to include women as well?

POPE: Deus benedicte tutti homine et tutti dame.

PRELATE: With your permission, Your Holiness. It would perhaps be better if you could make a more general and all-inclusive blessing.

POPE: Deus benedicte tutti homine, tutti dame, et tutti fruitti.

PRELATE: Pardon me, Your Holiness. It is almost ten o'clock. It would be well if you withdrew and prepared for your audience.

POPE: Preparare pro audiencia?

PRELATE: So that Your Holiness might not miss the opportunity to make an entrance.

POPE: Bonus. *(Exits)*

PRELATE: *(Showing in* MERCANTEGGINI, BRUNA, *and* GALAS*)* If you will be so kind as to wait here His Holiness will be with you in a moment.

(BRUNA weeps uncontrollably.)

MERCANTEGGINI: Bruna, why are you crying?

BRUNA: Because I'm so happy. *(Sobs loudly)*

(The POPE enters through a tiny door at the back. The music, lighting, and his stately bearing inspire awe. He ascends the steps to his throne and sits. Far off boys' voices evoke heaven.

The PRELATE signals for MERCANTEGGINI, BRUNA, *and* GALAS *to go forward in turn and kiss the POPE's ring. The POPE blesses each of them. For this BRUNA removes her coat revealing sackcloth and ashes, dons a crown of thorns, and crawls to the POPE on her knees, flagellating herself with a flail she takes from her bag. When LA GALAS goes forward proudly to kiss his ring he lowers it by degrees, forcing her to bow very low. She crosses herself with a gesture of contempt.)*

POPE: *(Rising and coming forward he places his hand on* BRUNA's *head)* Let us bless the mother. *(*BRUNA *falls to her knees as if she had just witnessed a miracle. Touching* MERCANTEGGINI's *forehead)* And let us also bless Commendatore Mercanteggini and his wife *(Touches the forehead of* GALAS*)*, whose musical art we know from having heard her on the radio. *(Smiles at* GALAS*)* We heard you sing Wagner's *Parsifal* and were deeply moved. It is for that reason that we wished to meet you. We only regret that you did not sing *Parsifal* in the original German. Wagner loses so much when translated into Italian.

GALAS: We were broadcasting for the Italian public. If we had sung in German only a very few would have understood us.

POPE: True. But Wagner's music should not be separated from his words. He wrote them both. They were born together and they are inseparable.

GALAS: I don't agree. Very little is lost in translation. In order to understand the depths of the music one must understand the sense of the words.

(The conversation becomes more animated.)

POPE: Your achievement in this opera is very great. All the greater perhaps because of all operas Wagner's are the most difficult to sing.

GALAS: Not really. The operas of the bel canto repertoire make far greater vocal demands. Wagner's operas are relatively easy.

POPE: But Wagner's operas were conceived on a far grander scale. His mythic heroes demand a greater emotional range.

GALAS: Nonsense. Why, there is more true feeling on any page of Donizetti, Rossini, Verdi, or Bellini than there is in all the bombast and rhetoric of the *Ring.*

POPE: I have always found that—

GALAS: *(Interrupting)* Of course you can yell your head off in these operas *(Shaking a finger under the* POPE'*s nose)* or you can sing them musically, which is quite a different matter. . . .

(POPE is flabbergasted. MERCANTEGGINI *pulls* GALAS *back, steps forward, and changes the subject for fear that* GALAS *might go too far.)*

MERCANTEGGINI: Your Holiness, have you read the article about the new grafitti they've excavated beneath the Baths of Caracolla? Your Holiness probably doesn't bother to read the papers except for the most important articles that your aides prepare for you.

POPE: We read the papers from cover to cover. Nothing escapes us. Not even your legal battles with the Pastaciutta Mills. Our nephew is president of that company. The newspapers never tire of disporting themselves with the Pucelli name. We would be grateful if you would quickly settle this matter out of court so that the Pope might be left in peace.

MERCANTEGGINI: *(Nodding "yes" aside to* GALAS*)* Your Holiness, we will do everything in our power to arrive at a settlement as quickly as possible.

(GALAS shakes her head no. POPE *gives* BRUNA *a rosary and offers his ring to be kissed, then gives* LA GALAS *a rosary and offers hand. With the rosary,* GALAS *lassoes his hand to prevent him from lowering it again, kisses the ring, and steps back with hands clasped angelically in prayer.)*

POPE: Have you brought umbrellas?

GALAS: No, why?

POPE: Because, if I may speak ex cathedra, it is going to rain.

(POPE dismisses them with a benediction and withdraws.)

GALAS: *(To* MERCANTEGGINI*)* Now I want you to understand that it is you who promised the Pope. I didn't promise the Pope anything. Come Bruna.

MERCANTEGGINI: Now now, Magda.

(Exit BRUNA before them on her knees, then GALAS *and* MERCANTEGGINI. *They are shown out by the* PRELATE, *who reenters.)*

GALAS: *(As* MERCANTEGGINI *hustles her out)* Besides this has absolutely nothing whatsoever to do with the Pope.

(They are gone. POPE *reenters.)*

POPE: That woman is more fatiguing than a mission from Salt Lake City.

PRELATE: *(Sending up his brows a little)* Orthodox.

POPE: I'm not used to being flatly contradicted.

PRELATE: Where do you find the patience?

POPE: The martyrs are ever before me. Misericordia! This lawsuit could be the worst scandal since the fall of Innocent XVI. And this morning we have detected rat droppings among the papyrus plants.

PRELATE: They come up from the Tiber.

POPE: Are there any more audiences today?

PRELATE: That was the last.

POPE: Good. Disinfect our finger and the ring.

(PRELATE takes out a can of aerosol disinfectant and sprays the POPE's finger and ring as lights fade.)

Scene 5: *The Rome Opera.*

(A view of an opera box as seen from behind the spectators. The box plays upstage and forms a kind of proscenium for the silhouetted figures of the spectators while the performance of the opera is in progress. Downstage of the box, the backstage scenes are played. During the scene change we hear GALAS *singing the "Casta Diva" and the final Act One duet between Pollione and Adalgisa is heard as the lights come up on the silhouetted tableau vivant of the spectators' backs in the box. There are incidental movements of fans, programs, opera glasses, egret feathers, and the sparkle of jewels in the darkness. As the duet finishes and the curtain call is heard on tape the people in the back mime applauding, as the light wipes vertically to indicate the rise and fall of the grand curtain. The people then assume the more casual attitudes of intermission, but do not move. As the last applause dies away,* LA GALAS *flies onto the stage in her Norma costume, pursued by* MERCANTEGGINI *and attended by* BRUNA *in great consternation.)*

MERCANTEGGINI: But you must finish the performance!

GALAS: I can't! I wish to god I could. But I can't. The voice . . . the voice is slipping.

MERCANTEGGINI: Slipping?

GALAS: Yes slipping! Slipping! The voice will not obey.

MERCANTEGGINI: *(Growing more and more alarmed)* How can that be?

GALAS: I told you, sometimes the voice obeys and sometimes it will not. Tonight it will not!

MERCANTEGGINI: You're speaking of your voice as though it had a will of its own.

GALAS: *(With horror)* It has! It does! Tonight it will not obey.

MERCANTEGGINI: You've got to get hold of yourself. It's your voice. You must command it.

GALAS: *(In a hoarse whisper)* It's no use.

MERCANTEGGINI: We demanded a million lire for this performance. You must go on.

GALAS: *(Weeping)* I can't! I can't! I can't!

BRUNA: *(Quietly aside to* MERCANTEGGINI*)* Leave her alone. When the voice goes it is no use to call it back. Believe me, if she could finish the performance tonight, she would.

(There is a knock at the door.)

VOICE: *(Off)* Cinque minuti.

MERCANTEGGINI: What shall I tell them? That you don't want to risk being a flop?

GALAS: If I go back out there it will be worse than a flop. It will be a musical fiasco.

MERCANTEGGINI: Very well, I'll tell them to send on a replacement. *(Exits)*

GALAS: Where is my voice, Bruna? I call it and call it but it will not answer.

BRUNA: Only a happy bird can sing.

(A tumult of voices is heard off. GHINGHERI, FRITALINI, *and* MERCANTEGGINI *enter arguing.)*

GHINGHERI: *(Ranting)* This is impossible! Completely impossible! We have given *Norma* a thousand times and we never have this!

FRITALINI: *(Echoing in falsetto)* Impossible! Completely impossible!

MERCANTEGGINI: Well, there's a first time for everything. Send in the replacement.

GHINGHERI: *(A note of hysteria creeping into the voice)* That's just it! Don't you understand? There is no replacement!

MERCANTEGGINI: No replacement?

FRITALINI: No replacement!

MERCANTEGGINI: How is that possible? Why don't you have a replacement?

GHINGHERI: *(Shrill and screaming)* I don't know why we don't have a replacement! WE JUST DON'T HAVE A REPLACEMENT!

MERCANTEGGINI: Magdalena, they don't have a replacement.

GALAS: I heard him.

MERCANTEGGINI: What should we do?

GALAS: We'll have to cancel.

GHINGHERI: Have to cancel?

FRITALINI: Have to cancel?

GHINGHERI: Cancel is completely wrong! Cancel is impossible!

FRITALINI: Impossible!

(A tall tenor, FRANCO COGLIONES, *enters weeping in the Roman garb of Pollione.)*

GHINGHERI: What's the matter with you?

COGLIONES: *(Crying like a baby)* She kicked me in the shins!

GALAS: Imagine me kicking a big strong man like you in the shins.

*(*COGLIONES *cries.)*

GHINGHERI: Shut up, you idiot. *(To* GALAS*)* The President of Italy is sitting out there. Do you want to ruin me, the Rome Opera, La Scala, and your own career all in one stroke?

GALAS: I'm sorry. But I have no voice.

GHINGHERI: *(Savagely)* No voice? So what's new, Mrs. Galas? You never had a voice! But that never stopped you before.

GALAS: WHAT?

GHINGHERI: I know why you don't want to continue. You don't dare. You were lousy out there and everyone knew it.

GALAS: Lousy? You called my performance lousy?

GHINGHERI: There were boos after the "Casta Diva" and the stage crew found radishes among your roses. It appears your vanity is more important than your music.

GALAS: I'll fracture your skull you worm! (LA GALAS *draws a dagger from her belt and attacks* GHINGHERI. MERCANTEGGINI *and* BRUNA *prevent her.* FRITALINI *screams and hides behind* GHINGHERI) I'll kill him! I'll kill him! I'LL KILL HIM!

(BRUNA *drags* LA GALAS *off amid the tumult.)*

MERCANTEGGINI: *(Mockingly to* GHINGHERI *as he exits)* Well, you have your scandal.

GHINGHERI: I should have known! I never wanted to let that woman sing in the first place. *(Gravely)* Give me a few minutes to inform the President personally and then go make the announcement. Tell them that Madame Galas has left the opera house.

(They exit at opposite doors. The announcement is heard in Italian over the public address system. The crowd greets this news with an uproar of boos and jeers. The figures in the box at the rear stand and gesticulate. The gentlemen help the ladies on with their wraps as the houselights come up and Act I ends.)

(Curtain.)

ACT II

Scene 1: *The Yacht.*

(At rise the sea chanty from the opening of Act Two of Ponchielli's La Gioconda *is sung severally and variously by sailors.)*

SAILORS:
　　Ho! He! Ho! He! Fissa il timone!
　　Ho! He! Ho! He! Fissa! Fissa!
　　Ho! He! Ho! He! Issa artimone!
　　Issa!
　　La ciurma ov'è?
　　Ho! He! Ho! He!

OTHER SAILORS:
　　Siam nel fondo più profondo
　　Della nave, della cala,
　　dove il vento furibondo
　　spreca i fischi e infrange l'ala.
　　Siam nel fondo più profondo. *(Etc.)*

BOYS:
　　La, la, la, la, etc.
　　Siam qui sui culmini, siam sulla borda.
　　Siam sulle tremule scale di corda.

SAILORS: Ho! He! *(Etc.)*

OTHER SAILORS: Ah! *(Etc.)*

BOYS: Guardate gli agili mozzi saltar, guardate *(Etc.)*

SAILORS: Ho! He! *(Etc.)* La, la, la *(Etc.)*

OTHER SAILORS: Ah! *(Etc.)* La, la, la! *(Etc.)*

BOYS: Noi gli scoiattoli siamo del mar. Siam gli scoiattoli *(Etc.)* Ah!

SAILORS: Ho! He! Ho! Ah! *(Etc.)*

OTHER SAILORS: Ah! La, la, la *(Etc.)* Ah!

(Exit SAILORS. *Enter* BRUNA, *as Greek chorus)*

BRUNA: Would that my mistress had never accepted the invitation to cruise on Odysseus's yacht. Would that she had never walked out on her performance at the Rome Opera. Would that she had not granted the press so many interviews. Better she had drowned in the wine-dark sea than that these things had come to pass.

ODYSSEUS: *(Off)* Poop deck! *(Enter* GALAS *laughing,* MERCANTEGGINI, ARISTOTLE ODYSSEUS, *and his wife* ATHINA*)* I hope you will enjoy cruising on my yacht as much as I do. Traveling this way, bounded only by the sea, the sky, the elements, imparts a godlike sense of freedom.

MERCANTEGGINI: Maybe so. But the immensity of it all restores one's sense of scale. We are reminded that Man and his endeavors are but a minute twitching in the infinite universe.

ODYSSEUS: We are all the more heroic for it. Every man struggles with an adversary knowing he must eventually lose.

GALAS: What adversary is that?

ODYSSEUS: Time.

GALAS: Ah, but we have this one great advantage. We know our foe; our foe does not know us. That is our triumph and our curse.

MERCANTEGGINI: *(To* ATHINA*)* I almost forgot. We brought our hostess a little gift.

ATHINA: You really shouldn't have.

MERCANTEGGINI: Ah, but we wanted to. *(Gives her a box)* Go ahead and open it.

ATHINA: *(Looking inside the box)* What is it?

MERCANTEGGINI: It's a necklace of shark's teeth. We bought it in the airport. Let's put it on. *(*ATHINA *does so.)* Very becoming. *(To* ODYSSEUS*)* Don't you think?

ODYSSEUS: Exquisite. Shark's teeth are you, my dear. And before I forget, I have a little something for Magdalena. *(He takes out a jewelry box, opens it, and removes a necklace of polished green stones. He places them around* GALAS*'s neck. She gasps)* Cabochon emeralds. They were reputedly worn by Helene when she was abducted to Troy.

GALAS: They're lovely.

MERCANTEGGINI: *(To* ATHINA, *pointing to her necklace)* They're supposed to be sacred to pygmies. At least that's what the saleslady said. *(To* ODYSSEUS*)* Do you have anything for seasickness?

ODYSSEUS: I have some Dramamine in my medicine chest. Come with me and I'll get you some. *(Then to* GALAS*)* Ah, there on the starboard side. That little village, Ithaca. My namesake's birthplace and mine as well.

GALAS: I didn't know you were from Ithaca.

ODYSSEUS: This afternoon we'll drop anchor and go ashore. I want to show you the church where my parents were married. Come, my friend, and I'll get you some Dramamine. Look there! A flying fish! Did you see it?

*(*ODYSSEUS *laughs heartily and exits with* MERCANTEGGINI.*)*

GALAS: I am so looking forward to this little sightseeing trip. Perhaps it will give us a chance to get to know each other better.

ATHINA: I won't be going.

GALAS: Why not?

ATHINA: I've taken that tour before. Many times. I'm sorry.

GALAS: I'm disappointed. But I understand. If you've seen it all before. It will be the first time for me.

ATHINA: Yes, and I've heard all Soc's stories a thousand times over. Frankly I'm a little tired of them.

GALAS: *(Taking her hand)* I hope we'll be great friends.

ATHINA: *(Looking her straight in the eye)* Of course we will. Why shouldn't we be? *(Exits)*

GALAS: Bruna, what should I wear? Madame Blini designed me so many outfits I don't know where to start. I'll have to change ten times a day if I expect to wear them all. *(Starts off but pauses when she hears* BRUNA'*s foreboding tone)*

BRUNA: Sackcloth and modesty. Ashes and silence. Things that shadow and conceal. You should think of nothing else.

GALAS: Nonsense. A woman should always arrive last and wearing the least. *(Exits)*

BRUNA: *(Following her out)* Do not go ashore today. Stay in. Hide yourself.

(Reenter ODYSSEUS *and* MERCANTEGGINI.*)*

MERCANTEGGINI: Our family lost a lot of our factories during the war. But afterwards we built them up again. Bricks never go out of style. That's how we made our fortune.

ODYSSEUS: *(Chuckling)* I was completely wiped out in twenty-nine and then again under the Germans. But every time I started again from scratch. It's easy to make millions—once you know how.

MERCANTEGGINI: But even with millions I still watch every penny. It's something that's ingrained in me.

ODYSSEUS: You don't mean to say you're penny wise and pound foolish?

MERCANTEGGINI: I wouldn't say that. But I am a man who husbands his wealth.

ODYSSEUS: Indeed you are. Your wife is a treasure.

MERCANTEGGINI: Ah yes, Magdalena is a great gal. My family practically disowned me when I married her. Eventually I gave up the family business to handle her career. Everything I knew about selling bricks I put into selling her voice. And it worked. Maria Magdalena Mercanteggini Galas is now the highest-paid singer in the world. Not to mention the most famous.

ODYSSEUS: Not to mention the best?

MERCANTEGGINI: That too. Of course the best.

(Enter ILKA WINTERHALTER *smoking a cigar.)*

ILKA: Look at this, boys. Maria has really come out!

(Enter GALAS. *She has changed into a white silk jumpsuit with big roses printed all over it.* BRUNA *looks on like a fate.)*

GALAS: How do you like it?

ODYSSEUS: Ravishing! Ravishing!

GALAS: Thank you. Giovanni, what do you think?

MERCANTEGGINI: Is this supposed to be a joke?

GALAS: What do you mean?

MERCANTEGGINI: Isn't it just a trifle vulgar?

GALAS: Madame Blini said it was perfect for sightseeing.

MERCANTEGGINI: You want to see the sights, not be a sight. You're not going to let people see you in that.

ILKA: Isn't she divine? Isn't she just ta-hoo ta-hoo divine? There's an aura about her.

MERCANTEGGINI: *(Aside to* GALAS*)* Who is that horrible woman?

GALAS: Shh. That's Ilka Winterhalter. Be very nice to her. She's doing my profile for *Time* magazine.

ILKA: Magdalena, tell me, dear, how do you feel now that you've finally sung at La Scala?

GALAS: Oh, La Scala, wonderful theater, wonderful, but then, I am nearsighted, you see, all theaters look alike to me.

ILKA: Some of your critics say you have a wobbly voice.

GALAS: *(Snarling)* Well, it happens to be a trill!

ILKA: You're hypnotic. You're a priestess. A high priestess. Being in your presence is an almost mystic experience.

GALAS: *(To* MERCANTEGGINI*)* Soc says I look ravished in it.

MERCANTEGGINI: Madame Blini should be shot.

ODYSSEUS: Drop the anchors! Let's disembark. Let's live, my friends. You want to live, don't you Magdalena?

GALAS: Yes, I do.

ODYSSEUS: I hope so, because I am only interested in people who want to live.

GALAS: I do want to live. I do want to live. I do.

ODYSSEUS: What about you Baptista? Do you want to live?

MERCANTEGGINI: Aaaagh.

ODYSSEUS: Then since we are all in agreement, let's live! *(As they exit down the gangway,* ODYSSEUS*'s voice is heard trailing off.)* Let's live! Let's live! Let's live!

(Enter ATHINA ODYSSEUS *and* HÜRE VON HOYDEN.*)*

VON HOYDEN: I'm sure I don't know what you're talking about.

ATHINA: Do you think I'm blind? Do you think I can't see what's been going on under my very nose?

VON HOYDEN: You're mistaken. I don't like husbands. But I like wives even less. Here, take back these jewels he gave me. They were yours, I believe, and probably false. *(Drops a necklace, bracelet, and ring into* ATHINA*'s hand)*

ATHINA: *(Flinging them into the sea)* I don't want them.

VON HOYDEN: *(Gasps)* If I'd known you were going to fling them into the sea I never would have given them back. If you didn't want them you should have let me keep them. *(Looking over the side)* Oh well, there goes my old age insurance.

ATHINA: I want you to keep your hands off my husband.

VON HOYDEN: And what makes you think I've had my hands on your husband?

ATHINA: He took you ashore to show you the village where he was born, didn't he?

VON HOYDEN: Yes.

ATHINA: And you went to meet Krakitoukitifanipoulous, the hierophant of the island?

VON HOYDEN: Yes.

ATHINA: And you knelt before him to receive his blessing?

VON HOYDEN: Soc told you all this?

ATHINA: He didn't have to. It's the same routine with every woman he seduces. You got the treatment, honey. So I know the rest.

VON HOYDEN: He knows how to make a woman feel like a woman. But when he's through with you he throws you away like a used condom.

ATHINA: How dare you speak like that to me?

VON HOYDEN: I didn't mean you.

ATHINA: If you don't break off this affair with my husband I'm going to sue him for divorce and name you as correspondent.

VON HOYDEN: You're wasting your time being jealous of me. He's already lost interest. It's the Greek opera singer who fascinates him now.

ATHINA: Galas?

VON HOYDEN: They've gone ashore to meet Krapatoukifanny . . . Krafticulo . . . Kooka tafi . . .

ATHINA: Krakitoukitifanipoulous?

VON HOYDEN: That guy. To receive his blessing. She's the one you'd better watch out for.

ATHINA: I'm not worried. She's safely in the custody of her husband. *(The Sailors' Chorus is heard again)* Do you hear that? They're returning from the island. Go do something with yourself before the soirée tonight. Perhaps you can snag another victim.

VON HOYDEN: You know, you could open clams with that tongue of yours.

ATHINA: If I see you anywhere near my husband tonight I'm going to put you off this yacht.

VON HOYDEN: We'll be hundreds of knots out to sea.

ATHINA: Exactly.

(Exit VON HOYDEN. *Enter* ODYSSEUS *laughing,* MERCANTEGGINI, *and* GALAS. ILKA *and* BRUNA *enter and exit holding hands.)*

GALAS: *(To* ODYSSEUS*)* Thank you for a lovely afternoon.

ODYSSEUS: That was nothing, Magdalena. Tonight after we have dined there will be a masquerade. We're all to come in costume.

GALAS: But what will I wear?

ODYSSEUS: Surprise me.

GALAS: But I didn't bring a costume.

ODYSSEUS: Improvise! Use your imagination. I'm sure you'll come up with something.

ATHINA: Come, Soc. Hadn't we better leave our guests alone to freshen up for dinner?

ODYSSEUS: But of course! I daresay tonight you will dine as you have never dined before. I have four chefs—one Greek, one French, one Italian, and one Chinese.

MERCANTEGGINI: I have no appetite.

ODYSSEUS: An appetite for food is an appetite for life. You'll find something to tweak you. My cooks are as great artists in their own realm as our Magdalena is in hers. *(To* GALAS, *kissing her hand and staring deeply into her eyes)* Until dinner then, divine one. *(Exits with* ATHINA*)*

MERCANTEGGINI: Now it's a masquerade! What next? Do these people do anything besides party morning, noon, and night?

GALAS: Aren't you happy?

MERCANTEGGINI: Do you care?

GALAS: Of course I care. I want you to enjoy yourself.

MERCANTEGGINI: That's about all I *am* enjoying. You practically ignored me all afternoon.

GALAS: Did I? There were so many things to see and do I guess I just got carried away.

MERCANTEGGINI: And when we went to see that bishop or whatever he was . . .

GALAS: *(Transported)* Krakitoukitifanipoulous.

MERCANTEGGINI: It gave me a funny feeling the way the two of you knelt before him to receive his blessing. It was almost as if he were marrying you.

GALAS: You're not Greek. You don't understand these things. How could you?

MERCANTEGGINI: And then when we heard on the radio that the Pope had died it was like an omen.

GALAS: The Pope died? I didn't hear that.

MERCANTEGGINI: What do you mean you didn't hear it? I told you myself.

GALAS: Then it's really true? The Pope is dead?

MERCANTEGGINI: Yes, the Pope is dead.

GALAS: Good. Now you don't have to keep that promise you made him. We can go back to court.

MERCANTEGGINI: Really Magdalena, I'm surprised at you. Shouldn't you be thinking about the Pope's death rather than your lawsuit?

GALAS: I don't care that for the Pope. *(Snaps her fingers)* Remember I am Greek Orthodox. To me he's just another bishop.

MERCANTEGGINI: But the Bishop of Rome—

GALAS: *(Interrupting)* I do not recognize Rome and I do not recognize the Pope.

MERCANTEGGINI: But think of your Italian public. . . .

GALAS: My Italian public are a bunch of savages. Imagine, after that unfortunate Rome cancellation, smearing our entire villa with excrement!

MERCANTEGGINI: To them he's like God on earth. They consider him infallible.

GALAS: In matters of dogma he may be infallible, but in matters musical I found him quite fallible. Him and his Wagner! The Pope should mind his own business and not go sticking his nose in my affairs.

MERCANTEGGINI: Magda, darling, I'm not a religious man, but really, what a way to speak of the Pope!

GALAS: Well, really, whose side are you on anyway? Mine or the Pope's?

MERCANTEGGINI: All right! All right! But I want you to know that this goes against everything I believe in. Squabbling in court is an utterly squalid and shabby way to conduct one's life. I don't see what you are trying to prove.

GALAS: It's the principle of the thing. Now please, let's go in to dinner.

MERCANTEGGINI: Very well, if you want to drag this sordid mess on and on, go ahead. We'll go back to court.

(He storms out. LA GALAS *follows dejectedly. Music.)*

BRUNA: *(Enters as before to express foreboding)* A little love is like a light breeze on a lovely day that fills the sails and moves the ship along. A lot of love is like a gale that hastens progress but rocks the boat. A great love is like a storm that tosses the vessel this way and that with no rhyme or reason until the passengers are ill and all capsize. Better a little love than a lot. Better a small love than a great.

(It is now evening. Latin music is heard. Japanese lanterns are lighted. ODYSSEUS, ATHINA, VON HOYDEN, ILKA, *and other* GUESTS *enter dancing in a conga line in masquerade costumes. They break and dance in couples.)*

ODYSSEUS: *(Removing his mask)* But where is La Galas and Mercanteggini?
GALAS: *(Reenters in gown, with vizard, followed by* MERCANTEGGINI*)* Here I am.
ODYSSEUS: You look like a Greek goddess. But then, you are, after all, Greek.
GALAS: I thought Iphigenia.
ODYSSEUS: Iphigenia. Of course Iphigenia. I will steer the yacht toward Tauris if you so desire.
GALAS: Don't go out of your way.
ODYSSEUS: *(Noticing* MERCANTEGGINI *standing alone looking over the rail)* What's this? Baptista undisguised? You should know better than to be yourself at this kind of a gathering!
MERCANTEGGINI: If you don't mind I think I'll skip the costume party. I have a bit of a headache. I'll just stay up here on the deck and take the air.
ODYSSEUS: If you insist.
MERCANTEGGINI: I do.
ODYSSEUS: But here's a costume for you if you change your mind. *(Gives him a box)*
MERCANTEGGINI: How do you know it will fit?
ODYSSEUS: It's a one size fits all affair. Magdalena, do you ever go in for popular music?
GALAS: Hot jazz, no. Rumbas, things like that, yes.
ODYSSEUS: We must go dancing. I will instruct the orchestra to play nothing but rumbas. And now friends, how about a little game of hide-and-seek? *(All cheer)* Athina, you're it.
ATHINA: But I was it last time.

*(*GUESTS *laugh and scurry out at different doors.* ATHINA *leans against the wall and covers her eyes and counts to* 100. MERCANTEGGINI *sits upstage with his back to the audience and looks out to sea.)*

MERCANTEGGINI: And these are supposed to be mature adults? It's as though they're in an endless childhood.
ATHINA: Ninety-seven, ninety-eight, ninety-nine, one hundred. Here I come, ready or not. *(Exits)*

*(*GUESTS *cross and recross the stage as they play hide-and-seek in their masquerade costumes.)*

ILKA: *(Crossing with* ODYSSEUS*)* Isn't Galas divine? Isn't she just ta-hoo ta-hoo divine?
ODYSSEUS: I find her a suitable object for worship.
ILKA: Do you? Do you really? I'm doing a profile on her for *Time* magazine. I want to show the public what she's really like.
ODYSSEUS: *(Chuckles)* That's something I'd like to discover for myself.
ILKA: You too, eh? It looks like we may end up rivals.

*(*ILKA *and* ODYSSEUS *laugh and exit. Sounds of a rumba are heard off mingled with the* GUESTS' *laughter. Occasionally* GUESTS *in masquerade costumes cross the stage. A couple of* SAILORS *wander on holding hands.* VON HOYDEN *approaches them and the three of them begin to make love.)*

MERCANTEGGINI: *(Watching appalled)* What is this, a masquerade or an orgy? I'd better go find Magdalena. *(Exits)*

SAILOR: I can't do it.

VON HOYDEN: *(Drunkenly)* What do you mean can't? You don't want to or you're too drunk?

ATHINA: *(Enters calling)* Soc? Soc? Have any of you seen my husband?

SAILOR: No, ma'am.

VON HOYDEN: Don't look at me. I can't swim.

MERCANTEGGINI: *(Enters in a state of great agitation, to* ATHINA*)* Have you seen my wife? I can't find her anywhere.

ATHINA: No I haven't. Have you seen my husband?

MERCANTEGGINI: No, I'm sorry.

ATHINA: *(Exiting)* Soc? Soc?

MERCANTEGGINI: *(Looking at* VON HOYDEN *and* SAILORS *making it)* These people are disgusting. They're like animals. I'm in a pigsty! *(*ILKA *crosses in a pig mask. A passenger in gorilla costume passes with cocktail in hand)* Excuse me, have you seen my wife? *(*ILKA *snorts and exits. To other* GUEST*)* Pardon, have you seen my wife?

(Each time he asks a guest this question they laugh a nightmarish laugh and exit. Weird laughter is heard coming from all sides.

Enter Athina, nude, except for her hair which falls below her waist, partially covering her body. She is weeping.)

ATHINA: You have lost your Magdalena.

MERCANTEGGINI: What?

ATHINA: I came upon them in the dark. They had hidden in the lifeboat. I heard sounds and lifted up the tarp. And there the two great fishes lay, flopping in the net. Then twisting, turning head to tail, I heard her laugh and say, "It will open up my throat!" And then I heard her sing—a song such as I've never heard before. Her voice grew loud and mingled with the sound of wind and waves. It was as though a bird that had long been caged escaped and flew away. It soared and dipped and circled o'er these stinking fish.

MERCANTEGGINI: *(Beside himself)* It was dark. Are you sure it wasn't someone else?

ATHINA: I knew them by the wetness of their skin and the shimmer of her jewels. *(Exits wailing)*

MERCANTEGGINI: *(To a* SAILOR*)* Give me that bottle there. I need a drink. *(He drinks wildly, recklessly)* Let's have a party.

(He opens the box ODYSSEUS *gave him and takes out a Pagliacci costume. He puts it on, smears his face with clown white, muttering unintelligibly all the while. Then we hear Caruso's voice singing the aria "Vesti la Giubba" from Pagliacci.* MERCANTEG-GINI *lip-syncs the aria and gestures accordingly.* GALAS *and* ODYSSEUS *enter drunk. They watch him through to the end of the aria.)*

ODYSSEUS: *(Applauding)* Bravo! Bravo! It seems Giovanni Baptista has decided to join the party.

MERCANTEGGINI: *(Glaring at him murderously)* From what I've heard, it's you who've decided to join the party. *(Seizing* MAGDALENA*)* You, what have you done, huh? You pig, you're shit!

GALAS: You're drunk.

MERCANTEGGINI: Yeah? Well I'll be sober tomorrow. But you'll still be shit.

ODYSSEUS: You don't understand Magdalena. She's looking for a father figure.

MERCANTEGGINI: Who asked you, you rancid piece of pork?

ODYSSEUS: Well, if you're going to be a sore loser.

GALAS: Stop it! Stop it both of you!

MERCANTEGGINI: Now the sow is bellowing! That's what you are! You're a sow and you're a boar.

GALAS: Get away from me, you horrible old man. I hate you! I hate you! I hate you!

MERCANTEGGINI: I'll get a pistol and shoot you two Greeks dead.

GALAS: Well, I'll get a shotgun and kill you first!

ODYSSEUS: Come away Magdalena. You don't need this.

MERCANTEGGINI: I built your career! You're nothing without me.

GALAS: *(Laughs incredulously)* Oh, ho ho!

ODYSSEUS: Yes, we have a word for a man who lives off his woman's earnings—pimp!

MERCANTEGGINI: I do not live off her career. I have millions of my own, *millions!*

ODYSSEUS: Magdalena means more to me than all the money in the world. I'll buy her from you. How much do you want for her? One million? Two million? Name your price. I'll write you a check.

MERCANTEGGINI: Will you know what to do with her? I doubt it.

(The following three speeches are spoken together, three times in a round, meant to evoke an operatic trio.)

MERCANTEGGINI: I'm the one who built your career. You were nothing before me and you'll be nothing after me. . . .

GALAS: Twelve years, twelve years. You must let me go. I want to live! . . .

ODYSSEUS: She wants to live! Let her live! . . .

MERCANTEGGINI: All these years, I have lived only to expand her fame and her prestige. I never thought of myself.

ODYSSEUS: Ah, go back to your bricks. That was more your line. I am only interested in bouyant things, things that float. Come Magdalena. In the future, man will travel at the speed of light and this great ass will be sitting there on his pile of bricks. *(He exits.* LA GALAS *goes to follow him)*

MERCANTEGGINI: So you're really leaving me for that repulsive pile of putrescent flesh?

GALAS: *(Turns back)* Yes.

MERCANTEGGINI: Then there's nothing else to say, is there?

GALAS: Only . . .

MERCANTEGGINI: Yes?

GALAS: Will you still be my business manager?

MERCANTEGGINI: *(With disbelief)* What?!!

GALAS: Will you still handle my career?

MERCANTEGGINI: Your career is over as far as I'm concerned.

(GALAS stalks off. Music. MERCANTEGGINI *weeps, sits. Enter* ILKA.*)*

ILKA: *(On seeing him weeping)* Is something wrong?

MERCANTEGGINI: I have just received word that someone I loved has died.

ILKA: Oh, that's too bad. I'm sorry you're not feeling better. I was kinda hoping you could help me with something.

MERCANTEGGINI: What do you want?

ILKA: Well, I'm writing a profile on Magdalena for *Time* magazine. I'd like to help my readers distinguish the real Magdalena from the legends that spring up about her. We all know Magdalena the artist. But what about Magdalena, the woman.

MERCANTEGGINI: What do you want to know?

ILKA: Well, her spectacular weight loss, for example. She went, if you'll pardon my saying so, from two hundred and fifteen pounds to one hundred and thirty-five in a little over a year. I'm sure every woman in America would like to know how she did it.

MERCANTEGGINI: She swallowed a tapeworm.

ILKA: *(Shocked)* A tapeworm?

MERCANTEGGINI: Yes, she took a tapeworm. Didn't you know that?

ILKA: Well, I heard rumors of course, but I was never certain. . . .

MERCANTEGGINI: Well, you know she always had an enormous appetite. She could never control it.

ILKA: Really?

MERCANTEGGINI: Sure. Why in Greece during the war she even sang to the soldiers for food. And she'd eat it all herself.

ILKA: *(Writing more and more furiously)* Really? It was that bad, huh?

MERCANTEGGINI: Oh terrible, terrible. With an appetite like that dieting is just no use. So she went to a doctor who gave her the egg of a tapeworm. He got it out of the ass of an infected patient.

ILKA: That's incredible! Are you sure?

MERCANTEGGINI: I ought to know. I'm her husband.

(Blackout.)

Scene 2: *Galas's apartment, Paris.*

(At rise Galas stands silhouetted against the window with her back to the audience, looking out. Enter Bruna.)

GALAS: Has the postman arrived yet, Bruna?

BRUNA: You know he hasn't. You've done nothing but stand and look out that window all afternoon.

GALAS: Do you smell tar?

BRUNA: *(Sniffs)* No, madam.

GALAS: It's very strange, I smell tar. That postman comes later and later every day.

BRUNA: There's a new man on. He needs time to learn his route.

(Doorbell rings.)

GALAS: There's the bell. Bruna, see who it is.

BRUNA: *(Returning)* Miss Von Hoyden to see you. *(Exits)*

(VON HOYDEN enters wearing a sari.)

GALAS: *(Embracing her and kissing both cheeks.)* Hüre!

VON HOYDEN: Magda, sweetie, long time no see.

GALAS: It is a long time, isn't it? Where have you been?

VON HOYDEN: *(Throwing herself into a chair)* Oh Indya, Indya!

GALAS: Have you heard from Soc?

VON HOYDEN: God, no. I have a maharaja now. How have you been?

GALAS: Ah, well, you know, I'm never really well.

VON HOYDEN: What's wrong?

GALAS: Nothing's wrong, really. It's just that nothing's right, if you understand me.

VON HOYDEN: Aren't you happy?

GALAS: Happy? Now that's too much to ask. I live on—that's about it.

VON HOYDEN: But you've had it all. Think of how many other people live and have nothing.

GALAS: To have nothing isn't so bad. To have everything and lose it—now that isn't funny.

VON HOYDEN: Do you know what I think, Maggie? I think you take men too seriously.

GALAS: In what way?

VON HOYDEN: Well, you know, most men can't help themselves.

GALAS: What do you mean?

HOYDEN: I mean they're men and there's very little that can be done about it.

GALAS: To me a man has always been a thing apart. To love is akin to worship.

VON HOYDEN: But one must keep one's eyes wide open about the reasons one is loved in return.

GALAS: Reasons? There are always so many reasons for everything. People are always so fast to invent reasons, especially where they do not exist. So many reasons.

VON HOYDEN: Soc, for instance, loves fame.

GALAS: Fame?

VON HOYDEN: No woman could ever be famous enough for him. That's why he remarried.

GALAS: I gave up my career for him.

VON HOYDEN: That was the very thing he loved.

GALAS: Then you think I've lost him?

VON HOYDEN: Not if you learn how to play the other woman.

GALAS: I'm afraid that role is not in my repertoire.

VON HOYDEN: And why not? All women are actresses at heart.

GALAS: I have always wanted to be loved completely and for myself alone. I could never play second fiddle. I must be the first woman. That, I believe, is the true meaning of the term, prima donna.

VON HOYDEN: Ah, but the other woman has certain advantages.

GALAS: What possible advantages could she have?

VON HOYDEN: For one thing, the wife is always jealous of the other woman, because she feels the other woman is getting the best part of the man. But the other woman is never jealous of the wife. All you have to do is learn to wait.

GALAS: But what do I do from morning to night while I'm waiting for him to call?

VON HOYDEN: Amuse yourself. Play cards. Gossip. Spend money on clothes. Accept dinner invitations. You're a lady of leisure and that's a luxury.

GALAS: I go crazy when I'm not working.

VON HOYDEN: Now take my maharaja for instance. Don't you dare. He has nine wives. That's enough to form an all-wife baseball team. (GALAS *laughs*) But he prefers to spend his time with me. But I have to be patient. My turn doesn't come around that often. But when it does it's a great relief to him. I enjoy my freedom.

GALAS: *(Her face turns into a tragic mask)* That's it. I hate freedom. First I belonged to my mother, then I belonged to my husband, then I belonged to my art, and now I don't belong to anyone.

VON HOYDEN: It's time to belong to yourself. Well, I'm off. Shopping, then lunch with the girls.

GALAS: *(Quietly)* Hell.

VON HOYDEN: What was that?

GALAS: Oh, nothing.

VON HOYDEN: Good-bye, sweetie, and remember you're a free woman. Cheer up. How about a little smile? *(LA GALAS forces a smile)* That's the Magdalena I like to see. Au revoir, chérie.

GALAS: *(Embracing her)* Good-bye. *(Exit VON HOYDEN. LA GALAS sniffs the air)* There's that tar again. *(She returns to her vigil at the window. BRUNA reenters)* Has the postman arrived *yet*, Bruna?

BRUNA: There's some good news for you.

GALAS: *(Eagerly)* Good news? What is it? Quickly!

BRUNA: You've won your lawsuit against the Pastaciutta Mills.

GALAS: *(Suddenly morose)* Is that all?

BRUNA: And there's an invitation to a dinner party at the Finzi-Continis tonight.

GALAS: Short notice.

BRUNA: They sent it to the Villa Mercanteggini by mistake. Commendatore Mercanteggini forwarded it.

GALAS: Thoughtful of him.

BRUNA: There's still time to go if you want to.

GALAS: You know I've never been able to stand the Finzi-Continis.

BRUNA: It might do you good to go out for a change.

GALAS: Do you think?

BRUNA: A little conversation and admiration might be just the thing you need to put the roses in your cheeks.

GALAS: "The roses in my cheeks." Where do you pick up expressions like that?

BRUNA: *(Going off into a spasm)* I don't know. I suppose my mother used to say it. Didn't your mother have any little expressions like that?

GALAS: I don't know. *(Comforting BRUNA)* I suppose she did. *(Glancing in the mirror)* Gilding the lily.

BRUNA: What's that?

GALAS: She used to say, "Gilding the lily." I remember once when I was a little girl I went into my mother's room and I saw her standing before the mirror applying mascara with a tiny brush. I said, "Mamma, what are you doing?" and she said, "I'm gilding the lily, dear, gilding the lily." For years I thought applying mascara was *called* gilding the lily. You know even today I never apply mascara that I don't think, "I'm gilding the lily."

BRUNA: If you want to go to that dinner party tonight there's still time to gild the lily.

GALAS: What if Soc calls?

BRUNA: *(As if on the phone)* I'm sorry, madam is not at home. May I take a message, please?

GALAS: Perhaps it would be better not to seem to be always waiting.

BRUNA: Shall I lay out your silk moiré?

GALAS: Where was I last seen in it? Check the file.

BRUNA: *(Consulting the file)* Winston Churchill, Prince Rainier and Grace, Ilka Winterhalter.

GALAS: It's safe. They're all either dead or in Monte Carlo.

BRUNA: Tonight you will appear in public and show the world you do not care what your rivals may say about you.

GALAS: Rivals? I have no rivals. Thank heaven I have not. When other singers sing the rôles that I sing the way I sing them, when they appear as I appear, do as I do, act as I act—then they can call themselves my rivals, and not until then.

BRUNA: Yes, madam. I know you do not fear any rivals.

GALAS: No, I do not fear them. Because I haven't any, you see.

BRUNA: Yes, madam, of course.

GALAS: *(Becoming more insistent)* On the contrary. I can sing the rôles they sing. I have sung them. These so-called rivals of mine say that they sing a lot of operas, but what I see is that they sing a very few. *(With a weary tone)* They sing *Aïda,* they sing *La Boheme,* they sing *Carmen.* And they sing these same operas over and over again, year in and year out. I do not take it easy. *(Dressing herself behind a screen)* I work hard, and I work a lot, bringing to life a Medea, an Anna Bolena, an I Puritani, and when one develops a new rôle—new! I mean they are new to the public. They are really very old. As I was saying— when one develops a new rôle, one loses months of work, months of money, months of time. Because I cannot accept another job—pardon me for using the vulgar expression, "job," but you know I do not gain any salary while I'm preparing a new work. And when one brings to life a new rôle, one also runs the risk of being a flop. Aha! Yes! Believe me, I could go out there and yell my head off in *Aïda,* but to sing a work musically, note by note, no more, no less, according to the composer's intentions, that is quite a different matter. So, it may sound a bit immodest. I hope you will understand me when I say that I have no rivals. Many enemies *(Coming out from behind the screen fully dressed in a formal gown),* but no rivals. Have I forgotten anything?

BRUNA: No, madam.

(LA GALAS goes to the mirror and plays with her stole before it. Each different way she arranges her stole suggests a different role in her repertoire.)

GALAS: Don't wait up for me tonight, Bruna. Here I go. *(She reaches the door, stops dead in her tracks, and stands there frozen for a long moment)* I can't face it. I can't, oh no, I can't face it. Bruna, are you doing anything tonight?

BRUNA: I was planning to go to the cinema.

GALAS: Are you going with someone?

BRUNA: No, I'm going alone.

GALAS: Oh, stay with me tonight, Bruna, we'll have a nice game of cards.

BRUNA: But tonight is my only night off, madam.

GALAS: Oh stay with me. Oh, what fun we'll have! I'll bet there's something nice on television.

BRUNA: But there is a new James Bond picture, madam, and I have a little crush on Sean Connery.

GALAS: Please stay with me tonight, Bruna. *(BRUNA still isn't convinced)* I'm afraid to be alone tonight. *(Seizing her arm)* I'm feeling a little depressed.

BRUNA: Very well, madam.

GALAS: Thank you, Bruna, and Bruna, would you call me Magdalena?

BRUNA: No madam, I am sorry. I wouldn't feel right doing that. *(Exits)*

GALAS: Oh, what fun we'll have tonight, Bruna. I need some good news.

BRUNA: *(Reenters with the dog)* Madam, your dog is dead.

GALAS: Ah toy, poor toy. My baby, my baby. *(Takes the dog)* How many moonlight rendezvous you saw. How many jet planes you peed on. How many pairs of expensive pumps you chewed up and destroyed. Oh, the secrets you knew. *(GALAS lays down the dog on her vanity and withdraws her hand suddenly in horror)* I used to replace them when they got old or died. Wouldn't it be wonderful if we could do that with people? When Soc remarried I saw no future for myself anymore. But even later, when he grew tired of the widow of the American President, and came back to me, it was never the same. I have always wanted to be loved completely, and for myself alone.

BRUNA: Your public loves you.

GALAS: The public, the public. When I sing well they applaud, and when I do not they boo and jeer. That's the public. Pah! You know, it's very strange, but there are certain nights when the public thinks that I am giving a great performance, but I do not feel that way at all. On such nights all compliments embarrass me. And yet there are certain other nights when I feel that the performance is going particularly well, and that I have attained a kind of perfection, but then the public does not agree. This is what haunts me.

BRUNA: A great artist is acknowledged but never understood. The voice is like the juice of a fruit: they squeeze it and throw the skin away.

(Phone rings. BRUNA *goes to answer it.)*

GALAS: Oh well, there are singers and then there are artists, and you see I speak deliberately of both. The singer sings notes, but the artist makes manifest what lies behind the notes, behind the gestures. That is the difference.

BRUNA: *(Reenters)* Madam, it is a call from Ithaca. Aristotle Plato Socrates Odysseus is dead.

GALAS: *(Stricken, assumes the postures of Greek tragedy)* Tell them I'm not at home. I don't even want to speak to them. *(Looks about the room as though she does not recognize the place)* Well, it seems I must find my joy in my music again. To live is to suffer, to endure pain. Anyone who says differently is a liar. People should tell their children that! *(Exits behind screen, laughing wildly)* Oh well, I was never really popular. I really wanted to be a dentist. What difference would it have made? Life is the same for every human being on this earth. The only difference is the weapons used against one and the weapons one uses in turn. What you want and what you're willing to do to get it, that is personality. Personality plus circumstance equals fate. *(LA GALAS reenters in a kimono. The pose and gestures suggest Madame Butterfly.* BRUNA *ties the obi)* Bruna, do you know where I put the fan that was given to me by the female impersonator of the Kabuki theater?

(BRUNA goes to fetch the fan. LA GALAS enters more fully into the character of Butterfly. BRUNA *reenters, looks on horrified at* GALAS's *mad behavior.)*

BRUNA: Here it is, madam.

GALAS: You see, the fan *(Snaps open the fan)* conceals a knife *(Draws knife from fan)*—the perfect weapon for a female impersonator. Bruna?

BRUNA: Yes, madam?

GALAS: Would you sing the "Vissi d'arte" to me? *(She blindfolds BRUNA with a glove.* BRUNA *moves her lips hesitatingly and sings the "Vissi d'arte." We hear the full orchestra. LA GALAS kneels in prayer)* What do I do from morning to night if I don't have my career? I have no family, I have no husband, I have no babies, I have no lover, I have no dog, I have no voice, and there's nothing good on television tonight. What do I do, what do I do from morning to night? I can't just sit around and play cards or gossip—I'm not the type. *(Suddenly her gaze falls on the fan. She looks to heaven as if for permission, smiles, takes fan, rises, opens fan, and exits toward the screen. Before she disappears behind the screen, she looks back at* BRUNA *and smiles in affirmation. She throws a scarf over the screen, then raises her hand with the dagger)* Grazie, Bruna.

(Her hand comes down with great force. As the last notes of the "Vissi d'arte" fade away, the scarf is dragged down behind the screen. Pounding on the door is heard, and the door being broken down. MERCANTEGGINI *rushes onto the stage, sees* BRUNA *blindfolded, looks behind the screen, and cries out.)*

MERCANTEGGINI: Magdalena? What has happened here?

(Tableau vivant as the lights fade slowly.)

Curtain

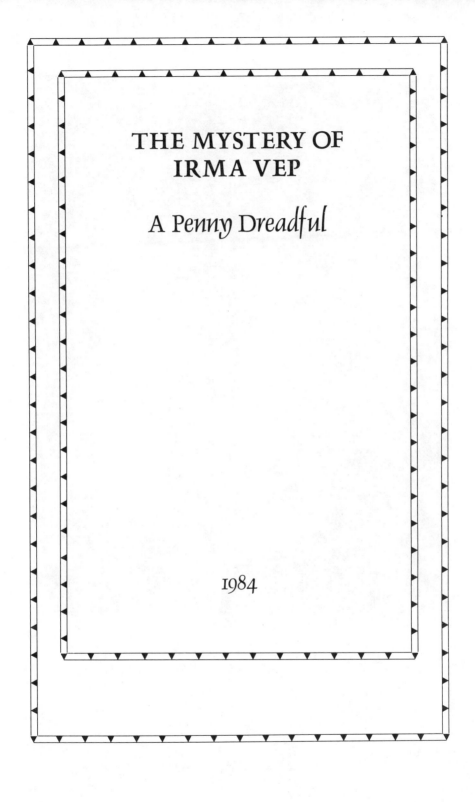

THE MYSTERY OF
IRMA VEP

A Penny Dreadful

1984

Charles Ludlam & Everett Quinton in
The Mystery of Irma Vep (Anita & Steve Shevett)

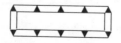

Cast of Characters

LADY ENID HILLCREST
LORD EDGAR HILLCREST
NICODEMUS UNDERWOOD
JANE TWISDEN
AN INTRUDER
ALCAZAR
PEV AMRI
IRMA VEP

The Mystery of Irma Vep is a full-length quick-change act. All roles are portrayed by two performers.

ACT I

Scene 1: *The library drawing room of Mandacrest, the Hillcrest estate near Hampstead Heath, between the wars.*

(The study is a large room with French doors at the back that open out on a garden. There is a desk and chair. A fireplace with a mantel over which is a portrait of Lady Irma in her bloom. Two deep armchairs flank the fireplace. There are signs that the Hillcrests have traveled: African masks and a painted Japanese screen. There is a bookcase with Morocco-bound volumes and doors left and right. At rise NICODEMUS *enters from the garden, through the French doors, carrying a basket. His left leg is deformed and the sole of his shoe is built up with wood.* JANE *is arranging flowers in a bowl.)*

JANE: Watch what you're doing! You're soaking wet! Don't track mud in here!
NICODEMUS: It's God's good rain, my girl.
JANE: It's the devil's rain. That's what it is!

(Lightning flashes, then thunder is heard.)

NICODEMUS: Would you rather the drought went on and on? It's thankful you
    should be. And that mightily.
JANE: And don't clump so with that wooden leg. You'll wake Lady Enid.
NICODEMUS: And wasn't it to save Lord Edgar from the wolf that me leg got
    mangled so? I should think she'd be glad to hear me clump after what I did
    for him.
JANE: That was a long time ago. Lady Enid doesn't know anything about it.
NICODEMUS: She'll find out soon enough.
JANE: Now, now, Nicodemus, I won't have you frightening Lord Edgar's new
    bride with your wolf tales.
NICODEMUS: And the sooner she does find out the better, I say!
JANE: Hush. Your tongue will dig your grave, Nicodemus. There are some
    things better left unsaid.
NICODEMUS: Pah! It's a free country, ain't it?
JANE: Shhhh!
NICODEMUS: Well, ain't it?
JANE: If Lord Edgar hears you you'll see how free it is. You'll find yourself
    without a situation.

NICODEMUS: That's a little bit too free for me. I'll bite me tongue.

JANE: We must stand by Lord Edgar. I'm afraid he'll be needing us now more than ever.

NICODEMUS: Why now more than ever? I'd say the worst was over. He's finally accepted the fact that Miss Irma's in her grave.

JANE: Don't talk like that. I can't bear the thought of her in a grave. She was always so afraid of the dark.

NICODEMUS: He's accepted it and you must too. Life has begun again for him. He mourned a more than respectable length of time and now he's brought home a new Lady Hillcrest.

JANE: That's just it. That's just the very thing! I don't think Lady Enid will ever make a fit mistress for Mandacrest.

NICODEMUS: And why not?

JANE: She's so, so . . . common. She'll never live up to the high standard set by Lady Irma.

NICODEMUS: That, my girl, is not for you or me to decide.

JANE: I can't stand the thought of taking orders from that vulgarian.

NICODEMUS: Come come, I won't have you talking that way about Lady Enid.

JANE: Lady Irma had a commanding presence and her manners were impeccable.

NICODEMUS: It takes more to please a man than fancy manners.

JANE: I would think a man—a *real* man—would find nothing more pleasing than fine breeding and savoir fair.

NICODEMUS: If that French means what I think it does you'd better wash your mouth out with soap. Here's eggs and milk. The turtle was laying rather well today.

JANE: And where's the cream?

NICODEMUS: I skimmed it.

JANE: Again? Ah, you're incorrigible.

NICODEMUS: In what?

JANE: Now what will I tell Lord Edgar when he wants cream for his tea, huh?

NICODEMUS: Tell him what you like.

(Lightning and a clap of thunder.)

JANE: *(Shrieks)* Ahhh!

NICODEMUS: There there. Don't be skeered. Nicodemus is here to protect you. *(Tries to put his arm around her)*

JANE: *(Eluding his embrace)* Keep your hands to yourself. You smell like a stable.

NICODEMUS: If you slept in a stable you'd smell like one too.

JANE: Keep your distance.

NICODEMUS: Someday, Janey my girl, you're going to smile on me.

JANE: Yeah, when hell freezes over and little devils go ice-skating.

NICODEMUS: If I was cleaned up and had a new white collar and smelled of bay rum and Florida water you'd think different.

JANE: Don't you get any ideas about me. You are beneath me and beneath me you're going to stay.

NICODEMUS: Someday you might want to get beneath me.

JANE: UGH! How dare you speak to me in such manner? I've had education.

NICODEMUS: What education have you ever had?

JANE: I've read Bunyan's *Pilgrim's Progress* from cover to cover, the Holy Bible, the almanac, and several back issues of *Godey's Lady's Book*.

NICODEMUS: Well I've read the *Swineherd's Manual* from kiver to kiver.

JANE: *(Contemptuously)* Hurmph!

NICODEMUS: You got no reason to look down your nose at me, miss. We're cut from the same bolt o' goods.

JANE: Don't go giving yourself airs. Go on back to your pigsty before I say something I'll be sorry for.

NICODEMUS: I'm not leaving until you give me a kiss.

JANE: I'll see you hanged first.

NICODEMUS: *(Chasing her around the room)* Give me a little kiss and then I'll show you how I'm hung.

JANE: Get away from me you beast with your double entendres.

NICODEMUS: Double what?

(Thunder, footsteps above.)

JANE: Now you've done it. You've waked Lady Enid. Go quick before she sees you in the house.

NICODEMUS: What's she gettin' up now for? It's just about evening.

JANE: That's her way. She sleeps all day and she's up all night.

NICODEMUS: It's them city ways of hers. Lord Edgar told me she'd been on the stage.

JANE: *(Shocked)* The stage! Ugh! How disgusting!

NICODEMUS: To think, a real live actress here at Mandacrest!

JANE: Yes, it's utterly degrading. But she is the mistress of the house now and we must adjust to her ways.

NICODEMUS: That's not what I meant. I think Lord Edgar has really done well for himself.

JANE: You men are all alike. You're so easily taken in. *(Footsteps)* I hear her footsteps. Go!

NICODEMUS: But I want to get a look at her.

JANE: She's just an ordinary woman and she doesn't need you gawking at her. Go on back to your pigsty.

NICODEMUS: I found better company there than ever I found at Mandacrest. *(Exits)*

LADY ENID'S VOICE: *(Off)* Jane, were you talking to someone?

JANE: Just Nicodemus. He came to bring the eggs.

LADY ENID: *(Off)* Is he gone?

JANE: Yes, Lady Enid.

LADY ENID: Has the sun set?

JANE: It's pouring down rain, your ladyship. There's very little out there that could be called sun.

LADY ENID: Draw the draperies and light a fire. I'm coming down.

JANE: Ah Lord, my work is never done. *(Draws the draperies across the French door, cutting off the view of the garden. She takes a quick look at herself in the mirror; fans herself with her handkerchief; straightens her hair and collar.)*

LADY ENID: Ah, you've made the room warm and cheery. Thank you, Jane.

JANE: Can I fix you a nice cup of tea?

LADY ENID: If it's no trouble.

JANE: *(Sternly)* That's what I'm here for.

LADY ENID: Is Lord Edgar about?

JANE: He was up and out at the crack of dawn.

LADY ENID: Out? Out where?

JANE: He goes riding in the morning. It's a custom with him. *(Teakettle whistles off)* Ah, there's the kettle calling. *(Exits)*

(LADY ENID looks about the room and examines the paintings and books. She looks out the French doors into the garden and out to the moors beyond. Then the portrait over the mantel catches her attention. She stands before it and stares at it a long time.)

JANE: *(Returning with the tea things)* How do you take it?
LADY ENID: I beg your pardon?
JANE: Your tea, miss.
LADY ENID: Plain.
JANE: *(Incredulous)* No cream or sugar?
LADY ENID: No, quite plain.
JANE: That's queer.
LADY ENID: Queer?
JANE: Tea ain't much without cream and sugar.
LADY ENID: I'm on an eternal diet. The stage you know.
JANE: But that's all behind you now.
LADY ENID: *(With a sigh)* Yes, I suppose it is. But the habit's ingrained. I shall probably refuse bread and potatoes 'til I die. *(Indicating the portrait)* Who is that woman?
JANE: Why, that's Lady Hillcrest. . . . I mean, that's the last Lady Hillcrest.
LADY ENID: She was very beautiful, wasn't she?
JANE: There will never be another woman who's her equal—oh, I beg your pardon, miss.
LADY ENID: That's all right, Jane. You were very fond of her, weren't you?
JANE: *(Bringing her a cup of tea)* She was like a part of meself, miss.
LADY ENID: I see. *(Sits and sips tea. Sharp reaction to the tea)* You do make strong tea, don't you?
JANE: *(Indignant)* When I makes tea I makes tea. And when I makes water I makes water.
LADY ENID: God send you don't make them in one pot.
JANE: *(Beat. Then realizing that a joke was made at her expense)* Hurmph!
LADY ENID: You don't like me, do you, Jane?
JANE: I don't hate you.
LADY ENID: I should hope not! That would be a terrible thing, wouldn't it? If you hated me and we had to live here together.
JANE: Yes, I suppose it would. I said I don't hate you.
LADY ENID: You don't hate me. But you don't like me.
JANE: I'm not used to you. You'll take getting used to.
LADY ENID: *(Shivers)* I felt a chill. A cat walked over my grave.
JANE: Isn't there a draft there, where you're sitting, Lady Enid?
LADY ENID: Yes, there is a little. Perhaps you'd better close the French doors.
JANE: Did Nicodemus leave them open again? If I've told him once I've told him a thousand times . . . Why, isn't that the master coming over there?
LADY ENID: *(Quickly)* Where? *(Gets up)* Yes, it's he. *(Hiding behind the curtain)* Stand back! Don't let him see us.
JANE: What's that he's carrying? Arms full of heather and he's dragging something behind.
LADY ENID: Dragging something?
JANE: It looks like a big animal. Why, I believe he's killed the wolf.
LADY ENID: *(Nervously)* Wolf?

JANE: The wolf that's been killing our lambs. Well we'll all sleep better too without that devil howling all night.

LADY ENID: He killed a wolf?

JANE: Yes, and he's brought the carcass back with him.

LADY ENID: Is it dead? Is it really dead?

JANE: It's dead and it won't get any deader.

LADY ENID: Which way is he coming?

JANE: He's taking the path by the pyracanthas.

LADY ENID: He's done that before. But will he take the footbridge?

JANE: That's just what I was asking meself. He's getting closer—no he's turned off—he's going the long way 'round and through the ivy arches.

LADY ENID: Then he's still not over it.

JANE: Ah, you can't blame him for not taking the footbridge after what happened there.

LADY ENID: They cling to their dead a long time at Mandacrest.

JANE: Nay, I think it's the dead that cling to us. It's as if they just don't want to let go. Like they can't bear to leave us behind. *(Comes back to herself abruptly)* The master will be wanting his dinner. *(Turning at the door)* How do you like your meat, miss?

LADY ENID: Well done.

JANE: No red meat?

LADY ENID: Not for me.

JANE: See, there's another difference. Miss Irma liked it bloody. *(Exits)*

LADY ENID: *(Turns sharply and looks at the portrait)* Don't look at me like that. I didn't take him away from you, you know. Someone was apt to take your place sooner or later. It happened to be me. I know how you must feel seeing us so happy under your very nose. But there's nothing to be done about it, old girl. Life must go on.

LORD EDGAR: *(Enters with arms full of heather, dragging wolf carcass as described)* Rough weather.

LADY ENID: *(Rushing to EDGAR and planting a kiss on his lips)* Edgar, darling, you're back.

LORD EDGAR: Please, Enid, not in front of . . .

LADY ENID: In front of who? There's no one looking. *(Pauses)* Unless you mean her. *(Points to the painting)*

LORD EDGAR: It does seem a bit odd. I mean kissing right in front of her.

LADY ENID: She looks vaguely sinister.

LORD EDGAR: Please, Enid. She's dead.

LADY ENID: Perhaps that's the reason.

LORD EDGAR: Let's don't talk about her.

LADY ENID: Yes, let's don't.

LORD EDGAR: Are you quite comfortable?

LADY ENID: Yes, quite. Jane doesn't like me but I think I'll win her over.

LORD EDGAR: I hope you'll like it here.

LADY ENID: I'm sure I will. Oh, Edgar, Edgar.

LORD EDGAR: Oh, Enid, Enid.

LADY ENID: Oh Wedgar, Wedgar, Wedgar.

LORD EDGAR: Oh Wenid, Wenid, Wenid.

LADY ENID: *(With a qualm)* Edgar.

LORD EDGAR: *(Slightly reprimanding)* Enid.

LADY ENID: *(Reassured)* Edgar.

LORD EDGAR: *(Condescendingly)* Enid.

LADY ENID: *(Snuggling his chest, with a sigh)* Edgar Edgar Edgar.

LORD EDGAR: *(Comforting and comfortable)* Enid Enid Enid.

LADY ENID: *(Passionately)* Edgar!

LORD EDGAR: *(Aroused)* Enid!

LADY ENID: *(More passionately)* Edgar!

LORD EDGAR: *(More passionately)* Enid!

LADY ENID: *(Rapturously)* Edgar!

LORD EDGAR: *(Likewise)* Enid!

LADY ENID: *(Climatically)* Edgar!!

LORD EDGAR: *(Orgasmically)* Enid!!

LADY ENID: *(Cooing)* Edgar.

LORD EDGAR: *(Drowsily)* Enid.

LADY ENID: Edgar?

LORD EDGAR: Enid.

LADY ENID: Take the painting down.

LORD EDGAR: I couldn't do that.

LADY ENID: Why not?

LORD EDGAR: I just couldn't.

LADY ENID: She's been dead three years.

LORD EDGAR: Yes, I know, but . . .

LADY ENID: Let's make a fresh start. Forget about the past.

LORD EDGAR: I want to, Enid, believe me, I do.

LADY ENID: We'll never feel comfortable with her watching every move we make.

LORD EDGAR: No, I suppose not.

LADY ENID: Then why not put her things away in a chest somewhere or make a little shrine where you can visit her once in a while? But not our home.

LORD EDGAR: You're right of course. I know you are. It's just that . . .

LADY ENID: What?

LORD EDGAR: She made me promise that I would always keep a flame burning before her picture.

LADY ENID: What nonsense.

LORD EDGAR: I tell you she made me promise.

LADY ENID: Blow it out.

LORD EDGAR: I couldn't break my word.

LADY ENID: I thought you belonged to me now. That we belonged to each other.

LORD EDGAR: We do, but that was before we met.

LADY ENID: Which means more to you? Your love for me or your promise to her?

LORD EDGAR: Enid, please. Don't put it that way.

LADY ENID: Which is it, Edgar? Which will it be?

LORD EDGAR: Please don't make me choose.

LADY ENID: Do you love me?

LORD EDGAR: How can you doubt it?

LADY ENID: Then the choice is already made. Blow it out!

LORD EDGAR: Dare I? *(Blows out the candle)*

LADY ENID: You see, nothing happened.

LORD EDGAR: Weird that we thought it would.

(They laugh.)

LADY ENID: And now, darling, as to this matter of dragging dead animals into the drawing room—it's really got to stop.

LORD EDGAR: I say, you're really out to reform me, aren't you?

LADY ENID: Just a little.

LORD EDGAR: I'll have Nicodemus tend to it. Why don't you change for dinner?

LADY ENID: Good. I'm famished.

LORD EDGAR: Don't be long.

LADY ENID: I won't, I promise. *(Exits)*

LORD EDGAR: *(Goes to the painting)* Forgive me, Irma, please. Please forgive me!

(Enter NICODEMUS.*)*

NICODEMUS: Where is the new lady?

LORD EDGAR: Changing. You know how slow women are.

NICODEMUS: So you've finally killed the beast, eh, Master Edgar.

LORD EDGAR: Yes, I've killed it. It will rage no more.

NICODEMUS: But what about the beast within? Is that through with raging?

LORD EDGAR: It's resting peacefully at the moment. That's about the most we can expect, don't you think?

NICODEMUS: You're a man of will, you are, Edgar Hillcrest.

LORD EDGAR: Nicodemus, take the guts out and burn it.

NICODEMUS: Don't you want to save the skin?

LORD EDGAR: No, burn every hide and hair of it.

NICODEMUS: And the ashes? What should I do with them?

LORD EDGAR: Scatter them on the heath.

NICODEMUS: And let the wind take up its howling?

LORD EDGAR: Then throw them in the mill run.

NICODEMUS: After her?

LORD EDGAR: Yes, after her. And Nicodemus . . .

NICODEMUS: Yes, Master Edgar?

LORD EDGAR: Take down the painting.

NICODEMUS: And what do you want me to do with it?

LORD EDGAR: Burn it with the wolf. *(Exits)*

*(*UNDERWOOD *goes toward the mantel and tries to take down the painting. Enter* JANE.*)*

JANE: And what do you think you're doing?

NICODEMUS: The master wants the painting down.

JANE: You can't do that. You can't take Lady Irma!

NICODEMUS: I can and I will. It's the master's orders.

JANE: Stop it! Stop it! Don't touch that picture. Ahgh! The sanctuary light's gone out. Oh God, this will never do.

NICODEMUS: Don't blame me. It was out when I came in. Lord Edgar must have extinguished it.

JANE: *(Indicating the carcass)* And what's this here?

NICODEMUS: You've got eyes in your head to see with. It's the wolf. He's killed the wolf.

JANE: Glory be! Is it possible?

NICODEMUS: It's cause for rejoicing.

JANE: *(Approaching the carcass warily)* It's no rejoicing there'll be this night, Nicodemus Underwood. He's killed the wrong wolf.

(Blackout.)

Scene 2

(The scene is as before. It is late evening. The household is asleep. Jane is stoking the last embers of the fire. Lady Enid enters silently in her dressing gown. She stands over Jane, whose back is to her, and watches. Jane suddenly becomes aware of her presence and, frightened, gasps. This in turn frightens Lady Enid, who gasps also.)

LADY ENID: I didn't mean to frighten you.

JANE: I didn't mean to frighten you either. You shouldn't creep up on a person like that.

LADY ENID: I'm sorry, Jane. You have lived here a considerable time. Did you not say sixteen years?

JANE: Eighteen, miss. I came when the mistress was married, to wait on her; after she died, the master retained me as his housekeeper. Though I knew him from childhood. I was raised at the Frambly Parsonage.

LADY ENID: Indeed.

(Long silence between them.)

JANE: Ah, times have greatly changed since then!

LADY ENID: Yes, you've seen a good many alterations, I suppose?

JANE: I have: and troubles too.

LADY ENID: The Hillcrests are a very old family, aren't they?

JANE: Oh, Lord, yes. Why the Hillcrests go back to . . . back to . . . well, I don't know exactly who. But they've been descending for centuries.

LADY ENID: Lord Edgar told me he was an only child.

JANE: Yes, a strange flower upon the old solid wood of the family tree.

LADY ENID: Was he always so fond of hunting, even as a child?

JANE: Nay, he only took that up after the mistress passed away. Oh, but that's a long story. I won't be after boring you with it.

LADY ENID: Oh, do go on, Jane. Everything about Lord Edgar fascinates me.

JANE: Where is himself?

LADY ENID: Sleeping soundly. Jane, it will be an act of charity to tell me something of the family history. I know I shall not be able to rest if I go to bed, so be good enough to sit and chat for an hour.

JANE: Oh, certainly, miss! I'll just fetch a little sewing and then I'll sit as long as you please. Listen to that wind! It's an ungodly night. Can I get you a hot toddy to drive out the cold?

LADY ENID: If you're having one.

JANE: Sure I loves me toddy and me toddy loves me.

(She crosses to the table, gets her sewing, and pours out two toddies from a pan she has nestled among the embers. She gives one drink to LADY ENID and settles into the chair opposite her before the fire.
    Howling sound.)

LADY ENID: That wind!

JANE: That's not the wind. That's a wolf howling.

LADY ENID: It seems you've been troubled by wolves of late.

JANE: Not wolves. It's one wolf in particular. Victor.

LADY ENID: Victor?

JANE: He was captured as a pup and tamed. But his heart was savage. Miss Irma kept him as a pet.

LADY ENID: Like a dog.

JANE: He was bigger than a dog, so big the boy used to ride about on his back. Though Victor didn't like that much, I can tell you. Though he bore it for the mistress's sake, for it was to her he belonged. His happiest hours were spent stretched out at Miss Irma's feet, his huge purple tongue lolling out of his mouth. He never left her side the whole time she was carrying. Lord Edgar locked him out when it came time for her to deliver. And when he heard her labor pains, he howled.

LADY ENID: Lord Edgar told me that he'd had a son but that he died when he was still a child.

JANE: Ah, there's a tragic story, miss. But your toddy's gettin' cold. Finish that and I'll fix you another.

LADY ENID: (Drains her cup and passes it to JANE) He was taken off with chicken pox, wasn't he?

JANE: Chicken pox? Now who told you that?

LADY ENID: No one told me. I was just supposing.

JANE: If Lord Edgar told you it was chicken pox, then chicken pox it was. We'd better leave it at chicken pox.

LADY ENID: No, really, he didn't tell me anything. The chicken pox was pure conjecture.

JANE: It's understandable that he didn't go into it. It's not an easy subject to talk about. Here's your toddy.

LADY ENID: Thanks.

JANE: And here's one for me.

LADY ENID: I'd like to know the true history, if you don't mind relating it.

JANE: (The toddy loosening her tongue) One clear winter day Victor and the boy went out to the heath to play in the new-fallen snow. The wolf came back without the boy. We waited. We watched. We called ourselves hoarse. And at dusk we found him in the mill run, dead. His throat had been torn apart.

LADY ENID: Horrible.

JANE: Lord Edgar wanted Victor destroyed. But Lady Irma fought against it. She said it wasn't Vic had done it.

LADY ENID: Perhaps it wasn't.

JANE: His throat was torn. What else could it have been? They fought bitterly over it. He said she loved the wolf more than her own child. But I think it was the double loss she dreaded, for when Victor was gone she'd have nothing, you see. When the master came to shoot Victor, Lady Irma turned him loose upon the heath and drove him away with stones, crying, "Run, Vic, run, and never come back!" I don't think the poor beast understood what happened because he still comes back to this day, looking for Lady Irma.

LADY ENID: Poor Victor. Poor boy. Poor Irma.

JANE: Poor Lord Edgar.

LADY ENID: Yes, poor poor Lord Edgar!

JANE: But here's the strangest part of all.

LADY ENID: Yes?

JANE: The fresh snow is like a map. I traced their tracks meself. Victor's trail turned off. The boy was killed by a wolf that left human tracks in the snow.

LADY ENID: Human? You mean the boy was murdered?

JANE: But that takes us to the subject of werewolves.

LADY ENID: Werewolves?

JANE: Humans who take the form of a wolf at night.

LADY ENID: But that's just superstition.

JANE: Yes, superstition, the realm beyond the explainable where science is powerless. Of course everything pointed to Victor. The boy fell down and skinned his knee. He let the loving beast lick his wound. He tasted blood. The killer was aroused. He turned on the child and sank his fangs into its tender neck. A perfectly logical explanation. But then there were those tracks in the snow. Wouldn't it be convenient for a werewolf to have a real wolf to blame it on?

LADY ENID: Didn't you show them to anyone? The tracks, I mean.

JANE: Ah, they wouldn't listen. They said they were my tracks. That I'd made them meself. I didn't push it, miss, or they'd have packed me off to Dottyville. It's hard to convince people of the supernatural. Most people have enough trouble believing in the natural.

LADY ENID: Of course you're right. But those footprints.

JANE: I wish I had 'em here as evidence. But where are the snows of yesteryear? And that's the werewolf's greatest alibi—people don't believe in him. Well miss, I must be gettin' meself to bed. My rheumatism is starting to act up again.

LADY ENID: Leave the light, Jane. I think I'll stay up and read a while.

JANE: Here's a good book for you. It's the master's treatise on ancient Egyptian mythology.

LADY ENID: Thanks!

JANE: Don't stay up too late now. We're having kippers and kidneys for breakfast and I know you wouldn't want to miss that.

LADY ENID: Jane, what was the boy's name?

JANE: Didn't you know? That was Victor too. Good night, Lady Enid. *(Exits)*

LADY ENID: *(Sits in chair with her back to the glass doors and reads. The shadow of the stranger can be seen through the sheer organdy curtains illuminated intermittently by flashes of lightning. A bony, almost skeletal hand feels for a latch. It drums its fingernails against the windowpane.)* What—what was it? Real or a delusion? Oh God, what was it? *(Suddenly a single pane of the French door shatters. The bony hand reaches in through the curtains and opens the latch. A gaunt figure enters the room slowly. A ray of light strikes the pallid face. He fixes her with a stare)* Who are you? What do you want? *(The clock chimes one. The* INTRUDER *emits a hissing sound)* What do you want? Oh God, what do you want of me?

(She tries to run to the door but the INTRUDER *catches her by her long hair and, winding it around his bony fingers, drags her back toward the mantel. She takes roses from the vase and presses their thorns into his eyes. The* INTRUDER *groans and releases her. She runs across the room. He follows her. She stabs him with scissors from Jane's sewing basket.* INTRUDER *staggers back and falls through open door down right.* LADY ENID *crosses to the mantel and tries to get control of herself. She sighs with relief.* INTRUDER *reenters and clapping his hand over her mouth drags her to the door, locks it, then crosses up center to the double doors where shriek follows strangled shriek as he seizes her neck in his fanglike teeth and a hideous sucking noise follows.* LADY ENID

emits a high-pitched scream made at the back of the throat by drawing the breath in. Running footsteps are heard off.)

LORD EDGAR: *(Off right)* Did you hear a scream, Jane?

JANE: *(Off right)* I did. Where was it?

LORD EDGAR: *(Off)* God knows. It sounded so near yet far away. I got up and got dressed as soon as I heard it.

JANE: *(Off. No pause)* All is still now.

LORD EDGAR: *(Off)* Yes, but unless I was dreaming there was a scream.

JANE: We couldn't both have dreamed it.

LORD EDGAR: Where's Lady Enid?

JANE: Isn't she with you?

(LADY ENID emits another high-pitched scream.)

LORD EDGAR: There it is again. Search the house! Search the house. Where did it come from? Can you tell? *(LADY ENID screams again as before)* Good God! There it is again! *(He tries the door stage right. But it will not open)* Enid! Enid! Are you in there? Speak for heaven's sake! Speak! Good God, we must force the door. *(They beat on the door)* Get the crowbar.

JANE: Where is it?

LORD EDGAR: In the cellar. Hurry! Hurry! Run! Run! Enid! Oh Enid!

JANE: Here it is.

(Edgar forces the door open and bursts into the room.)

NICODEMUS: *(Voice off, up center)* Lady Enid! Lady Enid! Oh God no! Lady Enid! *(NICODEMUS enters carrying the limp body of LADY ENID. Her long hair hangs down covering her face. There are several drops of blood on her nightgown)* Help oh help oh heaven oh help! *(He carries her body out the door stage right)* Now where the blue hell am I bringing her, beyond the veil?

LORD EDGAR: *(Following them)* What is it? What's happened? Who's done this thing to you?

NICODEMUS: *(Reentering)* Who or what? I saw something moving in the heath.

LORD EDGAR: Something? What kind of something?

NICODEMUS: Dog's skull. Dog's body. Its glazing eyes staring out of death candle to shake and bend my soul. *(Suddenly something with a horrible face appears at the window. It lets out a frightening earsplitting sound and then laughing bangs against the windowpanes. NICODEMUS growls in a hoarsened raspy voice)* There! There it is.

(The thing emits a shrill laugh like the sound of electronic feedback.)

LORD EDGAR: Lord help us!

NICODEMUS: Be it whatever thing it may—I'll follow it!

LORD EDGAR: No! No! Do not!

NICODEMUS: I must! I will!

LORD EDGAR: Not without a gun! Don't be a fool!

NICODEMUS: Let whoever will come with me—I'll follow this dread form! *(Exits)*

LORD EDGAR: Wait for me you fool! *(Takes a gun from off the wall)*

NICODEMUS: *(Voice off)* I see it! I see it! It goes down the wall and through the wisterias.

LORD EDGAR: It's dark down there. There isn't any moon. *(There are animal sounds, the sounds of a struggle, and then a few agonized cries. The doors fly open and a human leg, one that had formerly belonged to* NICODEMUS, *is thrown in)* Great Scott! *(He rushes out. And is heard calling off)* Which way? Which way?

NICODEMUS: *(Voice off)* Over here. Help! Oh help me!

(There is the sound of shots off.)

JANE: *(Sticking her head in through the door stage right)* Was them shots I heard?

LADY ENID: *(Off)* Jane. Jane.

JANE: Yes Lady Enid.

LADY ENID: Come. I need you. I'm afraid to be alone.

JANE: I'll come and I'll bring the ghost candle to light your agony. It's the curse of the Druids, that's what it is. The druidy Druids. *(Withdraws)*

(Footsteps and the sound of something dragging.)

NICODEMUS: *(Entering up center)* I saw it. I touched it. I struggled with it. It was cold and clammy like a corpse. It can't be human.

LORD EDGAR: *(Entering under* NICODEMUS*'s arm)* Not human? No, of course not human. You said it was a dog.

NICODEMUS: Then it looked like a wolf, then it looked like a woman! It tore off me leg and started chewing on it.

LORD EDGAR: Great Scott! It can't be.

NICODEMUS: If it hadn't been wood I swear it would have eaten it.

LORD EDGAR: No!

NICODEMUS: Yes! Yes! Ghoul! Chewer of corpses! And all the while it made this disgusting sucking sound. It sucked the very marrow from me bones. I can feel it now. It's very near. Bride bed. Child bed. Bed of death! She comes, pale vampire, through storm her eyes, her bat sails bloodying the sea! Mouth to her mouth's kiss! Her eyes on me to strike me down. I felt the green fairy's fang.

(Howling off.)

LORD EDGAR: What was that?

NICODEMUS: Just a wolf.

LORD EDGAR: No! It's Victor! Victor come back to haunt me! *(Starts out)* Give me that pistol there. This time I'll get him! *(Fur at the door)* Look! There it is now! It won't escape this time.

NICODEMUS: *(Clinging to his leg)* No! Master, do not go! There is no help for it!

(Keening lament is heard on the wind.)

LORD EDGAR: Let go of my leg. Goblin damned, I'll send your soul to hell! *(Exits)*

NICODEMUS: No! Master! Master! It's Irma, Irma Vep! A ghost woman with ashes on her breath, alone, crying in the rain.

(Shots, running footsteps, and howling heard off.)

JANE: *(Rushing in)* What's all this yelling? You'll wake the dead.

NICODEMUS: The master's at it again—hunting.

JANE: Is it wolves again?

NICODEMUS: This time he's sure its Victor.

JANE: Victor?

NICODEMUS: That's what he says!

JANE: Well, don't just stand there gawking! Go after him! Be some help!

NICODEMUS: Oh no. Not me! There's something on that heath that would make your blood run cold.

JANE: Ah, you big sissy. If you don't go to his aid I'll go meself.

NICODEMUS: Oh, very well, woman. Wait until I screw in me leg. *(He goes off, screws it in noisily, returns)*

JANE: It seems that more than your leg got bitten off. There's also been a loss of virility. *(She takes a gun down off the wall)*

NICODEMUS: Now don't go playing with firearms, miss. That's a man's tool you've got in your hands. *(They struggle for the gun)*

JANE: Let go! Let go! Get out of my way. Lord Edgar needs me.

(The gun goes off and the bullet hits the painting. The painting bleeds.)

NICODEMUS: Now see what you've done. You've shot Lady Irma. The painting is bleeding! *(Wrests the gun from her grasp and exits in the same direction as Lord Edgar)* Lord Edgar!

JANE: *(Calling after him)* Down past the mill run and out onto the moors. The other way, Nicodemus! The other way! Take the shortcut through the cedar grove. Faster. Faster, Nicodemus! Faster!

LADY ENID: *(Enters slowly)* Where is Lord Edgar?

JANE: He's searching the moors. He thinks he's seen Victor.

LADY ENID: The wolf or the boy?

JANE: Both.

(Blackout.)

Scene 3

LORD EDGAR: Can you tell me how it happened, Enid dearest?

LADY ENID: Jane and I sat up late, she regaling me with tales of Mandacrest, its history, legends, and such. As the hour grew late I prepared myself for bed as is my wont. When I had completed my beauty ritual I went straight to our bedchamber and discovered that you had fallen asleep over a book. I crawled in beside you. But unable to sleep myself got up again and came downstairs. As there were some embers of the fire still aglow, I instructed Jane to leave the light when she went to bed, which she did. Then I sat in that chair and began reading your treatise on lycanthropy and the dynasties of Egypt. There was a light rain, as you will recall. Then it turned to hail. And as I read I listened to the patter of the hailstones on the windowpanes. It was during that chapter on how the priests of Egypt perfected the art of mummification to the point that the Princess Pev Amri was preserved in a state of suspended animation and was known as She Who Sleeps . . .

LORD EDGAR: . . . but Will One Day Wake.

LADY ENID: Yes, that's it! She Who Sleeps but Will One Day Wake. And how her tomb was guarded by Anubis the jackal-headed god. But that her tomb has never been found.

LORD EDGAR: That is what is generally believed.

LADY ENID: Then suddenly the pattering at the window caught my attention, for the hail had stopped but the pattering went on. The glass shattered. I turned. It was in the room. I think I screamed. But I couldn't run away! I couldn't run away! It caught me by the hair and then . . . I can tell no more! I can tell no more!

LORD EDGAR: You seem to have hurt your neck. There is a wound there.

LADY ENID: Wound?!! I feel so weak. I feel so faint. As though I had almost bled to death.

LORD EDGAR: But you couldn't have bled very much. There were no more than five little drops of blood on your dressing gown. Now, you'd better get some sleep.

LADY ENID: No sleep! No sleep for me! I shall never sleep again! Sleep is dead. Sleep is dead. She hath murthered sleep. I dare not be alone to sleep. Don't leave me alone. Don't ever leave me alone again. For sleep is dead. Sleep is dead. *(Off)* Who murthered sleep?

LORD EDGAR: Jane will sit with you. *(Leans out the door and speaks to* JANE *off)* Take care of her Jane.

JANE: *(Voice off)* There there, Lady Enid. Easy does it. Here we go.

LORD EDGAR: Good girl, Jane.

(Enter NICODEMUS *up center.)*

NICODEMUS: Is Lady Enid alive?

LORD EDGAR: She is weak and will sleep long. *(Sighs)*

NICODEMUS: You sigh. . . . Some fearful thoughts, I fear, oppress your heart.

LORD EDGAR: Hush. Hush. She may overhear.

NICODEMUS: Lord Edgar, look at that portrait.

LORD EDGAR: Why, that's blood, isn't it?

NICODEMUS: You must muse upon it.

LORD EDGAR: No, no. I do wish, and yet I dread . . .

NICODEMUS: What?

LORD EDGAR: To say something to you all. But not here—not now—tomorrow.

NICODEMUS: The daylight is coming quickly on.

LORD EDGAR: I will sit up until sunrise. You can fetch my powder flask and bullets. And if you please, reload the pistols.

NICODEMUS: Lady Enid is all right, I presume.

LORD EDGAR: Yes, but her mind appears to be much disturbed.

NICODEMUS: From bodily weakness, I daresay.

LORD EDGAR: But why should she be bodily weak? She was strong and well but a few hours ago. The glow of youth and health was on her cheeks. Is it possible that she should become bodily weak in a single night? Nicodemus, sit down. You know that I am not a superstitious man.

NICODEMUS: You certainly are not.

LORD EDGAR: And yet I have never been so absolutely staggered as I am by the occurrences of this night.

NICODEMUS: Say on.

LORD EDGAR: I have a frightful, a hideous suspicion which I fear to mention to anyone lest it be laughed to scorn.

NICODEMUS: I am lost in wonder.

LORD EDGAR: Nicodemus, swear to me that you will never repeat to anyone the dreadful suggestion I am about to make.

NICODEMUS: I swear.

LORD EDGAR: Nicodemus, you have heard of the dreadful superstition which, in some countries, is extremely rife, wherein it is believed that there are beings who never die.

NICODEMUS: Never die?

LORD EDGAR: In a word you have heard of a . . . heard of a . . . oh God in heaven! I dread to pronounce the word, though I heard you speak it not three hours past. Dare I say? . . . Dare I say? . . .

NICODEMUS: Vampyre?

LORD EDGAR: You have said it. You have said it. Nosferatu. But swear to me once more that you will not repeat it to anyone.

NICODEMUS: Be assured I shall not. I am far from wishing to keep up in anyone's mind suspicions which I would fain, very fain refute.

LORD EDGAR: Then let me confide the worst of my fears, Nicodemus.

NICODEMUS: Speak it. Let me hear.

LORD EDGAR: I believe the vampire . . . is one of us.

NICODEMUS: (Uttering a groan of almost exquisite anguish) One of us? Oh God! Oh God! Do not too readily yield belief to so dreadful a supposition, I pray you.

LORD EDGAR: Nicodemus, within a fortnight I shall embark for Cairo. There I will organize an expedition to Geza and certain obscure Numidian ruins in the south.

NICODEMUS: Are you taking Lady Enid?

LORD EDGAR: No, I fear that in her delicate mental state the trip might be too much for her. I will arrange for her to rest in a private sanatorium. Look after Mandacrest until I return. I believe the desert holds some secret. I feel it calling to me. I believe I shall find some answer out there among its pyramids and sacred mummies. At least I know I shall be far away from her.

NICODEMUS: From Lady Enid?

LORD EDGAR: No, from Lady Irma. For Nicodemus, it is she I believe has extended her life by feasting on human gore.

NICODEMUS: Say not so!

LORD EDGAR: Irma could never accept the idea of death and decay. She was always seeking consolation in the study of spiritualism and reincarnation. After a while it became an obsession with her. Even on her deathbed she swore she would come back.

NICODEMUS: Do you think she will come again?

LORD EDGAR: I know not. But I almost hope she may. For I would fain speak to her.

NICODEMUS: It is said that if one burns a love letter from a lover who has died at the third crowing of the cock on Saint Swithin's Day, you will see the lover ever so briefly.

LORD EDGAR: More superstition.

NICODEMUS: Very like. Very like. Yet after the occurrences of this night I can scarcely distinguish truth from fancy. (Cock crows off) There's the cock. 'Twill soon be dawn. Damnéd spirits all, that in crossways and floods have burial, already to their wormy beds have gone, for fear lest day should look their shames upon.

LORD EDGAR: (Amazed) Nicodemus, you know your Shakespeare!

NICODEMUS: I paraphrase. (Exits)

(The cock crows again.)

LORD EDGAR: The second crowing of the cock. *(Takes out letters bound with a ribbon)* Irma's letters. Of course it's ridiculous . . . but what harm can it do? I'd best part with them anyway. *(Quotes)* "In all the world. In all the world. One thing I know to be true. You'd best be off with the old love before you're on with the new." *(Burns letter before painting. Cock crows. Painting flies out. A woman's face appears in the painting. She screams)* Irma!

(Curtain.)

ACT II

Scene 1: *Various places in Egypt.*

LORD EDGAR: Ah Egypt! It looks exactly as I pictured it! I have a presentiment that we shall find the tomb intact in the valley of Bîbân–el Mulûk.

ALCAZAR: Osiris hear you!

LORD EDGAR: This invocation is certainly permissible opposite the ancient Diospolis Magna. But we have failed so often. The treasure seekers have always been ahead of us.

ALCAZAR: In recent years our work has been made doubly difficult by the activities of certain political groups seeking to halt the flow of antiquities from out of the country. These armed bandits use this high moral purpose to seize any and all treasures. And this, after the excavators have spent a great deal of time and money to unearth them.

LORD EDGAR: If we can but find an untouched tomb that can yield up to us its treasures inviolate!

ALCAZAR: I can spare you the disappointments of places I know to be quite empty because the contents have been removed and sold for a good price long ago. I believe I can take you to a syrinx that has never been discovered by the miserable little jackals who take it into their heads to scratch among the tombs.

LORD EDGAR: The idea fascinates me. But to excavate an unopened tomb—not to mention the difficulties of locating one—would require manpower and organizational abilities almost equal to those the Pharaohs employed to seal it.

ALCAZAR: I can place at your disposal a hundred intrepid fellahs, who, incited by baksheesh and a whip of hippopotamus hide, would dig down into the bowels of the earth with their fingernails. We might tempt them to bring to light some buried sphinx, to clear away the obstructions before a temple, to open a tomb . . .

LORD EDGAR: *(Smiles dubiously)* Hmmm.

ALCAZAR: I perceive that you are not a mere tourist and that commonplace curiosities would have no charm for you. So I shall show you a tomb that has escaped the treasure seekers. Long it has lain unknown to any but myself. It is a prize I have guarded for one who should prove worthy of it.

LORD EDGAR: And for which you will make me pay a round sum.

ALCAZAR: I will not deny that I hope to make money. I unearth pharaohs and sell them to people. Pharaohs are getting scarce these days. The article is in demand but it is no longer manufactured.

LORD EDGAR: Let's not beat about the bush. How much do you want?

ALCAZAR: For a tomb that no human hand has disturbed since the priests rolled the rocks before the entrance three thousand years ago, would it be too much to ask a thousand guineas?

LORD EDGAR: A thousand guineas!

ALCAZAR: A mere nothing. After all, the tomb may contain gold in the lump, necklaces of pearls and diamonds, earrings of carbuncle formed from the urine of lynxes, sapphire seals, ancient idols of precious metals; why, the currency of the time, that by itself would bring a good price.

LORD EDGAR: *(Aside)* Artful scoundrel! He knows perfectly well that such things are not to be found in Egyptian sepulchers.

ALCAZAR: Well, my lord, does the bargain suit you?

LORD EDGAR: Yes, we will call it a thousand guineas. If the tomb has never been touched and nothing—not even a stone—has been disturbed by the levers of the excavators, and on condition that we can carry everything away.

ALCAZAR: I accept. You can risk the banknotes and gold without fear. It seems your prayer has been answered.

LORD EDGAR: Perhaps we are rejoicing too soon and are about to experience the same disappointments encountered by Belzoni when he believed he was the first to enter the tomb of Menepha Seti. He, after having passed through a maze of corridors, pits, and chambers, found only an empty sarcophagus with a broken lid, for the treasure seekers had attained the royal tomb by mining through the rocks from the other direction.

ALCAZAR: Oh no! This tomb is too far removed for those accursed moles to have found their way there. I have lived many years in the valley of the kings and my eyes have become as piercing as those of the sacred hawks perched on the entablatures of the temples. For years I have not so much as dared to cast a glance in that direction, fearing to arouse the suspicions of the violators of the tombs. This way, my lord.

(They exit. The lights fade and come up somewhere in the tomb. It is very dark. From time to time some detail emerges from the darkness in the light of their lanterns.)

LORD EDGAR: The deuce! Are we going down to the center of the earth? The heat increases to such a degree that we cannot be far from the infernal regions.

ALCAZAR: It is a pit, milord. What's to be done?

LORD EDGAR: We must lower ourselves on ropes. *(Echo)* These cursed Egyptians were so cunning about hiding the entrances of their burial burrows. They could not think of enough ways to puzzle poor people. One can imagine them laughing beforehand at the downcast faces of the excavators.

ALCAZAR: Another dead end.

LORD EDGAR: It looks like they've beaten us this round. Rap on the floor and listen for a hollow sound. *(They do so. After much rapping the wall gives back a hollow sound)* Help me to remove this block. It's a bit low. We'll have to crawl on our faces.

ALCAZAR: Oy! *(They do so)* Look there, milord.

LORD EDGAR: The familiar personages of the psychostasia with Osiris as judge. *(Stands)* Well well, my dear Alcazar. So far you have kept your part of the bargain. We are indeed the first human beings who have entered here since the dead, whoever he may be, was abandoned to eternity and oblivion in the tomb.

ALCAZAR: Oh, he must have been a very powerful personage, a prince of the royal household at least.

LORD EDGAR: I will tell you after I decipher his cartouche.

ALCAZAR: But first let us enter the most beautiful room of all, the room the ancient Egyptians called the Golden Room.

LORD EDGAR: Really, I have some compunction of conscience about disturbing the last rest of this poor unknown mortal who felt so sure that he would rest in peace until the end of the world. Our visit will be a most unwelcome one to the host of this mansion.

ALCAZAR: You'll be wanting a proper introduction and I have lived long enough among the Pharaohs to make you one. I know how to present you to the illustrious inhabitant of this subterranean palace.

LORD EDGAR: Look, a five-toed footprint in the dust.

ALCAZAR: Footprint?

LORD EDGAR: It looks as though it were made yesterday.

ALCAZAR: How can that be?

LORD EDGAR: It must have been the last footprint made by the last slave leaving the burial chamber thirty-five hundred years ago. There has not been a breath of air in here to disturb it. Why, mighty civilizations have risen and fallen since this footprint was made. Their pomp, their power, their monuments of stone have not lasted as long as this insignificant footprint in the dust.

(Sarcophagus revealed.)

ALCAZAR: My lord! My lord! The sarcophagus is intact!

LORD EDGAR: Is it possible, my dear Alcazar—is it intact? *(Examines the sarcophagus then exclaims rapturously)* Incredible good fortune! Marvelous chance! Priceless treasure!

ALCAZAR: I asked too little. This my lord has robbed me.

LORD EDGAR: There there, Alcazar. A bargain is a bargain. Here are the vases that held the viscera of the mummy contained in the sarcophagus. Nothing has been touched in this palace of death since the day when the mummy, in its coffins and cerements, had been laid upon its couch of basalt.

ALCAZAR: Observe that these are not the usual funerary offerings.

LORD EDGAR: Don't touch it! Touch nothing! It might crumble. First I must decipher this cartouche. "She Who Sleeps but Will One Day Wake." A lotus sarcophagus. Hmmmm. Notice that the lotus motif recurs, as well as the ankh, emblem of eternal life. Must you smoke those nasty musk-scented cigarettes? There's little enough air in here as it is.

ALCAZAR: Shall we open the sarcophagus?

LORD EDGAR: Certainly. But take care not to injure the lid when opening it, for I want to remove this monument and make a present of it to the British Museum.

(They remove the cover.)

ALCAZAR: A woman! A woman!

LORD EDGAR: Astonishing novelty! The necropolis of the queens is situated farther off, in a gorge of the mountains. The tombs of the queens are very simple. Let me decipher the cartouche. "She Who Sleeps but Will One Day Wake."

ALCAZAR: *(Pointing to the butt)* This is a very primitive hieroglyph.

LORD EDGAR: It's a little behind.

ALCAZAR: It's almost more than I can believe.

LORD EDGAR: It's *altogether* more than *I* can believe.

ALCAZAR: What? You see these things before your very eyes and still you do not believe?

LORD EDGAR: The women of the East have always been considered inferior to the men, even after death. The greater part of these tombs, violated at very remote epochs, have served as receptacles for deformed mummies, rudely embalmed, that still exhibit traces of leprosy and elephantiasis. By what means, by what miracle of substitution, had this woman's coffin found its way into this royal sarcophagus, in the midst of this palatial crypt, worthy of the most illustrious and powerful of the Pharaohs? This unsettles all of my opinions and theories and contradicts the most reliable authorities on the subject of the Egyptian funeral rites so uniform in every respect for thousands of years.

ALCAZAR: We have no doubt alighted on some mystery, some obscure point lost to history. Had some ambitious woman usurped the tomb as she had the throne?

LORD EDGAR: What a charming custom. To bury a young woman with all the coquettish arsenal of her toilette about her. For there can be no doubt that it is a young woman enveloped in these bands of linen stained yellow with age and essences.

ALCAZAR: Compared with the ancient Egyptians we are veritable barbarians: dragging out a mere animal existence. We no longer have any delicacy of sentiment connected with death. What tenderness, what regret, what love are revealed in this devoted attention, this unlimited precaution, this vain solicitude that no one would ever witness, the affection lavished upon an insensible corpse, these efforts to snatch from destruction an adored form, and to present it to the soul intact upon the great day of the resurrection.

LORD EDGAR: Someday we may attain to such heights of civilization and refinement of feeling. In the meantime let us disrobe this young beauty, more than three thousand years old, with all the delicacy possible.

ALCAZAR: Poor lady, profane eyes are about to rest upon charms unknown to love itself, perhaps.

LORD EDGAR: Strange. I feel embarrassed at not having the proper costume in which to present myself before a royal mummy.

ALCAZAR: There is no time here. In this tomb, far away from the banal stupidities of the modern world, we might just as well be in ancient Egypt on the day this cherished being was entrusted to eternity.

(They unwrap the mummy's hand, which holds a scroll.)

LORD EDGAR: Extraordinary! In most cases mummification is accomplished by the use of bitumen and natron. Here, the body, prepared by a longer, safer, and more costly process, has preserved the elasticity of the skin, the grain of the epidermis, and a color that is almost natural. It has the fine hue of a new Florentine bronze and the warm amber tint of Titian.

ALCAZAR: By the knees of Amon Ra—behold—there is a scroll clasped in her hand!

LORD EDGAR: *(Gently unrolls the scroll)* Bring that electric torch here. "She Who Sleeps but Will One Day Wake." It is the same cartouche unmistakably. *(Reads on silently, then mutters)* Good god! It can't be! It can't be!

ALCAZAR: What does it say?

LORD EDGAR: *(Awed)* It is the formula to revive the princess. To return her to life once more.

ALCAZAR: But surely you don't . . .

LORD EDGAR: It's more than I can believe at the moment, Alcazar. But something inside me wants to believe. *(He reads more)* Well! This is simple enough. These caskets and bottles and bowls contain the ingredients in the formula. *(Reads)* The priest must wear certain vestments and douse the lid with wine. The wine in these bottles has dried up over the centuries. Oh drat! I have no wine. I am an abstainer.

ALCAZAR: *(Produces a bottle of wine from his pocket)* I have wine. Very good wine. And although it is a Madeira, of somewhat more recent vintage, I believe it may suffice. The wine may very well be the least important element in the formula.

LORD EDGAR: *(Reads)* It says here that the priest must be alone with the mummy when the soul is called back from the underworld.

ALCAZAR: Permit me to withdraw and leave you alone with your newfound lady friend. But before I go, may I make one request?

LORD EDGAR: Certainly, Alcazar, what is it?

ALCAZAR: Leave some wine for the return trip.

LORD EDGAR: I'll use only what is absolutely necessary to complete the ritual.

ALCAZAR: Thank you. *(Exits backwards making a salaam as he goes out)*

LORD EDGAR: *(Dresses himself in the costume of the Egyptian priest. Lights the charcoal braziers in the perfuming pans on either side of the sarcophagus. And intones the following invocation)* Katara katara katara rana! Ecbatana Ecbatana Soumouft! Soumouft! Fahata fahata Habebe! Oh Habebe! Oh Habebe! Habebe tay! *(He gently unwraps the mummy as the music swells)*

PEV AMRI: *(Flutters her eyelashes and opens her eyes)* Habebe? Habebe tay?

LORD EDGAR: *(Cries out)* Oh God!

PEV AMRI: *(Dances, then)* Fahouta bala bala mem fou ha ram sahadi Karnak!

LORD EDGAR: Oh exquisite! Exquisite beauty!

PEV AMRI: Han fu bazaar danbazaar.

LORD EDGAR: Forgive me divine one, but your spoken language is lost on me.

PEV AMRI: Mabrouka. Geza. *(Laughs, then looking into Sarcophagus and touching herself)* Ankh! Ankh!

LORD EDGAR: *(Exclaims)* Ankh! Life! Ankh! Life! Life!

PEV AMRI: Ankh . . . life?

LORD EDGAR: Ankh . . . life.

PEV AMRI: Life. Life!

LORD EDGAR: Life!

PEV AMRI: *(Writhing indicates stiffness of spine)* Cairo! Cairo! Practor! [*(If audience hisses)* Asp!]

LORD EDGAR: Those lips. Silent for three thousand years now beg to be kissed. But do I dare? *(Kisses her)*

PEV AMRI: *(She slaps him)* Puna kha fo ha na ba bhouna. *(Makes gesture that she is hungry)* Bhouna! Bhouna!

LORD EDGAR: Hungry? Of course you must be hungry after not having eaten in three millennia. I'll get you food. A loaf of bread, a jug of wine, a book of verse, and thou beside me in the wilderness and wilderness is paradise enow! *(Kisses her hand and runs out to get Alcazar)*

PEV AMRI: Amon! Amon Ra! Amenhotep. Memphis. Geza. Aswan. Hatshepshut. Toot 'n come in! *(Sniffs)* Sphinx! *(Scurries back into the mummy case, closes the door after her)*

LORD EDGAR: Alcazar! Alcazar! She's hungry! She wants food!

ALCAZAR: *(Off)* She wants? Surely you don't mean . . .

LORD EDGAR: Yes it's true! It's true! She's alive! She's alive. In flesh and blood.

ALCAZAR: My boy you have stayed too long in the tomb. Your mind is playing tricks on you.

LORD EDGAR: Come if you don't believe me. See for yourself. *(He rushes onto the stage.* ALCAZAR *follows behind somewhat slowly and dubiously. He is obviously totally unconvinced)* Where is she? She's gone. She was here a minute ago.

ALCAZAR: Akh—naten!

LORD EDGAR: I tell you she spoke! I kissed those divine lips. Look! She gave me this ring!

ALCAZAR: We must leave before dawn. If they find us looting the tomb they will report us to the authorities.

LORD EDGAR: But she's alive, I tell you, alive! *(Calling)* Princess! Princess, where are you? Where are you, Pev Amri? Pev!

ALCAZAR: *(Goes to the sarcophagus and opens it slowly)* Is this what you are looking for?

(Inside the sarcophagus stands a mummy as before, only this time the wrappings have been partially removed revealing a hideously decomposed face through the dried flesh of which the skull protrudes.)

LORD EDGAR: *(Screams)* No! It can't be! It can't be! Pev. Pev. I should never have summoned you, Alcazar. It broke the spell and sent her back to the underworld.

ALCAZAR: The hour grows late. We must leave before dawn. Pack up whatever you want to take along.

LORD EDGAR: I must take her with me. I must find a way to bring her back again. If it's the last thing I do, I'll bring her back again!

ALCAZAR: Let us remove the sarcophagus. The most dangerous part is over. Rain is what we have to fear now.

(They carry out the mummy case. Lights fade.)

Scene 2: *Mandacrest.*

(The time is autumn. Jane is dusting the mummy case. Nicodemus looks on.)

NICODEMUS: It was a devil of a time we had getting it in here. The thing must weigh a ton.

JANE: Did you bring Lady Enid's trunk upstairs?

NICODEMUS: Yes.

JANE: Where is she?

NICODEMUS: Alone with her secrets: old feather fans, tasseled dance cards powdered with musk, a gaud of amber beads locked away in her drawer. A program from Antoine's when she appeared with Bonita Bainbridge in *The Farfelu of Seville.*

JANE: It's the paralysis of the insane. She sleeps all day and she's up all night.

NICODEMUS: That was always her way.

JANE: She's got terrible insomnia.

NICODEMUS: Can't remember a thing, eh?

JANE: And when she's up—she walks.

NICODEMUS: And why shouldn't she walk? It's daft she is, not crippled.

JANE: I haven't slept a wink since they brought her home a week ago.

NICODEMUS: You're doing the work of three people.

JANE: I asked Lord Edgar if I could get a slight raise in pay and he said he'd consider it.

NICODEMUS: And to think of you having to beg from these swine. I'm the only one who knows what you are. Why don't you trust me more? What have you got up your nose against me?

JANE: *(Crosses to the mirror)* Come to the glass, Nicodemus, and I'll show you what you should wish. Do you mark those two lines between your eyes? And those thick brows that instead of rising, arched, sink in the middle? And that couple of black fiends, so deeply buried, who never open their windows boldly, but lurk glinting under them, like devil's spies? Wish and learn to smooth away the surly wrinkles, to raise your lids frankly, and change the fiends to confident, innocent angels, suspecting and doubting nothing, and always seeing friends where they are not sure of foes. Don't get the expression of a vicious cur that appears to know the kicks it gets are its desert, and yet hates all the world, as well as the kicker, for what it suffers.

NICODEMUS: In other words, I must wish for Edgar Hillcrest's great blue eyes and even forehead. I do, but that won't help me to them. I was abandoned. Found on the doorstep of a London doss house. My own mother didn't want me.

JANE: Who knows but your father was emperor of China and your mother was an Indian queen, each of them able to buy up Mandacrest with one week's income. And you were kidnapped by wicked sailors and brought to England. Were I in your place, I would frame high notions of my birth, and the thought of what I was should give me courage and dignity.

NICODEMUS: Thank you, Janey. In the future while I'm shoveling shit I'll try to think of myself as a prince in disguise.

JANE: *(Looking out of the door windows)* Why don't you do some washin' and combin' and go to the village and visit that dairy maid you've taken a fancy to?

NICODEMUS: She's a cute little baggage but she smells of cheese.

JANE: It's a good night for wooing for the moon is full. *(Bell off)* There's the bell. The mistress wants me. *(Exits)*

NICODEMUS: The moon is full? *(Goes upstage and looks out through the doors)* A full moon. *(He begins to make jerky movements)* A full moooooon! *(The word moon trails off into a howl as* NICODEMUS *with his back to the audience raises one arm, which has become a wolf's paw)* No! No! No! Oh God! God help me! Don't let it happen! It's the moooooon! Mooooooooon! *(He turns to the audience. His face has become that of a wolf. He tears off his jacket to reveal a furry torso. He runs about the stage on his tiptoes with his knees bent. He sniffs, scratches, lifts his leg against a piece of furniture, howls, and runs out leaving his jacket on the floor)*

JANE: *(Enters)* Nicodemus, Lady Enid wants to have a word with you. *(Sees the door left open)* He's gone and he's left the door wide open again. God, he'll never change.

(There is the sound of a wolf howling in the distance.)

LADY ENID: *(Enters)* Do you hear that? First you think it's a wolf. Then you tell yourself it's the wind. But you know that it's a soul in pain. *(Crosses to the fireplace)* Get that flower out of here!

JANE: I thought it looked so lovely.

LADY ENID: I can stand neither its color nor its scent. Take it away.

JANE: It's the last rose of summer.

([LADY ENID] *takes down a dulcimer, lays it across her lap, and begins to play "The Last Rose of Summer." * JANE *takes the flowers out and returns with another dulcimer. She sits on the other side of the fireplace and joins* LADY ENID *in a duet.*)

LADY ENID: *(Staring at the portrait over the mantel)* Who is that woman?

JANE: Why that's yourself, Lady Enid.

LADY ENID: No, no, that's not me. She's a virgin.

JANE: It was painted a long time ago.

LADY ENID: She still has her illusions. She still has her faith. No, that isn't me.

JANE: Virginity is the balloon in the carnival of life. It vanishes with the first prick.

LADY ENID: *(Stops playing abruptly)* In all of England I don't believe I could have married into a situation so completely removed from the stir of society. A perfect misanthropist's heaven—and Lord Edgar and I are such a perfect pair to divide the desolation between us.

JANE: It's a refuge, it is, from the chatter of tongues.

LADY ENID: Mine eyes itch. Doth that bode weeping?

JANE: Maybe you've got something in your eye, Lady Enid.

LADY ENID: Where is Nicodemus? I want to have a word with him.

JANE: I'm afraid that's not possible, Lady Enid.

LADY ENID: And why not? Send for Nicodemus. I demand to see him at once.

JANE: Nicodemus can't come, Lady Enid. For obvious reasons.

LADY ENID: Obvious reasons? *(The light dawns)* Oh! Oh! For obvious reasons. Oh I see. In that case, I'll go to him.

JANE: Are you fond of Nicodemus?

LADY ENID: Fond of Nicodemus? Sometimes I feel that I am Nicodemus. That Nicodemus and I are one and the same person.

JANE: Now, now, Lady Enid, what have you got up your sleeve?

LADY ENID: Up my sleeve? Up my sleeve? *(She looks up her sleeve. Her own hand comes out in a clawlike gesture. She screams)*

JANE: Don't be frightened, Lady Enid. That's your own hand.

LADY ENID: I frighten myself sometimes. Jane, I fear that Lord Edgar and I are drifting apart. It's a terrible thing to marry an Egyptologist and find out he's hung up on his mummy. [*(If audience hisses)* That wind!]

JANE: He's an incurable romantic. If you really want to please him, you should try to appeal to that side of his nature. I have a lovely old dress you could wear. It's a family heirloom. It's full of nostalgia.

LADY ENID: We could have it cleaned.

JANE: I'll lay it out in your room. Wear it tonight. It's sure to get a strong reaction.

LADY ENID: Thank you, Jane. *(Exit* JANE. LADY ENID *picks up dulcimer, plays "Skip to My Lou."* LORD EDGAR *enters)* Edgar, darling, where have you been?

LORD EDGAR: I've been to the jewelers.

LADY ENID: To buy jewelry?

LORD EDGAR: No, bullets. Silver bullets. The young dairymaid in the village was found badly mauled. It seems the werewolf has struck again. I must go to the morgue.

LADY ENID: Oh Edgar. Why don't you just go and live at the morgue instead of making a morgue of our home. *(She flings out)*

LORD EDGAR: *(Calling after her)* Enid. Enid darling. Please be reasonable.

(NICODEMUS appears in the door windows up. He has blood on his hand.)

NICODEMUS: Lord Edgar.

LORD EDGAR: Nicodemus. I'll be needing your help tonight. The werewolf has struck again. This time, the cur must die.

NICODEMUS: Must he die? Is there no other help for him? Can't he be put away somewhere where he could receive therapy? Perhaps someday science will discover a cure for what he has.

LORD EDGAR: There is only one cure for what he has. The barrel of a gun and a silver bullet. *(Exits)*

NICODEMUS: Oh miserable me. Must I, like Tancred in *Jerusalem Delivered,* ever injure what I love beyond all else? Unloved I lived. Unloved I die. My only crime was having been born.

(Enter JANE.)

JANE: And who are you talking to, Nicodemus Underwood.

NICODEMUS: Myself. The only one who'll listen.

JANE: Did you see the milkmaid tonight, Nicodemus?

NICODEMUS: The milkmaid, oh, the milkmaid. Would that I had never seen the milkmaid.

JANE: There's blood on your hand. Did you hurt yourself?

NICODEMUS: No. It's her blood. The blood of the tender maid you spoke of. The werewolf got her.

JANE: Werewolf?

NICODEMUS: Yes, you know, a person who dons the skin of a wolf in the full of the moon and turns into a wolf to prowl at night. A woman is usually the victim. It makes a horrible story.

JANE: And where is it now, this hound of hell?

NICODEMUS: Wipe from my hand the blood you see with your dainty little hankie, and behold the mark of Cain.

JANE: *(Spits on her hankie and wipes some of the blood from NICODEMUS's palm. She gasps and jumps back)* The Pentagram! When did this happen to you?

NICODEMUS: Tonight, in the full of the moon! I turned into a wolf! And took the life of the only fair creature who'd ever shown me any love.

JANE: But the moon is still full. How come you're not a wolf now?

NICODEMUS: I'm in remission since a cloud passed over the moon.

JANE: Unspeakable horror!

NICODEMUS: Unspeakable shame! For I fear what I may do next. For it is the thing I love I kill. And I love you Janey, with all my heart.

JANE: No you don't. It's just infatuation tinged with lust.

NICODEMUS: And I love Lady Enid!

JANE: Lady Enid?

NICODEMUS: Yes. I'd have never dared confess it until this moment. But now I fear I may be some danger to her person. All must out!

JANE: Run away, Nicodemus. Run away and never come back!

NICODEMUS: Where shall I go? I've never known any life but Mandacrest! I have no money, no luggage!

JANE: Go upstairs to my room. On the table by my bed you will find a copy of Lord Lytton's *Zanoni.* In it I have saved a few pounds. Take them. You may need them.

NICODEMUS: Thank you, Janey. *(Exits)*

JANE: Sufficient unto the night are the horrors thereof. *(Falls on knees and prays)* Please god, don't let anything happen to Lord Edgar, don't let anything happen to Lady Enid, and please god, don't let anything happen to me!

LADY ENID: *(Enters in a different frock)* How do I look?

JANE: Lovely, Lady Enid. It's sure to put Lord Edgar into a romantic mood. This dress was always his favorite.

LADY ENID: Are you sure he really likes it?

JANE: Positive. He's even worn it himself when in an antic mood, in younger, happier days. *(Exit)*

LADY ENID: *(Goes over to the mantel and looks up at the portrait)* Well any man who dresses up as a woman can't be all bad! *(To herself in the portrait)* If you continue at this rate you'll be an even greater actress than Bonita Bainbridge!

VOICE: *(Off left, moans twice, then)* Help me. Help me! Turn the figurine. Turn the figurine!

(LADY ENID moves an ornament on the fireplace, triggering a sliding panel. The bookcase slides back, revealing a cage. She jumps back, startled. A shrouded figure appears within the cage.)

LADY ENID: Who are you? What are you doing in there?

VOICE: They keep me here! I'm their prisoner! They torture me! Please help me! Help me!

LADY ENID: Who? Who tortures you?

VOICE: Edgar! Edgar tortures me!

LADY ENID: You poor thing. Who are you?

VOICE: Why, I'm his wife, Irma.

LADY ENID: Irma!

VOICE: Irma Vep! The first Lady Hillcrest.

LADY ENID: But I thought you were dead!

IRMA: That's what they want you to think! That's what they want everyone to think!

LADY ENID: Why have they put you here?

IRMA: There are jewels hidden in the house. I alone know where they are. But I'll never tell! For if I tell, they'll kill me! If you help me, I'll tell you where the jewels are, and I'll share them with you.

LADY ENID: Poor woman! Of course I'll help you. But this cage is locked!

IRMA: Jane has the key! Steal it from her! But don't tell her you've seen me! Don't tell anyone! Not Jane. Not Nicodemus! Not Lord Edgar! *(Footsteps are heard)* I hear someone coming. Turn the figurine! And please, please, remember me! Remember me!

LADY ENID: Remember you? Of course I'll remember you! How could I forget you. You poor darling. Poor, poor darling! *(Turns the figurine. The bookcase starts to close and sticks.* ENID *struggles with the figurine. The bookcase closes fully as* LORD EDGAR *enters)*

LORD EDGAR: Enid!

LADY ENID: *(Turning)* Edgar.

LORD EDGAR: Where did you get that dress?

LADY ENID: Do you like it?

LORD EDGAR: Like it? I hate it! I despise it! I loathe it! *(Tears the dress)* Take it off! Take it off!

LADY ENID: But Edgar! I only wanted to please you!

LORD EDGAR: Please me? You wanted to torture me! You wanted to make me suffer! I'll never forgive you for this, Enid. Never!

LADY ENID: But Edgar! I only wanted to be nearer to you!

LORD EDGAR: You've only driven me further away. I'd rather see you locked away in rags in the deepest, darkest dungeon I could find than see you in that dress!

LADY ENID: No!

LORD EDGAR: Take it off, I said! You're making me hate you!

LADY ENID: What are you saying?

LORD EDGAR: It was her dress.

LADY ENID: *Her* dress?

LORD EDGAR: Irma's!

LADY ENID: Jane didn't tell me that!

LORD EDGAR: Jane told you to wear that? She should have known better. She knows how it upsets me to see the dress Irma wore the night she died!

LADY ENID: Died? But she . . . she didn't . . .

LORD EDGAR: Didn't what?

LADY ENID: *(Catching herself)* . . . die in this dress, did she?

LORD EDGAR: Oh don't talk about it anymore! You'll only make me hate you more. *(Tears her dress.* LADY ENID *bursts into tears and runs to the door)* Stop, Enid! I'm sorry. I didn't mean it.

LADY ENID: You don't love me and you never have.

LORD EDGAR: You're wrong! I love no one else but you.

LADY ENID: Then why, why, why must we go on living here as brother and sister? Why don't you live with me as a wife?

LORD EDGAR: Because of the terror I feel of *her* . . .

LADY ENID: Terror?

LORD EDGAR: Yes, terror! Terror! A terror so great that I've never been able to communicate it to anyone.

LADY ENID: Even your wife?

LORD EDGAR: Very well, then, I'll tell you. Sometimes I see her standing before me as big as life.

LADY ENID: How does she look?

LORD EDGAR: Oh, very well. Exactly as she did when I saw her last, three years ago.

LADY ENID: Three years ago?

LORD EDGAR: She won't let me go. I'm her prisoner.

LADY ENID: *She* won't let *you* go?

LORD EDGAR: No, I realize it's useless.

LADY ENID: That woman has an unearthly power over you, Edgar.

LORD EDGAR: Yes, yes, she's horrible. I'll never get rid of her.

LADY ENID: But you have gotten rid of her. On your trip to Egypt. You said you'd found something in the tomb that had made you forget all about her.

LORD EDGAR: Don't talk about it. Or think of it, even. There was no help for me there. I can feel it in my bones. I didn't get rid of it out there either.

LADY ENID: Of what? What do you mean?

LORD EDGAR: I mean the horror. The fantastic hold on my mind, on my soul.

LADY ENID: But you said it was over.

LORD EDGAR: No no, that's just the thing. It isn't.

LADY ENID: Not over?

LORD EDGAR: No Enid, it's not over, and I'm afraid it never will be.

LADY ENID: *(In a strangled voice)* Are you saying then that in your heart of hearts you'll never be able to forget this woman?

LORD EDGAR: She comes toward me and puts her arms around me. Then she presses her lips to mine.

LADY ENID: To kiss you?

LORD EDGAR: As if to kiss me—but she doesn't kiss. She sucks.

LADY ENID: Sucks?

LORD EDGAR: She sucks my breath until I feel I'm suffocating. *(Turns blue)*

LADY ENID: Good God! Edgar! You're sick! You're much sicker than you thought. Than either of us thought.

LORD EDGAR: *(Clutching at his throat)* Yes! Yes! I can't breathe! I'm suffocating, and her fingers are tightening! Tightening around my throat. Help me. Help me.

LADY ENID: Oh, my dear Lord Edgar! Then you've been suffering in silence all this time and you've never told me anything about it?

LORD EDGAR: I couldn't tell you. I couldn't speak the unspeakable, name the unnameable. *(Gasps for breath)* And her fingers are tightening. Tightening more and more. Help me! Help me!

LADY ENID: Nicodemus! *(Runs off calling)* Nicodemus.

NICODEMUS: *(Off)* You called, Lady Enid?

LADY ENID: *(Off)* Yes please, please help me. Lord Edgar is having an attack. *(She weeps)*

NICODEMUS: *(Off)* There there, Lady Enid. Calm yourself.

LADY ENID: *(Off)* Oh please, hurry, hurry!

NICODEMUS: *(Off)* Stay here. I'll go to him. *(Enters)* There there, Lord Edgar. Doing poorly? Have you got the horrors again?

LORD EDGAR: *(Rolling about on the floor, clutching his throat)* Yes, yes, the horrors. It's her. I'll never be free of her.

NICODEMUS: *(Offering his flask)* Here you go. You must fight fire with fire and spirits with spirits!

LORD EDGAR: No, I won't break my rule. You know I am an abstainer.

NICODEMUS: Oh well then, in that case . . . *(Drinks himself)*

LORD EDGAR: *(Seeing this)* On second thought, maybe just a drop.

NICODEMUS: *(Passing him the flask)* For medicinal purposes only. *(LORD EDGAR drinks)* Feeling better?

LORD EDGAR: Yes, much. Thanks. Nicodemus, stay with Lady Enid tonight. There's a wolf about, and I don't want her left alone. *(Exits up center)*

NICODEMUS: No, no, Lord Edgar. Not that! Don't ask me that! Anything but that! Horror. Horror. Horror. For I fear the gibbous moon. Oh horror! Oh horror!

JANE: *(Enters with wolfsbane)* Did you find the money?

NICODEMUS: Yes, thank you Janey.

JANE: Now go, Nicodemus. I've never liked you, but I've never wished you any harm. May god help you!

NICODEMUS: Thank you, Janey. This is the only kindness anyone has ever shown me.

JANE: Ah, be off with you. I have to put up wolfsbane against you.

NICODEMUS: I understand. *(Exits)*

(JANE *hangs up wolfsbane around the room.* LADY ENID *enters.*)

LADY ENID: Where's Lord Edgar?

JANE: He's gone out, after the wolf.

LADY ENID: Is he hunting wolves again, with one of his villainous old guns?

JANE: I think he took a horse pistol.

LADY ENID: The blackguard.

JANE: Now, Lady Enid, I won't have you talking this way about Lord Edgar.

LADY ENID: *(Seizing her by the wrist)* When a woman loves a man she should be willing to do anything for him. Cut off her little finger at the middle joint there. *(Twisting* JANE's *finger)*

JANE: *(Loudly)* Ow!

LADY ENID: Or cut off her dainty hand at the wrist.

JANE: Please, let go. You're hurting me!

LADY ENID: Or lop off her pretty little ear. *(Twists her ear and takes keys)*

JANE: Ow! Ow! Ow! Please stop!

LADY ENID: When you're willing to do those things for Lord Edgar then entertain thoughts of loving him. Otherwise back off. *(Releases her)*

JANE: *(Rubbing her wrist)* Now look. You've left red marks on my wrist. You've got a devil in you. That's what it is. You know I'm nothing to Lord Edgar. I have no more hold over his heart than you have. It's Irma he loves! Irma Vep. It's no use our fighting over the same man . . . when he's in love with a dead woman.

LADY ENID: You scandalous little hypocrite! Are you not afraid of being carried away bodily whenever you mention the devil's name? I warn you to refrain from provoking me or I will ask your abduction as a special favor. *(JANE goes to leave)* Stop, Jane! Look here. I'll show you how far I've progressed in the Black Art. *(Taking down a book from the shelf)* I shall soon be competent to make a clear house of it. The red cow didn't die by chance, and your rheumatism can hardly be reckoned among providential visitations!

JANE: Oh wicked! Wicked! May the Lord deliver us from evil!

LADY ENID: No, reprobate! You are a castaway. Be off, or I'll hurt you seriously. I'll have you all modeled in wax and clay; and the first who passes the limits I fix, shall . . . I'll not say what he shall be done to . . . but you'll see! Go—I'm looking at you.

JANE: *(Trembling with sincere horror, hurries out praying and ejaculating)* Wicked! Wicked!

LADY ENID: *(Laughing)* Wicked, perhaps. But I have the keys! *(She approaches the bookcase. She turns the figurine. The bookcase slides)* Psst! Psst! Irma! Irma darling. Are you there?

IRMA: Where else would I be? Did you get the key?

LADY ENID: Yes, I have it.

IRMA: Open the door. Quickly. Quickly!

LADY ENID: But I don't know which one it is.

IRMA: Quickly! Quickly! Before someone comes.

LADY ENID: *(Trying one key after another)* Well there are so many of them.

IRMA: Quickly! Save me! Save me!

LADY ENID: *(Opening the door)* Ah, there, Irma dearest. You're free.

(IRMA *flies out of the door shrieking like a madwoman. She seizes* ENID *by the throat, turns her back to the audience, and leans over her.* ENID *sinks to her knees.*)

IRMA: *(Calmly)* Oh triple fool! Did you not know that Irma Vep is "vampire" anagrammatized!

LADY ENID: *(Reaches up and rips off* IRMA*'s face, which is a rubber mask, revealing the other player)* Edgar?

JANE: No, Jane!

LADY ENID: Jane! You?

JANE: Yes, I did it! I killed the child, and Irma too! I was the vampire, feeding on the lifeblood of my own jealousy! No more will I eat the bitter crust of charity, nor serve a vain mistress!

LADY ENID: You? You killed her?

JANE: Yes I killed her, and I'll kill again. I'd kill any woman who stood in my way.

LADY ENID: You're mad.

JANE: Mad? Mad? *(She laughs maniacally)* Perhaps I am. Love is a kind of madness. And hatred is a bottomless cup, and I will drink the dregs.

(Pulls out a meat cleaver and attacks ENID. ENID, *who has backed over to the mummy case, deftly opens the door as* JANE *runs at her.* JANE *goes into the mummy case.* ENID *slams the door and holds it shut. We hear* JANE *pounding within the mummy case.)*

LADY ENID: *(Crying out)* Help me! Nicodemus! Edgar! Someone! Anyone! Help me!

EDGAR: *(Rushes in)* Enid, what is it?

LADY ENID: *(Hysterically)* She's in the mummy case. She's in the mummy case. You can hear her rapping.

(The rapping stops.)

EDGAR: I don't hear anything.

LADY ENID: I found it all out. Jane killed Irma, and the child! Irma Vep is "vampire" anagrammatized.

EDGAR: Enid, I think your mind is affected.

LADY ENID: No, it's Jane. Jane is mad. Mad, I tell you. She attacked me with a meat-ax. She's in the mummy case. Call Scotland Yard.

EDGAR: Nonsense, Enid. *(Goes to open the mummy case)*

LADY ENID: What are you going to do?

EDGAR: I'm going to open the mummy case.

LADY ENID: No, don't open the mummy case.

EDGAR: I'm going to open the mummy case. Stand back.

LADY ENID: Don't open the mummy case.

EDGAR: I'm going to open the mummy case.

LADY ENID: Don't open the mummy case. Don't open it. Don't open it. Don't
. . .

EDGAR: *(Opens the mummy case)* See Enid? The mummy case is perfectly empty.

LADY ENID: *(Somewhat mollified)* Well, she was in there a moment ago. *(The lights begin to dim)* The lights. The lights are dimming. The lights. The lights are dimming. *(The lights come back up)*

EDGAR: Nonsense, Enid. The lights are not dimming. Come and sit by the fire.

(Lights dim again.)

LADY ENID: The lights are dimming.

EDGAR: *(He escorts her to chair)* If you don't stop, Enid, they'll put you back in the sanatorium and they'll never let you out again.

LADY ENID: *(In a tiny voice)* The lights are dimming.

EDGAR: *(Infuriated)* Stop it, Enid! Stop it stop it stop it stop it! I don't want to hear you say that again!

LADY ENID: *(Turns to the audience and silently mouths the words "The lights are dimming.")*

EDGAR: There's the good girl. There's the good girl. Go on, play your dulcimer like the good girl. Play with your dulcimer, Enid. *(Crosses to the door to exit)* And I'll have Jane fix you a nice hot cup of tea.

LADY ENID: *(Winces)*

EDGAR: Tch tch tch! *(Exits)*

LADY ENID: *(Begins to play "The Last Rose of Summer" on her dulcimer as ominous music swells)* Is it possible my mind is affected? And yet I saw it with my very eyes. *(There is a tapping at the window, as in Act I)* There it is again! Oh god. Oh god in heaven. There it is again. The rapping! The rapping! As if someone gently tapping. *(She takes the poker from the fireside and approaches the French doors stealthily and flies through them, brandishing the poker)* Tapping at my chamber door!

NICODEMUS: *(Off)* Hey Lady Enid! What's going on? *(Poking his head through the door)* What's going on here? *(Ducks out)*

LADY ENID: *(Appearing at the door)* Oh Nicodemus. I heard a rapping, a rapping, as if someone gently tapping, tapping at my chamber door! *(She ducks out)*

NICODEMUS: *(Popping in)* There there, Lady Enid. 'Tis the wind and nothing more. *(Ducks out)*

LADY ENID: *(Popping in)* Oh Nicodemus, I was so frightened, so terribly, terribly frightened!

NICODEMUS: *(His arm comes through the door, pats her shoulder)* There there, Lady Enid. I'll never let any harm come to you.

LADY ENID: *(Kissing his hand)* Thank you, Nicodemus. Thank you.

NICODEMUS: There there. *(His hand is withdrawn and reappears as a wolf's hand. Pats her cheek and squeezes her breast)* There there.

LADY ENID: *(Reenters the room, closing the French doors behind her)* It's so good to know he's there! Is it possible my mind is affected? Or can I trust my senses five? I saw it with my very eyes. And yet, the mummy case is perfectly empty! *(Opens the mummy case)*

(JANE in her maid's uniform once again, comes running out of the mummy case shrieking and wielding a meat-ax. ENID screams and runs out the door, slamming it behind her. The corner of her robe sticks out through the closed door.)

JANE: *(Flies to the door, finds it locked, and rants)* Open the door. Open the door, Lady Enid. It's just a matter of time before I get in, you know. It was the same way when I killed Lady Irma. She was all alone in the house the night I strangled her.

LADY ENID: *(Off)* No no! You're horrible!

JANE: And Victor, the little bastard. I drowned him in the mill run.

LADY ENID: *(Off)* No!

JANE: You should have seen the bubbles coming out of his ugly little nose.

LADY ENID: *(Off)* How could you? How could you?

JANE: Ah, glorious death. Glorious, glorious death! *(NICODEMUS, as werewolf, bursts through French doors)* Victor!

Everett Quinton & Charles Ludlam in
The Mystery of Irma Vep (Anita & Steve Shevett)

([NICODEMUS] grabs JANE by the throat and drags her out the way he came in, howling. He staggers back through the door with only her dress, and humps it. Suddenly, realizing the dress is empty, he throws it down and wheels about confusedly. He sees Enid's robe caught in the door and crosses to it, clumping all the way with his wooden leg, lifts the hem of her robe, sniffs it, turns to the door, and raps three times.)

LADY ENID: *(Off)* Edgar, is that you?

(EDGAR rushes in and fires shots. The werewolf falls and turns into NICODEMUS.)

NICODEMUS: Each man kills the thing he loves. The coward does it with a kiss, the brave man with a sword. Yet, Nicodemus did love.

LORD EDGAR: Nicodemus, Nicodemus, I've killed you. In earnest.

NICODEMUS: Thank you. *(Dies)*

LORD EDGAR: The poor man is dead. From his fair and unpolluted flesh may violets spring! Bury him on the moors he loved so well, and may his soul ascend to heaven, for he lived in hell!

(Blackout.)

Scene 3

(Lights up on LADY ENID *and* LORD EDGAR. EDGAR *is sitting in his chair.* ENID *is standing beside him.)*

LADY ENID: Poor Nicodemus. Poor Victor. Poor Irma. Poor Jane! Somehow it just doesn't make sense.

LORD EDGAR: Enid, there are more things on heaven and earth than are dreamed of in our philosophies! Enid, I had an uncanny experience in Egypt. And I've written it all up in a treatise, which I expect will cause some stir. My very reputation as an Egyptologist would hang in the balance. I've been warned by all my colleagues not to publish it, but I must. They say that it couldn't have happened. That an ancient mummy, a hideously shriveled, decayed object, could not have survived the ages and been brought to life by spells and incantations. And yet I saw it with my very eyes! I must tell the world, even if it ruins my reputation! For I believe that we all lived before, in another time, in another age, and that you and I were lovers in ancient Egypt, thirty-five hundred years ago. She was so like you. You are so like her. Oh Enid, Enid!

LADY ENID: Stop! I can't bear it! I can't go on. Oh, you poor, poor man!

LORD EDGAR: What do you mean, Enid?

LADY ENID: Oh, stop. You're making me weep so terribly! I've done a terrible thing. I fear you'll never forgive me for it.

LORD EDGAR: What are you talking about?

LADY ENID: It was me in the tomb, Edgar.

LORD EDGAR: You? Impossible. But you were away in a sanatorium.

LADY ENID: No, I wasn't. I feigned madness. Alcazar is my father! He is actually Professor Lionel Cuncliff of Cambridge University.

LORD EDGAR: Not *the* Lionel Cuncliff! The leading Egyptologist and sarco-phagologist.

LADY ENID: Yes, your old rival.

LORD EDGAR: Old Cuncliff your father? That's impossible! You couldn't have been in Egypt!

LADY ENID: If you could only believe that I did it for you, to win you away from . . . her. If I could make you believe that our love was destined, I thought I could bind you to me. But my father used it for his own purposes—to make a fool of you. To discredit you before the academic community and the world! He had never forgiven you for having won the Yolanda Sonabend fellowship he had so counted on. Can you ever forgive me?

LORD EDGAR: I can't believe that you pulled it off! How did you get in the tomb?

LADY ENID: The tomb was actually an Egyptian restaurant that had been closed quite a number of years. I simply came in through the kitchen.

LORD EDGAR: You little witch!

LADY ENID: We had only a few days to make it look like a tomb. We used a decorator from the theater. Oh, the hours he spent polishing that floor. It gave us quite a turn when you discovered that footprint. But by then you wanted to believe so much, you convinced yourself. Can you ever forgive me?

LORD EDGAR: Forgive you? I want to thank you. You've freed me at last. Somehow I've come to realize that we are all God's creatures every one of us. Big Victor and little Victor too.

LADY ENID: You can say that.

LORD EDGAR: I mean it. Oh God, I've been so selfish.

LADY ENID: Me too. But we can make it all up somehow.

LADY ENID: There's a hard day's work ahead of us Enid.

LADY ENID: But on the seventh day we'll rest.

LORD EDGAR: *(Quietly, very moved)* And in that stillness perhaps we'll hear the spirits visiting.

LADY ENID: *(In a whisper)* Spirits?

LORD EDGAR: *(As before)* Yes, perhaps they'll be all around us—those we've lost.

LADY ENID: Big Victor and little Victor too?

LORD EDGAR: Yes, it may be that now and then throughout our lives we may still catch glimpses of them. *(Ardently)* If only I knew where to look. Where should I look, Enid?

LADY ENID: *(Going to the doors and opening them)* Out there through the fog—beyond the moors. *(Reaches out her hand to him and beckons him to come)*

LORD EDGAR: *(His eyes fixed on her, he moves toward her slowly)* Beyond the moors?

LADY ENID: And upward . . .

LORD EDGAR: Yes, yes, upward.

LADY ENID: Toward the stars and toward that great silence.

LORD EDGAR: *(Taking her hand in his)* Thank you.

(They stand in the doorway with their backs to us, looking up as the lights fade to darkness.)

The End

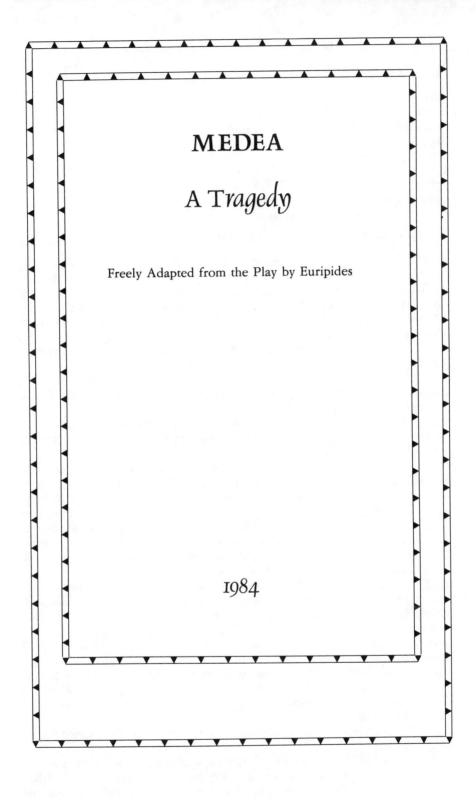

MEDEA

A Tragedy

Freely Adapted from the Play by Euripides

1984

Cast of Characters

MEDEA
JASON
TWO CHILDREN
KREON, *King of Korinth*
AEGEUS, *King of Athens*
NURSE
TUTOR
MESSENGER
KHORUS OF KORINTHIAN WOMEN

Scene: *In front of Medea's house in Korinth.*

NURSE: *(Entering from house)* Would that the axes had never cut the firs to make the planks to build the ship that sailed the sea to bring Jason to the land of Kolchis! Would that that ship, the *Argo,* had gone down in the wine-dark sea than that this hero should have stolen the Golden Fleece! For then my mistress, Medea, would never have seen Jason and fallen in love with him! And in her passion, would not have killed her brothers and betrayed her father, to help him escape! She would not have had children by him! And would never have known the pain of losing him to a younger woman!

MEDEA: *(Voice within the house)* I wish I would die! I want only to die!

NURSE: *(To the audience)* Do you hear that? Her grief is terrible! For it is no ordinary woman lamenting within the house!

MEDEA: *(Within)* I wish a lightning bolt would come down from the blue sky and strike my skull, splitting it, and splattering my brains on the hard ground! Oh, let me die! Let me die! Is it too much to ask that I die?

NURSE: *(To the audience)* Since you're new in these parts, I'll tell you. The woman in this house you hear lamenting is Medea! A barbarian princess whose father was a sorcerer. She was brought back to Greece by Jason and the Argonauts, after their first expedition against the barbarians of the East. Her grief is boundless. And she, being a foreign woman, it is impossible to comfort her. So there you have it. There's no use standing there gawking! I see a crowd is already gathering! Go and watch, if you wish. You won't shame her! She'll play out her tragedy in public if need be!

MEDEA: I hate you children! Children of a hateful mother! And I hate your father! Damn this house and everyone in it! *(Enter* MEDEA, *disheveled with grief)*

NURSE: Can you blame the children for what their father did? Be reasonable, Medea!

MEDEA: You be reasonable if you like. I'll be what I please, and what I am. I don't know what a Greek woman would do in my case, but women of my race are somewhat rash! You Greeks are idiots with your fatalism and your democracy! You institutionalize your mediocrity and make a virtue of it! We don't accept our fate so easily where I come from, nor do we consider it an advantage to be in the majority!

NURSE: What's the use of struggling against something that was destined before you were born?

MEDEA: Destined? I'm not so sure it's destined. The stars impel but they do not compel. I'm not afraid to take responsibility for my actions, be they what they may! And as for the majority, why should they rule? I'd rather follow one exceptional man than a herd of mediocrities!

NURSE: Oh, I pity you! Great people have great pride and great tempers! They think they're free to do what they please, but they're slaves of every mood. It is better to be a good neighbor among equals and grow old in a humble way! To endure in moderation than to die great!

MEDEA: Oh where is the lightning? Why doesn't it split open my head? What good is life? I would gladly leave this miserable existence behind me! Great Artemis, look what I have suffered from a hateful husband! And now he's taken to bed a young girl with small breasts and narrow hips! And they laugh at me as they make love! I can hear them laughing! My father, my brothers, my endless exile! Hated in my own country! Where will I turn? There is no turning back! I must do what comes next, step by step. There is no choice! I must do what comes next! *(Shrieks and hurls herself on the ground and rolls around)*

NURSE: I heard a shriek! Medea brings down curses on herself and him who betrayed her!

MEDEA: Women of Korinth! I know you think bad of me. I tend to be solitary, undemocratic by nature, unfriendly, strange, alone! I've never really been a friend or neighbor to any of you. It's hard for a foreigner to adapt to strange new ways. But even in my country we try to be good neighbors. Now I'm not fit for company. I'm like a dead woman walking in a barren place. I look and I look, but I see no friends anywhere! I see only judges' faces! But if you had my cause, women, and I hope you never do, you might feel a bit out of place yourselves. I married for love! I didn't buy my husband. And now I've lost him for love! Marriage is not an easy thing for a woman. A man takes his pleasure where he will, and a woman must take it lying down! Men say we have it easy. We stay at home; they fight all the wars. But I say I would rather stand three times in the front line of battle than bear one child! Of course, I can only speak for myself. This country is your home. You can enjoy life and friendship. But I am abandoned! An alien, who had nothing but her husband, and now has nothing! I'm something he brought home, a souvenir from a foreign land. I have no relatives who'll take me in. I only ask you one thing, women: help me to get even!

NURSE: *(Aside to* MEDEA*)* Medea, quiet! You're making a scene! Look: I see King Kreon coming!

KREON: *(Enters)* Medea, I have tried to be patient with you and give you the benefit of the doubt. But again today I have reports of you. You make threats against my daughter and your husband. You say rash things against me in public, which is politically embarrassing. Therefore you must go! It is my decree. Prepare to leave at once!

MEDEA: All is lost! Am I to have no inch of earth? Maggots, insects, snails, vile things have some part of the earth to crawl upon, but I have none. Kreon, why do you banish me?

KREON: I am not afraid to admit, I'm afraid of you! You're a shrewd and clever woman, practiced in the black arts and all forms of evil magic! You're enraged at having lost your husband's love. You blame my daughter and me, too. An ounce of prevention is worth a pound of cure. I mean to be rid of you before you do some harm!

MEDEA: This is not the first time I've suffered for having been clever. People should hope their children be born idiots so they suffer less! Let them all be dolts and live in a fool's paradise! Intelligent people find pain everywhere. It's no fun being intelligent! You tell your ideas to fools, they think you a fool in turn. And if you tell your ideas to those with a reputation for learning, they hate and envy you for them. Being clever, I know too well how this happens. Oh, to play dumb, to know how to be stupid, doltish, thick: that would be a gift of the gods. So you're afraid of me, Kreon. What harm can I do to you? And why should I hate you? You and your daughter have the man you want. I hate him, yes, but why should I hold it against you?

KREON: Hmmmm.

MEDEA: I'll go further! I wish you well! I wish you health, happiness! I hope the marriage prospers! I hope they live happily ever after! I hope they're lucky! I hope they're happy! Please let me stay! You won't hear a peep out of me! I know how to be a good loser. You'll see.

KREON: This all sounds very good, but I don't trust you. I would rather deal with a wild woman who rages and lashes out than with a secret enemy who knows how to be silent and wait!

MEDEA: I beg of you! On my knees!

KREON: You're wasting your breath.

MEDEA: On my face! *(Lies on the ground)* I kiss your foot! *(She kisses his foot)*

KREON: Stop it! Stop it! Nothing you can do will change my mind!

MEDEA: Look at me, Kreon! Have you ever seen anything more docile? *(She takes his foot and places it on her head)*

KREON: Enough of this disgusting display!

MEDEA: Will you drive me out, then, and show me no mercy?

KREON: I wish only to protect my family and my country.

MEDEA: *(Stricken)* My country! That's bitter. Oh Gods, what an evil thing is love! Evil the things I did for it!

KREON: Love is not evil. But those who love sometimes are.

MEDEA: I'll remember that. In fact, I'll never forget you said it!

KREON: Go, this is painful! Don't make me force you!

MEDEA: Painful for you, but what about me? Am I to be spared no pain?

KREON: You'll be removed by force.

MEDEA: Not that! Anything but that! No Kreon, I beg you!

KREON: Woman, you seem to thrive on scandal. You could have gone quietly, but now I see a crowd is gathering. You will have to be dragged out in front of everyone.

MEDEA: I will go! I will go!

KREON: Then why are you clinging to my hand?

MEDEA: I ask only this day! To make some preparations. And provision for my children, since their father doesn't care about them. You have children of your own. You must understand this! I don't care about myself. It's the children I fear for.

KREON: I have often shown mercy and regretted it later.

MEDEA: All I ask is one day! One turn of the world! One rising and setting of the sun! A lifetime to a mayfly. Nothing to a man. Kreon, you are old. You've had so many days. Can you not just spare me one?

KREON: Very well. One day to pack up your things, make a few plans. But if you stay any longer, you die! That is my fixed word and I won't go back on it. Even as I say it I fear I am making a mistake. And yet I suppose there's not much harm you can do in a day. *(Exit)*

MEDEA: *(Starts to chuckle, a low, rattling, distant sound, deep in her throat. It grows louder and louder until she's convulsed with spasms of laughter)* Fool! Fool! You'll rue this day you gave me! You'll see what can be done in a day! I degraded myself before you. I kissed your foot. I stuck out my tongue and licked between your toes, like a mutt! Like a bitch! You've given me one day, one day to carve you up. One day to make dead bodies of you, my husband, and your daughter. *(She laughs)* How little you knew me, Kreon! To believe I would lower myself before you unless I had a reason for it! And now, decisions, decisions! There are many ways by which death may be dealt them. Shall I stab them with a sword? Slip poison into their food? Or shall I simply take a scarf and strangle them? But this I know! I must live to glory in their death and not be caught! I must find some means of escape, some little hole a snake could crawl through. Until then, like a spider I spin my web, and wait!

KHORUS: Oh pitiful Medea! The Gods are cruel! Oh woe! With no place to turn, no one to help. Who will come to your rescue? Medea, a virtuoso in suffering, can teach us all a lesson in despair!

MEDEA: Come Medea, and hatch a plot. Remember your grandfather was a God. Helius! Come schemer, you must have a trick or two up your sleeve! The Greeks say that women aren't much good. Well I say they can be much evil! Much, much evil!

KHORUS: Flow backward rivers! Time reverse! Begin again this dreadful history! Rewrite life not as it is but as it should be! Let life conform to our ideals and stand corrected!

JASON: *(Enters)* Medea, I pity you as I pity the village idiot! If you'd kept your mouth shut you could have kept your home. But no, you have to rant and rave, make threats, and cause a scene. And what good have you done? I begged Kreon to let you stay. And he was agreeable. But you made it impossible for him. The one thing political figures cannot take is embarrassment. And you've been an embarrassment ever since you came here. There's nothing to be done. And so I've come to make some provision for you so you and the children won't be utterly penniless in exile.

MEDEA: This is the pits. The dregs. The slime. The bottom of the barrel! You coward! You call yourself a man? You should have that thing between your legs cut off!

JASON: And now obscenity! This is inexcusable. I don't like your attitude, Medea. I don't like your attitude one bit! And after all I've done for you!

MEDEA: You know my motto: all or nothing!

JASON: Yes, I know it. I've heard it often enough. And now that you can't have all you will have nothing! This all-or-nothing attitude is foolishness!

MEDEA: Foolishness, yes! It was foolish, I suppose, to poison the great serpent that guarded the Golden Fleece and help you steal it, thereby profaning the Gods of my own country. Running off with you and killing my brother, dismembering him and strewing his limbs upon the sea, so that my father in pursuit must stop and do obsequious grief to each and every part. That slowed him down, hah? And then, when your uncle Pelius tried to keep your inheritance from you, I convinced his daughters I could rejuvenate him with herbs and incantations if they would but kill him and dismember his body according to my instructions! And then I left the unsuspecting daughters with their father's blood on their hands!

JASON: That crime did not advance me as you had hoped, but led us both into exile!

MEDEA: But I tried! You can't say I didn't try! And now where do I go? Back to my father? Or should I go to Pelius's daughters and ask them for sanctuary?

These things I did for you, Jason, for love of you, have left me nowhere to go. I've burned my bridges behind me. And now you have cast me out!

JASON: And what about what I've done for you, Medea? Took you from a barbaric land and tried to civilize you. I see you're not grateful for it.

MEDEA: Civilize me? Is that what they call it now? And what about the children I bore you? They were the direct result of this civilizing, as I recall it.

JASON: Oh God, if only men could find another way to beget children, they could do away with women altogether!

MEDEA: But they can't! And as long as they must proceed in the old-fashioned way, certain standards of behavior ought to be upheld. You didn't have to remarry behind my back. You could have discussed it with me first.

JASON: I'm sure you would have been very helpful in your advice.

MEDEA: I know it's because you're ashamed of me, ashamed of having a foreign wife.

JASON: It wasn't for a woman that I left you, Medea. I was passionately in love with you. Only fools fall passionately in love more than once. No, it was not for a woman! It was to secure my political position in this country that I married Kreon's daughter. To secure our future and the future of our sons.

MEDEA: You're telling me I've had good fortune and should be happy for it.

JASON: Sometimes it's painful to do what is good for you.

MEDEA: You insult me! You have a home! I have no one and nowhere!

JASON: You brought it on yourself.

MEDEA: How did I bring it on myself? Did I betray my husband? Did I sleep with another man?

JASON: You cursed the King's family!

MEDEA: How can I curse, I who am a curse?

JASON: I'm not going to stand here and mince words with you. I did what I did for the children and yourself. And now you've ruined it. Discretion is the greater part of valor, Medea. At least I'll be able to provide you with introductions to some friends who can help you when you go away.

MEDEA: Friends of yours are no friends of mine! I'll never take a thing from you, so don't bother to offer it.

JASON: The Gods are my witness that I tried to help you, but you refused it. You've pushed me away. And you're the one who's going to suffer for it!

MEDEA: Go! Your bride is waiting with spread legs! She'll be jealous of you spending so much time with another woman. Go stick your nose in it!

JASON: Medea, you disgust me. *(Exits)*

KHORUS: There's no hatred worse than that between those who had once loved!

(Enter AEGEUS, King of Athens, an old friend of Medea.)

AEGEUS: Medea! Greetings! Let us embrace, my dear old friend!

MEDEA: Oh greetings, Aegeus, son of King Pandion! What brings you here?

AEGEUS: I have just visited the oracle of Phoebus.

MEDEA: Why?

AEGEUS: I went to find out how I might get children.

MEDEA: At your age you must ask an oracle a question like that?

AEGEUS: Medea, this is no joking matter! I am childless!

MEDEA: Have you a wife?

AEGEUS: Yes.

MEDEA: And what did the oracle tell you?

AEGEUS: Words too wise for me to understand their meaning.

MEDEA: May I inquire what the God replied?

AEGEUS: You may. For someone must interpret it.

MEDEA: What was the message then? Tell me, if you don't mind my hearing it.

AEGEUS: I am not to loosen the hanging foot of the wineskin.

MEDEA: Until you have done something, or . . . ?

AEGEUS: Until I return home.

MEDEA: Well it sounds like good advice at any rate.

AEGEUS: But why so sad, Medea? Why downcast of eye and pale of cheek?

MEDEA: My husband has hurt me.

AEGEUS: What do you mean? How has he caused you grief?

MEDEA: Jason wrongs me though I never injured him.

AEGEUS: In what way? Be more specific.

MEDEA: He's taken another wife and cast me out.

AEGEUS: Surely he wouldn't do a thing like that.

MEDEA: But he has! Once dear, I am now abandoned.

AEGEUS: Did he fall in love? Or is he tired of you?

MEDEA: He fell madly in love, this traitor.

AEGEUS: Perhaps you're better rid of him.

MEDEA: He has fallen in love with power!

AEGEUS: Power?

MEDEA: He's married Kreon's daughter.

AEGEUS: Ah, Medea. I understand your grief.

MEDEA: I am ruined, and worse than that, I am banished!

AEGEUS: Banished? Who banished you?

MEDEA: Kreon drives me into exile.

AEGEUS: But surely Jason does not consent? I cannot approve of this.

MEDEA: He pretends not to, but he lets it happen. Ah, Aegeus, I beg you on my knees to have pity on me, have pity on your poor old friend. Exile is a bitter thing. Give me asylum in your country and I will end your childlessness, for I know drugs that can work miracles!

AEGEUS: I will take you in, for your sake and for my own, as I want children. I'll never let anyone harm you, no matter what!

MEDEA: Do you give me your word on this? No matter what?

AEGEUS: Don't you trust me?

MEDEA: I trust you, but I am hated everywhere! The house of Pelius and Kreon also. My own father would like to get his hands on me! I'll need some protection. No matter what.

AEGEUS: I'd never give you up to your enemies, but if you must have an oath, name the Gods and I'll swear.

MEDEA: Swear by the earth, the heavens, and Helius, my father's father, and name together all the Gods!

AEGEUS: What shall I swear?

MEDEA: That you will never cast me out from your land, no matter how many of my enemies shall demand me! You will never in your life hand me over!

AEGEUS: I swear! By the sun god Helius, by the heaven, the earth, and all the Gods, I will protect you always!

(They clasp hands. A thunderclap is heard.)

MEDEA: The Gods have heard you!

AEGEUS: Farewell then.

MEDEA: Farewell until tomorrow.

(AEGEUS *goes out.*)

MEDEA: Sun god Helius! I see the light! The way is clear! To be kind to your friends and merciless with your enemies: that is justice. The will of the stronger: that is justice. Now I know I have some refuge from which I can view their destruction and laugh! And now, to make my peace with Jason! There's to be a wedding. And I have some gifts to send! A robe of gold and a diadem to fit the King's daughter. A wedding gown to be her shroud! (MEDEA *laughs maniacally, then suddenly stops.*) Where is that lightning bolt? I wish it would come and kill me before I do what comes next! Nurse, bring my children to me! Come my children, come my little ones! It's twilight. Twilight brings the bird to the nest and the child to the arms of its mother. So said Sappho. How would she know? Come, come children! Let me gaze into your innocent eyes! What do I see there? I see his eyes! Jason's eyes! As long as these children live, my blood is mixed with his!

NURSE: No, Medea, no! You cannot do that! There is no animal in nature that would harm its own young!

MEDEA: Then I'll be like no other animal in nature. You haven't suffered as I have.

NURSE: But how could you find it in your heart to kill your own children?

MEDEA: It is a way to hurt my husband.

NURSE: In so doing you will hurt yourself.

MEDEA: I'm not afraid of pain. I'm used to it. Go! Bring Jason to me! And I, with soft words, will lure him into my trap! This you will do if you love me, if you are truly a woman!

(NURSE *exits.*)

KHORUS: Medea, we beg of you! Do not murder your babes! Be not the murderess of your babes! Do not murder your little ones! For if you kill them it is your own blood you spill!

MEDEA: Yes! My own blood! And Jason's!

JASON: *(Enters)* I have come at your request, although I am almost out of patience with you. What is it you want now, woman?

MEDEA: Jason, I want to apologize. I was foolish not to understand the wisdom of the course you've taken. I thought it over, and I said to myself, Why am I so mad? Why am I so angry? Jason knows what he's doing. It was a shrewd decision to marry a Princess. My own children will have Princes for brothers! We'll have wealth, power, influence! And I was such a little silly wanting to go and spoil it all. Can you forgive me, Jason? You know what women are, how weak, how helpless, how irrational. I was mad and I admit it. I should have helped you in this triumph, celebrated this new marriage, waited on the bride, and taken pleasure in it. I admit that I was wrong. I see things more clearly now. *(Turns to the house)* Children! Come, welcome your father! Say good-bye to him. And let's make peace! See Jason, I'm not angry anymore. Hold out your hands to your father, children. As you will after long life, at his grave. Our quarrel is over. Why do my eyes fill with tears?

NURSE: *(Enters)* My eyes too fill up with tears.

JASON: I forgive you, Medea. Your jealousy was quite natural. Any woman would feel the way you did if her husband took a secret love. But I'm glad to see you talking sense at last. And as for the children, I have made ample provision for them. Why are you weeping? Aren't you pleased to hear that you shall want for nothing when you leave?

MEDEA: I was thinking of the children.

JASON: Yes, and do not worry. I'll look after them.

MEDEA: I won't. It's not that I don't believe you, but women are frail things, prone to weeping.

JASON: Why should you grieve for your children?

MEDEA: I am their mother. I do not fear exile, but I beg you, ask Kreon not to banish the children!

JASON: I'll try, but I doubt that it will be of any use.

MEDEA: Then tell your wife to beg her father on their behalf.

JASON: Very well. She would do anything for me.

MEDEA: If she's like the rest of us women, she will. And I will help you to convince her. I will send her gifts, wedding gifts, that will far surpass anything else currently in fashion. A fine spun veil, a golden veil and a golden wreath, to bind her head. The children will bring them to her. Nurse! Bring me that beautiful dress. This should please her, and please her well. A handsome husband for her bed, a golden wreath to bind her head. A shimmering veil with threads of gold given to my father by Helius of old. Here children, take these wedding presents to little Kreusa and tell her I hope she likes them.

JASON: Medea, this is too much! These are a King's treasures! The House of Kreon has gold enough. Don't give it away! You have more need of money than she has now.

MEDEA: I have no use for gowns of gold. Black is my color. I'd do anything to sway her on my children's behalf. I would not stop at gold. I'd give my life! Go, children! Be suppliants to your father's new wife. Beg her not to let you be banished! And give her this raiment. Carry it carefully! Don't touch the gold, or it might tarnish. Gently, gently! There you go. Off, my brave little messengers. Come back and tell me what happens.

(Exit JASON, NURSE, and CHILDREN carrying gifts.)

KHORUS: Now there is no hope for the children's lives. No hope! No hope! They will soon be murderers. And Medea will weep for her little ones. She will weep blood!

TUTOR: *(Enters with CHILDREN)* Medea, I have good news! The Princess was well pleased with the gifts you sent. She has reprieved your boys. They need not go into exile.

MEDEA: Oh I am lost, I'm lost!

TUTOR: Why this downcast eye? Why the tear-stained cheeks? It is good news, is it not?

MEDEA: Oh, I am lost, lost!

TUTOR: But the children are safe!

MEDEA: Safe? Oh God! What have I done? There is no turning back. I planned it and my children have done it. They are murderers with me! They could have been saved. But now it is too late! The gold wreath is on her head, she wraps the sheer veil about her naked shoulders. She walks through the marble halls casting side glances into polished mirrors. Did you hear a scream? Was it real or did I imagine it? I thought I heard her scream. Listen! *(Pause)* Did you not hear it? Yes yes! It was her voice. It is too late. I and my boys are lost.

TUTOR: Have courage, Medea. Someday your boys will find you and bring you home. As long as they live there is hope for you.

MEDEA: My boys shall bring me home? Home? Where is that?

TUTOR: You are not the first to be parted from your children. Accept your fate.

MEDEA: Yes, that's what I'll do. Go bring the children to me. *(TUTOR brings* CHILDREN *from the house.)* Children, children! We will soon be far apart. Come, give your mother a kiss. Oh, these dear little lips! Most beautiful eyes. Let me look one last time into those beautiful eyes. I see the blue sea in those eyes. They're his eyes! Jason's eyes! As long as these children live, my blood is mixed with his. No, I must not do it! I cannot harm my babies! I won't do it. I'll protect them. I'll take them with me. I'll raise them. I'll see them become young men. What am I, mad? To let my enemies go free? Am I a bitch, lapping at its pups? Or am I Medea, Princess of Kolchis? Ah, but I see the nurse coming, out of breath. What news, good woman? What have you to tell?

NURSE: Oh horror horror horror! Medea, run for your life! You have done a dreadful deed!

MEDEA: What is it? What's happened?

NURSE: The Princess is dead and Kreon, too! Murdered! You, you have murdered them!

MEDEA: Ah, you've brought good news! From the way you moaned and groaned, I thought something was amiss.

MESSENGER: What, are you out of your mind? Are you mad, woman? You've outraged the royal house, and you enjoy it? Know you no fear?

MEDEA: Relax, my friend. Take your time. Tell your tale slowly. I'll enjoy it all the more if you say they died in agony.

MESSENGER: When your children came to the house of Kreon bearing gifts, all were pleased and amazed that you had had a change of heart. The whole court talked of nothing else. At first, the Princess scarcely noticed the fine gifts you sent. She couldn't take her eyes off Jason. I think she was disgusted by the children's coming there to beg. She turned away from them in a bad temper. But Jason begged her to receive them and the gifts, at which she softened her hard looks and considered the gifts with an indifferent eye. But when she saw the veil of gold and wreath to match she couldn't restrain herself. She drew the robe around her, and put the golden wreath on her curly head, and arranged her hair in a gleaming mirror, and smiled at her image in it. Then she rose from her chair and walked through the rooms strutting and showing off her finery. Then suddenly her face turned pale. She staggered back. Her legs trembled. She fell onto a chair. An aged servant cried out, Good God! Then she began to foam at the mouth, and her eyes rolled back, and the blood flew from her face. She let out a huge shriek, a savage cry. The women ran through the hall like a flock of birds frightened at the twang of a bow. The whole palace echoed with running footsteps, like a racetrack. Then with a terrible groan she came to herself. The wreath of gold resting on her head burst into flame. She ran through the palace like a human torch. The golden veil, too, burst into flame and cooked her flesh as she ran. She tried to rip the diadem away, but the flesh came with it. Part of her face was disfigured. Her eyeballs popped from their sockets, and from her mouth oozed blood and fire mixed together. And like pine pitch it dripped down on her charred breasts. By now the bones were visible. And like a hideous skeleton dancing in the flames her teeth were poison fangs. Then Kreon came and fell upon the corpse as if to snuff the fire out, and wept, My poor child! And as his tears fell on her charred bones, they sputtered and made steam. He shrieked, Who has destroyed you? Who has robbed me of what I held most dear? Oh let me die with you, my child! But when he was through with weeping and wailing, he tried to raise himself to his feet. But as the ivy clings to the twigs of the laurel so he stuck to that veil of gold and struggled fearfully. And as he tried to pull himself off she pulled him down. The harder he tugged, the more his ancient flesh was ripped from its bones. Until he, unhappy man, gave up the ghost and fell down into that same pool of molten tar, flesh, innards, and excrement.

MEDEA: *(Sighs)* Ahh. I feel as though a great weight had been lifted from me. I feel light. I feel merry. You've told good news well. I'll never forget you for this. You'll be rewarded.

NURSE: Medea, you will never escape from punishment for this. You've brought a sorrow on yourself.

MEDEA: Life is but a shadow. Death is a great light. Oh, that I who've known such grief should know such happiness at last! The sun has set on Kreon and his daughter forever. They are no more, but I can still feel the rays of the sun on my face. This must be pure happiness, a joy few mortals ever know. *(She laughs long and wildly. Then suddenly she gasps)* I see a chasm yawning before me, a great abyss. Oh God, will I have the strength to do what comes next? It is too cruel. I can't bear it! To be a comedian on the stage of life! We mortals suffer while the Gods laugh. Come Medea, don't be a coward! Forget you are their mother just this once. Act now and weep later. *(She rushes into the house.)*

NURSE: No, no! Don't do it, Medea! You'll regret it the rest of your life!

CHILDREN: No, Mother! Aagh!

NURSE: Oh heart of flint! You can kill your own flesh and blood. Hell hath no fury like a woman's scorn.

JASON: *(Enters)* You, woman! Where is Medea? Is she still here or has she fled? Does she think she can commit murder and get away with it? I don't care what happens to her now, for I've come to save my boys! To smuggle them out of the country before Kreon's men come for them. For they will pay for their mother's evil deeds!

NURSE: Oh unhappy man! Your sorrows have only begun.

JASON: What? Does she plan to kill me too?

NURSE: Worse, worse than that.

JASON: Break down the door! And drag Medea out! I want my children before she can do harm to them!

(They batter at the gates of the house. MEDEA appears at the door.)

MEDEA: Who is knocking at the door of my house? What do you want? Why have you come here?

JASON: Monster Medea! I want my sons!

MEDEA: Don't come near me. You dare not touch me. Sun god Helius protects me. He sent a chariot for me. I'm coming! I'm coming! Say what you have to say. I haven't long.

JASON: Vile woman! How on earth did you contrive these things? I wish you were dead. I should have killed you when I met you. You're a monster, not a woman. A destructive witch! Give me back my boys!

MEDEA: Give them to you? No, never! I'll let you see them only. No one wounds this proud heart that doesn't pay for it. *(She shows him the dead bodies of the* CHILDREN. JASON *groans and retches.)* Here they are, Jason. This is the way I want you to remember them always.

JASON: Oh my children! What a wicked mother you had.

MEDEA: They died of a disease they caught from you, Jason.

JASON: It was not my hatred that destroyed them.

MEDEA: No, it was your love for little Kreusa.

JASON: And for that you killed them?

MEDEA: Do you think love is so small a thing for a woman?

JASON: Are you completely evil?

MEDEA: I killed them because I hated you more than I loved them, and I wanted to make you suffer.

JASON: But you're suffering, too, I see. These dead children bring down curses on you!

MEDEA: The Gods know who is to blame.

JASON: Yes, the Gods know, and they know your vile heart!

MEDEA: Go ahead and hate me. But I'm tired of listening to you. And I'm late. The one day Kreon granted me is almost up. And I fear I overstay my welcome.

JASON: Give me the bodies that I may at least give them a decent burial.

MEDEA: No. I will bury them myself, in my own way. So that no enemy may touch them by digging up their graves. And I will establish, in the land of Korinth, a holy feast and sacrifice each year forever to atone for this guilt. And now I go to Aegeus's house, where I will find a strange welcome, while you will die in obscurity, a ludicrous death, when a piece of your ship's rotted timber falls on your head and lays you flat. Until that day, Jason, savor the bitter taste of my love!

JASON: May a fury avenge these children's blood on you and tear you to pieces.

MEDEA: Do you think the Gods heed the prayers of traitors?

JASON: I hate you. Murderess of my children!

MEDEA: Go bury your bride.

JASON: I go, and I mourn my children, too.

MEDEA: You don't feel it yet. Wait for the future. Then it will dawn on you.

JASON: Oh, my children, I loved them so.

MEDEA: I loved them. You did not.

JASON: You killed them! How can you say you loved them?

MEDEA: I killed them to hurt you, Jason.

JASON: Oh let me kiss my children's lips!

MEDEA: Now you want to kiss their lips. But when you had the chance you rejected them.

JASON: Let me touch their delicate flesh!

MEDEA: You're wasting your breath, Jason.

JASON: Oh God! Punish this murderess, this monster, this hateful woman, murderess of children! I will never stop calling upon the Gods to punish you. You've killed my boys! You won't let me touch them or bury them! I wish I had never begot them, to see them slaughtered by their mother!

MEDEA: No more talk. My chariot has come.

(She lifts the CHILDREN, *takes them into the chariot with her. The wheels of the chariot turn. The wind comes up. Her cape billows behind her. The house and all below drift away. We see only* MEDEA *in her chariot drawn by dragons, flying through the clouds.)*

JASON: Do you feel no guilt? No shame?

MEDEA: Why should I feel guilt or shame? I am not responsible for these. I am not responsible for my actions. They were destined before I was born! *(She laughs a little dubiously as the curtain falls.)*

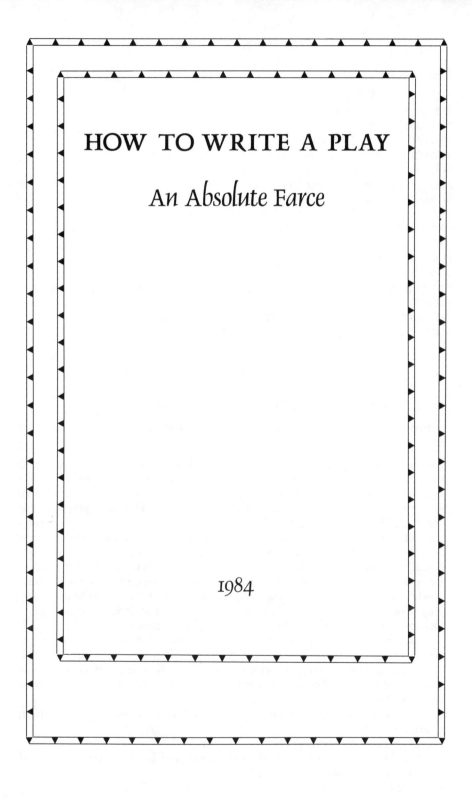

HOW TO WRITE A PLAY

An Absolute Farce

1984

Cast of Characters

CHARLES, *a playwright*
EVERETT, *his roommate and man Friday*
NATALIE, *his maid*
UNITED PARCEL DELIVERY MAN
MADAME WONG, *macrobiotic cook*
MR. POUSSY, *composer*
MRS. HORNBLATT, *a neighbor*
ROSALIE, *her daughter*
CLAUDIA, *a friend*
ORVILLE TITWILLY, *balloon folder*
JOUJOUKA, *a belly dancer*
FIRE DEPARTMENT
GAY SENIORS
GENERALISIMO JULIO CARRAGUA FANFARRON, *a South American general*
MIGUEL, *his assistant and translator*
THE EMPEROR AND EMPRESS OF HUMIDIA
A GORILLA

ACT I

Scene: *The apartment-studio of Charles, a playwright.*

(CHARLES *enters in his pajamas, stretches, yawns, and goes to the window and looks out.*)

CHARLES: Ah! Beautiful day. Perfect day. And today is the day I'm going to write a play. But first I'll quickly take care of a few things. (*Looks over his extensive plant collection*) Make some coffee. Ah, the stipelia has a new bud. I've got to water the bilbergia nutans. (*Gets watering can*) The ophiopogon needs repotting, BUT—NOT TODAY! Because today is the day I'm going to write a play. First feed the fish. (*Sighs*) And the birds. They really need water changes. Not today. Not today. I've got to write a play. Their cages need cleaning but not today. Brush my teeth. Comb what's left of my hair. Shave—not today. I've got to write a play. I've got to write a play. My face needs a rest anyway. (*Looks in mirror*) The poor thing looks exhausted. Between shaving and mugging it really gets a workout. (*Commanding himself in the mirror*) Write a play! Do you hear me? Write a play! You've put it off long enough. (*Meekly*) I'll try. (*Sits at typewriter. Business of getting comfortable, adjusting the light, the chair, the typewriter, the paper*) The light is perfect. The chair is comfortable. The paper is clean. (*Raises his fingers as if to type*) The light is too perfect. The chair is too comfortable. The paper is too clean. (*Stares at the blank sheet of paper in the typewriter*)
EVERETT: (*Enters with two long swatches of fabric trailing behind*) Good morning Charles.
CHARLES: Good morning Everett.
EVERETT: I can't make up my mind. Which of these fabrics do you think would be best for Salammbô's first entrance veil?
CHARLES: I think this one.
EVERETT: Good. I'll use the other.

CHARLES: Then why did you ask me?

EVERETT: Because you have absolutely no taste. And if you like it, then the other one must be the right choice.

CHARLES: Thanks.

EVERETT: Thank *you.*

CHARLES: By the way. We're not doing *Salammbô* next.

EVERETT: We're not?

CHARLES: No. There isn't time.

EVERETT: Well, I'm certainly glad you told me. I was just about to shop the fabrics. What are we going to do?

CHARLES: I'm not sure.

EVERETT: Well, you'd better make up your mind. You only have three weeks to get it on.

CHARLES: I know. I just didn't feel that three weeks was enough to stage *Salammbô.* The splendor of the ancient world. The battle scenes. For that, we need at least four weeks.

EVERETT: Larry already put the casting notice in the trades.

CHARLES: We'll just have to have someone meet them at the theater, take their pix and res, and tell them I will consider them for the fall.

EVERETT: All right. But I was really looking forward to costuming the barbarians.

CHARLES: Elaborate?

EVERETT: No. I think in costuming muscle men less is more.

CHARLES: You've got something there.

EVERETT: *(Dreamily)* Armies of men without false modesty of *any* kind.

CHARLES: Next season. And now I've got to write. So if I could have it quiet.

EVERETT: You mean I can't even play an opera?

CHARLES: *(Thinks a moment)* Well, an opera might not be too bad. It might even help.

EVERETT: Good. *(Puts record on. The opera is the* William Tell Overture *by Rossini)*

CHARLES: *(Tries to write but jangled by the music)* No opera. I just can't work.

EVERETT: *(Taking off the record)* All right. I don't know why you hate opera.

CHARLES: I don't hate opera. I go whether I need the sleep or not. It's just that it *demands* to be listened to. And I've got to write a play.

EVERETT: I've got to work in here.

CHARLES: You do?

EVERETT: Yes. I've got to work somewhere.

CHARLES: All right. If you're quiet.

EVERETT: *(Begins ripping seams.* CHARLES *gives him a withering look)* I'm taking this costume apart since we're not doing *Salammbô.*

CHARLES: Leave it. We'll do *Salammbô*—someday. Now Everett, I can't impress upon you enough that I've got to have absolute quiet to work. I mean silence.

EVERETT: *(Shouts)* All right! All right! *(Puts work away and starts to tiptoe across the room. His shoes squeak.* CHARLES *gives him a look)* New shoes!

CHARLES: Shhhh. Please. *(*EVERETT *removes his shoes and tiptoes. The bones in his toes crack. Doorbell)* Who can that be?

EVERETT: *(Goes to intercom)* Hello?

INTERCOM: *(Singsong)* Natalie.

EVERETT: It's Natalie.

CHARLES: Oh no. Today is her day.

EVERETT: You told her to come today.

CHARLES: I forgot all about it.

EVERETT: Shall I send her away?

CHARLES: We can't do that. Let her come. The place is a mess. It needs her.

(Knock at the door. EVERETT *lets in* NATALIE, *a cleaning woman of heroic proportions.)*

NATALIE: You forgot I was coming.

CHARLES: No, of course not.

NATALIE: You want me to come another time?

CHARLES: Ummm. No no. We need you. Go ahead. I'm glad you're here. I always work better in a clean environment. *(Starts to type)*

NATALIE: *(Changes and brings out a vacuum cleaner)* What's he doing? *(Turns on vacuum)*

EVERETT: He's writing a play.

NATALIE: What?

EVERETT: *(Over vacuum)* He's writing a play.

NATALIE: *(Shouting)* He's what?

EVERETT: *(Shouting)* HE'S WRITING A PLAY!

NATALIE: *(Turning off the vacuum cleaner)* I'm sorry. I couldn't hear you. What did you say he's doing?

EVERETT: He's writing a play.

NATALIE: Writing a play! He is something. Yes he is.

EVERETT: He's something all right.

NATALIE: How does he do it?

EVERETT: Do what?

NATALIE: Write all those plays. I don't like writing. I don't even like to read. You're something, you are.

CHARLES: *(Feebly, sheepishly)* Thank you Natalie.

NATALIE: *(Slaps him on the back and starts the vacuum)* I don't know how you do it. Move your feet. *(She vacuums under his feet. Phone rings.* NATALIE *answers without turning off the vacuum cleaner)* Hello! *(Shouts)* Speak up, I can't hear you! How's that? Wait a minute. Wait a minute. *(She turns off the vacuum)* It's for you. *(Gives phone to* CHARLES*)*

CHARLES: Hello. *(*NATALIE *turns the vacuum back on)* HELLO. I can't hear you. Just a minute. Natalie turn off the vacuum cleaner.

NATALIE: What?

CHARLES: Turn off the vacuum cleaner!

NATALIE: What?

CHARLES: Natalie.

NATALIE: *(Turns off the vacuum cleaner and crosses to* CHARLES*)* Now what was it you wanted?

CHARLES: *(Quietly)* Turn the vacuum cleaner off.

NATALIE: It's off.

CHARLES: Don't vacuum anymore. This is an important phone call from my manager. Hello. Yes. The play? Oh, it's coming along. Yes. I'm writing it now. Well, I don't have anything down on paper yet. But I've been thinking about it a lot. You know, thinking is part of the process too. Yes, I know, three weeks. Yes. Or else we have to give the forty thousand dollars back. I know. Don't worry. I'm writing it now. *(Doorbell)* Oh, now who is it?

EVERETT: *(Enters and crosses the stage)* I'll get it. You just keep writing. *(At the intercom)* Hello? Hello? I can't hear you! Speak up! Parnell? I don't know any Parnell. Oh, parcel! Oh, United Parcel! Oh, come right up. *(To* CHARLES*)* Were you expecting a package?

CHARLES: No.

EVERETT: I wonder what it is. How's the writing coming?

CHARLES: I've almost got a title.

(Knock at the door. EVERETT *goes, opens the door.)*

UNITED PARCEL MAN: *(Enters)* Package for Robert Ludlum.

EVERETT: Are you sure you don't mean Charles Ludlam?

UNITED PARCEL MAN: Whatever. Sign here.

EVERETT: He wants you to sign.

CHARLES: *(Gets up, crosses to* UNITED PARCEL MAN, *and signs)*

EVERETT: *(Aside)* You've got to give him something.

CHARLES: I don't think you have to tip mailmen.

EVERETT: *(Looking over the* UNITED PARCEL MAN*)* Oh I think you really should.

CHARLES: *(Searches for wallet, tips* PARCEL MAN *ten cents)*

UNITED PARCEL MAN: Here, keep it. You need it more than I do. *(Exits)*

CHARLES: I wonder what's inside. *(Shakes package)*

EVERETT: Open it!

CHARLES: *(Opens package)* Oh God!

EVERETT: What is it?

CHARLES: Plays. Dozens of them.

EVERETT: Do you think they're any good?

CHARLES: *(Opening one or two)* They all have characters named Gillian and Sandy.

EVERETT: Oh, here's a life of Benjamin Franklin!

CHARLES: Really? Maybe . . . no.

EVERETT: Well give it a chance. Why don't we read the opening scene together. You read Benjamin Franklin. And I'll read . . . *(In a sick voice)* Sandy?

CHARLES: Forget it. I've got to write. Someone's got to keep the torch of culture alive.

EVERETT: That's a mixed metaphor.

CHARLES: They're my metaphors and I'll mix them if I please.

EVERETT: Don't get testy.

CHARLES: I'm sorry. It's just that I've got to write this play.

EVERETT: Well, write it! Who's stopping you?

CHARLES: I feel faint.

EVERETT: No wonder. You haven't eaten a thing today. You're working too hard.

CHARLES: I can't stop to eat. There's no time for that.

EVERETT: Do you want me to go out and get you something?

CHARLES: No! I've taken care of it. I've hired a macrobiotic cook to come in and prepare my meals for me while I'm writing so that I don't have to go out or even think about it. Nothing must take me away from my work, do you hear? Nothing. And a macrobiotic diet lends itself perfectly to intellectual work.

EVERETT: Why?

CHARLES: Human culture evolved simultaneously with the development of cereal grain. The grain of rice is exactly the same shape as the human brain.

EVERETT: That explains a lot of things.

(Doorbell.)

CHARLES: That must be Madame Wong now. Would you get it? I've got to keep writing.

EVERETT: Certainly. *(At intercom)* Hello?

INTERCOM: Madame Wong.

EVERETT: Come in. *(Buzzes)* It's Madame Wong.

CHARLES: Good. What I need right now is brown rice, sautéed vegetables, and seaweed. Great bowls of slimy seaweed. Yum yum.

EVERETT: Seaweed? Ech. Repulsive.

(Sound of a gong. The door opens. MADAME WONG *enters in a dragon lady dress with a slit up the side and fuck-me pumps. She carries with her an enormous bunch of celery.)*

CHARLES: Madame Wong, it's wonderful to see you again. I hope you can work in our kitchen.

MADAME WONG: *(Looking deeply into his eyes)* Central nervous system badly damaged.

CHARLES: I don't doubt it.

MADAME WONG: *(Looking closely at* EVERETT*)* River no good.

EVERETT: River?

CHARLES: Liver.

EVERETT: Oh, liver!

MADAME WONG: Need to eat seaweed, much seaweed.

CHARLES: The kitchen is this way. If you need anything, just yell. *(Shows* MADAME WONG *off right. Sees* EVERETT *leaving)* Where are you going?

EVERETT: Out for bacon and eggs.

(Knock at the door.)

CHARLES: Would you see who that is? I've got to write this play.

EVERETT: Certainly. Who is it?

VOICE OUTSIDE THE DOOR: I am Mr. Poussy. I want to see Mr. Ludlam.

EVERETT: In reference to what?

VOICE OUTSIDE THE DOOR: It's a most urgent matter.

EVERETT: What's wrong?

VOICE OUTSIDE THE DOOR: It's a matter of life and death, I tell you!

EVERETT: Charles, it's a Mr. Poussy. He says it's a matter of life and death. He says it's urgent.

CHARLES: It's always urgent for them. That doesn't mean it's urgent for me.

VOICE OUTSIDE THE DOOR: Please. Please. I must see Mr. Ludlam. His whole career may depend on it.

EVERETT: Charles, he says your whole career may depend on it. I think you'd better see him. It sounds important.

CHARLES: Ask him what it is. I can't see him now.

EVERETT: He can't see you now, but if you'll just tell me what it is, I'll pass the message on.

VOICE OUTSIDE THE DOOR: I have composed a song. And if Mr. Ludlam would only sing it in one of his shows I'm sure it would be a great success. Show it to Mr. Ludlam and ask him what he thinks of it.

EVERETT: I'll show it to him. He wants you to sing his song in one of your shows.

CHARLES: *(With a sigh)* Let me see it.

"If you'd only studied yoga you could kiss your ass good-bye."

This is asinine. *(Hands it back to* EVERETT *who takes it to the door)*

POUSSY: What did he think?

EVERETT: He says your song is asinine.

POUSSY: How can that be? Perhaps he needs to hear the arrangement. You must let me see him. Let me play it for him. I'm sure he'll change his mind.

EVERETT: He wants to play you the arrangement.

CHARLES: No no no no no!

EVERETT: He says no.

CHARLES: Oh, I've got to take a break. *(Exits)*

(Doorbell.)

EVERETT: Yes? Who is it?

VOICE ON INTERCOM: Flowers.

EVERETT: Send them up.

CHARLES: *(Calling off)* Who is that?

EVERETT: *(Calls back)* Flowers.

CHARLES: Flowers?

EVERETT: That's what he said.

(Knock at the door. The U.P.S. MAN *comes in with an enormous bouquet of roses.)*

UNITED PARCEL MAN: Sign here.

EVERETT: One moment please. *(Takes the sheet to the next room to* CHARLES*)*

(The U.P.S. MAN *stands waiting.* MR. POUSSY *sneaks in through the open door.)*

POUSSY: *(To* U.P.S. MAN*)* That's quite a bouquet of flowers.

UNITED PARCEL MAN: Big.

POUSSY: Who are they from?

UNITED PARCEL MAN: There isn't any card.

POUSSY: What? No card? Can you imagine? Spending that much on flowers and not even telling who it's from?

UNITED PARCEL MAN: You'd be surprised how many people do that.

POUSSY: *(Aside)* It's a shame to let all those flowers go to waste. *(He takes out a little card, signs his name, and slips it in)*

EVERETT: *(Reenters with the sheet, gives it to the* U.P.S. MAN, *and hands him a dollar)*

UNITED PARCEL MAN: Thanks a lot. You're a nice guy, not like that other cheapskate. *(Exits)*

POUSSY: Really, if you just give me another chance to speak to Mr. Ludlam. I know his style. I know just the kind of material he wants. Believe me, I'm sure that I can write on the level of his taste.

EVERETT: Is that up or down from your usual level?

POUSSY: No, I think we're really of a mind. Here's some other material. Could you please put in a good word for me?

EVERETT: I'm sorry. I'm sorry. He said your work is asinine and I don't think it's wise to push it. We don't accept unsolicited manuscripts. Now would you please go?

POUSSY: If I could just have a word with him. I'll wait outside.

EVERETT: I really think you're wasting your time.

POUSSY: No trouble at all. I'm sure it will be worth it. *(Goes out)*

EVERETT: *(Closes the door after him)*

CHARLES: *(Enters)* So many flowers. Did I die or did I win the Kentucky Derby? Who are they from?

EVERETT: I don't know. Look at the card. *(Takes card out of the bouquet and hands it to* CHARLES*)*

CHARLES: "With sincere admiration, Ima Pussy."

EVERETT: *(Correcting him)* Poussy.

CHARLES: Poussy? Who is that?

EVERETT: It's that composer.

CHARLES: Oh dear. I feel guilty. I wouldn't even see him. These flowers are simply gorgeous. He was so generous and I was so stingy with my time. *(Smells the flowers)* But what's this? *(Removes a jewelry case from the bouquet. Opens it and gasps)* It's a necklace, earrings, bracelet, and ring. An incredible matched set. You don't see paste like this anymore. Costume jewelry of this quality costs a fortune. This isn't that shit they wear in *Cage aux Folles* that screams drag queen. This is a copy of a Harry Winston.

EVERETT: Let me see that. There's something inscribed on the back: "To the divine Galas, from her willing slave, Harry Winston."

CHARLES: Harry Winston's been dead for years.

EVERETT: Charles, this isn't a copy. This jewelry is real!

CHARLES: *(Almost drops the jewelry, as though it had suddenly turned hot in his hands)* Real! Why a set of rocks like this must be worth several hundred thousand dollars! Do you know how much junk jewelry I could buy with that?

EVERETT: I think your junk jewelry days are behind you. You've got the real thing there, honey.

CHARLES: No, I'd be terrified to wear anything of this value. Compared to this stuff, my life wouldn't be worth a plug nickel. People have been decapitated for a fourteen-karat-gold-plated chain. Are you sure they're not diamelles?

EVERETT: *(Inserting a jeweler's loupe into his eye)* No, these are the real thing. And you've got some emeralds and rubies thrown in there for good measure.

CHARLES: God, I feel terrible about having been so rude to Mr. Pussy.

EVERETT: Poussy.

CHARLES: Maybe his song wasn't so bad after all. We could change it around a little bit. *(Trying on the necklace and earrings)* I really should keep an eye out for new material.

EVERETT: Let me try it on.

CHARLES: Later, if you're good.

EVERETT: He's still waiting outside. He's a terrible bore but perhaps you should see him.

CHARLES: You're right. I can't put it off another minute. But I've got to get back to my writing! Leave me alone with him for about five minutes, and then come in and say that I have another appointment and that it's very important and I mustn't keep it waiting.

EVERETT: Ah yes. The usual treatment for bores.

CHARLES: Yes. Exactly. Send Mr. Pussy in.

EVERETT: Poussy. Mr. Poussy, Mr. Ludlam will see you now.

CHARLES: Come right in Mr. Poussy.

POUSSY: How do you do? I know that you didn't care for my . . .

CHARLES: Care for it? I found it fascinating! Sit down Mr. Pussy.

POUSSY: Poussy. Ima Poussy.

CHARLES: Oh don't say that. I'm sure you're wonderful once you get to know you.

POUSSY: But but I mean, I uh . . .

CHARLES: Sit down. Sit down you naughty boy! *(Referring to the stack of manuscript pages in* MR. POUSSY's *hands)* Are these all your songs? Shame on you, you've been holding out on me!

POUSSY: Holding out on you?

CHARLES: Thought you could get away without showing me more of your work, did you?

POUSSY: I should say so, after you said my song was asinine!

CHARLES: Asinine? I said asinine? You must have misunderstood. I said it was . . . absolutely sublime!

POUSSY: *(Astonished)* Really?

CHARLES: But before we go on, I want to thank you for these lovely flowers.

POUSSY: *(Momentarily puzzled)* Flowers? *(Then realizing)* Oh. Oh. Yes, the flowers. Oh. Oh it was nothing!

CHARLES: Nothing? How could you say that? It was very extravagant of you. Look at this necklace. These earrings. This ring. This bracelet! See, I've put them on.

POUSSY: Yes, so it seems.

CHARLES: This ruby is really magnificent.

POUSSY: Ruby? That's what it is all right. You can imagine what a thing like that costs.

CHARLES: I can! Believe me, I appreciate it.

POUSSY: Jewels like that cost a small fortune.

EVERETT: They do?

CHARLES: Of course they do. I knew that.

POUSSY: You could feed a family for three years on what a ring like that costs.

EVERETT: *(Aside to* CHARLES*)* This is disgusting!

CHARLES: Well I just want you to know that I appreciate it. It just shows that the person who gave it is extremely generous.

POUSSY: He certainly was. Now getting back to my song . . .

MADAME WONG: Runch is leady!

CHARLES: It is? Oh wonderful. I'll help you serve. Mr. Pussy, you must stay for lunch. *(Exits to kitchen)*

POUSSY: *(Calling after him)* Poussy!

EVERETT: *(Turning on* MR. POUSSY*)* All right, what gives? What are you up to?

POUSSY: Up to? I'm sure I don't know what you mean.

EVERETT: I'll tell you what I mean. You're in love with Charles. And you're making a play for him.

POUSSY: I'm what?

EVERETT: You're in love with him. Don't try to deny it.

POUSSY: My friend, I think you've gotten the wrong impression!

EVERETT: Don't you lie to me, Pussy.

POUSSY: Poussy! Ima Poussy!

EVERETT: I'll say you are! You'd just better keep away from him if you know what's good for you, or I'll kill you. I'll kill you.

POUSSY: Surely you have the wrong impression.

EVERETT: I have the wrong impression! You're going to get an impression all right. From my fist. If I see you so much as touch him, I'll break every bone in your body.

POUSSY: Whatever gives you the idea that I'm in love with Ludlam? I'm not queer.

CHARLES: *(Sweeps back into the room)* I'm so sorry to have left you alone so long.

POUSSY: That's all right.

CHARLES: Now we can have our little tête-à-tête.

EVERETT: *(Aside to* POUSSY*)* Watch it, Pussy.

POUSSY: *(Aside)* My interest in Mr. Ludlam is purely professional.

CHARLES: Now where were we?

POUSSY: You said my song was . . .

CHARLES: Ah, your song! It was brilliant. Those lyrics! You're another Cole Porter!

POUSSY: Thank you! *(Turns to* EVERETT, *aside)* And you thought he said it was asinine.

CHARLES: But I think it needs a little tightening up. I think we could rework it a bit.

POUSSY: *(Somewhat put out)* I don't know! I . . .

CHARLES: It needs . . . a little . . . wit. That's it! Something witty! It needs wittier lyrics, and maybe a different tune. That's all.

POUSSY: But the form—

CHARLES: *(Interrupting)* Form it's got. And it has the advantage of brevity. But perhaps with some castanets, something to liven it up a bit. Something about it is, I don't know, how do you say, flat. Don't get me wrong, the song is brilliant. But it's a little ahead of its time. It's trendy but without seeming new. It's avant-garde and old hat at the same time. It's . . . it's a puzzle, that's what it is. But I'm sure something could be done with it.

EVERETT: Charles, don't forget your three o'clock appointment.

CHARLES: Oh, I'm terribly sorry, Mr. Poussy, but I have to interrupt our meeting. I have another appointment.

POUSSY: That's all right. I'll wait.

CHARLES: No no. No need to wait. This may go on a very long time.

POUSSY: Oh I don't mind. I have nothing better to do.

CHARLES: Oh, but I couldn't possibly dream of wasting your valuable time.

POUSSY: No no, really, I don't mind.

CHARLES: But the woman's a terrible bore! This meeting may go on for hours! It's impossible to get rid of her once she gets here.

POUSSY: A bore you say? Let her come in. When she sees you're busy with me she'll get the idea and go away.

CHARLES: No no no. I have to see her privately.

POUSSY: What's the bore's name?

CHARLES: Mrs. Traherne.

POUSSY: Oh I know her. Mrs. Traherne is an old friend of mine.

CHARLES: No no. This is a different Mrs. Traherne. She's a terrible bore.

POUSSY: I'll just wait in the next room. *(Exits)*

CHARLES: Will he ever leave? Well I can't worry about it now. I've got to write this play. He can wait in the next room forever for all I care.

POUSSY: *(Reappearing)* I have a solution for you. I'll wait in the next room. I'll give you about five minutes with her. Then I'll pretend to have just arrived and you tell them that it's some bore you have an appointment with.

CHARLES: Brilliant idea! You do that.

POUSSY: *(Exits into the next room)*

CHARLES: *(Sits down to write; begins typing furiously. Knock at the door)* Good god! Not again! *(Gets up and goes to the door)*

MRS. HORNBLATT: Mr. Ludlam? It's your neighbor Mrs. Hornblatt, from downstairs.

CHARLES: Mrs. Hornblatt, you caught me at an awkward moment. I'm busy. I really can't see you now.

MRS. HORNBLATT: *(Putting her foot in the door)* This won't take but a minute. Remember I told you about my daughter? Well she's back from nursing school and I thought you might give her an audition. She's a triple threat, you know. I'm sure you could use her in one of your plays.

CHARLES: I really don't think . . .

MRS. HORNBLATT: She's multitalented. She studied ballet, acrobatic, and tap, and she can play the kazoo. It's really cute when she plays the kazoo.

CHARLES: I'm sure it is, Mrs. Hornblatt, but you caught me at a bad time.

MRS. HORNBLATT: You're such a nice man. I know you'll love my daughter. To know her is to love her. Couldn't you just see a little bit of her routine? I won't take no for an answer.

CHARLES: All right. I'll see her briefly.

MRS. HORNBLATT: Come in, Rosalie, and meet the big man. She's awful cute, Mr. Ludlam. You'll see. She's another Shirley Temple.

CHARLES: Shirley . . . *(ROSALIE enters, a very good-looking adult dressed in Mary Janes and a jumper with a bow in her hair. It is obvious that her mother is preventing her from making the transition from child "star.")* What the . . . ?

MRS. HORNBLATT: If you need a little girl, she's perfect. She's a little well developed for her age.

CHARLES: What does she do?

MRS. HORNBLATT: She does the new math tap routine.

CHARLES: How does it go? Let's see it.

MRS. HORNBLATT: How much is two and two, Rosalie?

ROSALIE: *(Beats the ground with one foot four times)*

MRS. HORNBLATT: Four! Right! Very good! How much is five plus three, Rosalie?

ROSALIE: *(Paws the ground seven times)*

MRS. HORNBLATT: One more.

ROSALIE: *(Paws the ground one time)*

MRS. HORNBLATT: Eight! Right! How much is—

CHARLES: *(Shouts)* That's enough! This is pathetic! It's a little elementary, don't you think, Mrs. Hornblatt?

MRS. HORNBLATT: Wait! Wait! You haven't seen the gazintas!

CHARLES: The gazintas? What are they?

MRS. HORNBLATT: Watch. Rosalie, tell me how many times three gazinta nine.

ROSALIE: *(Taps her foot against the floor three times)*

CHARLES: Mrs. Hornblatt, have you considered family counseling? There's something terribly wrong here.

MRS. HORNBLATT: Wait! Wait! You haven't heard her sing . . .

CHARLES: She sings, too?

MRS. HORNBLATT: Like a bird! Sing, Rosalie. Sing!

([MRS. HORNBLATT hands ROSALIE a baby bottle. ROSALIE takes a swig and]
begins to sing "Old Man River" [while gargling].)

CHARLES: Mrs. Hornblatt! Mrs. Hornblatt! Stop! Stop, Rosalie!

MRS. HORNBLATT: Do you think you can do anything for her?

CHARLES: Perhaps, Mrs. Hornblatt. I'd like to speak to Rosalie alone for a moment. Would you mind waiting in the next room?

MRS. HORNBLATT: I could use a glass of water.

CHARLES: The kitchen is right through there.

MRS. HORNBLATT: Oh, don't bother. I'll help myself. *(Exits)*

CHARLES: *(To* ROSALIE*)* Rosalie! How old are you?

ROSALIE: *(She starts to tap her foot)*

CHARLES: Rosalie, stop that! Speak to me! How old are you?

ROSALIE: Twenty-six.

CHARLES: How long have you wanted to be in show business?

ROSALIE: Do you want the truth?

CHARLES: Truth is the safest lie, Rosalie.

ROSALIE: I don't. I never wanted to. I do it for mama.

CHARLES: What do *you* want, Rosalie?

ROSALIE: What do I want?

CHARLES: Yes. What do you want out of life?

ROSALIE: Mama thinks that I should—

CHARLES: Never mind what mama thinks. What do you want, Rosalie?

ROSALIE: I don't know. I just want to make mama happy.

CHARLES: Rosalie, something tells me that you're utterly miserable.

ROSALIE: I am. But don't tell mama. It would break her heart. I only want mama to be happy.

CHARLES: Rosalie, I think you'd better start doing something to make Rosalie happy or one day you're going to take a hatchet and bury it in mama's head, and that wouldn't be nice, would it?

ROSALIE: No.

CHARLES: Rosalie, I'm going to give you a part in my play, not because I think you'll succeed, but because I think you'll fail, and then you'll be free, Rosalie. Free of mama forever.

ROSALIE: Thank you. But tell me one thing.

CHARLES: Yes?

ROSALIE: How did you know?

CHARLES: Know what?

ROSALIE: About the hatchet.

CHARLES: I'm a playwright. I know people.

MRS. HORNBLATT: *(Entering)* That was the best glass of water I've ever had in my life! It was really delicious. The water in my apartment doesn't taste that good.

CHARLES: Mrs. Hornblatt, I think I see great potential in your daughter. And I'm going to give her a part in my new show. *(Aside)* Whatever that may be, and if I ever get it written. Now if you'll excuse me, I have to get back to work.

MRS. HORNBLATT: Mr. Ludlam, you've made me the happiest woman in the world. Come Rosalie. Are you happy, Rosalie? One for yes, two for no.

ROSALIE: *(Taps her foot once)*

POUSSY: *(Pops his head in)* Excuse me, Mr. Ludlam, but I believe we had a three-fifteen appointment.

MRS. HORNBLATT: *(Seeing* POUSSY*)* Ima!

POUSSY: Frieda!

MRS. HORNBLATT: So where have you been?

POUSSY: Frieda, let me explain!

MRS. HORNBLATT: I don't want to hear any explanations. Fifteen years ago you went out to buy a bottle of horseradish for the gefilte fish and you never came back! I've been waiting, Ima. It's been a long time to be without horseradish. Where is the horseradish, Ima?

POUSSY: Frieda darling, there were extenuating circumstances.

MRS. HORNBLATT: You heel, you beast, you deserter!

POUSSY: I had to leave you, Frieda. You were always melancholy. You had a head like a melon and a face like a collie.

[*(*CHARLES *types this line.)*]

MRS. HORNBLATT: When I married you you promised me big things!

POUSSY: I fooled you, didn't I?

ROSALIE: *(Wailing)* Mama! Who is this man?

MRS. HORNBLATT: This is your father, dear, the no-good SOB.

POUSSY: Frieda, let me explain!

EVERETT: Could you two please step outside? Mr. Ludlam has got to write a play.

(They exit, all talking at once.)

ROSALIE: *(Wails)* Mama! Papa! Stop it!

CHARLES: *(Collapsing in front of the typewriter)* Oh, god. I've got to write a play. Time is running out. I haven't accomplished anything today.

EVERETT: *(With heavy sarcasm)* Planning to do a musical?

CHARLES: No, why?

EVERETT: I saw the way you threw yourself at that composer.

CHARLES: Don't be ridiculous. The man has been most generous. The least I can do is hear him out.

EVERETT: Huh!

CHARLES: Now I've got to write. I've really got to write. I can't put it off another minute.

(The doorbell rings again. CHARLES *groans.)*

EVERETT: I'll get it. Hello?

INTERCOM: Claudia.

CHARLES: Claudia? Oh thank god! Claudia! She's always good for moral support.

CLAUDIA: *(Bursts into the room, an explosion of haute couture)* Charles darling! How is my little genius today? Creating another masterpiece for the dramatic stage?

*(*EVERETT *exits.)*

CHARLES: Claudia my pet, it doesn't look good. I'm trying desperately to write but the world seems to militate against it.

CLAUDIA: Well darling, I have fabulous news for you.

CHARLES: Really? What kind of good news?

CLAUDIA: Career news, darling. You're made. I've found the patron that we've all been waiting for. The man's a perfect dream! And he wants to give you heaps of money to just do anything you want with in the theater.

CHARLES: Claudia, how can this be?

CLAUDIA: I know it's unbelievable, but there it is. He's a South American millionaire, Generalisimo Julio Carragua Fanfarron.

CHARLES: Generalisimo?

CLAUDIA: Yes, he's a general from Uruguay. Perhaps you've heard of him. He was involved in that coup d'état. They deposed some communist or other and installed a liberal fascist.

CHARLES: Oh did they? It's so hard to keep up.

CLAUDIA: But anyway. It seems he's absconded with half the national treasury and it's burning a hole in his pocket. He's going to write you an enormous check to finance your next theatrical production. But he wants to give it to you in person. He wants to meet you, you understand.

CHARLES: Oh that's, well of course, I'd be happy to meet him. When does he want to get together?

CLAUDIA: Well that's the thing. He's only in town for twenty-four hours and he wants to see you tonight.

CHARLES: Tonight? But I have to write this play! I'm working against an incredible deadline.

CLAUDIA: I know darling, but first things first. You know you never do enough fundraising, and this is one of those rare opportunities where a patron of extraordinary taste and vision is coming forward. The least you can do is meet him halfway.

CHARLES: You're right, of course. How on earth am I ever going to get this play written? I suppose I can just forget about writing this evening and take him out to dinner.

CLAUDIA: I think it might be better if you saw him here.

CHARLES: Here? Why?

CLAUDIA: There is this one little catch. He saw *Galas* and absolutely loved it, but he doesn't realize that you are a man. Now if you could just get in drag and see him—

CHARLES: *(Interrupting)* Out of the question! That would be absolutely impossible.

CLAUDIA: Just long enough for him to give you the check.

CHARLES: I'll never pull it off. He'd see right through it.

CLAUDIA: Nonsense. You've played that role hundreds of times. And think of the thrill it would give him.

CHARLES: Why doesn't he know I'm a man? I thought that was part of the thrill of it.

CLAUDIA: Well he doesn't speak English that well, and who knows? You've devoted your life to creating illusions. Why shatter his? The man is offering you enough money to run your theater for a year. I think the least you can do is put your art above personal considerations.

CHARLES: Well now that you've put it that way, I'll do it.

EVERETT: *(Bursts into the room)* Oh no, look at this. They printed your home address by mistake in the trade papers, and we're being deluged with vaudeville acts hoping for an audition. The lobby is a mob scene.

CLAUDIA: What are you going to do?

CHARLES: There's nothing else to do. I'll see them. Send them up one at a time.

EVERETT: Do you think that's wise?

CHARLES: Oh let's just see them and get it over with. There are a lot of them, you say?

EVERETT: It seems like an endless number. But I'll try to screen them and only send up the most promising numbers.

CHARLES: Thank you.

NATALIE: You're holding auditions? Would you let me try out for you? I think I have everything you would ever want in a performer.

CHARLES: That seems possible. What do you do?

NATALIE: I do a queen of burlesque number.

CHARLES: No!

NATALIE: Yes! It goes something like this. *(She sings)*
I'm a G-string girl.
Just a G-string girl.
I bump I bump I bump.
I grind I grind I grind.
I'm plea-he-heasingly plump
And I know what's on your mind.
So come on boys
You're too old for toys
You're ready for the real thing now!
How do you like it?

CHARLES: Well, I don't know. I think—

NATALIE: *(Interrupting)* Well wait. You haven't seen the second chorus. [*(Beginning to strip)*]
I'm a G-string girl.
Just a G-string girl.
I bump I bump I bump.
I grind I grind I grind.
I bump and I bump
I grind and I grind
I drive you out of your mind.
I'm a G-string girl.
Just a G-string girl.
Oh I bump I bump I bump
I grind I grind I grind . . .

CHARLES: No, no, Natalie, Natalie, I don't think, I don't think . . .

NATALIE: *(Continues)*
I'm a G-string girl.
Just a G-string girl.
I bump I bump I bump
I grind I grind I grind . . .

CHARLES: Natalie, no! I don't think you're what we're looking for. You're too . . .

NATALIE: Yes?

CHARLES: You're too . . . Irish.

NATALIE: Irish?

CHARLES: Yes. You're too Irish. I think we need someone more ethnic.

NATALIE: That's all my whole life has been. Nothing but rejections. And you're no different from the rest. I'm not a slave, you know. I have an artistic soul. If I can't be in show business, I don't want to live. I'm going to end it all. And I'm going to end it right now.

CHARLES: No Natalie, don't do it!

NATALIE: I don't care. Good-bye, cruel world! *(She runs to the window to jump out and starts to jump through the window, gets stuck)*

EVERETT: *(At the door)* Orville Titwilly, balloon folder.

ORVILLE: *(Enters)* Hi kids! What kind of fun are we going to have today? *(Then in a kid's voice)* Balloon fun, Uncle Orville!

(He starts to blow up balloons and make animals of them. He throws balloons into the audience and tells them to blow them all up. NATALIE *is screaming in the window.* CHARLES *runs desperately back and forth between* ORVILLE *and* NATALIE.*)*

CHARLES: Claudia, do something! She's stuck!

CLAUDIA: What should I do?

CHARLES: I don't know. Get some Vaseline! Call the super! Do something!

CLAUDIA: Right. *(Exits)*

EVERETT: *(Announces at the door)* Joujouka! Passion flower of the Middle East.

(Belly dance music begins and the belly dancer does a number. ORVILLE *meanwhile continues his balloon act.* MADAME WONG *begins to serve macrobiotic food and gives what appears to be a karate demonstration at the same time. The* UNITED PARCEL DELIVERY MAN *comes with a package.)*

UNITED PARCEL MAN: *(Shouting over the din)* Package for you.

*(*LUDLAM *signs.)*

EVERETT: What is it?

CHARLES: More scripts.

EVERETT: Charles, Charles, the gay senior citizens are here. They want to know if you would say a word to them.

CHARLES: Can't you tell them that I'm holding auditions? I'm trying to write a play. I can't see them now.

EVERETT: It's too late. They're here. You may as well see them. They consider you to be a great sex symbol.

CHARLES: Oh well, I'll try to squeeze them in.

CLAUDIA: *(Enters with* FIRE DEPARTMENT*)*

FIREMAN: There's a fire in the next apartment. We have to go through your window.

CHARLES: I'm afraid that's not possible. There's a woman stuck in the window.

EVERETT: The gay seniors are here.

*(*GAY SENIORS *run in screaming, "Oh, Charlie," and start ripping* CHARLES's *clothes off. He clutches desperately at his typewriter trying to type a few words. The* GAY SENIORS *rip his clothes off as he screams amid the din.)*

CHARLES: CAN'T YOU PEOPLE SEE I'M TRYING TO WRITE A PLAY?

(Curtain.)

End of Act I

ACT II

Later that evening.

(EVERETT *goes to the door and admits* CLAUDIA.)

CLAUDIA: Where is he? Is he in drag yet?

EVERETT: He's dressing.

CLAUDIA: Well he'd better hurry. The generalisimo is on his way. He's just looking for a parking space.

EVERETT: Carragua Fanfarron?

CLAUDIA: The same.

EVERETT: He's really resisting this tooth and nail.

CLAUDIA: Good heavens, I don't see why! He's got a fish nibbling at the hook. All he has to do is pull him in.

EVERETT: So it seems. But he always has these moral qualms.

CLAUDIA: Perhaps if you talked to him.

EVERETT: I'll try. *(Doorbell)* Yes?

INTERCOM: General Carragua Fanfarron.

EVERETT: He's here.

CLAUDIA: Go warn Charles and tell him whatever he does not to give it away. And get that check!

EVERETT: *(Crosses to door to the bedroom)* Charles, he's here.

CHARLES: *(Off)* Come! Quickly! Zip me up!

(EVERETT exits. Knock at the door.)

CLAUDIA: *(Opens the door, shows in* GENERALISIMO *accompanied by a man in uniform who carries a huge bouquet)* Oh, this way, General. Won't you come in?

GENERALISIMO: *(With a Spanish accent so thick you could fill tacos with it)* Bueno. I come een? Señora Claudia, I kees your hand. Ees she here? Ees she een?

CLAUDIA: She? Oh, yes, she! She's een. I mean in.

GENERALISIMO: *(To* EVERETT, *snapping his fingers)* You! Mr. Butler! Mr. Butler!

EVERETT: *(Puzzled)* Mr. Butler? I'm Mr. Quinton.

GENERALISIMO: Garçon! Boy! You! Over here.

EVERETT: I beg your pardon. Are you referring to me?

GENERALISIMO: Who you theenk I mean? I no mean me! Pendejo! Go tell your meestrees I am arrive for.

EVERETT: Sure General. *(Calls off)* Magdalena darling, the general is here. Here she is, General.

CHARLES: *(Enters in full drag in an evening gown, wearing all the jewels he received in the first act, the hair done in incredibly chic do. The impression is dazzling)*

GENERALISIMO: Ah! Ees sight to make eyes sore!

CHARLES: Señor Fanfarron?

CLAUDIA: Magdalena, this is Generalisimo Julio Carragua O'Brien Figueroa Gonzales de Jesús Fanfarron.

GENERALISIMO: A sus órdenes. Your servant, señorita.

CHARLES: General, I'm overcome.

GENERALISIMO: No no. Ees I am come over!

CHARLES: Of course. And who is this gentleman?

GENERALISIMO: Ees me interpreter.

CHARLES: Charmed, I'm sure.

GENERALISIMO: Al contrario! Ees me am charmed for. Miguel! Las flores, por favor. *(*MIGUEL *hands* CHARLES *large bouquet)* Permeet me, I give leetle flowers for grand lady.

CHARLES: *(Accepting the flowers)* Why General, you shouldn't have.

GENERALISIMO: *(He gives smaller bouquet to* CLAUDIA*)* And also for other lady I geeve flowers. Ees not so big like other one, but not so hard to carry. Miguel! Wait for me outside, yes?

MIGUEL: Sí, mi general. *(Exits)*

CHARLES: These flowers are lovely, General. I adore them.

GENERALISIMO: Ees nothing.

CLAUDIA: *(With a little sarcasm, smelling her little bouquet)* Me too. I adore them.

GENERALISIMO: Ees nothing.

CLAUDIA: *(Looking at the little bouquet)* Well, not quite. But almost.

GENERALISIMO: I throw these bosoms at your feet, for you are like a bosom. You are almost like a real bosom.

CLAUDIA: Bosoms?

CHARLES: Blossoms, Generalisimo. Blossoms.

GENERALISIMO: Ah sí, blossom! You are like a blossom, like a real blossom.

CHARLES: Oh you flatterer you.

GENERALISIMO: And now, weeth permeet me, you should go, Señora Claudia, and leave we two alone, yes?

CLAUDIA: I was just going.

CHARLES: *(Alarmed)* Señora Claudia. Permit you should go no!

GENERALISIMO: *(Polite but firm)* You go now yes?

CLAUDIA: I go now, yes!

CHARLES: You go now no! *(Aside to* CLAUDIA*)* You can't leave me alone with this barbarian!

CLAUDIA: *(Aside)* I'm afraid you have to fight your own battles, dear. Don't do anything I wouldn't do.

CHARLES: *(Aside)* Deserter!

CLAUDIA: Until we meet again, General.

GENERALISIMO: Good. You no come back, right?

CLAUDIA: Now that you put it that way . . . right. *(Aside to* CHARLES*)* Remember the Alamo. *(Exits)*

GENERALISIMO: Ees you and me alone together here at last for.

CHARLES: For? That for worries me. Please sit down, General.

GENERALISIMO: I no can seet because of pain I feel.

CHARLES: Hemorrhoids?

GENERALISIMO: No. You geeve me beeg pain in the corazón.

CHARLES: General, what's wrong? You seem distraught.

GENERALISIMO: Ees because you ees weeth me here alone. *(He dares to speak his inmost heart, advancing on her)* I love you Magdalena. I love you!

CHARLES: Be careful General. Fools rush in where angels fear to tread. This could be dangerous.

GENERALISIMO: Fear? I am no knowing fear! Danger ees for me like eating frijoles. Een my country I am ess-minister of war.

CHARLES: General, you minister of war! I had no idea. This is an honor.

GENERALISIMO: No, ess! Ess!

CHARLES: Ess? I'm afraid I don't understand you, General. What is "ess"?

GENERALISIMO: Ess-minister. I no more minister now.

CHARLES: *(Compassionately)* Oh I'm sorry. What are you there now?

GENERALISIMO: Een my country? What I am now?

CHARLES: Yes, what are you now?

GENERALISIMO: Creemeenal. If I return they shoot me.

CHARLES: What?

GENERALISIMO: I face firing squad. Ees no problem. I no go back.

CHARLES: But General, why would they want to shoot you?

GENERALISIMO: I take money from treasury and lose at roulette.

CHARLES: You lost money from the national treasury at roulette! Why did you do that?

GENERALISIMO: Ees very unlucky for me always. But maybe I lucky in love! For you, Magdalena, I weel do anything. Ees for you with me here alone, my heart is beeg with love for you. But your beauty ees bigger than my heart. For you I wear my heart on.

CHARLES: Hard-on?

GENERALISIMO: Sí, I wear my heart on my sleeve for you.

CHARLES: Oh, oh, I see. That's very sentimental of you.

GENERALISIMO: Sí, ees sentimental. Ees for you I am a . . . how you say, how you say . . . One moment please. *(He goes to the door)* Miguel!

MIGUEL: Sí, mi general!

GENERALISIMO: Cómo se dice esclavo en inglés?

MIGUEL: Slave, mi general.

GENERALISIMO: Ah sí, sí. Gracias, Miguel.

MIGUEL: Sí, mi general. *(Exits)*

GENERALISIMO: I am slave for you, Magdalena. I am throwing myself at your . . . at your . . . Miguel!

MIGUEL: Sí, mi general.

GENERALISIMO: Cómo se dice piedes en inglés?

MIGUEL: Feet, mi general.

GENERALISIMO: Gracias, Miguel.

MIGUEL: De nada, mi general.

GENERALISIMO: I am throwing myself at your feet. I geeve you all I have.

CHARLES: Thank you, General.

GENERALISIMO: When I think of you, I lose my appetite. You make me seeck, seeck in heart. I go hungry for you.

CHARLES: General, you go hungry? I'm sure you don't even know the meaning of the word.

GENERALISIMO: Sí, sí. I know meaning of word. Before I was reech general, I was poor teacher.

CHARLES: Teacher?

GENERALISIMO: Yes. I geeve Eenglish lessons.

CHARLES: You mean you used to speak English?

GENERALISIMO: Sí, sí. Een my country I speak Eenglish fluently, but when I come here I no speak so good. Can you believe that?

CHARLES: *(Laughing)* Yes, I can believe it!

GENERALISIMO: Sí.

CHARLES: Sí, sí. But do sit down, General.

GENERALISIMO: No seet. No seet. I am a rodillas for you.

CHARLES: Arro . . . what was that, General?

GENERALISIMO: A rodillas!

CHARLES: Rhodesia?

GENERALISIMO: Miguel!

CHARLES: Here we go again.

MIGUEL: Sí, mi general.

GENERALISIMO: Cómo se dice en inglés a rodillas?

MIGUEL: On my knees, mi general.

GENERALISIMO: Thank you, Miguel.

MIGUEL: De nada, mi general.

GENERALISIMO: I am on my knees . . .

CHARLES: I get the idea, General.

GENERALISIMO: Where ees your bedroon?

CHARLES: *(Taken aback)* My what?

GENERALISIMO: Tell me. Tell me this meenute! Where is your bedroon?

CHARLES: General, isn't that a rather personal question?

GENERALISIMO: My mouth make love to you. I no can help it. For beautiful woman I must take to bedroon. Ees uh, ees uh, ees cómo altar. Miguel! Cómo se dice altar en inglés?

MIGUEL: Altar, mi general.

GENERALISIMO: Ees bedroon ees altar for to worship diva.

CHARLES: General, you certainly have a way with words!

GENERALISIMO: Ees love ees an universal language, no? Ahh, what beautiful reeng on feenger. What beautiful jewels all over you.

CHARLES: Oh this is just a piece of junk.

GENERALISIMO: Junk? Junk? Miguel!

CHARLES: Maybe I can help you out. It's just a trinket.

GENERALISIMO: Miguel, qué significa "justatrinket?"

MIGUEL: Justatrinket?

CHARLES: *(Calling off to* MIGUEL*)* Miguel, I was just telling the general that this ring is *(Enunciating very clearly)* just a trinket.

MIGUEL: Mi general. La señora dice que el anillo no vale nada.

GENERALISIMO: No vale nada? Ees no worth nothing?

CHARLES: No General. I wear it for sentimental reasons. It was my mother's.

GENERALISIMO: Eet was who? Ees no your mother! I geeve thees reeng to you!

CHARLES: You!

GENERALISIMO: I send een beeg bouquet flowers.

CHARLES: You sent it? *(Drawing in his breath sharply)* That pig Poussy! How dare he stoop to such a low-down trick? What gall. And to think I was actually going to listen to those songs of his! Wait till I get my hands on him.

GENERALISIMO: For why you so angry? You like reeng, no?

CHARLES: I like ring yes! I thought you meant the *other* ring. But I had no idea it was you who sent these beautiful jewels! How can I ever thank you for them?

GENERALISIMO: I tell you how you thank me for them. By go weeth me to bedroon now, no?

CHARLES: General, I don't know that I could do that now! We were planning to have dinner.

GENERALISIMO: Before deener we have appetizer.

CHARLES: No no, General, but perhaps after dinner we might have dessert.

GENERALISIMO: Oh ho ho! I see! We have dessert! I love you. I love you!

CHARLES: You love me? Ah General, I don't know how to break this to you, but I think it's all wrong, you and me. We are from different worlds, General.

GENERALISIMO: Ees one world. Ees beautiful world. Because you are een eet. I love you. And because I love you, I breeng more jewels. And later I geeve you something beeger yet!

CHARLES: General! You're bragging!

GENERALISIMO: I geeve you . . . beeg check, no?

CHARLES: You give me big check? Yes! Yes! Sí! Sí sí, mi general.

GENERALISIMO: But first we have dessert!

CHARLES: *(Evading his advances)* Oh General! You certainly do have a big appetite, but no no no no! I think you're a naughty boy. You want to eat your dessert before your main course.

GENERALISIMO: I want to eet everything I see! You, appetizer, dessert, and main course too! Ees because I love you, I love you.

CHARLES: No no General, don't say that.

GENERALISIMO: I say it because eet ees true!

CHARLES: General, I have no choice but to give you back these jewels. I have no right to accept them.

GENERALISIMO: Why for? For why you no accept them?

CHARLES: Because I can never never love you, General.

GENERALISIMO: *(Incensed)* What deed you say? *(He leaps up)*

CHARLES: I can never love you, for I love someone else.

GENERALISIMO: Who ees he? Who ees he?

CHARLES: Oh, well you wouldn't know him.

GENERALISIMO: Some other man?

CHARLES: Yes, definitely. Some other man. Not you.

GENERALISIMO: You love preetty man?

CHARLES: Yes, pretty man. Very pretty man.

GENERALISIMO: He exeest, thees man?

CHARLES: Yes, I'm afraid so, General. Please try to understand. I must love another as long as he lives.

GENERALISIMO: As long as he leeves? Ah, no problem! I kill heen! I kill heen!

CHARLES: No, General! You mustn't kill heen! It's not his fault.

GENERALISIMO: I no care! I no care! I die I tell you. You make me seeck, Magdalena, seeck in mi corazón!

EVERETT: *(Enters)*

CHARLES: *(To* EVERETT*)* How am I ever going to get this play written?

EVERETT: Charles, please don't be alarmed, but guess who's coming to dinner?

CHARLES: Sidney Poitier?

EVERETT: Close. The Emperor and Empress of Humidia.

CHARLES: The Emperor and Empress of Humidia? But they're not due until July first. And everybody knows that thirty days hath September, April, June, and . . . *(Gasp. Doorbell)* Oh my god! It's them!

GENERALISIMO: Who ees them?

CHARLES: It's the other guests for dinner, General.

GENERALISIMO: What other guests? We have dinner alone.

CHARLES: Oh no, General. We're having several dignitaries from the new African nation of Humidia. Humidia, land of chocolates.

GENERALISIMO: Land of chocolates?

(Knock at the door.)

CHARLES: Why that must be *the* chocolates now!

EVERETT: *(Opens the door and admits the* EMPEROR *and* EMPRESS OF HUMIDIA*)* Welcome, Your Highnesses. It's an honor to receive you here.

EMPEROR: *(Speaking with highly cultivated Oxford English accent)* It is an honor to be admitted into the home to see how a typical American lives.

EMPRESS: Balala fa ha bala. Fo twa. Hic bey na bala bala foo.

EMPEROR: My wife expresses her sincere regards and admiration and hopes to perhaps exchange a few recipes while she's here.

EVERETT: I have a fabulous recipe for tuna-noodle casserole that I think you'd love.

EMPEROR: *(To the* EMPRESS*)* Pom hwa click twa foo foo bala tuna-noodle casserole bala bala pot kabuna.

EMPRESS: Nim click twa Kenya mbutu Tanganika hippo potamkin zebra pot.

EMPEROR: The Empress would be pleased to teach you her recipe for zebra testicles.

EVERETT: You don't have to twist my arm. I don't get good zebra testicles that often.

EMPEROR: Very good. Is the renowned comic playwright of your country, Mr. Ludlam, here?

EVERETT: *(Turning to look at* CHARLES *who is still in drag)* He's not here at the moment, but we're expecting him at any minute.

EMPEROR: And who is this?

EVERETT: Er, ah, this is his sister, Magdalena.

EMPEROR: Sister?

EVERETT: Yes, his twin sister. They were separated at birth.

EMPEROR: Separated?

EVERETT: Yes, they were Siamese twins. They were joined at the crotch.

(The EMPEROR *and* EMPRESS *exchange a look.)*

EMPRESS: Tan in buk tu quada crotch?

EMPEROR: Banta fala baktu pu zambisi gnu.

EMPRESS: Ah, ah! *(Nods in understanding)* Kabada freefu ngthtq.

EMPEROR: We have brought presentation gift of pet for Mr. Ludlam.

EVERETT: How thoughtful. Mr. Ludlam is a great animal lover.

EMPEROR: It is a pygmy gorilla.

EMPRESS: *(Pulls on a leash and a* GORILLA *bounds in)*

EVERETT: Oh, it's adorable!

*(*GORILLA *jumps into* EVERETT*'s arms.)*

EMPEROR: This is pygmy gorilla.

EVERETT: *(Continuing the introductions)* This is Generalisimo Fanfarron of Uruguay. *(Puts* GORILLA *out on terrace)*

EMPEROR: *(Alarmed)* This is impossible! We have broken diplomatic relations with Uruguay!

CHARLES: That's quite all right, I'm sure. So has the generalisimo. He's in exile.

EMPEROR: In that case, I'm very pleased to meet you.

GENERALISIMO: The pleasure's all mine. You didn't by any chance bring any chocolates along with you, did you?

EMPEROR: Ah yes, certainly. Here. How foolish of me. I almost forgot. *(Gives him a great block of chocolate wrapped in a zebra skin)*

CHARLES: Now, now, now. You'll all spoil your appetites. We'll save this for dessert.

GENERALISIMO: *(Aside)* Ah yes. Dessert. Do not forget you promised me my dessert.

CHARLES: *(Aside)* Don't worry, General. You'll get your just deserts.

EMPRESS: Kuna kuna.

CHARLES: I beg your pardon?

EMPRESS: Kuna kuna butu butaka rumba png.

EMPEROR: My wife is looking forward to sampling your typical American cuisine.

MADAME WONG: *(Enters)* Kombu daikon noodle soup is served.

EVERETT: *(Shudders)*

CHARLES: Yum-yum. Won't you all be seated? This is Madame Wong, my cook. I hope you won't be too disappointed, but I've been eating in the Japanese manner lately.

EMPEROR: Really? Why?

CHARLES: Well, we all find that eating simple macrobiotic foods keeps us slender.

NATALIE: *(Enters)* Did someone say dinner?

CHARLES: *(To EVERETT, aside)* Natalie! What's she doing here?

EVERETT: She's been in my room, recuperating. I couldn't just send her home after the traumatic experience she had this afternoon. Let her stay to dinner. What harm could it do?

CHARLES: Well I hope there's enough to go round. *(Takes MADAME WONG aside)* Madame Wong, there seem to be a few extra people for dinner. I hope you can stretch the menu.

MADAME WONG: *(Takes enormous piece of rubbery seaweed and stretches it like rubber band)* More seaweed. *(Exits)*

CHARLES: *(To EVERETT)* How am I ever going to get this play written?

EVERETT: *(To CHARLES)* Never mind that. How are you going to get out of drag and be two people at once?

GENERALISIMO: You! Butler! Butler!

EVERETT: *(To CHARLES)* I do wish he'd stop calling me that.

CHARLES: General, this is not my butler. This is my, er, ah, friend, Everett Quinton.

GENERALISIMO: *(Suspicious)* Friend? What kind of friend?

CHARLES: Oooh, an old friend! Just an old friend.

EVERETT: That's one way of putting it. *(Doorbell)* Hello?

VOICE: Joujouka.

EVERETT: Charles, it's that belly dancer who auditioned this afternoon. We told her to come back this evening.

CHARLES: Oh no! I mean, oh great! Just in the nick of time. We seem to have another representative. From the Arab bloc. *(Opens door. JOUJOUKA enters)* Miss OPEC. With her there's never an energy crisis. Now if you'll excuse us, she's going to slip into something a little more comfortable. You may talk among yourselves. *(Escorts JOUJOUKA into bedroom)*

EMPEROR: Mr. Ludlam's sister is fascinating. Fascinating!

EMPRESS: Twa bat nkruma mobutu ntzake shange baraka dashiki drag queen.

EMPEROR: Bidet zambisi poi poi fu egg egg kumbaya.

EMPRESS: Twa twa in fu fu twa twa.

(By now the others have all been listening intently to their conversation.)

EMPEROR: My wife was remarking that Mr. Ludlam's sister had a regal bearing. She could be a queen in our country.

EVERETT: She could be a queen in our country, too.

(JOUJOUKA enters, dancing.)

GENERALISIMO: How long you know Magdalena?

EVERETT: Oh, years and years.

GENERALISIMO: She tell me she loves pretty man.

EVERETT: *(Flattered)* Did she?

GENERALISIMO: You know heen, pretty man?

EVERETT: Well, I don't want to be immodest, but I would imagine I know who she means.

GENERALISIMO: You know who she means?

EVERETT: Yes, I have a pretty good idea.

GENERALISIMO: I want to know heen, pretty man.

EVERETT: Well, I could tell you who he is . . . I don't want to appear vain.

GENERALISIMO: You know who he ees?

EVERETT: Yes, I think I do.

GENERALISIMO: You could tell me who ees pretty man?

EVERETT: Yes I could.

GENERALISIMO: You weel tell me?

EVERETT: Yes I weel. General, why do you want to know?

GENERALISIMO: I want to know because I no see pretty man here.

EVERETT: *(Indignantly)* Thanks a lot.

GENERALISIMO: You tell me? You tell me who ees pretty man?

EVERETT: You really want to know, General?

GENERALISIMO: Yes, I be most grateful for knowing.

EVERETT: Well this may come as a big surprise to you, General, but the pretty man happens to be . . . you'll never believe this in a million years. Do you really want to know. *(Laughing)* Ha ha ha.

GENERALISIMO: Sí sí sí, I want to know. Ha ha ha. Because I want to keel heen.

EVERETT: *(Alarmed)* Ah ha ha ha. *(Laughing out of the other side of his face)* Ha ha ha ha.

GENERALISIMO: Who ees? Who ees?

EVERETT: It's ah, er, ah . . .

GENERALISIMO: Who ees thees man in love with Magdalena?

EVERETT: It is Poussy! Ima Poussy!

GENERALISIMO: You a what?

EVERETT: No no. Ima. Ima Poussy.

GENERALISIMO: You a poussy?

EVERETT: No. Ima. That's his name. Ima.

[*(Knock at the door.)*]

GENERALISIMO: Oh, Ima Poussy. Ima Poussy. Poussy sera hombre muerto. Poussy no vive un día mas. *(Infuriated, raging)* Yo mataré a Poussy!

(Knock at the door.)

NATALIE: I'll get it. It's Ima Poussy.

GENERALISIMO: *(Drawing his sword)* Poussy? Ima Poussy? I keel heen, I tell you. I keel heen!

POUSSY: Is Mr. Ludlam here?

EVERETT: No no. He's not here.

GENERALISIMO: *(Crossing to the door)* You are Señor Poussy?

POUSSY: Yes yes, I am.

EVERETT: Yes, that's right. He's Mr. Poussy. He is. He is.

GENERALISIMO: I'm glad to meet you.

POUSSY: The pleasure is all mine.

GENERALISIMO: Because I going to keel you. I want to keel you, you understand. I tear you limb from limb. I break your head. I rip out your heart and feed it to dog. I keel you! I keel you!

EVERETT: For god's sake, General, no!

GENERALISIMO: You stay out of thees, Queentown. *(Grabbing* POUSSY *by the lapels)* You dead man, Poussy. You dead man.

POUSSY: Help! Help!

CHARLES: *(Entering)* What's the matter? What is going on here?

POUSSY: This gentleman seems to, has a wrong impression . . .

CHARLES: *(To* POUSSY*)* You have your nerve coming back here! How dare you show your face around here after that cheap trick with the flowers?

POUSSY: But I brought my other songs!

CHARLES: Your song is asinine. Do you hear! Asinine!

EVERETT: Yes, your song is asinine.

GENERALISIMO: Sí, your song ees aseenine.

CHARLES: Get out, Mr. Poussy.

POUSSY: But I . . . but I . . .

EVERETT: You heard what he said. Get out!

GENERALISIMO: Sí sí. Get out!

(They push him out the door, all shouting, "Out! Get out!")

POUSSY: *(Popping back in)* This is an insane asylum! That's what it is! An insane asylum!

(They push him out the door, all shouting, "Out! Get out!")

GENERALISIMO: Oh, thank you Magdalena. You do thees for me.

CHARLES: For you?

GENERALISIMO: Sí sí. *(Throws himself on his knees in front of her)* Gracias, Magdalena, gracias.

POUSSY: *(Pokes his head back in again)* Excuse me.

CHARLES: Not you again!

POUSSY: I forgot my umbrella.

(Everyone descends on him again yelling, "Get out! Get out!")

CHARLES: Now please let us have dinner in peace.

EMPEROR: But where is your brother?

CHARLES: *(Puzzled)* My brother?

EMPEROR: Your brother Charles.

CHARLES: My brother Charles? Oh yes! My brother Charles! Of course! My brother Charles. How stupid of me. Yes. My brother Charles. My brother Charles. It seems he's been detained. He'll be here any minute. Why don't we begin without him?

EMPRESS: Buk nwa butu caca nala nala bung.

EMPEROR: Well, I don't want to do anything impolite, but we are rather hungry.

CHARLES: No no, I think it best that we start without him.

EMPEROR: Very well. I do hope he's able to make it. We had a very important matter to discuss with him concerning the State Department tour of his company in Humidia.

EVERETT: How is the weather in Humidia?

EMPEROR: Damp. Very damp. It's the rainy season in Humidia. There's tremendous flooding.

EVERETT: Like New Jersey.

EMPEROR: Yes. Humidia is very much like New Jersey.

EMPRESS: Twa twa? Click bung fu? Conga?

EMPEROR: Bantu fwa mikbu click New Jersey fu bongo bongo Humidia twa.

EMPRESS: Twa fu click mikbu New Jersey bantu fu bongo bongo Humidia. *(She laughs)* Ha ha ha ha ha ha.

EMPEROR: My wife finds you very witty. Pass the salt?

CHARLES: Certainly. *(Passes salt)*

GENERALISIMO: Pass the pepper.

CHARLES: Pass the seaweed.

(By now the guests at dinner are the following: CHARLES *in drag as Magdalena,* EVERETT, GENERALISIMO, EMPEROR *and* EMPRESS OF HUMIDIA, NATALIE, *and* MADAME WONG. *A silence falls over the table. Then suddenly they all speak at once. Then they stop, chuckle, and all say in unison, "After you!" Then they all speak at once again, stop, laugh, and say "After you!" again. They all speak in unison again, each in his own language.)*

EMPEROR: But where is Mr. Ludlam? It's getting late. *(Doorbell)* Oh, maybe this is he!

CHARLES: Maybe . . . but I doubt it.

GENERALISIMO: *(To* EMPEROR OF HUMIDIA*)* This Mr. Ludlam, ees pretty man?

CHARLES: Oh he's a great beauty.

EMPEROR: In our country, we find him unbelievably funny looking.

CHARLES: *(Choking on his soup)* Is he? Well. I've always found him to be extremely attractive.

GENERALISIMO: You find heen attractive?

CHARLES: Yes, I think he's very, very good-looking.

GENERALISIMO: *(Under his breath)* Then I keel heen. I keel heen!

CHARLES: Please, General, he's my brother!

GENERALISIMO: Ah, sí sí. Ees your brother. Ha ha.

CHARLES: *(To* EVERETT, *aside)* This dinner party seems to be growing at an alarming rate, and I have got to write a play! *(Goes to the door)*

ORVILLE: *(Poking his head in the door)* Mr. Ludlam, could I have a word with you?

ALL AT DINNER TABLE: Mr. Ludlam?

CHARLES: *(Clutching at a straw)* Here he is everybody! America's foremost comic playwright, Charles Ludlam! What a thrill! Can you believe it?

ORVILLE: *(Going over to the table)* Er, ah, I'm not, what do you mean? There must be some mistake!

CHARLES: *(Aside to* ORVILLE*)* Shut up you idiot! *(Aloud)* Here he is, a real genius!

ORVILLE: But I'm not . . .

CHARLES: *(Aside)* Quiet, you imbecile! *(Aloud)* One of the great minds of the theater!

ORVILLE: What . . . what are you . . . what do you mean? I don't understand. I don't understand anything.

CHARLES: *(Aside)* Shut up, blockhead! *(Aloud)* A man whose profound understanding of human nature has made him a modern bard!
ORVILLE: *(Babbling almost like an idiot)* But but I er ah, um, I er um—
CHARLES: *(Interrupting)* A man with a consummate ear for dialogue. Here he is, Mr. Eloquence himself, Charles Ludlam!

(Everyone at the table applauds and begins showering ORVILLE *with congratulations.* ORVILLE *continues to protest feebly. The doorbell rings.* CHARLES *goes to the door.* MRS. HORNBLATT *puts her foot in the door.)*

MRS. HORNBLATT: Oh, Mr. Ludlam!

(Everyone at the table suddenly becomes silent, turns sharply toward the door, and says in chorus, "Mr. Ludlam?")

CHARLES: *(In agony, to* MRS. HORNBLATT*)* Please Mrs. Hornblatt, Mr. Ludlam is busy!
MRS. HORNBLATT: Oh Mr. Ludlam, I know that's you! I just want to talk to you for a moment.
CHARLES: *(Aside)* Please, please, keep your voice down. Perhaps we could speak in private out on the terrace.
MRS. HORNBLATT: Sure, Mr. Ludlam.
CHARLES: As I said, Mr. Ludlam is busy right now.

([MRS. HORNBLATT *and* ROSALIE *enter.* CHARLES] *shows* [MRS. HORNBLATT] *out onto the terrace where the pygmy* GORILLA *has been chained, quickly closes the door locking her out on the terrace. She protests but in pantomime, since we cannot hear her through the door. The* GORILLA *breaks his chain, seizes her, and begins to hump her. She begins to protest. The* GORILLA *picks her up King Kong style and begins to carry her over the balustrade. She screams in pantomime for help.* CHARLES *observes her coolly and draws the drapery.)*

ORVILLE: *(Protesting loudly)* But I'm not her brother!
GENERALISIMO: *(Leaps to his feet, as on a spring)* You no her brother?
ORVILLE: No no. I am not her brother.
GENERALISIMO: *(Raging like a bull)* Ees pretty man ees no your brother? I keel heen! I keel heen!
ORVILLE: *(Looking terrified)* No no! Help! You have made a mistake! I'm not Charles Ludlam! I am Orville Titwilly, humble balloon folder.
GENERALISIMO: Ha ha! Ees just what I theenk. I keel you! I keel you! You love her, so you must die!
CHARLES: *(Rushing between them)* No no, Generalisimo. You've made a terrible mistake. He doesn't love me.
GENERALISIMO: He no love you?
CHARLES: No, he no love me. He love this girl here, Rosalie!
ORVILLE: I do?
CHARLES: Yes, you do!
GENERALISIMO: *(To* ROSALIE*)* How long you know heen?
ROSALIE: *(Begins to paw the ground)*
CHARLES: Stop that, Rosalie! You two, quickly . . . They were just about to elope! And who are we to stand in the way of true love?
ROSALIE: But I hardly know him.
CHARLES: Rosalie, this is your chance. Run away and start a new life.
ROSALIE: But what about mama?

CHARLES: Mama has her hands full. You'll never have to put up with any more of her monkey business. Run away, Rosalie. This is your one chance of happiness. Don't be afraid. Give yourself to love. Go. *(To* ORVILLE*)* Orville, take this girl out of here and be good to her. If I ever hear of you giving her any harm, you'll answer to me. Go. *(He shoves them out the door)*

MADAME WONG: How you like seaweed?

EMPEROR: Scrumptious. But I must confess I have one qualm about the macrobiotic diet. I have an incurable sweet tooth.

MADAME WONG: Ah so! Sweet tooth say yes but wisdom tooth say no.

EVERETT: But I have a surprise for you all! I baked a cake in your honor!

*(*EVERETT *brings in a huge multilayer cake, places it on the table. They are all about to eat when* NATALIE *bursts out of the cake in a G-string and pasties, throws herself down on her back on the table with an apple in her mouth.)*

EMPRESS: *(Shrieks in horror)* Buktu bantu watusi mau-mau. Mundugomore. Twa twa twa!

EMPEROR: *(Leaping up, outraged)* These people are cannibals! Come, Sheeba! Let us be singled from the barbarous. The State Department will hear of this. *(They storm out)*

GENERALISIMO: Ah, Magdalena, when weel you and me be alone once more? In bedroon.

CHARLES: General, I have a terrible confession to make. I don't think that you and I would be a great success in the bedroon.

GENERALISIMO: Ah, you are wrong. I know you are.

CHARLES: No, Generalisimo. I don't think I'm what you want, because . . . I don't know how to break this to you, General. I'm not the Magdalena of your dreams. I'm a man. I'm Charles Ludlam. *(He pulls off his wig)*

GENERALISIMO: *(Laughing wickedly with a twinkle in his eye)* Ha ha ha ha! I knew that! What you theenk, I beeg buffoon? I love you. I love you!

EVERETT: *(Going insane with jealousy)* I keel heen! I keel heen!

MADAME WONG: Stop! Stop! You! Callagua Fanfallon! You are under allest! *(She pulls out a revolver)*

GENERALISIMO: Arrest?

MADAME WONG: Leechie for the sky!

GENERALISIMO: *(Putting his hands up over his head)* What for ees meaning of thees?

MADAME WONG: I am Madame Wong of C.I.A. You have secret documents. We have reason to believe you are involved in attempt to sabotage presidential face-lift!

GENERALISIMO: You knew? Ees not to worry. President can no more have face-lift. Next time have to lower body instead.

MADAME WONG: This will come out in Congressional investigation. You leave playwright alone! He need time to finish play.

CHARLES: Madame Wong is wight, I mean, right!

MADAME WONG: You know THE Madame Wong. Yes, Generalisimo, many years go you make love young Chinee girl and leave with broken heart. I that girl. Many years I wait to even score. I have many connection.

GENERALISIMO: Madame Wong, maybe we could peeck up where we left off?

MADAME WONG: Is too late. I have no choice but to take you to Szechuan Fire.

GENERALISIMO: *(Horrified)* Set me on fire?

MADAME WONG: No, Szechuan Fire Chinese restaurant, where I will hear your proposition. Good-bye evlybody.

GENERALISIMO: Adiós.

(They go out.)

CHARLES: Madame Wong working for the C.I.A.? I had no idea.

EVERETT: You heard what she said about her connections. Madame Wong has the biggest Tong in China.

CHARLES: Oh my God! I've got to write this play! I can't do it! The deadline is up, and I'm completely dry. I'm burned out. It's writer's block. I haven't got an idea in my head! There've just been too many distractions! *(He collapses in despair)*

EVERETT: Why don't you just write about all the distractions and interruptions that happen to you when you're trying to write a play?

CHARLES: *(Brightening)* That's a brilliant idea! I'll do it! *(He sits down at the typewriter, threads it with a piece of paper, and with a faraway look in his eye, begins to giggle and type.)*

[*(Phone rings. Buzzer sounds.* William Tell Overture *plays.* MRS. HORNBLATT *bursts in at the door.)*]

MRS. HORNBLATT: Mr. Ludlam?

([The noise and madness continue. CHARLES *continues giggling and typing] as the lights fade.)*

End of Play

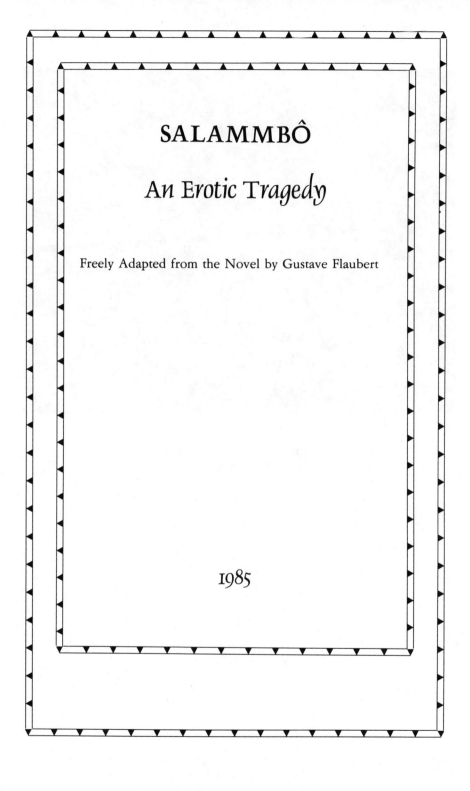

SALAMMBÔ

An Erotic Tragedy

Freely Adapted from the Novel by Gustave Flaubert

1985

Barbarians before the city walls in
Salammbô (Anita & Steve Shevett)

Cast of Characters

SALAMMBÔ, *priestess of the moon*
TAANACH, *her nurse*
MATHO, *the barbarian*
SPENDIUS, *a Greek, freed from slavery by Matho and loyal to him*
HAMILCAR BARCA, *Suffete of Carthage, father to Salammbô*
NARR'HAVAS, *King of Numidia, suitor to Salammbô*
SCHAHABARIM, *an old eunuch priest*
HANNO, *a decadent Suffete who suffers from overweight and leprosy*
BARBARIANS
CARTHAGINIANS
PRIESTS
PRIESTESSES
GUARDS
SLAVES

ACT I

Scene 1: *Hamilcar's gardens.*

(BARBARIAN MERCENARIES *are feasting.*)

MATHO: Three days we've been waiting and still Hamilcar has not paid us!
FIRST BARBARIAN: Has he already forgotten that we saved his precious Carthage for him?
SECOND BARBARIAN: They're going to cheat us!
THIRD BARBARIAN: Do you think he hired soldiers and means not to pay them?
FOURTH BARBARIAN: I broke my leg fighting for this city.
FIRST BARBARIAN: And I my arm.
SECOND BARBARIAN: I lost an eye!
THIRD BARBARIAN: I lost my teeth.
FOURTH BARBARIAN: I broke a nail. We served well as mercenary soldiers, soldiers of fortune and good ones, too.
THIRD BARBARIAN: Soldiers, yes, but without fortune.
FIRST BARBARIAN: Out of luck? Out of luck do you say? (*Grabs him drunkenly*) I'll punch your nose. (*Others prevent him, put cup of wine in his hand*)
THIRD BARBARIAN: We've earned our pay. Where is it?
OTHER BARBARIANS: Yes, where is it?
THIRD BARBARIAN: Bring us wine, meat, and women!

(*Others take up the chant.*)

BARBARIANS: Wine meat women! Wine meat women! Wine meat women!
FIRST BARBARIAN: Just wine and meat for me, thanks.

(*They make indecent wagers. They hold drinking contests. They immerse their heads in amphorae of wine. Some advance on lewd women making obscene gestures. Others strip naked like gladiators and wrestle in the midst of the feast.*
   A plaintive song rising and falling, strong and soft, is heard off: voices of slaves from the ergastulum.)

FIRST BARBARIAN: Listen! What is that song?

SECOND BARBARIAN: It sounds like the fluttering of the wings of a wounded bird.

NARR'HAVAS: *(To* MATHO*)* Warrior, what is your country and what your name? I have seen you fight and among the bold, boldest of all.

MATHO: And you, your name, the place of your birth? You struggled by my side, no one more bold than thee.

NARR'HAVAS: My name is Narr'Havas, and the Numid land my country.

MATHO: My place of birth was arid Libya. My name is Matho.

NARR'HAVAS: Among soldiers I grew.

MATHO: And I hunting the lion; yet son of a shepherd.

NARR'HAVAS: I am a king, but let us be friends.

MATHO: And sit side by side.

NARR'HAVAS: And drink a toast.

VOICES OF SLAVES: *(From the ergastulum, as before)*

FIRST BARBARIAN: What? This plaintive chant breaks again upon our hearing.

MATHO: Who are those unfortunates whose voices thus implore us?

NARR'HAVAS: Let's give them little worry.

MATHO: On this triumphal day, who calls upon us?

NARR'HAVAS: In peace, keep thy sword and have no scruple in leaving Hamilcar's slaves in their dungeon.

MATHO: Slaves?

NARR'HAVAS: Yes, it is the voice of the slaves, imprisoned in the ergastulum. What makes them cry out is the odor of meats they smell from afar and the perfume of the wine.

MATHO: Slaves, say you? I know no slaves wherever I may be. *(To his men)* Come! *(He heads his followers and exits)*

FIRST BARBARIAN: Let's free them! Free the slaves!

SECOND BARBARIAN: Free them! Free them!

THIRD BARBARIAN: Free them! Highday! Highday!

NARR'HAVAS: *(Laughing)* Slaves are not men. Why leave the table for them!

(They free the SLAVES, *who run riot,* [*including* SPENDIUS, *who faints*]*.)*

AUTHORITATUS: *(To the* MERCENARIES*)* Friends, the one who delivers this slave is strong, he is just and bravest of all, and if Carthage today, abjuring her vow, keeps her gold, the price of blood spent for her, if for vengeance a chief we must have, let it be he!

MATHO: [*(To* SPENDIUS*)*] Calm yourself! Dry your tears. Bow to a happier fate. Join us. Take part in the feast. Ask at once to drink and fight.

SPENDIUS: *(Standing aside from the others and kissing the* BARBARIANS' *hands. Then raises his arms. Chains dangle from his wrists)* All hail! First to thee Baal Eschmoun, liberator, whom the people of my country call Aesculapius! Hail! Ye genii of the springs! of the light! and of the woods! and ye gods, hidden beneath the mountains and in the caverns of the earth! and ye strong men in shining armor, who have released me! *(He bows, shows his back)*

BARBARIAN: Behold the weals left by the lash.

MATHO: Who are you, man?

SPENDIUS: My name is Spendius. I was captured by the Carthaginians during the battle of the Aegation Islands. I speak Greek, Ligurian, and Phoenician.

MATHO: Take this cup and drink.

SPENDIUS: But what is this? I thought that surely you, a victorious army, would be drinking from the Golden Cups of the Sacred Legion! For to the victorious it is a privilege, a sacerdotal honor, to drink from them.

MATHO: Yes, we have risked our lives for the honor of drinking from the sacred cups. But the detested Legion withholds them from us.

SPENDIUS: I remember. Only the Senate drinks from these venerated and sacred cups of gold. The Senate, jealous, keeps them within its treasure trove.

THIRD BARBARIAN: The slave said that they were deposited with the Syssites.

BARBARIAN: Who the hell are the Syssites?

THIRD BARBARIAN: Companies of merchants who eat in common.

BARBARIAN: Oh! I always wondered!

THIRD BARBARIAN: But at this hour all the members of the Syssites sleep.

MATHO: Let them be awaked! Should we, a victorious army, be without honor?

BARBARIANS: No!

MATHO: Let us drink from the Golden Cups of the Sacred Legion!

OTHER BARBARIANS: Yes! Yes! The cups! The cups! Bring us the cups!

NARR'HAVAS: No! Fear Baal, this is an impious thing!

SPENDIUS: Greece is my country, and there there is nothing a conqueror may not have.

ALL: The cups! The wine! The cups! The wine!

(Et cetera. They cause a general commotion and take up the chant, "The cups! The cups! The cups!" pounding on the table and beating their feet on the floor in rhythm to the chant.)

NARR'HAVAS: Hanno in the name of the Senate now comes.

(HANNO enters.)

HANNO: Soldiers of fortune! Sons of victory! Saviors of Carthage! No honor is too great for you, nor any too great glory.

BARBARIANS: 'Tis true! Hurrah! The cups! The cups! Give us the cups!

HANNO: Hear me! If it were just a question of your bravery, you certainly merit the cups.

BARBARIANS: True, true.

HANNO: But the Golden Cups of the Sacred Legion are private property.

BARBARIANS: No, Carthage belongs to us.

HANNO: Go camp outside the city walls and you'll be paid!

SPENDIUS: You lie! Sewer of Moloch!

HANNO: By Tanit and Moloch you shall repent of this. *(Exits)*

BARBARIANS: Scum! Scum! Scum! The cups! The cups! Give us the cups!

SPENDIUS: They are locked in the temple.

BARBARIAN: Let the temple be opened!

NARR'HAVAS: Do not arouse the rancor of their jealous gods!

SPENDIUS: Pleasant gods, that would trouble valiant men. And these gods without thee would depart captive for Rome.

SOLDIERS: Vengeance!

NARR'HAVAS: *(Frightened)* The gods of Carthage never tire of drinking human blood.

MATHO: We'll give them blood to drink, and hot blood, too! Do you bring us the gold cups won by our blood in twenty battles?

SOLDIERS: Our pay!

BARBARIAN: Carthage belongs to us.

BARBARIAN: We've been tricked.

MATHO: They outrage us! Let Carthage tremble.
SOLDIERS: Axes! Torches! Anything!
SPENDIUS: Scum! You have cheated us!
SOLDIERS: *(Cry)* Scum! You have cheated us! *(Et cetera)*

(The BARBARIANS *resume the feast, though somewhat uneasily. Suddenly a* LARGE NEGRO *begins to roll around beating his limbs against the ground frantically. His eyes bulge, his neck contorts, and he foams at the mouth.)*

SECOND BARBARIAN: What's wrong with him?
THIRD BARBARIAN: He looks as though he's been poisoned.
FIRST BARBARIAN: He's been poisoned!
BARBARIANS: Poisoned!
THIRD BARBARIAN: They poisoned him!
FIRST BARBARIAN: The wine! The wine's been poisoned. They've poisoned us so they don't have to pay us.
SECOND BARBARIAN: Kill the wine bearers!
BARBARIANS: *(Generally)* Kill them! Kill them! *(They kill the wine bearers)*
MATHO: You shouldn't have done that.
SECOND BARBARIAN: If you can locate a speck of sand in the center of the sun, then you can tell me what to do!
LARGE NEGRO: That was good stuff!
THIRD BARBARIAN: It's Hamilcar's fault!
FOURTH BARBARIAN: Hamilcar has cheated us.
FIRST BARBARIAN: Burn his gardens!
THIRD BARBARIAN: Get his elephants!
SECOND BARBARIAN: Cut off their trunks!
FIRST BARBARIAN: Look in this pool.
SECOND BARBARIAN: Fishes with jewels in their gills.
FIRST BARBARIAN: Catch them.
SECOND BARBARIAN: Kill them.
THIRD BARBARIAN: Cook them.
FOURTH BARBARIAN: Eat them.
NARR'HAVAS: No no! These fish are the property of the Barca family. They are descendants of the primordial eel-pout which hatched the mystic egg wherein the goddess was concealed.

*(*BARBARIANS *kill and eat the fishes. The jingling of bells is heard approaching.)*

FOURTH BARBARIAN: Listen! What is that sound?
THIRD BARBARIAN: I hear bells.
SECOND BARBARIAN: Bells?
THIRD BARBARIAN: Bells.

(Enter the eunuch priest, [SCHAHABARIM,] *his white robe sewn with bells.)*

NARR'HAVAS: It is the eunuch priest of the temple of Tanit. It is the high priest of the moon.
MATHO: Eunuch priest?
NARR'HAVAS: Yes, he castrated himself, the better to serve the goddess.
BARBARIANS: Ooooh!

(Then SALAMMBÔ *enters in veils, robes, and jewels. She goes to the sacred pool. She carries a small ebony lyre.)*

SALAMMBÔ: Where are the sacred sturgeon? Dead? Dead! All dead. No longer will you come when I call or take watermelon seeds from my hands. In the depths of your eyes rolled the mystery of Tanit. Siv! Sivon! Tammouz! Eluol! Tischiri! Zabar! I call your names which are the names of the months, but you do not answer. Ah Goddess, have pity on me!

(The soldiers crowd around her.)

MATHO: What is she saying?

FIRST BARBARIAN: Her eyes seem to penetrate far away beyond terrestrial space.

SECOND BARBARIAN: The moon makes her look very pale.

THIRD BARBARIAN: The gods seem to envelop her like a subtle mist.

FOURTH BARBARIAN: Who is she?

MATHO: I do not know! But I saw her last night, at the summit of the temple, praying to the stars.

NARR'HAVAS: The mere look of Tanit is less and no more. This is the daughter of Hamilcar—'tis Salammbô.

SALAMMBÔ: What have you done? What have you done? For your enjoyment we have provided meat, oil, and malobathrum from the storehouses. I even had oxen brought from Hecatompylos and I sent hunters into the desert that you might have all sorts of game. Where do you think you are? In a conquered city? Or the palace of a master? Hamilcar, the Suffete, my father, servitor of the Baalim! Your weapons reek with the blood of his slaves. Why I ought to give you boys a good tongue-lashing! Alas! Carthage, sad city. No longer have you heroes to defend you, but mercenaries who can be bought and sold like slaves.

(She begins to chant in a strange tongue. As SALAMMBÔ sings, they slowly fall under her spell and begin to applaud.)

MATHO: Great heaven! I see in her eyes the supernatural. I hear in her voice something of the gods.

SALAMMBÔ: Oh deiess, forgive us.

NARR'HAVAS: No, fear nothing, oh virgin! 'Tis with great love we look on a divinity who reigns in her native land.

(MATHO leans toward her. She pours him wine into a gold cup in a gesture of reconciliation with the army.)

SALAMMBÔ: Soldier, drink! Take this cup by my own hand filled. May this toast serve as an alliance between your army and Carthage. Soldier, drink and be gay!

(MATHO goes to drink.)

A GAUL: *(Slapping him on the back)* Ha! Ha! Ha! Congratulations!

MATHO: What do you mean?

GAUL: Ha! Ha! Ha! *(Slaps him on the back again)*

MATHO: Speak!

GAUL: The gods be with you! When is the wedding?

MATHO: What wedding?

GAUL: Yours. For among my people, when a woman offers wine to a warrior, she also offers him her bed.

MATHO: *(Emptying the glass)* I drink to Salammbô and accept the augury.

NARR'HAVAS: I have loved her for a day and more. Understand me well.

MATHO: I love her: and forever!

(NARR'HAVAS *pulls a javelin from out of his belt and hurls it at* MATHO, *pinning his hand to the table.*)

MATHO: (*Pulls it out as though it were nothing. Because he is unarmed he picks up a table and hurls it at* NARR'HAVAS *and cries out*) Coward!

(*The crowd rushes between the two enraged men. Screeching and chattering is heard*)

TAANACH: Listen mistress—high above in the trees they have frightened the apes sacred to the moon. Let us withdraw into the temple.

SALAMMBÔ: Far away you can hear the lazy slaves masturbating on the balustrade. You are right, Taanach. Let us be singled from the barbarous.

(SALAMMBÔ, TAANACH, *and* SCHAHABARIM *withdraw into the temple.* MATHO *throws himself against the door to no avail.* SPENDIUS *rends his tunic with his teeth. He begins to bind up* MATHO's *wound.*)

MATHO: Get away from me.

SPENDIUS: No. You're bleeding. (*Binds the wound*)

MATHO: Leave me! Leave me alone!

SPENDIUS: No! You freed me from the ergastulum. I am yours. You are my master. Command me.

MATHO: I don't want you. You're scrawny, you're a weakling.

SPENDIUS: Don't hate me for it. I have lived in the palace, and I know how to enter it, between the stones, like a viper. I know where the ingots of gold are hid, and I know the passage to the tombs.

MATHO: What of it?

SPENDIUS: The heart beats faster at the thought of such priceless things. Ahh, what wealth, and the men who possess it do not even have weapons to defend it. Gold, pearls, diamonds, hyacinth stones, and stones of chalcedony—they shall be yours. Come, let's take them.

MATHO: No! The curse of Moloch weighs upon me. I felt it in her eyes. Where is she?

SPENDIUS: I do not see her. But there, on the steps of the temple, is the Numidian prince, Narr'Havas.

MATHO: (*Trembling*) The spear! The spear! Give me the spear! I will kill him!

SPENDIUS: (*Restraining him*) Not yet.

MATHO: (*Continues to watch the palace*)

SPENDIUS: Master, you are suffering. What is it? Tell me. (*Shakes him by the shoulders*) Master! Master!

MATHO: (*In a deep voice*) Listen! It is the wrath of the gods. The daughter of Hamilcar pursues me. I fear her, Spendius! (*He clutches his heart, his eyes starting from his head, like a child terrified by a phantom*) Help me. I am ill. Perhaps you know of stronger gods or a more compelling invocation.

SPENDIUS: For what purpose?

MATHO: (*Striking his head with his fists*) To free me from her! I believe I am a victim she has promised to her gods. She holds me bound by a chain that cannot be seen. If I walk, she is beside me. When I pause, she stops. Her eyes burn me. I hear her voice. She has become my soul! And yet there is an ocean between us. She is far away. I cannot reach her. Her beauty is like a veil, a mist of light. Sometimes I think I never saw her, that she has no existence, that it was all a dream. *(He weeps in despair)*

SPENDIUS: Be strong, my master. Call upon your will, and implore the gods no longer. They do not heed the cries of men. You're crying like a coward! Are you not ashamed that a mere woman can make you suffer so?

MATHO: Am I a child? Believe you that I weaken at the sight of women's faces, and at the sound of their songs? We kept them at Drapanum to sweep out our stables. I have fucked them under crumbling walls while the catapults vibrated. But that woman, Spendius, she!

SPENDIUS: If she were not the daughter of Hamilcar . . .

MATHO: No! She is unlike any other daughter of man. Her eyes under her great curved eyebrows are like suns beneath triumphal arches. Remember when she appeared how all the lamps paled? And between the diamonds of her collar glimpses of her nipples shone resplendently. And how the odor of perfumes floated behind her as from a temple. She was more fragrant than wine, more terrible than death. But I desire her. I must have her. I am dying for her. The thought of holding her in my arms fills me with a frenzy of rapture. And yet I hate her! Spendius, I want to overcome her! How can I do it? I could sell myself to become her slave. You were her slave. You could see her. Tell me, does she go out on the terrace of her palace every night? Ah, the stones must thrill under her sandals, and the stars themselves bend down to gaze at her. *(He falls back in an excess of passion, moaning like a wounded bull)*

SPENDIUS: Up, master. Awake! We're going to see her.

MATHO: *(Somewhat dazed)* Where are we going?

SPENDIUS: Through the sewers, via the aquaduct, and into the Temple of Tanit!

Scene 2: *Salammbô's chamber.*

(Salammbô enters supported by a female slave, Taanach, who carries an iron perfuming pan.)

SALAMMBÔ: *(Extends her arms, throws back her head, and addresses the crescent moon plaintively as if calling someone)* O Rabetna! Tanit! By the hidden symbols and the ringing bells . . . by the furrows of the earth, ever silent, ever fruitful . . . O Goddess of the shadowy sea and the blue shore, O queen of the humid world and of all things damp and moist, all hail! *(Sways her body three times and falls facedown. TAANACH quickly lifts her)* O my goddess moon! How lightly you sail through the impalpable ether like a mastless galley. Why do you constantly change your forms? As you wax and wane the eyes of cats lengthen or grow short and the leopards change their spots. Women scream your name in the pangs of childbirth. Thou causeth the wine to ferment, the corpse to putrify, and pearls to form at the bottom of the sea. But you are a frightful mistress too. You bring bad dreams and during the period of your rejuvenescence the sacred apes fall ill. O Tanit, do you not love me? I have gazed on you so often. But, no, you ignore me, you go on in your azure, you float in your violet immensity, while I . . . I must remain on the motionless earth. Taanach, take your nebal and play softly on the silver string, for my heart is sad. *(Gets into bed. TAANACH lifts a triangular ebony harp, bigger than herself, and plays with both hands)* Hush!

TAANACH: What is it, mistress? If a breeze but blow, or a cloud pass, you are vexed and disturbed.

Charles Ludlam & Everett Quinton in
Salammbô (Anita & Steve Shevett)

SALAMMBÔ: I know not.

TAANACH: You have exhausted yourself by praying too long.

SALAMMBÔ: Oh! Taanach! Would that I could dissolve myself in prayer like a flower in wine!

TAANACH: Perhaps it is the scent of the perfumes?

SALAMMBÔ: No, the spirit of the gods dwells in sweet odors.

TAANACH: Or perhaps you miss your father who has gone into the Amber country beyond the pillars of Melkarth?

SALAMMBÔ: I don't care if he ever comes back!

TAANACH: But, mistress, when he returns you must choose, as was his will, a husband from among the sons of the Elders; and your unrest will vanish in the arms of your husband.

SALAMMBÔ: Why? All the sons of the Elders I have ever seen horrified me. They had coarse limbs and laughed like wild beasts.

TAANACH: When your mother died your father did not want you to enter the college of priestesses. He wanted you to make a good marriage.

SALAMMBÔ: An "alliance," he called it. An alliance that would serve his political ends.

TAANACH: Least of all did he want you acquainted with Tanit, goddess of the moon. But now it is too late. Since your dear mother's death you have lived alone in the palace. You have grown up amid abstinences, fasts, and purifications. You have always been surrounded by exquisite and solemn things . . . your body saturated with perfumes . . . your soul filled with prayers. You have not tasted wine, or eaten meat, or touched an unclean animal. Neither have you ever beheld an obscene image or set foot in the house of death.

SALAMMBÔ: Taanach, sometimes a feeling emanates from the innermost depths of my being, like hot flushes, heavier than the vapors arising from a volcano. . . . O Mother! *(Falls panting on her ivory couch. Moaning exquisitely)* Ah!

TAANACH: What is it, mistress?

SALAMMBÔ: *(As before)* I know not!

TAANACH: *(Places a collar around* SALAMMBÔ*'s neck)* Mistress, here, wear this.

SALAMMBÔ: *(Looking up at her half dazed)* What's this?

TAANACH: A collar of amber and dolphins' teeth to banish terrors.

SALAMMBÔ: *(In a voice almost inaudible)* Go and bring Schahabarim to me.

TAANACH: *(Strikes a gong then pauses)* Listen, mistress, he is coming. Do you not recognize the tinkling of the little gold bells he wears on the hem of his robe?

(SCHAHABARIM enters. He is a wizened old priest with deep wrinkles and sunken eyes. His face is yellow, his head oblique.)

SCHAHABARIM: Speak! What do you wish?

TAANACH: It is Salammbô, O holy one. She is obsessed with vague terrors.

SCHAHABARIM: What is the problem?

TAANACH: She is troubled by Tanit. She longs to know the goddess, to penetrate the profundities of her dogma, to see the veil.

SCHAHABARIM: The veil?

TAANACH: The magnificent veil, known as the Zaïmph, wherein rests the destiny of Carthage.

SCHAHABARIM: It is forbidden even to behold the veil, let alone touch or possess it.

TAANACH: An influence of the moon must have descended on her. For whenever that planet wanes she becomes feeble, languishing all day, only reviving at night; during an eclipse she almost died.

SCHAHABARIM: I fear the jealous Rabbetna is revenging herself on this chaste maiden because she was withheld from immolation.

TAANACH: It is true she prays only to Tanit.

SCHAHABARIM: It was to avoid the confusion of contradictory cults that we taught her to worship the goddess in her sidereal manifestation. But the other gods must be given their due.

SALAMMBÔ: *(Cries out in a kind of delirium)* The veil! The veil!

SCHAHABARIM: She dreams of what is forbidden.

TAANACH: The allure of the Zaïmph is all the stronger because it is vague. It is the outgrowth of faith strengthened by imagination.

SCHAHABARIM: Too much intimacy with the gods leads to heresy. She should never have been withheld from the flames. It was a sacrilege.

TAANACH: It was you who educated her. Speak to her now.

SCHAHABARIM: Hamilcar, her father, has ordered me to tell her no more.

SALAMMBÔ: *(Calls faintly)* Schahabarim?

SCHAHABARIM: *(Goes to her couch and standing over her)* What is it you wish? Speak!

SALAMMBÔ: I hoped . . . you almost promised me . . . Why do you despise me? What have I neglected in the rites? You are my teacher, and you have said that there is no one more learned in the mysteries of the goddess than I; but there are some of which you have not yet told me; is not this true, O holy one?

SCHAHABARIM: No! I have nothing more to teach you.

SALAMMBÔ: A spirit impels me to this adoration. I have climbed the steps of Eschmoun—god of the planets and intelligences; I have slept under the golden olive tree of Melkarth—patron of all Tyrian colonies; I have opened the gates of Baal-Khamoun—medium of light and fertilization; I have made sacrifices to the subterranean Kabiri—to the gods of the winds, the rivers, the woods, and the mountains. But they are all too far away, too insensible, too high—do you understand? But Tanit mingles with my life, she becomes my soul, and I tremble with internal dartings. I feel I am about to hear her voice, behold her face; a brightness dazzles me, then I fall back again into the shadows.

(SCHAHABARIM *is silent.* SALAMMBÔ *implores him with beseeching glances.*)

SCHAHABARIM: Dismiss your slave. She is not of our race. (SALAMMBÔ *claps her hands.* TAANACH *withdraws.* SCHAHABARIM *raises one arm in the air*) Before the gods only darkness existed, and a breath stirred, heavy and indistinct, like the consciousness of a man in a dream: it contracted itself, creating Desire and Fog; from Desire and Fog proceeded primitive matter. This was a primordial slime, black, icy, profound, containing insensible monsters, incoherent parts of forms to be born, such as are painted on the walls of the sanctuaries. Then matter condensed and became an egg. The egg broke: one half formed the earth, the other half the firmament. The sun, the moon, the winds, and the clouds appeared as well as earthquakes, tornadoes, tidal waves, volcanic eruptions, hurricanes, meteor showers, lightning bolts, and at a crash of thunder the sentient animals awoke.

SALAMMBÔ: What a hullabaloo!

SCHAHABARIM: Then Eschmoun unrolled himself in the starry sphere! Khamoun shone brilliantly in the sun; Melkarth with his arms pushed him beyond Gades; the Kabiri descended into the volcanoes, and Rabbetna, like one who nourishes, leaned over the world, pouring forth her light like milk, and her night like a mantle.

SALAMMBÔ: And then . . . ?

SCHAHABARIM: She inspires and governs the loves of men.

SALAMMBÔ: (*Dreamily*) The loves of men!

SCHAHABARIM: She is the soul of Carthage. Although her influence reaches over all, it is here she dwells, beneath the Sacred Veil.

SALAMMBÔ: I shall see her, shall I not, O holy one? You will take me to her? For a long time I have hesitated: now the desire to see her form devours me. Pity me; comfort me! Let us go to the temple!

SCHAHABARIM: (*Repulsing her with a vehement gesture full of pride*) Never! The very wish is a crime! Do you not know that to look upon her is death? The hermaphrodite Baals unveil only to us who are men in understanding and women in weakness. Your desire is sacrilege. Be satisfied with the knowledge that is already yours. (*Looks down on* SALAMMBÔ *sobbing with indignation, fear and humiliation and smiles a gloating, almost imperceptible, smile*)

(*Horses' hooves are heard in the distance, and horns.*)

SCHAHABARIM: What is that sound? There is a cloud of dust on the horizon.

TAANACH: (*Enters running terrified and throws herself on her face*) Priestess! Priestess! The Barbarian army is advancing on Carthage!

Scene 3: *Within the Temple of Tanit.*

SPENDIUS: Follow me.

MATHO: We've climbed walls. We swam the aqueduct. Where have you brought me?

SPENDIUS: To the Temple of Tanit. Would you see your soldiers victorious?

Carthage in flames? Would you see at your feet this imperious woman who has tortured your heart? Stolen your soul?

MATHO: See Salammbô once more? Yes, perhaps, then die.

SPENDIUS: Master, there is, in the sanctuary of Tanit, a mysterious veil, fallen from heaven, that covers the goddess.

MATHO: I know that.

SPENDIUS: Who possesses this veil is a god on earth. It is because Carthage possesses it that Carthage is great.

MATHO: What of it?

SPENDIUS: I have brought you here to take this veil.

(The walls of the sanctuary open. SPENDIUS *and* MATHO *hide. Enter* SCHAHABA-RIM *and* PRIESTS *worshipping, blindfolded. They carry on a cross a crucified lion.)*

SCHAHABARIM: Anaito, Derceto, Mylitta, O Rabetna, Baalet, Tyratha! O Tanit, goddess of the world, from the depths of space throw down your moonbeams upon Carthage, the city thou lovest. Come and receive, O mistress of heaven, with incense the honey mixed with the wine.

PRIESTS: Anaito, Derceto, Mylitta, O Rabetna, Baalet, Tyratha, Tanit!

SPENDIUS: *(Aside)* A crucified lion!

MATHO: What kind of people are they that crucify lions?

(Dance of the sacred maidens optional.)

SCHAHABARIM: Then let us open the gates of the dreaded sanctuary. Let us adore the mantle that Tanit threw upon her mysterious symbol. The veil—the sacred Zaïmph, guardian of Carthage. But first let us be blindfolded for the veil is so holy it is a crime to behold it; to touch it is death.

SPENDIUS: What, do you fear death?

MATHO: I fear the gods whom I honor in my heart.

(Gongs—sacred music—march. The sanctuary opens revealing the idol of Tanit covered by the sacred veil. MATHO *and* SPENDIUS *enter furtively. The* PRIESTS *don blind-folds and go into the sanctuary. The walls close after them.)*

SCHAHABARIM: *(And* PRIESTS, *backs to audience)* Anaitas, Derceto, Mylitta—O Rabetna, Baalet, Tyratha, O Tanit. Pray all adore this veil, wherein is the soul of the gods, the mysterious Zaïmph made from a fiery star.

PRIESTS and SCHAHABARIM: O Rabetna, Baalet, Tyratha.

SPENDIUS: May the Zaïmph be resplendent in your hands.

MATHO: Go get someone else. I will not aid in such an abominable crime!

PRIESTS: Anaitis, Derceto, Mylitta!

SCHAHABARIM: Pray all, for in this veil lies the greatness of Carthage. Honor! Fortune! Victory!

SPENDIUS: Did you hear that?

MATHO: I don't want to commit a sacrilege. Yet if I but possess the veil . . . We will go on!

SCHAHABARIM: Pray all, this veil is terrible—for the goddess has decreed that it is a crime to behold it, to touch it is death. O Rabetna! Baalet! Tyratha!

SCHAHABARIM and PRIESTS: Anaitis, Derceto, Mylitta!

SCHAHABARIM: Tanit—mirror of the world. We glorify thee. Carthage entreats thy light, Goddess excellently bright!

MATHO: I feel sick. My heart. This is wrong what we're doing.

(Knock at the temple doors.)

SPENDIUS: Shhhh.

(They hide again.)

SCHAHABARIM: Who knocks thus at the sanctuary? Who dares disturb the sacred mystery? *(To* PRIEST*)* Remove your blindfold.

PRIEST: 'Tis Salammbô!

SCHAHABARIM: Salammbô!

MATHO: Salammbô, great god!

SCHAHABARIM: Close the gates of the dreaded sanctuary.

*(*SPENDIUS *disappears* [*behind the walls*]. MATHO *remains hidden.* TAANACH *enters.)*

SCHAHABARIM: Speak! What is it now?

TAANACH: It is Salammbô, O holy one. For three days she has not slept or eaten.

(Enter SALAMMBÔ, *disquieted.)*

SCHAHABARIM: Oh daughter of Hamilcar, what wouldst thou?

SALAMMBÔ: Blessed pontiff, soften the heart of the goddess. Her anger weighs upon me.

SCHAHABARIM: Amid perfumes, amid prayers, until now your days were simple and pure. How did you anger the goddess?

SALAMMBÔ: I know not. Everything weighs upon me and oppresses me.

SCHAHABARIM: I follow thy great soul. In your heart beats the agonies of which Carthage is the victim.

SALAMMBÔ: It may be. The insolent barbarian camps beneath our walls. In the shadows of the night I hear voices, like nothing terrestrial, speaking words of horrible vent.

SCHAHABARIM: You hear voices?

SALAMMBÔ: Yes, I hear voices far away saying: Salammbô, save the veil of Carthage. Save the veil of Carthage. This sacred veil, O Father, I would see it, press it to my bosom, kiss it, adore it.

SCHAHABARIM: You go to an abyss!

SALAMMBÔ: Take me to the sanctuary! Come!

SCHAHABARIM: Never! The very wish is a crime! Go, profane priestess. Go! Go! Go! Go! Go! Go! Go!

(Exit TAANACH *with* SALAMMBÔ *who sobs with indignation, fear, and humiliation, leaving the doors of the sanctuary open.)*

PRIEST: She is gone.

*(*SCHAHABARIM *and* PRIESTS *genuflect before the Zaïmph and, turning, exit.)*

MATHO: Oh I'm dying. I'm dying here. This is impossible what we are doing. An attempt like this is unthought of—why, the very inadequacy of the means to prevent it show that it was deemed impossible. Inspired terrors, more than walls, defend such sanctuaries. We're going to die.

SPENDIUS: Someday, yes. But not today.

MATHO: Spendius? Spendius, where are you?

SPENDIUS: Behind the sanctuary walls. Strike the gong!

MATHO: No! They'll hear us! *(Murmurs placatingly as if trying to appease someone who is angry)* Excuse us, Tanit. Excuse us, Salammbô. Don't be angry, goddess. We're only borrowing your veil. When Carthage falls we will bring it back. *(Forces back sanctuary walls with his brute strength. Light comes up on the veil. It hangs by the corners and drapes under the face of the goddess)*

SPENDIUS: Ah! Behold her! Behold her!

MATHO: The veil! It is at the same time bluish—like night; yellow—like dawn; and crimson—like the sun; harmonious, diaphanous, glittering, and light. This is the mantle of the goddess, the sacred Zaïmph, which no one might behold! Take it!

(SPENDIUS unfastens the veil, which sinks to the ground.)

SPENDIUS: That wasn't difficult, was it? Let us go!

(MATHO lifts it by placing one hand under it. Then he puts his head through the opening in the middle of it and completely envelops himself in it, spreading out his arms the better to contemplate its splendor.)

MATHO: *(Stands panting, his eyes riveted on the pavement)* But what if I now go to her? I no longer need fear her beauty! Behold, I am more than a man! I can traverse flames! I can walk on the sea! Salammbô! Salammbô! I am thy master!

(Footsteps draw near. A PRIEST enters. SPENDIUS quickly sinks two daggers into his sides. When he falls his head rings upon the stone pavement. They pause, motionless, and listen. The sound of the wind is heard. SPENDIUS washes his bloodstained hands in a fountain. They run. A cynocephalus runs beside them tugging at the veil. A man recoils in the darkness.)

SPENDIUS: *(Whispers)* Hide the Zaïmph.

MATHO: *(Repeats again and again)* Where is she? I must see her; take me to her.

SPENDIUS: It is madness. She will summon her slaves, and, in spite of your strength, you will be slain!

MATHO: I feel omnipotent. Like a god himself. Take me to her, I tell you. Take me to her! *(He threatens SPENDIUS who, alarmed by the violence of his passion, acquiesces. Suddenly SALAMMBÔ'S bed, shrouded in mosquito netting, floats in. An enormous mosquito buzzes. SALAMMBÔ is asleep)* Is this a dream? *(MATHO approaches the bed, holding the lamp at arm's length. The airy mosquito nettings catch fire)*

SALAMMBÔ: *(Awakening)* Great consoler, god young and charming, tell me by what name they worship thee.

MATHO: The one thou thinkest some forgiving god is only a mortal who adores thee.

SALAMMBÔ: *(Drawing back terrified)* Who art thou then if not a god? I have already seen, as if in a dream, the fire in thine eyes, terrible yet gentle. Speak!

MATHO: I am the mercenary whose cup thou didst fill in the gardens of Hamilcar; a soldier, a barbarian. In the camp, they obey me. I have conquered thy gods. I am more than a man. I can dare both Carthage and Rome, and assume the royal bandlet. Come to me, I love thee more than life, virgin who meltest my soul. Take this nuptial garment.

SALAMMBÔ: What is it?

MATHO: It is the veil of Tanit.

SALAMMBÔ: *(Crying out)* The veil of Tanit? *(Supporting herself on her hands she leans tremblingly over the side of the couch)*

MATHO: I have sought it for you in the depths of the sanctuary.

SALAMMBÔ: Let me see it.

MATHO: Behold! *(He shows her the veil)* You remember then? In the night you came in my dreams, but I could not divine the mute command in your eyes.

SALAMMBÔ: Nearer, nearer.

MATHO: Drown my soul in the sweetness of your breath. Let my lips be crushed in kissing your hands. I love you.

SALAMMBÔ: Give it to me. *(MATHO embraces her)* Oh horror. My blood freezes in my veins. Oh Tanit has punished my impious desires. Help! Help!

MATHO: Come. You must follow me, or if you do not desire to go I will remain. It makes no difference.

SALAMMBÔ: Come to me Taanach, Schahabarim! Help! Help!

MATHO: Salammbô, I beg of you!

SPENDIUS: Fly! They are coming!

(TAANACH and GUARDS rush in. GUARDS go to kill MATHO.)

SALAMMBÔ: Do not touch him! It is the mantle of the goddess! *(SPENDIUS quickly gets under the veil for protection. GUARDS and TAANACH avert their eyes and shrink back. SALAMMBÔ comes forward out of the corner into which she had retreated and extending her bare arm curses him)* Malediction on you, who have plundered Tanit! Hate, vengeance, massacre, and sorrow! May Gurzil, god of battles, rend you! May Mastiman, god of death, strangle you! And may the Other—whom I dare not name—burn you! And may Crepitus, god of flatulence, blast you!

MATHO: *(Utters a cry like one wounded by a spear)* Aieough!

SALAMMBÔ: *(Repeats again and again)* Go, sacrilegious, infamous, accursed. Go! Go!

(MATHO and SPENDIUS exit arrogantly with the veil.)

SCHAHABARIM: *(Enters)* What is it? What has happened?

TAANACH: Someone has taken from the Temple of Moloch the treasure of Carthage! They have stolen the veil of Tanit.

SCHAHABARIM: But that is impossible! Everyone knows it is a crime to behold it. To touch it is death. We must retake the veil, for in it lies the fate of Carthage.

SALAMMBÔ: How can we? How can we retake the veil when it is a crime to behold it to touch it is death?

TAANACH: The barbarian gained entrance to Salammbô's chamber.

SCHAHABARIM: It is likely that she has been defiled by him. Salammbô, tell me, did the barbarian touch you?

SALAMMBÔ: *(Looks at him but does not answer)*

TAANACH: She is in shock. Look there. The gold chain that joins her ankles has not been broken. It is clear that there has been nothing improper. The daughter of Hamilcar is still a virgin.

SCHAHABARIM: *(Looks up at the sky)* Behold! It is an eclipse of the moon! Tanit hides her face in shame. It is an evil omen.

SALAMMBÔ: What does it mean, Schahabarim?

SCHAHABARIM: Let us go make sacrifice. The loss of the veil portends the fall of Carthage.

(The moon disappears in shadow. TAANACH screams and SALAMMBÔ faints.)

Scene 4: *The Council of Elders.*

HAMILCAR: Are these to be the last evil days of Carthage? As I entered the port a crowd followed my galley along the flagstones shouting, "Welcome! Greeting! Hail, Eye of Khamoun! Oh, deliver us! It is the fault of the Rich! They desire your death! Guard yourself, Barca!" Then on the shore I recognized the vessels I had formerly commanded. They lay on the shore, leaning over on their sides, with their poops high in the air, displaying their bulging prows covered with gilding and mystic symbols. The chimeras had lost their wings, the Pataecian gods their arms, the bulls their silver horns; yet all, though half defaced, inert and rotten, were full of associations, and still exhaled the aroma of past voyages; now like disabled soldiers who again meet their old commander, these old vessels seemed to say to me, "Here we are! 'Tis we! And you also—you are vanquished!" *(Falls to his knees)* Oh Gods! If only Hanno had not arrived too late on the morning of the battle of the Aegatian Islands! *(Rises to his feet)* And I come home and find awaiting me the tales of all that happened since the conclusion of the peace: the demands of the soldiers; the refusal of the Elders to pay them. And I have no doubt there will be more to hear tonight at the Assembly of the Elders in the Temple of Moloch.

(Enter HANNO *and* SCHAHABARIM. *As they enter they salute* HAMILCAR *and kiss his hands.)*

HAMILCAR: Hail to the grand council.

HANNO and SCHAHABARIM: Hail Hamilcar Barca!

HAMILCAR: Long life to you.

SCHAHABARIM: And to your ancestors.

HAMILCAR: And now, pray tell me, Priest of Moloch, what is the state of the republic since I was away at war? Speak, O high priest of Tanit.

SCHAHABARIM: The mercenaries are revolting.

HANNO: They certainly are.

SCHAHABARIM: They besiege our walls. They use catapults to hurl our own dead at us. Infection is spreading. We don't know how much longer we can hold out.

HAMILCAR: Did you pay them?

HANNO: Pay them? No. Inflation is so bad that I now pay more for a pair of slaves than I used to pay for a pair of elephants.

HAMILCAR: Inform us rather how you steered your galleys into the Roman fleet?

HANNO: I was driven by the wind out of my course.

HAMILCAR: You are like a rhinoceros treading on his dung. You expose your own folly! Be silent!

HANNO: It was you who failed to join forces with us. We waited but you never came.

HAMILCAR: You should have stood out from the coast. What prevented you? Oh! I forgot . . . the elephants are afraid of the sea!

*(*SCHAHABARIM *laughs.)*

HANNO: Please! Please! My leprosy was acting up as the result of a chill I received during the siege of Hecatopylos. *(His hand drops off. He weeps)*

SCHAHABARIM: Hamilcar, Carthage supplicates you. Take command of the army. Think of the dire peril we are in.

HAMILCAR: Is Tanit favorable? You hesitate. You fall silent. You drop your eyes. *(To* SCHAHABARIM*)* Speak venerable pontiff, keeper of the sacred veil, the soul of the gods.

SCHAHABARIM: The veil of Tanit, the sacred Zaïmph, is in the barbarian camp.

HAMILCAR: Great Gods!

SCHAHABARIM: Their chief came here to ravish it.

HAMILCAR: It is impossible to defeat those who possess the veil.

HANNO: It is a matter of delicacy. He does not wish to afflict his daughter! Since she takes her lovers from amongst the barbarians.

HAMILCAR: *(Wheels about, stunned)* What? Schahabarim, what is he saying?

(HANNO sniggers.)

SCHAHABARIM: He was seen leaving her bedchamber one morning in the month of Tammouz.

HANNO: He is the thief of the Zaïmph. A very handsome man. More muscular than Hamilcar.

HAMILCAR: *(Jerks off his tiara and hurls it to the ground where it shatters)* By the hundred torches of your intelligences! By the eight fires of the Kabiri! By the stars! By the meteors! And by the volcanoes! By all that which burns! By the thirst of the desert! By the salt of the sea! By the cavern of Hadrumetum, the realm of Souls! By the extermination! By the ashes of your sons, and the ashes of the brothers of your ancestors, with which I now commingle my own! You, the hundred Councillors of Carthage, have lied in accusing my daughter! And I, Hamilcar Barca, Suffete of the Sea, Chief of the Rich and Ruler of the people, before Moloch with the Bull's head, I swear . . . that I will not even speak of it to her! *(Pause)* You name me your chief on any conditions I set?

HANNO and SCHAHABARIM: *(Terrified)* Yes. Any condition! But you must save us!

HAMILCAR: Anything I ask?

HANNO and SCHAHABARIM: Yes!

HAMILCAR: You give me absolute command?

HANNO and SCHAHABARIM: Yes. Yes.

HAMILCAR: Then I accept.

SCHAHABARIM: May the Gods protect you.

HAMILCAR: *(Angry)* To cruel Moloch I vow a cruel and bloody sacrifice.

HANNO: *(Alarmed)* No, no! For pity's sake, do not speak!

HAMILCAR: Yes. A human sacrifice . . . from every citizen of Carthage, his firstborn male child to be hurled into the flames and burned alive on the Altar of Moloch!

HANNO: Oh horror! Horror! Our sons! O Gods! Our sons!

SCHAHABARIM: *(Praying)* Be Moloch happy, happy with our tears.

(HANNO and SCHAHABARIM exit.)

Scene 5: *Salammbô's chamber.*

SALAMMBÔ: All hail, Eye of Baalim! Triumph! Glory! Peace! Contentment! Wealth! A long time has my heart been sad, and the household languished, but the master who returns is like Tammouz restored to life; and under thy gaze, O Father, joyousness and a new existence will expand over all! *(Taking a little oblong vase from* TAANACH's *hands)* Drink a full draft of the welcome cup prepared by thy servant.

HAMILCAR: *(Taking the vase, mechanically)* Benediction on thee! *(Scrutinizes her keenly)*

SALAMMBÔ: *(Stammers out)* Thou hast been told, O Father!

HAMILCAR: *(In a low voice)* Yes! I know! *(Aside)* Is this a confession? Or does she merely allude to the Barbarians? *(To* SALAMMBÔ*)* Somewhat embarrassing, but perhaps I can dispel . . .

SALAMMBÔ: O Father! Thou canst never repair that which is irreparable! *(*HAMILCAR *starts back so violently that* SALAMMBÔ *is frightened.* SALAMMBÔ *cries out)* Mercy!

*(*HAMILCAR *lowers his head, searches her face.* SALAMMBÔ, *panting, buries her face in her bosom, crushed by his austere scrutiny. Hamilcar lifts his fists over her. She shrieks and falls back. Taanach presses herself between them.)*

HAMILCAR: So it is true. It is true. *(Turns on his heels and exits)*

*(*SCHAHABARIM *enters.)*

SCHAHABARIM: The souls of the dead resolve themselves into the moon as do the corpses into the earth. Their tears compose her humidity; it is a dark abode full of mire, wrecks, and tempests.

SALAMMBÔ: What will become of me?

SCHAHABARIM: At first you will languish, light as vapor that floats on the waves; and after trials and most prolonged agonies, you will enter the center of the sun, the very source of intelligence!

SALAMMBÔ: Is it out of shame that she is vanquished that you do not mention Tanit but refer to the goddess by the commonplace name of moon?

SCHAHABARIM: No! No! She draws from the sun all her fruitfulness! Have you not seen her wandering around him like an amorous woman who runs after a man in a field? Light is greater than darkness. Day is greater than night!

SALAMMBÔ: How do you know that?

SCHAHABARIM: I have judged that Baal is supreme by the position of the sun above the moon. The orb is only his reflection and visage.

SALAMMBÔ: *(Rapturously)* Tell me more! Tell me more!

SCHAHABARIM: If you promise never to reveal it, I will tell you a secret.

SALAMMBÔ: *(Rapturously)* I promise! I swear. Tell me, oh tell me more!

SCHAHABARIM: I no longer believe that the earth is shaped like a pinecone; I believe it to be round, and eternally falling in space with such prodigious velocity that no one can perceive its fall. I perceive even in the heavens the misfortunes of the sacrilege against Tanit. The Suffete your father is in grave danger. He is assailed by three armies commanded by Matho. Because Matho possesses the veil he has become King of the Barbarians. The fate of Carthage depends on you alone.

SALAMMBÔ: On me? What can I do?

SCHAHABARIM: *(With a smile of disdain)* Never will you consent!

SALAMMBÔ: What do you mean?

SCHAHABARIM: You must go to the Barbarians' camp and bring back the Zaïmph.

SALAMMBÔ: *(Sinks down shuddering throughout her entire frame)* Then I must die for Carthage.

SCHAHABARIM: Not necessarily. You might obtain the veil and not perish. The

Grand Council has openly hurled invectives at your father. You must save his good name, his honor won in many battles. You have sinned. Make reparation for your crime. Rabetna commands this sacrifice.

(Screams are heard, off.)

SALAMMBÔ: What is that sound?

SCHAHABARIM: To appease Moloch, each Elder has agreed to sacrifice his firstborn male child. Are you ready to go to Matho? Or shall I tell your father that you abandon him?

SALAMMBÔ: I need an augury. Let me consult the sacred python. [*(TAANACH enters with the python in a basket)*] O holy reptile, how bodes it for Carthage? *(Python coughs, collapses)* It's dying! I will go. I will demand that Matho give back the veil!

SCHAHABARIM: Claim it.

SALAMMBÔ: But if he should refuse? *(The priest smiles)* Yes. What then?

SCHAHABARIM: You will be alone with him.

SALAMMBÔ: And then?

SCHAHABARIM: Alone in his tent.

SALAMMBÔ: And what then?

SCHAHABARIM: *(Biting his lips)* If you are to die, it will be later, much later! Fear nothing; and whatever he attempts, do not call out. Do not be frightened! You must be humble, you understand, and submissive to his desire, for it is ordained of heaven!

SALAMMBÔ: *(Hides her face in her veil)* I am afraid of Matho. Sometimes the gods descend into the bodies of men. Is he not Moloch? O sacred and annointed eunuch, if only you would accompany me!

SCHAHABARIM: No! Kneel, raise your left hand and keep the right one extended: Oh Goddess, I swear to bring back to Carthage the veil of Tanit.

SALAMMBÔ: *(Tremblingly)* Oh Goddess, I swear to bring back to Carthage the veil of Tanit.

SCHAHABARIM: When the peacock crows, look under the myrtle for a man with two horses. You must fast yourself for three days. Here is a map of the roads you must take to reach Matho's tent. You may take Taanach with you.

SALAMMBÔ: May the gods bless and keep you, Schahabarim.

(SCHAHABARIM exits. Enter TAANACH.)

TAANACH: What are you looking at?

SALAMMBÔ: Taanach, the doves of Carthage are flying away.

TAANACH: You know that every year at this season they migrate to the Mountain of Eryx in Sicily, there to nest about the Temple of Venus!

SALAMMBÔ: See, see how they go—high above the sea, like a white cloud driven by the wind. *(Drops her head)*

TAANACH: But, mistress, they will return.

SALAMMBÔ: Yes! I know it.

TAANACH: And you will see them again.

SALAMMBÔ: *(Sighs)* Perhaps.

TAANACH: Are you ready for the sacred rites?

SALAMMBÔ: Yes.

TAANACH: Here, the High Priestess has sent you this.

SALAMMBÔ: *(Absently)* What is it?

TAANACH: Something liquid yet coagulated.

SALAMMBÔ: Ah. It is the blood of a black dog, strangled by barren women on a winter night amid the ruins of a sepulcher. *(Dips her finger and rubs some behind her ears.* TAANACH *drinks off the rest)* Make me magnificent.

TAANACH: I learned from a Hindoo slave how to dress the hair of courtesans.

SALAMMBÔ: Did they also teach you about love?

TAANACH: Love like music is an art. It gives emotion of the same order, as delicate, as vibrating, perhaps even more intense.

SALAMMBÔ: I am sure I have no talent for it.

TAANACH: You play upon the lyre. You know its every rhythm and subtlety.

SALAMMBÔ: Taanach, did you see the barbarian who stole the veil? Was he handsome or ugly? No, don't tell me. I don't care.

TAANACH: I didn't get a good look at him, mistress.

SALAMMBÔ: My sandals. Ah, Taanach, I would like to have extraordinary adventures.

TAANACH: Everything is extraordinary and nothing is. The days pass. One day is like another.

SALAMMBÔ: It didn't used to be so. In the olden days the gods descended to earth to love mortal women. But if the gods will descend no more, if they are dead or too old or too tired . . . Taanach, will I also die without having seen one who is a little more than a man? A hero who will bring tragic events into my life?

TAANACH: You should live and be happy.

SALAMMBÔ: If I can't have a life I want to have a fate.

TAANACH: What bracelet?

SALAMMBÔ: All of them. I will wear them all. *(Piles jewelry on)* If someone were to adore me, I am sure I would take pleasure in making him suffer until he died of it.

TAANACH: Perhaps you should whip a slave. That always makes you feel better.

SALAMMBÔ: Taanach, this is no time for frivolity. Well, perhaps just a small slave. *(*SMALL SLAVE *enters and is whipped)* This slave is too skinny. Bring me a mesomorph. *(*MESOMORPH *enters)* Now that's more like it. *(*MESOMORPH *is whipped to the point of delight)* My headache's gone! *(*SLAVE *exits)* Taanach, shave the swell of my delta that in the eyes of men I may have the nudity of a statue. *(*TAANACH *kneels between her legs and does so)* Now tint me! Perfume me! Powder me! Quickly! Quickly!

TAANACH: *(Growls)* Well! Well! Mistress . . . you have no one waiting for you.

SALAMMBÔ: Yes! Someone waits for me.

TAANACH: What do you order me to do, mistress, should you remain away? *(*SALAMMBÔ *sobs)* Do not go! When you were a little one and wept, I held you to my heart and suckled you, and made you laugh by tickling you with my nipples.

SALAMMBÔ: I am sure I remember nothing of the kind!

TAANACH: *(Striking her withered breasts)* Mistress, you sucked them dry! Now I am old! I can do nothing for you! You do not love me anymore! You hide your troubles from me, you despise your nurse! *(Tears roll down her face and into the scars of her tatooing)*

SALAMMBÔ: No no. There there. Be comforted. I love you, old ape.

TAANACH: *(With the smiles of an old ape, continues her task)* You will not be fairer the day of your bridal.

SALAMMBÔ: *(In a reverie)* My bridal! *(The crowing of a peacock is heard off)* Quick. See, under the myrtles, if there be not a man with two horses.

TAANACH: *(Looks off the terrace upstage then turns back to* SALAMMBÔ*)* He is there. Mistress! The cypress shadow falls to your left. It is a presage of death! *(*SALAMMBÔ *turns and exits.* TAANACH *throws herself on the floor and tears her face with her fingernails)* Take me with you! Take me with you! Take me with you!
SALAMMBÔ: *(Reenters)* Come.

(They exit. Curtain.)

ACT II

Scene 1: *The Barbarian's Tent.*

NARR'HAVAS: Matho, sorry about that little incident with the spear. I was drunk.
MATHO: Don't worry about it. *(They kiss their thumbs and press them together.* NARR'HAVAS *exits)* Spendius, they have made me head of the army.
SPENDIUS: Some army. Men with beastlike profiles, grinning with idiotic laughter—wretches ravaged by hideous diseases, deformed pygmies, mulattoes of doubtful sex, albinos whose red eyes blink in the sun. Stammering out unintelligible sounds, they put their fingers in their mouths to show that they are hungry.
MATHO: In the land of the blind, the one-eyed man is king. And it has fallen on my shoulders to lead this human wreckage against Carthage. But take heart: we still have a few good men. And it's a lucky thing that Narr'Havas joined us with the Numidian troops.
SPENDIUS: What brings him here I wonder? Is it to betray us or Carthage?
MATHO: Nonsense. Did you not see how he kissed his thumbs as a sign of allegiance?
BARBARIANS: Wine meat women gold! Wine meat women gold!
SPENDIUS: Listen! The drunken Barbarians grow restless! They demand wine, meat, and gold.
BARBARIANS: *(Rave)*
SPENDIUS: They cry out for women. They are raving in a hundred languages!
BARBARIANS: *(Moan)*
SPENDIUS: *(Exits, then returns)* The men have begun to use the boys as women. They rouge their lips and cheeks with the blood of the dying slaves and sodomize them on the broken spears.
MATHO: Can you blame them? I'm so horny my nuts are up around my ears. I could fuck a dog!
SPENDIUS: No need to do that. Maybe we could help each other out.
MATHO: You sure don't waste any time.
SPENDIUS: Where I come from people think nothing of it.
MATHO: The other day when you were bathing I noticed you had a nice ass.
SPENDIUS: You know, with your profile you could be a Greek.

*(*MATHO *takes* SPENDIUS *in his arms and drops the tent flap. There are a few sounds of lust, which quickly subside into snores. Commotion off.)*

BARBARIAN: Matho, there are two women in the camp. They wish to see you.
MATHO: Send them in.
SALAMMBÔ: Conduct me to his tent. I wish it.
BARBARIAN: Follow me. *(He shows* SALAMMBÔ *into the tent)*

TAANACH: Spendius, do you recognize me?

SPENDIUS: Taanach!

TAANACH: I have brought you these flamingoes' tongues all wrapped in a hippopotamus hide.

SPENDIUS: You're adorable.

(They slip out behind the tent.)

MATHO: Who are you? *(*SALAMMBÔ *lets out a little cry)* What brings you here? Why do you come?

SALAMMBÔ: *(Pointing to the Zaïmph)* To take it. *(She pulls off her veils.* MATHO *recoils terrified)* Give it to me!

MATHO: *(Does not answer. He merely stares at her completely overcome. Like a child he touches the upper part of her bosom with the tip of his finger)* You? You! *(His bosom heaves. His teeth chatter. Taking her by the wrists and drawing her to him he sits down on a lion skin and holds her between his knees)* How beautiful you are! How beautiful you are! I desire to envelop you. Absorb you. Drink you.

SALAMMBÔ: *(Repelled, has to restrain herself from screaming. She averts her face and tries to shake her wrists loose from his grasp)*

MATHO: *(Dilates his nostrils and inhales deeply)* You smell of honey, pepper, incense, roses—with another odor still.

SALAMMBÔ: What have I done to you that you should desire my death?

MATHO: Your death?

SALAMMBÔ: I saw you one night in the flames of my burning gardens, between the steaming cups and my slaughtered slaves. You were in a rage; you bounded toward me like a ferocious animal and made me run away! Then terror came to Carthage. The burning of cities, the massacre of soldiers. It is you who ruined our cities! It is you who killed our men. I hate you! I loathe you! I abhor you! You gnaw at me like remorse! You nauseate me like the plague! I despise you, do you hear? Despise you!

MATHO: How did you find your way here?

SALAMMBÔ: I followed your trail of fires and corpses as if I walked behind Moloch himself. You barbarian.

MATHO: Hey, watch that! My mother was a barbarian! *(*MATHO *bounds up full of pride)*

SALAMMBÔ: As if your sacrilege were not enough you came to me in my sleep dressed as a woman wearing the Zaïmph itself. Your words I did not understand. But I knew that you wanted to drag me down toward something horrible at the bottom of an abyss.

MATHO: *(Wringing his hands cries out)* No! No! It was to give the Zaïmph back to you. For it seemed to me that the goddess moon had left the veil for you alone to wear.

SALAMMBÔ: Blasphemy!

MATHO: No, no! I worship you. Are you not omnipotent, immaculate, radiant, and beautiful even as the moon? Unless, perhaps, you are the moon?

SALAMMBÔ: I, the moon!

MATHO: Oh, come near! Come near! Fear nothing. What is Carthage to me? The whole herd of Carthaginians stumble about as though lost in the dust of your sandals. All of their treasures are as nothing compared to your lips and the whiteness of your shoulders. I only want to pull down the walls of Carthage that I might come near to you and possess you. I crush men's skulls like shells. I throw myself down on the broken spears. The catapult is powerless to kill me. I fear not fetters, the ax, or the cross. I can see your eyes in the flames of their funeral pyres, and I can hear your voice in the crash of cymbals. I turn around and you are not there. And I go on fighting!

SALAMMBÔ: *(Rises and goes over to the Zaïmph and raises her hands to seize it)*

MATHO: *(Crying out)* What are you doing?

SALAMMBÔ: I am going back to Carthage with the Zaïmph.

MATHO: *(Stammering)* You? Return with it to Carthage? *(Grinding his teeth)* You return with it to Carthage! Ah! You came to take the Zaïmph, to conquer me, then to disappear! No! No! You belong to me! And no one can now tear you from me! Ah! I have not forgotten the insolence of your large tranquil eyes and how you crushed me with your proud beauty. It is my turn now! You are my captive, my slave, my servant! Call if you will on your father and his army, the Elders, the Rich, and your entire accursed people! Your people! What kind of people are they who crucify lions? I am the master of three hundred thousand soldiers. I will overthrow your town and burn all its temples. Your ships shall float on waves of blood. Not a single house, stone, or palm tree will remain. And if men fail me I will draw the bears from the mountains and turn the lions upon your people. Do not seek to fly or I shall kill you! *(Sobs suddenly suffocate him, and he sinks down before her)* Ah! forgive me! I am a wretch viler than the scorpions, the mud, or the dust. Trample me, if only I can feel your feet. Curse me, if only I can hear your voice. Do not go. Have pity. I love you. I love you! *(Puts his arm around her waist, looks up at her face, tears rolling down his cheeks. SALAMMBÔ, overcome, faints, and falls back on the lions' skins. MATHO seizes her in a frantic embrace. Her gold chain snaps. The two ends fly apart. The Zaïmph falls and envelops her. He kisses all her fingers, her arms, her feet, and the long tresses of her hair from end to end, and then buries his nose between her legs)*

SALAMMBÔ: *(Exclaims)* Moloch, thou burnest me! *(She lies back and moans in what may be either agony or ecstasy)*

MATHO: Take the Zaïmph! How can I resist? Take me with it also! I will renounce everything! Beyond Gades, twenty days' journey by the sea, there is an island covered with gold dust, with verdure, and birds. On the mountains flowers full of smoking perfume swing like eternal censers; in citron trees taller than cedars, milk-white serpents with the diamonds of their jaws toss the fruit to the ground. The air is so soft that you cannot die. Aye, I will seek it; you shall see this haven. We shall live in crystal grottoes hewn out at the foot of the hills. No one inhabits this country; I shall become king.

SALAMMBÔ: You are nothing! You are lower than a slave! You are as dirt under my feet! You are not fit to place your tongue between my toes!

MATHO: *(Groveling at her feet and kissing her feet)* You are right!

(The moon appears gliding through the clouds outside of the tent.)

SALAMMBÔ: The moon, Tanit! She sees us! *(She turns her head away, ashamed)*

MATHO: *(Looking up at the moon)* Ah, what nights I have spent in contemplating her. She seemed to me a veil which hid your face; you looked at me through it; memories of you were mingled with her rays. Then I could see you there no more. *(He weeps freely on her bosom, sleeps)*

SALAMMBÔ: *(Aside)* So this is he, the formidable man who makes all Carthage tremble! *(SALAMMBÔ disengages herself. She looks with shame at the broken chain between her legs. Lamenting cries come from afar in the darkness. SALAMMBÔ sees a dagger, and seizing the shaft of the weapon, she raises it as if to kill him. MATHO partially opens his eyes and kisses her hand that holds the dagger. The dagger drops.*

There are shouts outside. MATHO *lifts the tent cloth and sees a conflagration beyond. Trumpets sound)*

MENS' VOICES: *(Off)* Matho! Matho! Come! Hamilcar is burning the camps!

MATHO: *([Covers her with blankets,] exits in one bound)*

SALAMMBÔ: *[(Makes up pallet as if she were still in it, begins to leave with the Zaïmph.)]*

TAANACH: *(Enters)* I saw everything!

SALAMMBÔ: *(Gasps)* Taanach!

TAANACH: Ah, why have not the Baals granted me this mercy? They would have spared me the pain of cursing you!

SALAMMBÔ: *(Draws herself quickly back)* You seem to me something horrible! Like a larva! Or a phantom!

TAANACH: I shall soon be one hundred years old.

SALAMMBÔ: I am not a child! I shall soon be thirteen. And a half.

TAANACH: Not for one single day have I despaired of Carthage! But now all is ended! All is lost! The Gods curse her! And they curse you, who have ruined and dishonored her!

SALAMMBÔ: *(Parts her lips as though to speak, but* TAANACH *interrupts her)*

TAANACH: Ahhh, I was there! I saw you panting with lust, like a prostitute, and when he told you of his passion, you permitted him to kiss your hands! But if the madness of your unchastity impelled you, at least you could have done as the wild beasts which hide themselves to couple, and not thus have displayed your shame almost before the very eyes of your father!

SALAMMBÔ: What?

TAANACH: Then you do not know that the two encampments are within sixty cubits of each other—that your Matho, from excess of audacious pride, has set up camp in front of Hamilcar. Your father is just there behind you, and if I could only have climbed up the pathway to the platform I could have cried, "Come now, see your daughter in the embrace of a Barbarian! She has put on the mantle of the Goddess to please him, and abandons her body to his lust. Oh! Sacrilegious one! Be accursed! Accursed! Accursed!

SALAMMBÔ: *(Draws back the flap of the tent and points off in the distance)* It is this way, is it not?

TAANACH: What matters that to you? Rather turn aside! Away! Or crush your face against the earth! It is a holy place, which your look would pollute! You wanton! You slut! You whore! But I am guilty too. For I have failed in my charge to keep you ever virgin.

SALAMMBÔ: Taanach, it was not for nothing that I came to the barbarian camp. I have reconquered the veil of Tanit! *[(Displays it)]*

TAANACH: Forgive me, my mistress. I have misjudged you.

SALAMMBÔ: Come, let us go.

TAANACH: Where are we going?

SALAMMBÔ: To Carthage, old woman! To Carthage!

(They exit. MATHO *reenters with* SPENDIUS.*)*

SPENDIUS: What do you plan to do with her? A woman in camp is an encumbrance.

MATHO: Hush! She's sleeping. You'll awaken her. *(He pats delicately the lions' skins spread out on the couch of palm branches, and calls out gently)* Salammbô? Salammbô! She answers not! *(He tears down a strip of canvas to admit the daylight and lets out a heartrending cry)* The Zaïmph is gone! *(He runs to the tent flap, calling*

Hanno at the Baths in *Salammbô* (Anita & Steve Shevett)

after her) Salammbô! Where are you? Salammbô! Priestess of the Moon! Where are you?

SPENDIUS: Maybe she's gone back to the moon.

MATHO: Then I'll to the moon to bring her back! *(He wails at the moon like a wild animal)* Salammbô! Moon! Salammbô!

Scene 2: HANNO *in the Baths.*

(He lies in a bathtub. Two youths massage his feet.)

HANNO: *(To a* SLAVE*)* You know that several barbarians have been taken prisoner. And here I sit racking my brains trying to think of some terrible new torture for them. *(To the boys)* Massage the feet more vigorously. The leprosy has them swollen.

SLAVE: More peacocks' tongues?

HANNO: Mmmmm. Mmmmmm. I really shouldn't but . . . *(Helps himself to some of the dainties proffered on an ox hide. Then to a* SLAVE *standing near to him writing on the palm of his hand)* Stop! Let them be brought to me! I wish to see them. *(Three* BARBARIANS *are pushed in)* Rejoice, light of the Baals! Your Suffete has exterminated the ravenous dogs. Benedictions on the Republic! Order prayers to be said! *(Looks at the captives and then bursts into laughter)* Ha! ha! ha! my braves of Sicca. You do not shout so loud today. It is I! Do you not recognize me? Hanno! Where then are your swords? What terrible men are these! *(Feigns to hide as if he experienced great fear)* You asked for horses, women, lands, magistracies, and doubtless also for priesthoods! Ah, well, I will give you plots of land and you shall never leave them. You shall be married to beautiful

young gallows. For your pay ingots of lead shall be melted in your mouths. And I will put you in the very best places, far up and exalted, among the clouds, near the eagles! *(The three weary* BARBARIANS *look at him without understanding what he says. Their heavy chains drag on the stones. A* BARBARIAN *spits in* HANNO's *face.* HANNO *screams at them indignantly)* On your knees! On your knees! Nine lashes for your boyfriend! *(*GUARD *takes* BARBARIAN *off)*
BARBARIAN: No! Take me! Take me!

(Sounds of whipping off. Screams of BARBARIAN. *Laughter of* HANNO. GUARD *brings* BARBARIAN *back.)*

HANNO: Now, kiss my ass! *(*BARBARIAN *hesitates.* GUARD *insists.* BARBARIAN *holds his nose, kisses* HANNO's *ass)* Jackals! Dirt! Vermin! Excrement! And do they reply? Enough! Silence! Let them be flayed alive! No! not now; presently! Oh! Demonades, how I suffer! Have the bricks reheated until they are red-hot.
DEMONADES: *(Holding out a golden cup from which steam arises)* Drink! a broth of vipers, that the strength of the serpents, born of the sun, may penetrate the marrow of your bones. And take courage! O reflection of the gods! You know, moreover, that a priest of Eschmoun watches the cruel stars around the dog whence you derive your malady. They pale like the spots on your skin; therefore you will not die.
HANNO: Ah, yes! That is true! I ought not to die of them! *(From his violet lips escapes a breath more nauseous than the exhalations of a corpse)* Perhaps you are right, Demonades. I feel stronger! Look, even now some of the ulcers are closed. See how I eat! *(Eats delicately but voraciously)* And imagining the cruel and unusual punishments to be showered upon these vanquished helps my digestion. *(Giggles then turns on the three captives and shoots a volley of insults at them in an unnatural voice)* Ah, traitors! Wretches! Infamous! Accursed! And you outraged me! Me! Hanno! Their services, the price of their blood as they have said. Their blood! Their blood! All shall perish! Not one shall be sold! It would be best to bring them to Carthage. No . . . without doubt I have not brought enough chains. . . . How many prisoners are there? Iddibal! Go ask Muthumbal. Go! No pity! And have all their hands cut off and brought to me in baskets! *(Distant cries are heard and the trumpeting of elephants)* What is that? Has the battle begun anew?
IDDIBAL: *(Enters panting and throws himself on his face at* HANNO's *feet)* The Carthaginian army have been crushed by their own elephants!
HANNO: Crushed by our own elephants? How is that possible?
IDDIBAL: In the ruins of their camp the Barbarians discovered a vat of petroleum doubtless left behind by the victorious army. With this bitumen they besmeared swine, set them on fire, and turned them loose toward Utica. The elephants, frenzied by these running flames, stampeded back upon the Carthaginians, ripped them with their tusks, trampled them beneath their massive feet, suffocated and crushed them.
HANNO: Why did they not retreat behind the city walls?
IDDIBAL: The Barbarians descended the hill behind the elephants. The Punic camp, being without entrenchments, was sacked at the first attack, and the Carthaginians found themselves crushed against the city gates, which were kept closed for fear of the Mercenaries. I have told it.
HANNO: *(Screams)* Help me out of this vapor bath! [*(They struggle to do so)*] No, idiots! Get me up quickly. Quickly! . . . Get away! My robe. Get my robe! *(A* NEGRO *who carries his umbrella whispers in his ear)* What then? *(*NEGRO

whispers again) Ah, well, kill them. *(The Ethiopian beheads the three captives with a single swipe of his blade. The three heads fall and clatter on the stones. The Suffete dips his hands in their blood and rubs it on his knees)* Human blood. Good for leprosy. *(Several* BARBARIANS *enter at the back unseen by* HANNO. *All* GUARDS *and* ATTENDANTS *flee.* HANNO *turns, sees* BARBARIANS *and calls for his captains)* Demonades, call my captains. *(In a hoarse whisper)* No! What are you going to do with me? I am rich! I will give you anything you want! You see well, I do not resist! I have always been complaisant!
BARBARIANS: Call Matho.

[*(The* BARBARIANS *carry in a giant cross.)*]

HANNO: Not the cross. I am dreaming. Not the cross!
MATHO: *(Enters)* Speak! What kind of people crucify lions?
HANNO: *(Pleading)* Spare me and I will deliver unto you Hamilcar. And we will both be kings!
MATHO: *(Turns away in disgust, signals the men to hasten)* Hurry up!

(They lay HANNO *on the cross.)*

HANNO: I hate Hamilcar. I will sacrifice him to you—you're not going to kill me, are you? *(Weeps bitterly)*
MATHO: Get on with it.
HANNO: *(Wailing)* No! No!
BARBARIAN: The ropes are not strong enough to raise him on it.
MATHO: Then nail him to it before it is erected.

(They begin driving the nails into HANNO's *hands and feet.)*

HANNO: *(Foaming and writhing like a sea beast)* You will all die more horribly than I! Do you hear me? I will be revenged for you will die more horribly! More horribly than I! *(*HANNO *screams and the sounds of nails being driven are heard as the lights fade)*

Scene 3: *Carthage.*

HAMILCAR: Triumph! Glory! Victory! Carthage is free and her ferocious enemies are dispersed and at an end. Of the sacred battalion the valor was in vain. Already our elephants were flying in the plain, when from heaven a sudden succor came. Yes, Tanit, appeased, forgetting her anger, spread over us her tutelary strength. Tanit spoke and fought for us!
SCHAHABARIM: Everywhere incense burns on the altar of the city. Oh! Tanit, may the fire consume a holocaust offering to thy divinity. Triumph, glory, and victory!
NARR'HAVAS: Hamilcar, in a foolish moment to the enemies of your country I promised help and aid; these bonds I detested once my anger gone, and thus came back to you. In the battle my zebras quickly joined your own.
HAMILCAR: *(Coldly)* I know not, O King, what price they will offer thee, but Hamilcar is not ungrateful.
NARR'HAVAS: The recompense, most charming, and the prize most rich, Hamilcar, are in thy power. *(Showing* SALAMMBÔ, *who appears)* Salammbô!
HAMILCAR: Salammbô!
SCHAHABARIM: Salammbô! *(*SALAMMBÔ *covered with black comes slowly)* What

mortal pallor, how touching and how lovely: coming thus with religious mien, not even lifting her eyes.

SALAMMBÔ: *(Still at back)* The prize to which you owe the victory was not the elephants, or the zebras, or the cavalry mounted on ostriches, but the great veil of Tanit which was reconquered. Here it is. *(She pulls back her mantle and the Zaïmph is seen)*

SCHAHABARIM: Oh, joy, hope, and pride, our good genius has returned. Salammbô, thou'rt blessed. *(Adoring the Zaïmph)* Anaitis! Derceto! Mylitta! Oy, Rabetna, Baalet, Tyratha!

NARR'HAVAS: *(Aside)* Matho no doubt is dead while deserving my anger!

HAMILCAR: *(To SALAMMBÔ)* What did you do?

SALAMMBÔ: Saved Carthage and my father!

HAMILCAR: *(Examines chains between her legs. Aside to SCHAHABARIM)* The golden chain is broken.

SCHAHABARIM: Better marry her off as quickly as possible.

(They look at NARR'HAVAS.)

HAMILCAR: Prince, you shall have my daughter's hand in marriage. Let Carthage and Numidia in nuptial bonds be joined.

SCHAHBARIM: *(Followed by PRIESTS, exits with the Zaïmph, which he holds with tongs in order to avoid touching it.)*

SALAMMBÔ: Father, must I be sacrificed?

HAMILCAR: Someday my daughter you shall rule the world!

SALAMMBÔ: And if I do not choose to rule the world?

(On come SPENDIUS, AUTHARITE, BARBARIAN CHIEFS, PRISONERS, and GUARDS)

SCHAHBARIM: *(Reenters)* Be accursed, sacrilegious bandits. Scoundrels, detestable wretches, to the cross, to the torture! Vengeance!

AUTHARITE: We know how to meet our fate and ask no sort of mercy. Without pity, had we been the conquerors, so send us now to death.

BARBARIAN: *(Pulling him back)* Are you crazy?

SPENDIUS: *(At the feet of HAMILCAR)* Noble Hamilcar, save me! These rags of purple I'll tear away, become again a slave. Oh! Pallor of death, let some other than myself now mock thee. Save me. Narr'Havas—save me, Salammbô.

AUTHARITE: Oh, shame . . . before a master, cowardly humiliant, and cowardly begging even to the traitor Narr'Havas.

HAMILCAR: Very well. Give me five Barbarians to be crucified and I will be appeased.

SPENDIUS: Can we have a minute to think it over?

HAMILCAR: You may confer among yourselves.

(They confer.)

SPENDIUS: We agree.

HAMILCAR: Good. I choose you.

SPENDIUS and BARBARIANS: *(Cry out)* No!

HAMILCAR: All to the death—let the crosses be raised.

(During the following scene crosses are seen slowly erected in the distance.)

MATHO: *(Rushing on, sword in hand)* Give me also mine.

SALAMMBÔ: Great Gods! I see him once more!

ALL: Matho!

SALAMMBÔ: Even in his horrible agony the lion is still terrible.

MATHO: Why these cries and this fright? What, you all fall back? Are you of me afraid? Fear nothing, for my strength is gone. *(Throws away his sword)* My sword is broken, also my heart.

HAMILCAR: Chain him. *(They do)*

SALAMMBÔ: *(Aside)* Oh, Gods, let me die; your victim is tired of suffering.

MATHO: *(To* HAMILCAR*)* Thou who hast not blushed to soil glory so great in buying this miserable king. *(To* NARR'HAVAS*)* Thou! Thou coward, who at the moment of victory deserted. *(To* SALAMMBÔ*)* Crowned courtesan who but yesterday belonged to me. Thou more than destiny fatal and cruel; oh, Salammbô, so false and so beautiful. *(Weeping)* Salammbô! Salammbô! *(With force)* I detest you. Oh, avenging Gods, keep your thunders ready. Gods of infernal depths, join in my anger, let only death and despair fall on their heads.

SCHAHABARIM: Gods infernal, spare us. To the torture.

SALAMMBÔ: *(Fearful)* To the torture.

HAMILCAR: No! Matho shall live one day longer. His blood shall redden the altar where you adore—Tanit!

SCHAHABARIM: What shouts of joy will go up to heaven.

HAMILCAR: Expiring he will see Carthage triumphant and the wedding of Narr'Havas in splendor and in pomp, to Salammbô, the one who rescued the veil of Tanit.

SALAMMBÔ: Oh great Gods!

NARR'HAVAS: Tomorrow you die.

MATHO: Good deliverance.

HAMILCAR: Thus it is that Hamilcar doth punish and reward.

Scene 4: *Salammbô's chamber.*

TAANACH: You live! Or do I see before me the shadow of a priestess? To my lips with your digits and their rings and cease your wandering in a land time forgot.

SALAMMBÔ: Back. The black torrent of my immaculate hair bathes my lonely body in horrid ice. And my hair, when laced with light becomes immortal! O woman, a kiss could kill me if beauty were not death. How am I to know under what spell and on what morning but dimly recalled by amnesiac eunuchs drenches the dying distance in lugubrious festivals? O frosty nurse, you have seen me go down to choose the lions to be crucified and when I pointed to the victim it licked my hands!

TAANACH: An omen!

SALAMMBÔ: Silence. Bring me the glass. *(*TAANACH *rolls in a huge mirror)* O mirror, cold water frozen with boredom in your frame. And my pallid lilies cast no reflection in the marble waters of the fountains. My hair in this do reminds me of those lions' manes. *(*TAANACH *averts her eyes)* Come since you dare not look at me. Comb it listlessly before the mirror.

TAANACH: If not myrrh in amber bottles would you prefer the essence sucked from funereal roses?

SALAMMBÔ: No perfumes. You know how I hate them. Would you have me drunk with fragrances? Not even flowers can make me forget my suffering.

I wish only to be sterile and cruel like armor and vases, artifacts of extinct civilizations.

TAANACH: Forgive me my queen. I am getting senile like the faded writings on an ancient book. My memory fails me.

SALAMMBÔ: The sun has already begun to descend and the crescent moon rises in another part of the sky.

TAANACH: The people love you, for you have restored the Zaïmph and saved your country. Therefore they have declared your wedding a national holiday. On the square, they await your appearance. The festival is to last all night. The death of Matho has been promised for the ceremony.

SALAMMBÔ: For months I have prayed daily for his death.

TAANACH: But how to slay him? Some suggested that they run molten lead into his bowels, others that he be tied to a tree and let a monkey beat his brains out with a stone, or that he be tied to a dromedary after having inserted into the various openings of his body flaxen wicks steeped in oils, and for their amusement he is to be paraded about, writhing under its fire, a human candelabrum blown about by the wind.

SALAMMBÔ: And what have they decided?

TAANACH: That he is to be flayed alive in the streets. But in order not to disappoint anyone he is to go from his prison to the square of Khamoun. The people have all let their fingernails grow long, the better to lacerate his flesh. You are fainting!

SALAMMBÔ: Oh Taanach, I do not want him to die. He was so innocent. A big kid. How do I look?

TAANACH: Truly beautiful. A human star. But there a lock of hair is out of place.

SALAMMBÔ: Do not touch me! Restrain the profanation of this gesture.

TAANACH: My child, you are so lovely and so terrible.

SALAMMBÔ: You were about to touch me, were you not?

TAANACH: I wish that I could be the one with whom you share your secrets— for whom do you, devoured by anguish, save your secret splendor and the vain mystery of your being?

SALAMMBÔ: Go close the shutters of my terrace. Shut out the sky. For the beautiful azure is everywhere. And I detest the beautiful azure. Now let us go.

TAANACH: Lamentable victim offered to its doom.

SALAMMBÔ: I await a thing unknown.

Scene 5: *Wedding of Salammbô.*

(The forum of Carthage. The crowd swarms about the terraces. All is noise and joy. The High Priests stand at the foot of the statue of Tanit.)

SCHAHABARIM: People, your gods join you in your happiness; they tremble with joy beyond bounds to the very heaven. Giving up her starry abode to deliver herself to your love. Praise Baal. Praise Moloch. Tanit, the goddess for whom I sacrificed my manhood, will soon be uncovered. *(The golden calf comes on, followed by three men admiring it in a lustful, ritual manner. [Another worshipper enters in drag. They struggle for position as the four form a daisy chain.])* Great Hamilcar approaches. Before heaven joins you together King Narr'Havas, with thou, our pride, Salammbô.

(SALAMMBÔ is carried on by dancing women. SALAMMBÔ performs the dance of the seven veils.)

SALAMMBÔ: *(To HAMILCAR)* Did my dancing please you?

HAMILCAR: Yes, very good, my daughter, we are well pleased.

SCHAHABARIM: We owe to Tanit a bloody sacrifice.

HAMILCAR: Bring forth the victim. Matho!

(Great emotion among the people. MATHO dragged in by the GUARDS is thrown before the statue of Tanit. He falls in front of SALAMMBÔ by the altar.)

ALL: Matho. Matho. Matho. Matho.

SALAMMBÔ: Oh protecting Gods.

SCHAHABARIM: *(Taking the sword)* Accept then this blood, O Tanit.

VOICE FROM THE CROWD: No, not the priest! The one who rescued the veil. Salammbô!

ALL: Salammbô! Salammbô! Salammbô! Salammbô!

HAMILCAR: Salammbô! O Gods on high.

SALAMMBÔ: *(Coming forward)* I hear what the people ordain.

HAMILCAR: What, and you would obey?

SALAMMBÔ: Give me the knife, O priest.

NARR'HAVAS: *(Trying to stop her)* Salammbô! No, my darling.

(She takes the sword and goes toward MATHO who is kneeling by the altar. He looks toward her, his eyes full of love. SALAMMBÔ makes a superhuman effort to lift the sword. Her arm falls.)

BARBARIAN: What, the sword escapes her?

ANOTHER BARBARIAN: Revenge Tanit, Salammbô!

SALAMMBÔ: At last, Matho, you are in my power. You are my captive, my slave. You asked me once what kind of people they are who crucify lions. Well, now I will show you what kind of woman Salammbô really is.

AUTHORITATUS: Strike!

MATHO: Strike!

SALAMMBÔ: *(Raising the sword)* Accept then this blood, O Tanit. And through this dew let thy anger be appeased—for all who touch thy sacred and saintly veil—must die. *(She strikes herself)*

MATHO: *(Breaking his bond and holding SALAMMBÔ in his arms)* Do not approach, for she is mine. Salammbô! I adore thee!

SALAMMBÔ: [*(Weakly)*] Matho!

MATHO: I am dying, Carthage.

SALAMMBÔ: Beyond Gades, twenty days' journey by the sea there is an island covered with gold dust, with verdure, and birds.

MATHO: No one inhabits this country.

SALAMMBÔ: We shall live in crystal grottoes hewn out at the foot of the hills.

MATHO: The air is so soft that you cannot die.

SALAMMBÔ: You shall be king. *(Dies)*

MATHO: No! Salammbô, don't leave me!

TAANACH: My mistress has slain herself. Why did she slay herself? She looked too long on the moon. I told her not to look on the moon. Only insane people worship the moon.

SCHAHABARIM: *(Picks up knife, stabs MATHO, [castrates him,] removes the heart, holds it up in one hand as it pulsates)* Thus dies Salammbô, high priestess, daughter of Hamilcar, for having touched the veil of Tanit.

THE ARTIFICIAL JUNGLE

A Suspense Thriller

1986

Domino night in *The Artificial Jungle*
(Anita & Steve Shevett)

Cast of Characters

ROXANNE NURDIGER, *Roxy for short*
CHESTER NURDIGER, *her husband, a lovable sap*
MRS. NURDIGER, *her mother-in-law*
ZACHARY SLADE, *a drifter and a smoothie*
FRANKIE SPINELLI, *a cop, somebody's brother-in-law*
MRS. MUNCIE

ACT I

(The scene is set in a pet shop on Manhattan's Lower East Side. It is not a well-kept shop, but rather a family affair with the owners living in the back of the store. Stacked birdcages, bubbling aquariums, and rodent cages create an atmosphere of general disorder. Large potted plants and lush foliage lend a tropical touch. The overall effect is one of denseness and kitsch exoticism. It is clear that these people are creatures of fantasy. Fishnets and other jungle and sea motifs are overlaid with five-and-ten-cent-store modern furniture. We sit in the back of the store and look out through the shop to the street where occasional passers-by stop and look in the window. Signs naming species and prices break up the otherwise tropical effect. A sign on the window spells Pet Shop backward.)

FRANKIE: That bird you sold me just won't talk.
CHESTER: It talked here. You heard it.
FRANKIE: Yeah, but it hasn't said a word since I got it home.
CHESTER: Give it time. Give it time.
FRANKIE: I've had it three weeks. And the damn bird doesn't say anything. It just sits there.
CHESTER: Sometimes they have to get used to the new environment.
FRANKIE: I guess. The kids are real disappointed. They keep asking me, When's the birdie gonna talk, Daddy? When's the birdie gonna talk? I feel like an asshole.
CHESTER: You better watch your language around it. You know the story of the old lady and the parrot. They pick up profanity.
FRANKIE: This one ain't pickin' up anything. It's just a dumb bird.
CHESTER: I can't understand it. It was talking here. Be patient. When the time comes it will talk.
FRANKIE: I hope so. I hate to think I wasted my money.
CHESTER: Maybe what you need is a train-your-bird-to-talk record.
FRANKIE: No.
CHESTER: Here, look at this. "Your bird, too, can be a star." Now, this side teaches it to say "Hello" and "Pretty Boy."
FRANKIE: What's on the other side?
CHESTER: "Polly Want a Cracker." Now that's a parrot classic! I'll tell you what—it's four ninety-eight, I'll give you a break on it. Four eighty-nine.
FRANKIE: You're a real sport.
CHESTER: You need any birdseed, anything like that?
FRANKIE: A small bag.
CHESTER: One small bag coming up. *(Places huge bag on counter)* You know, maybe your bird needs a more balanced diet. Have you thought of getting it some proso millet?

FRANKIE: No.

CHESTER: Sometimes this will get them talking right away.

FRANKIE: Well, try it.

CHESTER: Or maybe your bird is bored.

FRANKIE: Now that's a possibility.

CHESTER: We have a whole line of bird toys and amusements here. We've got a bird Ferris wheel. We got a bird mirror—he could admire himself. We got a bird dumbbell—he could pump up. And we got a bird . . . we got a bird . . . pipe. Now what the hell is that? [*(Tosses it back)*] Do you have *Parrots of the World?*

FRANKIE: No.

CHESTER: Look at this. Over one hundred full-color photographs of every parrot known to man. Oh, look at that one!

FRANKIE: Oh, that looks like Tweetheart!

CHESTER: Yeah, that looks like yours, doesn't it? I think you should get that for the kids. It's very educational.

FRANKIE: Well, you might as well throw that in too.

CHESTER: Throw that in. So, Frankie. Anything else I can get you?

FRANKIE: How about something in the way of a birdbath?

CHESTER: One birdbath coming up. [*(It's a dog dish)*] Let me add this up for you.

MRS. NURDIGER: *(Off)* Roxanne, did you clean the gerbils' cages?

ROXANNE: Yes.

MRS. NURDIGER: *(Off)* Did you feed the piranhas?

ROXANNE: *(Entering)* I'm doing it now.

FRANKIE: Hi, Roxanne.

ROXANNE: Aw hi yourself.

FRANKIE: Whatsamatter with her?

CHESTER: Oh she's got the rag on.

ROXANNE: Flake off.

CHESTER: Nice talk.

ROXANNE: Oh, leave me alone, will ya? I'm in no mood.

FRANKIE: She's been like this for weeks.

CHESTER: I don't know what's eating her. Women, you can't figure 'em. [*(Calculates on the back of a brown paper sack)*] That'll be forty-nine dollars and ninety-eight cents—eighty-nine cents. I'm giving you a break on the record. Oh! She's going to feed the piranhas. Don't miss this. *(*ROXANNE *lowers slab of meat into piranha tank, removes bloody bone, and disposes of it in kitchen)* My they were hungry.

FRANKIE: Maybe she's bored. Everybody needs a vacation once in a while.

CHESTER: Naw. I took her to the tropical fish show in Pittsburgh. And even that didn't snap her out of it.

ROXANNE: *(Looking at cages)* Ooooh, the rats had another litter.

FRANKIE: Maybe it's time you two thought about raising a family.

CHESTER: Look, we got baby rats. What do we need children for?

ROXANNE: Ooh wittle baby wats. Hewo babies. Hewo.

FRANKIE: *(They both look over at* ROXANNE*)* Think about it.

CHESTER: Yeah, yeah, I'll think about it.

FRANKIE: I gotta go.

CHESTER: You gonna play dominoes tonight?

FRANKIE: What is tonight?

CHESTER: Thursday.

FRANKIE: Right. I'll be here. Wednesday bowling, Thursday dominoes.

CHESTER: We're gonna be playing for blood tonight, baby.

FRANKIE: See you later.

CHESTER: See you later. Oh, Frankie, don't forget your change. *(Hands him a pittance)*

FRANKIE: See you later Roxanne.

ROXANNE: Not if I see you first. *(FRANKIE exits)* How could you have sold him that bird? You know it doesn't talk.

CHESTER: I didn't want to sell it to him. He insisted on buying it.

ROXANNE: It was a dirty trick to play on a pal.

CHESTER: I was trying to put one over on this rich dame. You know, making the bird talk by ventriloquism. Suddenly he came into the shop. I'm just about to clinch the deal when he horns in and says he wants to buy the bird for his kids. The rich dame bowed out. What could I do but sell it to him?

ROXANNE: You could have told him the truth.

CHESTER: Are you kidding? He's a cop. He'd probably arrest me.

ROXANNE: You're his best friend.

CHESTER: Listen, he's got more morals than he knows what to do with. He'd arrest his own mother for jaywalking. I didn't have the heart to tell him. It would ruin a beautiful friendship.

ROXANNE: Then take the bird back and give him a refund.

CHESTER: I hate to do it. It's not so much the bird as the money has a sentimental value to me.

ROXANNE: Chester, you're going to take that bird back and give him a refund. Because if you don't, I will.

CHESTER: All right, all right. I'll take the bird back. Give it a few more days. The bird might talk, you never know.

MRS. NURDIGER: *(Calling from off)* Roxanne, two portions of tubifex worms.

ROXANNE: Coming up! *(Sighs)*

CHESTER: Whatsamatter?

ROXANNE: Nothing.

CHESTER: It's something. You're not your old self. You walk around here mopin' and sighin'.

ROXANNE: You know I'm not nuts about handling tubifex worms. They give me the creeps.

CHESTER: You're sure that's all it is?

ROXANNE: Sure.

CHESTER: Maybe you're overworked.

ROXANNE: We could use some help around here.

CHESTER: It's always been a family business. I never thought of hiring anybody from the outside.

ROXANNE: Maybe just to handle the worms, clean the rat cages. You know— the disgusting stuff. You know I don't mind the birds and the tropical fish— they're pretty.

CHESTER: Okay. If it will make you happy, why not? Here. I'll put a sign in the window. *(Makes sign. Reads)* "Help wanted." *(Puts sign in window)* There. Are you satisfied?

MRS. NURDIGER: *(Voice off)* Roxanne, I need two dozen mouse pinks.

ROXANNE: *(Groans)* Mouse pinks! That's another thing. I just don't feature feeding baby mice to the snakes.

CHESTER: But that's what they eat.

ROXANNE: But their eyes aren't even open yet.

CHESTER: They was just born. They never know what hit 'em.

ROXANNE: It seems cruel.

CHESTER: That's the law of the jungle. Every animal preys on some other animal.

ROXANNE: What about vegetarians?

(ZACHARY SLADE walks by shop, sees the sign, and enters, unnoticed. He leafs through a book on the counter as the conversation continues.)

CHESTER: What, you think plants have no feelings? Just because they don't scream, they don't cry out when they're hurt? Believe me they feel plenty. In fact vegetables are probably more sensitive than people.

ROXANNE: Some people.

CHESTER: Every living thing lives off some other living thing. That's the law of the jungle.

ROXANNE: But why create an artificial jungle?

CHESTER: It's educational and amusing. What better occupation than to study nature—its beauty and its cruelty.

ZACHARY: *(Carrying the help wanted sign)* Excuse me, you're looking for help?

CHESTER: Yeah. You had any experience in the pet trade?

ZACHARY: I know tropicals.

CHESTER: Latin names?

ZACHARY: I can tell a Hyphessobrycon heterorhabdus from an astronotus ocellatus.

CHESTER: Very good, very good.

ROXANNE: What did he say?

CHESTER: He can tell an Oscar from a flag tetra.

ROXANNE: So he knows Latin. But can he change hamster cages?

ZACHARY: I've done my share of that. What's the deal?

ROXANNE: Long hours—low pay.

ZACHARY: I'll take it.

CHESTER: Well, you see, I'm seeing several other applicants. Come back tomorrow and I'll let you know.

ZACHARY: O.K. I'll come back tomorrow. *(Goes out)*

MRS. NURDIGER: *(Calls from off)* Roxanne, I need two portions of tubifex worms!

ROXANNE: What are you stallin' for? Call him back. Hire him.

CHESTER: I don't know anything about him. How do I know he'll work out?

ROXANNE: Try him and see, Chester. Because if you think I'm going to go on dishing up these disgusting worms you've got another think coming. I quit!

MRS. NURDIGER: *(Off)* Roxanne worms!

CHESTER: Roxanne, Mother needs worms.

ROXANNE: Let her get her own worms, Chester. I'm not putting my hands in that filth again.

CHESTER: Oh, all right, all right! I'll see if I can still catch him. *(Runs out)*

MRS. NURDIGER: *(Enters frantically)* Roxanne, I want two portions of tubifex worms and I'm tired of waiting! *(ROXANNE sits staring straight ahead ignoring the old lady)* Sulking again. I'll get them myself. *(Goes to refrigerator and opens dish and scoops out two dollops of worms and puts them in dixie cups, which she closes)* I do wish you'd snap out of it. *(Exits)*

(ROXANNE rises and begins restlessly prowling around the room, as if she were about to explode. CHESTER reenters with ZACHARY.)

CHESTER: Say, how old are you?

ZACHARY: Thirty-four.

CHESTER: That's a good age. I need somebody young to help me take care of my business. Young, but not a kid, if you know what I mean.

ZACHARY: Young, but not a kid. I guess that description fits me all right.

CHESTER: What's your name?

ZACHARY: Zachary, Zachary Slade. My friends call me Zack.

CHESTER: You got friends?

ZACHARY: What do you mean by that?

CHESTER: Nothing, it was just a joke. I'm Chester Nurdiger. *(They shake hands)* This is my wife, Roxanne. The little Nurdiger.

ZACHARY: Nice meeting you.

ROXANNE: How do you know? You haven't met me long enough to know whether it's nice or not.

CHESTER: Oh, here comes Mrs. Muncie to get the weekly rat for her boa constrictor. *(MRS. MUNCIE enters)* Hello, Mrs. Muncie.

MRS. MUNCIE: Hello, Chester.

CHESTER: We have a big fat rat for you today. *(Bags the rat)* Ninety-eight cents . . . a dollar for you.

MRS. MUNCIE: Thank you. Give my love to your mother. *(Exits)*

CHESTER: Bye, Mrs. Muncie. Great gal, Mrs. Muncie. I've got to go see my bird man, pick up a shipment of canaries. Roxanne will break you in. *(Exits)*

ROXANNE: You keep reptiles?

ZACHARY: Yeah, python, couple a boas.

ROXANNE: Well, you get a discount on rats here. Sorta makes up for the low pay—if you're into reptiles.

ZACHARY: Yeah, I'm into reptiles. *(Their eyes meet. She turns away. He slips up behind her and whispers in her ear)* Why did you marry this guy, anyway?

ROXANNE: *(Turns on him as if stung)* That's none of your business.

ZACHARY: Unless I make it mine.

ROXANNE: You've got some gall.

ZACHARY: A man who never makes a pass at a woman has to settle for the women who make passes at him.

MRS. NURDIGER: *(Voice off)* Roxanne, two tubifex.

ROXANNE: Get me a couple of portions of tubifex.

ZACHARY: Where are they?

ROXANNE: They're in the refrigerator—in a plastic container.

ZACHARY: *(Opens the refrigerator and screams)*

ROXANNE: *(Unruffled)* Something wrong?

ZACHARY: They moved.

ROXANNE: They should; they're alive. Or didn't you know? Say, how long have you been in the pet trade?

ZACHARY: I had a goldfish when I was a kid.

ROXANNE: You gotta be kidding! What about all those Latin names?

ZACHARY: You've got a very informative book out there on the rack and I'm a fast learner.

ROXANNE: Here, let me do that. *(She takes the tubifex to* MRS. NURDIGER*)* What makes you think I won't tell him you're a phony?

ZACHARY: You won't. Besides, I'm not a phony. I'm a jack-of-all-trades.

ROXANNE: And a master of none?

ZACHARY: Maybe, but I'm sure you'll find some use for me when he's not around. I've been everything from a golf caddy to an insurance salesman. I can give a Swedish massage and instructions on the mandolin. *(Comes up behind her and takes her in his arms)*

ROXANNE: Do you sell accident insurance?

ZACHARY: Why, is somebody going to have an accident?

ROXANNE: You never know.

ZACHARY: Don't you carry insurance?

ROXANNE: Oh yeah, public liability, collision, fire, and theft. *(Dreamily)* But I was thinking more along the lines of accident insurance. Chester is accident prone.

ZACHARY: I'll talk to him about it.

ROXANNE: Does he have to know? I mean, can't I just insure him without asking?

ZACHARY: You need his signature.

ROXANNE: I hate to alarm him.

ZACHARY: Whatsamatter? Afraid he'll find out he's worth more to you dead than alive?

(Enter CHESTER *with a crate of canaries.)*

CHESTER: What a bunch of canaries! There's not a bad singer in the lot. I'm sorry I was away so long. *(Kisses* ROXANNE*)* Are you cross with me?

ROXANNE: No.

CHESTER: I tell you, Roxanne, you've never seen such canaries, and all in perfect feather. You just want to love them to death. *(The birds sing)* Listen, they're singing. *(Whistles along with the canaries)* Wait till I show Mamma! *(Exits)* Mamma! Mamma!

ROXANNE: I hate him.

*(*CHESTER *reenters with* MRS. NURDIGER*.)*

MRS. NURDIGER: What varieties did he have?

CHESTER: They're all American Singers.

MRS. NURDIGER: I can hear it.

CHESTER: Oh, and Mamma, this is our new employee, Mr. Zachary Slade.

MRS. NURDIGER: How do you do, Mr. Slade.

ZACHARY: My friends call me Zack.

MRS. NURDIGER: Well, perhaps someday if we become friends I'll call you that too, Mr. Slade. Have you had much experience in the pet trade?

ZACHARY: *(Glances nervously at* ROXANNE*)* Well as a matter of fact I . . .

ROXANNE: Oh he's an expert. You don't have to worry about that.

CHESTER: That's right, Mamma. You should hear him rattle off those Latin names.

MRS. NURDIGER: Oh, I don't care about book learning. It's just that inexperienced people tend to be squeamish. Are you squeamish, Mr. Slade?

ZACHARY: Squeamish? No.

MRS. NURDIGER: Pet people have to handle a lot of things in the course of a day that would put most grown men into a dead faint. *(They all laugh—*ZACK *a little uneasily)* I hope you'll like working here. We don't make much money. But we have a lot of fun.

ZACHARY: Oh, I like it all right. But I can see room for improvement.

MRS. NURDIGER: Improvement? What kind of improvement?

ZACHARY: Well, your sign, for instance. It's a wonder you do any business at all with a sign like that.

CHESTER: What's wrong with the sign?

ZACHARY: It just says Pet Shop.

CHESTER: But that's what it is—a pet shop.

ZACHARY: Sure it is. But there are a million pet shops. But what makes this pet shop different from all the others? You need something to make this shop different and you need a neon sign to say so.

MRS. NURDIGER: Neon sign?

CHESTER: What's the point? The shop is open during the day. Neon shows up better at night.

ZACHARY: People will see it coming home from work. You could leave it on all night. Believe me it will give you presence here.

CHESTER: We've already been here for twenty-five years.

ZACHARY: All the more reason to make it new.

CHESTER: Look, I don't want us to look like one of those discount pet places. This is a family business. It has a personal touch. I know it isn't a slick operation. It may look a little like a jungle—but I like it that way.

MRS. NURDIGER: I'm afraid we're set in our ways, Mr. Slade.

ZACHARY: I'm not saying change the character of the place. But merchandise it. You like it like a jungle—good. Make other people like it too. You have to tell them what to think. Call it The Artificial Jungle and put it up there in neon light. Advertise it on television and believe me you'll make plenty.

MRS. NURDIGER: You certainly have a lot of ideas, Mr. Slade. *(Shop bell off. It's* FRANKIE*)* There's a customer. Would you get it, Roxanne. *(*ROXANNE *doesn't move)* Oh, all right, I'll go.

ZACHARY: Please, allow me.

MRS. NURDIGER: Oh, no, Mr. Slade, please don't bother. I'll take care of it.

ZACHARY: It's no bother. After all, what am I here for, but to take some of the burden off of you. *(Exits into shop)*

MRS. NURDIGER: What a nice young man.

ROXANNE: I don't like him.

CHESTER: Why on earth not?

ROXANNE: All he does is talk talk talk.

CHESTER: He was making a lot of sense just now.

ROXANNE: You should never have hired him.

CHESTER: You were the one who insisted.

ROXANNE: Me? Don't blame it on me.

MRS. NURDIGER: Now Roxanne, you know you've been asking for help with the dirty work. Look at the clock. It's almost closing time.

ZACHARY: *(Entering)* There's a gentleman here who wants to return a parrot.

CHESTER: Return a parrot? Oh that's no gentleman—that's Frankie Spinelli. Officer Spinelli, what can I do you for?

FRANKIE: *(Entering)* Take back this damn bird, will you, Chester.

CHESTER: I don't know, the store has a no return policy.

FRANKIE: But the damn bird won't talk.

CHESTER: It talked for me.

FRANKIE: Well, it won't talk for me.

CHESTER: How much will you pay me to take it off your hands?

FRANKIE: You know I'd almost be willing to pay you just to be rid of this lousy bird. *(Falling on his knees and pleading with mock tears)* Chester please—please, Chester, take back the bird Chester, have a heart Chester . . . Chester . . . *(Pretends to break down)*

CHESTER: *(Playing along)* Oh, all right. I can't stand to see a grown man cry. I really shouldn't, but as a favor to a friend . . . just this once . . . I'll take it back.

FRANKIE: *(Kissing his hands in mock gratitude)* Thank you! Thank you! *(Hands him the cage with the parrot)*

PARROT: *(As soon as it is in* CHESTER's *hands)* Gawk! Polly want a cracker.

FRANKIE: Goddamn! Did you hear that?

CHESTER: Frankie, please, your language, this bird is very impressionable.

FRANKIE: Give it here. I was wrong. I'll keep it.

CHESTER: No, Frankie, somehow I have a feeling this bird will only talk for me.

PARROT: Hiya handsome! Hiya handsome!

FRANKIE: Maybe I should take it home and give it another chance.

ROXANNE: Naw, you heard what he said, Frankie. It's a one-man bird.

PARROT: How much are the turtles?

FRANKIE: Shut up!

PARROT: Shut up! Shut up! Shut up!

FRANKIE: I can't figure it.

CHESTER: Come on. Don't let a bird brain get you down. Let's play some serious dominoes here. Frankie, this is my new employee, Zack Slade. Zack, this is Frankie Spinelli, my cousin. Aw hell, my best friend. *(*ZACK *and* FRANKIE *shake hands.)* Frankie is one of New York's finest.

ZACHARY: You've got guts. I couldn't cut it.

FRANKIE: Sometimes you find out you've got guts you didn't know you had.

CHESTER: Ah, you're beautiful. Say, Zack, why don't you stay and play dominoes with us?

ZACHARY: I don't know how to play.

CHESTER: Come on. Any idiot can learn. No offense meant. And there's dinner in it. This is our Thursday night ritual. We play dominoes and Mamma keeps a steady stream of food coming from the kitchen. When was the last time you had a square meal?

ZACHARY: If it's not an imposition.

CHESTER: If it's not an imposition! Zack, I think you're carrying this nice guy bit a little too far. Did you all hear that? Come on, kid. Make yourself at home. Roxanne, get the box of dominoes. Let's clear the table. Pull up a chair. *(They seat themselves around the table)* So Frankie, what's new? Anything exciting in the field of law enforcement?

FRANKIE: Well, if you want news, there was a real mess over at the Prince Hotel.

CHESTER: Mess, what mess? I saw there was a crowd over there this afternoon.

FRANKIE: They found a woman's body cut up in four pieces.

CHESTER: Cut up in four pieces. Now how would you do that? A wing and a breast or a leg and a thigh? *(Draws imaginary lines on* ROXANNE, *then, as she speaks, on himself)*

ROXANNE: Stop that!

MRS. NURDIGER: Horrible.

FRANKIE: They found the pieces in a trunk some guest had left behind.

ZACHARY: Have they caught the murderer?

FRANKIE: No, they don't have any idea who did it.

CHESTER: *(Laughs)*

ZACHARY: And who was the victim?

FRANKIE: I'm afraid they don't know that either.

MRS. NURDIGER: You mean they can't even identify the victim?

FRANKIE: Her identity is a little hard to establish. You see, the body was naked and the head was missing.

CHESTER: Perhaps it was mislaid.

MRS. NURDIGER: Please, don't joke about it. It gives me chills just thinking about this woman cut up in four pieces.

CHESTER: We can laugh because we are here surrounded by friends, safe and sound. You have to admit some of these crimes are so grotesque they are almost funny.

MRS. NURDIGER: To you, perhaps.

CHESTER: What about the man in Chinatown who found a woman's toe in his chow mein.

ROXANNE: How did they know it was a woman's toe?

CHESTER: The toenail was painted—red!

MRS. NURDIGER: *(Shudders)* Ehgh!

CHESTER: I read about a woman who bit into a piece of fried chicken and discovered it was a rat. She had a heart attack and died. But that's different I suppose. I mean it isn't murder.

ZACHARY: It's grisly nonetheless.

CHESTER: Where the devil do you think her head went? The woman who was quartered.

FRANKIE: We have no idea. It disappeared without a trace.

ZACHARY: Do many crimes go unpunished?

FRANKIE: Are you kidding? Stranglings, poisonings, drownings, and fatal falls—they disappear without a scream or so much as a drop of blood. And no weapon found. The police search. But they find no clues. And the murderer is walking around free as a bird.

PARROT: *(Screams, all jump with fright)*

CHESTER: Shut up.

FRANKIE: Freer than some, I might add. These are in cages.

MRS. NURDIGER: But surely they always make some slip.

FRANKIE: No—the fact is some of them don't. There are murderers among us and we never know who they are. Why, I'm sure some of us meet a murderer every day. He could be your barber, the butcher, or your dearest loved one.

MRS. NURDIGER: Oh nonsense! Enough of this talk. Are the police of no use at all, then?

FRANKIE: They're of use when they have clues. But when there are no clues—they can't do the impossible.

CHESTER: What do you think, Zack? Do you believe in the perfect crime? Do you think it's possible to commit a murder and get away with it?

ZACHARY: I think Frankie is trying to frighten us with his gruesome stories. If there are no clues and no bodies, how can we be so sure these crimes were actually committed? I'm sure your wife is not so gullible. What do you think, Mrs. Nurdiger?

ROXANNE: What no one knows does not exist.

MRS. NURDIGER: Good heavens! Let's talk about something else. What happened to your game of dominoes?

CHESTER: You're right, Mamma, we've forgotten to play. *(Dumps tiles. They shuffle and deal)*

MRS. NURDIGER: I'll serve the cold cuts. *(Shivers)* Oooh cold cuts. *(Exits)*

CHESTER: Here we go. We each take seven. Who's high? Double nine!—I'll be the first to go!

(They play as the curtain falls.)

ACT II

(As before, but the shop seems more lush. The piranha tank, in particular, has a new tropical look. CHESTER *is dressed in a Tarzan costume and* ZACHARY *videotapes him.* MRS. NURDIGER *and* ROXANNE *look on admiringly.)*

ZACHARY: Ready, Chester?

CHESTER: Do you think this leopard skin is too sexy?

ROXANNE: Not at all.

CHESTER: It doesn't make me look fat?

ZACHARY: You look svelte.

CHESTER: I wish we could get the new sign in.

ZACHARY: You know the new sign won't be ready until later. Which reminds me, you've got to pick it up this afternoon. Once it's up I'll get a shot of it to end the commercial. O.K., now let's do it. Ready, Chester?

CHESTER: I'm nervous.

ZACHARY: Don't be. Just remember to get all the information in. And give it lots of personality.

CHESTER: O.K. shoot.

ZACHARY: All right now. Lights. Camera. Action.

CHESTER: *(Lets out a Tarzan cry then speaks in an almost expressionless voice. He is no actor)* This is The Artificial Jungle. Bring love into your home with a cuddly pet or add a touch of the exotic with a home aquarium, tropical fish, a snake, lizard, or even a tarantula. We have everything you need to bring adventure into your living room. Or take home a cuddly hamster, rat, mouse, or gerbil. Whatever your choice we have all the accessories to turn your home into an artificial jungle too. Open six days a week except Sunday. Conveniently located at 966 Rivington Street in lower Manhattan.

MRS. NURDIGER: *(Having left during commercial, enters in a sarong)* I'm The Artificial Jungle mother. We have talking parrots too.

CHESTER: *(Lets out Tarzan cry again)*

MRS. NURDIGER: My son the orangutang.

ZACHARY: Cut! That's a good one.

CHESTER: Let's do it again. I mispronounced tarantula.

MRS. NURDIGER: Did you? I didn't notice.

CHESTER: I did. I said tarantyula.

ZACHARY: Nobody will notice.

CHESTER: You don't think?

ZACHARY: No. It was perfect.

CHESTER: If you say so. Did you hear that, Roxanne? Perfect! It was rather good.

ZACHARY: Now as soon as you pick up that sign I can get a shot of it for the end.

CHESTER: *(Changing out of costume)* I'll go right away. I can't wait to see that sign in the window.

ZACHARY: I'll take the old one down and spruce up the shop a bit before you get back.

CHESTER: Fine. Roxanne, you take care of customers. Give Mamma a rest.

ROXANNE: Don't worry, I've got everything under control.

CHESTER: *(Exits whistling)* See you later.

MRS. NURDIGER: Chester left his Tarzan costume on the floor. *(Folding it)* I'll put it away. He really was something in his Tarzan costume, wasn't he? *(Exits)*

ROXANNE: I can't stand it anymore.

ZACHARY: Be patient, Roxy, it won't be long now.

ROXANNE: How can I be patient laying next to him at night thinking about you. Wondering where you are, who you're with. Sometimes I think I'm going crazy.

ZACHARY: It isn't easy for me either, going home to a flophouse, laying on the bed counting the cracks in the ceiling and the roaches in the cracks. Trying to think of something else while all the time I can still smell you on me. You know I have a pair of your panties. I stole them. I always carry them with me. I caress them at night.

ROXANNE: Oh Zack, I'd do anything for you.

ZACHARY: Would you blow?

ROXANNE: Sure.

ZACHARY: I mean leave here, run away with me tonight.

ROXANNE: No, I couldn't.

MRS. NURDIGER: *(Enters to fuss with various shop items)*

ROXANNE: And the ram horn snails are fifty cents apiece. . . .

MRS. NURDIGER: *(Exits)*

ZACHARY: We could hit the road—live like a couple of bums.

ROXANNE: That's O.K. for kids. But we're at the age when we like our creature comforts. I can't run away and become a Gypsy. Not now. How I hate him. The mamma's boy.

ZACHARY: Why did you marry him?

ROXANNE: He's the only one who asked.

ZACHARY: You've gotta be kidding! A dame with your looks?

ROXANNE: Oh there were others. But they just didn't stand on ceremony. I got invited to a lot of parties. And I used to go. A lot of parties for two.

ZACHARY: I figured you'd been around the block.

ROXANNE: I didn't get these lips from suckin' doorknobs.

MRS. NURDIGER: *(Enters as before)*

ROXANNE: Here are the aquatic plants: the anacrus and the cabamba, the hydrophyla and the water sprite. They are priced as marked. You put them in a plastic bag and tie them off like this. *(Demonstrates)* Now here are the feeder goldfish.

MRS. NURDIGER: *(Exits)*

ZACHARY: You like me, don't you?

ROXANNE: Oh yes. I like you. I like you fine. You smell like a man. He smells like a bar of soap. Watch it!

MRS. NURDIGER: *(Enters)* I think the rats are in heat. Are either of you hungry? I could make lunch.

ROXANNE: No, wait for Chester.

MRS. NURDIGER: Then I'll just go to your room and watch my program. *(Exits)*

ROXANNE: Let's do it.

ZACHARY: What?

ROXANNE: What we talked about.

ZACHARY: You can fry for that.

ROXANNE: Not in New York State. There's a law against capital punishment.

ZACHARY: So you get life.

ROXANNE: Not if you do it right. You heard what Frankie said.

ZACHARY: But I've got nothing against this guy.

ROXANNE: No? Even though he's standing in our way? While you spend your lonely nights counting cracks, he's banging the woman you love.

ZACHARY: Now that you put it that way . . .

ROXANNE: We've all got to go someday. Death can be awaited or it can be induced. What's the difference when it comes when come it must?

ZACHARY: You talk as though it were perfectly all right.

ROXANNE: No one will know but you and me. We'll be the judges. We'll be the jury. No one will know but us. And what no one knows does not exist. Now kiss me, Zack. Kiss me till I bleed.

ZACHARY: You're like a wild animal.

ROXANNE: In an artificial jungle. *(They kiss.)*

(CHESTER'*s whistling is heard.)*

CHESTER: [*(Entering)*] Just wait until you get a load of this sign. Here, help me unpack it. Gently, gently. The thing cost an arm and a leg. It breaks if you look at it crosswise. *(Unpacks sign and displays it proudly)* Well, what do you think?

ZACHARY: You didn't tell me about the palm trees.

ROXANNE: Or the parrots.

CHESTER: They were my idea. Mamma! Mamma! Look at this.

MRS. NURDIGER: *(Enters)* Why Chester, it's lovely. Real artistic.

CHESTER: I can't wait to hang it in that window. I'm going to get a ladder.

MRS. NURDIGER: Have you eaten?

CHESTER: No.

MRS. NURDIGER: *(As they exit)* I saved you plenty.

ROXANNE: Do you have that insurance policy here?

ZACHARY: Yes. But how are we going to get him to sign?

ROXANNE: Leave that to me.

CHESTER: Here we go. *(Brings in ladder)*

ROXANNE: Oh, Chester, the reptile supplier was here, he wants you to sign this invoice.

CHESTER: Let me see that. I never sign anything without reading it first. *(Reads)* Iguanas—two, horned lizards—six, one was dead.

ROXANNE: He gave you credit.

CHESTER: Oh yes. Three skinks, baby boa, corn snake, indigo, turtles, red-eared sliders, box. Everything seems to be in order. *(Signs)* Here you go. *(Sets up ladder and starts to climb)*

ROXANNE: He wants you to sign two copies.

CHESTER: Isn't there a carbon there?

ROXANNE: Yes but he wants an extra one for his file.

CHESTER: Duplicate, triplicate, the paperwork expands but does anything more get accomplished? Where is it? *(Descends the ladder)*

ROXANNE: Here. *(She slides the top copy up just enough to leave room for him to sign. He signs and* ROXANNE *and* ZACHARY *exchange a look)*

CHESTER: *(Climbing the ladder again and taking down the old sign)* Out with the old and in with the new. *(Hangs the new sign in the window and almost falls—* ZACK *catches the ladder just in time)* Zack, hold the ladder. You wouldn't want me to fall and kill myself, would you?

ZACHARY: Of course not. *(Aside)* Now what did I go and do that for?

CHESTER: Here, Roxanne, plug it in. And be careful of those wires around the aquariums. Somebody could get electrocuted.

ROXANNE: *(Dipping the plug in water)* Here, you do it. I'm afraid.

CHESTER: All right. *(Plugs in sign, all the lights go out)* We must have blown a fuse. I'll have to go down to the basement. *(Exits with flashlight)*

ROXANNE: This is our chance. It's dark. Follow him downstairs and hit him over the head. It will look like he fell.

ZACHARY: What will I hit him with?

ROXANNE: *(Takes a decorative rock off the shelf)* Here's a rock.

ZACHARY: *(Takes rock and follows* CHESTER *out)* Let me help. Chester, be careful on those stairs in the dark!

(Loud blow is heard off.)

CHESTER: Ow!

ZACHARY: What happened?

MRS. NURDIGER: *(Entering)* What's the matter?

(The lights come on.)

CHESTER: *(Reentering with* ZACK*)* I seem to have hit my head on something. *(Shows lump)*

MRS. NURDIGER: You've got an egg on your head. Kiss and make better.

ROXANNE: *(Aside to* ZACHARY*)* You didn't hit him hard enough.

ZACHARY: I hit him with all my might.

ROXANNE: If we're going to do this we've got to do it right. No more slipups.

ZACHARY: He must have a head like a sledgehammer. Look at this rock. *(Shows rock broken in two pieces)*

MRS. NURDIGER: What did I tell you? There's going to be a lump. You lie down and I'll put some ice on it. *(She goes to kitchen.* CHESTER *lies down on bed.)*

ROXANNE: Did he see you do it?

ZACHARY: No, I don't think so. The lights were out. I hit him from behind.

ROXANNE: I'm telling you there can't be any more slipups.

ZACHARY: If you hate this guy so much why stick around? We could split. Hit the road. Live like a couple of Gypsies.

ROXANNE: Are you crazy? We've got him insured for a hundred grand. All we've got to do is cash him in.

ZACHARY: Never again.

ROXANNE: Listen, Zack, he's accident-prone. We have to plan it better, that's all. Throw 'em off our trail. Put the blame somewhere else.

ZACHARY: Like where?

ROXANNE: Like on the piranhas. They can strip a body in half an hour and they do a clean job. Nobody ever sent a piranha up the river.

ZACHARY: You're sick, lady.

ROXANNE: Love is the disease. And you gave it to me.

ZACHARY: Look, Roxy, you can't get away with it.

ROXANNE: We can if we do it right. Tonight after closing time I'll slip him a Mickey. There's a lot of stuff in the shop that he could take by accident. Run this insurance policy down to the corner and drop it in the mailbox. The last pickup is at six. It will be postmarked today. After midnight we'll cash him in.

ZACHARY: What do you think I am?

ROXANNE: Kiss me and I'll tell you. *(They kiss)* Kiss me harder. *(They kiss again)* Bite me. Make me bleed. *(They kiss until blood spurts)* You still wanna know what I think you are?

ZACHARY: Yeah?

ROXANNE: A killer. *(Licks a stamp and puts it on the letter)* Now mail this and come back right away. Tonight we're going to do it. And we're going to do it right.

MRS. NURDIGER: *(At* CHESTER's *bedside)* What happened to you?

CHESTER: *(Groans)* Ow, my head!

MRS. NURDIGER: Son, tell me, what did you do?

CHESTER: I must have hit my head on a pipe. It was dark. Then it was darker. Except for the little stars.

ZACHARY: *(Who has been overhearing this conversation with* ROXANNE*)* Do you think she's suspicious?

ROXANNE: No, she's a trusting old soul. It's almost closing time. Go and come back quickly, before I have to close up.

*(*ZACHARY *starts out the shop door with the stamped envelope containing the signed insurance policy.* MRS. NURDIGER *enters.* ZACHARY *hides the envelope behind his back.)*

MRS. NURDIGER: Go get into your nightie, Chester. You've had a hard day. Where are you going, Mr. Slade?

ZACHARY: I er was just going out to ah . . .

ROXANNE: Get some wine. I thought we ought to celebrate.

MRS. NURDIGER: Celebrate?

ROXANNE: Yes, the new piranha tank, the neon sign, The Artificial Jungle. It seems we have a lot to celebrate, don't we?

MRS. NURDIGER: *(Dubiously)* Yes, I suppose we do.

ROXANNE: And Mr. Slade, hurry back with that wine. And make sure it's the very best. My husband deserves nothing but the best. Here's some cash. There's a liquor store around the corner. Go. *(With hidden significance)* It's almost six o'clock.

MRS. NURDIGER: I'm worried about Chester. He may have a fractured skull.

ROXANNE: Don't worry yourself unnecessarily, Mother Nurdiger. He got a bump on the head, that's all.

MRS. NURDIGER: Perhaps Mr. Slade could go for a doctor. Or we could take him to Beth Israel.

ROXANNE: I'm sure he'll be all right after he's had a good night's sleep.

MRS. NURDIGER: But that's just it. I've heard that sometimes, if they fall asleep with a fractured skull—they don't wake up.

ROXANNE: *(Exchanges a significant look with* ZACHARY, *then looks at her watch)*

It's quarter to six. The liquor store is going to close. Hurry, Mr. Slade, and get that wine.

(ZACHARY stands frozen for a moment and then realizing she means the mail pickup, dashes out the door.)

MRS. NURDIGER: You don't think we should take him to the hospital?

ROXANNE: If he doesn't feel better by tomorrow, yes. But tomorrow his pain may be over and he'll be as good as new.

MRS. NURDIGER: I hope so. Did you see the size of that lump on his head? Poor Chester, he's always been accident-prone.

ROXANNE: Yes, accident-prone. You've always said that yourself, haven't you?

MRS. NURDIGER: Well, you know: He was dropped by his nurse, he was hit by a car, he was thrown by a horse, he fell off his bike and got a scar under his chin. He got a fishhook caught in his finger, he broke his arm, he broke his leg, he got a tooth knocked out in a fight, sprained his ankle, he sprained his neck, he almost drowned, he slipped on ice . . . he burned himself on an iron, he fell down the stairs, he's been bitten or stung by every kind of animal you can imagine, and now I'm afraid he's fractured his skull. God, when you come to think of it, he's probably the luckiest man alive.

ROXANNE: Lucky?

MRS. NURDIGER: To have survived all those accidents. Why any one of them would have been enough to kill him.

CHESTER: *(Groans)* Ow, my head!

MRS. NURDIGER: I'd better go look in on him *(Goes to CHESTER)*

(ZACHARY enters with bottle of wine.)

ROXANNE: Did you mail it?

ZACHARY: Yes, and as I was coming back I saw the mailman pick it up.

ROXANNE: Good, then we're in business.

ZACHARY: Here's the wine. The best they had.

ROXANNE: Chateau Lafite 1972. I hope that was a better year for wine than it was for me. That was the year I married him.

ZACHARY: Look, I'm getting cold feet. Let's stop this before it goes any further.

ROXANNE: Don't you want me?

ZACHARY: You know I do.

ROXANNE: Don't you want us to be together?

ZACHARY: I'm aching for it.

ROXANNE: Me too. Don't you see? This is the only way.

ZACHARY: Is that the only way? To kill a man for his pet shop and his wife?

ROXANNE: Wash your mouth out with soap. "Wife" is a dirty four-letter word. I'm his whore! I'm his maid!

ZACHARY: I don't care! That's your business. Yours and his. Leave me out of it!

ROXANNE: You don't care? Even when he comes home with the stink of liquor on his breath and beats me.

ZACHARY: He beats you? Chester? But he wouldn't hurt a fly.

ROXANNE: Not unless he happened to bore it to death.

ZACHARY: What if I go to jail?

ROXANNE: I'd wait for you. Wouldn't you wait for me?

ZACHARY: Yes, yes, yes.

ROXANNE: Now let's kiss and kill. *(They kiss.)*

PARROT: Gawk! Where's Roxanne? Where's Roxanne? Gawk! I spy! I spy!

ZACHARY: What was that? A parrot?

ROXANNE: That's just Chester playing. He's an amateur ventriloquist. That's how he sells birds that don't talk to suckers. He throws his voice into the bird and they buy. Of course we have a no refund policy.

ZACHARY: The birds don't talk, huh?

ROXANNE: No they're all too old to learn. In the shop they talk but when the people get them home they clam up.

ZACHARY: The little crook.

ROXANNE: Yeah, he's a little crook and a cheapskate too. I'm lucky if I get a new dress twice a year.

ZACHARY: Still you look hot.

ROXANNE: After we cash him in I'll look hotter. And it will be all yours, baby. All yours. *(They go to the living area behind shop)*

MRS. NURDIGER: *(Carrying a tray)* Chester is going to take his supper in bed.

ROXANNE: Yes, let us help you spoil him. Mr. Slade, bring that wine. I'll get some glasses.

MRS. NURDIGER: I'll get them.

ROXANNE: No, no, you let me do it. You're always waiting on us hand and foot. You go to Chester.

MRS. NURDIGER: Why, Roxanne, what's come over you? *(She goes to* CHESTER*)* Chester, we're going to have a little drink to celebrate the new sign. Here, put this ice pack on your head.

ROXANNE: This ought to do it.

ZACHARY: What's that?

ROXANNE: Malachite green. It's a cure for ich.

ZACHARY: Ich?

ROXANNE: Yeah, it's a disease in tropical fish. They get a white fuzz all over them. *(Reads label)* "Malachite green controls ich in tropical fish. CAUTION: Keep out of the reach of children. Also poisonous to baby fish and tetra species." Pour the wine. *(*ZACHARY *does so)* Now we have to make sure he gets this glass. *(She pours a dollop of malachite green into the glass intended for Chester)*

CHESTER: The new neon sign does look beautiful, doesn't it, Mamma?

MRS. NURDIGER: It looks real gorgeous.

CHESTER: And the custom-made decor piranha tank sure is swell too, isn't it?

MRS. NURDIGER: It's the prettiest piranha tank I've ever seen.

CHESTER: Me either. Oh, Mamma, I never thought such happiness could exist in this world.

MRS. NURDIGER: God has been good to us.

CHESTER: You know it's all Zack's doing. He's such a nice guy. He's really come to be like one of the family. Don't you feel that way too, Mamma?

MRS. NURDIGER: Yes, Chester, I do. Now you rest. Don't exert yourself unnecessarily because that may be a concussion.

CHESTER: Don't worry about it. You know I'm accident-prone. Did you see when that ladder started to go over? It's a good thing Zack was there to break my fall.

*(*ROXANNE *and* ZACHARY *enter with the tray of glasses into which the wine has been poured.)*

ROXANNE: *(Passing the glasses around)* May I propose a toast?

CHESTER: Yes, a toast! Roxanne, a toast! *(Winces)* Oooh, my head.

MRS. NURDIGER: Easy, Chester.

ROXANNE: To the new neon sign, to The Artificial Jungle, and to the piranhas!

(All raise glasses)

MRS. NURDIGER: To the piranhas? Why toast the piranhas?

CHESTER: Why not toast the piranhas, Mamma? That's a very good toast. To the piranhas, the king of the tetras.

ROXANNE: Tetras? Piranhas aren't tetras.

CHESTER: Oh yes they are! They are the greater tetras. And I drink to them! *(Goes to drink)*

ZACHARY: *(Stopping CHESTER from drinking)* Chester, there's some cork in your wine. Let me get you another glass. *(Takes CHESTER's glass and goes to the kitchen and pours him another)*

CHESTER: Cork? I didn't notice any. Zack is so thoughtful.

MRS. NURDIGER: He's a real gentleman.

ROXANNE: All he does is eat our food.

CHESTER: I don't know what you have against him, Roxanne. I wish you liked him better.

ZACHARY: Here's a fresh glass, Chester.

CHESTER: Thank you, Zack. That was very considerate. Now I forgot the toast. *(Raises his glass)* To our pet shop, The Artificial Jungle, wasn't that it, Roxanne?

ROXANNE: Yes, to our pet shop!

CHESTER: Say, that was good!

ZACHARY: You want to see the label?

CHESTER: All wines are the same. They just put the fancy label on to get your money. Chateau Lafite 1972. It's an omen! That was the year we were married!

MRS. NURDIGER: How's your head doing, sweetie?

CHESTER: Well it's still pretty sore. But it feels better since I've had this wine.

ROXANNE: Have another glass.

CHESTER: Don't mind if I do.

MRS. NURDIGER: Chester, honey, go easy on the wine. It may not be good after a bump on the head.

ROXANNE: It can't be bad if it lessens the pain. *(Refills CHESTER's glass)*

MRS. NURDIGER: All right, one more, but after that put it away. You know you have a tendency to overdo.

CHESTER: All right, Mamma, just one more for medicinal porpoises. *(Drinks)*

MRS. NURDIGER: Now why don't we all leave Chester alone to rest so that he'll be bright-eyed and bushy-tailed tomorrow.

(They leave the bedroom.)

ZACHARY: I'll be going.

ROXANNE: I'll let you out and lock up.

MRS. NURDIGER: I could use a good night's sleep myself. I just hope the garbage trucks don't wake me up at the crack of dawn.

ROXANNE: They won't if you turn off your hearing aid.

MRS. NURDIGER: That's a good idea. But then I won't be able to hear Chester if he calls out during the night.

ROXANNE: Don't worry. I'll be here to take care of him. I promise I'll wake you if there's any need.

MRS. NURDIGER: All right I'll turn my hearing aid off. I do tend to be a light sleeper. *(Turns off hearing aid)*

ZACHARY: Good night, Mrs. Nurdiger.

MRS. NURDIGER: *(Shouting)* How's that?

ZACHARY: *(Shouting likewise)* I said good night, Mrs. Nurdiger.

MRS. NURDIGER: What did you say? Oh, my, I can't hear a thing without my hearing aid. *(Turns it back on)* There, now what did you say?

ZACHARY: I said, good night, Mrs. Nurdiger.

MRS. NURDIGER: Good night, Mr. Slade. Zack. I'm calling you Zack, if it's all right with you. Because Chester says you're like one of the family. Do you like it?

ZACHARY: Yes, I like it, Mrs. Nurdiger. I like it fine.

MRS. NURDIGER: And I wish that from now on you'd call me Mother Nurdiger. Would you do that? For me?

ZACHARY: Yes, thank you, Mother Nurdiger.

MRS. NURDIGER: Now don't talk to me, I'm turning this thing off and going to bed. *(Turns off hearing aid and exits)*

ROXANNE: That's great. You've got the old lady eating out of the palm of your hand.

ZACHARY: That was a close one with the wine.

ROXANNE: Yeah we almost poisoned some perfectly good piranhas. But what's worse is we almost poisoned our alibi. I didn't know piranhas were tetras.

ZACHARY: You learn something every day. Now what are we going to do? We can't poison him.

ROXANNE: No. We'll have to smother him in his sleep. You go and come back in about half an hour. Tap on my window. By then I'll have him good and drunk; you'll be able to overpower him. I'll give you a signal. I'll whistle softly.

ZACHARY: What if he cries out and somebody comes to help him?

ROXANNE: Are you kidding? This is New York City. Go. *(Loudly)* Good night. And don't be late tomorrow. We've got a big fish delivery.

ZACHARY: O.K. Good night. Good night, Chester. *(Exits)*

CHESTER: Good night, Zack.

(ROXANNE goes back to the bedroom. CHESTER has been drinking all the wine and is now quite drunk and incoherent.)

ROXANNE: *(Softly)* Chester? Chester are you awake?

CHESTER: Yeah, c'mere, Roxanne. Gimme a big wet kiss.

ROXANNE: I don't want to.

CHESTER: Come on. *(Tries to grab her)*

ROXANNE: Not tonight, Chester. I have a headache.

CHESTER: So take an aspirin.

ROXANNE: Please, Chester, I'm not in the mood.

CHESTER: *(Drunkenly)* Let's have another glash of wine. A post to the tiranahs. Zzzzzzzzzz. *(He is asleep)*

ROXANNE: *(Softly)* Chester? *(Shakes him gently)* Chester? *(She pauses a moment to listen and then she whistles softly. There is no response. She lies there staring at the ceiling. We hear only the sound of CHESTER snoring. After a pause she whistles again softly. There is a light tapping at the window. She gets up and opens the window. ZACK climbs in)*

Black-Eyed Susan, Everett Quinton & Charles Ludlam in
The Artificial Jungle (Anita & Steve Shevett)

ZACHARY: Now what?
ROXANNE: Like we planned.
ZACHARY: Are you sure you want to go through with it?
ROXANNE: Sure I'm sure. Are you sure?
ZACHARY: I'm sure if you're sure.
ROXANNE: Then do it. Here's a pillow.
ZACHARY: *(Takes pillow and raises it over* CHESTER*'s sleeping face)* Here goes.
(Pauses) I can't go through with it.
ROXANNE: You've got to do it. We've come this far. We can't turn back now.
ZACHARY: I can't.
ROXANNE: Listen, Zack, we're on this train together and we're not getting off
until the last stop.
CHESTER: *(Suddenly waking and not fully realizing where he is sees* ZACK *standing
over him)* Hi, Zack, want shome more wine—Hey, Roxanne, get another glass.

A toast to . . . Hey, wait a minute. What time is it? I must have . . . What are you doing here? What are you doing? *(ZACHARY smothers CHESTER with the pillow)* Hey, Zack, cut it out! Ha! Ha! Stop it. That isn't funny. I can't breathe. I CAN'T BREATHE! Stop! Help! Zack! Roxanne, help me! Roxanne! *(He manages to get out from under the pillow and sees that ROXANNE is staring at him coldly)* Roxanne. Roxanne. *(ZACHARY holds the pillow over CHESTER's face again)* Mamma! Mamma! Roxanne! *(He coughs and we hear his muffled cries through the pillow. Finally the sounds fade and he stops. ROXANNE and ZACHARY exchange a look. She nods. ZACHARY removes the pillow from CHESTER's face. CHESTER jumps up and starts screaming again)* Help! Help! Aahhhgh! *(ZACHARY smothers him again. This time he dies)*

ROXANNE: Now let's get him into that piranha tank.
ZACHARY: I hope those piranhas are hungry.
ROXANNE: They should be. I haven't fed them in a week.

(With difficulty they lift CHESTER's body and lug it to the piranha tank. They lift him over it and, just as they are about to dump him in, a flashlight is seen through the pet shop window. Footsteps are heard. FRANKIE, the cop on the beat, in his uniform is outside. ROXANNE and ZACHARY quickly drop CHESTER on the floor. FRANKIE taps on the door. ZACHARY jumps back behind the shop door just as ROXANNE opens it.)

FRANKIE: I heard some sounds and saw you were awake. Did you know your bedroom window is open?
ROXANNE: I was just trying to get some air.
FRANKIE: *(Seeing CHESTER on the floor)* What happened to Chester?
ROXANNE: He polished off a whole bottle of wine.
FRANKIE: That's Chester. Never knows his limit. Let me help you get him into bed.
ROXANNE: I hate to put you to all this trouble.
FRANKIE: Oh it's no trouble. It's all in the line of duty. Besides Chester is a pal. Come on, you take his legs. Alley Ooop! God, he sure is loaded isn't he? It's like trying to lift a dead weight.
ROXANNE: Yeah, you can say that again.

(They lug him to the bed and tuck him in.)

FRANKIE: I guess there's nothing he can do but sleep it off. Good night, Chester. *(ROXANNE waves CHESTER's hand at FRANKIE. All this time ZACHARY has been hiding behind the open shop door. FRANKIE, as he starts to leave, shines his flashlight all over the door and then lets it come to rest on the lock and handle)* You should consider getting a better lock for this door—a police lock—there have been a lot of burglaries in the neighborhood lately. *(As he speaks he opens and closes the door revealing and concealing ZACHARY whom he just misses seeing)* Talk to Chester about it.
ROXANNE: Yeah, I'll talk to Chester about it.
FRANKIE: Good night, Roxanne.
ROXANNE: Good night, Frankie. *(She closes the door after him)*

(ZACHARY is plastered against the wall behind the door, frozen in terror. Just as he starts to move, FRANKIE reopens the door and pokes his head in.)

FRANKIE: Tell Chester—raw egg and tomato juice and a dash of tabasco sauce—good cure for a hangover.

ROXANNE: Yes.

FRANKIE: *(Closes door to leave then opens it again)* Or if all else fails—hair of the dog that bit him.

ROXANNE: Yeah, yeah. Hair of the dog. *(FRANKIE leaves and walks off. The sound of his whistling gradually fades in the distance)* It's clear. He's gone.

ZACHARY: What if he comes back?

ROXANNE: He won't. Now we've got to get him into that tank.

(They carry CHESTER to the piranha tank and dump him in. Sounds of the piranhas eating as the lights fade.)

ACT III

Several days later.

(ROXANNE is working around the shop. ZACHARY enters with a box.)

ROXANNE: Zack, the insurance money came through.

ZACHARY: Look, I bought you this. *(Slips a fur jacket over her shoulders)*

ROXANNE: Oh, Zack, is it mink?

ZACHARY: No, skunk.

ROXANNE: We're rich now, Zack. Everything has worked out just the way we planned.

ZACHARY: I just can't get over the way he looked when they fished him out of the piranha tank! I thought you said they did a clean job.

ROXANNE: They do. But Chester was only partially submerged. We had to make it look like an accident.

ZACHARY: His face was hideously eaten away. How's Mother Nurdiger?

ROXANNE: Oh, she's all right. She has her good days and her bad days.

ZACHARY: She really took it hard.

ROXANNE: Chester was her baby. Everytime she thinks of him or hears his name she starts that crying. Try not to mention him if you can avoid it.

MRS. NURDIGER: *(Enters)* Oh, Zack, you're here. Thank you so much for all your help in our troubled time. I just don't think I could have handled the funeral arrangements myself.

ZACHARY: Why should you have to?

MRS. NURDIGER: Oh, you're so kind. I don't know how to thank you. Not only for myself—but for Chester . . . Chester thanks you too. *(She weeps.)*

ROXANNE: *(Showing impatience)* What did I tell you?

ZACHARY: There there.

MRS. NURDIGER: I don't know what I would have done without you. Chester was right. You're like one of the family. *(Weeps)* Where are you going, Roxanne?

ROXANNE: I was just going to feed the piranhas.

MRS. NURDIGER: *(Recoils with horror)* The piranhas? Why should you feed them? I hate them! I hate them! They killed my baby! They killed my baby! *(She attacks the piranha tank, bursts into tears, and sinks to the floor, feebly beating on the tank with her fists and weeping)*

ROXANNE: Now, now, Mother Nurdiger, it wasn't their fault. They didn't know what they were doing.

MRS. NURDIGER: They're evil! Evil murderers! Evil murderers!

ZACHARY: They're just dumb animals. They kill by instinct. They have no moral sense.

ROXANNE: And no remorse.

MRS. NURDIGER: I could kill them with my bare hands. *(Goes to put her hands in the tank)*

ZACHARY: *(Stopping her in the nick of time)* I wouldn't do that if I were you.

MRS. NURDIGER: Why should they live when they killed my Chester. Chester! Oh. *(Weeps)*

ROXANNE: Oh, here comes Mrs. Muncie to buy the weekly rat for her boa constrictor. Come now, Mother Nurdiger, you don't want Mrs. Muncie to see you like this. Zack, help her to her room.

MRS. NURDIGER: Oh, you're so kind. I know that Chester is up in heaven looking down on your kindness. I know he's seen everything you've done. I know he blesses you both and he'll ask God to repay you for it.

(ZACHARY helps her off. MRS. MUNCIE enters the shop as in Act I. Because her shawl is over her head we do not see her face.)

ROXANNE: *(Waits on her)* The usual, Mrs. Muncie? *(MRS. MUNCIE nods)* We've got a beautiful rat for you today—nice and fat. *(She gets rat. ZACHARY reenters)*

ROXANNE: How is she?

ZACHARY: She's resting. Oh hello, and how are you today, Mrs. Muncie?

MRS. MUNCIE: *(Turns, it is CHESTER with part of his face eaten away)* As well as can be expected, Mr. Slade. And how are you?

ZACHARY: *(Frozen in horror)* Oh God! Oh God! It can't be!

ROXANNE: What is it?

ZACHARY: Look there! Look there! *(Points to MRS. MUNCIE)* Don't you see who it is?

ROXANNE: Yes, Zack, it's Mrs. Muncie.

ZACHARY: No! No! It's him! It's him! Chester! Chester!

MRS. MUNCIE: *(To ROXANNE)* The young man seems to have mistaken me for someone else.

ROXANNE: Here, Mrs. Muncie, take the rat—there'll be no charge today. *(Hurries her out of the shop)* Good day, Mrs. Muncie, good day! *(Slams the shop door and locks it)* What's gotten into you? You frightened that poor old lady half to death.

ZACHARY: Old lady? Old lady? *(Laughs insanely)* That was no old lady. It was Chester. Didn't you see how his face was eaten away by the piranhas?

ROXANNE: Zack, you've got to get hold of yourself. You're seeing things.

ZACHARY: No. No. I'm not seeing things! It was Chester, I tell you! It was Chester!

ROXANNE: *(In a hoarse whisper)* Quiet! Do you want to give us away? I'm going to close the shop. It's been a long day and we're all under a strain.

ZACHARY: I tell you it was Chester.

ROXANNE: Stop saying that. It was Mrs. Muncie. I hope she doesn't talk about it. It might arouse suspicions.

ZACHARY: I'm sorry—I must be losing my grip. I could have sworn I saw—

ROXANNE: *(Interrupting him)* Now that's enough about what you thought you saw. Go into my room and lie down for a while. I'll get you a good stiff drink.

ZACHARY: Yes, yes, that's what I need—a good stiff drink. *(He goes and lies on the bed, turns on the TV, and hears the first few lines from* CHESTER'S *Act II commercial before snapping it off. Roxanne pours a shot of whiskey, tosses it down, then brings him the bottle and shot glass. He quickly throws down three shots)*

ROXANNE: Feel steadier?

ZACHARY: Yeah. Give me another.

ROXANNE: That's enough. We can't take the risk of getting loaded and talking too much, now can we?

ZACHARY: No, no. What have you made me do? What have you made me do?

ROXANNE: What have *I* made you do?

ZACHARY: Yes, I killed the only person who ever gave me a break. I had nothing against him. It's all your fault.

ROXANNE: My fault? I like that! Did I force you to climb in the window? Did I put the pillow in your hand? Did I force you to hold that pillow over his face while he gasped and begged for air? Did I make you choke the life out of him?

ZACHARY: *(Covering his ears)* Stop! Stop! I don't want to hear any more!

ROXANNE: Well, you'd better hear and you'd better hear good. You're the one who did it. Do you hear me? You're the one. I helped you plan it. But that was all.

ZACHARY: Don't say that. Don't put it that way. I thought we were on this train together—right until the very last stop.

ROXANNE: Yeah, we're on it together; and we'd better stay on it just as long as we can. Because the last stop is the cemetery.

ZACHARY: I've got to have another drink.

ROXANNE: *(Taking the bottle away from him)* I said no more.

ZACHARY: I saw him. I saw him clear as day. And did you hear what he said to me? He asked me how I was!

ROXANNE: I tell you that was Mrs. Muncie. Come on now, Zack. Let's forget all that now. We've got each other, Zack, and that's all that matters. We've got each other—just the two of us—and nothing can ever come between us. *(Lying back on the bed behind him)* Make love to me, Zack, and let me make you forget everything that ever was for good. *(She reaches to draw him to her. He turns to kiss her, but it is* CHESTER*)*

ZACHARY: *(Screams)* Chester! It's Chester! *(He tries to strangle* CHESTER *who disappears. He is strangling* ROXANNE.*)* Leave me alone, Chester! Leave me alone! I'll kill you again! I'll kill you a thousand times and a thousand different ways!

ROXANNE: Zack, please, I can't breathe. Zack! Zack, please. My God! I don't dare call for help!

MRS. NURDIGER: *(Rushes in and sees* ZACHARY *strangling* ROXANNE*)* What is it? What happened?

ZACHARY: *(Raving at* ROXANNE *as he strangles her)* You're dead, Chester! Now you've got to lie down! Down in that grave we buried you in! Because you're dead, Chester! We killed you. We smothered you with your pillow and fed you to the piranhas! So lie down, Chester! You've got to lie down!

MRS. NURDIGER: You killed him? You killed my Chester. Murderers! Murderers! *(She staggers toward them.)* You killed my child. My poor little boy! Murderers! You murderers! Oh God, punish them! Punish them! *(Suddenly she is stricken and goes all crooked. She falls.* ZACHARY *releases* ROXANNE *and runs to her)* I can't . . . I can't . . .

ZACHARY: Mother Nurdiger?

ROXANNE: She's dead.

ZACHARY: No. She's had a stroke. She's paralyzed. Her eyes are alive and they are threatening us.

ROXANNE: May God turn her lips and tongue to stone.

(Blackout.)

ACT IV

It is a Thursday night—domino night—several months later.

ROXANNE: Where are you going?

ZACHARY: To get Mother Nurdiger.

ROXANNE: Can't you leave her in her room?

ZACHARY: Have you forgotten? It's domino night.

ROXANNE: Domino night! How long must we go on with that infernal ritual?

ZACHARY: I know it's a strain. But we agreed that it was best to maintain the appearance of normalcy.

ROXANNE: Normalcy! Normalcy! We killed him to escape the tedium of existence. Now we're even more mired in it.

ZACHARY: It's only Frankie—faithful Frankie. And we do owe him something, don't you think?

ROXANNE: *(With bitter irony)* Yes, I suppose we do.

ZACHARY: Because if he hadn't happened in on us it might have looked like murder. He was your witness that Chester was drunk and probably fell into the piranha tank and got himself killed. He was your airtight alibi.

ROXANNE: Airtight, yes.

ZACHARY: And it didn't hurt that he was an officer of the law.

ROXANNE: Yes, the law was on our side.

ZACHARY: And it's touching, his devotion to Mother Nurdiger.

ROXANNE: Yes, I know it's her he comes to see.

ZACHARY: So I'd better bring her out.

ROXANNE: I can't stand her eyes. They seem to be accusing us—damning us. She hates us. I know she'd tell everything if she could.

ZACHARY: Well, she can't. The paralysis is almost total. She can't move at all—except for her eyes.

ROXANNE: Her eyes! Her eyes! She's learned to make them speak and I know she accuses and damns us.

ZACHARY: It's almost time. Frankie will be here. I must get her.

ROXANNE: If you must—you must!

(ZACHARY goes to get MOTHER NURDIGER whom he carries in and places in her usual chair at the table. She doesn't move a muscle—except for her eyes.)

ZACHARY: Here she comes! There you go, right in your usual chair, Mother Nurdiger. Are you comfortable? I think she says yes.

ROXANNE: I suppose she imagines us abandoning ourselves to our lust—our lust!—some joke!

ZACHARY: Do you have to rub it in?

ROXANNE: We killed him so we could be together. But there hasn't been anything between us since he's been out of the way. You haven't touched me since he died.

ZACHARY: I can't. I can't. He's there. Always there.

ROXANNE: That first night I went out and walked the streets. I made it with the first man I met. And I've done it since and been paid for it. In doorways, in cars, and in hotel rooms. I tried to forget. But always I thought of the woman who was cut up in four pieces. I was afraid. But sometimes I wished for it. Are you listening? Did you hear what I said to you? Any man would be furious. Aren't you furious? Why don't you beat me? Or aren't you a man at all?

ZACHARY: I'm relieved. It takes the pressure off of me . . . the pressure to perform. *(He pauses then in alarm)* My God. We've dropped our guard completely. We've been talking freely in front of her.

ROXANNE: She's so silent, like a statue. It's so easy to forget she's there.

ZACHARY: Look, look at her eyes. Her eyes are full of hatred.

ROXANNE: *(Slightly mad)* No, no, not hatred. Sometimes I see great compassion in them. Her eyes speak to me. I understand the meaning of her every glance. I know she understands and has found it in her heart to forgive us. Isn't that right, Mother Nurdiger? You do forgive us, don't you? Look, her eyes are brimming over. She does forgive us. I know she does.

ZACHARY: No, you're deluding yourself. That's not a blessing you see in her eyes. It's a mother's curse. She is clinging to life in the hopes of seeing us punished. That's what keeps her going. Her hatred is keeping her alive and her desire for revenge.

ROXANNE: By God, I'll put those eyes out! *(She grabs an ice pick.)*

ZACHARY: No! Do you want to give us away? *(Struggles with her)* Drop that ice pick! Drop it!

(ROXANNE drops the ice pick.)

ROXANNE: So, you're afraid of being found out, you coward! I have a good mind to go to the police and tell them everything. It would be a relief. Yes, that's what I'll do. I'll go to the police right now. I'll tell them everything.

ZACHARY: You little fool! Are you crazy? You're not going anywhere.

ROXANNE: *(Raving)* Coward! Coward! Coward! Coward!

ZACHARY: Look, she's listening. She knows everything that goes on in this house. I can't stand it anymore. I'm going to tell the police myself!

ROXANNE: Go, see if I care!

ZACHARY: *(Putting on his jacket)* I will!

ROXANNE: Go ahead! Tell them how you killed him!

ZACHARY: You killed him too.

ROXANNE: No, no I didn't. I was out of my mind. I didn't know what I was doing!

ZACHARY: If his ghost came back it would strangle you first!

ROXANNE: Good! I wish it would. Anything would be better than dominoes every Thursday night and the same boring conversation.

ZACHARY: All right then! *(Storms out of the shop)*

ROXANNE: *(Sits still for a few moments and then begins to panic)* My God! He's really going to do it. We'll both go to prison for the rest of our lives! They'll put us in prison 'til we rot. No! No! No! *(Leaps to her feet and runs out into the street after him)* Zack! Zachary! No! No! Don't do it! I didn't mean what I said.

(The stage is left empty for a few moments as MRS. NURDIGER sits stone still, her eyes burning like cold fires in their sockets. ROXANNE and ZACHARY reenter.)

ZACHARY: I lost my nerve.

ROXANNE: I'm sorry. Oh God I'm sorry. What are we doing to ourselves? What are we doing to each other?

ZACHARY: Keep your voice down. We'll be caught. *(They crawl under the table)*

ROXANNE: *(In a strangled whisper)* Do you think anyone heard?

ZACHARY: *(Also in a hoarse whisper)* I don't know. I don't think so. I hope not.

(The sound of whistling is heard approaching, they both crouch like hunted animals, frozen in terror.)

ROXANNE: It's him—Frankie.

ZACHARY: Sometimes I think he knows. And that he's laughing at us.

ROXANNE: Don't be absurd. Why would he play with us? Please, let's not add him to our nightmares.

ZACHARY: You're right. Let's pull ourselves together. Act like nothing happened.

(They rise.)

FRANKIE: Hello, anybody home?

ROXANNE: Frankie.

FRANKIE: Domino night.

ZACHARY: Yes, domino night.

FRANKIE: You know I wouldn't let you down. And how is Mother Nurdiger doing? Ah, very well I see. In her usual chair, peaceful and contented. Surrounded by those she loves. And we all love you. Be brave. Look at her eyes. How expressive they are. She can say anything with her eyes.

ROXANNE: Here are the dominos.

FRANKIE: Won't you play for a change, Roxanne? Chester's chair looks so empty and sad. As if it missed him as much as we do.

ROXANNE: No, I couldn't. I have no mind for dominos.

ZACHARY: *(Changing the subject)* Do you have any news, Frankie? Anything exciting in the field of law enforcement? As Chester used to say.

FRANKIE: Well, they caught the ones who cut up that woman into four pieces. It was the husband and another woman.

ZACHARY: I thought there were no clues?

FRANKIE: There weren't. But these two were seized with a compulsion to confess. They turned on each other. (MRS. NURDIGER's *hand begins to rise)* Well, will you look at that! Her hand is moving! Very good, Mother Nurdiger! Very good! Look she's making movements as though she wants to write something. She wants to communicate something.

ROXANNE: My God!

ZACHARY: Steady . . . steady.

FRANKIE: What is it, Mother Nurdiger? What is it? Look there, she's forming letters on the table. *(Watching her hand and spelling the message out loud)* R-O-X . . . Roxanne! Yes, yes, don't bother with the rest. You've got to save your strength. A-N-D Z-A-C . . . and Zack. Yes, I got it. Go on. A-R-E . . . are, yes, K-I . . . Oh, I know . . . kind. Roxanne and Zack are kind. She's trying to tell you how grateful she is for the way you're taking care of her. Oh look, she's trying to write some more.

ROXANNE: She's like a statue coming to life.

ZACHARY: *(Taking hold of a meat cleaver)* By God, I'll cut her arm off.

FRANKIE: Come on, Mother Nurdiger, what are you trying to tell us? Oh, now your arm has fallen back to your side.

ROXANNE: She's turned to stone again.

ZACHARY: We're safe.

ROXANNE: For the moment.

FRANKIE: Well, shall we begin our game? I'll play for Mother Nurdiger. *(He dumps the tiles)* Now we each take seven. *(As they draw their tiles CHESTER rises from behind the table and sits in his chair)* Who's high?

CHESTER: Double nine. I'll be the first to go.

ZACHARY: *(Aside to ROXANNE)* He's there. He's there. Don't you see him?

ROXANNE: *(Desperately aside)* Will you be quiet. There's nobody there.

FRANKIE: Zack, it's your move.

CHESTER: That's right, it's your move, Zack.

ZACHARY: It's there. It's here. It's everywhere!

FRANKIE: What? Oh that fly. *(He follows the movements and buzzing of the fly with his head and eyes)* I'll get it. *(He swats the fly)*

ROXANNE: *(Screams)* No! No! Don't! Look what you did! *(Breaking down and crying)* You killed it. You killed this innocent fly. You killed it! You killed it. *(Sobs pathetically and uncontrollably)*

PARROT: Gawk! Hey, Zack, that isn't funny. Ha! Ha! I can't breathe! I CAN'T BREATHE. No! No! Help me Roxanne! Roxanne! Gawk! I can't breathe.

ZACHARY: I need a drink. *(Drinks)*

FRANKIE: The parrot! It almost sounds as if he were repeating . . .

ROXANNE: *(Steals FRANKIE's gun)* The murder scene? Is that what you were going to say, Officer Spinelli?

PARROT: Gawk! Roxanne, help me, I can't breathe!

ROXANNE: *(Fires on the parrot blowing it to bits)* And now for Mother Nurdiger.

ZACHARY: No, Roxy, don't! *(He rushes toward her, they struggle for the gun. It goes off. They both stand for a long moment looking at each other, stunned. ROXANNE slides down his body to the floor)* Oh my God, Roxy.

ROXANNE: It's the end of the line. Everybody off. *(Dies)*

FRANKIE: That was six. Give it up. I've gotta take you in.

ZACHARY: That's all right. *(Throws down the gun)* That drink I took was malachite green, a cure for ich, poisonous to piranhas, and deadly to little men like us. I'm dying. And I look up at the stars, the thousand unseeing eyes that look back on this little speck of dust we call the world, and I ask—What was my crime compared to your indifference. I committed a senseless murder. But in its very senselessness it is in harmony with the universe, which is itself senseless and ultimately stupid. In an aeon or two, who will be left to accuse me? *(Dies)*

FRANKIE: Poor Chester.

(The lights fade except for two tiny points of light on MOTHER NURDIGER's eyes.)

The End